The *Dictionary of North Carolina Biography*, the most comprehensive state project of its kind, will provide information on some four thousand notable North Carolinians whose accomplishments and occasional misdeeds span four centuries. Volume 5, P–S, includes 729 entries. The final volume is scheduled for publication in 1995.

The *Dictionary* contains the first comprehensive biographical information for many of these individuals. Included are native North Carolinians, no matter in what area they made their contributions, and non-natives whose contributions were made in North Carolina. All persons included are deceased.

Explorers, inventors, engineers, writers, chemists, business leaders, architects, artists, musicians, colonial leaders, military figures, national and state officials, and outstanding teachers and clergymen are among those recognized. And there are the infamous and eccentric—pirates, criminals, a hermit, and the man who weighed more than one thousand pounds. Averaging about eight hundred words, each sketch includes the full name of the subject, dates and places of birth and death (when known), family connections, a career description, and a bibliography. Most of the sketches are based on manuscript and contemporary printed sources that are rare or difficult to find. Some research was conducted in Europe.

William S. Powell has been working on the *Dictionary* since 1971 with the help of several hundred volunteer contributors.

Volume 5, P–S

DICTIONARY OF NORTH CAROLINA BIOGRAPHY

EDITED BY
WILLIAM S. POWELL

VOLUME 5 P–S

Dictionary of North Carolina Biography

Edited by William S. Powell

Volume 5 P–S

The University of North Carolina Press
Chapel Hill and London

Manufactured in the United States of America

Library of Congress Cataloging-in-Publication Data

Dictionary of North Carolina biography.
Includes bibliographical references.
1. North Carolina—Biography—Dictionaries.
I. Powell, William Stevens, 1919– .
CT252.D5 920'.0756 79-10106
ISBN 0-8078-1329-X (vol. 1)
ISBN 0-8078-1656-6 (vol. 2)
ISBN 0-8078-1806-2 (vol. 3)
ISBN 0-8078-1918-2 (vol. 4)
ISBN 0-8078-2100-4 (vol. 5)

The paper in this book meets the guidelines for permanence and durability of the Committee on Production Guidelines for Book Longevity of the Council on Library Resources.

98 97 96 95 94 5 4 3 2 1

In Memory of

Guion Griffis Johnson
11 April 1900–12 June 1989

Frontis Withers Johnson
31 October 1908–25 May 1990

Hugh Buckner Johnston, Jr.
11 April 1913–27 July 1990

Blackwell Pierce Robinson
4 April 1916–22 February 1991

Durward Turrentine Stokes
8 December 1908–14 June 1991

Sterling Aubrey Stoudemire
4 September 1902–26 May 1992

Nannie May Tilley
29 May 1899–4 October 1988

whose scholarly assistance contributed to the usefulness of the *Dictionary of North Carolina Biography*

Acknowledgments

I am grateful to the North Carolina Society of the Cincinnati for making a generous grant to the University of North Carolina Press to assist with the publication costs of this volume as it did for volumes two, three, and four; to the late George E. London for his interest and support; and to Armistead Maupin and other members of the Society for their continuing assistance. I would like to thank Stevie Champion, a copyeditor without parallel; my wife, Virginia Waldrop Powell, a skilled proofreader who also questions the text she reads; and Sandra Eisdorfer and C. David Perry at the University of North Carolina Press, each of whom made the *DNCB* more useful and reliable than when I turned the manuscript over to them. The staffs of the North Carolina Collection and the Humanities/General Reference section of the University of North Carolina Library aided in numerous ways as I sought elusive biographical information.

Most significant, however, is the debt owed to the many volunteer writers of the biographies in this work. They generously gave their time and talent to produce another volume in what has been hailed the best such work yet published for an American state.

Dictionary of North Carolina Biography

Pack, George Willis *(6 June 1831–31 Aug. 1906)*, lumber merchant and benefactor of the city of Asheville, was born in Fenner, Madison County, N.Y., of English ancestry. His forebears had settled in New Jersey in 1664 and for generations had been active in political and military affairs there and in New York. His father and grandfather were both named George Pack; his mother was Maria Lathrop of Connecticut. He was educated in the public schools of Peterboro, N.Y., and at age seventeen accompanied his father to Sanilac, Mich., in the midst of a vast forest area. His father's aim was to establish a lumbering business. Young Pack worked for his father for some years, then went into business on his own in 1854. His initiative and knowledge of all phases of forestry and lumbering led to quick success. Over the next thirty years he established a network of profitable firms and resided at various places in Michigan and Ohio. Eventually he settled in Cleveland, using that city as a base of operations for his many enterprises.

Pack first went to Asheville in 1884 and, attracted by the healthy climate of the growing town, chose it as his permanent home. In 1885 construction was completed on Manyoaks, his large mansion, which shortly became one of the showplaces of the mountain city. Soon thereafter he began his program of gifts to the city; over the next twenty years his contributions of land and money would aid many needy causes and provide educational, cultural, and welfare benefits for the people. His benefactions showed great foresight, and many are still evident in Asheville.

In 1892 Pack established a free kindergarten, donating the complete cost of land, construction, and a teacher's salary. In 1896 he bestowed $2,000 towards the erection of a monument to honor Zebulon B. Vance. In 1899 he purchased land and buildings on the site of Court Square for the Asheville Public Library; the library received both a permanent new home and income from rents on the existing buildings. The next year Pack gave land on College Street with the stipulation that the existing Buncombe County Courthouse be torn down and a new one constructed. The remaining land was to be made into a public square. In gratitude, local officials changed the library's name to Pack Memorial Public Library and the previous Court Square to Pack Square; both sites still bear his name.

Among his other contributions to the civic betterment of Asheville were funds to aid hospitals, the YMCA, orphans and widows, and veterans' organizations. He also deeded land for three city parks. These gifts were bestowed in his characteristically quiet manner, often by means of a brief note to city officials. They were always timely and of an enduring value, so that though an outsider he held a high place in Asheville hearts. The *Asheville Citizen* commented typically on 2 Jan. 1901: "We salute George W. Pack! If heaven has vouchsafed to any community a better citizen, the fame of him has not reached these parts."

In failing health, he spent his last days by the sea at Southhampton, Long Island. At the news of his death, Asheville observed a day of public mourning, with many offices closed and their doors draped in black. A representative from the city attended his funeral and burial in Cleveland, Ohio, on 4 Sept. 1906.

A Presbyterian, Pack married Frances Farnam of Milwaukee in 1854. The couple had three children: Charles L., a nationally known forester and conservationist, Mary, and Beulah. Two portraits are on view in Asheville, one at the Buncombe County Courthouse and one in Pack Memorial Public Library.

SEE: *Asheville Citizen*, 1 and 4 Sept. 1906, 8 Aug. 1926, 17 July 1960; *Life of George W. Pack* (privately printed, Cleveland, 1898); *The State*, 9 Oct., 18 Dec. 1943.

JAMES MEEHAN

Packer, Francis Herman *(13 Feb. 1873–13 July 1957)*, sculptor, was born in Munich. In the United States, he was a student of the sculptors Philip Martiny and Augustus Saint-Gaudens. By 1914 he was a resident of Rockville Centre, Long Island, N.Y., where he remained for the rest of his life.

Packer's work is well represented in North Carolina; it includes bronze statues of Ensign Worth Bagley (1907, Raleigh), Confederate senator and Attorney General George Davis (1910, Wilmington), Chief Justice Thomas Ruffin (1914, Raleigh), and General Nathanael Greene (1915, Guilford Courthouse National Military Park). The last is an equestrian figure. Packer's monument to the *Soldiers of the Confederacy* (1924), featuring two bronze figures, stands in Wilmington. He was commissioned in 1914 to execute a bust of Judge William Gaston, which was copied in marble from a plaster bust (now lost) that had been modeled from life by Robert Ball Hughes in 1831–34. The marble is now exhibited in the North Carolina Supreme Court Library, Raleigh. Packer visited North Carolina in connection with his professional commissions but never resided in the state.

Other works by Packer included *Nebraska* for the Louisiana Purchase Exposition at St. Louis (1904), the Congressional Medal honoring the Byrd Antarctic Expedition (1930–31), and various portrait sculptures.

Packer's wife, Julia Bucher, predeceased him and he left no immediate survivors. Friends described him as a gentle, artistic man who shunned public attention and insisted upon perfection in his sculptures.

SEE: *New York Times*, 15 July 1957; Lorado Taft, *The History of American Sculpture* (1930); *Who's Who in American Art*, vol. 1 (1935); *Who Was Who in America*, 3 (1966).

JOHN SANDERS

Page, Allison Francis (Frank) *(30 Aug. 1824–16 Oct. 1899)*, was born at Oaky Mount, a tobacco plantation in Wake County near Leesville, about twelve miles north of

Raleigh. He was of English ancestry, having descended from John Page who migrated to Virginia. Frank's father was Anderson Page, who married Mary Hayes. His paternal grandfather, Lewis Page (m. Sally Justice), and great-grandfather, Edward Page, came into the wild and hitherto untamed region of North Carolina and had been associated with Lewis and Clark, who made the brave trek westward. They were motivated not only by the desire for more land, but also for greater freedom from ritualistic worship than they had been allowed in the colony of Virginia.

Frank Page was born of an interesting family consisting of ten children. Anderson Page was financially able to send his children to college and several of them graduated, but Frank Page was not a college-bred man. His domineering, independent, pioneer nature led him into the vast virgin forests of North Carolina to harvest naval stores and operate huge lumbering outfits. He realized much wealth from his logging operations, rafting the timbers down the Cape Fear River to Fayetteville, his headquarters, and on to Wilmington, an important port of the Carolinas. Page became a citizen of no small means, only to lose one fortune and be $10,000 in debt in his middle fifties. Of tremendous physique, he possessed the immense strength and endurance that was typical of the rugged Page breed. He was an energetic builder and developer with an adventuresome nature—a statesman who desired to make America a great place to live in. Of a keen intellect, intensely religious, and a staunch prohibitionist, he was admired for his candid, just, and uncompromising opinions rendered freely in situations where others dared not speak up.

His home, known as Pages, was an example of some of the finest architecture of the era. Frank Page became the first mayor and postmaster of Cary, a small village about twelve miles west of Raleigh. He had an intense interest in education on behalf of the people of this town and was instrumental in founding the Cary Academy. The lumber used to build the two-story frame structure of the Cary school was prepared at his mill. Page had an active interest in politics, siding with the Whigs, who opposed slavery and secession of the South prior to the Civil War. Because he was such a great benefactor of the little town, many of the citizens wished to name it Page's Station, but he insisted that it be called Cary in honor of an outstanding prohibitionist whom he greatly admired.

In addition to the founding of Cary, Page is credited with establishing Aberdeen, in Moore County. Here he again became prosperous in logging the original pine forests and transported the logs on his own railroad. He located many sawmills and built two important railroads—one extended from Biscoe to Mount Gilead and the other from Aberdeen to Asheboro, towns in central North Carolina. He was a founder and philanthropist of the Methodist Home for Children in Raleigh. Desiring that the capital of his state should have a first-class hotel without a saloon, he constructed the Mansion Park Hotel. He was a large contributor in the building of churches for both whites and blacks wherever he went.

At age twenty-five, Page married Catherine Frances Raboteau (12 Nov. 1831–21 Aug. 1897), on 5 July 1849. She was the daughter of John Samuel and Esther Barclay Raboteau of Barclaysville, near Fayetteville. Her parents were of French Huguenot descent. The blend of her intellectual, refined nature with her husband's venturesome and determined characteristics afforded a unique home of great culture and refinement. Straightforward living, patterned after their interpretation of the Bible, was the order of their home. They applied vigorous moral rules —yet seasoned with a sense of humor, mutual love, and respect—in the upbringing of the family.

Some people attain an unquestionable place in the world and receive distinction because of their own achievements. Others seem to have greatness thrust upon them. There are still others who become known because of the outstanding progeny that they beget. These people appear to genetically sort out a favorable combination of traits for their children and then meticulously train and inspire their offspring to greatness in their home life and produce citizens of near-genius caliber. The latter of these combinations of circumstances appears to have been true of Allison Francis Page.

Catherine and Frank Page's eight children became internationally known as statesmen, educators, ministers, and businessmen: Walter Hines was a brilliant scholar, noted editor, and respected U.S. ambassador to Great Britain during the presidential administration of Woodrow Wilson; Robert Newton became an eminent legislator, congressman, and banker; Henry Allison was the U.S. food commissioner under Herbert Hoover during World War I and had important railroad connections, building the line between Aberdeen and High Point; Junius (Chris) Raboteau became a prominent businessman and benefactor of Aberdeen; John W. was a distinguished physician; Jesse became a prominent clergyman of the Methodist Episcopal Church, South; Emma Catherine taught Bible in the North Carolina College for Women at Greensboro for fifty years; Mary Esther was fondly known as the family historian and philanthropist; and Frank, a noted engineer and businessman, was the founder and executive vice-president of Wachovia Bank in Raleigh. He was chairman of the North Carolina Highway Commission under Governor Cameron Morrison, and during his term of office North Carolina earned the title of the "Good Roads State."

Page died in Raleigh and was buried in the family plot in Bethesda Cemetery near Aberdeen.

SEE: Samuel A. Ashe, ed., *Biographical History of North Carolina*, vol. 3 (1906); Tom Byrd and Evelyn Holland, *Cary's One Hundredth Anniversary* (1971); Burton J. Hendrick, *The Life and Letters of Walter H. Page* (1927); *North Carolina Biography*, vol. 3 (1941); *Who's Who in America*, vol. 10 (1918).

IRMA RAGAN HOLLAND

Page, Estelle Lawson *(22 Mar. 1907–7 May 1983)*, amateur golfer, was born in her mother's hometown of East Orange, N.J., but raised in Chapel Hill. She was the only child of Dr. Robert Baker and Estelle Adelaide Ward Lawson. Dr. Lawson was a 1900 graduate of The University of North Carolina, where he was a star baseball and football player; he pitched in the major leagues in 1901 and 1902.

The Lawsons returned to Chapel Hill in 1905, when he took a position at The University of North Carolina as baseball coach. The next year he became a professor of anatomy in the medical school, a position he held until his retirement in 1949. Mrs. Lawson was active in local civic and charitable affairs. Young Estelle attended Chapel Hill High School, where she played basketball and tennis. She briefly attended Salem College before transferring to The University of North Carolina, where she was graduated in 1928. At the university she was a member of Phi Beta Kappa and president of the Woman's Pan Hellenic Council. After graduation she worked briefly in the cost accounting department of Durham Hosiery Mills and as an occasional substitute teacher.

Estelle Lawson took up golf around 1930. Taught by her father, she quickly became the dominant player in the Carolinas and one of the best in the country. In 1931 she entered her first tournament and the next year won the Carolinas Amateur championship. She repeated as champion of that tournament in 1933 and 1934 and would eventually win it ten times between 1932 and 1947. Her most important victory came in 1937, when she won the U.S. Golf Association Women's Amateur Championship, held that year at the Memphis Country Club. In the thirty-six-hole match play final she defeated Patty Berg 7 and 6. At the end of 1937 she was runner-up in the Associated Press voting for outstanding U.S. female athlete; *Golf Magazine* voted her the outstanding woman golfer. The next year she again advanced to the national finals against Miss Berg but lost 6 and 5. Although Mrs. Page regularly advanced to the semifinals in the national championship, she never again made the finals.

She won the prestigious North and South tournament, held annually at Pinehurst, seven times—in 1935, 1937, 1939, 1940, 1941, 1944, and 1945. Her 1935 win in that tournament was the first victory by a southern woman. She also won the 1946 Southern Amateur, the first three North Carolina Women's Golf Association tournaments in 1950, 1951, and 1952, and numerous other, lesser tournaments.

Mrs. Page was a member of the U.S. Curtis Cup team, which played against the women's team representing Great Britain, in 1938 and 1948 and undoubtedly would have been named to additional teams had that tournament not been suspended for a decade due to World War II. She basically ended her tournament competition in 1955 after a thyroid operation, although she did make a few later appearances at Pinehurst. Mrs. Page ended her career with an unusually high total of seventeen authenticated holes-in-one. Although women's professional golf became established in the late 1940s, Mrs. Page declined to turn professional.

She was a founder of the North Carolina Women's Golf Association and served as its first president in 1950. She had previously been president of the Women's Southern Golf Association and was a member of the U.S. Golf Association Women's Committee. In 1963 she became a charter member of the North Carolina Sports Hall of Fame. She was also a member of the Carolinas Golf Hall of Fame and the New Jersey Sports Hall of Fame.

She married Chapel Hill native Junius Page, Jr., on 7 July 1936. Her husband, an executive with the Liggett and Myers Tobacco Company in Durham, was seriously wounded in World War II and awarded the Croix de Guerre. They had no children. Mrs. Page was a lifelong member of the Chapel of the Cross in Chapel Hill; she was buried in the old Chapel Hill Cemetery.

SEE: Peter Alliss, *The Who's Who of Golf* (1983); *Chapel Hill Weekly*, 15 Oct. 1937; *Durham Herald-Sun*, 11 Apr., 17 Oct. 1937; *Durham Morning Herald*, 11 Jan. 1948, 2 Sept. 1973; Page File (Alumni Office and North Carolina Collection, University of North Carolina, Chapel Hill); Raleigh *News and Observer*, 28 May 1933, 14 Apr., 24 Oct. 1935, 10 May 1936, 23 May, 29 Sept. 1937, 15 June 1950, 8 May 1983; Robert Scharf, ed., *Golf Magazine's Encyclopedia of Golf* (1973); *Yackety Yack*, 1928.

JIM L. SUMNER

Page, Frank *(22 Feb. 1875–20 Dec. 1934)*, banker, industrialist, railroad builder, and father of North Carolina's modern highway system, was born at Cary of French and English ancestry. His father was Allison Francis Page, a pioneer in the development of railroads, banking, and industry in the Sandhills section of central North Carolina. His mother was Catherine Raboteau Page. Upon completion of his preparatory education at Davis Military School, young Page entered The University of North Carolina for two years of study. He then joined his father and brothers in their far-flung business operations in Aberdeen.

On 17 June 1896 he married Ella Barringer Martin of Chapel Hill. They had three children: Allison Martin, who served with distinction in World War I before being fatally wounded at Belleau Wood; Clara Martin Page Harrison, whose husband, a prominent High Point physician, died of a strange malady apparently contracted while serving in the South Pacific area in World War II; and Frank Martin.

During World War I, Frank Page served in the U.S. Army Corps of Engineers with the rank of major in Europe. When he returned home, Governor Thomas W. Bickett prevailed upon him to undertake the chairmanship of the newly formed North Carolina Highway Commission, a post he held for ten years with distinction. In launching his state's Good Roads program, he managed the effort during its initial decade with skill and with never a hint of scandal.

Page served as president of the American Road Builders Association and of the American Association of State Highway Officials. He was chairman of the National Highway Safety Council by appointment of President Herbert Hoover. As one of five U.S. delegates selected by Calvin Coolidge, he represented his country at the Pan-American Road Congress in South America. He was a member of the State Public Works Advisory Board and the Raleigh Rotary Club. In 1923, The University of North Carolina awarded him the honorary degree of LL.D.

After retiring from the North Carolina Highway Commission chairmanship, Page joined the Wachovia Bank and Trust Company at Raleigh as vice-president; he remained in that position until his death.

A Methodist by affiliation, he was buried in the family plot in Old Bethesda Cemetery near Aberdeen. A bronze plaque commemorating his leadership in North Carolina's outstanding road building program is at the entrance to the Highway Building in Raleigh.

SEE: Daniel L. Grant, *Alumni History of the University of North Carolina* (1924); Winnie Ingram Richter, ed., *The Heritage of Montgomery County* (1981); Gary E. Trawick and Paul B. Wyche, *One Hundred Years, One Hundred Men* (1971); Capus Waynick, *North Carolina Roads and Their Builders* (1952); *Who's Who in the South* (1927).

HOLT MCPHERSON

Page, Hubbard Fulton *(11 Dec. 1873–23 Aug. 1957)*, folk poet, teacher, and composer, was born in northern Sampson County near the old Harnett County community of Averasboro. He was the son of Sion Cephas, a circuit-riding Baptist minister and farmer, and Johnnie Louise West Page. Young Page attended Buies Creek Academy, then taught Greek, Bible, and Latin there in 1902–3. In 1905 he was graduated from Wake Forest College. After this time he returned to school and in 1911 received the master of arts degree from Harvard University. For two academic years (1911–12 and 1912–13) he was assistant professor of English at Texas Christian University, where *The Horned Frog*, the student yearbook, referred to him as "fast becoming a poet of renown."

In the summer of 1913 Page returned to North Carolina and taught for three years at Buies Creek Academy, where one of his devoted students was Tar Heel playwright Paul Green, who lived on a nearby farm. From 1916 to 1926 Page served as assistant professor of English at Texas A&M University. He then taught for one year (1927–28) at Mississippi College. In 1930 he went back once again to Buies Creek to teach at Campbell Junior College (formerly an academy), where he remained on the faculty until his retirement in 1947.

Known as an eccentric, Page cared little for appearances—as his rumpled clothing and mop of flaring reddish hair attested. He was sometimes the object of derisive laughter from students or townspeople because of his absent-mindedness or his mannerisms during lectures, from which students slipped away when he continued declaiming long after the bell to end class. On 20 Aug. 1925, at age fifty-one, he married Orilla Ellen Viers, a young woman thirty-one years his junior whom he had met in Florida where she had gone with her parents from West Virginia to pick strawberries. She talked him into returning to Harnett County during the year 1926–27 to farm, a project about which she said afterward "I was sorry I thought of [it]," and he soon resumed his teaching career. They had nine children, the last being born when Page was seventy-one.

In a 1980 interview, Paul Green said that Professor Page had been a major influence on his career. "I don't recall that we ever talked much about drama, except for *Hamlet*, but it was his great enthusiasm for his teaching and for literature that excited me and made me respect him," Green said.

During his lifetime, Page's best-known work was a collection of verse called *Lyrics and Legends of the Cape Fear Country*, published in 1932. In this volume he set a number of local folktales into verse, paid tribute to occupational types such as riverboat men and lumberjacks, and transcribed the lyrics and tunes of several Negro songs and spirituals. The book contains many references to the Highland Scottish heritage of the Upper Cape Fear region. Also, quite a few of the poems are written in Negro dialect. A second book of poems, *The Threshold*, published posthumously in 1963, is largely romantic, sentimental, and reminiscent. Many of its selections deal, once again, with the landscape and people of the Cape Fear River valley. According to Green, most of what Professor Page wrote was imitative verse, patterned after the work of Robert Burns and John Charles McNeil. Page was restricted by his use of rhyme and his images were sometimes incorrect, but he had a very great enthusiasm for his subject matter, Green said, just as he did for his teaching. Page's poetry has been discussed and represented in *Who's Who in American Poets* and in Richard Walser's *North Carolina Poets* (1951). A considerable number of his poems remain in manuscript and have never been published. For Campbell he wrote an "Alma Mater," which was used as the college song until the early 1970s.

His children included five sons—Brenton C. (d. 1947), Elmer Fulton (d. 1951), Ronald (of Fayetteville), Fordyce (of Hawaii), and Embert (of Denver, Colo.)—and four daughters—Ellen (m. J. H. Mincey, of Burlington), Edna Lee (m. B. R. Matthews, of Marietta, Ga.), Doris (m. John Lupton, of White Plains, Md.), and Virginia (m. the Reverend Jack W. Robbins, of Sulphur Springs, Tex.).

Page died in his sleep at his home in Buies Creek and was buried in Greenwood Cemetery, Dunn.

SEE: Paul Green, personal contact, 3 Feb. 1980; *The Horned Frog* (Texas Christian University, 1912); Hubbard F. Page, *Lyrics and Legends of the Cape Fear Country* (1932) and *The Threshold and Other Poems* (1963); J. Winston Pearce, *Campbell College: Big Miracle at Little Buies Creek* (1976); Raleigh *News and Observer*, 23 Aug. 1957; Virginia Page Robbins, personal contact, 9 Feb. 1980; David H. Stewart (Chairman, English Department, Texas A&M University) to the author, 4 Sept. 1979; *Texas Christian University Bulletin*, May 1912; Richard Walser, *North Carolina Poets* (1951).

E. T. MALONE, JR.

Page, Robert Newton *(26 Oct. 1859–3 Oct. 1933)*, businessman and congressman, was born in Wake County at what was then commonly known as Page's, or Page's Station, but which is today the city of Cary. His father, Allison Francis Page, owned extensive timberlands in the area and engaged in lumbering. Although he owned a number of slaves in the 1850s, the elder Page disliked slavery and, like many of the yeoman class in his district, only reluctantly supported the secession movement of 1860–61. Robert's mother, Catherine Frances Raboteau Page, a native of Fayetteville, was well educated by the standards of the day, having attended private female academies in Raleigh and Louisburg.

In 1880 Allison Francis Page and his family, which by this time included five sons and three daughters, moved to Aberdeen, Moore County, where eventually they developed substantial business holdings. Indeed, the Page family pioneered in the economic development of the Sandhills section of the state.

Robert was the second born of the five Page brothers, all of whom achieved success in one capacity or another. Walter Hines (1855–1918), the eldest brother, became a well-known journalist and author but is best remembered as the U.S. ambassador to Great Britain during World War I. Henry (1862–1935) served in the state legislature from 1913 to 1918 and as wartime state food administrator. Junius (1865–1938) became a prominent Aberdeen businessman whose career was largely devoted to the supervision of family-controlled railroad, lumbering, and banking enterprises. Frank (1875–1934), the youngest brother, was the able chairman of the North Carolina Highway Commission in the 1920s and subsequently executive vice-president of the Wachovia Bank and Trust Company.

Robert Page was educated at Cary Academy, which his father helped to found, and at the Bingham Military Academy in Mebane. In his early business career he was associated with several of the family enterprises, being at one time or another general manager of the Page Lumber Company and an official of the Aberdeen and Asheboro Railroad Company. In the late 1890s he moved to the town of Biscoe in Montgomery County and in 1901–3 represented Montgomery in the lower house of the General Assembly.

In 1902, Page, a Democrat, was elected to Congress from the Seventh Congressional District. He served a total of seven terms in Congress (1903–17), where his most important committee assignment was as a member of the powerful Appropriations Committee.

As a congressman, Page supported President Woodrow Wilson's domestic program. He voted, for example, for the Underwood Tariff (1913), the Federal Reserve Act (1913), and the Clayton Anti-Trust Act (1914). But he was among those Democratic congressmen from rural constituencies in the South and West who, led principally by Congressman Claude Kitchen of North Carolina, opposed the president's preparedness program and criticized his neutrality policies. In 1916 Page, among others, sought unsuccessfully to reduce the expenditures provided for in the administration-supported naval appropriations bill. In the same year he complained in a letter to his constituents that Wilson's policy of allowing private bankers to extend loans to belligerent powers had "destroyed the semblance even of neutrality . . . and will probably lead us into the war." Page again found himself at odds with the president when the McLemore Resolution, warning American citizens to refrain from traveling on armed belligerent ships, was before the House. Although he personally favored such a congressional warning, Page, motivated largely by a reluctance to break party ranks and to embarrass Wilson, finally capitulated to the president's wishes by voting to table the resolution.

Page's view on Wilson's preparedness and neutrality policies contrasted sharply with those of his brother Walter Hines Page, the staunchly Anglophile ambassador to Great Britain. More significantly, however, Robert's failure to support the president wholeheartedly during critical times alienated many of the voters of the Seventh Congressional District. Declaring that he could not follow the president's leadership, as seemingly demanded by his constituents, without violating his "self-respect and intellectual integrity," Page announced in March 1916 that he would not seek reelection.

He retired from Congress in 1917 and returned to Biscoe. In May of that year, a month after America's entry into World War I, Governor Thomas W. Bickett appointed him a member of the North Carolina Council of Defense, in which capacity he served throughout the war. Page's last attempt at public office came in 1920, when he challenged Cameron Morrison and O. Max Gardner in the Democratic gubernatorial primary. His platform, which endorsed a highway development program, increased expenditures for education, and expanded public health services, bespoke progressive principles. At the same time, however, he campaigned as the business candidate, stressing economy and efficiency in state government. His advocacy of "Industrial Democracy," or corporate profit-sharing with employees, alienated many businessmen who otherwise might have voted for him. Lacking adequate press support and an effective statewide political organization—and less colorful than Morrison and less affable than Gardner—Page waged a losing battle almost from the start of the campaign. He was eliminated in the first primary, in which he carried only eleven of the state's one hundred counties, and in the runoff Morrison defeated Gardner.

Soon afterwards Page moved to Southern Pines and shortly thereafter to Aberdeen, where from 1927 until his death he was president of the Page Trust Company.

Robert Page was a member of the Methodist Episcopal Church, South, and for thirty-five years served as chairman of the board of trustees of the Methodist Orphanage in Raleigh. He was also a trustee of the North Carolina College of Agriculture and Mechanic Arts and, in 1931–32, president of the North Carolina Banker's Association. On 20 June 1888 he married Flora Shaw of Manly, and the couple had four children: Robert N., Jr., Thaddeus, Richard, and Kate. Page was buried in Old Bethesda Cemetery near Aberdeen.

SEE: Alex M. Arnett, *Claude Kitchen and the Wilson War Policies* (1937); *Biog. Dir. Am. Cong.* (1950); John M. Cooper, Jr., *The Vanity of Power: American Isolationism and the First World War, 1914–1917* (1969); Burton J. Hendrick, *The Life and Letters of Walter H. Page* (1924); *North Carolina Biography*, vol. 6 (1919); Robert Newton Page Papers (Manuscript Department, Duke University Library, Durham); Raleigh *News and Observer*, 4 Oct. 1933.

NATHANIEL F. MAGRUDER

Page, Thaddeus Shaw *(3 Nov. 1890–5 Sept. 1973)*, automobile distributor, congressional secretary, and federal archivist, was born in Aberdeen, the son of Flora Eliza Shaw and Robert Newton Page, who had careers in lumbering, railroading, politics, and banking. An uncle, Walter Hines Page, was a journalist and President Woodrow Wilson's ambassador to Great Britain during World War I. Thad's formal education came from attendance at Fishburne Military School in Waynesboro, Va. (1904–8), and The University of North Carolina (1908–12), where his training included one-half year of law. In Raleigh, on 29 Oct. 1913, he married Martha (Patsy) Macon Hinton. They had two sons: Thaddeus Shaw, Jr. (b. 1917), and John Hinton (1921–41).

As a college baseball star, Thad Page's initial yen was for a career in professional baseball. From this he was dissuaded by his father, then beginning his sixth successive term as a Democratic representative in Congress, who appointed Thad his personal secretary. In this capacity the son served until his father declined to run for renomination in 1916. Young Page then entered the world of business, setting up in Charlotte the Page Motor Company, a wholesale and retail automobile agency (1916–19). Then, for a year (1919–20), he was sales manager of the Winston-Salem automobile agency of W. I. Young and Company. This position he relinquished in order to assist in the management of what turned out to be his father's unsuccessful campaign (1920) for the governorship of North Carolina. Following a year's association with the Sandhills peach growers' cooperative association (1921), Thaddeus Page swung back into the orbit of automobile sales. After seven years (1921–27) as general manager of the H. A. Page Company in Aberdeen he became owner and manager of the Ford Motor Company's outlet, the Hamlet Motor Company, in Hamlet (1927–30).

In 1930 Page left the world of business amid increasing intimations of the Great Depression and with the opportunity of aiding in the management of the successful campaign of Josiah W. Bailey as the Democratic candidate for U.S. senator from North Carolina. Page's efficiency was recognized by his appointment (1931) as Bailey's private secretary. In this position, as he later summarized it, he "handled correspondence, did some research work, and conducted relations with constituents, newspaper correspondents, and Government departments."

The name of Thad Page was sent by President Franklin D. Roosevelt on 8 July 1935 to the Senate to fill the post of administrative secretary in the newly created National Archives of the United States. Unanimously confirmed on 20 July, he began his new duties on 28 August. His experience on Capitol Hill stood him in good stead in his new position in the executive branch. Here he initially (1935–46) conducted relations with the Congress, press, and public; prepared budget justifications; edited publications; and arranged exhibits. Later, as director of the Legislative Service (1947–54), he operated a legislative reference service for the benefit of members, committees, and officials of Congress. Still later, as chief archivist of the Legislative, Judicial, and Diplomatic Records Division (1954–60), he was responsible for the accessioning, repair, description, servicing, and safety of archives received from the Congress, the courts, and the Departments of State and Justice. Special assignments included the secretaryships of the National Archives Council (1936–50), the National Archives Trust Fund Board (1936–50), and the board of trustees of the Franklin D. Roosevelt Library (1952–60). Page had contributed measurably to the principles and procedures that underlay the success of the pioneering National Archives establishment. Age forced his involuntary retirement from federal service in 1960. Unwilling, however, to face inactivity, he formed a connection with the Gem Realty Corporation of Alexandria, Va. in 1961; this he maintained until an eye condition forced him to terminate the association in 1964.

In politics Page was a Democrat, in religion a Presbyterian. He was deacon or elder in each of the following congregations: Presbyterian Church of Hamlet; Church of the Pilgrims, Washington, D.C.; Calvary and Westminster, both in Alexandria, Va. So active was he in the Westminster church that he was affectionately dubbed Mr. Presbyterian. Potomac Presbytery of the Synod of Virginia sent him as a commissioner to the Ninety-eighth General Assembly of the Presbyterian Church of the United States at Charlotte, 24–29 Apr. 1958, and also to the Ninety-ninth General Assembly in Atlanta, Ga., 23–28 Apr. 1959.

He maintained memberships in Kappa Alpha fraternity and the North Carolina State Society of Washington, D.C., as well as in the professional Society of American Archivists. The *American Archivist* journal for April 1950 includes Page's moving memorial to R. D. W. Connor, first archivist of the United States. Like Connor's, Page's capacity for friendship was unlimited. In physical appearance there was no distinguishing mark except a close-cropped mustache; at age fifty-seven he reported his weight as 153 pounds and his height as five feet, ten inches. No portrait is known to exist. He died in Circle Terrace Hospital, Alexandria, Va., and was buried in Bethesda Cemetery near Aberdeen.

SEE: Alexandria, Va., *Gazette*, 6 Sept. 1973; *American Archivist* (April 1950, October 1973); Application for Federal Employment, no date (National Personnel Records Center, St. Louis); *Biog. Dir. Am. Cong.* (1950); Employee Record Card, 1935–60 (Personnel Office, National Archives and Records Service, Washington, D.C.); Daniel L. Grant, *Alumni History of the University of North Carolina* (1924); Mrs. Thad Page, personal contact, February 1974; Thaddeus Shaw Page Papers (Southern Historical Collection, University of North Carolina, Chapel Hill); Raleigh *News and Observer*, 9 July 1935, 30 Oct. 1963; *Register of the National Archives* (1937); *Washington Star-News*, 6 Sept. 1973; *Who's Who in America* (1954–55).

W. NEIL FRANKLIN

Page, Walter Hines *(15 Aug. 1855–21 Dec. 1918)*, editor, author, educational reformer, and ambassador, was born in Wake County in the area that became Cary. He was the eldest of eight children of Allison Francis and Catherine Frances Raboteau Page. His father, an enterprising businessman, later moved to Moore County, where he engaged in lumbering, railroad building, and the development of Pinehurst. Growing up in Cary, Page received his education at a local academy, the Bingham School, Trinity College, and Randolph-Macon College, from which he was graduated in 1875. After training for a career in higher education, which included graduate study among the first group of Fellows of the Johns Hopkins University and summer teaching at The University of North Carolina, Page turned to journalism. Within four years he progressed from the editorship of a daily newspaper in St. Joseph, Mo., to a reporter's job on the *New York World* and finally to starting his own weekly, the *State Chronicle*, in Raleigh in 1883.

With the *State Chronicle* Page established himself as a spokesman for a modified version of Henry Grady's "New South" viewpoint, likewise stressing economic development and sectional reconciliation but laying greatest emphasis on improved education. Though he chafed at the cultural and political torpor of his native state, he suppressed most of his criticism until after he had left North Carolina, when he sent back a series of letters blasting domination by "mummies." Scant earnings in Raleigh and hopes for a brighter career in New York led Page to turn the *State Chronicle* over to Josephus Daniels in 1885. Thereafter, despite frequent visits and much speaking and writing about the South, he remained an expatriate, spending the rest of his life in the North and abroad.

Page rose rapidly in metropolitan journalism, particularly when he entered the magazine field after working again for New York newspapers. In 1891 he became editor of the *Forum*, a monthly nonfiction journal that he made a vital sounding board for current opinion and a pioneer in investigative reporting. After losing control of the *Forum* in 1895, Page moved to Boston, where he worked as a book editor for Houghton, Mifflin, and Company and successively as assistant editor and editor of the *Atlantic Monthly*. With the *Atlantic* he repeated his earlier feat of enlivening a magazine through increased emphasis on public affairs and timely reporting. Page returned to New York in 1899 to work briefly with S. S. McClure before joining Frank N. Doubleday the same year in founding the publishing firm Doubleday, Page, and Company. As a book publisher, he helped the house (now Doubleday and Company) become one of the giants of the industry by attracting such popular authors as Ellen Glasgow, Thomas Dixon, and Booker T. Washington. In 1900 he began his own monthly magazine, *World's Work*, which broke new ground in news coverage and the use of photography. Page remained with the firm until 1913, when he became U.S. ambassador to the Court of St. James's and passed the *World's Work* editorship on to his son Arthur.

Demanding though his journalistic career was, Page maintained extensive outside interests and involvements. An early literary vocation persisted and he published three books, including a pseudonymous novel, *The Southerner* (1909). But success as a writer eluded him in his lifetime and came only with Burton J. Hendrick's posthumous *Life and Letters of Walter Hines Page* (1922–25). Various business ventures, often with members of his family, likewise brought profits but not great wealth. Page's biggest successes outside his profession came in educational reform and amateur politics, both of which involved his native South. Even before his *State Chronicle* editorship, he had singled out education as the South's surest means to overcome poverty and backwardness, and he persisted in preaching that gospel in his magazines and frequent speeches. He gave his most famous speech, "The Rebuilding of Old Commonwealths," at Greensboro in 1896 to kick off the public school campaign led by his friends Edwin A. Alderman and Charles D. McIver. He later played an important part on the Southern Education Board, which directed similar campaigns throughout the South, the General Education Board, and the Hookworm Commission, both of which dispensed massive Rockefeller benefactions. In all, Page established himself between 1896 and 1913 as perhaps America's leading educational propagandist and mediator between the South and the rest of the country. His political involvements sprang in part from his magazine work but more from his concern for sectional reconciliation, particularly when he promoted the presidential candidacy in 1912 of his old acquaintance and fellow southern expatriate, Woodrow Wilson. An original Wilson backer, Page narrowly missed a Cabinet post but received instead the appointment as ambassador to Great Britain.

Though inexperienced in foreign affairs, Page proved a successful peacetime ambassador who promoted Anglo-American cooperation much as he had earlier labored for sectional reconciliation, often operating outside formal diplomatic channels. The high point of his ambassadorship came during the first year, when he helped resolve controversies with the British over Mexico and Panama Canal tolls. A grateful President Wilson set up a special private fund to defray Page's expenses and allow him to remain in London. With the outbreak of World War I his influence eroded because of his passionate championship of the Allies. During the first two years of the war Page directed a fusillade of letters and cables at Wilson urging actions tantamount to intervention on the Allied side. He soon lost the administration's confidence and was sidelined in important dealings, being allowed to remain at his post mainly due to the inconvenience of replacing him.

Page had the satisfaction of witnessing the United States enter World War I in 1917, and he subsequently enjoyed doing what he could to facilitate comradeship in arms. In the spring of 1918 his health failed from hypertension, and he barely survived the voyage homeward that fall after relinquishing his post. Page died at Pinehurst and was buried in the family plot in the Old Bethesda Cemetery near Aberdeen. He was survived by his wife, Willia Alice Wilson Page, whom he had married in 1880; his three sons, Ralph Walter, Arthur Wilson, and Frank Copeland; and his daughter, Katharine Page Loring. Also surviving were his three sisters and four brothers, including former U.S. Representative Robert N. Page and Frank Page, who later served as North Carolina Highway commissioner. Numerous posthumous honors commemorated his work, most notably a tablet in Westminster Abbey and the naming of the school of international relations at Johns Hopkins after him. The first two volumes of Page's *Life and Letters* became the third ranking nonfiction best-seller in 1923.

SEE: John Milton Cooper, Jr., *Walter Hines Page: The Southerner as American* (1977); Ross Gregory, *Walter Hines Page: Ambassador to the Court of St. James's* (1970); Burton J. Hendrick, *The Life and Letters of Walter Hines Page*, 3 vols. (1922–25), and *The Training of an American: The Earlier Life and Letters of Walter Hines Page* (1928); Walter Hines Page Papers (Houghton Library, Harvard University and Randolph-Macon College Library, Ashland, Va.).

JOHN M. COOPER

Paine, Robert *(12 Nov. 1799–19 Oct. 1882)*, Methodist Episcopal clergyman, was born in Person County, the son of James Paine, who was educated at The University of North Carolina and served as clerk of the Person County Court, and his wife Nancy A. Williams. James's father, Robert, and his grandfather, Dr. James Paine, of English ancestry, also lived in what is now Person County. In 1814 the family moved to Giles County, Tenn. Although Robert Paine's formal education was limited, he acquired some knowledge of Latin, Greek, Hebrew, and French. In 1817, after a camp meeting experience, he was converted, and on 1 Oct. 1818 he was admitted to the itinerant ministry at the Tennessee Conference of the Methodist Episcopal church at Nashville. In 1821, at Salem, Tenn., he was ordained a deacon by Bishop William McKendree, the first native American Methodist bishop, and in 1823 was ordained an elder by McKendree at Huntsville, Ala. From 1829 to 1846 Paine was president of La Grange College, in northern Alabama, an institution that in 1855 became Florence Wesleyan University at Florence, Ala. In 1845, at Louisville, Ky., he was one of the "founding fathers" of the Methodist Episcopal Church, South.

In 1846, at the General Conference of the Methodist Episcopal Church, South, at Petersburg, Va., Paine and William Capers (1790–1855) were elected bishops on the second ballot. Paine was ordained the sixteenth bishop of the church on 14 May 1846 at Washington Street Church, Petersburg, and his family moved to Aberdeen, Miss. He was a delegate to or presiding officer at conferences (district, annual, or general) in Alabama, Arkansas, Florida, Georgia, Kentucky, Louisiana, Maryland, Mississippi, Missouri, North Carolina (Charlotte and Fayetteville), South Carolina, Tennessee, Texas, Virginia, and West Virginia; he presided over the Indian Territory Conference and the German Mission Conference; and he helped organize the Colored Methodist Episcopal Church in America at Jackson, Tenn., in 1870. In 1849 he had supervised California as a "foreign" mission. In a letter of request for retirement in 1882 he asserted that he had been a member of every General Conference of the church from 1828 to that date. On the eve of the election of Abraham Lincoln, he conferred with President James Buchanan at the White House about conditions in the South.

Paine and several of his episcopal colleagues of the church in the South were "planter-preachers." By 1844 he owned extensive property in Davidson County, Tenn., and Franklin County, Ala. Even before the 1844 General Conference, at which the church split into the Methodist Episcopal church and the Methodist Episcopal Church, South, his views were those of the "Southern Aristocracy." The family occupied a large mansion built in 1847 by Mrs. Paine's uncle in Aberdeen, Miss. (near Matubba and Jefferson Street), a dwelling owned in 1966 by Thomas Fite Paine, a descendant. Paine himself supervised his 3,100-acre plantation and fifty-two slaves. Usually he arranged his episcopal tours in the winter months to permit direct supervision of his farming operations. In 1860 his plantation yielded 5,000 bushels of corn, 310 bales of cotton, 800 bushels of sweet potatoes, and smaller amounts of wheat, rye, oats, and Irish potatoes. In the war years he seldom left Mississippi. The end of the war found Paine's fortunes diminished and the episcopacy reduced to six men; thus, Paine increased his tours of the Southern conferences.

In 1842 Wesleyan University in Middletown, Conn., conferred on him the degree of doctor of divinity; later the University of Nashville awarded him the master of arts degree. Paine was the author of *Notes of Life* and *Life and Times of William McKendree, Bishop of the Methodist Episcopal Church* (1869), the latter required reading for ministerial candidates for fifty years in the Methodist Episcopal Church, South. In 1823 Paine married Susanna Beck, daughter of John E. Beck and granddaughter of General James Robertson, Tennessee pioneer; they had two sons, John E. Beck and James S. In 1837 Paine married Amanda Shaw; no children were born to this union. In 1839 he married Mary Eliza Millwater and they had seven children: Robert, John Emory, George W., William, Sarah Felix, Ludie, and Mary. The bishop was interred at Aberdeen, Miss.; portraits of him are in standard Methodist histories.

SEE: Emory S. Bucke, ed., *The History of American Methodism*, 3 vols. (1964); W. H. Daniels, *History of Methodism* (1879); *Guide to North Carolina Historical Highway Markers* (1964); Hilary T. Hudson, *The Methodist Armor* (1887); A. B. Hyde, *The Story of Methodism* (1887); James Lee, Naphtali Luccock, and J. M. Dixon, *The Illustrated History of*

Methodism (1900); *Methodist History* (October 1968, October 1970, January, October 1971); *Methodist Magazine* (April 1964); R. H. Rivers, *The Life of Robert Paine, D.D.* (1884).

GRADY L. E. CARROLL

Paine, Robert Treat *(18 Feb. 1812–8 Feb. 1872)*, lawyer, shipper, and politician, was born in Edenton. Little is known of his ancestry but the family was apparently well-to-do. He was graduated from Washington (now Trinity) College in Hartford, Conn., read law privately after the custom of the day, and practiced in his native Chowan County. At times he also operated a shipyard and engaged in shipping.

A Whig in politics, Paine was a member of the House of Commons in the 1838, 1840, 1842, 1844, 1846, and 1848 sessions. In 1847 Whig Governor William A. Graham appointed him colonel of the North Carolina Volunteer Regiment, which saw duty in northern Mexico with General Zachery Taylor. It was in this capacity that Paine gained his greatest notoriety.

In the spring of 1846, when the War with Mexico erupted, North Carolinians enthusiastically rushed to arms. More volunteers came forward than the proposed regiment could possibly enroll. In July 1846 ten companies were drawn from the thirty-two available. Not until November 1846 did the War Department order the state regiment to muster. Then the terms of service were for the duration rather than for twelve months as previously announced. Also, by then political factionalism had crystallized. Whigs, including Governor Graham, had denounced "Mr. Polk's War," while averring to preserve the national honor despite the questionable origin of hostilities. This equivocation, combined with the change in enlistment conditions and the natural diminution of initial enthusiasm, presented North Carolina with a dilemma. When polled, only one company of those that had volunteered six months earlier agreed to enter Federal service. New volunteers were sought but were found to be exceedingly scarce. Not until the late summer of 1847 was the regiment whole and united in Mexico.

Likewise, the question of regimental command was politically sensitive. Robert Treat Paine, a partisan Whig legislator, had been Governor Graham's fourth choice for regimental colonel and was appointed amid bitter protests by North Carolina Democrats. This inauspicious beginning was a harbinger of things to come. The regiment was assigned to garrison duty in northern Mexico and never saw action against the enemy. Inactivity, miserable weather, and an unhealthful climate resulted in boredom and restlessness. Paine, an intransigent disciplinarian, proved to be an egotistical martinet. He employed a wooden horse and other forms of corporal punishment in order to maintain order. A large majority of the regiment's officers and men, in part inspired by political differences, despised Paine. They were joined in this sentiment by Virginia and Mississippi volunteers who were encamped with the North Carolinians.

On the nights of 14 and 15 August 1847, a mutinous disturbance directed towards Colonel Paine occurred. On 14 August privates from the Virginia, North Carolina, and Mississippi regiments invaded the North Carolina camp and partially destroyed the hated wooden horse located near Paine's tent. Spurred by this success, on 15 August several volunteers rocked the tent early in the evening. Later, after tattoo, an unruly crowd of noisy, swearing men entered the North Carolina camp and approached Paine's quarters. Armed with a pistol, the colonel emerged. The frightened crowd dispersed and refused to halt when Paine threatened to fire on them. A voice challenged him to "fire God damn you." He did, killing a North Carolina private, who happened to be an innocent bystander, and wounding another from Virginia. Subsequently, the controversial Paine received the backing of General John Ellis Wool, the ranking officer in the area, and was exonerated of wrongdoing by a court of inquiry; however, his reputation was irrevocably tarnished in the minds of many North Carolinians.

In time Paine's fortunes improved. President Zachery Taylor appointed him to the Mexican Claims Commission in March 1849, and he was an American (Know-Nothing) member of the U.S. House of Representatives from 1855 to 1857. In that capacity he was a moderate champion of Southern rights but voted against reopening the foreign slave trade.

In 1860 Paine, his wife Lavinia, their only child Sarah, and her husband William Thompson moved to the Mills Creek section of Austin County, Tex. There Paine and Thompson cultivated cotton on a large plantation. Paine died in Galveston and was interred in the Brenham Cemetery, Brenham, Tex.

SEE: *Biog. Dir. Am. Cong.* (1961); *Congressional Globe* (Thirty-fourth Congress); Robert T. Paine Papers (Southern Historical Collection, University of North Carolina, Chapel Hill); Max R. Williams, "William A. Graham, North Carolina Whig Party Leader, 1804–1849" (Ph.D. diss., University of North Carolina, 1965).

MAX R. WILLIAMS

Paine, Sidney Small *(26 Feb. 1887–29 Dec. 1972)*, cotton manufacturer, was born in Boston, Mass., the son of Sidney Borden and Mary Adams Small Paine. A 1908 graduate of Brown University, he became an engine oiler at the textile firm of Amoskeag Manufacturing Company in Manchester, N.H. After recovering from poliomyelitis, he determined to enter the ministry and attended Newton Theological Seminary in Newton, Mass. (1909–10) and the University of Chicago (1910–11). Convinced that this choice was not suitable for him, he became a machine operator with the Nonquit Spinning Company in New Bedford, Mass. (1911–13) and then a cotton classer at the Wamsutta Mills in the same place (1913–15). Following a year as night superintendent of a spinning company in Rhode Island, he was superintendent of the Lawton Mills in Connecticut from 1917 to 1921. Between 1921 and 1924 he was a consultant with the Cotton Research Company in Boston. In 1924 he organized and was president of the Textile Development Company with offices in Boston and Greensboro, N.C. Surveying all aspects of textile mill operations, his firm not only made recommendations for management but also supervised their implementation.

Before selling his company in 1934, Paine had been responsible for surveying over a thousand mills in the United States and abroad and in 1928 had also become president and director of the Tabardrey Manufacturing Company, in Haw River, where he remained until 1945. He more than doubled the capacity of Tabardrey and made it into one of the country's leading producers of corduroy. This company in 1945, together with others, merged to form the Cone Mills Corporation with some eighteen plants in the Carolinas and Alabama. Paine was vice-president (1946–51) and director (1946–52). In 1933 he became president and director of the Asheville Cotton Mills, serving until 1947 and also as chairman of the board until 1949. From 1933 to 1946 he was president of the Eno Cotton Mills, Hillsborough, and afterwards, until

1949, also chairman of the board. To the mills in Asheville and Hillsborough he brought greater management efficiency and improved procedures.

As a longtime resident of Greensboro, Paine was active in such local organizations as the Salvation Army, the Juvenile Court Commission, and the City Government Reorganization Survey Commission. Late in life he became a self-taught wood-carver and a teacher of wood carving, especially at the Orthopedic Hospital in Greensboro. To his church, Holy Trinity Episcopal Church, he contributed a carved pulpit, lectern, bishop's chair, litany desk, credence table, communion rail, large organ screen, and wall carving of the Last Supper. For his wood carving he received the O. Henry Award for Artistic Achievement.

Paine's wife, whom he married in 1909, was the former Audrey Lydia Lake. They were the parents of Sidney Lake, Audrey (Mrs. John J. Slattery), and Barbara (Mrs. Wilbur J. Harrell). He died in Greensboro.

SEE: *Greensboro Daily News*, 30 Dec. 1972; *Nat. Cyc. Am. Biog.*, vol. 57 (1977 [portrait]); *Who's Who in the South and Southwest* (1950).

WILLIAM S. POWELL

Palin, John *(d. 1737)*, chief justice, was born in Pasquotank County, perhaps the son of Henry Palin, who lived in the region in 1685. The Palin family, one of the first to settle in northeastern North Carolina, resided in the Pasquotank region of the old county of Albemarle.

Palin served as an attorney in 1713. Then, as regimental captain of the provincial militia, he was ordered by Governor Charles Eden to send volunteers to South Carolina in order to assist one Colonel Hastings in fighting the Indian rebellion of 25 May 1715. Palin was appointed justice of the peace and an assistant to the chief justice of the General Court in the Chowan Precinct of the county of Albemarle on 1 Nov. 1716. From 1718 to 1719 he served as escheat general. In October 1719 he was appointed associate justice of the General Court, with Frederick Jones presiding as chief justice.

Palin was reappointed justice of the peace in 1724 and also served as acting solicitor general. He sat on the Governor's Council of the province from 1725 to 1728, having been appointed by Sir Richard Everard on 17 July 1725, who was under the authority of the Lords Proprietors. Palin served again on the Council in 1730. He returned to the General Court in 1726 as associate justice. In 1729 he presided as a judge of the Court of Chancery. Governor George Burrington appointed him chief justice of the General Court on 27 July 1731 to succeed William Smith, who vacated the position upon returning to England. During the same year, he was nominated treasurer of Pasquotank. Palin served as chief justice until the following year, resigning on 18 Oct. 1732 for reasons of health. He was succeeded in the position by William Little. Palin served one term in the General Assembly after his election in 1734.

Palin was married in 1728 to Sarah Bull, also of Pasquotank, and had two children: Mary (b. 1729) and John (1732–55). He was active in the Church of England, serving as a church warden in 1717 and later as a vestryman of the South-West Parish, Pasquotank Precinct. He died in Pasquotank County, leaving as his estate a small plantation and fourteen Negro slaves.

SEE: J. Bryan Grimes, ed., *Abstract of North Carolina Wills* (1910); J. R. B. Hathaway, ed., *North Carolina Historical and Genealogical Register*, vol. 2 (1900); William L. Saunders, ed., *Colonial Records of North Carolina*, vol. 3 (1886); Charles L. Van Noppen Papers (Manuscript Department, Duke University Library, Durham).

MARK S. CUMMINGS

Palmer, John C. *(ca. 1800–1893)*, silversmith, daguerreotyper, and churchman, was the son of John B. and Sarah Rich Palmer. The Palmers had moved from New Jersey to Rowan County, where they were involved in a number of land transactions. John C. Palmer, one of four children, learned the art of silversmithing from John Y. Savage in Raleigh. It was during his years of apprenticeship that he became an active member of the Edenton Street Methodist Church.

The silversmith was still in Raleigh in 1826, but sometime thereabout he left Raleigh to work for a time in Oxford, Granville County, and in Haywood, Chatham County. On 16 Oct. 1827 Palmer—whose middle name could not be determined—married Maryann (or Mary Anne) Hampton, daughter of the silversmith William Hampton of Salisbury and sister of James Brandon Hampton and Mrs. Philo White (Mary Hampton). Palmer and his brother-in-law, James B. Hampton, operated a jewelers' and watch repair firm in Salisbury known as Hampton and Palmer from 1830 until Hampton's death in 1832. Two years later, on 9 Aug. 1834, Palmer was advertising a branch business in Concord, with the Concord office being operated by a Mr. Bagby of Lynchburg, Va. The two men combined the jewelry and watch repair trades, and Palmer made silver to order.

On 23 Oct. 1840 John Palmer advertised in the *Western Carolinian* (Charlotte) that he planned to sell at auction most of his household furniture and move from Salisbury to Raleigh. By 18 Nov. 1840 he had returned to Raleigh and was operating a jewelry business and watch repair shop in a new building erected by Richard Smith on Fayetteville Street. By 1845 he had added a daguerreotype gallery to his business operation. Two years later, in 1847, Palmer acquired a partner, Walter J. Ramsay. Upon the partnership's dissolution in 1855, Palmer purchased Ramsay's interest and continued the business until he retired in 1889. Palmer was listed in the Raleigh *Register* of 30 Mar. 1859 as one of the directors of the North Carolina Institution for the Education of the Deaf and Dumb, and of the Blind. The craftsman, who had been instrumental in the organization of a Methodist church in Salisbury, resumed his activity in the Edenton Street Methodist Church after returning to Raleigh.

Palmer was married twice, but the death dates of both wives are in question. The frequent occurrence of "Mary Palmer" in county records and newspapers causes confusion. There was in the *Western Carolinian* of 17 Jan. 1840 this notice: "Departed this life at Hillsborough very suddenly on the 9th inst. Mrs. Mary A. Palmer in the 60th year of her age." The name *Mary* was common in the family of Martin Palmer of Hillsborough, and it cannot be determined whether or not this was the first Mrs. John C. Palmer. The *Charlotte Democrat* of 22 Aug. 1871 carried a notice of the death of Mary Ann Hampton Palmer in Raleigh; another source noted that she was "age 60 years 8 months 8 days." The *Carolina Watchman* of 4 Mar. 1875 announced John C. Palmer's marriage on 25 Feb. 1875 to Mrs. Mary Aphia Young of Chatham County. The fact that both wives were named *Mary* adds to the dilemma.

Palmer died in 1893 at the home of Mrs. M. J. Brown on North Person Street. The funeral service was conducted at his church and burial was in the City Cemetery. Palmer's grave, evidently unmarked, is believed to be in the family plot where Charles W. Palmer and his wife

Sarah J. Palmer were also buried. Their relationship to John C. Palmer has not been determined. No survivors are named in Palmer's obituary and apparently there were no surviving children or spouse. In Raleigh during his final years he was affectionately called "Uncle Johnny."

In partnerships with other craftsmen and working alone, John C. Palmer handcrafted much silver flatware of exceptionally fine quality during his long life; many pieces have been identified in the Salisbury and Raleigh areas—all over the state, in fact—and undoubtedly other pieces will eventually come to light.

SEE: *Carolina Watchman* (Salisbury), 23 Aug. 1834, 4 Mar. 1875; *Charlotte Democrat*, 22 Aug. 1871; George Barton Cutten and Mary Reynolds Peacock, *Silversmiths of North Carolina, 1696–1850* (1973); Elizabeth Norris, Elizabeth Reid Murray, and James S. Brawley, personal contact; *North Carolina Standard*, 25 Nov. 1840, 24 Sept. 1845, 24 Nov. 1847; Raleigh *News and Observer*, 17 Nov. 1893; Rowan County Deed Books and Marriage Bonds (Rowan County Courthouse, Salisbury).

MARY REYNOLDS PEACOCK

Palmer, Paul *(d. 1742?)*, General Baptist clergyman and a founding father of Baptists in the upper South, is traditionally said to have been a native of Maryland, to have been baptized in Delaware, ordained in Connecticut, and called to the ministry in New Jersey and Maryland, and to have ended his days in North Carolina. None of this tradition, which owes its existence to Morgan Edwards, the Calvinist Baptist historian, has ever been verified. Edwards, while touring American Baptist churches and gathering historical data on the eve of the American Revolution, did not visit the General Baptist churches in eastern North Carolina that grew out of Palmer's ministry, nor did he interview their clergy, who would have given him more accurate particulars of Palmer's life than he seems to have been able to collect.

Palmer's earliest known appearance is in the records of York County, Va. Shortly after May 1717 he married Martha Hansford Hill, the widow of Samuel Hill, mother of two small children, and keeper of a house of ordinary entertainment on the York road. She died during the first year of the marriage, and by May 1718 her brothers John and Charles Hansford had taken into their care her children by Hill and had assumed control of the ordinary. They also seized some of Palmer's property, including his fiddle and slave. Palmer's creditors followed in the wake of the Hansford brothers and commenced suits to recover debts from him, whereupon he decamped and withdrew into North Carolina.

Sometime before March 1719 Palmer established himself in Perquimans Precinct and married the well-to-do and twice widowed Joanna Taylor Jeffreys Peterson, stepdaughter of Benjamin Laker. It is unknown when Palmer embraced Quaker principles, but from 1719 until 1722 he was affiliated with the Perquimans Monthly Meeting of Friends. In July 1722 he requested a certificate of clearness from the meeting without asking that the certificate be sent to another meeting. Consequently, one supposes that it was in 1722 that Palmer fell under the influence of General Baptist doctrine.

The General Baptists were distinguished from their Calvinist brethren, the Particular Baptists, by their doctrine that held the life and death of Jesus to have been effective generally for the redemption of all of mankind who repented of past sins and believed in him, not merely for a particular few who had been elected for redemption out of the whole mass of fallen humanity. Such doctrines were not embraced casually, and they must have been carefully examined by Palmer during the years he held Quaker views.

Palmer had opportunity to discuss doctrine with General Baptist ministers in Virginia, with North Carolina Baptists who predated him, and with Baptists coming into the province from the northern colonies. Possibly Palmer had access to General Baptist expository works that had belonged to Benjamin Laker or that had been sent to North Carolina after his death by London General Baptists in 1702. The inventory of the Palmer plantation house in Perquimans made after the death of Palmer's daughter included a small library of about thirty books. How many, if any, of these books had originally been Laker's, how many had been sent from London in 1702, or how many had been Palmer's originally is beyond speculation, for the inventory does not report the titles of the books.

If Palmer was not influenced by the Virginia Baptists during the period of his conversion, he was in communion with them shortly thereafter. The General Baptist churches there (located in Prince George, Surry, and Isle of Wight counties) were under the general superintendence of Robert Norden, formerly of Warbleton in Sussex (England) who had been ordained as messenger to Virginia in 1714. (The office of messenger, a sort of diocesan bishop among the General Baptists, was conferred by the imposition of hands of at least two other, but preferably three, messengers; was held for life; and empowered the holder to gather and establish churches, to make annual visitations of the churches, to settle unsettled congregations, to determine orthodoxy of doctrine, to ordain deacons, ministers, and elders, and to strengthen the hands of ministers.) Since Norden's ordination as messenger was specifically to Virginia, it is likely that he exercised no general superintendence over North Carolina. It is probable, however, that with or without the assistance of Richard Jones, elder of the Surry and Isle of Wight churches, he ordained Palmer shortly after his immersion.

Palmer's earliest work was in the four precincts north of Albemarle Sound, where there was already an established Baptist presence. Besides the old group that had been led by Benjamin Laker in Perquimans Precinct, there was a pocket of General Baptists in Chowan, where two of them had sat on the vestry of St. Paul's parish in 1714. Northeastern Pasquotank, which never had been penetrated successfully by the Quakers, proved to be highly receptive to Baptist doctrine, while neighboring Currituck was home in 1718 to a lifelong Baptist physician whose six adult children had not been christened as infants. From his center on Lakers Creek in southwestern Perquimans Precinct, Palmer journeyed into the other three precincts preaching, baptizing, and laying his hands on the newly converted.

In northwestern Chowan near the Chowan Indian town, Palmer found a community with a large population of settlers from Nansemond County, Va., where there was a persistent tradition of religious dissent from the established church. Some had arrived in the area prior to the Tuscarora Indian war in 1711–15. Others came into the area upon the cessation of hostilities. Giles Rainsford, missionary from the Society for the Propagation of the Gospel in Foreign Parts, preached here in 1714 and complained that though vast crowds came to hear him, his auditory expressed little or no devotion in time of divine service. Perhaps in part to correct this situation, and in part to accommodate the growing population, the vestry of St. Paul's parish built a chapel of ease in the area and appointed a reader in 1719. Palmer had his earliest success in this community. It was presumably due to his preaching that Thomas Roundtree, a member of St. Paul's vestry, "turned anabaptist" at the end of 1726, much to the consternation of his fellow vestrymen, who summoned Roundtree to explain the matter. When a second vestryman, John Jordan, likewise joined the General Baptist church at Indian Town Creek in 1728, he asked to be excused from the vestry on account of age, wisely saying nothing about his having joined the General Baptists. Palmer is traditionally said to have "gathered" this church in Chowan Precinct in 1727, but the contemporary account written in 1729 says that he "settled" it—a term that normally means that the congregation already existed but in an unsettled condition.

While working with the Chowan congregation Palmer discovered the length to which malice in a community could go. At the end of January 1728 John Dunning, who lived in the neighborhood of the General Baptist church at Indian Town Creek, put out the report that Palmer had tried to seduce his wife, Rebecca. When the report came to the ears of Palmer, he publicly denounced Mrs. Dunning as a notorious liar and a woman of lewd life who had indecently exposed herself to him in an unsuccessful attempt to seduce him. The Dunnings then sued Palmer for defamation and caused a summons to be left at his house in Perquimans Precinct in his absence. When the General Court sat in July 1728 Palmer, presumably still absent from home, did not appear in court to defend himself. Under the technicality of default by nonappearance, the Dunnings were granted a writ whereby £500 of Palmer's goods could be seized and sold if Palmer did not appear at the October court to answer the Dunnings. Sometime during the next three months Palmer called on the Dunnings, with the result that Dunning voluntarily retracted his accusation in open court at the October session (*Retraxit propria personas*, as the docket has it).

While Palmer worked with the congregation in Chowan, he concurrently visited and preached in northeastern Pasquotank Precinct. On 15 Oct. 1729 William Burgess petitioned the precinct court to register his dwelling as a meeting place for a Baptist congregation gathered in the precinct. At the same time, Palmer, who had signed the petition with Burgess and six others, appeared before the court and subscribed the oaths prescribed for dissenting ministers desiring protection under the Toleration Act of 1689. The inference is that this was a small congregation recently gathered by Palmer in the face of local opposition sufficiently strong to make necessary an appeal to the court for protection under the Toleration Act. The Pasquotank congregation was probably half the size of the one in Chowan.

Confronted with the problem of securing resident ministers for the congregations, Palmer turned his thoughts to the Rhode Island General Baptists of whose work and reputation he had learned. The Chowan congregation wrote the Reverend John Comer, the Calvinist pastor of a General Baptist church in Newport at the end of summer 1729; twelve men of the congregation signed the letter, presumably as guarantors for a salary to be subscribed in the event a minister could be found for them. Comer received the letter on 27 Sept. 1729. On 2 November Comer was visited by Constant Devotion, presumably a kinsman of the two Massachusetts Baptist clergymen, Ebenezer and John Devotion. A few days later, on 7 Nov. 1729, Comer made his reply to the Chowan church. His diary entries reveal neither the topic of his conversation with Constant Devotion nor the nature of his reply to the Chowan church. Since, however, Devotion shortly afterwards went to North Carolina where he is found in Albemarle County General Baptist centers in company with Palmer, and subsequently in General Baptist centers in the Roanoke and Tar River valleys in company with William Surginer, one takes it that Comer discussed with Devotion the work in North Carolina at the time of his visit in November 1729 and that Devotion went to the colony (in whatever capacity—private church member, exhorter, or minister) either on account of, or with knowledge of, that work. In December 1729 Comer, who was gathering information on American Baptists, opened a correspondence directly with Palmer. By a happy circumstance the yearly meeting of the New England General Baptists had met at Newport earlier in 1729; thirty-two elders, deacons, and representatives of fourteen churches in Rhode Island, Massachusetts, Connecticut, and New York had attended. Comer apparently described the yearly meeting to Palmer with the result that Palmer, accustomed only to the small Virginia–North Carolina yearly meeting, was invigorated and inspired by the account.

Nothing is known of Palmer's education. He wrote a legible hand casually and well-formed hand carefully. He had been taught surveying and held an appointment as surveyor for Albemarle County under deputation of the provincial surveyor general. It is doubtful, however, that Palmer was educated to the standard of many of the northern Baptist clergy. Nonetheless, he prepared for publication a manuscript entitled "Christ the Predestinated and Elected" and sent it to Comer early in 1730. He then decided to make a personal tour of the northern churches and by the autumn of that year set sail for Boston. Palmer seems to have visited the churches in Massachusetts and Connecticut first. Then, at the beginning of October, he visited and preached in Rhode Island, and at the end of the month he was at Piscataqua, N.J. At the latter place he joined Elder John Drake in ordaining to the ministry a young man named Henry Lovell who had already been active as a preaching brother. Shortly afterwards, when charges were made that Lovell, prior to his conversion, had been a runaway indentured servant who had taken up life with another man's wife (presumably meaning that he had married a divorced woman whose husband was still alive), Palmer, Comer, Drake, Elder Daniel Wightman, and all who had endorsed Lovell, or had aided in his ordination, fell under harsh criticism from the churches in West New Jersey for having failed to perform the necessary scrutiny of the candidate's life. Palmer completed his tour among the General Baptists by following an overland route that would have taken him from New Jersey to New York, Pennsylvania, Maryland, and Virginia. He presumably arrived home again during the year 1731, but the absence of any reference to Palmer in surviving North Carolina records for the whole of the year 1731 and the first eleven months of 1732 leaves the date of his return to the province in question.

During the year 1733 Palmer lived in his usual quiet way as a planter, minister, and surveyor in Albemarle County. The year 1734, however, opened the last, remarkable phase of the clergyman's life. In the summer of that year Palmer and his wife executed a joint deed of gift settling their real and personal property on their two children, Martha Ann and Samuel, aged about fourteen and twelve respectively. This preparatory measure left Palmer free to face the considerable personal dangers of a much enlarged ministry that is known to have taken him into Beaufort, Hyde, Craven, Onslow, and New Hanover precincts in Bath County, and into South Carolina and Maryland. It is singular that he restricted his ministry to the sounds, rivers, and creeks of the outer coastal plain of North Carolina at the very time that the inner coastal plain was being settled, and settled to a large degree from those General Baptist centers served by his friend Richard Jones in Virginia—Surry and Isle of Wight counties. It is almost as if a division of labor had been agreed upon at the 1734 yearly meeting of Virginia and North Carolina churches, with Palmer committing himself to a ministry on the seaboard while leaving the Roanoke and Tar River basin frontier to another or to others or to God. In April 1734 Constant Devotion was in company with Palmer, and one is much struck by the fact that it is shortly thereafter that Devotion is to be found with William Surginer in the Roanoke River valley on the eve of the blossoming of General Baptist churches in that area.

At the end of 1734 the General Baptists in South Carolina invited Palmer to go to Charleston to preach to them at the yearly meeting of South Carolina Baptists to be held on 8–9 Feb. 1735. As a very small minority who shared an endowed meetinghouse with a Calvinist majority, the General Baptists in Charleston had little opportunity to hear any other than Calvinist doctrine—hence their invitation to Palmer. They sent the invitation with neither the knowledge nor the consent of the Calvinist majority. As a result, when Palmer arrived in Charleston he found himself silenced by a pulpit filled both days by unsympathetic Calvinists who refused to yield to him. Angered by this treatment, the General Baptist minority (from whose families had come much of the endowment for the church in Charleston) went into consultation with Palmer. He described Rhode Island to them as "having Great plenty of ministering brethren," and at his suggestion, they wrote to the elders, deacons, and brethren in Newport asking assistance in obtaining a pastor for their congregation. No pastor was furnished from Rhode Island, however, and the congregation was settled in 1736 by Elder Robert Ingram, who allied them with the General Assembly of General Baptists in London. In 1739 the Assembly ordained Henry Heywood messenger to South Carolina. It is possible that Palmer visited Charleston again before his death, meeting Ingram or Heywood or both.

In the autumn of 1735 Palmer sailed to Maryland to console, instruct, and advise the General Baptists in that province. Stopping at Indian River in August, he attended the court for Somerset County, took the oaths required of a dissenting minister, and registered six places in the county (the easternmost ones now in Sussex County, Del.) as sites of Baptist meetings. From here he seems to have sailed to Wilmington, Del., then crossed overland by the post road to another General Baptist center that had been established at Chestnut Ridge, northwest of Baltimore. This community is traditionally said to have been served sometime prior to Palmer's advent by George Eaglesfield. This presumably would have been prior to 1725, in which year Eaglesfield left Philadelphia for ordination as pastor to the congregation at Middletown, N.J. Eaglesfield, as a mere licensed preacher rather than an ordained minister, had been unable to perform the ceremony of baptism and laying on of hands, and his converts had had to be sent to Philadelphia for administration of those ordinances, as the Baptists term them (rather than sacraments). Palmer did not labor under those difficulties, and he baptized converts at Chestnut Ridge. By October 1735 he was home again in Perquimans Precinct, where he stayed for the rest of the year.

The remaining four years of Palmer's life were spent in a continuing circuit through the precincts of Bath County and up into Maryland—preaching, baptizing and laying on hands, gathering congregations, ordaining exhorters and ministers, and exercising a general supervision over all. In fact, his ministry took on the characteristics of the office of messenger. He had purchased a tract of land on Town Creek in New Hanover Precinct (now Brunswick County) before the end of 1734. He is known from contemporary records to have gathered a congregation from Broad Creek, Flea Point, and Greens Creek in present Pamlico County, another from Goose Creek in Beaufort and Pamlico counties, one from Pungo River in Beaufort and Hyde counties, and yet another from Swift Creek in present Pitt and northern Craven counties. On the south side of Neuse River he preached and baptized at Hancock Creek and in the area of Brice Creek; on the upper reaches of the river he made conversions among the settlers of Contentnea Creek. In Onslow County he gathered a church on New River, some families from Chowan church having moved to that place. A generation after his death a place where he had baptized in Trent River near Deep Gully (in present Jones County) was still known variously as "Paul Palmer's Landing" and "Paul Palmer's Dipping Hole."

Early in 1738 Palmer prepared to take his ministry into the two principal towns of New Bern and Edenton. In March he purchased Lot 112 in the former town, and in April he purchased Lots 161 and 162 in the latter. Simultaneously in April 1738 Palmer contracted with John Pratt, millwright and house carpenter, to build for him in Edenton and at his plantation in Perquimans Precinct, two identical, small, shingle-roofed, wooden-chimneyed, one-and-a-half-story houses measuring fifteen by twenty feet. It is probable that Palmer contracted for a similar structure in New Bern, and it is likely he intended these to be General Baptist centers, serving both as meeting place and as accommodation for traveling ministers. (One notices that Richard Bevan of Hyde County bequeathed in 1744 his dwelling house and plantation for the use of traveling Baptist ministers in that county.)

Late in 1738 Palmer sought an effective means of countering opposition to his ministry in the southeastern precincts by securing so broad a protection under the Toleration Act as would render unnecessary an appeal to every local court with jurisdiction over the area in which he preached. The result was a license (October 1738) allowing him to preach as a dissenting minister in any precinct in the province. This step might have been in specific response to the reaction of antagonistic magistrates in Craven Precinct to his having gathered his converts there into a church, for by May 1739 his critics in Craven were complaining that an exhorter and a minister whom Palmer had ordained (Francis Ayres and William Fulsher) were creating public disturbances by their "misbehaving speeches." Subsequently Palmer's churches in that area, having been repulsed by the court for the counties of Beaufort and Hyde and repelled by the Craven County Court when attempting to register their meeting places, took their cue from Palmer's 1738 maneuver by successfully appealing directly to Chief Justice Montgomery for protection under the Toleration Act.

In the autumn of 1739, Palmer was obliged to return from his work in the southeastern precincts to his home in Perquimans. His son, Samuel, died on 24 Nov. 1739, very nearly on his eighteenth birthday. Palmer preached his burial sermon upon the text in *Proverbs*, "I love them that love; and those that seek me early shall find me."

In the spring of the following year, Palmer sailed for the last time up the Atlantic coast of Maryland to Indian River. His ministry there had come so near to fruition that the church members planned to build a meetinghouse on a half-acre of land at the Healing Spring on the west side of Swann Gut. On 1 May 1740 Palmer addressed a letter to the clerk of court for Somerset County, Md., asking that this place and a private dwelling be registered as places of public worship for his congregations there. From Indian River, Palmer went to the General Baptist congregation at Chestnut Ridge, northwest of Baltimore. On this occasion his preaching and baptizing seems to have aroused the anger of a local magistrate. On 29 Jan. 1742 Palmer was obliged by William Young, a justice of the peace, to appear at the March term of the Baltimore County Court to answer such allegations as should be made against him by the justice. Two of his converts, William Talbot and John Sumner, acted as sureties for Palmer's appearance. When the case was called in court, however, neither Palmer nor his sureties appeared, and the six witnesses against him were discharged. Palmer appears at some point to have informed Henry Lovell (the young man whose ordination in 1730 by Palmer and others had caused such an outcry in the Jersies) of the work at Chestnut Ridge and to have interested him in undertaking the pastoral care of the congregation there. In view of the reaction by the civil authorities to Palmer's ministry in the county, Lovell, who organized the church under a formal constitution in July 1742, appealed (with success) to the Baltimore County Court at its August 1742 term for protection under the Toleration Act.

No more is heard of Palmer after his 1740–42 trip to Maryland. His wife purchased land in her own name in June 1743 so she was publicly recognized as a feme sole, rather than feme covert, by that date. One assumes, therefore, that Palmer died in Maryland in 1742 or immediately upon his departure from that place. No clear statement of the fact of his death, however, has been found.

Palmer's reputation has swung from one extreme to the other. His journal was probably contained in the "Several old Pockett Books" inventoried with the other contents of his house following the death of his daughter. Had those little memorandum books survived, we might be far better able to assess with accuracy the effect of Palmer's life. As it is, only a few fragments, some legal proceedings, and a smattering of contemporary remarks remain to help his successors understand him. Morgan Edwards, the Calvinist Baptist historian writing in 1772–73, described Palmer as the father of the General Baptists in North Carolina (whom he viewed as wrongheaded, of no spiritual account, and stumbling blocks in the paths of divine grace). Wittingly or unwittingly Edwards played the role of blackguard to Palmer's posthumous reputation. "He was not so happy," says Edwards in the voice of Mrs. Candor, "as to leave a good character behind him."

Writing in 1930, George W. Paschal redeemed Palmer's reputation, pointing out the enormous debt that all Baptists in the state owe to him. In view of the fact that Palmer took up and continued the work of others, that his ministry in North Carolina was restricted to the outer coastal plain, and that the work of the General Baptists in the inner coastal plain was separate from his ministry, it may be inexact to call him the father of General Baptists in the state. On the other hand, in view of the facts that the General Baptist churches founded independently of Palmer in the inner coastal plain were all destroyed by the particular form of Calvinism that swept into that area during the Great Awakening, and that most of Palmer's congregations in the outer coastal plain were perseveringly faithful to the doctrine of general provision taught by Palmer, it must be conceded that the Free Will Baptist churches (as the General Baptists came to be called) owe a debt both of doctrine and survivorship to the churches and clergy raised up under Palmer.

Of Palmer's family, little is known with certainty. His son, Samuel, had died in 1739 at age eighteen, and his widow, Joanna, died in 1747 at age sixty-one. His daughter, Martha Ann, married Walter Kippin (d. 1754), a New York merchant in the coastal trade who settled in Edenton in 1746; by him she had a son named Samuel born in 1749 and a daughter named Joanna (familiarly called Ann and Nancy) born in February 1751. Martha Ann Palmer Kippin died early in 1759 leaving the two children in possession of a very handsome estate. By John Hodgson (d. 1774), Palmer's granddaughter Joanna Kippin had in 1774 two daughters, Elizabeth (named for Hodgson's mother) and Sarah (named for his aunt, Sarah Eelbeck). By 15 July 1775 she had become the second wife of Edward Benbury of Edenton. Samuel Kippin sold part of his Perquimans County lands in 1772, and nothing more is heard of him thereafter.

Of others of the Palmer family in the province, it is possible that Nathaniel Palmer who died in Perquimans Precinct early in 1728 (and of whose estate Paul Palmer was administrator) was a brother or other near kinsman. The second Samuel Palmer of Perquimans Precinct who was licensed to build a house of ordinary entertainment on the courthouse lot in October 1739 and who died on 4 Dec. 1739, ten days after the death of Paul Palmer's son Samuel, might have been a kinsman as well.

SEE: Archival sources: From the Hall of Records, Annapolis, Md., the proceedings of the Somerset County court at August term, 1735, and March term 1739/40, and the proceedings of the Baltimore County court at March term, 1741/41; from the North Carolina State Archives, Raleigh, dockets, civil action papers, criminal action papers, 1719–42, of the General Court in the Colonial Court Records, and court minutes, deeds, wills, and estate records from Perquimans, Pasquotank, and Chowan counties; and from the Virginia State Archives, Richmond, York County Court Orders and Wills, 1716–20, Parts I and II; C. Edwin Barrows, ed., "Diary of John Comer," vol. 8, *Collections of the Rhode Island Historical Society* (1893); J. R. B. Hathaway, ed., *North Carolina Historical and Genealogical Register*, vol. 3 (July 1903); George W. Paschal, *History of North Carolina Baptists, 1663–1805* (1930).

GEORGE STEVENSON

Palmer, Robert *(1724–ca. 1790)*, was a native of Scotland who entered royal service as a purser in England in 1750. In June 1753 he received a royal commission under the sign manual as surveyor general of North Carolina, and on 8 November he took his oaths of office in the colony and assumed the post of collector of the Port of Bath as well. With such influential positions, Palmer began a rapid rise within North Carolina politics and society. He was named justice for the New Bern district of the supreme court in March 1756 and justice of the peace for Beaufort County in 1760. In April 1762 he was elected to the General Assembly from Bath, and on 27 Aug. 1764 he took his seat on the royal Council of the province, having been earlier nominated by Governor Arthur Dobbs.

In July 1764 Palmer purchased a fine house in Bath from the Lockhart family for £1,012. Edmund Fanning would later say it was one of the best-furnished houses in North Carolina. Noted for its massive chimneys, the dwelling stands today.

Palmer served ably on the Council under William Tryon's administration, and the governor looked upon him as a trusted adviser. He appointed Palmer a commissioner for drawing the Cherokee boundary agreement in May 1767 and made him adjutant with the rank of lieutenant general for the first Regulator expedition in 1768. At the close of 1770 Tryon named him provincial secretary and crown clerk; Palmer, in turn, designated his only son William to be his deputy.

When the backcountry erupted into renewed Regulator conflict early in 1771, Palmer, as colonel of the Beaufort militia, was ordered to march. Tryon appointed him an aide de camp, and Palmer participated in the Battle of Alamance on 16 May 1771. The day after the battle he was one of those who urged Tryon to issue a general pardon to all Regulators who laid down their arms and took oaths of allegiance.

Late in 1771 Palmer returned to England in poor health, claiming that he needed the air of the mother country to recover. He resigned his North Carolina offices over to his son. During the Revolutionary War Palmer never heard from his son, who had sworn an oath to support the Patriot cause. In July 1785 Palmer received word that William was dead, and the following month he returned to North Carolina. In fact, his son was not dead but in extremely poor health, having been driven to drink (as Palmer told the Loyalist Claims Commission) by the harassment of North Carolina rebels who thought him too loyal to the Crown. Within a few months William was dead, and all of the Palmer property in North Carolina was confiscated. Robert returned to England.

Later in England, when making claims for his losses, Palmer valued his North Carolina holdings at £10,000 sterling. He had owned fifty slaves and valued the surveyor generalship at £600 sterling per annum and the collectorship of Bath at £200. In 1788 the Loyalist Claims Commission made a settlement on him of £762 plus £300 per annum for his lifetime.

SEE: English Records, Loyalist Claims (North Carolina State Archives, Raleigh); William L. Saunders, ed., *Colonial Records of North Carolina*, vols. 5–9 (1887–90).

WILLIAM S. PRICE, JR.

Papathakes, George. *See* **Patterson, George.**

Paris, John *(1 Sept. 1809–6 Oct. 1883)*, Methodist Protestant clergyman, Confederate chaplain, and author, was born in that part of Orange County that became Alamance in 1849, the son of Henry and Mary Johnston Paris. There appears to be no record of his education, but in 1842 at the annual conference he received deacon's orders in the Methodist Protestant church in North Carolina. At some unknown time he apparently was awarded the honorary doctor of divinity degree, as in later life he was referred to as Dr. Paris.

Under the direction of the president of the conference, he was assigned to the Roanoke Circuit early in 1843, but in November he became an associate pastor in the Guilford Circuit. In 1846, at his own request, he was left without an appointment, when he probably engaged in mission work or in writing. He was a delegate to the General Conference of the church in 1846, and in 1849 he published a *History of the Methodist Protestant Church: Giving a General View of the Causes and Events that Led to the Organization of that Church.* In 1850 he was again a delegate to the General Conference and in 1852 he moved to Virginia. In the latter year he brought out his second book, *Baptism, Its Mode, Its Design and Its Subjects, considered as an ordinance of the Church of Christ*, in Baltimore. Apparently a third book, of which no copy may have survived, was published; in 1860 B. W. Wellons, editor of the *Christian Sun*, was the author of *The Christians, South, Not Unitarians in Sentiment: A Reply to Rev. John Paris' book, Entitled "Unitarianism Exposed, As It Exists In the Christian Church, &c."*

On 11 July 1862 Paris was commissioned chaplain of the Fifty-fourth Regiment of North Carolina Troops, perhaps one of the oldest chaplains in Confederate service. He was considered by the men with whom he served, however, to be one of the most efficient chaplains. Paris participated in military action to a greater extent than was expected of chaplains and he suffered the same hardships as the men. In addition, it was reported that he "walked hundreds and hundreds of miles to preach to the soldiers."

In February 1864, twenty-two Confederate deserters were hanged at a hastily constructed gallows at the brigade's encampment on the south side of the Neuse River about a mile from Kinston. Paris's diary for 5 February records that men named Jones and Haskett were sentenced by a court martial to be hanged, having been "found in the enemy's lines in arms against us." After visiting them in their confinement, the chaplain wrote: "They were the most hardened and unfeeling men I ever encountered and met their fate with apparent indifference." On the eleventh he visited five more convicted deserters whom he found "in Great distress apparently." On the following day in the prison he baptized John L. Stanley and William Irving, shortly before they were taken to the gallows, while five others "made confession of penitence at the gallows." On Sunday, 14 February, Paris visited each of the thirteen men who were to be hanged the following day. He also visited two others, newly convicted, and heard their sentences read to them. "They insisted they should not be hanged as they had been persuaded to do so [that is, join the enemy]." On the morning of the fifteenth he baptized eight of the prisoners just before they were taken to the gallows.

The group of thirteen revealed the names of the Union men who had "induced" them to desert, and Paris turned a list of them in to the commanding general's headquarters. His diary records that the condemned men were then "arranged on the scaffold and all were ushered into Eternity at a given signal." It was further noted that some women and children, presumably relatives, were present at the hanging and that they were deeply moved by the scene.

On Monday morning, 22 February, the chaplain met and prayed with the two most recently convicted men—one named Kellam, who "professed to be prepared for death," and another named Hill, who was "calm and said he was not afraid to die." Some of these men, all of whom were recently Confederate soldiers, had joined the North Carolina Union Volunteers but were captured on 1 February in a Confederate drive on enemy-held New Bern. After these several days of hangings, Paris preached a long and impassioned sermon at the regimental encampment site on the south side of the Neuse River about a mile from Kinston, taking as his text verses 3–5, chapter 27, of the gospel according to St. Matthew, concerning Judas's betrayal of Christ for money. While he dramatically explained that the deserters had been lured by Union soldiers from their sworn allegiance for a few pieces of silver, he also made a strong appeal for renewed patriotism and a drive to Confederate victory. The men who witnessed the hanging and heard the sermon probably never forgot it. The sermon apparently was delivered extemporaneously, as Paris spent the next two days writing it down "by request" and then revising it. Soon afterwards it was printed in Greensboro and widely distributed. It bore the title *A Sermon: Preached Before Brig.-Gen. Hoke's Brigade, At Kinston, N.C., on the 28th of February, 1864, By Rev. John Paris, Chaplain Fifty-Fourth Regiment N.C. Troops, Upon the Death of Twenty Two Men, Who Had Been Executed in the Presence of the Brigade for the Crime of Desertion*. In the North there was criticism of Union leaders for permitting Confederate deserters to serve in Federal units, thereby risking capture and such a fate as this.

After the war Paris reestablished his North Carolina affiliations and became pastor of Methodist Protestant churches in the Albemarle Circuit of the state. He was a delegate to the General Conferences of 1866, 1870, 1874, 1877, and 1879; in the latter year he was president. In 1881 the needs of the church in La Grange were such that he served it as well as his regular churches a hundred miles distant. Finally, during the last year of his life, he served only the La Grange Mission.

While a chaplain Paris kept a detailed diary and from its entries the sketch of the Fifty-fourth Regiment was largely compiled for publication in Walter Clark's five-volume history of North Carolina troops. His diary and other unpublished writings are in the Southern Historical Collection at The University of North Carolina. The diary is noteworthy for its record of casualties. Paris remained a loyal Confederate for the rest of his days. To the periodical, *Our Living and Our Dead*, he contributed a fourteen-part "Soldier's History of the War." The first installment was dated from Enfield, 1868, but it appeared in the issues of the magazine between December 1874 and March 1876. To the *Southern Historical Monthly* in January and February 1876, he also contributed a two-part article, "Causes Which Produced the War." Another book by him, *The Methodist Protestant Manual: A Concise Treatise Upon the Principles of the Government of the Methodist Protestant Church*, was published in Baltimore in 1878.

Paris's first wife was a Miss Bellamy of Edgecombe County who died shortly after their marriage. On 19 Dec. 1849 he married Maria Yancey of Mecklenburg County, Va., and they became the parents of eight children. On 5 Mar. 1864 he noted that he had just received the first letters from two of his children, Mary Ellen and John. Suffering a chronic illness in his last years, he nevertheless continued his work until shortly before his death when he went to Buffalo Springs, a health resort in Virginia. He died there in the family of his father-in-law and was buried at La Grange, Lenoir County, N.C.

SEE: Richard Bardolph, "Confederate Dilemma: North Carolina and the Deserter Problem, Part II," *North Carolina Historical Review* 66 (April 1989); John G. Barrett, *The Civil War in North Carolina* (1963); J. Elwood Carroll, *History of the North Carolina Annual Conference of the Methodist Protestant Church* (1939); *Civil War Times Illustrated* 19 (August 1980); Walter Clark, ed., *Histories of the Several Regiments and Battalions from North Carolina*, vols. 3–4 (1901 [portrait]); *Confederate Veteran* 11 (April 1903); *Minutes of the Proceedings of the 58th Session of the North Carolina Annual Conference of the Methodist Protestant Church* (1884); John Paris Papers (Southern Historical Collection, University of North Carolina, Chapel Hill); Wilmington *Star*, 28 Apr. 1864.

WILLIAM S. POWELL

Park, John Asley *(19 Nov. 1885–15 Mar. 1956)*, journalist, was born in Raleigh, the son of Benjamin Franklin and Frances Beavers Park. His ancestral lines extended from Scotland and Ireland on his father's side, and from Great Britain and France on his mother's. John Quincy Adams was a prominent American of his mother's family. With early schooling in Raleigh, Park entered the North Carolina State College of Agriculture and Engineering (now North Carolina State University) and was graduated in 1905 at age nineteen with a degree in mechanical engineering.

His professional career began in 1906, when he was a teller in a Raleigh bank; he soon left to become manager of the Carolina Machine and Garage Company. Park was a pioneer automobile owner, and in 1908 he drove the first automobile from Raleigh to Morehead City, a trip of less than 150 miles that took two days and one night and required the building of several temporary bridges. This interest gave him the opportunity to help write the first vehicle laws for North Carolina, and forty years later he served by gubernatorial appointment on the state's Advisory Committee on Highway Safety.

Newspapers were the major interest of Park's life, however. He bought the *Raleigh Times*, an afternoon daily, in 1911 and was its editor and publisher until that paper was sold to the *News and Observer* forty-four years later (1955). Over the years he also owned papers in Fayetteville, New Bern, and Greenville and was the owner and publisher of *Turner's Almanac*.

If John Park had one hobby, it was travel. When just out of college, he signed on a cattle boat to Europe; his two companions were O. Max Gardner, later governor of North Carolina, and Robert R. Reynolds, later U.S. senator. Subsequent travel took him to Europe five times; to Central America, three times; to South America, twice; as well as to Alaska, Greenland, Newfoundland, North Africa, Labrador, and most of the continental United States. Incident to his journeys, he was an early passenger (1949) on small jets and was a guest of the government on the speedy trial run of the *Leviathan* from Boston to Cuba. The readers of his newspaper were treated to interesting reports on all of those trips.

A by-product of one visit to Germany (1947) was a project that attracted international attention. After a twelve-year-old girl asked Park for "something to read," he returned home and promoted the collection of books for shipment abroad. More than five million books and magazines were sent through his book aid program, for which he had the continuous cooperation of General Lucius D. Clay and Captain Eddie Rickenbacker.

The editorial page of the *Raleigh Times* was described as "expressing conservative political and economic views," but those views did not limit his crusades on behalf of such causes as the enforcement of the prohibition laws, his attacks on professional gambling and petty racketeering, and his advocacy of the council-manager form of government for Raleigh. He was a strong believer in the national defense against ideologies conflicting with those of the United States. A classic line appeared in one of his editorials in the early days of the Korean War: "I believe in peace at any price—even to fighting for it."

John Park was closely allied with the Rotary Club of Raleigh (charter member, president, and district governor), North Carolina Press Association, Southern Newspaper Publishers' Association, Carolina-Virginia Highway Association, chamber of commerce, community chest, YMCA, Civic Music Association, Boy Scout Council, Executives' Club, Wake County Sunday School Association, Sons of Confederate Veterans, and Sons of the American Revolution. In all of these organizations he held high offices and served on important committees. He was for many years chairman of the Wake County Board of Education, and during World War I he was chairman of War Savings for Wake County. In the same period (1917–18) he was a member of the Selective Service Board and a representative of the Government Intelligence Service. For a number of years, he was a member of the board of trustees of North Carolina State College.

Park was a lifelong Methodist. His first affiliation was with the Edenton Street Methodist Church, which he served as superintendent of the Sunday school and as a member of the Board of Stewards. In later years, he joined the Hayes-Barton Methodist Church, where he became a trustee and onetime chairman of the Board of Stewards.

He married, on 23 Dec. 1909, Lily Helen Pair of Kenly, and they had four children: John A., Jr., Albert P., Ben F., and Elizabeth (Mrs. Mark G. Lynch). Park died at age seventy at his home in Raleigh. Funeral services were held at the Hayes-Barton Methodist Church, and interment followed in Oakwood Cemetery.

John Park was an indefatigable worker, often at his desk before sunrise and remaining until after 5:00 P.M. Most of his weekday evenings were spent at community meetings. He was a respected citizen of Raleigh and elsewhere, enjoying a wide reputation through his multiple contacts in Rotary and his association with journalists around the state.

SEE: *Asheville Citizen*, 19 Mar. 1956; Ben F. Park, Raleigh (private paper); Raleigh *News and Observer*, 24 Jan. 1942, 16, 25, 28 Mar. 1956.

C. SYLVESTER GREEN

Parker, Francis Marion *(21 Sept. 1827–18 Jan. 1905)*, Confederate officer, was one of nine children of Theophilus Parker (1775–1849), an Edgecombe County merchant, planter, and president of the Bank of Tarboro, and Mary Irwin Toole Parker (1787–1858). He was a descendant of John Haywood, surveyor for Lord Granville.

Parker was educated at the Lovejoy Academy in Raleigh, the Caldwell Institute, and a private school in Valle Crucis. On 17 Dec. 1851 he married Sally Tartt Philips (22 Mar. 1835–22 Sept. 1906), daughter of Dr. James J. Philips, a prominent Edgecombe County physician, and Harriet Burt Philips. Following his marriage, Parker began running a plantation in the Glenview Community in Halifax County, between Enfield and Whitakers. Through his association with his kinsman, Governor Henry Toole Clark, and with Colonel Michael Hoke, Parker became active in the Democratic party.

In the fall of 1859, in the aftermath of the John Brown Raid, Parker helped to organize a local military company, the Enfield Blues, later known (following the Battle of Bethel) as the Bethel Regiment. The company was enrolled for active duty in April 1861, after President Abraham Lincoln called on North Carolina to provide troops to coerce the seceded states; it eventually became Company I, First North Carolina Regiment. Parker enlisted on 19 April and was appointed second lieutenant; on 1 September he was promoted to the rank of captain. Six weeks later, he was appointed colonel of the newly organized Thirtieth North Carolina Regiment of Volunteers.

On 31 May 1862 the Thirtieth Regiment fought in the Battle of Seven Pines and afterwards in the Seven Days' Battle around Richmond. Parker participated in the Battle of South Mountain and, on 17 Sept. 1862, distinguished himself in the Battle of Bloody Lane at Sharpsburg, where he was temporarily disabled by a minié ball in his head.

Parker saw duty in the Battle of Fredericksburg, and at Chancellorsville he merited recognition for his dramatic advance on the field and capture of a large number of prisoners. The Thirtieth Regiment accompanied General Robert E. Lee in the invasion of Pennsylvania and advanced farther northwards than any other Confederate regiment; it occupied the Federal barracks at Carlisle. Parker was again wounded in the Battle of Gettysburg but was able to participate in the Battle of the Wilderness and in the charge of Ramseur's Brigade at Spottsylvania, where he received a wound that disqualified him from further active service. He was placed in command of the Confederate post in Raleigh and remained there until the end of the war.

One of his superior officers referred to Parker as "the courteous and refined colonel of the regiment . . . a brave, cool, and excellent officer . . . ever observant of his duties to the cause and to his command. He was severely wounded in nearly every important engagement in which he participated."

After the war Parker, whose health had been greatly affected by his wounds on the battlefield, operated his plantation and reared nine children: Mary (Mrs. John Battle; 1853–1935), James Philips (1855–1942), Theophilus (1857–1920), Harriet Burt (Mrs. Peter A. Spruill; 1860–1926), Haywood (1864–1945), Francis Marion, Jr. (1867–1914), Sally Philips (1870–1964), Kate Drane (1873–1962), and Dr. Frederick Marshall (1875–1939).

Colonel Parker was named a brigadier general of the North Carolina Division of the United Confederate Veterans. The Frank M. Parker Chapter, United Daughters of the Confederacy (UDC), No. 1096, in Enfield, chartered on 24 Aug. 1907, was named in honor of the area's most distinguished Confederate soldier. His daughters, Sally and Kate, were charter members of the UDC chapter. On the day following Parker's death, members of the North Carolina legislature heard several eulogies on his life and career and adjourned in honor jointly of his memory and the birthday anniversary of General Lee.

Parker was a member of the Protestant Episcopal church and a Mason. He was buried in the Calvary Episcopal Church Cemetery, Tarboro.

SEE: W. C. Allen, *History of Halifax County* (1918); Samuel A. Ashe, ed., *Biographical History of North Carolina*, vol. 7 (1908); Louis H. Manarin, comp., *North Carolina Troops, 1861–1865: A Roster*, vol. 3 (1971); Helen Parker to Ralph Hardee Rives, 13 Dec. 1978; *The* (Enfield) *Pointer*, 10 Feb. 1905; *The* (Enfield) *Progress*, 13 June 1913; Records and papers of the Frank M. Parker Chapter, No. 1096 (United Daughters of the Confederacy, Enfield).

RALPH HARDEE RIVES

Parker, John Johnston *(20 Nov. 1885–17 Mar. 1958)*, lawyer, politician, and jurist, was born in Monroe, the eldest of four children and the brother of World War I hero Samuel Iredell Parker, first recipient of the army's three highest decorations for valor. His well-educated mother, Frances Ann Johnston, from Edenton, was descended from William Bradford of Plymouth Colony, Mass., a line of early North Carolina governors, and Associate Justice James Iredell of the U.S. Supreme Court (1790–99). The daughter of an Episcopal clergyman, she married John Daniel Parker, a Baptist-turned-Episcopalian, who eked out a living as an independent grocer.

The ambitious, thrifty, and self-reliant young Parker worked his way through The University of North Carolina, where maverick philosophy professor Horace H. Williams materially contributed to his intellectual development and cosmopolitan outlook. At Chapel Hill Parker won numerous academic honors and prizes, became student government leader, actively opposed the undemocratic fraternities, and began a long oratorical career. He received his A.B. degree in 1907 and the LL.B. in 1908.

Six feet tall with gray-blue eyes, Parker was somewhat reserved and possessed a deep sense of dignity and morality. His vast capacity for tedious, demanding work was offset by a genial personality and a wry sense of humor. He married Maria Burgwin Maffitt of an old and prominent Wilmington family on 23 Nov. 1910. An innately private person, she devoted herself to raising two sons and a daughter: Sara Burgwin (Mrs. Rufus Montgomery Ward, b. 1911), John J., Jr. (b. 1914), and Francis Iredell (b. 1923). John, Jr., a promising law student, died on 4 July 1941 of injuries suffered in an automobile accident.

Following legal apprenticeship in 1908 with David Stern in Greensboro and another year of practice alone in his hometown, Parker formed a partnership with A. M. Stack in Monroe (1910–19), becoming a senior partner in the firm of Stack, Parker, and Craig (1919–22). In 1922 he moved to Charlotte where, until 1925, he headed the firm of Parker, Stewart, McRae, and Bobbitt. Both firms developed large general civil and criminal practices in North Carolina and South Carolina although public service corporations were never numbered among their clients. Parker, a skilled advocate, argued cases in state and federal trial and appellate courts, including the U.S. Supreme Court. His regional reputation as a criminal lawyer led to his appointment as special assistant to the U.S. attorney general (1923–24), in which capacity he prosecuted several hard-fought war fraud cases.

The son of Democratic parents, Parker joined the Republican party in 1908. He cast his lot with the dominant "lily-white" and anti-Bryan "business respectables" faction that sought to promote and represent the state's nascent industrial interests. The youthful Parker climbed the orthodox political ladder—manager of John Motley Morehead's successful 1908 campaign for Congress, Seventh District congressional nominee against Democratic incumbent Robert N. Page (1910), candidate for attorney general (1916), gubernatorial contender (1920), and member of the GOP National Committee and delegate-at-large to the Republican National Convention (1924). In his vigorous but losing (42.8 percent) 1920 campaign against Cameron Morrison, he advocated woman suffrage, protectionism, and opposition to the League of Nations treaty, and, at the state level, a variety of progressive programs: an income tax, a workmen's compensation law, protective legislation for women and children in industry, collective bargaining and a voluntary state labor arbitration system, improved highway and educational systems, and a more powerful and centralized executive branch. To the traditional race-baiting strategy of the state's Democratic party, he responded that the largely disenfranchised "negro as a class does not desire to enter politics. The Republican party of North Carolina does not desire him to do so."

President Calvin Coolidge gave Parker a recess appointment to the U.S. Court of Appeals for the Fourth Circuit (to succeed Charles A. Woods, deceased) on 3 Oct. 1925 and a lifetime appointment on 14 Dec. 1925. In the wake of Hoover's 1928 electoral triumph in North Carolina, the forty-four-year-old jurist was considered for the solicitor and attorney generalships and for appointment to the Law Enforcement and Observance Commission before nomination to a Supreme Court vacancy caused by Edward T. Sanford's death. The nomination on 21 Mar. 1930 reflected political, sectional, and jurisprudential considerations. Parker's four-year judicial record of 184 written opinions received little publicity, but his single decision in *United Mine Workers of America [UMW] v. Red Jacket Consolidated Coal and Coke Co.* (18 F. 2d 839 [1927]) ignited massive opposition from organized labor and their allies in the Senate who perceived it as further legitimating the legality of yellow-dog employment contracts. Although the constitutionality of such contracts was not at issue, the scope of a sweeping injunction against UMW organizing efforts was involved. And Parker upheld that portion enjoining the union from even "persuading" employees to break their nonunion contracts. Such "persuasion" indicated an "unlawful purpose" as laid down in landmark Supreme Court decisions issued in 1917 and 1921 and in a 1925 decision of his own circuit court. In addition Walter White, then acting director of the NAACP, led a frenetic grassroots lobbying campaign against the nomination. Although no evidence of racism appeared in his judicial opinions, the association assailed Parker for his political statement of a decade earlier. These two interest groups, combined with other factors, caused the Senate to deny his confirmation (41–39) on 7 May 1930. Parker continued a fruitless quest for a place on the high court by launching major campaigns in 1941, 1942–43, 1945, and 1954.

On the Court of Appeals, Parker sat with such distinguished colleagues as John C. Rose, Morris A. Soper, and Simon E. Sobeloff of Baltimore, Armistead M. Dobie of Virginia, and Clement F. Haynsworth, Jr., of South Carolina. He heard more than 4,000 arguments during his thirty-two years as appellate judge and wrote opinions in approximately 1,500 cases found in volumes 8–253 of the *Federal Reporter, Second Series*. These opinions reflect an ability to grasp complicated issues of fact and law and to apply logically his philosophy of law. That philosophy was based on the major premise that society was an ever-changing organism and law the life principle of that organism. Law was thus "not a static thing," Parker said, in *Marshall v. Manese* (85 F. 2d 944, 948 [1936]), "bound down by prior decisions and legislative enactments. It is based on reason, arises out of the life of the people, and must change as the conditions of that life change."

He eschewed the role of "judicial legislator"; recognition of legislators as preeminent lawmakers and of the subordinate place of an intermediate appellate court in the judicial hierarchy guided his work (cf. *United States v. Appalachian Coals, Inc.*, 1 F. Supp. 339, 349 [1932]). But where ambiguity or gaps in law existed, Parker's opinions manifested his broad humanitarianism, reliance upon the "rule of reason," and belief that constitutions should be interpreted as charters of government not as contracts.

On the controverted relationship between government and the economy he regarded it as "unthinkable that the public should be left at the mercy of private individuals as to matters which affect the public welfare." Government must protect free people from economic tyranny. Even in the 1920s, he upheld exercises of state police powers as against challenges based on the due process clause of the Fourteenth Amendment (*Suncrest Lumber Co. v. North Carolina Park Commission*, 30 F. 2d 121 [1929]) and the constitution's contract clause (*Carolina and North Western Railway Co. v. Town of Lincolnton*, 33 F. 2d 719 [1929]). With the exception of gold clause cases (*Machen v. United States*, 87 F. 2d 594 [1937]), landmark New Deal regulatory legislation generally passed early muster under Parker's broad conception of the general welfare clause (*Greenwood County, South Carolina v. Duke Power Co.*, 81 F. 2d. 986 [1936]), the commerce clause (*Virginian Railway Co. v. System Federation #40*, 84 F. 2d 641 [1936]; contra, *Burco, Inc. v. Whitworth*, 81 F. 2d 721 [1936]), and federal bankruptcy power (*Bradford v. Fahey*, 76 F. 2d 628

[1935]). He believed that government must be a liberating not an oppressive force in economic life. Resolution of conflicts between property and government demanded of judges not self-restraint to the extent of abdication of duty, but rather the application of law and reason to prevent arbitrariness. Judges must compel public officials to act justly in taking privately owned property for public use (*United States v. Twin City Power Co.*, 215 F. 2d 592 [1954]) and in regulating and fixing the price of its products (*Hope Natural Gas Co. v. Federal Power Commission*, 134 F. 2d 287 [1943]).

Major issues of civil liberties and rights came before Judge Parker in the 1940s and 1950s. He typically applied various reason-based pragmatic "balancing" tests to the former category. In voiding West Virginia's compulsory flag salute law, Parker balanced religious freedom of Jehovah's Witnesses against the compelling nature of the state's interest in enforcing a secular regulation (*Barnett v. West Virginia Board of Education*, 47 F. Supp. 251 [1942]). But when those asserting First Amendment rights were members of a Communist conspiracy, "nothing in the Constitution or in any sound political theory . . . forbids [government] to take effective action . . . to protect itself from being overthrown by force and violence" notwithstanding the absence of a "clear and present danger" (*Frankfeld v. United States*, 198 F. 2d 679, 682 [1952]; *Scales v. United States*, 227 F. 2d 587 [1955]). In criminal appeals Parker proved no supporter of the Bill of Rights "incorporation" theory. He consistently treated alleged procedural errors with the due process–based "fair trial" rule (*Cary v. Brady*, 125 F. 2d 253 [1942]). And his sympathy for "dual federalism" was reflected in repeated attempts to restrict the use of habeas corpus writs as vehicles of appeal from final decisions of the highest state courts (*Stonebreaker v. Smyth*, 163 F. 2d 499 [1947]).

His last decade on the bench confronted Parker with a rising volume of race relations cases. Racial disenfranchisement resulting from state "white primary" laws and practices were enjoined as clearly discriminatory under the Fourteenth and Fifteenth amendments (*Rice v. Elmore*, 165 F. 2d 387 [1947]; *Baskin v. Brown*, 174 F. 2d 391 [1949]). Although the equal protection clause barred state racial discrimination, Parker believed that "if equal service is accorded . . . reasonable regulations based on public custom and a desire to avoid disturbances of the public peace should be sustained." Strictly applying this "separate but equal" standard in the light of reason, Parker struck down as racially discriminatory a municipal zoning ordinance (*Deans v. City of Richmond*, 37 F. 2d 712 [1930], public school teachers' salary schedules (*Alston v. School Board of Norfolk*, 112 F. 2d 992 [1940]), and union collective bargaining and seniority strategies (*Brotherhood of Locomotive Firemen and Engineers v. Tunstall*, 163 F. 2d 289 [1947]; *Dillard v. C and O Railway Co.*, 199 F. 2d 948 [1952]). But in *Briggs v. Elliot* (98 F. Supp. 529 [1951]) he resisted going beyond that standard long endorsed by the Supreme Court to find South Carolina's legally segregated public schools unconstitutional per se. Reversed by the Supreme Court in *Brown v. Board of Education of Topeka* (1954), Parker immediately complied and construed that decision as meaning "the Constitution does not require integration; it merely forbids discrimination. It does not forbid segregation as it occurs as the result of voluntary action, but forbids the use of governmental powers to enforce segregation" (*Briggs v. Elliot*, 132 F. Supp. 776 [1955]). This often-reiterated statement of interpretation and conciliation would, Parker hoped, promote "amicable adjustment" of the heated desegregation question on the basis of what he called a "spirit of Christianity."

As acting or regular presiding judge for twenty-eight years, he was administrator of his circuit as well as a member of the national policy-making Judicial Conference of the United States. From 1941 to 1958 he served on sixteen Conference committees, including the Advisory Committee, and chaired those on punishment for crime, court reporting, habeas corpus, pretrial, venue and jurisdiction, appeals from interlocutory orders, and administration of the criminal laws. His efforts aided enactment of the Administrative Office of the U.S. Court Act of 1939, the Federal Court Reporters Act of 1944, the Federal Youth Corrections Act of 1950, and the Interlocutory Appeals Act of 1958. They also contributed to preservation of broad federal diversity of citizenship jurisdiction and to compensation of counsel and public defenders for indigent defendants posthumously provided by law.

Parker was active in the American Law Institute and the American Bar Association (ABA). His service on ABA committees began in 1931 (Jurisprudence and Law Reform, 1931–33) and largely reflected an abiding interest in judicial administration, criminal law (council member, Section on Criminal Law, 1945–53), and a subsequently developed concern with international law and relations. As leader in the Section of Judicial Administration (council member, 1934–38, 1942–58; chairman, 1937–38; chairman, Special Committee on Improving the Administration of Justice, 1940–46) and in the Judicial Conference (1930–58), and as judicial adviser to the U.S. high commissioner for Germany (1949), he promoted judicial reforms to strengthen an independent judiciary and protect its functions by means of judge-centered courts. Thus his enduring legacy included diminution of popular influence over courts, enhancement of institutional autonomy of the judiciary as a coordinate branch of government, unification, simplification and centralization of intrajudiciary procedures and administration, and assertion of judge control over court proceedings.

From numerous platforms, Parker advanced his optimistic view that Americans as individuals and as a nation could, if they would, surmount all obstacles and master their environment. His own life, the postbellum recovery and industrialization of his native state, and the rise of the United States as a world power served to reinforce his idealism. As a member of The University of North Carolina Board of Trustees (1921–58) and as a firm supporter of the North Carolina College for Negroes in Durham, founded and led by his longtime friend James E. Shepard, he worked to provide the state's youth with low-tuition, higher educational opportunities in the belief that the "source of all wealth is to be found in the intelligence of the people." He denounced the "parsimonious policy" of the General Assembly of North Carolina before its Appropriation Committee in the depths of the Great Depression. That policy, he said, would drive "the more ambitious to seek an education elsewhere and probably to live elsewhere." In 1930 he served as a member of the board's presidential search committee that nominated Frank Porter Graham. Thereafter Parker became one of the president's stalwart supporters although differing with Graham's absolutist interpretation of free speech. But when the president waged battle with the medical school's anti-Semitic admissions quota system in 1933, he sided with Graham. Together with board colleagues O. Max Gardner, Josephus Daniels, and Cameron Morrison, Parker led and defended consolidation of the university system in the 1930s. As war clouds loomed in June 1940, he urged preparedness, and the board adopted his resolution to establish a military training program at Chapel Hill. Then in the 1950s the judge urged racial integration of the professional schools; after *Brown II* in

1955, he called on the board to reverse its segregation policies forthwith.

Parker also served his state as a member of the North Carolina Constitutional Commission (1931–32), to which he was appointed by Governor Gardner. The new constitution proposed by the commission gave recognition to the need for a modern state government capable of positive action in conserving natural resources and regulating industry and commerce. It reflected Parker's administrative thought through provisions for flexible legislative taxing power, a stronger executive with budget and veto powers as well as an appointed council of state, and a unified judicial system under control of the chief justice of the supreme court.

In addition, Judge Parker performed important extrajudicial services for the nation. By appointment of President Franklin D. Roosevelt in late 1943, he sat with Judge Learned Hand (CA2) and Joseph C. Hutcheson, Jr. (CA5), on the Advisory Board on Just Compensation to the War Shipping Administration, which drafted rules used to fix compensation paid for requisitioned vessels. Appointment by President Harry S Truman as alternate member for the United States of the International Military Tribunal at Nuremberg, Germany (1945–46), attested to Parker's rising prominence as a spokesman for "internationalism." At the trial, he materially contributed to development of the critical "conspiracy" issue in the tribunal's final judgment. Subsequently, as chairman of the American Bar Association Committee on Offenses against the Law of Nations (1946–51), he regarded the trial as "strengthening immeasurably the foundation of international law." His idealism led him to perceive America's postwar mission as that of building a new world order based on such law, incorporating the basic principles of this country's constitutional structure and endowed with force. Thus he became an early advocate of a United Nations (UN) organization, led by the United States and equipped with military capabilities. His interest resulted in election to the UN's International Law Commission in 1953, a post that he declined on constitutional grounds (cf. U.S. Constitution, Art. I, Sec. 9). As the Cold War waxed, he publicly warned against Communist-bloc military power, warmly endorsed aid to Greece and Turkey in 1947, and supported both universal military training and collective security arrangements such as the North Atlantic Treaty Organization. Isolationism manifested in the Bricker Amendment to limit the president's power to make treaties and to enter into executive agreements evoked sharp public criticism from the judge. As delegate of the ABA's International and Comparative Law Section (1952–54; member of its council, 1955–58) and in testimony before Congress, Parker actively opposed the measure that he regarded "as the most dangerous" since FDR's court-packing bill. Nevertheless, in *United States v. Capps* (204 F. 2d 655 [1953]) he held that inherent presidential power to make executive agreements was limited by express constitutional grants of power to Congress, especially when Congress had enacted laws on the basis of such grants.

Parker was a devout and biblically knowledgeable member of the Protestant Episcopal church. He served as a Sunday school teacher, vestryman, and delegate to the 1937 General Convention of the Episcopal church. He was an Episcopal lay representative to the National Study Conference of the Commission on a Just and Durable Peace of the Federal Council of Churches at Cleveland, Ohio, in early 1945. Chaired by John Foster Dulles, the conference sought to promote "world-mindedness" among American Protestants and to encourage congregational support for international cooperation as represented by the then-emerging United Nations organization. In November 1957 he became chairman of the General Crusade Committee of the Billy Graham Charlotte Crusade. To that committee, Judge Parker declared that peace among people and nations could be achieved only "through the cleansing of the hearts of men and women throughout the world and instilling in them a sense of responsibility to Almighty God and to the ideals and standards of human brotherhood."

He died in active judicial service at Washington, D.C., and was buried in Charlotte's Elmwood Cemetery.

SEE: William C. Burris, "John J. Parker and Supreme Court Policy: A Case Study of Judicial Controls" (Diss., University of North Carolina, Chapel Hill, 1965); Peter G. Fish, "Guarding the Judicial Ramparts: John J. Parker and the Administration of Justice," *Justice System Journal* 3 (1977); "In Memoriam Honorable John Johnston Parker, 1885–1958: Proceedings in the United States Court of Appeals for the Fourth Circuit, April 22, 1958," *Federal Reporter, Second Series* 253 (1958); Harold K. Medina, "John Johnston Parker, 1885–1958," *North Carolina Law Review* 38 (1960); John Johnston Parker Papers (Southern Historical Collection, University of North Carolina, Chapel Hill); John J. Parker, *American Constitution and World Order Based on Law* (1953) and *Democracy in Government* (1940); "John J. Parker: Senior Circuit Judge: Fourth Circuit," *American Bar Association Journal* 32 (1946); Richard L. Watson, Jr., "The Defeat of Judge Parker: A Study in Pressure Group Politics," *Mississippi Valley Historical Review* 50 (1963).

PETER G. FISH

Parker, Joseph *(d. 1791 or 1792),* General Baptist (now Free Will Baptist) clergyman, founded churches in Halifax, Pitt, Greene, and Lenoir counties. According to tradition, he was a member and probable pastor of the General Baptist church in Chowan County in 1727, founded and pastored a church in Hertford County about 1735, pastored the church called Lower Fishing Creek in Edgecombe (now Halifax) County from 1748 to 1756, and then moved to the south of Tar River. George W. Paschal suggested that Parker was the son of a man of the same forename and that he married the daughter (Sarah Welch) of another member of the 1727 Chowan church. Some elements of this tradition have been accepted for more than a century and a half, and one is very reluctant to offer an exposition of Parker's life contrary to it.

Nevertheless, Joseph Parker was the son of a prosperous planter named Francis Parker and his wife Elizabeth who came with other families from Surry, Nansemond, and Isle of Wight counties, Va., through Bertie County into the Roanoke and Tar river valleys in North Carolina during the 1720s. The numerous Parkers who were members of the 1727 Chowan County General Baptist church might or might not have been related, but there appears to be no reason in fact to connect either Joseph Parker or his father Francis directly with that church or with the ministry of Paul Palmer. On the other hand, this family of Parkers had by 1727 settled on Deep Creek on the south of Roanoke River below Kehukee Swamp, which brought them within the sphere of influence of William Surginer and other General Baptist families who had come from Isle of Wight County, Va., into the Roanoke River valley. Sometime before 1735 the family had moved farther south to the lower, or southeastern, portion of Fishing Creek on Tar River, at which time young Joseph Parker held the office of constable of the district.

It is not known under whose influence he was converted to Baptist doctrine or who immersed him in baptism. Such education as he had, he got as an adult, learning to read and write sometime between 1735 and 1740, so his conversion was presumably through hearing rather than reading. Since Parker purchased a New Testament in 1741 from the estate of Henry West, one assumes that he had leanings towards a religious life by that date. In the spring of 1742, the Lower Fishing Creek community was visited by Constant Devotion, a Rhode Island Baptist who had been with Paul Palmer in 1734 and had joined William Surginer at Kehukee Swamp in the late 1730s. While at Lower Fishing Creek in May 1742, Devotion witnessed two deeds made by Parker's father, Francis Parker, so he is known to have had contact with the family of Joseph Parker. Little is known of Devotion other than that he was active in Baptist circles in Rhode Island and North Carolina, but whether as an exhorter or as a preacher is unclear. Whatever his role had been in establishing General Baptist congregations in colonial Edgecombe County, it came to an end when he was killed by a fall from his mare at Fishing Creek on 8 June 1742. One supposes Devotion played a role in the conversion of Parker.

Parker presumably attended meetings at the General Baptist church established at Kehukee Swamp by William Surginer about 1742. Parker was at Kehukee in November 1745, for he witnessed a deed from Surginer to William Andrews at this time. One supposes, too, that Parker had been baptized by Surginer at Kehukee, and that he was licensed by the church there to preach prior to his actual ordination. Further, Parker seems to have attended the yearly meetings of the General Baptist churches for he learned something of Paul Palmer's work in the eastern counties. In 1747 Parker was joined at Lower Fishing Creek by Palmer's disciple and successor, Josiah Hart. In 1748 the General Baptist church called Lower Fishing Creek (in contradistinction to the church called Fishing Creek upstream in Bute County) was constituted, and Parker was ordained its pastor. There can be little doubt that either Surginer or Hart was officiating elder for both the constitution of the church and the ordination of Parker. In 1748 Hart went north to Roanoke River to join Surginer at Kehukee, but he continued to return to Tar River and Lower Fishing Creek to assist Parker at intervals. In the spring of 1749, for example, Hart was back at Lower Fishing Creek where he baptized Charles Daniel, and he returned in August 1753 to ordain Daniel as assistant to Joseph Parker.

At the beginning of 1753, Parker, who had purchased and sold tracts of land in Edgecombe from as early as 1742, commenced negotiations with the agents of Lord Granville's land office for the purchase of a square mile of land in the area of his church on Lower Fishing Creek, but the acquisition of Daniel as his assistant in August of that year freed Parker to visit some of the churches to the southward that had resulted from Palmer's ministry in the late 1730s. At Stony Creek in present Wayne County, northeast of the town of Goldsboro, he found a General Baptist church pastored by George Graham, who had been ordained by Palmer about 1739, and to the east at Swift Creek in northwestern Craven County he found another pastored by Joseph Willis, who had been ordained by Graham and William Fulsher. (Fulsher, like Graham, had been ordained by Palmer at the close of the 1730s.) It was in the area between these two General Baptist centers, present northern Lenoir and southern Greene counties, that Parker was to devote most of his ministry. His initial reception there was warm and the field promising. As a result, on Christmas Day, 1756, Parker purchased one hundred acres in the area where he gathered his first church in Greene County, Little Creek, lying between Great and Little Contentnea creeks.

While Parker was busy at Neuse River establishing a new ministry, forces greater than he were at work among the General Baptist churches he had left on the Roanoke and Tar rivers. On the heels of William Surginer's death in February 1750, a pair of Surginer's recently ordained preachers at the upper Fishing Creek church (subsequently called Reedy Creek, Warren County) embraced the Calvinist doctrine of divine election of particular individuals to eternal salvation to the exclusion of the remainder of humanity. This doctrine was antithetical to the General Baptist doctrine of general provision that held the death of Jesus to have been efficacious for the salvation of any of mankind who believed in him and repented of their sins. By 1751 at least one member of Surginer's original church, Kehukee, had fallen under the influence of the newly imported doctrine. These ministers, or others, appealed to the Philadelphia Association of Baptists to send clergy south to strengthen their hands. That association had been a voluntary coming together of Baptists, both Arminian and Calvinist, for common benefit. In 1742, however, the organization adopted a Calvinist creed as the standard of orthodoxy, and the particular form of Calvinism that developed among its constituent churches was greatly heightened by the Great Awakening. Like Whitfield, they believed themselves justified in going uninvited into other ministers' churches, and they followed Whitfield's example of denouncing as unregenerated, hypocrites, or wolves in sheep's clothing those clergy who were opposed to their practices and theology. The Philadelphia Association sent the Reverend John Gano to look into conditions in the Carolinas in 1754. Gano stopped in the Roanoke River valley long enough to examine General Baptist clergy and laity alike, and to assure many of both that they were neither walking in the paths of grace nor among the elect of God. The following year, having received Gano's report, the Philadelphia Association sent two ministers, Benjamin Miller and Peter Peterson Vanhorn, on a special mission to rescue the southern churches from General Baptist "error." The two Calvinist missionaries arrived on Roanoke River at the very time that the two senior General Baptist ministers of the area were absent: legal affairs had obliged Josiah Hart to return to Tyrrell County (where he died prior to the spring of 1758), and Joseph Parker was engaged on his mission to Neuse River.

Miller and Vanhorn astutely began their work of expunging General Baptist "error" by persuading to their views the young clergymen who had not yet turned Calvinist (for example, Surginer's successor at Kehukee was only twenty-two when he was ordained in 1750, as was Parker's assistant when he was ordained in 1753). The newly converted pastors then led a minority of their church members in forming a new church on Calvinist lines, leaving their previous General Baptist congregations to get along as best they could without pastoral care. This meant that those congregations without a pastor to administer communion and preside over the washing of the saints' feet, to baptize and lay on hands, to maintain orderly discipline in the churches, and to ordain successor clergy were doomed to extinction. Even those who held onto their meetinghouses or, as at Toisnot, contested Calvinist occupation of their places of meeting, were unable to survive indefinitely without pastors. At Parker's church, Lower Fishing Creek, his young assistant, Charles Daniel, stopped preaching and walked out in 1756 with six members, formed a new Calvinist church with himself as pastor, and built a new meetinghouse in 1757, calling it thereafter the church at

Daniel's Meetinghouse. Having done not quite enough, Daniel then helped the pastor of the General Baptist church at Falls of Tar River constitute a new Calvinist church there, consisting of the pastor and five members, on 3 Dec. 1757.

In the interim Miller and Vanhorn progressed southwards towards Neuse River on their mission. At Stony Creek they converted Palmer's disciple, George Graham, who withdrew with some members to form a new Calvinist Baptist church at adjacent Bear Creek; in this case the General Baptist church at Stony Creek survived, owing perhaps to the efforts of the nearby Joseph Parker. The two Calvinist missionaries had similar success with Palmer's church at Swift Creek, Craven County, where they proselyted (the term is the one used by the Calvinist Baptist historian, Morgan Edwards) the pastor, two women of his family, and twelve other General Baptists to form a new Calvinist Baptist church there. The two Philadelphians had no luck at all with Joseph Parker, nor with Palmer's disciple William Fulsher at Pungo in Beaufort County, Palmer's convert John Winfield in Hyde County, nor William Harris, also in Hyde County, who had been ordained by Graham and Fulsher just prior to the missionaries' advent.

To the north of Albemarle Sound, however, Palmer's church in Pasquotank County divided doctrinally in 1757 when the pastor (son of the original pastor and Palmer's old friend, William Burgess) led out his son and ten other members and built them a new meetinghouse at his own expense. They were constituted a Calvinist Baptist church on 20 Jan. 1758 by Joseph Parker's former assistant at Lower Fishing Creek, Charles Daniel. This state of affairs was discovered by Parker in the summer of 1758 when he visited the General Baptist church in Pasquotank and baptized Henry Abbott (who, too, embraced Calvinist views in the following decade). What Parker probably did not know is that the General Baptist churches in the northern colonies, toured by Palmer in 1730, had experienced a similar onslaught after 1742 with the result that many of them were "dissolved" while Calvinist churches were constituted in their stead. What Parker must have known, on the other hand, is that Calvinist doctrine had been introduced into the church in Isle of Wight County and that the ministers there wrote to the Philadelphia Association at the end of 1756 requesting a delegation be sent to examine their foundations and settle their doctrine in conformity with the orthodoxy of Philadelphia. If there was a yearly meeting of the Virginia and North Carolina General Baptist churches held in 1758, it was the last in Parker's lifetime. Thereafter, the yearly meetings would have included only Joseph Parker's churches in Greene, Pitt, and Lenoir counties, Palmer's churches in the Albemarle-Pamlico peninsula pastored by William Fulsher, William Harris, and John Winfield, and, presumably, the church at Meherrin in Hertford County pastored by William Parker.

Parker, unable to counter the effects of Calvinism in the Roanoke-Tar river area or to impede its progress among the clergy, but able to stem its spread into his newly evangelized territory at Neuse River, sold in 1758 his interest in the square mile of land on Fishing Creek for which he had made an entry in Lord Granville's land office in 1753. He then moved permanently to the Neuse River area and purchased more land there. (It is unlikely that the deaths of Parker's father in 1757 and brother Simon—whose will was witnessed by Charles Daniel—in 1758 had anything to do with his permanent move to Neuse River.)

Parker's initial work in the Neuse River basin carried him from his center at Little Contentnea Creek to Swift Creek in Pitt and Craven counties, where he regained some ground from the Calvinists. Immediately to his northeast, on the headwaters of Swift Creek, he gathered a congregation at Gum Swamp (southwest of Winterville). From here he traveled in 1762 north of Tar River and preached the doctrine of general provision to the Conetoe settlements and to families living in the area of Flat Swamp (where the counties of Pitt, Edgecombe, and Martin share a common boundary). The ground here was contested by ministers from the Calvinist Baptist church at Toisnot Swamp who commenced preaching at Flat Swamp in 1766. Parker seems to have found a disciple at Flat Swamp, however, for when the Calvinist Baptist church was constituted in 1776, two ordinands offered themselves, and one of them, John Stancill, was discovered to hold Arminian views. He was rejected for ordination. Parker is said to have preached here perhaps a couple of times a year during the latter part of his life, and it is entirely possible that he ordained Stancill when the Calvinists refused to do so. Stancill has been described by the Calvinist Baptist historians as a "tolerably arch, cunning, and insinuating" man. By his preaching in the neighborhood, Stancill carried away many members from the Calvinists "with his craft." Parker's successor, James Roach, reaped in this field sown by Parker and Stancill by gathering a General Baptist church at Conetoe in 1798. Similarly, Parker's ministry near the mouth of Swift Creek in Craven County is now known to have borne immediate fruit, but the churches at Little Swift Creek, Clayroot, and Kitts Swamp were gathered after Parker's death by his successors.

At the time that Parker was preaching in the Conetoe settlements, he did not neglect other areas. Tradition says that he preached occasionally to the Meherrin General Baptist church in Hertford County pastored by William Parker. The pastor at Meherrin has been supposed a cousin to Joseph Parker, but on no very good authority, and Joseph Parker has been suggested as founder of the church on no authority at all. William Parker is known to have been pastor at Meherrin as early as 1773, but how long before that year is unknown. It is possible that Joseph Parker preached a few times at Meherrin during the course of his life, though it is unlikely that actual evidence for the claim will ever appear. The church at Meherrin remained steadfast to General Baptist principles through the life of William Parker, who died in 1794. The church was reported in 1790 as having one hundred members. After William Parker's funeral, Lemuel Burkitt, pastor of the Calvinist Baptist church at Kehukee, examined the congregation, pronounced "a small number" to be among the elect of God, and organized those few into a Calvinist Baptist church in 1794. As usual in such cases, the larger General Baptist congregation at Meherrin withered away without pastoral care.

The tradition that Parker journeyed from his church at Little Creek to preach to the church at Pungo from time to time is probably more soundly grounded. The sites of yearly meetings usually moved from church to church, and it is reasonable to suppose that Parker would have attended, and preached at, the yearly meetings held in Beaufort and Hyde counties. It is unlikely, however, that the eastern churches formed part of his ministry.

It is clear that he preached a general invitation to salvation south of Contentnea Creek in the area of present northern Lenoir County during the same period he visited the Conetoe settlements. It is assumed that Parker gathered his congregations at Wheat Swamp and Luzon Swamp, northwest and north of Kinston, prior to the American Revolution, but the total absence of surviving county records and church records alike places this assumption of date beyond either confirmation or denial. His three congregations at Gum Swamp, Wheat Swamp, and Luzon Swamp apparently existed for the duration of Parker's life as branches of Little Creek, as the church on Little Contentnea Creek was called. Since both Morgan Edwards (1772–73) and John Asplund (1790) were unable to gather information on absolutely every Baptist church in North Carolina, the fact that both of them report Parker's only church as "Contantony" or "Quotankney" may or may not suggest that Parker's church was one with three branches within a radius of ten miles. The life Parker lived, passing in turn week after week from one congregation to another, must have paralleled almost precisely the life of the circa 1810 "monthly pastor" with four substantial churches described by David Benedict in the fourth chapter of his *Fifty Years among the Baptists*. Though Parker had a grant of land on Little Contentnea Creek and is known to have purchased and sold various tracts there, he is said to have spent his last years in straightened circumstances domiciled at Wheat Swamp, rather than at Little Contentnea Creek. One assumes this move from southern Greene to northern Lenoir County to have taken place towards the end of the Revolutionary War, for by 1785 the Calvinist Baptists from Toisnot had penetrated Greene County and had gathered a church (named Meadow) on the headwaters of Little Contentnea Creek in the extreme northern end of the county. In the spring of 1791 they gathered a second church named Little Contentnea. One takes it, then, that Parker's influence here had waned or that he had departed for Lenoir County by 1785.

Parker is said to have been a broad-faced, square-built man of about five feet, eight inches tall with an animated style of preaching. He had married by 1749, but of his wife, Lucia, her forename alone is known (and that, from a 1749 deed). They are not known to have had any children. Both Joseph Parker and his wife appear to have been living in 1790 when the Dobbs County census was taken. He died in the next year or two and was buried without memorial stone in Robert Witherington's burial ground at Wheat Swamp. Parker's successor, both to his churches and to his spirit, was Elder James Roach.

The Free Will Baptists in North Carolina (as the General Baptists came to be called early in the following century) very nearly owe their continued life to Parker, and through them the Disciples of Christ are indebted to him. In his life Parker merged the General Baptist tradition received in the inner coastal plain from Virginia and the tradition received in the outer coastal plain from Paul Palmer. It is probable that had Parker not, in his long ministry of nearly fifty years, remained faithful to the doctrine he had inherited form the seventeenth century, those teachings would not have survived, as they have, in churches throughout the southern and southwestern states to the end of the twentieth century.

SEE: Lemuel Burkitt and Jesse Read, *Concise History of the Kehukee Baptist Association* (1803); Morgan Edwards, "Materials Toward a History of the Baptists of North Carolina" (Furman MSS) and "Tour . . . to the Baptists of North Carolina, 1772–1773" (Crozer MSS) (Microfilm, North Carolina Collection, University of North Carolina, Chapel Hill); Thad F. Harrison and J. M. Barfield, *History of the Free Will Baptists of North Carolina* (1898); Margaret M. Hofmann, *Province of North Carolina, 1663–1729, Abstracts of Land Patents* (1979), *Colony of North Carolina, 1735–1775, Abstracts of Land Patents*, 2 vols. (1982), and *Abstracts of Deeds, Edgecombe Precinct, Edgecombe County, North Carolina* (1969); Manuscript land records in the Land Grant Office, Secretary of State, Raleigh; and, in the North Carolina State Archives, Dobbs County Index to Deeds, 1746–1880, and Craven County Deeds, vol. 1, 1745–72, folio 73.

GEORGE STEVENSON

Parker, Robert Hunt *(15 Feb. 1892–10 Nov. 1969)*, chief justice of the North Carolina Supreme Court, was recognized as an eminent jurist, scholar in history, the classics, and common law, and orator, and as a fearless champion of the average citizen. He was an outspoken conservative in the areas of race, politics, and public morality and, as a result of his innate command of language, he was one of the most highly quotable public figures of his day. Tall, somewhat austere in appearance, impeccably dressed, silver-haired in later years, the epitome of dignity at all times, Parker was referred to as "all judge [Washington *Daily News*, 27 Jan. 1966], "a judge's judge" [*Charlotte Observer*, 12 Nov. 1968], and a "law and order" man long before the phrase became a cliché of political candidates.

Parker was the only son of Romulus Bragg Parker (3 June 1856–31 July 1939), a prominent landowner and businessman of Enfield, and his first wife, Victory Coleman Hunt Parker (10 Nov. 1857–21 July 1912). Educated at the Enfield High School, The University of North Carolina, the University of Virginia (B.A., 1912), Wake Forest Law School, and the University of Virginia Law School, he was admitted to the North Carolina bar in the summer of 1914, approximately a year before receiving his LL.B. degree from the University of Virginia Law School. In 1958 he was awarded the honorary doctor of laws degree from The University of North Carolina.

During World War I Parker served as field artillery officer in the cavalry, attached to the adjutant general's office in France for nearly seventeen months. After the war he practiced law in Enfield and Roanoke Rapids, and in 1923–24 he represented Halifax County in the General Assembly. This began a career of public service in North Carolina that led from solicitor, superior court judge, supreme court associate justice, supreme court senior justice, and, finally, to chief justice of the supreme court. Parker was the third native son of Halifax County to serve as chief justice in the twentieth century.

"Judge Parker," as he was affectionately known in later years, served as solicitor of the Third Judicial District from 1924 to 1932, when he was appointed to the superior court, having been chosen by the district judicial committee to fill the unexpired term of the late superior court judge Garland Midyette of Jackson. Parker was reelected for three eight-year terms in 1934, 1942, and 1950. As a superior court judge, he was given special assignments involving election violations, tax dodgers, mob violence, and several notorious criminal and civil cases.

In 1952 he ran for the supreme court and became the first person in North Carolina history to unseat a state supreme court justice at the polls; this was the last time that anyone reached the high court bench other than by appointment. Upon the retirement of Chief Justice Emery Denny in 1966, Governor Dan K. Moore named Parker to replace him and, in 1968, Justice Parker was reelected for an eight-year term.

During Parker's seventeen years on the North Carolina Supreme Court, twenty-three of his opinions were selected for inclusion in the *American Law Reports*. Among the landmark cases in which his opinions gained state and national attention was *State v. Goldberg* (1964), in which he affirmed the conviction of professional gamblers on several counts of conspiring to bribe college basketball players. In 1968 he upheld a permanent injunction against commercial diving operations involving three Confederate blockade-runners in the coastal waters off New Hanover County. During his tenure, the state's judicial system underwent wide-ranging reform and substantial enlargement with the creation of an intermediate state court of appeals and a district court system below the superior courts. In this period, the responsibilities of the state's chief justice and of the administrative staff increased significantly.

Parker gained the title of the "Fighting Chief Justice" because no fight was too difficult or too unpopular for him to wage when he felt that North Carolina's heritage was being threatened. He insisted that judges did not make law but, rather, were interpreters of the constitution and should follow the doctrine of *stare decisis*.

He was a member of the Commission to Study Improvements in the Administration of Justice in North Carolina (1947–49) and a member and later chairman of the Judicial Council. Unlike many former chief justices, Parker was an extremely popular public speaker throughout the state. His courtly manner and strong sense of integrity and decorum, and the fact that he was "predictably honest," caused him to be in great demand as an orator and his stirring patriotic addresses were widely acclaimed. He made his last public appearance one month prior to his death when he addressed the North Carolina Bar Association.

Parker was a member of several veterans' organizations including the American Legion, the "40 and 8," and the Veterans of Foreign Wars. An honorary member of the Society of the Cincinnati, he served on the Confederate Centennial Commission and the Governor Richard Caswell Memorial Commission. He was a member of the Episcopal church.

On 28 Nov. 1925 Parker married Mrs. Rie Alston Williams Rand (21 May 1888–12 Aug. 1976) of Greensboro. They had no children. Chief Justice and Mrs. Parker were buried in Elmwood Cemetery, Enfield, near the grave of Governor John Branch, one of Parker's favorite heroes.

SEE: Joseph Branch, "Presentation Address at Ceremonies for the Presentation of a Portrait of the Late Chief Justice Robert Hunt Parker to the Supreme Court of North Carolina" (typescript, 15 Dec. 1972, North Carolina Collection, University of North Carolina, Chapel Hill); *Enfield Progress*, 27 Jan. 1966, 13 Nov. 1969; Greenville *Daily Reflector*, 11, 13 Nov. 1969; Judge R. Hunt Parker's Papers and Scrapbooks (possession of Mrs. Rom B. Parker, Jr., and Rom B. Parker III, Enfield); Raleigh *News and Observer*, 11–13 Nov. 1969; Rocky Mount *Sunday Telegram*, 4 Sept. 1966.

RALPH HARDEE RIVES

Parker, Surry *(1 Dec. 1866–21 Apr. 1942)*, designer and builder of steam logging machinery and founder of Pinetown, was born in Nansemond County, Va., the son of Confederate Captain George Thomas Parker, of Gates County, and Eunice Katharine Riddick Parker. Parker's ancestors had lived in Gates County since 1740. Surry Parker was educated at Suffolk Military Academy, but because of difficult conditions after the Civil War he left school at age seventeen to work as a locomotive fireman and later as a locomotive engineer for the Roanoke Railroad and Lumber Company. He continued on his own, however, to study mechanical engineering, his chief talent and interest.

By 1893 Parker established his own business, in which he designed and built labor-saving steam logging machinery, excavating and dredging machinery, and engines for driving piles and hoisting machinery (e.g., cranes, derricks, and winches). He built the town of Pinetown in Beaufort County around his shops, from which many mechanics trained by him branched out on their own. Among these men was Sam Jones of Hyde County, who went on to found the Berkley Machine Works and Foundry Company of Norfolk, Va.

At the turn of the century Pinetown had a population of approximately five hundred, consisting of Parker employees and their families. Parker brought in a doctor for the community and hired teachers for the elementary school that he built. He also built a general store, three churches, and an "opera house," where theatrical productions and early silent movies were shown, and established a lending library in his home for the townspeople. Prior to World War I, the equipment built in Pinetown was sold throughout the logging states of the East and in South America. Parker patented several machine parts. Always looking towards the future, he worked on plans for such things as a machine-driven airplane and an escape hatch for submarines.

The first person to own an automobile in Beaufort County, Parker was an early advocate of good roads; he was one of the first highway commissioners in Beaufort. In addition, he built the railroad between Plymouth and Washington, which later became part of the Norfolk Southern Railway system.

In his later life Parker became southern manager of the Stave and Timber Corporation, the lumber division of the Arbuckle Sugar and Coffee Company, of New York, which had large interests in the Dismal Swamp area of North Carolina and Virginia. During the Great Depression he returned to building logging machinery at the Surry Parker Machine Works in Norfolk County, Va., and continued this work until his death in Norfolk. He was buried in Cedar Hill Cemetery, Suffolk, Va.

Parker was a member of the American Forestry Association, the Brotherhood of Locomotive Engineers, the Masonic order, and the Methodist church. He was married three times: to Ida Jane Whaley, by whom he had one daughter, Katharine Isabel; to Mary Shepard Odom, by whom he had five children: Mary Shepard, Elizabeth Walton, Surry, Jr. (died in infancy), Margaret Byrd Riddick, and Jane Odom; and to Patty Borland Odom, his second wife's sister.

SEE: [Business catalogue], *Surry Parker, Pine Town, North Carolina Designer and Builder of Labor-Saving Machinery For Handling Logs, Excavating and Dredging Machinery, Engines For Driving Piles, Cranes, Derricks, Winches, Hoisting Machinery, Manufacturer of Logging Tools, Works* (1912); [Business postcard], Logging Machinery Pictured; [Business stationery], "Surry Parker, Designer & Builder Steam Logging Machines and High Grade Hoisting Engines For All Purposes Established 1893, Pine Town, N.C."; *The Independent* (Elizabeth City), 22 June 1911; Weymouth P. Jordan, comp., *North Carolina Troops, 1861–1865: A Roster*, vol. 4 (1973); Ursula Fogleman Loy and Pauline Marion Worthy, *Washington and the Pamlico* (1976); *State* magazine, 7 July 1951; U.S. Patent Office, Surry Parker, 623, 733 Patented 25 Apr. 1899, Bolster for Logging Car Frames.

B. W. C. ROBERTS
JANE PARKER BOSMAN

Parker, Thomas Bradley *(2 Jan. 1851–10 Feb. 1934)*, agriculturalist, farm leader, and public servant, was born in Goldsboro, the son of William Right and Nancy Parker Parker. He had no formal education beyond the third grade but was self-taught. His daughter, Katharine Parker Freeman, recalled that he paid for German lessons with milk and absorbed learning "like a sponge absorbs water."

Farming was his main occupation, and he owned a truck and dairy farm four miles from Goldsboro, the present site of Cherry Hospital. His farming methods were scientific, and he encouraged diversified agriculture. Parker was an authority on alfalfa culture and fertilization. A frequent contributor to the *Progressive Farmer*, he encouraged the development of commercial peach and apple orchards in the Sandhills and Brushy Mountains of North Carolina.

Parker's interest in farming led him to play an active role in the Farmers' Alliance, a national protest organization, informally labeled the Southern Alliance. He held a number of important posts in the North Carolina State Farmers' Alliance, including business agent (1896–1907) and secretary-treasurer (1899–1907). Elected vice-president in 1913, he functioned as president during the annual meeting. Parker was president of the state alliance from August 1927 until August 1929. Elected state alliance lecturer in 1928, he worked in that office until his death in 1933. Thomas Parker served the alliance longer than any other official.

The State Farmers' Alliance encouraged farmers to seek public office, and Parker was elected to the North Carolina House of Representatives in 1896. Unlike most alliancemen who affiliated with the People's party after 1893, he remained a loyal Democrat. His legislative career was short-lived as he moved from Wayne County to Hillsborough in 1897. Later he resided in Raleigh.

Parker's outstanding service was in the field of agricultural extension. He was the first director of the Division of Co-Operative Experiments, which was started in 1908, and continued this work as director of Farmers' Institutes and Demonstration Work. One of his accomplishments was to organize Boys' Corn Clubs, which encouraged youth to increase the productivity of acres planted in corn. Corn clubs were forerunners of the 4-H Club. In 1918 Parker became the first superintendent of Warehouses in North Carolina and in that office promoted the building of warehouses. He retired from public office in 1920 but continued his activities in the State Farmers' Alliance.

For more than sixty years Parker was a member of the Neuse Lodge No. 6 of the Odd Fellows in Goldsboro. A Baptist, he was a deacon in every church in which he held membership—in Goldsboro, Hillsborough, and Raleigh. He was liberal in both his religious and racial attitudes.

On 8 Dec. 1874 he married Penelope Alderman. Parker's death occurred seven months after that of his wife. He was survived by five children: William A., Emma (Mrs. Charles E. Maddry), John H., Frank, and Katharine (Mrs. L. E. M. Freeman). Funeral services were held in the First Baptist Church, Raleigh, on 11 Feb. 1934, and Parker was buried in Montlawn Cemetery.

SEE: *Biennial Report of the North Carolina Department of Agriculture* (1920); *Biennial Report of William A. Graham, Commissioner of Agriculture* (1909–13); Elias Carr Papers (Carolina Manuscript Collection, East Carolina University, Greenville); John L. Cheney, Jr., ed., *North Carolina Government, 1585–1979* (1981); Katharine Parker Freeman to Lala C. Steelman, 4, 22 Dec. 1980; T. B. Parker, "Annual Report of Farmers' Institutes," *Bulletin of the North Carolina Department of Agriculture* (1916); *Proceedings of the North Carolina Farmers' State Alliance* (1889–1933); Raleigh *News and Observer*, 11 Feb. 1934 [portrait].

LALA CARR STEELMAN

Parrish, Edward James *(20 Oct. 1846–22 Oct. 1922)*, tobacco merchant and manufacturer, pioneering tobacco company executive assigned to Japan, and Durham business and civic leader, was born near Round Hill post office in Orange (now Durham) County, the son of D. C. and R. A. Ward Parrish. He married Rosa Bryan of Haywood, Chatham County on 5 Oct. 1870. They had one daughter, Lily Virginia.

Parrish figured prominently in the enterprises that established a major tobacco marketing and manufacturing center in Durham during the 1870s and 1880s. He was reared on a farm and served with the Confederate army during the last six months of the Civil War. His first occupations after the war were those of a petty merchant and state government worker. In 1871, while operating a grocery and confectionery store in Durham, he became a part-time auctioneer in the first tobacco warehouse to be opened in that city. Two years later he formed a partnership with J. E. Lyons to acquire a warehouse and to become a full-time tobacco merchant. This initial venture proved to be ill-timed, since the panic of 1873 forced the partners to close almost immediately. Parrish in association with various partners persisted, however, opening still other warehouses and building an ever more lucrative tobacco trade over the next decade. In 1886 he acquired a manufacturing plant, producing a tobacco product called "Pride of Durham."

But these were rough-and-tumble years when another Durham firm, W. Duke and Sons, was bowling over competition as it made its way towards the formation of the giant trust known as the American Tobacco Company. In this setting, Parrish suffered misfortunes that destroyed his hopes of building his own tobacco empire. First, his warehouse and other key facilities were destroyed by fire. Then, along with several notables in Durham's business community, he lost heavily in a financial upheaval that was remembered locally as "Black Friday." These reverses in no way tarnished Parrish's reputation as an able tobacco man, and he was able to continue his operations for a number of years. Yet he appears to have incurred debts that made him receptive to an offer tendered in 1899 by the American Tobacco Company. For an annual salary of $15,000 he was to go to Japan where, as vice-president of Murai Brothers Company, Ltd., he would represent American Tobacco's majority interests in the Japanese firm.

Parrish's job was to preserve the American Tobacco Company's stake in an increasingly valuable Japanese market at a time when nationalist sentiment was demanding an end to foreign intrusions. Sales of American cigarettes had started in Japan under a system whereby the Japanese were prohibited by treaty from assessing more than nominal tariff rates. In 1899, however, Japan was freed from this prohibition and acted promptly to adopt a new tariff structure that promised to give infant Japanese firms a monopoly of the home market. Faced with these potentially ruinous circumstances, the American Tobacco Company found a Japanese firm in need of capital to finance its ambitions to expand into a variety of enterprises, bought enough stock to control the firm, and appointed Parrish to oversee the tobacco operations. In effect, American Tobacco had found a way to circumvent Japan's tariff barrier. To Parrish fell the responsibility of making the company's investment pay.

Under Parrish's direction Murai Brothers augmented its production with a new factory modeled along the lines of one that had recently been completed in Durham. The techniques of modern advertising that had worked so successfully in the United States were transferred to Japan and adapted to the requirements of that market.

And care was lavished on the development of a network for the distribution of the Murai Brothers brands. In this work Parrish proved remarkably sensitive to Japanese feelings. Against all advice from others in Japan's foreign business community, for example, he allowed the financial transactions associated with the cigarette trade to be handled solely by native banks. Moreover, though startled by business practices that were quite different from those of Durham, he managed to adapt his ways to the local scene. In short, Parrish seems to have been largely responsible for the manufacturing and sales strategies that effectively defeated Japan's intent of turning the tobacco trade over to its own nationals. Cigarette sales in 1901 realized a net profit of $626,039 on a total capital investment of $5 million, and the figures for the next three years were even more gratifying.

But profits such as those realized by the Murai Brothers and its Japanese competitors did not escape for long the attention of a government that was anxious to expand its revenues. After studying European precedents, Japanese officials indicated a determination to seek the parliament's approval of a government tobacco monopoly. Although elements of Japan's tobacco industry were inclined to oppose the monopoly scheme, Parrish advised his New York office against this line. His prediction was that the government would inevitably win and that opposition would only stir ill will, which would be costly to American Tobacco. New York apparently agreed. In any event, by 1902 James B. Duke had formed a new international combine—the British-American Tobacco Company—and his interests in Asian markets were beginning to focus on China. Thus, from 1902 to 1904 Parrish turned his attention to the liquidation of his company's holdings. He was successful in saving for the company its claim to certain cigarette brand names that were becoming profitable in the China market. Further, while his firm and the Murai Brothers suffered financial loss by the government's takeover, Parrish's negotiating skills seem to have contributed to keeping these in the neighborhood of $350,000. At one point, Parrish had reported, both he and the Murai family had expected to be "skinned alive."

Parrish returned to New York and Durham with praise coming from all quarters. Throughout his stay in Japan his work had been followed closely by James B. Duke, who offered him the choice of a position in New York or another foreign assignment. The Murai family presented him with a $5,000 gift on his departure, and both the American and British ministers to Japan testified to his skills as a negotiator. Perhaps the most unexpected decoration was the Emperor Meiji's award of the Third Order of the Sacred Treasure. Parrish was not tempted, however, to continue in the tobacco trade. At fifty-eight he made his home on a farm near Durham and became active in that city's civic and business community.

As we become increasingly aware of how entwined our own lives are with those beyond America's borders, Parrish's career suggests the role of North Carolina's tobacco industry in the making of an interdependent world.

SEE: Samuel A. Ashe, ed., *Biographical History of North Carolina*, vol. 8 (1917); Robert F. Durden, "Tar Heel Tobacconist in Tokyo, 1899–1904," *North Carolina Historical Review* 53 (October 1976); Leonard Wilson, ed., *Makers of America* (1916).

BURTON F. BEERS

Parsley, Eliza Hall Nutt (Hallie) *(13 Aug. 1842–11 June 1920)*, founder of the North Carolina Division of the United Daughters of the Confederacy (UDC), was born in Wilmington, the daughter of Louise and Henry Nutt. She was educated at St. Mary's School in Raleigh. On 2 Sept. 1862 she married William Murdock Parsley, a captain in the Confederate army. He was wounded three times during the war and was sent home to recuperate. Near Richmond, Va., a few days before the surrender at Appomattox, by then a lieutenant colonel, he was fatally wounded. Mrs. Parsley and their two young daughters, Amanda and Janie, were then refuging at Sleepy Hollow in Bladen County but soon returned to Wilmington. There she spent the remainder of her life, supporting herself and her daughters by teaching. In 1894 she opened her own school for small children at 619 Orange Street.

During the war Hallie Parsley had been occupied in caring for wounded soldiers and in offering what comfort she could to suffering friends and neighbors. After the war she continued her service to others, largely through the Confederate Memorial Association of Wilmington. Among other things, the members undertook to decorate the graves of the seven hundred Confederate dead there.

There were similar organizations elsewhere in the state and the members learned of the United Daughters of the Confederacy that had been established in other states. Mrs. Parsley was named chairman of a committee to inquire about the purpose of this body, and from the original chapter in Nashville, Tenn., she received information, a charter, and authority to establish units in North Carolina. In December 1894 she organized the Cape Fear Chapter of the UDC, and in April 1897 she formed the UDC's North Carolina Division. Mrs. Parsley was the division's first president, a post she held for two years. She soon became a public figure, advising women who wanted to create new chapters, traveling frequently throughout the state and elsewhere on behalf of the UDC. Her goal was to inspire love for the Southern states and to teach that Southern soldiers were heroes and not traitors. "In her speeches," it was said, "her soft voice was always animated by the love and devotion in her heart to the young soldier-husband who did not return." She also was involved in arranging the production of amateur plays, pageants, and musicals in Wilmington in the 1890s.

Mrs. Parsley spent her final years at her home on Red Cross Street, Wilmington, receiving friends and admirers. It was said that, like countless Confederate widows, she always dressed in black, her straight hair parted in the middle and combed back. When out of doors she wore a small black bonnet with a long crepe veil at the back. An Episcopalian, she was buried in Oakdale Cemetery, Wilmington.

SEE: Lucy London Anderson, *North Carolina Women of the Confederacy* (1926); *Charlotte Observer*, 25 Apr. 1937; *Confederate Veterans Magazine*, 3–4, 6, 8–11, 15, 19, 23, 25, 28, 36, 38 [consult index] (1895–1930); Eliza Hall Parsley Papers (Southern Historical Collection, University of North Carolina Library, Chapel Hill); Louis H. Manarin, comp., *North Carolina Troops, 1861–1865: A Roster*, vol. 3 (1971); *Minutes of the Twenty-fourth Annual Convention of the United Daughters of the Confederacy . . . New Bern* (1920); Raleigh *News and Observer*, 14 Sept. 1937; Lou Rogers, *Tar Heel Women* (1949) and "Eliza Nutt Parsley," *We the People* 3 (November 1945); *Wilmington Morning Star*, 12–13 June 1920; Tony P. Wrenn, *Wilmington, North Carolina: An Architectural and Historical Portrait* (1984).

WILLIAM S. POWELL

Parson, Donald *(10 Jan. 1882–29 Dec. 1961)*, poet, author, and authority on the game of bridge, was born in Washington, D.C., the son of William Edwin and Anna Rebecca Naille Parson. He was graduated *cum laude* from Harvard University in 1905 and received the master's degree the following year. In 1906 he became sales manager of the Youngstown [Ohio] Car Manufacturing Company but soon opened an automobile agency in that city. In 1914 he went to Pinehurst, N.C., to play golf and in 1915 built a home there. He also had a summer home in Brooklin, Maine.

During World War I Parson served in the army, first as an enlisted man and then as a captain attached to the General Staff in Washington in the military intelligence branch. Promoted to subsection chief, he later served as assistant to the divisional commander. In World War II he joined the navy and when the submarine menace was at its height, he was given command of a Coast Guard picket boat on patrol between Canadian waters and Norfolk, Va.

Parson's early poems appeared in various periodicals including *Wings*, *Talaria*, *Singing Quill*, *American Weave*, *Nature Magazine*, and *Poetry Review*, the latter an English publication. His poem, "The Natural Bridge," received an award in the Elberta Clark Walker Memorial Nature Poetry Contest in 1939. Parson's first volume of poetry, *Behold the Man and Other Poems*, appeared in 1931, followed by *Glass Flowers* (1936) and *Surely the Author* (1944). *Glass Flowers* was also printed in England in 1939. After years of research in libraries, art galleries, and museums in the United States and abroad, he published *Portraits of Keats* in 1954. This one-volume book brought together all of the known portraits and physical descriptions of the English poet, John Keats.

A highly respected scholar, Parson was also a sportsman who enjoyed golfing, yachting, and angling. In Pinehurst he was president of the Tin Whistles, a men's golfing organization. He was also a noted bridge expert and wrote a column on bridge, "Tricky Tricks," which he began as a contribution to the *Pinehurst Outlook*. His last literary work was *Fall of the Cards* (1959), a collection of his Tricky Tricks columns, which was described as "a witty collection of stories centering on intellectual problems at the bridge table."

On 5 Oct. 1907 he married Frances Maria Arrel of Youngstown, Ohio. They were the parents of George Arrel (1911–81), William Edwin (1913–29), Frances (Mrs. Albert D. Hunt, 1914–79), and Donald, Jr. (1916). Parson died at his home in Pinehurst and was buried in Mount Hope Cemetery.

SEE: W. J. Burke and Will D. Howe, *American Authors and Books* (1972); Stanton A. Coblentz, comp., *Music Makers: An Anthology of Recent American Poetry* (1945); William Coyle, ed., *Ohio Authors and Their Books* (1962); Dust jacket of *Surely the Author* (possession of William S. Powell); *Fiftieth Anniversary Report of the Harvard Class of 1905* (1955); *Harvard, Class of 1905, Twenty-fifth Anniversary Report* (1930); *Nature Magazine* 33 (April 1940); *New York Times*, 30 Dec. 1961; Southern Pines *Pilot*, 4 Jan. 1962.

WILLIAM S. POWELL

Paschal, George Washington *(7 July 1869–13 June 1956)*, classical philologist, educator, and historian, was born on a farm near Siler City, the son of Richard Bray and Matilda Schmidt Paschal. His father was sheriff of Chatham County during the Civil War. His great-great-grandfather, Henry Bray, was one of the Regulators who brought charges against Edmund Fanning for collecting illegal fees for registering deeds. Paschal's identical twin brother, Robert Lee, was a prominent educator in Forth Worth, Tex.

George Paschal received most of his early instruction from his sister. The reopening in 1881 of Mount Vernon Springs Academy, which was within walking distance of his home, made a more formal education possible. He attended the academy five months out of the year for four years, working on the farm the remainder of the time. He was graduated in 1886. Lacking money for college, Paschal worked three years in Greensboro before entering Wake Forest College in 1889. It was while he was editor of the *Wake Forest Student*, a literary magazine that his writing ability became evident. The A.B. degree was conferred in 1892.

That fall Paschal entered the University of Chicago for graduate study and after completing the residence requirements for the Ph.D. returned to Wake Forest in 1896 as assistant professor of Latin and Greek. He was a Fellow in Greek at Chicago during the year 1899–1900 and received his doctoral degree at the end of the year. In 1900 Paschal was named associate professor of Latin and Greek at Wake Forest and in 1911 he became a full professor. From 1927 until his retirement in 1940 he was a professor of Greek. For several years he taught Greek at the University of Chicago's summer sessions.

Although teaching the classics was his principal responsibility, Paschal served Wake Forest in many other ways as well. At various times he taught courses in English, history, and mathematics. From 1901 to 1919 he was curator of the library, and during much of that period he was "Collector for the College," writing letters to and visiting those who owed money to the institution. Early in the century he began serving as the admissions examiner and as the college's first registrar, a position he held until 1926. For many years he was director of athletics, personally bearing complete financial responsibility for the teams. His interest in intercollegiate sports never waned.

Soon after completing his doctoral dissertation, Paschal became contributing editor of the *State Democrat*, a newspaper published in Raleigh. From 1912 to 1920 he was contributing editor of the *State Journal*, another Raleigh paper, and during World War I his front-page summary of the war news was a regular feature. From 1931 to 1940 he was editorial writer for the *Biblical Recorder*, a Baptist weekly published in Raleigh, and contributed 8,000 words of copy per week in addition to all the editorials. From 1938 to 1939 he was acting editor. At various times Paschal also contributed articles to the *North Carolina Historical Review*, *Encyclopedia Britannica*, *Review and Expositor*, and *Baptist Quarterly Review*.

Widely recognized as the premier historian of North Carolina Baptists, Paschal was the author of *A History of North Carolina Baptists* (vol. 1, 1930; vol. 2, 1955) and *A History of Wake Forest COllege* (vol. 1, 1935; vols. 2–3, 1943). He also wrote *A Study of Quintus of Smyrna* (1904), *A History of Printing in North Carolina* (1946), which emphasized the Edwards and Broughton Company, and an unpublished manuscript for a three-volume history of the Foreign Mission Board of the Southern Baptist Convention. He was coeditor with E. E. Folk of *A Young Man's Visions—An Old Man's Dreams* (1956), the poems of Benjamin F. Sledd.

For many years Paschal was a member of the Advisory Committee on Historical Markers for the State Department of Archives and History. In 1932 he was president of the State Literary and Historical Association. He also served as a trustee of Chowan College, a vice-president of the Baptist State Convention of North Carolina, and a member of the Historical Commission of the Southern Baptist Convention, the board of the State Hospital at Goldsboro, and the council of the town of Wake Forest. Paschal was a member of the American Philological Association, Phi Beta Kappa, and the Democratic party. He was a deacon in the Wake Forest Baptist Church.

On 21 Dec. 1905 Paschal married, in Dillon, S.C., Laura Allen, a graduate of Greenville Woman's College and the daughter of Joel I. Allen of Marion County, S.C. The Paschals' ten children, all of whom earned at least one degree from Wake Forest, were Robert Allen, Laura Helen, Catherine, Paul Shorey, and Harry Edward, all of whom remained in Wake Forest; George Washington, Jr., of Raleigh; Richard, of Reidsville; Ruth (Mrs. Emmett S. Lupton), of Alamance; Joel Francis, of Durham; and Mary, of Raleigh. George Paschal was buried in the Wake Forest Cemetery.

SEE: *Annual of the Baptist State Convention of North Carolina* (1958 [portrait]); *Biblical Recorder*, 12 May 1951, 23 June (portrait), 7 July 1956; *Director of American Scholars: A Biographical Director* (1951); George Washington Paschal Papers (Baptist Historical Collection, Wake Forest University, Winston-Salem); Raleigh *News and Observer*, 3 July 1949; William L. Saunders, ed., *Colonial Records of North Carolina*, vols. 7–8 (1890); *Wake Forest Magazine* (April 1956 [portrait]); Winston-Salem *Journal-Sentinel*, 10 July 1955 (portrait).

HENRY S. STROUPE

Paschall, Joshua Ernest *(9 Aug. 1896–6 Nov. 1974)*, banker, lawyer, and legislator, was born near Black Creek in Wilson County. The son of Joshua Walter and Sallie Poole Paschall, he attended the public schools of Wilson County and Atlantic Christian College (1914–18), from which he received the A.B. degree. In the summer of 1917 he had attended The University of North Carolina. Paschall was on active duty in the U.S. Naval Reserve Force in 1918 and 1919, completing his inactive service in 1921. He was commissioned a second lieutenant in the North Carolina National Guard in 1922.

In 1919 he entered the banking profession as a runner and a transit clerk for Branch Bank, becoming a teller in 1920. After working in other banks he returned to Branch Bank, becoming assistant cashier (1933), vice-president (1942), cashier and director (1943), and ultimately president (1 Jan. 1953), a post he held until his retirement in 1964. Afterwards, he continued to serve as director and on committees on finance, investments, and trusts. During his presidency, the operations and facilities of Branch Bank were expanded greatly, deposits increased, and the policy of the bank became more liberal in support of the financial needs of individuals and businesses in the communities served. Confidence in the bank was maintained by continuing the relative conservatism of Branch Bank in the banking community and by the open and humane personality of Paschall, whose personal goal in life was to be of service to people in every possible way. He was also a director of Wilson Savings and Loan Association and its president from 1944 until his death.

Paschall's professional activities went beyond Branch Bank and benefited the banking community as a whole. He was instrumental in organizing the Wilson County Chapter of the American Institute of Banking. One of its first graduates, he was an instructor for several of its courses and remained active in the institute during his banking career. He was also chairman of Group II of the North Carolina Bankers Association and served as president of the state organization in 1960–61. In 1961 Governor Terry Sanford appointed him to membership on the North Carolina Banking Commission (1961–65).

Paschall's interest in law originated in its value for certain fields of banking. He enrolled in a course in law in 1923 and received an LL.B. degree from American Extension University, Los Angeles, in 1926. For two years, beginning in 1929, he studied law in a night school conducted by retired superior court judge George P. Pell in Rocky Mount, and in 1931 he passed the bar examination given by the North Carolina Supreme Court. He was a member of the American Bar Association, North Carolina State Bar, Inc., Wilson County Bar, and American Judicature Society. After retiring from Branch Bank in 1964, Paschall entered the practice of law.

Upon his retirement, various friends urged Paschall to seek election to the North Carolina House of Representatives for the Fifteenth District (Wilson and Johnston counties). He served in the legislature for four terms (1965–72) and sat on numerous committees, including Appropriations, Finance, Banks and Banking (vice-chairman), Corporations, Education, Higher Education, Water Resources and Control, Judiciary No. 1, Rules, Conservation and Development, Highway Safety (chairman), Propositions and Grievances (vice-chairman), and House Committee on Trustees of The University of North Carolina (chairman). In addition, he served on the Special Study Committee on the Uniform Commercial Code (1964), whose cause he championed; the Special Committee on Redistricting the House of Representatives (1965); and the Special Study Commission of Reorganizing the Conservation and Development Department (1967–68). At the time of his death, he was chairman of the Wilson County Democratic Executive Committee. He maintained a perfect election voting record by leaving the hospital to vote on the day of his death.

From the 1920s Paschall served Atlantic Christian College (later Barton College), the object of a lifelong loyalty. Keeping the books for the College Office, he and his wife lived on campus for two years. In later years, he served as a member and vice-chairman of the board of trustees, a member of the board's executive committee, and chairman of its finance committee. In 1961 he was awarded the LL.D. degree, and in 1971 he received the Alumnus of the Year Award.

Paschall was a member of First Christian Church in Wilson from his college days until his death. He participated in many civic activities, including the work of the Wilson Chamber of Commerce (president, 1945), United Fund (chairman, 1960), North Carolina Citizens Committee for Better Schools (1961), Wilson Planning and Zoning Commission (1964–65), and board of directors of the Coastal Plains Development Association (president, 1965–66). He also was a member of the Wilson Rotary Club, Loyal Order of Moose, Wilson Elks Club, Newcomen Society in North America, National Society of State Legislators, American Legion (post commander, 1935–36), and American Cancer Society (local chairman).

Paschall married Claire Hodges of Lenoir County (near Mount Olive) on 18 Dec. 1919. They had a daughter, Julia Daly (Mrs. Charles W. Mauze), and a son, James E., who became a major general in the U.S. Air Force. Joshua Paschall was buried in Maplewood Cemetery, Wilson.

SEE: *Atlantic Christian College Alumni News*, April 1961; Autobiographical sketch (possession of Mrs. Ruby Paschall Shackleford, Wilson); Vidette Bass, *Branch: A Tradition with a Future* (1962); Biographical sketches and clippings (possession of Miss Sadie Greene, Wilson); Sadie Greene, Wilson, personal contact; Joshua E.

Paschall to Capital Hill Publishing Company, Oklahoma City, 3 Nov. 1972; Raleigh *News and Observer*, 12 July 1959; Jack Satchwell, Wilson, personal contact; Ruby Paschall Shackleford, Wilson, personal contact; *Smithfield Herald*, 16 Feb. 1968; *Who's Who in America* (1965); *Who's Who in the South and Southwest* (1967–68); *Wilson Daily Times*, 6 Nov. 1974.

WALTER W. ANDERSON, JR.

Pasteur, Charles *(d. 29 Dec. 1793)*, physician, legislator, and local official, was a descendant of Huguenots who emigrated from their native Geneva, Switzerland, arriving in Williamsburg, Va., in 1700. Some of the family were among the Huguenots who settled in Bath, N.C., in 1705. Charles, who was in Halifax, N.C., by 1767, may have been the son of Charles Pasteur who died in Henrico County, Va., in 1736. A physician and apothecary, he frequently furnished state troops with medical supplies during the American Revolution. He represented the borough of Halifax in the House of Commons in 1785 and was sheriff of the county in 1787. He also served as a judge at county fairs and was examiner of claims of disabled veterans. Pasteur was frequently involved in the sale of land and other property. A tavern in Halifax in which he had an interest (or perhaps even owned) appears to have been operated by one Jacob Johnson, perhaps the father of Andrew Johnson; Jacob left in 1793, the year Raleigh was established and where Johnson worked at a tavern. President Andrew Johnson was born in Raleigh in 1808.

The 1784 census of Halifax County indicates that Pasteur held thirty-one slaves, while the 1790 census indicates that that number had grown to thirty-three.

Pasteur's wife, whom he married in 1771, was Martha, daughter of John McKinnie. They were the parents of Martha (m. William Lane in Wake County in 1793), Mary (m. Charles Gilmour), Frances (m. James Clark), John James, Anne McKinnie, Sarah Elizabeth (m. Nathaniel Judkins), and perhaps Nancy (m. one Morgan). The fact that his will was dated the day before his death suggests that his final illness may have come suddenly. His will mentions medicine, shop apparatus, and a number of medical books. There is evidence to indicate that he was Anglican. When the trustees of The University of North Carolina sought subscriptions in 1793 for the establishment of the university, Pasteur was a generous donor.

SEE: Kemp P. Battle, *History of the University of North Carolina*, vol. 1 (1907); Walter Clark, ed., *State Records of North Carolina*, vols. 12–13, 15, 18, 20–21, 26 (1895–1905); Halifax *North Carolina Journal*, 1 Jan., 5 Mar. 1794; Margaret Hoffmann, *Genealogical Abstracts of Wills, 1758 through 1824, Halifax County* (1970); *William and Mary Quarterly* 8 (April 1895).

JOHN MERCER THORP, JR.

Pasteur, Thomas *(1757–29 July 1806)*, career army officer, was from Halifax and perhaps was a brother of Charles Pasteur. On 15 July 1777 he was commissioned an ensign in the Fourth Regiment of the North Carolina Continental Line. After a promotion to lieutenant late in 1777, he was transferred to the First Regiment during the consolidation of the state's Continental Line at Valley Forge early in the summer of 1778. During the 1780 action in Charles Town, S.C., he was captured by British forces and remained a prisoner until his exchange on 14 June 1781. Pasteur returned to the Fourth Regiment in October 1782 and served as paymaster until the end of the war. Remaining in the military service, he retired as a major in 1803. In 1787 he bought one hundred acres of land in Halifax County. A deed dated 1789 indicates that his wife's given name was Margaret but nothing has been found to indicate that there were children.

The 1784 Halifax County census lists Thomas Pasteur, one female, and five blacks. The 1790 census of the same county, however, records a family consisting of himself, four females, and one other free person. The latter probably was the Molly Gordon who indentured herself to him on 10 Oct. 1787 for ninety-nine years. Pasteur was a Mason and a member of the Royal White Lodge in Halifax. He died in Buncombe County.

SEE: Walter Clark, ed., *State Records of North Carolina*, vols. 13, 15–17, 22 (1789–1907); Raleigh *Register*, 15 Sept. 1806; *Roster of Soldiers from North Carolina in the American Revolution* (1932); F. G. Speidel, *North Carolina Masons in the American Revolution* (1975).

JOHN MERCER THORP, JR.

Pasteur, William *(fl. 1770s)*, physician and Revolutionary War administrator, may have been a brother of Dr. Charles Pasteur. He served as a surgeon for the Second Regiment of the North Carolina Continental Line from 1 Sept. 1775 to June 1776, after which he became paymaster of the Fourth Regiment. In 1778 he advertised a number of recently imported medicines for sale in New Bern. Throughout the war Pasteur was active in the procurement of both medicines and munitions for the troops. He was also authorized by the General Assembly to oversee the printing and distribution of state treasury notes. In the late eighteenth century he resided in New Bern.

SEE: Walter Clark, ed., *State Records of North Carolina*, vols. 11, 13–15, 22 (1895–1907); New Bern *North Carolina Gazette*, 6 Mar. 1778; *Roster of Soldiers from North Carolina in the American Revolution* (1932); William L. Saunders, ed., *Colonial Records of North Carolina*, vol. 10 (1890).

JOHN MERCER THORP, JR.

Pate, Zebulon Vance *(2 May 1866–17 Aug. 1941)*, businessmen, merchant, banker, landowner, and farmer of Scotland County, which was a part of Richmond County at the time of his birth, was born on the Thoroughgood Pate plantation near Gibson. He was the third child of George Thoroughgood (1836–1922) and Mary Ann Adams Pate (1840–1920), the latter of Marlboro County, S.C. His siblings were Dr. WIlliam Thoroughgood (1860–1917), James Franklin (b. 1864), Artemus Ward (1868–1928), Charles Thomas (1870–1943), Annie Jane (Mrs. John A. McGregor, 1872–1948), George Mary (1877–1944), Duncan Alpheus (1882–1944), and Sallie Adams (1883–94).

Pate's business interests, including banking and investing, railroads, manufacturing, and trade, occupied much of his efforts. In 1882, at age sixteen, he went to work for John F. McNair (whose daughter he later married) in a Laurel Hill general store, and in 1900 he bought the store and established the firm of Z. V. Pate, Inc. In 1935 the firm expanded to include his stores in Purvis, Osborne, and Gibson. He was president and treasurer of the family business until his death. In 1923 Z. V. Pate General Merchandise in Laurel Hill was advertised in a Charlotte newspaper as "one of the largest stores under one roof between Richmond and Atlanta."

At his death Pate was president of the McNair Investment Company, director of the Commercial State Bank

(Laurel Hill and Hamlet) and the Bank of Gibson, and director and vice-president of the State Bank of Laurinburg. His financial investments included an interest in railroads. In 1909 he had been treasurer of the Laurinburg and Southern Railroad Company, which line ran from Johns to Raeford.

His ties with local manufacturing firms were many. He served as president of the Liberty Manufacturing Company (Red Springs), chairman of the board of directors of Waverly Mills, Inc., vice-president of John F. McNair, Inc., and of Laurinburg Oil Company, and treasurer of the Dixie Guano Company. At his death he was president of the Robeson Manufacturing Company (Lumberton), president and manager of Dixie Guano, and an officer of the Laurinburg Milling Company.

Pate's commercial responsibilities involved three local companies. At his death he was president of Pate's Supply Company (Pembroke), the Dundarrach Trading Company, and the Hamlet Gin and Supply Company.

As a landowner and farmer he was known for having turned to profit the fruit, vegetable, and cotton crops from the Sandhills property of Joe's Creek Farm. During his life he owned land in Richmond, Scotland, Robeson, and Hoke counties, and in Marlboro County, S.C.

Pate was educated at public schools in (then) Richmond County and Marlboro County, S.C. He lived in Laurel Hill from 1884 until 1921, when he moved to Laurinburg. He belonged to the Laurel Hill Presbyterian Church from July 1889 until he joined the First Presbyterian Church of Laurinburg in September 1923.

On 27 Dec. 1893 he married Sallie Patterson McNair (22 May 1869–4 June 1934), daughter of John F. and Mary Jane Lytch McNair, of Laurel Hill. They had four children: John McNair (1896–1924), Edwin, Sarah (Mrs. William Bartel Townsend), and Mary (Mrs. John Duncan Currie). The surviving son, Edwin, a state senator when his father died, had been active in the family business and was then vice-president of the corporation.

In politics Page was affiliated with the Democratic party. He died at his home on Church Street and was buried two days later in Hillside Cemetery, Laurinburg.

SEE: *Charlotte News*, 18 Aug. 1941; *Charlotte Observer*, 19 Aug. 1923, 19, 26 Aug. 1941; G. F. Kirkpatrick, *Historical Sketches of Laurel Hill and Smyrna Presbyterian Churches* (1931); Laurinburg *Exchange*, 15 May 1924, 21 Aug. 1941 [portrait]; *North Carolina Biography*, vol. 3 (1929 [portrait]), vol. 3 (1956); Julia Claire Pate, *Pate-Adams-Newton and Allied Families* (1958).

EVA MURPHY

Paton, David *(23 May 1801–25 Mar. 1882)*, architect, the third of twelve children of John (1772–1842) and Elenor Roper Paton, was born in Edinburgh, Scotland. He attended the University of Edinburgh (1820–24) and was trained as a builder and architect by his father, an extensive builder in Edinburgh. David Paton gained much experience in the design of business and residential structures in the New Town of Edinburgh, where construction was in stone and the neoclassical style dominated design. He worked from November 1829 to May 1830 as an assistant in the London office of John Soane (later Sir John Soane), then the leading English architect.

After leaving Soane's office, Paton returned to Scotland, then sailed for America "with a view to the more active prosecution of his profession there." He reached New York on 30 July 1833 and began to search for employment among the architects of the city, including the leading firm of Ithiel Town and Alexander Jackson Davis.

After the North Carolina State House burned on 21 June 1831, the General Assembly late in 1832 had decided to rebuild on the old site, using stone as the principal building material. The initial plan of the capitol was provided by William Nichols, then of Alabama, who as state architect had greatly enlarged and improved the statehouse in 1820–24, and by his son and agent, William Nichols, Jr. In June 1833 the building commissioners approved the Nichols plan, which was an enlarged and improved version of the statehouse plan. In July they dispensed with the services of the Nicholses and immediately engaged the New York architectural firm of Town and Davis, which modified and improved the Nichols plan, then already in the course of execution. The building superintendents resigned in mid-1834, and the commissioners asked Ithiel Town to find a replacement. He chose David Paton, whose professional experience, especially in stone construction, ideally fitted him for the task. On behalf of the commissioners, Town on 10 Sept. 1834 contracted with Paton—for three dollars a day—to take over the superintendence of the stonecutting and masonry, as well as of the remainder of the project if the commissioners wished it.

When Paton reached Raleigh and began work on 16 Sept. 1834, the exterior walls of the capitol were forty feet high and the general plan was considered well settled. He was immediately made clerk of the works with the entire superintendence of the project as the building commissioners' employee. (Under a direct arrangement with Town and Davis and acting as its employee, he undertook to do concurrently much of the architectural detail work as well.) He kept the extensive labor accounts for all employees, who by 1837 numbered more than 330. By reorganizing the work force, he achieved economies in supervision.

Paton soon gained the confidence of the building commissioners, who accepted his suggestions for modifications in the plan that they had agreed upon with Town. Professionally much offended by that experience, Town withdrew his firm from the project. The commissioners in March 1835 made Paton their architect as well as superintendent, and henceforth he had complete responsibility for the design and construction of the capitol.

Although the basic features and dimensions of the Nichols–Town and Davis plan were well settled by the time Paton took over, he was able to make a number of significant changes. He made the first floor offices and corridors fireproof by spanning them with masonry groin vaults, introduced the galleried opening between the first and second floor levels in the rotunda, moved the supreme court and library rooms from the second to the third floor and introduced their domed and toplit vestibules, redesigned the east and west wings to provide more offices and committee rooms, added public galleries at the third-floor level in the legislative chambers, and effected several other improvements in the plans for the interior. These changes had the effect of making the building more functional without a sacrifice—and often with a gain—in architectural elegance. He eliminated some of the intended exterior decorative details of the pediments, the blocking course of the north and south flanks, and the dome. Paton supervised the execution of the upper third of the exterior walls, the porticoes, the dome and its drum, and all of the interior of the capitol, and therefore he is due much credit for the quality of the work even when it was carried out to the designs of others.

In addition to his work on the building site, Paton made annual trips to Philadelphia and sometimes to New York to consult other architects, observe other major public buildings under construction, engage craftsmen, and procure fittings and equipment not available locally.

For most of the nearly six years he worked on the capitol, Paton was well regarded by the building commissioners and citizens of Raleigh. The commissioners increased his salary progressively from three to five dollars a day, effective 1 Feb. 1837. By early 1840, however, tensions between Paton and the commissioners—exacerbated if not initiated by his demands for more pay—became unsupportable and he was dismissed on 23 May 1840 as the capitol neared completion. Throughout much of his time in Raleigh and for many years after he left North Carolina, Paton futilely pursued his probably meritorious claim for additional compensation. He contended that his services as architect were over and above those called for by his initial contract with the state as construction superintendent and were performed from March 1835 onwards based on the commissioners' promise of extra compensation.

Paton's duties with the state allowed him no time for remunerative private professional work. In 1835, however, he provided without compensation plans for the buildings of the Caldwell Institute, a Presbyterian-sponsored classical school for boys, which the trustees gratefully adopted. In 1839–40 he gave advice about contemplated alterations to buildings of The University of North Carolina, including covering their exterior brick walls with a protective cement wash. In 1837 Paton declined the post of master builder of the U.S. Arsenal at Fayetteville.

Paton left Raleigh for New York in June 1840 and journeyed to Scotland that fall. After working for several years in Edinburgh, where he seems not to have opened an architectural practice in his own name, Paton returned to the United States in 1849. He settled in the city of Brooklyn, where his only certain employment for the remainder of his career was as an instructor of architectural and mechanical drawing in technical institutes in Brooklyn and New York City. Although Paton had a professional office, documentation or family tradition of a substantial architectural practice has not been found. Disabled by a paralytic stroke about 1875, Paton had to decline an invitation in 1878 to advise on a plan for a governor's mansion for North Carolina. His work on the North Carolina state capitol done by the time he was thirty-nine, Paton never fulfilled the promise of that significant early achievement.

Paton married first (on 23 Jan. 1829) Mary Nichol, of Scotland, who died early in 1833. They had one daughter, Eleanor Murray (1830–1902), who remained in Scotland and married John Wyld of Glasgow. Paton married second Diana (or Anna) Bertie Gaskin Farrow (d. 30 June 1875) of Washington, N.C., on 2 Aug. 1837. They had one son and seven daughters. A daughter, Agnes Charlotte (1845–1921), came to live with her mother's family in North Carolina, married C. E. Foy of New Bern, and has descendants living in the eastern part of the state.

David Paton never became a U.S. citizen. He died in Brooklyn, where he was buried in Cypress Hill Cemetery.

SEE: Samuel A. Ashe, *David Paton: Architect of the North Carolina State Capitol* (1909); David Paton Papers (North Carolina State Archives, Raleigh).

JOHN L. SANDERS

Patrick, John Tyrant *(11 Nov. 1852–7 Dec. 1918)*, journalist and resort developer, was born in Wadesboro, the youngest of six children of William H. and Margaret A. Campbell Patrick. The Civil War interrupted his formal education, but he later commented that the printing office where he served an apprenticeship and the newspaper were important sources of training. At age seventeen he added to his family's income by traveling around the country as a retail confectioner and presenting magic lantern shows. In 1877, as a delegate and a reporter, he attended a meeting in Charleston of businessmen supporting the completion of the Cheraw and Salisbury Railroad between Wadesboro and Cheraw. By 1878 he was proprietor and editor of the *Pee Dee Herald* in Wadesboro, as well as the owner of a general store and a captain in the State Guard. He also was selling building lots in Wadesboro and, as secretary of the Dixie Agricultural and Mechanical Association, he arranged the first annual fair in the town.

Recognizing the potentials of Anson County to appeal to northern farmers, businessmen, and tourists, he began distributing publicity releases to northern newspapers pointing out the availability of inexpensive and fertile land. Governor Thomas J. Jarvis learned of the enthusiasm being generated by Patrick's efforts and the matter of immigration began to be discussed. A group of around two hundred families organized to purchase 20,000 acres of land that Patrick consented to secure for them. The State Board of Agriculture, Immigration, and Statistics became interested, and the governor named Patrick to be North Carolina's first general immigration agent. In July 1883 he became head of the Department of Immigration.

Dr. George H. Sadelson, a physician from Lockport, N.Y., settled in Moore County and began to praise the healthful qualities of the longleaf pine belt of the Sandhills. Patrick had relatives in the community and, in consultation with residents there, developed plans for a health resort. After conferring with the U.S. Department of Agriculture, he learned that the climate and soil of the Sandhills were similar to those of France and Italy where grape- and peach-growing flourished. Public health officials in Washington also agreed with Dr. Sadelson that the area's climate and air were beneficial to persons suffering from pulmonary and other respiratory diseases. After carefully considering several sites and in consultation with the newly enlarged Seaboard Air-Line Railway, Patrick used his own resources in March 1884 to purchase 675 acres in Moore County. He organized the New England Manufacturing, Mining, and Estate Company and laid out a town first called Vineland but soon renamed Southern Pines. Securing the recommendation of physicians in New England and the Middle Atlantic states, he issued brochures and other material to attract newcomers.

With Edward G. Stevens and Company of Clinton, Mass., serving as real estate agent, the Southern Pines Resort Company was also formed. A hotel, the Patrick House, was opened and guests began arriving before the end of 1884. The railroad offered special fares to those who wanted to visit the site when considering a move. By 1910 Southern Pines had become one of the state's most popular recreation centers.

Even as Patrick launched one town, he took steps to start another. In March 1885 south of Southern Pines he bought 772 acres of land that at first was called Patrick Plantation but became the winter resort of Pinebluff. Here he built his own home and soon had a printing office where he issued newspapers, pamphlets, and brochures. His *Southern Home-Seekers' Guide* was widely circulated in the North. A similar publication was *Our Sunny Home*, but he also used the columns of the *Bulletin* of the Board of Agriculture to publicize the Sandhills.

As the state's immigration agent, Patrick designated a number of subagents in several northern states and by 1886 was able to report that 125 northern newspapers and some 30 subagents were engaged. Each paid his own expenses but received a commission on the sale of land. The state sent exhibitions to ten fairs in New York, New Jersey, and Pennsylvania in 1885. Patrick also frequently toured the North himself, sometimes speaking at public meetings and enlivening the occasion with minstrel shows that accompanied him. It was observed that Patrick "was no verbal firebrand by Southern standards of the 1880s, but he spoke articulately and sensibly." In 1886 a Northern-Born Settlers' Convention was held in Raleigh to enable newcomers to exchange views and to generate publicity to induce others to come.

In July 1887 Patrick reported to the Board of Agriculture that a new resort, Avoca in Bertie County, had been established, and the next year it was announced that two men from New Jersey had established a silk mill in Wadesboro. Due in large measure to Patrick's efforts, a few French grape growers settled in the region as well as a great number of Scottish crofters. But more notable were large numbers of visitors and settlers from the North, many of whom brought capital for investment. In 1887 it was estimated that more than $500,000 from other states had been invested in farmland, manufacturing, mining, and town properties. This produced in excess of $260,000 in revenue, largely from property taxes. The state of North Carolina spent less than $3,000 in salaries for Patrick and his clerk, office expenses, travel, and printing.

When James W. Tufts of Boston arrived in the Sandhills in 1895, Patrick was on hand to guide him around so that Tufts might select the site of the future Pinehurst. The success of his own ventures made Patrick a source of advice and guidance for others; he assisted in such town projects as Roseland in Moore County, Peachland in Anson County, Vaughn in Warren County, Southmont in Davidson County, and Patrick in South Carolina.

For his success Patrick was commended not only in the state but also by progressive leaders elsewhere. Newspapers in Virginia recommended that officials there seek his advice. In 1889 he was named chairman of the executive committee and special commissioner in charge of planning exhibitions for the Southern Inter-State Immigration Convention in Montgomery, Ala. The Winston-Salem Southbound Railroad was largely the product of his genius for development and promotion.

Other interests also claimed Patrick's attention. He championed the cause of North Carolina's Confederate veterans, helping them secure the state's first substantial pension system for disabled and destitute veterans. Confederate President Jefferson Davis commended him for his work on behalf of the veterans. On several occasions Patrick served as manager of the state fair, and in 1892 he was in charge of the exposition marking Raleigh's centennial.

Poor health in the early 1890s caused Patrick to relinquish some of his work, but by 1896 he was fully recovered. For fifteen years he was industrial agent of the Seaboard Air-Line Railway, and for five years he held the same post with the Southern Pacific Railroad with headquarters in Houston, Tex. After returning from Texas he acquired and developed extensive property in the Chimney Rock area of Rutherford County and was largely responsible for building the excellent highway from Asheville to Charlotte by way of Chimney Rock.

Although he became less active after the turn of the century, he made occasional trips to the North, especially to Maine where he served as president of the Southern Pines Maine Association. His interest in Southern Pines at home also continued—he brought Japanese merchants from San Francisco to establish a Japanese art store and a Belgian artist to do landscape and portrait painting. One of his last projects was a colonization and industrial scheme called "Hope Isle" to relocate a number of blacks on some sea islands between Savannah and Norfolk. He planned to raise $1.5 million to purchase 4,000 acres for a new town with industries, churches, schools, and a civic center.

Temperate in his eating and drinking, Patrick was an early advocate of natural foods. He was a Democrat and a member of the Methodist church and supported vocational education. In 1881 he married Hattie Elizabeth Patterson of Patterson Springs, Cleveland County, and they were the parents of two daughters and a son. Patrick died at the Southland Hotel in Southern Pines and was buried in the family plot at East View Cemetery, Wadesboro. An oil portrait of him hangs in the Pinebluff town hall. His papers and correspondence were stored for many years in Southern Pines but have now been lost or destroyed.

SEE: Aberdeen *Sandhill Citizen*, 13 Dec. 1918, 19 June, 4 Sept. 1975, 13 May 1976; *Biennial Report of the Department of Immigration* (1887–88); Carthage *Moore County News*, 19 Feb. 1975; Mary L. Medley, *History of Anson County, North Carolina, 1750–1976* (1976); Moore County Deed and Will Books (Moore County Courthouse, Carthage); *North Carolina Biography*, vol. 6 (1919); North Carolina Board of Agriculture *Bulletin* (January, August, November 1886); John T. Patrick Scrapbook (North Carolina Collection, University of North Carolina, Chapel Hill); Mrs. Sadie Bilyeu Patrick, personal contact, 10 Jan. 1976; Raleigh *News and Observer*, 9 Dec. 1918; Southern Pines, *Pilot*, 24 Nov. 1944, 18 Nov. 1949; Wadesboro *Pee Dee Herald*, 14 June 1876, 10, 24 Jan., 14 Mar., 9 May 1877; Wadesboro *Messenger and Intelligencer*, 12 Dec. 1918, 7 Oct. 1949; Manly Wade Wellman, *The County of Moore, 1847–1947* (1962).

CHARLES H. BOWMAN, JR.

Patten, John *(1733–1 Aug. 1787)*, planter and Revolutionary soldier, was born in New England around 1733 and moved to North Carolina from Wells, Mass. He established himself on a plantation on the south bank of the Pamlico River about six miles from the site of Washington. On 26 Oct. 1766 he married Ann Caldom, daughter of Churchill Caldom. Patten and his wife had two children, a son and a daughter.

At the Battle of Alamance on 16 May 1771, he served as a captain of a company of Beaufort County volunteers in the regiment of Colonel William Thompson. Four years later he represented Beaufort County in the Third Provincial Congress, which sat at Hillsborough during August–September 1775. On 1 September, when the congress appointed officers of the First and Second North Carolina Continental regiments, Patten was named major for the Second Regiment. He served in Virginia under Colonel Robert Howe when Howe went to the aid of the Virginians against Lord Dunmore. On 10 Apr. 1776 Patten was promoted to lieutenant colonel and in June served with his regiment at Charleston, S.C., when that town was besieged by the British.

In the spring of 1777 the North Carolina Continentals were sent northwards to reinforce the primary American army under General George Washington, which they joined at Morristown, N.J. Patten was present at the Battles of Brandywine and Germantown. On 22 November, when the Second and Third North Carolina regiments were consolidated and designated the Second Regiment, he was promoted to colonel and given the command of the unit. He spent the dreadful winter of 1777–78 at Valley Forge, and on 28 June 1778 he and his men fought in the Battle of Monmouth Court House. Patten was stationed in the New York highlands during the summer and fall of 1778. In late 1779 the North Carolina Continental regiments were detached from Washington's army and ordered south to aid Major General Benjamin Lincoln, arriving at Charleston on 19 Feb. 1780. When the city fell to the British on 12 May 1780, Patten was taken prisoner with 301 of his men. An attack of fever led to his being paroled.

John Patten was mustered out of the army on 1 Jan. 1783. After the war he lived rather quietly on his plantation until his death.

SEE: Walter Clark, ed., *State Records of North Carolina*, vols. 11–12 (1895); Hugh F. Rankin, *North Carolina Continentals* (1971); William L. Saunders, ed., *Colonial Records of North Carolina*, vols. 9–10 (1890); Charles L. Van Noppen Papers (Manuscript Department, Duke University Library, Durham).

HUGH F. RANKIN

Patterson, Andrew Henry *(28 Sept. 1870–9 Sept. 1928)*, scientist and professor, was born in Salem, the son of Colonel Rufus Lenoir and Mary Elizabeth Fries Patterson. He was graduated from The University of North Carolina in 1891 and received A.B. (1892) and M.A. (1893) degrees from Harvard University. After working briefly as an electrical engineer with Westinghouse Electric Manufacturing Company, he joined the faculty at the University of Georgia in 1894. While at Georgia he took a year's leave for graduate study at the University of Berlin and Cambridge University. He returned and taught physics and astronomy until 1908, when he became professor of physics at The University of North Carolina for the remainder of his life.

From 1911 Patterson was also dean of the school of applied science. On leave from the university in 1915–16, he was connected with the American Machine and Foundry Company, in New York, which was engaged in manufacturing munitions. In 1927 the University of Georgia granted him the honorary Sc.D. degree. He was a Fellow of the American Association for the Advancement of Science and a member of the American Meteorological Society, American Physical Society, Society for the Advancement of Engineering Education, North Carolina Academy of Science, and Elisha Mitchell Scientific Society and served as president of the latter two organizations. Among his contributions were studies of X-rays, high tension phenomena, lightning discharges, and atomic structure. As a supporter of intellectual freedom, he was effective in the fight to permit the study of evolution in North Carolina. An advocate of high athletic standards and ideals in southern colleges and universities, Patterson was a founder of the Southern Intercollegiate Athletic Association.

His wife was Eleanor, daughter of Eben Alexander, professor of Greek at The University of North Carolina. Their children were Mary Fries and Howard Alexander. An Episcopalian, Andrew Patterson was sometime senior warden of the Chapel of the Cross in Chapel Hill; he was buried in the Moravian Cemetery, Winston-Salem.

SEE: *Durham Morning Herald*, 11 Sept. 1928; *Georgia Alumni Review* 15 (January 1936); *Journal of the Elisha Mitchell Scientific Society* 45 (November 1929 [portrait]); *Nat. Cyc. Am. Biog.* 21 (1931 [portrait]); Raleigh *News and Observer*, 16 Sept. 1928; University of North Carolina, *Alumni Review* 17 (October 1928 [portrait]); *Who Was Who in America*, vol. 1 (1943).

WILLIAM S. POWELL

Patterson, George *(b. George Papathakes; 1828–10 Dec. 1901)*, clergyman, was born in Boston, Mass., of Greek-American parentage. His father was Petro Papathakes, a native of Greece and member of the Greek Orthodox faith, and his mother Louisa Miles, a Unitarian of Massachusetts. At his baptism his surname was changed from Papathakes to its English equivalent, Patterson. Patterson received his early education at Nashotah House in Wisconsin and later attended The University of North Carolina. In 1850 he received permission to take his pastoral training in North Carolina. In 1852 Bishop Levi Silliman Ives ordained him deacon in North Carolina, and in 1856 Bishop Thomas Atkinson ordained him priest. In his early years he adopted a vow of celibacy, a promise that he maintained throughout his life.

During his first year in the church, Patterson served as rector of the church at Plymouth. From 1852 to 1861 he was a missionary to the slaves belonging to Josiah Collins, owner of the massive Somerset Plantation in Washington County. Near the onset of the Civil War, he joined the Confederate cause as chaplain of the Third North Carolina Regiment. As a result of his devout service, late in the war he was made post chaplain at the Chimboraze Hospital in Richmond.

Following the Civil War he located in Wilmington, where he served successively as rector of two Episcopal churches, including eleven years at St. James's from 1870 to 1881. During the following year he moved to Tennessee to be financial agent for the University of the South at Sewanee. He then spent four years as a missionary in Tyler, Tex., before returning to Tennessee, where he finished his career (1885–1901) as a beloved rector of Grace Church in Memphis. He was awarded an honorary degree by The University of North Carolina (1877) and the University of the South (1895).

Despite his origins, Patterson became a devotee of the South and of the institution of slavery. His views on slavery were revealed in a pamphlet, entitled *The Scripture Doctrine with Regard to Slavery*, that he published anonymously in Pennsylvania in 1856. In the pamphlet Patterson asked "Is slavery a sin?" and attempted to argue in the negative by citing dozens of passages from the Old and the New Testament that seemed to provide at least scriptural approval of the practice. The piece became one of the more prominently known defenses of slavery.

SEE: Thomas Frank Gailor, *Rev. George Patterson, D.D.* (1902); J. G. de Roulhac Hamilton, "George Patterson, North Carolinian by Adoption," *North Carolina Historical Review* 30 (April 1953); Frederic E. Lloyd, ed., *American Church Clergy and Parish Directory* (1898).

LARRY E. TISE

Patterson, Gilbert Brown *(29 May 1863–26 Jan. 1922)*, lawyer, legislator, and teacher, was born near Maxton in Robeson County, the son of Gilbert and Margaret Patterson. He attended Shoe Heel Academy in Shoe Heel (now Maxton), Laurinburg High School, and The University of North Carolina, from which he was graduated in 1886. Patterson then taught in Elizabeth City and studied law

(1886–89). He was admitted to the bar in 1890 and began practice in Maxton.

In 1898 Patterson was a Red Shirt leader in the campaign that returned North Carolina to the Democratic party after the tremendous Populist surge in the 1890s. He served in the General Assembly from 1899 to 1901. In 1902, as a candidate for nomination to Congress from the Sixth District, he sought to unseat John Dillard Bellamy of Wilmington. E. J. Hale of Fayetteville and Joe A. Brown of Chadbourn were also contenders, but at the convention in Fayetteville the contest became a fight between the Bellamy and Patterson forces. The voting continued until well past midnight, with Bellamy always leading. Some delegates left disgusted and disgruntled, but the supporters of the two leaders continued to work. Finally at 7:00 A.M. the following day, Brown threw his support to Patterson, who won the nomination by twenty-five votes. Patterson was elected in 1902 and again in 1904.

Patterson returned to his law practice in Maxton in 1907. In the same year he married Mrs. Mattie McNair Evans. One of the most respected lawyers in Robeson County, he influenced many with his opinions. He took part in two controversial causes in Robeson. The county was by far the largest in the state, and from time to time some part of Robeson wished to secede and become a separate county or to be annexed to a neighboring county. In 1911 one of the bitterest fights concluded with the creation of Hoke County. Patterson was one of the leaders of the antidivisionists.

In 1920 he was on the opposite side of the campaign. The leaders in several towns led the divisionist movement while Patterson was running for the state senate. Each town hoped to be the seat of the new county. Lumberton, the county seat, and Fairmont were the only large towns that voted against division, but the small towns and rural areas opposed it. L. R. Varser was elected to the senate, and the antidivisional candidates won seats in the General Assembly. This was Patterson's last campaign.

Gilbert Brown Patterson was a large landholder, a Master Mason and a Shriner, and for many years a ruling elder in the Presbyterian church. He was honored posthumously by his hometown of Maxton with the naming of the Gilbert Patterson Memorial Library, which opened in 1927.

SEE: *Biog. Dir. Am. Cong.* (1961); Daniel L. Grant, *Alumni History of the University of North Carolina* (1924); *The* (Lumberton) *Robesonian*, 26 Feb. 1951; *Who Was Who in America* (1963).

MAUD THOMAS SMITH

Patterson, Jesse Lindsay *(16 May 1858–26 Nov. 1922)*, attorney, was born in Greensboro, the son of Rufus Lenoir and Marie Louise Morehead Patterson. His mother was the daughter of John Motley Morehead, governor of North Carolina from 1841 to 1845. His father was the son of Samuel Finley Patterson (1799–1874), a native of Rockbridge County, Va., who settled in Wilkesboro and had a prominent career in the political life of the state.

Patterson received his elementary education in the primary schools of Salem and in 1872 enrolled in the prestigious Finley High School in Lenoir. At that time the school was operated by Captain E. W. Faucette. Two years later Lindsay Patterson entered Davidson College, where he was graduated (1878) with the B.A. degree, ranking second in his class. At Davidson he was active in numerous campus organizations and was a recognized leader. Principal among his interests was membership in the Phi Society.

Having determined to enter the legal profession, Patterson went to Chapel Hill to read law and attend the lectures of Judge W. H. Battle. Later he moved to Greensboro and for two years studied under two famous judges: Robert P. Dick and John H. Dillard. In the summer of 1881 he was admitted to the North Carolina bar and immediately located in Winston, where he practiced law for forty-one years.

For two years (1882–84) Patterson was solicitor of the Forsyth County Criminal Court and established himself as an able attorney, one who specialized "in the science of law." From that period of service his professional status was continuously enhanced, and for nearly forty years he was one of the most respected and honored members of the Forsyth County bar. He became affiliated with legal groups at the local, state, and national levels.

Politically, Patterson was an independent, which explains his lack of political appointments and positions. Only twice was he found to have any political status. In 1896 he was a delegate to the "Sound Money" Democratic convention at Indianapolis which nominated John M. Palmer for president and Simon B. Buckner for vice-president. The regular Democratic convention, held in Chicago during 21–23 June, nominated former President Grover Cleveland. Cleveland won the election by a vote of 277 to 145 in the electoral college, defeating Benjamin Harrison, the Republican nominee. The Sound Money Democrats and other splinter parties polled 285,297 popular votes out of a grand total of more than 12 million. Patterson's second political venture was no more successful. In 1902 he ran as an independent against incumbent congressman William Walton Kitchin of the Fifth District, a contest won easily by Kitchin.

Patterson's first law partner was Charles Yates. When Yates left the state, Patterson formed a partnership with Judge E. B. Jones, an association that dissolved after a dozen years when Judge Jones was elected to the bench. For the rest of his life he practiced independently and enjoyed a lucrative, prestigious practice throughout western North Carolina.

The capping legal experience in Patterson's career came in 1901, when he was defense attorney in the impeachment trial of two supreme court members, Chief Justice David M. Furches and Justice Robert M. Douglass. The justices were Republicans and party lines showed in the charges against them, charges judged sufficient by a Democratic General Assembly. It was to the credit of Patterson and his associates in the trial that the justices were acquitted of all charges. Patterson's summation speech to the North Carolina Senate has long been regarded as one of the greatest literary presentations that body has ever heard. It is still read by students of the law.

An even earlier famous case had brought Patterson local and statewide recognition. He was the successful counsel in the case of *Whitfield v. Byrd* (158 N.C. 451), which established title to the Pilot Mountain (the knob, not the town) after a long trial and several arguments before the state supreme court.

Patterson married, on 6 Sept. 1888, Lucy Bramlette Patterson (1865–1942; no relation), of Philadelphia, the daughter of Colonel William Houston and Cornelia Humes Graham Patterson. The Pattersons had no children.

Lindsay Patterson was stricken in the fall of 1919 and died in a Statesville sanitarium three years later. Funeral services were held in Statesville at the home of his sister, Mrs. A. L. Coble, with interment at the Chapel of Rest in Caldwell County's Happy Valley.

During his entire career Patterson had found time for only two activities outside his practice of law. He served for two terms as a trustee of The University of North Carolina, which proved a pleasant experience for him and highly helpful to the school he respected and appreciated. In his home community he was an active member of the First Presbyterian Church; a longtime elder, he was concerned with many lay phases of the church.

Young lawyers in Winston-Salem found Patterson a willing and gracious counselor. He exhibited to them not only talent but also the life pattern of high ethics that one associate labeled "the very soul of honor." When the December 1922 term of the Forsyth County Superior Court convened, five lawyers, all trained in his office, shared in a memorial to Patterson.

SEE: Samuel A. Ashe, ed., *Biographical History of North Carolina*, vol. 5 (1906); Davidson College, *Alumni Directory* (no date); *Greensboro Daily News*, 28 Nov. 1922; North Carolina Bar Association, *Proceedings* 25 (1923); *North Carolina Biography*, vol. 5 (1919); *Who Was Who in America*, vol. 1 (1943).

C. SYLVESTER GREEN

Patterson, Lucy Bramlette Patterson *(22 Aug. 1865–20 June 1942)*, organizational leader, literary figure, and Republican national committeewoman, was born at Castle Rock, her mother's family home in Tazewell, Tenn., the daughter of Colonel William Houston and Cornelia Humes Graham Patterson. Her paternal grandfather, Major General Robert Patterson who had fought in the War of 1812, the Mexican War, and the Civil War on the Union side, lived in Philadelphia. She was graduated in 1882 from Salem Academy, where her mother had also gone to school; there she met her future husband, a promising young lawyer, J. Lindsay Patterson, who became a distinguished attorney, a trustee of The University of North Carolina (like his father and grandfather before him), and prominent throughout the state. They were married on 6 Sept. 1888. The Pattersons had no children of their own but reared two young nieces, Margaret and Catherine Miller, who were two of the three daughters of Mrs. Patterson's sister.

In 1924 Lucy Patterson built a vacation home in Russellville that she named "Long Hope Hill." From this point she wrote articles on her special interests and research, continuing a practice begun in her early life and founded, it is thought, on the habits of her father and other family members who have left some records of their literary pursuits. Beginning in 1904 or earlier she wrote for the *Progressive Farmer*; columns carrying her picture, and often sketches to illustrate her stories, appeared under various titles, including "Just a Bit of Eden" (6 Jan. 1912), "Southern Little Gardens" (3 Mar. 1917, 14 Jan., 25 Feb. 1922), "Winter on Long Hope Hill" (31 Jan. 1925), "Winter Hints on Books and Beauty" (29 Jan. 1927), "What Makes a Girl or Woman Charming" (29 Apr. 1930), and "Here Are Flowers You Will Enjoy" (15–31 July 1931). There were probably other column titles, for many of the clippings to be found in her files now preserved in the Manuscript Department of Duke University Library are unidentified; her page in the *Progressive Farmer* appeared from about 1904 to 1918. Other columns were published in the *Charlotte Observer* under the title "Days of the Right Hand" (3 Sept. 1905; 17 Sept., 9, 16 Dec. 1906; 20 Jan., 24 Mar., 7 July, 11 Aug. 1907) and "Observations of an Early American Capitalist" (11 Aug. 1907). An article seemingly related to this last column, "Sketch and Diary of General Patterson," appeared in the *Journal of American History*, evidently just before 1 Dec. 1907, when it is alluded to in one of her columns in the *Charlotte Observer*; her writing for this newspaper goes back at least to December 1903, when she filled in at Christmas while columnist J. P. B. was on a two-week vacation.

In the Winston-Salem *Journal-Sentinel* her regular column "Just One Thing and Another" appeared for a time, one bearing the date Sunday, 28 June 1931. Two unidentified published stories, "Mrs. Jackson in Washington" and "Mrs. Jackson's Tobacco Factory," are evidently parts of a serial showing the heroine as the Honorable Mrs. Jackson, secretary of state, and in other leadership roles that seem to be a continuation of one of the themes that runs through Mrs. Patterson's columns, that of woman's rights and opportunities in business, the arts, and politics. In addition to her work as a writer she drew others from the few in the state who from 1888 to 1919 were active in literary pursuits; her home, Bramlette, became a center for them, the high point being her annual house party. Her role as a gracious hostess may also have been patterned after that of her forebears; the novel *Captain Macklin* by Richard Harding Davis is based in part on the character, home, and guests entertained by General Robert Patterson, Lucy B. Patterson's grandfather. Her father was writing his memoirs at the time of his death; in Mrs. Patterson's files some of his writing and art work, especially woodcut designs on letter paper, give insight into his tastes and talents as well as his interests as a social leader and host.

Lucy Patterson is perhaps best remembered for her annual award for literary achievement in the state, the Patterson Memorial Cup, a massive three-handled gold-plated on sterling silver loving cup set with forty-nine precious stones from North Carolina mines. Thirteen writers received the award from 1905 to 1933, when their engraved names filled up all the available space on the sides of the cup and it was retired to the Hall of History (now North Carolina Museum of History). In 1930 it was replaced by the Mayflower Society Cup, established through the State Literary and Historical Association as the Patterson Cup had been. Awardees of the Patterson Cup include the poet John Charles McNeill, who received the cup from the hand of President Theodore Roosevelt on a visit to Raleigh (19 Oct. 1905); the Honorable Samuel A'Court Ashe (1908); Horace Kephart (1913); and Josephus Daniels (1922). This award, her writing, and her close ties with other writers earned for her the sobriquet "Inspirer of Tar Heel Writers" to add to that of "Our Patroness" from a grateful editorial writer and "Our Lady of Letters" from a *Charlotte Observer* correspondent. The latter title was used in a story about her appearing in *Sky-Land Magazine* (September 1914).

During the reconstruction period after World War I, Mrs. Patterson visited the Balkan countries and wrote letters home describing her experiences, some of which are preserved with her papers. She became acquainted with the royal family of Rumania and was later entertained by Queen Marie; she was decorated by King Alexander of Yugoslavia for her work in Serbia and was made an honorary member of Kola Sestara, an organization for the relief of war widows and orphans. She traveled widely all during her life, beginning with a trip to Egypt as a young girl; in her mid-sixties, she spent a winter in Moscow. Throughout the years she had widespread interests: she was the organizing president and president for the first three years (1902–5) of the State Federation of Women's Clubs; organizing regent (1902) of the Centennial Chapter of Salem, later renamed the General Joseph Winston Chapter, Daughters of the American

Revolution (DAR); and the first North Carolinian to be elected vice-president general of the National Society DAR, serving two terms (1906–9).

In 1907, as president of the Southern Woman's Interstate Association for the Betterment of Public Schools, she spoke at the Tenth Annual Conference for Education in the South held at Pinehurst; in 1913, as chairman of the Interstate Boone Trail Association, she saw to completion the marking of Daniel Boone's trail from North Carolina through Tennessee to Kentucky; and in 1915 she was chairman of the newly organized Forsyth Moonlight (Night School) Association, which enlisted volunteers as teachers in an adult education program. She was state chairman of several national committees, including the Jamestown Historical Commission, Shakespeare Ter-Centenary Celebration, and Work for Relief in Belgium. The North Carolina exhibit at Jamestown won one of the three silver medals for excellence; the medal is now owned by the North Carolina Literary and Historical Association, of which Mrs. Patterson once served as president. A description of the exhibit by Miss Mary Hilliard Hinton in the *North Carolina Booklet* for 1907 includes a tribute to Mrs. Patterson in which she is credited in large measure with the planning and much of the execution in arranging the exhibition.

In 1922 Lucy Patterson campaigned actively, though unsuccessfully, in the Fifth Congressional District against Major Charles M. Stedman, a Democrat; she upheld the reasonableness of the Republican tariff, arguing for its help to wages; emphasized her support of action to make the tax burden lighter; and urged especially the need for and justice of having women in diplomatic and consular positions. An effective party worker on the national level, she served on the Republican National Executive Committee from about 1923 until her death—a period of almost twenty years—first as an associate member and later as national committeewoman from North Carolina.

After a five-week illness Mrs. Patterson died at Winston-Salem and was buried at Bethesda Cemetery between Russellville and Morristown, Tenn. She had been for many years an active member of the First Presbyterian Church of Winston-Salem.

SEE: Samuel A. Ashe, ed., *Cyclopedia of Eminent and Representative Men of the Carolinas* (1892) and "J. Lindsay Patterson," *Biographical History of North Carolina*, vol. 2 (1905); Gertrude S. Carroway, *Carolina Crusaders*, vol. 2 (1941 [2 portraits]); Hampton L. Carson, *A History of the Historical Society of Pennsylvania*, vols. 1–2 (1910); *Charlotte Observer*, 21 June 1942; "Colonel Joseph Winston Chapter," *DAR in N.C.: Seventy-five Years of Service* (1975); Henry Howard Eddy, "Patterson and Mayflower Cups Served to Stimulate State's Literary Talent," Raleigh *News and Observer*, 16 Mar. 1947 [cups pictured]; John Charles McNeill, Introduction: The Patterson Memorial Cup and Presentation of the Patterson Memorial Cup, *Lyrics From Cotton-Land* (1922 [cup pictured]); "Marking Daniel Boone's Trail," *DAR Magazine*, April 1914; Mrs. E. E. Moffitt, "Biographical, Genealogical, and Historical: Mrs. Lindsay Patterson," *North Carolina Notebook* 12 (July 1912); "The Old Patterson Mansion, The Master and His Guests," *Pennsylvania Magazine of History and Biography*, 39:1 (1915); "Palmyra in the Happy Valley, Home of the Family of J. Lindsay Patterson," *North Carolina Booklet* 12 (July 1912 [home pictured]); Lucy Bramlette Patterson and/or Mrs. Lindsay Patterson, "Dear Salem" (April 1918 [seven illustrations]), "What the Society of Little Gardens Has Accomplished in the South" (October 1917), and "A North Carolina Country Home: Bramlett" (ca. 1920), *House Beautiful*; Mrs. Lindsay Patterson Papers (with Samuel Finley Patterson Papers, Manuscript Department, Duke University Library, Durham); Philadelphia *North American*, 12 Mar. 1905 (microform, Free Library of Philadelphia); Celia Myrover Robinson, "The Patterson Family: Lucy Bramlette Patterson and Her Forebears," Charlotte *Daily Observer*, 10 Nov. 1907; Lou Rogers, "Unusual N.C. Women of the New South," *Tar Heel Women* (1949 [portrait]); "Treasures of An Old Attic," no date, and "Thanksgiving Day in Dixie," New York *Evening Post*, 19 Oct. 1911; "Women Prominent in the Literary and Cultural Life of North Carolina," *Sky-Land Magazine*, 1 Sept. 1914 [portrait]; *Who Was Who in America, 1607–1896*; *Who's Who in America* (1924 ed. through 1941 ed.).

CLARA HAMLETT ROBERTSON

Patterson, Rufus Lenoir *(22 June 1830–15 July 1879)*, manufacturer and entrepreneur, was a member of a distinguished North Carolina family of Scotch-Irish ancestry. Born at Palmyra in the Happy Valley of the Yadkin in Caldwell County, he was the oldest son of Samuel Finley Patterson, a wealthy planter and prominent North Carolina politician. His mother, Phebe Caroline Jones Patterson, was the daughter of Edmund Jones and the sister of Edmund W. Jones, both respected politicians in Wilkes and later Caldwell County. Rufus's brother, Samuel Ledgerwood Patterson, was a planter and politician who served his state for a time as commissioner of agriculture.

During his childhood Rufus Patterson lived both on the Palmyra plantation and in Raleigh, where his father had to take up residence as state treasurer and later as president of the Raleigh and Gaston Railroad Company. He attended the Raleigh Academy and then the school of the Reverend T. S. W. Mott, an Episcopal minister, in Caldwell County. At The University of North Carolina, he was a popular student, winning election to several offices including the marshalship. After graduating in 1851, he studied law under John A. Gilmer, although he never practiced that profession.

In 1852 Patterson married Marie Louise Morehead, daughter of Governor John M. Morehead. After spending a few months at Palmyra, Rufus decided that he preferred business to the agricultural world and moved to Greensboro to study banking under his wife's uncle, Jesse H. Lindsay. Soon, with the financial aid of his father-in-law, he went into business for himself, becoming owner and manager of a cotton, flour, and paper mill in Salem. He also became active in county politics, serving as chairman of the Forsyth County Court from 1855 to 1860 and as mayor of Salem for several years.

A Jacksonian Democrat before the Civil War, Patterson became disillusioned with his party after the 1860 convention in Charleston. As a delegate, he discouraged secession but to no avail. He finally decided to vote for John Bell, hoping to establish "a *Union* sentiment in North Carolina." As he explained in a letter to Colonel I. W. Alspaugh on 3 Oct. 1860: "I am a Union man. I am unwilling to see our country ruined because a Bl'k Rep. President is elected. . . . I am for giving him a trial. If he commits no overt act which would amount to a clear, wilful & palpable violation of our rights, I am for submitting to his government." Patterson believed that the issue of the expansion of slavery into the territories was a mere abstraction, not worth the cost of a civil war. However, in 1861, as a delegate to the North Carolina Constitutional Convention, he voted for and signed the state's ordinance of secession.

In 1862, after the death of his wife, Patterson sold his

Salem mills and returned to Caldwell County to manage his father's cotton factory in the town of Patterson. He remained at this job until the business was burned by Union troops in 1865. During the war, though not active in politics, he supported the original secessionists and criticized the Conservative party headed by Governor Zebulon Vance. In 1862, for example, he praised the Southern cause and Southern victories and denounced the conservatives, whom he accused of "crying out . . . for the old Union that Lincoln might confiscate the property of the *rich* & give it to the *loyal* poor." By May 1865, however, he was attacking the Jefferson Davis government as "the most corrupt despotism that ever *tried* to exist"; he proclaimed his "thanks . . . to a merciful and just Providence" that that government had "ceased for all time." As a delegate to the 1865 constitutional convention, he was a member of the Conservative party and a staunch supporter of Jonathan Worth, an old-line Whig and longtime ally of Vance. This 1865 office was the last one Patterson held.

In 1864 he married Mary E. Fries, the daughter of Francis Fries, a successful Salem manufacturer and merchant who pioneered in textiles and machinery development. After the war Patterson returned to Salem, entering into business with H. W. Fries. At the time of his death, Patterson, along with Fries, owned several cotton and paper mills and a general merchandising firm. Patterson also had an interest in railroad development, which is probably why he became a moderate Republican. He actively supported internal improvements, especially the Western and Northwestern North Carolina railroads. He was a director of both lines and treasurer of the latter, as well as a director of the North Carolina Railroad Company. In addition, Patterson took a lively interest in his alma mater, serving as a trustee from 1874 and contributing a good deal of money to its postwar construction projects.

Patterson raised a large and distinguished family. He had five children by his first wife: the eldest died in infancy, Jesse Lindsay became a prominent lawyer, Carrier F. married Judge A. L. Coble, Lettie W. was wed to Colonel Frank H. Fries, and Louis Morehead died in adolescence. He and his second wife had six children: Frank F., a newspaperman for the *Baltimore Sun*; Samuel F., a Baltimore cotton manufacturer; Andrew H., a professor of physics at the University of Georgia; Rufus L., Jr., an inventor and businessman based in New York City; John L., a cotton manufacturer in Roanoke Rapids; and Edmond V., who was in the cotton commission business in New York City. His fourth son from his second marriage was the most outstanding. Rufus Lenoir Patterson founded the American Machine and Foundry Company at the turn of the century and with his invention of a machine to weigh, pack, stamp, and label smoking tobacco, he built the company into a million-dollar business. He then merged with and became a vice-president in charge of manufacturing for the American Tobacco Company.

Although Patterson was reared in the Episcopal church, he was received as a full member of the Moravian church by confirmation on 16 June 1878. On his death, services were held at the Moravian church and burial was in the family burying grounds in the Salem Woodland Cemetery beside the remains of his first wife. Rufus Patterson was said to be "strikingly handsome," a description confirmed by his portrait in Samuel A. Ashe's *Biographical History*.

SEE: Samuel A. Ashe, ed., *Biographical History of North Carolina*, vol. 2 (1905 [portrait]); Jones and Patterson Family Papers (Southern Historical Collection, University of North Carolina, Chapel Hill); J. G. McCormick, "Personnel of the Convention of 1861," *James Sprunt Historical Monographs*, No. 1 (1900); Patterson Papers (North Carolina State Archives, Raleigh); Samuel Finley Patterson Papers (Manuscript Department, Duke University Library, Durham).

ROBERTA SUE ALEXANDER

Patterson, Rufus Lenoir, Jr. *(11 July 1872–11 Apr. 1943)*, inventor and businessman, was born in Salem, the son of lawyer, planter, and paper mill owner Rufus Lenoir (1830–79) and his second wife Mary Elizabeth Fries Patterson (1844–1927), the daughter of textile pioneer Francis Fries. He attended the Moravian Boys School and the Winston graded school, worked briefly for the Roanoke and Southern Railroad, and in 1889 enrolled at The University of North Carolina.

Patterson left the university after one year to work with William H. Kerr, an inventor of Concord, who manufactured a machine to produce tobacco bags. In 1891 Patterson traveled to England to introduce Kerr's machine and remained there two years to study machine design. After his return in 1893, he divided his time between Baltimore, Md., where Kerr had established his firm, and Durham, where Patterson was associated with the Golden Belt Manufacturing Company, the firm that produced and operated the Kerr bagging machines.

In 1893 Patterson organized the Automatic Packing and Labelling Company to develop his first invention, the Patterson Packer, a machine that automatically weighed, packed, stamped, and labeled smoking tobacco. This machine brought Patterson to the attention of James B. Duke of the American Tobacco Company. After viewing the Patterson Packer, Duke reportedly said, "Ding it, your machines are all right, but I also must have you." In 1898, at age twenty-six, Patterson joined the New York office of Duke's firm as supervisor of all its machinery, including his own packer. He became secretary of the company in 1900 and vice-president in charge of manufacturing in 1901.

In 1900 Patterson organized the American Machine and Foundry Company, a subsidiary of the American Tobacco Company, and in 1901 established two other corporations, the International Cigar Machinery Company and the Standard Tobacco Stemmer Company. When American Machine and Foundry became an independent corporation in 1912, Patterson remained president; he held that position until 1941, when he became chairman of the board of directors. By 1920 American Machine and Foundry and its subsidiaries produced must of the machinery used in the tobacco industry, including the automatic cigar maker developed by Patterson at a cost of $5 million. The company then diversified into other areas of automatic packaging, beginning with the standard bread wrapper in 1924. By 1935 Rufus Lenoir Patterson was one of the eight highest-paid executives in the country.

Although he lived most of his later years in New York City, Patterson remained loyal to his native state and was an active member of both the Southern Society and the North Carolina Society. In 1930 he joined with John M. Morehead in presenting the Morehead-Patterson Bell Tower to The University of North Carolina. In 1925 Patterson was decorated with the French Legion of Honor in recognition of his service as chairman of the Fourth Liberty Loan Drive and in 1935 was awarded an honorary doctor of laws degree by The University of North Carolina.

In November 1895 he married Margaret Morehead, granddaughter of Governor John M. Morehead. They had a son Morehead, who succeeded his father as president of American Machine and Foundry, and a daughter, Lucy Lathrop (Mrs. Casimir deRham). A portrait of Patterson, painted by Sir William Orpen in 1920, hangs in the Rufus L. Patterson Tobacco Engineering Center in Richmond, Va.

SEE: Samuel A. Ashe, ed., *Biographical History of North Carolina*, vol. 2 (1905); Rufus Lenoir Patterson Papers (Southern Historical Collection, University of North Carolina, Chapel Hill); "Rufus Lenoir Patterson's Cigar Machine," *Fortune* (June 1930).

ELLEN BARRIER NEAL

Patterson, Samuel Finley *(11 Mar. 1799–20 Jan. 1874)*, planter and politician, was born in Rockbridge County, Va., of Scotch-Irish parents. In 1811 he moved to Wilkesboro to live with his uncle. There he became a clerk in the store of Waugh and Finley until he turned twenty-one and began his own business, which he pursued until 1840. In 1848, in a village that was named for him, he started—along with Edmund Jones, his brother-in-law, and James C. Harper—the first industry of any importance in Caldwell County: a cotton factory.

At this time, however, Patterson was more interested in politics. At age twenty-two he won the position of engrossing clerk of the House of Commons and for fourteen years thereafter he continued to be elected to some clerkship in the state legislature. In 1835 he became chief clerk of the senate, and from 1835 to 1837 he served as treasurer of North Carolina. He was a Whig with a strong interest in internal improvements, a concern that was strengthened while he was president of the Raleigh and Gaston Railroad in its early stages of growth from 1840 to 1845.

Patterson married Phebe Caroline Jones, the daughter of General Edmund Jones and the granddaughter of General William Jones, both planters and politicians from Wilkes and later Caldwell County. When his father-in-law died in 1845, Patterson moved to his wife's family home, Palmyra, in the Happy Valley of the Yadkin River in Caldwell County, to engage in farming and politics, careers that occupied him for the remainder of his life. The year he returned to Caldwell County, he was elected chairman of the county court, a post he held until the court was dissolved and a new court structure was created by the state legislature in 1868. He also served in the state senate in 1846 and 1848. During the latter term, as chairman of the Committee on Internal Improvements, he wrote the bill chartering the North Carolina Railroad Company. Patterson again served Caldwell in 1854 as a member of the House of Commons, in 1864 as a state senator, and in 1866 as a delegate to the second session of the state's constitutional convention.

As a Whig, he originally opposed secession. And after the Civil War, in a letter to his son Rufus, he claimed that he was "content with a return to the old government under which *I* never felt that I was opposed." But during the war he was loyal to his state and rejoiced over Southern victories. After the war, he joined the Conservative and later the Democratic party, attending the 1866 Philadelphia Peace Convention which supported Andrew Johnson and his policies as opposed to the Republicans. In 1868 he was nominated by the Democrats for the office of superintendent of public works but was defeated, as were the rest of his party's nominees. After that, he essentially retired from public life, returning to Palmyra.

Patterson also held several less important offices during his lifetime, including clerk of the superior court, justice of the peace, and, in 1839, Indian commissioner. He was also a brigadier general and later a major general in the state militia and thus became known as General Patterson. In addition, he served as a trustee of The University of North Carolina. In 1828 he became a junior grand warden of the Grand Lodge of Masons in North Carolina; in 1830 and 1831 he was deputy grand master and in 1833 and 1834 grand master. Patterson was active in the Episcopal church, serving as a lay reader, warden, and vestryman for many years. In 1871 he attended the General Convention of the church in Baltimore as a lay delegate from the North Carolina Diocesan Convention.

Though entrenched in public life, Patterson also loved farming. He constantly read and contributed to agricultural journals; at Palmyra, he introduced new seeds, improved implements, and experimented with better methods of cultivation. His home was a showplace in the county. He remodeled it in the 1850s, adding two wings, a dining room and pantries, and a large staircase. On the plantation he also had a blacksmith and carpenter shop, a shoe shop, and a loom room. Both of his sons became successful and prominent North Carolinians, Rufus L., as a manufacturer and entrepreneur, and Samuel L., as a planter-politician and onetime commissioner of agriculture.

Patterson died at his home and was buried in the family cemetery in Caldwell County.

SEE: Nancy Alexander, *Here I Will Dwell* (1956); Samuel A. Ashe, ed., *Biographical History of North Carolina*, vol. 2 (1905 [portrait]); Thomas Felix Hickerson, *Happy Valley* (1940); Jones and Patterson Family Papers (Southern Historical Collection, University of North Carolina, Chapel Hill); Patterson Papers (North Carolina State Archives, Raleigh); John H. Wheeler, ed., *Reminiscences and Memoirs of North Carolina and Eminent North Carolinians* (1884).

ROBERTA SUE ALEXANDER

Patterson, Samuel Legerwood *(6 Mar. 1850–14 Sept. 1918)*, farmer and legislator, was born at Palmyra, the family home located in the Yadkin River valley in Caldwell County, the son of Samuel Finley and Phebe Caroline Jones Patterson. His father, a farmer, financier, and businessman, was a member of the state house of representatives and the senate, state treasurer, and president of the Raleigh and Gaston Railroad for five years. Samuel L. Patterson was educated at Faucette's school, Bingham's, and Wilson's Academy. He entered The University of North Carolina in 1867 but the school closed the following year. He then attended the University of Virginia for one year before taking a clerking job in Salem. On 17 Apr. 1873 he married Mary S. Senseman, the daughter of a Moravian minister from Indiana.

Although a Republican, Patterson was appointed county commissioner and district superintendent of the census in a Democratic county. He served in the state house of representatives in 1891 and 1898 and in the state senate in 1893; in the legislature he was chairman of the committee on agriculture and was a member of many other committees. He was also a trustee of The University of North Carolina. Patterson was commissioner of agriculture from 1895 to 1897, when he was removed by the Fusion party. He was reappointed in 1899 and then elected by popular vote through 1908. Patterson Hall at North Carolina State University is named in his honor.

SEE: Samuel A. Ashe, ed., *Biographical History of North Carolina*, vol. 2 (1905); C. Beauregard, *North Carolina's Glorious Victory* (1898); A. M. Fountain, *Place Names on*

State College Campus (1956); Daniel L. Grant, *Alumni History of the University of North Carolina* (1924); *Prominent People of North Carolina* (1906); W. F. Tomlinson, *State Officers and General Assembly of North Carolina* (1893).

CHARLES S. POWELL IV

Pattillo, Henry *(1726–1801)*, pioneer Presbyterian minister, educator, and Patriot in North Carolina, was born in Balermic, Scotland, the son of George and Jane Pattillo. He had two brothers, George and William, and several sisters whose names are unknown. Except that young Henry was educated by his deeply religious parents to a degree above most of his Scottish contemporaries, nothing more is known about his youth until he arrived in Virginia with his brother George about 1740.

Henry Pattillo worked in a mercantile establishment until he became dissatisfied with that occupation, then became a schoolteacher. While thus engaged, he constantly felt the call to become a Christian minister and, in 1750, began planning to obtain the higher education he considered necessary for that purpose. He actually started on a journey to Philadelphia to start his theological training when he was stricken with pleurisy and was forced to remain in Virginia. During his long convalescence, the young ministerial aspirant was invited by the venerable Presbyterian educator, Samuel Davies, to reside in his home and study in his school. Pattillo intended to complete his studies at the College of New Jersey (later Princeton University), of which Davies had become the head, but he fell in love with Mary Anderson and married her in 1755. Supporting his family by teaching school in Hanover County, Va., and living with extreme economy, Pattillo continued to study with Davies until 1758, obtaining the equivalent of a college education.

In 1755 the Presbyterian Synod of New York had established the Presbytery of Hanover, and on 29 Sept. 1785 this body licensed Pattillo as a Presbyterian minister. The licentiate then began his trials required by the church for ordination. These consisted of delivering various sermons, lectures, and exegeses before the Presbytery and being examined by that body on the subjects of ontology, pneumatics, ethics, rhetoric, geography, and astronomy, and on his religious experiences. Having passed all requirements satisfactorily, Pattillo was ordained into the ministry of the Presbyterian church in September 1758.

Pattillo immediately accepted a call to become the resident minister of the congregations at Willis, the Byrd, and Buck Island churches in Virginia. He labored with these congregations for four years, then accepted a call to the Cumberland, Harris Creek, and Deep Creek churches, also in Virginia. After a stay of two years, the minister moved to Orange County, N.C., in 1765, to become the pastor of the Hawfields, Eno, and Little River churches.

In his new location, the minister not only officiated so influentially as a clergyman that he became known respectfully as "Father Pattillo," but he also began a classical school for men in his home. The success of this school inspired the teacher to continue it in Bute and Granville counties when he left the Orange churches after a nine-year ministry. The school became widely known and among its pupils were Nathaniel Rochester, Charles Pettigrew, and William Blount.

Pattillo was engaged in his pastoral work in Orange County when the War of the Regulation took place. Deploring the violent tactics of its participants, the clergyman and several of his colleagues wrote a letter to Governor William Tryon stating that they would use their influence to discourage the growth of the movement. They also sent a letter to the churches in their presbytery urging that a peaceful means be sought to settle governmental controversies. These protests were in vain but the governor remembered the effort, and when he went to Hillsborough in 1768 at the head of the militia, Pattillo was one of the clergymen requested to preach to the troops on the Sabbath.

In 1770 Pattillo joined David Caldwell, Hugh McAden, Joseph Alexander, Hezekiah Balch, and James Creswell in the organization of the Presbytery of Orange, a new division of the Presbyterian church. In 1780 he accepted the pastorate of the Granville County churches at Nutbush and Grassy Creek.

Despite the unhappy events of the Regulation, Pattillo continued his interest in the political life of the colony. Having moved to Bute County (present-day Franklin and Warren counties) after he left Orange and before he located in Granville, he was elected a county delegate to the Third Provincial Congress, which met at Hillsborough in 1775, and made chaplain of that body after it convened. He was also assigned to serve on a committee with Richard Caswell and Maurice Moore to explain to the former Regulators that the oath of loyalty Governor Tryon forced them to take under military duress was not morally binding and did not prevent them from joining the Patriots in their struggle for independence of Great Britain. In addition, Pattillo was made a member of the Provincial Council for the Halifax District. In 1771 he had been named a trustee of Queen's College, and in 1776 he became a trustee of Granville Hall. He also participated in a movement to establish Warrenton Academy.

As a testimony to his general influence, the Transylvania Company offered Pattillo a gift of 640 acres of its western land on condition that he settle on it, but he refused, though doubtless appreciated, the offer. In 1784 the minister's Granville parishioners presented him with a 300-acre farm on Spicemarrow Creek on condition that he remain their pastor permanently, and Pattillo lived there with his family until his death.

While engaged in political affairs, the clergyman did not neglect his ministry or his educational projects. In 1787 he published a treatise on Christian conduct entitled *The Plain Planter's Family Assistant; Containing an Address to Husbands and Wives, Children and Servants; With Some Helps for Instruction by Catechisms; and Examples of Devotion for Families: With a Brief Paraphrase on the Lord's Prayer*. In the same year Hampden-Sydney College awarded him an honorary master of arts degree in recognition of his accomplishments. He published a book of his sermons (1788), which included homilies entitled "The Divisions Among Us" and "An Address to the Deists," as well as *A Geographical Catechism* (1796), a textbook on geography written in question-and-answer style, the first publication of its kind in North Carolina.

No portrait of Pattillo is known. However, he was described by a contemporary as a large man with coarse features but with a commanding voice, impressive delivery, and usually a cheerful demeanor. Although his strength failed in his later years and he suffered severe financial reverses, Pattillo continued to work on behalf of Christian evangelism even in old age. In 1801 he went to Dinwiddie County, Va., to conduct a series of services and died there while thus engaged. Presumably he was buried in that area although the location of his final resting place is unknown. A commemorative service was held in the Granville churches for the departed pastor on which occasion the Reverend Drury Lacy included the following statement in his eulogy: "Thus he closed his life on a preaching tour, being far advanced in his 75th year, which doubtless does honor to his character, and should serve to stimulate all his younger brethren in the ministry to follow his example, and be willing to spend, and be spent in the cause of their Saviour, and in the cause of religion."

SEE: Samuel A. Ashe, ed., *Biographical History of North Carolina*, vol. 3 (1906); William Henry Foote, *Sketches of North Carolina, Historical and Biographical* (1846); Pattillo Papers (Union Theological Seminary, Richmond, Va.); William M. E. Rachal, "Early Minutes of Hanover Presbytery," *Virginia Magazine of History and Biography* 63 (January 1955); William Buell Sprague, *Annals of the American Pulpit*, vol. 3 (1858); Durward T. Stokes, "Henry Pattillo in North Carolina," *North Carolina Historical Review* 44 (October 1967); Herbert Snipes Turner, *Church in the Old Fields* (1962).

DURWARD T. STOKES

Patton, James Washington *(13 Feb. 1803–26 Dec. 1861)*, contractor and merchant, was born in Wilkes County to James, an Irish immigrant and pioneer to the Yadkin River area, and Anne Reynolds Patton of Wilkes County. When James was four, the family moved to Buncombe County outside of Asheville. There he was educated at Newton Academy and lived in and around Asheville the remainder of his life.

A prominent merchant, Patton is noted for having used his "social position and wealth" as a "power for the good in his section of the country." To increase commerce, he proposed and helped complete an east-west thoroughfare in Asheville. With the help of construction workers employed in his business, the road was finished and named Patton Avenue. From his father Patton inherited the Eagle Hotel, one of the first hotels in Asheville. He later expanded his resort interests and built another hotel in Warm Springs.

Patton donated the land on which Trinity Episcopal Church in Asheville now stands and helped open the church in 1841, serving on the first vestry. He was a member of Asheville's first board of commissioners (1841) and served as the presiding justice in the Buncombe County Court of Pleas and Quarter Sessions for many years.

Clara Walton of Burke County was his first wife by whom he had two sons, James Alfred and William Augustus; both died in the disease-ridden army camps of the Confederate army. Patton's second wife was Henrietta Kerr of Charleston, S.C., by whom he had two children, Fanny Louisa and Thomas Walton. Fanny was a founder of Mission Hospital in Asheville. Thomas Walton had a distinguished military career and held numerous political offices in Asheville, including that of mayor.

It is to the credit of James W. Patton and Charlotte Kerry, his sister-in-law from Charleston, that Beaucatcher Mountain has its characteristic name. Charlotte strolled on the mountain with her beaux, and her brother-in-law teased her, dubbing the mountain "Charlotte's Beaucatcher."

SEE: *Biographical Sketch of Thomas Walton Patton, 1841–1907* (1907 [portrait]); Virginia T. Lathrop, "A Century of Roots" (a paper presented to the Review Club; Pack Library, Asheville); Laura Macmillan, *The North Carolina Portrait Index* (1963); F. A. Sondley, *History of Buncombe County*, 2 vols. (1930 [portrait]).

AGNES R. BURHOE

Patton, James Welch *(28 Sept. 1900–17 May 1973)*, educator, archivist, and historian, was born in Murfreesboro, Tenn., the son of James Wesley and Elizabeth Welch Patton. He received his college preparatory training at Hawkins School in nearby Gallatin and attended Vanderbilt University, from which he was graduated in 1924 with a bachelor of arts degree and membership in Phi Beta Kappa. The University of North Carolina awarded him a master's degree in 1925 and a Ph.D. in 1929.

Patton began his teaching career at Georgia State Woman's College (now Valdosta State College) (1925–27), then spent a year as associate professor of history at The Citadel (1929–30) and as a member of the faculty of Wittenburg College in Springfield, Ohio (1930–31). From 1931 to 1942 he was chairman of the Department of History of Converse College in Spartanburg, S.C. In 1942 he accepted the chairmanship of the Department of History and Political Science at North Carolina State College (now North Carolina State University).

In Chapel Hill, Patton's interest in southern history and record of scholarship brought him the respect and lasting friendship of J. G. de Roulhac Hamilton, his major professor. Upon Professor Hamilton's retirement in 1948, Patton was invited to succeed him as director of the Southern Historical Collection, the manuscript repository at The University of North Carolina. For many years thereafter Patton canvassed the southern states in search of manuscripts, and through these travels he became familiar with the entire South, but especially with North Carolina, South Carolina, and Tennessee.

Patton also held a professorship in The University of North Carolina's Department of History, and during his later years with the Southern Historical Collection he taught one class in North Carolina history each term. On retiring from administrative duties in 1967, he joined the Department of History and for four years taught a full load of courses in North Carolina history. At age seventy, still active and vigorous, he continued to teach for two additional years on a reduced schedule. His full retirement began in May 1973, less than ten days before his death.

As an archivist James Patton was a man of established reputation. He delivered papers at several meetings of the Society of American Archivists and in 1959 was elected a Fellow of the society. He also was known as a conscientious teacher and a careful scholar. His mastery of detail and his extraordinary memory were marvels to colleagues and students alike, and the quality of his scholarship is evident in his writings. *Unionism and Reconstruction in Tennessee* was published by The University of North Carolina Press in 1934 and *Women of the Confederacy*, written jointly with Francis Butler Simkins, appeared in 1936. In addition, he contributed numerous articles and reviews to professional journals and was a contributor to both the *Dictionary of American Biography* and the *Dictionary of American History*. He was editor of the three-volume *Messages, Addresses, and Public Papers of Governor Luther H. Hodges* and of the *Minutes of the Greenville Ladies' Association in Aid of the Confederate Army*.

Few historians have invested more of their time and talents in their professional associations. When the Historical Society of North Carolina was reorganized in 1945, Patton became a charter member and was elected to its first Executive Council; in 1966 he was chosen president. Three other associations profited from his presidential leadership—the South Carolina Historical Association in 1939, the Southern Historical Association in 1956, and the North Carolina Literary and Historical Association in 1964. He was also an active member of the American Historical Association and the Organization of American Historians.

It can be said of James Welch Patton that he was a loyal

son of his native region and of his adopted state. His mind was filled with the history of the South and of North Carolina, and he shared this knowledge willingly. As an individual he was a kind and devoted friend to those who knew him. His work as a scholar, particularly in providing scholarly resources for others, stands as a lasting contribution to historical research.

Patton's death came quietly in his sleep during a visit to Charleston, S.C., with his wife, Carlotta Peterson Patton, a native of that city. The Pattons had married in June 1930. In addition to his wife, a daughter, Emilie Patton deLuca, and two grandchildren, Anne Randolph deLuca and James Patton deLuca, survived him. Patton was an active member of the Episcopal church. Funeral services were held at the Chapel of the Cross in Chapel Hill, with interment in the New Chapel Hill Cemetery.

SEE: Anna Brooke Allan, "James Welch Patton," *Journal of Southern History* 39 (August 1973); *Chapel Hill Newspaper*, 18, 22 May 1973; *Chapel Hill Weekly*, 30 July 1948, 22 Nov. 1955, 12 Nov. 1956; Raleigh *News and Observer*, 10 Sept. 1967; *Who Was Who in America*, vol. 6 (1976).

J. ISAAC COPELAND

Patton, Sadie Smathers *(28 Sept. 1886–2 Jan. 1975)*, local historian, was born in Henderson County, the daughter of John Wesley and Mary Rickman Smathers. She was educated by private tutors and read law under a Hendersonville attorney. As senior court reporter she served in most of the counties of western North Carolina. Active in numerous local and regional historical and patriotic organizations, she was a founder and trustee of the Cherokee Historical Association, producer of the outdoor drama, *Unto These Hills*. From 1941 to 1957 she was a member of the executive board of the North Carolina Department of Archives and History.

Sadie Patton was the author of *Ghost Stories and Legends of the Mountains* (1935), *The Story of Henderson County* (1947), *Sketches of Polk County History* (1950), *Saint James Episcopal Church, Hendersonville* (1953?), *Buncombe to Mecklenburg: Speculation Lands* (1955), and *The Kingdom of the Happy Land* (1957).

Her husband was Preston Fidelia Patton and they had an adopted son. She was buried in Calvary Churchyard, Fletcher.

SEE: *Asheville Citizen-Times*, 25 Apr. 1954, 6 Apr. 1958, 9 June 1958; *North Carolina Biography*, vol. 3 (1956); William S. Powell, ed., *North Carolina Lives* (1962).

GEORGE MYERS STEPHENS

Paul, Hiram Voss *(8 Feb. 1848–ca. 1900)*, poet, author, editor, and journalist, was born in New Bern of Scotch-Irish ancestry. His forefathers, the McCotters and the Pauls, were among the first settlers of Albemarle County in 1663.

The son of a Baptist pastor in New Bern, the Reverend Hiram Voss Paul, he attended New Bern Academy and Lenoir Institute. His mother died in 1864 and his father in 1865. Although his father had intended for him to be a minister and had already made provisions with Braxton Craven for him to enter Trinity College, his guardian took little interest in his education and revoked the Craven contract. Paul was instead apprenticed to John Spellman, a printer and the editor and proprietor of the *New Berne Commercial*. He did, however, start studying theology with the Reverend Edward M. Forbes, D.D., rector of Christ Church, New Bern, in 1869. The same year, a volume of his poems was published in New Bern.

In 1871 Paul went to visit his uncle in New York City and stayed for three years. While there, he worked for the business firms of Lang, Little, and Hillman and Moses Dow and established a journal, entitled *Evolutionist*, that was devoted to the Evangelical Temperance Alliance. His journal offices were destroyed by fire in the latter part of 1872. During this period, one of his poems, "Alone," fell into the hands of Mrs. Sarah Josepha Hale, who had it published in *Waverly Magazine*. Soon his poems, sketches, and stories were appearing in what his biographer, the Reverend James Dike, called "some of the best magazines and journals." At this time, he also resumed his theological studies with the Reverend Charles F. Deems.

After traveling much from 1872 to 1877, Paul returned to North Carolina and pursued a career as a journalist. During the next few years, he was editor of the *Daily Evening Dispatch* in Raleigh, the *Evening Post*, probably also in Raleigh, and the *North Carolina Prohibitionist*. The mission of the *Dispatch* was the vindication of the interests of North Carolina against foreign railroad syndicates and the paper was an inveterate opponent of the sale of the state's interest in the Western North Carolina Railroad. The paper's owners, although originally against the sale, changed their minds, putting them at odds with Paul, and they did not renew his contract. He then turned to editing the *Evening Post* with Major William Hearne. The *Post* was a Democratic paper devoted largely to promoting the candidacies of Daniel G. Fowle and Julian S. Carr for governor and lieutenant governor respectively.

In the early 1880s Paul founded the *Durham Workman*, a newspaper that served as an organ for the Knights of Labor. Generally considered Durham's first historian, Paul was the author of *History of the Town of Durham: Embracing Biographical Sketches and Engravings of the Leading Business Men of Durham*, published in 1884 by Edwards and Broughton Company. The book included a business directory of Durham plus an appendix of information on the cultivation, curing, and manufacturing of tobacco in North Carolina. J. Dike wrote a biography of Paul for the volume.

Later years found Paul still living in Durham and working for a Mrs. B. Davis, a dealer in clothing, shoes, and dry goods at 117 West Main Street. In September 1899 Paul, who was facing great personal and financial hardship, wrote a letter to Washington Duke asking him to arrange for Paul's daughter, Anne, to enter a musical conservatory. He told Duke, in the letter dated 12 September, that the sicknesses and deaths of his wife, son, and brother had left him so in debt that he had had to stop his daughter's musical training. Though he gave his assurance that he would pay her tuition as soon as he was out of debt, Duke refused Paul the favor. Obviously upset, Paul told Duke that he was "leaving him with his conscience and his God."

Paul apparently left Durham or died about 1900.

SEE: H. M. Douty, "Early Labor Organization in North Carolina, 1880–1900," *South Atlantic Quarterly* 34 (July 1935); Washington Duke Papers (Manuscript Department, Duke University Library, Durham); Hiram Voss Paul, *History of the Town of Durham: Embracing Biographical Sketches and Engravings of the Leading Business Men of Durham* (1884).

PATRICIA J. MILLER

Payne, Anne Blackwell *(15 Oct. 1887–5 Mar. 1969)*, poet, was the daughter of Charles M. and Margaret Justice Sparrow Payne. Anne, called "Annie" until she grew up, was born in Concord, where her father was a Presbyterian minister. When his daughter was six months old, Dr. Payne accepted a call to the First Presbyterian Church of Washington, N.C., where both he and his wife had relatives. Anne Payne's roots were so deep in Washington that she was never reconciled to the fact that her actual birth had occurred in Concord.

After attending local schools Anne was sent to Flora MacDonald College, a Presbyterian institution in Red Springs. Two years later she returned to Washington to teach in the new graded schools and to be a companion to her mother, now a widow. Following her mother's death Anne went to New York, where she lived for years with a friend from Wilmington, Kathryn Worth. (Kathryn eventually became a successful writer of teenage novels, including *The Middle Button*, *They Loved to Laugh*, and others.)

Anne Payne had been writing verse all her life. At Columbia University she undertook the serious study of poetry—its history, structure, and style. She enjoyed her work and her contacts with John Erskine, Carl Van Doren, and Horace Gregory. Particularly she profited from her study in craftsmanship with Joseph Auslander, Pulitzer Prize–winning poet in the twenties. Under his tutelage she became adept in the art of song and sonnet.

She joined the Writer's Club at Columbia as well as the Poetry Society of America, through which she won several awards. Many periodicals bought her poetry, including *Century Magazine*, *Good Housekeeping*, *Virginia Quarterly Review*, *The Youths' Companion*, *Commonweal*, *Living Church*, and *Contemporary Verse*. The *Boston Herald*, New York *Herald*, and *New York Times* provided steady markets, and for more than a quarter of a century her poems were seen frequently on the editorial page of the *New York Times*.

In 1930 The University of North Carolina Press published *Released*, by Anne Blackwell Payne. This was the first book of poetry brought out by that press, and it was widely and favorably reviewed. Miss Payne's gentle, gracious, and delightful personality now became better known in her native state. Although she wrote prolifically for thirty-odd years after *Released* appeared, no second volume was ever published since books of poetry are notoriously poor money-makers.

Anne Blackwell Payne was widely anthologized, however, particularly in collections of poetry for children, as she had a gift for communicating with young people. She wrote much of this verse for her niece and nephew, Mary and Tim, the children of her brother, Thomas Sparrow Payne of Washington. For many years she spent her summers at Thomas's home on the Pamlico River. During World War II Anne left New York and went to live in Wilmington, where she ran a library for the Federal Housing Administration.

When she was invited to make her home with her double first cousin, Dr. Thomas Sparrow, she moved to Charlotte, where Sparrow was a prominent surgeon. As his hostess-housekeeper she lived in Charlotte for some years before her death there. She was buried in Oakdale Cemetery, Washington.

SEE: *Greensboro Daily News*, 18 May 1930; *North Carolina Authors: A Selective Handbook* (1952); Raleigh *News and Observer*, 29 May 1927, 17 Nov. 1929, 18 May 1930.

PAULINE WORTHY

Payne, Bruce Ryburn *(18 Feb. 1874–21 Apr. 1937)*, college president, was born in the Mull Grove community of Catawba County, the son of Jordan Nathaniel and Barbara Anne Eliza Warlick Payne. The elder Payne was a teacher and a Methodist minister who, though licensed, was never ordained. Young Payne received his preparation for college at the Patton School of Morganton, entered Trinity College (now Duke University) in 1892, and was graduated with a bachelor of arts degree in 1896.

Payne had made plans to study medicine, but on leaving college he accepted the position of principal of Morganton Academy and soon decided upon a career in education. After teaching in Morganton for three years, in the last of which he also held the office of superintendent of schools for Burke County, Payne in 1899 returned to Durham to teach in the local high school. While teaching he took advantage of the opportunity to continue his studies at Trinity. He received a master's degree in 1902 and in the fall of that year enrolled at Teachers College, Columbia University, where he was awarded a Ph.D. degree in 1904.

Payne taught for a year at the College of William and Mary and then moved to the University of Virginia, where he was professor of secondary education and later head of the summer session. At the university his instructional load at one time or another included courses in philosophy, psychology, logic, and ethics—all in addition to education. When Payne was placed in charge of the summer session, he was apparently given a free hand because substantial reorganization soon took place. The course offerings were expanded to include a generous number in the field of arts and sciences, university officials agreed to accept credit for the courses offered, and the summer session became an integral part of the university's program.

Payne's association with the University of Virginia lasted only five years, yet his influence on the state may well have been greater even than on the university. In close cooperation with the State Board of Education and the State Board of Examiners, he worked to prepare a course of study for the public schools; not content with this, he urged the establishment of more and better high schools. When classes were not in session, Payne and a colleague would frequently start out separately, crossing the state to reach citizens in every area, and speak before interested groups about the importance of a high school education. Their talks stressed such basic issues as sanitation, adequate school buildings and equipment, and the necessity for cooperation between school and home.

In January 1911 Payne accepted with considerable reluctance the invitation to become president of George Peabody College for Teachers in Nashville, Tenn. Peabody Normal School of the University of Nashville had been closed in 1909, with plans made to move the institution to a new campus in another part of the city and to give it a new name, George Peabody College for Teachers. Payne's responsibility was to raise the money needed to match a $1.5 million gift from the Peabody Education Fund, plan for and supervise the development of the new campus, and select a faculty. In an amazing display of ability, he was able in a few decades to make Peabody the most influential institution in the South for the training of teachers and one of the three or four most influential in the nation.

Payne's study at Teachers College had brought him in touch with a group of leading educational theorists—Paul Monroe, John Dewey, and Edward L. Thorndike, plus Frank M. McMurry, who was his major professor. Although these men had made an impression on him, Payne was one to chart his own course. The faculty selected for Peabody College included able educators, as one might expect, but in addition there were sound scholars in mathematics, history, English, geography, psychology, and languages. Furthermore, the courses offered reflected Payne's commitment to the liberal arts as fundamental in the preparation of teachers.

Any description of Payne calls forth memories of a restless, energetic, and determined man—one frequently thought of as aloof, yet in reality warm and humane. If he appeared to be distant it was because his mind was preoccupied with thoughts of the college and the education of America's children, both black and white. In less than three decades, almost single-handedly, he brought the assets of the college from $2 million to $8 million and saw the enrollment, including summer school, reach more than four thousand. Payne was a man of medium height and stocky build. Ingrained in him was a love of beauty and a deep, unemotional religious faith. His appreciation of beauty is reflected in the buildings and grounds of Peabody College, in both of which he took a personal interest. And his writings—particularly those messages addressed to the graduating classes—reveal his awareness of the beautiful in literature, nature, and art, and the importance of religion in his daily life.

Payne married Lula Carr of Kinston in 1897, and they were the parents of a son, Maxwell Carr, who became a successful Nashville businessman. Throughout life Payne was active in civic and religious affairs, and at the time of his death he was the Nashville chairman of a committee seeking additional endowment funds for Fisk University. O. C. Carmichael, vice-chancellor of Vanderbilt, said of him that "few . . . in the South have achieved so distinguished a career of service to education"; Thomas E. Jones, president of Fisk, referred to Payne as "not only a great educator, but a great humanitarian" and one whose "educational philosophy extended to all the people." Trinity College (1917), Miami University (1920), and Columbia University (1929) conferred honorary degrees upon him.

Payne died suddenly of a heart attack. Funeral services were conducted in Peabody's Social-Religious Building by his pastor, Dr. Costen J. Harrell of West End Methodist Church, assisted by Dr. W. F. Powell, pastor of the First Baptist Church. Interment was in Mount Olivet Cemetery, Nashville.

SEE: Philip Alexander Bruce, *History of the University of Virginia, 1819–1919*, vol. 5 (1922); *DAB*, vol. 11 (1958); "Messages of the Late Bruce Ryburn Payne to the Graduating Classes and Alumni of George Peabody College," *Peabody Reflector and Alumni News* 18 (1945); *Nashville Banner*, 22 Apr. 1937; *Nashville Tennessean*, 4 Dec. 1927, 22–23 Apr. 1937; *Nat. Cyc. Am. Biog.*, vol. 32 (1945); *New York Times*, 22 Apr. 1937; "Our Greatest Industry," *Peabody Reflector and Alumni News* 4 (1931); "President Bruce R. Payne," *Peabody Reflector and Alumni News* 10 (1937 [portrait]); *Who Was Who in America*, vol. 1 (1942).

J. ISAAC COPELAND

Payton, Boyd Ellsworth *(21 Apr. 1908–1 Sept. 1984)*, labor organizer and executive, was born in Dobbin, W.Va., the son of James William, a timber contractor, and Mary Sidonna King Payton. As a youth growing up in Garrett County, Md., where the family had moved when he was two, Payton had aspired to be a minister; but, following graduation from Oakdale High School in 1926, he began working in the Chemical Division of the Celanese Corporation of America plant in Cumberland, Md. During his seventeen-year career with the company, he established the Celanese Benefit Club to assist employees in financial need and helped organize Celanese Local No. 1874 of the Textile Workers Union of America (TWUA) in 1936. As president of the 11,000-member local in 1941, he supported the company's hiring of black workers to compensate for the wartime labor shortage; but he lost the next election because of this support. Nevertheless, he was elected president of the Maryland and District of Columbia Congress of Industrial Organizations Council in 1942.

The next year the TWUA named Payton an international representative and assigned him to Lynchburg, Va., as regional director for Virginia, West Virginia, and Maryland. He served as president of the Virginia State CIO Council (1944–47) and as an international vice-president of the TWUA (1948–64). In 1953 the TWUA promoted him to director of the eleven-state southern region with headquarters in Charlotte. During a strike of city bus workers in 1957, Payton, appointed by the mayor to be his labor adviser, succeeded in persuading both parties to accept a compromise settlement.

In November 1958 Payton went to Henderson to assist in negotiations between TWUA Locals No. 578 and 584 and the management of the Harriet-Henderson Mills. The situation had become polarized as the company demanded substantial revisions to the existing contract, parts of which had been in effect since 1943. After the entire work force struck, the company used strikebreakers to reopen the mills in February 1959. In the following month, there were reports of sixteen bombings; more than 150 arrests were made, and Payton himself was assaulted. Governor Luther Hodges unsuccessfully tried to mediate the dispute, which he later described as "a blot" on the state "in which just about everyone was at fault." Union members increasingly felt that the textile industry was using the situation to subvert all unions, and they particularly resented the role of the state, through the Highway Patrol and the National Guard, in protecting the strikebreakers.

On 15 June Payton, two other union officials, and five union members were indicted for conspiracy to dynamite a Carolina Power and Light Company substation and to destroy two mill buildings. The sole evidence against Payton was a telephone call he took for his assistant in which he warned the caller, as he did everyone, that the phone was probably bugged. The caller, Harold Aaron, admitted in court that he was a paid informant for the State Bureau of Investigation (SBI), but his testimony as chief prosecution witness convinced the jury that all eight defendants were guilty.

In his book on the case, *Scapegoat: Prejudice/Politics/Prison*, Payton described a conversation he had with Aaron in 1966 in which Aaron admitted to having been coached by the SBI to give false testimony against Payton. According to Payton, Aaron agreed to meet him in Washington, D.C., the following day and tell his story to a reporter. The next and final news Payton had of him, however, was of his confinement to the psychiatric ward of the Veterans Hospital in Durham.

As a result of Aaron's courtroom testimony, Payton was sentenced to a six- to ten-year prison term. After exhausting all avenues for appeal, he and the others went to prison in November 1960. Shortly thereafter Payton failed a lie detector test, but such people as evangelist Billy Graham, author Harry Golden, and Burlington Mills president Spencer Love continued to assert his innocence to the new governor, Terry Sanford. In July 1961 Sanford reduced the sentences of the men, and Payton was released in August after having served nine months.

Sanford eventually pardoned Payton—but not the others—on his last day in office, 31 Dec. 1964.

Upon his release, the Textile Workers Union made Payton an assistant to the national organizing director and later director of the Upper South Region. In the years before his pardon, Payton found his effectiveness as an organizer greatly diminished; consequently, he resigned in 1964 and took a job conducting tours for foreign trade unionists under the sponsorship of the U.S. Departments of Labor and State. Within a month, Congressman William M. Tuck of Virginia succeeded in having Payton fired when he protested the use of an "ex-con" in such a position. After Payton received his pardon, the Labor Department hired him, and he served in various administrative posts in the Neighborhood Youth Corps and the Manpower Administration before retiring in 1977.

Payton married Katherine (Kitty) Jardine Harvey (1908–73) in 1932, and they had three daughters: Patricia, Sandra, and Nancy. An active member of the Presbyterian church, he taught Sunday school and served as an elder of Forest Hills Presbyterian Church in Charlotte. He died in Charlotte and was buried in Sharon Memorial Park.

SEE: Lisa S. Fisher, "Union Solidarity in a Southern State: The Henderson, North Carolina Strike, 1958–1961" (M.A. thesis, University of North Carolina at Charlotte, 1990); Luther H. Hodges, *Businessman in the Statehouse* (1962); Boyd E. Payton, *Scapegoat: Prejudice/Politics/Prison* (1970); Boyd Ellsworth Payton Papers (Atkins Library, University of North Carolina at Charlotte, and Duke University Library, Durham); *Pineville Pioneer*, 10 November 1982.

ROBIN BRABHAM

Peace, Samuel Thomas *(13 July 1879–1 Nov. 1964)*, banker, author, and historian, was born near Oxford, the son of Alexander Smith and Ella Grandy Peace. His father, an attorney, was descended from Joseph and Sarah Mass Peace, who settled at Tabbs Creek in the Kittrell Springs area shortly after the Tuscarora Indian massacre of 1713. These were the first known settlers of the land now comprising Vance County.

Peace received his preparatory education at Horner School in Oxford in 1893 and 1897. Between these terms, he was employed as bookkeeper with the firm of J. C. Cooper and Son. In 1899 Peace participated in the organization of the Bank of Chapel Hill and served as its first cashier. He entered The University of North Carolina in 1901 and was active in student publications and the Kappa Alpha fraternity.

In 1905 Peace participated in the organization of the First National Bank in Henderson, where he permanently settled. From 1899 to 1935 he served as president of eleven corporations, several of which he organized. These included the First National Bank of Henderson, the Roanoke Bank and Trust Company of Roanoke Rapids, and the Corbitt Company of Henderson, which manufactured heavy-duty trucks.

In 1931 Peace published at his own expense the first of a series of "Christmas cards." This volume, entitled *Leaves of Leisure*, contained whimsical stories, poems, and anecdotes written by Peace and sent to friends as a Christmas gift. Similar volumes were published and distributed from 1932 to 1949. The stories are chiefly humorous in tone, though many are poignant. They treat subjects of local color and tradition as well as the author's personal experiences in a small North Carolina town of the period. The writings, which include numerous passages in dialect, exhibit a particular aptitude for coining or recording memorable local expressions for universal experiences. One of the stories describes in detail a backwoods black gathering near the state boundary whose participants were from both North Carolina and Virginia. The ancient narrator, lamenting that the party did not equal the rousings of his youth, sums it up as a case of "Too much Virginia and too little grape."

In addition to the Christmas cards, Peace published *Me and Ole' Kate* (1957), a further collection of stories. In 1955 he brought out *Zeb's Black Baby*, a history of the region that comprises Vance County from the colonial period. This volume has had numerous editions and remains the standard work for history of the area.

Peace was extremely popular as a dinner speaker and entertainer in Vance and surrounding counties. At age eighty, he organized the Mockingbird Combo, a musical group with which he performed on the harmonica at civic, charitable, and political events. On these occasions, he would delight audiences with his impromptu wit and humorous anecdotes between renditions of popular songs.

On 8 Dec. 1909 Peace married Willie Closs Parker, daughter of W. Scott and Lucy Closs Parker. Mrs. Peace was a local historian and philanthropist. The couple had three children: Samuel Thomas, Jr., Closs Peace Wardlaw, and Anne Peace Rawls. Peace was a member of the First Methodist Church of Henderson, the Democratic party, the Rotary Club, and the Order of Freemasons. He died in Henderson and was buried in Elmwood Cemetery.

SEE: Daniel L. Grant, *Alumni History of the University of North Carolina* (1924); *Henderson Daily Dispatch*, 2 Nov. 1964; Subject's own works.

GEORGE T. BLACKBURN II

Peace, William *(7 Mar. 1773–11 July 1865)*, merchant and philanthropist, Presbyterian layman, and founder of Peace Institute, was born in Granville County. His father, John Peace, was a wealthy planter; his mother was Margaret Scott. Little is known of his early life, but he is believed to have been in the first class of The University of North Carolina; leaving before graduation, he went to Raleigh in 1796.

Four years after Raleigh was established, William and his brother Joseph opened a mercantile business on Fayetteville Street. After Joseph's death in 1842, William became sole owner, earning the title of "merchant prince." During the War of 1812, he served as lieutenant and later captain of the militia. After the war he was a commissioner of city government at the time the old governor's mansion was constructed in 1816. The building was used as the mansion until the end of the Civil War, and in 1876 it was converted into a public school.

For forty-five years Peace was director of the Bank of the State and the Bank of North Carolina. He acted as chief trustee of the Rex Hospital Fund, which had been left by John Rex to aid in the development of the Raleigh community. Peace was active in civic affairs and the advancement of education. In 1830 he purchased the original Raleigh Academy building and equipment, served as treasurer, and advanced funds to meet deficits in order to keep the school open until 1855.

Peace petitioned Orange Presbytery to establish a Presbyterian church in Raleigh and, when on 21 Jan. 1816 the First Presbyterian Church was organized, he was one of the charter ruling elders. In 1858 he, together with other zealous Presbyterians, obtained the charter for a female seminary intended "to have for its object the thoro education of young ladies, not only in the substantial branches of knowledge but also in those which are elegant and ornamental." To this purpose he subscribed $10,000 (one-third of the cost) and donated the land for the establishment of a woman's college, which was named Peace Institute (now Peace College) in his honor. The original building was partially constructed in 1860, but during the war it was occupied as a Confederate hospital (on 6 June 1862) and later it was used by the Freedmen's Bureau. Thus, Peace Institute did not open as a school until 1872, seven years after Peace's death. The street bordering Peace Institute on the south was also named for William Peace.

Peace never married. At the time of his death, in the early days of Reconstruction, he was residing at the home of Governor W. W. Holden, where he had lived for many years, and at age ninety-two he was the oldest citizen of Raleigh. William and Joseph Peace were buried side by side near the center of the Old City Cemetery on New Bern Avenue. The graves are circumscribed by a wall several feet high and the inscriptions on the stones are very weatherworn. A heavy marble slab giving Peace's name and the date of his birth and death covers his grave.

Several portraits of William Peace exist. One oil painting by William Garl Browne was executed in 1857, when Peace was eighty-five. Presented to Peace Institute by Governor Holden, it hangs in the chapel of Peace College.

SEE: Moses N. Amis, *Historical Raleigh from Its Foundation in 1792* (1902); Samuel A. Ashe, ed., *Biographical History of North Carolina*, vol. 6 (1907); Hope S. Chamberlain, *History of Wake County, North Carolina* (1922); Charles H. Hamlin, *Ninety Bits of North Carolina Biography* (1946); Marshall D. Haywood, *Builders of the Old North State* (1968); Guion G. Johnson, *Antebellum North Carolina* (1937); Raleigh *News and Observer*, 19 June 1966; Sidney Ann Wilson, *Personae: History of Peace College* (1972); James R. Young, *Peace Institute, Its History and Ownership as Shown by Its Charter* (no date).

MRS. S. DAVID FRAZIER

Peacock, Dred *(12 Apr. 1864–10 Mar. 1934)*, college president and attorney, was born in Stantonsburg of English and Scottish ancestry, the son of Dr. C. C. and Eva Heath Peacock. An outstanding student at old Trinity College and a member of Phi Beta Kappa, he received the A.B. degree in 1887, the A.M. in 1888, and the Litt.D. in 1889. In 1887 he married Ellas Carr of Trinity, where the school was located, near High Point.

Peacock accepted a position at Greensboro College as professor of Latin and then served the school as president from 1894 to 1902, when he retired. Afterwards he became involved in furniture manufacturing and insurance at High Point. His love of learning prompted him to read law and he passed the North Carolina bar examination in 1912. A successful attorney, Peacock represented numerous prominent clients including McClellan Stores Corporation, of which he was an organizer and a director. He took a lively interest in educational and religious matters and, as a Democrat, in state and local government.

Peacock's avocation was the study of the French Revolution. A natural scholar, he gathered one of the finest libraries on that period—it remained intact at the home of his daughter, Mrs. J. Everett Marsh, in High Point. At the time of his death, Peacock was a member of the boards of trustees of Duke University and Greensboro College as well as chairman of the Guilford County Board of Education.

SEE: Samuel A. Ashe, ed., *Biographical History of North Carolina*, vol. 7 (1908 [portrait]); North Carolina Bar Association, *Proceedings* 36 (1934); *Prominent People of North Carolina* (1906); *Trinity Alumni Register* 2 (1916); *Who Was Who in America*, vol. 1 (1943).

HOLT MCPHERSON

Pearce, Samuel *(20 May 1807–25 Dec. 1878)*, cartographer, was born in St. Mary's Parish, Truro, County Cornwall, in Great Britain. The fourth son of a saddler, John Pearce, and his wife Sarah Salmon Pearce, he was probably educated at the grammar school in Truro. At an early age Pearce came to the United States and settled briefly in Virginia, where he was ordained to the ministry in the Methodist church. From 1840 to 1845 he was assigned to various circuits in the North Carolina Conference, and in 1846 he was appointed to the Hillsborough Circuit, Raleigh District. In 1848 he ended his days as a circuit rider (though he remained a Methodist pastor all his life) by "locating" in Hillsborough, where he occupied the house formerly belonging to Signer William Hooper. Pearce opened a school in Hillsborough in 1848 and a bookstore in 1851. As a bookseller he acted as agent for publishers in Boston, New York, Richmond, and Charleston and eventually was one of the principal distributors for Calvin H. Wiley's *North Carolina Reader*.

Through Wiley, Pearce became interested in producing an authoritative map of North Carolina. As early as 1852 Wiley and Pearce, with William Dewey Cooke, began gathering data for their projected map, but by 1854 Wiley withdrew from the project. Three years later Cooke and Pearce produced their map, but under the title of *Cooke's New Map of North Carolina*, Pearce's name appearing without explanation in the lower right corner of the map. When in 1858 Cooke had the map republished by the well-known firm of Joseph H. Colton in New York, he dropped Pearce's name entirely. Two years later Cooke left North Carolina for Georgia, and Pearce determined to bring out his own map of the state. At the end of the Civil War, Pearce announced his forthcoming map in the *Hillsborough Recorder* from early October 1865 until the end of February 1866. His design called for the map to measure 48 by 70 inches and to be ornamented in the borders with North Carolina vignettes and portraits of such notables as President Andrew Johnson and Governor David L. Swain. When the map appeared, it did so under the title *Pearce's New Map of the State of North Carolina*, measured 58 by 83 inches, and was decorated in the border with vignettes of North Carolina and Virginia buildings and scenes lithographed by Harline and Hensel of Philadelphia and printed by Hayes and Zell. The decorations included in an inset the illustration from John H. Wheeler's 1851 *Historical Sketches of North Carolina* of Theodor de Bry's depiction of the landing of the English at Roanoke Island in 1584. Pearce's partner in financing publication of the map, printed in soft, bright tones, was R. W. Best of Raleigh. The year of publication does not appear on the map; Levi Branson's *Business Directory* for 1867/68 reports the publication date as 1860, surely a misprint for 1866. The map, mounted on a roller, was ideal for use in the public schools.

For the next few years Pearce was obliged to bring out new editions as the General Assembly erected new counties (Dare, 1870; Swain, 1871; Pamlico and Graham, 1873). His edition of 1871 (copyrighted in 1870) appeared under the same title as the first edition but was reduced in size to 39½ by 55½. This edition was printed by H. H. Lloyd and Company of New York and included as insets a map of the United States and the eastern and western hemispheres. This edition was financed by Pearce alone, apparently from proceeds of sales of the first edition.

When it became necessary to bring out another edition almost immediately after release of the second, Pearce turned to Alfred Williams, the Raleigh stationer, for help in financing it. Williams thus acquired a share of the copyright. The 1872 edition (copyrighted in 1871) was again printed by H. H. Lloyd and Company and was further reduced in size to 30½ by 58 inches. The U.S. map and the hemispheres were replaced by comparative data from the 1860 and 1870 censuses and points of altitude on the railroads of the state. As had the 1871 edition, the 1872 edition retained the original title of 1866.

Presumably Alfred Williams acquired full title to the copyright he and Pearce jointly owned, for in 1873 he instructed H. H. Lloyd and Son (as the firm was now called) to alter the plates, bringing out a new edition in that year measuring 35 by 60 inches and titled *Williams' New Map of the State of North Carolina*. This edition is recognizably the work of Pearce, and the title should be understood to signify proprietorship and not authorship. Pearce died of paralysis five years later in Charlotte, where he and his family had moved. His death brought to an end the long line of North Carolina's independent, local cartographers that had commenced with John Lawson in 1709 and had included Edward Moseley (1733), William Churton and John Collet (1770), Jonathan Price and John Strother (1808), Robert H. B. Brazier (1833), and William Dewey Cooke (1857). Although there were additional maps of the state made by local cartographers, they were produced as part of the cartographers' function as geological officers of the state. Otherwise, authoritative maps of North Carolina were thereafter produced routinely by professional cartographic firms drawing on data gathered by the U.S. Geological Survey.

Of Pearce's family, only the forename of his wife, Mary A., a native of North Carolina, is known. Their daughter, Ann B. J. Pearce, married James W. Turrentine of Orange County in 1863.

SEE: Census of 1850, Orange County, N.C., Hillsborough (Family #367); *Hillsborough Recorder*, 20 Dec. 1848, 12 Dec. 1849, 10 July 1850, 19 Feb., 17 Dec. 1851, 18 Oct. 1865–28 Feb. 1866; Maps mentioned in the sketch (editions of 1866, 1871, and 1872 in the North Carolina State Archives, Raleigh; Edition of 1873 [*Williams' New Map*] in Library of Congress, Washington, D.C.); *Minutes of the Annual Conferences of the Methodist Episcopal Church, South, 1845–1852*; Orange County Deed Book 37, pp. 155–56, and Deed Book 40, p. 162; St. Mary's Parish Register, Truro, County Cornwall; Calvin H. Wiley Papers (North Carolina State Archives, Raleigh).

GEORGE STEVENSON

Pearce, Thomas *(fl. 1672)*, Council member, served on the Council of the North Carolina colony (then called Albemarle) as of 26 Apr. 1672, when he and other Council members signed a letter to the Lords Proprietors and instructions for Governor Peter Carteret, who was to deliver the letter.

Nothing more is known of this Thomas Pearce. Although an individual bearing the name collected quit rents in the colony in 1685, nothing indicates whether or not he was the former Council member. A Thomas Pearce (Peirce), son of John Peirce and member of the Assembly in the early 1700s, was only three years old in 1672. Several individuals bearing the name were in Virginia during the period, but none has been identified as the Albemarle Council member.

SEE: William S. Powell, ed., *Y^e Countie of Albemarle in Carolina* (1958).

MATTIE ERMA E. PARKER

Pearsall, Thomas Jenkins *(11 Feb. 1903–5 May 1981)*, legislator, attorney, businessman, and farmer, was born in Rocky Mount, the son of Leon F. and Maryetta Jenkins Pearsall. He was educated in the public schools of Rocky Mount until his senior year in high school, when he went to Georgia Military Academy for the year 1922–23. He entered The University of North Carolina in the fall of 1923 and the law school two years later; he was graduated in 1927 and began to practice law in Rocky Mount. Pearsall's first venture into politics in 1928 resulted in his election as solicitor of the local Recorder's Court, a post he held until 1933. In 1940 he was appointed to the legislative seat vacated at the death of the incumbent, William E. Fenner, two days after he had been elected to his fourth term. Thereafter Pearsall was elected to three successive terms, serving a total of four terms from 1941 until 1947; he was speaker of the state house of representatives in 1947.

Following the U.S. Supreme Court decision in the case of *Brown v. Board of Education* in 1954, Governor William B. Umstead named a Special Advisory Committee on Education of which Pearsall was chairman. This committee recommended "that North Carolina try to find means of meeting the requirements of the Supreme Court's decision within our present school system before consideration is given to abandoning or materially altering it." In March 1955 the General Assembly adopted a pupil assignment plan affirming that local school boards had power over the enrollment and assignment of children in the public schools. In July 1956 a special session of the General Assembly adopted the "Pearsall Plan" embodying in a constitutional amendment provisions for paying education expense grants from state or local funds for the private schooling of children assigned against the wishes of parents or guardians to an integrated school. Reaction was mixed, no tuition money was granted, and in 1966 the Pearsall Plan was declared to be unconstitutional, although it had not been used in a single school system. The plan, however, is often said to have softened the blow and to have enabled the state to carry out desegregation with "a minimum amount of tension."

Pearsall was active in the reorganization of the consolidated University of North Carolina as well as the establishment of North Carolina Wesleyan College at Rocky Mount. He was chairman of the board of the Roanoke Island Historical Association, a member of the board of governors of the Research Triangle Institute, and a trustee of the Children's Home Society, the Rocky Mount public schools, and the Asheville School for Boys. He also managed the M. C. Braswell Company (inherited by his wife), which held 22,000 acres in Nash, Edgecombe, Martin, and Halifax counties devoted to farming, timber production, and a warehouse enterprise. It was through this connection that he became active in the American Farm Bureau and the American Farm Managers Association; in addition, he was president of the Citizens Savings and Loan Association in Rocky Mount and a director of the Planters National Bank and Trust Company. He often was mentioned as a candidate for governor but declined to give it serious consideration.

In 1930 Pearsall married Emily Elizabeth Braswell and they became the parents of two sons, Thomas J., Jr., and Mack Braswell. He was a member and sometime senior warden of the Church of the Good Shepherd in Rocky Mount and was buried in Pineview Cemetery.

SEE: *Durham Morning Herald*, 8 Feb. 1948; *North Carolina Manual* (1941–47); Raleigh *News and Observer*, 10 Aug. 1952, 7 Nov. 1976, 6–7 May 1981.

CAROLYN ROFF

Pearson, Charles Chilton *(1879–26 Nov. 1956)*, teacher, administrator, and scholar, was born in Richmond County, Va. He received the M.A. degree from Richmond College in 1904, completed one year of graduate study at Columbia University, and received a Ph.D. from Yale. After teaching at Yale and at Washington and Lee, he joined the faculty of Wake Forest College in 1916. In 1917 he was made professor of social sciences and chairman of the department, positions he held until his retirement in 1952. He was a Harrison Research Fellow at the University of Pennsylvania (1925–26) and visiting professor of history for many summers at Trinity College and the University of Virginia.

A noted teacher, Pearson conducted classes in history, government, economics, and sociology. He demanded diligent work, rigorous analysis, and precise thinking, but his courses were always popular. He encouraged scholarly research and to that end devoted much effort, time, and money towards improving the college library in his own and other disciplines. A longtime chairman of the faculty committees on the library and graduate study, Pearson inspired many students to pursue graduate work, especially in history, at Wake Forest and elsewhere. His former students include historians and educators in many other fields, along with administrators, writers, lawyers, physicians, and people in various walks of life. Among his students who were also members of the Political Science Club were Irving Carlyle, W. J. Cash, Christopher Crittenden, and Forest C. Clonts.

Although chairman of one of the largest departments on campus, Pearson found time for many quasi-administrative activities in the area of student life. He established the college bookstore and sundry shop and ran it for several years. He was the first chairman of the fraternity council, a successful debate coach, and sponsor of the influential Political Science Club. Interested in athletics throughout his life, he introduced golf to Wake Forest, organized the area's first golf course, and saw the game become a major intercollegiate sport.

An inveterate scholar, Pearson always gathered research materials—especially on the history of Virginia—during summer trips and other travel. His publications included articles in the Wake Forest College *Bulletin* and the *South Atlantic Quarterly*, thirty-two sketches in the *Dictionary of American Biography*, and a 1932 report to the Virginia General Assembly. He was the author of a handbook on patriotism for the National Security League during World War I; *The Readjuster Movement in Virginia* (1917); and, posthumously, *Liquor and Anti-Liquor in Virginia, 1619–1919* (1967).

Pearson was a Baptist, a Mason, a member of Phi Beta Kappa, and a charter member of the Historical Society of North Carolina. As a young man he traveled in Europe and the American West and spent some time on a Texas ranch. A campus character, he was known by the nickname "Skinny" because of his physical appearance and his idiosyncrasies remain legend in the folklore of Wake Forest. In 1933 he married Sarah Cullom, the daughter of religion professor W. R. Cullom, and they had one daughter, Virginia Chilton. Pearson retired as head of the Department of Social Sciences in 1952 and continued his research and activities on campus until his death in the town of Wake Forest.

SEE: C. C. Pearson Papers (Baptist Historical Collection, Wake Forest University, Winston-Salem); Wake Forest College, *Alumni News* 23 (October 1952); *Wake Forest Student Magazine* 62 (1948–49), 66 (1950–51), 72 (1956–57).

J. EDWIN HENDRICKS

Pearson, James Larkin *(13 Sept. 1879–27 Aug. 1981)*, poet and printer, was born of English and Scotch-Irish ancestry in a log cabin on Berry's Mountain three miles from Boomer in Wilkes County, the oldest of two sons of William Thomas and Mary Louise McNeill Pearson, unlettered laborers constantly moving from one rented farm to the next. At age four, while riding with his father in an ox cart one bitter January day, upon being asked if he was cold, the child replied, "My fingers an' my toes, / My feet an' my hands, / Are jist as cold as / Ye ever see'd a man's." From ages seven to fifteen, he attended the rural schools for a few weeks each winter, but his education came primarily from reading. Pearson once said that he could never remember when he did not plan to be a poet. During his workday on the farm, he always took along a notepad and, in the tradition of Robert Burns, jotted down stanzas as he plowed the mountain soil. He considered "The Vision," written when he was twelve, his first "finished" poem. In 1896 the *Blue Ridge Times* at Parsonville in Wilkes County printed some of his work, and the *New York Independent* in December 1900 paid him eight dollars for "The Song of the Star of Bethlehem." Thereafter Pearson thought of himself as a professional poet.

From farming he turned to carpentry, then at age twenty-one learned to set type for the *Republican Patriot* across the mountain in Jefferson. He soon started his own paper *Paper Talk* and intermittently edited, published, and worked for a number of newspapers in the area, notably the *Yellow Jacket* of Moravian Falls, whose owner R. Don Laws sent him to Washington, D.C., in 1903 as correspondent for his lucrative political journal. For a few months in 1907 he was with the *Charlotte Observer* and there became acquainted with the North Carolina poet John Charles McNeill.

In Charlotte on 1 May 1907 he married Laws's sister-in-law, Cora Wallace, whom he had chosen for his wife seven years before. Like him, she was a writer and a printer but her activities were much restricted because of poor health both before and after marriage. The couple returned home, opened a print shop, and the following year hand-set *Castle Gates*, Pearson's first little book of poetry. An infant named Blanche Rose was stillborn. In 1910 he began publishing the *Fool-Killer*, a monthly intended, according to Pearson who wrote most of the copy, "to make a fellow laugh right big and to cram a truth down his throat while his mouth was open." At fifteen cents a year, it grew rapidly in circulation, up to 50,000 at one point, and brought Pearson a measure of prosperity. In 1916 operation of the paper was transferred to a fifty-acre farm near Boomer. But over the years, the hopeless illness of his wife and his constant bedside attention lessened his enthusiasm for the satiric comment that was responsible for the success of the venture. Its fortunes declined and its last number was published in 1929.

Meanwhile, his bachelor brother John Milton Pearson had died on 29 Apr. 1923. In the same year the Pearsons adopted a daughter, Agnes Vivian. In 1924 he brought out the 274-page *Pearson's Poems*, the second of five books of his poetry to come from his one-man printing and publishing office.

Though frustrated in his efforts to be published commercially, Pearson was not unknown. The prominent American novelist Upton Sinclair praised him in *Money Writes~!* (1927) and later in *Another Pamela* (1950) used Pearson as the basis for the character of a bucolic poet. Sinclair also urged him to seek a wide audience and introduced him to the *New York Times*, which accepted a number of his poems, including "Fifty Acres" (27 June 1930), destined to be his signature and the title poem of his next little book, *Fifty Acres and Other Selected Poems* (1933). His "discovery" by North Carolina began at this time, and soon he was being honored as much "for his simplicity, sincerity and poverty, as for his melodious verses." His wife died (see "Bereft") on 17 June 1934. On 4 December of that year, upon being invited by Frank Graham to be on the program at the annual meeting of the North Carolina Literary and Historical Association in Raleigh, Pearson spoke of his life as poet and read some of his verse. So impressive was his presentation that the *News and Observer* was prompted to note editorially: "More than any other living North Carolinian he has put the life of the people into poetry, made it tangible and beautiful and easily seen."

The public recognition he had so long sought did not dispel the loneliness he experienced after his wife's death. By January 1937 he had moved his print shop to Lincolnton and was publishing the short-lived *Literary South*, but soon he was back in Wilkes County. His marriage on 6 Apr. 1939 to Eleanor Louise Fox, whom he had met four years earlier at a writers' conference in Black Mountain, brought about his move to her home in the village of Guilford College, where he was pleasantly established for the next twenty-one years. There he printed the last two of his series of self-published books, *Plowed Ground: Humorous and Dialect Poems* (1949) and *Early Harvest: The First Experimental Poems of a Self-Taught Farm Boy* (1953). On 4 Aug. 1953, in accordance with the unanimous recommendation of the Awards Committee of the North Carolina Literary and Historical Association, Governor William B. Umstead, following the resignation of Arthur Talmage Abernethy, appointed Pearson as the official poet laureate of North Carolina during an impressive ceremony at the capitol in Raleigh.

After the death of his second wife on 27 Apr. 1962, Pearson went back to Wilkes County to live with his adopted daughter Agnes (Mrs. Albert Eller). He died in North Wilksboro seventeen days before his one hundred and second birthday and was buried in the family plot at the Moravian Falls Cemetery. On his tombstone were prominently lettered the words "Printer and Poet." His printing press, personal library, manuscripts, and oil portrait (1970) by Joe King are housed in the James Larkin Pearson Building at Wilkes Community College. Pearson was a Republican and religious nonconformist. Poems such as "Fifty Acres," "Homer in a Garden," "Choice," "More Than Power," "Lincoln," and "Erosion" are lyrical, optimistic, and traditional in form and meter, his dialect verse simple and lighthearted. *Selected Poems* (1960) and *"My Fingers and My Toes"* (1971) were well-received collections from commercial publishers.

SEE: *Autobiographical Sketch of James Larkin Pearson* (ca. 1919); Autobiography (incomplete), 39 installments published weekly, *Wilkes Record* (July 1964–April 1965); Bernadette Hoyle, *Tar Heel Writers I Know* (1956); Ruth Linney, "James Larkin Pearson," *Greensboro Daily News*, 22 Oct. 1933; Raymond Lowery, "Tar Heel of the Week," *News and Observer* (Raleigh), 10 June 1951; *North Carolina Authors* (1952); Richard Walser, ed., *Poets of North Carolina* (1963); *Who's Who in America*, 1934–35 to 1946–47.

RICHARD WALSER

Pearson, Jesse A. *(1776–March 1823)*, legislator, planter, and major general of militia in the War of 1812, was born in Rowan County. He was the son of Richmond Pearson, Patriot leader and soldier in the American Revolution, who moved to North Carolina in the early 1770s and later settled in the forks of the Yadkin at the site of the present town of Cooleemee in Davie County. His mother's maiden name was Sara Haden. Jesse A. Pearson was a brother of congressman Joseph Pearson and a half brother of Richmond Mumford Pearson, chief justice of the North Carolina Supreme Court.

Jesse A. Pearson, a Federalist, served in the House of Commons of the General Assembly of North Carolina (1807–8 and 1812–15) and in the North Carolina Senate (1816). He was an ardent supporter of the need for a convention to revise the 1776 state constitution, a document that gave eastern counties almost complete control of the General Assembly. To keep this control, politicians in the east fought the creation of western and Piedmont counties. This controversy over the county basis for representation and the agitation for constitutional reform led Pearson to introduce a resolution in the 1808 session proposing moving the capital to Fayetteville (the location western legislators wanted) and the calling of a constitutional convention. Introduced the last day of the session, Pearson's proposal to link the relocation of the state capital with constitutional reform was tabled, but it reflected the determination of the west for greater equality in the state government.

In 1814 Colonel Jesse A. Pearson was sent with North Carolina militia under the command of Brigadier General Joseph Graham against the Creek Indians in Alabama. Pearson's militia forces began assembling in Salisbury in January 1814 but arrived in Alabama after the Battle of Horseshoe Bend and Jackson's victory over the Indians. Pearson's men remained near the junction of the Coosa and Tuscaloosa rivers, where more than six hundred Creeks surrendered.

The Indian village where the surrender occurred was called "Cooleeme" and the Creek tribe involved was the "Kulimi." In the Creek language the word perhaps means "the place where the white oaks grew." After his return home, Pearson named his plantation "Cooleemee Hill."

In 1817 Jesse Pearson sold his 2,500-acre Cooleemee Hill plantation on the Yadkin River in Davie County to Peter Hairston of Stokes County. The same year he became very involved in an undertaking to make the Yadkin River navigable for freight and passenger boats. The overall plan, proposed by Archibald Murphey, included river and canal links with the Cape Fear and thence to Wilmington. Pearson, Murphey, and some fifteen other stockholders from North Carolina and Virginia formed the Yadkin Navigation Company with an authorized capital of $25,000. The state appropriated $25,000. Pearson served in a managerial capacity. Despite expert engineering aid and extensive construction, the project failed. The rocky shoals in the riverbed and the effects of the panic of 1819 were impossible to overcome.

In connection with the Yadkin River project, Pearson also helped organize the Clinton Town Company in 1818. The company bought from Joseph Pearson 327 acres in the "the Point" where the South Yadkin River joins the Yadkin and laid out the planned town of Clinton. Forty-six lots were sold. But the panic of 1819 and the failure to make the Yadkin navigable doomed the plan; nothing was ever built there. Most of the land was resold to Joseph Pearson at a greatly reduced price.

After selling his Cooleemee Hill plantation, Jesse A. and Elizabeth Pearson moved to Mocksville and probably built the house, since renovated and enlarged, still standing at 419 Salisbury Street. They had considerable business interests and property in and near the town.

Pearson was married twice. His first wife was Ann Steele, of Salisbury, whom he married on 13 Feb. 1804; she died on 4 Oct. 1804 at age twenty. His second wife, whom he married on 6 Sept. 1810, was Elizabeth Causey Wilson, widow of Hugh Wilson of Mocksville; she died in 1861. No children were born to these marriages.

Said to have been "sudden and quick in a quarrel," Pearson once fought a duel with General Montfort Stokes in which Stokes was wounded. As a young man, he was an avid horse-racing fan and was at one time one of the managers of the Jockey Club of Salisbury and a promoter of the Salisbury races and sweepstakes. He died from injuries received when he was thrown from his horse while returning from Colonel Francis Locke's funeral near Salisbury. Archibald Murphey described him as one of his "fondest Friends and one of the most Correct Gentlemen in North Carolina." In 1859 John Foard, a kinsman and friend, erected a marker to his memory in the Pearson graveyard in southern Davie County.

SEE: William H. Hoyt, ed., *The Papers of Archibald Murphey* (1914); McCubbins Papers (Rowan County Library, Salisbury); Martin Collection (Davie County Library, Mocksville); *North Carolina Biography*, vol. 2 (1919); Eugene J. Pearson, *The Pearson Family, 10th–20th Century* (1978); Jethro Rumple, *History of Rowan County* (1881); Henry M. Wagstaff, ed., *The Papers of John Steele* (1924); James W. Wall, *History of Davie County* (1969); John H. Wheeler, *Historical Sketches of North Carolina* (1851) and ed., *Reminiscences and Memoirs of North Carolina* (1883–84).

JAMES W. WALL

Pearson, Joseph *(ca. 1778–27 Oct. 1834)*, congressman, lawyer, legislator, and planter, was born in Rowan County. He was the son of Richmond Pearson, Patriot leader and soldier in the American Revolution, who moved to North Carolina in the early 1770s and later settled in the forks of the Yadkin at the site of the present town of Cooleemee in Davie County. His mother's name was Sara Haden. Joseph Pearson was a brother of Jesse A. Pearson, legislator, planter, and War of 1812 officer, and a half brother of Richmond Mumford Pearson, chief justice of the North Carolina Supreme Court. Joseph Pearson received his early education at the Academy of Sciences in Iredell County where he was taught by the Reverend James Hall. He probably attended Clio's Nursery, also taught by Hall. Pearson practiced law in Salisbury.

Joseph Pearson was a staunch and uncompromising Federalist, a conservative, and a strong supporter of the Constitution and effective national government. He represented the borough of Salisbury in the House of Commons in the North Carolina General Assembly in 1804 and 1805 and was elected to the U.S. House of Representatives from the Tenth (western) District (Rowan, Mecklenburg, and Cabarrus counties) in 1809. Until 1813 he was one of the three Federalists of twelve congressmen from North Carolina. Described as one "ready to make good his words by his acts," he challenged Democratic congressman John George Jackson to a duel in 1809. Jackson, wounded on the second fire, recovered but remained partially disabled from the wound.

In the late summer of 1812 Congressman Pearson, who had been very critical of President James Madison's foreign policy, joined John Steele of Salisbury and others in a peace party movement to "dump" Madison. Pearson bitterly opposed the War of 1812 and voted against the declaration of war and taxes and appropriations to support the war effort. He declared the war to be "impolitic and disastrous" and in March 1813 wrote, "I hope the career of folly, imbecility, and ambition is nearly at an end —if it is not, I fear the liberties of the country will be the sacrifice."

The people of his congressional district held conflicting views of the war. A mass meeting in Salisbury denounced it as "unwise, premature, and unnecessary," whereas a prowar mass meeting of his constituents in Charlotte scathingly condemned Pearson's stand. After the 1810 census the Republican-controlled General Assembly gerrymandered the congressional district, and Pearson barely won reelection in 1813; he was defeated in 1815.

In the congressional debates regarding the relocation of the national capital following the burning of Washington on 24 Aug. 1814 by the British, Pearson spoke forcefully and effectively against removal. He deserves a major share of the credit for the close affirmative vote in the House of Representatives to keep Washington the seat of the national government.

Joseph Pearson's brother, Jesse A. Pearson, was one of the leaders of the undertaking begun in 1818 to make the Yadkin River navigable for freight and passenger boats. Joseph Pearson sold 327 acres of land in "the Point" where the South Yadkin River joins the Yadkin for a proposed town site. After the project failed, he repurchased most of this land.

Pearson was married three times. His first wife was Ann McLinn, whom he married in January 1806; she died in September of the same year at age twenty. In 1811 he married Eleanor (or Ellen) Brent, who died on 29 March 1818; two daughters were born to this marriage. His third wife was Catherine Worthington, a sister-in-law of the distinguished statesman William Gaston. Joseph and Catherine Pearson had four children. Pearson died in Salisbury and was buried in the Pearson graveyard in southern Davie County.

SEE: Ethel S. Arnett, *Mrs. James Madison: The Incomparable Dolley* (1972); *Biog. Dir. Am. Cong.* (1950); James S. Brawley, *The Rowan Story* (1953); William Henry Foote, *Sketches of North Carolina* (1846); Hugh T. Lefler and A. R. Newsome, *North Carolina: The History of a Southern State* (1954); McCubbins Papers (Rowan County Library, Salisbury); Martin Collection (Davie County Library, Mocksville); Eugene J. Pearson, *The Pearson Family, 10th–20th Century* (1978); Jethro Rumple, *History of Rowan County* (1881); Henry M. Wagstaff, ed., *The Papers of John Steele* (1924); James W. Wall, *History of Davie County* (1969); John H. Wheeler, *Historical Sketches of North Carolina* (1851).

JAMES W. WALL

Pearson, Richmond *(26 Jan. 1852–12 Sept. 1923)*, legislator, congressman, and diplomat, was born at Richmond Hill, the Pearson family home in Yadkin County. His parents were Richmond Mumford, chief justice of the North Carolina Supreme Court, and Margaret McClung Williams Pearson, daughter of U.S. senator and diplomat John Williams of Tennessee. Pearson's eldest sister, Ellen

Brent, married Daniel G. Fowle, a governor of North Carolina (1889–91).

Pearson attended Horner School in Oxford and Princeton University, where he was valedictorian of his graduating class in 1872 and received a master of arts degree in 1875. He returned to North Carolina in 1872 to study law under his father and was admitted to the North Carolina bar in 1874. On 19 June of the same year President Ulysses S. Grant appointed Pearson U.S. consul to Verviers and Liege, Belgium. He resigned the consulate on 22 Apr. 1877 and began to practice law in partnership with John D. Davis in St. Louis, Mo., but was forced to abandon the practice to go back to North Carolina when his father died in 1878.

Pearson was elected as a Democrat from Buncombe County to the North Carolina House of Representatives for the 1885 and 1887 sessions. While in the legislature he was involved in two challenges to duels that were widely publicized. In April and May 1886 Pearson challenged General Johnstone Jones and R. Y. McAden in connection with Pearson's opposition to the Buncombe County Stock Law of 1885. Both challenges were declined.

After changing his political party, Pearson was elected as a Republican from the Ninth Congressional District to the U.S. House of Representatives in 1894 and 1896. He lost the race in 1898 but successfully contested the honesty of the election and unseated his Democratic opponent, William T. Crawford, in a court decision of May 1900. Pearson had been a supporter of the Republican-Populist fusion of 1894, but fusion governor Daniel Russell denounced Pearson for the tactics he employed in the Crawford controversy.

President Theodore Roosevelt appointed Pearson U.S. consul to Genoa, Italy, on 10 Dec. 1901. A year later he was made envoy extraordinary and minister plenipotentiary to Persia, and in 1907 he was appointed to the same position in Greece and Montenegro. He held the latter post for two years before retiring to his home in Asheville, also named Richmond Hill. Pearson was well served in his role of diplomat by his knowledge of the French, German, and Italian languages.

Pearson became discouraged when his friend Theodore Roosevelt failed to win the Republican nomination for president at the Chicago convention of 1912, but he supported Roosevelt in his bid for the presidency as the Progressive party's nominee. After Roosevelt's defeat in the general election, Pearson no longer participated in partisan politics.

In 1882 Pearson married Gabrielle Thomas, daughter of James Thomas, Jr., one of the wealthiest tobacco planters in Virginia. The Pearsons had four children, two of whom lived to maturity. Richmond, Jr., died in infancy, and another son, also named Richmond, died of scarlet fever at age sixteen. A daughter, Marjorie, and a son, Thomas, outlived their parents. Pearson died at Richmond Hill after an acute illness of two weeks and was buried in Riverside Cemetery, Asheville.

SEE: Samuel A. Ashe, ed., *Cyclopedia of Eminent and Representative Men of the Carolinas* (1892); *Biog. Dir. Am. Cong.* (1961); *Greensboro Daily News*, 13 Sept. 1923; *Legislative Biographical Sketch Book, Session 1887, North Carolina* (1887); Gary E. Trawick and Paul B. Wyche, *One Hundred Years, One Hundred Men* (1971); *Who Was Who in America*, vol. 1 (1942).

BRENDA MARKS EAGLES

Pearson, Richmond Mumford *(28 June 1805–5 Jan. 1878)*, jurist and law teacher of note, was born at his father's home, Richmond Hill, in Rowan (now Davie) County. He was the son of Revolutionary War veteran Colonel Richmond Pearson, who had moved from his native Virginia after the war, settled in the forks of the Yadkin River, and established himself as a successful merchant, mill owner, and planter. His mother, Elizabeth Mumford Pearson, was the daughter of Robinson Mumford, a former officer in the British navy, who had come to North Carolina following a period of residence in Jamaica. She was descended from the elder William Brewster of New England.

For several years prior to the death of his father in 1819, young Pearson was primarily under the care and supervision of his half brother Joseph, a U.S. congressman who resided near Washington, D.C. During these formative years in the nation's capital, the future chief justice of North Carolina is known to have attended a Roman Catholic school and to have been baptized in that faith by Archbishop John Carroll. It is reasonable to assume that the ambiance of Washington's social and political activity imbued young Pearson with the desire to enter public life. Returning to North Carolina in his early teens, he completed his college preparation at the Statesville Academy under the stern tutelage of the Reverend John Mushat.

In 1820 Pearson entered The University of North Carolina. There he is said to have "devoted but little time to the beauties of poetry and the elegancies of polite literature." Instead, he studied avidly the histories of Greece, Rome, and England, with special emphasis on the long, painful evolution of the law in both its philosophical and practical aspects. In 1823 he received the A.B. degree, sharing first honors in a graduating class of twenty-eight members. Soon after his gradation, Pearson entered the law school of Judge Leonard Henderson near Williamsboro in Granville County. Among his fellow students at Henderson's school was William Horn Battle, who in later years would become his chief rival as the preeminent legal educator in North Carolina. Pearson was licensed in 1826 and began a law practice in Salisbury, where he soon established a reputation for hard work and careful attention to detail.

In 1829 Pearson entered public life as a representative from Rowan County to the state House of Commons, where he served until 1832. In 1835 he was defeated in a bid for a congressional seat. During the following year he was elected a judge of the superior court, and as he rode the circuits he won acclaim for his ability as a trial judge. Twelve years later, in 1848, the Democratic General Assembly elected Whig Pearson to fill the seat of Justice Joseph J. Daniel on the state supreme court, and on 30 Jan. 1849 the new justice took the oath of office before Governor Charles Manly. A decade later, following the death of Chief Justice Frederick Nash, Pearson was named to that post.

Although his reputation was made in his judicial career, Richmond M. Pearson was also prominent because of his law school. Originally opened in Mocksville about 1836, this school was moved some ten years later to Richmond Hill in present-day Yadkin County when Pearson acquired a sizable plantation on the Yadkin River. There the law school continued to operate with conspicuous success until his death more than three decades later, with spring and fall sessions alternating regularly with the terms of the supreme court.

As a teacher of the law Pearson employed a rigorous Socratic method involving intensive discussion and examination of both the law and its underlying principles. Instruction was offered both to those students who were studying for their county court licenses, and to those more advanced students preparing for practice in the superior courts. In addition to attending lectures and participating in discussions, students were expected to read deeply and repetitively the works of certain American and English legal authorities, especially the writings of the seventeenth-century English jurist, Sir Edward Coke.

Pearson himself claimed to have instructed "more than a thousand law students" at Mocksville and Richmond Hill, and many of these achieved distinction in the legal and political life of North Carolina and the nation. Three of his students, Thomas Settle, William P. Bynum, and William T. Faircloth, later served with him as associate justices of the North Carolina Supreme Court. After his death, three other students, Alphonso C. Avery, David M. Furches, and William Alexander Hoke, were also elevated to the supreme court bench. Indeed, Faircloth and Hoke went on to become chief justices, following in the footsteps of their mentor. Three of Judge Pearson's students, Daniel G. Fowle, John W. Ellis, and Robert B. Glenn, became governors of North Carolina and at least three others, John Steele Henderson, Joseph J. Martin, and William H. H. Cowles, became U.S. congressmen. A student from Mississippi, Jacob Thompson, served as secretary of the interior under President James Buchanan. In addition to these, many Pearson students distinguished themselves as superior court judges and as members of both houses of the North Carolina legislature.

Pearson is, of course, best remembered for his supreme court opinions, which reflect his learning in the law, his keen intellect, the strength of his convictions, and his ability to penetrate quickly to the heart of a question. He used many everyday, down-to-earth illustrations in his opinions and expressed them with clarity and forcefulness.

During the Civil War, his decisions in exemption and habeas corpus cases raised storms of protest in North Carolina and throughout the South. Time after time, he asserted the rights of the individual and the sanctity of contract over the dictates of military necessity, holding that the conscription laws of 1862 had exempted those engaged in certain occupations and had provided to all men the clear option of furnishing able-bodied substitutes in lieu of military service. Confederate authorities, he argued, had no right to violate and abrogate these laws. Over and over again he issued the writ of habeas corpus when men seeking release from military service applied to him for exemption from conscription. The interpretation of conscription and exemption laws occupied much time of the justices, both while court was in recess and in full session. Pearson's colleagues tended to side with him in the early months of the war but the tide shifted as time passed. In 1864, when the Confederacy suspended the writ of habeas corpus, Pearson refused to uphold the suspension and continued his practice of releasing many individuals who applied to him for relief.

It was widely known that Pearson, a staunch Federalist and old-line Whig, had previously opposed the nullification movement of the 1830s, and that he had similarly set his face against the secession movement and the dissolution of the Union. Many detractors now saw in his actions a deliberate attempt to betray the South by undermining its military might, but all evidence indicates that his actions were, instead, based on sincere moral, legal, and constitutional convictions.

A key case, involving one Edward S. Walton, who had furnished a substitute early in the war but who was conscripted in 1864, received much publicity. The other two members of the court held that the amended law, making Walton subject to the draft, was constitutional. Pearson cast a dissenting vote, reasoning that when Walton furnished a substitute there had been a binding contract, a contract that the Confederate Congress had no power to violate. Therefore, he said, Walton should continue to be exempt from service. The *Carolina Watchman* quoted the reaction of the Wilmington *Journal* to Person's position: "So uniform has been his course, so well known and decided are his proclivities, that, no matter what the case may be, the public are always prepared for the same result—a decision against the Confederate government." Despite the controversy surrounding his decisions, however, the fact remains that most North Carolinians retained their confidence in the chief justice.

When, after the war, all offices were vacated, Pearson was promptly reelected to his judicial post. Early in 1866 he was apparently considered by President Andrew Johnson for appointment to the U.S. Supreme Court but was not nominated. Deceived in his hopes of reaching the federal supreme court bench, Pearson continued to serve as chief justice of North Carolina until 1868, when all offices were again vacated by congressional reconstruction. Once more he was reelected chief justice, having secured the nominations of both the Republican and Conservative parties for the post.

In 1868 Pearson, having identified himself with the Republican party, issued a statement setting forth his reasons for supporting Ulysses S. Grant for president of the United States. A protest in reply to the active political stand of Pearson, and other judges, was prepared under the leadership of Bartholomew F. Moore and signed by 107 other lawyers including A. S. Merrimon, Thomas Bragg, and Z. B. Vance; it was published in the 19 April issue of the Raleigh *Sentinel*. In their statement, the lawyers questioned the wisdom of permitting the judiciary to engage in political activity. As a consequence, the supreme court, on 8 June, took steps to prevent those of the protestors who practiced before the supreme court from again appearing there. Initially, the rule was served on only Moore, Thomas Bragg, and E. G. Haywood; after those affected disavowed any intention of holding the court in contempt, the rule was discharged on 19 June.

In 1870, during the Kirk-Holden war, Pearson issued writs of habeas corpus for A. G. Moore and others held by military authorities. Governor W. W. Holden wrote to the chief justice and, after explaining that Alamance County was in a state of insurrection, took the position that public interest required that no military prisoners be surrendered to civil authorities. Petitioners called for an attachment against George W. Kirk, a military official, because of his failure to make returns to the writs; they also sought an additional writ to the sheriff of some county commanding him to take the prisoners from Kirk. Pearson's response held that Holden's reply should be considered part of the proceeding. He held further that the governor could not suspend the writ of habeas corpus but that Kirk had sufficient reason not to make returns. Pearson took the position that Kirk was acting under authority and orders of Holden, his commander in chief. He refused to take steps to assure enforcement of the writ, only referring the writ to the marshal of the superior court for enforcement, but with instructions to exhibit it to the governor; if the governor thereafter ordered the petitioner to be delivered to the marshal, well and good; if not, Pearson explained, the power of the judiciary was "exhausted." In many quarters Pearson was now denounced for abandoning the principle that he had often propounded during the Civil War: "Let justice be done though the heavens fall."

As chief justice of the state supreme court, Pearson was constitutionally bound to preside over the impeachment trial of Governor Holden. In carrying out this duty he was at least outwardly impartial, but many believed that he sympathized with the governor and it was rumored that he privately advised those handling Holden's case. For a time there was a real danger that Pearson would be swept from office with Holden. Pearson himself feared impeachment and actually went so far as to prepare a defense. This he sent to the senate, where it was rejected. Support for Pearson by his former law students supposedly influenced the decision against impeachment.

It was during the time of Governor Holden's impeachment and his own threatened impeachment that Pearson was most stridently accused of excessive drinking and relentless ambition, although these accusations were by no means new. They had been made previously in 1848 at the time of his elevation to the supreme court and in 1859 upon his becoming chief justice. The Raleigh *Sentinel* was especially vocal in its denunciations of Pearson. On 16 Jan. 1871, for example, it called for his impeachment and alleged habitual public drunkenness as a prime justification. The charge of religious skepticism was also leveled at Pearson, though as an adult he was at least nominally an Episcopalian and, while in Raleigh, attended Christ Church.

Pearson was married twice. His first wife, whom he wed on 12 June 1832, was Margaret McClung Williams, daughter of U.S. senator John Williams of Tennessee. Unfortunately, the first Mrs. Pearson, like the second, seems never to have been happy with the rather isolated and rustic existence at Richmond Hill. Moreover, she was tragically afflicted with a progressive and apparently congenital insanity which, during the last two years of her life, loomed darkly over the household. Correspondence between Pearson, doctors, members of the family, and friends is full of concern for Mrs. Pearson's health. Efforts were made to cure her, both at home and in Philadelphia, but to no avail. She died at Richmond Hill on 27 Dec. 1855, at age forty-two. The immediate cause of her death was deemed paralysis, which began in the hand but spread "until it was supposed to have reached the heart, when it resulted in sudden dissolution."

Pearson's marriage to Margaret McClung Williams had produced ten children. Eight of these children were alive at the time of their mother's death, but only three survived past their father's death some twenty-two years later. His daughter Ellen Brent married Daniel G. Fowle in 1856 but died in 1862, long before he became governor of North Carolina in 1889. Another daughter, Mary Williams, married E. Hayne Davis and took up residence near Statesville. A son of the chief justice, Richmond, was active in Republican politics in the late nineteenth and early twentieth centuries as a prominent legislator, congressman, and diplomat. He died at his Asheville home, Richmond Hill, on 12 Sept. 1923.

Pearson's second wife was Mary McDowell Bynum, widow of General John Gray Bynum and daughter of Captain Charles McDowell of Quaker Meadows in Burke County, near Morganton. They were married at Quaker Meadows on 22 Sept. 1859. It was during the following year that the present home at Richmond Hill was built, replacing the log structure that had been Pearson's home during his first marriage. For nearly two decades the second Mrs. Pearson assisted in the management of the household, plantation, and law school at Richmond Hill, but soon after her husband's death she moved her place of residence to Morganton. There she remained until her own death in 1886.

On 5 Jan. 1878 Pearson was in a buggy on the way to Winston, planning to get the train there to return to Raleigh for the January term of court. There is no indication that he had been recently ill. The law school had been conducted normally during the preceding fall term, and plans had already been made for the spring term to come. Well before reaching Winston, however, he was already dying, and he quietly passed away soon after his arrival there. The *People's Press* of Salem carried the following account of his death in its issue of 10 January: "The community was painfully startled by the announcement, on Saturday last, that Judge Pearson had arrived at Winston in a dying condition, from acute paralysis of the brain. He had left home in the regular mail buggy, with no one but the driver, and was stricken when but a few miles from home, the driver failed to arouse him and in his condition he was lifted from the buggy in Winston and carried to his room in Wilson's Hotel. All attention was given to him by kind friends, but he sank rapidly, and gently breathed his last at thirty-five minutes past 10 o'clock Saturday night."

Following a period of confusion as to when and where the funeral and burial would be held, the remains of the chief justice were taken to Raleigh. Pearson lay in state in the rotunda of the state capitol prior to funeral services on the afternoon of 9 January at Christ Episcopal Church, conducted by the Right Reverend Theodore Lyman. Burial followed in Raleigh's Oakwood Cemetery. In 1881 an impressive monument was erected at his grave by an association of lawyers, most of whom had studied under the chief justice. Inscribed thereon, under the seal of the North Carolina Supreme Court, are these words: "His epitaph is written by his own hand in the North Carolina Reports."

SEE: Wilson Angley, "Richmond M. Pearson and the Richmond Hill Law School," 1978 (North Carolina State Archives, Raleigh); Samuel A. Ashe, ed., *Biographical History of North Carolina*, vol. 5 (1906); Daniel Moreau Barringer Papers and Richmond M. Pearson Papers (Southern Historical Collection, University of North Carolina, Chapel Hill); *DAB*, vol. 7 (1934); Daniel L. Grant, ed., *Alumni History of the University of North Carolina* (1924); James Albert Hutchens, "The Chief-Justiceship and Public Career of Richmond M. Pearson, 1861–1871" (M.A. thesis, University of North Carolina, 1960); Memroy F. Mitchell, *Legal Aspects of Conscription and Exemption in North Carolina, 1861–1865* (1965); North Carolina Supreme Court Reports, 1848–78 (North Carolina State Archives, Raleigh); "Proceedings in Memory of Richmond Pearson," *North Carolina Reports* 78 (7 Jan. 1878); *Raleigh Daily Telegram*, 18 Mar. 1871; Raleigh *News* and Raleigh *News and Observer*, 8–10 Jan. 1878; Raleigh *Register*, 9 Jan. 1856; Salem *People's Press*, 10 Jan. 1878; Salisbury *Carolina Watchman*, 14 Mar. 1864; Tombstone inscriptions, Oakwood Cemetery, Raleigh; Will of Richmond M. Pearson (Yadkin County Estates Papers, North Carolina State Archives, Raleigh).

MEMORY F. MITCHELL

Pearson, Robert Caldwell *(9 Dec. 1807–18 Nov. 1867)*, merchant, postmaster, bank and railroad president, Democratic leader, jurist, and gold mine and flour mill owner, was born at the family plantation, Silvercreek, on Silver Creek, near Morganton, in Burke County. His parents were Isaac (1778–1857) and Elizabeth Caldwell Pearson; she was the daughter of Robert Caldwell, Sr., and Elizabeth Snell Caldwell.

Around 1817 Robert left Silvercreek to live with his uncle, John Caldwell, to be tutored in mathematics, the classics, Greek, and Latin. He later attended the Morganton Academy, of which he was a trustee by 1845. Pearson was interested in providing excellent educations for the young scholars of the day. All of his sons (except the youngest, who was nine at the beginning of the Civil War) attended The University of North Carolina. One son, William Simpson Pearson, who was prepared for college by Dr. Alexander Wilson, entered Davidson College at age thirteen and The University of North Carolina at fourteen; he was graduated with honors from the university in 1868 at age eighteen.

Robert clerked in John Caldwell's store, which was located on the town square. This experience became the basis for beginning his career as a merchant. After his marriage he operated his own store on the square in Morganton.

Gold mining was flourishing in North Carolina when Robert Caldwell Pearson and his brother both owned mines. These later became part of larger mining interests in the state.

One of Robert's earliest civic achievements was the donation of a log cabin and land near Spruce Pine to serve as the courthouse until a more suitable structure could be erected in Morganton. Within a short time, R. C. Pearson, Thomas Walton, Sr., Frank Glass, Colonel Isaac Avery, and David Corpening obtained a contract for the courthouse (with builder Joseph Binney), levied the taxes, and supervised completion.

In 1844 Pearson became president of the Morganton branch of the Bank of the State of North Carolina, a position he held until 1860, when Thomas G. Walton assumed the presidency. John H. Wheeler noted in his *Reminiscences* that Pearson was a skillful financier.

Transportation was a major concern throughout the state, and Pearson was one of the Burke County delegates to a general convention "to consider and recommend a general system of Internal Improvements, by Railroads, for the State." The General Assembly ratified an act to incorporate the Western North Carolina Railway with the existing railroad. At this time, Pearson organized the first stockholders' meeting of the Western North Carolina Railway in Salisbury. In his *Reminiscences* Wheeler states that Pearson was "the stay and backbone of the belt of counties between Rowan and Buncombe. What Morehead was to the Central, so was Pearson to the Western Railroad." Pearson was elected the first president of the Western North Carolina Railway.

Pearson was married to Jane Sophronia Tate on 18 Mar. 1834 in the old Presbyterian Meeting House by a Reverend Mr. Stillman. The couple lived in a house across from the courthouse on the Morganton town square; later this structure was partially torn down and became a business establishment. Pearson and his wife had five sons and three daughters: Robert Caldwell Jr., James, Duncan Cameron, William Simpson, John Henry, Ann Elizabeth, Jane Sophronia, and Laura.

A local Democratic leader, Pearson held several county offices. For many years before and during the Civil War, he was the leading magistrate in Burke County. In 1833 he had been a justice of the Burke County Court of Pleas and Quarter Sessions and had served as postmaster in Morganton for several years before the war.

Pearson was a strict Presbyterian and assumed prominent leadership in church affairs. He was buried in the churchyard of the new Presbyterian church in Morganton.

SEE: Samuel A. Ashe, ed., *Biographical History of North Carolina*, 8 (1908 [portrait]); Eugene J. Pearson, *The Pearson Family, 10th–20th Century* (1978); "Robert Caldwell Pearson," undated newspaper clipping (North Carolina Collection, University of North Carolina, Chapel Hill); Edward W. Phifer, Jr., *Burke: The History of a North Carolina County, 1777–1920* (1977); William S. Stoney, *Historical Sketches of Grace Church, Morganton* (1935); Thomas George Walter, *Sketches of Pioneers in Burke County History* (1984).

JEAN CAMERON POLAND

Pearson, Thomas *(24 June 1893–16 Apr. 1963)*, international economic adviser, was born at the family home, Richmond Hill, in Asheville, the son of Richmond and Gabrielle Thomas Pearson. His grandfather was Richmond Mumford Pearson, chief justice of the North Carolina Supreme Court during the Civil War. He attended St. Paul's School, Concord, N.H., and was a 1915 graduate of Princeton University.

Pearson worked for the American International Corporation in New York between 1916 and 1920, except for service in France as a captain in the U.S. Army (1917–19) during World War I. After the war he was the foreign trade editor of the *New York Evening Post* (1920–21). From 1922 to 1927 he was in Persia with a group that took over the finances of the government by request and operated them during that period. From 1929 to 1936 Pearson was with the International Chamber of Commerce in Paris, an organization established after the war to improve world business conditions and the prospects for world peace. In 1937 President Franklin D. Roosevelt appointed him deputy receiver of customs in the Dominican Republic to help supervise repayment of a $25 million U.S. loan. In 1941 he was named to the board of directors of the National Bank of Haiti. Returning to the Dominican Republic in 1948, he was director of the department of economic research for the Central Bank of the Republic.

During his long stay in the Caribbean, Pearson became an authority on the culture and social customs of the people and was instrumental in establishing the Dominican-American Cultural Institute. He retired from foreign service in 1951 and returned to Asheville. Pearson never married; his only survivor was a sister, Marjorie Pearson, who had helped him to restore Richmond Hill. He was buried in Riverside Cemetery, Asheville.

SEE: *Asheville Citizen*, 17 Apr. 1963; *Who Was Who in America, 1961–1968* (1968).

ROBERT O. CONWAY

Pearson, Thomas Gilbert *(10 Nov. 1873–3 Sept. 1943)*, ornithologist and wildlife conservationist, was born in Tuscola, Ill., the son of Thomas Barnard and Mary Eliott Pearson. A Quaker farm family, the Pearsons moved to Indiana and then in 1882 to Archer, Fla., where they grew citrus fruit. Stimulated by the wildlife in rural Alachua County, Gilbert Pearson taught himself ornithology and taxidermy. In 1891 he entered Guilford College, where he earned six years of education, including two preparatory years, by donating a collection of bird eggs and mounted birds to the school's museum and serving as its curator. From field trips in North Carolina, Virginia, and Florida, he returned with a wide variety of specimens and built what was described as the "largest scientific collection of bird-eggs in the South." Some of his eggs were exhibited at the World's Columbian Exposition in Chicago in 1893. He wrote articles for bird magazines and joined the American Ornithologists' Union (AOU).

During at least one summer in Archer, Pearson operated a business as a naturalist and taxidermist, specializing in birds and eggs. Distressed by the killing of birds for their plumage, he wrote a circular, "Echoes From Bird Land; An Appeal to Women" (1895), in which he urged women to stop wearing bird feathers and stuffed bird bodies on their clothes. The circular was distributed in North Carolina by the Woman's Christian Temperance Union.

After earning a B.S. degree at Guilford College in 1897, Pearson enrolled at The University of North Carolina. He supported himself in Chapel Hill by working as an assistant in the office of the state geologist, who let him concentrate on biological studies. In 1899 he received his second B.S. degree and returned to Guilford College as professor of biology. In 1901 he became professor of biology and geology at the State Normal and Industrial School for Women. During the summer before his first classes, he studied botany at Harvard. In the same year he published his first book, *Stories of Bird Life*. Soon afterwards he received a letter from William Dutcher, chairman of the bird protection committee of the AOU, which was trying to persuade all the states to adopt laws protecting birds. Dutcher suggested that Pearson found a state Audubon society to sponsor a bill in North Carolina incorporating the main features of the AOU's "model law."

In 1902, at Pearson's instigation, the Audubon Society of North Carolina (ASNC) was formed. Pearson was elected secretary. Aware of the absence of a means of enforcing laws protecting wildlife in North Carolina, he combined in a single bill the ASNC's proposals for protecting birds and provisions authorizing it to enforce not only the regulations of the bill but also the numerous local game laws of the state. He visited Governor Charles Brantley Aycock and won his support; he also addressed the house of representatives in behalf of the bill. When the bill was adopted in 1903, the ASNC became the first state game commission in the South and Pearson, at age twenty-nine, became the first commissioner.

In 1905, when the National Association of Audubon Societies (NAAS) was incorporated in New York, Pearson was elected secretary. Anticipating this development, he had already obtained leave from teaching duties at the State Normal and Industrial School. He then divided his time between the NAAS and the ASNC. Except for brief service each summer for several years in the Summer School of the South, where he began teaching in 1902, he never again held a professorship. Promoting the Audubon movement was his major occupation for the next thirty years.

For six years, 1903–9, Pearson had considerable success in enforcing the bird and game laws of North Carolina and in protecting coastal nesting sites. Furthermore, by cultivating legislative committees, he managed to assure the defeat of bills that he viewed as harmful to wildlife and the passage of bills that he regarded as beneficial. But his successes caused resentment, especially in Beaufort and Currituck counties, where the hunting of waterfowl had economic and political importance. In the General Assembly in 1909 a bill to remove those two counties from the jurisdiction of the ASNC was taken from the committees friendly to Pearson, amended to include fifty more counties, and passed. The ASNC was left with forty-six counties, too few for it to be effective any longer.

Pearson, his pioneering leadership repudiated in North Carolina, turned his full-time attention to the national movement. In 1910 he was elected president of the National Association of State Game Wardens and Commissioners. After William Dutcher, president of the NAAS, suffered a stroke in October of the same year, the board of directors bestowed executive power on Secretary Pearson. In 1911 he resigned from his office in the ASNC and moved to New York. Upon Dutcher's death in 1920, Pearson became president of the NAAS. He held that position until he resigned in 1934.

In the NAAS Pearson encouraged national and international efforts to obtain legal protection for birds. He successfully lobbied for a provision in the Tariff of 1913 prohibiting the importation of plumage of wild birds except for scientific and educational purposes. He worked for passage of the Weeks-McLean Migratory Bird Act (1913) and served on the secretary of agriculture's advisory committee for implementing the act. He supported the Migratory Bird Treaty (1916) between the United States and Great Britain and became a member of the advisory board to enforce it. In 1928 he became chairman of the National Committee on Wildlife Legislation, which backed passage of the Migratory Bird Conservation Act (1929), authorizing appropriations for the establishment of bird refuges.

The NAAS provided warden service that national and state governments failed to provide. It guarded Pelican Island and the Everglades in Florida, Lower Klamath Lake in Oregon and California, hundreds of square miles of marshes and islands in Louisiana, and nesting areas along the Atlantic coastline. It opposed the draining of lakes and marshes important to wildlife, fought against the construction of dams that would flood wildlife habitats, and aided in the protection of mammals, including the buffalo and the prong-horned antelope. And it sought the adoption of state laws protecting birds and mammals wherever they seemed threatened.

In 1922 Pearson founded the International Committee for Bird Preservation. He served as president until 1938 and thereafter as chairman of the U.S. section and the Pan-American section. An international conference for bird protection sponsored by the committee in 1928 called for, among other actions, an international convention on oil pollution of navigable waters.

A talented lecturer and fund-raiser, Pearson estimated in 1937 that he had spoken to more than 3,000 audiences in behalf of birds and other wildlife. In most of the states and in numerous foreign countries, he had lectured, organized, lobbied, and advised. By 1934, under his leadership, the NAAS had distributed 270 million pages of printed information on birds and 54 million pictures in color. Its magazine, *Bird-Lore*, had influenced young and old alike. Membership in Junior Audubon clubs rose from less than 10,000 in 1910 to more than 5 million in 1934. Pearson was credited with developing the NAAS into "the largest organization in the world interested in the protection of wild life."

Throughout his career, Pearson retained his special interest in North Carolina, which he spoke of as "the State of my adoption." In 1919 the ASNC joined with the state Geological and Economic Survey and the state museum to publish *Birds of North Carolina*, by Pearson, Clement S. Brimley, and Herbert H. Brimley. Pearson also drew on his studies and observations in North Carolina in writing most of his other books, which included *The Bird Study Book* (1917) and *Tales From Birdland* (1918). In addition, he edited *Birds of America* (1917, 3 vols.) and *Portraits and Habits of Our Birds* (1920–21, 2 vols.) and contributed to the National Geographic Society publication, *The Book of Birds* (1937, 2 vols.). The University of North Carolina awarded him an honorary LL.D. degree in 1924.

In 1911, and every two years thereafter until success was achieved, the ASNC sponsored a bill to establish a new state game commission, with state wardens. It was finally set up in 1927 by an act that abolished ASNC.

On 17 June 1902 Pearson married Elsie Weatherly, a

graduate of the State Normal and Industrial School for Women. They had three children: Elizabeth, Thomas Gilbert, Jr., and William Theodore. Pearson belonged to the Boone and Crockett Club and the Explorers Club of America. After his death in New York City, funeral services were held in the Central Presbyterian Church. His body was cremated and the remains were buried in Greensboro.

SEE: *Audubon Magazine* (January–February, September–October [portrait], November–December 1943); Audubon Societies Papers (New York Public Library); *Auk* (April 1947); *Bird-Lore* (November–December 1934 [portrait]); *DAB*, Supp. 3 (1973); Dorothy Lloyd Gilbert, "T. Gilbert Pearson and Guilford College," *Guilford College Bulletin* (January 1944); *Nat. Cyc. Am. Biog.*, vols. D and 33 (1934–47); *New York Times*, 5 Sept. 1943 (portrait); Oliver H. Orr, Jr., *Saving American Birds* (1992); T. Gilbert Pearson, *Adventures in Bird Protection, an Autobiography* (1937 [portrait]); *Who Was Who in America*, vol. 2 (1950).

OLIVER H. ORR, JR.

Pearson, William Simpson *(9 Oct. 1849–11 Dec. 1920)*, author, was born in Morganton, Burke County. His parents were Robert Caldwell (9 Dec. 1807–18 Nov. 1867) and Jane Sophronia Tate Pearson (27 June 1807–24 July 1877), both born in Morganton. Pearson was a relative of Governor Tod R. Caldwell and Robert Caldwell, a shipowner from Derry, Ireland, who went to Philadelphia in 1763. Pearson's formal education began in Morganton and was continued in Melville, Alamance County. After his preparation for college by Dr. Alexander Wilson, he entered Davidson College at age fifteen. One year later he transferred to The University of North Carolina, where he received an A.B. degree with honors in 1868.

Later that year Pearson was made a Grant elector and a messenger of the vote, and in 1873 he served as the U.S. consul at Palermo, Italy. After editing the *Asheville Pioneer* in 1874 and 1875, he was an aide to Governor Curtis H. Brogden and a commissioner of the state for the Western North Carolina Railroad. During his term (1875–77) as a commissioner, Pearson initiated the practice of having convicts work on the mountain section of the railroad, established a telegraph line in western North Carolina, placed the town of Newton on the main line, and inaugurated a system of cheap excursions in western North Carolina.

In 1880 Pearson began practicing law, and in 1881 his political novel, *Monon Ou; or, Well Nigh Reconstructed*, was published. This novel demonstrated his expertise in political history. During the remainder of his life, Pearson held numerous positions including commissioner of the state hospital at Morganton (1877–82), computer in the supervising architect's office (1883–85), state attorney for the Eastern Building and Loan Association (1893–98), editor of the *Farmers' Friend and Morganton Herald* (1897–1901), referee in bankruptcy (1898–1904), Bryan elector (1900), state senator from the Thirty-fourth District (1905), and trustee of The University of North Carolina (1905–7).

Pearson married Bettie Venable Michaux on 7 June 1882, and they became the parents of five children: Susie, Paul, Ada, Richard, and Grace. He was a Chi Phi at The University of North Carolina, a Master Mason, a member of the Junior Order of United American Mechanics, a vestryman of Grace Episcopal Church in Morganton, and a Republican.

SEE Samuel A. Ashe, ed., *Biographical History of North Carolina*, vol. 7 (1908 [portrait]); *Asheville Citizen-Times*, 26 May 1972; Daniel L. Grant, ed., *Alumni History of the University of North Carolina* (1924); *Greensboro Daily News*, 19 Oct. 1930; Membership records (First Presbyterian Church, Morganton); Membership records (Grace Episcopal Church, Morganton); *Nat. Cyc. Am. Biog.* 18 (1922).

ANTHONY G. CARRAWAY

Peattie, Elia (Maria Cahill) W. *(15 Jan. 1862–12 July 1935)*, writer, journalist, and lecturer, was born in Kalamazoo, Mich., the oldest of five daughters of Frederick and Amanda Maria Cahill Wilkerson. She and her four sisters—Kate, Gertrude, Bertha, and Hazel—were ninth-generation Americans. The family early moved to Chicago, where she went to school through the sixth grade, then went to work setting type in her father's print shop. After a six years' courtship, on 10 May 1883 she married Robert Burns Peattie, a newspaperman born in 1857 to immigrant Scottish parents.

Elia Peattie became art and society editor of the *Chicago Tribune*, then a reporter. From 1888 to 1896 she and her husband were employed by the *Omaha World-Herald*. Returning to Chicago, Elia was literary critic for the *Tribune* (1901–17). For many years her husband was associated with the *New York Times*. About 1899, she first journeyed to Tryon seeking a mild winter climate for her son Donald Culross, whose health was delicate in his boyhood. In spite of frequent and prolonged visits thereafter, often staying with Charles and Emma Payne Erskine, the Peattie family did not settle in Tryon permanently until after World War I. Elia and Robert were active in community life, organized a little theater group, and spearheaded the purchase of Pearson's Falls as a conservation project.

Elia W. Peattie, a tall, commanding woman, lectured and traveled widely. She could, it is said, "fight like an Indian" for causes in which she believed. She published some thirty titles: travel, history, novels, short stories, poetry, drama, and books for young readers. Among the last are *Azalea, the Story of a Girl in the Blue Ridge Mountains* (1912) and its three sequels, *Annie Laurie and Azalea* (1913), *Azalea at Sunset Gap* (1914), and *Azalea's Silver Web* (1915). The Peatties' four children were Edward Cahill; Barbara Culross (Mrs. Ralph Erskine); Roderick, the well-known geographer; and Donald Culross, the famed naturalist. Elia was an Episcopalian and a Democrat. She died at Westhill, her son Roderick's farm in Vermont, and was buried in Tryon, where on her tombstone are these words: "She ate of life as if 'twere fruit."

SEE: *Asheville Citizen*, 13 July 1935; Sadie Smathers Patton, *Sketches of Polk County History* (1950); Donald Culross Peattie, *The Road of a Naturalist* (1941); Roderick Peattie, *The Incurable Romantic* (1941); *Who Was Who in America*, vol. 1 (1942).

RICHARD WALSER

Peck, Clara Jane Thornton *(1 Mar. 1862–15 June 1926)*, nurse, the daughter of John and Jane Thornton, was born in Stroud, Gloucestershire, England. When she was about ten, her family moved to Pittsburgh, Pa., where she attended the public schools and was graduated in voice from the Pershing School of Music. For several years she was a member of the choir and a soloist at St. Peter's Episcopal Church.

During early womanhood she met and on 19 Sept. 1883 married Delbert Stephen Peck of Cleveland, Ohio. They became the parents of Howard Thornton (who died young), Saza Hendrick, and Cora Bliss. In 1898 the family moved to Greensboro, N.C., to be near Mrs. Peck's parents, who had moved there in hopes that a change of climate would restore John Thornton's health. The father died in 1899, however, and soon afterwards Delbert Peck died of pneumonia.

Clara Peck, in considering ways of supporting herself and her two small daughters, turned to her natural instinct to care for the ill. There was no source of nurse's training immediately available, but in 1901 local physicians opened the Greensboro Hospital and accepted her for training. She soon became the institution's first matron and began voluntarily to visit patients in their rooms. General practitioners, recognizing her skills, called on her to care for patients with unusual illnesses.

Soon after entering a home to serve as a nurse, she came to be regarded as a friend and adviser. In homes where the mother was ill and there were children to be cared for, she often took the children to her own home until other arrangements could be made. Her public-spirited service filled a community need at a time when no public agency existed to provide help. In 1909 a group of women in Greensboro organized the District Nurse and Relief Association and volunteered their services, contributed financial support, and employed Mrs. Peck as the first district nurse in the town. Within three years she reported that she had answered 7,750 calls for assistance. She came to be called "Mother Peck" by those whom she helped and, indeed, by the citizens of Greensboro.

Before long it was discovered that many people at various economic levels were suffering from tuberculosis. Women of the town opened a six-room cottage as a hospital and named Mother Peck as nurse and general manager. She also visited homes throughout the community to minister to the sick who could not be accommodated in the hospital. Visits to local schools as a health nurse helped to alert citizens to the need for a tax-supported public health department and a sanatorium for tubercular patients. For several years the District Nurse and Relief Committee, with Mother Peck to direct the work, provided tuberculosis control in Greensboro. She went to a specialized sanatorium to receive training in the care of such patients and then played a leading role in securing county support for erecting a sanatorium. It was opened in 1923 as the first such county-supported institution in North Carolina. She was able to convince persons with the disease in its early stages to receive treatment, and after thirty-two years the program was so successful that the hospital site and buildings were no longer needed for this purpose. The Guilford Technical Institute took it over as a training center.

During the influenza epidemics of 1918 and 1920 the District Nurse and Relief Association offered its nursing staff to the relief organization of the Greensboro Chapter of the Red Cross, and Mother Peck extended her already full schedule to include care for those who fell victim to this new illness.

Having worked for "the rich and the poor, the sick and the fallen" in and around Greensboro for almost a quarter of a century, Mother Peck retired with the gratitude of the community. Numerous tokens of appreciation were extended on the occasion and a little later the Clara J. Peck Elementary School was named in her honor. She died suddenly and was buried in Green Hill Cemetery, Greensboro. She was survived by two daughters.

SEE: Family records (possession of Cora Peck, Greensboro); *Greensboro Daily News*, 16 June 1926 (portrait), 25 Feb. 1960; Greensboro Public Library, biographical clipping file; Greensboro Tuberculosis Association, *Greensboro Battles a Disease, 1909–1959* (1959?); Guilford County Health Department files.

ETHEL STEPHENS ARNETT

Peebles, Robert Bruce *(21 July 1840–29 June 1916)*, legislator and judge, the son of Ethelred J. and Lucretia Tyner Peebles, was born at Moorfield, his father's plantation in Northampton County. After attending Horner School in Oxford, he entered The University of North Carolina in 1859. At Chapel Hill Peebles earned high honors but left to join the Confederate army before receiving a degree. Entering the army as a private in Company E, Fiftieth North Carolina Regiment, he soon was promoted to company lieutenant; afterwards he became adjutant of the Thirty-fifth Regiment. During the war he saw action at Petersburg, Drury's Lane, and Bermuda Hundred in Virginia and at Plymouth, N.C. At Five Forks he was made assistant adjutant general of General Matt Ransom's brigade.

At the end of the war Peebles returned to Chapel Hill to complete his studies and to read law under Judge William H. Battle. Settling in his native county, he established a practice in Jackson and became county attorney. He was elected as a Democrat to the General Assembly of 1866–67 and again in 1883, but this election was contested and after serving for a brief time he was obliged to step down. He was returned to the legislature for the sessions of 1891 and 1895, however. From 1874 to 1903 he served as a trustee of The University of North Carolina, and in 1902 he was elected a judge of the superior court, a position he held until his death.

In 1875 Peebles married Margaret Cameron, daughter of Paul C. Cameron, a prominent planter and businessman of Orange County. They were the parents of a daughter, Annie Ruffin Peebles. A lifelong member of the Episcopal Church of the Saviour, Jackson, he died in Hillsborough and was buried in the churchyard at St. Matthew's Church.

SEE: Samuel A. Ashe, ed., *Biographical History of North Carolina*, vol. 4 (1906 [portrait]); John L. Cheney, Jr., ed., *North Carolina Government, 1585–1979* (1981); Daniel L. Grant, *Alumni History of the University of North Carolina* (1924); *North Carolina Bar Association Report* (1917); Northampton County Bicentennial Committee, *Footprints in Northampton* (1976); J. C. Tomlinson, *Assembly Sketch Book, Session 1883* (1883).

JAMES ELLIOTT MOORE

Peele, Herbert Evans *(24 Apr. 1882–2 Dec. 1952)*, newspaper editor and publisher and radio executive, was born in rural Halifax County at Crowell's Crossroads, the son of the Reverend Robert Evans and Adelaide Whitehouse Peele. His early education was sporadic and varied in public schools in North Carolina and South Carolina where his father served as a Baptist pastor. He was graduated from high school at Mullins, S.C. in 1900. At age eighteen he entered Wake Forest College, Wake Forest. Stringent financial limitations required that he "go to school a while, work a while." Following his first year of college, he taught for five years in South Carolina. In the fall of 1906 he returned to Wake Forest and completed his academic work, graduating (1908) with a bachelor of arts degree *magna cum laude*.

Two careers appealed to Peele: teaching and journalism. He held his first newspaper job as a printer's devil on the *Timmonsville* (S.C.) *Enterprise* (1904). There he really got "printer's ink on his hands," and the lure of the newspaper won over teaching. He may have worked on other newspapers at odd times and in between sessions at college, but his first full-time newspaper connection was a summer job with a paper in Lumberton in 1905.

Peele taught in Florence, S.C., for two years (1908–10), then spent one year (1910–11) in Andrews, N.C., as superintendent of schools. In 1911 he negotiated the lease and ultimate purchase of a weekly newspaper in Elizabeth City, *The Tar Heel*. Thus began a location and an occupation that continued for the rest of his life—forty-one years.

It would be interesting to know why Peele changed the name of the paper in 1912 from *The Tar Heel* to *The Advance*. It is possible that the campus newspaper at The University of North Carolina made prior claim to the name, but more likely he wanted a new name to make it more *his* paper. *The Advance* operated as a local weekly, until about 1918, when it became *The Daily Advance* and was published each weekday afternoon. Under that name it became an effervescent and indomitable influence in northeastern North Carolina. Peele's province was not limited to Elizabeth City and Pasquotank County, for a hundred miles around, throughout the coastal region and west of it, he claimed an undying concern and exerted a continuing influence for progress.

In 1949 Peele sold the paper and thereafter devoted his full attention to an adjunct journalist project, radio station WGAI, which he had purchased several years earlier. He believed that the media, too, should inform as well as entertain its listeners.

On both the paper and the radio, Herbert Peele practiced a type of journalism that was informal, intimate, and scrupulously accurate and kind. His standards for himself and his staff were high and exacting. For both media he did a very personal column headed "Peelings"—with a heavy sprinkling of the first-person pronoun, unabashed references to "Miss Kate," his wife, and their joint interests, and his friends in Elizabeth City and around three states.

His editorials were widely read and as widely quoted by other editors, who recognized him as a deliberate but calm crusader for many causes that meant progress for his section of the state. Peele pleaded for good roads. He wanted adequate air service in the new age. He believed growth could come only with good schools. He found much along the coast, especially on the Outer Banks of North Carolina, that deserved preservation. He was interested in its history from the "Lost Colony" to the Wright brothers' memorial. Peele served for a number of years as a trustee of Wake Forest College, his alma mater, and was always cordially interested in its alumni association.

It was to all of these concerns that he dedicated his subtle, studied capacity for communication. It was his commitment to enhance the Albemarle region that earned him the affectionate title, "Mr. Albemarle." The Albemarle of 1911 was an isolated, inaccessible area as far as North Carolina was concerned. A journey from Elizabeth City to Raleigh was best done by going first to Norfolk, Va. Herbert Peele turned the whole picture around. Long bridges across wide rivers and sounds connected good highways west. Airports provided quick travel. The Albemarle became an accessible, integral part of the state, and he lived to see his handiwork. As virtually a one-man chamber of commerce and a masterful publicist, he drew attention to the region. State and local governments and private investment contributed to the changes.

Peele remained a soft-spoken, mild-mannered man, known to thousands whether they had ever seen him or met him. They knew his ideals and objectives; they knew he was promoting their causes, and they loved him for it. His church was Blackwell Memorial Baptist, which he found many ways to serve; Peele gave his presence and his means to its program. The Rotary Club of Elizabeth City knew him as one who truly put "Service Above Self." A charter member, he held many offices, including president, and often attended district conferences and intercity meetings.

In the North Carolina Press Association, he was a familiar figure, twice its vice-president (1929–30, 1941–42), once its president (1946–47). His fellow editors admired him and the principles of good journalism he exemplified. In 1933 Governor J. C. B. Ehringhaus appointed him secretary-treasurer of the North Carolina Railroad, and he served in that post through 1937.

Up and down the streets of Elizabeth City Peele was known, hailed, and respected. On his death an editorial in the *Asheville Citizen* commented, "It is not too much to add that there was scarcely any newspaper executive in North Carolina who enjoyed to quite the same degree the confidence of other Tar Heel publishers." His staff gave him an intense loyalty, and he inspired in them a high level of journalism.

Peele married, in June 1913, Kate Ford of Mullins, S.C., in a ceremony performed at Meredith College, Raleigh, where she was an art teacher. They had two sons: John (d. 1946) and Thomas. Miss Kate was almost as well known as her husband; every day she worked by his side. It was "their" newspaper, "their" radio station. They complemented each other in extraordinary fashion. She was walking to work with him that early morning in December when he died suddenly at age seventy. Funeral services were held at Christ Church (Episcopal), whose rector assisted Peele's own Baptist pastor in the service. Burial followed in the Hollywood Cemetery, Elizabeth City. Several years after his death, his widow edited and published *Mr. Albemarle: Some Quotations from Herbert Peele's Editorials and Peelings* (1955).

SEE: Elizabeth City *Daily Advance*, 3 Dec. 1952; *North Carolina Biography*, vol. 4 (1941); Pasquotank-Chowan Library, Elizabeth City (clipping file); Kate Ford Peele, *Mr. Albemarle* (1955); Raleigh *News and Observer*, 3 Dec. 1952; *Who's Who in the South and Southwest* (1952).

C. SYLVESTER GREEN

Peele, William Joseph *(31 Jan. 1855–27 Mar. 1919)*, lawyer and cultural leader, was born near Jackson in Northampton County, the youngest of fourteen children of Isaac (1807–91) and Nancy Thompson Cobb Peele (1812–78). He was the brother of John Hardy (b. 1829), Mary Elizabeth (Mrs. C. C. Hardee, 1831–1922), Thomas Moseley (1833–41), Benjamin Evans (b. 1834), Frances (1836–1916), William Isaac (1837–91), Joseph Richard (1840–41), Henrietta Hannah (Mrs. William L. Fetcher, b. 1841), Elizabeth Rebecca (Mrs. Samuel N. Buxton, 1845–1928), Rennie (Mrs. James H. Buxton, b. 1847), Susan Alice (b. 1849), Isaac Edward (b. 1851), and Robert Evans (b. 1852), father of Herbert Peele, a newspaper editor of Elizabeth City. Isaac Peele, whose father Dr. John Peele was a book-reading Quaker, moved from Virginia first to a farm near Rich Square and later to another three miles north of Jackson.

William Joseph Peele attended Bush Horn Academy, and in 1875, upon the reopening of The University of North Carolina, became a freshman at Chapel Hill, financed there by his two Buxton brothers-in-law. He studied the classics and was graduated in 1879, realizing full well that he had not been prepared to earn a living. His senior essay was on the necessity of reform, and it became his lifelong theme. Based on his impecunious predicament in the moneyless late 1870s, Peele became convinced that North Carolina could no longer ignore the need for industrial education. He studied law in Jackson and then in Raleigh, where he obtained his license and formed a partnership with Ernest P. Maynard.

In 1884 Peele founded the Watauga Club, a group of young men whose primary goal soon became the establishment of an industrial school for the training of farmers, mechanics, and manufacturers. Three members of the club—Arthur Winslow, Walter Hines Page, and Peele—memorialized the General Assembly early in 1885 to create an institution for instruction in "wood-work, mining, metallurgy, practical agriculture and in such other branches of industrial education as may be deemed expedient." Many of Peele's Wataugans appeared before the Legislative Committee on Education to argue in favor of the proposal. Thomas Dixon, Jr., a member of the club, helped push the bill through the house. Later Peele wrote of how, "with the powerful assistance of many others," it became law, but "not without considerable difficulty. Some opposed it because they were fossils and oppose everything; some feared it would ultimately draw the Land Scrip Fund away from the University." The latter fear was justified. Two years later Peele's Wataugans and Leonidas L. Polk's organized farmers saw to it that the fund was transferred from the university, and in 1888 the cornerstone was laid for the first building of the North Carolina College of Agriculture and Mechanic Arts (now North Carolina State University).

Peele was active on many other fronts. He promoted the first chair of history at The University of North Carolina and after serving (1891–97) on the board of trustees, he acted in a similar capacity for the North Carolina College of Agriculture and Mechanics beginning in 1899. In 1897 he formed the North Carolina Publishing Society to bring out *Lives of Distinguished North Carolinians*, which he compiled. His other books were *Index to the Law of Exemptions in North Carolina of Homestead and Personal Property* (1892) and *Civil Government of North Carolina and the United States* (1907). In 1901 he helped organize the State Literary and Historical Association and was chairman of the committee to draft its constitution. The next year he was involved in the Roanoke Island Celebration Committee. Peele drew up one of the first lists of North Carolina books. In 1903 he wrote the bill for the establishment of the North Carolina Historical Commission, was primarily responsible for nursing it through the General Assembly, was appointed by Governor Charles B. Aycock as one of its first five members, served as its first chairman, and remained on the commission until his death.

On 4 Sept. 1909, after a twenty-one-year courtship, Peele married Elizabeth Bellamy of Raleigh. He was a Baptist and a Democrat. In 1969 an oil portrait of Peele by Jacques Busbee hanging in Peele Hall, a classroom building on the North Carolina State University campus named in his honor, was stolen and slashed by vandals.

In spite of his many interests, Peele led a lonely life. His renowned eloquence and felicitous literary style were placed in the service of a more history-conscious, more cultured, and more prosperous North Carolina. "One could not conceive of Peele as a careless, frolicsome boy; he was always old," wrote his friend Robert W. Winston. "Great sums of money simply terrified him! He could not understand how people got rich honestly." In truth, Peele was preeminently a philosopher, a dreamer, and a planner.

SEE: Grady L. E. Carroll, *They Lived in Raleigh*, 2 vols. (1977); Family records (possession of Henry M. Shaw, Raleigh); David A. Lockmiller, *History of the North Carolina State College* (1939 [portrait]); *The Need of an Industrial School in North Carolina . . . A Memorial to the General Assembly by the Watauga Club* (1885); W. J. Peele, "A History of the Agricultural and Mechanical College," *North Carolina Teacher* 6 (September 1888); William Joseph Peele Papers (Southern Historical Collection, University of North Carolina, Chapel Hill); Raleigh *News and Observer*, 24 Aug. 1899; *Raleigh Times*, 24 Mar. 1970.

RICHARD WALSER

Peele, William Walter *(26 Nov. 1881–1 July 1959)*, Methodist clergyman and educator, was born at Gibson, the son of Andrew and Nora Jane Gibson Peele. He received a bachelor of arts degree at Trinity College (now Duke University) in 1903 and was elected to Phi Beta Kappa.

In 1906 Peele was ordained to the ministry of the Methodist Episcopal Church, South. From 1903 to 1906 he served as professor of mathematics and from 1906 to 1909 as president of Rutherford College (established in 1853 in Burke County as Rutherford Academy; later the academy and Weaver College merged with Brevard College). After leaving Rutherford he was headmaster of Trinity Park School, the preparatory school of Trinity College, and professor of biblical literature at Trinity. He returned to the pastorate and from 1918 to 1923 served as pastor of Edenton Street Methodist Church in Raleigh and Trinity Methodist Church in Durham. In 1928 Peele transferred to the Western North Carolina Annual Conference and became pastor of the First Methodist Church in Charlotte, serving until 1937. He was the presiding elder of the Greensboro District from 1937 to 1938.

In 1938 he was elected bishop at the last General Conference of the Methodist Episcopal Church, South, which united with the Methodist Episcopal church and the Methodist Protestant church to form the Methodist church at the United Conference in Kansas City, Mo. (26 Apr.–10 May 1939). He was assigned to the Richmond Area, which included Virginia and North Carolina (fifty-six eastern counties), then elected president of the Council of Bishops. Peele was the only pastor of Edenton Street Church to be elected to the episcopacy since the church was founded in 1811. Peele served the church as vice-president of the foreign division of the Board of Missions; chairman of the Commission on Army and Navy Chaplains, Commission on Camp Activities, and Methodist Commission on Overseas Relief; and president of the North Carolina Council of Churches. He received honorary degrees from Duke University and Randolph-Macon College.

Peele married Elizabeth Lytch of Laurinburg in 1911, but they had no children. At his retirement in 1952 he was succeeded in the Richmond Area by Bishop Paul Neff Garber (1899–1972), onetime professor of church history at Duke University. He died at Laurinburg and was buried in a family cemetery near the Peele home.

SEE: E. S. Bucke, *The History of American Methodism*, vol. 3 (1964); Elmer T. Clark, *Methodism in Western North Carolina* (1966); *Edenton Street in Methodism, 1811–1961* (1961); *Journal of the North Carolina Conference* (1960); *North Carolina Christian Advocate*, 16 July 1959; William S. Powell, *Higher Education in North Carolina* (1964).

GRADY L. E. CARROLL

Pegg, Herbert Dale *(11 May 1889–13 May 1974)*, teacher, farmer, and conservationist, was born on the headwaters of Deep River in Guilford County, the eldest son of Jabez Gardner and Ellen Gray Pegg. As a boy he attended Millwood, a one-room district school in Deep River township, and worked on his father's farm, not only acquiring a sound knowledge of the three R's and of agricultural techniques but also developing an abiding interest in fields, forests, and streams. He was a student at Whitsett Institute from 1907 to 1910 and Wake Forest College (now Wake Forest University) from 1910 to 1915. Though he took a law degree in addition to a bachelor's degree at Wake Forest, he was always more interested in teaching and farming than in the practice of law. In fact, he had accepted a position in the North Carolina public school system before leaving Wake Forest and taught in Davie and Madison counties until the United States entered World War I in 1917.

Pegg joined the navy and served as ensign until discharged in the spring of 1919. Returning to the public school system, he was a teacher and principal at Candor High School until 1924. During these five years he also helped with the construction of a new school building at Candor, completed the work for an M.A. degree at The University of North Carolina, and married Mayme Kate Carter, of Moore County, a graduate of the Woman's College in Greensboro, who taught at Candor High.

Though he remained in the public school system for four more years, his interest in field and forest was growing, and he began buying land between the Sandy Ridge and Deep River communities, near where he was born and where most of his forebears had lived over more than two centuries. He wanted to go to the land but was not sure that he should. In the spring of 1928 he decided to return to The University of North Carolina and earn a doctorate in history before making a final decision. That summer, when he and Kate moved to Chapel Hill, he began his studies under R. D. W. Connor and she took a teaching position in the local high school. In 1931, when he had completed work for the Ph.D., the Great Depression was on and good teaching positions were scarce. Pegg built a brick house on his land near the center of Deep River township and settled into the business of growing corn, clover, wheat, soybeans, and melons, and, more important, of enriching his fields and managing his forests and streams. He often said that one of the most important things one could do in this world was to improve some segment, however small, of the physical environment, for life and society would depend increasingly on the products of field, forest, and stream as populations grew, the supplies of oil and coal dwindled, and industrial and nuclear waste accumulated.

Absorbed as he became in farming and conservation, however, his interest in history and the education of young people never waned. During the 1960s Pegg did additional work on his doctoral dissertation and published it in 1969 under the title of *The Whig Party in North Carolina*. At the same time he and Kate, ever conscious of the financial problems they had faced as students, decided to leave most of their modest properties for a scholarship fund for needy and deserving boys and girls in the predominantly rural areas of nine counties in the central Piedmont. Holders of Herbert Dale Pegg and Mayme Kate Carter Pegg Scholarships may attend either the Chapel Hill or the Greensboro branch of The University of North Carolina. He died in the Wesley Long Hospital in Greensboro and was buried in the cemetery at the Sandy Ridge Methodist Church.

SEE: *Greensboro Daily News*, 23 May 1974; History Department Records, 4, 11 Dec. 1929, 10 Nov. 1938 (University of North Carolina Archives, Chapel Hill); William W. Pegg, Sr., *Something of the Story of Deep River* (1980); *Record of the University of North Carolina: Undergraduate Bulletin* (1982); *Yackety Yack*, vol. 91 (1981).

CARL H. PEGG

Peirce (Pearce, Perse, Pierce), Thomas *(8 Sept. 1669–Feb. or Mar. 1731/32)*, Assembly member and prominent Quaker, was the son of John and Mary Peirce, who were living in the North Carolina colony by 1679. His maternal grandfather was Joseph Scott, a member of the Council in 1673 and one of the first North Carolina converts to the Quaker faith. Peirce's parents also were Quakers. Like Scott and his wife Mary, they were among the earliest members of the Perquimans Monthly Meeting.

Thomas Peirce was the eldest of six children, one of whom died in early childhood. His father died in 1682, leaving his wife with five children, including an infant a few months old. The surviving children were Thomas, John, Joseph, Rebekah, and Mary. In 1683 the widowed mother married William Bundy, a neighboring Quaker. Bundy died in 1692, and later that year Thomas's mother married Nicholas Simmons. By that time Thomas himself was married. His mother lived until 1724.

Probably about 1703 Peirce was a member of the lower house of the Assembly, representing Pamlico Precinct, which was in the county of Bath. During the session he and a fellow member from Pamlico, William Barrow, petitioned the deputy governor and Council requesting lower quit rents and more favorable terms for purchasing land in Pamlico than were then in effect. The Council's action on the petition is not known. In 1708 Peirce again held a seat in the Assembly. In that session he was appointed to the important committee on the public accounts. Although other details of his career in the Assembly are not known, it is safe to say that Peirce, a devout Quaker, was deeply involved in the struggles between Anglicans and dissenters that provided the chief issues in those sessions.

Like his parents and grandparents, Peirce took an active part in the Perquimans Monthly Meeting. He served on many committees appointed to settle differences between members or to handle other matters. At times he also served as overseer and often he was appointed to present the state of the monthly meeting to the quarterly meeting. For many years he kept the records of the Perquimans meeting, and in 1727 he and two others were appointed to transcribe the old records into a new book, which they did. He was among the Perquimans members who had property distrained in 1707, probably because he, like many other Quakers, had refused to pay tithes to support the Anglican church.

Although Peirce was living in Pamlico Precinct during his service in the Assembly, he resided in Perquimans Precinct before and after that period and remained a member of the Perquimans Monthly Meeting during it. He owned a plantation of three hundred acres in Perquimans, which he had inherited from his father, and he acquired additional land, some of which was in the county of Bath.

Peirce and his wife, Mary Kent, had six children, the eldest of whom was born in 1691. The children were John, Thomas, Ann, Mary, Sarah, and Joseph. All except Ann lived to adulthood. John married Sarah Chapman, by whom he had five children. Thomas, Jr., who was married twice, had six children by his first wife, Mary Copeland, but none by his second wife, Isabel. Peirce's older daughter, Mary, married Peter Jones, Jr., by whom she had five children. His younger daughter, Sarah, was married twice—first to George Sutton and second to John Williams. She had at least one child, Nathaniel Sutton. Peirce's youngest child, Joseph, also was married twice. His first wife, Penelope Tomes, died about a year after her marriage. His second wife, Alice, bore him three children.

Thomas Peirce died between 11 Feb. 1731/32, when he made his will, and 30 Mar. 1732, when the will was probated. He was survived by his wife Mary and three of his children—Thomas, Joseph, and Mary. He no doubt was buried on his plantation in a "burying ground" that he set aside for the family in his will, where his parents and his dead children had been interred.

SEE: Albemarle Book of Warrants and Surveys (1681–1706), Albemarle County Papers (1678–1739), Colonial Court Records, Perquimans Births, Marriages, Deaths, and Peirce Family Wills (North Carolina State Archives, Raleigh); J. Bryan Grimes, ed., *Abstract of North Carolina Wills* (1910); J. R. B. Hathaway, ed., *North Carolina Historical and Genealogical Register* (1900–1903); William W. Hinshaw, comp., *Encyclopedia of American Quaker Genealogy* (1936–50); Minutes and Records of the Perquimans Monthly Meeting of the Society of Friends in North Carolina, 1680–1762 (Guilford College Library, Greensboro); Mattie Erma Edwards Parker, ed., *North Carolina Higher-Court Minutes, 1670–1696* (1971); William L. Saunders, ed., *Colonial Records of North Carolina*, vol. 2 (1886).

MATTIE ERMA E. PARKER

Pelham, Charles *(12 Mar. 1835–18 Jan. 1908)*, Confederate officer, Alabama judge, Republican congressman, and District of Columbia lawyer, was born in Person County. His grandparents, Major Charles and Isabella Atkinson Pelham, left Virginia after the American Revolution to settle in Mason County, Ky., where his father, Dr. Atkinson Pelham (1797–1880), was born. Perhaps because of Atkinson family roots in North Carolina, Dr. Pelham began a medical practice in Person County and in 1833 married Martha M. McGehee (1808–76), daughter of William and Elizabeth Clay McGehee, Carolinians who migrated to Alabama. In 1838, with their first child Charles and still younger son William, the Pelhams followed to Benton (later Calhoun) County, Ala., and located in the Alexandria neighborhood near Jacksonville (the county seat until displaced by Anniston).

The Pelham offspring, increased by a daughter and four sons born in Alabama, had the benefit of local schooling and paternal encouragement. Charles may have been influenced towards the law by the proximity of Thomas A. Walker, a Jacksonville lawyer and circuit court judge who was married to the children's aunt Sarah. By 1858, at age twenty-three, Pelham had read enough law to gain admission to the bar at Talladega, court seat of adjoining Talladega County, where noted J. L. M. Curry was then a leader.

Eleven days after Alabama seceded, Charles Pelham married, on 22 Jan. 1861 at Louisville, Ky., Margaret Louise Johnston (1836–83), daughter of Judge George W. and Rosalinda E. Talmadge Johnston. Charles's brother William, who had been graduated from old Oglethorpe University in 1859, quickly entered the Calhoun State Guards and was sent to Fort Morgan. Their brother John, then in his final year at the U.S. Military Academy, broke away for a meteoric Confederate artillery career that ended in 1863 in his death as a major, "the gallant Pelham." Charles, joined by the fourth brother, Peter, an Oglethorpe student, enlisted at Talladega on 1 Apr. 1862. They went into the Fifty-first Alabama Partisan Rangers, a fighting regiment organized by Colonel (later brigadier general and postwar U.S. senator) John Tyler Morgan. Into this mounted unit, also known as the Fifty-first Alabama Cavalry, soon came William Pelham and eventually the teenage Pelham brothers, Samuel C. and Thomas A. The more mature Charles and William drew commissions as second lieutenants. William in Company A was captured, but Charles in Company C was promoted to first lieutenant and at the war's end was paroled at Talladega on 16 May 1865.

In resuming a legal career there, Charles Pelham seems to have gained rapport with Lewis Eliphalet Parsons, Sr., or certainly with his son, L. E., Jr. The senior happened to be the Talladega resident whom President Andrew Johnson tapped in June 1865 to be provisional governor of Alabama. Lawyer Pelham, becoming one of the founders of the Republican party in Alabama, was in 1868 elected judge of the Tenth Alabama Judicial Circuit and while still on the bench in 1872 was elected to the Forty-third U.S. Congress (4 Mar. 1873–3 Mar. 1875). Placed on the District of Columbia Committee in the U.S. House of Representatives, he proved assertive in introducing, reporting, and supporting liberal legislation for the District. When added to a select committee on the Washington Monument, he reported on a bill for a monument to Washington's mother. When the Alabama Republican party was being denounced for dishonesty or fraud, Pelham rose in the House to its defense.

In what L. E. Parsons, Jr., termed the terrible and bloody campaign of 1874, the Republicans lost Alabama. Failing to be renominated, Pelham turned to full-time legal work as a member of the District of Columbia bar, dealing particularly with claims. In 1887, when he published his 233-page compendium of *Hints and Helps to Lawyers, Applicants for Positions in the Civil Service, and All Others Having Business of Any Kind with the Government at Washington City*, he practiced in the firm of Pelham, Reid, and Stevenson.

In 1889 Pelham in vain sought from Secretary of the Treasury William Windom some position where he could be of service to the Republican party, to the government, and to the country "and at the same time earn a salary sufficient to pay for a modest living in this City." In the 1890s he did indeed shift his residence to nearby Virginia. For a decade, from 1897 until his final resignation on 20 Apr. 1907, he held somewhat tenuously to minor assignments with the Treasury Department in Washington.

His two children were born in Calhoun County, Ala., during and just after the Civil War: Martha Rose (31 Mar. 1862) and John Charles (23 Aug. 1865). After he was graduated from Columbia University with two law degrees in 1888, John Charles Pelham pursued a successful legal career at Anniston; he was already judge of the Seventeenth Judicial Circuit in Alabama before his father retired and left Washington. Less than a year after that move, Charles Pelham, aged nearly seventy-three, died at Poulan, Worth County, in South Georgia. This was the community where his Confederate veteran brother, known locally as Major Peter Pelham (1840–1924), had been established since the 1880s. The marble slab in Poulan Cemetery identifying the grave of "Charles Pelham of Alabama, Born in Person Co. N.C." enjoins, "Let me lie where I fall."

SEE: *Biog. Dir. Am. Cong.* (1961); Wm. K. Boyd, *Boyd's Directory of the District of Columbia* (1876–1907); *Compiled Service Records of Confederate Soldiers Who Served in Orga-*

nizations from the State of Alabama, Fifty-first Partisan Rangers (National Archives microcopy 311, roll 347); *Congressional Record* and *Journal of the House of Representatives of the United States*, 43d Congress, 1st and 2d sessions (1873–75); Charles G. Milham, *Gallant Pelham* (1959); Thomas McAdory Owen, *History of Alabama and Dictionary of Alabama Biography*, vol. 4 (1921); Charles Pelham application file (1889) and appointment file (1897–1907) (General Records of the U.S. Department of the Treasury, National Archives); Mrs. Roger Williams, data from a Bible once owned by Dr. Atkinson Pelham, copied at pp. 126–27 of *Report of the Genealogical Records Committee, District of Columbia Daughters of the American Revolution, 1934–36* (typescript vol. 29, pt. 3, Library, National Society DAR).

H. B. FANT

Pelley, William Dudley *(12 Mar. 1890–30 June 1965)*, journalist, novelist, promoter of mystical and political teachings, and founder of the Silver Shirt Legion and the Christian party, was born in Lynn, Mass., the son of William G. A. Pelley, a Methodist minister, and Grace Goodale Pelley. He dropped out of high school and worked in his father's tissue paper manufacturing company until he was twenty-one; he then was associated with a succession of small newspapers in New England. After receiving considerable notice for his short stories published in popular magazines, he was commissioned during World War I by the Methodist Episcopal church to survey foreign missions in the Far East and to write a series of reports for the church's publications. While in the Orient, he was sent by the International YMCA to eastern Russia and Siberia to scout for locations for proposed canteens. Thus he was in Russia as troops from several nations sought to contain the Bolsheviks. Concluding that the entire World War I had been a result of machinations of the Jews to establish Russia as a Jewish homeland, Pelley dated his anti-Semitism from his Siberian experiences.

Upon his return to the United States, Pelley resumed his literary career; this led to the editorship of at least fifteen magazine titles, a dozen books, and hundreds of short stories, articles, and religious and political tracts. His second book, *The Fog* (1921), is said to have sold nearly 100,000 copies; the third, *Drag*, was made into a motion picture featuring Lon Chaney. For several years Pelley lived near Hollywood, writing movie scripts and investing in several business ventures. He claimed that on the night of 29 May 1929, while lying in his cottage on the side of the Sierra Madre Mountains, he suddenly felt himself "quitting" his body and for seven minutes he communed with departed friends "behind the beyond." When he returned to his mortal body, he found that he could receive messages from "clairaudient voices." He later reported that while he was on a train passing through the Mohave Desert, Christ appeared to him and promised to give him wisdom as the circumstances demanded. From that time on, Pelley called Jesus "My Elder Brother."

His story, "Seven Minutes in Eternity—Amazing Experience That Made Me Over," caused a sensation when it appeared in *American Magazine* (March 1929). Some readers were offended by what they considered a hoax; others believed his story and became followers when he established the League of the Liberation and began publishing his mystical teachings through the *New Liberator*, organ of the league. Reportedly, 476 assemblies or study groups sprang up around the country. In search for an appropriate location for a college at which he could impart his "renovated Christian religion," Pelley moved to Asheville in 1932, chartered the Foundation for Christian Economics, and started Galahad College, a sort of "spiritual clinic for people troubled by religious and psychical problems." The school operated only one summer, after which Pelley published his lectures and enrolled hundreds of persons in a correspondence course.

Increasingly, Pelley's magazine and other publications assumed a political and racial tone. The anti-Semitism and anticommunism expressed during World War I again was asserted, and he viewed the election of Franklin D. Roosevelt (whom he called a "Dutch Jew") as evidence that "Dark Forces"—which he now identified as Jews and communists—were conspiring to set up a dictatorship in the United States. On the day following Adolf Hitler's induction as chancellor of Germany, Pelley announced formation of the Silver Shirt Legion of America (chartered the following year in Delaware), an "American Aryan Militia" ostensibly to "foster, promote, and develop political patriotic principles." It is probable that the league—whose members wore a silver shirt with the letter "L" (for liberation) on the shoulder, a tie, blue corduroy trousers, a service hat, and leggings—reached a membership of no more than 25,000 at any one time until it disbanded in 1940. The press and congressional committees, however, exaggerated its strength, and Pelley, who was investigated for pro-Nazi activities beginning in 1934, gloried in his notoriety. The league was strongest in California and Washington State.

In 1935 Pelley formed a political arm for the Silver Shirts, the Christian party, which espoused establishment of a "Christian Commonwealth" in which the assets of the nation would be taken over and run as a giant corporation. Each newborn would be given one share, and individuals could earn additional shares by contributing significantly to the welfare of the nation. One city in each state would be set aside as a "Beth-Haven" in which Jews would reside. The next year the Christian party was admitted to the ticket in only one state, Washington, where the chief of the Silver Shirts and his running mate, Willard M. Kemp, received only 1,598 votes. Pelley charged that a Jewish-instigated conspiracy plugged the handles of the voting machines in many Washington polling places and blocked his party from the ballot in the other states.

From 1932 to 1941 Pelley maintained his headquarters in Asheville, from where he shipped tons of materials to followers around the country. His business and publications were conducted under a confusing number of names, and following his payment of a fine and acceptance of a suspended sentence in 1935 for violating North Carolina's blue-sky laws relating to the sale of stock, an increasing number of persons suspected his motives. He had little following in North Carolina and was virtually ostracized in Asheville, so in 1941 he moved his operations to Noblesville, Ind. On several occasions the state of North Carolina had attempted unsuccessfully to jail him for violating his parole by publishing pro-Fascist materials, but in 1942 he was convicted of sedition in a federal court and sentenced to fifteen years in prison. Following his parole in 1950, he returned to Noblesville and devoted the remainder of his life to writing on psychical phenomena, extrasensory perception, and reincarnation, and to publishing and distributing these materials to the membership of his Soulcraft Fellowship, of which 104 local study groups were said to have been organized. He was buried in Noblesville Cemetery.

Pelley married Marion Harriet Stone in 1911, and they had three children: Harriet, who died in childhood; Adelaide, who married Melford Pearson; and William Ernest.

After divorcing Marion in 1936, Pelley married Helen Hansmann. That marriage also ended in divorce, and in 1956 he married Agnes Henderson, who survived him.

SEE: H. G. Jones, "The Younger Brother of Christ" (typescript, 1981, North Carolina Collection, University of North Carolina, Chapel Hill); Adelaide Pelley Pearson to H. G. Jones, 22 Oct. 1981; William Dudley Pelley, *The Door to Revelation: An Autobiography* (1939); Donnell Byerly Portzline, "William Dudley Pelley and the Silver Shirt Legion of America" (Ed.D. diss., Ball State University, 1965); *Who's Who in America* (1924–25).

H. G. JONES

Pemisapan (Wingina) *(d. 1 June 1586)*, was king, or head man, of the Algonquian (or Algonkin)-speaking Indians on Roanoke Island and the opposite mainland when Sir Walter Raleigh was seeking to establish an English colony on the North Carolina coast. The Indian king was first mentioned by Arthur Barlowe in 1584 in his report to Raleigh concerning his and Philip Amadas's exploration or fact-finding mission. The explorers conversed and traded with Granganimeo, brother of King Wingina, who was said to be some distance away at "the main village" recuperating from wounds he had received in a fight with the chief of a neighboring country.

Soon after Raleigh's first colony, with Ralph Lane as governor, had settled on Roanoke Island in 1585, King Wingina took the name of Pemisapan. At first relations between him and the English were friendly, but friendship turned to enmity when the English exploited and subjugated the Indians through the threat of their superior weaponry and the natives' superstitions. Pemisapan and his great men considered several schemes to throw off the English yoke of oppression, and Lane came to regard him as a serious threat to the well-being of his colony. Rather than confronting the English alone with his small band of warriors from Roanoke and Dasemunkepeuc on the mainland near present Manns Harbor, Pemisapan sought the assistance of stronger tribes.

When Lane visited King Menatonon, the strong king of the Chowanocs on the Chowan River, in the spring of 1586, he learned that Pemisapan's emissaries had preceded him. However, he also learned that Menatonon had not been moved by his intrigues. But the Moratocs, a weaker group, were frightened when warned that the English planned to kill them. When Lane sought to explore the Roanoke River upon which they lived, they abandoned their villages and retired with their food into the interior.

When Lane and his men returned safely from Chowanoc and Moratoc, a disappointed Pemisapan gathered up his people at Roanoke and retired with them to the village of Dasemunkepeuc on the mainland, leaving the English to plant and tend their own crops and catch their own fish.

About this time Pemisapan's father, Ensenore, a man of great influence as "an advisor and prophet," died, leaving his son unrestrained. Forthwith Pemisapan began formulating plans to unite the coastal tribes in one great effort to destroy the English. Largely because of Menatonon's advice King Okisko of the Weapemeocs declined to be enticed by the promise of much copper to join him. Skiko, Menatonon's son who was held hostage by the English at Roanoke, told Lane of Pemisapan's plot, and Lane decided that the troublemaker should be destroyed.

On the morning of 1 June 1586, Lane and twenty-five of his men crossed over Croatan Sound in his largest boat and a canoe about three miles to Dasemunkepeuc. They hailed one of Pemisapan's men who was standing watch at the shore, and the man carried a message from Lane to his chief. The Englishmen were on their way to Croatoan and had stopped to complain about one of Pemisapan's men who had sought to free a prisoner.

Pemisapan and seven or eight of his great men and their followers came down to the shore. Whereupon Lane gave the watchword "Christ our victory" and his men shot into the group of Indians. Pemisapan was hit by a pistol ball and fell to the ground as if mortally wounded. But shortly he "started up and ran away as though he had not been touched." As he ran he was shot through the buttocks by one Kelly or Gavin ("mine Irish boy") with a petronel, a large cavalry pistol. The crippled chief then was chased into a woods and killed by Thomas Hariot and Edward Nugent, another Irishman. Soon they returned to the company with the king's head.

Although Lane may have prevented an Indian assault on the English at Roanoke, Pemisapan's followers became enemies unto death, perhaps costing the lives of some later arrivals at Roanoke Island.

SEE: David B. Quinn, *Roanoke Voyages*, 2 vols. (1955).

F. ROY JOHNSON

Pender, David *(1874–22 Sept. 1950)*, grocer and businessman, was born in Tarboro, the son of Robert W. and Martha Wallace Pender and the nephew of General W. D. Pender. His father was a cotton commission merchant. Educated in the schools of Edgecombe and Warren counties, Pender at age twelve began work as a helper in a Tarboro grocery store and undertook to learn everything he could about the business. In 1893 he went to New York and worked in several large department stores before returning to Tarboro.

At twenty-four he packed his belongings, took his modest savings, and moved to Norfolk, Va., where he found a job in a grocery store owned by two partners. In addition to his wages Pender received a quarter share of the annual profits, but soon the owners decided to sell their business. Borrowing the money to acquire it, Pender became the proprietor. By catering to the needs of his customers, keeping his store clean and attractive, and offering friendly service, he succeeded even in the face of cutthroat competition intended to drive him out of business. On 29 Jan. 1900 he incorporated as the D. Pender Grocery Company and soon opened other outlets in Norfolk and, in time, elsewhere in Virginia and in North Carolina. His central store on Granby Street was probably the largest grocery store in the United States.

By 1922 Pender owned seventy-five stores and passed the million-dollar mark in sales. He also formed the Pender-Dillworth Company, Inc., an independent wholesale establishment, opened his own bakery and restaurant, and organized the Norfolk Delivery Corporation. In 1926 he disposed of his business interests, including 244 grocery stores, to a syndicate. In time the D. Pender stores became a part of the Colonial Stores, Inc. After selling his business, Pender established the Southgate Brokerage Company, which he soon turned over to his son. He then undertook a program of public service, serving as head of the Naval YMCA, president of the Norfolk Merchants Association, and president of the Norfolk General Hospital, among other roles.

In 1902 Pender married Mellie Whitehurst of Tarboro, and they became the parents of David, Jr., and Elizabeth. He was buried in Forest Lawn Cemetery, Norfolk.

SEE: David Pender, "What I learned in a Tarboro Grocery," *American Magazine* (January 1922 [portrait]); Raleigh *News and Observer*, 21 May 1933, 26 Sept. 1950; *State* magazine, 15 Apr. 1939 (portrait).

WILLIAM S. POWELL

Pender, Josiah Solomon *(11 Mar. 1819–25 Oct. 1864)*, poet, artist, army officer, and Confederate blockade-runner, was the son of Solomon and Mary Batts Pender of the Tarboro area of Edgecombe County, both of whom were descended from substantial families resident there since late colonial days. He received his early education at the Hickory Grove Academy, of which his father was a cofounder in 1831, and entered the U.S. Military Academy on 1 July 1835 but withdrew voluntarily on 2 Feb. 1836 because of his unwillingness to adapt to the military life. After attending The University of North Carolina in 1838–39, he studied painting in Paris and Rome. He remained in eastern North Carolina for a time before marrying and working for several years in Petersburg, Va.

Pender's artistic talent was solicited in 1840 for the painting of several decorative flags to enliven the locomotive *Brunswick* and its cars for their splendid dedicatory run over the historic new railroad between Wilmington and Weldon on 9 March of that year. There still exist at least six identified portraits that he painted during his career, the most notable being a life-size one of his father, who died on 8 Sept. 1852. The painting of his schooners *Alma* and *Lady Davis* demonstrate his skill with other subjects, while his surviving letters and poems reveal a cultivated and ingenious intellect.

Following in the footsteps of his father, who served as treasurer (1832–45) of Concord Lodge No. 58, Ancient, Free, and Accepted Masons, of Tarboro, Josiah Pender undoubtedly became a Mason in 1840, but the official records of that period have been lost. By 1852 he was filling the office of junior warden, and in 1853 senior warden. The Franklin Lodge No. 109 at Beaufort mentioned him as master pro tempore for one of its meetings as early as 1854, but his peripatetic business life affected his regular attendance even after he established his home in Beaufort and transferred his membership from the Concord Lodge in 1856.

When North Carolina was challenged to support the American war against Mexico, Pender returned to Tarboro and volunteered on 23 Dec. 1846 in Captain Louis D. Wilson's Company A, First North Carolina Volunteer Regiment. He was elected second lieutenant on 5 January and was mustered into the U.S. Army at Wilmington on 8 January. Appointed acting assistant commissary of Companies A and E on 14 February, he left for northern Mexico the next day on the schooner *E. S. Powell.*

On 16 Aug. 1847 Pender was "Disch.[d] Dishonorably by order of the Commanding General," the choleric General John Ellis Wool, who presumed that he had been involved in a prank subjecting Wool to public ridicule. But no compliment to Pender's character could have surpassed the elegant sword presented to him by his military associates bearing this inscription: "Presented to Josiah S. Pender by his company as a token of respect and confidence in him as a commander. August 16, 1847."

He again reported for active duty on 24 December after having taken his case directly to Washington, D.C., and having been reinstated with the rank of first lieutenant by direct orders from President James Knox Polk and his secretary of war. January–March 1848 found Pender "attending on Court of Inquiry at Saltillo." On 31 May 1848 he tendered his resignation at Fort Monroe in Virginia and withdrew from further military duty. At that period of his life he was described as being 6′1½″ in height, handsome in person, distinguished in dress, and courtly in manner.

In 1850 Pender moved his family from Petersburg to the large plantation owned by his father on Hendrick's Creek near Tarboro, where he pursued the profession of artist and operated a successful jewelry business. His frequent trips to Beaufort and increasing fondness for all aspects of the coastal life resulted in his subsequent purchase of three steamships for carrying on trade between the ports of Beaufort, New Bern, Bermuda, and New York. In 1854 he purchased from John H. Neal a part of residential Lot 2 in New Town, followed gradually by some 10,000 acres of land on the North River in Carteret County.

In 1856 he bought his favorite oceanfront hotel, the Atlantic House, which had been erected in 1851, had served as the Hammond Military Hospital (1862–65), and was destroyed by a hurricane in 1879. It was then connected with the mainland by a good bridge and possessed an unusually handsome dining room that featured fine seafood and imported wines. Because his family accompanied him frequently on his trips to Bermuda, he also purchased a cottage in Hamilton. In 1858, the same year that the railroad was completed between Goldsboro and Beaufort, he became involved in a lawsuit because of the carelessness of his shipmaster, James Robbins, on a run to New York, but most of the details of his business career vanished among the private papers taken after his death by his brother Joseph J. B. Pender, who himself died in 1868.

When it appeared that a civil war was imminent, Josiah Pender raised and completely outfitted at his own expense a company of about fifty friends and neighbors (including his eldest son Walter, who held the rank of first lieutenant and was accidentally shot to death the next year while instructing troops in the use of the bayonet), known first as the "Old Topsail Riflemen." On 11 Apr. 1861, the day before the historic attack on Fort Sumter, they marched without official orders upon the unsuspecting Federal officer at Fort Macon, provided him with the railroad fare for an immediate return to the North, and replaced the Stars and Stripes with an improvised flag showing a green pine tree with a coiled rattlesnake at its foot.

Governor John W. Ellis ordered the Goldsboro Rifles, the Guilford Grays, the Orange Guards, and the Wilson Light Infantry (they left home on 18 April) to proceed immediately to the support of Pender, who formally volunteered on 13 April and was commissioned on 16 May as captain of Company G, Tenth North Carolina State Troops (First Artillery) Regiment, Confederate States of America. This company appears to have been known variously as the "Beaufort Harbor Guards" and "Pender's Battery" for some time after being placed under Confederate command on 20 August and ordered to the Bogue Banks on 29 August.

At a general court martial convened at Morehead City on 30 Nov. 1861, Captain Pender was charged (1) with having been absent without leave "from his camp on Bogue Island" between 5 and 20 November, and (2) that he did "falsely state to Col. M. J. White . . . that he had obtained a leave of absence from Brig. Gen'l Hill" at Fort Macon. Commandant White testified that General Daniel H. Hill had "issued no such orders," and General Order No. 21 was issued on 19 December to dismiss Captain Pender from the state service, followed ten days later by Order No. 24 from Richmond dismissing him from the Confederate service.

There is no evidence that Pender ever questioned the

decision of the court martial or that his ardor for the Confederate cause was thereby diminished. He undoubtedly felt that his action was justified because of a critical domestic situation and the absence of military activity at his post. Because of his impending dismissal, he was able to remain near his terminally ill wife's bedside in Beaufort, where he received the official notice on the day of her burial. Colonel Lawrence O'Bryan Branch, nephew of Governor John Branch, expressed the opinion of many distinguished North Carolinians when, without questioning the report of the court martial, he described Pender on 18 Apr. 1862 as "brave enterprising and intelligent, and devotedly anxious for the success of the Cause." He also hoped that "the President can, Compatibly with his sense of duty, place him in service" because the Confederacy was "at this time greatly in need of active and enterprising officers to carry on partizan operations against the enemy."

But Josiah Pender had already involved himself and his ships in something that would prove far more advantageous to the Confederate war effort, the running of the blockade then being implemented in Carolina waters by the U.S. Navy. Before the taking of Beaufort and the formal surrender of Fort Macon on 26 Apr. 1862, he had transferred his family and his base of operations to Hamilton on the island of Bermuda. The *Alma* was lost in 1863, but the *Advance* and the *Columbia* (renamed *Lady Davis*) were still active at the time of his unexpected death. The steamships *Pearl* and *Cornubia* were also involved in some of Pender's operations.

In August 1863 Pender and his second wife are known to have visited Halifax, Nova Scotia, on the *Lord Clyde* in company with colonial Secretary and Mrs. Miles Gerald Keon and Archbishop Thomas Louis Connolly of Bermuda, after which he steamed for England with a load of merchandise while his wife proceeded toward Wilmington on the *Advance* with the intention of bearing her anticipated child in the home of her parents at Oak Grove in Edgecombe County. The officer in command of the vessel was so intimidated by the large number of enemy ships that he hesitated to order the final run through the Federal blockade until his small but resolute mistress pointed a pistol at his head and threatened him with an immediately fatal alternative.

It had been Pender's intention to renovate his ravaged home and to bring his family back to Beaufort after the war, but he contracted yellow fever on his last voyage and died in the Atlantic House in October 1864. He was buried beside his first wife near the First Baptist Church. His second wife and the children were then in Edgecombe County, but the three daughters decided subsequently to live with their maternal aunt, Mrs. Jeremiah B. Jeter, whose husband was pastor (1852–70) of the Grace Street Baptist Church in Richmond.

On 25 Jan. 1842, at Petersburg, Pender married Maria Louise Williams (25 Jan. 1826–18 Dec. 1861), daughter of Henry Williams and his wife Amintia Dunn Thurston, by whom he had nine children: Victor Edwin (13–23 Nov. 1842), Walter Henry (12 Sept. 1844–23 Oct. 1862), Paul Solomon (2 Sept. 1847–2 Jan. 1905, m. on 23 Nov. 1871 Annie Eliza Thorogood [1850–86], and on 20 Dec. 1888 Lucy Jane Overstreet [1864–1946]), Kate Dunn (8 Oct. 1849–10 Dec. 1875, m. on 14 July 1868 Joshua Clifton Pender), India Louise (12 Sept. 1851–4 June 1852), Josiah Solomon, Jr. (12 Oct. 1853–1 July 1854), Mary America (15 Sept. 1855–18 Mar. 1942, m. on 13 Sept. 1876 Charles Frederick Sugg [13 Feb. 1854–11 Dec. 1933]), Marie Louise (7 May 1859–28 May 1921, m. on 5 Aug. 1879 Rev. Henry Allen Tupper, Jr. [22 June 1856–29 Sept. 1927]), and Edwin Graham (10 Sept. 1860–1 Mar. 1861).

On 23 Sept. 1862, nearly a year after the death and burial of his first wife at Beaufort, Josiah Solomon Pender married Laura Melvina Pender (20 Sept. 1840–6 Nov. 1918), daughter of Louis Coe Pender and his wife Mary Martha Hyman of Oak Grove plantation in Edgecombe County. They had one child, Josiah Keon (19 Oct. 1863–9 Oct. 1881), who spent his brief life there. Mrs. Pender was in greatly reduced financial circumstances for some years after the Civil War, but she subsequently married Captain Charles Betts Cook and had two additional children.

SEE: Jean B. Kell, *Historic Beaufort, North Carolina* (1977); Bill Stancil, "Suited to Command," *State* magazine, September 1974; J. Kelly Turner and John L. Bridgers, Jr., *History of Edgecombe County* (1977).

HUGH BUCKNER JOHNSTON

Pender, William Dorsey *(6 Feb. 1834–18 July 1863)*, Confederate soldier, was born in that part of Edgecombe County that became Wilson County in 1855, the son of James and Sarah Routh Pender. He received his early education in the common schools of the county and worked as a clerk in his brother's store in Tarboro before receiving, at age sixteen, an appointment to the U.S. Military Academy. On his graduation from the academy in 1854, Pender stood nineteenth in a class of forty-six. He was first commissioned in the artillery, but in 1855 he secured a transfer to the First Dragoons and three years later was promoted to the rank of first lieutenant.

From 1856 to 1860 Pender saw service on the frontier in New Mexico, California, Oregon, and Washington Territory. During this tour of duty, on 3 Mar. 1859, he married Mary Francis Shepperd, the sister of a classmate at West Point and daughter of Congressman Augustine H. Shepperd of Good Spring, N.C. The couple had three children: Samuel Turner, William D., and Stephen Lee, the last born four months after Pender's death.

Prior to the outbreak of the Civil War (and the secession of North Carolina), Pender resigned his commission in the U.S. Army and offered his services to the Confederacy, with the rank of captain in the Provisional Army. After temporary duties as a recruiting officer in Maryland (Baltimore), and then as an instructor of recruits at Camp Mangum (Raleigh) in his native state, he was elected colonel of the Third North Carolina Regiment on 16 May 1861. On 15 August he was transferred to the Sixth North Carolina. Under his command this regiment fought well during the Peninsular Campaign of 1862. For brilliant leadership at the Battle of Seven Pines he was promoted to brigadier general and assigned to command a brigade in A. P. Hill's division.

Pender ably led his brigade in the Seven Days' fighting before Richmond, at Cedar Mountain, Second Manassas, Harper's Ferry, Sharpsburg, Fredericksburg, and Chancellorsville. He was wounded at least five times, but he never relinquished his command. On 27 May 1863 he was promoted to major general. Though only twenty-nine at the time, Pender was considered one of the ablest generals in the Army of Northern Virginia. At Gettysburg he commanded a division in Robert E. Lee's newly formed Third Corps. On the second day of the battle, however, he was severely wounded in the leg and had to be evacuated to Staunton, Va., where he died after the amputation of his shattered leg. General Lee wrote: "His promise and usefulness as an officer were only equaled by the purity of excellence of his private life." Like many soldiers in the Civil War, Pender underwent a profound religious conversion, and the men who served under him were greatly influenced by his example. His body was taken to North Carolina and buried in the yard of Calvary Church, Tarboro.

SEE: Walter Clark, ed., *Histories of the Several Regiments and Battalions from North Carolina*, vols. 1–2 (1901); *DAB*, vol. 14 (1934); Clement A. Evans, ed., *Confederate Military History*, vol. 4 (1899); Douglas S. Freeman, *Lee's Lieutenants*, vols. 1–3 (1942); William W. Hassler, ed., *The General to His Lady: The Civil War Letters of William Dorsey Pender to Fanny Pender* (1965); Richard W. Iobst, *The Bloody Sixth* (1965); William J. Peele, ed., *Lives of Distinguished North Carolinians* (1898); Martin Schenck, *Up Came Hill: The Story of the Light Division and Its Leaders* (1958); Jon L. Wakelyn, *Biographical Dictionary of the Confederacy* (1977).

JOHN G. BARRETT

Pendleton, Andrew Lewis *(4 Nov. 1860–28 Feb. 1951)*, physician, druggist, and banker, was born at Nixonton, Pasquotank County, the son of Andrew Lewis and Mary Frances Cartwright Pendleton. Pioneer settlers from Virginia in the Albemarle region, the Pendletons came from Warwick and Lancashire, England, in the seventeenth century. The younger Pendleton's earliest childhood recollections were of the Union occupation of the community where his family lived. Enemy troops requisitioned large quantities of flour from his father's mill and later when the elder Pendleton was arrested for treason because of his loyalty to the Confederacy, his son was sent to live with his grandparents so that he could attend William Gaither's school for boys in Hertford. The trial was made a test case and the defendant was acquitted. One of the defense lawyers was W. N. H. Smith, afterwards chief justice of the North Carolina Supreme Court.

Pendleton was educated in Benbury's School and at Tillett's, both in Elizabeth City. As a youth he carried the mail from Elizabeth City to Norfolk and worked in a drugstore owned and operated by Dr. Julian Wood. In the store he began to study medical books and to receive training from Wood. This led him to enroll in the University of Maryland and after a year to enter the Jefferson Medical College in Philadelphia, from which he was graduated with the M.D. degree in 1884. His first practice was established at Coinjock, Currituck County, but after a short time he moved to Key West, Fla., where his brother Charles published a daily newspaper. Pendleton opened a drugstore in Key West and also served as acting marine surgeon and quarantine officer at Fort Jefferson on Dry Tortugas, inspecting all vessels entering U.S. waters in order to control the dreaded yellow fever. Pendleton also performed some civic duties in Key West, notably as a member of the commission charged with building a new courthouse.

Due to Charles's failing health, the brothers returned to Elizabeth City; Dr. Pendleton became county health officer and engaged in general practice. He also undertook postgraduate study to specialize in the treatment of the eye, ear, nose, and throat. A hotel overlooking the Pasquotank River that he had inherited from his father required his attention and he became its manager. He also acquired the Standard Pharmacy and shortly afterwards retired from the practice of medicine to devote full time to business. From the pharmacy he developed the Standard Drug Company, a wholesale business. Later it was of considerable satisfaction to him to recall that when the Wright brothers were in Elizabeth City en route to Kitty Hawk, they purchased some supplies from him.

Civic duties continued to hold his interest and he was chairman of the district Democratic Congressional Committee, president of the Board of Aldermen, and chairman of the Municipal Utilities Commission. During the administration of President Woodrow Wilson, Pendleton also was postmaster of Elizabeth City. In business he organized and was president of the Carolina Banking and Trust Company and of the Pasquotank Investment Corporation.

An Episcopalian, Pendleton served for many terms as vestryman and as warden of Christ Church. A Mason and a Shriner, he was also a member of the Elks. In 1910 he married Hazel Williams Evans, and they became the parents of four children: Mary Frances (Mrs. George London), Hazel Evans (Mrs. G. Potter Dixon), Andrew Lewis IV (m. Dorothy Jones), and Nancy Ross (Mrs. E. P. Owens). He was buried in Hollywood Cemetery, Elizabeth City.

SEE: Thomas R. Butchko, *On the Shores of the Pasquotank* (1989); Elizabeth City *Daily Advance*, 1 Mar. 1951; Family papers (possession of the author); *Year Book: Pasquotank Historical Society* 1 (1954–55 [portrait]).

GEORGE ELLIOT LONDON

Penick, Edwin Anderson *(4 Apr. 1887–6 Apr. 1959)*, bishop of the Protestant Episcopal church of the Diocese of North Carolina, was born in Frankfort, Ky., the son of Edwin Anderson and Mary Atchinson Shipman Penick. His father was an Episcopal priest. After careful training at home and in local schools he attended the University of the South, where he was awarded the A.B. in 1908; he received the A.M. from Harvard University in 1909 and was graduated from the Theological Seminary of Virginia in 1912. In 1922 Penick was awarded the honorary D.D. degree from both the University of the South and the Virginia Seminary. The University of North Carolina honored him an LL.D. in 1948. Penick married Caroline Inglesby Dial on 20 June 1917, and they had three children: Edwin Anderson, who became a college professor: Dr. George Dial, a pathologist; and the Reverend Charles Inglesby.

After his graduation from the seminary, Penick was ordained to the diaconate in 1912 and to the priesthood in 1913. He was rector of St. Paul's Church, Bennettsville, S.C. (1912–14) and the Church of the Good Shepherd, Columbia, S.C. (1914–17). During World War I he was civilian chaplain of the Episcopal Church War Commission, Camp Jackson, S.C. (February–September 1918), then served as first lieutenant in the Chaplain's Corps, U.S. Army, until 1919, when he became rector of St. Peter's Church, Charlotte. He was consecrated bishop coadjutor to Bishop Joseph Blount Cheshire of the Episcopal Diocese of North Carolina on 15 Oct. 1922 and succeeded to the bishopric on 27 Dec. 1923.

Bishop Penick served for thirty-seven years as coadjutor and bishop of North Carolina. When elected coadjutor he was the youngest member of the House of Bishops, and at the time of his death he was senior in service in that body; he had served as its vice-president from 1946 to 1952.

Bishop Penick had a calm manner. As one of his close associates put it, he did not say much but what he said was worth listening to and heeding. He began each day by reading a page of the Greek New Testament. Deeply involved in secular as well as religious education, he was a trustee of the University of the South; chairman of the board of trustees of St. Mary's College, Raleigh; president of the board of trustees of St. Augustine's College, where he was active on the campus particularly at the opening and closing of each school year; and president of the board of managers of the Thompson Orphanage. He was especially influential in increasing the role and importance of the Women's Auxiliary in the life of the church and made every effort to further the service of the Good Samaritan Hospital in Charlotte and St. Agnes Hospital in Raleigh. Bishop Penick was the founder and first president of the North Carolina Council of Churches and was chairman of the North Carolina Commission of Interracial Cooperation.

In addition to supporting higher education at St. Mary's, St. Augustine's, and Vade Mecum, Penick urged the development of a students' assistance program on the campus of The University of North Carolina. In 1926 the first director, Andrew Milstead, was named; he was followed by Thomas A. Wright, who later became bishop. This program was later expanded to colleges in Raleigh, Greensboro, and Charlotte.

As a young man Penick was active in sports and won the tennis championship of his state. He was a member of the social fraternity Alpha Tau Omega and of the scholastic society Phi Beta Kappa. He was an honorary Rotarian and a Democrat. In April 1964 the Edwin A. Penick Home for the Aged in Southern Pines became a reality, a proper monument for this man who spent his life working for the welfare of others. He was buried in Oakwood Cemetery, Raleigh.

SEE: *Nat. Cyc. Am. Biog.*, vol. 43 (1961); *North Carolina Churchman* 49, no. 6 (June 1959); *Who's Who in America* (1958); *Who Was Who in America*, vol. 3 (1960).

STERLING A. STOUDEMIRE

Penn, Charles Ashby *(29 Nov. 1868–22 Oct. 1931)*, tobacco manufacturer and corporate executive, was born at Penn's Store in Patrick County, Va., the son of Frank Reid and Annie Spencer Penn. In 1874 his father moved the family to Reidsville and in partnership with his brother S. C. Penn established the F. R. Penn Tobacco Company to manufacture both chewing and smoking tobacco. Popular plug brands produced by the Penns were Penn's Natural Leaf and Penn's Red Jay, and their leading smoking tobacco labels were Gold Crumbs and Queen Quality.

Charles Penn was educated in the local schools and attended Bingham School in Orange County. Interested in tobacco manufacturing from an early age, he joined his father's company and later formed a partnership with J. N. Watt in Watt, Penn, and Company, which was eventually purchased by his father. In 1911 the American Tobacco trust bought F. R. Penn and Company, and the next year a government antitrust unit forced the monopoly to be divided. Penn was appointed a director of the American Tobacco Company on 2 Mar. 1913 and moved to New York, where he became assistant to the production manager. By 1916 he had perfected the blend for a new cigarette that became Lucky Strike, one of the all-time leading brands in the world. Lucky Strike was initially produced in Brooklyn, N.Y., but Penn suggested that a new factory be constructed in Reidsville, N.C., his hometown. For many years the cigarette was inseparably identified with Reidsville, the "Lucky City." On 23 June 1916 Penn was appointed vice-president of manufacturing for the American Tobacco Company. By 1923 he headed the leaf department as well as manufacturing and was named a director and vice-president of the American Cigar Company, a subsidiary of American Tobacco. Penn is credited with creating the famous Lucky Strike advertising slogan "It's toasted!"

Although Penn had an apartment on Park Avenue in New York City, he always considered Reidsville his home and contributed in numerous ways to its development. He was the founder and the major benefactor of the Annie Penn Memorial Hospital, which still provides excellent health care for the community, and he organized the Pennrose Country Club and golf course. For several years he served as a trustee of The University of North Carolina.

On 1 May 1906 Penn married Stella Clarke Edrington of Fort Worth, Tex., and they had three sons and one daughter: Edrington Spencer, Charles Ashby, Jr., Frank Reid, and Virginia Anne. Edrington, a graduate of The University of North Carolina, became president of the Carolina-Virginia Tobacco Company. Frank R. Penn III, who also was graduated from the university, succeeded his brother as president of the Carolina-Virginia Tobacco Company and served in the North Carolina Senate (1967–69).

After a short illness, Charles Penn died at St. Luke's Hospital, N.Y. His body was returned to his home by private railroad coach for burial at Greenview Cemetery. At the time of his death he was characterized as the "first citizen" of Reidsville, and his funeral, the largest ever held in the community, attracted thousands of mourners. Tributes were published in newspapers throughout North Carolina and in New York City. His portrait may be seen at the headquarters of the American Tobacco Company in Reidsville.

SEE: Charles H. Hamlin, *Ninety Bits of North Carolina Biography* (1946); *North Carolina Biography*, vol. 4 (1956); *North Carolina Manual* (1969); *Reidsville Review*, 23, 26 Oct. 1931; *"Sold American!"—The First Fifty Years, 1904–1954* (1954); *Who's Who in the South and Southwest* (1956).

LINDLEY S. BUTLER

Penn, John *(6 May 1740–14 Sept. 1788)*, Revolutionary statesman and signer of the Declaration of Independence, was born near Port Royal in Caroline County, Va., the only son of Moses and Catherine Taylor Penn. Moses Penn did not place a high priority on formal education, so his son received only a few years of instruction at a local school. When John was eighteen, his father died, leaving him a comfortable estate. Thereafter, Edmund Pendleton, young Penn's kinsman and neighbor, offered him the use of his library. Penn studied law under Pendleton's guidance and at age twenty-one was admitted to the bar in Caroline County, where he practiced law for the next twelve years.

Penn married Susannah Lyme of Granville County, N.C., on 28 July 1763. No doubt family ties influenced the Penns' move to North Carolina in 1774. John Penn purchased a farm in the northern part of Granville County near present Stovall. The following year he was elected to the Third Provincial Congress, which met at Hillsborough on 20 Aug. 1775. An active member of the Congress, Penn was elected to succeed Richard Caswell as delegate to the Continental Congress; Caswell had resigned to become the treasurer for the Southern District of North Carolina. The original congressional delegation (William Hooper, Joseph Hewes, and Richard Caswell) were all easterners who had supported Governor William Tryon against the Regulators. Penn's election was clearly an attempt to appease backcountry leaders like Penn's neighbor and political supporter, Thomas Person. Although Penn frequently disagreed with Hooper and Hewes on political questions, he shared their hope for reconciliation with Great Britain. Penn was the first of the three to favor independence. Writing to Thomas Person on 14 Feb. 1776, he advocated foreign alliances even if the consequence was total separation from the mother country. By March all three delegates believed that independence was inevitable.

Penn and Hooper returned to North Carolina to attend the Fourth Provincial Congress at Halifax and to receive instructions. They arrived in Halifax on 15 April, three days after the Congress had voted to instruct their Continental delegates to vote for independence. Penn was reelected to the Continental Congress but remained in Halifax until the Provincial Congress adjourned. He returned to Philadelphia in June and with Hewes cast North Carolina's vote for independence on 2 July.

In December 1776 the Fifth Provincial Congress appointed Thomas Burke to Penn's seat in the Continental Congress. But when the first Assembly under the new state constitution met the following April, Penn, who was a member of the lower house, won the seat held by Joseph Hewes. The bitterly contested election was influenced by charges that Hewes, an Edenton merchant, had been neglecting his congressional duties to engage in a profitable trade as commissioned agent of the Congress's Secret Committee.

Although Penn never attained prominence as a member of the Continental Congress, he attended the proceedings for 1,038 days, longer than any other North Carolina delegate during the Revolutionary War, and served on fourteen committees and eight standing boards. Believing that a permanent union was necessary, he signed the Articles of Confederation on 16 July 1778. Along with the other North Carolina delegates he consistently voted with the southern bloc.

Criticism that Penn neglected his congressional duties seems on the whole unjustified. The correspondence of the North Carolina delegates who served with him provides no basis for the charge beyond a December 1778 letter from Thomas Burke to Governor Richard Caswell describing the "gaiety and Dissipation, public Assemblies every fortnight and private Balls every night." Burke concluded, "In all such business as this we propose that Mr. Penn shall represent the whole state." In 1779 Henry Laurens challenged Penn to a duel. As he assisted the elderly Laurens across a street on the way to the dueling ground, Penn proposed that their plans be abandoned. Laurens agreed but continued to disdain Penn's politics and abilities. Later that year Charles Thomson, secretary of the Congress, reported that Laurens answered Penn in debate singing, "Poor little Penny Poor little Penny."

The British victory at Camden on 16 Aug. 1780 paved the way for invasion of North Carolina. The military threat led to a crisis in government. The constitution did not provide the governor with adequate emergency power, and at Governor Abner Nash's request the Assembly created a three-man Board of War with control of military affairs consisting of Penn, Colonel Alexander Martin, and Oroondates Davis. They met at Hillsborough in September 1780. Since the other two members were absent during most of the board's four-month existence, Penn acted alone much of the time. The board was primarily involved in equipping and supplying the North Carolina militia and General Nathanael Greene's army operating in North Carolina; it provided energetic leadership during the crisis, coordinating military activities and securing provisions and transporting them to the armies. The Assembly abolished the board in January 1781 after complaints from military officers who resented civilian interference with military affairs and from Governor Nash, who claimed that the board had usurped his authority.

Five months later Penn was elected to the governor's Council. He was president of the Council during the closing months of the war, when the Council met frequently with Governor Thomas Burke. After two years on the Council Penn was defeated for reelection in 1783. The following year Robert Morris appointed him receiver of taxes for the Confederation in North Carolina, but Penn resigned the office within a month of his appointment.

Penn was buried at his home near Island Creek in Granville County. In 1894 his remains were reinterred at Guilford Courthouse National Military Park. Two children, William and Lucy, survived. An etching of John Penn by H. B. Hall is in the Emmet Collection, New York Public Library.

SEE: Samuel A. Ashe, ed., *Biographical History of North Carolina* 8 (1917); Edmund C. Burnett, *Letters of the Members of the Continental Congress*, vols. 1–4 (1921–31); Walter Clark, ed., *State Records of North Carolina*, vols. 11, 13–14, 16, 22, 24 (1895–1907); *DAB*, vol. 14 (1929); W. C. Ford, ed., *Journals of the Continental Congress*, 34 vols. (1904–37); David T. Morgan and William J. Schmidt, "From Economic Sanctions to Political Separation: The North Carolina Delegation to the Continental Congress, 1774–1776," *North Carolina Historical Review* 52 (1968); David T. Morgan and William J. Schmidt, *North Carolinians in the Continental Congress* (1976); "John Penn Sketch" (Southern Historical Collection, University of North Carolina, Chapel Hill); William L. Saunders, ed., *Colonial Records of North Carolina*, vol. 10 (1890); Woodson T. White, "The Taylor Family," *William and Mary College Quarterly* 12 (1903).

GEORGE TROXLER

Penn, Thomas Jefferson (Jeff) *(24 Feb. 1875–7 Jan. 1946)*, investment broker, farmer, and philanthropist, was the son of Frank Reid and Annie Spencer Penn of Penn's Store, Patrick County, Va. In 1874 his father moved the family to Reidsville, where he formed a business partnership with his brother, Samuel C. Penn, and established the F. R. Penn Tobacco Company for the purpose of manufacturing chewing and smoking tobacco. Born and reared in Reidsville, Jefferson Penn attended the local schools and the University of Virginia. He then became a salesman for his father's tobacco company and for a time was located on the Pacific Coast. Following the purchase of F. R. Penn Tobacco Company by the American Tobacco trust, Penn decided to become an investment broker and joined the New York Stock Exchange.

In 1912, while in New York, Penn began purchasing land near Reidsville which he named Corn Jug Farm and where he began developing a Holstein dairy herd. Over the next decade he bought additional tracts, bringing the total to six hundred acres. In Buffalo, N.Y., he met Genevieve Schoellkopf von Berg, who became his first wife. After her death he married her cousin Beatrice (Betsy) Schoellkopf, daughter of Arthur Schoellkopf, the developer of electric power at Niagra Falls, on 9 Oct. 1923 in New York. Although he had a house in Buffalo, the Penns chose to live at the dairy farm near Reidsville and began construction of a twenty-seven-room stone and log country home designed by architect Harry C. Ingalls of New York. The property was named Chinqua-Penn Plantation and an additional three hundred acres was added to the original farm. The grounds were landscaped by Gordon Hurleman of Switzerland. Jeff and Betsy Penn embarked on a series of European and world tours, purchasing a number of art objects that they sent to Chinqua-Penn; they gradually accumulated a considerable collection. On the farm Penn began to develop a prize herd of Black Angus cattle and also grew tobacco.

The Penns contributed to a number of local charities. They made major donations to the Reidsville Community Chest, the local Boy and Girl Scout programs, the American Red Cross, the North Scales Street Christian Church, the local Masonic lodge, the Jeff and Betsy Penn Foundation, and the Annie Penn Memorial Hospital. Betsy Penn was particularly interested in the Girl Scouts and was responsible for the creation of the Chinqua-Penn Girl Scout Camp near Reidsville. Jeff Penn was chairman of the county Committee on Economic Development, a member of the Reidsville Industrial Committee and of the county school board, and chairman of the board of directors of the First National Bank of Reidsville. He was a thirty-second-degree Mason and a member of the Oasis Temple of the Order of the Shrine. In 1942 he published a family memoir, *My Black Mammy*.

After the death of her husband at Hot Springs, Va., Betsy Penn continued community philanthropic work. On 20 Oct. 1959 she gave Chinqua-Penn Plantation to The University of North Carolina, retaining lifetime residence rights. Soon the Betsy-Jeff Penn 4-H Conference Center and summer camp were established on the original Corn Jug Farm property. North Carolina State University administered the conference center and the plantation's agricultural activities, which included a tobacco research station and the herd of Black Angus cattle. Upon the death of Betsy Penn on 21 Feb. 1965 at age eighty-three, the plantation house, the art collections, and surrounding grounds were placed under the care of the University of North Carolina, Greensboro. Just over a year later the estate was opened to the public. Portraits of the Penns were on display at Chinqua-Penn Plantation.

SEE: Charles H. Hamlin, *Ninety Bits of North Carolina Biography* (1946); Margaret M. Holt, *Chinqua-Penn Plantation* (1968); *North Carolina Biography*, vol. 4 (1956); Penn Family (Vertical file, Reidsville Public Library); Rockingham County Deeds and Wills; *Reidsville Review*, 7 Jan. 1946, 22 Feb. 1965.

LINDLEY S. BUTLER

Pennington, John L. *(May 1829–14 July 1900)*, newspaper editor and governor of the Dakota Territory, was born in Wake County, N.C. The names of his parents seem not to be recorded, but he probably was the son of John Pennington of Wake County who had two sons under age five at the time of the 1830 census; or perhaps of Smith Pennington of the same county who also had two sons under five. In either case, his father was a native of Virginia and his mother of North Carolina. His only education seems to have been in a local school after which he served an apprenticeship on the Raleigh *Star*, an attractive, highly regarded newspaper with features far advanced for the times.

Unsubstantiated accounts of his life record that in 1856 he established a newspaper, the *Columbian*, in Columbia, S.C., but no evidence has been found that any such newspaper was ever published there. Soon afterwards, however, he became editor of the New Bern *Progress*, established in 1858. It had daily and weekly editions, announced that it published telegraph reports furnished by the American Press Association "from all quarters of the globe," and stressed both local and state news. The 1860 census of Craven County includes the name of the thirty-year-old editor, his twenty-four-year-old wife, Kate A., and a two-year-old daughter, Kate D. His household also consisted of a printer and two printer's apprentices. Among other local benefits, his newspaper advocated improved schools for New Bern, and with the approach of the Civil War it anticipated an early Southern victory. On 20 Sept. 1861 Governor Henry T. Clark commissioned Pennington a first lieutenant in a battery of heavy artillery formed in Craven County but because of ill health he resigned on 17 July 1862.

New Bern fell to the invading enemy in March 1862, and when Pennington returned from his brief military duty his newspaper was reestablished in Raleigh as the *Daily Progress*, continuing the same volume and numbering as the New Bern paper. In 1862–63 Pennington alone was shown as the publisher, but in 1864–65 "Pennington and Co." was indicated as publisher; after 10 Mar. 1866 it was in the hands of Guthrie and Orr, the latter, Captain H. E. Orr, having previously had the editorial management, probably while Pennington was in the army. Pennington early recognized that the North was fighting "to *elevate*" blacks while the South was fighting "to retain" them "and defend our homes." During the war Pennington advocated peace without reunion of the two sections and expressed the belief that such was the desire of people on both sides. He advocated the naming of commissioners to agree upon peace terms, a subject on which he corresponded with President Jefferson Davis. He also advocated a strong Home Guard in every county to apprehend all deserters on the same day so that they could not escape from one county to the next.

In 1865, at the end of the war, Pennington served on a Raleigh committee to draw up resolutions following the assassination of Abraham Lincoln to be presented to newly arrived General William T. Sherman. He also announced for his newspaper that "we shall give a zealous and cordial support to the views and principles of the great National Union Party and endeavor at all times to perform our whole duty to the State and country." This party was the forerunner of the Republican party. Pennington soon left North Carolina for Alabama where, regarded as a carpetbagger, he served in the state senate from Lee County as a member of the Reconstruction legislature during the sessions of 1868, 1871–72, 1872–73, and 1873. On friendly terms with George E. Spencer of New York, another carpetbagger in Alabama, Pennington supported Spencer's campaign for the U.S. Senate; Spencer then brought his supporter's name to the attention of the president.

President Ulysses S. Grant named Pennington governor of the Dakota Territory and he served from January 1874 to May 1878. Pennington's first wife—and perhaps his daughter as well—apparently was no longer living, as he was accompanied to his new post by his wife Amanda and children, Lulu, sixteen; Mary R., fourteen; and John L., Jr., twelve. All except the son, who was born in Alabama, were natives of North Carolina. They lived in Yankton, the capital of the territory. His household according to the 1880 census also consisted of a male and a female servant, both aged twenty-one, the latter born in Michigan, the former in Wisconsin. In Yankton Pennington built a two-story brick home for himself and three brick rental houses, all of which still stand.

The previous governor had been ineffective so Pennington set about to make improvements. He presented a very progressive program to his first legislature to reduce interest rates, to extend rail service, to seek appropriations for a capitol building, and to provide relief for farmers. His program met with initial success, but a plague of grasshoppers destroyed crops for several years. The discovery of gold on land occupied by Indians led to extensive conflict, and a scheme by land speculators to divide the Dakota Territory produced political unrest. Pennington's plans came to naught and he was not reappointed at the expiration of his term in 1878. He was, however, named by President Rutherford B. Hayes to be internal revenue collector for Dakota. Although out of office, Pennington remained interested in territorial affairs and attended the constitutional convention in 1883, while in 1887 he was active in a movement for unified statehood. Returning to his first love in 1885, he established a weekly, the *Telegram*, in Yankton which he continued until he returned to Alabama in 1891 following the death of his wife.

In 1900 the census of Calhoun County, Ala., recorded Pennington as a resident in the household of his daughter Lulu, her husband Alex J. Adair, and their six children at Oxford, Ala. Adair and Pennington owned the newspaper, *Alabama Home*, of which Pennington was editor. He died after an illness of several months, and his funeral was held at the Presbyterian church; he was buried in the Oxford city cemetery, where two adjoining graves are marked Adair [a child] and Pennington [an adult].

SEE: *Anniston Republic*, 14 Jul. 1900; *City Directory of Anniston, Oxanna, and Oxford* [Ala.] (1896; 1900–1901); Bernie Hunhoff, Yankton, S.D., to William S. Powell, 10 Jan. 1992; Louis H. Manarin, comp., *North Carolina Troops, 1861–1865: A Roster*, vol. 1 (1966); Harold D. Moser, "Reaction to the Emancipation Proclamation," *North Carolina Historical Review* 44 (January 1967); Elizabeth Reid Murray, *Wake: Capital County of North Carolina*, vol. 1 (1983); *N. W. Ayer & Sons American Newspaper Annual* (1887); Lynwood E. Oyos, ed., *Over a Century of Leadership: South Dakota Territorial and State Governors* (1987 [portrait]); John L. Pennington, *Get Up A Club!! Daily and Weekly Progress* (broadside, North Carolina Collection, University of North Carolina Library [1865]); L. L. Polk, *Handbook of North Carolina* (1879); Doane Robinson, *Encyclopedia of South Dakota* (1925); Alan D. Watson, *A History of New Bern and Craven County* (1987); Mary Westcott and Allene Ramage, comp., *A Checklist of United States Newspapers*, pt. 4 (1936); Richard E. Yates, "Governor Vance and the Peace Movement," *North Carolina Historical Review* 27 (January 1940).

WILLIAM S. POWELL

Pennington, William *(1738–15 Mar. 1829)*, colonial official in North Carolina and master of ceremonies at the Hot Wells, Clifton, near Bristol, England, was probably the son of a Bristol merchant and member of an ancient family resident there. He may have had a classical education, as a letter written in 1801, quoting a ballad, said, "Mr. Pennington will see an allusion to an Epigram of Martial in the first stanza."

He went to North Carolina with William Tryon in 1764, when Tryon was appointed lieutenant governor of the colony. Pennington was named comptroller of customs at the port of Brunswick, then the colony's leading port, and was so diligent in performing his duties that Tryon later wrote that "he acquitted himself faithfully and becomingly in the execution of his office." His responsibilities included collecting customs duties and inspecting ships in search of cargoes on which duties had not been paid. In March 1765 Pennington was a member of the board of inquiry charged with investigating the death of Lieutenant Thomas Whitehurst, a British naval officer, in a duel with a seaman.

In February 1766, during the course of colonial resistance to Parliament's Stamp Act, a delegation sought Pennington in the governor's house but Tryon, by then the governor, refused to permit them to take him. The next day between four hundred and five hundred men gathered and threatened to remove Pennington by force. Pennington offered to leave, declaring to the governor that "whatever Oaths might be imposed on Him, he should consider them as Acts of Compulsion and not of free Will." In spite of Tryon's intention to protect him, Pennington volunteered to resign his office and accompany the men. They took him into the town and obliged him and other officials to sign an oath not to enforce the Stamp Act. On 3 Mar. 1766, however, Pennington was restored to his office by the governor.

When Tryon left for his new post as governor of New York on 1 July 1771, he gave his fine house on the outskirts of Brunswick to Pennington. It is not clear how long Pennington remained in North Carolina, but on 12 Aug. 1776 Tryon reported that his friend had rendered nearly twelve years of faithful duty when he was driven from office. This suggests that Pennington remained at least until 1776. The American Revolution began that year, and in trying to persuade the British government to assist him, Tryon said that Pennington "is now left without friend or Relation in England."

There are references to Pennington as a colonel and as having fought against the Americans in the Revolutionary War. He probably was not the Captain Pennington of the Guards, however, who fatally wounded the Honorable J. Talmash (Tollemache), brother of the Earl of Dysart, in a duel in New York in November 1777, although the *Virginia Gazette* (21 Nov. 1777) does not give Pennington's full name.

Pennington was captured by the Americans in or near New York on 16 July 1781, but at some time before January 1783 he left America for England. It is reported that aboard ship he met another Englishman who was returning home to try to locate relatives last seen many years before. The new acquaintance became ill and in spite of Pennington's nursing care, he died soon after preparing a will leaving everything to Pennington. Once in England Pennington searched for and found the man's relatives and then destroyed the will so that they might inherit his property.

In 1785 Pennington was acting as master of ceremonies at the Clifton Hot Wells near Bristol, having been "inducted" into the position "under the patronage of the Archbishop of Tuam and the Bishop of Cloyne [both of Ireland], and with the unanimous voice of a numerous circle of nobility and gentry." Clifton Hot Wells was a popular spa fifteen miles from the better-known Bath. It was the function of the master of ceremonies to arrange balls, entertainments, and other amusements for the pleasure of the wealthy and the titled elite of the day. One of his acquaintances observed, "We are all in the right to love Mr. Pennington, 'tis for all our credit to love him." Another said, "He has won all our hearts here, and his charming wife will do the same with his friends wherever they are." As a mark of his position, the master wore a gold medallion hanging from a blue ribbon around his neck. For nearly thirty years Pennington ably operated a dignified, socially correct, and popular resort. The waters of the wells were believed to have medicinal qualities, and many of the patrons sought to improve their health as well as to be entertained.

On 27 Dec. 1792 Pennington married Penelope Sophia Weston (1752–1827), an attractive, popular lady who had declined many offers of marriage; she perhaps was the daughter of Edward and Penelope Weston and related to a number of people in high positions. She was a close friend of numerous highly regarded people but was especially attached to Hester Lynch Thrale Piozzi and well acquainted with Samuel Johnson; her correspondence with a wide range of friends has been published. Mrs. Tryon was one of Sophia's admirers, Mrs. Piozzi wrote a mutual friend. (Penelope Pennington appears to have been called Sophia by her close friends.)

William Pennington, having suffered from gout since 1793, became seriously ill in 1813 and resigned his position, but his successor proved to be ineffective. After a stay at Weymouth and the return of better health, Pennington resumed his old post for a time. He died in his ninety-first year.

In her will drawn on 30 May 1818, Margaret Wake Tryon, widow of Governor Tryon, bequeathed fifty pounds to Penelope Pennington, while to Penelope and William together she left all of her real property in Sloane Street, Chelsea, occupied at the time by Lady Skipwith. Pennington's own will, proved 7 Apr. 1829, is in the Public Record Office, London (Prob. 11/1756/310).

SEE: Edward A. Bloom and Lillian D. Bloom, eds., *The Piozzi Letters*, 2 vols. (1991); Walter Clark, ed., *State Records of North Carolina*, vol. 15 (1898); *Gentleman's Magazine*, Supplement for the Year 1792 and March 1829; Mary Hyde, *The Thrales of Streatham Park* (1977); Oswald G. Knapp, ed., *The Intimate Letters of Hester Piozzi and Penelope Pennington, 1788–1821* (1914); Lawrence Lee, "Days of Defiance," *North Carolina Historical Review* 43 (April 1966); Patrick McGrath, ed., *Bristol in the Eighteenth Century* (1972); William S. Powell, ed., *The Correspondence of William Tryon and Other Selected Papers*, 2 vols. (1980–81); Lorenzo Sabine, *Biographical Sketches of Loyalists of the American Revolution*, 2 (1864); William L. Saunders, ed., *Colonial Records of North Carolina*, 7 (1890); John Tearle, *Mrs. Piozzi's Tall Young Beau, William Augustus Conway* (1991).

WILLIAM S. POWELL

Percival, William *(fl. 1853–60)*, architect and civil engineer, was said to have been a British army officer who retired with the rank of cornet. According to his advertisements he had professional architectural training and by 1858 more than sixteen years of practical experience in Europe, Canada, and the United States in both public and private building. The Royal Institute of British Architects has no record of him; nor does the Ministry of Defence Library in London, which has army lists of the period, have any record of an officer by that name in the Royal Artillery or the Royal Engineers, which were the technical arms of the period. He completed several engineering commissions in Virginia prior to opening an architectural and engineering office in Richmond in 1855. Among them were the Keysville and Christiansville Plank Road, the Richmond and Danville Railroad, and a private railroad for William Allen of Surry County, Va.

In 1855 he received an award for his architectural drawings from the Virginia Mechanics Institute of Richmond. During the year 1856–57 he was an instructor in design at the institute, and the term ended in May 1857 with an exhibition of the work of Percival's thirty pupils.

In 1857 Percival formed a partnership with John Grant in Richmond and obtained architectural commissions for the First Baptist Church in Raleigh and New East and New West buildings on the campus of The University of North Carolina. They opened a branch office in Raleigh in January 1858 but the partnership apparently was dissolved that May. Thereafter Percival devoted his energies to new commissions in North Carolina. He negotiated contracts with Rufus S. Tucker, William M. Boylan, and William S. Battle. Construction on the Tucker villa began in the spring of 1858 and was soon followed by construction of The University of North Carolina buildings in June and the Boylan mansion in September 1858. Construction on the villa for William S. Battle in Tarboro probably began a few months later.

Meanwhile, Percival received a contract for the Caswell County courthouse and exhibited the design for it at the North Carolina State Fair in October 1858. The architect also installed water closets in the state capitol in Raleigh. Percival's work continued to flourish as construction began on Carter B. Harrison's villa in Raleigh (1859), the Calvary Episcopal Church in Tarboro (1860), and the First Baptist Church in Hillsborough (1860).

Percival's architectural designs followed the mandate established in the writings of Andrew Jackson Downing (1815–53) and as seen in the North Carolina work of Richard Upjohn (1802–78), Ithiel Town (1784–1844), and Alexander Jackson Davis (1803–92). His drawings, watercolors, sketches of English pastoral scenes, and engineering plans were consistent winners at the state fairs of 1858 and 1859, and he was acclaimed for his use of North Carolina sandstone, the material for most of his important structures in the state. His Baptist church in Raleigh and the Episcopal church in Tarboro are in the Greek Revival style expounded by Upjohn, notably in the exposed interior roof structure. New East and New West buildings on the campus of the university were inspired by the classical state capitol by Town, and the Davis design of Blandwood in Greensboro for Governor John Motley Morehead was a prototype in the Italianate style for the five houses by Percival: Montfort Hall in Raleigh for William Montfort Boylan, The Barracks for William S. Battle, and the William L. Dozier houses at Tarboro (the latter attributed to Percival by Arthur J. P. Edwards, who surveyed the area for the North Carolina Division of Archives and History), and the Carter B. Harrison and Rufus Sylvester Tucker houses (both demolished).

The dates of Percival's birth and death are unknown, and his career prior to 1853 and after 1860 remains a mystery. He does not appear in the census returns for either Virginia or North Carolina and no obituary for him has been found.

SEE: Catherine W. Bishir, *North Carolina Architecture* (1990); William B. Bushong, "William Percival: An English Architect in the Old North State, 1857–1860," *North Carolina Historical Review* 57 (July 1980); Archibald Henderson, *Campus of the First State University* (1949); Elizabeth Reid Murray, *Wake: Capital County of North Carolina*, vol. 1 (1983); Raleigh, *North Carolina Standard*, 1857–60; Raleigh *Register*, 1857–60; Raleigh, *Spirit of the Age*, 1857–60; *Richmond Daily Dispatch*, 1855–57; Richmond *Enquirer*, 1855–57; Tarboro *Southerner*, 1859–60; Tompkins Family Papers (Virginia Historical Society, Richmond); R. S. Tucker to contractors Thomas Briggs and James Dodd (letter owned by Willis Briggs, Raleigh); Elizabeth Waugh and Ralph Mills, *North Carolina's Capital: Raleigh* (1967); Lawrence Wodehouse, "William Percival, Architect," *North Carolina Architect* 14 (November 1967).

WILLIAM B. BUSHONG
LAWRENCE WODEHOUSE

Perry, Alice Threatt *(8 Feb. 1870–14 Sept. 1966)*, pioneer registered nurse in North Carolina, Spanish-American War veteran, commander of the North Carolina Department of United Spanish War Veterans, and trustee of Wingate College, was born near Dudley in Chesterfield County, S.C. Her early life on the family farm instilled in her a penchant for hard work and an empathy for the sick and needy that endured throughout her life. At age twenty-one, while nursing a sick friend, the attending physician suggested nurse's training to her. She entered Asheville Normal School and earned her tuition by nursing sick students; later she completed her training in the Orange Memorial Hospital, Orange, N.J., receiving her license in 1897.

With the declaration of war against Spain in 1898, Alice Threatt volunteered for the U.S. Army Nurses Corps for service in Cuba. She was stationed briefly at Fort Meyer, Va., then ordered to Cuba but was diverted en route to an army hospital in Albany, Ga., where troops for the regiment she was to join were being sent as they returned from Cuba.

After her release from service in 1900, she became the first registered nurse in private practice in Charlotte, under the sponsorship of Drs. E. C. Register, John R. Irwin, Charles Meisenheimer, and Robert L. Gibbon, who were engaged in an effort to "educate" people on the value of using trained nurses for private duty. For five years she worked in many homes, in the Charlotte Sanatorium, and in St. Peter's Hospital, where at times she served as acting superintendent.

After a brief stay in St. Louis, Mo., she returned to her native Chesterfield County to nurse an invalid aunt. The scarcity of physicians in that rural area and the great need for professional help led her to convert her aunt's home in Pageland into a private hospital known as Alice Threatt's Clinic, which she operated for six years. Following the death of her aunt, she closed the clinic and worked for ten years in Oklahoma City, becoming assistant superintendent of the Rolater Hospital.

In 1904 she helped to organize the veterans of the Spanish-American War and thereafter regularly attended their conventions. In 1956 she was elected the first and only woman commander of the North Carolina Department of United Spanish War Veterans. She was the last survivor of the Spanish War Nurses Corps in the United States.

In the 1920s while on a trip, Alice Threatt befriended two Confederate veterans on their way to a reunion. One of them, William M. Perry, was so impressed by her kindness that a correspondence developed, leading to their marriage in 1924. For the next fourteen years they resided in Wingate, traveled extensively, and attended both Confederate and Spanish-American veterans' reunions. In 1932 she succeeded her husband as a member of the board of trustees of Wingate College, where she served for more than a quarter of a century. Mindful of her own early struggle for training, she assisted many worthy but impoverished students in acquiring an education, often financing them through senior college after they had been graduated from Wingate. Mrs. Perry was active in various organizations of the Baptist church and for fifteen years was a regular participant at the Baptist summer retreat at Ridgecrest.

Possessing a commanding personality, she was a competent nurse, administrator, and trustee yet, despite the public recognition accorded her, retained an abiding concern for the ill and the destitute. Without children of her own she became the foster mother of hundreds fortunate enough to pass her way and was known throughout life by the simple appellation of "Miss Alice." In politics she was a Democrat. At age ninety-two she suffered a cerebral hemorrhage that resulted in partial paralysis. She died from the infirmities of advanced years in the Veterans Hospital in Salisbury and was buried in the Wingate cemetery.

SEE: *Charity and Children*, 3 Aug. 1961.

PERCIVAL PERRY

Perry, Louise Anderson Merrimon *(20 Aug. 1878–8 Aug. 1962)*, ophthalmologist and malacologist, was born in Asheville, the daughter of Emory H. and Rachel Augusta Hendrick Merrimon. From a large and prominent family, she was called "Lillie" as a child. After studying medicine she was licensed in 1899 to practice in North Carolina and the following year in Ohio. In Asheville, however, for fifteen years she served a flourishing eye, ear, and throat practice in association with Dr. H. H. Briggs. In 1918 she married Nelson R. Perry, a tobacconist, and with him established a winter home at Sanibel Island in the Gulf of Mexico off the southwestern coast of Florida. Nevertheless, they remained in Asheville until 1926, when they settled permanently on the isolated Florida island. During the first winter there, she became fascinated by the area's wide variety of seashells and began studying them as a hobby. In time she produced the definitive work on that subject, *Marine Shells of the Southwest Coast of Florida*, published as a 200-page book by the Paleontological Institution in Ithaca, N.Y., in 1940. A second edition of 318 pages appeared in 1955.

Although she relinquished her regular medical practice after moving to Florida, Dr. Perry freely gave her services to residents of the island. During World War II, after the death of her husband, she returned to Asheville to practice full-time; she made her home at the Battery Park Hotel, where she died. Although she and her husband had no children, he had a son from a previous marriage and Dr. Perry regarded his children as her grandchildren. She was buried in Greenwood Cemetery, Orlando, Fla.

SEE: *Asheville Citizen-Times*, 23 Feb. 1941, 9 Aug. 1962; Death certificate (Buncombe County Courthouse, Asheville); Theodore Pratt, "Shell Shock," *Saturday Evening Post*, 22 Feb. 1941 (portrait); Schnorrenberg Papers (Southern Historical Collection, University of North Carolina, Chapel Hill [portraits]); *Transactions of the Medical Society of the State of North Carolina* (1899).

MICHAEL HAWKINS

Perry, Oliver Hazard *(1819–3 Jan. 1885)*, state librarian, held that office from March 1854 until 1868. In that capacity he compiled two catalogues of the state library and one catalogue of the supreme court library. As the first published guides of the two collections, they provided increased organization of and access to the books.

Perry had a variety of other interests, including service from 1855 until 1859 as deputy clerk of the state supreme court. In 1860 O. H. Perry and Company of Raleigh republished the 1714 edition of John Lawson's *History of Carolina*. Perry also served as supervising agent for the North Carolina State Life Insurance Company. An avid Baptist, he wrote numerous articles for the Raleigh *Biblical Recorder* and in 1875 penned *Truth Vindicated, With Reference to the Book of Job*, also published by the *Biblical Recorder*. Perry died in Raleigh and was buried in Oakwood Cemetery.

SEE: *Biblical Recorder*, 7 Jan. 1885; "Bro. O. H. Perry," *North Carolina Baptist Almanac* 1 (1886); O. H. Perry, *Catalogue of Books Belonging to the North Carolina State Library* (1854, 1866) and *Catalogue of the North Carolina Law Library, Supreme Court Room* (1866); Raleigh *Daily News*,

3 Jan. 1874; Raleigh *Farmer and Mechanic*, 7 Jan. 1885; Raleigh *News and Observer*, 4 Jan. 1885.

MAURY YORK

Perry, Samuel L. *(b. 1849)*, teacher and civil rights activist, resided in Chatham County as the slave of William Perry. Following emancipation he moved to LaGrange in Lenoir County, where he directed the exodus movement from eastern North Carolina in Lenoir, Wayne, Greene, Pitt, and Jones counties. This movement reflected a response pattern involving the movement of blacks from the rural South to the West and North, beginning as early as 1879. It was motivated by the return of ex-Confederates to power, the abridgment of suffrage, unjust treatment in the courts, unfair and sometimes cruel treatment by landlords and merchants, and rumors of economic opportunities in other parts of the country.

Perry's activities had their beginning in 1872, when he and others around him saw leaflets distributed by the Union Pacific Railroad advertising cheap western land. Although he began to talk about forming a colony to be settled somewhere along the railroad, nothing came of these early discussions. With the withdrawal of Federal troops from the South in 1877, however, blacks became more uncertain of their future there and the prospect of cheap land became more and more appealing. Peter C. Williams, a minister, joined Perry to act for a body of blacks formed in 1879 in Goldsboro to look into the prospects offered in Kansas, Nebraska, and Colorado. Each member of the group contributed twenty-five cents, and with a total of fifty-four dollars the two men set off to find land. In September they were in Washington, D.C., trying without success to get the support of the National Emigration Aid Society. It may have been here that Perry focused his efforts on Indiana, because at this time the Baltimore and Ohio Railroad was promoting a movement to that state.

Through Perry's work more than four hundred North Carolina blacks moved to Indiana. But soon it became apparent that blacks were unwelcome there. Also, Perry later reported, the Baltimore and Ohio Railroad did not pay him what had been promised, and in both Indianapolis and Greencastle his efforts were rebuffed. Indiana Democrats saw in this influx of people a Republican move to carry the next election. It was about this time that folders promoting Kansas were distributed and Perry turned his attention there.

Blacks were poorly treated in their new surroundings, often lacking proper housing and adequate food. They complained that Perry had made extravagant promises in order to entice them to leave North Carolina. Cheap land, of course, was an inducement, but free railroad tickets, suits of new clothes, high wages, and even white wives were also mentioned.

The role played by Perry, nevertheless, entailed many responsibilities. He provided emigrants information regarding opportunities for work at the points of destination, the names of contact persons there, and assistance with transportation. On occasion he secured financial aid for the emigrants from the Emigrant Aid Society and from churches and individuals in the Washington, D.C., and Indianapolis, Ind., areas. It was largely through his efforts that 220 poor blacks reached Shelbyville, Ind., late in 1879. Soon after 40 more were sent to Washington, D.C., and 763 reached Indiana; in Indianapolis it was reported that a total of 1,135 eventually arrived in the state. Estimates of those who went to Kansas from North Carolina apparently are not available.

Many white southerners became alarmed over the movement of blacks and the prospect of ever-increasing numbers emigrating. Various methods were tried to keep them on the land as laborers, including enforcement of vagrancy and labor contract laws, enactment of legislation imposing penalties for enticing laborers away, and establishment of systems of peonage by which blacks were hired out by the county in order to pay the fine for a crime or to pay a debt. Perry's continuing involvement was perceived as having an unsettling and negative impact on the labor force. Thus, upon returning to LaGrange in 1879, after one of many trips out of the state assisting emigrants, Perry was surprised when he was arrested for forging a school order in the amount of fifty-four dollars. The order was actually signed by one Aaron Perry, who was jailed briefly and released on a straw bail. The school committee awaited the return of Samuel L. Perry. At the trial he was accused of writing the order and signing the names of committee members. Unlike the orders that Perry previously had routinely signed as a teacher, the handwriting in this document—upon inspection—demonstrated that it had been forged. Although the evidence presented at the trial did not incriminate Perry, an official declaration of his innocence was not affirmed. The forgery accusation was a harassment tactic. After the trial Perry hurriedly left LaGrange and settled in Washington, D.C.

In 1880 a Senate select committee was established to determine the causes of the massive emigration of blacks from the South to northern and western cities. Numerous individuals, one of whom was Perry, appeared before the committee. While testifying he presented two signed statements that focused on his trial in LaGrange the previous year. These were then sent, at Perry's request, to some persons who had attended the trial; they were asked whether they felt Perry's trial had been fair. The first statement received by the committee in response was signed by thirteen people, including the justice of the peace. The consensus was that Perry's trial had been "bogus" and the signers deplored the absence of evidence against him. Further, they indicated that they had known him for several years and believed him to be innocent of making out school orders and forging signatures. Finally, they indicated that they believed the forgery charges against Perry were drawn because of his involvement in the exodus movement rather than because of the school orders alleged to have been forged. A second statement signed by five LaGrange residents, including the mayor and former constable, reported that Perry had taught school in LaGrange for several years and that he was regarded as trustworthy and reliable. The signers of both documents were identified as white.

Beyond this nothing further has been discovered about the life of Samuel Perry. A clearly unsympathetic Shelbyville, Ind., newspaper described him as a "short, thickset Negro, with a pair of fine check pants, and large fashionable boots, upon an enormous pair of pedal extremities."

SEE: Robert G. Athearn, *In Search of Canaan: Black Migration to Kansas, 1879–80* (1978); John Hope Franklin, *From Slavery to Freedom: A History of Negro Americans* (1980); Talmage C. Johnson and Charles R. Holloman, *The Story of Kinston and Lenoir County* (1954); *Report and Testimony of the Select Committee of the United States Senate to Investigate the Causes of the Removal of the Negroes from the Southern States to Northern States* (1880).

ODELL UZZELL

Perry, William Joel *(5 Oct. 1877–28 Aug. 1954)*, physician, planter, businessman, and state senator, was born in Union County, near Ames (now Wingate), the fifth of nine children of William Marion and Martha Moore Perry. His forebears on each side served in the Revolutionary War and were among the earliest settlers of the region. His father, a Confederate veteran, farmer, and skilled mechanic, established a milling complex in Ames in 1892 and, eager to provide better educational opportunities for his children, was one of the founders of the Wingate School in 1896. Young Perry grew up on his father's farm, attended the Marshville Academy, and in 1898 was one of three students who were graduated in the first class at Wingate, where he had gained distinction as a debater.

Perry entered the Atlanta College of Physicians and Surgeons (now part of Emory University) and was graduated with the M.D. degree in 1900. He began medical practice in Taxahaw, near Lancaster County, S.C., but in 1905, at the request of a number of prominent citizens of Chesterfield County, moved there. In 1905 and again in 1907 he received graduate medical training in the New York Polyclinic Medical School and Hospital.

Resuming his practice in Chesterfield, he became active in the economic life of the community, entering partnerships in several mercantile establishments and serving as a bank director. He helped usher in the automobile age by purchasing the first automobile in Chesterfield in 1908 and later developed several automotive garages in the area. Perry acquired farms and became an active promoter of agricultural interests. In a county devoted primarily to the cultivation of cotton, he constantly experimented with new crops and with new methods for growing them.

Law and politics rivaled his interest in medicine, and he was elected to the state house of representatives in 1922 and 1924 and served as senator from 1927 to 1930. His primary efforts in the General Assembly were in behalf of improving public schools, farm-to-market roads, the medical college, and the state's charitable and penal institutions. Perry was singularly responsible for the defeat of a bill providing for a bond issue for paving intercity highways in the 1920s on the grounds that concrete highways were in an experimental stage and that through delay South Carolina could profit from the mistakes of others and ultimately build a better system for one-third less cost, wisdom borne out by subsequent developments. An ardent Democrat, he made the only speech in the county in behalf of the unpopular Democratic presidential nominee, Alfred E. Smith, in 1928.

These wide interests did not divert him from the practice of medicine, for which he was best remembered. Skilled in surgery and obstetrics, his practice covered a radius of twenty miles and extended into neighboring Anson County, N.C. Regarding his practice more as a mission to heal the sick and relieve suffering, he refused to send statements of accounts, trusting his patients to pay him when they could. His supreme effort came in the great influenza epidemic of 1918, which partially wrecked his health. A coronary, suffered under the strain of World War II, forced his retirement in 1945. He was a member of the Chesterfield County Medical Society, which honored him at a testimonial dinner in 1953, the South Carolina Medical Association, the American Medical Association, and the Masonic order.

An excellent public speaker and a delightful raconteur, Perry had the gift for being at ease whether in the hut of the humblest tenant farmer or among his peers on the senate floor. Passionately devoted to education, he served as chairman of the local school board and often made loans to worthy students for their college education. His empathy for the disadvantaged was legendary.

In 1899 he married Martha V. Griffin, daughter of Enoch W. and Margaret Bivens Griffin, of Wingate, who died in 1905. In 1907 he married Essie Burns Buchanan, eldest daughter of Miriam DeLoss Melton and Jesse Burns Buchanan, a planter and former mayor of Chesterfield, and they had three sons: William Louis and Jeremiah Buchanan, who followed him in the practice of medicine, and Percival, who became professor of history at Wake Forest University. He died of a cerebral hemorrhage at his home in Chesterfield and was buried in the Chesterfield cemetery. An oil portrait by Stanislav Rembski, painted three months prior to his death, is in possession of his son in Winston-Salem.

SEE: *Chesterfield Advertiser*, 2 Sept. 1954; J. Wilson Gibbs, *Legislative Manual of South Carolina* (1927); Family records (possession of the author).

PERCIVAL PERRY

Perry, William Marion *(25 May 1847–24 May 1938)*, Confederate veteran, farmer, millwright, merchant, banker, and a founder of Wingate College and the town of Wingate, was born on Niggerhead Creek, in Union County, the third of seven children of Jeremiah and Elizabeth Griffin Perry. Forebears on each ancestral side had served in the Revolution and settled in the county. William Marion Perry spent his early years on his father's farm without opportunities for education, a circumstance that greatly influenced him in later life.

Too young to enlist at the beginning of the Civil War, he was apprenticed to work in a bayonet factory in Wadesboro until his enlistment at age seventeen in August 1864 in the Second North Carolina Junior Reserves, Company F. Later transferred to a regular regiment, he served principally in eastern North Carolina guarding the railroad that was the lifeline for General Robert E. Lee's army in Virginia.

Returning home after the war, he married Martha Emmaline Moore, daughter of Samuel Rode and Mary Ross Moore, in September 1866, and they had nine children prior to her death in 1888. In October 1868 his parents gave him 70 acres of timberland on which he constructed a log house; he moved in in January 1870, before he had completed the roof or hung the doors. During the next twenty-six years he farmed and purchased an additional 225 acres and cleared 100 for farming. He also developed other skills: he used the metallurgical knowledge gained in the bayonet factory to become a blacksmith and wheelwright for the community; he made a pair of forceps in his shop and served as the local "dentist," extracting teeth for his neighbors; and he was a cobbler and a carpenter.

Perry's early ambition in life was to become a physician. Denied educational opportunities as a youth, he was determined to provide them for his children. The only schools available locally were subscription schools, taught irregularly for brief intervals. In 1890, following the death of his first wife, he married Katherine M. Rushing, a schoolteacher, and with her support resolved to abandon farming and enter the milling business in Marshville, where his children could attend the academy. When these plans went awry, his brother-in-law, G. M. Stewart, aware of his mechanical skills, offered to sell him a choice block of land at a minimal price if he would move to Ames Turnout on the railroad and enter a partnership with him. Perry agreed provided they would build a school for the community.

In 1895 the Union Baptist Association was searching for a site for an Associational school. Stewart offered to give the Association ten acres of land, with a spring on it, and Perry offered to saw the lumber gratuitously at his mill from logs contributed by people in the community. The school, named Wingate in honor of a former president of Wake Forest College, was opened in the fall of 1896. In the same year Perry built one of the first houses in the new town that developed around the school. In 1901 the town was incorporated and its name changed from Ames to Wingate.

In addition to the lumber mill and cotton gin, established in 1892, Perry and Stewart developed a corn and flour mill and a general merchandise store. In 1896 Perry added a planer mill, specifically to dress the lumber for the new school. In 1909 they organized, with others, the State Bank of Wingate, with Perry as vice-president, a position he held until his death. Although limited in resources, the bank survived the economic collapse of 1929.

A man of quiet temperament, sound judgment, and genial good humor, Perry never sought the limelight but was content with his service to others. He assisted many students in obtaining an education by boarding them in his home and extending them loans in time of need. He regarded the Wingate School as his lifework and remained an ardent supporter, serving for many years on the board of trustees and as chairman of its building committee for a new brick building in 1911. When the state public school system of the 1920s threatened the existence of the private academies, he supported the conversion of the Wingate School to a junior college in 1923 to assure its perpetuity.

After the death of his second wife in 1921, he married Alice Threatt, a registered nurse, in 1924. He died at his home from advanced years and gradual heart failure and was buried in the Wingate cemetery. He was a lifelong member of Meadow Branch Baptist Church, the Democratic party, and the Masonic order. All by his first wife were his children Clarence, Cora, Julia, James, William (who realized his father's ambition by becoming a physician), Mary, Wilma, and Martha.

SEE: Mary Perry Beddingfield and Wilma Perry Dry, personal contacts, various dates, 1970–78; *Charlotte Observer*, 25 May 1938; Hubert I. Hester, *The Wingate Story* (1972); Perry Family Bible and other records (possession of Percival Perry); *Monroe Enquirer*, 1 Feb. 1912; *Monroe Journal*, 12 Feb. 1929, 20 Nov. 1936, 10 Jan. 1969.

PERCIVAL PERRY

Person, Alice Morgan *(28 July 1840–12 June 1913)*, businesswoman and medicine show performer, was born in Petersburg, Va., the daughter of Samuel and Esther Morgan. In December 1857 she married Joseph Arrington Person and moved to Franklinton, N.C., where he was a prosperous farmer. After he was paralyzed by a stroke in the 1860s, she supported their seven children by making and selling a proprietary medicine, marketed as "Mrs. Joe Person's Remedy." The recipe, she claimed, was given to her mother by an "old Indian" and was "composed entirely of plants growing in the woods around the house." The medicine was said to be effective against a host of ills, among them scrofula, catarrh, rheumatism, cancer, heart disease, colic, and indigestion. It was also billed as an antidote to drunkenness.

After her husband's death in 1883, Mrs. Person "went on the road advertising, selling, drumming, talking." In Raleigh she staged a "public test" at Yarborough House, a downtown hotel, to demonstrate the curative powers of the remedy. She traveled across the state in her horse-drawn rig laden with the cure-all. Her procedure was the same in each county. She would make the county seat her headquarters, hire a double team and "good, reliable white driver," visit every country store, and stop at every house on the wayside with an organ or piano, staying the night wherever she was welcome.

By 1903 the business had outgrown home manufacture and she moved it to Charlotte, establishing a plant with Charles R. Jones as her financial partner. The product, initially marketed only in the Carolinas and Virginia, was in time sold up and down the eastern seaboard and as far west as Texas. According to a promotional circular, the remedy's adherents included former governor W. W. Holden, prominent judges, doctors, and pharmacists. Mrs. Person, on the basis of her popular personal appearances, made several records for the Victor Talking Machine Company in Camden, N.J. In 1898 an eastern North Carolina newspaper called her the "best known woman in the State."

A writer for the *Charlotte Observer* neatly described Mrs. Person in March 1913: "Her whole air, her quick, positive speech, the straight look of her eyes, the knowing way in which she unconsciously sizes one up, the frank grasp of her chubby hand, even the active movement of a body that is so big it ought to be cumbersome, tell of the independence which has made her career." The reporter was particularly struck by her business acumen, sensing a "strange feeling in talking to Mrs. Person that she is more than two parts man."

Three months later Mrs. Person, just short of age seventy-three, died in Santa Fe, N.Mex., en route to California and Alaska. By faith she was an Episcopalian, though she never identified closely with the church. She was survived by two daughters, Mrs. W. A. Harris of Wake Forest and Miss Josie Person of Hickory, and two sons, W. M. Person of Louisburg and R. M. Person of Charlotte. A sixty-six-page typescript copy of her autobiography, entitled "Banny's Book," is among her papers deposited in the Southern Historical Collection.

SEE: *Charlotte Observer*, 16 Mar., 13 June 1913; *Franklin Times* (Louisburg, N.C.), 1 Apr. 1898; *Halifax* (Va.) *Record-Advertiser*, 30 Mar. 1972; Alice M. (Mrs. Joe) Person Papers (Southern Historical Collection, University of North Carolina, Chapel Hill); "Mrs. Joe Person's Remedy" (Charlotte, no date; Pamphlet Collection, Duke University Library, Durham).

MICHAEL HILL

Person, Benjamin Thomas *(16 Sept. 1833–2 Jan. 1916)*, physician, legislator, and postmaster, was a son of Thomas and Sally Tarver Person of Greene County. Details of his youth and education are unavailable. He enlisted on 17 Mar. 1862 in Company H, Ninth North Carolina (First Cavalry) Regiment, Confederate States of America, and was promoted to first lieutenant on 23 July 1863. He served until General Robert E. Lee's surrender but declined to apply for a parole. From 26 May to 25 June 1866 he represented Wayne County in the North Carolina Constitutional Convention. After living and practicing medicine for many years in the Stantonsburg area, he was by 1896 in Wilson, which he served as postmaster from 24 Mar. 1903 to 1 June 1914. For a brief period he had also represented Wilson County in the state house of representatives (6 Jan.–9 Mar. 1897).

"Dr. Tom" became something of a legend in Wilson and adjacent counties, particularly after leading several ex-Confederates into Goldsboro, then one seat of the

Federal Army of Occupation, and shooting on a public street with his Colt revolver a certain Andrew Wilson, whose misbehavior among the local people had caused them to suspect him of being an informer. On the fatal day, about daylight, Wilson ambushed and almost killed a young hired hand on the Coley farm, having mistaken him for ex-cavalryman Frank Coley, who had been active in protecting his friends and neighbors from the foraging Yankees. Within an hour three or four Blue Rangers were in pursuit. They came upon Wilson in Goldsboro at the point of crossing of the two railroads. In a rapid exchange of fire their leader, Tom Person, left Wilson dying on the steps of a store as they galloped rapidly out of town with a band of Federal cavalry in hot pursuit.

For two or three years Dr. Tom was forced to keep on the move among friends and relatives between Contentnea Creek and Nahunta Swamp, and he had several hairbreadth escapes during the repeated searches of military patrols. The Federal authorities finally abandoned their efforts, and he soon married (26 Apr. 1871) Elizabeth Kennedy Ruffin (13 Oct. 1833–28 Jan. 1906), daughter of William Lee and Sidney Delzell Crawford Kennedy of Greene County and widow of Etheldred Francis (Dred) Ruffin, who had given his life in the Confederate service. She and her two husbands were buried in Maplewood Cemetery, Wilson. There were children by both of her marriages, but the Persons were Thomas L., William Kennedy, and Sally, who married William Edwin Bardin of the Eureka area.

SEE: John L. Cheney, Jr., *North Carolina Government, 1585–1974* (1975); *Wilson Daily Times*, 12 Feb. 1952, 6 July 1963; J. M. Hollowell, "War-Time Reminiscences" (manuscript).

HUGH BUCKNER JOHNSTON

Person, Thomas *(19 Jan. 1733–16 Nov. 1800)*, philanthropist, surveyor, sheriff, justice, landed proprietor, member of the General Assembly and Provincial Congress, and brigadier general in the American Revolution, was born in Surry County, Va., and moved to North Carolina with his parents, William and Ann Person. Thomas grew up in Granville (present-day Warren) County and established his seat at Goshen in Granville; he spent his entire life in the Warren-Granville area.

Early in his career Person became a surveyor for Earl Granville. He was noted for the accuracy of his surveys and commitment to his work and, as he became acquainted with the best lands, he was able to accumulate a handsome estate. In 1788 he listed for taxation 82,358 acres in Granville, Halifax, Warren, Franklin, Orange, Caswell, Guilford, Rockingham, Anson, and Wake counties, N.C., and in Davidson, Sumner, and Greene counties, Tenn. On 24 June 1765 he married Jeanna Thomas (b. 15 Sept. 1739). She died after 1810, when Granville County records show a deed of gift from Jeanna Person to John W. Philpott (whom she had appointed in September 1805 as her attorney to collect all debts due her). Thomas and Jeanna Person had no children.

The first record of Person's appearance in public life is on 6 July 1756, when at age twenty-three he was recommended as a justice of the peace for Granville. Thus began a long and illustrious life of public service, which included being sheriff of Granville County (appointed 1762) and representing Granville in the General Assembly (first in October 1764) almost continuously for thirty years.

He was a member of all provincial conventions and congresses, which took the place of the Assembly from 1774 to 1776, and served on the most important committees, including those that drafted the Bill of Rights (of its twelve clauses for the protection of individual rights, eleven were embodied in the first ten amendments of the U.S. Constitution) and the state constitution (which remained in force for fifty-nine years without change). On 9 Sept. 1775 Person was chosen to serve on the Provincial Council—the executive head of the state. He and Willie Jones of Halifax were of the more progressive element, which favored a simpler government more directly responsible to the people. He also served on the Council of Safety, which replaced the Provincial Council.

One of his important services to the state was as a leader of the Antifederalist party in the convention of 1788, which was called to consider the federal constitution. This party was ultra-democratic and advocated a federal government of limited power in order to protect the interests of the states against the centralizing tendency evident in the new constitution. Person feared the federal power to tax, and although the new consitution was adopted at the Fayetteville convention in November 1789, Person, "true to his convictions and game to the last, voted nay."

His most valuable service was as a member of the General Assembly for some thirty years. There he was always an Argus-eyed guardian of the rights of the people; no form of what he thought injustice, illegality, or graft could escape his sharp eye or pass without protest. He was especially quick to attack whatever savored of injustice or class legislation. He served on the most important committees, usually as chairman. In 1784 he was chairman of the whole. Some of the committees on which he served were concerned with public accounts, military matters, privileges and elections, finance, propositions and grievances, depredations of Tories, manufacture of iron, defense, location of the capital, affairs of the North Carolina Continental Line, paper money, revenue, Indian affairs, raising regular troops and regulating the commissary department, bills of attainer, debts due to and from the public land grants, vesting power in the Continental Congress to levy duties, claims and depreciation, trial of impeachment, proposed revision of the constitution, the Virginia boundary, and confiscated property.

An individual of prominence, such as Person, was, of course, envied and criticized. Such was the case when John Ashe accused him of perjury in the Assembly in 1769. When Person was tried at the December 1770 session, the investigating committee, headed by John Campbell, reported that "there is not any one of the charges or allegations—in any matter supported," but that they were exhibited "through malice and envy, with design to injure the character and reputation of the said Thomas Person." It was ordered that this report be published in the newspaper of the day.

When abuse by colonial officials led to the Regulator movement in North Carolina, Thomas Person was one of the leaders in this effort to secure redress of grievances from the government. Although he did not participate in the Battle of Alamance, he was seized on the order of Governor William Tryon and imprisoned at Hillsborough in the care of the Reverend George Micklejohn. Realizing that certain papers at home would incriminate him if found by Tryon, he promised his jailer he would return by daybreak if he were permitted to leave during the night. Person was considered a man of such honor that Micklejohn consented to his request, and he was soon on his way to Goshen, his home in Granville County. There he secured his bonds and money in a brick kiln, removed from his desk stacks of papers, which he burned, and managed to return in time to keep his promise to the clergyman. The following morning his estate was invaded by Tryon's troops, who hacked open his desk (this historic desk is now owned by The University of North Carolina) but discovered no evidence; instead, they found only ashes of the papers they had hoped to seize. The soldiers hurried to Hillsborough and questioned Micklejohn concerning whether Person had left the prison the night before. Micklejohn's reply was, "I supped and breakfasted with him."

It is said that Person was among those most feared by Tryon and that when amnesty was offered to the Regulators who would take the oath of allegiance to the king, he and a few others were excepted. During the three weeks when he was in irons in Hillsborough, he was marched to the gallows and back again. Surviving this experience, he became one of the early leaders in the American Revolution and was appointed brigadier general on 22 Apr. 1776.

Stephen B. Weeks states that by sheer weight of character alone, General Person made himself a necessity to the colony. According to Weeks, when on 12 Apr. 1776 at Halifax, North Carolina became the first colony to make a formal proposal for a declaration of independence, this proposal—though evidence will not be found to settle this point beyond dispute—was as much the work of Thomas Person as of any other man. No student of North Carolina history, Weeks maintains, will dare to claim that such an honor could belong by right of work done to any other man or that any other citizen of the state was more worthy of this great and signal honor.

Person, a man of wealth, was generous with his fortune and promoted education. During the war he placed his property at the service of the state. He loaned Governor Thomas Burke $50,000, "to be replaced or paid by warrant which I did not issue." He assisted in securing a charter for The University of North Carolina in 1789 and was a member of its first board of trustees (1789–95). Though the university had been chartered, no money had been provided by the state and an effort was being made to open its doors to students. Person made substantial donations at a time when hard money was almost unattainable. Person Hall at The University of North Carolina was named in his honor, as were streets in Raleigh and Fayetteville, and Person County. It is believed that Person's ordinary was built by him and was in operation on or before 1764 (in that year he obtained a "lycense" to keep an ordinary at Butterwood in Bute County). It was restored by the Littleton Woman's Club.

He died in Franklin County at the home of his sister Martha (wife of Major Francis Taylor) while on his way from Raleigh to Goshen. He was buried at Personton on Hub Quarter Creek in Warren County, now covered by the waters of Lake Gaston.

SEE: W. C. Allen, *History of Halifax County* (1918); Samuel A. Ashe, *History of North Carolina*, vol. 1 (1908), and ed., *Biographical History of North Carolina*, vol. 7 (1908); Bute County Records, Estate Papers, Granville County Records, and Warren County Records (North Carolina State Archives, Raleigh); John L. Cheney, Jr., *North Carolina Government, 1585–1979* (1981); Walter Clark, ed., *State Records of North Carolina*, vols. 11 (1895), 13–15 (1896–98), 17 (1899), 19 (1901), 22–23 (1907, 1904); Raleigh *Register*, 25 Nov. 1800; William L. Saunders, ed., *Colonial Records of North Carolina*, vols. 6 (1888), 8–10 (1890); George F. Walker, *Person Lineage* (1951); Manly Wade Wellman, *The County of Warren, North Carolina, 1586–1917* (1959); John H. Wheeler, *Historical Sketches of North Carolina* (1851).

SUE DOSSETT SKINNER

Person, William *(1700–11 Nov. 1770)*, county justice, vestryman, commissioner, sheriff, militia officer, and planter, was the son of John Person (ca. 1660–1738) and his wife Mary (ca. 1670–pre-1721), the daughter of Thomas Partridge of Surry County, Va. His parents were married on 10 Jan. 1692. William was born in Isle of Wight County, Va., and later lived in Surry County before migrating to North Carolina. He was one of the first settlers to secure acreage for a great plantation in the area of Edgecombe (later Granville, Bute, and present-day Warren) County. Family tradition says that he mortared together fieldstones for the dwelling his patent required him to build and that the stream beside the dwelling was thereafter known as Stonehouse Creek. The house was still standing in 1993.

When the Granville precinct of Edgecombe became a county in 1746 and the new government was organized, William Person was its first sheriff; he was also elected a county commissioner along with Francis Stringer, James Maclewean, and William Eaton. Person was a vestryman, as had been his father (of the Old Brick Church in Isle of Wight County, Va.), and was lieutenant colonel of a regiment of Granville militia of which William Eaton was colonel and James Paine, major. He was named a justice for the county in 1756. The recipient of numerous royal grants through Lord Granville, he owned extensive acreage.

Person and his wife Ann (d. 1781) had five children: Thomas (9 Jan. 1733–16 Nov. 1800, m. Joanna Thomas in 1765), William (30 Nov. 1734–1778, m. Martha Eaton), Mary Ann (6 May 1736–pre-1819, m. George Little of Hertford County), Benjamin (13 Feb. 1737–1771, m. Lucretia Browne), and Martha (6 Oct. 1752–25 Jan. 1836, m. Peterson Thorp, then Francis Taylor).

SEE: References cited for Thomas Person.

SUE DOSSETT SKINNER

Person, William *(30 Nov. 1734–1778)*, planter and member of the colonial Assembly and Provincial Congress, the son of William and Ann Person, was born in Surry County, Va. When he was a small child, he moved with his parents to North Carolina and spent his life in Granville (later Bute and now Warren) County. Among his large landholdings were six grants from Earl Granville.

William Person succeeded his brother, Benjamin, on 16 Dec. 1771 as representative of Bute County in the colonial Assembly and was reelected for three successive sessions, serving until 1774. He then became a member of the first four Provincial congresses, which held sessions at New Bern in 1774 and 1775, at Hillsborough in 1775, and at Halifax in 1776. In the latter body he held a variety of committee posts. In addition, he was a justice of the Bute County Court.

On 2 Sept. 1759 in Granville County he married Martha Eaton (b. 1742), the daughter of Colonel William and Martha Rives Eaton. Their children were Sarah (b. 30 July 1760, m. William Vaughan), Martha (b. 19 Jan. 1763, m. William Johnson), William (19 July 1765–1857, m. Elizabeth Holman), Thomas (b. 17 Feb. 1768), Mary (b. 15 Dec. 1771, m. one Williams), and Benjamin Eaton (b. 5 Mar. 1774). Person died in Bute County.

SEE: References cited for Thomas Person.

SUE DOSSETT SKINNER

Peter, John Frederick *(19 May 1746–19 July 1813)*, musician, composer, teacher, and minister, was born of German parents in Heerendyck, Holland, where his father, John Frederick Peter, was a Moravian pastor. His mother was Susannah Peter. Before coming to America, young Peter received excellent musical training, and while a student at the theological seminary in Barby, Saxony, from 1765 to 1769, he began his lifelong habit of copying the works of noted German composers. Some of his beautifully written transcripts are now the only existing copies.

By 1770, when he joined the Moravian colony at Bethlehem, Pa., Peter was a brilliant and accomplished musician; that summer he composed a solo for strings and organ. He later directed performances of works by Bach, Handel, and Graun and developed a full orchestra which played symphonies by Haydn, Mozart, and their contemporaries.

Peter went to Bethlehem as assistant superintendent of the unmarried men. After the Brethren's House was turned into a Continental hospital, he was called to Salem, N.C., where he arrived in June 1780 and was ordained as a Moravian deacon on 16 September. He preached and performed many other duties in addition to his musical activities.

Under his leadership, the Collegium Musicum Salem was organized in 1786 and soon became the foremost musical society in the early history of North Carolina. It had at its disposal one of the largest and most diversified libraries of secular music in America. Peter's six quintets for two violins, two violas, and cello, composed at Salem in 1789, have been acclaimed as the earliest extant chamber works written in America and the most important compositions in the history of early American music. Although these works followed the classical tradition, they displayed considerable harmonic freedom and boldness in modulation. During his ten years at Salem, Peter also composed thirty interesting and effective anthems and four soprano solos. He left Salem in August 1790 and in 1793 again took charge of the musical activities in Bethlehem, Pa. There he directed in 1811 the first complete American performance of Haydn's *Creation*.

For more than a century after his death, Peter's musical compositions were largely forgotten, but in recent years they have received national recognition on account of scholarly research and publications in the field of early Moravian music. He now occupies a prominent position in American musical history.

He married Catharine Leinbach (1755–1830), a soprano singer of Salem, in 1786. There were no children. Peter continued his musical career until the day of his death; he was buried in the Old Moravian Cemetery at Bethlehem.

SEE: Adelaide L. Fries, ed., *Records of the Moravians of North Carolina*, vol. 4 (1930); Donald Mc. McCorkle, "The Collegium Musicum Salem: Its Music, Musicians, and Importance," *North Carolina Historical Review* 33 (October 1956); Moravian Archives (Bethlehem, Pa., and Winston-Salem, N.C.).

FRANK P. CAUBLE

Pettigrew, Charles *(20 Mar. 1744–8 Apr. 1807)*, clergyman, planter, and educator, was born on the Pennsylvania frontier, the sixth of eleven children and the third son of James and Mary Cochran Pettigrew, both immigrants from Northern Ireland. The family possessed some slender means, and James had received a degree of medical education, a combination with which he set out to make his way in the New World. Leaving the exposed Pennsylvania frontier after General Edward Braddock's defeat, the Pettigrews moved to Lunenburg County, Va., where it was apparently decided that Charles was to receive all the education the family could afford. Presbyterian by faith, the father selected clergymen to teach his son, among them James Waddel and Henry Pattillo. From Virginia the family migrated to Granville County, N.C., and eventually to South Carolina, where their wanderings ceased. James Pettigrew was a Patriot during the American Revolution and frequently attended the wounded in spite of his advanced age. Some of the South Carolina family later changed the spelling of the surname to Pettigru.

Charles Pettigrew remained behind in Granville County when his parents moved to South Carolina in 1768. After teaching in a small school for the children of the Macons and the Hawkinses for about seven years, he was appointed by Governor Josiah Martin as schoolmaster at Edenton, an important colonial town. At this time Pettigrew became an Anglican. He served as assistant to the Reverend Daniel Earl at St. Paul's Church and in 1774 went to England, where he was ordained deacon and priest by the bishops of London and Rochester. He returned to Edenton on 20 May 1775.

As the waves of revolution broke over the state, Pettigrew became a moderate Patriot. He preached appropriate sermons to patriotic assemblages but was insufficiently fiery to appease the powerful Blount family, one member of whom seems to have arranged that he be drafted for military service in spite of his clerical standing. Pettigrew served for a few weeks in the spring of 1780 and was then able to secure his release by "having produced Zachariah Carter an able bodied man in his Room." During the war, he was named rector of St. Paul's Church, with which he continued to be loosely affiliated until his death. From 1790 to 1794 he participated in a movement to organize the former Anglican church into the Episcopal Diocese of North Carolina, promoting together with the Reverend Nathaniel Blount four conventions for this purpose. In 1794, at Tarboro, he was elected bishop of the proposed diocese. Unfortunately for the church, he failed to attend the next two triennial conventions at either one of which he would have been consecrated bishop, and at the time of his death there was neither bishop nor diocese in the state.

Pettigrew was more fortunate as a planter. In 1781 he purchased land in Tyrrell County to which he gradually added; eventually he owned two plantations on which he grew rice, wheat, and corn, and whose timber he made into shingles and barrels for sale. His neighbors, the Collins family, formed the Lake Company together with Nathaniel Allen and Samuel Dickinson, draining the swamps, building canals to connect Lake Phelps with the Scuppernong River and thence to Albemarle Sound, and erecting mills and threshing machinery, allowing Pettigrew their use. Beginning with nine slaves who were the property of his first wife, Pettigrew more than tripled their number by the time of his death. From a poor frontier boy, he became the owner of two plantations in North Carolina, eight hundred acres of land in Tennessee, thirty-four slaves, a chapel, and a good house that he built (it was still standing in the 1990s), and he possessed what he described to a cousin as "more than a Competency."

Apparently taught some medicine by his father, Pettigrew considered himself a "quack" and frequently prescribed for friends as well as himself; he intended that his oldest son become a physician. He was interested in education, serving on the first board of trustees of The University of North Carolina until he became disgusted with the rampant deism there. A Federalist in politics, he detested both Thomas Jefferson and Tom Paine. There are extant a number of his sermons, a good deal of his poetry, and some hymns that he wrote, displaying some degree of literary talent.

Pettigrew was twice married, first to Mary (Polly) Blount of Mulberry Hill, an heiress by whom he had two sons: John who died in an epidemic in 1799, and Ebenezer. Polly died in childbirth in 1786. Pettigrew secondly married Mary Lockhart in 1794, an apparently happy union. There were no children. John and Ebenezer were enrolled by their father in the first session (1795) held at The University of North Carolina, and their letters home are among the treasures of the university's archives. Pettigrew also encouraged various nephews to continue their education in the church or in medicine. Pettigrew died of general ill health and was buried in the Blount cemetery at Mulberry Hill by the side of his first wife. His son Ebenezer moved the remains in 1831 to the new family cemetery at Bonanza Plantation on Lake Phelps. A memorial plaque may be viewed in St. Paul's Church. His portrait, in clerical garb, has been reproduced in *The Pettigrew Papers*, vol. 1.

SEE: Samuel A. Ashe, ed., *Biographical History of North Carolina*, vol. 6 (1907); DAB, vol. 7 (1934); Sarah M. Lemmon, "Genesis of the Protestant Episcopal Diocese of North Carolina, 1801–1823," *North Carolina Historical Review* 29 (1952), *Parson Pettigrew of the "Old Church": 1744–1807* (1970), and ed., *The Pettigrew Papers*, 2 vols. (1971, 1988 [portrait]); William B. Sprague, *Annals of the American Pulpit*, vol. 5 (1859).

SARAH MCCULLOH LEMMON

Pettigrew, Ebenezer *(10 Mar. 1783–8 July 1848)*, planter, U.S. congressman, and state senator, was born near Edenton of Irish and Scottish ancestry, the son of the Reverend Charles Pettigrew, planter and first bishop-elect of the Protestant Episcopal church in the Diocese of North Carolina, and Mary Blount, of Mulberry Hill, wealthy sister of the Revolutionary patriot Colonel James Blount. His mother having died in childbirth (1786), he was reared by his stepmother Mary Lockhart (m. 1794) and, after the death of his older brother John in 1799, by a somewhat grim and ultraconservative father. Following a brief stay in the preparatory division of the new University of North Carolina (1795–97) and further study at the Edenton Academy, he was withdrawn from school by his father in 1803 to assume responsibilities at the plantation in Washington County.

Following his father's death in 1807, Pettigrew cared for his stepmother until her death in 1833 at Belgrade, the family plantation, and himself developed a second plantation and house, Bonarva, at Lake Phelps. His business flourished through fanatical hard work as he grew rice and wheat, cut lumber and shingles, and sold them in Baltimore, Philadelphia, New York, and occasionally Boston. While a bachelor he enjoyed traveling to visit his friends Thomas B. Haughton and James Iredell, Jr., at Princeton and his business associates in the larger cities; but following his marriage in 1815 to his cousin, Ann Blount Shepard of New Bern, he devoted his attention to his wife, his business, and his children. Always somewhat introverted and opposed to frivolity, he became even more so following the death of his wife in childbirth in 1830. The couple had nine children, of whom five lived to maturity: Charles Lockhart, William Shepard who entered the ministry, James Johnston who became a Confederate general and was killed in the Civil War, Mary Blount, and Ann Blount Shepard.

Pettigrew, always a conservative, was elected to the state senate for two terms (1809–10) and to the U.S. Congress (1835–37) as a Whig, defeating the Jacksonian incumbent Thomas H. Hall. His political career was undistinguished, his melancholy demeanor and taciturnity unfitting him for politics. As a planter he was more successful. In addition to Belgrade and Bonarva, he developed a third plantation, Magnolia, all in the same vicinity. Lands, books, houses, cash, and over ninety slaves at the time of his death amounted to a substantial sum. In spite of his accumulated wealth, he lived simply and condemned the fashionable follies of the Josiah Collins family at adjoining Somerset plantation.

Pettigrew was buried in the family cemetery. The two vast collections of family papers reveal in minute detail the social mobility of four generations of Pettigrews, concluding with the final collapse of their position after the Civil War destroyed the slave-based plantation system.

SEE: *Biog. Dir. Am. Cong.* (1950); John L. Cheney, Jr., *North Carolina Government, 1585–1974* (1975); Sarah McCulloh Lemmon, *Parson Pettigrew of the Old Church* (1970) and ed., *The Pettigrew Papers*, vols. 1–2 (1971, 1988 [portrait]); Pettigrew Family Papers (North Carolina State Archives, Raleigh, and Southern Historical Collection, University of North Carolina, Chapel Hill); Bennett H. Wall, "Ebenezer Pettigrew: An Economic Study of an Ante-Bellum Planter" (Ph.D. diss., University of North Carolina, 1946), "Medical Care of Ebenezer Pettigrew's Slaves," *Miss. Valley Hist. Review* 37 (1950), and "The Founding of the Pettigrew Plantations," *North Carolina Historical Review* 27 (1950).

SARAH MCCULLOH LEMMON

Pettigrew, James Johnston *(4 July 1828–17 July 1863)*, lawyer, scholar, and Confederate general, was born at Bonarva in Tyrrell County, eighth of the nine children of Ebenezer and Ann Blount Shepard Pettigrew. He was educated at Bingham's Academy near Hillsborough and entered The University of North Carolina at age fourteen. Highly gifted intellectually, his academic prowess was a tradition at Chapel Hill for many decades. He made a rating of "excellent" in every subject taken in four years and was graduated as valedictorian of the class of 1847.

Pettigrew was a particularly talented mathematician and upon graduation was appointed a professor at the National Observatory by President James K. Polk and Secretary of the Navy John Y. Mason, both alumni of The University of North Carolina. Although esteemed by the head of the observatory, the oceanographer Matthew F. Maury, Pettigrew left after six months to study law. From January 1850 to August 1852 he was in Europe. He studied at the University of Berlin and traveled over most of Western Europe, visiting on foot and on horseback many regions not frequented by tourists. In the course of his travels he acquired a deep romantic identification with the Latin peoples, particularly the Italians and the Spanish. Pettigrew's European study was subsidized by James C. Johnston, of Hayes, his father's friend for whom he had been named. Subsequently, when Pettigrew was thirty, Johnston made him a gift of $50,000 so that he might devote his talents to public service.

On his return from Europe Pettigrew was made a junior law partner of James Louis Petigru at Charleston, S.C. Petigru, Ebenezer Pettigrew's first cousin, was one of the leading attorneys of the country and also the most notable "Union man" of South Carolina. From 1852 to 1861 James Pettigrew was a resident of Charleston. Related through Petigru to many prominent families in the city, he took an active part in the social and public life of the area and was noted for his intellectual pursuits and romantic temperament. Pettigrew was proficient in at least four European languages as well as in Hebrew and Arabic, which he taught himself with the intention of writing a history of the Spanish Moors, whose chivalry and civilizing influence upon Europe he admired. He was said to be an accomplished musician and his mathematical ability was proverbial.

By the time of the Civil War Pettigrew was also an able, self-taught military engineer and artillerist. His chivalric gestures were frequent and unaffected. For example, he resigned as secretary of the U.S. Legation at Madrid when entreated to do so by the wife of a candidate for the office. He visited Cuba intending to take part in an expected revolt on that island. And several times he risked his life to nurse the sick and relieve the poor during epidemics. His subsequent career was a model of modest heroism. Pettigrew never married, although his name was linked by matchmakers to those of several notable South Carolina ladies at various times.

Elected to the South Carolina House of Representatives in 1856, Pettigrew rendered his most notable service in his presentation of a minority report that marshaled the arguments against reopening the foreign slave trade, a measure that had been endorsed by the governor and a legislative committee. (See the *Report of the Minority of the Special Committee of Seven, to Whom Was Referred So Much of Governor Adams' Message No. 1 As Relates to Slavery and the Slave Trade*, published at Columbia in 1857 and Charleston in 1858.) This paper was reprinted in *DeBow's Review*, attracted national attention, and together with Pettigrew's role as second in a duel in which a popular young editor was killed, secured his defeat at the next election.

Never an enthusiastic secessionist, Pettigrew had nevertheless become convinced from his association with Massachusetts students in Berlin that a sectional war in America was inevitable. He also believed that the war would be a long, massive, and desperate affair, not the short, decisive campaign that was commonly expected. To prepare himself he took an active part in the South Carolina militia throughout the 1850s. In 1859, when war broke out in Italy against the Austrians, Pettigrew hastened to Europe to fight for the liberty of the Italians and to experience war firsthand. He presented himself to Camillo B. di Cavour as an unpaid volunteer for the front, but hostilities ended before he saw action. He spent some time studying tactics and logistics with French officers, however, and after returning to Charleston was in demand as an instructor for the numerous active militia companies formed there in the months preceding the Civil War. He also published anonymously in *Russell's Magazine* (vol. 6, March 1860) a satire of the ineffectiveness of the militia together with recommendations for improvement.

As a result of his second trip to Europe he wrote a book entitled *Notes on Spain and the Spaniards in the Summer of 1859, With a Glance at Sardinia* (1861). Published privately amidst the distraction of Fort Sumter, it attracted little attention at the time but has been praised since by every critic who has read it. Ludwig Lewisohn, for instance, described it as "as interesting a volume of its kind as one can well imagine." The book is at the same time a travel account, an exploration of Spanish history, and a defense of the Spanish against Anglo-Saxon prejudices. It exhibits an intimate knowledge of the life of all classes as well as an attractive style, a capacity for humor, and a profound sympathy for Spanish temperament and traditions. Many of the Spanish characteristics he celebrated—individualism, personal pride, democratic manners, particularism, loyalty, devoutness, disdain for capitalist and utilitarian values—were not irrelevant to what he perceived to be the virtues of the Southern states in contrast to the Northern states, Great Britain, and Germany.

At the secession of South Carolina Pettigrew was appointed chief military aide of Governor Francis W. Pickens and elected colonel of the First Regiment of Rifles. It was Pettigrew who, early in the morning of 27 Dec. 1860, shortly after the Federal forces at Charleston were withdrawn inside Fort Sumter, carried to the Federal commander the governor's demand that the status quo ante be restored. The same day Pettigrew occupied the abandoned Castle Pinckney, and he remained on duty with the forces in Charleston harbor until the surrender of Sumter the next April. Declining several commissions and an invitation to go to Raleigh and electioneer for a high appointment in the North Carolina forces, Pettigrew went to Virginia as a private in the Hampton Legion. Nevertheless, he soon accepted election as colonel of the Twenty-second North Carolina Regiment, organized for regular Confederate service in August 1861. From September 1861 to March 1862 he was stationed on the lower Potomac.

Conspicuous for his ability and energy, Pettigrew was several times recommended for promotion to brigadier general. In a characteristic gesture he repeatedly declined the position, even after an interview with President Jefferson Davis, stating that no one should command a brigade who had not previously led men in action. Then at the beginning of the Peninsula campaign he accepted the commission and became one of the few general officers at that early period who had been neither a U.S. Army officer nor an influential politician. During the Battle of Seven Pines, on 31 May 1862, Pettigrew received a rifle ball through his throat and shoulder while advancing on an enemy position. Refusing to allow men to leave the ranks to carry him to the rear "because from the amount of bleeding I thought the wound to be fatal, [and] it was useless to take men from the field for that purpose," he barely escaped bleeding to death before his wounds were bandaged by a fellow officer. During a Federal counterattack he was shot again in the arm and bayoneted in the leg while he lay on the ground. Reported dead in the Confederacy, Pettigrew was picked up from the field the next morning by Federals, made prisoner, and gradually recuperated from his wounds. When exchanged he was assigned to command a brigade consisting of the Eleventh, Twenty-sixth, Forty-fourth, Forty-seventh, and Fifty-second North Carolina regiments. With these troops Pettigrew fought in a number of small battles in eastern North Carolina between September 1862 and the spring of 1863, including a successful independent action at Blount's Creek on 9 May in which he repulsed a Federal raiding column of superior force. During this period Governor Zebulon B. Vance and the state's members of the Confederate Congress petitioned unsuccessfully for Pettigrew to be assigned command in North Carolina. Highly regarded by both rank and file, Pettigrew deliberately set an example of patriotic sacrifice and cheerful endurance of privation. He lived on privates' fare and allowed himself no leave from duty.

In May 1863 Pettigrew's brigade joined the Army of Northern Virginia for the Pennsylvania campaign. On 1 July, in one of the bloodiest assaults of the war, Pettigrew's brigade drove some of the best Federal units from their position on McPherson's Ridge on the outskirts of Gettysburg. The division commander, Henry Heth, was wounded, and during the next two days of the Battle of

Gettysburg Pettigrew commanded his own and three other brigades. On the third day the severely reduced division, under Pettigrew, took part in the dramatic, unsuccessful, and controversial assault known to history as Pickett's Charge. In this attack Pettigrew's horse was hit and he was wounded in the hand; he was said to have been one of the last men to return to the Confederate lines. At Gettysburg Pettigrew's own brigade had the highest casualties of any in the army. During the retreat from Pennsylvania, at the Falling Waters just north of the Potomac early in the morning of 14 July, Pettigrew was shot in the stomach in a melee with a straggling Federal cavalry unit that had ridden into his resting troops by error. Pettigrew refused the immobilization that was the only hope of saving his life, commenting that he had rather die than be captured again. Remaining with the army, he was carried eighteen miles to Bunker Hill, (West) Va., where he died three days later at 6:25 A.M. at age thirty-five.

Slender, fair-complexioned, with piercing eyes and a conspicuously high forehead, modest, and ascetic, Pettigrew was dedicated to his society and his duties with a medieval intensity. A portrait in uniform hangs in the Southern Historical Collection at The University of North Carolina, and a prewar likeness appears in James Petigru Carson, *Life, Letters, and Speeches of James Louis Petigru* (1920). An Episcopalian, actually though not formally devout, Pettigrew was widely read in theology and expressed in his book considerable sympathy for Spanish Catholicism. He was buried at Raleigh on a day of public mourning and after the war was reinterred in the family ground at Bonarva.

Pettigrew's high intellect and chivalric temperament made a deep impression on his contemporaries. Scientist Matthew F. Maury called him "the most promising young man of the South." James Louis Petigru spoke of an intellect greater than John C. Calhoun's. English-born Collett Leventhorpe, who served in Pettigrew's brigade, remarked that he never met a man "who fitted more entirely my 'beau ideal' of the patriot, the soldier, the man of genius, and the accomplished gentleman." The South Carolina scholar William Henry Trescot wrote that Pettigrew alone was evidence that the Southern cause was "not wholly wrong." Cornelia Phillips Spencer said that there were many in North Carolina "who believed he was the good genius of the cause—he was the coming man who should yet guide us to victory." Douglas Southall Freeman wrote that for no officer who served with the Army of Northern Virginia so briefly were there so many praises while living and so many laments when dead. A well-informed student of the Old South, Clement Eaton found that "in no other Southerner did romantic ideals show to greater advantage than in James Johnston Pettigrew."

SEE: Sarah McCulloh Lemmon, ed., *The Pettigrew Papers*, vol. 2 (1988); Pettigrew Family Papers (North Carolina State Archives, Raleigh, and Southern Historical Collection, University of North Carolina, Chapel Hill); Clyde Wilson, "Carolina Cavalier: The Life of James Johnston Pettigrew" (Ph.D. diss., 1971, University of North Carolina), *Carolina Cavalier: The Life and Mind of James Johnston Pettigrew* (1990), and "The Most Promising Young Man of the South: James J. Pettigrew," *Civil War Times Illustrated* 40 (February 1973). (The sketches of Pettigrew in the *Dictionary of American Biography* and in Ezra J. Warner, *Generals in Gray*, contain minor inaccuracies.)

CLYDE WILSON

Pettigrew, William Shepard *(3 Oct. 1818–27 July 1900)*, planter and clergyman, was born at Bonarva plantation on Lake Scuppernong (now Lake Phelps) in Tyrrell County, the son of Ebenezer and Ann Blount Shepard Pettigrew. He was the older brother of James Johnston Pettigrew and the grandson of the Reverend Charles Pettigrew, first bishop-elect of the Protestant Episcopal church in North Carolina.

Pettigrew received his preparatory schooling at Hillsborough Academy. He attended The University of North Carolina from 1834 to 1837, studied law, and was awarded the A.M. degree in 1838. In 1837 he settled in Washington County at Belgrade, one of the Pettigrew plantations that was given to him on his twenty-first birthday by his father. Magnolia plantation, in nearby Tyrrell County, was a bequest to Pettigrew on his father's death in 1848. Pettigrew remained a planter on Belgrade and Magnolia plantations until Federal occupation of his home counties in 1863. Due to his poor health, summers during the planter years were often spent at the Virginia hot springs. During these and other absences he left the management of the plantations to two Negro slave foremen, Moses and Henry. Correspondence between Pettigrew and the foremen through a white intermediary is included in the Pettigrew Family Papers in the Southern Historical Collection at Chapel Hill.

A member of the North Carolina Secession Convention, Pettigrew was a former Whig who had opposed secession but became a secessionist when Abraham Lincoln issued his call for troops. Pettigrew joined the Senior Reserves of Edgecombe County in 1864. After the war he returned to the plantations and engaged for several years in various tenant arrangements that proved unsuccessful due largely to the depressed economy. He was ultimately forced to sell both plantations to pay his mounting debts and taxes.

On 31 Jan. 1869 Pettigrew was ordained a deacon in the Protestant Episcopal church at St. James's Church in Wilmington, and for a short time he officiated at St. David's Church in Scuppernong, where he had been a lay reader for two years. On 12 June 1870 Pettigrew was ordained a priest at St. James's Church, and in the same year he became rector of the Church of the Holy Innocents in Henderson and of St. John's Church in Williamsboro. In 1878 he resigned from the Henderson church and accepted the parish of the Chapel of the Good Shepherd in Ridgeway. He took over a mission at Middleburg in 1884 and served it, as well as the Williamsboro and Ridgeway parishes, until his death.

Pettigrew never married; a courtship disappointment at age twenty-seven permanently confirmed him in bachelorhood. He died at age eighty-one at the rectory in Ridgeway and was buried the following day in the nearby churchyard.

SEE: Daniel L. Grant, *Alumni History of the University of North Carolina* (1924); Sarah McCulloh Lemmon, ed., *The Pettigrew Papers*, vols. 1–2 (1971, 1988 [portrait]); John G. McCormick, *Personnel of the Convention of 1861* (1900); Pettigrew Family Papers (Southern Historical Collection, University of North Carolina Library, Chapel Hill); Protestant Episcopal Church *Journal* (1901).

BRENDA MARKS EAGLES

Petty, Annie Florence *(27 Aug. 1871–7 Dec. 1962)*, pioneer North Carolina librarian was born in the Bush Hill community (now Archdale), Randolph County, the daughter of William Clinton, a successful businessman, and Mary Victoria Petty. She was the fifth of seven children in a Quaker family, one in which books and a desire for knowledge were deemed important and religion was a part of everyday life. At the close of the Civil War, her father began to manufacture building supplies such as sashes, doors, blinds, and mantels; he also was engaged in building construction.

Annie Petty received a sound education at New Garden Boarding School and Guilford College, where she earned a degree in 1894. The following year she was employed as a teacher in Red Springs, then joined the staff of the State Normal and Industrial School in Greensboro (now the University of North Carolina at Greensboro). Though her title was that of librarian, as Miss Petty once explained, her duties were more nearly those of a general utility person because she found herself receiving and sorting mail, signing for express packages, and ringing the bell for the change of classes. The library was located in the Administration Building in a room of modest size; there were shelves around its walls and six tables to accommodate readers.

During the academic year 1898–99 Miss Petty attended the Library School of Drexel Institute in Philadelphia; after completing her studies she returned to Greensboro, where she remained as librarian for more than two decades. Active in efforts to promote libraries and library service beyond institutional boundaries, she was in 1904 one of the seven people—three women and four men—who founded the North Carolina Library Association, and she was promptly made a member of the executive committee. When the American Library Association and the North Carolina Library Association met jointly in Asheville in 1907, Annie Petty was elected second vice-president of the state association during its business session. In November 1908 she was elected president, and in 1913, at the annual meeting held that year in the town of Washington, she was reelected to that office.

On 8 Mar. 1909, while she was serving her first presidential term, the North Carolina legislature ratified a bill establishing the North Carolina Library Commission. Miss Petty was appointed to the commission in April 1918 at the recommendation of the North Carolina Library Association. In its issue for June 1918 the *North Carolina Library Bulletin* referred to the appointment as a peculiarly fitting one, stating that Annie Petty was not only North Carolina's first trained librarian but also had been identified closely with every movement for library development in the state, including the establishment of the Library Commission. She was reappointed for another three-year term in 1921 but resigned in September to accept the position of associate secretary for the commission. In her new work Miss Petty used her energy and intelligence to publicize the need for improved library service and to enlist citizen support. Indeed, one of the things in which she must have taken considerable pride was the beginning of bookmobile service to rural areas.

In 1933 Annie Petty retired and returned to the family home that she shared with her sister Mary in Greensboro. There she attended the First Friends Meeting, though her membership remained at Springfield Friends Meeting near High Point. At one time she was secretary of the North Carolina Friends Historical Society. Miss Petty was buried in the Springfield Meeting Cemetery. She was survived by two nephews, David and James Petty.

SEE: Eugenia Babylon, "History of the North Carolina Library Commission" (M.S. in L.S. thesis, University of North Carolina, Chapel Hill, 1955); Delta Kappa Gamma, *Some Pioneer Women Teachers of North Carolina* (1955); "Editorial Notes," *North Carolina Library Bulletin* 3 (1918); *Greensboro Daily News* (obituary), 8 Dec. 1962; Headstone marker, Springfield Meeting Cemetery, High Point; Elizabeth Holder, "History of the Library of the Woman's College of the University of North Carolina, 1892–1945" (M.S. in L.S. thesis, University of North Carolina, Chapel Hill, 1955); North Carolina Library Commission, *Fifth Annual Report, 1917–1918*; "Pioneer Educators Still Enjoy Campus Life," Raleigh *News and Observer*, 27 Jan. 1952; Louis R. Wilson, "The North Carolina Library Association, 1904–1909," *North Carolina Libraries* 13 (1954), and "The North Carolina Library Commission, 1908–1949," *North Carolina Libraries* 8 (1949).

J. ISAAC COPELAND

Petty, Mary Maria *(10 Nov. 1863–1 Jan. 1958)*, chemist and educator, was the pioneer woman chemist in North Carolina. Born in the Quaker community of Bush Hill (since 1887, Archdale), she was the third of seven children of William Clinton and Mary Victoria Petty. Her father's family was from Kentucky, her grandfather and his mother, a Macy, from Nantucket, Mass., and her mother's family, the Hayworths, had gone to Philadelphia with William Penn. William Clinton, though a farmer, had—perhaps more to his interest—made the first power loom shuttles for the South's cotton mills, invented a device to fit the shoes of Confederate soldiers with wooden pegs, and, in 1866, began to produce building supplies, the only business of its kind in a large area. Later he was the contractor for the old Trinity College buildings.

Mary Petty was first educated in a school in Bush Hill built by members of the community to supplement the three-month public schools and staffed by teachers from New Garden Boarding School (now Guilford College), Trinity College (Duke University), Haverford College, and other institutions from as far away as Indiana. She transferred to New Garden School, and in 1881 her father took her and a friend, Gertrude Mendenhall (who later was her faculty colleague for many years at Greensboro), by train and by ship, to Wellesley College. She received a bachelor's degree in chemistry in 1885, at a time when higher education for women was not at all widespread and emphasis on science in their education almost unheard of. Later she did graduate work at Bryn Mawr (1895–96) and in summer schools at Harvard, Cornell, and the University of California.

She first filled the chair—or, as she described it, the settee—of mathematics at Statesville College (later Mitchell College), and after a period in a Philadelphia hospital in 1888 was called to be one of the founding members of the faculty of Guilford College, where she taught mathematics, botany, history, Latin, and English literature. In 1893, one year after the opening of the State Industrial and Normal College (later the Woman's College of The University of North Carolina and then the University of North Carolina at Greensboro), she returned again from medical treatment in Philadelphia to join its faculty to teach physics, chemistry, and mathematics and in 1903 became head of the Department of Chemistry. She was the first female member of the American Chemical Society in North Carolina, was responsible for setting up the first chemistry laboratory for women in the state, and ultimately planned and saw built several buildings for chemistry as the institution grew. She set high standards for her students in this field opening to women and had to struggle to see that these standards were maintained. Her lectures were down-to-earth, exciting, inviting; she sent her classes to the Pomona clay pits to bring back the material to make crystals of alum; and soap—good soap! —was made with infectious enthusiasm. She succeeded in painting a broad background of the science for her students, but also in drawing many of them into the field for a career, contemporaries with Madame Curie.

Mary Petty retired in 1934, but for two more decades was active in the Woman's College, with an office in the administration building, as chairman of the social committee that she had many years before originated; her enthusiasm in planning activities for the faculty was legendary. In 1936 she was named the first woman trustee of Guilford College. In 1920 she had been one of three North Carolina delegates to the World Conference of Friends in London on world peace and was again a delegate to a similar conference in 1937. She was an organizer and then president of the Greensboro Women's Club, the first secretary of the North Carolina Federation of Women's Clubs, and for many years recording clerk of the North Carolina Yearly Meeting of Friends.

Never married, she lived at the family home in Archdale with other unmarried or widowed brothers and sisters in the summer, and on Ashe Street in Greensboro during the winter. Death came quietly for her at the Oakdale Nursing Home near Greensboro, and she was buried in Springfield Cemetery, near her childhood home.

SEE: Class of 1885, *Annals of the Class of 1885, Wellesley College*, 1930, 1935, Wellesley, Mass.; *Faculty Memorials, University of North Carolina at Greensboro*, 15 Apr. 1958; *Guilford College Bulletin*, January 1958; Raleigh *News and Observer*, 27 Jan. 1952.

MAURICE M. BURSEY
WILLIAM J. MEYERHOFFER

Petty, William Oscar *(13 Nov. 1845–28 Sept. 1926)*, educational administrator and clergyman, was the third child and oldest son of Charles and Harriett Lunsford Petty of Stafford County, Va. His boyhood was spent in nearby Fauquier County—to which his family had moved shortly after Petty's birth—where he attained the rudiments of an elementary education in the community schools of that region of the Old Dominion.

Following a term of service in the Army of Virginia as a private in Company G, Virginia Cavalry (the famed Mosby Raiders), Petty attended Richmond College for two years and Columbian College (now George Washington University) for three years. Meanwhile, the devastation of the Civil War, together with the early death of his father, had left him responsible for the welfare of his mother and five brothers and sisters—a responsibility that both interrupted the steady progress of his educational pursuits and contributed to later periods of chronic ill health.

Petty served as pastor of churches in the vicinities of Germantown, Montross, and Frostburg, Md. (1875–83). In September 1883 he moved to Louisville, Ky., where he spent one year in studies at the Southern Baptist Theological Seminary. Thereafter, for some eleven years he served as a pastor and missionary laborer among churches in the Santee, Welsh Neck, Broad River, and York Baptist associations in South Carolina, supplementing his meager income by teaching in local schools and academies. For the last thirty years of his life he engaged in schoolwork in Louisa County, Va., until his failing health made this no longer possible.

During his tenure as principal of York Academy in York, S.C., Petty was elected to the presidency of Chowan Female Institute (16 June 1896). The one year he spent at Chowan was marred by controversy between him and the Reverend Samuel Saunders, pastor of the Murfreesboro Baptist Church, whom the trustees of the institute had elected as an "associate to the president." Saunders eventually brought charges against Petty before the institute's board of trustees, accusing him of "setting me and my wife aside without cause"; employing a pedo-Baptist teacher; giving preference to the hiring of a less competent teacher over a more competent one; and seeking to justify himself by circulating slanders and attempting to divide the Murfreesboro church against Saunders. While passing no judgment on the merits of the charges preferred against him, the board of trustees requested and received Petty's resignation on 26 May 1897.

Petty married Annabel Veirs, of Calloway County, Mo., on 3 June 1879. They had four children: Herbert St. Clair (d. in infancy), Grace L. (m. Luther L. Fonville), Lydia Clare (m. Stanley Atwood Bowles), and Oscar Veirs. He was interred in Oakland Cemetery, Louisa, Va.

SEE: "Minutes of Board of Trustees, Chowan College," June 1896–Aug. 1897; *Religious Herald* (obituary), 23 Dec. 1926; Samuel Saunders to Board of Trustees of Chowan Female Institute, 12 Jan. 1897 (Trustee Record Books, Chowan College); George Braxton Taylor, *Virginia Baptist Ministers* (6th ser., 1935); J. F. Weishampel, Jr., *History of Baptist Churches in Maryland Connected with the Maryland Baptist Union Association* (1885).

R. HARGUS TAYLOR

Peyton, Benjamin *(ca. 1700–1748)*, colonial official and legislator, was born in Gloucester County, Va., the son of Robert Peyton. His grandfather, Robert Peyton, who settled in Virginia prior to 1680, was the son of Thomas and Elizabeth Yelverton Peyton of Rougham, County Norfolk, England. With the death of Sir John Peyton of Isleham without heirs in 1721, John Peyton of Gloucester County, Va., first cousin to Benjamin Peyton of Beaufort County, N.C., inherited the baronetcy.

Benjamin Peyton with his father and his brother Robert moved to North Carolina prior to 1728 and settled in what was then Beaufort Precinct of Bath County. There is some indication in the fragmentary records of Gloucester County that the elder Peyton was in financial difficulty. In 1731 Benjamin Peyton was a justice of Beaufort-Hyde and was listed as provost marshal or sheriff for Bath County, which at the time extended from the Albemarle to the Cape Fear. In 1738, when the precincts comprising it were themselves made counties, Bath County ceased to exist. At a session of the Assembly in 1731, Peyton was accused of having erased the name of the duly elected representative from New Bern Town and of having inserted the name of another person. In 1733 Mosely Vail, the clerk of the Assembly, complained that the register of Beaufort-Hyde having died, Benjamin Peyton had taken the writings and books belonging to that office, pretending to have a commission from the governor for the same, and carried them from the town of Bath against the law. Both of these accusations against Peyton probably involved his performance of his duties as chief officer or marshal of the county of Bath. Vail went on to describe Peyton as a person of ill fame and character. Whether or not this opinion was justified, Benjamin Peyton was elected to the Assembly from Beaufort County in 1739, a position to which he continued to be elected until his death. In 1745 he also was a commissioner of Bath Town and colonel of the county militia.

Benjamin Peyton resided at The Garrison, a plantation on Durham's Creek on the south side of the Pamlico. When he made his will on 30 Sept. 1746, he stated that he intended going on an ocean voyage. Peyton died in

Beaufort County. His will, probated late in that year, mentioned his wife, five daughters, his sloop *Savannah*, then on a trip to Boston, and the tract of land in Gloucester County, Va., that his father had formerly lived on.

Peyton married Eleanor (surname unknown), who had been married previously to a Mr. Bell. As Eleanor Peyton she left a will in Beaufort County, dated 1751 and probated in 1753. Benjamin and Eleanor Peyton were the parents of five daughters: Mary, Elizabeth, Sarah, Eleanor, and Grace. Mary married Captain Henry Snoad in the lifetime of her father. Elizabeth married first her cousin John Peyton Porter and second the Reverend Alexander Stewart. The daughters Sarah, Eleanor, and Grace are said to have married respectively, Thomas Bonner, William Tripp, and Lionel Reading.

SEE: John Burke, *Extinct and Dormant Baronetcies of England, Ireland, and Scotland* (1841); Walter Clark, ed., *State Records of North Carolina*, vols. 22–23 (1907); William A. Crozier, *Virginia Heraldica* (1908); Horace E. Hayden, *Virginia Genealogies* (1891); C. Wingate Reed, *Beaufort County* (1962); William L. Saunders, ed., *Colonial Records of North Carolina*, vols. 3–4 (1886).

CLAIBORNE T. SMITH, JR.

Peyton, John Lewis *(15 Sept. 1824–21 May 1896)*, European agent for the state of North Carolina (1861–65), lawyer, and author, was born near Staunton, Va., the son of John Howe and Anne Lewis Peyton. One of his great-grandfathers, Colonel William Preston, died of wounds received some years before at the Battle of Guilford Court House. Peyton attended the Virginia Military Institute and was graduated from the University of Virginia in 1844 with a law degree. He was practicing at Staunton when Secretary of State Daniel Webster sent him to Europe on a secret mission to England, France, and Austria.

During the period 1853–56 Peyton lived in Chicago, where he contributed to a number of periodicals and was assistant editor of W. W. Dannenhower's *Literary Budget*. He also was active in the National Guard with the rank of lieutenant colonel. At the recommendation of Stephen A. Douglas, President Franklin Pierce appointed him federal district attorney of Utah but because of ill health he declined the post and in 1856 settled again in Staunton. As a Whig he supported the Bell-Everett presidential ticket in 1860. An opponent of secession, he considered the election of Abraham Lincoln to be no cause for alarm. Following the secession of Virginia, however, he helped organize and largely equip a regiment of which he was made colonel, but because of physical infirmities he was unable to serve.

In the late summer of 1861, while drilling troops, he was appointed North Carolina's agent abroad by Governor Henry T. Clark and on 26 October sailed by way of Bermuda from Charleston aboard the Confederate man-of-war, *Nashville*. He landed at Southampton on 21 November and joined other Confederate agents and English sympathizers of rank and influence in London. They promptly set about to secure support and recognition of the Confederacy from Great Britain and felt that they might have succeeded if the home government had been more supportive at a critical time. Peyton remained in England at the end of the war and retired to the Island of Guernsey. He declined to renounce his claim to American citizenship in order to accept appointment to office in Guernsey and in 1876 returned to Staunton. Peyton was widely published, writing on such a variety of subjects as the trade of China, recollections of the Far West, and a history of Augusta County, Va.

He was married in 1855 to Henrietta, daughter of Colonel John Washington of Lenoir County, N.C. She was a niece of Governor William A. Graham and an aunt of Congressman William A. B. Branch. The Peytons were the parents of an only son, Lawrence Washington Howe. John Lewis Peyton died at his home, Steephill, near Staunton.

SEE: S. Austin Allibone, *A Critical Dictionary of English Literature*, vol. 2 (1899); *DAB*, vol. 7 (1934); *Nat. Cyc. Am. Biog.*, vol. 4 (1895 [portrait]); John Lewis Peyton, *The American Crisis; or, Pages from the Note-Book of a State Agent During the Civil War* (1867); *Who Was Who in America*, vol. 1 (1967).

WILLIAM S. POWELL

Pfohl, Bernard Jacob *(13 Sept. 1866–5 Dec. 1960)*, church musician, was the oldest son of Christian Thomas and Margaret Siewers Pfohl and the brother of Bishop John Kenneth Pfohl and Dr. Samuel Frederick Pfohl. In 1881 he was graduated from Salem Boys School, which his great-grandfather, the Reverend Christian Thomas Pfohl, had come from Saxony to Salem in 1791 to head and where his grandfather, the Reverend Samuel Thomas Pfohl, also had taught.

B. J. Pfohl began his business career at age fourteen when he went to work at the F. and H. Fries Cotton and Woolen Mills, where his father was in charge of the office. At thirty-two he became secretary of the Fries Manufacturing and Power Company, which was bought by Southern Public Utilities Company in 1913. Pfohl continued with this company as office manager, a position he retained when Southern Public Utilities was bought by Duke Power Company in 1935. Pfohl remained head of the office staff until his retirement in February 1958, shortly after his ninety-first birthday.

It was his leadership and long service in the Moravian Church Band that made Pfohl so well known and well loved by many generations of North Carolinians. As a young boy he began to play in the Home Moravian Church band and at seventeen became its leader. In 1889 he was made director of the Easter Band (the combined bands of the various Moravian churches, which played together in the graveyard for the famous dawn service). Under his constant care and direction for the next fifty-six years, this group grew from ten to more than five hundred players, the largest organization of its kind in the world. "Mr. B. J.," as he was affectionately known to his "band boys," rehearsed throughout the year a small segment of the large band and gave concerts during the summer on Salem Square. For that group he arranged secular music and for all the church bands he arranged the old Moravian chorales and other hymns. Dr. Douglas L. Rights, writing on the fifty-year celebration of Pfohl's directorship, praised "his patient and persistent leadership. . . . To be a bandman under him means more than musical training. It means a strong impartation of moral and cultural qualities. . . . Some impress of living character is seen wherever we find his boys." In addition to the band parts booklets of Moravian hymns, Mr. B. J. published a history of the organization, *The Salem Band* (1953).

From the time of his confirmation at age fifteen until his death at ninety-four, Pfohl was a devoted member of the Home Moravian Church, serving it chiefly through his work with the church band but also, for a time, as a member of the Board of Central Elders of Salem Congregation. He was one of the founders of the Wachovia Historical Society in 1897 and a charter member of the Winston-Salem Kiwanis Club. In 1956 Moravian College (Bethlehem, Pa.) conferred on him the honorary doctor of humane letters degree.

On 21 Feb. 1901 Pfohl married Sarah Elizabeth Traeger, and they had three children: Joseph Thomas, Henry Clauder, and Katherine Adelaide, all of whom became professional musicians. B. J. Pfohl died in Winston-Salem, where he had spent all of his life, and was buried in God's Acre, the Moravian cemetery.

SEE: Anna W. Bair (personal recollections); "Memoir of Bernard Jacob Pfohl" (Moravian Church Archives, Winston-Salem); *North Carolina Biography*, vol. 5 (1919); *Winston-Salem Journal-Sentinel* (numerous articles and portraits).

ANNA WITHERS BAIR

Pfohl, John Kenneth *(13 Aug. 1874–27 Nov. 1967)*, was the 229th bishop of the worldwide Moravian church and the 167th bishop of the Renewed Moravian church. For thirty-one years he proclaimed "The Lord is Risen" to open the Easter sunrise service of the Home Moravian Church in Winston-Salem, to which the congregation waiting outside in Salem Square responded, "The Lord is risen, indeed." The services were first carried by the local radio station, WSJS, in 1932, then by CBS and NBC radio networks; they were subsequently sent overseas by the Voice of America and during World War II the broadcasts were heard by America's armed forces. At one time, more people heard the sunrise services than any other religious service in the world.

Bishop John Kenneth Pfohl was "a son of the Moravian Church." His ancestry went back to the founding days of the Ancient Unitas Fratrum (Unity of Brethren of Bohemia), and his forebears in the Renewed Unity were largely engaged in the service of the church. Two great-great-grandfathers were ministers; one of them was a missionary to the West Indies. Two great-grandfathers were ministers in the Wachovia Tract—the first settlement of the Moravians in North Carolina. His grandfather was a minister as well as the treasurer of Salem Congregation, where his father was an elder for twenty-three years.

John Kenneth was the fifth child of six born to Christian Thomas and Margaret Siewers Pfohl. He attended Aunt Sophia Pfohl's School, Salem Boys School, and Moravian College; he received an A.B. degree from The University of North Carolina in 1898 and a B.D. degree from the Moravian Theological Seminary at Bethlehem, Pa., in 1900. Pfohl's first service to the church was as a teacher. He was the first principal of Clemmons School, which opened in October 1900. While there he met Bessie (Harriet Elizabeth) Whittington, of East Bend, who was the music teacher for the lower grades. They were married on 21 Aug. 1901, and she immediately joined him in his work for the church. During this period he also was ordained a deacon of the Moravian church on 15 Sept. 1901 by Bishop Edward Rondthaler. In July 1903 he received his first pastorate, at Christ Church in Salem, where he served for a little more than five years; he was ordained a presbyter at the Triennial Provincial Synod of 1905 by Bishop Rondthaler. On 1 Nov. 1908 he was transferred to the Home Church, where he served as pastor for almost twenty-six years.

In 1912 Pfohl began to hold dinner meetings in his home to which he invited community leaders from the two neighboring towns and the participants formed the Cosmos Club, which provided the impetus for the consolidation of Winston and Salem in 1913. In 1914 he was a delegate to the General Synod at Herrnhut, Germany. In 1922 he attended the Unity Conference and took part in its important postwar deliberations.

He was elected to the Southern Provincial Elders' Conference in 1920 and succeeded Bishop Rondthaler as president in 1929, thereby making him chairman of all the Provincial boards. After Rondthaler's death, a special Provincial Synod was held on 14 Apr. 1931, and Pfohl was elected bishop on the first ballot. He was consecrated on 26 Apr. 1931. On 2 May of the same year he became the pastor of Salem Congregation. He attended the General Synod of 1931 as bishop and as delegate of the Southern Province of the Moravian church. During much of World War II, with the church's Continental Province unable to function, Bishop Pfohl was the actual executive head of the worldwide Moravian church. When the Foreign Missionary Society of the Moravian Church, South, was formed on 29 Apr. 1923, Pfohl became its first president, a position he held until 1935, when Dr. Edmund Schwarze took over.

Pfohl received a doctor of divinity degree from Moravian College in Bethlehem (1921) and an honorary D.D. from The University of North Carolina (June 1940). He was president of the Salem College trustees, a trustee of Moravian College and Seminary, president of the North Carolina Council of Churches, and president of the Winston-Salem Ministerial Association.

In November 1953, at age seventy-nine and after having served for twenty-four years as president of the Provincial Elders' Conference of the Southern Province, Pfohl asked to be relieved of that office. He expressed a "hope and purpose to continue" serving the church, including performing his duties as senior pastor of Salem Congregation.

For forty-five years Bishop and Mrs. Pfohl hosted a New Year's Vespers in their home for all Moravian ministers and their wives from the Southern Province; they held their last vespers in 1964. As much a tradition as the Easter sunrise service for Pfohl were the annual love feasts for employees and trainees of Goodwill Industries. He conducted them for thirty years, missing his first one in 1965 because of a broken hip. The bishop believed that the church should be a powerful influence in the community—and he used his office to see that it was. In the 1940s and 1950s it was widely accepted that community projects had to be cleared first with the mayor of Winston-Salem, then with Pfohl, and finally with the people. Told about this, the bishop laughed and said, "Thank the Lord someone has to feel they must consult God's church. As long as they come to me, we will do our best to guide them correctly." His acceptance by all areas of the community was reflected in an introduction by a Jewish merchant ("Here, I want you to meet *our* Bishop") and by the honorary D.D. conferred on him in June 1966 by Wake Forest University, a Baptist institution.

To be opposed to Bishop Pfohl on a public question was, according to an old friend, "an invigorating intellectual experience." He had a great love for his state and spoke appreciatively of the fact that at one time he was the oldest living alumnus of The University of North Carolina. Pfohl also loved history—both the history of the church and the history of Salem. In answer to the complaint that the Moravian church was the "hard-to-understand" church, he wrote an eight-page pamphlet in which he packed a brief history of the church, what the church stood for, and its distinguishing characteristics. One minister reported, "Those eight pages reached more people for the Moravian Church than a thousand sermons." From it grew the book *The Moravian Church: Yesterday and Today* (1926), of which he was coauthor with

Dr. Adelaide L. Fries, archivist of the Moravian Church, South. As senior pastor of the Salem Congregation he wrote the annual "Memorabilia" delivered on New Year's recounting the principal events of the past year.

Possessing an almost photographic memory, he could recite unbelievable portions of Scriptures flawlessly. Music was also a vital part of his life, and he had a rich, baritone voice that he used not only for preaching but also for singing God's praise. In his early years he often ended a morning sermon with a solo. Music often brought the Pfohl family together in his home and he played the flute at musical gatherings. He had a wonderful sense of humor and a joyous quality to his laughter. All who knew him remember "the twinkle in his eye and the wink he gave to a point that hit home." This humor enabled him as an administrator to relieve tense situations as well as "marked the down-to-earth humanity of this great saint of God."

At age ninety-three Bishop Pfohl died at his home just a short walk from the entrance of God's Acre, the Moravian graveyard, where he was buried. His portrait, painted by Otto John Hershel, was presented by the artist on 5 May 1946 to the Home Moravian Church to hang in the church office. Pfohl and his wife, who died on 23 Nov. 1971, had six children: Margaret Elizabeth (Mrs. Edmund Campbell) of Arlington, Va.; Mary Dorothea (Mrs. Vernon Lassiter) of St. Petersburg, Fla.; Ruth Whittington (Mrs. Roy Grams) of Whittier, Calif.; John Kenneth Pfohl, Jr., of Roswell, Ga.; James Kenneth Pfohl of Reston, Va.; and Donald Lawrence Pfohl, who died on 16 Sept. 1940.

SEE: Adelaide L. Fries and John K. Pfohl, *The Moravian Church, Yesterday and Today* (1926); Rt. Rev. Kenneth G. Hamilton, *History of the Moravian Church, 1722–1957* (1967); James C. Hughes, *Remarks at the Funeral of Bishop John Kenneth Pfohl* (1967); Rt. Rev. Edward Rondthaler, *Memorabilia of Fifty Years, 1877–1927* (1928); *Winston-Salem Journal-Sentinel*, 27–29 Nov. 1967.

JOHN THOM SPACH

Pfohl, Samuel Frederick *(29 May 1871–18 Jan. 1961)*, the beloved and highly venerated "Doctor Fred" of Salem, was a practicing physician who continually served the citizens of Winston-Salem and Forsyth County for sixty-three of his eighty-nine years. Born the fourth of six children to Christian Thomas and Margaret Siewers Pfohl, he was a direct descendant of two of Salem's pioneer Moravian families. His mother taught at Salem Academy and Salem College from 1859 to 1865. Baptized when he was three months old, he confirmed his Christian faith on 14 Nov. 1886, at age fifteen, and joined the Home Moravian Church. Pfohl began his education at Salem Boys School, where he was a serious, scholarly student. For a brief period he worked as a carpenter, but with the encouragement of his close friend and cousin, Dr. Nathaniel Siewers, he entered the medical school of the University of Pennsylvania, from which he was graduated in 1893 at age twenty-two. Believing that his medical knowledge was inadequate, he remained at the university for another year and received two diplomas. Although an internship was not required in those days, he served on the staff of the Boston Emergency Hospital for three years to gain clinical experience. Then, at the request of Dr. Siewers, he returned to Salem to begin practicing in September 1897.

Pfohl's services as a physician in North Carolina date from the horse-and-buggy days, and he frequently operated by lantern light with his patients on kitchen tables. He delivered hundreds of babies for the families of the then two towns, Winston and Salem, and there came to be an uncountable number of male citizens of the consolidated city who bore the name of Frederick Pfohl in his honor and for the affection their parents felt for this gentle, unselfish man. Since opening his first office in his parents' house, Pfohl always worked out of his home. After building his residence on South Main Street in Salem in 1913, he opened his office there in order to spend as much time as possible with his family.

On 14 Jan. 1903 he married Rose Hoffman Haas at the home of her relatives in Washington, D.C. A native of Woodstock, Va., she was an attractive, red-haired nurse at the University of Maryland when she brought a patient from Baltimore to the Twin City Hospital of Brookstown Avenue in Winston for treatment and there met the quiet, skillful doctor for the first time. They had three children: William Frederick, Richard Haas, and Virginia.

When Dr. Pfohl was inclined to enter military service at the time of World War I, townspeople persuaded him to remain at his practice in Salem. He always answered the call where he was needed most, as when he gave up his surgical practice, his first professional love, to become a general practitioner. He was a member of the City Memorial Hospital staff from the day it opened in 1914. Pfohl was one of the first members of the Forsyth County Medical Association, as well as a member of state and national associations. For a number of years he served as a county physician, and from 1917 to 1957 he was the physician for Salem Academy and Salem College; he was also a trustee at both institutions. It is believed that he brought the first electrocardiograph machine to Winston-Salem following his return to the University of Pennsylvania for advanced training in 1931. Although a general practitioner, Pfohl did a great deal of work in cardiology, and he practiced in obstetrics until he was in his fifties.

Stories of his generosity are numerous and consistent with his character. He often paid for the medicine that he prescribed for hospital charity patients. He is known to have taken blankets from his home and given them to needy patients. He always made low charges and never sent bills or used collectors. A modest, reticent man, Pfohl shunned publicity and this led a newspaper reporter to observe: "Though he was a man of few words, he conveyed love, understanding, and selflessness in service which can be described, not as a profession, but as a ministry." He read and studied to keep abreast of the latest information and techniques, which caused one intern to tell a relative that he was ashamed because he knew Dr. Pfohl spent more time in study than he did. A reluctant conversationalist, Pfohl was asked by a Salem medical student why he did not talk more; reportedly he replied: "What I don't say, I don't have to take back." His unique sense of humor, when it did reveal itself by spoken word, often delighted and surprised his patients. He once informed a charming, but talkative female patient that he had declined her offer to be his blood donor during an illness because he was afraid that if he received her blood, he would start talking and never stop!

The one certain way to make this quiet man speak was to mention Roan Mountain; then his love for nature and especially trees revealed itself in knowledgeable, enthusiastic words. The native rhododendron gardens at the summit of the western North Carolina mountain had been the object of many family excursions throughout the days of horseback and the early Ford automobile. It was not unusual for Salem students to find Pfohl on campus standing in silent admiration before a tree whose majestic fall or spring beauty had caught his eye.

Despite failing health, he continued his practice until a

month before his death, when he was admitted to City Memorial Hospital. He died only a few hours after the medical staff of the hospital adopted a resolution honoring him for more than sixty years of service to the community. Pfohl was buried in the Moravian graveyard, God's Acre, of the Home Church on 20 January. His portrait, painted by George Lynch in 1972, was hung in the Craig Conference Room of the Forsyth County Memorial Hospital.

Bernard J. Pfohl, Dr. Pfohl's older brother, was the band director at the Home Moravian Church for more than fifty years and advanced the Easter Band from about a half dozen to over four hundred instruments. John Kenneth Pfohl, Pfohl's younger brother, was a Moravian bishop of the Southern Province and devoted a lifetime to the promotion of religion. After fifty-four years of marriage, Rose Haas Pfohl died on 21 Feb. 1957. William Frederick Pfohl, Dr. Pfohl's eldest son, died on 30 Sept. 1949; and Richard Haas Pfohl died on 5 May 1971. Surviving him were his daughter Virginia and three grandchildren.

SEE: "Memoir of Brother Samuel Frederick Pfohl" (Church Office, Home Moravian Church, Winston-Salem); Dorothy R. Niflong, *Brethren with Stethoscopes* (1965); Raleigh *News and Observer*, 19 Jan. 1961; *Winston-Salem Journal-Sentinel*, 18–20 Jan. 1961.

JOHN THOM SPACH

Phenney, George *(d. April 1737)*, governor of the Bahama Islands, customs collector in the southern colonies, and Council member, served effectively in the Bahamas from 1721 to 1727, between the two administrations of the famous Woodes Rogers. He was efficient and well liked; his wife also was popular and acted as courier on at least one occasion, taking letters from the governor to London. After leaving the governorship, he was accused of impropriety in court martialing an officer against whom he had a grudge and confining him in a dungeon for eighteen months. There also was fear that his actions might contribute to the return of pirates to the islands.

On 3 Dec. 1731 Phenney sought appointment as surveyor general of customs for the Southern District in America as well as a seat on the councils of those colonies. His appointment came on 24 Feb. 1732, when he was also named to the councils of Virginia and South Carolina; membership on the North Carolina Council, in which he took an active part, was added on 30 Nov. 1733. Phenney took up residence in North Carolina, although the date of his arrival in the colony is unknown. The fate of his first wife is also unknown, yet his marriage to Penelope Golland Lovick, the stepdaughter of Governor Charles Eden, took place in North Carolina after 25 June 1734. Eden had died on 26 Mar. 1722 at Eden House on the west bank of Chowan River, across from Edenton. Penelope Golland became one of the wealthiest women in the province and was for a long time mistress of Eden House, Governor Eden's wife having died on 4 Jan. 1716 at age thirty-nine.

Eden House, noted for its "splendid hospitality" and the "refined society generally assembled there," became the residence of Phenney and his new wife. Penelope, incidentally, was married four times: first to Colonel William Maule; second to Captain John Lovick, secretary of the province, at one time sole owner of Roanoke Island; third to George Phenney; and finally to Governor Gabriel Johnston. Johnston governed the colony for eighteen years (1734–52), longer than any other governor—Proprietary, royal, or state.

The Southern District for which Phenney was surveyor general of customs consisted of Pennsylvania, Maryland, Virginia, North Carolina, South Carolina, the Bahama Islands, and Jamaica. Perhaps he regarded North Carolina as a central location. His will, dated 23 June 1736, was probated on 23 June 1737. The bulk of his estate was left to his wife with provision for a then unborn child. In fact, she gave birth to a son about four months before Phenney's death. The *Virginia Gazette* of 6 May 1737 reported that the death of this son a short while before "afflicted him so much, that it occasioned his Death."

SEE: *Calendar of State Papers, Colonial Series, America and West Indies*, vols. 32–40 (1933–39); Michael Craton, *A History of the Bahamas* (1962); J. Bryan Grimes, ed., *North Carolina Wills and Inventories* (1912); Cyrus H. Karraker, *Piracy Was a Business* (1953); Robert E. Lee, *Blackbeard the Pirate* (1974); William L. Saunders, ed., *Colonial Records of North Carolina*, vol. 3 (1886); William A. Shaw, ed., *Calendar of Treasury Books and Papers*, vol. 2 (1898).

ROBERT E. LEE

Phifer, Edward William (Ned), Jr. *(13 Aug. 1910–19 Feb. 1980)*, surgeon and historian, was born in Morganton, the son of Edward William and Susan Presnell Phifer. Following graduation from Morganton High School in 1928, he entered Davidson College and received an A.B. degree in 1932. Phifer studied medicine at The University of North Carolina (1933–35) and at Harvard University, where he obtained his M.D. in 1937. After a period as an intern at Yale–New Haven Hospital in New Haven, Conn. (1937–38), and a surgical residency at Long Island College Hospital in Brooklyn, N.Y. (1939–42), he entered military service. From October 1942 to November 1945 Phifer served in the U.S. Army Medical Corps as captain and then major, with twenty-eight months in the African and Italian campaigns, working with a general hospital and auxiliary surgical group.

Son of a well-known surgeon and chief of staff of Grace Hospital in Morganton, the young doctor returned to his hometown to practice surgery; he, too, served as chief of staff of Grace Hospital. He was president of the Burke County Medical Society (1949), charter member and (in 1956) president of the North Carolina Surgical Association, a Fellow of the American College of Surgeons, diplomate of the American Board of Surgery, a trustee of the Regional Health Council of Eastern Appalachia; surgeon of the Southern Railway System; and member of the Society of Southern Railway Surgeons. He belonged to Phi Chi medical fraternity.

Edward W. Phifer, Jr., M.D., was also Edward W. Phifer, Jr., historian. An avocation grew into a full-time occupation following retirement from the practice of surgery early in 1979. His first published article appeared in the *North Carolina Historical Review* in January 1959. This essay, "Certain Aspects of Medical Practice in the Ante-Bellum Era," was followed by others: "Champagne at Brindletown: The Story of the Burke County Gold Rush, 1829–1835"; "Money, Banking, and Burke County in the Ante-Bellum Era"; "Saga of a Burke County Family," a three-part study of the Averys; and "Religion in the Raw: Cyclone Mack in Burke County, August–September, 1920." In 1963 he received the Southern Historical Association's biennial Ramsdell Award for the best article in the *Journal of Southern History*; the winning essay, entitled "Slavery in Microcosm; Burke County, North Carolina," appeared in the May 1962 issue. Phifer was also the author of *Burke: The History of a North Carolina County*, published in 1977 as part of the county's bicentennial observance. From this book, the North Carolina Division of Archives and History published a pamphlet for its county history series.

Publishing was only one facet of Dr. Phifer's historical interests. A leader in founding the Burke County Historical Society in February 1959, he was elected its first president. On 22 Apr. 1961 he was chosen to serve as vice-president of the Western North Carolina Historical Association; in the fall of 1972 he was elected a member of the council of the Historical Society of North Carolina, and four years later, vice-president; and on 9 Nov. 1979 he was chosen president of the North Carolina Literary and Historical Association. Governor Terry Sanford named him to the executive board of the State Department of Archives and History on 16 July 1963, and Governor Robert W. Scott reappointed him on 22 Aug. 1969. Phifer served on that board (later known as the North Carolina Historical Commission) until 9 June 1975. In the summer of 1978 he accepted appointment to a five-year term as a member of the Advisory Editorial Committee of the *North Carolina Historical Review*. Phifer became a member of the North Carolina Society of the Cincinnati in 1967 and a member of the Courthouse Restoration Commission in Burke County in 1974.

His service went beyond the fields of medicine and history. A member of the board of trustees of Davidson College (1961–69), Phifer sat on its executive committee. In 1958 he was made a trustee of the Morganton-Burke Public Library, a post he held until his death. He was elected to the board of education for the Morganton City Schools for the years 1967–69. A leader in the founding of Western Piedmont Community College in Morganton, Phifer was the first chairman of its board of trustees and was again serving in that capacity at the time of his death. His service as a member was unbroken.

The Morganton surgeon was one of a small group who brought professional baseball to his hometown in the 1940s, when the Morganton Aggies was formed. The team played for several years. Phifer was president of the Morganton Kiwanis Club (1963), director (1967) and vice-president (1968–69) of the Burke County Chamber of Commerce (1967), treasurer of the Burke County Democratic Executive Committee (1963–64, 1974), and director of Dacotah Cotton Mills, Lexington, and of the Morganton branch of the North Carolina National Bank. In 1963 he was named Morganton's Man of the Year.

On 5 Nov. 1938 Phifer married a nursing graduate of Yale University, Mary Adair Edwards of Orlando, Fla. They had a son, Edward W. Phifer III, and five daughters: Adair (Mrs. John W. Crute, Jr.), Susan (Mrs. George Dean Johnson, Jr.), Mary Phifer Frye, Nancy Welcome, and Martha Avery, who died in 1976.

Dr. Phifer died after an illness of several months. His funeral was held at Morganton's First Presbyterian Church, which he had served as an elder. He was buried in Forest Hill Cemetery, Morganton.

SEE: *Biennial Reports*, State Department of Archives and History (1962–64, 1968–70) and North Carolina Division of Archives and History (1974–76); Wake Bridges, "Historian: Burke Surgeon Makes Switch," *Hickory Daily Record*, 18 Jan. 1979; "Burke Surgeon, Historian Dies," *Hickory Daily Record*, 20 Feb. 1980; Adair Phifer Crute (Raleigh), personal contact; "Noted Doctor-Historian Dies," Morganton *News-Herald*, 20 Feb. 1980; *North Carolina Historical Review* and *Carolina Comments* (various issues).

MEMORY F. MITCHELL

Phifer, Martin (or Fifer, Fiffer, Phieffer, Pheiffer, Phyfer, Pfifer) *(18 Oct. 1720–18 Jan. 1791)*, planter, colonial militia officer (major), colonial assemblyman, member of the North Carolina House of Commons, and justice of Mecklenburg County Court, was a native of Switzerland. Tradition has it that he was born in the canton of Berne, but better evidence indicates that he came from the village of Hafelfingen, district of Homburg, canton of Basel. He sailed from Rotterdam in 1736 on the *Harle* and landed in Philadelphia. Sometime between 1751 and 1756 he migrated from Pennsylvania to North Carolina and settled on Big Cold Water Creek (before 1750 located in Bladen, after 1750 in Anson, and after 1 Feb. 1763 in Mecklenburg County). On 1 Oct. 1745 he had married Margaret Blackwelder (1722–1803), a native of Holland who may also have sailed on the *Harle*.

In North Carolina Martin Phifer prospered and advanced rapidly in politics, in wealth, and in the militia. From the mid-1750s to the early 1760s he served the colony as a commissary officer provisioning the Indians who cooperated with the settlers during the intermittent raids associated with the French and Indian War. He was also elected to the lower house of the Assembly and was seated on 6 Feb. 1764. During the Regulator uprising he was a loyal supporter of the colonial government. In 1767, when Governor William Tryon made his celebrated march from Salisbury to the Cherokee nation to survey the boundary line, he halted for the night of 22 May at the plantation of Major Phifer, who was continuing to serve as one of his officers. Also, when the militia was called out in August-September 1768 because of unrest at Hillsborough, Governor Tryon was quartered periodically at Major Phifer's home and used his plantation as a rallying point for the militiamen. This plantation continued to be the site for holding the general muster of the Mecklenburg Regiment until at least 1779.

Phifer continued to serve in the lower house of the colonial Assembly (1764–68, 1773–75) and in the House of Commons of the new state (December 1776–77). In 1773 he cosponsored, with Griffith Rutherford, a bill to establish a new county from western Rowan (in 1777 it was finally established as Burke County) and, with John Davidson, sponsored a bill to establish a "Public Seminary of Learning in the Western part of this Province [North Carolina]." In an ordinance passed in the convention of 1776 (this probably refers to the last Provincial Congress of 1776), Martin Phifer was appointed one of the eighteen justices of Mecklenburg County Court of Pleas and Quarter Sessions.

Martin and Margaret Blackwelder Phifer had three children: John (1747–78), Caleb (1749–1811), and Martin, Jr. (1756–1837). Major Phifer was a Protestant and his biographers state that he was of the Lutheran denomination. It is of interest to note that he had fast friends in the Moravian settlements and, with his wife, visited Bethabara and Bethania on at least three occasions: sometime prior to 9 Nov. 1762, on that date, and on 12 May 1770. At the time he made his will in 1789, he owned eighteen slaves, a gristmill, and three plantations. One plantation, Red Hill, was located on the western outskirts of present Concord between U.S. 29 and North Carolina 49. A second, five miles west of Concord on Buffalo Creek, was inherited by his son Caleb, and a third plantation, Cold Water, where he himself lived and died was located on Cold Water Creek about 3–4 miles due east of the center of Concord off North Carolina 73. Phifer also had landholdings on Mecklin's Fork of Lyles Creek in present Catawba County that he divided equitably between his heirs. He was buried "at the Phifer graveyard, three miles from Concord near the old road leading from Charlotte to Salisbury."

SEE: Walter Clark, ed., *State Records of North Carolina*, vols. 11–12, 22–23 (1895–1904); A. B. Faust and G. M. Brumbaugh, *List of Swiss Emigrants in the Eighteenth Century to the American Colonies* (1968); Adelaide L. Fries, ed., *Records of the Moravians in North Carolina*, vol. 1 (1922); Charles H. Phifer, *Genealogy and History of the Phifer Family* (1910); Major Martin Phifer [Sr.], will, 1789 (Mecklenburg County Courthouse, book 1, p. 37); William S. Powell et al., comps. and eds., *The Regulators in North Carolina* (1971); William L. Saunders, ed., *Colonial Records of North Carolina*, vols. 5–7, 9–10 (1887–90); Ralph B. Strassburger, ed., *Pennsylvania German Pioneers: A Publication of the Original Lists of Arrivals in the Port of Philadelphia from 1727 to 1808* (1934).

E. W. PHIFER, JR.
NANCY W. PHIFER

Phifer, Martin, Jr. (see Martin Phifer for name variations) *(25 Mar. 1756–12 Nov. 1837)*, planter, soldier, millwright, and huntsman, was born at his father's plantation, Cold Water, which at that time was located in Anson County but after 1762 in Mecklenburg and after 1792 in Cabarrus County. He was the third son of Martin Phifer, who had recently migrated from Pennsylvania, and his wife, Margaret Blackwelder Phifer, a lady of German descent. Young Phifer was educated at the same school with his two older brothers, John and Caleb.

On 15 Apr. 1776, by act of the Fourth Provincial Congress, he was appointed to the rank of captain and "ordered by the State of North Carolina to raise the second troop of light Dragoons." Three such companies of light horse were authorized, although they were not mentioned in the resolves from the Continental Congress. After raising the troop he marched it to Charleston but arrived two or three days after the British attack on Sullivans Island (28 June 1776). Some months later his troop (Independent Company of North Carolina Light Horse in Continental Service) was transferred to the northern army. It remained there until the spring of 1778, when it was discharged by the Board of War for lack of horses, equipment, and provisions. (Captain Phifer's appointment is listed as extending from March 1777 to April 1780, but these dates do not coincide with his pension deposition of 1832.)

From his father Phifer inherited Cold Water plantation and two-thirds of a tract of land on Mecklin's Fork and Lyle's Creek in present Catawba County. He also received military land warrants for 1,149 acres in present Tennessee and purchased two large grants (2,373 acres and 5,000 acres) in the "Middle District" (probably present Bedford County) of that present state. In addition to farming, he operated successfully as a millwright, "being regarded as the most skillful in that trade of anyone in that country." In politics he was an anti-Jacksonian and in religion he was a Protestant of the Lutheran denomination. He did, it is interesting to note, maintain a friendly relationship with the Swiss Moravians at Salem since he is known to have visited them at least once (23 July 1778).

"In personal appearance," says one biographer, "Martin had much to be admired. He was six feet in height, of great strength and vigor . . . and was considered the best looking of his father's children and the handsomest man in all that part of the country. Of his domestic character, frugality was not a part of it, and on the reception of his friends, his house was open to all." When President George Washington toured the South in the spring and early summer of 1791, he lodged on the night of 29 May at Major Martin Phifer's residence, an estimated twenty-two miles from Charlotte on the road to Salisbury.

On 5 Nov. 1778 he married Elizabeth Locke (1758–91), daughter of General Matthew Locke of Rowan County. The children of this marriage were John, George, Mary, Margaret, and Ann. When Captain Phifer's brother John died suddenly in 1778, Martin moved from his father's house at Cold Water to Red Hill, his brother's home on the old road from Salisbury to Charlotte, about three miles west of Concord off the present Poplar Tent road, in order to care for John's family. When his father became infirm, he moved back to Cold Water and remained there for many years after his father's death. In his last years he lived with his son John at the Black Jacks, a plantation adjoining Red Hill, where he died at 9:00 A.M. According to Society of Cincinnati records, Martin Phifer, Jr., was the last surviving officer of the North Carolina Continental Line.

SEE: Walter Clark, ed., *State Records of North Carolina*, vol. 24 (1905); Curtis Carroll Davis, *Revolution's Godchild* (1976); Douglas Southall Freeman, *George Washington: A Biography* (1954); Adelaide L. Fries, ed., *Records of the Moravians in North Carolina*, vol. 1 (1922); Francis B. Heitman, *Historical Register of Officers of the Continental Army during the War of the Revolution* (1893); Military Land Warrants, Continental Line (North Carolina Secretary of State's Office); Military Service Records (National Archives, Washington, D.C.); Charles H. Phifer, *Genealogy and History of the Phifer Family* (1910); Hugh F. Rankin, *The North Carolina Continentals* (1971); John H. Wheeler, ed., *Reminiscences and Memoirs of North Carolina and Eminent North Carolineans* (1966).

E. W. PHIFER, JR.
NANCY W. PHIFER

Phifer, Robert Fulenwider *(19 Nov. 1849–16 Oct. 1928)*, first benefactor of the North Carolina Museum of Art, was born in Concord, the fifth of seven children. His father was Caleb Phifer, a prosperous merchant involved in the cotton trade, railroads, and other commercial enterprises; his mother was Mary Adeline Ramsour of Lincolnton. His great-grandfather, Martin Phifer, Jr., a large landowner and millwright, was personally visited at his home, Red Hill in Mecklenburg County, by General George Washington on his southern tour in 1791. His grandfather, John (Jack) Phifer, a merchant in Concord, represented Cabarrus County in the North Carolina Senate and House of Commons.

In September 1863, at age fourteen, Phifer entered Davidson College, where he made excellent grades in all subjects except deportment and had a reputation as a lively youth. Two and a half years later, in December 1865, he left Davidson when the faculty and his parents turned down his request to take an "irregular course." Thereafter Phifer engaged in merchandising in Newberry, S.C., as a planter and cotton buyer. He was a good businessman, made excellent financial investments, and became a man of substantial means.

In 1881, on the advice of physicians, he gave up business and went to New Orleans for several years. It was probably there that he acquired his taste for beauty, for his principal interests became painting, travel, and golf. He studied art both in London and Paris and once on a two-year trip around the world, he spent six months traveling and painting with a band of Japanese artists. After leaving New Orleans, Phifer took up residence in

New York City, where he joined the Salmagundi Club and the Calumet Club, two men's societies composed of artists and art enthusiasts. He acquired works of many members of the Salmagundi Club for his own collection.

In his later years Phifer became very concerned with finding a home for his paintings, a place where they would be well cared for and where many people would benefit from them. He sought a group that would not only take care of his collection but also use it as a basis for forming an art museum in the state; however, no such group seemed to exist. The towns of Concord and Charlotte were approached, but he was apprehensive about how the art would be maintained as neither of these towns had an art museum. In 1927, after reading an article in the *Magazine of Art* about the formation of the North Carolina State Art Society, which in that year received its charter, Phifer wrote to John J. Blair, director of School House Planning (now the State Department of Public Instruction), the first president of the Art Society and a personal friend. In his letter, Phifer told Blair that he wished to find a home for his collection and inquired about the society's organization and facilities for displaying and caring for art works. Blair responded with enthusiasm and arranged an exhibition of part of the Phifer Collection at the 1927 State Fair. This exhibit was well received by the public. Later that year Phifer sent ten paintings for the annual meeting of the Art Society.

The exchange of letters between Phifer and Blair continued, and in October 1927 Phifer put clauses in his will bequeathing his art collection to the Art Society with additional funds, held in trust, to become available under certain conditions. A letter written from a sanatorium in Battle Creek, Mich., on 28 Dec. 1927 informed Blair of the changes in his will in regard to his art collection and also his concern for his failing health. A few weeks before his death Phifer wrote in a shaky but still fine hand, "I feel now that any pictures I may leave the Art Society will be properly shown. . . . I wish the Society great success."

One year after his death, when the Art Society was informed of its share in Phifer's estate, Dr. Clarence Poe, then chairman of the executive committee for the North Carolina Art Society, stated that the final settlement of Phifer's estate assured a minimum of one-quarter of a million dollars for the State Art Museum, with the possibility that the amount might greatly exceed this figure.

Though he had never mentioned bequeathing anything other than his art works to the Art Society, the major portion of Phifer's estate, with a net worth of $1,172,834 according to a transfer tax appraisal filed in New York on 29 Aug. 1929, was to be placed in a trust for four principal beneficiaries who were all close relatives. Should these relatives leave no heirs, the North Carolina Art Society was to inherit their share of the Phifer trust. Eventually, all four portions of this trust, with its considerable interest, did pass into the hands of the Art Society. In 1960 the society presented the Phifer Collection to the state of North Carolina so that it now belongs to the North Carolina Museum of Art. In accordance with Phifer's will, the trust, still administered by the Art Society, has been and will continue to be used only for the purchase of works of art. For many years the trust Phifer left, both monetary and in his personal art collection, was the backbone of the Art Society, holding it together in its struggle to bring art to the people of North Carolina.

Phifer never married. He died in Battle Creek, Mich., and was buried in the Memorial Garden of the First Presbyterian Church, Concord.

SEE: Ola Maie Foushee, *Art in North Carolina: Episodes and Developments, 1585–1970* (1972); "Last Will and Testament of Robert F. Phifer" (North Carolina Collection, University of North Carolina, Chapel Hill); Raleigh *News and Observer*, 30–31 Aug. 1929, 17 Nov. 1968; *Robert F. Phifer Collection* (1973); George E. Wilson, *Genealogy and History of the Phifer Family* (1910).

ADAIR PHIFER CRUTE

Philips, Abraham *(25 June 1755–23 Mar. 1836)*, militia general and state legislator, was born in England and settled in northern Guilford (now Rockingham) County by 1778. His home, which was still standing in the late 1970s, was located on Great Rockhouse Creek, where he eventually had a 700–acre plantation and by 1830 a total of thirty-one slaves. In addition, Philips owned 800 acres in other tracts in the county, and in 1789, for his Revolutionary War service, he received 1,500 acres on the Big Hatcher River in the future state of Tennessee.

In the Revolution Philips served in the county militia as a sergeant, an ensign, and finally a captain in command of a company. In March 1781, when General Nathanael Greene's army was encamped in the county at Speedwell Furnace on Troublesome Creek, Philips was a scout and guide for Colonel William Washington's cavalry. In the fall of 1781 the county militia was recruited in the campaign commanded by General Griffith Rutherford that forced the British to evacuate Wilmington. In this campaign Philips was captain of his company; in a brief narrative he wrote about his experiences, he mentioned being in five skirmishes with Tories. He remained a militia officer after the war and by November 1810 had become colonel in command of the Rockingham County regiment. In May 1811 he was elected brigadier general of the Fourth Division and served until his resignation in 1817.

By February 1783 Philips was deputy surveyor of Guilford County, and in December 1785 he was named a commissioner to survey a line to divide Guilford County to create the new county of Rockingham. He was elected county surveyor of Rockingham at the first court in February 1786 and served in this position for many years, surveying the earliest towns in Rockingham County, Leaksville (1795) and Wentworth (1799). Appointed a county justice on the first court, he was a justice for over forty years. Through the years Philips was on a number of important county commissions, among them the commissions responsible for the promotion of the county seat at Wentworth, for construction of the courthouse and jail, and for establishing the county poorhouse. In 1807 he was elected chairman of the county court.

On the state level Philips had a long and worthy political career. He was a delegate to both state conventions to consider ratification of the federal Constitution. The Rockingham County delegation was anti-Federalist and consistently opposed ratification. Philips was elected to the state House of Commons for three terms (1788–90) and to the North Carolina Senate for nine sessions (1797–99, 1801–3, 1812–14). In the General Assembly he served on the committee of propositions and grievances and of privileges and elections. A Jacksonian Democrat, he was a presidential elector in 1828.

On 9 Dec. 1784 Philips married Cynthia Lanier (1761–1837) of Guilford County, and they had six children: Mary (Polly), Pleasant, Charles, Elizabeth, Isaac, and James. With the exception of Polly, who married and lived in Rockingham County, the children emigrated to Georgia and later to Russell County, Ala. Philips died at his home and was buried in a marked grave nearby.

SEE: Robert W. Carter, Jr., "Old Sandy Cross Homes and Families," *Journal of Rockingham County History and Genealogy* 1 (October 1976); Betty Cartwright and Lillian Gardner, *North Carolina Land Grants in Tennessee, 1778–1791* (1958); John L. Cheney, Jr., ed., *North Carolina Government, 1584–1974* (1975); Walter Clark, ed., *State Records of North Carolina*, vols. 21–22 (1903–7); Guilford County Deeds; Abraham Philips Journal, 1781 (Miscellaneous Revolutionary Papers, Library of Congress); Rockingham County Deeds and Wills; U.S. Census 1810, 1830; S. F. Webster and Linda Vernon, eds., *Early Families of the N.C. Counties of Rockingham and Stokes with Revolutionary Service* (1977).

LINDLEY S. BUTLER

Philips, James Jones *(12 Mar. 1798–10 Apr. 1874)*, physician and planter, was born in Edgecombe County, the son of Frederick and Sally Tartt Philips and the grandson of Hartwell Philips, who moved from Surry County, Va., and settled on Swift Creek in Edgecombe in 1763. Hartwell Philips married in North Carolina Pheraby Jones, the daughter of James Jones of Halifax County.

Frederick Philips, the father of Dr. Philips, represented Edgecombe in the General Assembly in 1797 and was at times a schoolteacher and county surveyor. On 22 July 1830 he advertised "The Hickory Grove Academy" in the Tarboro *Free Press* being four miles from Teat's Bridge. The terms of tuition were six dollars for five months of reading, writing, and arithmetic and twelve dollars for students who wished to study surveying. In a letter, dated Manor Hill 16 Sept. 1815, Frederick Philips wrote his cousin Joseph Philips of Sugar Tree Grove near Nashville, Tenn., that his son James, then eighteen, was attending the academy in Tarboro and was a good scholar. He added that James expected to finish his Latin Studies that year and would then go to Raleigh to complete his education.

James Philips decided to become a physician and entered the office of a neighbor, Dr. Cullen Battle, as a medical student. He later attended a series of medical lectures at the University of Pennsylvania. About this time his father had had financial reverses and sold his last remaining slave, a valuable carpenter, to finance his son's attendance at the lectures in Philadelphia.

It is not known when Dr. Philips returned to his native county to practice. However, he had become established by 1822, as he was in that year one of the physicians involved in the so-called North Carolina Accident, a smallpox epidemic in the town of Tarboro and the surrounding county. In 1821 the Vaccine Institute, established in Baltimore by the federal government in 1813, had appointed Dr. John F. Ward as agent for Edgecombe County. In December 1821 Ward was accidentally sent some material containing small pox instead of cow pox. Ward vaccinated several persons and gave some of the material to James Philips and other physicians who did likewise. Philips and Ward soon saw that the patients vaccinated showed mild cases of smallpox. They obtained the proper vaccine from physicians in neighboring areas and vaccinated as many persons as they knew had been exposed to those improperly vaccinated. In spite of their efforts, fifty people in the county contacted small pox and several died. As a result of the public reaction and through the efforts of the North Carolina delegation in Congress, the Vaccine Institute was unfortunately closed.

Over the years, Philips developed a reputation as a physician of unusual skill and enjoyed a large practice in Edgecombe and the surrounding counties. He himself had several students living in his home as apprentices, including Dr. Newsome J. Pittman of Tarboro, a Dr. Reid, and Dr. Franklin J. Hart.

In the first half of the nineteenth century, it was a rare physician who could support a family on his practice alone. James Philips was as well known as a planter as a doctor. He was one of the earliest in the state to advocate the use of fertilizer and his efforts on his own plantation were met with marked success. In 1852 he addressed the Edgecombe Agricultural Society on the application of chemistry to agriculture. In a newspaper controversy with Dr. Elisha Mitchell of Chapel Hill regarding soil analysis, his views were considered to be more thoughtful and progressive.

In 1827 Philips bought a plantation five miles northeast of present-day Rocky Mount and established his residence there; he named the place Mount Moriah. The doctor was active in Masonic circles, and in 1827 the North Carolina Assembly established a Masonic lodge called "Mount Moriah" on the lands of James J. Philips. It is not known how long the lodge was in operation, but the hall was later used as a schoolhouse. In 1850 the house was considerably enlarged.

On 23 Apr. 1834 Philips married Harriet Amanda Burt, the daughter of William Burt of Hilliardston, Nash County, and his wife Susan Sims. Dr. and Mrs. Philips had five sons and five daughters who reached maturity. The oldest son, Frederick of Tarboro, was for many years a superior court judge. The second son, James, was killed in the Civil War at age nineteen. Of the other sons, Joseph B. represented Nash County in the legislature for several sessions, and John and Walter resided in Edgecombe County. Sallie, the oldest daughter, married Frank Parker, later a colonel in the Confederate army. Susan married J. J. Battle and Elizabeth wed G. C. Battle. Harriet, another daughter, married Benjamin Bunn of Nash County, a member of Congress. Laura became the wife of John Peter Arrington, of Nash County, son of Congressman Archibald Hunter Arrington. Dr. Philips and his wife were both buried in the family cemetery at Mount Moriah.

SEE: William W. Boddie, "The Philips Family," in *Southside Virginia Families* (1956); James Jones Philips Papers (Southern Historical Collection, University of North Carolina, Chapel Hill); Walter Everett Philips, "Memoirs" (mimeographed, Southern Historical Collection, University of North Carolina, Chapel Hill); S. S. Satchwell, *Memorial Address* read before the Medical Society of North Carolina (1892).

CLAIBORNE T. SMITH, JR.

Phillips, Charles *(20 July 1822–10 May 1889)*, professor of engineering and mathematics and Presbyterian minister, was born in Harlem, N.Y., the oldest of three children of James and Julia Middagh Vermeule Phillips. His father operated a successful school for boys in Harlem; his mother was a member of a Dutch family long established in New Jersey. There is some evidence that James and his brother Samuel Field Phillips, sons of a Church of England rector, changed their surname from Postlethwaite to Phillips when they emigrated from England to New York in 1818.

Charles Phillips moved with his family to Chapel Hill in 1826, when his father was appointed to the chair of mathematics and natural philosophy at The University of North Carolina. He received his A.B. degree from the university, where he was a member of the Dialectic Society in 1841, sharing first honors in his class with his younger brother Samuel Field. A wide range of interests complicated his decision about a choice of professions. Phillips first read medicine for a time with Chapel Hill physician William Jones. Deciding on a career in the ministry, he entered Princeton Theological Seminary in the summer of 1843. Problems with his health and subsequent pressure from family and friends led to a decision to postpone his religious training, and in July 1844 Phillips accepted a call from President David L. Swain to return to The University of North Carolina as his father's assistant. In that year he also received his M.A. degree from the university. Phillips held a position as tutor of mathematics, with a specialization in applied math, until 1853, when he was elected to the newly established chair of civil engineering. He spent the summer and fall of that year in study at Harvard College and assumed his post in January 1854. In 1860 he was named professor of mathematics. For many years Phillips served as secretary of the faculty, assisted in the preparation of the annual catalogue, and wrote newspaper articles about university affairs. He was also author of a textbook entitled *A Manual of Plane and Spherical Trigonometry; With Some of Its Applications* (1857).

Even after he was well established in a successful teaching career, Phillips's commitment to the ministry remained vital. In December 1857 he was licensed to preach by the Presbytery of Orange and on 14 Apr. 1866 he was ordained at Orange County's New Hope Church, which had long been under the pastoral charge of his father. From 1857 to 1868 he served as stated supply for the Chapel Hill Presbyterian Church. Phillips also contributed his time as teacher and superintendent of the church Sunday school and, with his wife, inaugurated a Negro Sunday school. At the commencement of 1868, his contributions to his church and community were recognized when he was awarded a doctor of divinity degree by The University of North Carolina.

With the reorganization of the university by the state's Reconstruction government in 1868, Phillips was dismissed from the faculty. In February 1869 he found a position as professor of mathematics at Davidson College. Together with other clerical members of the faculty, he was also designated stated supply by the congregation of the Davidson College church. When in 1875 The University of North Carolina reopened (due in large part to the determined efforts of his sister Cornelia Ann Phillips Spencer), Phillips was invited to return as professor of mathematics. During the first year of his second association with the university, he served as chairman of the faculty. Also in 1876 he received an LL.D. degree from Davidson College. In 1879 the rheumatic gout that had plagued him for many years forced his retirement from the faculty. He then became professor emeritus of mathematics, the first individual to have that title bestowed upon him by the trustees.

Phillips married the former Laura Caroline Battle, youngest child of Edgecombe County businessman Joel Battle and Mary (Pretty Polly) Johnson and sister of judge and professor of law William Horn Battle. Their union in December 1847 marked the first time a college tutor had married; this infraction of the rules was, however, tolerated and the ban on such marriages was subsequently dropped. The couple had eight children: Julia Vermeule, Charles, Mary, James Tifton, William Battle, Alexander, Lucy, and Susie.

A virtual invalid for the eleven years preceding his death, Phillips left Chapel Hill in the company of his wife and youngest daughter on 29 Apr. 1889 to live with his sons William and Alexander in Birmingham, Ala. He died en route at the Columbia, S.C., home of his daughter Mary (Mrs. John S.) Verner and was interred in the family plot in Chapel Hill. On his death the family home was sold to the Presbyterian church and became its manse. A portrait of Phillips is at the University of North Carolina in Chapel Hill.

SEE: Richard H. Battle, "Memoir of Rev. Charles Phillips," *N.C. University Magazine*, n.s. 10 (1891); Hope S. Chamberlain, *Old Days in Chapel Hill* (1926); Daniel L. Grant, *Alumni History of The University of North Carolina* (1924); Cornelia Spencer Love, *When Chapel Hill Was a Village* (1976); Charles Phillips Papers (Southern Historical Collection, University of North Carolina, Chapel Hill); Lucy Phillips Russell, *A Rare Pattern* (1957); Phillips Russell, *These Old Stone Walls* (1972); *Sketches of the History of the University of North Carolina, Together with a Catalogue of Officers and Students, 1789–1889* (1889); Cornelia Phillips Spencer, "Old Times in Chapel Hill, No. XII: The College Tutor," *N.C. University Magazine*, n.s. 8 (1889); "University Notes," 15 May 1889 (Clipping File, North Carolina Collection, University of North Carolina, Chapel Hill); "University Record," *N.C. University Magazine*, n.s. 8 (1889).

KATHERINE F. MARTIN

Phillips, Fitzroy Donald *(23 May 1893–19 July 1982)*, attorney and judge, was born in Laurinburg, the son of Robert D., a lumberman, and Anna McLean Phillips, a first cousin of Governor Angus W. McLean. He received his early education in the public schools of Florida, where the Phillips family engaged in manufacturing and merchandising lumber. After attending the Georgia Military Academy, Phillips entered the University of Georgia in 1911, studied at the University of Florida for a brief time in 1913, and enrolled as a law student at The University of North Carolina for the year 1913–14. In both Georgia and Chapel Hill he was a member of Kappa Sigma fraternity, and at The University of North Carolina he also played football—he was the last surviving member of the team of 1913. Although he had not completed the law course, he applied to the state law board; after examination, he was admitted to the state bar in 1914. He returned to Laurinburg and entered the practice of law with W. S. Thomas in 1915.

In May 1917 Phillips volunteered for military service and in September was commissioned second lieutenant in the infantry. Ordered overseas, he saw action on five fronts. While attached to the 125th Infantry, 32nd Division, in the region of the Alsace-Lorraine, he took part in the Battle of Chateau Thierry. He later was in battles in the Soissons sector and on the Meuse. At the Argonne offensive, he fought for twenty-one days in a continuous battle. He was awarded the Croix de Guerre by the French government and cited by the American commander for bravery. In 1919 he was discharged following service with the Army of Occupation.

Phillips returned to Rockingham, where he discovered that he had been elected mayor in his absence. He filled this post for two years before resuming his law practice with Thomas. When his partner was elected clerk of court, Phillips formed a new partnership with J. C. Sedberry in Rockingham for the general practice of law. In 1923 he was elected solicitor of the Thirteenth Judicial District, composed of Richmond, Anson, Union, Scotland, Moore, and Stanly counties—a post he held for twelve years. In 1934 he was elected a superior court judge and remained in that post until his retirement in 1962. Except for the time in Nuremberg, Phillips served his district for twenty-eight years.

In 1946–47, after World War II, the United States participated in the International Military Tribunal that tried twenty-two Nazis in Nuremberg. President Harry S Truman designated F. Donald Phillips one of the judges. The jurists were divided into six courts of three judges each with four alternate judges. Sitting at the head of his court, Phillips tried all of the war criminals at Nuremberg assigned to it; nineteen were convicted and twelve were sentenced to death.

A Democrat, a member of the Methodist church, and an active Mason, Phillips was married on 12 Nov. 1925 to Octavia S. Scales, daughter of Walter Leak and Panthier Stauback Scales of Rockingham. They were the parents of two children, F. Donald, Jr., and Octavia Scales. He died in Rockingham and was buried in Eastside Cemetery.

SEE: Daniel L. Grant, *Alumni History of the University of North Carolina* (1924); Hamlet *News-Messenger*, 6 Nov. 1951, 22 Jan. 1960; *North Carolina Biography*, vol. 3 (1929 [portrait]); Judge and Mrs. Phillips, personal contact; Raleigh *News and Observer*, 20 July 1982; Records of the American Legion, North Carolina Adjutant (Raleigh).

F. CRAIG WILLIS

Phillips, Guy Berryman *(26 Nov. 1890–11 Feb. 1968),* educator, was born in rural Randolph County, southwest of Asheboro, the eldest child of Jessie Lee and Fannie Polk Waddell Phillips. A successful farmer, Jessie Lee Phillips had visions of education for his children and moved in 1899 from his original homeplace to a newly acquired farm near the village of Trinity, the original site of the school that later became Trinity College and in 1924 became Duke University.

Guy Phillips's elementary and secondary education were acquired in the local schools at Trinity, and he was the sole graduate of the high school in the class of 1909. His high school years were marked by many extracurricular activities, especially baseball. His leadership was evidenced by a high scholastic record and participation in many school projects. In 1909 he enrolled in a 188-member freshman class at The University of North Carolina. Four years later (1913) he was graduated with a bachelor of arts, one of 76 classmates who received a degree that year.

His first teaching post was at the Raleigh High School, where he taught English and coached the football and baseball teams, one of his teams winning a state championship at Chapel Hill; he also coached championship debating teams. In the summer of 1916 Phillips became superintendent of the city schools of Oxford and for four years (1916–20) provided superior educational and community leadership in that Granville County town. The Bank of Oxford lured him from schoolwork for a short tenure. He was assistant cashier of the bank until February 1921, when he accepted an invitation to become principal of the Greensboro High School. In 1924 he went to Salisbury as superintendent of city schools and then returned to Greensboro as head of the city's school system where he served for seven years (1929–36).

From the beginning of his career Guy Phillips attracted statewide attention as a public school educator. He attended graduate schools at the University of Chicago and Teachers College of Columbia University, N.Y., where he earned a master of arts in education in 1942. Ten years later High Point College awarded him an honorary doctor of literature degree (1952).

Invited to return to The University of North Carolina in 1936, he became professor of education and held the post for the rest of his life. Phillips was given a special assignment to revitalize relationships between the university and the state's public school system. In addition to his regular duties as superintendent of schools in Salisbury and Greensboro, he had taught and directed the summer session of Catwaba College and subsequently taught similar sessions at the University of North Carolina at Greensboro (then called Woman's College) and later at The University of North Carolina. His background in both high school and college levels equipped him for his work at Chapel Hill, a position in which he soon became known as "Mr. North Carolina Public Education."

Among his many services over the years, Phillips organized the North Carolina High School Athletic Association (1920) and was executive director for twelve years (1920–32). From the beginning he was active in the North Carolina Education Association (board of directors, 1920–56; president, 1934–35) and was a life member of the National Education Association, attending the annual sessions of both groups and serving on many of their committees.

Three gubernatorial appointments provided a broader base for his interests and leadership. He was a member of Governor Angus McLean's Commission to Study Problems of Negro Education in North Carolina (1927) and of Governor Clyde Hoey's Commission on Education (1937), serving as executive secretary and editor of its formal report to the governor. In 1957 Governor Luther Hodges appointed him to the State Board of Education, a post he held until his death, where he was chairman of the Policy Commission. He was also by special appointment a founder and member of the board of directors of the Learning Institute of North Carolina (1963).

During his long tenure at The University of North Carolina, he served in many capacities: respected counselor and assistant to the presidents and chancellors, director of the Teacher-Placement Bureau, adviser in the General College, director of the Summer Session, acting director of Admissions (1941–45), and executive officer of the College for War Training (1943–46). The School of Education was discontinued in 1933 but reestablished in 1948, when Guy Phillips was unanimously chosen dean and served for six years (1948–54), earning for the school recognition by the National Council for the Accreditation of Teacher Education. His superb leadership showed itself in the multiple acknowledgments accorded both his undergraduate and graduate programs in education. Upon retiring from the deanship in 1954, he continued to teach educational administration for seven years and during that period directed seventeen doctoral dissertations. Through those years he remained active in the work of the National Association of Public School Administrators, which he had helped organize in the early 1940s.

A group of his colleagues summarized Guy Phillips's accomplishments by listing the following improvements in the public education system of North Carolina: lengthening of the school term to nine months, addition of the twelfth year, establishment of a school bus transportation system, consolidation of schools, training of laymen to serve as school board members, establishment of the United Forces for Education which initiated much of the basic educational legislation of the previous two decades in North Carolina, professional training and improvement of school administrators, raising the basic salary scale for teachers and other school personnel, reduction of the teacher-pupil load, involvement of laymen and college teachers with professional educators in a statewide study of the school curriculum and teacher education, a new form of certification for teachers that emphasized subject matter preparation and institutional responsibility, establishment of the State Department of

Community Colleges, responsible and effective attention to problems of desegregation in the schools, and responsible and effective utilization of federal aid in the public schools.

Conspicuous among his early educational activities was the organization of the North Carolina State School Board Association. For thirty years he was both executive secretary-treasurer and editor of its bulletin or a consultant to the group. With a reputation as a good writer, his contributions were mainly limited to educational journals, although he participated in more than thirty surveys of state school systems and himself wrote many of the reports.

As a speaker Phillips traveled all over the state to address educational gatherings. In one way or another he continually emphasized public education and insisted that the schools meet the demands of the times, present and future. He was an avid worker in civic groups in all the places he lived and became at one time a national member of the Board of Advisers of the Boy Scouts of America. In Greensboro he was a member of the Recreation Commission (1930f.) and in Chapel Hill he was civilian defense coordinator (1940–45).

For several years he was a director of the North Carolina Association for the Blind and the North Carolina Conference for Social Services, and for the latter group he served as state chairman for the preparation of the North Carolina Report for the White House Conference on Children and Youth.

From his early years Guy Phillips was an ardent churchman. He taught in Methodist Sunday schools (1909–66) and served in multiple capacities in the lay leadership of his church, both locally and at the Conference level.

He married, on 17 June 1917 in Timmonsville, S.C., Annie Elizabeth Craig, then of Monroe, a graduate of Meredith College and the daughter of a distinguished Baptist minister and a niece of Locke Craige, a governor of North Carolina. She was born in Ahoskie (1895) and died in Greensboro (18 Sept. 1975) at age eighty. Guy and Annie Phillips had five children: Helen (Mrs. A. W. Graham), Guy Berryman, Jr., Charles C., Andrew Craig, and Robert L. All of the children were graduated from The University of North Carolina.

Phillips retired in 1961 and moved to Greensboro in 1966. He died in Greensboro and was interred in the Chapel Hill Cemetery.

SEE: Data sheet, Alumni Office, University of North Carolina, Chapel Hill; Daniel L. Grant, *Alumni History of the University of North Carolina* (1924); In Memoriam, State Board of Education (5 Apr. 1968); In Memoriam by five professors (colleagues) at the University of North Carolina, Chapel Hill: A. K. King (chairman), John B. Chase, Jr., J. Minor Gwynn, R. B. House, and Arnold Perry; Obituaries: *New York Times*, 13 Feb. 1968, *Greensboro Daily News* and other North Carolina dailies, 12 Feb. 1968.

C. SYLVESTER GREEN

Phillips, James *(22 Apr. 1792–11 Mar. 1867)*, educator and clergyman, was born at Nevenden, Essex, England, a small village about twenty miles northeast of London. He was the second of the three sons of the Reverend Richard Phillips, rector of the parish, and Susan Meade Phillips. James's mother died when he was about seven, and in 1800 his father moved to Roche, Cornwall, where he married again and James's older brother, John, died. There were children by Richard Phillips's second marriage, and conflict with their stepmother drove James and his remaining brother, Samuel, from the home. The break was so complete that neither James nor Samuel ever saw their father again. Samuel entered the British navy, and James worked as a bookkeeper in Plymouth, an important seaport during the war with Napoleon then in progress. James soon taught Latin in a boys' school, meanwhile studying higher mathematics on his own. While living in Plymouth, he once saw Napoleon pacing the deck of the *Bellerphon* just before he was carried into exile on St. Helena.

Following Samuel's discharge from the navy at the end of the war in 1815, the two Phillips brothers emigrated to the United States. Arriving in New York, they soon found employment as teachers in a boys' school and within a few months established their own private academy for boys in Harlem, then a separate town from New York City. In 1821 James Phillips married Judith Vermeule of Plainfield, N.J. A well-educated young woman, who had been taught Latin, Greek, and French, she was a descendant on both sides of old, prominent Dutch families of New York and New Jersey.

In 1826 Phillips became professor of mathematics and natural philosophy at The University of North Carolina. After about 1835 most of his teaching was in mathematics. An industrious scholar and an exacting teacher, he wrote out in full many of the lectures he gave his advanced classes, reporting in clear, elegant prose the results of the latest research. He was the author of a textbook, *Elements of the Conic Section* (1828). A sturdy, heavy-built man with an iron constitution, he was feared by students because of his burly appearance and brusque speech as well as his reputation—deserved or not—for skill in fencing and the use of the single stick. The knotted walking stick he habitually carried was a thing of awe.

In 1832 Phillips joined the Presbyterian church and soon became active as a lay preacher. In 1833 he was licensed to preach by Orange Presbytery and in due time was ordained and installed as minister of the New Hope Presbyterian Church, located about seven miles outside of Chapel Hill. He shared the work of the university chapel with Professor Elisha Mitchell and spent much of his summer vacations making evangelizing tours across the state. He studied theology, as he had mathematics, on his own, reading the standard works in the field, and became a recognized scholar in divinity. In 1851 The University of North Carolina honored him with the D.D. degree. Apparently Phillips was not a political activist, but his sympathies seemingly lay with the Whigs.

At about 9 o'clock one morning, as he was waiting to begin a class in geometry, Phillips fell dead in his classroom. He was buried in the Chapel Hill Cemetery. His carefully chosen library, mostly theological, was later donated to the university by his daughter. An oil portrait of Phillips by William Garl Brown, signed and dated 1859, is owned by the Dialectic Society of The University of North Carolina.

Each of the three Phillips children played a significant role in the history of the state. The oldest, Mrs. Cornelia Phillips Spencer (1825–1908), was a writer of note and has been given much credit for the reopening of The University of North Carolina (1875) after Reconstruction. The second, Charles Phillips (d. 1889), was a Presbyterian minister and taught mathematics at both The University of North Carolina and Davidson College and engineering at The University of North Carolina. The youngest, Samuel Field Phillips (d. 1903), was an attorney and legal educator. He served as state auditor during the first term (1862–65) of Governor Zebulon B. Vance and as U.S. solicitor general under President Ulysses S. Grant.

SEE: Kemp P. Battle, *History of the University of North Carolina*, vol. 1 (1907); Hope Summerell Chamberlain, *Old Days in Chapel Hill: Being the Life and Letters of Cornelia Phillips Spencer* (1926); Charles Phillips Papers and Cornelia Phillips Spencer Papers (Southern Historical Collection, University of North Carolina, Chapel Hill, and North Carolina State Archives, Raleigh); Charles Phillips Russell, *The Woman Who Rang the Bell: The Story of Cornelia Phillips Spencer* (1949); L. R. Wilson, ed., *Selected Papers of Cornelia Phillips Spencer* (1953).

W. CONARD GASS

Phillips, Samuel Field *(25 Feb. 1824–18 Nov. 1903)*, solicitor general of the United States and Republican political leader during Reconstruction, was born in Harlem, N.Y., the son of the Reverend James Phillips, a native of England, and Judith Vermeule Phillips of Plainfield, N.J. In 1826 the family moved to Chapel Hill, N.C., where James Phillips accepted a professorship of mathematics, which he held until his death in 1867. Samuel, along with his brother Charles and sister Cornelia (later Cornelia Phillips Spencer), was tutored by his parents at home. He then entered The University of North Carolina, graduating with first honors in 1841 at age seventeen. After studying law under President David L. Swain and then at the newly established university law school, he was admitted to the bar and began a practice in Chapel Hill as soon as he came of age in 1845.

Phillips was married twice, first in 1848 to Frances Lucas, of Chapel Hill, who bore him eight children before her death in 1883. One son and four daughters survived him. His second wife, whom he married in 1889, was Sarah Maury of Washington, D.C. She died in 1902.

According to his associates Phillips possessed a brilliant, reflective mind and a dispassionate temperament. His legal practice got off to a slow start in Chapel Hill, but he quickly developed into one of the most successful and respected lawyers in the state. From 1854 to 1859 he taught in the university law school. At the same time he embarked on a political career of some distinction. A Whig in politics, he was elected to the House of Commons in 1856 and 1858 and took an influential part in its proceedings. He opposed secession but accepted the decision when it was made. During the war he served on the state Court of (War) Claims, and when that body was superseded by the office of state auditor, he became its first incumbent. He was again elected to the House of Commons in 1864 and 1865 and unanimously chosen speaker in the latter year. Elected also to the constitutional convention of 1865, he was one of its leading members.

The advent of congressional Reconstruction caused Phillips some indecision. As a consistent Whig he never affiliated with the Democratic party, but he refrained from joining the Republicans formally until 1870. Instead, he devoted himself to his growing law practice. He moved to Raleigh in 1867 after forming a partnership with R. H. Battle; a later partner was Augustus S. Merrimon. From 1866 to 1871 Phillips was official reporter of the state supreme court. In 1870 he served on a three-man panel appointed to investigate alleged frauds in the state government.

On joining the Republican party, Phillips was at once admitted to its inner councils. He received the nomination for attorney general in 1870 but was narrowly defeated in a race that also saw the Democrats win control of the legislature. The next year he was elected to the legislature from Wake County (he had previously represented Orange), becoming Republican house leader. During the successful 1871 and 1872 campaigns, he served as chairman of the Republican state executive committee. In the same years, as an assistant federal district attorney, he also prosecuted Ku Klux Klan cases before the circuit court in Raleigh. In part because of this experience, he received an appointment as solicitor general of the United States late in 1872, necessitating a move to Washington, D.C.

Phillips's capability as solicitor general was attested by his long tenure of twelve years under four Republican presidents. With the return of a Democratic administration in 1885, he took up a lucrative private law practice in Washington before the Supreme Court and lesser tribunals. As solicitor general Phillips had been overruled as the Supreme Court dismantled much of the civil rights legislation enacted by Congress during Reconstruction. As a private practitioner one of his most important cases was *Plessy v. Ferguson* (1896), in which he and his former North Carolina associate, Albion W. Tourgée, unsuccessfully fought the separate-but-equal doctrine relating to public accommodations for Negroes.

He retired from practice about 1900 and died in Washington three years later. He was buried in Chapel Hill. Phillips was a lifelong Presbyterian.

SEE: R. H. Battle, "Hon. Samuel Field Phillips, LL.D.," *North Carolina Law Journal* 1 (January 1904); Hope Summerell Chamberlain, *Old Days in Chapel Hill: Being the Life and Letters of Cornelia Phillips Spencer* (1926); Charles Phillips Russell, *The Woman Who Rang the Bell: The Story of Cornelia Phillips Spencer* (1949 [portrait]); Cornelia Phillips Spencer Papers, Battle Family Papers, and Charles Phillips Papers (Southern Historical Collection, University of North Carolina, Chapel Hill).

ALLEN W. TRELEASE

Phillips, Sylvanus *(April 1775–31 Oct. 1830)*, pioneer Arkansas settler and land speculator, was born in Jackson township, Union County. No record of his family origin or early life is known prior to his settlement in Arkansas at the mouth of the St. Francis River in 1797. In 1799, when Indian troubles threatened, Phillips moved to Arkansas Post, remaining there for a number of years. As one of the earliest Americans in the area, he was intimately involved in land speculations after 1803, often in association with the St. Louis land speculator William Russell. His name appears prominently in *The Territorial Papers of the United States* usually in connection with land deals. Although not involved in the grossest frauds of the day, his relations with Russell were not entirely legitimate.

His most famous development was the town of Helena, plotted in 1820 by Nicholas Rightor and William Russell and named after Phillips's daughter. Located where Crowley's Ridge meets the Mississippi River, Helena enjoyed a modest prosperity and an unenviable reputation. Stories of its wickedness were commonly reported by eastern travelers to Arkansas, most notably G. W. Featherstonhaugh, who, however, never visited the town.

Phillips held a number of offices, including a term on the Territorial Council and as clerk of the county named after him; he was commonly addressed as Colonel Phillips, presumably a militia appointment. In politics he was associated with the Conway faction in opposition to Territorial Secretary Robert Crittenden. He was twice married in Arkansas: to Phebe Dunn on September 1808 and to Rebecca Kendrick on 25 Aug. 1812. He died at his home near Helena and was buried there.

SEE: Clarence Edwin Carter, ed., *The Territorial Papers of the United States: The Territory of Arkansas, 1819–1825*, vols. 19–20 (1952, 1954); G. W. Featherstonhaugh, *Excursion Through the Slave States* (1844); Little Rock *Arkansas Gazette*, 10 Nov. 1830; Josiah H. Shinn, *Pioneers and Makers of Arkansas* (1908); Ted R. Worley, "Helena on the Mississippi," *Arkansas Historical Quarterly* 13 (1954).

MICHAEL B. DOUGAN

Phillips, William Battle *(4 July 1857–8 June 1918)*, mining engineer and educator, was the first recipient of an earned Ph.D. degree from The University of North Carolina. He was born in Chapel Hill, the son of Charles Phillips, professor of mathematics at The University of North Carolina, and Laura Caroline Battle Phillips. He was educated at local schools and at the Bingham School in Asheville; he earned the Ph.B. in 1877, delivering a senior oration on "Women in Politics." Remaining in Chapel Hill to take a position as chemist (1877–82) with the Agricultural Experiment Station then located there, he was also professor of chemistry in 1879 for the university's Normal School, the recently established summer school for teachers. Phillips began graduate work in 1881 under Francis P. Venable, presenting a dissertation entitled "Part I: Rate of Reversion in Superphosphates from Red Navassa Rock; Part II: North Carolina Phosphates" in 1883; it would seem that his association as chemist with the Navassa Guano Company (1882–85) in Wilmington led him to the subject, which was pertinent to the production of agricultural fertilizers.

The expansion of the university in 1885 to provide a broader program in the agricultural and mechanical arts included an appointment for Phillips to the chair of agricultural chemistry, mineralogy, metallurgy, and mining. Because facilities were not ready to begin instruction in these areas immediately, he studied for a year at the famous mining school at Freiburg, Saxony, to fill in gaps in his knowledge, returning to take up his position in 1886. There had been criticism of his appointment on the basis of both his age and his inexperience in mining, but the university mounted a spirited defense of Phillips and of others attacked by interests not in favor of maintaining this program at Chapel Hill. Those interests were eventually successful, and with the withdrawal of land-grant support from Chapel Hill in 1888, his chair disappeared.

Phillips moved to Birmingham, Ala., and established the firm of Claghorn and Phillips, consulting in mining, chemistry, and assaying from 1888 to 1892; his work was critical to the ongoing development of the iron and steel industry of Birmingham. From 1890 to 1892 he was also professor of chemistry and metallurgy at the University of Alabama. Next he was chemist for the Tennessee Coal, Iron, and Railway Company (1892–98) in Birmingham, and in 1898–1900 he was editor of the *Engineering and Mining Journal*, *American Manufacturer*, and *Iron World*.

In 1900 Phillips began a long association with the University of Texas, serving as professor of field and economic geology from 1900 to 1914 and as director of the University of Texas Mining Survey from 1901 to 1905 and of the Bureau of Economic Geology and Technology from 1909 to 1914. From 1914 to 1916 he was president of the Colorado School of Mines. In 1916 he returned to Texas, where he died two years later in Houston.

Phillips contributed more than three hundred scientific articles to various publications. Monographs representative of his longer works are *Iron Making in Alabama* (1898, 1912); *Texas Petroleum* (1901), written many years before the discoveries at Spindletop that led to the great expansion of the oil industry there; and *The Mineral Resources of Texas* (1910). He was profoundly interested in science education in the South and remained an adviser to The University of North Carolina on that subject almost all of his life.

He married Minerva Ruffin McNeill, the daughter of George II and Elizabeth Drury McNeill, in Fayetteville, N.C., on 8 Oct. 1879. They had three sons: William Battle, Jr., Drury McNeill, and Laurance Vermeule. His second marriage was to Angie Isabel Miller, the daughter of John Martin and Mary Angelina Nichols Miller, in Columbia, S.C., on 21 Jan. 1908.

SEE: Kemp P. Battle, *History of the University of North Carolina*, vol. 2 (1912); Maurice M. Bursey, *Carolina Chemists: University of North Carolina Chemistry Department* (1982); *Journal of the Elisha Mitchell Scientific Society* (1884); Thomas M. Owen, *History of Alabama and Dictionary of Alabama Biography*, vol. 4 (1921); *Who Was Who in America*, vol. 1 (1949).

MAURICE M. BURSEY

Philpott, Harvey Cloyd *(6 Apr. 1909–19 Aug. 1961)*, manufacturer, legislator, and lieutenant governor, was born in Bassett, Va., the son of Benjamin Cabell, Sr., and Daisy Hundley Philpott. The family moved to Lexington, N.C., in 1920, when the elder Philpott purchased a bankrupt furniture plant. As a young man, Cloyd helped his father in the family business and attended Lexington High School. He also attended Eastman Business College and was graduated from Virginia Military Institute in 1929. Entering the furniture business, he became president and chairman of the board of the United Furniture Corporation and of the Philpott Furniture Corporation of Lexington. As a member of the Southern Furniture Manufacturer's Association, he served a term as its president. In 1956 he was named Furniture Man of the Year at the American Furniture Mart.

Philpott once stated that his interest in politics began with his election in 1934 to the Lexington School Board, where he served until 1945; he was chairman of the board from 1943 to 1945. During all of these years he demonstrated concern for the promotion of education throughout the state. He was a trustee of Wake Forest College and chairman of the Committee of One Hundred for the development of Campbell College.

During the period 1945–49 he was mayor of Lexington and from 1949 to 1956 he was a member of the Lexington Utilities Committee. He also served on the board of directors of the Commercial Bank of Lexington and the Mutual Savings and Loan Association in Lexington. In 1953 he was elected to the state house of representatives, in which he served until 1959. In the house he was a member of the Pearsall Committee and chairman (1958) of the Commission on the Reorganization of State Government. Though conscious of the business interests in the state, Philpott was not a strict conservative and was known in the General Assembly as a man who voted his convictions. He was instrumental in the enactment of the state minimum wage law, though business urged its defeat.

In November 1960 Philpott was elected lieutenant governor, defeating the Republican candidate by more than 230,000 votes. He died in office at age fifty-two and was buried in Forest Hill Memorial Park, Lexington.

In 1931 Philpott married Frances Adelaide Thompson of Lexington, and they became the parents of two daughters, Kathleen (Mrs. Harry V. Anderson, Jr.) and Betty Joe, and a son, Harvey Cloyd, Jr.

SEE: *Greensboro Daily News*, 20–22 Aug. 1961; *North Carolina Baptist State Convention Minutes* (1961); *North Carolina Manual* (1959); William S. Powell, ed., *North Carolina Lives* (1962); Raleigh *News and Observer*, 20–22 Aug. 1961; *We the People of North Carolina*, September 1961; *Who Was Who in America* (1968).

DAVID CALEP WRIGHT III

Phipps, Luther James *(20 Mar. 1898–1 Oct. 1969)*, lawyer, layman, and civic and political leader, was born on an Orange County farm to Connie Weaver and Charles Reid Phipps, attended schools in nearby Chapel Hill, and was graduated from The University of North Carolina in 1922 with a B.S. degree in civil engineering. He then studied law there for two years before beginning his forty-five-year career as a practicing attorney and judge in local courts.

While a student at the university in 1918, he joined the Student Army Training Corps and served in the U.S. Army Infantry. He returned to his studies in Chapel Hill with a Julian Carr Fellowship. Phipps held many offices in student government, was tapped for membership in the Order of the Golden Fleece (the highest campus honorary and leadership organization), and was secretary of Phi Beta Kappa honorary scholarship fraternity. In 1922 he was president of his graduating class and received the Major Cain Prize in Mathematics at commencement exercises. In addition, he was a member of Phi Gamma Delta social fraternity and Phi Alpha Delta law fraternity. Throughout his career he was active in the alumni affairs of his alma mater—both as permanent secretary of the Class of 1922 and as an ardent partisan of the university and its leadership.

Twice he was the judge of the Chapel Hill Recorder's Court (1933–39 and 1964–68). He also was appointed as the first judge of the Orange County Recorder's Court at Hillsborough on its creation in 1947 and served on that bench until 1963. In 1969 he was elected as one of the four judges of the newly created Fifteenth District Court for Orange, Chatham, and Alamance counties. He was sitting on that court when he suffered a mild attack of angina on 3 Sept. 1969, and he died about three weeks later.

Throughout his career Judge Phipps was active in Democratic party politics in Orange County, serving as county Democratic executive committee chairman for a number of years. When former university president Dr. Frank P. Graham ran in 1950 for election in his own right to his appointive post as U.S. senator from North Carolina, Phipps was one of his most active campaign leaders in that hotly contested primary election battle. In 1963 he was appointed by Governor Terry Sanford to serve as Orange County's representative in the General Assembly, succeeding J. W. Umstead, Jr., who resigned because of poor health.

Of his many civic affiliations, his earliest was as a charter member of Chapel Hill Post No. 6 of the American Legion. In that veterans' group he held almost every local and district office before serving as commander of the legion's North Carolina Department—the elected head of the more than 60,000-member statewide organization. His other primary interest was the University Baptist Church of Chapel Hill, where he was chairman of the Board of Deacons for many years and church moderator at the time of his death.

Many honors came to Phipps through his lifetime in the university community—especially because of his constant involvement in almost every phase of local and civic activities. He was for many years the attorney for the town of Carrboro and for the Chapel Hill–Carrboro Merchants Association. For thirty-nine years he was an active member of the Chapel Hill Rotary Club, serving as president in 1938–39 and as international service chairman for many years until his death. His colleagues in the County Bar Association honored him in 1968 with a silver bowl in recognition of his "41 years of integrity and honor" in the practice of law. He was general chairman of the Orange County Bicentennial celebration in the fall of 1952, an original member and chairman of the Historic Hillsborough Commission, and a founding member and director of the Chapel Hill Historical Society.

In other service areas, he had been Orange County district chairman for the Boy Scouts of America and the recipient of the highest volunteer award given to Scouters—the Silver Beaver. He was chairman of the Orange County Morehead Scholarship Committee and a member of the Aubrey Lee Brooks Scholarship Committee for The University of North Carolina. Among his varied hobby interests were stamp and coin collecting and bird study.

At his death a local editor noted Phipps's conservative instincts and "fierce patriotism" but added: "He saw the law not only as a deterrent to our darker impulses and a restraint on our baser conduct, but as a living, constructive force that could help to shape a better society. . . . He was a man of rock-like principles and he stood as squarely on them as anyone we have ever known. He loved family, God, and the Democratic Party with a passion that is increasingly rare in our times." Chancellor Emeritus Robert B. House of The University of North Carolina wrote of Phipps: "I have never known a man with higher ideals or with a quieter, steadier loyalty to those ideals."

Phipps married, on 23 June 1924, Vivian Jane Lassiter, of Aulander, who survived him. They had two daughters, Vivian Lassiter (Mrs. Edward G. Bond of Edenton) and Jamesina Dana (Mrs. William Dean Gordon of Greensboro).

SEE: *Chapel Hill Weekly*, 23 Jan. 1961, 23 June 1963, 1 Oct. 1969; *Durham Morning Herald*, 25 June 1963; Daniel L. Grant, *Alumni History of the University of North Carolina* (1924); Stephen E. Massengill, *Biographical Directory of the General Assembly of North Carolina, 1963–1978* (1979); *North Carolina Biography*, vol. 4 (1941); *North Carolina Manual* (1963); William S. Powell, ed., *North Carolina Lives* (1962); *Who's Who in the South and Southwest* (1963).

ROLAND GIDUZ

Pickens, Israel *(30 Jan. 1780–24 Apr. 1827)*, lawyer, congressman, governor of Alabama, and senator, was born in Mecklenburg (now Cabarrus) County near Beattie's Ford across the Catawba River. He was the son of Captain Samuel, a slave owner and veteran of the Revolutionary War, and Jane Carrigan Pickens. The family was of French Huguenot descent. Israel was educated under the Reverend John Robinson in a classical school at Poplar Tent Church and studied law at Jefferson College, Cannonsville, Pa.

In 1802 young Pickens moved to Morganton, Burke County, where he began to practice law and soon became involved in the politics of western North Carolina. As a Democrat, he served in the state senate in 1808 and 1809 before his election to three terms in the U.S. Congress from 1811 to 1817. During the War of 1812 he was a staunch supporter of President James Madison's war measures and was a friend and political ally of William R. King, with whom he shared the same "Congressional mess" at Claxton's Hotel on Capitol Hill. Pickens voted with the narrow majority of the House and of the North

Carolina delegation for the internal improvements bill passed in late 1816. Earlier he had supported the rechartering of the Bank of the United States, reflecting the tone of his ardent "mountaineer" Democratic outlook. In the final session of the Fourteenth Congress, he was chairman of the committee on public expenditures.

Pickens did not seek reelection and by mid-1818 he joined a stream of North Carolinians moving to the new Alabama and Mississippi territories. He settled in Hale County, Ala., not far from his former fellow congressman-friend from North Carolina, William King. Pickens was appointed a register of the land office, named president of the Tombigbee Bank, and selected as a delegate from Washington County to the convention that voted statehood for Alabama. He was elected governor by "anti-Crawford" forces in 1821 and reelected in 1823. King, also a member of the statehood convention, won a seat in the U.S. Senate the year after Pickens became governor. Much credit for organizing the machinery of government for the state and chartering the University of Alabama is given to Pickens. In 1826 he was named to fill a vacancy in the Senate and served from February to November, when a successor was chosen. By then he was suffering from tuberculosis and declined a federal judgeship for the Alabama district; instead, he went to Cuba where he hoped his health might improve. He died at Matanzas, Cuba, however, and was buried there. His remains were later moved to a family cemetery near Greensboro, Ala.

Pickens had other interests as well. It probably was merely as a hobby that he engaged in scientific research, but he invented a lunar dial.

A Presbyterian, Pickens was married in 1814 to Martha Orilla, daughter of General William Lenoir. They became the parents of Julia (m. Lieutenant C. S. Howe, U.S. Army), Andrew Lenoir (m. Caroline Gordon), and Israel, Jr. (m. Eliza Nelson).

SEE: *Biog. Dir. Am. Cong.* (1971); John L. Cheney, Jr., ed., *North Carolina Government, 1585-1974* (1975); *DAB*, vol. 7 (1934); William S. Harris, "Governor Pickens of Alabama," *The Land We Love* 1 (June 1866); Albert B. Moore, *History of Alabama and Her People*, vol. 1 (1927); Thomas M. Owen, *History of Alabama and Dictionary of Alabama Biography*, vol. 4 (1921); Edward W. Phifer, *Burke: History of a North Carolina County* (1977).

ROY PARKER, JR.

Pickett, Albert James *(13 Aug. 1810–28 Oct. 1858)*, planter and historian, was born in Anson County, the youngest of three children of Colonel William Raiford and France Dickson Pickett. The Pickett family, of Scottish, English, and French origin, was prominent in the politics and military annals of Virginia and North Carolina from colonial times. Colonel William Pickett was sheriff and tax assessor-collector of Anson County and served his district in the state legislature. In 1818 he settled at Autauga, Ala., where he became a cotton planter and operator of trading posts in Creek Indian country. He also served with distinction in both houses of the Alabama legislature.

Growing up in a frontier environment, with Creeks and Indian traders as his closest companions, young Pickett had little opportunity locally for formal education. For two years, however, he attended private academies in Massachusetts and Virginia and for a brief period in 1830 read law in the office of his brother, William, a magistrate of the Sixth Judicial District of Alabama. Not finding the legal profession to his liking, Pickett abandoned his studies and for several years tried his hand as a journalist. He worked on various newspapers, including the Alabama *Journal*, which was owned by his brother-in-law, General Mosely Baker.

In 1832 Pickett married Sarah Smith Harris, daughter of William Harris, a leading planter. Sarah's dowry was an estate of 1,100 acres known as Forest Farm. The couple settled there and developed the land into a fine cotton plantation and home for their twelve children. Pickett immersed himself in the manifold tasks of plantation management. He diversified his crops to include dairy and vegetable products and rice and experimented with new strains of plants. One of the first Alabama planters to practice scientific farming, he wrote articles for the *Southern Cultivator* and other agricultural journals.

An intelligent man of stocky build and a stern visage that belied a jovial personality, Pickett was highly respected by his neighbors and was called upon frequently to assume leadership roles in civic affairs. Deeply concerned with economic matters and with free public education, he maintained an extensive correspondence with local officials across the state. Although he took the lead in opposing abolitionist sentiment in Alabama, Pickett worked to secure passage of bills designed to prevent the importation of additional slaves. A lifelong Jacksonian Democrat, he spoke at patriotic rallies against the Nullifiers. At the time of the expulsion of the Creeks, he served as acting assistant adjutant general to Governor Clement C. Clay. In 1853 Pickett was proposed as a candidate for governor, but he declined the honor in order to devote his energies to his plantation and his writing.

Pickett is remembered chiefly as a major southern historian, as a founder of the Alabama Historical Society, and as the collector of important manuscripts essential to research in the history of the Gulf states. His principal work, published in 1851, was the *History of Alabama*. Essentially an account of the evolution of Alabama from Hernando de Soto's expedition in 1538 to statehood in 1819, the book stressed frontier developments and military annals. Although poorly organized and written in an awkward style, the work was remarkably free of bias, even when Pickett dealt with controversial subjects. It was based on sound research in manuscript sources and on personal reminiscences dictated to the author by pioneer settlers. More than a century after publication, Pickett's *History of Alabama* is still the starting place for research in the colonial and territorial history of Alabama.

Although plagued by chronic ill health, Pickett labored at additional historical writings. A massive history of the Southwest was well under way when he died suddenly while on a visit to his plantation. He was buried in Oakwood Cemetery, Montgomery, Ala.

SEE: Crawford M. Jackson, *Brief Biographical Sketch of the Late Col. Albert James Pickett of Alabama* (1859); Marie Bankhead Owen, "Albert James Pickett: Alabama's First Historian," *Alabama Historical Quarterly* 1 (Spring 1930); Albert James Pickett, *History of Alabama and Incidentally of Georgia and Mississippi, from the Earliest Period* (1896 [portrait]) and "The Red Lands of Alabama," *Southern Cultivator* 5 (January, June 1847); Albert James Pickett Papers (Alabama Department of Archives and History, Montgomery).

HERBERT H. LANG

Pierce, Ovid Williams, Jr. *(1 Oct. 1910–9 Dec. 1989)*, author and college teacher, was born in Weldon, the son of Ovid Williams, a well-to-do farmer, and Minnie Deans Pierce, and the grandson of a country doctor. In 1932 he was graduated from Duke University, where he was a member of Phi Beta Kappa and editor of *The Archive*. Returning home, he lived with his family for a few years before entering Harvard. In Cambridge he studied literature under G. L. Kittridge and J. L. Lowes and creative writing under Robert S. Hillyer, Pulitzer Prize–winning poet. Here Pierce wrote some of his first stories and received a master's degree in English in 1936. Returning to Weldon, he worked on a novel for several years before entering the army counterintelligence corps and serving in Latin America. Years later he related that a novel he was writing about his war experiences was stolen while he was in service and never recovered.

After World War II Pierce taught creative writing at Southern Methodist University and wrote several stories for the *Southwest Review*. He accepted a similar post in 1949 at Tulane, where he taught until 1953, the year in which his first novel, *The Plantation*, was published. Afterwards he lived for a time in England, France, and Spain. In 1956 he became writer-in-residence at East Carolina College, in Greenville, and taught courses in creative writing and literature. He also served as faculty adviser to *The Rebel*, the campus literary magazine that he founded in 1957.

Pierce became noted for his cavalier attitude towards teaching. His nonchalance about his classes is suggested by a story he enjoyed telling—that his department chairman "always told me only when and where but never what to teach, knowing full well I'd talk about the Civil War anyhow." When Mac Hyman, author of *No Time for Sergeants*, asked for teaching tips, Pierce gave him instructions on how to "spend the whole . . . hour without even mentioning the subject." His students often were disappointed that an author of such renown offered them so little of substance.

Many students were nevertheless inspired by Pierce's joviality, easy manner, courtliness, and image as the quintessential country gentleman. The deep impression he made resulted in numerous lifelong friendships, especially among his literary magazine and fraternity advisees.

During the twenty years he was on the East Carolina faculty he divided his time between a Greenville apartment and The Plantation, his farm at Pierce's Crossroads near Enfield. In the mid-1950s he completed the restoration of the nineteenth-century two-story house on his farm and furnished it with southern primitive antiques, European objets d'art, seventeenth- and eighteenth-century oil portraits, old engravings and maps, his own watercolors, and books. This rural retreat captured the flavor of the antebellum period of which he was especially fond. Here he entertained countless guests, particularly literary figures, East Carolina College colleagues and students, and his Doubleday editor, LeBaron (Lee) Barker.

Doubleday published three novels completed while he was at East Carolina: *On a Lonesome Porch* (1960), *The Devil's Half* (1968), and *The Wedding Guest* (1974). In 1976 The University of North Carolina Press brought out *Old Man's Gold and Other Stories*, an anthology of stories that had previously appeared in *Southwest Review*. Retiring from East Carolina in 1976, Pierce lived at The Plantation, but after a short time he sold his farm and returned to Greenville, where he completed his last three novels: *Judge Buell's Legacy* (1985), *The Story of Cabbage Green* (1987), and, left in manuscript at his death, "Lost Boy Found."

Pierce's native Roanoke River valley provided inspiration and background for his novels, which together portray the region from the post–Civil War era to the 1950s. His eastern North Carolina landscapes, handling of characters' dialogue and dialects, and prose style won acclaim from major literary critics. Twice he received the Sir Walter Raleigh Award for fiction and in 1969 he won the North Carolina Award for Literature. The O. Max Gardner Award citation that he received in 1973 noted that he had "produced, with artistry and integrity, an authoritative portrait of the South."

Having suffered from declining health for several years, Pierce died of cardiac arrest at Pitt Memorial Hospital. He was buried in Cedarwood Cemetery, Weldon. Portraits hang in the Kappa Alpha fraternity house, in the Manuscript Department of the library, and in the English Department at East Carolina University, Greenville.

SEE: William Blackburn, *Love, Boy: The Letters of Mac Hyman* (1969); Mary Jo Jackson Bratton, *East Carolina University: The Formative Years, 1907–1982* (1986); *Contemporary Authors*, vol. 4 (1981); John D. Ebbs, Jr., "Ovid Williams Pierce, Jr.: Nomination for the O. Max Gardner Award" (1973); Greenville *Daily Reflector*, 9 Dec. 1987; Erwin Hester and Douglas J. McMillan, *Cultural Change in Eastern North Carolina as Reflected in Some of the Novels of Inglis Fletcher and Ovid Pierce* (1973); Ovid W. Pierce Papers (Manuscript Collection, Duke University Library, Durham, and East Carolina University Library, Greenville); *Time*, 2 Mar. 1953, 20 June 1960; Richard Walser and E. T. Malone, Jr., *Literary North Carolina* (1986).

W. KEATS SPARROW

Pierson, William Whatley *(30 Feb. 1890–23 Apr. 1966)*, scholar, university professor, and administrator, was born in Brundige, Ala., the eldest son of Dr. William Whatley, a surgeon, and Minto Anglin Pierson. After preliminary education with tutors and in local private and public schools, he attended the State Normal School in Troy (Ph.B., 1908), the University of Alabama (A.B., 1910; A.M., 1911), and Columbia University (A.M., 1912; Ph.D., 1916). Travel and study abroad included research in Peru, Chile, Argentina, Brazil, Portugal, Spain, and France as a Kenan Traveling Professor and, as an associate of the Carnegie Institute of Washington and the Carnegie Foundation of New York, respectively, in Venezuela in 1928 and 1940. Pierson earned doctoral degrees *honoris causa* from Boston University (1943), Washington and Lee University (1949), and the University of North Carolina at Greensboro (1963), fittingly the first honorary degree conferred by that institution under its new title.

Pierson's principal teaching was at The University of North Carolina, where he was successively instructor, assistant professor, and professor of history and government (1915–35); professor of political science (1936–57) and head of that department (1936–42); and Kenan professor (1957–63). In his capacity as administrator, he was first of all dean of the Graduate School at Chapel Hill (1930–57). He also served in the university system as acting chancellor of the Woman's College in Greensboro (1956–57, 1960) and acting director of the Board of Higher Education (1960). Furthermore, he guided in the formation of a graduate curriculum at the North Carolina College (later North Carolina Central University) in Durham and prevailed upon the state legislature to establish a graduate school there in 1939, serving as its first dean and later its co-dean. From 1954 to 1964 he was a key member of its board of trustees.

Beyond North Carolina's borders Pierson was active in numerous regional and national agencies concerned with postbachelaureate education. His most important role was in the pivotal Association of American Universities, where he served on the Committee on Classification (1933–48) and was executive secretary (1943–48). Regionally, he was a two-term president of the Conference of Deans of Southern Graduate Schools, member of the Executive Council and the Committee on Instruction in Higher Education of the Southern Association of Colleges and Universities (1945–52), vice-president (1951–52) and president (1953) of the Southern University Conference, and chairman of the Administrative Committee of the Southern Fellowships Fund (throughout its existence, 1954–63). As part of his work in these agencies he wrote many reports and synoptic recommendations that are preserved in their several journals or proceedings. Typical of these is "Organization of a Graduate School within the University," *Journal of the Proceedings and Addresses of the 37th Conference, Association of American Universities* (1933).

As a scholar, Pierson pursued constitutional history and political theory in the United States and in Hispanic America. His chief book-length publications are *Texas v. White: A Study in Legal History* (1916); *American Ideals*, edited jointly with Norman Foerster (1917); *Hispanic-American History: A Syllabus* (4 eds., 1921–27); and *Governments of Latin-America*, with Federico G. Gil (1957). Among his articles in learned journals are "The Sovereign State of North Carolina: 1787–1789," *Proceedings of the North Carolina Literary and Historical Association* (1916); "The Joint Committee on the Conduct of the Civil War," *American Historical Review* (1917); "Is There a Republican Form of Government?," *North Carolina Law Review* (1923); "The Political Influence of an Inter-Oceanic Canal," *Hispanic-American Historical Review* (1926); "Scientific and Interpretive History," *North Carolina Historical Review* (1926); "Institutional History of the Cuban Intendencia," *James Sprunt Historical Studies* (1926–27); "Foreign Influences on Venezuelan Political Thought," *Hispanic-American Historical Review* (1935); "Pathology of Democracy in Latin America," *American Political Science Review* (1950); and "Which Is Superior—The Supreme Court or the Constitution,?" *Congressional Record* (1956).

Pierson also was an associate editor of the *Hispanic-American Historical Review* (1920–26, 1928–34); editor of the Inter-American Historical Series of The University of North Carolina Press; a member or corresponding member of Sigma Alpha Epsilon, Phi Beta Kappa, the Chapel Hill Rotary Club (president, 1949–50), the Hispanic Society of America, and the Academie Nacional de la Historia de Venezuela.

In religion Pierson was a Methodist. He was married twice: to Henrietta Elizabeth Brase in New York in 1916 (divorced in 1942) and to Mary Bynum Holmes in Mount Olive, N.C., in 1945. At the time of his retirement in 1963, he moved to Mount Olive and, upon his death three years later, was buried in Maplewood Cemetery. He was survived by Mary Bynum Holmes Pierson and no children.

Pierson's career spanned a period of explosive growth in the number of institutions of higher learning in the nation and especially in the southern region. His leadership contributed greatly to the achievement of orderly growth rather than a chaotic proliferation of programs leading to master's and doctoral degrees. In this way a firm foundation was laid for the South to attain a standard of excellence in postbachelaureate education previously aspired to only by a few universities in the North and the East.

SEE: *American Men of Science*, vol. 5 (1962); *Dictionary of American Scholars* (1951); *Nat. Cyc. Am. Biog.*, vol. 51 (1969 [portrait]); Mary Bynum Holmes Pierson, *Graduate Work in the South* (1947); *Who's Who in America*, vol. 32 (1962–63).

CHARLES B. ROBSON

Piggot, Aaron Snowden *(1822–13 Feb. 1869)*, physician, dentist, chemist, and professor, was born in Philadelphia, the son of the Reverend Dr. Robert Piggot, stipple engraver and Episcopal clergyman, and his wife Rebecca S[nowden?]. He received the doctor of physic degree in 1845 from the University of Maryland, from which he also held the master's degree. His inaugural dissertation was on "Congestion."

Piggot practiced medicine and was professor of anatomy and physiology in Washington University, Baltimore, from 1848 to 1851 and at Baltimore College of Dental Surgery from 1858 to 1861. In the 1850s he was an analytical chemist and a mining consultant. He was coeditor of the *American Journal of Dental Science* (1856, 1867–69) and professor of chemistry at the Baltimore College of Dental Surgery (1865–69). His textbook, *Dental Chemistry and Metallurgy as Applied to the Study and Practice of Dental Surgery* (1854), was a pioneer in its field. Piggot also was the author of *Art of Mining and Preparing Ores* (1858). His books and papers on medical and dental subjects as well as on metallurgy (copper, gold, and silver particularly) were published in the United States and in England. As an expert on metals, he was engaged by the state of North Carolina to prepare *Geological and Mineralogical Reports of Mecklenburg Gold and Copper Mines* (1860). He contributed literary essays and reviews to the *Knickerbocker Magazine, Southern Quarterly Review, Southern Literary Messenger*, and *Harper's Magazine*. Between June 1856 and June 1857 he was the author of a series of five articles on great epidemics published in *Harper's New Monthly Magazine*.

Early in the Civil War Dr. Piggot cast his lot with the South to work for the Confederate States of America Nitre and Mining Bureau; in 1862 he supervised the construction of the works for smelting lead, copper, and zinc at Petersburg, Va. On 19 July 1862 he was appointed surgeon in the Confederate service, but on 13 Jan. 1863 he was in Lexington, N.C., en route to Georgia to inspect the work of the Nitre and Mining Bureau.

Because of the large quantity of medicinal herbs produced in western North Carolina, the state in May 1863 began to construct a laboratory near Lincolnton to produce medicines for the Confederacy. A new brick building was completed by August and Piggot was employed to supervise the production. He moved his family to Lincolnton, where they attended the local Episcopal church. A botanical garden was laid out and among other plants it grew poppies for the manufacture of opium. Piggot was either captured or surrendered at Lincolnton on 27 Apr. 1865 and took the required oath of allegiance on 24 July. Soon afterwards he returned to his home in Baltimore, where he became professor of chemistry at the Baltimore College of Dental Surgery. He died suddenly four years later at age forty-seven when he was returning home from inspecting a mica mine in Spottsylvania County, Va. He had married Margaret Moore in Baltimore on 13 Oct. 1845, and they were the parents of four children. One of them was Cameron Piggot, M.D. (b. 1856), who taught chemistry first at Johns Hopkins and afterwards at the University of the South, where he was also dean of the Academic Faculty.

SEE: S. Austin Allibone, *A Critical Dictionary of English Literature and British and American Authors*, vol. 2 (1872); Baltimore County Marriage Licenses, 1839–46 (Hall of Records, Annapolis, Md.); *Confederate States Medical and Surgical Journal*, vol. 1 (July, November 1864); Eugene F. Cordell, *Medical Annals of Maryland, 1799–1899* (1903); Wyndham D. Miles, ed., *American Chemists and Chemical Engineers* (1976); John R. Quinan, *Medical Annals of Balti-*

more from 1608 to 1880 (1884); John T. Scharf, *History of Baltimore City and County* (1881); *War of the Rebellion: A Compilation of the Official Records of the Union and Confederate Armies*, ser. 4, vol. 3, p. 1074 (1900).

WILLIAM S. POWELL

Pigott, Emeline Jamison *(15 Dec. 1836–26 May 1919)*, Confederate spy, was born in Carteret County, the daughter of Levi and Eliza Dennis Pigott, both from families with roots deep in the area. At the time of the Civil War, the Pigotts lived on a farm along Calico Creek directly across from the present Morehead City cemetery. The site then served as a camping ground for Confederate soldiers, and Emeline saw at close hand the hardships the soldiers faced. She quickly became involved in the Southern cause.

She fell in love with Stokes MacRae, a private, and refused many invitations from Confederate officers for social affairs he could not attend. There still exists an invitation sent to her for a New Year's Eve ball to be held in Beaufort by the Twenty-sixth Regiment of North Carolina Troops in 1861. MacRae was killed in the Battle of Gettysburg, and his body was never identified. After his death, Emeline became even more active in war service. She nursed the sick and injured and was in New Bern when the town fell. She left on the last train and spent an extended period in Kinston as a nurse until she had to leave that community, too. She then went to Concord, where she became friendly with a Mrs. Brett, the widow of a chaplain of the Northern army. The two women worked their way through Union lines, sometimes on foot and sometimes by cart, until they reached the Pigott farm. Mrs. Brett made her home there and later married a family relative.

When Northern soldiers were stationed on the Pigott farm, it became the task of Emeline to entertain the officers in the evenings so that her brother-in-law, Rufus Bell, could carry food to Southern soldiers who were hiding in the woods nearby. She also served as a courier, taking medicine, food, and mail to predetermined drop points for the Southern forces to pick up. Emeline hid the provisions under her hoop skirt.

Once she was arrested in Beaufort while attempting to take war information to the Southern troops. Actually, the information had been planted because the Northern authorities suspected Emeline's activities. She was traveling with her brother-in-law, and he was searched first for the incriminating documents the pair was suspected of carrying. When authorities found nothing, they sent a black woman to search Emeline. In an effort to gain time, she refused to allow the black woman to search her and insisted that a white woman whom she knew be found. By the time the white woman arrived, Emeline had swallowed the incriminating evidence and torn all the mail to bits so that it could not be read.

She was taken to prison in New Bern but was allowed to spend a night at home on the way, and the authorities even permitted her cousin, Mrs. Levi Woodburg Pigott, to accompany her. She was incarcerated for about a month, and conditions at the prison were very bad. One night, an attempt was made to kill the two women by pouring chloroform into their room. Fortunately, Emeline was awake, and she and her cousin took turns breathing through a broken window pane until the fumes dissipated. Finally, they were able to get the attention of a guard stationed outside who gave them aid.

For unexplained reasons, Emeline was never brought to trial, although she was taken to court day after day. If she had been tried, she probably would have been sentenced to death as a spy. After the attempt on her life, she sent for the two men in Beaufort who had given her the false information that led to her arrest. She told them that if she died in prison, they would die too, and that threat led the men to arrange her release. She was never arrested again, although she was watched closely and her home was searched repeatedly. Emeline continued to help the Confederate cause in every way she could.

After the war, she organized the Morehead City chapter of the United Daughters of the Confederacy, and it was named in her honor. In addition, a street in Morehead City was called Emeline Place. She lived her entire life in Morehead City and was buried in the family cemetery near the grave of an unknown Confederate soldier. Emeline had tended the grave throughout her life as an act of continuing devotion to the Confederate cause. She never married.

SEE: Lucy Worth London, *North Carolina Women of the Confederacy* (1928); Mildred Wallace, "The Sacrifice or Daring of a Southern Woman During the War Between the States," Benjamin Royal Papers (Southern Historical Collection, University of North Carolina, Chapel Hill).

RUTH ROYAL BARNES

Pilmore, Joseph (or Pillmore, Pilmoor, Pilmoore) *(31 Oct. 1739–24 July 1825)*, clergyman, was born in Tadmouth, Yorkshire, England, to parents who were members of the Church of England. At sixteen he became acquainted with John Wesley (1703–91), founder of the Methodist church, and was converted under his influence; he was educated at Wesley's Kingswood School near Bristol and acquired some knowledge of Latin, Greek, and Hebrew. His early itinerant ministry was in Wales and Cornwall.

In 1769 at the Methodist Conference at Leeds, Pilmore and Richard Boardman volunteered for missionary work in the American colonies and arrived at Gloucester Point, N.J., on 21 Oct. 1769. Until May 1772 the two men alternated in preaching in Philadelphia and New York for four-month periods; on 26 May 1772 Pilmore left on a journey that was to take him to Georgia. He traveled through the German counties of Pennsylvania and the northern counties of Maryland to Baltimore, Annapolis, Norfolk, Portsmouth, Williamsburg, and Yorktown. In December 1772 he preached the first real Methodist sermon ever delivered in North Carolina at Currituck Court House and realized the "unparalleled opportunities" open to the Christian evangelists in these places. He also visited Edenton, New Bern, and Wilmington. His ministry in each place was brief but excellent. After reaching Savannah, Ga., in February 1773 and staying eleven days, he returned to Philadelphia over the same route. In January 1774 Pilmore and Boardman returned to England.

The years 1774 through 1784 were "silent years" for Pilmore; he received no Methodist appointments and was stationed at London, Norwich Circuit, Edinburgh, Dublin, Nottingham, Edinburgh, and York. Then, returning to America, he was ordained a deacon and priest of the new Protestant Episcopal church in the United States on 27 and 29 November 1785. The remaining years of his ministry, until retirement from the rectorate in 1821, were spent in Philadelphia, Oxford (now Lawndale), and Lower Dublin (now Torresdale). His body was interred in a vault beneath the floor of the Sunday school room of St. Paul's Church, Philadelphia.

Pilmore served as vice-president of the Philadelphia Bible Society and of the Society of the Protestant Episcopal Church for the Advancement of Christianity in Pennsylvania. In 1807 the University of Pennsylvania awarded him the honorary doctor of divinity degree. In 1790 Pilmore married Mary Benezet Wood, formerly of Georgia; some writers state that he married twice; however, there appears to be no extant record of the name of a second wife.

The Journal of Joseph Pilmore: Methodist Itinerant, For the Years August 1, 1769 to January 2, 1774 was edited by the Reverend Frederick E. Maser and Howard T. Maag and published for the first time in 1969 by the Historical Society of the Philadelphia Annual Conference of the United Methodist church. At the order of the Society of the Sons of St. George's, Philadelphia, John Neagle painted a portrait of Pilmore that was loaned to St. George's United Methodist Church, Philadelphia. The Joseph Pilmore Bicentennial Celebration was held at Currituck Court House in September 1972 with Frederick E. Maser and others as principal speakers under the sponsorship of the Commission on Archives and History of the North Carolina Annual Conference of the United Methodist church. The Pilmoor Memorial United Methodist Church is located in the Elizabeth City district of the denomination.

SEE: Emory Stevens Bucke, ed., *History of American Methodism*, 3 vols. (1964); Frank E. Maser and Howard T. Maag, eds., *The Journal of Joseph Pilmore* (1969); Louise T. Stahl, *Lest We Forget* (no date); William Warren Sweet, *Men of Zeal* (1935).

GRADY L. E. CARROLL

Pinchot, Gifford *(11 Aug. 1865–4 Oct. 1946)*, forester and politician, was born in Simsbury, Conn., the eldest son of James W. and Mary Jane Eno Pinchot. James was a wealthy manufacturer and partner in the firm, Pinchot, Warren and Company in New York City. One of four children, Pinchot was named after Sanford Gifford, a noted American landscape painter. He was raised in Milford, Pa., his father's birthplace. In 1885, the year after his graduation from Phillips Exeter Academy in New Hampshire, he entered Yale College, where he studied botany, geology, and meteorology; he was graduated in 1889. Pinchot developed an interest in forestry and went to London to study with Sir Dietrich Brandis, the leading forester of the day. At this time there was no organized school of forestry in the United States. Brandis sent Pinchot to the French Forestry School at Nancy, where he studied silviculture and forest economics in 1889–90. He became the first American to choose forestry as a profession.

In the 1890s George W. Vanderbilt began purchasing large tracts of land in the North Carolina mountains for the construction of his residence, Biltmore House. At the suggestion of his landscape architect, Frederick Law Olmsted, Vanderbilt hired Pinchot, America's first trained forester, to devise a plan for managing Biltmore Forest and to prepare an exhibition of the forest for the World's Columbian Exposition in Chicago. Upon his arrival at Biltmore on 2 Feb. 1892, Pinchot found the forest in poor condition after many years of neglect. Although his forest management was subject only to Vanderbilt's control, Pinchot's work was affected by the purpose of the estate as a residence. He and Vanderbilt established three goals for this pioneering work: to promote the profitable production of timber, to establish a constant annual yield, and to improve the general condition of the forest.

In order to do an efficient job, Pinchot made an extensive topographical survey of the estate. He divided the forest into ninety-two units of forty-two acres each. These tracts were examined and relevant silvicultural data were entered into a card catalogue. Pinchot began his forest enhancement by making improvement cuttings. Although sure of the scientific and educational advantages of careful timber cuttings, he doubted that the lumber produced by this method could compete with that provided by traditional lumbering techniques. However, Pinchot was fortunate in finding a good market for cordwood and sawed lumber and thus had a favorable financial balance in his first year. Along with a successful exhibition and a pamphlet prepared for the World's Columbian Exposition in 1893, Pinchot drew considerable publicity to the advantages of practical scientific forestry in America.

In 1894 Pinchot discovered the Pink Beds, a three-thousand-acre valley of rhododendron and mountain laurel in nearby Transylvania County. At his recommendation, Vanderbilt purchased this land and consolidated it with other tracts to create the Pisgah Forest. Pinchot remained at Biltmore until 1895, when he suggested that Vanderbilt hire Carl A. Schenck as resident forester. Schenck, a German forester, established the Biltmore Forest School, the first school of forestry in the United States.

Pinchot worked as a forestry consultant throughout the country. In 1897 he took a post with the U.S. Forest Service to make a survey of U.S. forest reserves. As part of his report, Pinchot suggested that a government forest service be established to protect and control forest reserves. In 1898 he accepted an appointment as head of the U.S. Forest Service with the title of forester, an office located in the Department of Agriculture.

During the Theodore Roosevelt administration, Pinchot moved control of U.S. forests to the Bureau of Forestry. Roosevelt strongly supported Pinchot's conservationist measures, as the two became very close friends. However, William Howard Taft, Roosevelt's successor, did not hold the same views. Days before Taft's inauguration, Roosevelt, Pinchot, and James Garfield, secretary of the interior, withdrew some four million acres of public lands from private use. Under Taft, Garfield was succeeded by Ralph Ballinger, a rival of Pinchot. Although Ballinger was not an anticonservationist, his ideas were very different from Pinchot's strict views. Pinchot accused Ballinger of trying to give government lands to the power trust. In the dispute Taft sided with Ballinger and fired Pinchot on 7 Jan. 1910 for disrespect to the president and official insubordination.

Pinchot returned to the private sector as a forestry consultant. On 15 Aug. 1914 he married Cornelia Bryce at Roslyn, Long Island, the bride's home. Theodore Roosevelt attended the wedding. At this time, Pinchot became extremely interested in politics. In 1914 he ran for the U.S. Senate as a Progressive but was defeated by Boies Penrose. Pinchot left the Progressives to become a Republican. In March 1918 he became Pennsylvania state forestry commissioner under Governor William Sproul. In 1922 Pinchot was elected governor of Pennsylvania and served from 1923 to 1927. In the fall of 1923 he was a candidate for one of the statewide delegates to the 1924 presidential nominating convention. As governor, he felt confident and did not campaign. But due to his criticism of the national administration, Pinchot lost support in the urban areas and was defeated by Ralph B. Strassburger.

Pinchot ran unsuccessfully in the 1926 Republican primary for the U.S. Senate. Again, he showed strength in the rural areas but was soundly defeated in urban centers, such as Philadelphia. In 1930 Pinchot was elected governor of Pennsylvania for a second time and served in the period 1931–35. He did not align himself with the regular party organization when he ran for the U.S. Senate for a third time in 1934. The Republican party saw Pinchot as an enemy of industry and not a Republican at heart. He was defeated in the primary by incumbent David Reed. Pinchot was virtually a man without a party; however, he continued to voice his choice of candidates.

During the last ten years of his life, Pinchot fought every action against forestry and conservation. He was a consultant to Franklin D. Roosevelt and Harry S Truman. In 1935 he began an autobiography that covered the years until his dismissal from the U.S. Forest Service in 1910. After ten years of hard work, he finished one day before his eightieth birthday. *Breaking New Ground*, a defense of Pinchot's views on forestry and his side of the Ballinger controversy, was published posthumously in 1947.

Following the funeral on the lawn of his home, Grey Towers, Pinchot was buried in Milford Cemetery, Milford, Pa. He was survived by his only son, Gifford Bryce Pinchot (b. 22 Dec. 1915). The state of Pennsylvania never erected a statue of Governor Pinchot but more appropriately dedicated a two-thousand-acre state park in his name. Similarly, the Sierra Club dedicated a large redwood tree located in California's Muir Woods to Gifford Pinchot, a longtime advocate of conservation.

SEE: M. Nelson McGreary, *Gifford Pinchot: Forester-Politician* (1950); Gifford Pinchot, *Breaking New Ground* (1947); Harold T. Pinkett, "Gifford Pinchot at Biltmore," *North Carolina Historical Review* 34 (July 1957), and *Gifford Pinchot, Private and Public Forester* (1970); Nancy Rorie, *Historical Studies of Western North Carolina* (1977).

CHARLES B. KELLY

Pittman, Hobson Lafayette *(14 Jan. 1899–5 May 1972)*, painter and teacher, was born in Edgecombe County, where his father, Biscoe Pittman, was a merchant in the small community of Epworth. His mother, Alice Walston, was a native of Scotland Neck; she was a devoutly religious woman who had a strong influence on her son. Both parents came from families long settled in eastern North Carolina.

When young Pittman was six, the family moved to nearby Tarboro. Here he began the study of art and attended the local schools. In early life, however, Pittman considered the theater as a career. His father died when he was eleven and his mother when he was sixteen. At age eighteen Pittman went to Pennsylvania to make his home with his older sister, Juanita, who had married a resident of the Philadelphia area. From 1921 to 1922 he attended Pennsylvania State College before teaching for a short while in a one-room school in Chester County, Pa. This experience contributed to his later success as an art teacher.

Pittman resumed his education with studies at the Carnegie Institute of Technology (1925–26). From 1920 to 1931 he spent his summers in the art colony at Woodstock, N.Y., where he studied chiefly with Albert Heckman. During his formative years Pittman said he was influenced by the works of Hopper and Birchfield. He admired the painting of the nineteenth-century Frenchman, Odelon Redon, and of Antonello de Messina, who is said to have brought oil painting from Flanders to Italy. In 1928 Pittman made the first of his many trips to Europe. In 1956 he spent a year of study abroad after receiving a Guggenheim Fellowship, and late in life he traveled in the Orient and South America.

Pittman first painted in the cubist and expressionist veins, but as he approached his mid-thirties he developed a very personal style. He himself said that he painted not real objects but from reminiscences or memory. The first drawing he ever made was of his mother's bureau, and a painting done a few years before his death, entitled *Self Portrait*, depicts a bureau, flowers strewn on its top surface, against a blue sky flecked with clouds.

Typical of Pittman's major style are his paintings of interiors, either empty or peopled with what he described as "languid ladies," night-gowned or dressed in turn-of-the-century clothes. These rooms have many doors and windows, revealing bits of landscape which, be it a moonlit garden, an empty street, or the dusk of a summer evening, help set the mood for the picture. Critics of Pittman's work use the words *poetic, romantic, Victorian, stage setting*, or *southern*, but there is something more—there are paintings in which he conveys the sensation of hot weather; in others, the psychological feeling of recent death or departure. The actual themes of many paintings are widowhood, loneliness, or disappointment but at the same time they are not without hope and convey a subtle, wry humor. The South as Pittman captured it is not the conventional one of moonlight and magnolias but the distinct imprint, frozen in time and space, of that part of rural eastern North Carolina where he spent his childhood, that landscape, open and yet curiously intimate, of flat fields and densely wooded horizons. His friend and colleague, Francis Speight, described the "interiors" as "touched with genius" and was of the opinion that for these the artist would be best remembered.

Pittman became equally celebrated for his flower paintings and he treated flowers, particularly roses and anemones, as few modern painters have. Not only living flowers but also dead flowers intrigued him, and, as one critic put it, he was able to convey the "tension of a blossom bending on its stalk" and "the mystery of stems entering water."

This artist also excelled in watercolor and pastel. William Hull, who organized the retrospective of Pittman's work at Pennsylvania State University, is of the opinion that his forte was watercolor and that he was one of the masters of this medium. Late in life Pittman said that he best expressed himself in pastel. He felt that color was the most important aspect of painting, and it is appropriate that he has been described as a master colorist. It is interesting to observe the development in his sense of color throughout his lifework. The early paintings are dark and somber, whereas with maturity color is lighter and more vibrant. The large paintings done in his last years are more abstract than his usual style, thinly painted with bold strokes, canvases shimmering with color and light.

In Philadelphia art circles, Pittman was considered an unusually gifted teacher. He himself maintained that the best instruction an artist could have was observation of nature and study in museums. His teaching career began in 1931, when he became director of art at the Friends Central Day School near Philadelphia. From 1932 to 1965 he taught in the summer school at Pennsylvania State College. In 1945 Pittman began teaching and lecturing at the Philadelphia Museum of Art and in 1949 he became a member of the faculty of the prestigious Pennsylvania Academy of Fine Arts, the oldest art school in the world. He had the rare talent of aiding a student's development without leaving his own imprint. His teaching advanced his career in many ways. At Penn State he met Margaret Sanger, who was a friend for years. At the Philadelphia Museum he was associated with John Canady, later art critic of the *New York Times* who developed an appreciation of his work. In his later years his Philadelphia Museum lectures on the history of art were extremely popular.

During his lifetime, Pittman was the recipient of many honors. His work was exhibited in group and one-man shows all over the United States. In 1934 he was represented in the Nineteenth Biannale Exhibition in Venice and in 1946 his work appeared in a show of American art at the Tate Gallery in London. The show "Romantic Painting in America," held at the Museum of Modern Art in New York in 1943, also included some of his work. In 1953 the National Academy of Design elected Pittman to membership, and in 1960 he became an honorary member of the International Institute of Arts and Letters. In 1943 he won the Scheidt Memorial Prize at the Pennsylvania Academy of Fine Arts, and in 1960 he was the first recipient of the Brevoort-Eickemeyer prize at Columbia University. He received the Penn State Medal in 1963. In the same year the North Carolina Museum of Art in Raleigh honored Pittman with the first retrospective exhibition of his work; it was the third in the museum's series of exhibits devoted to prominent North Carolina artists. In 1968 he received the North Carolina Award in Fine Arts. Shortly after his death the museum of Penn State University organized a retrospective, entitled "The World of Hobson Pittman," that was shown at University Park and later at the Pennsylvania Academy of Fine Arts in Philadelphia.

In the last decade of his life Pittman had good and frequent press coverage in Philadelphia newspapers. The late Jane Hall, art editor of the Raleigh *News and Observer*, was a sympathetic critic of his work. Some years earlier he had been featured in *Life* magazine with colored reproductions of some of his paintings (1945), and afterwards *Life* commissioned him to paint scenes of Charleston, S.C. (1946). Clare Booth Luce, wife of the publisher of *Time-Life*, became a close friend.

In 1949 Pittman bought a carriage house with four acres in Bryn Mawr, a Main Line suburb near Philadelphia. Over the years he converted the structure into a comfortable residence, studio, and art gallery. Here were displayed the treasures he collected on his travels, representing art objects from varying cultures worldwide. The galleries were hung with his own paintings and those of favorite and particularly gifted students. The house, called Silver Beech, took its name from the magnificent beech tree near the front door. The four acres surrounding it were divided into small gardens by hedges and embellished with occasional statues, urns, and other garden ornaments—this gave the effect of the artists own "interior" paintings.

As he grew older, Pittman came to consider Silver Beech as an integral part of himself and was apprehensive that the collection would be dispersed after his death. He therefore made arrangements that the house and contents be conveyed to nearby Bryn Mawr College to be maintained as a museum.

Pittman's thrift was proverbial among his friends and he left, in addition to the house and its contents, a respectable estate. In his will certain paintings were left to various museums, and trusts were set up to benefit relatives for life; the residual legatees were the North Carolina Museum of Art, the Philadelphia Museum of Art, and the Pennsylvania Academy of Fine Arts.

Pittman died in the Bryn Mawr Hospital after a long illness. He was buried in Greenwood Cemetery, Tarboro. A few months before his death, he had spoken of Joseph M. W. Turner, the master colorist and innovator whose contribution to the development of painting has only recently been recognized. He observed, "I do not know where I will stand in the history of art but I do know that I will be only a small dot compared to the genius of Turner, and to think he was an Englishman!" Pittman may have been too modest in his comparison, but it may be said that it is no more surprising that Turner was an Englishman than Edgecombe County in the early years of the twentieth century produced an artist of international note.

Pittman's paintings are in many major museums in this country, including the Metropolitan Museum of Art and the Whitney Museum of American Art in New York, the Phillips Collection in Washington, D.C., the North Carolina Museum of Art in Raleigh, and the Ackland Art Museum in Chapel Hill. He is represented in many private collections, chiefly in Pennsylvania and North Carolina. A large collection of works by Pittman, including three self-portraits, along with his furniture and personal effects, is housed in the Blount-Bridgers House in Tarboro. Here a "loving museum" has been established by Pittman's niece and heir, Alyce Weeks Gordon Patrick. The Hobson Pittman Memorial Gallery, also located in the museum, often displays work by Pittman and his students.

A portrait of Pittman by his former student, Hiram Williams, afterwards head of the Department of Art, University of Florida, was displayed at Silver Beech. It was exhibited at the North Carolina Museum of Art in the show "North Carolina Collects" in 1967.

SEE: David S. Bundy, *Painting in the South, 1564–1980* (1983); *Hobson Pittman: Exhibition, November 7–27, 1970* (1970); *Hobson Pittman: Retrospective Exhibition, His Work since 1920* (1963); William Hull, *Catalogue, Retrospective, Penn State University and Academy of Fine Arts* (1972); *New York Times*, 26 Feb. 1933; *North Carolina Awards Commission* (1968); Raleigh *News and Observer*, 10, 19 Apr. 1953, 15 Oct. 1955, 26 June, 8 Oct. 1960, 4 Feb. 1963, 7 May 1972; Tarboro *Daily Southerner*, 15 Nov. 1982; *Who Was Who in America*, vol. 5 (1973); *Who's Who in American Art* (1970).

CLAIBORNE T. SMITH, JR.

Pittman, Newsom Jones *(9 Aug. 1818–14 May 1893)*, physician, surgeon, and gynecologist, was born in Halifax County, the son of John and Catherine Jones Pittman. He was graduated in medicine from the University of Pennsylvania in 1839 and in 1849–52 studied in medical clinics in Europe, primarily in London, Berlin, and Paris. While in Paris he was president of the American Medical Society of Paris. Pittman practiced in Falls of Tar River (Rocky Mount) until he left for Europe and afterwards until his death in Tarboro. Active in the North Carolina Medical Society, he served as vice-president (1852–54) and president (1860–61).

In medical annals Pittman was noted for successful operations in five cases of lithotomy and one of lithotrity. In 1861 he was appointed surgeon in Lawrence O'B. Branch's brigade and served until he was captured with the Confederate forces that surrendered at New Bern the following year. In 1866 he was elected chairman of the State Medical Board of Examiners, a post he filled for six years. His professional publications appeared in the *Transactions* of the North Carolina State Medical Society. In 1877 Pittman was first vice-president of the American Medical Association (AMA), and in 1881 he was a delegate to the International Medical Congress in London from the AMA. Also in 1881 he was a delegate to the British Medical Association. He was a member of the Society of Science, Letters, and Art in London.

Pittman was also engaged in agriculture and livestock

raising and developed large herds of Shropshire sheep and Devon and Jersey cattle. He was a Master Mason and an Episcopalian. His first wife, whom he married in 1858, was Mary Ann Streeter. They were the parents of two daughters, Kate (1859–73) and Minerva (1860–1940). Mrs. Pittman died in 1861, and in 1867 he married Mrs. Mary Eliza Battle Dancy. They were the parents of Eliza (1868–89) and Cornelia (1874–1954), who married John W. B. Battle. Pittman was buried in Calvary Episcopal churchyard, Tarboro.

SEE: *North Carolina Medical Journal* (1893); Pittman Family Papers (possession of Dr. Newsom Pittman Battle, Rocky Mount); *Tarboro Southerner*, 18 May 1893; *Transactions of the Medical Society of the State of North Carolina* 17 (1886), (1894), (1917).

WILLIAM S. POWELL

Pittman, Thomas Merritt *(24 Nov. 1857–8 Feb. 1932),* lawyer and judge, was born in Franklin County near the town of Louisburg to Alfred H. and Elizabeth Alston Neathery Pittman. He attended the local common schools and Belford Academy in Franklin County.

Orphaned at fourteen, Pittman ended his formal education and went to work in the foundries of Charlotte. While in his teens he became a skilled artisan at the Mecklenburg Iron Works and at seventeen was foreman at the Carolina Agricultural Works, the largest ironworks in Charlotte. He spent his evenings studying the decisions of noted jurists. Pittman's precocity attracted the attention of the law firm of Guion and Flemming, which permitted him to read law in its offices. Admitted to the North Carolina bar in June 1878, while still in his minority, Pittman began his law career in Charlotte. He was admitted to the South Carolina bar in April 1881.

Pittman began the general practice of law in Henderson after his marriage in June 1883 to Mrs. Harriet Thrower Lassiter, a native of Henderson. Appointed examiner in equity for the Western District of North Carolina, he also served as general counsel for Vance County and the Bank of Henderson and worked for many years after 1901 as city attorney of Henderson. He was the first president of the Charlotte Street Railway Company but retired before the line had been completed.

Pittman was vice-president of the North Carolina State Bar Association for the 1911–12 session and beginning in 1909 chaired the legislative committee to investigate and report on the Torrens system of land registration. The Torrens Land Act, drafted by Pittman's committee, became law in 1919.

A deacon and Sunday school superintendent of the Henderson Baptist Church, Pittman became vice-president of the North Carolina Baptist State Convention and of the American Baptist Historical Society in Philadelphia. In addition, he held various other state and local church offices. He wrote "The Preparation of Baptist Work in North Carolina" and promoted the publication of the *Baptist Historical Papers*.

Pittman was an avid amateur historian and assembled a large collection of North Carolina historical documents, pamphlets, and books. A prolific writer and speaker, he published essays on "The Revolutionary Congresses of North Carolina," "Willie Jones, Democrat," "John Porter and the Cary Rebellion," "John Penn: One of the North Carolina Signers of the Declaration of Independence," "Lemuel Burkitt," and "Nathaniel Macon." He wrote a biographical sketch of Governor W. W. Holden for Samuel A. Ashe's *Biographical History of North Carolina* and a sketch of John Penn for the *North Carolina Booklet*. His study of North Carolina during the period 1832–42 won the Julian S. Carr essay prize. Pittman was a charter member of the North Carolina Literary and Historical Association and served as its president in 1925–26. Beginning in 1911 he was a member of the North Carolina Historical Commission and headed that group from 1923 until his death.

A Democrat, Pittman accepted Governor Cameron Morrison's appointment in 1923 to the superior court judgeship, but chronic asthma forced him to resign the following year. Pittman's wife Harriet had died in 1918. Their children were Thomas Merritt, Jr., and Elizabeth Pittman Davis. On 16 Oct. 1923 Pittman married Elizabeth N. Briggs of Raleigh. He died at age seventy-four at his home in Henderson after a brief critical illness.

SEE: *Annual of the North Carolina Baptist State Convention* (1932); *North Carolina Biography*, vol. 4 (1919); Thomas Merritt Pittman Papers (Southern Historical Collection, University of North Carolina, Chapel Hill); *Proceedings of the North Carolina Bar Association* (1932); *Prominent People of North Carolina* (1906); Raleigh *News and Observer*, 9 Feb. 1932.

BRENDA MARKS EAGLES

Plater (or Plato), Richard *(d. ca. September 1705),* General Court justice, attorney general, comptroller of the customs, and clerk of the Council, probably was from Norfolk County, England, where his mother, Dorothy Plater, was living in 1705. He was said by a contemporary resident of North Carolina to have come to that colony from Virginia or Maryland. He may have been the Richard Plater who arrived in Maryland in 1666, the only individual bearing the name who has been located in the available records of Maryland or Virginia.

Plater had settled in the North Carolina colony, then called Albemarle, by 4 Feb. 1687/88, when he witnessed the will of a resident of Pasquotank Precinct. The move may have been influenced by the presence of relatives in Albemarle, as he appears to have been the brother-in-law of Henry Palin and the brother of Mary Clark, widow of John Clark. His relation, if any, to several colonists bearing the Plater name has not been determined.

By February 1690/91 Plater was clerk of the county court of Albemarle, then the highest court of law in the colony. By the following May he was clerk of the Council. He was replaced in those positions by September 1694. In November 1694 he took the oath as customs collector for Pasquotank and Perquimans precincts, serving as deputy for Francis Tomes, customs collector for the colony. In November 1695 he became comptroller of customs, a position equal in rank to that of collector and with duties overlapping the collector's to a degree. The lack of clear delineation of duties and remuneration led to disputes between Plater and Tomes, which eventually were resolved by the General Court. Plater's tenure as comptroller lasted at least through 1697.

In October 1696 Plater took the oath as attorney general. In that position he handled two important suits brought in the General Court on behalf of the Lords Proprietors on the claim that substantial sums were due the Proprietors from the estate of the recently deceased Seth Sothel, former governor of the colony. The suits were eventually dismissed on grounds stemming from Sothel's status as a Proprietor as well as governor.

In July 1700 Plater took office as a justice of the General Court. He sat on the court through July 1703. During that period he continued to hold office as attorney general, stepping down from the bench to conduct cases, as was the custom in that day. While he was a judge, as well as earlier, he also practiced before the court as a private attorney. His public career seems to have ended about July 1703, although he appeared twice before the court as a private attorney in 1704.

Plater lived in Pasquotank Precinct, where presumably he owned land, although no record of his holdings has been located. It is not known whether he was married. He died about September 1705, when he made his will, which was probated the following January. He bequeathed property that he owned in England to his mother, Dorothy Plater of Linn in the County of Norfolk, England, and to a Madam Sarah Beacher of the County of Bucks, England. With the exception of bequests of clothing to his three slaves and small sums of money to four North Carolina residents, apparently unrelated to him, he left his North Carolina estate to Anthony Hatch, whose relation, if any, is not known.

SEE: J. Bryan Grimes, ed., *Abstract of North Carolina Wills* (1910); J. R. B. Hathaway, ed., *North Carolina Historical and Genealogical Register* (1900–1903); Mary Weeks Lambeth, *Memories and Records of Eastern North Carolina* (1957); North Carolina State Archives (Raleigh), particularly Colonial Court Records (boxes 148, 192), Council Minutes, Wills, Inventories (1677–1701), and Will of Richard Plater (24 Jan. 1705/6); Mattie Erma Edwards Parker, ed., *North Carolina Higher-Court Records, 1670–1696* and *1697–1701* (1968, 1971); William S. Price, Jr., ed., *North Carolina Higher-Court Records, 1702–1708* (1974); Gust Skordas, ed., *Early Settlers of Maryland* . . . (1968).

MATTIE ERMA E. PARKER

Plummer, Kemp *(1769–19 Jan. 1826)*, host, lawyer, and political leader, was a native of the Mobjack Bay area of Gloucester County, Va. Some sources list his birth date as 1767. His grandfather, William Plummer I, emigrated from England early in the eighteenth century and settled in Middlesex County, Va., where he married Elizabeth (Betsy) Kemp, descendant of Richard Kemp, deputy governor of Virginia for a year (1644–45). Kemp's father, William II, moved to Gloucester County and married Mary Hayes. Their children were William III, Mary, Anne, Elizabeth, Hannah (who married Nathaniel Macon in 1783), and Kemp (namesake of an uncle who had been a major in the French and Indian War). William II died in 1774, and about 1778 Mary Hayes Plummer moved her family to North Carolina.

Kemp Plummer attended Hampden-Sydney College, graduating with the first class to receive diplomas from that new school in 1786. He then read law with Chancellor George Wythe at the College of William and Mary before being licensed to join the bar in Warrenton. The 1790 census reported him in Warren, unmarried, and the owner of thirty-eight slaves. Four years later he married Susanna Martin (1776–1838), daughter of William Martin of Granville County and a granddaughter of Nicholas Long, commissary general of North Carolina during the Revolution. The young lawyer represented his county in the House of Commons the year he married, 1794.

As a lawyer Kemp Plummer practiced in all the counties surrounding Warren, becoming immensely popular with his clients and associates. He was known as "the honest lawyer." His singing and story-telling abilities, his generosity, and his convivial disposition attracted all classes. The hospitality of the Plummer home drew friends from far and wide; the dinner parties and balls were legendary in the upper Roanoke area. By 1815 Plummer had become a dominant spirit in the "Warren Junto," the close-knit collection of politicians who lived in and around Warrenton. Nathaniel Macon, James Turner, Weldon Edwards, William Hawkins, and William Miller were a few of the luminaries of the group. Together they dominated the political life of North Carolina during the era of the Virginia Dynasty.

In the decade after the War of 1812 Kemp Plummer reached the threshold of great power. He represented Warren in the state Senate in 1815 and 1816. In Raleigh he became chairman of James Monroe's campaign organization in North Carolina. After Monroe's election, he was dispenser of Republican patronage in the state. He was a leader in Masonic and Episcopal affairs. In 1817 he was appointed a trustee of The University of North Carolina, a prestigious position he held for the rest of his life. His friends were the dominant group in the General Assembly. In 1820 they offered Plummer the governorship, but Kemp Plummer's large family and style of living made it impossible for him to accept the honor. His livelihood depended on his legal practice, and he could not afford a move to Raleigh and the governor's mansion.

Kemp and Susanna Plummer had a large family. Among the children were Anne, Mary, Henry, William, Austin, Bettie, Lucy, Kemp, Alfred, Susanna, and Thomas. One of their most illustrious grandchildren was Kemp Plummer Battle, president of The University of North Carolina (1876–91). Kemp, Sr., developed gout in his middle fifties and died soon afterwards. The *Warrenton Republican* mourned, "He was the glory of our little world, the pride of the village." Susanna lived on twelve more years. Three years after her death the citizens of Warrenton purchased the old Plummer home for the Warrenton Female College.

SEE: Kemp P. Battle, "Kemp Plummer," Hampden-Sydney *Kaleidoscope* (1900), and *Memories of an Old Time Tar Heel* (1945); J. B. Boddie, *Southside Virginia Families*, vol. 1 (1966); J. G. de Roulhac Hamilton, *Papers of Thomas Ruffin*, vol. 1 (1920); L. W. Montgomery, *Sketches of Old Warrenton* (1924); Raleigh *Register* and *North Carolina Gazette*, 27 Jan. 1826; L. G. Tyler, *Encyclopedia of Virginia Biography*, vol. 4 (1915); F. A. Virkus, ed., *Compendium of American Genealogy*, vol. 7 (1942).

DANIEL M. MCFARLAND

Plyler, Alva Washington *(14 Sept. 1867–28 June 1956)*, Methodist minister and editor, was born in Iredell County, the son of Robert Conrad and Mary L. Kimball Plyler and the identical twin of Marion Timothy Plyler. He married Grace Davis Barnhardt on 20 July 1911, and they became the parents of three daughters, the eldest of whom died at birth. Mary, the second child, also died at an early age. Helen married Richard Maxwell, Jr.

A. W. Plyler was educated at Trinity College and pursued graduate studies at the University of Chicago. Honorary degrees were conferred on him by Asbury College and Duke University. He entered the ministry in 1892 in the Western North Carolina Conference of the Methodist Episcopal Church, South. Plyler served pastorates at Hot Springs, Pineville, Winston-Salem, Waxhaw, Asheboro, Weaverville, Charlotte, Lexington, Wadesboro, and Greensboro. He also was presiding elder of the Asheville, Salisbury, and Greensboro districts.

Plyler became editor of the *North Carolina Christian Advocate* in 1921 and was joined by his brother as coeditor in 1928. He served in this capacity until his retirement in 1945. He was a member of the Editorial Council of the Religious Press of America; a member and president of the Southern Methodist Press Association; a member of Omicron Delta Kappa, Phi Beta Kappa Associates, and Duke University Varsity Club; a trustee of the Lake Junaluska Methodist Assembly and Brevard College; and a member of the joint board for the sesquicentennial celebration of American Methodism. He represented the Western North Carolina Conference as a delegate at six General Conferences of the church, the Ecumenical Methodist Conference in Atlanta, and the Uniting Conference in 1939.

He was the author of *The Iron Duke of the Methodist Itinerancy* (1925) and coauthor of four other literary productions.

SEE: Nolan B. Harmon, ed., *The Encyclopedia of World Methodism* (1974); *Journal of the Western North Carolina Conference of the Methodist Church* (1956).

LOUISE L. QUEEN

Plyler, Marion Timothy *(14 Sept. 1867–24 Mar. 1954)*, Methodist minister and editor, was born in Iredell County, the son of Robert Conrad and Mary L. Kimball Plyler, and the twin brother of A. W. Plyler. He married Epie Duncan Smith on 20 June 1900, and they had nine children: Edle Mern, Ruth, Leroy S., Marion T., Jr., Conrad N., Eppie Duncan (Mrs. Willis Van Wagoner), Mern (Mrs. James R. Anthony), Grace (Mrs. J. A. McLean), and Eleanor K. (Mrs. Wasson Baird). The two oldest children, Edle Mern and Ruth, died at ages four and three respectively.

M. T. Plyler received the A.B. degree from Trinity College and M.A. degrees from Trinity and The University of North Carolina; he pursued graduate studies at the University of Chicago. Both The University of North Carolina and Duke University awarded him honorary degrees. He entered the traveling ministry in the North Carolina Conference of the Methodist Episcopal Church, South, in 1892 and served pastorates at Carteret Circuit, Wilmington, Murfreesboro, Grifton Circuit, Plymouth, Louisburg, and Chapel Hill. He also was presiding elder of the Elizabeth City, Durham, and Raleigh districts.

In 1928 Plyler became joint editor and business manager of the *North Carolina Christian Advocate*, where he served until his retirement. For a number of years he was president of the Board of Managers of the Conference Pastors' School, and he was elected as a delegate from the North Carolina Conference to three General Conferences of the church. He was buried in Maplewood Cemetery, Durham.

SEE: Nolan B. Harmon, ed., *The Encyclopedia of World Methodism* (1974); *Journal of the North Carolina Conference of the Methodist Church* (1954).

LOUISE L. QUEEN

Poe, Clarence Hamilton *(10 Jan. 1881–8 Oct. 1964)*, editor, publisher, and author, was born on his father's small cotton farm near the town of Gulf, Chatham County, the only son of William Baxter (1839–1907) and Susan Dismukes Poe (1846–1911). Prominent in the maternal ancestry was Augustine Shepperd (1792–1864), of Surry and Forsyth counties, who served nine terms in Congress between 1827 and 1851, in the later years as a Whig.

What little formal education Poe received was chiefly in a one-room country school known as Rocky Branch School, which was in operation three to four months of each year, plus one year of high school in Greensboro. However, he read eagerly and was encouraged by his mother, a former teacher, to develop his talent for writing. At age sixteen he went to Raleigh to work as associate editor for the *Progressive Farmer*, a weekly paper that had been founded in Winston in 1886 by Colonel Leonidas Lafayette Polk. Poe became editor on 4 July 1899. In 1903 he purchased the paper and together with Dr. B. W. Kilgore, Josiah William Bailey, Dr. C. W. Burkett, and T. B. Parker organized the Agricultural Publishing Company, the name of which was later changed to the Progressive Farmer Company. Poe served as president from the firm's inception until January 1954, after which he served as senior editor and board chairman until his death. The headquarters of the company were moved to Birmingham, Ala., in 1911, but Poe continued to direct its operations from his Raleigh office. Between 1903 and 1930, fourteen other farm papers were bought or merged into *Progressive Farmer*; its circulation expanded from 5,000 to 1,400,000, and *Progressive Farmer* became the dominant farm publication in the South and one of the strongest in the United States.

Poe studied agricultural and social conditions abroad on trips to Europe in 1908 and 1912 and on a trip around the world in 1910–11. He was the author of *Cotton: Its Cultivation, Marketing and Manufacture*, with C. W. Burkett (1906); *A Southerner in Europe* (1908); *Where Half the World Is Waking Up* (1912); *Life and Speeches of Charles B. Aycock*, with R. D. W. Connor (1912); *How Farmers Cooperate and Double Profits* (1915); *True Tales of the South at War* (1961); and *My First Eighty Years* (1963).

In the field of agriculture he was a member of the State Board of Agriculture (1913–31), Advisory Council of the U.S. Department of Agriculture (1933), and National Commission on Farm Tenancy (1934); president of the State Farmers' Convention (1919–20), State Dairymen's Association (1929–30), North Carolina Forestry Foundation (1935–40), National Agricultural Conference (1936), and American Country Life Association (1940–41); and master of the North Carolina State Grange (1929–30). In 1936–45 he represented American agriculture on the Federal Board for Vocational Education. Poe received the Distinguished Service Award from the National Future Farmers of America (1911), North Carolina State College (1935), Southern Agricultural Workers (1942), North Carolina State Grange (1947), National 4-H Congress (1951), American Association of Agricultural College Editors (1952), and North Carolina Farm Bureau (1955). In 1949 he was granted honorary membership in Alpha Zeta, the national agricultural fraternity; in 1964 he received the Award of National Convocation of the Church in Town and Country; and in 1966 he was named to the North Carolina Agricultural Hall of Fame.

In the field of education, he was a trustee of Wake Forest College (1915–47); chairman, executive committee of the board of trustees, North Carolina State College of Agriculture and Engineering (1916–31); member, executive committee, and chairman, Agriculture Committee, Trustees of the Consolidated University of North Carolina (1931–55); and member, board of advisers, Institute of Public Affairs, University of Virginia (1927–32). He also served as a member of the Raleigh School Board. He received honorary degrees from Wake Forest College (doctor of literature, 1914); The University of North Carolina (doctor of laws, 1928); Washington College (Maryland) (doctor of laws, 1929), Clemson Agricultural College (doctor of science, 1937), and North Carolina State College (doctor of agricultural education, 1951).

The great variety of his interests is indicated by other numerous activities and awards. He was president of the State Press Association (1913–14), North Carolina Conference for Social Service (1913–15), and State Literary and Historical Association (1914–15). In 1925–64 he was an elector of the Hall of Fame; in 1926–60, director of the North Carolina State Art Society (also part-time chairman of its executive committee); and in 1933–35, head of the North Carolina Rural Electrification Authority. He was a member of the Raleigh Board of Managers of the Wachovia Bank and Trust Company (1924–33), Commission to Draft a Revision of the State Constitution (1931–32), State Planning Board (1935), National Advisory Committee of National Youth Administration (1935–43), National Committee on Hospital Care (1944–46), North Carolina Hospital and Medical Care Commission (1944–55 [vice-chairman, 1945–55]), Jackson-Johnson-Polk Monument Commission (1947–48), Commission on Health Needs of the Nation (1951–52), International Development Advisory Board (known as the Rockefeller Commission, 1951–55), State Art Commission (1951–61), and State Commission on Racial Segregation in the Schools (1954–55). In addition, he was chairman of the State Committee that secured ratification of five constitutional amendments (1936), National Advisory Committee on Rural Electrification (1936), and Southern Governors' Campaign for Balanced Prosperity in the South (1940–43).

In World War I he was a member of the Executive Committee of State Food and Fuel Administration and the War Savings Committee. In World War II he was a member of the North Carolina Council of National Defense, State Council of Civilian Defense, and National Committee to Defend America by Aiding the Allies, as well as chairman of Executive Committee of the North Carolina Farm Manpower Commission.

Poe twice won the Patterson Cup Award for best North Carolina book of the year (1909, 1912). He was named Citizen of the Year by the North Carolina Citizens' Association (1955). Other honors included the Distinguished Service Award from The University of North Carolina School of Medicine (1957) and from the National Council of Churches of Christ (1964), the World Peace Award from the American Freedom Association (1962), and the North Carolina Award for Distinguished Public Service (1964).

Goldsboro editor Henry Belk said: "If one were asked to name the North Carolinian who has made the greatest contribution to progress and enlightenment, to education and health and improved living, most would name Dr. Poe." Similarly, Virginius Dabney, Richmond, Va., editor, observed: "If a list were drawn up of the half-dozen men who have done most for the South since 1900, it would have to include Dr. Clarence Poe."

For years Poe conducted extensive dairy, tobacco, cotton, and poultry production operations on his 800-acre Longview Farm. He also served as president (1937–55) and board chairman (1938–64) of Longview Gardens, Inc., a suburban real estate firm that sold residential lots and built and operated a neighborhood shopping center. Poe's leisure activities included horseback riding, landscaping, and gardening. He held membership in the First Baptist Church, Raleigh Rotary Club, Watauga Club (longtime president), and Sandwich Club.

He married, in Raleigh on 29 May 1912, Alice Varina, daughter of Charles B. Aycock, former governor of North Carolina (1901–5). They had three children: Charles Aycock, Raleigh attorney; William D., edition editor of the *Progressive Farmer* (d. 1958); and Jean Shepperd, who married Gordon Smith, Jr. Clarence Poe had one sister, Daisy Poe Moore, of Gulf. He died in Raleigh at age eighty-three, still writing his column for the *Progressive Farmer* and working on his eighth book.

SEE: *Better Crops with Plant Food* 44 (September 1960); *Congressional Record*, 4 Feb. 1954; Joseph A. Cote, "Crusading Editor, 1881–1964" (doctoral diss., University of Georgia, 1976) and "Clarence Hamilton Poe: The Formative Years, 1899–1917" (master's thesis, East Carolina University, 1969); *Greensboro Daily News*, 9 May 1958; *Nat. Cyc. Am. Biog.*, vol. 52 (1970); Raleigh *News and Observer*, 24 Feb. 1952, 9 Oct. 1964; Richmond *Times-Dispatch*, 4 Jan. 1954; *Who Was Who in America*, vol. 4 (1968).

CHARLES AYCOCK POE

Pogue, Joseph Ezekiel, Jr. *(6 June 1887–17 Dec. 1971)*, geologist, petroleum engineer, and economist, was born in Raleigh, the son of Joseph Ezekiel and Henrietta Kramer Pogue. After preparatory education in Raleigh, he entered The University of North Carolina and was graduated with A.B. (1906) and M.A. (1907) degrees. An honor student, he was elected to Phi Beta Kappa in his junior year; the university yearbook, the *Yackety Yack*, said of him: "He was a scholar, a ripe one and a good one." He was a member of Sigma Zi and Alpha Tau Omega social fraternity. Pogue was awarded the Southerland Fellowship in chemistry for a year of graduate study; his master's thesis on the Cid Mining District in Davidson County received the Kerr Prize and was later published in the *North Carolina Geological and Economic Survey* (1910). Between 1906 and 1907 he also worked as an assistant geologist for the North Carolina Geological Survey. Continuing graduate study at Yale University, he earned the Ph.D. degree in geology in 1909.

Also in 1909 Pogue joined the Smithsonian Institution as assistant curator and remained there until 1913, except for a year as a special student at the University of Heidelberg in 1911. After a year (1913–14) as an associate geologist with the U.S. Geological Survey, he joined the faculty of Northwestern University as an associate professor (1914–17). He returned to the Smithsonian in 1917 as a mineral technician and in 1918 was named assistant director of the Bureau of Oil Conservation in the U.S. Fuel Administration.

Pogue married Grace Needham, of Washington, D.C., on 17 Apr. 1919. After World War I he joined the Sinclair Oil Corporation, but in 1921 he established his own consulting engineering firm and for the next fifteen years was active in petroleum explorations in the United States and abroad.

In 1936, when Winthrop W. Aldrich, then head of the Chase National Bank, decided to establish a petroleum department in the bank, he brought Pogue in as a vice-president of Chase to organize and head the new department. From 1936 until his resignation in 1949, Pogue was a key figure in an increasingly important area of the bank's interests. He knew the petroleum field and the people in it as few men did; as one colleague put it: "He was an unreplaceable liaison between the oil industry and the financial community."

During World War II Pogue served the government in a number of capacities relating to the petroleum industry, among them assistant to the chairman, Petroleum Industry War Council; member of the National Oil Policy Committee; and adviser to the Economic Committee, Petroleum Industry War Council. Although he no longer held a full-time position with the Chase National Bank after 1949, he remained a valued consultant on petroleum matters until 1957. During this period he served for ten years (1949–59) on the board of directors of Gulf Oil Company.

Throughout his career, Pogue maintained a keen interest in the advancement of knowledge in his profession.

He was a Fellow of the Geological Society of America and a member of the American Statistical Association, American Association of Petroleum Geologists, American Petroleum Institute, American Economics Association, American Institute of Mining and Metallurgy, American Society of Automotive Engineers, and American Society of Mechanical Engineers.

He published numerous books and articles on geological subjects and various facets of the petroleum industry, including *The Turquoise* (1915), *Prices of Petroleum and Its Products during the War* (1919), and *Economic Structure of the American Petroleum Industry* (1936); he was coauthor of *Energy Resources of the United States* (1919) and *Capital Formation in the Petroleum Industry* (1952). His articles appeared in *Atlantic Monthly*, proceedings of the American Statistical Association, proceedings of the Smithsonian Institution, bulletins of the National Museum, *American Journal of Science*, *Journal of Geology*, *National Geographic*, *Scientific Monthly*, and other periodicals.

The University of North Carolina awarded Pogue an honorary doctor of science degree in 1963, when he was cited as "a geologist and mineralogist of international distinction." Devoted to the university, he was a regular and generous contributor and he made the University of North Carolina at Chapel Hill the principal beneficiary of his large estate. Dr. and Mrs. Pogue had no children and his widow, Grace Pogue, who had come to share his love for the university, left the residual estate to the university upon her death on 8 Mar. 1973. Their $11 million dollar gift was the largest ever received by the University of North Carolina at Chapel Hill. In 1930 Mrs. Pogue had established a student loan fund at the university in honor of her husband. He once described her as his "Secretary, Statistical Assistant, and General Advisor . . . a financial expert in her own right."

During the 1960s the Pogues maintained three homes—one on Park Avenue in New York City, one at Port Jefferson, N.Y., and the third at Mountain Lake, Lake Wales, Fla. Both Dr. and Mrs. Pogue died in Florida, where in their later years they lived almost year-round.

SEE: *Chapel Hill Weekly*, 10 Dec. 1976; Daniel L. Grant, *Alumni History of the University of North Carolina* (1924); *North Carolina Biography*, vol. 5 (1919); Joseph E. Pogue Papers (Southern Historical Collection, University of North Carolina, Chapel Hill); Joseph E. Pogue, Jr., *Writings*, 5 vols. (North Carolina Collection, University of North Carolina, Chapel Hill); Raleigh *News and Observer*, 20 Mar. 1927, 5 June 1963, 19 Dec. 1971, 11 Dec. 1976; *Who's Who in the South and Southwest* (1973); *Who Was Who in America*, vol. 8 (1985).

J. CARLYLE SITTERSON

Polk, James Knox *(2 Nov. 1795–15 June 1849)*, eleventh president of the United States and oldest of the ten children of Samuel and Jane Knox Polk, was born in Mecklenburg County, south of Charlotte on a bend of the Little Sugar Creek. Samuel Polk was a good provider; his lands were productive and the family's home, though built of logs, was of the type that denoted a measure of prosperity. The Polks were of Scotch-Irish descent. The first members of the family had arrived in the New World in the late seventeenth century and settled on Maryland's Eastern Shore; by 1753 they had moved to North Carolina to the area that became Mecklenburg County. Land was cleared on Sugar Creek, cabins were built, and, as in Maryland, the Polks—along with families who moved with them—gave support to the organizing of Presbyterian congregations.

In 1790 James K. Polk's grandfather, Ezekiel, was appointed a deputy surveyor of land grants in the western country and for a brief time moved his family to Tennessee, a region then known as the Southwest Territory. The adventure lingered in Ezekiel's mind, and in 1803 he returned to Tennessee, this time taking with him the married children and their families; only Samuel's family remained in Mecklenburg. The Polks settled in Middle Tennessee in the fertile valley of the Duck River, now a part of Maury County. It was not long before Sam Polk saw the possibilities of economic gain by moving to Tennessee, and in the fall of 1806, after crops had been gathered, he began the westward trek. The distance to the new home was approximately five hundred miles, with a large segment of the route leading across mountainous terrain; along the entire route the road was rough and in places hardly more than a trail. Six weeks of travel were required before the Samuel Polks were united with their relatives.

It was in Maury County that James Polk spent a part of his childhood and adolescent years and reached young manhood. Young Polk had attended school briefly before leaving North Carolina, but the details are not known. His school attendance probably amounted to no more than a few sessions at an old field school, but in view of the fact that his father was a man of comfortable means, one can safely assume that he would have required that his son be taught to read and write. A neighbor recalled having seen "Little Jimmy Polk . . . [passing] along [the] road often to school, barefooted, with his breeches rolled up to his knees." But Polk was small for his age, frequently sick, and, worst of all, unable to hold his own in vigorous sports. The cause of his illnesses was diagnosed as gallstones, and in the fall of 1812 he and his father made the trip to Danville, Ky., for surgery to be performed by Dr. Ephraim McDowell, the best-known surgeon living west of the mountains. After recuperation Polk returned home feeling greatly improved, yet his health was never to be robust.

In July 1813, when almost eighteen, Polk was enrolled in a Presbyterian academy located a few miles south of Columbia, Tenn. The teacher was the Reverend Robert Henderson, a man well prepared to offer his students a sound introduction to a classical education. The following year Polk entered an academy in Murfreesboro conducted by Samuel P. Black, which, like the previous school, was also under Presbyterian influence though it had a larger student enrollment and a broader curriculum. Course offerings quite naturally included Greek and Latin, but instruction was also available in mathematics, geography, natural and moral philosophy, astronomy, belles-lettres, and logic. Polk was blessed with a good mind of which he made full use; in fact, by the end of the year 1815 he had established himself as a superior student and was prepared to apply for admission to The University of North Carolina. The choice of a school for further study must have been easy because there were Polk relatives who lived near Chapel Hill, and his father's cousin, Colonel William Polk, was a trustee of the university. James Polk passed the test for admission and indeed performed so well that he was admitted to the sophomore class. He began his studies in January 1816 and was graduated with honors in June 1818.

Polk was not well at the time of graduation and delayed his return home until October. At some time during this enforced delay he made the decision to study law and enter politics. After a short visit with family and relatives he moved to Nashville to read law in the office of Felix Grundy. With Grundy's support he was elected clerk of the state senate, a position that afforded him an opportunity to meet many of Tennessee's leading citizens. He assumed this office in 1819 and was reelected in 1820 and 1822. In 1820 he received his license to practice and was then free to devote the time between the brief legislative sessions to the law practice he had established in Columbia, his hometown.

In 1823 Polk announced his candidacy for the Tennessee legislature, issuing a challenge to a veteran incumbent. In view of his opponent's strength, he campaigned vigorously in all parts of the county and was able to win the election by a comfortable margin. Polk served in the house for only one term, but within that brief time he established himself as an able legislator and a superior debater. Undoubtedly, the greatest benefit he derived from this experience was the lasting friendship formed with Andrew Jackson.

During the summer of 1824 there were frequent conferences and exchanges of letters that involved Polk, Grundy, and other Jackson supporters, and by August it was clear that Polk would be a candidate to represent Tennessee's Sixth Congressional District in the U.S. House of Representatives. Once this decision was made he campaigned relentlessly and won the nomination and election over a field of five Democratic candidates.

Polk was a member of Congress from 4 Mar. 1825 to 3 Mar. 1839, and for the Twenty-fourth and Twenty-fifth Congresses he was elected Speaker, a position in which he displayed strong leadership and extraordinary political skill by his ability to enforce party discipline. Polk gave vigorous support to Jacksonian political doctrines and was openly and frankly a party leader—the first Speaker to be so regarded.

By 1837 Tennessee's Democratic party was in disarray, and Polk, the most successful of the party's leaders, was persuaded to run for governor. The announcement of his candidacy came in the summer of 1838, while he was on a visit home during the congressional recess. From that date until the election in July 1839 Polk campaigned in every section of the state and won by the small majority of 2,462 votes. The Whigs blamed their defeat on Polk's unprecedented campaigning, and an analysis of the campaign justifies this conclusion. As governor, Polk functioned as a party leader, seeking to maintain harmony and give guidance to party members in dealing with the questions of banking and internal improvements. Soon he was being mentioned as a possible vice-presidential candidate, and his ambition for higher office was undoubtedly related to his failure to bring heavier pressure upon recalcitrant Democrats.

Polk ran for reelection in 1841 but was defeated by the Whig candidate, James C. Jones, and again in 1843 was defeated by Jones. The margin of defeat was narrow in both elections. Following the second defeat Polk embarked on an amazing comeback that was to result in his nomination for president on the ninth ballot at the Democratic convention held in Baltimore in May 1844, making him the nation's first "dark horse" candidate. "While . . . far from being the unknown that the Tennessee Whigs tried to make him out, the idea of him as a presidential possibility required some getting used to, by Whigs and Democrats alike." Polk's political ability had been recognized and his loyalty to the Democratic party rewarded. In the November election he defeated Henry Clay, the Whig candidate, by a narrow margin.

Polk was forty-nine years old and the youngest of any of his predecessors when inaugurated on 4 Mar. 1845. Though party faithfulness had contributed much to his success, once elected president he made clear his intention to dictate policies rather than to follow. To his friend and future cabinet member, Cave Johnson, he wrote on 21 Dec. 1844, "I intend to be *myself* President of the U.S." And this he did, even rejecting on several occasions the advice of his mentor, Andrew Jackson. Upon assuming office he set four goals for his administration: to lower the tariff, to provide an independent Treasury, to settle the Oregon boundary dispute, and to acquire California. When he left the White House, each of these had been realized. Polk's policy of expansion added more than 500,000 square miles of territory to the United States, and his statements in opposition to European interference in American affairs—a specific example of which is his message to Congress, delivered 2 Dec. 1845—are frequently referred to as the "Polk Doctrine."

Few presidents have been more successful in attaining their goals. In spite of the fact that during his administration the nation was involved in a war with Mexico, a territorial dispute with Great Britain, and the issues of slavery, the bank, and the tariff, Polk has emerged in the light of history as "a sound statesman, an unusually capable executive, and an unwavering patriot." He was conscientious to the extreme, and if his executive ability showed weakness, it was that he regarded it as a duty that he "supervise the whole operations of the Government." His position in American history was long underrated, and unjustly so, but in a poll of fifty-five leading American historians conducted in 1948, Polk was ranked with Theodore Roosevelt, Grover Cleveland, and John Adams as one of the nation's four near-great presidents.

Polk was a man lacking personal magnetism. He commanded respect, yet generated neither liking nor awe, and in fact had none of the capacity for comradery so much a part of most politicians. Cave Johnson, a fellow Tennessean, appears to have been the only man with whom he ever formed a relaxed friendship. Descriptions of Polk indicate that he was solidly built, a bit under middle height, and carried himself with military bearing—perhaps a bit awkwardly. His head was small and his mop of unruly black hair, flecked with gray, was brushed away from his broad forehead. His eyes were a penetrating gray, his mouth appeared stern, and his countenance—which frequently gave the appearance of sadness—was sometimes lightened by a friendly smile.

Polk had little of the native gift of speaking, but, through training that had been started under the Reverend Mr. Henderson and then improved by practice, he developed a style that was to make him one of Tennessee's most celebrated campaign orators. His manner was sufficiently dignified to satisfy the educated townspeople, his speeches were full of information, and his arguments were logically developed. Equally important, he had learned to use wit and sarcasm to bring shouts of approval from the rural folk. This was accomplished without waving of arms; instead, with an expressive face he used sly glances and grimaces to drive home innuendoes that delighted his listeners.

On 1 Jan. 1824 James K. Polk married Sarah Childress of Murfreesboro, the daughter of Major Joel Childress, who had been a wealthy merchant, tavern keeper, planter, and land speculator. The wedding was a major social event in Middle Tennessee. Though never described as beautiful, Sarah was vivacious, intelligent, and at her best in social gatherings; in addition, her careful training at home had made her a charming hostess. Like her mother-in-law, she was a devout and strict Presbyterian. Polk regularly attended church services with his wife while at home and in Washington, but on those rare occasions when Sarah was sick or they were separated by travel he attended a Methodist service. Near the end of his life he was baptized and received into membership of the Methodist church. The Polks had no children, but throughout their married life nieces and nephews traveled with them or paid them lengthy visits.

Polk retained his affection for The University of North Carolina. One of his rare vacations was a trip made to Chapel Hill in the late spring of 1847 when he returned for the university's commencement exercises, with Mrs. Polk and one of her nieces accompanying him. The account of this trip as related in his diary reveals the closeness of his attachment to his alma mater.

As 4 Mar. 1849 was on Sunday, the inauguration of General Zachary Taylor was delayed until the following day. The Polks left Washington on the sixth by boat on a trip that was to be made by boat and train and would take them by way of Wilmington, Charleston, Mobile, New Orleans, up the Mississippi to Memphis and into the Ohio and Cumberland rivers to Nashville, arriving on 2 April. Four years in office and the lengthy trip to Tennessee left Polk exhausted. He had purchased a home in Nashville, once owned by Felix Grundy, where he had planned to spend his remaining years in dignified retirement. But ill-health and overwork had taken their toll. He was buried in the garden of his Nashville residence, and in 1893 his remains, with those of this wife, were removed to the capitol grounds and placed in a tomb designed by William Strickland.

SEE: *Biog. Dir. Am. Cong.* (1961); Jerry C. Cashion, "James Knox Polk and North Carolina" (North Carolina State Archives, Raleigh); *DAB*, vol. 8 (1935); James K. Polk, *Polk: The Diary of a President, 1845–1849*, ed. Allen Nevins (1952); Arthur M. Schlesinger, "The U.S. Presidents," *Life* 25 (1948); Charles G. Sellers, Jr., *James K. Polk: Jacksonian, 1795–1843* (1957), *James K. Polk, Continentalist, 1843–1846* (1966), and "Jim Polk Goes to Chapel Hill," *North Carolina Historical Review* 29 (1952); Mrs. Jean B. Waggener (Director, Archives and Manuscripts, Tennessee State Library and Archives) to the author, 11 Mar. 1982.

J. ISAAC COPELAND

Polk, Leonidas *(10 Apr. 1806–14 June 1864)*, Episcopal bishop and Confederate corps commander, was born in Raleigh. His father, William Polk, distinguished himself as a soldier in the American Revolution (at Brandywine, Germantown, and Camden), maintained a close relationship with Andrew Jackson, and contributed to the advancement of education in North Carolina. His mother, Sarah Hawkins, was the sister of North Carolina Governor William Hawkins. Many members of the Polk family settled in Tennessee and by 1840 held a "commanding position."

Leonidas Polk attended The University of North Carolina for two years (1821–23) before entering the U.S. Military Academy. There he roomed with Albert Sidney Johnston, developed a close friendship with Jefferson Davis, and achieved a commendable academic record. During his final year, Dr. Charles P. McIlvaine, a newly assigned chaplain, converted Polk to the Episcopal church. After only six months service, Polk resigned his commission and entered the Virginia Theological Seminary. He was ordained deacon in April 1830 and priest in May 1831. In 1830 he married Frances Ann Devereux, the daughter of John Devereux of Raleigh. They became the parents of eight children: Alexander Hamilton, Frances Devereux, Katherine, Sarah, Susan R., Elizabeth D., William Mecklenburg, and Lucia. After a short assignment as assistant rector in Richmond, he resigned because of poor health and traveled and studied. In 1834 he assumed his duties at St. Peter's Parish in Columbia, Tenn., surrounded by his relations.

In 1838 Polk was consecrated missionary bishop of the Southwest. This extensive area of scattered settlements comprised the states of Arkansas, Texas, Mississippi, Alabama, Louisiana, and a section of the Indian Territory. During the first six months of 1839, he familiarized himself with the region, having "travelled 5,000 miles, preached 44 sermons, baptized 14, confirmed 41, consecrated one church and laid the cornerstone of another." "It is in extent about equal to all of France." His journeys on horseback across most of the lower South gave him a knowledge of the area rivaled by few of the Confederate high command.

Polk settled in Louisiana in 1841, having been consecrated bishop of Louisiana in that year. For twelve years he attempted unsuccessfully to manage a vast sugar plantation at Bayou la Fourche while performing his ecclesiastical duties. For the four hundred slaves Polk controlled at Leighton, he proved to be an enlightened master, marrying them with ceremony in the "big house" and establishing a Sunday school on the place. In 1849 cholera swept away one hundred slaves, and in 1854 Polk lost the plantation because of heavy debts.

In the five years preceding the Civil War, Polk's chief concern was the establishment of the University of the South. To supply the Episcopal clergy for the Middle South and to educate properly the lay leadership, he labored to raise funds adequate to erect "a university which would rival the establishment at Harvard or Yale." Through the assistance of Bishop Stephen Elliott and many others, about ten thousand acres were purchased at Sewanee, Tenn., and on 19 Oct. 1860 Polk laid the cornerstone for the university.

In the spring of 1861 President Jefferson Davis and many other Southerners urged him to enter the Confederate army. Despite his lack of military experience, Polk accepted the appointment as major general, considering it "a call of Providence." Passionately committed to the Confederacy, he felt that it was his duty to enlist in times when "constitutional liberty seems to have fled." Polk's presence was an emotional asset to the Confederacy throughout the war and offset his limitations as a commander.

In the summer and fall of 1861 he accepted responsibility for the defense of the Mississippi River, the importance of which he continually stressed. Despite successes with the occupation of Columbus in September and the defeat of Ulysses S. Grant's force at Belmont in November, Polk's efforts failed, largely because of Albert Sidney Johnston's insistence on the consolidation of the western forces of the Confederacy. Polk resigned in November 1861, when Johnston withdrew five thousand men from Columbus, but was placated by Davis.

At Shiloh Polk earned a reputation for courage and displayed an ineptitude for logistics. During the invasion of Kentucky in 1862, he upheld his combat record but worked at cross purposes with his commander, Braxton Bragg, thereby helping to undermine the campaign. Commissioned lieutenant general in October, Polk succeeded in fielding a corps noted for high morale and dogged fighting. At Murfreesboro in December 1862 his corps sustained frightful losses and accomplished little with repeated frontal attacks. The spring of 1863 found Polk continually quarreling with Bragg and urging Davis to have Bragg replaced. The Bragg-Polk controversy raged following Chickamauga, and Davis settled the irreconcilable conflict by sending Polk to Mississippi. Polk's actions at Chickamauga were open to criticism but hardly justified Bragg's demand for a court-martial.

Following the disaster at Chattanooga in November 1863, Polk rejoined the army now commanded by his friend Joseph Johnston. Under Johnston, Polk proved himself to be an able, competent corps commander. His corps maneuvered well and fought well. The end came at Pine Mountain in June 1864. Polk and his staff were observing the enemy lines when Union artillerymen spotted them. Polk ordered his staff off the hill but remained for a last look. A shell from a ten pounder hit him, killing him instantly.

The Army of Tennessee mourned Polk's loss. He had inspired the army for three years by his example and was loved by his men. His fellow corps commander, William J. Hardee, wept when he learned of Polk's death. The loss of this experienced corps commander hurt the chances of the Army of Tennessee in the heavy fighting around Atlanta. One young Confederate felt that "a fair investigation of his record in the army as a general and in the church as a priest makes it evident that there was a very eloquent, earnest bishop, spoiled to make an ordinary general." Another soldier, a Tennessean who fought under Polk for three years, stated, "'Bishop Polk' was ever a favorite with the army, and when any position was to be held, and it was known that 'Bishop Polk' was there, we knew and felt that 'all was well.'"

Leonidas Polk was buried first in Augusta, Ga., and later in Christ Church Cathedral, New Orleans. Three portraits of him may be found in the University of the South.

SEE: Joseph B. Cheshire, *The Church of the Confederate States* (1912); Beth G. Crabtree and James W. Patton, eds., *Journal of a Secesh Lady* (1979); J. H. Parks, *General Leonidas Polk, C.S.A.* (1962); William S. Perry, *The Episcopate in America* (1895); Leonidas Polk Papers, Gale and Polk Family Papers, and George Washington Polk Papers (Southern Historical Collection, University of North Carolina, Chapel Hill); Leonidas Polk Manuscript (Manuscript Department, Duke University Library, Durham); Leonidas Polk Papers (University of the South, Sewanee, Tenn.).

N. C. HUGHES, JR.

Polk, Leonidas LaFayette *(24 Apr. 1837–11 June 1892)*, agrarian leader, was born in Anson County, the only child of Andrew Polk and his second wife, Serena Autry. The father was a middle-class farmer who practiced diversified agriculture—cotton, corn, oats, cattle, hogs—and at the time of his death owned thirty-two slaves. The mother died two years after her husband, when Leonidas was fifteen. In sharing the estate with three half brothers he received 353 acres and seven slaves. He attended neighborhood schools, read widely, and benefited from the guidance of several sympathetic, responsible adults. Certain that he wanted to be a "gentleman farmer," the young man enrolled at Davidson College in 1855 and completed with distinction one year as a special student. He then returned to Anson, married, received 300 more acres of land on approaching his majority, and developed a keen interest in politics.

As an ardent Union Whig he was elected to the state House of Commons in 1860. After President Abraham Lincoln's call for troops against the South the following spring, Polk declared himself "for resistance to the bitter end." He led a joint house-senate committee in the creation of a state militia; commissioned a colonel, he performed the delicate task of applying compulsory service legislation in his home county. In May 1862 he transferred to the Twenty-sixth North Carolina Regiment (as a private, then sergeant-major) commanded by Colonel Zebulon B. Vance. After Vance's election as governor, however, Polk joined the Forty-third Regiment (as a second lieutenant), in which he served until returned to the legislature in 1864. After the war he also won election to the constitutional convention that restored North Carolina to the Union. For the next eight years he devoted his energies chiefly to restoring his war-ravaged property and caring for his growing family. At length he opened a country store, started the weekly *Ansonian*, and, as the new Carolina Central Railroad approached his farm, sold lots, attracted settlers, and incorporated the town of Polkton.

The appearance of his paper's first number in 1874 signaled Polk's return to public affairs. He advocated Zeb Vance for governor two years hence for conservatism over radicalism, and he championed diversification—"raise your own bread and meat"—while condemning the one-crop—"all cotton"—system. It was his conviction that the Grange, of which he was a leader, could exemplify necessary education and cooperation. Together, and with Governor Vance's backing, they initiated action resulting in a state Department of Agriculture in 1877 with Polk as commissioner. Utilizing a tax on commercial fertilizers, the agency quickly became a prototype for five other southern states. Following Vance's election to the U.S. Senate, however, the department's conservative governing board so crippled the agency that Polk resigned in 1880. Shortly afterwards he joined the daily Raleigh *News*.

As a roving reporter he campaigned for development of the state's resources and revealed himself as a strongly partisan Democrat. In 1881 he efficiently managed the state fair; in 1883 he exerted strong influence towards the reorganization of the state Board of Agriculture. But three business ventures he launched in the early eighties failed. Polk then returned to journalism and agricultural leadership as he began the weekly *Progressive Farmer* on 10 Feb. 1886. He strove to make the paper of practical value to farm families, encouraged farmers to organize clubs to advance their interests, and insisted that the annual federal land-grant fund under the Morrill Act be transferred from The University of North Carolina to a separate institution that would teach "practical" subjects. Each goal was attained. When the North Carolina College of Agriculture and Mechanic Arts was established at Raleigh in 1887, Polk's prime role became apparent. Leaders of his denomination then called upon him to push through a long-dormant project to create a Baptist school for girls—ultimately Meredith College in Raleigh.

The farmers' club movement initiated by Polk made North Carolina receptive to the Farmers' Alliance in 1887. Since the Grange had declined and farmer grievances were mounting, this predominantly southern organization had great appeal. Facilitated by Polk, the Alliance rapidly gained thousands of members and impressive strength over the next four years. First came the North Carolina Farmers' Association, formed in connection with the struggle for the agricultural college. Several months later, in Atlanta, the Inter-State Farmers' Association, a group of southern farm leaders, elected Polk president by acclamation and repeated their action at Raleigh in 1888 and at Montgomery in 1889. Both organizations were absorbed by the great Farmers' Alliance. Following a year as first vice-president and another as chairman of the executive committee, Polk in 1889 became president of the two-million-member Alliance and was reelected in 1890 and 1891. Farm distress was acute during these years. He and other officers, with headquarters in Washington, D.C., planned, organized, corresponded, published, lobbied, and exhorted. But their opposition—the industrial and financial interests of the Northeast and Midwest—seemed unyielding.

Polk participated vigorously in the political campaigns of the early nineties. Endowed with personal warmth, great energy, and oratorical skill, he traveled by train to almost every state in behalf of the farmers' cause. He elaborated the Alliance's panacea for agriculture's ills, the "sub-treasury plan"; he fervently called for an end to North-South sectionalism. The focal point in the West was Kansas, where the new People's party (Populists) threatened to combine with the minority Democrats to overthrow the Republicans. Polk made two speaking trips to Kansas in 1890 and still another the next year. As in the West, the political power of the Farmers' Alliance in the South became formidable. The Negro issue, however, dictated that the Alliance endeavor to control the Democratic majority rather than form a third party, which might result in a Republican victory. When the Kansas Republicans lost in the elections of 1890, and hundreds of Alliance-backed candidates won in both the West and the South, the farmers' revolt gained national attention. "We are here to stay," said Polk. "This great reform movement will not cease until it has impressed itself indelibly in the nation's history."

As leader of the Alliance, largest of the many organizations campaigning for the farmer and the laborer, Polk himself drew much notice. At the annual meetings of the Alliance at Ocala, Fla., in 1890 and at Indianapolis in 1891, third-party speculation was rampant and his name was often mentioned in that connection. By the latter year he was convinced that neither major party would legislate for farm relief. Indeed, Congress had defeated a vital "free silver" bill and refused even to discuss the sub-treasury plan. Polk therefore saw his plain duty: to do all in his power to promote the success of the now national People's party. Already he had been bitterly attacked by both the Kansas Republicans and the North Carolina "Bourbon Democrats." But "Alliance Democrats" in his home state scored heavily in 1890, enacted the following year the most progressive legislation since antebellum times, and in 1892 held the balance of political power.

Thousands of Tar Heel farmers enlisted with Polk in the People's party in 1892. Yet more thousands who admired him—more conservative, fearful of a third party, aware of their strength—stayed with the Democratic party. Marion Butler, young president of the State Alliance, proposed fusion of Democrats and Populists in state politics. Polk naturally opposed the plan: "I cannot give such a policy my endorsement. . . . I am an out and out People's Party man." Both rejoiced, nonetheless, when the Democratic state convention nominated for governor an outstanding allianceman, Elias Carr, over the incumbent Bourbon, Thomas M. Holt.

Nationally the first landmark of 1892 was St. Louis, where 1,200 delegates from many reform organizations assembled on 22 February to agree on a platform and arrange for a subsequent People's party convention. Polk served as permanent chairman and conferred at length with other Populist leaders. The body then made the site Omaha and the date 4 July; 1,776 delegates were authorized to nominate the third-party ticket. By spring, sentiment began to crystallize on the nomination of Polk for president. His leadership of the Alliance, acceptability to diverse reform groups, and crusade against sectionalism combined to sway many minds. He was willing and zealous. So strongly did his *Progressive Farmer* on 24 May favor the Populists, however, that the State Alliance executive committee objected; as official organ the paper was required to be nonpartisan. Whereupon Polk, possibly misunderstanding, submitted his paper's resignation. This trying decision, the realization that the Bourbon Democrats would support the Alliance Democrats against the Populists in North Carolina, overwork and overstrain, and the aggravation of a physical ailment of four years finally overcame him. He died in the Garfield Memorial Hospital, Washington, and was buried the next day in Oakwood Cemetery, Raleigh.

L. L. Polk was a great-great-grandson of William Polk of Carlisle, Pa., common ancestor of the North Carolina Polks, and a second cousin to Leonidas Polk, churchman, educator, and Confederate officer. He married Sarah Pamela Gaddy of Anson County on 23 Sept. 1857. They had six daughters and a son who died in infancy. The daughters who bore children were Juanita Polk Denmark and Carrie Polk Browder.

SEE: Stuart Noblin, *L. L. Polk* (1949 [portraits]); W. J. Peele, *North Carolina Baptist Almanac* (1893); Clarence Poe, *Colonel Polk* (1926); L. L. Polk Papers (Southern Historical Collection, University of North Carolina, Chapel Hill); Raleigh *News and Observer*, 29 July 1926.

STUART NOBLIN

Polk, Lucius Eugene *(10 July 1833–1 Dec. 1892)*, probably the ablest brigade commander in the Confederate Army of Tennessee, was born in Salisbury, the son of Dr. William Julius and Mary Rebecca Long Polk, the grandson of Colonel William Polk, and the nephew of Lieutenant General Leonidas Polk. In 1835 Lucius Polk's parents moved to Maury County, Tenn., to join other members of the family who collectively dominated this rich, fertile center of the state. After graduation from the University of Virginia in 1852, Polk became a cotton planter in Phillips County, Ark.

When war broke out, Lucius Polk volunteered as a private in Company B, Fifteenth Arkansas Regiment. As a member of the "Yell Rifles" he came under the command of Captain (later Major General) Patrick R. Cleburne. The two were devoted to each other and Cleburne prized Polk as a subordinate. They served together throughout the war until Polk's wounds forced his retirement. Polk quickly rose in rank to lieutenant. He won recognition for bravery and ability at Shiloh, where he was wounded. A few days later he became colonel of the Fifteenth Arkansas as Cleburne moved to brigade commander.

In the Kentucky campaign in the fall of 1862, Polk excelled although "scalped" by a minié ball in the Battle of Richmond in August and wounded again at Perryville in October. On 13 Dec. 1862 the Confederate War Department commissioned him brigadier general, and later that month he led Cleburne's old brigade into battle at Murfreesboro. Beginning with Murfreesboro and continuing through the Battles of Chickamauga and Missionary Ridge, Polk received continual praise not only from Cleburne but also from his corps and army commanders. Polk's enlisted men and others throughout the army echoed the compliments of their superiors. Sam Watkins described Lucius Polk in 1864 as a man "with long black hair that curled, a gentle and attractive black eye that seemed to sparkle with love rather than chivalry, and were it not for a young moustache and goatee that he usually wore, he would have passed for a beautiful girl. In his manner he was as simple and guileless as a child, and generous almost to a fault."

An incredibly successful brigade commander, he inspired confidence and that confidence inspired victory and determination. Polk's brigade (consisting of the First and Fifteenth Arkansas, Second and Forty-eighth Tennessee, and Fifth Confederate regiments) was the pride of Cleburne's division and that division was the pride of William J. Hardee's corps and the Army of Tennessee. Characteristically, in late June 1864, during the Atlanta campaign, Polk's brigade held the most exposed position in the Confederate line. The enemy opened a furious cannonade, killing many of Polk's men and virtually severing Polk's leg. This fourth wound ended his service.

Polk returned to Maury County and after the war, although crippled, resumed farming. A staunch Democrat, he was elected a delegate to the National Convention in 1884 and entered the Tennessee Senate in 1887.

During the war (19 Aug. 1863) Polk married his cousin, Sallie Moore Polk. They were the parents of five children. He was buried in St. John's Churchyard, just west of Columbia, Tenn.

SEE: Mary P. Branch, *Memoirs of a Southern Woman* (1912); I. A. Bucke, *Cleburne and His Command* (1908); Clement A. Evans, *Confederate Military History*, vol. 10 (1899 [portrait]); James C. Nisbet, *Four Years on the Firing Line* (1914); W. H. Polk, *Polk Family and Kinsmen* (1912).

N. C. HUGHES, JR.

Polk, Sarah Hawkins *(6 Mar. 1784–10 Dec. 1843)*, businesswoman and community leader, of Warren County, was one of thirteen children of Philemon Hawkins, Jr., and Lucy Davis Hawkins. Her father was a noted Patriot during the Revolution, as was her grandfather, Philemon Hawkins, Sr. One of her brothers, William, served as governor of North Carolina during the War of 1812; another, John D., was a member of the state senate and a trustee of The University of North Carolina.

Little is known about her early life, but Sarah Hawkins obviously received a good education for a woman of her day. On 1 Jan. 1801 she married a widower, Colonel William Polk, who was a respected and well-known Revolutionary War veteran. Colonel Polk had moved to Raleigh the year before, and he and his second wife became leaders in the social and civil life of the capital city. Several accounts relate an incident that occurred at a subscription ball held in 1807. When the managers of the ball assigned a socially inferior partner to Mrs. Polk, her husband felt insulted and angry; but she calmed Colonel Polk, telling him that some of the people only wanted to annoy him. She danced with the man and, in the words of Kemp P. Battle, showed "the excellent sense which distinguished her."

Mrs. Polk was noted for her business acumen and her intelligence. Following her husband's death in 1834, she inherited land, slaves, and stock. She herself bought at auction the tanyard sold by the executors of John Rex of Raleigh in 1839. Her ability was attested to by her husband who, naming her sole executrix of his will, said, "I have entire confidence, in her integrity, intelligence prudence and parental regard, for our children."

There is conflicting evidence as to the origin of the idea for the experimental railroad to haul granite from the quarry to build the state capitol. For example, Joseph Gales, in his reminiscences, said he conceived the plan. Several sources, however, including David L. Swain, credit Mrs. Polk with having first advanced the suggestion. William Peck, too, an incorporator of the experimental railroad, undoubtedly attributed the idea to her; when in June 1840 a gala three-day celebration was held in Raleigh to commemorate the completion of both the capitol and the Raleigh and Gaston Railroad, he made one of the toasts to "The distinguished female who suggested the construction of the Raleigh Experimental Rail Road; the first ever seen in North Carolina—She well deserves a name among the benefactors of our State." Colonel Polk had been one of the incorporators, and whether or not Mrs. Polk actually first thought of the railroad, she was evidently concerned about the road and its functioning.

Interest in The University of North Carolina led Sarah Polk and several other women to present a pair of globes to the university. She was a leader in the operation of the Raleigh Female Benevolent Society, chartered in December 1821 for the purpose of aiding "distressed females, who may be considered fit objects of charity." For many years the society operated a school for female orphans, and during her lifetime Sarah Polk was active in its program, holding the office of first directress.

When Mrs. Polk died, the Raleigh *Register* reported that "the loss of this lady will be deeply felt, not only by her numerous family and personal friends, but by the community at large. To domestic merits of the most valuable and endearing kind, she added an indefatigable and intelligent devotion to objects of public beneficence; and her name is conspicuous in the annals of the foundation and management of various important charitable establishments."

The Polks had several children: Lucius Junius, who married Mary Ann Eastin in the White House during the administration of Andrew Jackson; Leonidas, bishop of Louisiana and an officer in the Confederate army who was killed in the Battle of Pine Mountain in 1864; Rufus King, who predeceased his mother; George Washington; Susan Spratt; and Andrew Jackson.

Sarah Hawkins Polk was buried in Raleigh's City Cemetery. Inscribed on her tombstone is the epitaph, "Her relative duties were performed with exemplary fidelity."

SEE: Samuel A. Ashe, ed., *Biographical History of North Carolina*, vols. 2 (1905), 5 (1906) (sketches of William Polk and various members of the Hawkins family); Kemp P. Battle, *The Early History of Raleigh . . . A Centennial Address . . . October 18, 1892*; Charter of Raleigh Female Benevolent Society in Legislative Papers, 1821, Minutes of Experimental Railroad and Wills of William Polk and Sarah Polk, and Wake County Tax Lists, 1837–43 (North Carolina State Archives, Raleigh); Dr. R. B. Haywood, "Recollections of Raleigh" (manuscript owned by Marshall Delancey Haywood, Jr., Raleigh); William H. Hoyt, ed., *The Papers of Archibald D. Murphey*, vol. 2 (1914) (sketch of William Polk); ; Raleigh *Register*, 8 Jan. 1838, 7, 10 Feb., 16 June 1840; 12 Dec. 1843; David L. Swain, *Early Times in Raleigh* (1867).

MEMORY F. MITCHELL

Polk, Thomas *(1732–25 Jan. 1794)*, Revolutionary officer, planter, and politician, was the great-grandson of Robert Bruce Polk, an immigrant from Northern Ireland who settled in Maryland sometime before 1687. Thomas was born to William and Margaret Taylor Polk around 1732 in Cumberland County, Pa., to which his father had moved from Maryland. In 1753, along with two of his brothers, Thomas moved to Anson County, N.C. Two years later he married Susanna Spratt, and they became the parents of eight children: Thomas, William, Ezekiel, Charles, Margaret, Mary, Martha, and James.

Through a combination of personal qualities and a relatively superior education, Polk quickly achieved a position of leadership in the community. In 1765 he led settlers in a rather violent local movement, which became known as the War on Sugar Creek, against Henry Eustace McCulloh, the land agent for George Selwyn. After promoting the establishment of Mecklenburg County and the town of Charlotte, he became a justice of the peace for the county, a commissioner, and the first treasurer for the town. Polk represented Mecklenburg County in the House of Commons from 1766 to 1771 and in 1773–74. As a captain of militia Polk aided Governor William Tryon in his expedition against the Regulators. In 1772 he was engaged as a surveyor in establishing the North Carolina–South Carolina boundary line.

Thomas Polk was active during the Revolutionary crisis, involved in such things as shaping the public mind, intimidating the Loyalists, and drafting and adopting the Mecklenburg Resolves of 31 May 1775. This document declared null and void all commissions granted by the Crown and provided for a reorganization of county government. As a member of the Third Provincial Congress, he sat on a committee that established a temporary state government. In December 1775, as a colonel of militia, he participated in the "Snow Campaign" against Loyalists in upcountry South Carolina.

When the Fourth North Carolina Continental Regiment was formed, Polk was appointed its colonel. The regiment first joined Brigadier General James Moore in the Lower Cape Fear before marching north in the spring of 1777 to reinforce the main army of General George Washington. He participated in the Battle of Brandywine and was at Valley Forge. In February 1778 he returned to North Carolina in an attempt to gather supplies and recruits for his command. He had hoped to be promoted to brigadier general to succeed Francis Nash, who had been killed at Germantown, but he was passed over. This disappointment, coupled with the consolidation of the Fourth Regiment with the Second, led him to resign his commission on 26 June and become a civilian once again.

Nevertheless, Polk returned to military life in the summer of 1780, when he accepted two appointments, the first as commissary general of purchases for North Carolina and commissary of purchases for the Continental troops under General Horatio Gates, newly appointed commanding general of the Southern Department. The other appointment came from the provincial Board of War and made him superintendent commissary for the Salisbury District. When Lord Charles Cornwallis invaded the state, Polk was active in the resistance and often pledged his own credit in securing supplies. But his talents were spread too thin, and he became angry when there were accusations that his "conduct was deemed doubtful and suspicious." Thus he resigned the post, although he did continue to serve for a while under Nathanael Greene, who succeeded Gates. Polk, who was held in high esteem by Greene, was appointed brigadier general in the spring of 1781, but the Assembly gave him a commission as "colonel commandant" which Polk refused to accept although he continued his duties until relieved in May.

In 1783 and 1784 the General Assembly elected Polk to the Council of State, and in 1786, delegate to the Continental Congress; there is no record of his attendance at the Congress. He was also a promoter and trustee for Queen's College (1771) and served in a similar capacity for Liberty Hall (1777) and Salisbury (1784) academies. By 1790 he owned much land and forty-seven slaves. When George Washington made his southern tour in 1791, Polk served as his host in Charlotte. Polk died at his home there.

SEE: Walter Clark, ed., *State Records of North Carolina*, vols. 11–13, 16–18, 20, 22 (1895–1900); *DAB*, vol. 8 (1935); William L. Saunders, ed., *Colonial Records of North Carolina*, vols. 6–10 (1888–90); Hugh F. Rankin, *North Carolina Continentals* (1971).

HUGH F. RANKIN

Polk, Thomas Gilchrist *(22 Feb. 1791–1869)*, political figure and general of militia, was born in Mecklenburg County, the eldest child of Colonel William and Griselda Gilchrist Polk. Among his prominent relatives were his brother, Dr. William Julius Polk, his half brothers Lieutenant General Leonidas Polk and Colonel Rufus K. Polk, and a second cousin, President James K. Polk. In 1805 he entered The University of North Carolina, where he was a member of the Dialectic Society and was graduated in 1809. Afterwards he studied law and in 1816 was granted a master of arts degree. Though trained for and admitted to the bar, he was quite wealthy and never practiced.

During the legislative sessions of 1823, 1824, and 1825 Polk represented Mecklenburg County in the House of Commons. About 1826 he moved to Salisbury and there married Mary Eloise Trotter; they became the parents of Mary Adelaide (Mrs. George Davis), Jane (Mrs. A. Buchelle), William, Richard, Emily C., and Thomas G. In Salisbury, Polk represented Rowan County in the House of Commons in the sessions of 1829, 1830, 1831, and 1832, during which he earned a reputation as an effective public speaker. He was one of three candidates for governor in 1832, but since none of the three received a majority of the vote, the legislature elected David L. Swain. Polk reentered public life as the state senator from Rowan County for the terms 1835 and 1836.

In Salisbury Polk also became president of the Rowan Auxiliary of the American Colonization Society and captain of the Salisbury Light Infantry. Later he was elected major general of the Fourth Division of the North Carolina militia over Brigadier General John N. Phifer of Cabarrus County. Polk advocated internal improvements and in a long address in Salisbury in November 1833 deplored the massive immigration from the state due to the lack of good roads and urged a state program of internal improvements.

He also was a member of the board of trustees of The University of North Carolina during the period 1831–39. His retirement from that board followed his move to La Grange, Tenn., in 1838, where he remained only a short while before settling in Holly Springs, Miss. The 1840 census there indicates that he owned eighty slaves. Thereafter he declined an opportunity to become a candidate for governor of Mississippi.

During the War with Mexico he was recommended for appointment as a brigadier general and consented to serve, but his cousin, President James K. Polk, declined to permit the appointment because of their family relationship. The last known official record of him occurs in the 1860 census, when he was a resident of the city of Holly Springs, Miss., and identified as a farmer owning extensive real estate and personal property.

SEE: James S. Brawley, *The Rowan Story, 1753–1953* (1953); John L. Cheney, Jr., ed. *North Carolina Government, 1585–1979* (1981); Davis and Walker Family Papers (Southern Historical Collection, University of North Carolina, Chapel Hill); Dialectic Society, *Catalogue of the Members of the Dialectic Society* (1890); Hattie S. Goodman, *The Knox Family* (1905); Daniel L. Grant, *Alumni History of the University of North Carolina* (1924); Laura MacMillan, *North Carolina Portrait Index* (1963); W. H. Polk, *Polk Family and Kinsmen* (no date); *Salisbury Post*, 4 May 1969.

ROGER N. KIRKMAN

Polk, William *(9 July 1758–14 Jan. 1834)*, hero of the Revolution, banker, and political leader, was born in Mecklenburg County. He was a descendant of Scots-Irish emigrants who went to the Eastern Shore of Maryland in the early eighteenth century. His paternal grandparents were William and Margaret Polk. Thomas Polk, his father, moved to Sugar Creek, near the Catawba, about 1753 and soon married Susanna Spratt, whose parents had recently moved to the area from Pennsylvania. Thomas and Susanna had eight children, of whom William was the oldest. Thomas represented Mecklenburg in the General Assembly and saw service in the Revolution.

William Polk was attending Queen's College in Charlotte when the rebellion against England began, and he was a witness of the Mecklenburg Convention in May 1775. Though only seventeen, he joined a South Carolina regiment as a second lieutenant and fought in the Palmetto state against Tories; he was wounded at the Battle of Canebrake on 22 Dec. 1775. After eleven months of recuperation he was commissioned a major in the Continental service, and in March 1777 he joined a regiment at Halifax and marched from there to join George Washington's forces in New Jersey. In September he fought in the Battle of Brandywine and in October his jawbone was shattered at Germantown. During the winter he was hospitalized at Valley Forge before being sent home to do recruiting during most of 1778 and 1779. The year 1780 found him again on duty in South Carolina, where he participated in the August Camden campaign and the retreat back into his home area and on to Guildford Court House by the following March. By May 1781 he was back in South Carolina, now a lieutenant colonel under Thomas Sumter. He was present at Eutaw Springs on 8 September when his brother was killed.

After the war Polk was a leader in the formation of the Society of the Cincinnati in North Carolina. In 1783 the General Assembly appointed him surveyor general of the district around present-day Nashville, Tenn., and the young veteran moved there to take up his duties. Twice he was elected to represent Davidson County in the North Carolina House of Commons. While in the future Tennessee, he made many contacts and acquired large tracts of land in his own right.

Returning to Mecklenburg in 1786, he represented his native county in the House of Commons in 1787, 1790, and 1791. In the latter year he was Federalist candidate for speaker of the Assembly and was regarded as one of the leading Federalists in the state. In October 1789 he married Griselda Gilchrist, a granddaughter of Robert Jones, Jr., colonial attorney general under Governors Arthur Dobbs and William Tryon. During this period the young couple had two sons: Thomas Gilchrist (b. 1791) and William Julius (b. 1793). The colonel was a trustee of The University of North Carolina from 1790 until his death and served as president of the trustees from 1802 to 1805. In March 1791 he was appointed federal collector of internal revenue for his native state, a job he held until 1808. The first Mrs. Polk died in 1799 and shortly afterwards Polk moved to the state capital. About the same time he was elected grand master of the state Masonic order, serving from December 1799 to December 1802.

On New Year's Day 1801 Polk married Sarah Hawkins, daughter of Colonel Philemon Hawkins, Jr., of Warren. Of their eleven children, one son, Leonidas, became an Episcopal bishop and a lieutenant general in the Confederate army. Daughter Mary married George E. Badger and Susan married Kenneth Rayner. Both in-laws were later leading Whigs.

During the Jefferson, Madison, and Monroe administrations Polk was a leader of the opposition in North Carolina and a man of growing prestige. Federalists in the Assembly nominated him as their candidate for governor in 1802, but he was defeated by John Baptist Ashe, 103 to 49. He became first president of the State Bank in 1811 and held that post for eight years. When the War of 1812 began, the state's delegation in Congress offered Polk command of a North Carolina regiment with the rank of brigadier general but he declined the honor, being opposed to the war with England as were most Federalists. Only after the British burned Washington did he give up his opposition to the conflict. The wartime governor of the state was William Hawkins, Polk's brother-in-law.

Near the end of the war, in 1814, Assembly Republicans could not agree on a successor to Governor Hawkins and Federalists tried to capitalize on this division and elect Polk. After the Assembly voted, Federalists claimed that Polk received more votes than either Republican candidate but the Republicans quickly combined their count and announced William Miller to be the victor. Polk's supporters believed that the results were fraudulent but were forced to accept the decision.

Honored as Raleigh's most illustrious citizen, Polk was busy with speaking engagements and public meetings during his later years. He was active in the American Colonization Society. A forceful advocate of constitutional reform and internal improvements, he headed in 1826 a company to develop navigation on the Neuse River. Feeling that John Quincy Adams was responsible for the death of federalism, he worked hard to keep Adams out of the White House. He was a leader of the Jackson-Calhoun movement in 1824 and 1828. In 1827 there was another brief attempt to have the Assembly elect him governor. By 1832 Polk developed second thoughts about Old Hickory's dictatorial ways and tried to head off Jackson's choice for his running mate by supporting the Barbour movement against Martin Van Buren.

William Polk died at home at age seventy-five and was buried in the Morgan Street Cemetery. Both North Carolina and Tennessee have counties named for the Revolutionary hero, and in World War I a tank camp outside Raleigh bore his name.

SEE: Samuel A. Ashe, ed., *Biographical History of North Carolina*, vol. 2 (1905); D. H. Gilpatrick, *Jeffersonian Democracy in North Carolina, 1789–1816* (1967); W. S. Hoffmann, *Andrew Jackson and North Carolina Politics* (1971); W. H. Hoyt, ed., *Papers of Archibald D. Murphey*, vol. 2 (1914); Sarah McCulloh Lemmon, "Dissent in North Carolina during the War of 1812," *North Carolina Historical Review* 49 (1972); A. R. Newsome, *Presidential Election of 1824 in North Carolina* (1939); William Polk Papers (North Carolina State Archives, Raleigh); William Polk, "Autobiography of Colonel William Polk" (manuscript, Library of Congress).

DANIEL M. MCFARLAND

Polk, William Tannahill *(12 Mar. 1896–16 Oct. 1955)*, editor, author, and lawyer, was born in Warrenton of Scots-Irish ancestry. His father, Tasker Polk, was a lawyer, orator, poet, and the nephew of President James Knox Polk. His mother was Elisa Tannahill Jones Polk, a housewife and artist; she was descended from Edward Jones (ca. 1698–1751) and Abigail Sugars Jones, two of the earliest settlers in present-day Warren County. He attended the Miss Lucy Hawkins School, widely known throughout the state, and Warrenton High School, operated by John Graham, both private schools. At age seventeen he entered The University of North Carolina, where he received an A.B. degree in 1917. At Chapel Hill he was a member of Golden Fleece honorary society, Phi Beta Kappa, and Zeta Psi. In his freshman year, he broke an ankle playing baseball and while in the infirmary wrote a story that won a prize. He started writing for the *Tar Heel*, later becoming managing editor and then editor; he also wrote university news for the state papers. Polk studied journalism at Columbia University and read a set of books called *The Library of Original Sources*, to which he ascribed most of his education. Afterwards he took law courses at Harvard, rooming during his first year in an attic with Albert Coates, Thomas Wolfe, and Thomas S. Kittrell.

During World War I Polk entered the army as a private (1917) and was promoted to second lieutenant. After receiving his license to practice law from the court where Walter Clark was chief justice, he joined his father in the firm of Polk and Polk (1922–28) and then practiced in the firm of Polk and Gibbs (1928–42). In addition to his legal work, he wrote book reviews, poetry, magazine articles, and short stories. Most of his short stories appeared in *Story Magazine*. One, "The Patriot," was reprinted in O'Brien's *Best Short Stories of 1930*. "The Fallen Angel" and "The Hunter's Moon" were published in *North Carolina in the Short Story*, edited by Richard Walser. The first short story that he wrote after college, entitled "Croix de Cuisine," was about the army; *Collier's* bought it for $400 and changed the title to "So Long, Lilly." "The Hated Helper" appeared in the *South Atlantic Quarterly*. His book, *Southern Accent*, was an immediate success. Dr. Clarence Poe, editor of the *Progressive Farmer*, said, "William Polk was one of the best interpreters of Southern life that we have had in this generation. And he was one of the wisest in his thinking about what should be done about our present problems in North Carolina and the South."

Polk was mayor of Warrenton (1935–42) and for a time president of the Warren County Memorial Library and of the State Literary and Historical Association, chairman of the North Carolina Editorial Writers Conference and of the North Carolina Citizens' Library Movement, and director of the North Carolina State Art Society and of the North Carolina Social Service Conference.

In December 1941 he joined the staff of the *Greensboro Daily News* as editorial writer and associate editor. In Greensboro his major civic contribution was in service on the board of directors of the public library. He served as president of the board at one time and was one of the founders of Friends of the Library. Polk was president of the Greensboro chapter of the university alumni. He was a member of the Greensboro Civitan Club, the Watauga Club of Raleigh, and the board of directors of the North Carolina Conference for Social Service.

During a cruise around the world in 1931, he met Marion Campbell Gunn, of Canada, whom he married on 30 June 1931 in Toronto, Ontario. They had two daughters: Marion Knox, a composer, and Catherine Ross. William T. Polk was a member of the Episcopal church and a Democrat. A portrait by Warren Brendt is owned by the Greensboro Public Library. At the time of his death in Washington, D.C., he was attending a conference of the National Editorial Writers Association. He was buried in Fairview Cemetery, Warrenton.

SEE: Daniel L. Grant, *Alumni History of the University of North Carolina* (1924); *Greensboro Daily News*, 17 Oct. 1955; Bernadette Hoyle, *Tar Heel Writers I Know* (1956); *North Carolina Authors: A Selective Handbook* (1952); Mrs. William T. Polk and Mrs. John G. Mitchell (sister of William T. Polk), personal contact; Raleigh *News and Observer*, 6 Feb. 1938; *Who's Who in the South and Southwest* (1956).

PANTHEA M. TWITTY

Pollard, John Henry Mingo *(10 Feb. 1855–2 Aug. 1908)*, Episcopal clergyman, was born in Lunenburg County, Va. He read for orders in Petersburg, Va., under the direction of the Reverend Giles B. Cooke, John D. Keiley, and the Reverend Thomas Spencer. On 28 June 1878 Pollard was ordained deacon by Bishop F. M. Whittle in the chapel of the Theological Seminary of Virginia. Eight years later, on 14 Dec. 1886, Bishop Whittle ordained him priest in St. Paul's Church, Norfolk, Va.

Pollard's first assignment was as deacon in charge of the black congregation attached to Christ Church, Alexandria. In 1880 he became assistant minister at St. Stephen's Church, Petersburg, where he remained for three years. The next four years he spent as deacon in charge of the mission of Holy Innocents, Norfolk. In 1887 Pollard moved to the Diocese of South Carolina to be assistant minister of St. Mark's Church, Charleston; the next year he became rector. Pollard went to South Carolina at the height of a controversy that had divided that diocese since 1875: the right of the black clergy and laity to have a seat and a vote in the diocesan conventions. Pollard maintained that since his parish had fulfilled all of the canonical requirements for full membership in the diocesan convention, he and his parish were entitled to all rights and privileges of the convention. He was supported in his stand by his Bishop, William B. W. Howe, who had held this position from the first. The question was settled in 1889 by a compromise that admitted St. Mark's Church into union with the convention but put all other black churches and missions in a separate convocation under the bishop. In 1890 Bishop Howe placed Pollard in charge of all black missions in the Charleston district.

After eleven years in South Carolina, Pollard was called to the Diocese of North Carolina on 1 Feb. 1898 to be "Archdeacon for Work Among Colored People." One of the significant contributions he made as archdeacon was in the field of education. In his opinion, a most effective means of improving the work among blacks was through parochial schools. Pollard believed that "neither the State nor the Church can be safe in the hands of ignorant people." It was the duty of the church "to remove the cloud of ignorance now hanging over this large class of our population." In addition to promoting existing parochial schools, he established in 1900 a "Farming and Training School" in connection with St. Anna's Mission at Littleton. Pollard's work received recognition outside the Diocese of North Carolina in 1903, when he addressed the Missionary Council of the Episcopal church in Washington on his church's work for southern blacks. In 1907 he was appointed field secretary for a year to the Board of Missions.

Pollard married Julia May Evans, by whom he had two daughters and six sons. One of his sons, George C., distinguished himself as a lay missionary and teacher in Louisburg. He was principal of St. Matthias's parochial school from 1902 until it ceased to operate in the late 1930s. Following the archdeacon's death, Bishop Joseph B. Cheshire characterized him as "a man of real ability, of sound judgment, of tact, of a singularly well-balanced character; a good preacher, and one who commanded the respect of all." Pollard was buried in Mount Hope Cemetery, Raleigh.

SEE: *Journals of the Annual Councils of the Diocese of Virginia* (1878–86); *Journals of the Diocese of North Carolina*

(1898–1909); *Lloyd's Clerical Directory for 1905* (1905); Albert Sidney Thomas, *A Historical Account of the Protestant Episcopal Church in South Carolina, 1820–1957* (1957).

LAWRENCE F. LONDON

Pollock, Cullen *(1697–1750)*, colonial official, was the son of acting governor Thomas Pollock by his first wife, Martha Cullen West Pollock, the second of their three sons and one daughter who lived to adulthood, Thomas, George, and Martha. Cullen and his brothers received much of their formal education in Boston, where their father had property and business connections. He also probably read law under his father. The three brothers benefited from their father's political and landowning interests in North Carolina; they held many colonial offices and owned large tracts of land themselves in Chowan, Bertie, Edgecombe, and Tyrrell precincts. Thomas Pollock II sat on the Council, while his brother Cullen was a member of the Assembly from Chowan and George was a successful merchant. Later Cullen served on the Council after his older brother retired.

As a child Cullen was a member of St. Paul's Parish in Edenton, but with its division in 1722 he became a vestryman of the South Shore Parish. When his father was acting governor, after the death of Governor Charles Eden, Cullen was appointed a judge of the General Court of Oyer and Terminer. He received another appointment as associate justice of the supreme court from royal governor Gabriel Johnston in 1734. He also held assorted minor offices and served for several terms as assemblyman for Chowan County. In 1733 he was made a member of the Council, a post he held for the remainder of his life.

The practice of factional politics is an ancient one in North Carolina; Governor Pollock had to wrestle with factions and so did his sons. The records reveal one incident involving violence, and when Cullen Pollock was summoned by Chief Justice Christopher Gale in October 1722 to answer charges that he had beaten and abused Thomas Cooke "very notoriously"—and which was proved before the court—he was fined forty shillings and required to post a security bond of twenty pounds on condition that if he behaved himself until the third day of the next General Court, the sentence would be voided. Pollock complied with these terms, but he appeared in court on other occasions for minor misdeeds. He also was involved in disputes over land claimed by Christoph von Graffenried and the Palatines who established New Bern.

Pollock married his cousin, Frances West, and they were the parents of two sons, George and Cullen, and three daughters, Martha, Frances, and Mary. He instructed the executors of his will that his minor children should have as good an education as could be had in the province after which his two young sons should be sent to Boston for further study until they were eighteen.

SEE: Walter Clark, ed., *State Records of North Carolina*, vols. 11, 22, 25 (1896–1907); R. D. W. Connor, *History of North Carolina: The Colonial and Revolutionary Periods, 1584–1783* (1919); J. Bryan Grimes, ed., *North Carolina Wills and Inventories* (1912); J. R. B. Hathaway, ed., *North Carolina Historical and Genealogical Register*, vol. 1 (1900); Hugh T. Lefler and William S. Powell, *Colonial North Carolina: A History* (1973); Pollock-Devereux Papers (North Carolina State Archives, Raleigh); Pollock, Devereux, and Hinsdale Family Papers (Manuscript Department, Duke University Library, Durham); William L. Saunders, ed., *Colonial Records of North Carolina*, vols. 1–5 (1886–87).

VERNON O. STUMPF

Pollock, John Alfred *(1 Nov. 1844–11 Nov. 1932)*, physician, legislator, and novelist, was born at Stones Bay, Onslow County, of Scottish descent, the son of W. A. J. Pollock, also a physician, and his wife, Olive Branch Humphrey. In 1850 the family moved to Kinston, where his father operated a drugstore. In addition to studying drugs and pharmacy under his father, young Pollock received a thorough classical education at the Kinston Academy. He enlisted in the Third Regiment of cavalry in October 1862 and served throughout the Civil War; he was paroled at Greensboro on 30 Apr. 1865 as a "hospital clerk." Returning to Kinston, he again worked in the family pharmacy until, having decided to study medicine, he enrolled in the medical department of New York University from which he was graduated in 1876.

After establishing a medical practice in Kinston, Pollock served as medical examiner for the town and Lenoir County, lectured on physiology and hygiene in colleges and institutes, was an early advocate of preventive medicine, wrote many papers on hygiene, and served as captain of the local unit of the state militia. Interested in education, he appeared before the General Assembly on behalf of local schools and he served as a school trustee. A number of young men received early medical training under his supervision and were reported to have done well when they attended college.

Dr. Pollock also participated in the organization of the first fire company in Kinston and served on the board of alderman. He was elected to the state senate in 1902 by a very large majority and was active in the nomination of W. W. Kitchin for governor. In 1909 he became a member of the governor's staff as surgeon general of the National Guard, from which he retired with the rank of brigadier general. Pollock was an active churchman as well, having joined the Baptist church soon after the Civil War; he taught Sunday school and served as church treasurer.

Pollock read widely and was especially interested in history. Writing under the pseudonym Ronleigh de Conval, he was the author of the 403-page novel, *The Fair Lady of Halifax*. Its setting was eastern North Carolina in the first half of the eighteenth century.

On 8 Jan. 1867 he married Agnes Jones of Kinston, and they became the parents of three children: Mozelle, Raymond, and Emily. He was a member of the Baptist church and was buried in Kinston.

SEE: Samuel A. Ashe, ed., *Cyclopedia of Eminent and Representative Men of the Carolinas*, vol. 2 (1892); Clement A. Evans, ed., *Confederate Military History*, vol. 4 (1899); Louis H. Manarin, comp., *North Carolina Troops, 1861–1865: A Roster*, vol. 2 (1968); *Prominent People of North Carolina* (1906); Raleigh *News and Observer*, 14 Nov. 1932; *Transactions of the Medical Society of North Carolina*, 80th annual sess. (1933).

WILLIAM S. POWELL

Pollock, Thomas *(6 May 1654-August 1722)*, lawyer, planter, colonial official, and acting governor of the colony of North Carolina, was a native of Glasgow, Scotland, and a descendant of Pollok of Balgra, Renfrewshire, Scotland, who, according to legend, saved the life of James IV of Scotland from an attack by a wild boar. Thomas Pollock settled first in Maryland but moved to North Carolina in 1683 as the deputy of Lord Proprietor Carteret and long served as the agent of both Carteret and Lord Proprietor Beaufort. For over thirty years Pollock held numerous military and civil offices under the colonial government. He was a member of the governor's

Council for a longer term than any other person. Further, he served ably on the first vestry of St. Paul's Parish, Edenton, and in 1701 contributed money towards the construction of a new church building, which was completed in 1705.

In addition to practicing law, Pollock was a merchant and also carried on extensive planting operations. He eventually owned about one hundred slaves, and from the time of his arrival in the colony to his death he accumulated large tracts of land along the Chowan, Roanoke, and Trent rivers. One of his plantations in Bertie County included 40,000 acres. He also owned two lots in Bath and New Bern. The town of New Bern was rebuilt largely under his leadership after the Tuscarora Indian war (1711–15).

Well educated, wealthy, and closely identified with the Proprietary and royal interests, Pollock was in full sympathy with the ideals and ambitions of the privileged classes of the colony. An ardent supporter of the Church of England, he disliked all Dissenters but was especially opposed to the Quakers, whose theology he detested and whose politics he distrusted. In the Glover-Cary dispute (1708) over whether Quakers should be required to swear, rather than affirm, allegiance to the English sovereign as a condition for holding public office, he supported acting Governor William Glover in opposition to the Quakers and their political allies under the leadership of Thomas Cary. After Cary's triumph Pollock followed Glover into exile in Virginia. During Cary's Rebellion (1711) against Governor Edward Hyde, Pollock was Hyde's principal lieutenant. A firm believer in law and order, Pollock was imprisoned soon after his arrival in the colony for opposing the illegal activities of Seth Sothel, governor from 1682 to 1689, who openly accepted bribes, arbitrarily deprived citizens of their freedom, and unlawfully seized their property.

Upon the death on 8 Sept. 1712 of Governor Edward Hyde, Pollock as president of the Council became acting governor and served for about two years until the arrival of Governor Charles Eden in 1714. As governor, Pollock succeeded in uniting the colony's quarreling factions and with the aid of troops from South Carolina vigorously prosecuted the war against the Tuscarora that had begun in 1711. Pollock again became acting governor upon the death on 17 Mar. 1722 of Governor Eden and served until his own death some five months later.

Pollock's first wife was Martha Cullen West (1663–1701), apparently a native of England; she was the widow of Robert West and a daughter of Thomas Cullen, colonial official, planter, and Indian trader, who had come to North Carolina from Dover, England, about 1669. Of the children of Thomas and Martha Cullen West Pollock, two sets of twins died in infancy. One daughter, Martha (1694–1719?), and three sons, Thomas (1695–1733), Cullen (1697–1750), and George (1699–1736), lived to adulthood. Governor Thomas Pollock's grandson, Thomas Pollock III (1731–77), married Eunice Edwards (1743–1822), a daughter of Jonathan Edwards, the famous New England minister. Frances (1771–1849), daughter of Thomas and Eunice Edwards Pollock, married John Devereux, a native of Ireland, who acquired a reputation as a financial wizard. Of their three children, Frances Ann Devereux (1807–76) became the wife of Leonidas Polk (1806–64), Episcopal bishop and Confederate general, and Thomas Pollock Devereux (1793–1869) was a lawyer, planter, and from 1826 to 1839 reporter of the North Carolina Supreme Court.

Governor Thomas Pollock's second wife was Esther Wilkinson (d. 1716), widow of Colonel William Wilkinson; they had no children together. Pollock's residences included a plantation on Salmon Creek and Balgra, his plantation on Queen Anne's Creek, where he was buried. His remains were later moved to St. Paul's Church, Edenton.

SEE: Samuel A. Ashe, *History of North Carolina*, vol. 1 (1908), and ed., *Biographical History of North Carolina*, vol. 1 (1905); R. D. W. Connor, *History of North Carolina: The Colonial and Revolutionary Periods, 1584–1783* (1919); Beth G. Crabtree and James W. Patton, eds., *"Journal of a Secesh Lady": The Diary of Catherine Ann Devereux Edmonston, 1860–1866* (1979); Stuart Hall Hill Papers (Southern Historical Collection, University of North Carolina, Chapel Hill); E. Lawrence Lee, *Indian Wars in North Carolina, 1663–1763* (1963); Hugh T. Lefler and William S. Powell, *Colonial North Carolina: A History* (1973); Pollock Papers, Pollock-Devereux Papers, and John Devereux Papers (North Carolina State Archives, Raleigh); Blackwell P. Robinson, *North Carolina Guide* (1955).

W. CONARD GASS

Pomeroy, Warren Lewis *(31 Aug. 1822–post 1866)*, bookseller and publisher, was born in Suffield, Conn. As the town is on the Massachusetts-Connecticut border and was considered to be in Massachusetts until 1749, he has been referred to as a native of Massachusetts. He may have been born just north of the boundary between the two states. He was the son of Israel and Lydia Lewis Pomeroy. He had a brother Calvin (1816–89), who went to Alabama. The Pomeroys were of a Puritan family that settled in the New England colonies in 1630. The 1840 census for Connecticut records Warren Pomeroy as a resident of the town of Somers (very near Suffield) in a family consisting of five males and two females, including himself and his wife. Two members of the family were employed in agriculture.

In 1849 Warren had a bookstore in Raleigh where he remained throughout the Civil War, still operating his business in 1866. His bookshop was on Fayetteville Street by 1850. In 1851 he was among the Raleigh merchants signing an agreement to collect interest on unpaid debts. He appears to have been a civic-minded man and in 1852 invested in the construction of plank roads. In 1856 school superintendent Calvin H. Wiley informed David L. Swain, president of The University of North Carolina, that the collection and publication of colonial and other eighteenth-century records of North Carolina would be useful to the schools of the state and that Pomeroy would publish them.

As a publisher Pomeroy supported the issuing of several worthwhile North Carolina books. In 1854 he was responsible for the appearance of Mary Bayard Clarke's *Wood-Notes; or, Carolina Carols: A Collection of North Carolina Poetry* in two volumes. They were actually printed in New York by John F. Trow, but they bore the imprint of Pomeroy in Raleigh. In the same year he issued *A Digest of Reported Cases Determined in the Supreme Court of North Carolina, from the Year 1845 (December) to the Year 1853 (August)*, prepared by Hamilton C. Jones. The latter was printed in Raleigh by W. W. Holden at his printing establishment.

In 1866 it was reported that Pomeroy had available copies of Ebenezer Emmons's mineralogical report of the state. He also distributed Wiley's *North-Carolina Reader*, widely used as a public school textbook. In February 1863 Pomeroy sent Mrs. Martha P. Mangum a number of books, enclosing a bill, but since books were scarce he asked her to return any that she did not want.

It was circulated in New England that Pomeroy accumulated considerable property but lost it all "through the disasters of the Rebellion." He was said to have returned to the North for a time after the Civil War but later was again in the South, where trace of him was lost by his New England acquaintances.

SEE: Census of Connecticut, 1840 (microfilm, North Carolina State Library, Raleigh); J. G. de Roulhac Hamilton, ed., *Correspondence of Jonathan Worth*, vol. 1 (1909) and *Papers of William Alexander Graham*, vol. 4 (1961); Elizabeth Reid Murray, *Wake: Capital County of North Carolina* (1983); Albert A. Pomeroy, *History and Genealogy of the Pomeroy Family, Part Three* (1922); William W. Rodman, "A Study in Heredity: The Pomeroys in America," *New England and Yale Review* 51 (September 1889); Henry T. Shanks, ed., *The Papers of Willie Person Mangum*, vol. 5 (1956).

WILLIAM S. POWELL

Pool, Bettie Freshwater *(23 Dec. 1860–12 May 1928)*, teacher, writer, and novelist, was born on the Pool plantation in Pasquotank County, one of nine children of George Decatur and Elizabeth Fletcher Pool. Her father was a local politician and prominent farmer and her mother was the daughter of Aaron and Bettie Freshwater Fletcher. Two of her brothers, Walter Freshwater Pool and Judge Charles Carroll Pool, were prominent Republicans in the state and were candidates for Congress in the First District. She also was the niece of the Reconstruction president of The University of North Carolina, Solomon Pool, and of John Pool, a congressman. While still an infant, Bettie Pool was permanently disfigured when a careless nurse dropped her to the floor, and as a result she was unable to attend college. She received her education at a school on the family plantation where she was born.

While still quite young she was referred to as "The Little Story Teller," and her gift for storytelling remained with her all her life. Her first book, *The Eyrie and Other Southern Stories*, published in New York in 1905, was a collection of tales about her family's home neighborhood. Her next book, *Under Brazilian Skies*, appeared in 1908; it was a novel whose setting probably was influenced by a trip to Brazil that one of her kinsmen made in 1889. She also was a songwriter and one of her compositions, "Carolina, A Song," was so well received that many urged its adoption as the state song. It was published in the April 1909 issue of the *North Carolina Booklet*. That year a bill was introduced in the state senate to make "Carolina" the official state song. It was entered in the senate journal but nothing further came of the proposal.

It was also in 1909 that Bettie Pool contributed an article on Theodosia Burr to the *Booklet*, and in 1915 she published a 335-page book, *Literature in the Albemarle*, which became the work most closely identified with her. In it she attempted to gather much of the literary work of residents of the Albemarle area, past and present. Many of the selections, not surprisingly, failed to attain high literary standards, but the book contains selections and biographical sketches not found elsewhere. Her final work, which appeared in 1918, was a collection of songs entitled *America's Battle Cry and Other New War Songs Set to Old Familiar Tunes*. Other songs that she wrote included "I Love Thee, Carolina" and "My Love Is All Around Thee." Most of the music for her songs was written by a cousin, Mrs. Lilla Pool Price.

Bettie Pool spent most of her adult life supporting herself and a sister, Patty, by operating a private school at her home on Dyer Street in Elizabeth City. She was an Episcopalian and a Republican and never married. She was buried in the Pool family cemetery.

SEE: Elizabeth City *Daily Advance*, 14 May 1928, and *Independent*, 18 May 1928; *Library of Southern Literature*, vol. 15 (1910); Pasquotank Historical Society, *Yearbook*, vol. 1 (1954–55 [portrait]); Bettie Freshwater Pool, *Literature in the Albemarle* (1915); Pool Family Scrapbook (Southern Historical Collection, University of North Carolina, Chapel Hill).

B. CULPEPPER JENNETTE, JR.

Pool, Eliza Anne *(12 Nov. 1849–25 Nov. 1935)*, teacher, was born in Oxford, the daughter of Thomas Wyatt and Sarah Dorothy Hicks Pool. She attended the schools of Oxford and achieved such an outstanding record in Latin that Professor James Horner of the Horner Military Institute in Oxford invited her to study Latin with his class of boys. Her first employment was as a teacher in the Oxford Orphanage for a short time, and then she taught for two years in the Reidsville schools. Returning to Oxford, she taught briefly at Hobgood's School for Girls. In 1886 she moved to Raleigh and thereafter devoted forty-five years to the teaching profession. During summer vacations she attended The University of North Carolina, Amherst, Columbia University, and other schools and at one time took two years (1924–25) off to attend the Sorbonne in Paris and study in Switzerland and Germany. She became proficient in ancient Greek and read modern Greek, Spanish, and Italian; she spoke French and German as fluently as she did English.

Eliza Pool taught in and was principal of several schools in Raleigh, including the Murphey School and the Wiley School, and then taught Romance languages in the Raleigh High School. For a year she was lady principal of St. Mary's Junior College in Raleigh. In June 1926 she was chosen North Carolina's most outstanding teacher and represented the state at the Philadelphia Sesquicentennial Celebration, at which she and a teacher from each of the other forty-eight states received gold medals. It was in 1926 that the Raleigh Township School Committee named the public school at Caraleigh Mills the Eliza A. Pool School. In 1927 an oil portrait of Miss Pool was presented to the Hugh Morson High School.

Miss Pool was an Episcopalian and taught Sunday school at Christ Church in Raleigh. She was buried in Oakwood Cemetery.

SEE: Grady L. E. Carroll, Sr., *They Lived In Raleigh*, vol. 2 (1977); E. C. Hicks, Jr. (Wilmington), personal contact; Raleigh *News and Observer*, 26–27 Nov. 1935, 23 Jan. 1949.

WILLIAM S. POWELL

Pool, John *(16 June 1826–16 Aug. 1884)*, U.S. senator, was born on a plantation near Elizabeth City, the son of Solomon and Martha Gaskins Pool. After receiving his early education at home, he entered The University of North Carolina, where he was graduated with honors in 1847. In the same year he was admitted to the bar and put out his shingle in Elizabeth City. Although he practiced law for a livelihood, he preferred public life and politics.

A Whig since his boyhood, Pool won election to the state senate in 1856 and reelection in 1858. In 1860 North Carolina Whigs, calling themselves the Opposition party since the national Whig party had been dissolved by the slavery issue, nominated Pool for governor on a platform of union and an end to sectional agitation. But political emotions were high in this, the year of the election of a "Black Republican" to the presidency. Despite a vigorous campaign by Pool, whose ability in debate was impressive, he lost the election to John W. Ellis, the Southern Rights candidate, by a mere six thousand votes. After the election of Abraham Lincoln, Pool worked to prevent the secession of the state from the Union; when North Carolina finally seceded in May 1861, he quietly retired to his plantation, determined not to take part in any way in the Civil War.

When the peace movement flowered under William W. Holden's leadership in 1864, Pool, having moved to Bertie County, reentered politics and won election to the state senate on a platform seeking separate-state action to end the war. He quickly emerged as the leading peace advocate in the General Assembly, and in late 1864 he introduced a set of resolutions to end immediately the state's participation in the war. These resolutions, however, failed at passage.

After the war Pool served in the convention of 1865, which had been called as a prerequisite for the restoration of the state to the Union under President Andrew Johnson's plan of Reconstruction. Because of his prominence as a conservative Unionist during the war, he was sent to the U.S. Senate by the Whig-dominated General Assembly elected in late 1865. He never took his seat in the Senate, since Congress rejected all of the Southern representatives chosen under Johnson's scheme of Reconstruction. Already Pool had soured on the president's diluted brand of Unionism, which seemed to him to be a sellout to former "rebels."

After the tide turned against the president's conservative reconstruction policy in the North, Pool, along with Holden and three other anti-Johnson men, visited Washington in December 1866 and conferred with Radical leader Thaddeus Stevens on Reconstruction affairs. Impressed by the power of Congress and its determination to impose black suffrage on the former Confederate states, Pool and Holden rushed home to organize a state Republican party, based on support for Congress, before outsiders gained control of the new voters for radical or corrupt purposes. In joining the Republican party he admitted that in part he was motivated by a fear that estates would be confiscated, either directly or indirectly through taxation, and divided among the blacks unless conservative Unionists like himself accepted the political changes demanded by Congress and controlled the course of reconstruction in the state. Although his efforts to set the fledgling Republican party on a conservative course failed, he campaigned in 1868 for the Holden ticket and the ratification of the so-called black-and-tan constitution. After the Republicans swept to victory in the election, the General Assembly selected him again for the U.S. Senate. He was seated and served in that body until 4 Mar. 1873.

In the Senate Pool took a leading role in securing legislation to suppress Ku Klux Klan terror in the South. He also worked for the removal of the Fourteenth Amendment disabilities that had been imposed on selected former Confederates. At home he used his influence to obtain the passage of the Shoffner bill, empowering the governor (in this case, Holden) to declare any Klan-infested county in a state of insurrection and to employ the militia to suppress terrorist groups. When Klan activity became intense in Alamance and Caswell counties in 1870, Governor Holden met on 8 June with leading North Carolina Republicans to seek advice on the implementation of the Shoffner Act. At this meeting Pool advocated stern measures against the Klan, specifically recommending that selected state troops be dispatched immediately to the afflicted counties with orders to suppress the terrorists without regard to court proceedings. He allegedly recommended (a charge he later denied) that the governor should form military commissions, as had been done successfully in Arkansas, to try arrested Klansmen.

Holden accepted Pool's advice, although he later abandoned the plan of holding military trials. As it turned out, the implementation of the senator's program of action against the Klan resulted in the Kirk-Holden war and the governor's impeachment and removal from office. In the wake of this political upheaval, the state senate appointed a committee to inquire into Pool's conduct in the episode. After a brief investigation the committee reported that he was guilty of misconduct in the affair. But the dominant conservatives in the senate, realizing that the passage of a resolution censuring Pool would make them open to charges of partisanship, permitted the committee's report to die a silent death.

In a surprisingly close vote in the General Assembly, Pool failed to be reelected to the U.S. Senate in 1873. However, he remained in Washington to practice law, only returning to North Carolina in 1876 to fill a brief appointment as superintendent of public instruction. He then moved to Washington, where he spent the rest of his life. Pool turned against the Republican party when President Rutherford B. Hayes abandoned the regular Republicans (or Unionists) in the South in an effort to obtain conservative support. In the presidential election of 1880 Pool attempted to persuade disillusioned Southern Republicans to vote for W. S. Hancock, the Democratic candidate. He died of a heart disease in Washington.

Pool was twice married, first to Narcissa Sawyer and then, upon her death, to Mary Elizabeth Mebane of Bertie County. By each wife, he was the father of a son and a daughter.

SEE: *DAB*, vol. 5 (1961); Graham *Alamance Gleaner*, 21 Aug. 1884; J. G. de Roulhac Hamilton, *Reconstruction in North Carolina* (1914), and ed., *Correspondence of Jonathan Worth*, 2 vols. (1909); Rutherford B. Hayes Papers (Hayes Memorial Library, Fremont, Ohio); *Memoirs of W. W. Holden* (1911); *New York Times*, 17 Aug. 1884; Allen W. Trelease, *White Terror: The Ku Klux Klan Conspiracy and Southern Reconstruction* (1971); Richard L. Zuber, *Jonathan Worth: A Biography of a Southern Unionist* (1965).

WILLIAM C. HARRIS

Pool, Solomon *(21 Apr. 1832–8 Apr. 1901)*, educator, University of North Carolina president, and clergyman, was born at Elmwood on the Pasquotank, the Pool plantation near Elizabeth City. His father, Solomon Pool, was a wealthy slaveholding planter of English descent, from a family prominent in northeastern North Carolina since 1679. His mother, Martha Gaskins Pool, was of French Huguenot ancestry. She died when Solomon was five; his father had died earlier. Young Solomon was raised on the plantation by his older brother, George Decatur Pool, a farmer who became active in the Republican party. Solomon had two brothers of note: John, who became a U.S. senator, and William Gaskins, a physician.

Pool prepared for college in Elizabeth City and entered The University of North Carolina in 1849 at age seventeen. He was graduated in 1853, the second honor student in a class of fifty-nine. While in Chapel Hill, he was a member of the Philanthropic Society. In December 1853 he became tutor of mathematics at the university, and in 1856 he received an honorary alumni master's degree. In 1861 he was promoted to adjunct professor of math and held the position for six years. In 1866 Pool took a leave of absence to accept a more lucrative position ($5,000 per year) as U.S. deputy appraiser in North Carolina, with the agreement that the floundering university would not be obligated to reemploy him until he was needed.

Pool accepted the presidency of the university in 1869 and was permitted to keep his appraiser's job at the same time. Reconstruction governor William W. Holden had taken charge of the university's board of trustees to ensure that someone with the appropriate Republican affiliations would be chosen president. At thirty-seven, Pool seemed to fit their specifications and was hired for $1,500 per year. Although brought up within the realm of slavery, Pool rejected its basic ideas.

While Pool was president, the university continued its postwar deterioration. Buildings were neglected and overgrown, and campus trees were cut down for firewood. Pool incurred the wrath of many North Carolinians by, among other things, charging that the university was ruled too much by the landed eastern aristocracy and said that if no white students came to fill classes, he would enroll blacks. He concluded that it was "better to close it [the university] than have a nursery of treason to foster and perpetuate the feelings of disloyalty." A group of Carolinians against Pool, headed by Cornelia Phillips Spencer, succeeded in blackening his name; even today, Pool is missing from many university histories although his ideas of egalitarianism and the consolidation of all state universities became a reality in the twentieth century.

In January 1871 Pool addressed alumni and friends of the university, pleading for money to pay off the university's debts. However, it was too late—the trustees decided that the institution should close on 1 Feb. 1871 and Pool's title was taken away by a court order. He then became principal of a school in Cary for three years.

Pool converted to the Methodist Episcopal church in Elizabeth City at age fourteen and became licensed to preach in 1856. He was ordained deacon at Raleigh in 1862 and elder at Fayetteville in 1865. He preached once a month at the college chapel while in Chapel Hill and was often called upon to preach in various North Carolina cities after he left the university. In 1885 Pool was received into the North Carolina Conference of the church and was sent to Smithfield. He was transferred frequently, filling in wherever he was needed, to towns such as Charlotte, Greensboro, Concord, and Camden.

Pool married Cornelia Kirkland of Chapel Hill in 1856; she was the daughter of Joseph and Martha Kirkland. The Pools had six sons and two daughters: Edward, Clarence, Warren, Clifton, Eugene, Theodore, Cornelia, and Lillie.

On 2 Sept. 1896, while ending a revival sermon at South Mills in Camden County, Pool was stricken with paralysis. He recovered partially but remained in poor health and died five years later in Greensboro.

SEE: Alumni Files (University of North Carolina, Chapel Hill); Samuel A. Ashe, ed., *Cyclopedia of Eminent and Representative Men of the Carolinas* (1892); Kemp P. Battle, *History of the University of North Carolina* (1912); *Chapel Hill Newspaper*, 15 July 1973; Thomas N. Ivey, ed., *Handbook of the Methodist Episcopal Church, South, In North Carolina and Almanac for 1902* (1901); *Journal of the North Carolina Annual Conference of the Methodist Episcopal Church, South* (1900); Ralph I. Pool, "Pool Family of Pasquotank, North Carolina" (no date); Raleigh *News and Observer*, 3 Sept. 1950; Van Noppen Papers (Manuscript Department, Duke University Library, Durham).

DIANA DRU DOWDY

Pool, Stephen Decatur *(1819–21 Dec. 1901)*, newspaper and magazine editor, educator, and politician, was born in Elizabeth City, the son of Joshua and Ann (Nancy) Lowry Pool. An obituary notice reported that he was "born to comparative poverty" but "rose by marriage with a wealthy heiress, to the crest of the wave of prosperity." It was under the guidance of Charles R. Kinney, attorney and president of the Elizabeth City branch of the Bank of North Carolina, that Pool undertook the study of law, but it is not clear that he ever practiced.

In September 1849 he was principal of the Elizabeth City Academy, and later his wife joined him as head of the Female Department. In 1850 he opened a night school for young men and apprentices whose daytime work prevented them from attending a day school. He offered reading, writing, arithmetic, grammar, and geography at five dollars for an eleven-week period. In 1851 a military school, under the direction of a graduate of the Virginia Military Institute, was added to the academy. In the academic department there were two teachers and sixty pupils. The school flourished and after a time it was moved to a larger building.

While operating the academy, Pool in 1850 also became editor of *The Old North State*, an Elizabeth City newspaper. During the next few years the masthead listed him in various positions, including printer, editor, proprietor. But after 1854 there was a different editor and proprietor, and finally in 1855 the paper ceased publication for "pecuniary considerations." Pool was a Whig, but the editor of the competing paper, Lucien D. Starke of the *Democratic Pioneer*, was a Democrat. The two men feuded through the columns of their papers as well as in person, and on one occasion Starke attacked Pool with a cane and challenged him to a duel. Pool rebuffed the challenge because of his wife and six children and his deep indebtedness. A topic of lively discussion was slavery. Although he was a Unionist, Pool thought that each state had a right to be slave or free as it chose, while Starke favored the extension of the Missouri Compromise line.

For the benefit of the academy, Pool also delivered public lectures. In February 1852, for example, he announced that in March he would speak on "the Ptolemaic and Copernician theories of the structure of the universe" to raise funds to purchase equipment. If enough interest were shown, he said, this would be the first in a series of lectures. During the period October–December 1852 Pool, recorded as residing in Pasquotank County, was clerk of the House of Commons. Later he moved to Carteret County, where he taught in a female seminary.

At age forty-two Pool was commissioned captain of Company H, Tenth Regiment of North Carolina Troops, to rank from 16 May 1861. He was captured at Fort Macon on 26 Apr. 1862 but paroled and exchanged in August. On 1 October of that year he was promoted to lieutenant colonel and in September 1863 to colonel. In a move that was not unknown among military men, he represented Carteret County in the House of Commons for brief sessions in 1864 and 1865. In the spring of 1865 he commanded the First Sub District, Department of North Carolina.

Returning home after the war, Pool became editor of the New Bern *Daily Journal of Commerce* from 1866 to 1875 and of the weekly edition from 1866 to 1876. An able editor, he became a charter member of the North Carolina Press Association and was present at its first meeting in Goldsboro in May 1873. During the period just before the election of 1870, he published the *Campaign Anti-Radical* in New Bern. Also in New Bern in 1873–74 he published *Our Living and Our Dead* as a weekly in newspaper format for the North Carolina Branch of the Southern Historical Society and then as a monthly in magazine format in 1874–76. Its purpose was to present war reminiscences, registers of North Carolina troops, miscellaneous sketches, diaries, letters from correspondents, state news, and literary contributions. In 1876 the *Southern Historical Monthly* appeared as the successor to *Our Living and Our Dead*. Between 1874 and 1876, under a Raleigh imprint, Pool also edited the monthly *North Carolina Journal of Education* which appeared in three volumes.

In 1874, as a Conservative candidate, he was elected superintendent of public instruction, one of the first state Democratic officials to be elected after the war. Under a Republican administration, he served from 1 Jan. 1875 to 30 June 1876. Pool was charged with irregularities in the management of funds provided by the Peabody Education Board and forced to resign. He was accused of using some of the fund, which he intended to return, to purchase a home for himself. Later in the year or in 1877 he moved to New Orleans, where his son, Stephen D., Jr., was a highly regarded newspaper editor. The elder Pool was listed in New Orleans city directories from 1877 through 1887. His last years were spent largely in farming. He lived across Lake Pontchartrain from New Orleans in Tangipahoa Parish on the Mississippi border. He died and was buried in Osyka, Miss.

Pool's wife was Caroline S. Lockwood and their children were James Harrell (1842), John Lockwood (1843), Henry Clay (1845), Stephen D., Jr. (1847), Dora or Theodora (1849), Mary and Carlton F. (1851), and Caroline S. (1854).

SEE: Ray M. Atchison, "*Our Living and Our Dead*: A Post-Bellum North Carolina Magazine of Literature and History," *North Carolina Historical Review* 40 (October 1963); Thomas R. Butchko, *On the Shores of the Pasquotank* (1989); John L. Cheney, Jr., ed., *North Carolina Government, 1585–1979* (1981); R. D. W. Connor, *North Carolina: Rebuilding an Ancient Commonwealth*, vol. 2 (1929); Elizabeth City *North Carolinian*, 2 Jan. 1902; William A. Griffin, *Ante-Bellum Elizabeth City: The History of a Canal Town* (1970); J. G. de Roulhac Hamilton, *History of North Carolina*, vol. 3, *North Carolina Since 1860* (1919); Louis H. Manarin, comp., *North Carolina Troops, 1861–1865: A Roster*, vol. 1 (1966); *New Orleans Times-Democrat*, 22 Dec. 1901; M. C. S. Noble, *A History of the Public Schools of North Carolina* (1930); Stephen B. Weeks Scrapbook, vol. 8 (North Carolina Collection, University of North Carolina, Chapel Hill).

WILLIAM S. POWELL

Pool, Stephen Decatur, Jr. *(11 Nov. 1847–8 Feb. 1892)*, Confederate soldier, lawyer, and journalist, was born in Elizabeth City, the son of Stephen D. and Caroline S. Lockwood Pool. Educated in a local private school, perhaps for at least some of the time in one operated by members of his family, including his father, he was at work as a printer at age thirteen, helping his father publish a newspaper. In October 1864 in Wayne County, where his family then lived and shortly before his seventeenth birthday, he enlisted in the Tenth Regiment of North Carolina Troops, commanded by his father, a colonel. He was appointed acting sergeant-major in January or February 1865.

At the end of the war Pool moved to New Bern, where he assisted his father in the publication of the *New Bern Journal of Commerce* until 1869. In January 1870 he went to New Orleans to work in the composition room of the *Picayune*, but in 1873 he returned to New Bern to purchase the newspaper on which he had formerly worked. At the same time he studied law under Major John Hughes and practiced until 1876, when he returned to New Orleans. There he set type on the *Bulletin* and the *Democrat* and served as telegraph editor of the latter until the two were consolidated as the *Times-Democrat* in 1881. Pool then became news editor of the new paper, and after two years he became night editor and deputy manager. On occasion, during the absence of the editor-in-chief, Pool was manager of the paper.

Pool was known for his understanding of state and national politics and for his excellent taste in typography. He was described by a fellow journalist as "calm in his judgments and prompt in his decisions." The *New York Times* considered him to be "one of the ablest newspaper men in the South."

In 1878 Pool married Jeanne B. Guireud of New Orleans and they became the parents of six children. Unlike many of his relatives, he was a Democrat. He died in New Orleans of pneumonia after returning from Atlanta, where he became ill while attending a meeting of the Southern Press Association.

SEE: Louis H. Manarin, comp., *North Carolina Troops, 1861–1865: A Roster*, vol. 3 (1966); *New York Times*, 9 Feb. 1892; Stephen B. Weeks Scrapbook, vol. 8 (North Carolina Collection, University of North Carolina, Chapel Hill).

B. CULPEPPER JENNETTE, JR.

Pool, Walter Freshwater *(10 Oct. 1850–25 Aug. 1883)*, lawyer, politician, and congressman, was born at Elm Grove plantation in Pasquotank County, the son of George Decatur and Elizabeth Fletcher Pool. His father was a prominent farmer and minor officeholder in the county. One of his brothers was Judge Charles Carroll Pool, a Republican politician; his sister was Bettie Freshwater Pool, a writer and a teacher. He was a nephew of Solomon Pool, president of The University of North Carolina during Reconstruction, and of John Pool, unsuccessful Whig candidate for governor in 1860 and U.S. senator. Like other members of his family, young Pool attended a school on the plantation and at age seventeen entered the sophomore class at The University of North Carolina (1869–70). In 1870 his parents moved to Elizabeth City, where he read law and was admitted to the bar in 1873.

Inspired through his study of law, Walter Pool became known throughout the First District as an intelligent lawyer and a brilliant orator. It was largely these traits that influenced the district Republicans to nominate him for Congress, although Pool was only twenty-four at the time of the 1876 election. He lost the race but continued to practice law in Elizabeth City until 1883, when he ran for Congress and defeated the Democratic candidate, Major Louis C. Latham. Pool's personal popularity was cited as the key to his victory in a solid Democratic district. Throughout the campaign, Pool suffered from ill health and following the election traveled to Hot Springs, Ark., to recuperate. Returning to Elizabeth City, he became ill again and died at age thirty-two. Members of both political parties paid tribute to him. Technically he served as a member of the Forty-eighth Congress from 4 Mar. to 25 Aug. 1883, but in fact the Congress had not assembled prior to his death.

Pool, an Episcopalian, was buried in the family cemetery in Pasquotank County. A monument was erected at his grave by an act of Congress.

SEE: *Biog. Dir. Am. Cong.* (1961); Daniel L. Grant, *Alumni History of the University of North Carolina* (1924); Pool

Family Scrapbook (Southern Historical Collection, University of North Carolina, Chapel Hill); Bettie Freshwater Pool, *Literature in the Albemarle* (1915 [portrait]).

B. CULPEPPER JENNETTE, JR.

Poole, Charlie Clay *(22 Mar. 1892–21 May 1931)*, pioneer country music recording artist, banjoist, singer, and entertainer, was born in Randolph County, the son of Philip, whose father was an Irish immigrant, and Betty Johnson Poole. Both parents were mill workers in Haw River, Alamance County, where they had moved from Iredell County. Young Poole apparently developed a strong interest in music while still a small child. Due to his poor rural background he could not afford formal musical training, so he made himself a banjo out of a gourd and taught himself to play. It was only after he had gone to work in a local textile mill that he bought himself a real banjo for $1.50.

The exact source of Poole's unique three-finger picking style is not known although it is possible that he learned to pick in a rolling style by listening to the early recordings of such classical artists as Fred Van Epes, violinist, and Vess Ossman, banjoist, who were popular in the pre–World War I era. A childhood accident while playing baseball left him with partially deformed fingers on his right hand, which probably contributed to the development of the three-finger style. Whatever the cause, his method of playing was certainly ahead of its time. After working long hours at night at the Leaksville Cotton Mill in his early twenties, Poole saved just over $200, bought a Gibson banjo, and quit, never to work in a mill again. He joined with Norman Woodlief, guitarist, Lonnie Austin, who played anything but mostly fiddle, Haman Newman, left-hand tenor banjo, Mae Weeks Mabes, pianist, and Posey Rorrer, fiddler, to form a band.

About 1917 or 1918 Charlie Poole combined his talents with those of Posey Rorrer (1891–1936), a fiddler from Franklin County, Va., to form the North Carolina Ramblers as a string band. Poole later married Rorrer's sister and both he and Rorrer moved to Spray, N.C., in 1920.

Between 1920 and 1925 Poole and Rorrer began to achieve a substantial reputation over a wide area. The combination of Poole's three-finger banjo playing and Rorrer's old-time fiddling began to make them popular at square dances, corn shuckings, and parties. Two guitarists, Clarence Foust, a childhood friend of Poole, and Norman Woodlief, a resident of Spray, began to accompany Poole and Rorrer on their musical excursions. The addition of these two men as well as others gave the band a more complete sound. By 1924 the North Carolina Ramblers were giving concerts over a wide area of the Southeast, including Virginia, West Virginia, Ohio, Kentucky, and Tennessee.

In June 1925 the Ramblers went to New York City to make their first records. Recorded country music was still in its infancy, with only a handful of records having been released by various mountain musicians. On 27 July 1925 the North Carolina Ramblers cut four sides for the Columbia Record Company. Their first release was Columbia 15038-D, "Don't Let Your Deal Go Down Blues / Can I Sleep In Your Barn Tonight Mister." The success of this record, which sold 102,451 copies, was a clear indication of their popularity since the average sales for a Columbia country music record of that time was about 5,000.

Each year between 1926 and 1931 the Ramblers returned to Columbia studios to make records, cutting a total of more than seventy sides; in addition, Poole made records for the Paramount and Brunswick record companies in 1929. By 1931 the North Carolina Ramblers had sold almost one million records. The songs recorded by Charlie Poole during this five-year period have now become standards among Blue Grass and Country Music musicians. They include "White House Blues," "Budded Roses," "If I Lose," "There'll Come a Time," and others. Poole's three-finger banjo style was also highly influential in the development of the three-finger style used in Blue Grass Music long after his time.

A Columbia record catalogue published early in 1927 well described Charlie Poole and the North Carolina Ramblers: "Charlie Poole is unquestionably the best known banjo picker and singer in the Carolinas. A dance in North Carolina, Virginia, or Kentucky isn't a dance unless Charlie and the North Carolina Ramblers supply the pep. People everywhere dance all night when these favorites supply the music."

The personnel of the North Carolina Ramblers changed on several occasions and came to include Lonnie Austin and Odell Smith, fiddlers from Leaksville, and Roy Harvey, guitarist of Beckley, W.Va. The band played theater circuits, schoolhouses, and fiddler's conventions and from 1928 to 1930 presented live radio shows in Virginia and Pennsylvania.

In the early months of 1931 a movie company in Hollywood hired Poole and the North Carolina Ramblers to play the music for a western movie. However, on 21 May, a few weeks before he was to leave for California, Poole suffered a fatal heart attack in Spray at the home of his sister, Sarah Elizabeth Seaver. He was thirty-nine.

Poole was married twice: in 1911 to Maude Gibson from Henderson (from whom he later was divorced) and on 11 Dec. 1920 to Lou Emma Rorrer, who died on 11 Dec. 1967. By his first wife he had one son, James Clay Poole.

SEE: Bob Artis, *Bluegrass* (1975); *Charlie Poole*, vols. 1–3 (County Records, Floyd, Va.); Steven D. Price, *Old as the Hills: The Story of Bluegrass Music* (1975); Rocky Mount, Va., *Franklin County Gazette*, 1926; Clifford K. Rorrer, *Charlie Poole and the North Carolina Ramblers* (1968) and *Rambling Blues: The Life and Songs of Charlie Poole* (1982).

CLIFFORD KINNEY RORRER

Poole, David Scott *(3 Aug. 1858–20 Apr. 1955)*, newspaperman, legislator, and teacher, was born in Montgomery County, the oldest of eight children of William R. and Mary Eliza Ray Poole. He was educated at Jackson Springs Academy in Moore County from 1868 to 1880. While teaching school during the winter, an occupation that he continued intermittently for many years, Poole also learned the printer's trade. He began his editorial career about 1894 in Red Springs, where he established the *Scotch Scion*, and he moved around the state until 1915, when he began editing the *Hoke County Journal* in Raeford. Poole was active in the political and religious life of Raeford, where he served as mayor and justice of the peace and was a lay leader in the Presbyterian church.

His religious beliefs were sincere though conservative. Darwin's theory of evolution disturbed him, and he determined to protect his state from such heresy. Campaigning on an antievolution platform, Poole was elected to the North Carolina House of Representatives in 1924 as a Democrat from Hoke County. In 1925 he introduced what became known as "the Poole bill" prohibiting the teaching of Darwinism in the public schools. The controversy that followed the introduction of his bill split the state. After heated exchanges between opposing sides in the legislature (which produced such memorable quips as Sam Ervin's remark that passing the bill would only help absolve monkeys from all responsibility for the human race), the bill was defeated, 67–46. This was a significant defeat for antievolutionists nationwide, for North Carolina was a key state in their program.

In 1927 Poole introduced a second antievolution bill, this one written largely by Thomas C. Bowie, which was more extreme than the first. It forbade the teaching of any theory that contradicted the biblical story of creation and provided penalties for teachers who did so. The bill died in committee, and that controversy disappeared from the state legislature. Poole served for an uneventful third term in the house.

He married Margaret Lenora Holliday on 28 Sept. 1884; she died in November 1948. They had five children: William L., Mrs. Luke Bethune, Mrs. A. K. Currie, Maude, and Mrs. Hugh Lowe. In addition to his religious and political affiliations, Poole was a Mason. He died at age ninety-six and was buried in Raeford Cemetery.

SEE: Willard B. Gatewood, Jr., *Preachers, Pedagogues, and Politicians* (1966) and ed., *Controversy in the Twenties: Fundamentalism, Modernism, and Evolution* (1969); *North Carolina Manual* (1929); Raleigh *News and Observer*, 21 Apr. 1955; Southern Pines *Pilot*, 29 Apr. 1955.

ALICE R. COTTEN

Poole, Jesse Robert (Bob) *(10 Apr. 1916–24 Jan. 1978)*, broadcaster and humorist, was born in Stoneville, the youngest of seven children of Thomas Phillip and Myrtle Roberts Poole. He often referred to himself as "Mrs. Poole's youngest son," one of the titles he was to assume for life. After graduating as valedictorian of Stoneville High School in 1933, Poole received a scholarship to Guilford College in Greensboro. In 1934, while still in school, he went to work for WBIG radio, then in its rising days under the directorship of Major Edney Ridge. After two years at Guilford, he attended The University of North Carolina, but on weekends he would hitchhike to Greensboro to tape spots and broadcast at the radio station.

Having once considered law school, Poole changed his mind after graduating during the Great Depression. He went to New York City to work in a show called "A Southern Boy and a Southern Girl" for radio station WNEW. As the "southern boy," Poole played alongside Dinah Shore, who was the "southern girl." The station's management felt that Poole's southern accent was a bit too pronounced, however, and dismissed him from the assignment, unwittingly launching him into a new phase of his career.

With World War II in its early stages, Poole went to Kingsport, Tenn., and joined the U.S. Navy, serving for four years. Sent to the Naval Air Station in New Orleans, he began to broadcast a U.S. Navy program called "Sky Wave to Victory" over radio station WWL in New Orleans. After three years of broadcasting with the navy, Poole received a discharge but remained on the station staff as a full-time broadcaster. It was here that "Poole's Paradise" was born. With Robert Taylor as narrator, Poole presented celebrities of the period and was accompanied by then-unknown members of WWL's studio orchestra, including such greats as Al Hirt and Pete Fountain.

Poole's affection for easy rhythm led him to include performances by the New Orleans Symphony on Poole's Paradise. When he discovered that his friend, the symphony's first violinist, was going to a party, Poole decided to crash the affair. The hostess was to become his wife, Gloria. She was the daughter of Harry Rothchild, who operated an antique business in New Orleans, and Mrs. W. F. Hoffecker. The Pooles had three children: Michelle, Randolph, and Kyle.

To oblige his father-in-law, Poole spent a year in the antique business but then returned to radio. He broadcast an early morning talk show over WWL radio and became famous not only in Louisiana but in Canada as well. Induced to move to New York, Poole completed a contract with radio station WOR of New York for an hour-long daily show, beamed by the network coast to coast to 515 radio stations in the country.

Poole became known not only for his trademark corny jokes and cheerful booming baritone voice but also for candid interviews with stars like Bob Hope, Frank Sinatra, Perry Como, Don Knots, and Andy Griffith. Poole was voted "Disc Jockey's Favorite Disc Jockey" in 1949 and 1950. In 1949 American Radio Listeners voted Poole "Radio Mirror's Favorite Disc Jockey Award." Not long afterwards, Poole began to write an article for Macfadden Publications, in New York, which published the piece in *Radio* and *TV Mirror* magazine.

Ready to return to North Carolina and to the Piedmont, Poole left New York City in 1952. By then, however, he had already won the coveted "America's Favorite Disc Jockey" award given by John Lester's nationally syndicated radio and TV column.

Returning to station WBIG, Poole established a morning talk show which he began by whistling his theme song, "Paradise." The show, Poole's Paradise, aired for twenty-five years and consistently maintained the highest audience appeal ratings for any age of any show in the area.

The town of Stoneville, Poole's birthplace, awarded him a "Certificate of Meritorious Proclamation" during its Centennial celebration, officially dubbing him the "Duke of Stoneville." The title, which Poole had unofficially assumed many years before, lingered during his broadcast of the first Greater Greensboro Open in North Carolina and still later when he accepted the Heart Fund Appreciation Award for service to the American Heart Association.

As a member of the Greensboro Jaycees, Civitans, and Rotary, Poole was active in the United Fund, Polio, Christmas Seal, and Easter Seal drives. He received "Keys to the City" from Dallas, Tex., Charleston, S.C., and Greensboro. On 25 Sept. 1962 Greensboro citizens turned out by the thousands for "Bob Poole Day." On 4 Jan. 1965 Governor Terry Sanford appointed him ambassador extraordinary in the Order of the Long Leaf Pine.

In 1964 Poole suffered a crushed vertebra in an automobile accident and was hospitalized for a month. His health continued to fail when, in 1973, he had a series of heart attacks and a collapsed lung. The final broadcast of Poole's Paradise took place on the morning of 21 Dec. 1977 at WBIG. His epitaph at Forest Lawn Cemetery in Greensboro closed Poole's life with the same words he used to say good-bye every day of his career, "Take care of you, for me."

SEE: *Greensboro Daily News*, 25–26 Jan. 1977, 24 Jan. 1978, 2 Sept. 1977, 26 Jan. 1978; Dr. Clyde A. Milner (Guilford College, Greensboro), Mrs. Robert Poole (Greensboro), and Kip Poole (Greensboro), personal contact; *Muse Magazine*, November 1972.

F. CRAIG WILLIS

Pope, Liston *(6 Sept. 1909–15 Apr. 1974)*, clergyman, theological educator, and ecumenist, was born in Thomasville, one of three children of Robie Lester and Dora Vivian Younts Pope. His sisters were Mildred (Mrs. Frank H. Wood) and Evelyn (Mrs. Weldon Royal). The father, a banker, was prominent in the state's financial circles, a longtime city councilman, and onetime mayor of his home city; served one term in the North Carolina House of Representatives; and received an honorary doctor of humane letters degree from High Point College. Robie Pope died in 1963 and his wife in 1968. Liston Pope described his father as "a North Carolina banker with a conscience" and his mentor in a life dedicated to the study of social problems from the Christian point of view.

Young Pope was graduated from Thomasville High School in 1925 and Duke University, with a bachelor of arts degree, in 1929. During those years he established a reputation as a thoughtful scholar and an astute and vocal communicator. He was active in many spheres of campus leadership, especially those emphasizing religious themes. Upon completion of his undergraduate work, he returned to Thomasville and spent fifteen months working in the field of insurance. Then in the fall of 1930, he returned to Duke and enrolled in the School of Religion, where he received a bachelor of divinity degree in 1932.

After Duke, where he had distinguished himself for his perspectives in the social sciences, he sought a "frontline experience" and became associate minister of the 2,500-member Wesley Memorial Methodist Church in High Point with the popular and erudite Dr. G. Ray Jordan, who was quoted as saying he hired Pope "because he wanted some practical experience before he went further." In High Point Pope first immersed himself in issues dealing with the acute social needs of low-income people and the social problems arising in the factories and businesses where they worked. After three years (1932–35) at Wesley Memorial, he attracted church leaders in New Haven, Conn.

Called to the pastorate of the Humphrey Street Congregational Church in New Haven, Pope was ordained in the Congregational ministry (1935) and remained at Humphrey Street for three years (1935–38). Immediately he began a connection with Yale University that lasted for thirty-eight years. He simultaneously was enrolled in the Graduate School of Yale as a candidate for the degree of doctor of philosophy, conferred in 1940. His doctoral thesis was a study of the interrelation of religion and economics as specifically revealed in Gastonia and Gaston County. This thesis, published under the title *Millhands and Preachers* (1940), was long used as a textbook in social ethics courses at many prestigious universities and seminaries.

Pope joined the faculty of Yale University as a lecturer in social ethics (1938–39), assistant professor (1939–44), associate professor (1944–47), Gilbert L. Stark Professor of Social Ethics (1947–73), and dean of the Yale Divinity School (1949–62). During his deanship the Divinity School nearly doubled the number of its teachers and its physical equipment, and established new scholarships and internships. When he retired from teaching in 1973, he gave Yale his extensive collection of books on social ethics and provided endowment funds to assure that the collection was kept up-to-date. In appreciation of his many personal and professional contributions, he was signally honored at the 1973 Yale Divinity School convocation. His collection there is known as the Dean Liston Pope Divinity School Library of Yale University.

When Pope became dean, he was only forty years old, succeeding the noted Dr. Luther A. Weigle. He took to that post a liberal Protestantism that combined sociological and theological emphases generated through more than fifteen years of study and work in the two fields. In that posture he was an admirable successor to the same liberal leadership for which the Yale school had long been noted. He found a podium for his thoughts as chairman of the Industrial Relations Division of the Federal Council of Churches of Christ in America, and of the National Religion and Labor Foundation. He insisted upon mutuality of responsibility on the part of both labor and the Christian conscience.

During the late thirties and early forties he arbitrated many disputes, especially in the men's clothing industry, and was instrumental in reorganizing (1937) the New Haven Labor College, where he frequently taught. From 1945 to 1948, he was a lecturer at the Presbyterian Institute of Industrial Relations in New York City. That institute was designed to take twenty carefully selected students through a month's intensive study of labor relations. His activities in the noted Political Action Committee, of which he was a onetime chairman, catapulted him into a controversial limelight that did not terminate with his resignation because of a so-called clash of personalities.

Principal among the lectureships he held were the Alden Tuthill at Chicago Theological Seminary (1945), the Merrick at Ohio Wesleyan University (1950), the Wallace at Macalester College (1950), the Gray at Duke University (1952), the Shaffer at Northwestern University (1954), and the Finch at High Point College (1960). He was awarded the John Addison Porter Prize at Yale (1940) for his book *Millhands and Preachers*.

Pope received honorary degrees from Duke (doctor of divinity, 1951), Boston University (doctor of sacred theology, 1950), Coe College (doctor of humane letters, 1953), Bradley University (doctor of humane letters, 1957), Grinnell College (doctor of divinity, 1957), University of Geneva (doctor of theology (1959), Bucknell University (doctor of divinity, 1960), and Rollins College (doctor of divinity, 1960).

In addition to teaching in Yale Divinity School, Pope was also a Fellow of Saybrook College of Yale. He also was an expansive reader and researcher especially in the field of social ethics, from which came several books of unusual merit: *Labor's Relation to Church and Community* (1947), which he edited, and *The Kingdom Beyond Caste* (1957). Pope was editor of *Social Action Magazine* (1944–48) and a frequent contributor of thought-provoking articles to such journals as the *Saturday Review of Literature*, *Christianity and Crisis*, the *New York Times*, and other periodicals of comparable stature, in addition to numerous festschrifts and symposia.

In 1961 Pope went back to Thomasville for a sabbatical year. He rented a downtown office, where he spent much of his time researching and writing a series of articles for early publication in scholarly magazines and books.

Among his multiple community, civic, and church connections he was a trustee of the Phelps-Stokes Fund of Vassar College and of Franklin and Marshall College and a director of the Nanking Board of Founders and of the Yale University Press. He was president of the board of directors of the Prospect Hill School for Girls in New Haven (1953–55, 1959–60) and a member and chairman of the executive committee of the American Association of Theological Schools and of the National Council of Religion in Higher Education. Pope also was a Julius Rosenwald Fellow and a Phelps-Stokes Visitor to Africa (1949), chairman of the National Advisory Committee of the Student Young Men's Christian Association (1950–

52), and director of the Rockefeller Brothers Theological Fellowship Programs. He held membership in several fraternities, including the prestigious Phi Beta Kappa and Omicron Delta Kappa as well as Phi Delta Theta and Sigma Upsilon, and in the Morys Club and the Yale Club in New York and the Faculty Club in New Haven.

Through his church affiliations Pope served as chairman of the Congregational Council for Social Action (1950–52), member of the Interseminary Committee of the National Council of Churches (1955–57), Congregational delegate to the National Council of Churches (1949–60), and member of the Central Committee and the Executive Committee of the World Council of Churches (1954–73). He was one of the principal speakers at the Third Assembly of the World Council in New Delhi, India (November 1961).

Pope was an erudite scholar who retained his sense of social responsibility and made it a point through countless speaking engagements, as well as through teaching and writing, to show the Christian message pertinent to the problems of human society. He was a great apostle of faith and tolerance who knew no compromise with wrong and believed that the modern church had a message of hope for a confused world. With such a message he was a popular preacher on college and university campuses and at various conferences and religious gatherings. He remained a warm, personable individual who won and treasured many friendships.

Pope was married first (3 Feb. 1934) to Bennie Howell Purvis, of Durham, herself a graduate of Duke (1933). They had three children: Mary Anna (Mrs. Clement Barbey), Liston, Jr., and Bennie Allison. Bennie Pope died on 13 Nov. 1967 and was buried in the family plot in Thomasville. Pope then married Mrs. Gerd Thoreson, of Trondheim, Sweden, in 1972. He had met her when he was on sabbatical in Spain during the previous year. When Pope retired from Yale in May 1973, they moved to Trondheim, and he was "enjoying his retirement, resting and rocking, in a house with a terrace overlooking a fiord." But illness stalked the last year of his life, and he died in Trondheim at age sixty-four. A funeral service was held at Yale the following week, and interment was at Thomasville in late April. He was survived by his wife, his three children, and his sister, a Mrs. Wood.

SEE: Data Files (Duke University Alumni Office, Durham); *Greensboro Daily News*, 20 May 1961, 19 Apr. 1974; *New Haven* (Conn.) *Register*, 16 Jan. 1949; William S. Powell, ed., *North Carolina Lives* (1962); *Thomasville Times*, 19 Apr. 1974.

C. SYLVESTER GREEN

Porter, Edmund *(ca. 1685–1737)*, colonial official, was born in Lower Norfolk County, Va., the son of John Porter (d. 1712) and his wife Mary. He was the brother of John Porter, a leading figure in the pro-Cary forces during Cary's Rebellion. A strong Cary supporter in his own right, he was exempt from pardon because of his role. Governor Edward Hyde considered Porter to be "as useful for any wicked purpose as the others." John Porter, Edmund's father, escaped to England, but Edmund was one of five men who were captured in Virginia. They were sent to England late in 1711 on board the British man-of-war *Reserve* to stand trial for their role in the rebellion. After a year of intermittent hearings in London before the Lords Proprietors, Porter and his friends were released for lack of sufficient evidence. In July 1712 Hyde issued a general pardon to all participants in Cary's Rebellion with five exceptions; Edmund Porter and his brother were two of those excepted.

On 30 July 1717, as "son and heir of John Porter of North Carolina," Edmund sold land in Princess Anne County, Va. Styled "Merchant," he sold land in Chowan County near Bluff Point in 1718. There are no records pertaining to him for the next seven years, when he was probably out of the colony. Reported in May 1725 as having come to North Carolina from the West Indies, he soon was named a judge of the colony's Admiralty Court and late in the year he was elected to the Assembly from Chowan County.

A vocal critic of Governor Sir Richard Everard, and thus a natural ally of former Governor George Burrington, Porter was one of three men selected by the Assembly to carry its protests against Everard to London in 1726. His hostilities towards the governor peaked in October 1726 with his indictment for having assaulted Everard on the streets of Edenton the previous July. However, at Everard's request, all charges were dismissed in August 1728. Throughout the Proprietary years Porter and Burrington remained close friends, and in 1730, when it became clear that Burrington would be North Carolina's first royal governor, he nominated Porter to be on the initial Council of State. Porter was sworn as a councillor on 9 Mar. 1731.

Before 1731 had ended Porter and Burrington became stronger enemies than they had been friends previously. Burrington felt that Porter was becoming increasingly allied with John Baptista Ashe, and he bitterly resented it. The governor began encouraging raucous demonstrations in the Admiralty courtroom and openly insulted Porter at Council meetings. Early in 1732 he suspended Porter from his judgeship. When Porter appeared before the governor and seven other councillors to present a written defense of Burrington's charges, the governor took the document from his hand and dropped it into a roaring fireplace behind him. Burrington then demanded a vote to suspend Porter from the Council. The suspension tally was four to three, with two votes in the majority coming from men only recently appointed to the Council (under questionable circumstances) by Burrington.

Porter sought to fight his suspensions, and many political associates in the colony supported him with numerous petitions to the Board of Trade in London. Against Burrington's active opposition, Porter was elected to the lower house from Chowan in 1733; there he ranked second only to Edward Moseley in popularity. In July he was authorized to express the Assembly's gratitude to William Smith returning from England where he had been to protest Burrington's executive actions.

When Gabriel Johnston succeeded Burrington as governor late in 1734, he brought with him a commission returning Porter to the Council. Porter took his oaths on 16 Jan. 1735. In October of the next year he was restored to his admiralty judgeship. A regular attendant to his official duties, Porter died somewhat suddenly late in 1737. He left no children by his wife, Elizabeth.

SEE: John B. Boddie, *Historical Southern Families*, vol. 8 (1964); John L. Cheney, Jr., ed., *North Carolina Government, 1585–1979* (1981); William S. Price, Jr., "A Strange Incident in George Burrington's Royal Governorship," *North Carolina Historical Review* 51 (1974), and ed., *North Carolina Higher-Court Minutes, 1709–1723* (1977); William L. Saunders, ed., *Colonial Records of North Carolina*, vols. 1–4 (1886).

WILLIAM S. PRICE, JR.
CLAIBORNE T. SMITH, JR.

Porter, John *(1663–1712),* colonial official and ringleader of Cary's Rebellion, was born in that part of Lower Norfolk County, Va., which after 1691 became the county of Princess Anne. He was the son of John Porter, who with an elder brother with the identical name, appeared in Virginia by 1642. The two brothers were differentiated in the records as Sr. and Jr., respectively. There is strong evidence that they were the sons of one Edmund Porter and of the family of Porter of Tapenhall, Parish of Claines, Worcestershire, England. The two brothers were early converts to Quakerism. In 1663 the elder John, elected a member from Lower Norfolk, was dismissed from the House of Burgesses for being a Quaker. Colonel John Sidney, sheriff of Lower Norfolk, in December 1662 fined several persons, among them his own daughter, Mrs. John Porter, Jr., two hundred pounds of tobacco for holding a Quaker meeting. John Porter, Sr., died without issue in 1675.

John, the younger, and his son John, moved in 1691 to North Carolina, where the son, referred to in the records of the Albemarle as John Porter, Jr., early assumed a prominent role as a merchant and political figure. He was appointed attorney general by Governor John Harvey in 1694 to replace William Wilkinson and qualified before the court. He seems to have served until Governor Henderson Walker took office in 1695. Porter's father died in 1697, as thereafter the designation of junior was dropped. John Porter was a General Court justice and speaker of the Assembly in 1697 and was a member of the Court of the Admiralty in 1705.

In early North Carolina the Quakers and the Dissenters had great influence. In 1704 there was much unrest when the Proprietary government decided to establish the Church of England and to require all officeholders to take the oath of Supremacy to Queen Anne, passed by Parliament in 1702. John Porter does not seem to have been a Quaker and took the required oath. However, it is noteworthy that the Reverend John Urmstone, a contemporary Anglican missionary, described him as a "known villain, the son of a Quaker, and he one in disguise." Porter was at least sympathetic to the faith of his father and in 1706 was sent to England by the Quakers of the Albemarle to present their grievances to the Lords Proprietors.

Successful in his mission, John Porter returned to North Carolina in October 1707 with introductions that provided for the removal of the deputy governor Thomas Cary, then at odds with the Quakers. There was also the provision for the appointment of five new deputies or councillors and for the election by the new Council of a president to act as governor in the place of Cary. On his return, Porter found that Thomas Cary had left the colony and that William Glover had already been elected president by the existing Council. Glover was thought to be amenable by the Quakers so John Porter called together the newly appointed Council and persuaded its members to reelect William Glover president. Although the instructions under which Porter acted required the presence of Thomas Cary and the former Council to make the election legal, he concealed this important fact. When John Porter found that he could not control Glover, who began to insist on oaths, he revealed the conditions listed in the instructions that he had kept secret and insisted that the election of William Glover had been illegal.

At this juncture the former governor, Thomas Cary, reappeared, joined forces with the Quakers, deposed Glover, and ruled the colony for two years, the period known in the history of North Carolina as Cary's Rebellion. John Porter was a member of Cary's Council from 1708 to 1711. With the arrival of Edward Hyde, appointed governor by the Proprietors, Cary and the Quakers lost control, and Cary, John Porter, and others were declared traitors. Porter escaped capture and in the words of Hyde, "went in a great runne to England" where he died in exile shortly afterwards.

John Porter's role in Cary's Rebellion has been the subject of controversy. As early as 1879 the Honorable George Davis, a descendant, attempted to rehabilitate Porter's reputation in a speech before the Literary and Scientific Society of Wilmington. Davis felt that John Porter had been the victim of party rancor. The historian Samuel A. Ashe, also a descendant, tended to put Porter in a favorable light and argued that Porter, as the builder of the original St. Paul's Church in Chowan, the first such building in North Carolina, could hardly be against the Anglican establishment. A John Porter was a contractor for the building, but as there were at least three men by that name in North Carolina at the time, it is not certain which John Porter was involved.

John Porter resided at Bluff Point on Albemarle Sound, in what is now eastern Chowan County. The will of John Porter, merchant of the county of Albemarle, was probated by John Thomas, mayor of Bridgwater in Somerset, England, on 7 Aug. 1712. The surname of his wife Mary is not known. She continued to live in Chowan until her death late in 1717. Her will lists many pages of personal property, unusual for North Carolina at such an early date. John and Mary Porter had five children who survived to maturity. Their three sons, Edmund, John, and Joshua, maintained the prominence of the family in the political life of the colony. Sarah, the oldest daughter, married first John Lillington and second Seth Pilkington. Both husbands were residents of the town of Bath. The youngest daughter, Elizabeth, married first Thomas Fry of London and Bath and second Dr. Patrick Maule. Dr. Maule, brother of William Maule, was an early resident of Bath. A member of the Assembly in 1726 and described as a "man of learning and plentiful fortune," he served as deputy judge of the Admiralty for Bath under his brother-in-law, Edmund Porter.

Of the sons, Joshua Porter was a justice of Beaufort-Hyde and a member of the colonial Assembly in 1726. He married first Catherine, the widow successively of his father's old adversary William Glover and Tobias Knight. With his second wife, Dorothy, the daughter of Robert Peyton, he had a son, John Peyton Porter, and a daughter, Elizabeth. Joshua Porter died in Beaufort in 1734.

SEE: Samuel A. Ashe, ed., *Biographical History of North Carolina*, vol. 2 (1905); John B. Boddie, *Historical Southern Families*, vol. 8 (1964); John L. Cheney, Jr., ed., *North Carolina Government, 1585–1979* (1981); J. Bryan Grimes, ed., *Abstract of North Carolina Wills* (1912); William S. Price, ed., *Colonial Records of North Carolina*, 2d ser., vols. 4–5 (1974); William L. Saunders, ed., *Colonial Records of North Carolina*, vol. 2 (1886).

CLAIBORNE T. SMITH, JR.

Porter, John *(ca. 1690–1727),* legislator, was the son of John Porter (d. 1712). He moved from Chowan County to the area around Bath Town at an early date. In the Tuscarora uprising in 1711, the home of John Porter at the head of Chocowinity Bay is said to have been the first to sustain the Indian attack. Porter and his brother-in-law, Dr. Patrick Maule, were able to repulse the Indians and the family escaped by boat.

John Porter was a member of the Assembly from Beaufort in 1715–16. Active in the town of Bath in 1715, he was a trustee of the town and of the library and a vestryman of St. Thomas Parish. In 1718 Porter followed Governor Charles Eden to Chowan County when Eden moved the government there from Bath. Returning to Beaufort, Porter again represented that county in the Assembly in 1723. Shortly afterwards he joined his wife's connections, the Lillington-Moseley-Ashe clan, in their move to the Cape Fear section. John Porter died late in 1727 and his will was probated in January 1728.

Porter married Sarah, the daughter of Colonel Alexander Lillington and a sister of the John Lillington who married John Porter's sister Sarah. They were the parents of two children, John and Sarah. His widow Sarah survived him for many years and was mentioned in the will of her brother-in-law, Edward Moseley, in 1749. Porter's Neck on Masonboro Sound in the present New Hanover County derives its name from either this John Porter or his son of the same name.

SEE: John B. Boddie, *Historical Southern Families*, vol. 8 (1964); John L. Cheney, Jr., ed., *North Carolina Government, 1585–1979* (1981); Herbert R. Paschal, Jr., *A History of Colonial Bath* (1955).

CLAIBORNE T. SMITH, JR.

Porter, John *(ca. 1710–43)*, legislator, was born in Bath, the son of John Porter and Sarah Lillington and the third of the name to be prominent in the politics of colonial North Carolina. Mentioned as "nephew John Porter of Cape Fear" in the will of Edmund Porter in Chowan in 1737, he, in 1739, petitioned for a confirmation of title to 1,200 acres of land at Bluff Point in Chowan which had been in his family's possession for thirty-four years.

John Porter was recommended for the Council as early as 1730, but probably due to the enmity that developed between Governor George Burrington and the Moore family connection, no action was ever taken. Representing New Hanover in the Assembly in 1733, he was a justice in 1738 and an original commissioner of the new town of Wilmington in 1740. Porter was again elected to the Assembly in 1742 but died sometime late in 1743, when a new writ of election was issued.

John Porter married Elizabeth, the daughter of Colonel Maurice Moore. In 1736 his father-in-law conveyed to him one-half of his interest in the town of Brunswick. Porter and his wife were the parents of two children; Mary and John Swann. Mary was the first wife of her cousin Samuel Ashe, later governor of the state, and the mother of three sons. John Swann, the last of his name in North Carolina, died unmarried at Rocky Point, New Hanover County, in 1770. He left his estate to members of the Ashe family.

SEE: John B. Boddie, *Historical Southern Families*, vol. 8 (1964); John L. Cheney, Jr., ed., *North Carolina Government, 1585–1979* (1981); Lawrence Lee, *The Lower Cape Fear in Colonial Days* (1965); William L. Saunders, ed., *Colonial Records of North Carolina*, vol. 3 (1890).

CLAIBORNE T. SMITH, JR.

Porter, William Sydney (O. Henry) *(11 Sept. 1862–5 June 1910)*, American author of short stories, was born in Greensboro of English and Dutch ancestry. He was the son of Algernon Sidney, a physician, and Mary Jane Virginia Swaim Porter. Porter's great-uncle, Jonathan Worth, was governor of North Carolina from 1865 to 1868. Born of a respectable middle-class stock, he was reared and educated by Miss Evelina Porter, his aunt. At age fifteen, he quit school and began work as a clerk and as a pharmacist's apprentice in his Uncle Clark's drugstore. For reasons of unsatisfactory health and unfavorable home conditions, he left for La Salle County, Tex., in 1882, where he identified with the robust life of ranching that was to give an atmosphere and flavor to some of his later writings.

Within two years, he was in Austin working as a bookkeeper for a real estate firm. At the end of two years he accepted the position of assistant compiling draftsman for the General Land Office (January 1887–January 1891); later he became a paying and receiving teller in the First National Bank of Austin (1891–94). As a supplementary source of income during these years, he began writing free-lance sketches. Before resigning his position at the bank, he became editor and co-owner of a humorous weekly, *The Rolling Stone*. After its demise in 1895, he joined the *Houston Daily Post* staff as the columnist of "Some Postscripts," as a reporter, and as an occasional cartoonist.

In February 1896, after being indicted for the alleged embezzlement of bank funds during his employ as a teller at the First National Bank, he left Houston for Austin to stand trial. En route, he fled to New Orleans and later to Honduras. News of his wife's terminal illness in 1897 prompted his immediate return to Austin. His trial was postponed until after her death on 25 July 1897. The following February he was tried, convicted, and sentenced to imprisonment in the Ohio Penitentiary at Columbus for five years. He entered the prison on 25 Apr. 1898 and was released, after three years and three months for good behavior, on 24 July 1901. During his confinement, his jobs as a night druggist in the prison hospital and later as a secretary to the steward offered him spare time for writing. While in prison, his first short story, "The Miracle of Lava Canyon," was published by S. S. McClure and Company of New York on 18 Sept. 1898. For this and the stories that followed, he used such pen names as Oliver Henry, S. H. Peters, James L. Bliss, T. B. Dowd, and Howard Clark to conceal his identity. But upon release from prison, William Sydney Porter chose to emerge as O. Henry.

With confidence in himself as a writer, he arrived in New York during the spring of 1902. His chief quest was to obtain first-hand material of the city for his short stories, but it was not until 1904 that his stories were to reflect in a marked degree his new environment. The intervening tales continued to deal with the West or Southwest as well as Central or South America. His first book, *Cabbages and Kings* (1904), was a collection of stories that revealed a first-hand acquaintance with coastal Latin America. During his most prolific period (1904–5), he published a total of 115 short stories. All but 21 appeared in the columns of the *New York World*, and all but 16 dealt in some manner with New York City. With the publication of his second book, *The Four Million* (1906), he was hailed as the discoverer of romance in the streets of New York. Like most of his stories, the tales in this collection deal with the commonplace and arrive at a surprise ending through sheer coincidence. Each succeeding year until 1911 was marked by the publication of two collections of his stories. *Heart of the West* (1907) presented a fascinating collection of 19 stories about the West and the Texas range. *The Trimmed Lamp* (1907) established his right to be called the knight of the shop girl. Following these came *The Voice of the City* and *The Gentle Grafter* (1908), *Roads of Destiny* and *Options* (1909), and *Strictly Business* and *Whirligigs* (1910). *Strictly Business* contains "A Municipal Report," the last story published before his death. *Whirligigs*, published posthumously, contains

"The Ransom of Red Chief," perhaps his funniest story. Later posthumous volumes included *Sixes and Sevens* (1911), *Rolling Stones* (1912), *Waifs and Strays* (1917), *O. Henryana* (1920), and *O. Henry Encore* (1936). *Sixes and Sevens* contains his last complete work, "Let Me Feel Your Pulse," which is the most autobiographical. In the *O. Henry Encore*, a collection of his *Houston Post* sketches, are to be found his two favorite motifs: the situation of the impostor or wearer of a disguise, and the idea of fate as the one unavoidable reality of life.

Porter died of diabetes and cirrhosis of the liver in the Polyclinic Hospital in New York. Interment followed on 7 June in Asheville. He was married twice: on 5 July 1887 to Athol Estes and on 27 Nov. 1907 to Sara Coleman of Asheville. Athol bore him one daughter, Margaret Worth, in 1889. As a tribute to Porter's contributions to American literature, the Society of Arts and Letters, in 1918, founded the O. Henry Memorial Award to be awarded annually to the author of the best American short story.

SEE: Eugene Current-Garcia, *O. Henry* (1965); Robert H. Davis and Arthur B. Maurice, *The Caliph of Bagdad* (1931); Addison Hibbard, ed., *Stories of the South* (1931); Gerald Langford, *Alias O. Henry* (1957); C. Alphonso Smith, *O. Henry Biography* (1916).

EDGAR E. MACDONALD

Pory, John *(March 1572–March 1636)*, explorer, newsletter writer, and geographer, was born at Butters Hall, Thompson, Norfolk, England. The son of William Pory, he was graduated in 1592 from Gonville and Caius College, Cambridge, where for a brief time he was instructor in Greek. He studied and worked with Richard Hakluyt and assisted Hakluyt in the preparation of *The Voyages . . . of the English Nation*, published in 1600. In the same year Pory's own *Geographical Historie of Africa* was published, a work that was consulted by Shakespeare and other contemporary writers and that was the basis of English information on Africa and attitudes towards blacks for several centuries.

Pory served in Parliament during the period 1605–11, was a grantee of the Virginia Company of London in 1609, traveled abroad for several years, and was employed in the English Embassy in Constantinople for three years. He was secretary of the Virginia colony from 1619 to 1621 and while in Jamestown served as speaker of the first American legislature, organizing it along the lines of the House of Commons. In January and February 1622, while awaiting passage home, he explored the Chowan River area in modern North Carolina. He described what he saw there in glowing terms, reported that the Indians wanted to engage in trade with the English, and predicted that when the region was settled it would be a profitable place for agriculture and the production of naval stores in the vast pine forests that he discovered.

Much of Pory's life was spent as a newsletter writer in the employ of prominent Englishmen; this was before and at the time of the first appearance of a printed newspaper in England. Among other topics, he wrote about the Thirty Years' War and social and political conditions. He was also employed at court on several occasions and returned to Jamestown in 1624 in connection with an investigation of the Virginia Company. He was the author of several other published works of a geographic and religious nature. Pory was buried in the churchyard in the village of Sutton St. Edmunds, Lincolnshire, where his family apparently had originated and where he had relatives.

SEE: William S. Powell, *John Pory, 1572–1636: The Life and Letters of a Man of Many Parts* (1977).

WILLIAM S. POWELL

Post, James Francis *(24 Feb. 1851–5 Jan. 1918)*, railroad official and a native of Wilmington, was the son of James Francis and Mary A. Russell Post. His father was born in New Jersey and moved in 1849 to Wilmington, where he became one of the first men to devote himself exclusively to the practice of architecture in North Carolina. He enlisted in the Confederate army and served throughout the Civil War as a lieutenant, having charge of the fortifications in the harbor. Later he was the architect of City Hall, St. Paul's Lutheran Church, the John D. Bellamy mansion, and other buildings in Wilmington.

The younger Post was educated in the public schools and at Wilmington Academy. At age nineteen he entered the railroad service as a freight clerk of the Wilmington and Weldon Railroad, a part of the Atlantic Coast Line system. He held various positions in the company and was treasurer of the entire system for the last sixteen years of his life.

A Methodist, Post was superintendent of the Sunday school at Grace Church for twenty-five years, a magistrate for ten years, and at one time acting mayor. Interested in education, he was chairman of the Wilmington School Board and a trustee of the Agricultural School for Negroes and for the State Normal School for Women. He was a member of St. John's Masonic Lodge, Woodmen of the World, Knights of Pythias, Cape Fear Club, and Cape Fear Country Club. He also was a member of the Society of Railway Financial Officials of America, an honorary Fellow of the American Geological Society, and a member of the National Society of Political Economy.

On 6 Apr. 1876 Post married Sarah Virginia Jacobs of Wilmington. They had seven children: Virginia who died at age four, Robert E., James Francis, William N., Mary Russell, Julia B., and Lydia. Lydia became Mrs. Herbert Scott Snead and Mary married G. M. M. James. Post lived at 112 North Seventh Street in Wilmington. His funeral was held from Grace Methodist Church and he was buried in Oakdale Cemetery, Wilmington.

SEE: *Lower Cape Fear Historical Society Handbook* (1970); *North Carolina Biography*, vol. 5 (1919); Wilmington *Star*, 6 Jan. 1918.

LEORA HIATT MCEACHERN

Postlethwaite. *See* **Phillips, Charles.**

Poteat, Edwin McNeill *(6 Feb. 1861–25 June 1937)*, clergyman and educator, was born near Yanceyville in Caswell County, the youngest of three children of James and Julia A. McNeill Poteat. His siblings were William Louis, president of Wake Forest College (1905–27), and Ida, a teacher at Meredith College. James Poteat was a substantial planter.

Edwin McNeill Poteat received a B.A. degree from Wake Forest College in 1881 and the D.D. in 1894. He was graduated from Southern Baptist Theological Seminary, Louisville, Ky., in 1885, after his ordination to the Baptist ministry the previous year. His first pastorate was the Baptist church at Chapel Hill, from which he resigned in 1886 to become for a few months assistant professor of ancient languages at Wake Forest. From 1886 to 1888 he was a graduate student in psychology and philosophy at Johns Hopkins University. While in Baltimore, he served as acting pastor of Lee Street Baptist

Church. He spent the summer of 1888 in graduate study under Otto Pfleiderer at the University of Berlin, Germany.

Beginning in 1888 Poteat was for a decade pastor of Calvary Church, New Haven, Conn., and a special student at Yale University. In 1898 he became pastor of Memorial Baptist Church in Philadelphia, Pa., serving until 1903, when he accepted the presidency of Furman University, Greenville, S.C. Poteat received the LL.D. degree from the University of South Carolina, Columbia, in 1906 and from Baylor University, Waco, Tex., in 1907. Among his contributions to Furman was the enlargement of facilities for teaching the sciences and emphasis on combining the teaching of Christianity and the sciences. Finding administrative duties "continually growing more irksome," he resigned in 1918 to become platform representative of the Laymen's Missionary Movement and the Interchurch World Movement. Poteat had become widely known as a speaker. The editor of the *Baptist Courier* (1 July 1937) declared that "At the Baptist World Alliance in Philadelphia, 1911, Dr. Poteat proved to be . . . the most popular speaker in the program, and was the only one, we believe, who was implored from all parts of the audience to continue after he had closed."

From 1919 to 1921 Poteat was departmental executive secretary of the General Board of Promotion of the Northern Baptist Convention. In 1921, while visiting his two eldest sons who were missionaries in China, the University of Shanghai invited him to become professor of philosophy and ethics. Poteat held the post for six years. After his return to the United States in 1927, he was interim pastor of the First Baptist Church, Richmond, Va. Two years later he became pastor of Second Baptist Church in Atlanta, Ga. From 1931 to 1934 he taught ethics and comparative religion at Mercer University in Macon, Ga. In 1934 he returned to Furman as professor of ethics and remained on the faculty until his death.

At various times in his career Poteat was a member of the board of managers of the American Baptist Missionary Union and a member of the Baptist Publication Society. He was recording secretary of the American Baptist Education Society, trustee of the Southern Baptist Theological Seminary, life member of the American Bible Society, and president of the Southern Baptist Educational Association. He was a Democrat. His published works include *The Religion of the Lord's Prayer* (1914), *A Campaign Handbook for Christian Education* (1918), *The Withered Fig Tree: Studies in Stewardship* (1921), and *The Scandal of the Cross: Studies in the Death of Jesus* (1928).

On 24 Oct. 1889 Poteat married Harriet Hale Gordon, daughter of Adoniram Judson Gordon, pastor of Clarendon Street Church, Boston, Mass. Their children, with 1937 addresses for some, were Gordon, en route from Shanghai to join the faculty of Crozer Seminary, Chester, Pa.; Edwin McNeill, Jr., pastor of Pullen Memorial Church, Raleigh; John Robinson, Cleveland, Ohio; Priscilla Isabella Graves; James Douglass, Duke University; Clarissa Hale; and Arthur Barron (deceased). Poteat's first wife died in 1919. In China in 1925 he married Harriet Helen Brittingham, a missionary of the Northern Baptist Convention from Mount Vernon, N.Y.

He died in Durham and was buried in the Furman University plot in Springwood Cemetery, Greenville, S.C.

SEE: Robert Norman Daniel, *Furman University: A History* (1951 [portrait]); *Encyclopedia of Southern Baptists*, vol. 2 (1958); *The Furman Bulletin: Edwin McNeill Poteat Memorial Number* (November 1937 [portrait]); Greenville, S.C., *Baptist Courier* (1 July 1937); W. J. McGlothlin, *Baptist Beginnings in Education: A History of Furman University* (1926); Raleigh *Biblical Recorder* (30 June 1937); *Who Was Who in America, 1897–1942*, vol. 1 (1943).

HENRY S. STROUPE

Poteat, Edwin McNeill, Jr. *(20 Nov. 1892–17 Dec. 1955)*, Baptist clergyman, missionary, college president, and writer, was born in New Haven, Conn., the second of eight children of Edwin McNeill and Harriett Hale Gordon Poteat. His father, a Baptist clergyman, was for many years president of Furman University; an uncle, Dr. William Louis Poteat, was longtime president of Wake Forest College. Following attendance at Furman Fitting School, young Poteat entered Furman University, where he received A.B. (1912) and A.M. (1913) degrees. His master's degree in theology was from the Southern Baptist Theological Seminary (1916). Honorary degrees were awarded by Wake Forest (1933), Duke (1936), Hillsdale College (1940), The University of North Carolina (1946), and Colgate (1947).

Following his graduation from the seminary, Poteat was a traveling secretary for the student volunteer movement in New York (1916–17). In August 1917 he left for China as a Southern Baptist missionary. Until 1926 he served in Kaifeng, Honan, China, where he preached; built, with a Belgian architect and a Chinese contractor, a large compound consisting of a church, school, and residences; and, in his words, "Worried through a siege, ran into street corner beheadings and hunted ducks and wild swan near the city walls. Escaped in 1926 in zero weather in a freight car with a shivering but cheerful family when the revolution hit our city." Poteat's warnings of the potential danger to the work with the rise of the Nationalist movement and the Bolshevist influence were not taken seriously by the officers of the Foreign Mission Board. He and the board had differences in several areas; for example, the board felt that Poteat was too fascinated with studying the Chinese language when he should be pursuing other activities and it opposed his ecumenical efforts. After fleeing from Kaifeng, however, Poteat continued his work under the auspices of the board as professor of philosophy and ethics at the University of Shanghai until 1929.

In September 1929, following a trip home by way of Siberia and Europe, Poteat moved to Raleigh to assume the pastorate of Pullen Memorial Baptist Church. His brilliant sermons attracted large congregations of nonmembers as well as members of the church. In 1937 he was called to the Euclid Avenue Baptist Church in Cleveland, Ohio, where he remained until his selection as president of Colgate-Rochester Divinity School in Rochester, N.Y. Poteat moved to Rochester early in 1944 and served until 1948. In the spring of that year he suffered what he referred to as a combination of a coronary and "intestinal gremlins"; because of his health, he was advised to relinquish his administrative duties. His successor at Pullen Memorial having resigned, Poteat was again called by that church and returned to Raleigh in the late fall of 1948. His second term of service ended when he collapsed from a coronary occlusion on his way to perform a wedding at the church; death followed soon after his arrival at the hospital.

Poteat was noted for his versatility. A man of many talents, he was a musician of note: he was an organist, had a superior tenor voice, and wrote words and music to several hymns and anthems. Among those published were "Eternal God Whose Searching Eye Doth Scan," which was used at the opening session of the World Council of Churches meeting in Amsterdam in 1948; "In the End of the Sabbath" (1938); "Jesus Our Joy of Living Hearts" (1950); and "Indifference" (1942). His books include *The Reverend John Doe D.D.* (1934); *Thunder Over Sinai* (1936); *The Social Manifesto of Jesus* (1937); *Centurion*, a dramatic poem (1938); *These Shared His Passions* (1938); *These Shared His Cross* (1939); *These Shared His Power* (1941); *Four Freedoms and God* (1943); *Over the Sea the Sky*, a book of poetry (1945); *Last Reprieve?* (1945); *Parables Crisis* (1950); *God Makes the Difference* (1951); and *Mandate to Humanity* (1953). He contributed to *Harper's*, *Saturday Review of Literature*, *Christian Century*, and numerous other periodicals. He also wrote the exposition of Psalms 42–89 for the *Interpreters' Bible*.

He was an athlete of unusual ability. While in China he was star pitcher on the All-American baseball team. He once defeated political columnist Walter Lippman in a tennis match, and he served as trainer for a challenger for the world wrestling championship in 1916.

An Independent in politics, Poteat was active in the pacifist movement and was a founder and longtime president of Protestants and Other Americans United for Separation of Church and State. He served as a trustee (vice-chairman of the board, 1949) of Shaw University and received gubernatorial appointments to the North Carolina Commission on Displaced Persons, the Board of Charities and Public Welfare, and the Commission of Five to Study State Hospitals. He supported various liberal causes and worked for the rights of blacks, conscientious objectors, and others in minority positions. Poteat was the first clergyman to be invited to address the American Association for the Advancement of Science (1946).

He married Wilma Hardman of Commerce, Ga., on 27 June 1918. They had four children: William Hardman, Harriett Alden, who predeceased her father, Elizabeth McNeill, and Haley Gordon.

In an editorial of 19 December 1955, the day of Poteat's funeral, the Raleigh *News and Observer* observed: "it is hard to associate with death one who in his goodness and his wit, his courage and his charm was as gay a saint as ever walked our streets." Burial at Montlawn, Raleigh, followed funeral services at Pullen Memorial. There is a portrait of Poteat in the chapel of Pullen Memorial Baptist Church.

SEE: E. McNeill Poteat Papers (Southern Historical Collection, Unviersity of North Carolina, Chapel Hill); Raleigh *News and Observer*, 18–19 Dec. 1955; *Who Was Who in America, 1951–1960*.

MEMORY F. MITCHELL

Poteat, Hubert McNeill *(12 Dec. 1886–29 Jan. 1958)*, college professor, musician, author, and Shriner, was born at Wake Forest to William Louis and Emma James Purefoy Poteat. His early education was eclectic, and his principal instructor was his maternal grandmother, who operated a private school. The fundamental knowledge he received through her tutoring enabled him to enter Wake Forest College, from which he received the A.B. degree in 1906. Serving as instructor in Latin at the college for the next two years, he also earned the A.M. degree (1908).

While a student at Wake Forest, he developed interests that would dominate his later life. Study of the classics led to a doctorate. His proficiency in music was considerably advanced. Although he studied the violin, he did not often play this instrument, much preferring the organ. By 1905 he was ready to play at the inauguration of his father as president of Wake Forest College. As an athlete, Poteat won the singles and doubles Southern Inter-Collegiate Tennis Championships at Atlanta in 1907. Later he turned to the less strenuous game of golf, which, although he called it "the invention of the devil and perpetrated by his followers," he played every afternoon. His participation in Masonry began with his induction as entered apprentice by the Wake Forest Lodge on 21 Jan. 1908.

Also in 1908 he began studies towards a doctorate at Columbia University. Satisfactory academic progress did not prevent frequent attendance at the theater and the opera. Having thus been diverted but not interrupted, he was granted the Ph.D. degree in 1912 and immediately began to develop the characteristic features of his adult career. That year, after marrying Essie Moore Morgan on 26 June, he returned to Wake Forest College as professor of Latin. Poteat remained in this post, later serving as chairman of the department, until 1956, when the college was moved to Winston-Salem.

Poteat undertook scholarly writing soon after his academic appointment. In spite of administrative duties and the direction of the Glee Club (1912–23), he published a series of volumes consisting of colorfully, although scholarly, annotated texts and translations. They included *Repetition in Latin Poetry* (1912), *Selected Letters of Cicero* (1916, revised 1931), *Practical Hymnology* (1921), *Selected Epigrams of Martial* (1931), *Selected Letters of Pliny* (1937), *T. Livius Narrator: Selections from Livy* (1938), and a translation of Cicero's *Brutus: On the Nature of the Gods, On Divination, On Duties* (1950). These were interspersed with numerous journal articles. His professional activities also included a term as president of the Classical Association of the Mid-West and South in 1938. During summer sessions from 1924 to 1942 he taught at Columbia University.

Enthusiasm for Masonry and the Shrine in particular led him to the post of grand master of the Grand Lodge of North Carolina in 1923, to the honorary thirty-third degree, Knights Templars, to election as outer guard of the Imperial Shrine, and finally to the highest Shrine office, that of imperial potentate of North America, which he assumed at a meeting in Los Angeles in June 1950 and held during the next thirteen months.

Music was an ever-present interest. For about forty years he served as organist and choir director in the Wake Forest Baptist Church, Wake Forest. He gave many recitals on the organ and occasional vocal solos (while in New York he had been a member of the Brick Presbyterian Church choir and a soloist at the Church of the Intercession). In organ recitals he especially enjoyed playing transcriptions of more massive orchestral works, notably those of Wagner.

His outstanding achievements in these various fields were the result of a robust and even boisterous personality, a penetrating intellect, and a state of complete conviction. No one ever remained long in doubt about his opinions, which he expressed freely and pungently. Academically, as well as otherwise, he was a perfectionist, concentrating especially on purity and accuracy in the use of English. He spoke widely in the South, generally on causes he promoted from time to time. He was especially aroused by what he saw as a growing trend in the public schools towards vocational training and away from the humanities. He also held a violent dislike for "gospel hymns," which he called "jig tunes." When playing more traditional hymns, however, he spiritedly insisted that the congregation should not drag its singing.

Being near the statutory retirement age, in declining health, and somewhat resentful when the college moved to Winston-Salem, he chose to retire early and to remain at Wake Forest. On 29 Jan. 1958 he suffered a stroke and died the same day; two days later he was buried in the cemetery at Wake Forest. He was survived by his widow and two sons, Hubert McNeill, Jr., and William Morgan.

SEE: *Men of Achievement in the Carolinas* (1952 [portrait]); John S. Ramond, *Among Southern Baptists* (1936); *Who's Who in the South and Southwest* (1952); *Who Was Who in America*, vol. 3 (1960). See also scattered references in *Wake Forest Student* and *Old Gold and Black.*

C. P. WEST

Poteat, Ida Isabella *(15 Dec. 1858–1 Feb. 1940)*, artist, teacher, craftsman, and patron of art, was born at Forest Home near Yanceyville in Caswell County, the daughter of James and Julia A. McNeill Poteat. She received early education locally and at the Raleigh Female Seminary, then studied at the New York School of Fine and Applied Arts, the Cooper Union Art School in New York, and the School of Applied Design in Philadelphia. In New York she was a private pupil of William M. Chase, president of the Society of American Artists. Among her other teachers were Robert Henri, Charles Parsons, and Louis Mounier.

For a time she was an art instructor at Oxford Seminary in Oxford, Granville County, but with the opening on 27 Sept. 1899 of the Baptist Female University in Raleigh (now Meredith College), she joined the faculty as professor of art, a position she held until her death more than forty years later. Ida Poteat taught and inspired hundreds of young people both as students at Meredith College and in private classes, one of whom was the artist Francis Speight. Of her, Speight wrote: "Not only did she encourage us to appreciate fine forms and colors, but she encouraged us also to see beauty in humble things."

In 1924 the faculty at Meredith College established a lasting tradition of presenting a stage production of "Alice in Wonderland" every four years. Much to the delight of students and the public, the faculty played leading roles. Ida Poteat designed the costumes and made fantastic masks. Of a more serious nature, she also had designed the seal adopted by the college in 1909.

A devout Baptist, she was the sister of William Louis and E. McNeill Poteat. A portrait of her hangs in Poteat Hall on the Meredith campus. She was buried in the family cemetery near Yanceyville.

SEE: *The Acorn* (student publication, Meredith College, Raleigh) 22 (October 1940 [portrait]); *Annual of the North Carolina Baptist State Convention* (1940 [portrait]); Peter H. Falk, ed., *Who Was Who in American Art* (1985); Mary Lynch Johnson, *A History of Meredith College* (1972); *Meredith College Quarterly Bulletin*, ser. 34 (November 1940); Raleigh *News and Observer*, 16 Dec. 1938, 2 Feb., 16 Dec. 1940.

WILLIAM S. POWELL

Poteat, William Louis *(20 Oct. 1856–12 Mar. 1938)*, educator, was born in Caswell County, the son of James and Julia A. McNeill Poteat. He was taught by a governess and then entered the village academy at Yanceyville. In 1877 he was graduated from Wake Forest College with a B.A. degree, and in 1889 he received an M.A. degree from Wake Forest. Later he was awarded LL.D. degrees by Baylor, The University of North Carolina, Brown, and Duke and the Litt.D. degree by Mercer. In addition, Poteat went to the University of Berlin in 1888 and attended a course at the Marine Biological Laboratory, Woods Hole, Mass., in 1893.

A year after his graduation from Wake Forest, the trustees elected him as a tutor; and although he had begun to read law, his acceptance of this position determined his lifework. By 1881 he was an assistant professor of natural science and by 1883, a full professor of biology. Poteat introduced the laboratory method—as opposed to the recitation method—in the teaching of biology. He was the first person in the South to do this. Continuing to play a prominent role in the development of Wake Forest and Meredith colleges, he was elected president of Wake Forest College in 1905 and served until 1927—longer than any other president in the history of the college.

Poteat was a pioneer in the acceptance of the Darwinian theory of evolution. When the evolution controversy spread through the South in the early twenties, he became a focal point among Baptists and North Carolinians. He defended the teaching of evolution as the "divine method of creation" and believed that this perspective was in harmony with the fundamental tenets of the Baptists. Poteat helped to defeat the bill introduced in the state legislature in 1925 to prevent the teaching of Darwinism in North Carolina schools.

Involved in many social movements and organizations, Poteat was a member of the North Carolina Conference for Social Service (president), Southern Baptist Education Association (president, three terms), North Carolina Anti-Saloon League (president), Council of Church Schools of the South (president), North Carolina Reconstruction Commission, North Carolina Academy of Sciences (president), and many other organizations. He was a popular lecturer on religion, science, temperance, and education. Besides his numerous contributions to the *Biblical Recorder*, scientific publications, and other periodicals, Poteat was the author of *Laboratory and Pulpit* (1901), *The New Peace* (1915), *Can a Man Be a Christian Today?* (1925), and *Stop Light* (1935).

Poteat married Emma James Purefoy of Wake Forest on 24 June 1881. Their children were Hubert McNeill, Louie (Mrs. Wheeler Martin, Jr.), and Helen Purefoy Stallings Marshall.

Shortly after his eighty-first birthday, Poteat was stricken with paralysis. Within a short time he was able to regain partial use of his limbs, but he died quietly at his home in Wake Forest. His funeral was conducted in the Wake Forest Baptist Church and burial was in the cemetery at Wake Forest.

SEE: G. A. Hendricks, "William Louis Poteat," *Encyclopedia of Southern Baptists*, vol. 2 (1958); Suzanne Cameron Linder, *William Louis Poteat: Prophet of Progress* (1966 [portraits]); William Louis Poteat Papers (Baptist Historical Collection, Wake Forest University, Winston-Salem, N.C. [portraits]); Lou Rogers, "Dr. William Louis Poteat," *We the People*, November 1946; Gary E. Trawick and Paul B. Wyche, *One Hundred Years, One Hundred Men* (1971).

JOHN R. WOODARD

Potter, Henry *(5 Jan. 1766–20 Dec. 1857)*, lawyer, federal judge, and supporter of education, was born in Mecklenburg County, Va., of English ancestry. His father was John Potter, a planter and substantial property owner who moved to Granville County, N.C., when Henry was a child. The elder Potter was active in the Granville area, serving as a vestryman and justice of the peace. His wife was the widow Mary Howard Hawkins. Henry was one of six children raised in affluent circumstances, but little is known of his early education. During the inception of the new republic he spent two and one-half years in Philadelphia, where he coupled academic and perhaps legal studies with an active interest in and acquaintance with prominent national political figures.

About 1790 Potter returned to North Carolina and settled in Raleigh, where he immediately established a successful legal practice and became a conspicuous public figure. A supporter of Thomas Jefferson, he came to the president's attention in May 1801, when Nathaniel Macon successfully urged his candidacy for the judgeship of the U.S. Fifth Circuit Court, created under the Federalist-inspired Judiciary Act of 1801. Potter's commission was dated 9 May. He had held this position less than a year when Jefferson nominated him on 6 Apr. 1802 to be federal district court judge for North Carolina in place of the deceased John Sitgreaves. The following day the Senate confirmed the appointment.

During his fifty-five years of district court service Potter presided over cases involving counterfeiting, the Admiralty, bankruptcy, and federal crimes. Perhaps his most important contribution as a judge came early in his career in the case of *Coventry v. Davie,* whose central issues paralleled closely questions raised in the more celebrated case of *Martin v. Hunter Lessee* (1 Wheaton 304). Potter's charge to the jury was apparently instrumental in the jury's decision to deny the claims of the heirs of Lord Granville to an immense corridor of land running from the Atlantic Ocean to the Mississippi River through parts of the states of Virginia and North Carolina.

In addition to his judicial duties Potter engaged in a variety of political, public, and private pursuits. In 1816 he supported James Monroe for the presidency and eight years later he was an organizer on behalf of Andrew Jackson. Potter, William Polk, and Archibald D. Murphey foiled attempts by the supporters of William H. Crawford to deliver North Carolina's presidential electoral votes to the Georgia senator. Potter also provided important legal services to North Carolina beyond his judgeship. In 1819, along with Bartlett Yancey and Justice John L. Taylor, he revised the North Carolina statutes. The two-volume edition, primarily the work of Potter, appeared in 1821 and represents a landmark in North Carolina legal history. Also of importance was Potter's pioneering manual on the conduct of justices of the peace, entitled *Duties of the Justice of the Peace* (1816), which urged statewide order and uniformity in the conduct of that important office.

Potter served several terms as a commissioner for the city of Raleigh, acted as one of the commissioners in 1813 to erect an executive residence for the governor, and served on another commission in 1833 to sell several parcels of state land and procure stone for the capitol. He was also a distinguished and active supporter of education. Beginning in 1799 and continuing for over half a century he was a trustee and veteran fund-raiser for The University of North Carolina. In addition, he was a trustee of Pomona Academy, located northwest of Raleigh, and was one of the original trustees of the Raleigh Academy, which opened in July 1804. Potter was also an active Mason, a subscriber to the State Bank of North Carolina, and one of the founders of Raleigh's Brick Presbyterian Church.

Near his sixtieth birthday Potter moved his home from Raleigh to Chelsea, an estate near Fayetteville. There he engaged in agricultural activities assisted by a small number of slaves. Potter was married on 24 Jan. 1799, in Raleigh, to Sylvia Williams Easton, the daughter of James Easton, a native of Hartford, Conn., who was a major in the North Carolina militia and a Raleigh merchant. Of the couple's ten children, six lived to adulthood. Potter was buried with his wife, who died on 25 Oct. 1853, at Cross Creek Cemetery, Fayetteville. A portrait hangs in the federal courthouse in Fayetteville.

SEE: Willis G. Briggs, *Henry Potter, 1766–1857* (1953); Free and Slave Schedules, Sixth Census of the United States, Cumberland County, N.C.; *Newbern Gazette,* 8 Dec. 1798; *North Carolina Journal,* 9 Jan. 1793, 1 Aug. 1796; Henry T. Shanks, ed., *The Papers of Willie Person Mangum,* vol. 1 (1950); John H. Wheeler, *Historical Sketches of North Carolina,* vol. 2 (1851); Louis R. Wilson and Hugh T. Lefler, eds., *A Documentary History of the University of North Carolina, 1776–1799,* vol. 2 (1953). The case files of Potter's court, a few of his decisions, and charges to juries can be found in the Federal Records Center, East Point, Ga. A small collection of Potter manuscripts is held by the North Carolina State Archives, Raleigh.

KERMIT L. HALL

Potter, Robert *(June 1800?–2 Mar. 1842),* lawyer and politician, was born in Granville County, the son of Thomas and Susan Walker Potter. Thomas Potter is said to have been a member of a family of substantial merchants and farmers and a man of good character but no financial success. His son Robert later wrote of him with respect and affection. The mother evidently died while the son was a child.

Nothing is known of the schools Robert Potter attended, but he later demonstrated good knowledge of the classics and fluent command of the English language, with unusual oratorical ability. Appointed a midshipman at age fifteen, he spent six years in naval service along the Atlantic coast and in the West Indies. He resigned from the navy in March 1821 and returned to North Carolina, studying law in the office of Thomas Burgess of Halifax, quickly passing the bar examination, and beginning practice.

In 1824 Potter ran for election as the representative of the borough of Halifax in the North Carolina House of Commons in opposition to the incumbent Jesse A. Bynum, another young lawyer. The spirited campaign seems to have been characterized by personalities and factionalism rather than issues. Bynum was declared the winner, but Potter charged that the count was fraudulent and challenged his opponent to a duel. Bynum refused to fight on the grounds that Potter was not a gentleman. The two men again sought the seat in 1825, and their rivalry provoked a fight more like a brawl than a duel. Both were arrested, placed under peace bond, and published denunciations of each other. No election for borough representative was held that year.

In 1826 Potter was a candidate for the third time and won. Although a new and youthful member of the General Assembly of 1826–27, he introduced one of the more notable bills of the session and made one of the more sensational speeches. He proposed that the state borrow $220,000 to establish and support a "political college," in reality an agricultural school and academy where poor but intelligent boys selected from each county would devote three years to working on the farm and studying agriculture, the art of war, political economy, and morality. They were then to spend another three years teaching at assigned positions in the state. Potter supported his bill in a long and unusual speech critical of North Carolina and its officials, especially three members of Congress whom he denounced by name. Although as chairman of the committee on education he later reported favorably on the bill, it failed to pass.

In 1827 Potter moved from Halifax back to his native

county of Granville, publishing a denunciation of Halifax and of his law teacher and former friend, Burgess. He married Isabella Taylor, of a prominent family of Granville. In August 1828 he ran for election as a member of the House of Commons in an election marked by bitter criticism of the three banks of the state. The banks, whose charters were soon to expire, had begun to curtail activities and call in loans, and the resulting financial stringency aroused hostility. Banking thus became the principal issue in the legislative session of 1828–29, with Potter among those wishing to punish the bank's officers and stockholders. He proposed to confiscate the assets of the banks and to indict the officers for violation of charters through excessive note issues, suspension of specie payments, and usurious rates. Another legislator proposed to establish a new bank wholly controlled by the state government, its assets to be those confiscated from the former banks and the credit of the state. Supporters of the banks and fiscal conservatives combined to defeat both measures.

In August 1829 Potter enlarged his field of operations by winning election as the representative to Congress from his district. As a congressman he continued his hostility to banks, introducing a resolution, which failed to pass, declaring that a national bank was unconstitutional and paper money unwise.

In 1831 Potter was elected to Congress without opposition. He and his wife lived near Oxford, the county seat, and had two children, Susan and Robert. This apparently happy situation ended on Sunday, 28 Aug. 1831, when Potter assaulted and castrated two men, charging that his wife was guilty of infidelity with both of them. One was her cousin, a minister in his fifties; the other was a nephew of her stepmother, a youth of seventeen. News of the action created a sensation in North Carolina.

Potter was charged with mayhem on the younger man; he pleaded guilty and was imprisoned for six months and fined $1,000. Indictment for the attack on the older man was deferred on the grounds that the victim might die. He recovered, and in March 1832 Potter was tried for assault with a deadly weapon. Again pleading guilty, he was sentenced to two years in prison and required to post a peace bond when released. The judge ordered that his confinement be in Hillsborough rather than Oxford for safety. Potter resigned his seat in Congress in November 1831.

While in jail in Hillsborough, Potter wrote a lengthy "Address to the People of Granville County" justifying his conduct and declaring that his prosecution and punishment were politically motivated. He was then indicted for libel of the judge, but the case was never brought to trial.

When Potter's prison term was up in March 1834, he took the oath of insolvency and was released without payment of his fine. He soon ran again for the House of Commons in a campaign marked by violence between his supporters and his opponents and efforts of his brother-in-law to kill him. His victory under the circumstances was a remarkable demonstration of his popularity in his home county.

In the General Assembly of 1834–35 Potter's eligibility was challenged, since his recent oath of insolvency indicated that he lacked the one-hundred-acre freehold required for members of the house. The investigating committee sustained him as the owner of an adequate piece of land even though insolvent because a mortgage prevented sale of the property. The most noteworthy legislation of the session was the passage of a bill providing for the call of a convention to revise the state constitution. Potter's vote in opposition followed Granville County tradition but was uncharacteristically conservative. He took no prominent part in legislation and kept silent when the legislature heard and granted his wife's petition for divorce, change of name, and custody of their children. Late in the session Potter became involved in a gambling episode, charged his opponent with cheating, pocketed the money he had lost, and in the ensuing scuffle drew a pistol to defend himself. On 2 Jan. 1835 he was expelled from the North Carolina House of Commons.

In the summer of 1835 Potter went to Texas, arriving in Nacogdoches in time to participate in the Texas Revolution. He became a member of the Nacogdoches Independent Volunteers but soon resigned to request and receive a colonel's commission with letters of marque and reprisal. In February 1836 he was one of four men elected to represent Nacogdoches in a plenary convention. He was thus a member of the body that declared the independence of Texas, drafted a constitution, and formed a provisional government. His experience in legislative bodies and his forceful personality made him a leader, and he was appointed secretary of the navy in the government of provisional president David G. Burnet. He set out for Galveston to inspect the little Texas navy, on the way assisting a party of settlers fleeing to Galveston in fear of the Mexicans. Potter was appointed commander of the port of Galveston. After the Battle of San Jacinto he disagreed with Sam Houston on a number of points, and his brief service as secretary of the navy ended when Houston was elected president in September 1836.

Potter retired to private life, spent a year farming on the Sabine River, and built a home at what is now Potter's Point on Caddo Lake, then in Red River, now Marion County, where he farmed and practiced law. Living with him was Mrs. Harriet Moore Page, one of the refugees he helped to reach Galveston. She was a member of a respectable family who had moved to Texas, but she described her husband Solomon Page as a drunken ne'er-do-well who did not support her. She later claimed that Potter said her marriage was invalid by Texas law and that he and she were married by bond. She and Potter lived together as man and wife and had two children; her brother went to Caddo Lake to live with them. Their home was in a thinly settled area beset by lawlessness. Potter at one time tried to quell a mob and win a trial for a man it had captured. He was not successful in preventing the lynching, but he won recognition through his oratory and he was twice elected a member of the Texas Senate, serving in the Fifth (1840–41) and Sixth (1841–42) Congress.

In the meantime Potter had become involved in a frontier feud with a neighbor, William Pinckney Rose. The two men were leaders of rival factions ostensibly endeavoring to preserve order and prevent crime but also each seeking control. Rose was charged with murder, and Potter took a group of men to Rose's home to arrest him, failing to find him. Early the next morning, Rose and his supporters surrounded Potter's home. Potter, waking, attempted to escape by diving into the lake and swimming under water, but when his head emerged he was shot and killed. His body was recovered and buried at Potter's Point. Rose and several of his followers were tried for murder, but the case was dismissed for lack of evidence.

Potter was survived by Mrs. Page and two children, one of whom soon died in an accident. Potter's divorced wife died before he did; their two children survived the parents but died unmarried. Potter made a will the month before his death leaving land and other property to Mrs. Page and substantial bequests of land, including his homestead, to other women. While in Austin he wrote to Mrs. Page as "Mrs. Harriet Potter," but in his will he did not call her his wife or use the name Potter for her. She contested his will and initially obtained possession of the home they had occupied, but after many years the Texas court ruled that she was not legally married to Potter and that the will was valid.

In 1876 a county in Texas was named for Potter, and in 1928 the state of Texas had his remains moved to the State Cemetery in Austin and marked with a monument.

Robert Potter was a tall, slender man with dark hair and eyes. He was intelligent and industrious, with personal magnetism and compelling eloquence. His great ability was not matched by discipline and restraint, and his life was marked by extremes. He became notorious rather than noted, conspicuous rather than constructive. In spite of the prominent roles he played in North Carolina and Texas, he left no lasting achievements.

A portrait of Potter as a young man, oil on wood, was preserved by descendants of his sister, and a copy was made from it, oil on canvas. The copy was given to the North Carolina Historical Commission in 1930 and was probably the portrait hanging in the North Carolina capitol in 1945 (see Blanchard and Wellman, *The Life and Times of Sir Archie*). The present location of the portrait and the copy is unknown.

SEE: Potter's activities reported in the newspapers and in the *Journals of the House of Commons*; Pamphlet editions of his writings about Bynum and Halifax, the debate on his bill to punish the banks, and his "Address to the People of Granville County" (North Carolina Collection, University of North Carolina, Chapel Hill); Recollections of Mrs. Page (later Mrs. Ames) and other materials about Potter in the Samuel A. Asbury Papers (typed copies, Southern Historical Collection, University of North Carolina, and other repositories). See also Elizabeth A. C. Blanchard and Manly Wade Wellman, *The Life and Times of Sir Archie* (1958); Joseph Blount Cheshire, *Nonnulla* (1930); William A. Devin, "Robert Potter: An Uncommon American," a paper read before the Raleigh History Club, March 1948 (North Carolina Collection); Robert C. Shearer, *Robert Potter: Remarkable North Carolinian and Texan* (1951); Robert Watson Winston, "Robert Potter: Tar Heel and Texas Dare Devil," *South Atlantic Quarterly* 29 (April 1930).

CAROLYN A. WALLACE

Potts, James Manning *(14 July 1895–31 Jan. 1973)*, clergyman and author, was born at Como, the son of Reginald and Annie Christian Moore Potts. From Randolph-Macon College in Virginia he received a B.A. degree in 1917 and an M.A. degree in 1920; the college also awarded him an honorary doctor of divinity degree in 1935. After earning bachelor (1924) and master (1925) of theology degrees from Princeton Theological Seminary, he pursued additional study at the University of Virginia and the University of Chicago. In 1961 the Ewha Woman's University in Seoul, Korea, awarded him the Litt.D. degree.

After teaching high school courses in Richmond, Va., and service as a Fellow in apologetics and Christian ethics at the Princeton Theological Seminary in 1925, he was ordained to the ministry in the Methodist church in 1927. Between that year and 1944 he served churches in Richmond, Petersburg, and Roanoke, Va. From 1935 to 1940 he was district superintendent of the Richmond District, and from 1944 to 1948 he was associate director and publications editor of the Crusade for Christ. During the period 1948–56 he was editor of *The Upper Room Pulpit* and in the years 1948–67 of the *Upper Room* Radio and Television Parish. He was a delegate to many church conferences between 1938 and 1964 and was a member of the Uniting Conference of the three units of the Methodist Episcopal church. He also attended international and world conferences of the Methodist church.

Potts held memberships in the International Methodist Historical Society, the American Academy of Political and Social Science, the Southeastern Jurisdictional Historical Society, the World Methodist Council, and the Wesley Historical Society of London. He also was a member of church agencies on evangelism, broadcasting, film, and evangelism missions overseas.

He was the author of articles on the early history of Virginia Methodism and on devotional literature. He was co-author of *Love Abounds: A Profile of Harry Denman, A Modern Disciple* (1965) and editor of *Prayers of the Early Church*, *Prayers of the Middle Ages*, *Listening to the Saints*, *Letters of Francis Asbury*, *Selections from the Letters of John Wesley*, *Selections from the Letters of Francis Asbury*, *Selections from the Journal of John Woolman*, and the author of *Grace Sufficient* (1964). In April 1966 at the bicentennial celebration of American Methodism in Baltimore, he delivered an address on Methodist Bishop William Taylor, world missionary. From 1967 to 1970 he served as executive director of the Lake Junaluska Assembly, Lake Junaluska, N.C., where he was instrumental in establishing The Interpreter's House and the International Prayer Fellowship with headquarters on the Assembly grounds.

On 23 Dec. 1920 Potts married Agnes Wilson Wright and they became the parents of Annie Wilson, Reginald Harrell, James Manning, Joseph Christian, Katharine Coleman, and Agnes Withers. After spending his retirement years in Crystal River, Fla., he died in Tampa and was buried in Forest Lawn Cemetery, Richmond.

SEE: Emory S. Bucke, ed., *History of American Methodism*, vol. 3 (1964); Elmer T. Clark, *Forever Beginning, 1766–1966* (1967) and *Arthur James Moore: World Evangelist* (1960); *North Carolina Christian Advocate*, 14 May 1970; Randolph-Macon College Alumni Records (Ashland, Va.); *Who's Who in America* (1971); *Who's Who in the South and Southwest* (1969).

GRADY L. E. CARROLL, SR.

Pou, Edward William *(26 Oct. 1830–16 Nov. 1891)*, Reconstruction politician and legislator, was born in Orangeburg District, South Carolina, the oldest son of Joseph and Eliza Margaret Felder Pou. The Pous and the Felders had lived in South Carolina since the 1730s, but in 1834 Joseph Pou moved with his family to Talbotton, Ga., where he practiced law, eventually forming with Levi B. Smith the partnership of Smith and Pou. Edward W. Pou was graduated from the University of Georgia in 1851 and joined his father's law practice soon afterwards. About 1854 he married Lucy Carter, of Talbotton, by whom he had one child, Arthur, who subsequently altered the spelling of his surname to Pew. Upon the death of Lucy Carter Pou in 1858, Pou married in December 1859 Anna Maria Smith, daughter of the late James Hinton Smith and Nancy B. Smith of Tuskegee, Ala., but formerly of Johnston County, N.C.

At the opening of the Civil War, Pou accepted a commission in "Stephens' Rifles," Georgia militia, in July 1861 but seems to have had a short military career. By 1862 he was back in Tuskegee practicing law and attending to family affairs. His business ventures during the war years included a tannery operation (Persons and Pou) and niter production at Auburn, Ala., for the Confederate government. He continued his law practice in

Tuskegee until the close of 1866, when Pou moved with his wife, children, and mother-in-law to her property near Smithfield, N.C. To further his practice of law in the state, he secured letters of introduction to the members of the North Carolina Supreme Court and to Bartholomew Figures Moore.

As a young man, Pou had belonged to the Democratic party in Georgia. Some of his friends and relatives were surprised, therefore, when he announced in postbellum Alabama that he had favored emancipation before the Civil War and would have said so at the time had freedom of speech really been possible in the antebellum South. By May 1866 Pou seems to have won the confidence of the freedmen in Macon County, Ala., and these trends consistently characterized his political career in North Carolina. In April 1867 he addressed the Johnston County freedmen at Smithfield, urging them to support the National Republican party as the party that could, through compliance with the congressional Reconstruction acts, carry North Carolina back into the Union. In July of that year Pou attended the Union League's monster Fourth of July celebration in Raleigh and was one of the delegation appointed that day to go to Washington and secure Governor Jonathan Worth's removal from office.

In August 1867 Pou was elected a delegate from Johnston County to the Republican state convention and was subsequently elected a Republican representative from Johnston County to the 1868 and 1869 General Assembly. He was one of the trustees for the university newly appointed by Governor W. W. Holden under the constitution of 1868. After Holden was removed from office and his newspaper, the *Standard*, came to an end, Tod R. Caldwell and other party leaders consulted Pou in July 1871 on the feasibility of merging the *Carolina Era* and the *Telegram* to form a new Republican party organ (Pou having cast his support with the branch of the party rallying around Caldwell rather than Judge Thomas Settle and the friends of Holden). In the following spring Pou was one of those who joined with H. H. Helper and Daniel R. Goodloe in organizing the Liberal Republican party during the administration of Ulysses S. Grant. Consequently, in the presidential campaign of 1872, Pou campaigned for the Liberal Republican candidate, Horace Greeley, in Mitchell, Madison, Henderson, Polk, and Rutherford counties. Sometime after this campaign ended in Grant's reelection, Pou gave up politics altogether and by the early 1880s he had returned to the party of his youth as a Cleveland Democrat.

Pou occupied the remainder of his life with law and farming. His death, in fact, resulted from a fall from a platform of his barn. Pou was survived by the son of his first marriage, Arthur Pew (who remained in Georgia), and by his second wife and their children: James Hinton Pou (1861–1935), North Carolina legislator (house, 1885–87, and senate, 1889, 1893); Edward William Pou (1863–1934), U.S. representative from North Carolina, 1901–34; and Martha Temperance Pou (1870–1947).

SEE: Edward W. Pou (1830–91) Papers (North Carolina State Archives, Raleigh).

GEORGE STEVENSON

Pou, Edward William *(9 Sept. 1863–1 Apr. 1934)*, lawyer and congressman, was born in Tuskegee, Ala., the son of Edward William and Anna Maria Smith Pou. The family moved to Johnston County, N.C., in 1867 to land inherited by Mrs. Pou. Young Pou attended a school conducted by John L. Davis, was tutored in Greek and Latin by his parents, and attended The University of North Carolina during the period 1882–84. He taught school in 1884–85 while also reading law with his father and completed the law course at The University of North Carolina in 1885. Admitted to the bar in the same year, he began to practice in Smithfield with his brother, James H.

In 1886 Pou was chairman of the county Democratic executive committee and in 1888 he was a presidential elector. As solicitor of the Fourth Judicial District of North Carolina from 1890 to 1901, he was recognized as a vigorous prosecutor and a capable member of the bar. He was unsuccessful in his bid for Congress in 1896. In 1898 he became the law partner of Furnifold M. Simmons and joined him in the "White Supremacy" campaigns of 1898 and 1900.

Elected to Congress in 1900, Pou was returned at each succeeding election for the remainder of his life, usually without opposition. He served on the Ways and Means Committee for several sessions but was most effective as a member of the Rules Committee between 1911 and 1934. As chairman of the latter during 1917–21, he drew up and guided through the Congress legislation critical to the success of the war. Again as chairman of that committee he played an important role in the passage of legislation creating President Franklin D. Roosevelt's New Deal program.

Among the programs supported by Pou were stricter regulation of trusts, railroads, and banks; the reorganization of departments of government; and improved rural mail service. He also was a backer of bonuses for veterans of World War I. An advocate of state prohibition, he opposed federal control of alcoholic beverages.

Pou married Carrie Haughton Ihrie of Pittsboro and they became the parents of six children: two sons who died as infants; Edwin Smith, who was killed in France in 1918 during World War I; and Annie Ihrie, Margaret Atlee, and George Ross. He died of a heart attack in Washington and was accorded the rare honor of a funeral in the U.S. capitol. An Episcopalian, he was buried in Riverside Cemetery, Smithfield. He composed the inscription for his own tombstone: "I know not what record of sin may await me in the world to come, but this I do know: I was never mean enough to despise a man because he was poor, because he was ignorant, or because he was black."

SEE: *Biog. Dir. Am. Cong.* (1989); *DAB*, Supp. 1 (1944); *Nat. Cyc. Am. Biog.*, vol. 26 (1937 [portrait]); *North Carolina Biography*, vol. 3 (1941); *North Carolina Manual* (1933); *Proceedings of the 26th Annual Session of the North Carolina Bar Association* (1934); Raleigh *News and Observer*, 3–4 Apr. 1934; *Who Was Who in America*, vol. 1 (1943).

WILLIAM S. POWELL

Pou, James Hinton *(21 July 1861–29 July 1935)*, lawyer, politician, and Raleigh land developer, was born in Tuskegee, Ala., the middle son of Edward William and Anna Maria Smith Pou of Johnston County. The family moved to a farm in Johnston County that Pou's mother had inherited shortly after the Civil War. The elder Pou had studied classics at the University of Georgia and then became a lawyer. He practiced in Smithfield. Pou's older brother, Edward, attended The University of North Carolina and the Law School, but James was educated at home. He then read law under W. N. H. Smith and in 1885 was admitted to the bar.

In the period of Reconstruction politics Pou emerged as an active, articulate Democrat and served three terms in the General Assembly: in 1885 as a representative and in 1888 and 1892 as a senator. Although he was urged to pursue a career in politics, he chose to devote his time to his law practice.

Pou moved to Raleigh in 1898, and it was from there that he gained fame for his skills in criminal trials. But he acquired substance and power from his civil and corporate practice, which involved him in the industrialization and urbanization of the state and the South.

In 1905 Pou became a member of the board of the Raleigh Electric Company (became Carolina Power and Light Company in 1908). He served until 1911, when he was named the company's first general counsel, a position he held until his death. He also became a regular representative for Standard Oil of New Jersey and several other firms and with B. N. Duke was engaged in the expanding textile industry in North Carolina.

The motives that prompted Pou's involvement in suburban development undoubtedly grew from his abilities as a practical man of business, but that involvement had a profound effect on the physical and visual development of Raleigh. In 1906 the Glenwood Land Company with Pou as its president opened for development the first important planned early twentieth-century suburb in the capital city. Designed with all possible conveniences, Glenwood prospered and established a precedent for subsequent development, extending the traditional values of home and land ownership to the new, growing middle class while enhancing the city with an architecturally homogeneous and beautiful suburb. In 1911 Pou was head of the firm that created and promoted Bloomsbury and was then involved in Hayes-Barton, the next important suburb in northwestern Raleigh.

Pou's fame as a trial lawyer derived from his involvement in a series of famous cases including the Cole murder case in Rockingham County, the Peacock case in Johnston, the Lawrence case in Chatham, and the Libby Holman Reynolds case in Forsyth. It is said, however, that his ability as a speaker was based not on loud rhetoric but on the soundness of his argument, his wit, and his understanding of human psychology. These skills were demonstrated in the Founder's Day Speech he delivered at Trinity College in Durham on 2 Oct. 1917. Entitled "No Compromise Peace," it seems to summarize Pou's personal and public philosophy. Elegantly organized and rich in biblical and classical allusions, it is in a rhetorical style which uses vivid phraseology and strong contrasts, the most interesting being that between the government of Prussia which he called a government by force and the government of the United States which he called a government by fraternity. A deeply patriotic and moving speech, it gained circulation both within and outside the state.

Pou practiced law briefly with Senator Furnifold Simmons, with Fuller Staples, with his son-in-law, Josiah W. Bailey, and with his son, James H. Pou, Jr.

Pou married Annie Walker of Asheboro in 1889 and they had two children: James H., Jr., and Edith Walker, who married Josiah Bailey. Age did not diminish his activities and he remained a powerful and respected figure until his death.

SEE: B. N. Duke Papers and Van Noppen Papers (Manuscript Department, Duke University Library, Durham); Raleigh *News and Observer*, 30 July 1935; "Raleigh: Three Early Twentieth-Century Neighborhoods" (unpublished National Register Nomination, North Carolina Department of Cultural Resources, 1981); Jack Riley, *Carolina Power and Light Company: A Corporate Biography, 1908–1958* (1958).

CHARLOTTE VESTAL BROWN

Powell, Benjamin Edward *(28 Aug. 1905–11 Mar. 1981)*, librarian and teacher, was born in Sunbury, Gates County, the son of Willis Warren and Beatrice Franklin Powell. In 1922 he entered Trinity College, Durham, which became Duke University in 1924, and was graduated in 1926 with a major in history. He worked briefly in the university library; taught school and coached athletics in Bethel High School, Pitt County, during the year 1926–27; and then accepted a position on the Duke University library staff, where he soon became head of the circulation department. On leave of absence in 1929–30, he received a degree in library science from Columbia University.

At Duke, Powell planned, organized, and supervised the library move from the Trinity College library to the new General Library on the West Campus. After attending the Graduate Library School at the University of Chicago in 1934–35, he returned to Duke, but in 1937 he went to the University of Missouri, where he became head librarian. He received the doctorate in library science from the University of Chicago in 1946 and returned to Duke as university librarian, where he remained until his retirement in 1975. Frequently during those years Powell taught courses in the theory of library administration in the School of Library Science at The University of North Carolina.

Powell held numerous posts of professional significance: he was president of the American Library Association and of the Association of College and Research Libraries, consultant to college and research libraries and to the U.S. government, and an active member of committees and boards. He contributed to such journals as the *ALA Bulletin*, *College and Research Libraries*, and *Southeastern Librarian*. He made trips to Germany and England to study conditions there and to discuss topics of mutual concern. He also played key roles in the building of a new city library in Durham and integrating library service for all races.

During his administration, the Duke University library was enlarged twice and between 1946 and 1975 its holdings grew from 875,000 volumes to nearly 3 million and from 975,000 manuscripts to over 4.5 million. In 1972, under his guidance, the Duke University Archives became a part of the library. A completely automated library system covering serials, purchasing records, and the accounting system was established. An on-line ordering system and the preparation of a microfiche of serial titles also were completed under his direction.

Powell was married in 1940 to Elizabeth Graves of Scottsbluff, Nebr., and they became the parents of a daughter, Lisa Holland Powell. He was a Methodist and a Democrat. He was buried in Maplewood Cemetery, Durham.

SEE: *Durham Morning Herald*, 14 July 1958, 19 June 1960, 24 Aug. 1975, 12 Mar. 1981; William S. Powell, ed., *North Carolina Lives* (1962); *Who Was Who in America*, vol. 7 (1981); *Who's Who in the South and Southwest* (1967).

WILLIAM S. POWELL

Powell, Thomas Edward, Jr. *(6 July 1899–3 Dec. 1987)*, founder of the Carolina Biological Supply Company and related enterprises, was born in Warrenton, the son of Thomas Edward, Sr., and Clara Morton Bobbitt Powell. After attending public schools in Warren County, he earned an A.B. degree from Elon College (1919), an A.M. from The University of North Carolina (1923), and a Ph.D. in biology from Duke University (1930). Honorary doctor of science degrees were awarded by Elon College (1968) and Duke University (1987).

From 1919 to 1936 Powell taught biology and geology at Elon College, attaining the rank of professor in 1924. In 1918 he served for three months on active duty in the U.S. Army as a second lieutenant; he continued to serve in the army reserve, advancing to the rank of captain before resigning his commission in 1935.

While teaching at Elon and working towards the doctorate at Duke, Powell perceived the need for a biological supply house that could provide schools and colleges with their laboratory specimens. At the time, only two other businesses in the United States supplied specimens for classroom use—teachers were expected to collect their own protozoan, frogs, and animal skeletons. Powell began his business on a part-time basis in 1927 in a woodshed beside a pond at Elon College. Nine years later he resigned his teaching position to devote full time to management of the growing company. At the time of his death Carolina Biological Supply had operating units at Gladstone, Oreg.; Jonesport, Maine; Warrenton, N.C.; and two locations in Burlington. The company's 1,312-page catalogue listed over 30,000 items including over 90 types of fruit flies and fungi, 235 strains of algae, human and animal skeletons, laboratory equipment, books, scientific models, audiovisuals, charts, and computers.

As a pioneer supplier of biological materials, Carolina Biological made a number of innovations. It was the first to ship living protozoan cultures successfully. In 1940 it was the first biological supply company to inject preserved specimens with colored latex to highlight the circulatory system. The company formulated and produced three laboratory products that simplify complicated laboratory procedures: FlyNap—an anesthesia for drosophila flies; Formula 4–24, an easily managed fly growth medium; and Caro-Safe, a formaldehyde-free, odorless animal preservative. In addition, the company introduced slide strip, a method of preparing microscopic organisms in a plastic strip similar to a filmstrip.

In 1945 Powell founded Waubun Laboratories in Schriever, La., and in 1971 Rana Laboratories in Brownsville, Tex., as an operating division of Waubun. Powell and his children established a number of related companies. Biomedical Reference Laboratories, started in 1969 by three of his sons, was purchased in 1982 by Hoffman LaRoche for $165 million. At his death other Carolina Biological Supply subsidiaries or family-owned enterprises included Wolfe Sales Corporation, Bobbitt Laboratories, Cabisco Sports, Cabisco Teleproductions, Carolina Fitness and Health, and Geoscience Resources.

Powell served from 1934 to 1961 on the Alamance County Board of Education, and he was president of the North Carolina School Board Association from 1943 to 1945. He was instrumental in establishing the Duke University Marine Laboratory and with members of his family he created the Thomas E. Powell, Jr., Foundation, which contributes to the support of science programs at Elon College. At his death he was a member of Front Street United Methodist Church and the United Methodist Church of Macon, N.C.

In 1922 Powell married Sophia Maude Sharpe. They had four children: Sophia Maude (Mrs. Albert Eugene Wolf), Dr. Thomas E. III, John Sharpe, and Dr. James Bobbitt. After his wife's death in 1944, Powell married (1945) Annabelle Council, by whom he also had four children: William Council, Joseph Eugene, Dr. Samuel Christopher, and Dr. Annabelle Council Powell Guy.

As chairman of the Board of Carolina Biological Supply, Powell went to his office every day and was active in company management until the last three months of his life. He was buried in Magnolia Cemetery at Elon College.

SEE: Carolina Biological Supply clipping file; J. A. C. Dunn, "Thomas Powell, Jr., and the Business of Creepies and Crawlies," *Carolina Piedmont* (January 1988); Elon College clipping file; Denise Grady, "The Sears, Roebuck of Science," *Discover* (September 1982); Raleigh *News and Observer*, 4 Dec. 1987.

GEORGE W. TROXLER

Pratt, Eliza Jane *(5 Mar. 1902–13 May 1981)*, newspaper editor, congressional staff assistant, and member of the U.S. House of Representatives, was born in Morven, Anson County, one of seven children of James L., a farmer, and Lena Valetta Little Pratt. She attended public school in Morven until age nine, when her family moved to Raeford. In the fall of 1918 she transferred to Queens College from the Asheville Normal and Collegiate Institute. She remained at Queens for two years, leaving without a degree when her father became ill.

In 1923, as editor of the weekly Troy newspaper, the *Montgomerian*, Eliza Pratt met Eighth District congressman William C. Hammer while covering his speech in Candor during the town's peach festival. Hammer soon offered her a position in Washington as his administrative assistant. Beginning in 1924 she worked as staff assistant to Hammer and eventually for four other congressmen from the Eighth District.

Representative William O. Burgin, for whom Miss Pratt worked, died in April 1946 and the North Carolina Democratic Executive Committee nominated her in the special election to fill Burgin's term. During the five-week campaign that followed she paid all of her own expenses and was easily elected on 25 May 1946 as representative from the Eighth Congressional District. She was appointed to three committees: Pensions, Territories, and Flood Control. Congress adjourned in late summer and she was not a candidate for reelection, probably because of the illness and subsequent death of her mother.

From 1947 to 1951 she worked in the Office of Alien Property in Washington and from then until 1954 in the Department of Agriculture. In the latter year she joined the staff of the Library of Congress, where she remained through 1956. From 1957 to 1962 she was assistant to Representative A. Paul Kitchin from North Carolina's Eighth District. Returning to Anson County in 1963, she lived in Wadesboro, where she worked as director of public relations for the North Carolina Telephone Company for several years and remained active in Democratic politics.

Eliza Pratt lived during a period when women often set aside personal and professional goals to devote time and energy to their family. Although her public service was noteworthy, the needs of her parents and her devotion to them restricted her professional career. She died in Mercy Hospital, Charlotte, and was buried in the Raeford City Cemetery.

SEE: *Anson Record*, 11 May 1972, 19 May 1981; *Biog. Dir. Am. Cong.* (1989); *Charlotte Observer*, 16 May 1981; Mary Louise Medley, *History of Anson County* (1976); Eliza Jane Pratt Papers (Manuscript Collection, East Carolina University, Greenville, and Archives, Queens College, Charlotte); Raleigh *News and Observer*, 24 Apr., 23 June, 8 Oct. 1946; U.S. House of Representatives, *Women in Congress, 1917–1990* (1991); Washington *Times-Herald*, 13 June 1946.

ALICE R. COTTEN

Pratt, Joseph Hyde *(3 Feb. 1870–2 June 1942)*, geologist, conservationist, and state and local civic leader, was born in Hartford, Conn., the son of James Church and Jennie Abby Peck Pratt of the Peck and Hyde families of Norwich, Conn. Both parents were descendants of the Puritan settlers and New Englanders by birth, but James Pratt had strong Southern ties and served as a colonel in the Confederate army.

Joseph Pratt attended the Hartford public schools and the Sheffield School of Yale University. He carried with him to Yale a youthful interest in chemistry and mineralogy, and it was through his studies that he traveled to the western North Carolina mountains during the summer of 1892 with Dr. S. L. Penfield of Yale and North Carolina state geologist J. A. Holmes on a mineral collecting trip for the state exhibition at the Chicago World's Fair. After 1892 Pratt made frequent trips to the state. In 1893 he received his bachelor of philosophy degree at Yale and began graduate study in mineralogy, geology, and chemistry. During 1894 he was an assistant chemistry instructor at Yale and a mineralogy instructor at the Harvard summer school. He was awarded the Ph.D. degree in 1896.

Pratt gained recognition during the 1890s for many of his published studies and articles, an example of which was an 1895 report in the *American Journal of Science* that was described as "an elaborate and important piece of work." In the same year Pratt became an instructor in mineralogy at Yale.

Moving to North Carolina in 1897 to become assistant general manager of the Toxaway Company and to serve as a mineralogist for the North Carolina Geological Survey, he soon became state mineralogist, a post he held until 1906. In 1899 Pratt moved again, this time to Chapel Hill where he began teaching economic geology at The University of North Carolina. By 1900 he had over a hundred papers and several books in print, including his 300-page *Corundum and the Basic Magnesian Rocks of Western North Carolina* with J. V. Lewis of Rutgers. From 1899 to 1906 he was field geologist for the U.S. Geological Survey. Also in 1902 he was a special agent for the U.S. Census Bureau, and in 1906 he was appointed state geologist.

His work as state geologist resulted in the highlight of Pratt's career—the discovery of several minerals, including pirssonite, wellsite (with H. W. Foote), northupite, mitchellite, and rhodolite (with W. E. Hidden), the last being a gem mineral found only in North Carolina. Also in 1906 he was a member of the Commission of the Appalachian Forestry Reserve, a post that reflected Pratt's growing concern for the state's forests. He worked extensively for the passage of the Weeks Law, which authorized the acquisition of land for national forests. During this time he also began to push for state aid to improve road conditions and served for a while as secretary of the new State Highway Commission. Pratt also participated in the Buffalo, Jamestown, Charleston, Portland, and St. Louis expositions, where he sat on several committees and where his private mineral and gem collections won gold medals.

On 24 July 1917 Pratt, who had been in the state National Guard since 1913, entered the army. He had a distinguished career in World War I, eventually attaining the rank of colonel in command of the First Battalion of the 105th Engineers, succeeding Brigadier General H. B. Ferguson. He saw action on the front lines in Ypres sector, Flanders, and in Belgium; he was also at the Somme offensive and was part of the famous Thirtieth "Old Hickory" Division, the first to break the Hindenburg Line. Upon his discharge on 12 June 1919 he received the Distinguished Service Medal. Pratt's "War Diary," consisting of daily letters to his wife and son from 1918 to 1919, was published in book form some years later. But the war had taken its toll, and because of ill health he was hospitalized for three years and had to resign as state geologist in 1924 and from teaching in 1925.

Nevertheless, Pratt continued his vigorous leadership in organizations ranging from the North Carolina Symphony Society to the Chapel Hill Red Cross, to being regional engineer for the Civil Works Authority, the Federal Emergency Relief Administration, and the Resettlement Administration in the 1930s. He published on subjects ranging from peat and swamplands, to oystering, to using convict labor in building state roads. He continued his pioneering efforts on behalf of preserving forests, developing good roads, and establishing a state fisheries commission and belonged to numerous societies and professional bodies. He organized the Southern Forestry Congress, the North Carolina Forestry Association, and the Good Roads Association, among others.

In 1940 Pratt was honored as Chapel Hill's Most Valuable Citizen of the Year. In his later years he also occupied himself by collecting stamps and working for the Democratic party and the Episcopal church. Following his death, he was awarded an honorary doctorate of engineering from the North Carolina State College of Agriculture and Engineering. He had also received an honorary master of arts degree from Yale in 1923.

Pratt was married twice, first on 5 Apr. 1899 to Mary Dicus Bayley of Springfield, Ohio; they were the parents of Joseph, Jr. After her death he married, on 29 Aug. 1930, Harriet White Peters of Baltimore, Md.

SEE: Kemp P. Battle, *History of the University of North Carolina*, vol. 2 (1912); Archibald Henderson, "In Memoriam: Joseph Hyde Pratt" (delivered at the annual session of the North Carolina Society for the Preservation of Antiquities, 2 Dec. 1942); Jasper L. Stuckey, "Memorial of Joseph H. Pratt," reprinted from *American Mineralogist* (1943); *Who Was Who*, vol. 2 (1950).

CHARLES A. HERNDON III

Preddy, George Earl, Jr. *(5 Feb. 1919–25 Dec. 1944)*, Army Air Corps officer and highest ranking P-51 Mustang ace of World War II, was born in Greensboro, the son of George E., a railroad man employed by the Southern Railway, and Clara Noah Preddy. He was graduated from Greensboro High School at age sixteen by doubling up on his courses. Due to his small stature (5' 9", 125 lbs.), his desire to participate in sports was thwarted, but he took satisfaction in operating a concession stand, known as "The Mouse Hole," near the War Memorial Stadium in Greensboro. The year following his high school graduation, he worked in a cotton mill to pay his way to Guilford College, which he attended for two years. During this period he developed a yearning to fly and soloed in 1938 from a dirt strip at Vandalia; he spent the next two years barnstorming the state with his instructor, Bill Teague, also of Greensboro.

At age twenty he tried twice to enlist in the U.S. Naval Cadets but was rejected because of a curvature of the spine, his small size, and high blood pressure. He subsequently passed the enlistment requirements of the Army Air Corps in September 1940 but was told that all classes were filled. On the advice of the Air Corps he joined the National Guard and completed basic training at Fort Moultrie, S.C. Preddy received orders in April 1941 to report for primary flying school at Darr Aero Tech, Albany, Ga. He received his pilot's license and a commission as a second lieutenant at Craig Field, Ala., on 12 Dec. 1941. On the twenty-fourth he was assigned to the Forty-ninth Pursuit Group, Ninth Pursuit Squadron, with which he served for eight months in Darwin, Australia. The Forty-ninth flew Curtiss P-40s. Preddy named his first aircraft "Tar Heel" and flew it until he was hospitalized for four months after a midair collision on 12 July 1942. During this tour he had several encounters with Japanese aircraft but scored no victories.

On his release from the hospital, he was promoted to first lieutenant and shipped back to the United States, where he was assigned to the 352d Fighter Group, equipped with Republic P-47s. Preddy was promoted to captain on 5 Mar. 1943 and four months later shipped to Bodney, England, the permanent base for the 352d. He flew his first mission against the Luftwaffe on 14 September and scored his first victory on 1 December—a ME-109. During the succeeding seventeen months he served in the European Theater of Operations (ETO) and was officially credited with 26.83 aerial and 5.00 ground victories, making him the highest ranking ace in the ETO until his untimely death on Christmas Day 1944. His biggest day came on 5 Aug. 1944 when he destroyed 6 ME-109s in a dogfight while approaching Berlin. For this feat, he was awarded the Distinguished Service Cross. This record would be tied by another pilot in the ETO but never surpassed. Of the 31.83 victories Preddy scored, 29.83 were tallied while flying North American P-51s, each named "Crips 'A Mighty," one of his favorite expressions. On 28 Oct. 1944, following a thirty-day tour of the United States after his 6 August experience, he was made commanding officer of the 328th Fighter Squadron of the 352d Fighter Group.

On 23 Dec. 1944 his Fighter Group was transferred to the Continent to be based at Asch, Belgium. On Christmas Day Preddy, now a major, and a fellow pilot, Lieutenant James G. Carter, were on patrol near Liège, where he destroyed two ME-109s, his final victories. He received a report of an enemy aircraft strafing the U.S. troops and went down to drive off the enemy fighter. As the two pilots closed in on the fleeing fighter, U.S. ground troops opened up on the enemy plane. Preddy and his wingman flew into the ground fire and his plane sustained hits. The major was fatally wounded but survived long enough to force-land his crippled fighter.

Preddy had flown his 143d mission, with over 532 total hours of exposure. For his unselfish devotion to his nation and expertise in the performance of his job, he was awarded the Silver Star with oak leaf cluster, the Air Medal with seven oak leaf clusters, Distinguished Service Cross, Distinguished Flying Cross with eight oak leave clusters, and, posthumously, the Purple Heart and the Croix de Guerre by the government of Belgium. He was buried beside his brother, Lieutenant William R. Preddy, a fellow fighter pilot killed in action over Czechoslovakia on 17 Apr. 1945, in the U.S. military cemetery at Saint Avold, France.

Throughout his brief career George Preddy was noted for his willingness and his ability to assist new pilots to become as proficient as possible and to teach them how to survive. Of the many pilots who flew with him as wingmen, he lost only one. Contrary to the popular belief that most combat pilots were happy-go-lucky men, he was a very understanding and compassionate person, loved by all who served with him. Before he returned to duty following his thirty-day leave after his 6 Aug. 1944 mission, the Reverend E. H. Neece, pastor of West Market Street Methodist Church, Greensboro, asked him why he was returning to combat. Reportedly, Preddy replied:

Preacher, I must go back—
Back to do my part
Back to fly and give again
And I am not afraid
My plane may be shot away
But I shall not fall—
For I have wings—
Wings not of wood or steel or stuff
But wings of firmer kind—
Wings God gave my soul
Thank God for wings.

On 7 Dec. 1968 the city of Greensboro dedicated a portion of its southern interstate highway loop in memory of the Preddy brothers; the monument is enscribed: "This boulevard is named for Major George E. Preddy, Jr., and 1st Lt. William R. Preddy, Greensboro brothers who gave their lives for their country in World War II. *Dulce et decorum est pro patria mori.*"

SEE: John R. Beaman, Jr., "The Unknown Ace," *Journal of the American Historical Society* 14 (Winter 1969); Roger A. Freeman, *The Mighty Eighth* (1970); William N. Hess, *American Aces of World War II and Korea* (1968 [portrait]); Joseph W. Noah, *Wings God Gave My Soul* (1974); Samuel L. Sox, Jr., "Major George E. Preddy, Jr.," *Aero Album* 4 (Winter 1971).

SAMUEL L. SOX, JR.

Price, Charles *(26 July 1846–28 Sept. 1905)*, legislator and corporation lawyer, was born in Warrenton, the fourth child of John and Martha Reynolds Price, whose grandfather was a native of Scotland. His father, John Price, was a native of Raleigh but in early manhood moved to Warrenton and became a prosperous merchant.

Charles Price began school in Warrenton, becoming proficient in Latin and Greek under John S. Duggen and Henry Thompson, both eminent teachers. In the spring of 1864, at age seventeen, he joined a company of boys about the same age from Warren, Franklin, and Nash counties to become Company A of the first battalion of Junior Reserves. Afterwards Company A became part of the Seventh North Carolina Troops. As captain of his company Price participated in the engagements at Belfield, Kinston, and Bentonville.

A year after the surrender of Joseph E. Johnston's Confederate army at Greensboro, Price borrowed money to enter the law school of Chief Justice Richmond Pearson at Richmond Hill, Pearson's home in Yadkin County. He remained there for five sessions, not even returning home for vacations. After obtaining a license in June 1868, Price, on the advice of Judge Pearson, settled at Mocksville, where he fell into close company with John M. Clement, the leading attorney in Davie County, who gave young Price advice and encouragement. Price soon rose to prominence and was elected state senator from the Thirtieth District (composed of Rowan and Davie counties) and served in two sessions of the legislature. In 1875 Davie County elected him a delegate to the state constitutional convention as a Democrat; afterwards, he ably advocated the ratification of the amendments adopted by that convention. In the same election he was elected to the North Carolina House of Representatives, where he served in 1876 and 1877. In this session he was elected speaker of the house. Not long after the legislature adjourned in March 1877, he moved from Mocksville to Salisbury, where he resided until his death.

Price virtually abandoned politics after 1877 except to represent the Seventh District at the Democratic National

Convention held in Cincinnati in 1880. He devoted the last twenty-eight years of his life almost exclusively to practicing law, although in 1890 he was the Republican candidate for chief justice of the North Carolina Supreme Court. He had switched parties after the Prohibition election of 1881, which had split the Democrats.

In 1881 he was appointed counsel for the Western North Carolina Railroad and was the local counsel for the Richmond and Danville Railroad, both of which were incorporated into the Southern Railway in 1898. Later (1884) he became assistant to David Schenck, general counsel of the Richmond and Danville Railroad in North Carolina. For a few years he and Schenck were also counsel for the Charleston, Cincinnati, and Chicago Railroad Company. When Schenck retired and the various companies constituting the West Point Terminal System passed into the hands of the receivers, Price was put in charge of the legal business in North Carolina. In 1894 he was appointed division counsel of the Southern Railway Company in North Carolina, a position he held until his death.

In 1889 President Benjamin Harrison appointed Price U.S. district attorney for the Western District of North Carolina and he served for four years. But it was as an attorney that he gained his widest reputation, particularly in two cases. Price, contrary to general expectation, won the case of Julian versus the railroad, which went to the U.S. Supreme Court and gained for Price legal recognition throughout the country. His most notable triumph, however, was in two suits that he instituted against Stanly and Wilkes counties to require them to pay bonds in the amount of $100,000 each, issued by three counties in payment of subscriptions to stock in two railroads. The North Carolina Supreme Court in both cases had adjudged the bonds to be null and void. Price then brought suits in equity in the U.S. Circuit Court to enforce payment of the bonds. The validity of the bonds was sustained by the circuit courts; however, the Circuit Court of Appeals reversed the decision of the circuit courts and dismissed the bill. Price then filed a petition for a rehearing; his argument was so convincing that the court reversed its former decree and upheld the validity of the bonds. This decision was finally affirmed by the U.S. Supreme Court. These cases gave Price prominence throughout the United States, and in 1902 he was elected president of the North Carolina Bar Association, the last public position he held. He died at his home in Salisbury and was buried in the Chestnut Hill Cemetery.

Price was married twice. In 1871 he wed Annie Hobson, daughter of Mrs. Ann Hobson, of Davie County, who was a sister of Governor John M. Morehead. They had only one child, Augustus H. She died in 1876. In July 1878 he married Mary Roberts of Mobile, Ala.

SEE: Samuel A. Ashe, ed., *Cyclopedia of Eminent and Representative Men of the Carolinas*, vol. 2 (1892); Nat Atkinson and R. A. Shotwell, *Legislative Record, 1877* (1877); *Confederate Military History*, vol. 4 (1899); *North Carolina Bar Association Proceedings*, vol. 8 (1906); *North Carolina Biography*, vol. 4 (1929).

JAMES S. BRAWLEY

Price, Gwyn Brantley *(2 June 1900–27 May 1992)*, rural electrification advocate, was born in Clifton community, central Ashe County, the son of Avery Aster and Victoria Graybeal Price. He attended Jefferson High School in Jefferson and in 1919 Trinity College in Durham. After graduation from Emory and Henry College in Emory, Va., in 1924, he was principal of the Jefferson High School from 1924 to 1938, then worked briefly for the Agricultural Adjustment Administration and beginning in 1939 with the Farm Security Administration.

A dairy farmer, Price was a member of the Farmers Cooperative Council of North Carolina, the Yadkin Valley Dairy Cooperative, the Blue Ridge Electric Membership Corporation, and the Skyline Telephone Membership Corporation. He became chairman of the North Carolina Rural Electrification Authority (REA) in 1941, when only a fourth of the state's farms had electricity; when he left the agency in 1974, 97 percent had power. With Price's assistance, farmers obtained service from private companies or set up cooperatives. At the beginning of World War II Price was able to secure a large grant making it possible for the Jones-Onslow REA group to generate the electricity needed for the Camp LeJeune Marine base.

Once electricity was available, telephone service in rural areas became his next goal. In 1945 the General Assembly took steps to support this objective and placed its implementation under his supervision. He remained on the REA board of directors until 1974.

On 4 June 1925 Price married Pauline Shoaf, and they had two children: Joseph Gwyn, Jr., and Virginia Ruth. A member of the Methodist church and the Democratic party, he was buried in Ashelawn Memorial Gardens, Jefferson.

SEE: *North Carolina Biography*, vol. 4 (1929); *North Carolina Manual* (1969); Raleigh *News and Observer*, 19 Dec. 1954 [portrait], 29 May 1992.

WILLIAM S. POWELL

Price, Jonathan *(d. 23 May 1822)*, cartographer, son of Benjamin Price, moved into Pasquotank County from an unknown location with his sister and brothers shortly after the beginning of the American Revolution. Price requested to come under the care of the Pasquotank Monthly Meeting of Friends in 1781 and was received as a member in 1785. He and his siblings seem to have been given little more than the rudiments of education but were taught useful trades. Mathematically gifted, Price was interested in geography, surveying, navigation, and astronomy and had leanings towards botany. His brother John was trained as a bricklayer, while Price himself was taught house carpentry in addition to, apparently, surveying. Though Price agreed in March 1785 to teach an apprentice, Joseph Newby, the craft of house carpentry, his real interest and career lay with the surveyor's chain and transit.

Price's first opportunity to put his surveying skills to regular use came in March 1789, when he was named Pasquotank County surveyor. This appointment coincided with his determination to produce a new map of the state based on actual surveys of its boundaries and coastal waters. Price envisioned the map as properly demarcating the counties; delineating the shoals, inlets, sounds, and estuaries with their depths; and correctly displaying the roads, ferries, and fords throughout the state. He commenced mapping the area embraced in Edenton District in 1789. By 1792 he had completed enough of his projected work to be able to exhibit it to the General Assembly. On 25 Dec. 1792 he petitioned the Assembly for assistance in financing the work. At the same time, Nathaniel Christmas, who had returned from northern Georgia to Orange County, appeared with a similar petition and sample of his work. The Assembly agreed in January 1793 to lend Price £500 for three years. Of this sum, Price and Christmas, having agreed upon a collaboration, jointly borrowed £290 in October 1793 and began work on a map of the state.

At about this time Price came to the attention of John Gray Blount, presumably through Blount's brother Thomas, who had been in the Assembly when Price's petition was presented. Blount required the services of surveyors capable of integrating a multitude of surveys into a single comprehensive plan and of projecting numerous entries of land into a single tract covered by one survey. Price had done precisely this when laying out, as Pasquotank County surveyor, the forty land entries totaling 26,000 acres in Dismal Swamp belonging to a Blount rival, John Hamilton. Price gave up his office of county surveyor in 1794 for far more lucrative employment by the Blount family. John Gray Blount recognized Price's gifts as a topographic surveyor and encouraged him in the production of his new map of the state. When Price and Christmas finished their version of the map in 1795, the Blounts looked into the matter of getting it engraved for them in Philadelphia. It is extremely unlikely that this version was based on actual surveys of the entire state or that it satisfied the ideal described to the General Assembly by Price in 1792. More probably it was based in part on actual surveys, but in greater part on compilation of data projected cartographically.

Price abandoned the 1795 version of the map after meeting John Strother, a second topographic surveyor employed by Blount. Strother shared Price's conception of a map truly based on actual surveys in which every feature would be laid down with the precision of a surveyor's plat. The two agreed to join their talents to produce such a map. Under authority of the 1793 resolution, Price borrowed another £300 from the state treasurer in September 1795 (though he should have been allowed only £210). Presumably he took this sum for the purpose for which it had been authorized—completion of the state map. One supposes he found another way of financing the project later in 1795 with the publication of his *Description of Occacock Inlet*. This eight-page portolano was published at New Bern by François X. Martin and included Price's chart to illustrate his sailing directions engraved by William Johnston, a local silversmith. When, in December, Strother heard that Price had had a piece of work published, he leapt to the conclusion that Price had stolen a march and had published under his name alone some of their joint work. This misunderstanding was easily cleared up. It was not until 1798 that their joint work began to appear.

When Price was ready to publish the chart of the coastal survey he had made with Strother, he turned once more to William Johnston of New Bern to engrave the plates. When the chart came out in 1798, it was issued in two sheets, each measuring 14 by 23 inches, and carried the title, "To Navigators This Chart, Being an Actual Survey of the Sea Coast and Inland Navigation from Cape Henry to Cape Roman, is most Respectfully Inscribed by Price and Strother." A second chart meant specifically for the use of Cape Fear merchants was engraved for Price by William Barker of Philadelphia and published as a 13⅞- by 18¾-inch "Map of the Cape Fear River and Its Vicinity from the Frying Pan Shoals to Wilmington by Actual Survey, Addressed to the Commissioners of Navigation of Port Wilmington by Price and Strother." This chart was so satisfactory that Joshua Potts, a leading merchant of Wilmington, had it reengraved in a reduced version by John Scoles of New York and used it as a business card in his correspondence with European merchants. (Scoles, however, omitted the names of Price and Strother as authors of the chart.)

Work on the survey of the state progressed apace. Early in 1796 Price and Strother copyrighted it. After completing rough maps of nearly two-thirds of the state at a cost of $3,000, they successfully petitioned the General Assembly at the end of 1796 for an additional loan of £500. They announced forthcoming publication of, and opened subscriptions to, the map in June 1797. In December 1798 (when Strother had completed all the surveys he had engaged to prepare), the two men approached the Assembly for a further loan, having already borrowed £1,090 from the state. After the Assembly rose, a number of prominent members, including Blake Baker, David Stone, and William Richardson Davie, offered to advance, on the credit of expected sales, a loan of $1,000 towards engraving and publishing the map. In the end, the balance of cash needed to pay the engraver was put up by David Stone and Peter Browne, to whom the map is dedicated. (A final £100 loan was cadged out of the state treasurer by Price on 31 Dec. 1799.) In 1800 Price carried the final draft of the map to Philadelphia, where he remained from September until the spring of 1801 to oversee the engraving. When selecting an engraver for the chart of Cape Fear River, he had turned to one of the engravers employed by Matthew Carey in publishing his *General Atlas*. Now Price chose William Harrison, Jr., another engraver who was currently employed in that work. Harrison apparently engraved the manuscript just as it was given him, then pulled proofs for Price.

Sometime between Price's return to North Carolina in 1801 with the proofs and 1808 when the plates were corrected, Price, and perhaps others, read the map and marked engraver and author errors. William Christmas might have read the map in proof for Price. His 1812 obituary makes the claim that Christmas was the chief person employed in drawing Price and Strother's map. One wonders if the statement is based on a confusion of the role, if any, Christmas might have played in the version of the map prepared by his brother Nathaniel and Price in 1795 with the role, if any, he played in the completion of the version by Strother and Price in 1799. Errors in the original drawing smack of the untutored Price rather than the better-educated Christmas: Roan for Rowan, Iredel for Iredell, Tyrrel for Tyrrell, Edgecomb for Edgecombe, Nap Reads for Knap of Reeds, and so forth. Corrections were made in the proof, including alterations in two oddities: both the name and the boundaries of John Gray Blount's home county, Beaufort, were omitted from the 1801 proof, and the name of Ashe County was corrected from "Davie." Corrections to the plates were not engraved until 1808, in which year it was published under the dedicatory title, "To David Stone and Peter Brown Esqrs. this First Actual Survey of the State of North Carolina[,] Taken by the Subscribers[,] is Respectfully Dedicated by their Humble Servants Jona. Price, John Strother." The map was favorably reviewed by Aiken's *Atheneum* (London) in August 1808 and announced for sale by booksellers before the end of the year. Copies of the 28¾- by 59¼-inch map intended for the subscribers might have been colored professionally in Philadelphia, but copies subsequently furnished local booksellers were colored by Price, who kept a stock of the unfinished engraved sheets on hand for that purpose.

Because the state lent £1,190 for the creation of the map, it is easy to forget that this was not a public work but was a private undertaking by an essentially untutored, though gifted, man. It was generally recognized that a new map of the state was much wanted, for the last authoritative map of North Carolina had been John Collet's 1770 publication, and there was very little reliable topographical knowledge of the state at the end of the century. It is a measure of Price's intellect that he could conceive of both so comprehensive an undertaking and the means of bringing it to fruition. It is a measure of his ability that he actually completed, with the assistance of Strother, the herculean task of surveying the entire state, sounding and charting its coast, and laying down with such precision its watercourses, roads, towns, meetinghouses, and country seats of principal landowners. Its publication was hailed by American and European reviewers. Price's debt to the state was eventually transferred to The University of North Carolina, whose trustees, having first sued for recovery of the outstanding portion of the £1,190 debt, eventually forgave Price the unpaid balance.

Between the completion and the publication of Price and Strother's map, the U.S. Congress authorized a survey in 1806 of the most dangerous part of the North Carolina coast—Cape Hatteras to Cape Fear. Thomas Blount, one of the state's delegation, was probably consulted by Secretary of the Treasury Albert Gallatin in the choice of surveyors to perform the task. Gallatin named Jonathan Price, Thomas Coles, and William Tatham commissioners for the survey. Of Coles nothing is known. Tatham, on the other hand, had been educated at Cambridge, had arrived in Virginia in 1769, and had been active in Tennessee affairs from 1776 to 1795, except for a stay in Robeson County, N.C., from 1784 to 1792. Of an eccentric mental poise, Tatham had gone to Spain on behalf of one of those flirtatious intrigues indulged in by various leaders from the western country—one of which had cost William Blount his political career in 1797. After having been declared persona non grata in 1796, Tatham had left Spain for England, where he had remained for nearly a decade. In 1805 he returned to the United States and sought employment in Washington, D.C. Here his personal feelings and ambitions received a "painful stab" from Thomas Blount, who appears to have been responsible for the naming of Price in the commission and to have thwarted Tatham's effort to have himself named chief surveyor by Gallatin. The Blounts' protection rendered Price safe from the schemes of Tatham, who proved a hindrance rather than a help in surveying the coast. Tatham attempted to persuade Price to replace Coles with a surveyor of Tatham's own choosing, he appears to have felt that his superior academic credentials outweighed Price's superior ability, he was quarrelsome, and he spent his time fribbling on the edges of the survey.

Price and Coles successfully completed the survey during the weeks from the end of May to the end of September 1806 despite Tatham, tempestuous weather, and a hurricane that sank the two cutters used by them and destroyed Coles's papers, notes, and instruments. Their succinct narrative report was accompanied by a 24¾- by 35-inch manuscript, "Chart of the Coast of North Carolina between Cape Hatteras & Cape Fear From a Survey taken in the Year 1806 by Thomas Coles and Jonathan Price Pursuant to Act of Congress." (The chart was engraved for publication, and copies were offered for sale by North Carolina booksellers, though there are no known surviving examples of the engraved chart.) The draftsmanship of the manuscript chart forwarded to Secretary Gallatin, drawn to a scale of seven miles to the inch, exceeds Price's skill, though he is said to have understood drawing very well. It must have been drawn by someone whose talents had been given the necessary technical training: perhaps Thomas Coles, or the New Bern engraver William Johnston, or the architect William Nichols (whom Tatham had wished to engage as clerk to the survey). At the end of the survey, Price, perfectly capable of speaking his mind, relieved his feelings by expressing rather too freely his opinion of Tatham. This, too, must have been a "painful stab" to Tatham. He brought suit against Price, asking £1,000 damages. The jury found Price's words to have been actionable but meticulously fixed the damage to Tatham's reputation not at £1,000 but at precisely £37/10. Tatham, himself, to his credit as a gentleman, prevented the judgment from actually being executed against Price.

Price's next major surveys of a public nature were on behalf of the state. (He had been a member of the 1796–1803 commission to locate and mark the North Carolina–South Carolina boundary that never had been able to arrange a meeting with its South Carolina counterpart.) In 1815 the General Assembly, having been finally awakened to the necessity of giving its attention to internal improvements, erected a Board of Commissioners to Superintend Public Works. Price's patron, Peter Browne, was one of the commissioners, and when Price applied for the execution of some of the proposed public surveys, he was in 1818 awarded a contract for half the six surveys under consideration by the board. The commissioners especially wished to find a means of opening a direct communication from Roanoke River to Ocracoke Inlet; to concentrate the trade of Roanoke, Tar-Pamlico, and Neuse rivers at one place; and to open a communication from Neuse River to Beaufort Inlet. They were similarly anxious to improve the navigation of the Cape Fear and Yadkin rivers. The commissioners gave to Price as an assistant Woodson Clements (d. 1837), a young surveyor and later sheriff of Wake County, and sent them to examine the possibility of uniting the Uwharrie and Deep rivers by a navigable canal.

To this end Price and Clements ascertained the relative levels of the two rivers and explored the watercourses in the two river systems. The result was Price's manuscript topographic survey measuring 24⅓ by 28½ inches, "Plans and Sections of the Uwharee [*sic*] and Deep Rivers," completed in July 1818 (now hanging in the library of the executive mansion). From here, Price and Clements were sent by the commissioners to the northeastern section of the state, where they made four surveys: the country between the Roanoke and Tar rivers by a route from Conoho Creek to Tranters Creek, the country between the Pamlico and Roanoke rivers from the town of Washington to the mouth of Smithwick Creek, the country between Roanoke River at Plymouth to the head of navigation on Pungo River, and the country between the Pamlico and Neuse rivers by a route from Blounts Creek to Swift Creek. Though the text of Price and Clements's reports of their four surveys was published by the state printer in 1818 and again in the 1839 report of the Board of Internal Improvements, only one of the four manuscript maps of the project is known to have survived: the 35⅝- by 35⅝-inch survey of the country between Roanoke and Pungo rivers (in the North Carolina State Archives).

Price's other publicly commissioned works were undertaken on behalf of municipalities. The commissioners of New Bern, where he had moved from Pasquotank County, employed Price in 1809 to resurvey the town and renew the cornerstones of the squares. A few years later he combined this survey with one of 1806 that had laid out lots and streets on the property of the Dry family lying to the north of the town beyond Queen Street. The result was published about 1817 or shortly thereafter as "A Plan of the Town of New Bern and Dryborough With the Lands adjoining Contained within the bounds of the Original Grant to Danl. Richardson in 1713." Engraved by Allen Fitch, the 19¼- by 23-inch town plan was embellished with views of New Bern Academy, the Bank of New Bern, the State Bank of North Carolina, and the original building of Christ Church. After Price's death in

1822 his administrator, Joseph Bell, purchased the plate for ten dollars and had it further engraved with additional views of the recently completed Presbyterian church (1822) and the new Christ Church (1824). From the altered plates Bell struck fresh impressions. Of the original and second state of Price's plan of New Bern, neither of which bears a date, it is the post-1824 printing that is usually seen.

Between the date of Price's survey of New Bern and its publication, he was engaged by the commissioners of Beaufort to resurvey that town in May 1816. As late as 1951 his 21- by 32-inch manuscript plan of Beaufort was still being used by the corporation as the basis for town engineering work. Simultaneously with this survey, Price was employed to lay off the squares and streets of Lenoxville, a new town proposed to be established east of Beaufort. Never published, the original of Price's 12- by 16-inch manuscript plan of Lenoxville was given to the North Carolina Collection at Chapel Hill in 1958.

In his religious life Price remained active in Quaker affairs only from 1781 to 1797, but he seems to have embraced some of their principles permanently. In politics he was a Jeffersonian and unsuccessfully stood for election to the 1799 General Assembly. Intellectually his broad-ranging interests were reminiscent of the philosophes, though he shared neither their materialism nor their hedonism. In his private conversation he met opposing opinion with temper and candor, but without acrimony or malice. The overriding characteristic of his life is said to have been a true philanthropic benevolence. He took his slaves to Philadelphia and freed them, then visited them later in life and assured himself of their well-being. In his death he serves as a reminder of the caution, "Be careful what you pray for—you may get it." When the Presbyterians of New Bern announced their intention in 1818 of building a church in the town, Price jested that he had no wish to live any longer than until the Presbyterians, said to be too poor or too mean to build, completed the structure. His death followed the completion of the church by four months. Price appears to have been long predeceased by his wife, Susannah Morris, and their three children, Mary, Miriam, and Samuel.

SEE: *Edenton Gazette*, 8 Dec. 1809, 9 Feb. 1810; *Hall's Wilmington Gazette*, 8 June 1797; G. Melvin Herndon, "The 1806 Survey of the North Carolina Coast: Cape Hatteras to Cape Fear," *North Carolina Historical Review* 49 (July 1972); William Wade Hinshaw, ed., *Encyclopedia of American Quaker Genealogy*, vol. 1 (1936); William Henry Hoyt, ed., *Papers of Archibald D. Murphey*, vols. 1–2 (1914); Alice Barnwell Keith and others, eds., *John Gray Blount Papers*, vols. 2–4 (1959–82); New Bern *Carolina Centinel*, 1 June 1822; New Bern *Morning Herald*, 18 Nov., 9 Dec. 1808, 27 Nov. 1809; Mary Lindsay Thornton, "The Price and Strother 'First Actual Survey of North Carolina,'" *North Carolina Historical Review* 41 (October 1964). See also General Assembly Session Records, 1792, 1796, 1802; Treasurer's and Comptroller's Records, Journals and Ledgers, nos. 12, 19; Governor's Letter Books (Williams), no. 14; Pasquotank County Court Minutes, March Term 1785 and March Term 1789; Craven County Court Minutes, March Term 1807, and Civil Action Papers, 1806–8; Craven County Estates Records—Jonathan Price, 1822.

GEORGE STEVENSON

Price, Joseph Charles *(10 Feb. 1854–25 Oct. 1893)*, black educator, orator, and civil rights leader, was born in Elizabeth City to a free mother, Emily Pailin, and a slave father, Charles Dozier. When Dozier, a ship's carpenter, was sold and sent to Baltimore, Emily married David Price, whose surname Joseph took. During the Civil War, they moved to New Bern, which quickly became a haven for free blacks when it was occupied by Federal troops. In 1863 his mother enrolled him in St. Andrew's School, which had just been opened by James Walter Hood, the first black missionary to the South and later the bishop of the A.M.E. Zion Church. Price showed such promise as a student at this and other schools that in 1871 he was offered a position as principal of a black school in Wilson. He taught there until 1873, when he resumed his own education at Shaw University in Raleigh with the intention of becoming a lawyer. But he soon changed his mind and transferred to Lincoln University in Pennsylvania to study for the ministry in the A.M.E. Zion Church. He was graduated in 1879 and spent another two years at its theological seminary. During this period, he married Jennie Smallwood, a New Bern resident he had known since childhood. They were the parents of five children.

In 1881, soon after his ordination, Price was chosen as a delegate to the A.M.E. Ecumenical Conference in London. While there, Bishop Hood urged him to make a speaking tour of England and other parts of Europe to call attention to the plight of black education in the South and, more specifically, to raise funds to establish a black college in North Carolina. His effectiveness as an orator drew large crowds and resulted in contributions of almost $10,000. This, plus the support of white residents of Salisbury, enabled him to establish Livingstone College and to become its president in October 1882, when he was twenty-eight years old. (Originally called Zion Wesley College, its name was changed to that of the African explorer and missionary David Livingstone in 1885.) Sponsored by the A.M.E. Zion Church, Livingstone began with five students, three teachers, and a single two-story building, but it grew rapidly to become one of the South's most important liberal arts colleges for blacks. Though he encouraged the support of southern whites, such as Josephus Daniels, and philanthropists, such as Leland Stanford and Collis P. Huntington, Price felt that blacks themselves must bear the real responsibility for educating their race. In 1888 he stated that "Livingstone College stands before the world today as the most remarkable evidence of self-help among Negroes in this country."

Price's leadership of the college and his ability as an orator gained him national attention. In 1888 President Grover Cleveland asked him to serve as minister to Liberia, though he declined, saying he could do more for his people by remaining in Salisbury. In 1890 he was elected president of both the Afro-American League and the National Equal Rights Convention and named chairman of the Citizens' Equal Rights Association. But conflict among the groups and lack of financial support led to their decline soon afterwards. Like Booker T. Washington, Price believed that blacks' self-help through education and economic development was their best hope for solving the race problem, and he assured whites that social integration with them was not among their goals. But he was less conciliatory than Washington in demanding that the civil rights of blacks be upheld. Blacks were willing to cooperate and live peaceably with southern whites, but not at the cost of their own freedom of constitutional guarantees. "A compromise," he wrote, "that reverses the Declaration of Independence, nullifies the national constitution, and is contrary to the genius of this republic, ought not to be asked of any race living under the stars and stripes; and if asked, ought not to be granted."

Price's activist role in civil rights and black education

ended abruptly in 1893, when he contracted and died of Bright's disease at age thirty-nine. He was buried on the campus of Livingstone College. W. E. B. Du Bois, August Meier, and others felt that it was the leadership vacuum created by Price's death into which Booker T. Washington moved, and that had he lived, the influence and reputation of Price and of Livingstone College would have been as great or greater than that achieved by Washington and Tuskegee.

SEE: Annotated Bibliography of Joseph Charles Price (manuscript, Livingstone College Archives, Salisbury, 1956); *Charlotte Observer*, 17 Feb. 1970; *Durham Sun*, 31 Oct. 1970; *Greensboro Daily News*, 22 Feb. 1960; J. W. Hood, *One Hundred Years of the African Methodist Episcopal Zion Church* (1895 [portrait]); August Meier, *Negro Thought in America, 1880–1915: Racial Ideologies in the Age of Booker T. Washington* (1953); *North Carolina Teacher* 11 (November 1893); Stephen B. Weeks Scrapbook, vol. 10 (North Carolina Collection, University of North Carolina, Chapel Hill).

JOHN INSCOE

Price, Julian *(25 Nov. 1867–25 Oct. 1946)*, chairman of the board of the Jefferson Standard Life Insurance Company and philanthropist, was the son of Joseph Jones (1835–87) and Margaret Greene Hill Price (1847–1922) of Meherrin, Lunenburg County, Va. He was born near Richmond and received his formal education in a one-room schoolhouse. The village of Meherrin was a railroad stop, and it was with the railroad that Price found his first job. He once said that one of his first undertakings was cutting and selling wood to the railroad for use in wood-burning locomotives. On learning the Morse code he was employed as telegraph operator and dispatcher for the Southern Railway. In 1895 he moved to North Carolina with the railroad, first to Durham and shortly thereafter to Greensboro, where he was destined to become nationally known as an insurance executive, business and civic leader, and philanthropist.

In 1903 Price was a representative of the American Tobacco Company. But intrigued by the insurance business, he went to work for the Greensboro Life Insurance Company in 1905 and was called to the home office in 1909 as secretary and agency manager. When Jefferson Standard and Greensboro Life were consolidated in 1912, Julian Price became vice-president and agency manager. He was elected president of the company in 1919 and served until 28 Jan. 1946—a term of twenty-seven years. When he took over the presidency of Jefferson Standard, it had assets of $9.7 million and insurance in force of $81.6 million. When he left the presidency, the assets were $174.6, the insurance in force stood at $655 million, and Jefferson Standard ranked thirtieth among the nation's insurance companies.

During the administration of Governor Angus W. McLean (1924–28), Price, as head of the North Carolina Salary and Wage Commission, was instrumental in effecting a fair system of employment and pay for state employees. He became Governor McLean's most trusted financial adviser. Towards the end of McLean's term Price was strongly mentioned throughout the state for governor on the Democratic ticket but refused to have his name placed in nomination.

Shortly after World War I Price bought a majority interest in the *Greensboro Record* for $40,000; nine years later he sold this interest for $400,000. Subsequently, he became president of the Atlantic and Yadkin Railway and held that office until his death.

A Thirty-third degree Mason, an honorary member of the Patriotic Order Sons of America, and a life member of the Elks and of the Sons of Confederate Veterans, Price was also a past commander of the Knights Templar and a member of the Southern Society of New York. He was awarded a well-deserved honorary doctorate of laws degree at the sesquicentennial of The University of North Carolina on 13 Apr. 1946. During these ceremonies Frank Porter Graham, president of the university, characterized Julian Price as an "insurance executive and community builder who had a creative part in many business enterprises and philanthropic causes and who developed one of the largest life insurance companies in the southern states."

Price was one of the North Carolina business and professional leaders who chartered the Business Foundation at The University of North Carolina in July 1946. This foundation, working through the university, aided and promoted all types of education and research for business and industry.

On 22 Aug. 1897 Price married Ethel Clay (1874–1943), the daughter of Henry de Boisfeuillet (1843–97) and Harriet Field Clay (1850–1936). This happy marriage of forty-six years ended when Mrs. Price died on 26 Oct. 1943. They had two children, Kathleen Marshall (Mrs. Joseph McKinley Bryan) and Ralph Clay. In choosing a memorial for his wife Julian Price decided to honor her devout Roman Catholic faith, although he was not a Catholic. He personally chose an architect and a builder to copy a church that he admired. Price's legacy of $500,000 to build Our Lady of Grace Catholic Church in Greensboro was increased after his death by his two children when it became apparent that the original estimate was insufficient because of inflated costs.

Mrs. Kathleen Bryan Edwards, a granddaughter of Julian Price, relates two incidents that reveal his human side. The first concerns a man who approached Price in the lobby of the Jefferson Building when he was leaving for home after a busy day and asked him for ten dollars to buy a pair of shoes. When he asked the man what size he wore, he was amused to find that they wore the same size. Price promptly took off his own shoes, gave them to the man, and walked out to his car barefooted.

During World War II Guilford County was dry and this was hard on local Air Force base personnel. One officer inquired of the name of the local bootlegger and was told it was Price. He called Julian Price one Sunday afternoon and asked if he were the local source of liquor. Price asked what kind the captain wanted and when told, Johnny Walker, he asked the young officer, "Black or Red?" "Black," replied the stunned officer, who was then told to drive up in back of the house. The captain could hardly believe his luck when he tried to pay, for Price said, "No, no, young man, nothing is too good for our boys in the service." That afternoon the Air Force base was enthralled with the captain's awed description of how well the local bootlegger lived. They never knew that he had reached Greensboro's leading citizen, Julian Price, whose profession was much different from that of Price, the bootlegger.

Julian Price died as a result of injuries sustained in an automobile accident while en route to his mountain estate at Blowing Rock, on the eve of the third anniversary of the death of his beloved wife Ethel. In memory of their father his children established a professorship in life insurance at The University of North Carolina; funded with an original endowment of $80,000, it increased in value to $500,000 in the 1970s. Also, together with Jefferson Standard Life Insurance Company, they gave their father's estate in the mountains of western North Carolina to the U.S. government as a part of the Blue Ridge Parkway, which is called the Julian Price Memorial Park.

There are three portraits of Price. One, by North Carolina artist, Henry Rood, is owned by the Jefferson-Pilot Corporation. His daughter, Mrs. Joseph Bryan, owned a portrait by the noted artist Howard Chandler Christie. Another one, by M. D. Fox, was owned by Ralph C. Price, his son.

SEE: *Durham Morning Herald*, 28 Oct. 1946; *Greensboro Daily News*, 26 Oct. 1946; Julian Price Biography by Mary R. Taylor, in *The Jeffersonian*, November 1946; Records in possession of Mrs. Kathleen Bryan Edwards, granddaughter of Julian Price; *Who Was Who in America* (1950).

WM. A. BLOUNT STEWART

Price, Thomas Frederick *(19 Aug. 1860–12 Sept. 1919)*, first North Carolinian to be ordained a Roman Catholic priest and cofounder of the Maryknoll Missionaries, was born in Wilmington, eighth of the ten children of Alfred Lanier and Clarissa Bond Price. Alfred Price, a journalist and native of Beaufort County, joined at age twenty-one the staff of the then infant *New York Sun*. In 1843 he returned to Washington, N.C., as a reporter for the *Washington Republican* and a year later, at the invitation of citizens of Wilmington, moved there to found the *Wilmington Journal*, which he published as a weekly for seven years. In 1851 the *Journal* became the first daily paper in the state, and in 1860 it pioneered in the reporting of news by telegraph.

Clarissa Bond Price, who was reared a Methodist, attended school in Washington, N.C., and boarded at the home of Frederick Gallagher, where she met Al Price. The harmony of the Gallagher family life so impressed her that at age twenty she joined "their" Catholic church and thereafter was forever rejected by her parents and the entire Bond family. Al Price, an Episcopalian, surprised his wife and children on Christmas Day 1866 by also adopting the Catholic faith. Their son, Thomas Frederick, at age eight was one of the acolytes who served James Gibbons (later a cardinal) when he was installed the first vicar-apostolic of North Carolina at St. Thomas's Church, Dock Street, Wilmington (1868).

Thomas Frederick received his early education in the basement schoolroom of St. Thomas's. In September 1876 he left Wilmington by ship for St. Charles's College in Catonsville, Md., where, after surviving a shipwreck and a severe illness, he enrolled early in 1877 to begin his studies for the priesthood. A classmate was William O'Connell, later cardinal of Boston. Price completed his theological studies at St. Mary's Seminary, Baltimore.

Ordained on 20 June 1886 at St. Thomas's Church, Wilmington, by Bishop H. P. Northrop, Price was first assigned to North Carolina's oldest Catholic church, St. Paul's, New Bern, where he served as pastor for nine years. From there he was transferred to Sacred Heart Church, Raleigh, where in 1898 he founded an orphanage later known as Nazareth House. In 1897 he began a monthly magazine of apologetics called *Truth*, printing the first issue in the kitchen of his rectory. *Truth* had a wide circulation and in 1912 became the publication of the International Truth Society, at which time Thomas Frederick Price relinquished the editorship.

Price preached to missions throughout North Carolina in churches, on street corners, and in open fields. He was particularly interested in the conversion of blacks. Over time he developed many admirers among the Jewish communities and received from these friends lavish contributions for his church building projects in Goldsboro, Chinquapin, Halifax, Newton Grove, and Nazareth. At Nazareth, in conjunction with the orphanage, he developed (1902) a home mission center, the Apostolate of Secular Priests of North Carolina. The success of this venture was retarded by lack of men and money, but the purpose was later extensively developed by the Paulist Fathers, a religious home missionary order.

In 1904 Father Price discussed his mission methods at the first meeting of the Catholic Missionary Union held in Washington, D.C. It was at this conference that he first met Father James Anthony Walsh (later bishop) who was then director of the Propagation of the Faith in Boston. During a six-year correspondence these two men expanded the idea of an American Foreign Missionary seminary under the auspices of the Catholic University of America, with preparatory schools in major cities. They again met in 1910 at the International Eucharistic Congress assembled in Montreal, where their discussions dwelled on specifics for a Catholic Foreign Missionary Society of America. The plans were later endorsed by the American hierarchy, and on 29 June 1911 Pope Pius X gave his approval.

Temporary quarters for the organization were taken in Hawthorne, N.Y., until a permanent site could be purchased in Pocantico Hills. But when John D. Rockefeller offered a higher price for the land, the seller rescinded his agreement with the Catholic Foreign Missionary Society. Through subsequent civil action the society was awarded damages sufficient to purchase a site at Maryknoll, N.Y. Here established, and joined by the Maryknoll Sisters and another religious fraternity, the Maryknoll Missionaries became a renowned institution which in 1915 received the Decree of Praise from Rome. Meanwhile, Father Price was constantly on the road preaching missions throughout the country, recruiting young men for the society, and collecting funds to support the project.

Following World War I the first group of Maryknoll foreign missionary priests was ready for assignment to Yeungkong in southern China. In spite of his age, Thomas Price prevailed in his wish to accompany them. Within the year a combination of change of climate and primitive living conditions took their toll, and in 1919 an acute attack of appendicitis claimed his life at St. Paul's Hospital in Hong Kong. He was buried there in Happy Valley Cemetery, but in 1936 the remains were returned to Maryknoll and buried next to those of his friend and cofounder, Bishop Walsh, in the chapel crypt of the Mother House of the Missionary Society these two had formed. A portrait of Thomas Frederick Price hangs in the Mother House at Maryknoll, N.Y.

SEE: *DAB*, vol. 8 (1935); John C. Murrett, *The Story of Father Price* (1953) and *Tar Heel Apostle* (1944); *New Catholic Encyclopedia* (1967); Daniel Sargent, *All the Day Long* (1941).

D. F. GRANT

Price, Thomas Moore *(14 Jan. 1891–12 Sept. 1962)*, engineer, was born in Madison, the son of James Valentine and Pattie Frances Moore Price. He was graduated at Oak Ridge Military Institute at age seventeen and entered The University of North Carolina, where he was awarded the A.B. degree in 1912. After a year as principal of the high school at Rockford in Surry County, he returned to Chapel Hill and received the B.S. degree in civil engineering in 1915. His first employment was with a paving contractor in Greensboro, and after a year he became manager of two quarries operated by the Raleigh

Granite Company. During World War I he tried a number of times to enlist but was always rejected for health reasons. In the spring of 1919 Price left Raleigh for the West Coast, where he was employed by Henry Kaiser, a paving contractor.

Over a period of years Price was engaged in paving many miles of highway along the West Coast, particularly in southern California. Kaiser sent Price to Seattle to design and build what proved to be the first of more than a hundred gravel and sand plants that he designed. Among those with which he was associated were the Radum Plant near San Francisco and the Boulder, Bonneville, and Coulee Dam plants. The first of these was noted as producing 1,800 tons or 36 railroad cars hourly. As Kaiser's work expanded, he called upon Price to construct still larger and more productive sand and gravel plants. By studying the geology of an area, Price was able to locate productive sites. His work at Boulder Dam won national recognition and was completed two years ahead of schedule. Some of his work was described in an article he contributed to volume 109 of the *Transactions of the American Institute of Mechanical Engineers*.

Price was project manager for the construction of the Broadway vehicular tunnel through the Oakland Hills in California, and he managed the construction of the Delaware Aqueduct for the Board of Water Supply, New York City. He also was involved on the eve of World War II in the construction of new locks for the Panama Canal. In the spring of 1942 he was engaged in the construction of Kaiser's fully integrated steel plant in California to provide steel plates for ships. As in other instances, records were set for construction time. After the plant was completed Price was named works manager, and in 1944 he was vice-president in charge of the Iron and Steel Division of the Kaiser Company, Inc.

Price, accompanied by his brother, Wright, visited Venezuela in the spring of 1944 as a guest of the Venezuelan government. In the 1950s he went to New South Wales, Australia, to assist in the construction of the Snowy Mountain hydroelectric project and there developed a deep appreciation for the people and they for him. Price's contribution is recognized in the subsequent development by the Hamersley Iron Party, Limited, where a mountain in northwestern Australia, estimated to hold 500 million tons of iron ore, has been named Mount Tom Price. A coastal town, 182 miles north, to provide housing for works and shipping facilities was also named Tom Price.

In 1922 Price married Alice Bone of Red Bluff, Calif. They became the parents of a daughter, Shirley. When he lived in Raleigh, Price sang in the choir of the Episcopal Church of the Good Shepherd, and he was married in an Episcopal church. In his early life in Rockingham County, however, he attended the Presbyterian church. He was a devoted church worker, played the pipe organ, was president of the Oakland Symphony, and supported a school for boys in southern California. Throughout his life he retained an interest in North Carolina, following events in Chapel Hill and aiding in the rebuilding of the Presbyterian church in Wentworth.

SEE: Harold Coy, *The Prices and the Moores* (1944); H. H. Cunningham, *A Man Who Matched a Mountain* (n.p., n.d.); Daniel L. Grant, *Alumni History of the University of North Carolina* (1924); *New York Times*, 13 Sept. 1962.

WILLIAM S. POWELL

Prichard, John Lamb *(6 June 1811–13 Nov. 1862)*, clergyman, was the second of six children born to Enoch and Clarissa Gregory Prichard of Pasquotank County. His paternal great-great-grandfather, David Prichard, was a Welsh immigrant to Pasquotank Precinct. His maternal ancestry, of Scottish-English origin, had settled in New England prior to moving to the Albemarle region.

Bereft of a father at age nine, Prichard and his family then moved to the home of his maternal grandparents, the Willis Gregorys, in Camden County. There he was employed in work on the farm and later as an apprentice carpenter. Determined to pursue a formal education, Prichard enrolled in Wake Forest College in 1835, taking advantage of the institution's manual labor program to pay expenses and fees. He received the B.A. from Wake Forest in 1840 and was awarded a master of arts degree in 1843.

Prichard taught in the Hertford Academy, Murfreesboro, during the academic year 1840–41. However, he had also been conducting occasional religious services for several years and had been licensed to preach the gospel while a student at Wake Forest. Accordingly, he was induced to accept the pastoral care of First Baptist Church, Danville, Va., in November 1841. Ordained by the Danville church in March 1842, Prichard devoted the remainder of his years to the pastoral ministry, serving churches in Pittsylvania and Campbell counties in Virginia and in Caswell and New Hanover counties in North Carolina.

He served the following churches: First Baptist, Danville, 1842–52; Upper Banister, 1842–49; Bethany, 1843–52; Sandy Creek, 1843–45; and Mount Ararat, 1847. During the last year of his residence in Danville, he also kept monthly preaching appointments with the Baptist churches at Milton and Yanceyville, Caswell County. In February 1852 Prichard began a ministry of four years' duration with First Baptist Church, Lynchburg, where he is credited with having succeeded in restoring harmony among discordant elements of long standing within that congregation.

On 31 Jan. 1856 he returned to North Carolina to assume the pastoral care of Front Street Baptist Church (First Baptist Church), Wilmington. Here he labored diligently and sacrificially—especially in ministrations to the soldiers hospitalized in the city during the early months of the Civil War. Prichard fell victim to an epidemic of yellow fever that ravaged the port of Wilmington and vicinity during the autumn of 1862, having refused the pleas of family and friends to seek his own safety in order that he might minister to the needs of the sick and dying.

In denominational councils, Prichard is said to have been a persuasive advocate of those benevolent causes (missions, theological education, Sunday schools, and the like) towards which some of his fellow churchmen still maintained only lukewarm attitudes, at best. As preacher and pastor, he was characterized in the following manner by his biographer, James Dunn Hufham: "His sermons were carefully prepared, and delivered in the earnest and forcible manner characteristic of the man. They were plain, pointed, and practical, and free from the tinselry of rhetoric, and those extraneous ornaments which often give a preacher notoriety, and please without edifying his hearers. . . . As a pastor he had few superiors. His knowledge of human nature, his suavity of manner, his strong affections and active sympathies, and his untiring energies . . . peculiarly fitted him to shine in this sphere."

Prichard was twice married. On 1 Sept. 1842 he wed Mary Banks Hinton of Wake County. They had two children: Mary Hinton (m. Charles Elisha Taylor) and Robert Samuel. Mrs. Prichard died on 24 Nov. 1849. On 30 Oct.

1850 he married Jane Elizabeth Taylor, daughter of the Reverend James Barnett Taylor of Richmond, Va. John and Jane Prichard had five children: James Taylor (died in infancy), Annie Judson, John Lamb, George Taylor, and Jane Elizabeth Taylor (m. James Reynolds Duggan). Prichard's remains were interred in Oakdale Cemetery, Wilmington.

SEE: J. D. Hufham, *Memoir of Rev. John L. Prichard, Late Pastor of First Baptist Church, Wilmington, N.C.* (1867); J. D. Hufham, Obituary on J. L. Prichard, in *Minutes of the Twentieth Annual Session of the Union Baptist Association* (1863); Prichard Family Bibles (possession of Mrs. John Kerr, Jr., Warrenton, N.C.).

R. HARGUS TAYLOR

Primrose, William Stuart *(12 Nov. 1848–11 Apr. 1909),* businessman and North Carolina State College official, was born in Raleigh, the son of John and Eliza Tarbox Primrose. His father, a native of Scotland, was a merchant; his mother, a native of Hebron, Conn., went to Raleigh as tutor for the children of John Devereux. Young Primrose's earliest education was in Raleigh, after which he attended Davidson College for one year; otherwise, he was self-educated. As a young man he was assistant cashier of the State National Bank (1874–78), of which he later became a director. His interest in business inspired him to advocate and support the State Exposition of 1884, and he was elected president of the sponsoring body. When the North Carolina Home Insurance Company was organized, he was elected secretary and in 1885 he became president.

As a member of the influential Watauga Club in Raleigh, a group of the state's leading citizens who sought ways to advance North Carolina, Primrose is said to have been the first person to propose creation of what became North Carolina State College of Agriculture and Engineering. Because he did not have a college degree, he twice declined to be a candidate for president of the college. Nevertheless, he was a strong supporter of the institution and served as president of its board of trustees for twenty years. A building on the campus was named for him. He also served on the board of trustees of Peace Institute and of Davidson College.

Primrose, like his parents before him, joined the Presbyterian church as a youth. At age twenty-eight he became a ruling elder of Raleigh's First Presbyterian Church, a position he would fill for the remainder of his life. He also served as superintendent of the Sunday school and sang in the choir. He was an active Mason.

Primrose married Ella Williams, and they became the parents of six sons and a daughter: John Shelton, William S., Jr., Hugh Williams, Robert Owen, Henry Fries, Jesse Lindsay, and Helen (Mrs. R. Y. McPherson). After a funeral at the Presbyterian church, he was buried in Oakwood Cemetery, Raleigh.

SEE: Grady L. E. Carroll, Sr., *They Lived in Raleigh*, vol. 2 (1977); A. M. Fountain, *Place-Names on State College Campus* (1956); *North Carolina State Alumni News* 2 (May 1930 [portrait]); Papers in the possession of George London, Raleigh; Raleigh *News and Observer*, 29 Oct. 1984.

WILLIAM S. POWELL

Prince, Lillian Hughes *(17 June 1893–25 Feb. 1962),* actress, was born in Birmingham, Ala., the daughter of George Washington and Mary Lillian McTyeire Hughes, and attended the local schools. On 24 Nov. 1915 she married William Meade Prince, a New York illustrator. She began her acting career while the Princes were living at Swan Pond, their estate at Westport, Conn., in a pre-Revolutionary farmhouse that they had restored. In one of her first roles with the Westport Players she played a bridesmaid in a play starring Dorothy Gish. She studied acting with Harry Irvine at the Academy of Allied Arts in New York City and played a nine-week season at Irvine's Theater-in-the-Woods at Boothbay, Maine.

When the Princes moved to Chapel Hill in the 1930s, Lillian Prince became active in the Carolina Playmakers, appearing in thirty or more of their productions, including Paul Green's *The House of Connelly, The Little Foxes, Ah, Wilderness, Our Town*, and *The Madwoman of Chaillot* and such musicals as *Showboat, Oklahoma*, and *Spring for Sure*. She also worked with the organization for British War Relief.

After appearing in Chapel Hill in Howard Richardson's *Dark of the Moon*, Mrs. Prince joined the cast of the Shubert national touring company of the play in the demanding role of the "cunjer woman," which she played throughout the Northeast and the Midwest. In Chapel Hill she also sang roles in such Gilbert and Sullivan operettas as *The Pirates of Penzance* and *Pinafore*, and she performed with the Raleigh Little Theater in *Blithe Spirit*.

During the 1940s and 1950s Mrs. Prince played the role of Queen Elizabeth in Paul Green's outdoor drama, *The Lost Colony*, presented each year on Roanoke Island. The Princes had a house on the island and spent their summers near the theater with their beloved poodle, Zaza.

Mrs. Prince died in New York, survived by a sister, Mrs. Walter Barrett of New York City. She was buried in the Chapel Hill Cemetery. In her will she bequeathed considerable funds to the Carolina Playmakers, which had contributed extensively to her acting career.

SEE: *Chapel Hill Weekly*, 1 Mar., 5 Apr. 1962; *Durham Morning Herald*, 11 Nov. 1951; Raleigh *News and Observer*, 25 Feb. 1949; Walter Spearman, *The Carolina Playmakers: The First Fifty Years* (1970).

WALTER SPEARMAN

Prince, William Meade *(9 July 1893–10 Nov. 1951),* illustrator and author, was born in Roanoke, Va., the son of Robert Watson and Alice Wales Meade Prince. He was descended from Sir Richard Everard, the last governor of North Carolina under the Lords Proprietors, and from Bishop William E. Meade of Virginia.

At age five Prince moved to Chapel Hill and lived with his parents and his grandfather, Dr. William Meade, the Episcopal rector, until he was fifteen. After residing for a time in Birmingham, Ala., where he worked as a railway clerk, he moved to New York and studied at the New York School of Fine and Applied Arts (1913–15). There he won an illustration contest sponsored by *Collier's* magazine. His first illustration was done in black and white for a story by Harold Titus in *Red Book* in 1919. Prince illustrated the Negro stories of Roark Bradford and stories for many magazines (*Collier's, Saturday Evening Post, Red Book, Cosmopolitan*) by such authors as James Street, Phillip Wylie, Kathleen Norris, William Saroyan, and Arnold Bennett. He also did numerous advertising illustrations, including a series for Dodge cars.

In the 1930s Mr. and Mrs. Prince moved from their home in Westport, Conn., to Chapel Hill, and he became a lecturer in The University of North Carolina's Art Department, serving as head of the department during World War II. He made drawings and posters for the Committee to Defend America, the American Field Hospital Corps, and the USO, painting portraits of wounded soldiers and sailors. In 1942 Prince created the Sunday comic strip "Aladdin, Jr." He acted in several plays of the Carolina Playmakers with his wife Lillian and played Ananias Dare in Paul Green's outdoor drama, *The Lost Colony*.

In 1950 he wrote and illustrated a popular book about his experiences growing up in Chapel Hill, entitled *The Southern Part of Heaven*. A series of wood carvings of a circus parade by Carl Boettcher, based on his illustrations in the book, was installed at the Carolina Inn in Chapel Hill for a time, but in 1992 the carvings were moved to the new George Watts Hill Alumni Center. His series of portraits of university presidents and professors is also owned by the university.

In November 1951 Prince shot himself in the studio of his home in Chapel Hill. He was survived by his wife, Lillian Hughes, of Birmingham, Ala., whom he married on 24 Nov. 1915 and who died in New York in 1962. He was buried in the Chapel Hill Cemetery.

Prince was a member of the Chapel Hill Town Planning Board, State Planning Board, Building and Grounds Committee of The University of North Carolina, Virginia Museum of Fine Arts, Southern States Art League, North Carolina Artists Association, Sons of the American Revolution, Society of Illustrators, Artists and Writers Association, Players Club of New York, and Chapel Hill Country Club. In politics, he was a Democrat.

SEE: *Chapel Hill Weekly*, 16 Nov. 1951; *Charlotte Observer*, 21 Apr. 1940; *Greensboro Daily News*, 7 Sept. 1969; *North Carolina Authors: A Selective Handbook* (1952); Walter Spearman, *North Carolina Writers* (1949); *Who's Who in the South and Southwest* (1952).

WALTER SPEARMAN

Pritchard, George Moore *(4 Jan. 1886–24 Apr. 1955)*, congressman, district solicitor, and state legislator, was born in the community of Ivy, near Mars Hill, in Madison County, of Irish and Welsh ancestry. His father was Jeter Conley Pritchard, a U.S. senator and federal judge, and his mother was Augusta Lillian Ray. Young Pritchard attended public schools in Marshall and Washington, D.C., Emerson Institute in Washington, D.C., The University of North Carolina (1903–5), and the law department of the University of South Carolina (1907–8). Admitted to the bar in 1908, he practiced in Greenville, S.C., and was supervisor of the census for the Eighth Judicial District of South Carolina in 1910.

In 1911 Pritchard moved his family and practice to Marshall. He was elected a member of the board of trustees of The University of North Carolina for one term (1917) and served in the North Carolina House of Representatives from 1917 to 1919. Moving to Asheville in 1919, he was solicitor of the Nineteenth Judicial District (1919–22). Pritchard also served as chairman of the Buncombe County Republican Committee in 1928 and was elected as a Republican to the Seventy-first Congress (4 Mar. 1929–3 Mar. 1931). After foregoing renomination for membership in the lower house and an unsuccessful candidacy for election to the U.S. Senate in 1930, he returned to Asheville and resumed his private law practice.

A delegate to the Republican National Convention in 1932 and keynote speaker at the Republican State Convention in 1942, he was a leader of that party in Buncombe and Madison counties for many years. According to a letter dated 23 Nov. 1934, he was "The only Republican in the state who has been elected by the people to the three offices of Representative, Solicitor, and Congressman, and also honored as his party's candidate for the United States Senate." Although an unsuccessful Republican candidate for governor in 1948, he attracted considerable attention by demanding that the state use its surplus funds to build public schools.

Pritchard married Robenia Redmon on 19 Sept. 1911. Their children were Sarah (Mrs. Arthur Miller), Louise (Mrs. Neal), Helen (Mrs. Robert Viney), and Jeter C. Conley. He was a Presbyterian. His funeral was conducted from the Marshall Presbyterian Church in Marshall, where he had returned to live eight years earlier. Burial was in the Pritchard family cemetery.

SEE: Alumni Files (University of North Carolina, Chapel Hill); *Biog. Dir. Am. Cong.* (1950); *Congressional Record*, vol. 101, 84th Cong. (1955); Daniel L. Grant, *Alumni History of the University of North Carolina* (1924).

ROBERT L. CHERRY

Pritchard, Jesse Eli *(29 Nov. 1880–10 Aug. 1957)*, Methodist minister and administrator, was a native of Asheboro, the son of Isaiah Franklin and Nancy Ellen Conner Pritchard. Upon graduation from Western Maryland College in 1909, Pritchard enrolled in Westminster Theological Seminary, where he received the bachelor of divinity degree in 1912. Accepted on trial in the North Carolina Annual Conference of the Methodist Protestant church in November 1911, he was ordained an elder in November 1912 and assigned to the Halifax Circuit, where he remained until 1915. Afterwards he served churches in Thomasville (1915–16), Burlington (1916–21), Henderson (1921–26), Asheboro (1926–31), Winston-Salem (1931–34, 1940–41), Greensboro (1934–38), Ramseur (1941–45), and Mocksville (1945–46).

In 1938 Pritchard became president of the North Carolina Annual Conference of the Methodist Protestant church, a position he held for two years. He was a member of the church's General Board of Education from 1924 to 1928, serving as recording secretary. In 1932 Western Maryland College conferred on him the doctor of divinity degree. Pritchard served for a number of years as a trustee of High Point College and for twelve years as a trustee of the Methodist Children's Home of the Western North Carolina Methodist Conference in Winston-Salem. From 1934 to 1936 he was the editor of the *Methodist Protestant Herald*, published in Greensboro, the official church paper for the North Carolina Annual Conference.

Pritchard was a delegate to three General Conferences of the Methodist Protestant church, a delegate to the Uniting Conference of the Methodist church in Kansas City in 1939, and a delegate to the first Southeastern Jurisdictional Conference of the Methodist church. He was a charter member of the Asheboro Chamber of Commerce and Rotary Club and the Mocksville Rotary Club, and a life member of the North Carolina Society of County and Local Historians. Pritchard was a recognized authority on the history of the Methodist Protestant church in North Carolina, and his ability as an administrator within his denomination earned him the respect and esteem of church leaders statewide and nationally. His great wisdom and knowledge of church affairs, as well as his innate wit and talent as a conversationalist and pulpit speaker, endeared him to a great host of friends.

On 12 Dec. 1912, Pritchard married Laura Vestal of Siler City. Following his retirement in 1946, he resided in Asheboro. He was buried in Asheboro.

SEE: Mrs. C. W. Bates (Weaverville) and Mrs. J. E. Pritchard (Asheboro), personal contact; J. Elwood Carroll, *History of the North Carolina Annual Conference of the Methodist Protestant Church* (1939); Citation to Jesse Pritchard by the Asheboro Ministerial Association, 4 Mar. 1957; *Henderson Dispatch*, 27 July 1957; *Journal of the North Carolina Annual Conference of the Methodist Protestant Church*, scattered issues; *Who's Who in Methodism* (1952).

RALPH HARDEE RIVES

Pritchard, Jeter Conley *(12 July 1857–10 Apr. 1921)*, senator and judge, was born in Jonesboro, Tenn., the son of William H. and Elizabeth Brown Pritchard. Although he was seven years above the top age for enlistment in the Confederate army, the elder Pritchard enlisted as the paid substitute for Herman Cone, father of Ceasar and Moses Cone; he served throughout the war and after the surrender of Vicksburg contracted a fatal illness from which he died in Mobile, Ala. His widow, left to care for her family, apprenticed young Jeter at age twelve to a printer who also published the Jonesboro *Herald and Tribune*. Pritchard devoted himself to the tasks at hand and learned rapidly; at the end of his apprenticeship he became foreman of the *Union Flag and Commercial Advertiser*, another Jonesboro newspaper, where he remained until 1873. He studied at Martins Creek Academy, Erwin, Tenn., for two terms and then moved to Bakersville, N.C., where he became foreman of the weekly *Roan Mountain Republican*. Following further self-education, he became a partner in the newspaper and its associate editor.

In 1877 Pritchard's newspaper career came to an end when he moved to Madison County. There he farmed, operated a gristmill, and studied law under Colonel Pender A. McElroy. Pritchard moved to Marshall, the county seat, and began to practice law. He was a Republican elector in 1880 at age twenty-three, a member of the General Assembly in 1885, 1887, and 1891, and a delegate-at-large to the Republican National Convention at Minneapolis in 1892. In 1888 he was the Republican nominee for lieutenant governor of North Carolina, and in 1891 he was the Republican caucus nominee for U.S. senator. Elected president of the North Carolina Protective Tariff League in 1891, Pritchard used that body to seize control of the Republican party organization.

In 1895 the Republicans and Populists in the state legislature sent him to the U.S. Senate to complete the term of the late Senator Zebulon B. Vance. Pritchard had been one of the organizers of the "cooperative movement," which resulted in his election by factions of these two parties. He thus became the first Republican elected to the Senate from a southern state in twenty years. As the only southern Republican there, he was frequently consulted by President William McKinley on matters pertaining to the South, but he declined a cabinet appointment in the McKinley administration. Reelected for successive terms, he remained in the Senate until 1901. Election to his final term came following a bitter fight with Marion Butler, leader of the Populists. In Congress, Pritchard introduced the first bill for a Southern Forest Preserve which eventually resulted in the Great Smoky Mountains National Park.

Pritchard was state Republican chairman during the 1890s and again in 1902, and he served simultaneously as a member of the Republican National Committee for a number of years. He was a recognized leader in all councils and policies of his party and his political following was very large.

Appointed by President Theodore Roosevelt, Pritchard became an associate justice of the supreme court of the District of Columbia in 1903 and made an impressive record. The following year he was named judge of the Circuit Court of Appeals for the Fourth District. Soon after taking his seat on the bench, Judge Pritchard granted a writ of habeas corpus in the case of editor Josephus Daniels, who had been adjudged guilty of contempt of court by the district judge in Raleigh. Daniels was discharged and Pritchard's decision was widely hailed by the press, both domestic and foreign. He also made other significant decisions, some of which were appealed but uniformly sustained. He continued to serve until his death.

Pritchard was married in 1877 to Augusta L. Ray and they became the parents of three sons and a daughter—William D. (an army officer killed in the Philippines in 1904), George M., Thomas A., and Ida (Mrs. Thomas S. Rollins). Following the death in 1886 of his wife, Pritchard married Melissa Bowman by whom he had another son, J. McKinley. After the death of his second wife in 1902, Judge Pritchard married Lillian E. Saum in 1903. During World War I he spoke widely in support of Liberty Loan movements in Arkansas, Louisiana, Oklahoma, and Texas. He endorsed drives by the YMCA and the Red Cross.

Pritchard died in Asheville and was buried in Riverside Cemetery.

SEE: *Asheville Citizen*, 11 Apr. 1921, 1 May 1949, 7, 9 May 1967; *Biog. Dir. Am. Cong.* (1989); *Charlotte Observer*, 30 Aug. 1902; John L. Cheney, Jr., ed., *North Carolina Government, 1585–1979* (1981); *Federal Reporter*, vols. 129–272 (1904–21); London *Times*, 12 June 1904; D. C. Mangum, *Biographical Sketches of the Members of the Legislature of North Carolina, Session 1897* (1897); *New York Times*, 14 June 1904; *North Carolina Biography*, vol. 5 (1919); Jeter C. Pritchard Papers (Southern Historical Collection, University of North Carolina, Chapel Hill).

JOE L. MORGAN

Pritchard, Thomas Henderson *(8 Feb. 1832–May 1896)*, Baptist pastor and college president, was born in Charlotte, the son of Joseph Price and Eliza Hunter Henderson Pritchard. His father was a Baptist minister and a native of Charleston, S.C.; his mother was the daughter of Dr. Samuel and Margaret Dinkins Henderson of Mecklenburg County. After a short time the family moved to Mocksville, where young Tom attended the Mocksville Academy and was prepared for college by the Reverend Baxter Clegg, a Methodist minister. Pritchard was adopted by a wealthy bachelor uncle, Dr. William Davis Henderson, who sent him to Wake Forest College at age seventeen.

After Pritchard's second year of college Henderson married and left any further education up to his nephew. Pritchard left college at the end of his sophomore year and taught school in Nash County to enable him to return to Wake Forest. He then borrowed money and continued his education. While at Wake Forest College, Pritchard was president of the Philomathesian Literary Society (1853–54). A contemporary described him as a young man "bringing the joyfulness and energy of abounding health, and gracious manners, the uplifting influence of noble ambitions, literary tastes, with a readiness and fluency of speech which came to him by inheritance, and an optimism which clung to him." Pritchard had intended to study law but a revival at the college changed his whole life. He was baptized on 9 Sept. 1849 and soon after was licensed by the Wake Forest Baptist Church to preach. He received the B.A. degree from

Wake Forest in 1854. The board of the college then elected him to act as publicity agent for the college to stimulate interest in higher education for Baptist boys and to solicit scholarships and donations for the college.

After a year of traveling over the state as agent of the college, Pritchard decided that he wanted to return to the ministry. The Baptist church in Hertford, where he was living, requested his ordination. He was ordained as a minister on 9 Dec. 1855 and was immediately elected pastor of the Hertford Baptist Church, where he taught and preached for three years, earning enough to pay off the debts incurred in college. In 1858 Pritchard moved to Charlottesville, Va., and entered the University of Virginia to read theology with Dr. John A. Broadus. During the next year he supplied the pulpit of Dr. William F. Broaddus in Fredericksburg, Va., and in January 1860 he became pastor of Franklin Square Baptist Church in Baltimore, where he remained until July 1863, when he was imprisoned after an attempt to go South.

When he returned to North Carolina, Pritchard was appointed chaplain and colporteur to Gordon's Corps of the Army of Northern Virginia. He preached to the troops and was involved in the "Great Revival" that swept over the Confederate army in 1863. From the end of that year until June 1865, he filled the pulpit of the First Baptist Church of Raleigh in the absence of its pastor. In July 1865 he was called to the pastorate of the First Baptist Church of Petersburg, Va. He returned to the First Baptist Church, Raleigh, in February 1868. After eleven years, during which his congregation grew in membership from 240 to 515, he was elected president of Wake Forest College.

Pritchard assumed his duties as president of the college and as professor of "Moral and Intelligent Philosophy" in September 1878. His administration was characterized by a substantial increase in the student enrollment and endowment and in the completion of Wingate Memorial Hall. In 1882 he accepted the call of the Broadway Baptist Church in Louisville, Ky., retaining this charge until October 1884, when he accepted the call to the First Baptist Church of Wilmington. He remained in Wilmington until January 1893, when he accepted the call of Tryon Street (now First) Baptist Church in Charlotte, of which he was still pastor at the time of his death.

Pritchard was a trustee of The University of North Carolina, the Southern Baptist Theological Seminary, Louisville, Ky., and Wake Forest College. He served as chairman of the Board of Missions of the Baptist State Convention of North Carolina for seven years. He was associate editor of the *Biblical Recorder* and a frequent contributor to the *Recorder*, *Charity and Children*, *The Student*, and other publications. He was the author of a small book on infant baptism in 1871 and an enlarged edition in 1876. He prepared biographical sketches of North Carolina Baptists for Cathcart's *Baptist Encyclopedia*. Throughout life he was an ardent spokesman for education, and while in Raleigh he lent his talents to assist in the establishment of a college for agriculture and mechanics (now North Carolina State University). The University of North Carolina presented him with the D.D. degree in 1868.

On 18 Nov. 1858 he married Fannie Gulielma Brinson of New Bern. They had five children: Claudia (Mrs. Aaron Dallas Jenkins), William Broadus, Lauriston Levering, Thomas William, and Frances (Mrs. William Walter Holladay).

Pritchard died at the home of his son in New York City. His remains were taken to Charlotte, where a memorial service, attended by Baptist dignitaries and others, was held in the Tryon Street (now First) Baptist Church. After one of the largest funeral processions up to that time, Pritchard was buried in Elmwood Cemetery.

SEE: *Biblical Recorder*, 20 Dec. 1855, 27 May 1896; G. A. Hendricks, "Thomas Henderson Pritchard," *Encyclopedia of Southern Baptists*, vol. 2 (1958); *North Carolina Baptist State Convention Annual, 1896* [portrait]; Thomas Henderson Pritchard Biography File (Baptist Historical Collection, Wake Forest University, Winston-Salem) [portrait]; Raleigh *News and Observer*, 13 Feb. 1938; C. E. Taylor, comp., *General Catalogue of Wake Forest College, N.C., 1834–5–1891–2*.

JOHN R. WOODARD

Proffitt, Frank Noah *(1 June 1913–24 Nov. 1965)*, farmer, craftsman, and singer of traditional songs, was born in Laurel Bloomery, Tenn., the son of Wiley and Rebecca Alice Creed Proffitt. His paternal grandparents, John and Adeline Perdue Proffitt, moved to the Cracker Neck section of the eastern Tennessee mountains from Wilkes County, N.C., shortly after the Civil War. Frank's grandfather, John Proffitt, joined the Union army and was a member of the Thirteenth Tennessee Cavalry. His grandfather's brother, Benjamin Proffitt, fought on the Confederate side. When Frank was nine, the family moved back to North Carolina, to the Beaver Dam section of Watauga County, just a few miles below the Tennessee border. There Frank Proffitt lived the rest of his life.

During Proffitt's boyhood, life was very much like colonial pioneer days, when each family made nearly everything it used, including musical instruments. Music was a part of life. As a boy, Frank learned the old songs and ballads from his father, his grandfather, and his Uncle Noah and his Aunt Nancy Prather. He had little formal education, finishing sixth grade in a mountain school. All during his life, however, he read whatever he could find—and he had time to think and to wonder. He had a deep feeling for the ways and the songs of his forebears. Proffitt was sixteen when he walked barefooted across the mountains to see his first town—Mountain City, Tenn.

In 1937 Dr. Frank C. Brown of Duke University, on a collecting trip in Watauga County, recorded a few songs from Frank Proffitt. They appear in the *Frank C. Brown Collection of North Carolina Folklore*, published by the Duke University Press in 1952. From 1938 until his death Frank Proffitt was a close friend of Frank and Anne Warner and contributed more than a hundred songs to their collection: *Traditional American Folk Songs from the Frank and Anne Warner Collection*, published in 1984.

In the last few years of Proffitt's life—in the first half of the 1960s—he became to many a symbol for the newly awakened interest in the traditional singer. He was recognized as the source of the song "Hang Down Your Head, Tom Dooley," which catapulted the Kingston Trio to fame in 1959 (their recording of the song sold over three million copies) and is said to have begun the widespread interest in American folk music abroad. He made recordings for Folkways and for Folk-Legacy. From time to time he left his farming to sing at festivals, including the first Chicago Folk Festival (1961) and the Newport Folk Festival (1964), and at universities and colleges.

In 1961 and 1962 Proffitt was a staff member at Pinewoods Camp in Plymouth, Mass., run by the Country Dance and Song Society of America. His homemade dulcimers and fretless banjos were ordered by people near and far. At Alan Lomax's request, he made a gourd banjo like those used in the days of slavery for a film being made in Williamsburg, Va. Proffitt was featured in stories about folk music in *Time* magazine and other national publications. He was chosen by the governor of North Carolina to participate in North Carolina Day at the New York World's Fair in 1964. The state used his picture in a booklet encouraging summer visitors to come to North Carolina. *Sing Out* magazine (November 1965) published an article by him, "Good Memories For Me." His friends and admirers and correspondents—and visitors—were innumerable. When he died, leading newspapers across the country (including the *New York Times*) carried the story of Frank Proffitt and his music.

Proffitt married Bessie Mae Hicks, the daughter of Nathan and Rena Hicks of Beech Mountain. Nathan Hicks, too, was a maker of musical instruments and a singer. The Proffitts had six children: Oliver, who made a career in the U.S. Air Force; Ronald, a graduate of Berea College, with a Ph.D. in physics from the University of Kentucky; Franklin (Frank Jr.), a visiting artist under the aegis of the North Carolina Council of the Arts; Phyllis (Mrs. Lynn Hicks); Eddie; and Gerald.

Frank Proffitt was buried in the small private Milsap burying ground about a mile from his home. His headstone carries a line from one of his songs: "Going Across the Mountain, O, Fare You Well."

SEE: *Appalachian Journal* 1 (Autumn 1973); Jon Pankake and Paul Nelson, "Frank Proffitt Sings Folk Songs," a review of Proffitt's Folkways recording, *Little Sandy Review*, no. 22 (November 1961 [portrait]); *Frank Proffitt* (Folk-Legacy recording FSA-1), *Frank Proffitt Memorial Album* (Folk-Legacy recording FSA-36), and *Frank Proffitt Sings Folk Songs* (Folkways recording FA 2360); Frank Warner, "Frank Proffitt," *Sing Out* (October–November 1963); John Foster West, *The Ballad of Tom Dula* (1970).

ANNE WARNER

Prouty, William Frederick *(15 Aug. 1879–27 June 1949)*, geologist, university teacher, and administrator, was born on a farm near Putney, Vt., the third living child of Charles Eaton and Corintha Walker Prouty, both of English descent. After finishing the grammar grades in the Putney school, young Will Prouty left home at age fourteen to complete his preparatory schooling at Black River Academy at Ludlow, Vt., before entering Syracuse University at Syracuse, N.Y., where he lived in residence with his uncle and aunt, Mr. and Mrs. Frank Robinson Walker. Walker, a practicing attorney, later became head of the law school at Syracuse University. Prouty received his B.S. degree with honors in geology at Syracuse in 1903 and his M.S. in 1904, when he was also an instructor of geology.

After serving as assistant on the Geological Survey of Maryland during the summers of 1903 and 1904, Prouty entered Johns Hopkins University, from which he received a Ph.D. in 1906. Later that year, he accepted a position as associate professor of geology and mineralogy at the University of Alabama at Tuscaloosa, where he became head of the department in 1911. In addition to his teaching duties at the university, Prouty served as chief assistant geologist of the Geological Survey of Alabama, for which he compiled mappings in the vicinity of Birmingham that were largely instrumental in the discovery and later development of a thick iron seam; the utilization of its rich ores was of great significance in making that city the steel center of the South. During these years, he also did consulting work in Georgia, Tennessee, and Maryland, where his studies dealt largely with the availability and quality of iron, coal, graphite, and marble deposits. Prouty's extensive work with marble later established him as one of the country's leading experts on marble.

By the end of World War I, Professor Fred Prouty had determined to concentrate on teaching, his first love, despite the many opportunities offered him as a free-lance geological expert and oil prospector. Thus he became a dedicated teacher who prepared many of his students to become prominent in their fields of geology, both in this country and abroad. In 1919 he accepted a post at The University of North Carolina as professor of stratigraphical geology. Upon the death of Dr. Collier Cobb in 1932, he was named head of the Geology Department, a position he retained until his sudden death in 1949. From 1920 to 1924 he also was geologist for the North Carolina Geological Survey, and from 1922 to 1925 he served as paleontologist with the West Virginia Geological Survey. In 1938 he was named geologist on the Board of Consultants of the Tennessee Valley Authority, where he remained active until he died.

During World War II Prouty originated and supervised the teaching of map courses for the students of the V-12 ROTC units at Chapel Hill. For this work he received full recognition from the service officials on location and in Washington, as well as many letters of appreciation from his former students then overseas.

Prouty was the author of numerous articles appearing in scientific journals from 1907 to 1952, including a definitive work on a controversial subject, the "Carolina Bays and Their Origin," published posthumously in the *Bulletin of the Geological Society of America* (vol. 63, 1952), in which he established his modified meteoritic (air-shock wave) theory for the origin of the bays, a great many of which (such as those at White and Waccamaw lakes) appear throughout the coastal plain of North Carolina.

In 1909, while teaching at the University of Alabama, Prouty married Lucile W. Thorington (1884–1966), daughter of Judge William S. Thorington, who was at that time dean of the law school at Alabama. They had three sons: Frederick Morgan (1910–66), William Walker (b. 1912), and Chilton Eaton (b. 1914).

Prouty was a Fellow of the Geological Society of America and a member of the American Society for the Advancement of Science, Society of Economic Geologists, American Institute of Mining and Metallurgical Engineers, Seismographical Society of America, American Geophysical Union, American Meteorological Society, North Carolina Academy of Science, Elisha Mitchell Society, Carolina Geology Society, Phi Beta Kappa, Sigma Xi, Gamma Alpha, Phi Kappa Phi, Sigma Gamma Epsilon, Phi Delta Theta, the Order of Gimghoul, and the Rotary Club. He was a communicant of the Episcopal Chapel of the Cross in Chapel Hill and was a political independent. He died of a heart condition at Watts Hospital in Durham and was buried in the old Chapel Hill Cemetery.

SEE: Charles P. Berkey, "Memorial to William Frederick Prouty," *Proceedings Volume of the Geological Society of America, Annual Report for 1950* [portrait]; Mrs. William E. Butler, "Walker Genealogy" (possession of William W. Prouty, Chapel Hill); *Chapel Hill Weekly*, 1 July 1949, 19 Mar. 1957; *Charlotte Observer*, 29 June 1949; *Christian Science Monitor*, 16 Nov. 1948; *Daily Tar Heel*, 16 Nov. 1932, 13 Dec. 1933; *Durham Herald-Sun*, 25 July 1943; *Durham Morning Herald*, 29 June 1949; *Durham Sun*, 28 June 1949; *Greensboro Daily News*, 23 July 1937, 3 Feb. 1941, 29 June 1949; *Nat. Cyc. Am. Biog.*, vol. 38 (1953 [portrait]); Raleigh *News and Observer*, 29 June 1949; *New York Times*, 29 June 1949; *School and Society* 70 (9 July 1949) *Science* 110 (12

Aug. 1949); *Tar Heel*, 30 June 1949; *Who's Who in America*, vol. 25 (1948–49); *Winston-Salem Journal*, 29 June 1949.

WILLIAM WALKER PROUTY

Prudden, Emily C. *(13 June 1832–25 Dec. 1917)*, educator and missionary, established fifteen primary and secondary schools in western North Carolina in the late nineteenth and early twentieth centuries. At age fifty, she left her native Connecticut, where she had raised her late sister's orphaned children, to serve as housemother at Brainerd Institute in Chester, S.C. Her accomplishments over the next thirty years were all the more remarkable in light of the fact that from age seventeen she was deaf.

She began her work in North Carolina in 1884, when she acquired fifty acres at All Healing Springs in Gaston County. Her school there was known in time as Jones Seminary and later as Linwood College. In 1888 she established Lincoln Academy nearby for black females. From this beginning she went on to found schools at Blowing Rock, Connelly Springs, Saluda, Elk Park (one white, one black), Mill Springs, Cedar Valley, Lawndale, Brevard, and Tryon and one near Lenoir. The school at Lenoir was her greatest success. Oberlin Home and School, transferred to the care of the Woman's Home Missionary Society in 1903, was the direct forerunner of Pfeiffer College at Misenheimer.

The strategy she followed at Oberlin was the one she used elsewhere: to establish a school and after a few years transfer control to an organization better able financially than herself to keep it going. In this she worked closely with the American Missionary Association. Consequently, Prudden usually did not stay in one community more than two or three years. Upon retirement in 1909 she returned to Blowing Rock, site of her Skyland Institute founded in 1887. Prudden's remains were returned to Orange, Conn., for burial. In a eulogy, Congregationalist minister George Dickerman estimated that 10,000 students had passed through her schools over the years.

SEE: Barry M. Buxton, *A Village Tapestry: The History of Blowing Rock* (1989); Mary F. Floyd, "The Life and Work of Emily C. Prudden" (typescript, Pfeiffer College Library, no date); "Emily C. Prudden: An Autobiographical Sketch," *American Missionary* (March 1914); Christine L. Thomson, "An Invincible Schoolmarm," *State* magazine (March 1984).

MICHAEL HILL

Pruden, William Dossey *(2 Feb. 1847–27 Mar. 1918)*, lawyer, churchman, and Confederate officer, was born near Harrellsville, a son of Nathaniel and Martha Garrett Riddick Pruden. After attending Union Male Academy in his home community, he entered Trinity College in 1863. At age seventeen his studies were interrupted when he enlisted in the Confederate army during the last two years of the Civil War. He was promoted to second lieutenant of Company K, Seventieth Regiment of North Carolina troops under Colonel F. S. Armistead. Composed of Junior Reserves, this regiment served in eastern North Carolina and Virginia in 1864. It participated in the Battle of Kinston and won high praise for its conduct at the Battle of Bentonville, where Pruden was wounded. In April 1865 Pruden's regiment served as rear guard to General Joseph E. Johnston's forces as they passed through Raleigh. The Seventieth Regiment proceeded to Redcross in Randolph County and finally camped at Bush Hill, near Trinity College, where it remained until it was paroled on 2 May 1865.

Pruden entered the University of Virginia in 1865 and remained for two years. He then began to study law under Judge Richmond Pearson at the law school Pearson conducted at his home, Richmond Hill, in Yadkin County. Pruden was admitted to the bar in 1868. For a short time he practiced in Winton, the seat of his native county, before moving to Edenton. Soon after settling there, he formed a partnership with Major H. A. Gilliam, who later was appointed a judge of the superior court and moved to Raleigh. Pruden then established a partnership with C. S. Vann and still later practiced with W. B. Shaw, John G. Branch, and finally with his son, J. Norfleet Pruden. In time he came to be recognized as the leading lawyer in the Albemarle section and was associated with the most important litigation of his day and locality. Held in high esteem among his colleagues statewide, he was patient, studious, and attentive to his engagements. His integrity and devotion to truth, duty, and principle were apparent throughout his career. The courts respected him and juries believed him.

In 1872 he married Mary G. Norfleet, daughter of James Norfleet, a merchant of Edenton. They had three children: James Norfleet, Mary, and Margaret. His wife died in 1889 and three years later he married Annie A. Wood, daughter of Edward Wood, a farmer of Edenton. They had one son, William Dossey III.

Pruden was elected mayor of Edenton in May 1877 and served until 14 Dec. 1880, when he resigned. On 5 Jan. 1880 he was named legal adviser to the Chowan County Board of Commissioners, a post he held for thirty-eight years, until his death. In 1882 he also served as an examiner of candidates for the U.S. Military Academy. Pruden was a leader in the movement to organize the Bank of Edenton, which was chartered in October 1894 and opened early the next year. At its foundation he was a director, an original stockholder, and a first-day depositor.

In July 1886 Governor Alfred M. Scales appointed Pruden to the commission to rerun and mark the boundary between Currituck, Camden, and Gates counties and Virginia. The work of the commission lasted for two years and the report was submitted to the governor in December 1888. In 1889 Governor Daniel M. Fowle appointed Pruden to a commission to attend the annual meeting of the American Forestry Congress in Philadelphia. In addition, for twenty-five years prior to January 1909, he was division counsel for the Norfolk and Southern and the Atlantic Coast Line railroads.

Wake Forest College awarded him an honorary doctor of laws degree in 1891. An active churchman, Pruden was elected to the vestry of St. Paul's Church, Edenton, in 1897 and to the chancellorship of the Diocese of East Carolina; he served in both positions until his death. He also was frequently a delegate to the annual convention of the diocese. As a member of the Masonic order Pruden held a number of leadership posts. He was a member of the North Carolina Bar Association from its founding in 1899 (president, 1903) and served on the board of trustees of The University of North Carolina for two terms (1891–97, 1901–9).

In 1894 Pruden helped found and was a charter member of the Roanoke Colony Memorial Association and played a leading role in its activities. He held a number of offices in the organization, including that of president, and took the lead in the acquisition of property on Roanoke Island that later became the Fort Raleigh National Historic Site and the locale for the production of the outdoor drama, *The Lost Colony*.

An active, behind-the-scenes Democrat, Pruden neither held nor aspired to hold political office. He died in a hospital in Norfolk, Va., and was buried in St. Paul's Episcopal churchyard, Edenton. His descendants own a portrait of him and the Shepard-Pruden Memorial Library in Edenton recognizes his contributions to the community.

SEE: John Spencer Bassett Papers and Charles Van Noppen Papers (Manuscript Department, Duke University Library, Durham); Kemp P. Battle, *History of the University of North Carolina*, vol. 2 (1912); Chowan County Commissioners Book of Minutes (Courthouse, Edenton); Edenton Town Council Book of Minutes (Municipal Building, Edenton); *North Carolina Biography*, vols. 3 (1928), 4 (1941); William S. Powell, *Paradise Preserved* (1965); Pruden Family clippings (possession of Lina Pruden Mack, Edenton); William Dossey Pruden Papers (Southern Historical Collection, University of North Carolina, Chapel Hill); St. Paul's Church (Minutes of the Vestry, Edenton).

ELIZABETH H. COPELAND

Puckett, William Olin *(3 May 1906–3 June 1972)*, educator and biologist, was born in Cornelius, the son of William Lawrence and Mary Alice Washam Puckett. His family was of English, German, and Scottish descent and his earliest American ancestors arrived in Jamestown, Va., in 1619. Puckett was graduated as valedictorian of his class at Cornelius High School in 1923 and enrolled at nearby Davidson College, where he was an instructor of biology and was awarded a bachelor of arts degree in 1927. After receiving the master of arts degree from The University of North Carolina in 1931, he entered graduate school at Princeton University and served as a teaching Fellow; he received the master of arts and doctor of philosophy degrees in biology in 1934.

Puckett accepted a position as assistant professor of biology at Southwestern College, Memphis, Tenn., in 1935 but returned to Princeton later in the year. Puckett remained at Princeton for eleven years—as an instructor in biology (1935–40) and then assistant professor (1940–46). During World War II he was a research investigator for the Office of Scientific Research and Development, where he conducted significant studies in weapon trauma from 1943 to 1945. While at Princeton, Puckett quickly established his reputation as an authority in the science of vertebrate embryology and pioneered in the use of plastics to preserve biological specimens for study.

In 1946 he returned to Davidson College as chairman of the Department of Biology, a post he held until his retirement in 1971. Through his energetic leadership and teaching, he molded Davidson College into one of the foremost schools in the United States in premedical education. During his appointment as chairman of premedical studies and R. J. Reynolds Professor of Biology, Puckett taught and guided over 1,300 students to careers in medicine and influenced others to pursue research and teaching positions in the biological sciences. In recognition of his excellence in the field of biomedical education, he received the Thomas Jefferson Award in 1966 and was honored posthumously in the establishment of the W. Olin Puckett professorship in biology at Davidson College.

In addition to his educational work, Puckett engaged in research and published over forty articles dealing with his studies in embryology, comparative anatomy, radiation biology, endocrinology, and trauma. His work in developing transparent plastic preservatives for biological specimens represents one of his many lasting contributions to the science of zoology. As a member of the American Council on Education, Puckett was instrumental in preparing the critical 1954 report calling for increased funding and expansion of basic research in the United States during the decades following World War II and the Korean War. He was a member of the American Society of Zoologists, the American Association of Anatomists, Sigma Xi, Gamma Sigma Epsilon, Omicron Delta Kappa, and Sigma Chi and was elected president of the North Carolina Academy of Science in 1954. Puckett served as a ruling elder of the Davidson Presbyterian Church from 1958 to 1972.

He married Virginia Lewis House on 18 June 1942, and they were the parents of three children: Virginia Northington, John Lawrence, and James Butler. Puckett died in Huntersville and was buried in Mimosa Cemetery, Davidson.

SEE: Alumni Files (University of North Carolina, Chapel Hill); Davidson *Mecklenburg Gazette*, 8 June 1972; *Charlotte Observer*, 27, Dec. 1960; *Who Was Who in America*, vol. 5 (1973)

MARCUS B. SIMPSON, JR.

Pugh, Whitmell Hill *(1781–1834)*, physician, planter, and state legislator, was one of ten children born to William Scott and Winifred Hill Pugh of Bertie County. The Pughs, who had moved to Bertie County in the late 1720s from Chowan County, were a large and prominent family. Whitmell Pugh received medical training in North Carolina under Dr. Simmons J. Baker before attending the medical college of the University of Pennsylvania in Philadelphia. There he studied under Dr. Benjamin Rush and was graduated in 1804. While in Philadelphia, Pugh was a member of the Philadelphia Medical Society.

Returning to Bertie County, Pugh married his cousin Mary Whitmell Bryan Hill, the widow of John Hill, on 11 Mar. 1806. He resided at his wife's home, Woodville Plantation, in the village of Hotel (now Woodville). In addition to his medical practice, Pugh raised hogs on a large scale and hauled the meat to Richmond. In 1813, 1814, and 1815 he represented Bertie County in the House of Commons, and in 1816 and 1817 the legislature elected him a member of the Council of State.

In 1819 Pugh moved to Louisiana with his brother Augustin and half brother Thomas. The Pugh brothers settled in Lafourche Parish and established large cotton plantations. According to family tradition, it was at the urging of his wife that Pugh began planting sugarcane on his plantation, New Hope, in 1826. Pugh's brothers followed suit, and their sugar plantations flourished; the Pugh family became the most prominent in the parish and among the wealthiest in the state.

Pugh, who had retained his property in Bertie County, regularly visited North Carolina and sent his children there for their education. Pugh and his wife were the parents of four surviving children: Maria Augustus Hill, William Whitmell Hill, Harriet Eliza, and Mary Winifred Hill—all born in Bertie County. Harriet and Mary studied at the Moravian girls' academy in Salem, while William attended the Union Academy in Bertie County and The University of North Carolina. William resided at his father's Bertie County plantation before returning to Louisiana, where he became a wealthy planter and prominent political figure; he served in the state legislature and in the state constitutional convention of 1852.

Returning from a trip to North Carolina, Whitmell Pugh contracted pneumonia and died. He was buried at Madewood, Lafourche Parish, La., the plantation of his half brother Thomas. Mrs. Pugh died in 1854; both were

Episcopalians. Pugh's Bertie County home, Woodville, a handsome example of Federal-style architecture, still stands as a private residence.

SEE: John L. Cheney, Jr., ed., *North Carolina Government, 1585–1974* (1975); Stuart Hall Hill, "The Hill Family of Bertie, Martin, and Halifax Counties," vol. 3 (typescript, 1925, North Carolina Collection, University of North Carolina, Chapel Hill); Harnett T. Kane, *Plantation Parade* (1945); Charles Young Martin, *The Ancestors and Descendants of General Robert Campbell Martin and His Wife, Marty Winifred Hill Pugh* (1965); Whitmell Hill Pugh, *An Inaugural Essay on the Supposed Powers of Nature in the Cure of Disease; Submitted to the Examination of the Rev. John Andrews, D.D., Provost, the Trustees, and Medical Professors of the University of Pennsylvania, 6th day of June, 1804, for the Degree of Doctor of Medicine* (1804); J. Carlyle Sitterson, *Sugar Country: The Cane Sugar Industry in the South, 1753–1950* (1953).

J. MARSHALL BULLOCK

Pullen, John Turner *(1 Dec. 1852–2 May 1913)*, banker, philanthropist, author, church founder, and lay preacher, was born in Wake County, the son of Nancy A. (ca. 1828–31 Aug. 1888) and James D. Pullen (ca. 1820–15 Nov. 1887). His paternal grandparents were Elizabeth Smith (ca. 1792–25 May 1862), sister of early Raleigh merchants Richard and Benjamin Smith, from whose estates some of Pullen's inherited fortune eventually came, and her husband Turner Pullen (ca. 1780–21 Dec. 1867), sheriff of Wake County from 1823 to 1825 and justice of the Wake County Court from 1818. His father's brother was Richard Stanhope Pullen (18 Sept. 1822–23 June 1895), who donated Pullen Park to Raleigh and to the state gave the campuses that became North Carolina State University in Raleigh and (with R. T. Gray of Raleigh) the University of North Carolina at Greensboro.

John T. Pullen never married. He began his business career as clerk and then teller for the State National Bank in Raleigh. At the time he had the reputation, according to a contemporary, of being "the best field-shot in Raleigh, if not in the state, and one of the best at pool." He led what some termed a dissolute, intemperate, even "wild" life, although a close acquaintance later described him as merely "self-indulgent, rather than really bad." At some point he had become a member of the First Baptist Church, but in November 1881 that congregation in conference cited him to attend the next monthly conference "to answer to the church for unchristian like conduct towards the church in that he declined to conform to a rule of the church." Following his satisfactory hearing on 2 December, his life-style apparently changed completely, and he became known for his constant acts of charity and encouragement to the poor, the old, and those in prison. Now an active member of the church, he was elected an usher less than a year later and became both chairman of foreign missions and church clerk in 1883. The latter position he held until December 1884, when he organized the church's second mission church (the first was Raleigh's Tabernacle Baptist, formed in 1874) as the Third Baptist Church on South Fayetteville Street near the railroad crossing.

The new church, called by Senator Josiah W. Bailey "the happiest spot in Raleigh" because "the poor felt at home there in a degree that they could not feel in any other," relocated in 1892 to the corner of South and Fayetteville streets. It was then renamed the Fayetteville Street Baptist Church, although among Raleigh citizens it was almost universally called "John Pullen's church." He served on its first board of deacons, was superintendent of the Sunday school for the rest of his life, and, especially during intervals between regular pastors, served as lay preacher. At least once he personally paid a sizable remainder of the building debt. Immediately after his death, the congregation voted unanimously to change the name to the Pullen Memorial Baptist Church.

Similarly, when "John Pullen's bank" was mentioned, most residents of Raleigh knew the reference was to the Raleigh Savings Bank, organized in the mid-1880s, of which Pullen was the first cashier and eventually (ca. 1900) president. Josephus Daniels marveled, "He devoted more time to going into the homes of the very poor and the submerged and the wicked than to his bank. He never thought that his religion was helping the bank, but people had such confidence in him that widows and many others who had a few pennies they wished to save, would deposit their money in 'John Pullen's bank.'" A close friend, Dr. Clarence Poe, called him "virtually a one-man Salvation Army," declaring that of all his friends Pullen was the one who "most nearly deserved to be called a saint."

For three decades Pullen taught and was in charge of regular Sunday school classes at Central Prison. During part of that time he issued a magazine-type publication that he sent to prisoners all over the United States. In 1893 he helped organize St. Luke's Circle, an organization that provided housing for elderly women. He paid the rent for a succession of residential buildings for the women until they acquired their own house on South Street, prior to the construction of St. Luke's Home. From 1899 to 1913 he was the "mainspring," wrote a local reporter, "for an annual New Year's Day dinner at his church" for "the old people of Raleigh." In his will he left funds for continuing "the annual Old Folks Dinner," a bequest of $3,000 to St. Luke's Home, and another sum to provide "a weekly supper for the old ladies [there] such as I have been accustomed to have with them."

Pullen left a thousand dollars with his friend Livingston Johnson "to be used by him in giving away little books of the Bible." These, and small picture cards containing verses of scripture, Pullen was seen constantly to be handing to children, for whom his pockets also always bulged with candy and other treats. He was among the earliest contributors to the Methodist Orphanage in Raleigh at the time of its 1899 opening, and he was on a local chamber of commerce committee to raise funds for its support. Provision for the Methodist Orphanage and for the Thomasville Orphanage was made in his will.

Also provided for was Meredith College, with which he was associated from the time of its construction on the site that had been his home. He was among those who gave chapel talks, and he was a trustee from 1901 until his death, serving also as treasurer of the board. He personally underwrote tuition costs for some disadvantaged students and frequently visited the parlor and dining room of "the Club," a special self-help dormitory, after bringing "a treat of shad, steak, oysters, or chickens, with ice cream for dessert," according to one early alumna. "Kind Mr. Pullen" also provided money for carpeting their hall and stairway and lighting their parlor with gas.

Rex Hospital also benefited from his largesse. One of his last direct monetary gifts was made to its nurses' home and a sizable bequest was included in his will.

In the late 1890s Pullen helped organize a mission Sunday school in the village near Caraleigh Cotton Mills that developed into the Caraleigh Baptist Church, constituted in 1904. He was for some years a member of the home missions board of the Baptist State Convention. In addition to delivering sermons as a lay preacher, he was the author of several published commentaries on scripture, including *What Saith the Scripture?* and *Scripture Comments* (1900), and *Prayer and Its Answers from the Word of God*; the latter two works were reprinted in several editions by Clarence E. Mitchell, publisher, in the 1920s and 1930s.

For the last years of his life Pullen resided in the home of his niece and her husband, Kate Belvin and John William Harden, at 1519 Hillsborough Street, where he died after a short illness. On the day of his funeral at "his" church and his burial in Oakwood Cemetery, the banks and many local stores closed, factories shut down and silenced their whistles so that workers could attend the services, the Seaboard Railroad shops closed at noon to permit workmen to be present, and the state penitentiary permitted a representative group of prisoners to lay a wreath on his coffin. Three special streetcars transported children from all the Sunday schools of the city to the cemetery. The *Raleigh Times* and the *News and Observer* printed special articles about "the best loved citizen in Raleigh" every day for the unprecedented period of nearly two weeks. The Raleigh Baptist Association and the State Baptist Convention later published resolutions of tribute. A prominent member of the predominantly black First Baptist Church, Wilmington Street, Spanish-American War colonel James H. Young, noted that "the colored people, as well as his own race, [had] received unbounded favor and encouragement at [Pullen's] hands" and that he was "the friend of all people." A fellow banker and civic leader, Joseph G. Brown, recommended for his tombstone inscription, "Here lies John Pullen, who loved everybody and whom everybody loved." A local editorial declared, "Raleigh may not have had her greatest or wealthiest man as yet but she has had her best man."

SEE: W. P. Baker, "The First Forty-Five Years of Pullen Memorial Baptist Church" (manuscript, ca. 1947, Pullen Church Archives, Raleigh); Levi Branson, *Branson's North Carolina Business Directory, 1867–68, 1869, 1872*; Grady L. E. Carroll, *They Lived in Raleigh: Some Leading Personalities from 1792–1892* (1977); Hope Summerell Chamberlain, *History of Wake County* (1922); Josephus Daniels, *Editor in Politics* (1941); First Baptist Church, Raleigh, Minutes, November, December 1881 (Church Records, North Carolina State Archives, Raleigh); Alan DeLeon Gray, "The Social and Religious Contributions of the Methodist Orphanage, Raleigh, N.C., 1899–1940" (thesis, School of Religion, Duke University, Durham, 1941); Mary Lynch Johnson, *A History of Meredith College* (2d ed., 1972); Clarence Poe, *My First Eighty Years* (1963); Pullen family lot, Oakwood Cemetery, Raleigh; Raleigh city directories, 1875–76 through 1913; Raleigh *News and Observer*, 16 Nov. 1887, 1 Sept. 1888, 25 June 1895, 2–13 May 1913, 11 Jan. 1976; Raleigh *North Carolina Standard* (weekly), 18 Mar. 1863; Raleigh *Register* (semiweekly), 15 Sept. 1860; *Raleigh Times*, 1 Jan., 2–13 May 1913; Wake County Court Minutes and Wake County Estates Papers (North Carolina State Archives, Raleigh); Wake County Will Books (Wake County Court House, Raleigh).

ELIZABETH DAVIS REID MURRAY

Pullen, Richard Stanhope *(22 Sept. 1822–23 June 1895)*, businessman and philanthropist, was born on the modest plantation of his father, Turner Pullen, near Neuse Station, Wake County. His mother, Elizabeth Smith Pullen, was the sister of Richard and Benjamin Smith, prominent merchants in Raleigh's infant years. Nothing is known of his early life and education, for Stanhope Pullen (he preferred his middle name) diligently avoided conversations about himself. Presumably he received some schooling in local academies, but the keen business sense he exhibited as an adult appears to have come from his association with his uncle, Richard Smith.

In 1850 Pullen listed his occupation as merchant and seems to have been employed by Richard Smith, even though he continued to reside on his father's plantation a few miles north of Raleigh. Two years later his uncle died leaving his aunt, Penelope Smith, a comfortable estate but one encumbered with complex business arrangements. With no sons to turn to, Penelope prevailed upon her nephew, who moved to Raleigh and assumed control of her financial matters. Out of love and respect for his aunt and deceased uncle, Stanhope Pullen refused any wages for his services. Through the dark days of the Civil War and the financial woes of Reconstruction, he managed to hold the Smith fortune intact. Penelope Smith planned to reward her nephew with a cash bonus of $4,000 upon her death, but a family dispute erupted when her daughter and primary heir, Mary Jones (widow of Kimbrough Jones) entered into a contract to marry James T. Morehead. Horrified by the idea that Morehead would acquire any part of her estate, she changed her will in 1868 leaving nearly everything to her "faithful agent and friend Richard Stanhope Pullen who has served me very faithfully . . . and relieved me from many annoyances and troubles in my old age." From the bitterness of a family quarrel, Pullen emerged a wealthy man, a condition he turned to maximum advantage during the next quarter century.

Some years before a general prosperity returned to North Carolina, Pullen invested his available cash in Raleigh real estate. He followed a practice of developing neighborhoods by purchasing large squares of property, cutting streets through, and then donating the streets to the city. That approach allowed faster development than waiting for the city to buy or condemn land for roadways. Two of his most prominent neighborhoods included the fashionable residences along North Blount Street and along Elm Street in Oakwood, known for many years as "Pullentown." Other properties in and around Raleigh came into his possession, and by the early 1880s one could not travel very far in the capital without crossing land belonging to R. Stanhope Pullen.

Whether Pullen's great wealth activated his eccentricities or merely afforded him the luxury of indulging in them is difficult to say. His success lay in his initial evaluation of a business deal, for once he had made his investment, he never worried about profit or loss. Pullen detested the details of the business world and could never be prevailed upon to take the presidency or a seat on the board of directors of any corporation. By his own admission, he never lost, or intended to lose, a night's sleep over business. His personality was akin to that of an enlightened despot. To approach him for help often brought a stern rebuff, yet he always saw that his properties were kept in good repair. Complaining tenants quickly discovered that in a quiet and dignified manner the welcome mat had been withdrawn. Pullen's anonymous gifts to the poor and the needy were legendary, but the beggar who came to his door usually left in despair. Old acquaintances were often passed with no sign of recognition only to be greeted with great cordiality upon the next encounter. To those who knew him, "it was Mr. Pullen's way."

A kind and gentle man himself, Pullen was not one to tolerate inconsideration by others, particularly if he were the object of rudeness. On one occasion, a neighbor's dog persisted in moonlight serenades that kept Pullen from his slumber. Peaceful remonstrances to the cur's master failed, so he sought out the owner of the property, purchased his neighbor's house, and issued an ultimatum: the dog or the man had to go. When asked what had happened, Pullen wryly replied, "the tenant is still there, but the dog has changed his mind and decided to move."

While use of his wealth for the benefit of others gave him pleasure, Stanhope Pullen neither expected nor wanted overt expressions of appreciation for his gifts. Basically a shy man, he seemed embarrassed by such displays of emotion. In 1887, when he donated eighty acres to the city of Raleigh for a public park, he considered it gratuitous nonsense that it should be named in his honor. When he gave sixty acres of adjoining land for the North Carolina College of Agriculture and Mechanic Arts (now North Carolina State University), he was more careful. Approached by a delegation from the college and asked for a portrait to hang as a token of appreciation, Pullen, with a gleam in his eye, smiled and said pleasantly, "Well, they'll never get it. Good morning." So far as is known, he never allowed a portrait, photograph, or sketch of himself to be made. The college had to wait until Pullen's death to honor its benefactor through the construction of Pullen Hall.

Stanhope Pullen never married, but he was deeply concerned about young people, especially their education. Among his many charitable donations were timely gifts for Peace Institute (now Peace College) and the State College for Women at Greensboro (now the University of North Carolina at Greensboro). For many years his closest companion was a former slave named Washington Ligon, who worked as Pullen's man servant and handyman. Many years ago, old-timers in Raleigh recalled seeing "Old Wash" walking alongside his patron as they surveyed Pullen's estates. Periodically the stately gentleman would stop, point his gold headed cane, and "Old Wash" would dutifully mark the spot for a shrub or sapling. In the late 1880s Pullen arranged for his companion to purchase some property in the Method area near Raleigh, where he spent his remaining days. "Old Wash" died in 1893, two years before his benefactor and friend.

About fifteen years before his death Pullen affiliated with the Edenton Street Methodist Church, whose new structure he had helped to build. True to his character, he refused to be pressured into making a donation to the building fund, but when money ran out he simply inquired as to the balance necessary and wrote his check. Pullen remained a communicant of the church for the remainder of his life.

Curiously, because he owned numerous houses in Raleigh, Pullen resided for years in downtown boarding houses. In 1883 he and his nephew, John T. Pullen, moved into a large house at 213 East Edenton Street. There he lived until 1891, when the site was taken for use by the Baptist Female University (now Meredith College), located on the corner of Blount and Edenton streets. Stanhope Pullen spent the last years of his life with his niece, Lizzie Pullen Belvin, wife of Charles Belvin. He died at her residence and was buried in the western section of Oakwood Cemetery between Oakwood Avenue and Polk Street. The *News and Observer*, 25 June 1895, commented in a moving eulogy that Pullen's philanthropy "will tell the story of the liberal gifts of a plain, honest, unpretentious man, who wanted in a practical way to give happiness and rest to his fellow citizens of this and unborn generations."

SEE: Samuel A. Ashe, ed., *Biographical History of North Carolina*, vol. 6 (1907); Kemp P. Battle, *The Early History of Raleigh* (1893); Hope Summerell Chamberlain, *History of Wake County, North Carolina* (1922); *Chataigne's Raleigh Directory, 1875–76*; Deeds, Estates Papers, Wills (North Carolina State Archives, Raleigh); *Raleigh: Capital of North Carolina* (1942); *Raleigh Directory, 1880–1891*; Raleigh *News and Observer*, 25 June 1895.

JERRY L. CROSS

Purcell, Clare *(17 Nov. 1884–8 Feb. 1964)*, Methodist clergyman, was born at Columbia, Ala., the son of William Henry and Mary Callen Purcell. His ancestors were from eastern North Carolina. He received his undergraduate degree from Birmingham-Southern College in 1916 and a diploma in theology and the bachelor of divinity degree from Vanderbilt University Divinity School. In 1918–19 he was chaplain of the 131st Infantry, U.S. Army, American Expeditionary Force. Ordained deacon by Bishop Elijah E. Hoss and elder by Bishop James H. McCoy, he was assigned to a series of churches in Alabama until elected a bishop of the Methodist Episcopal Church, South, in 1938 and assigned to supervise the North Carolina, western North Carolina, South Carolina, and upper South Carolina conferences. Over the years his assignments changed, but North Carolina was a part of them until 1948, when he was assigned solely to Alabama. He retired in 1956.

Bishop Purcell was chairman of the Commission on World Service and Finance, chairman of the Commission on General Headquarters of the Methodist church, and a member of the Commission on Unification of the Methodist Episcopal church, the Methodist Episcopal Church, South, and the Methodist Protestant church. He also was president of the Council of Bishops and a frequent contributor to church periodicals. Purcell was awarded honorary degrees by Birmingham-Southern College, the University of Alabama, Duke University, and Emory University.

In 1910 he married Ida West, and they became the parents of William Wood-Rowe, John Robert, and Ida Claire.

SEE: Elmer T. Clark, *An Album of Methodist History* (1952 [portrait]) and *Methodism in Western North Carolina* (1966); C. Franklin Grill, *Methodism in the Upper Cape Fear Valley* (1966); *North Carolina Christian Advocate*, 20 Feb. 1964; *Who's Who in America*, vol. 26 (1950).

GRADY L. E. CARROLL

Purdie, Thomas J[ames?] *(22 June 1830–3 May 1863)*, Confederate officer, was born at Purdie Hall on the Cape Fear River in Bladen County, between Fayetteville and Elizabethtown, the second son of James B. (d. 1834) and Anna Maria Smith Purdie. His birthplace, a two-story brick Georgian-style house, still standing in 1992, was built by his grandfather. Little is known of his early life except in a few local accounts, such as a neighbor's diaries, indicating that he was a quiet, well-respected young man who collected books and helped tend his family's vast landholdings on both sides of the river. Family papers mention a special room for his library in a home he built for himself about 1855, several hundred yards upriver from Purdie Hall. This house, where he lived only a few years, was willed to his sister, Eliza Jane, who subsequently married William C. Dunham. The 1860 census reveals that Purdie was among the wealthiest men in the county.

Although Purdie appears not to have been mustering with the local militia, the Bladen Guards, he enlisted as a private in May 1861. The militia was called into state service at Wilmington on 15 June 1861 as Company K,

Eighth North Carolina Volunteers, and sent to nearby Camp Wyatt for training and outfitting. As a measure of the confidence he inspired and the leadership he displayed, Purdie was soon elected captain of the company. Following several promotions, he was a colonel by the end of 1862 and the Eighth Regiment had been redesignated the Eighteenth. With Purdie in command, it was attached to James H. Lane's Fourth Brigade under General Thomas J. (Stonewall) Jackson. The Eighteenth was sent by rail to Virginia in May 1862 and within a month became a part of Jackson's "foot cavalry."

In surviving Confederate records, Purdie is mentioned many times for his acts of courage and leadership. He was wounded at least twice, the last time fatally leading his regiment with saber drawn in its second predawn charge against a breastwork of twenty-eight Union cannons on Fairview Heights at Chancellorsville on 3 May 1863. Reports indicate that he was struck in the forehead from about seventy yards by a minié ball. Northern troops, momentarily retaking their position, stripped him of his revolver and braided officer's coat. Purdie's men recovered his body and saber in a third charge, however, which permanently captured the position. His body went by rail from Richmond to Wilmington and from there by steamer to his family's home.

As regimental commander of the Eighteenth, Purdie thought that his position was under attack by Union cavalry on the night of 2 May 1863 at the Battle of Chancellorsville, Va., when he issued orders directly resulting in the mistaken shooting of his own general, Stonewall Jackson. An account of the tragic error was written by Captain Alfred H. H. Tolar, who was commanding Purdie's old Company K of Bladen Guards.

"Under the circumstances, it would have been utterly impossible for anyone to know who fired the fatal bullet or bullets," Tolar wrote. "That the wounds were from the firing line of the 18th N.C. Troops, officers and men of that regiment will testify with regret. . . . Gen. Jackson and staff, accompanied by Gen. [A. P.] Hill and staff, rode down the turnpike in [front] of our line of battle, and coming closer to the enemy's lines than expected, were fired on from a regiment of [Union] infantry; and then some batteries of artillery turned loose with a heavy firing; sending shot and shell down the pike. The general and staff left the road and the two generals [Jackson and Hill] with staffs and couriers, came down on the 18th at a rapid gait. The night was calm and the tramp of horsemen advancing through a heavy forest at a rapid gait seemed to the average infantryman like a brigade of cavalry. Noting the approach of horsemen from the front and having been advised that the enemy was in front, with no line of pickets intervening to give the alarm [incorrect intelligence, since the Thirty-third North Carolina had been sent forward, unknown to the Eighteenth, as skirmishers at the end of a heated and often disarrayed all-day advance], the brave Col. Purdie gave the order, 'Fix bayonets, load, prepare for action!' as fast as the command could be given. When the supposed enemy was within 100 yards, perhaps, of our line, the colonel gave the command, 'Commence firing,' and from that moment on until notified by Maj. Harris [or Holland] of Gen. Jackson's staff that we were firing into our own men, the firing was kept up by the entire regiment with great rapidity. The horse of Maj. Holland [or Harris] was knocked down with a blow from the butt of a gun in the hands of Arthur S. Smith, Co. K, 18th N.C. Troops, and at that moment we were notified by the major of the sad mistake that had been made."

Concerning Purdie's execution of command in the heat of battle, there can be no doubt from available records that he was very competent. On 12 July 1862, after the battles of Mechanicsville and Malvern Hill, not long before Purdie took full command of the Eighteenth, Col. Robert H. Cowan wrote: "Where all behaved well it is difficult to make distinctions . . . still I desire to make special mention of my lieutenant-colonel, Thomas J. Purdie. He was everywhere in the thickest of the fight, cool and courageous, encouraging the men and directing them in their duty. His services were invaluable."

"I cannot speak in too high terms of the gallantry of Col. T. J. Purdie, [who] was slightly wounded," Brig. Gen. James H. Lane wrote in a 23 Dec. 1862 report to General Hill. Following Purdie's and Jackson's deaths, Lane wrote on 11 May 1863: "Never have I seen men fight more gallantly or bear fatigue and hardship more cheerfully. I shall always be proud of the noble bearing of my brigade in the Battle of Chancellorsville—the bloodiest in which it has ever taken part, where the 18th and 28th [North Carolina Troops] gallantly repulsed two night attacks made by vastly superior numbers. . . . Its gallantry has cost it many noble sacrifices and we are called upon to mourn the loss of . . . the gentle, but gallant and fearless Col. Purdie [who] was killed while urging forward his men."

One who attended Purdie's funeral paid tribute to him in the *North Carolina Presbyterian*: "Thinking it wrong for the gallant dead to pass away . . . when their deeds, founded in virtue, have merited the highest honors, I send you a brief history of the gallant Col. Thomas J. Purdie. 'One good deed dying tongueless murders a thousand that wait upon that.' The reticence natural to him concealed many latent virtues. . . . His benevolence was of the most unselfish kind, and he spared no pains to make all around him contented and happy. All the members of the 18th N.C. Troops will testify to his kindness, and at late hours of the night he would visit the tents to quell any disorder; his powers of persuasion were so great that he seldom had to use harsh means to bring a soldier to his duty."

Following a funeral service at Purdie Methodist Church near his home, Colonel Purdie, thirty-three and never married, was buried in the family cemetery on 10 May 1863, the same day that General Jackson died of complications from his wounds. Purdie's mother was still living at the time.

SEE: Bladen County Court Records (North Carolina State Archives, Raleigh); Lenoir Chambers, *Stonewall Jackson*, vol. 2 (1959); Walter Clark, ed., *Histories of the Several Regiments and Battalions from North Carolina*, vol. 2 (1901); Louis H. Manarin, comp., *North Carolina Troops, 1861–1865: A Roster*, vol. 1 (1966); *North Carolina Presbyterian*, 30 May 1863; *War of the Rebellion: A Compilation of the Official Records of the Union and Confederate Armies*, ser. 1, vols. 11, pt. 2 (1884), 12, pt. 2 (1885), 19, pt. 1 (1887), 21 (1888), 25, pt. 1 (1889).

JAMES L. PATE, JR.

Purefoy, James Simpson *(19 Feb. 1813–30 Mar. 1889)*, merchant and Baptist clergyman, was the youngest of three sons of the Reverend John and Mary Fort Purefoy near Forestville, Wake County. His paternal great-grandfather, Nicholas Purefoy, a French Huguenot refugee, had settled in Craven County following the revocation of the Edict of Nantes.

While little is known of Purefoy's boyhood, he appears to have received limited formal education. Yet he was an avid reader and able writer, as evidenced by the numerous letters and other communications that he contributed to the *Biblical Recorder*—the Raleigh weekly published under the auspices of the Baptist denomination. Moreover, he had acquired early habits of thrift, industry, and sound business management which he utilized to good advantage in succeeding years. His financial success as farmer and merchant enabled him to contribute liberally to various benevolent causes, while amassing a considerable estate that he bequeathed to his children and grandchildren. He retired from active involvement in the mercantile business in 1873, although maintaining a considerable interest in business affairs until the end of his life.

Purefoy joined the Wake Union Baptist Church, of which his father was pastor, in 1834. Thereafter, he displayed a keen interest in the affairs of the Baptist denomination. Ordained to the work of the gospel ministry on 1 Mar. 1842, he served throughout the succeeding years as pastor of churches in Wake, Granville, Franklin, and Warren counties, including Tabb's Creek (1842–47), Wake Union (1846–50, 1851–58, and 1862–63), Corinth (1849–73 and 1875–76), Perry's Chapel (1860–67), Enon (1869–71), Sharon (1861–62, 1868–69, and 1873), Brassfields (1871–75), and Stoney Hill (1886–89). His reports as historian for the Central Baptist Association (1876–88) contain a wealth of data regarding various individuals and churches of the region. He was a charter member of the North Carolina Baptist Historical Society and its first president (1885–88). The financial affairs of the Baptist State Convention were entrusted to him when he served as treasurer from 1842 to 1870.

It was through his connections with Wake Forest College as trustee, financial agent, and benefactor, however, that Purefoy accomplished his most significant work. As treasurer of the board of trustees, he exercised unusually sound judgment with his investments on behalf of the college. During the early years of the Civil War, he saved the institution from later bankruptcy by withholding a sizable portion of monies from investment in Confederate bonds. His work as financial agent prior to the war was instrumental in enabling the institution to erase a considerable indebtedness and to begin building a general endowment. He traveled throughout the Middle Atlantic and New England states during much of 1874–76, securing pledges of some $10,000 for the endowment. After 29 Apr. 1874, reports on the progress of this campaign—together with Purefoy's observations on the civic, cultural, political, and religious conditions of the regions he canvassed—were published almost weekly in the *Biblical Recorder*. A liberal financial supporter of Wake Forest throughout his life, he bequeathed an additional sum of $1,000 to the institution upon his death.

In December 1831 Purefoy married Mary Ransom Fort, the daughter of Foster Fort of Wake County. They became the parents of Addison Foster, Frederick Marion, Edgar Justin, John Knox, Emma E. (m. Phillip W. Johnson), and Isabella James (m. William Oscar Allen).

A portrait of Purefoy hangs in the reading room of the Ethel Taylor Crittenden Collection in Baptist History, Wake Forest University. He was buried in the town cemetery at Wake Forest.

SEE: George W. Paschal, *History of Wake Forest College*, vols. 1 (1935), 2–3 (1943); James S. Purefoy Papers (Ethel Taylor Crittenden Collection in Baptist History, Wake Forest University); Charles Elisha Taylor, "Life and Work of Elder James S. Purefoy," in *North Carolina Baptist Historical Papers* (July 1897); Wake County Deeds, Book B (Wake County Courthouse, Raleigh).

R. HARGUS TAYLOR

Purnell, Thomas Richard *(10 Aug. 1846–19 Dec. 1908)*, jurist, was born in Wilmington, the son of Thomas Richard and Eliza Ann Dudley Purnell. His grandparents were John and Sarah Purnell and Governor and Mrs. Edward B. Dudley. He was a great-grandson of the John Purnell who settled in North Carolina in 1780 and a descendant of John Haywood, one of the first settlers of Edgecombe County.

Purnell attended the Hillsborough Military Academy and at age sixteen enlisted in the Confederate army, serving as an orderly to General W. H. C. Whiting at Wilmington and later with a corps of topographical engineers in the Army of Northern Virginia. At the end of the war, he was paroled at Greensboro.

He was graduated from Trinity College with an A.B. degree in 1869 and an M.A. degree in 1872. After studying law under Robert Strange in Wilmington, he was admitted to the North Carolina bar in 1870. He practiced in Baltimore, Md., for a year and then in Salem, N.C., from 1871 to 1873.

Purnell had a long career in legal and public service in North Carolina. He was state librarian from 1873 to 1876, a state legislator in 1876–77, and a state senator in 1883–84. He ran for attorney general in 1892 and for solicitor of the Fourth Judicial District in 1894. From 1877 to 1897 he was commissioner of the U.S. Circuit Court of Appeals and an attorney in Raleigh. On 5 May 1897 he was appointed judge for the U.S. District Court in the Eastern District, where he served until his death.

On 11 Nov. 1870 he married Adelia E. Zevely, of Salem, the daughter of Dr. Alexander T. and Lucinda Blum Zevely. They were the parents of three daughters and a son. His funeral was held at the Episcopal Church of the Good Shepherd in Raleigh.

SEE: Harold Chase and others, comp. *Biographical Dictionary of the Federal Judiciary* (1976); Clement A. Evans, *Confederate Military History*, vol. 4 (1899); Raleigh *News and Observer*, 20 Dec. 1908; Harry Skinner, "Memorial to Thomas R. Purnell," *North Carolina Bar Association Proceedings* (1909); *Who Was Who in America* (1943).

ROSAMOND PUTZEL

Purviance, David *(14 Nov. 1766–19 Aug. 1847)*, minister, legislator, and church leader, was born in Iredell County, the son of John and Jane Wasson Purviance, but lived most of his adult life in Kentucky and Ohio. His father, known as "Colonel Purviance" in honor of military service in the Revolutionary War, had migrated from Pennsylvania to North Carolina in 1764 and was a justice of the peace. David Purviance attended an academy near Statesville run by the Reverend James Hall, a Presbyterian, but his stay at this school, popularly known as "Clio's Nursery," was disrupted during the Revolution by his failing health and the need for him to be at home. After the war he taught school for a while and worked in the town clerk's office in Salisbury. In 1789 he married Mary Ireland and two years later moved to Sumner County, Tenn. Because of Indian attacks in the area, during one of which his younger brother was killed, he moved again in 1792, this time to Bourbon County, Ky., where he began farming.

In 1797 Purviance was elected to the Kentucky legislature, where he served several terms, but was not elected as a delegate to the constitutional convention in 1799 because he opposed slavery and advocated gradual emancipation. As a member of the Cane Ridge Presbyterian Church he was deeply moved by the religious revival that began in the area in 1800. In 1804 he joined a group of ministers and laymen that withdrew from the Presbyterian church because they could not accept certain doctrines, especially predestination. Renouncing all creeds except the Bible, they adopted the name "Christian" and soon developed a new denomination known simply as the Christian church.

Purviance migrated to New Paris, Ohio, in 1807, where he established a church of this new denomination and served as its pastor for most of the rest of his life. He was first elected to the Ohio legislature in 1809, serving as state representative for one year and as state senator for six years (1810–16); he was again elected state representative in 1826. He worked to have a state penitentiary established, opposed laws restricting the rights of free blacks in Ohio, and supported the effort to have Miami University located at Oxford, Ohio, serving this institution as one of its trustees. In the 1840s he supported the Washingtonian temperance reform movement. He died and was buried near his home in New Paris, Ohio.

SEE: *DAB*, vol. 8 (1935); Robert Davidson, *History of the Presbyterian Church of Kentucky* (1847); Milo T. Morrill, *A History of the Christian Denomination in America, 1794–1911* (1912); Levi Purviance, *The Biography of Elder David Purviance* (1848); J. R. Rogers, *The Cane Ridge Meeting-house* (1910).

JOHN B. WEAVER

Purviance, Samuel Densmore *(7 Jan. 1774–ca. 1806)*, lawyer, state legislator, and congressman, was born at his family's home, Castle Fin House on Masonboro Sound, New Hanover County, near Wilmington, one of five children of Colonel William and Eleanor Purviance. In about 1754 William Purviance and two brothers, Samuel Densmore and Robert, had migrated to America from Ireland. William Settled in New Hanover County and his brothers in Baltimore, Md. They were grandsons of Jacques de Purviance, of Royan, Saintonge, France, a Huguenot who fled after the revocation of the Edict of Nantes in 1685 and settled in Ireland near the village of Castle Finn in County Donegal, Ulster.

Samuel D. Purviance was educated in a private school and later studied law. In January 1795 he was admitted to the bar by the Cumberland County Court and began to practice in Fayetteville. As the owner of a plantation on the west side of the Cape Fear River below Fayetteville, he also engaged in farming. In 1798 Purviance was elected to the North Carolina House of Commons, serving also in 1799. He won a seat in the state senate in 1801 and remained for one term. As a Federalist he was elected to the Eighth U.S. Congress, where he also served a single term in the House of Representatives from 1803 to 1805.

The exact circumstances of his death are not known. According to a letter written in 1859 by his son, Henry E., he died "somewhere on the Red River, Arkansas, about 1806 or 7."

In about 1792 he married Mary Brownlow (1775–23 Jan. 1801), daughter of John and Rebecca Evans Brownlow, of Fayetteville. They had four children: Julia Brownlow (died in infancy), Harry Edward (b. 19 Mar. 1794), Catherine Eleanor (b. 1796, m. Lawrence Fitzharris), and Mary (b. 1801, m. William Tams) of Philadelphia.

SEE: *Biog. Dir. Am. Cong.* (1961); Cumberland County Wills and Court Minutes (North Carolina State Archives, Raleigh); Genealogical information in the files of Mrs. Ida B. Kellam, Wilmington.

WILLIAM C. FIELDS

Puryear, Richard Clanselle *(9 Feb. 1801–30 July 1867)*, planter and congressman, was born in Mecklenburg, Va., the son of Richard and Sarah Shepherd Clanselle Puryear, both of French ancestry. About 1811 the family moved near Brookstown in Forsyth County, N.C., and began farming. The father died shortly afterwards, but young Richard received a good education, probably at home. He at first began studying medicine but soon afterwards determined to become a planter. He bought two tracts of land totaling 700 acres in Yadkin (now Surry) County and chose to reside on his estate, Shallowford, near Huntsville. Puryear became moderately successful; the census of 1860 listed him as owning thirty-two slaves and real estate worth $56,000.

Locally, Puryear served as a colonel in the state militia and as county magistrate. In 1838, 1844, 1846, and 1852 he was elected to represent Surry County in the House of Commons, and in 1840 he was sent to the state senate. The legislative journals show him to have been a dependable though unassertive legislator; nevertheless, his five terms of faithful attention to local problems seem to have entrenched him politically, for in March 1853 he went to the U.S. House of Representatives as a Whig. He was returned in 1854 but lost his bid for a third term because of his "unsoundness" on Southern rights in general and his opposition to the pro-South Kansas-Nebraska Act in particular.

During the secession crisis of 1860–61 Puryear favored the Union until Lincoln's call for troops to quell the Southern "rebellion" alienated almost all North Carolina Unionists. After secession a caucus of former Unionists, of which he was a prominent member, secured Puryear's election by the secession convention as a delegate to the Confederate Provisional Congress. During his year in this capacity he did little but attend and vote regularly. He obviously disliked the idea of national taxation, for he voted consistently for lower taxes and more exemptions. Otherwise he should be considered a strong supporter of the other war measures coming before Congress. He did not seek reelection, possibly because he felt that for the sake of victory the Confederate leadership would be willing to "build up a Monarchy upon the remains of our glorious Republic." After the war Puryear was a delegate to the Peace Congress in Philadelphia. At home he continued his planting activities until his death. He was buried in the family cemetery at Shallowford.

On 21 Nov. 1835 Puryear married Elizabeth Ann Clingman, daughter of Jacob and Jane Poindexter Clingman and sister of Thomas L. Clingman, whose ancestors had lived in Yadkin County since before the American Revolution. Their children were Jane Amanda, Sarah Ellen, Henry Shepherd, Elizabeth Patillo, Richard Clingman, and Thomas Lanier. The family was Episcopalian. Puryear's contemporaries considered him to be "a man of strong personality" and the "personification of what is peculiar and best in the character of a North Carolina gentleman of the old school."

SEE: *Biog. Dir. Am. Cong.* (1961); John L. Cheney, Jr., ed., *North Carolina Government, 1585–1979* (1981); Clingman-Puryear Papers (Southern Historical Collection, University of North Carolina, Chapel Hill); *Congressional Globe* (1853–57); *Journal of the Confederate Congress* (1904–5); *Journal of the Convention of 1861* (1861); *North Carolina House and Senate Journals* (1838–52); Z. V. Walser Papers (Southern Historical Collection, University of North Carolina, Chapel Hill [portrait]).

BUCK YEARNS

Pusey, Edwin Davis *(6 Jan. 1870–4 Jan. 1953)*, educator, was born at Princess Anne, Md., the son of Edwin and Katherine Ellen Davis Pusey. Tutored privately as a child, he entered Washington Academy, Princess Anne, in 1880 and after six years enrolled at St. John's College, Annapolis, from which he was graduated at age nineteen. He taught Latin and geography in Lancaster, Pa., for a year before returning to St. John's College, where he taught Latin and German (1890–1902). While there he earned a master's degree in classical languages (1892) and from Columbia University in New York he received a master's degree in education (1894). Between 1902 and 1924 he was principal of a high school and then superintendent of city schools in Laurinburg, Goldsboro, and Durham, in turn. He also taught education at The University of North Carolina during some summer terms. In 1919 St. John's College awarded him an honorary doctor of laws degree.

Leaving North Carolina, he taught briefly at Winthrop College in South Carolina and at the University of Georgia (1925–45), where he also became a dean. During his professional career Pusey was active in numerous educational organizations and was often elected to positions of leadership, particularly with the Southern Association of Colleges and Secondary Schools. He was editor of the *High School Quarterly* for a period and afterwards of *School and College*. While superintendent of city school systems in North Carolina, he worked to improve teaching standards, stressed the need for uniform school laws, and rendered special assistance to the Textbook Commission. While he was head of the Durham city schools he developed and published a model course of study that attracted considerable attention. In Georgia he drafted several school laws for the state.

During the Spanish-American War Pusey was a captain of infantry. An active Episcopalian, he served at both the parish and national levels. Over six feet tall and weighing around 230 pounds, he was a commanding figure and a popular public speaker, particularly on education and religion. He married Anita Mary Southgate and they had one daughter, Frances Southgate. After his wife's death he married Mrs. Bessie Payne Turner on 24 Aug. 1926.

SEE: *Athens Banner-Herald* (5 Jan. 1953); R. P. Brooks, *The University of Georgia under Sixteen Administrations, 1785–1955* (1956); *Who Was Who in America*, vol. 5 (1973).

C. SYLVESTER GREEN

Pyle, John *(8 Apr. 1723–1 Jan. 1804)*, was noted for his Loyalist activities during the American Revolution, which culminated in the massacre of a group of volunteers under his command by forces of Henry Lee and Andrew Pickens on 23 Feb. 1781. Pyle was born at Kennett in Chester County, Pa., the son of Dr. Samuel and Sarah Pyle. According to family tradition, he received his medical education in London prior to his marriage in June 1744 to Sarah Baldwin. About 1766 John and Sarah Pyle and their eight children migrated to North Carolina and settled in the Cane Creek community in Chatham County east of Snow Camp in modern Alamance County. Pyle soon became involved in the Regulator movement. The earliest evidence of his presence in North Carolina is a letter from Pyle to Colonel Edmund Fanning dated 17 Mar. 1766, in which Pyle apologized for publishing and spreading a "scandalous and Defaming" account of Fanning. Pyle signed a Regulator petition in August 1768 and in September the Hillsborough Superior Court failed to find a true bill against him when he was accused along with other Regulators of starting a riot.

In 1775 Pyle received a commission as colonel of Loyalist militia from Governor Josiah Martin and participated in the Moore's Creek campaign. Along with his son John, Jr., he was captured by the Patriots and imprisoned at Halifax. The Pyles and other prisoners whose presence in North Carolina endangered the Revolutionary movement were sent by the Provincial Congress to Virginia and Philadelphia. While being transported north, the Pyles escaped and returned to Chatham County. On 13 Dec. 1776 Pyle appeared before the North Carolina Provincial Congress, took an oath of loyalty to the state, and—upon giving bond—was permitted to return to his home.

In 1781 the proximity of Lord Cornwallis's army rekindled Pyle's Loyalist sentiments. In January and February of 1781 he raised three or four hundred Loyalists between Haw and Deep rivers and sent Cornwallis a request for an escort to Hillsborough. Cornwallis detached Banastre Tarleton with his cavalry and a small body of infantry with instructions to rendezvous with Pyle at a plantation a few miles from Hillsborough. On the afternoon of 23 Feb. 1781 Pyle's force was interrupted by the Continental cavalry of Henry Lee and militia commanded by Andrew Pickens as they were moving towards Hillsborough on the "Great Road" in the southern part of present Alamance County. Lee and Pickens had recrossed the Dan from Greene's base in Virginia. The Loyalists mistook Lee's legion, clad in short green jackets and plumed helmets, for Tarleton's dragoons, who wore similar attire. Lee, taking advantage of the deception, requested Pyle to move his force to the side of the narrow road and allow Lee's fatigued troops to pass. There are conflicting accounts of how the fighting began in the rear of Lee's column. Strong primary evidence indicates that Lee intended to bypass Pyle's force in order to surprise Tarleton, encamped two or three miles beyond. Once the deception was discovered, an orderly surrender was impossible and in ten minutes the battle was over. Casualty figures document only one casualty—a horse—but ninety-three bodies remained on the battlefield the next morning. Certainly many more dead and wounded were carried away by friends. According to local legend, John Pyle, badly injured, crawled into a nearby pond, where he concealed himself until rescued by friends. After recovering from his wounds, Pyle and his son surrendered to the local militia. Pyle earned the gratitude of the Whig militia by caring for their wounded. His property was saved from confiscation the following November when he was found not guilty of treason in the Chatham County court.

After the Revolution John Pyle returned to his farm and medical practice in the Cane Creek community. His will, dated 13 Jan. 1799, names eight children and indicates that his wife had died prior to the will.

SEE: Chatham County Court Minutes; Walter D. Clark, ed., *State Records of North Carolina*, vols. 10, 17–18, 22 (1895–1905); Lela Livingston, *Pyle Family History, 1594–1954* (no date); William S. Powell, James K. Huhta, and Thomas J. Farnham, *The Regulators in North Carolina: A Documentary History, 1759–1776* (1971); Carl Homer Pyle, *Colonel John Pyle and His People* (1970); George Troxler, *Pyle's Massacre, February 23, 1781* (1973).

GEORGE W. TROXLER

Quince, Parker *(12 Dec. 1743–1785)*, merchant, was the second son of Richard Quince and his wife, Mary. Richard emigrated from Ramsgate, England, to the Cape Fear about 1740, and became one of the leading merchants of Brunswick. He was justice of the peace of Brunswick County, churchwarden and vestryman of St. Philip's Parish, commissioner of the town of Brunswick, commissioner of pilotage for the Cape Fear River, and member of the safety committees of Brunswick County and the Wilmington District. He refused an appointment as judge of the Admiralty Court at Brunswick for the state of North Carolina. Richard Quince, Jr., and John Quince, brothers of Parker, were also active in public affairs. Richard, Jr., a merchant in Brunswick, was a justice of the peace for Brunswick County, served on the Brunswick County safety committee, and was first major in the Brunswick County Regiment at the outset of the Revolution. John Quince, merchant in Wilmington, was coroner and justice of the peace of New Hanover County, town commissioner of Wilmington, and member of the Wilmington safety committee.

Parker Quince first engaged in the mercantile trade in partnership with his father and brothers as Richard Quince and Sons and later with his brother Richard and with former Bostonian William Hill (1737–83), whose family also came from Ramsgate. His business was based in Brunswick until the onset of the Revolution, when the devastation of that town forced him to move his operations to Wilmington. Although appointed a justice of the peace for Brunswick County in 1769, Quince apparently preferred the pursuit of business to public service. The approach of the Revolution forced a revisal of his priorities, however. After Parliament passed the Boston Port Act in 1774, legislation designed by the British to punish Bostonians for the Tea Party of 1773, Quince volunteered to send supplies to Boston in his ship, *Penelope*, which he personally accompanied. In April 1775 he represented the town of Brunswick in the Second Provincial Congress and last Royal Assembly. He was also a member of the Brunswick County safety committee. In August 1775 Quince represented the county in the Third Provincial Congress, which appointed him second major in the county's regiment. The Fourth Provincial Congress assigned Quince—among others—to procure firearms in Brunswick County for the use of American troops. In the Fifth Provincial Congress in 1776, he once again represented the town of Brunswick and was appointed collector for the port of Brunswick by the Congress. Legislation in 1778 and 1783 designated Quince a commissioner to regulate pilotage and navigation on the Cape Fear River.

Quince used the proceeds of his successful mercantile trade to acquire a large landed estate. His holdings included Rose Hill, a plantation on the Northeast Cape Fear River where he resided, three other plantations in the Cape Fear area, Oak Island, a house in Wilmington known as The Lodge, and additional lots in Wilmington and Brunswick. The site of his house at Brunswick has been excavated and the foundations are open at the State Historic Site. He owned 110 slaves at his death. The bondsmen plus his landed property made Quince one of the richest men in Brunswick County.

Membership in St. Philip's Church attested to his Anglican religious persuasion. On 27 Oct. 1767 Quince married fifteen-year-old Susanna Hasell (22 July 1752–28 Sept. 1813), daughter of James, Jr., and Sarah Wright Hasell. They had three children: Richard (28 Aug. 1769–1809), Mary Sarah Washington (23 Sept. 1776–1 Oct. 1819), and William Soranzo (15 Nov. 1780–3 July 1844), who changed his name to William Soranzo Hasell. Parker Quince went to England, probably late in 1784, and was residing in Ironmonger Lane, London, at his death early in 1785.

SEE: Samuel A. Ashe, ed., *Biographical History of North Carolina*, vol. 3 (1905); Brunswick County Deeds, Books A–B (Bolivia); Walter Clark, ed., *State Records of North Carolina*, vols. 11–25 (1895–1906); William E. Craig (Twain Harte, Calif.) to William S. Powell, 17 Apr. 1989; New Hanover County Deeds, Book C–H (Wilmington); William L. Saunders, ed., *Colonial Records of North Carolina*, vols. 6–10 (1888–90).

ALAN D. WATSON

Quince, Richard *(1714–July 1778)*, merchant, planter, and jurist, was one of the most earnest and zealous Patriots of the Cape Fear region during the American Revolution. Baptized on 30 Mar. 1714 at St. Lawrence's Church, Thanet, near Ramsgate, England, he was the son of Richard Quince[y] (1682–?) and Jane Parker (1686–1773) and scion of a long-established and well-connected merchant family of London and the Isle of Thanet whose name had usually been spelled Quincey. About 1740 he settled in Brunswick Town, N.C., and maintained his connection with his merchant brother in Ramsgate, John Quince (1716–1801). A marriage soon afterwards with Mary (probably the widow of Thomas Gibson) produced three sons: Richard, Jr., Parker, and John. When Spanish ships shelled Brunswick in September 1748, Quince was one of those whose property was damaged.

Quince quickly became a successful merchant, ultimately owning several ships that carried on extensive trade with the other mainland colonies and the West Indies. In addition to his commercial activities in Brunswick, he also engaged in merchandising in Wilmington, where he maintained a second home. Further, he became extensively involved in planting, acquiring in 1770 Orton Plantation, which he continued to plant until his death and which remained in the family through Richard, Jr., until 1796.

Though the elder Richard Quince was unquestionably one of the most successful merchants and planters along the colonial Cape Fear River, it is his career of public service for which he is chiefly remembered. As early as 1745 he was a commissioner of the town of Brunswick. Later, he served for many years as a justice of the superior court and a judge of the vice-admiralty court. In addition, he served his church well for many years as warden at St. Philip's, Brunswick.

Quince performed his greatest service during the Revolutionary period. During the Stamp Act crisis of 1765–66, he organized the Sons of Liberty in the town of Brunswick and played a major role in events there. In the 1770s he was the leading member of the town's Committee of Correspondence, designed to create Revolutionary sentiment against the British. In 1774, with the closing of the port of Boston following the Boston Tea Party, he joined his son Parker and many other Lower Cape Fear merchants and planters in furnishing aid for the relief of Boston.

With the coming of the Revolution, Quince joined his sons Richard and John as a member of the Brunswick Committee of Public Safety, of which he became chairman. He also sat on the Wilmington District Committee of Safety and became active in military preparations, arming merchant ships and providing money from his own resources for the purchase of munitions. He contributed greatly to the organizing of the militia of Brunswick County, whose regiment his sons Richard served as first major and Parker as second major.

Quince did not live to see the outcome of the Revolution; he was buried in the churchyard of St. Philip's Church adjoining his Orton Plantation. His sons Richard and Parker (John died in 1775) continued their efforts to see the cause through to a successful conclusion. Doubtless the greatest personal loss for all of them during the war was their beloved Brunswick town, burned by British soldiers and marauding Tories.

Quince's descendants married into the leading families of the Cape Fear—Davis, Hasell, Moore, and Walker—and they achieved personal success and contributed to the public weal for generations.

SEE: Samuel A. Ashe, ed., *Biographical History of North Carolina*, vol. 6 (1905); Bishop's Transcripts, 1681–1720, Kent County, England (Archives at Canterbury Cathedral); Robert J. Cain, ed., *Records of the Executive Council, 1735–1754* (1988); John Drury, *The Heritage of Early American Houses* (1969); E. Lawrence Lee, *The Lower Cape Fear in Colonial Days* (1965); Leora H. McEachern and Isabel M. Williams, eds., *Wilmington–New Hanover Safety Committee Minutes, 1774–1776* (1974); William L. Saunders, ed., *Colonial Records of North Carolina*, vol. 10 (1890); James Sprunt, *Chronicles of the Cape Fear River* (1916).

JAMES M. CLIFTON

Quince, William Soranzo. *See* **Hasell, William Soranzo.**

Quinn, Dwight Wilson *(12 Sept. 1917–27 Feb. 1992)*, businessman and longtime legislator, was born in York, S.C., the son of William Lytle and Lucy Wilson Quinn. After attending the public schools of Kannapolis, N.C., he enrolled in night and correspondence classes to study business law, bookkeeping, accounting, business management, textiles, and related subjects. In 1944–45 he was in the U.S. Army. After working for a time as a printer in Kannapolis, Quinn by the late 1950s had become a supervisor and by 1979 a textile executive with the Cannon Mills.

From 1951 until his retirement, Quinn served successive terms in the North Carolina General Assembly for thirty-six years. Among other legislative assignments, he was chairman of the finance committee and served on the appropriations subcommittee on education. He also was a member of the employment security, local government, state government, federal and interstate cooperation, manufacturers and labor, and other committees. Quinn was a member (1959–60) and chairman (1961–62) of the Governor's Commission on Reorganization of State Government. For a time he was chairman and a member of the executive committee of the trustees of Appalachian State University. A Democrat, he was a delegate to the Democratic National Convention in 1960 and 1968. He was Man of the Year in Kannapolis in 1948 and received the National Distinguished Service Award for Outstanding Community Service from the Amvets organization in 1953. A Rotarian, a Mason, and a Shriner, he was also a member of the Lutheran church. On 23 Feb. 1936 he married Marian Elizabeth Isenhour, and they became the parents of a daughter, Linda Jo. Dwight Quinn died in Atlanta while visiting his daughter and was buried in Kannapolis.

SEE: Stephen E. Massengill, comp., *Biographical Directory of the General Assembly of North Carolina, 1963–1978* (1979); *North Carolina Manual* (1977); Raleigh *News and Observer*, 28 Feb. 1992; *Who's Who in the South and Southwest*, vol. 6 (1959).

WILLIAM S. POWELL

Rabun, William *(8 Apr. 1771–24 Oct. 1819)*, planter, Baptist lay leader, legislator, state senator, and governor of Georgia, was born in Halifax County of Scottish-English ancestry, the son of Matthew and Sarah Warren Rabun. The parents, William, and four sisters moved to Wilkes County, Ga., in 1785, when William was fourteen. In 1786 the Rabun family moved to an area later known as Horeb Baptist Church, four miles south of Powellton, in Greene (later Hancock) County, Ga. William probably was educated at local academies in both North Carolina and Georgia, but it is also likely that he received most of his formal education at home.

William Rabun, like his father, became a planter and a prominent Baptist layman at age seventeen and remained so throughout his life. William Northen reports that "he was a man of fine physique, tall and large, with no surplus flesh. He had brown hair and blue eyes, with a countenance full of kindness." Hancock was the county of his continuing residence and eventual death and burial. He married Mary Battle on 21 Nov. 1793, and their children included a son, John William, and six daughters.

From 1802 to 1810 Rabun was a justice of the Inferior Court for Hancock County, and in 1805 and 1806 he won a seat in the Georgia House of Representatives. Beginning in 1810, he served six one-year terms in the Georgia Senate, of which he was president from 1812 to 1816. In 1812 his plantation consisted of five hundred acres and he owned fifteen slaves. On 4 Mar. 1817, at age forty-five, he became, as president of the senate, ex officio governor of Georgia when Governor David B. Mitchell resigned to accept the post of U.S. agent to the Creek Indians offered to him by President James Madison. In November 1817 Rabun was elected governor by the General Assembly with a vote of 62 to 57, defeating John Clark by 5 votes. He never lost an election.

Governor Rabun, who died a few days before his term was to expire, served for two years in a period of considerable prosperity for Georgia: funds were appropriated for schools, roads, canals, and other waterways; the penal code was revised; the state penitentiary was completed; and a steamboat company was chartered. Also during his governorship there was a notable exchange of correspondence between Rabun and General Andrew Jackson concerning an attack on Cheha, an Indian village. And according to James Z. Rabun in Coleman and Gurr's *Dictionary of Georgia Biography*, "The continued smuggling of slaves from Africa into inlets on the Georgia coast made Rabun indignant. He denounced it and was pleased when the American Colonization Society in 1818 agreed to return a shipload of captives to Africa."

After a brief illness identified only as "a malignant autumn fever," Rabun died at home and was buried privately on his estate four miles south of Powellton in Hancock County. At the request of the state legislature, he was publicly eulogized by the Reverend Jesse Mercer (Rabun's friend and Georgia's leading Baptist minister at the time) at the Baptist church in Milledgeville, then the state capital, on 24 Nov. 1819. Rabun County, Ga., was formed and named in 1819 in honor of Governor William Rabun.

SEE: John Spencer Bassett, ed., *Correspondence of Andrew Jackson*, vol. 2 (1926–35); Kenneth Coleman and Charles Stephen Gurr, eds., *Dictionary of Georgia Biography*, vol. 2 (1983); *History of the Baptist Denomination in Georgia: With Biographical Compendium and Portrait Gallery of Baptist Ministers and Other Georgia Baptists* (1881); William J. Northen, ed., *Men of Mark in Georgia*, vol. 2 (1910; reprint, 1974); William Rabun Papers (Georgia Department of Archives and History, Atlanta); Robert Sobel and John

Raimo, eds., *Biographical Directory of the Governors of the United States*, vol. 1 (1978).

DOUGLAS J. MCMILLAN

Ragan, George Washington *(16 Sept. 1846–9 June 1936)*, textile manufacturer, was born in Gaston County, the son of Daniel Franklin and Harriet Frances Glenn Ragan. Self-educated, he is said to have joined in May 1864 the Junior Reserves, which became Company C of the Seventy-first Regiment of Confederate Troops, and to have seen service in eastern North Carolina and Virginia. Returning to the family farm, he remained until his father's death in 1872, when he began operating a series of nearby community stores before moving to Gastonia as a merchant in 1880.

In 1885 Ragan entered into a mercantile partnership with George A. Gray in the community of Lowell but after a year he returned to Gastonia. In 1887 he joined a group of other men, including Gray, to organize the town's first cotton mill and in 1890 he joined a small group to establish a bank, of which he was president and director for two years. Resigning from the bank in 1893, he joined others in creating a second mill, the Trenton Cotton Mills; he became its treasurer and, in effect, the chief executive officer. The mill was a success, but Ragan sold his interest in 1899 to undertake the organization of an even larger mill. In 1900 the Arlington Cotton Mills were established to produce combed cotton yarn of the finest quality and capable of competing with yarn heretofore produced only in the North. Ragan also was involved with mills in Charlotte and engaged in the development of real estate in both Gastonia and Charlotte.

A Presbyterian, Ragan was a donor to Davidson College, to a college in Georgia, and to the Presbyterian Orphans Home at Barium Springs, N.C. He married, first, Amanda Zoe Reid in 1883, and they became the parents of three daughters, only one of whom survived infancy. Following the death of his wife in 1891, he married Bettie Gibson Caldwell, and they became the parents of two sons and four daughters.

SEE: Samuel A. Ashe, ed., *Biographical History of North Carolina*, vol. 8 (1917); *Charlotte Observer*, 12 June 1936; *Confederate Veteran* 35 (February, August 1927); *Gaston Gazette*, 15 Oct. 1980; *Gastonia Gazette*, 4 Apr. 1965; James R. Young, *Textile Leaders of the South* (1963).

G. S. SELPH

Rains, Gabriel James *(4 June 1803–6 Aug. 1881)*, career soldier, Confederate general, and inventor, was born in New Bern, Craven County, the elder son of Gabriel M. and Hester Ambrose Rains. His brother, George Washington Rains, founded the Confederate gunpowder mill at Augusta, Ga. After his early education, Gabriel Rains entered West Point Military Academy on 1 July 1822. Graduating thirteenth in his class on 1 July 1827, he became second lieutenant of the Seventh Infantry Regiment and saw service in the West, mainly Indian Territory. On 28 Jan. 1834 he became a first lieutenant and on 25 Dec. 1837 he was promoted to captain.

In 1839 Rains took part in the Seminole War in Florida. Commanding a company of men at Fort King, he first began to experiment with explosives. The Indians harassed and beleaguered the garrison to such an extent that Rains in desperation rigged a live shell hidden under a blanket in the woods near a pond where the Indians went to get water. Some Indians set off the trap and were killed. Rains soon set a similar trap and when it was heard to explode, led a party of men out to investigate. It was discovered that the bomb had done no harm but as the group returned to the fort it was attacked by about a hundred Indians. Rains skillfully handled his men, however, and the Indians were repulsed though Rains himself was shot through the body and so badly wounded that announcements of his death were published. Nevertheless, he recovered and was promoted to brevet major on 28 Apr. 1840 for gallantry and meritorious conduct in the attack.

Upon returning to duty Rains served at posts in Louisiana and Florida and in the military occupation of Texas. In the Mexican War in 1846 he gave the deciding vote in a council of officers at Fort Brown against capitulation to General Ampudia. Rains participated in the defense of the fort and in the Battle of Rasaca de la Palma. Afterwards he was detailed to recruiting duty, at which he was quite successful. In 1849–50 Rains fought in a second Seminole War, and on 9 Mar. 1851 he was promoted to major of the Fourth Infantry Regiment. Sent to California the following year, he earned a reputation as an Indian fighter and on 5 June 1860 was made lieutenant colonel of the Fifth Infantry Regiment.

At the outbreak of the Civil War Rains resigned his commission on 31 July 1861 and offered his services to the Confederacy. He was commissioned a colonel in the Regular Confederate Army and on 23 Sept. 1861 was appointed brigadier general from North Carolina to rank from the same date (confirmed 13 Dec. 1861). Rains was then assigned to command the First Division of General John Magruder's army defending the Department of the Peninsula, which consisted of the Thirteenth and Twenty-sixth Alabama regiments and the Sixth and Twenty-third regiments. This command later became a brigade of General D. H. Hill's division. Rains commanded at Yorktown during the winter of 1861–62 and here continued his experiments with mines. He developed a type of subterranean mine (called "torpedoes") patterned after a design by Samuel Colt, and these were placed at a salient angle and other points along the earthworks that were considered to be accessible to the enemy. Rains even put mines in the nearby waters of the York River to discourage enemy naval operations.

When George B. McClellan's Union army finally forced the evacuation of the Yorktown defenses at the beginning of May 1862, Rains's brigade constituted part of the rear guard as the Confederate army retreated towards Richmond. His men hungry and exhausted from constant Union pursuit, Rains found outside Williamsburg a broken-down ammunition chest that contained several artillery shells fitted with percussion fuses. He had these quickly buried in the road. Pursuing Union cavalry trod on the shells and detonated them, causing a few casualties. Union troops entering the abandoned defenses of Yorktown also set off some of the mines Rains had left behind in the earthworks, causing about thirty casualties. All in all these devices made pursuing Union forces act with caution, and both the Northern press and General McClellan bitterly denounced their use as an improper means of warfare. McClellan described it as "the most murderous and barbarous conduct in placing torpedoes," and the Northern papers carried stories of booby traps being placed in wells, around houses, in bags of flour, in carpetbags, and what not. General Joseph E. Johnston, the Confederate army commander, read some of the stories in these newspapers and asked for comment from Rains. Rains, of course, took credit for the mines left in the works and placed in the road but denied using booby traps.

General James Longstreet, Rains's wing commander, in writing out orders for Rains's brigade on 11 May 1862, requested that Rains not use any more mines because he did not recognize it as a "proper or effective method of war." But Rains protested and went over Longstreet's head to report to Secretary of War George W. Randolph. Rains defended his use of explosive devices as a means to discourage a night attack by an enemy, to defend a weak point of a line, to check enemy pursuit, and so forth. General Hill, Rains's division commander, added an endorsement saying that he believed any means of destroying the enemy was legal in warfare. Secretary Randolph's decision on the matter was that such explosive devices were admissible to check pursuit, defend a work, or sink a ship, but were not allowable for the sole purpose of killing enemy soldiers. He further added that if Rains and Longstreet disagreed, Rains should yield to his superior or transfer to the river defenses, where the use of explosive devices was "clearly admissible."

On 31 May 1862 Rains participated in the Battle of Seven Pines outside Richmond, where his brigade brilliantly outflanked a Union position known as "Casey's Redoubt" and thus enabled the Confederate forces to sweep the Union troops from the field. Rains was unable to advance farther, however, and drew criticism from General Hill because of this. After the battle, Rains was transferred to the submarine defenses of the James and Appomattox rivers on 18 June 1862 to continue his experiments with explosives. During the summer he was briefly in charge of the defenses of the Cape Fear River in North Carolina, and on 16 Dec. 1862 he was assigned to head the Bureau of Conscription in Richmond. While in service here Rains began to formulate plans for the torpedo defense of Confederate ports. These were presented to President Jefferson Davis, who was much impressed and transferred Rains from the Bureau of Conscription on 25 May 1863 and directed him to put his plans into operation. Rains was first sent to Vicksburg, Miss., and then to Charleston, S.C., and Mobile, Ala. From then until the end of the war he worked to bolster the defenses of the major Southern ports with torpedoes and mines.

Rains was formally appointed chief of a newly created Torpedo Bureau on 17 June 1864 and remained in this position until the close of the war. Under his supervision torpedo factories were established at Richmond, Wilmington, Mobile, Charleston, and Savannah. His men filled beer kegs or barrels with gunpowder, fitted them with a percussion primer at each end, and then set them adrift to strike against an enemy vessel and explode. Other types were developed to be anchored to the harbor bottom and fired from a wire leading to shore. Rains also invented an autosubterranean explosive shell for land use, complete with a tin shield for protection against the rain. Despite the fact that leaders early in the war had objected to the use of mines on moral grounds, these devices were widely employed by the end of the conflict. Some 1,300 such shells were buried in the defenses of Richmond. In addition, Rains invented a machine for manufacturing gun caps.

His torpedoes were a great success. They provided an effective deterrent to Union naval attack, and they sank about fifty-eight Union vessels. Greater damage might have been done had the Confederacy been willing to put effort and money into torpedo defense earlier in the war. Perhaps Rains's greatest accomplishment in the use of explosives occurred on 9 Aug. 1864, when two of his agents exploded a bomb at the wharfs of Ulysses S. Grant's supply base at City Point, Va., causing a high loss of life and $4 million in damages.

After the war Rains lived for a time in Atlanta before moving to South Carolina, where he worked as a clerk from 1877 to 1880 in the Quartermaster's Department of the U.S. Army at Charleston. He died in Aiken, S.C. Rains had married Mary Jane McClellan, a granddaughter of Governor John Sevier. They had six children.

SEE: Walter Clark, ed., *Histories of the Several Regiments and Battalions from North Carolina*, vol. 4 (1901); Burke Davis, *Our Incredible Civil War* (1960); Jefferson Davis, *Rise and Fall of the Confederate Government*, vol. 2 (1881); Clement A. Evans, ed., *Confederate Military History*, vol. 4 (1899); Douglas S. Freeman, *Lee's Lieutenants*, vol. 1 (1944); Francis B. Heitman, *Historical Register of the United States Army*, vol. 1 (1890); Daniel H. Hill, *Bethel to Sharpsburg*, vol. 2 (1926); Ezra Warner, *Generals in Gray* (1959).

PAUL BRANCH

Rains, George Washington *(1817–21 Mar. 1898)*, army officer, educator, and author, was born in Craven County, the eighth child of Gabriel M. and Hester Ambrose Rains. He attended New Bern Academy and in 1838, after his parents had moved to Alabama, entered the U.S. Military Academy at West Point. In 1842 Rains was graduated third in a class of fifty-six. As a second lieutenant in the Corps of Engineers he was stationed first at Boston and then with the Fourth Artillery at Fort Monroe, Va. After a brief term as assistant professor of chemistry and geology at West Point, he saw action in the Mexican War in which he was brevetted major for gallant conduct. In 1847–48 he served as aide-de-camp to Generals Winfield Scott and Gideon Pillow and the following year was assigned to duty in New Orleans. He later fought in the Seminole War.

On 23 Apr. 1856 Rains married Frances Josephine Ramsell of New York. He was promoted to captain in 1856 but resigned the same year to become president of the Washington Iron Works and later the Highland Iron Works, both of which were located in Newburgh, N.Y. By 1861 he had obtained a number of patents for inventions relating to steam engines and boilers.

When the Civil War began, Rains enlisted in the Confederate army and was commissioned a major; a year later he was promoted to lieutenant colonel. Assigned the task of procuring gunpowder, Rains established government powder mills at Augusta, Ga., that produced 2,750,000 pounds of gunpowder during the Civil War. Rains was also put in charge of the collection of niter from caves in the South and published a pamphlet, *Notes on the Making of Saltpetre from the Earth of the Caves*. His efforts quickly led to the creation of the Nitre and Mining Bureau of the War Department.

After the war Rains remained in Augusta and became professor of chemistry at the Medical College of Georgia in August 1866. Eventually named dean of the college, he served on the faculty until 1894. He was the author of *Rudimentary Course of Analytical and Applied Chemistry* (1872) and *History of the Confederate Powder Works* (1882). Rains died in Newburgh, N.Y.

SEE: *Appleton's Cyclopedia of American Biography*, vol. 5 (1900); *DAB*, vol. 8 (1935); George McIver, "North Carolinians at West Point before the Civil War," *North Carolina Historical Review* 7 (1930); *North Carolina Presbyterian*, 16 May 1863; Jan L. Wakelyn, ed., *Biographical Dictionary of the Confederacy* (1977).

GEORGE D. TERRY

Rainsford, Giles *(b. 1679)*, Anglican clergyman, was born in Dublin, Ireland, the son of Mark Rainsford. A pensioner at Trinity College in Dublin on 2 Apr. 1695, he received an A.B. from Trinity in 1699 and an A.M. in 1705. Rainsford continued his education in England and was a fellow commoner at St. John's College, Cambridge, on 23 Mar. 1700. After his ordination by the bishop of London in 1702, he received the King's Bounty to go to Jamaica on 15 June of the same year. It is not known if he ever went to the West Indies and his record for the next several years is unclear.

On 8 Feb. 1711 Rainsford wrote the secretary of the Society for the Propagation of the Gospel in Foreign Parts from his charge in Bury in the county of Suffolk and asked for a position. In 1712 the society sent him to North Carolina as a general itinerant missionary. On 25 July Rainsford reported that he had reached his destination after a twelve-week passage from England to Hampton, Va. At Hampton he was befriended by a merchant, Edmond Kearney, who provided a horse for his journey to North Carolina. Kearney, a fellow Irishman, was the brother of Thomas Kearney, who founded the family of that name in North Carolina. At his new post, Rainsford was warmly received by Governor Edward Hyde. He divided Chowan Precinct with the incumbent, the Reverend John Urmston, taking the west shore "where there is no church but a vast tract of land to ride over."

From his letters to the officials in London and from the lists of books he requested to be sent him, Rainsford had an active and inquiring mind. After only a few months in his new home, he became interested in the Indians. He had several conferences with Thomas Hoyle, king of the Chowan Indians, who wished to become a Christian. Rainsford was surprised to find that the Indian had some idea of Noah's flood, which had been passed down by oral tradition or, as the king expressed it, "my father told me, I tell my son." The Indian king had some thought of sending his children to a school run by a Mr. Mashburn at Sarum on the border between Virginia and North Carolina. Rainsford was impressed with the instruction given there and in view of his own qualifications, this was high praise indeed.

Unfortunately, Rainsford came to North Carolina shortly after the Tuscarora war and conditions were unsettled. He was visited by a terrible "seasoning" and his life despaired of for some months. At least once he was captured by unfriendly Indians but was released. Early in 1713 the clergyman petitioned the governor of Virginia for a living in that colony for six months to recover. This was granted and he was assigned to Surry. The following year Rainsford became rector of the Lower Parish, Nansemond County, Va., and remained in that post for two years. He continued his interest in the Chowan Indians and seems to have visited his old mission area in North Carolina occasionally. On 19 Jan. 1715 Rainsford wrote to the London authorities that he had spent a total of five months in the Chowans' town and had almost mastered their language. He hoped to be able to minister to the Chowans at Fort Christiana, where the governor of Virginia was planning to move the tribe.

Rainsford returned to England for a visit in 1716. On 3 September of that year he received the King's Bounty to go to Maryland but returned to Virginia instead and became rector of St. Anne's Parish in Essex County. This did not meet with the approval of Governor Alexander Spotswood, who wished to present someone else. Rainsford, however, had the backing of both the vestry and Commissary James Blair. The argument became a test case, and an opinion obtained from the Inns of the Court in London was favorable to the vestry. Rainsford apparently remained at St. Anne's until 1720, when he moved to St. Paul's parish, Prince Georges County, Md. According to some accounts, he was in Culpepper County, Va., from 1718 to 1720; however, this county was not settled and organized until 1748. Rainsford was popular in Maryland. On 19 Apr. 1723 Governor Charles Calvert wrote the bishop of London that Rainsford was visiting England for his health and praised his character. The clergyman left St. Paul's four years later and returned to England for good. Rainsford married in Virginia in 1716 but there is no record of any children, and nothing is known of his later career.

SEE: Edward Lewis Goodwin, *Colonial Church in Virginia* (1927); Marshal D. Haywood, "Giles Rainsford," *Carolina Churchman*, July 1925; William W. Manross, *Fulham Papers in the Lambeth Palace Library* (1964); William L. Saunders, ed., *Colonial Records of N.C.* (1890), vols. 1–2 (1886).

CLAIBORNE T. SMITH, JR.

Raleigh (or Ralegh), Sir Walter *(1554?–19 Oct. 1618)*, courtier, sponsor of colonial enterprises, poet, and historian, was born at Fardel of a Devon, England, family, poor but with good connections. His father was Walter Ralegh; his mother, Katharine Champerowne, was previously the wife of Otto Gilbert, father of Humphrey Gilbert. Young Raleigh was taken to France by Devon mercenaries in Huguenot service and probably was there from 1568 to 1571. He returned to Oriel College, Lyons Inn, the Middle Temple, for rapid education from 1572 to 1576. Katherine Ashley, a relative, was close to Queen Elizabeth and is credited with edging both Gilbert and later his half brother Raleigh into the royal Court. Somehow Raleigh accumulated a little capital.

In 1578 Gilbert got a grant to explore and occupy lands not previously taken over by Europeans, meaning in fact eastern North America. Raleigh was given command of the *Falcon*, a former royal ship owned by the Hawkins firm of Plymouth. The expedition set out in November for North America by way of the Caribbean, but most of the ships turned back. *Falcon* went farthest, perhaps to the Cape Verdes, acted as a pirate, and crawled back leaking.

Gilbert next planned extensive colonies in Norumbega (New England) and Raleigh partnered him. Meanwhile, Raleigh was rising at Court, winning the queen's attention, getting handsome gifts, and also serving for a time as a soldier in Ireland, from which he wrote imposing letters for solving Irish problems. By 1582 he bought a new ship at Southampton, named it the *Bark Ralegh*, and prepared to go to reconnoiter the Gilbert objective. But Gilbert did not get away in that year, nor until 1583, by which time the queen forbade Raleigh to leave her to accompany him. Moreover, his ship returned very soon—allegedly because of inadequate stores on board. Gilbert claimed Newfoundland for England in August, but was himself drowned at sea after having to give up his exploring enterprise. As soon as Gilbert's associates ended their projects in 1584, Raleigh obtained from the queen a seven-year renewal of Gilbert's patent, which gave him a free hand to explore and colonize between Florida and Cape Breton.

A reconnaissance expedition under Philip Amadas and Arthur Barlowe brought news in September 1584 of the Carolina Outer Banks and Roanoke Island as well as two Indians, Manteo and Wanchese, to support hopes of successful colonization. Raleigh, influenced by Richard Hakluyt, wished to involve the queen and Parliament. He failed in both, though the queen allowed the name Virginia to be given to the newly discovered land, while members of Parliament (of whom Raleigh was one) rallied around the enterprise. Raleigh had a seal made as lord and governor of Virginia. He was not committed to long-term colonization, however. His expedition under Sir Richard Grenville (again he was not allowed to join it) was to leave Ralph Lane to try out the place as a base against Spain as war was looming, to make a survey of its resources (which Thomas Harriot and John White were to carry out), and to explore the hinterland.

The colony was less elaborate than planned because some ships were diverted to Newfoundland on a naval expedition. In July and August a settlement was made. Raleigh got good reports from Grenville in October 1585. The colony did much of what was expected of it, but supplies did not arrive—Raleigh's ship reached the Outer Banks and then Grenville's squadron with more supplies and men, but they were too late. Now the plan was for Raleigh to stand back so as to encourage and give some money to an independent group under White in order to settle a small community on Chesapeake Bay, a deep-water harbor. White's colonists duly made their way to America in 1587 but were left by the seamen at Roanoke Island, not Chesapeake Bay. Finding Grenville's small party gone and their own stores small, they sent John White back to Raleigh for aid. Why White did not return at once is not clear, but Raleigh and Grenville prepared a new squadron in 1588 to turn the bay into a base against Spain. But the ships were embodied in the royal navy awaiting the Spanish Armada, while Raleigh was busily engaged in defensive preparations; White's two supply pinnaces set out late and were overwhelmed by pirates off the Azores.

White returned totally disillusioned to take his place as a settler in Raleigh's other colony, that in counties Waterford and Cork in Ireland, built up successfully by his agents since 1586. Raleigh as captain of the guard was responsible for the queen's safety and played an active role against the Armada. After that he neglected North America. His patent remained good if the 1587 colony could be assumed to be alive, while White's brief visit to Roanoke Island in 1590 showed that some of its members had gone to Croatoan Island with friendly Indians. He doubtless hoped that when war had died down he could revive his concern with settlement in North America and renew contact with the settlers.

Raleigh had a distinguished position at Court, but his pride and capacity for quarreling, together with the death of powerful friends, the earl of Leicester and Sir Francis Walsingham, left him vulnerable, especially as the young earl of Essex was rising in favor. His secret marriage to Elizabeth Throckmorton, one of the queen's ladies in waiting, was disclosed in the summer of 1592, and his lies led to Raleigh's imprisonment in the Tower of London for a time, and to his disgrace, so that he retired to Sherborne to plan a comeback. Since 1587 he had been interested in the prospects of Guiana. A civilized, gold-rich people were supposed to live near the Orinoco River.

Raleigh hoped to enter the river with the assistance of local Indians and prospect for a base for an English colony as well as possible gold. With four ships he spent from February to September 1595 in his only American venture. He immobilized the Spanish at Trinidad, penetrated the delta of the Orinoco, and ascended the river, making friends with Arawak Indians as he went.

Exploring parties found indications of gold in various areas, while he himself ascended the Caroni Gorge but found no trace of El Dorado, the alleged ruler of the "empire," though Raleigh went home believing that there was gold accessible and that England might invade and colonize an area that would threaten Spanish Peru. At home he found little credence, though he published a tract on Guiana in glowing colors and continued to send exploring parties to the area. He did not, as he intended, visit Virginia on his way home. He was allowed to play a significant part in the attack on Cadiz in 1596 and won back some influence at Court.

He gradually resumed an interest in Virginia. Hakluyt was making propaganda for him in his *The Principal Navigations* (1598–1600), and perhaps 1599 saw the first of the small expeditions he sent to trade along the coast and he got news of the "Lost Colonists." In 1602 Samuel Mace explored the coast south of Cape Hatteras for him without success. In 1603 Bartholomew Gilbert lost his life off the Eastern Shore on another voyage. It seems likely that Mace in 1603 penetrated Chesapeake Bay, seized several Indians, and got some news of white men residing to the south of the bay, but this is not yet proved. Moreover, he took over sponsorship of a venture to the New England coast in 1602 under Bartholomew Gosnold that had aimed to set up a trading post on Elizabeth Island, and he authorized an expedition under Martin Pring to trade in Cape Cod Bay in 1603. As governor of Jersey (1600–1603), he had a post of some responsibility, but he failed to make friendly contact with the heir apparent, James VI of Scotland, who had been warned about his treacherous and arrogant character. When James succeeded to the throne in March 1603, Raleigh, unwisely, advocated stepping up war with Spain, which James was determined to end. He was accused, ironically, of plotting to depose James in favor of Spanish interests; in July he was imprisoned in the Tower of London. If news did arrive in September that the Lost Colony was still in existence, he could do nothing about it. His rights to North America and his offices were taken away, and the plot frame-up culminated in a show trial at Winchester in December at which he was sentenced to die as a traitor.

Raleigh was reprieved but not pardoned and remained prisoner in the Tower, where in 1605 he was joined by the eighth earl of Northumberland, an old friend in whose service Harriot now was. He kept contact with Virginia affairs, managed to maintain some trade with Guiana, and ingratiated himself with the queen and, as he grew up, the young Prince Henry. Since James would not release him, Raleigh worked at a history of the world and on chemical experiments. By 1614 a new secretary of state, Sir Ralph Winwood, induced James to release Raleigh to go gold hunting in Guiana, as he was short of money. Released in 1616, Raleigh found many willing to back his venture, he having become something of a legendary figure. No less than fourteen ships left the Irish coast in August 1617, under strict orders not to interfere with the Spanish. After arrival near the mouth of the Orinoco, Raleigh was too ill to go farther, but Lawrence Keymis was certain that he knew the location of a gold mine. A Spanish garrison was found at San Thome, and there was fighting in which Raleigh's eldest son, Walter, was killed. No gold mine was located and in March 1618 the parties returned, with nothing to show. The sentence, deferred since 1603, was revived on account of the breach with Spain, which threatened James's policies. Raleigh was beheaded on 19 October, making an eloquent speech from the scaffold and after his death becoming a popular hero as a patriot who stood up against Spain. For a time his wife kept his head in a velvet bag, but his body was interred in St. Margaret's Church, Westminster, London.

Raleigh had great gifts as a writer and poet and considerable statesmenlike insights, including his belief that

England should gain an overseas dominion. His confidence in the prospects of Virginia and Guiana were held firmly to the last. He was arrogant and, though he could play the courtier, was regarded as cynical and unorthodox in religion. He was greedy for office, power, and money and never got enough to meet his desires. But his tragic career, its heights and depths, fascinated contemporaries and his successors. He was intellectually and in action a genuine pioneer.

Raleigh and his wife were the parents of two sons, Walter (1593–1618) and Carew (1605–66). Raleigh may also have been the father of an illegitimate daughter.

SEE: J. H. Adamson and H. F. Folland, *The Shepherd of the Ocean: A Biography of Sir Walter Raleigh* (1969); Edward Edwards, *Life and Letters of Sir Walter Raleigh*, 2 vols. (1866); Stephen J. Greenblatt, *Sir Walter Ralegh: The Renaissance Man and His Roles* (1973); V. T. Harlow, ed., *The Discoverie of the Large and Bewtiful Empire of Guiana* (1928) and *Raleigh's Last Voyage* (1932); Robert Lacey, *Sir Walter Raleigh* (1973); Agnes A. Latham, *Poems of Sir Walter Ralegh* (1951); John Knox Laugton and Sidney Lee, "Sir Walter Ralegh (1552?–1618)," in *DNB*, vol. 16 (1922); Pierre Lefranc, *Sir Walter Raleigh: Ecrivain L'oeuvre et les Idées* (1968); David B. Quinn, ed., *The Roanoke Voyages, 1584–1590*, 2 vols. (1955), and *Sir Walter Raleigh and the British Empire* (1975); A. L. Rowse, *Ralegh and the Throckmortons* (1962); E. A. Strathmann, *Sir Walter Ralegh: A Study in Elizabethan Skepticism* (1951); Willard M. Wallace, *Sir Walter Raleigh* (1959); Norman L. Williams, *Sir Walter Raleigh* (1962).

DAVID B. QUINN

Ramcke, Frederick *(ca. 1760–29 Aug. 1800)*, physician, first appeared in North Carolina in 1783. His antecedents are unknown. His involvement in a large debt to a New York physician at the end of his life suggests a prior association with that city. His unusual surname has been subject to many interpretations. When J. R. B. Hathaway was publishing his genealogical quarterly in 1901, he conferred with another noted historian, Marshall DeLancey Haywood, on this subject, and they decided Ramcke was the correct spelling. The doctor settled initially in New Bern. On 10 Dec. 1783, as "practicioner of physik and surgery, usually residing in New Bern but at present in Edenton," he gave a power of attorney to William Righton to collect debts due the estate of Joseph Smith, the former husband of his wife. Ramcke had recently married Elizabeth Hardy, the daughter of Robert and Agnes Little Hardy of Edenton and the widow of Joseph Smith, a merchant in Edenton.

The public records in New Bern reveal nothing to throw light on Ramcke's residence there and undoubtedly his stay was brief. On 4 Aug. 1784 he advertised in the *North Carolina Gazette* in New Bern that he planned to leave town shortly and requested all those indebted to him to make immediate payment. Not long afterwards he moved to Edenton. He seems to have prospered in his new location, for, the Chowan deeds show, over the next fifteen years he purchased real estate, slaves, and expensive furniture. In 1790 Frederick Ramcke was living beside Captain Josiah Collins and maintained a shop next to his residence.

Less is known about Ramcke's professional life. It appears that a Dr. James Ward was his assistant from 1789 to 1798. In the latter year Ramcke and an Edenton colleague, Dr. John Beasley, found themselves in trouble with the community. Smallpox at the time was still a dreaded and often fatal disease. Although vaccination had been introduced in England from Turkey early in the eighteenth century, its use was not widespread at the century's end. It was dangerous and controversial. The two doctors had attempted to introduce it to the people of Edenton. Late in 1798 Blake Baker, then the attorney general of the state, prepared an indictment against the two men to be laid before the grand jury of the Edenton District. In the indictment Ramcke and Beasley were charged with maintaining a pesthouse for smallpox sufferers and "by force of arms innoculating divers persons." This episode was the subject of a sketch by Joseph B. Cheshire in his book *Nonnulla*, in which he referred to the physicians as medical martyrs. Cheshire could find no record that a grand jury had ever endorsed the bill. However, he commented that the fact that one was even drawn up was evidence that the progressive physicians had encountered opposition and prejudice in their efforts to control smallpox.

Ramcke soon had difficulties of a different kind. Economic troubles had surfaced. On 15 Apr. 1799 he sold some property at a loss to Dr. John Goodwin, of New York City, who had sued him for debt. An argument developed sometime in 1800 between Ramcke and Samuel Butler, a prosperous Edenton merchant. No clue has been found as to the cause. According to the custom of the time, though illegal, dueling was accepted as a manner of settling an altercation. On 15 August the two men were arrested as "being about to engage in a duel." Legal intervention did not cool tempers and the duel finally took place two weeks later. At the exchange of fire, Butler was wounded in the thigh. Both parties left the field apparently satisfied. Immediately afterwards, however, the doctor went into his shop and, in the words of the local newspaper, "by firing two pistols through his head, put a period to his life." If his fulsome obituary can be trusted, a gracious demeanor belied his troubled spirit. The Edenton paper lamented the "loss to the public in being bereaved of the services of a man of unblemished morals, untainted integrity, and singular probity and goodness."

On 19 Aug. 1800, after the initial encounter with Butler, Ramcke had made a will. It was written in a large, florid hand, reflecting no doubt his disturbed emotional state, and began with the phrase "calling to mind the uncertainity of life and being at this moment called upon to engage in a duel." He devised all his property to his wife, Elizabeth. She did not long survive him and died on 4 Dec. 1801. They were the parents of two children, Josiah Frederick and Anna Catherine. As there is no further record of them, they are presumed to have died young. By her first husband Elizabeth Ramcke had a son, Robert Hardy Smith, who lived until 1840.

SEE: Joseph B. Chesire, *Nonnulla* (1930); Chowan County Records (North Carolina State Archives, Raleigh); Elizabeth Vann Moore to the author; Lois Neal, *Abstract of Vital Records from Raleigh, N.C.: Newspapers*, vol. 1 (1979); *Post Angel or Universal Entertainment*, vol. 1, no. 2.

CLAIBORNE T. SMITH, JR.

Ramsaur, William Hoke *(13 Aug. 1890–28 May 1922)*, YMCA secretary, Student Volunteer Movement traveling secretary, Episcopal priest, and missionary, was born in China Grove of German and English ancestry. His father was Dr. George Alexander Ramsaur, a physician residing in Rowan County but a native of Lincoln County, where the Ramsaur family had settled prior to the American Revolution. His mother was Nancy Ellen Hoke Ramsaur, whose father, Colonel William James Hoke, entered Confederate service as captain of the Southern Stars and later commanded the Thirty-eighth Regiment of North Carolina Troops and whose mother, Georgiana Turner Sumner Hoke, was descended from Colonel Jethro Sumner (first cousin of Brigadier General Jethro Sumner) of the North Carolina Continental Line during the Revolutionary War.

Ramsaur was the second of six children and the eldest of four sons. Educated in the grade school of China Grove, he entered Catawba College at Newton in 1905 and spent two years studying to become a physician. He transferred to The University of North Carolina as a sophomore in 1907. Working to pay his expenses, he nevertheless found time as a senior to serve as president of the university YMCA and was graduated in 1910 with the A.B. degree. Having dedicated his life to Christ, he spent two years as secretary of the YMCA at the University of Alabama. Then in 1912, having enrolled as a member of the Student Volunteer Movement for Foreign Missions, he entered the junior class of Philadelphia Divinity School (Episcopal) to begin preparing for foreign service. From 1913 to 1915 he was engaged as a traveling secretary for the Student Volunteer Movement. Returning to the Divinity School, he served at a Philadelphia mission center and completed his theological course in 1917, graduating with highest honors and the bachelor of sacred theology degree.

Ordained to the diaconate of the Protestant Episcopal church on 2 Aug. 1914, Ramsaur was advanced to the priesthood on 15 July 1917. The Right Reverend Joseph Blount Chesire, bishop of the Diocese of North Carolina, who officiated at both ordinations, held in St. Luke's Church, Salisbury, later wrote of Ramsaur: "Among all the young men whom I have ordained to the Holy Ministry, I do not think there has been one who seemed to me to be of a finer type of young manhood, physically, mentally, and spiritually." Named priest-in-charge of the Church of the Messiah, Mayodan, during the summer of 1917, Ramsaur then returned to the Student Volunteer Movement as a traveling secretary (1917–18). In this service, cumulatively, he is said to have persuaded fifty or more young men to enter the Christian ministry. The summer of 1918 saw a happy and productive pastoral experience for Ramsaur as priest-in-charge of St. Andrew's Church, Greensboro. The fall of 1918 found him studying industrial trades (carpentry, bricklaying, and smithery) at Hampton Institute, Hampton, Va., in special preparation for forthcoming work in Africa.

While American forces were fighting in France during World War I, Ramsaur tried five times but failed to become a military chaplain. Then in patriotic desperation he decided to enlist as a private in the U.S. Army but after a soul-searching struggle of conscience bowed to the authority of Bishop Cheshire, who had overruled his decision. Ramsaur finally obtained an appointment, effective November 1918, as an Episcopal missionary to Liberia, West Africa, thus fulfilling his long-held, self-professed purpose to bring "the light of the life of Christ into Africa." At first he had aspired to evangelize the Moslems, since he deemed them the most difficult to win for Christ. Failing to find such an opportunity, he had offered himself for service in Africa and was eventually assigned to an area where Muhammadanism was making inroads among the Vai tribe.

After a visit in January 1919 to the Pro-Cathedral Church of the Nativity in Bethlehem, Pa., Ramsaur became a foreign missionary of that parish, which provided a modest salary and paid his expenses. Having sailed from the United States on 1 February, he arrived, via France and Spain, in Monrovia, Liberia, on 25 March. Settling eighty miles up the coast at Cape Mount, he engaged in educational, evangelistic, and practical work. Later that year he traveled five days by foot and one by train to Freetown, Sierra Leone, for a serious mastoid operation. Upon recovering, he trekked one thousand miles through the Liberian hinterland, visiting the Golah, Gbandee, Gezee, and Kimbuzee tribes. In his forceful report, "The Call of A Great Opportunity," published in the United States in September 1920, Ramsaur described the background, life, and needs of the peoples he had observed for two months. His call to action stirred Episcopalians throughout the United States.

On 2 May 1920 Ramsaur married Sarah E. Conway, a native of Gloucester City, N.J., who had served in Liberia as a nurse and medical practitioner for nearly seven years. Shortly after their marriage, the Reverend and Mrs. Ramsaur were stationed in the interior, across the lake from Cape Mount at Bendu, where they established the first mission outpost among the Vais.

During a six-month furlough in 1921 Ramsaur and his wife traveled widely through the eastern and midwestern United States, speaking and seeking funds for the industrial departments that he and Bishop W. H. Overs, bishop of Liberia, planned to develop at St. John's School, Cape Mount. During this period he required another mastoid operation, emergency surgery that saved his life. Though still weak, he and Mrs. Ramsaur sailed for Liberia on 3 December.

Shortly after arriving at Cape Mount, Sarah Ramsaur became ill and died on 22 Jan. 1922. Ramsaur bravely continued his work until April, when he contracted pneumonia. After an illness of six weeks and removal to Monrovia for treatment, his heart became affected and he died. His body was carried to Cape Mount for burial beside the grave of his wife.

Concerning his first landing at Monrovia, Ramsaur wrote a friend: "I think it was the happiest day of my life. Liberia! Yes, after years of earnest anticipation, and months of special preparation and patient waiting, I am here. . . . Of God's call to this field I have no doubt, and in spite of all my personal unfitness, I know he has work for me here."

His obituary in the Salisbury *Evening Post* (Rowan County) referred to Ramsaur as a "brilliant student and an able speaker," who was "well known in Salisbury as well as China Grove and Rowan County." Dr. Frank Porter Graham, writing in The University of North Carolina *Alumni Review*, declared, "In the death of William Hoke Ramsaur, the University has lost a noble son, the North American Student Movement a crusading volunteer, and the Christian civilization of the west a torchbearer who counted it an opportunity to lay down his life among the black folk of Africa. . . . Hoke Ramsaur had compressed noble and intense service within the years of his devoted youth. In him the University and religion have been extended and vindicated in heroic proportions. . . . (He was) honored and loved among all who knew him."

SEE: *Biographical Sketch of William Hoke Ramsaur* (1923); *Charlotte Observer*, 30 May 1922; Columbia, S.C., *The State*, 20 Aug. 1921; *Journal of the Diocese of North Carolina* (1915–23); *Letters of William Hoke Ramsaur* (1928); New York, *Spirit of Missions*, September 1920; *One Hundred Years of Nativity* (1962); Salisbury *Evening Post*, 29 May 1922; W. L. Sherrill, *Annals of Lincoln County, North Carolina* (1937).

WALSER H. ALLEN, JR.

Ramsay, James Graham *(1 Mar. 1823–10 Jan. 1903)*, physician and Confederate congressman, was born on his father's small plantation in Iredell County. Both parents, David and Margaret Graham Ramsay, were of Scotch-Irish descent. The Ramsays had emigrated in 1695 to Pennsylvania, and Dr. Ramsay's grandfather had moved to the Coddle Creek community in Iredell in 1766.

After obtaining his basic education in the local schools, young Ramsay entered Davidson College in 1838 and was graduated three years later. He taught school for a year, then studied medicine with his brother-in-law before entering the Jefferson Medical College in Philadelphia, where he was graduated in 1848. He opened an office near Cleveland in Rowan County, using part of his stately home, Palermo, for this purpose, and practiced there for the next fifty-one years. In 1849 he helped organize the first medical society in Rowan and was its first president. Ramsay also farmed on a small scale; the census of 1860 reported that he had real estate worth $10,000 and owned five slaves.

Ramsay was one of the more politically active men of his district. An excellent public speaker, he campaigned vigorously and faithfully for the Whig party and its candidates at each election. In 1856 he was sent to the state senate, where he served until 1864. In 1860 he supported the Bell-Everett ticket and was an ardent peace advocate until Abraham Lincoln's call for volunteers in April 1861 to quell the Southern rebellion. In 1863 Ramsay ran against the incumbent William Lander for a seat in the Confederate House of Representatives; he attacked Lander's strong support of the Davis administration and promised to work for an honorable peace if elected. Ramsay, who had the strong endorsement of W. W. Holden's Raleigh *Standard*, defeated Lander decisively.

In the Confederate Congress Ramsay was a member of the committees on the Medical Department and Naval Affairs. He seldom offered legislation of his own, but he voted so consistently to place state and individual rights over the needs of the Confederate war effort that his loyalty was suspect. He opposed higher taxes, extending conscription or limiting exemptions from military service, suspending the writ of habeas corpus, the impressment of farm produce for army use, and all other major administration measures. He worked consistently to force President Jefferson Davis to seek peace terms from the United States, and by April 1865 he favored a state convention to return North Carolina to the Union.

After the war Ramsay became an active Republican. In 1872 he was a presidential elector, and in 1882 he was returned to the senate for one term. President Rutherford B. Hayes offered him a diplomatic post in South America, but he declined the honor. Ramsay spent his last years in Salisbury with his son, and upon his death was interred in the cemetery of the Third Creek Presbyterian Church, near Cleveland, where he had been a ruling elder for forty-nine years.

The tall, spare physician was one of the best-read men of his community, and his contemporaries considered him "polished in his manners, precise but not still in his address, [and] . . . of fine conversational ability." In 1846 he married Sarah Foster of Davie County. Their children were Margaret F., Florence May, David W., James H., Edgar B., William G., Robert L., and Claudius C.

SEE: Samuel A. Ashe, ed., *Cyclopedia of Eminent and Representative Men of the Carolinas*, vol. 2 (1892); *Journal of the Confederate Congress*, vol. 7 (1902); *Journal of the Senate of North Carolina*, 1856–64, 1883–85; Salisbury *Daily Sun*, 10 Jan. 1903; *Salisbury Post*, 25 Aug. 1965; Z. V. Walser Papers (Southern Historical Collection, University of North Carolina, Chapel Hill [portrait]); Ezra Warner and Buck Yearns, *Biographical Register of the Confederate Congress* (1975).

BUCK YEARNS

Ramsay, John Andrew *(1836–27 Jan. 1909)*, land surveyor, civil engineer, Confederate soldier, and mayor of Salisbury, was born in Rowan County to Robert and Mary M. Walton Ramsay. Young Ramsay practiced the profession of land surveying and civil engineering until the outbreak of the Civil War. He then joined a battery of artillery known as the Rowan Artillery and on 8 May 1861 was elected its captain. The battery had no cannon at the time, so the company temporarily served as part of the Fourth North Carolina Infantry Regiment.

On 20 July 1861, at the request of Governor John W. Ellis, Ramsay turned over command of the company to Captain James Reilly, an officer with previous artillery experience, and accepted the assignment as first lieutenant of the company. The battery became Company D, Tenth North Carolina (First Artillery) Regiment, and was sent to Virginia, where it received its cannon. From here the battery served in General Joseph E. Johnston's Confederate army during the Peninsular campaign and later marched at the head of Stonewall Jackson's army arriving from the Shenandoah Valley to join Robert E. Lee's army at Richmond during the Seven Days' campaign. The battery was attached to General John B. Hood's famous "Texas" Division and was heavily engaged in the Second Manassas campaign.

On 30 Aug. 1862, the second day of the Battle of Second Manassas, Lieutenant Ramsay was wounded when a fragment of an enemy shell struck him on the right knee. Fortunately, the fragment caused only a contusion with no serious injury. In the Battle of Sharpsburg, 17 Sept. 1862, he commanded a section of the battery under the very eyes of General Robert E. Lee and at one point, while going into action, paused to identify with his field telescope a column of distant troops at Lee's request. Reilly's battery also participated in the Battle of Fredericksburg and, while serving with General James Longstreet's corps around Suffolk, took part in General D. H. Hill's unsuccessful siege of Washington, N.C., in April 1863. As a part of Major M. W. Henry's artillery battalion, the battery was engaged on the right flank at Gettysburg on 2 and 3 July 1863. On 7 Sept. 1863 Captain Reilly was promoted to the rank of major, and Ramsay succeeded him in command of the Rowan Artillery as captain. Ramsay's battery served as a part of Lieutenant Colonel John C. Haskell's artillery battalion throughout the Wilderness and Petersburg campaigns of 1864.

Granted a furlough on 1 Feb. 1865, Captain Ramsay went home and was not able to return to his battery before it surrendered with Lee at Appomattox. He was paroled at Salisbury on 19 June 1865. In the meantime, he had been given the post of chief of police of Salisbury by North Carolina's "Carpetbag" governor W. W. Holden in May. On 26 July 1865 he married Margaret L. (Maggie) Beall, the daughter of Burgess Beall of Davidson County and the widow of his cousin, Julius D. Ramsay. The couple made their home in Salisbury and once again Ramsay took up engineering and surveying. Among his accomplishments was the laying of one of the first sewers in the city, the designing of the original building of what was to be the Frank B. John School on Ellis Street, and the supervising of a gang of workers as superintendent of streets.

In 1879 Ramsay ran for the office of mayor on the ticket of the moderate wing of the Republican party and won. The following year he was reelected, but in 1881 he was defeated by the Democratic candidate, M. L.

Holmes. Ramsay won again in 1883. He worked to promote the education of the poor but at the time this was unpopular with the people, and he was defeated in the election of 1884, never to enter politics again. He returned to surveying and engineering until his death. He was buried in Chestnut Hills Cemetery, Salisbury.

SEE: James S. Brawley, *The Rowan Story, 1753–1953* (1953); Walter Clark, ed., *The Histories of the Several Regiments and Battalions from North Carolina*, vol. 1 (1901); Louis H. Manarin, comp., *North Carolina Troops, 1861–1865: A Roster*, vol. 1 (1966); John A. Ramsay Papers (Southern Historical Collection, University of North Carolina, Chapel Hill); Mrs. Patricia G. Rosenthal, History/Genealogy Librarian, Rowan Public Library, Salisbury; *Salisbury Sunday Post*, 24 Feb. 1974.

PAUL BRANCH

Ramseur, Stephen Dodson *(13 May 1837–20 Oct. 1864)*, Confederate soldier, was born in Lincolnton, the son of Jacob A. and Lucy Wilfong Ramseur. He attended school in Lincolnton and Milton and at age sixteen enrolled in Davidson College. Ramseur left Davidson in April 1856 to accept an appointment to the U.S. Military Academy, from which he was graduated on 1 July 1860 standing fourteen in a class of forty-one. Commissioned a second lieutenant, Third Artillery, he was stationed first at Fort Monroe, Va., and then for a short period in Washington, D.C. He was promoted to first lieutenant, Fourth Artillery, on 1 Feb. 1861 but never reported to his new command. Instead, he resigned his commission on 6 Apr. 1861 and offered his services to the Confederacy.

As captain of the Ellis Light Artillery, a Raleigh battery, he reported to General John Magruder at Yorktown, Va., in the spring of 1862. That April he was elected colonel of the Forty-ninth North Carolina, a regiment he led with distinction in the Seven Days' fighting before Richmond; though severely wounded at Malvern Hill, he refused to leave the field until the battle was over.

Ramseur was promoted to brigadier general on 1 Nov. 1862 and assigned a brigade in General Robert E. Lee's Second Corps. He led his brigade with distinction at Chancellorsville, Gettysburg, Wilderness, Spotsylvania, and Cold Harbor, suffering wounds on two occasions. During the Cold Harbor campaign he was promoted to the rank of major general and given a division. The promotion, which came on 1 June 1864, only one day after his twenty-seventh birthday, made him the youngest West Pointer to attain that rank in the Confederate army. Following Cold Harbor Ramseur served under Jubal Early at Lynchburg, participated in the Washington Raid, and fought against Philip H. Sheridan in the Shenandoah Valley. He was mortally wounded at Cedar Creek, Va., on 19 Oct. 1864. Taken prisoner, he died the next day at Sheridan's headquarters in Winchester. The day before he was wounded Ramseur learned of the birth of a daughter, Mary Dodson. He had married Ellen E. Richmond of Milton, N.C., on 22 Oct. 1863. His body was taken to Lincolnton for burial.

SEE: Mark M. Boatner, *The Civil War Dictionary* (1959); Walter Clark, ed., *Histories of the Several Regiments and Battalions from North Carolina*, vols. 1–5 (1901); *DAB*, vol. 15 (1934); Clement A. Evans, ed., *Confederate Military History*, vol. 4 (1899); Douglas S. Freeman, *Lee's Lieutenants*, vols. 1–3 (1942); Gary W. Gallagher, *Stephen Dodson Ramseur* (1985); Ezra J. Warner, *Generals in Gray* (1959 [portrait]).

JOHN G. BARRETT

Ramsey, Claude Swanson *(2 Mar. 1899–17 Oct. 1963)*, newspaper executive and political writer, was born in Burlington, the son of S. Clay and Lucy Pinckard Ramsey. As a youth he moved to Asheville with his family and began his newspaper career as a newsboy while still in grammar school. He sold copies of the *Asheville Gazette-News* (forerunner of the *Asheville Times*) in 1912 and became a reporter in 1917, his senior year at Asheville High School. Enlisting in the army in 1917, he served as a sergeant in the 113th Field Artillery, 30th Division, from the time it was formed until it was disbanded at the end of the war. He saw action in the St. Mihiel and Meuse-Argonne offensives and the Tourl and Woovre sectors and received four battle stars. He was graduated from the Saumur (France) Artillery School.

In 1919 Ramsey entered the University of Virginia, where he was sports editor of the university newspaper, *College Topics*, and a member of Sigma Nu fraternity. In 1920, however, he joined the news staff of the *Asheville Times* and three years later became sports editor, a post he held for two years.

Ramsey was sent to Raleigh to cover the regular session of the General Assembly in 1929, and he returned to report on the sessions of 1931, 1933, and 1935, as well as the special sessions of 1936 and 1938, for both the *Asheville Times* and the *Asheville Citizen-Times*. Although it was said that he was capable of handling any job in the newspaper plant save operating a linotype machine, it was in Raleigh that Ramsey's fascination with people and politics came to the fore. With an uncanny capacity for remembering names, faces, and facts, he came to know virtually everyone in public life in North Carolina. Many of these people became his close personal friends.

In 1939 he became North Carolina publications director for the United Brewers Foundation and made his home in Raleigh. In 1947, however, he once more joined the staff of the *Asheville Citizen-Times* to cover the General Assembly. Later in the year he was promoted to executive editor of the paper, a post he held until his death.

Known throughout the state for his work with the American Legion, Ramsey was district commander in 1936–38 and commander of the Kiffin Rockwell Post, Asheville, in 1937–38. He served as editor of the *North Carolina Legion News* and was chairman of the legion's publications committee as well as a member of its legislative committee. A member of the Thirtieth Division Association, composed of members of the World War I unit, he served as president in 1932. He was also a member of the Veterans of Foreign Wars and of the Veterans of World War I.

A Democrat, he served as Twelfth District secretary of the Democratic state conventions of 1956–58 and as a Democratic presidential elector in 1956. He was a director of the Associated Press Managing Editors Association from 1954 to 1957 and was elected president of the North Carolina Associated Press News Council in 1954.

In 1923 Ramsey married Nell Hendon, of Asheville, a native of Tuskegee, Ala. He was survived by his wife and four children: Claude S., Jr., James C., Mrs. William W. Dodge II, and Mrs. Adam Hardison.

SEE: *Asheville Citizen*, 28 Jan. 1939, 9 Nov. 1947, 18 Oct. 1963; Biographical sketch prepared by Claude S. Ramsey, Jr., in February 1963 (files of the newspaper in Asheville).

MARY COWLES

Ramsey, Darley Hiden *(24 Sept. 1891–18 Feb. 1966)*, editor, newspaper manager, historian, and scholar, was born in Gretna, Va., the son of Simeon Clay and Lucy Pinckard Ramsey of Ferrum, Va. In 1903 the family moved to Asheville, where Hiden was graduated at the top of his 1908 Asheville High School class. At the University of Virginia he made Phi Beta Kappa and was graduated with an A.B. in 1912 and an M.A. in 1913. Loss of an eye in a childhood mishap limited the sports he loved so well, but he made the golf team of Virginia Polytechnic Institute and after college dropped golf altogether. His outdoor interests focused on hunting, fishing, mountain climbing, seashells, ornithology, and other pursuits of a naturalist. His frequent companion in roaming the mountains of western North Carolina and of Canada was baseball's great Branch Rickey, along with industrialists and fellow newsmen.

His successful campaign, in association with a young men's club, to change Asheville's city administration from aldermanic to commission form led to his election as commissioner of public safety in the new administration at age twenty-four. Four years later he was defeated for reelection and moved to Winston-Salem briefly as its commissioner of safety. He returned to Asheville in 1920 as associate editor of the *Citizen* and spent the remainder of his life editing or managing first one and then both the Asheville daily newspapers. With two associates he bought the *Times*, which he edited until 1 Sept. 1925, when it was purchased by Don S. Elias. A year later he returned to the same staff as general manager. When the *Times* and the *Citizen* were consolidated in August 1930, he continued as general manager, and later also as vice-president, until his retirement in 1954. In addition to administrative responsibilities he served as the newspapers' chief editorial writer. When the North Carolina Press Association in 1940 first instituted its annual awards for journalistic excellence, Ramsey was cited for writing the best editorial of the year. The award-winning editorial dealt with conditions in the Negro hospital in Asheville.

His skill as a "paragraph" writer—concentrating a single concept into one brief, penetrating paragraph—led to a widespread adoption of that editorial style in the 1930s and resulted in his own items being frequently reprinted in other publications, especially the *Literary Digest*. Fellow journalists later elected him president of the North Carolina Press Association, and he served as treasurer of the School of Journalism Foundation at The University of North Carolina. The foundation was funded largely by gifts from newspapers in the state to upgrade the training of young news writers by supplementing faculty salaries in the School of Journalism.

Ramsey carried his convictions beyond the editorial pages into personal service to community and statewide causes. During World War I he worked as civilian aide to the adjutant general recruiting officer training candidates and as fuel administrator and war savings stamp chairman for Buncombe County. He served on the State Board of Education for eight years, and when the State Board of Higher Education was created in 1955, he became its first chairman, remaining on the board for four years. In addition, he was chairman of the North Carolina Rhodes Scholarship Committee.

His aid to education was cited when The University of North Carolina granted him the LL.D. degree in 1946 and again in 1952, when he received the honorary doctor of literature degree from Western Carolina College, which he had served as a trustee for ten years and nine years as board chairman. Asheville-Biltmore College named its new $850,000 library in September 1965 the D. Hiden Ramsey Library; on that occasion, Governor Dan K. Moore spoke of him as "a man who has dedicated his life to the pursuit of knowledge and the communication of ideas." On the same campus two years earlier, Ramsey had delivered a series of ten lectures on the history of western North Carolina.

Ramsey helped persuade the legislature to create a scholarship loan fund for prospective teachers and a money-saving self-insurance fund covering fire in state school buildings. He editorialized for greater interest in health careers, an idea that won statewide and national attention.

He was a Presbyterian, an active Democrat, and keynote speaker at the North Carolina Democratic Convention in Raleigh in 1940. Ramsey served as president of the North Carolina Railroad Company, North Carolina Society for Crippled Children, North Carolina Conference for Social Service, Asheville Chamber of Commerce, Civitan Club, Executives' Club, and Community Chest and as vice-president of the Medical Foundation of North Carolina. Chairman of the Sinking Fund Commission for seventeen years, he directed its 1936 debt-settlement near the end of the Great Depression. Both the Western North Carolina Historical Association and the North Carolina Society for the Preservation of Antiquities honored him in 1958 for persuading the state to restore the birthplace of Civil War governor Zebulon B. Vance at Reems Creek.

On 30 Jan. 1926 he married Mary Sumner, the daughter of Bynum Hillard (b. 23 July 1872 near Chimney Rock, Rutherford County) and Annie Mae Reynolds Sumner, who were married on 13 June 1895. Bynum Sumner, son of Frank A. and Mary Clark Sumner, moved in 1885 to Asheville, where he founded the B. H. Sumner and Son real estate firm and where he died in May 1945. The Ramseys had one son, D. Hiden, Jr. Darley Hiden Ramsey was buried in Riverside Cemetery, Asheville.

SEE: *Asheville Citizen*, 11 May 1952, 26 Sept. 1954, 1 July 1955, 8 Jan., 17 June 1959, 15 May 1960, 29 Sept. 1965, 19 Feb. 1966; *North Carolina Biography*, vol. 4 (1956); Gary Trawick and Paul Wyche, *One Hundred Years, One Hundred Men* (1971).

JACK RILEY

Randall, William George *(16 Nov. 1860–11 Dec. 1905)*, artist, was born near Table Rock in Upper Creek Township, Burke County, to John and Susan Webb Randall. John was from Buncombe County, where he and Susan lived for some time and where their daughters, Adeline and Elizabeth, were born before their son. From infancy William was left to the care of his widowed mother, who returned to Burke County, where her brother, Thomas Monroe Webb, lived and served at one time as sheriff.

The young boy early began to help his mother and sisters and plowed when he was hardly large and strong enough to "lift the plough around the end of the furrow." In his childhood he grew to love books and had as a teacher Miss Betty Craig, who fostered this love; she taught in a school held in the home of Dr. John McDowell on John's River. Afterwards he attended a Peabody school three miles from his home. Years later Randall was to paint a portrait of George Peabody, copied from a Mayall daguerreotype and now owned by the University of North Carolina at Greensboro. He continued to help the family and worked at odd jobs, farming, and brick making. At sixteen he entered the Table Rock Academy, opened by the Reverend Robert Logan Patton, who had recently returned from Amherst College. Patton encouraged young Will's talent for drawing and showed some of his work to Harvard geologists who were visiting

Table Rock. They sent him the first art materials (paper and crayons) that he had ever owned. He worked in the yard and garden of the Patton home and made a picture of Winnie, the little daughter. Later (ca. 1890) he did a charcoal drawing of Mr. Patton. Randall was interested not only in art but also in history and, asking many questions, he continued to learn from Patton. When he was seventeen and eighteen, Will taught at a free school in Lincoln County at Lowesville.

Determined to go to the state university, he set out in the fall of 1880 to walk to Chapel Hill from the home of his sister, Elizabeth, who had married a Beck of Burke County. Two nights on the way were spent with people known to Robert Patton. At Chapel Hill he was fortunate in being interviewed by the university president, Kemp P. Battle, who, in a short sketch written on 16 Dec. 1906, recalled him as a "pale-faced slender figure, modest and unassuming, but with determination in every feature." His uncle became his surety; Deems Fund money, later repaid in full, was borrowed. The Dialectic Society paid him for being librarian, the first year a salary had been given. In the Southern Historical Collection is a notebook he kept, with many drawings and illustrations, for a zoology course under Frederick Williams Simonds. Randall, who was graduated with high standing in the class of 1884, was class prophet, and James Lee Love was president and valedictorian. Randall's graduating speech on "North Carolina Folk Lore," a "humorous and able disquisition," met with "unusual applause." Later, when the university's enemies were requesting state legislators to cut appropriations because they said it catered only to students of well-to-do families, Randall wrote a beautiful tribute to the university and to Battle. "President Battle made me feel quite at home and I felt as if he had been waiting for the opportunity to make me welcome. . . . I knew the moment I saw his face that I would get sympathy and encouragement. . . . If a young man fails to get along at the University it is his own fault. It is not a rich man's college—it is the poor boy's college: and that State cannot spend money in any other way that will make such large returns." Battle called him "one of the worthiest of all the graduates of the University."

After graduation Randall took charge of the Marion academy, where he met Annie J. Goodloe, of Warrenton, who was an assistant at the school. They were married in 1885. She encouraged him to develop his artistic talent and, after teaching for two years "in accordance with his contract with the state when he secured a county appointment to the University," he went to New York to study at the National Academy of Design. The Right Reverend Theodore B. Lyman, bishop of the Protestant Episcopal Diocese of North Carolina, also encouraged him to study after seeing his work while he was in Marion. While studying at the National Academy he taught drawing and opened a studio but left in 1888 to teach mechanical and free-hand drawing and descriptive geometry at the University of South Carolina. Turning down the offer to become principal of a school in McKinney, Tex., he returned to his native state after a year, as his wife urged him to continue painting. Randall opened a studio in Raleigh in 1889 and did a great deal of portrait painting. Feeling that he needed a broader field, he went to Washington, D.C., in 1893 and had a studio in the Corcoran Building. Then he went to Paris to study and paint; he also traveled and studied in other cities on the Continent and in London. The *North Carolina University Magazine* of Jan. 1895 contains an article he wrote from Paris on 1 Dec. 1894 about the Thanksgiving dinner of the American Art Association. Randall went back to Washington, but the climate was too harsh for him and he returned to Raleigh. In the archives of the University of North Carolina at Greensboro is a copy of an address he gave to the North Carolina Teachers' Assembly at Asheville on 23 June 1896. Titled "The Relation of the Formative Arts to Liberal Education," it is particularly interesting today as now our state colleges do provide for the study of subjects as he wished for then: architecture, sculpture, and painting.

In 1898 Randall built a home on the crest of the Blue Ridge at Blowing Rock. For his health his physician sent him to the Southwest, where he spent several months at Sante Fe, N.Mex., but was not helped and so returned to Blowing Rock. On the back of a photograph of his wife in the archives at Greensboro is the statement that she served "as Registrar, English teacher, supply clerk around 1900 and for some years. Her husband, who died of T.B. while she was here, was an artist. . . . His studio was in the attic of Administration." Randall died at Blowing Rock and his body was taken to Washington, D.C., for burial in Glenwood Cemetery, 2219 Lincoln Road, NE, Lot 302 of Section D. His grave site is 11 and that of his wife, who died at age sixty-eight on 17 Apr. 1918, is 12. Also on the lot are the graves of a stillborn infant and William George Randall, Jr., age three. Another child who died as an infant is listed by Patton.

Randall did some landscape and genre painting, but it was in portraiture that he excelled. In the archives at Greensboro is an undated newspaper clipping that aptly describes his color as "good, in the pictures of men rich and warm, in those of women tender and delicate, all that is natural and correct." According to Patton, there are more than one hundred of his paintings owned by various people. Cuthbert Lee lists twelve portraits and a replica. The North Carolina Department of Cultural Resources has listed fifteen portraits owned by the state, some in storage, some hanging in state buildings in Raleigh. Five of these are also listed in Lee. The University of North Carolina owns nine, but the attribution of the three Mason ladies is questionable. At the University of North Carolina at Greensboro are seven portraits of men, all signed by him. There are four of young ladies that look like his work, but his signature is not discernible. The Greensboro Public Library owns a portrait.

A portrait of Randall, painted by a French artist when he was studying abroad, was presented by his niece, the late Mrs. Nana Beck Daugherty, of Jacksonville, Fla., to Oak Hill School on the Table Rock Road, with which the small Table Rock School he attended was consolidated. An unveiling was held on 16 Nov. 1943 with a display of all of his work that could be found. All known relatives were invited and some participated in the program.

SEE: Archives, including material sent by Mrs. Annie Goodloe Randall to Dr. William Cunningham Smith on 14 Sept. 1911 (Library, University of North Carolina, Greensboro); Biography File, Greensboro City Library; Cuthbert Lee, *Portrait Register* (1968); North Carolina Collection, Pack Memorial Public Library, Asheville; North Carolina Collection and Southern Historical Collection, University of North Carolina, Chapel Hill; R. L. Patton, *William George Randall Artist* (1960); Phillips Russell, *These Old Stone Walls* (1972).

CAROLINE HOLMES BIVINS

Raney, Richard Beverly *(7 Feb. 1860–8 Dec. 1909)*, hotel manager, insurance executive, and philanthropist, was born at Retreat, the family home in Granville County. Of English and Irish descent, he was the youngest of twelve children of Thomas Hall, a planter, and Eliza Partridge Baird Raney. His mother was the daughter of a clergyman from Mecklenburg County, Va.; his father was a direct descendant of John Speed, English historian and cartographer.

Raney attended the Fetter School in Kittrell until he was sixteen, when he was employed by Tredwell and Mallory, cotton factors in Norfolk. In 1878 he became a clerk at the Yarborough House, a noted Raleigh hotel. After gaining experience as a hotel cashier at Kimball House in Atlanta, he returned to Raleigh and leased the Yarborough House in 1883. He also was one of three partners who leased the Atlantic House in Morehead City, which he managed for a time. For fifteen years Raney served as general agent for North Carolina at the Penn Mutual Life Insurance Company and at the same time managed farms in Wake and Warren counties.

He held investments in the North Carolina Wagon Factory, the Raleigh Cotton Mills, the Caraleigh Cotton Mills, and the Caraleigh Phosphate Mills. He served on the board of directors of the South Piedmont Land and Manufacturing Company of Greensboro, the West End Hotel in Winston, and the Commercial and Farmers Bank of Raleigh. He was one of the organizers and a director of the Commercial National Bank and vice-president and director of the Standard Gas and Electric Company.

Raney's first wife, Olivia Blount Cowper, related to the Blount and Grimes families, died in 1896 in childbirth, less than two years after their marriage. As a memorial to her, Raney gave the three-story free circulating library to Raleigh. The Olivia Raney Library opened in January 1901 and provided not only a library but also an auditorium for musical and dramatic productions.

In 1903 Raney married Kate Whiting Denson, daughter of a Confederate officer who, before the Civil War, operated the Duplin Military Institute. Their children included Margaret, who married James Webb of Hillsborough; Richard Beverly, orthopedist and first professor of orthopedic surgery at The University of North Carolina; and Katharine Baird.

Raney died in Raleigh at age forty-nine. He was an active member of Christ Church and was buried in Oakwood Cemetery, Raleigh.

SEE: Samuel A. Ashe, ed., *Biographical History of North Carolina*, vol. 7 (1908), and *Cyclopedia of Eminent and Representative Men of the Carolinas*, vol. 2 (1892); Rosa R. Brandon, *Raney Days* (1974); *North Carolina Biography*, vols. 3 (1928), 4 (1919); *North Carolina Journal of Education* (March, April–May 1900); Raleigh *Evening Times*, 8–9, 15 Dec. 1909; Raleigh *News and Observer*, 9 Dec. 1909, 7 July 1963.

B. W. C. ROBERTS

Rankin, Alexander Martin *(29 Oct. 1857–23 Jan. 1940)*, Methodist Protestant lay leader and benefactor, manufacturer, and industrial pioneer, was identified with the activities of the Annual and General conferences of the Methodist Protestant church for forty years and was a prominent supporter of the Methodist Protestant Children's Home in High Point and High Point College. "Captain Rankin," as he was affectionately known, was the son of William Wharton and Louise Roach Rankin of Benaja, Rockingham County, and attended Yadkin College. For more than twenty years, he was a conductor on the Southern Railway System; later he was president of the Kearns Furniture Company, Carolina Casket Company, Tate Furniture Company, and Alma Furniture Company. He served as a member of the High Point City Council from 1905 to 1909 and as a director of the High Point Mantel and Table Company and the Bank of Randolph. He was also engaged in business enterprises in nearby Greensboro and Asheboro. Rankin suggested the "Century of Progress" observance that was held in High Point in 1938.

Captain Rankin took an active interest in the establishment and maintenance of the Methodist Protestant Children's Home in Denton and gave $500 when the home was later moved to High Point. He served as a trustee from the time the home opened until his death; after 1914, he was secretary-treasurer. In 1901 he was appointed to a ways and means committee to consider the establishment of a Methodist Protestant college in North Carolina, and in 1910 he was named a trustee of the North Carolina Conference Board of Education. He was instrumental in the founding of High Point College, gave $10,000 to it, and served as a trustee from 1924 until his death. He was also a trustee, and treasurer for more than twenty years, of the First Methodist Protestant Church of High Point. Rankin Memorial Methodist Church, founded about 1935 in High Point, was named in his honor.

Rankin attended ten General conferences of the Methodist Protestant church, beginning in 1903; for this distinction, he was honored at the General Conference of 1936 which met in High Point.

Rankin married, first, Mamie Belle Reece, who died in childbirth; they had one daughter who lived for only three years. In 1898 he married Lena May Blair, daughter of Joseph Addison and Martha White Blair of Asheboro. One of their children died young, but surviving were Margaret, Alexander M., Jr., Dorothy Lee, Robert Blair, and Jeanne Blair. Rankin died in High Point and was buried in Oakwood Cemetery.

SEE: J. Elwood Carroll, *History of the North Carolina Annual Conference of the Methodist Protestant Church* (1939); *High Point Enterprise*, 23 Jan. 1940; *Journal of the North Carolina Annual Conference of the Methodist Protestant Church, Our Church Record, The Methodist Protestant Herald*, and *The North Carolina Christian Advocate*, scattered issues; *North Carolina Biography*, vols. 3 (1928), 6 (1919).

RALPH HARDEE RIVES

Rankin, Robert Stanley *(17 Nov. 1899–4 June 1976)*, political science educator, was born in Tusculum, Tenn., the son of Thomas Samuel and Mary Isabel Coile Rankin. During World War I he served briefly as a sergeant. He was graduated from Tusculum College in 1920 and received a master of arts degree (1922) and a doctorate (1924) from Princeton University. Between 1924 and 1927 he taught history and political science at Tusculum College after which he joined the faculty of Duke University, where he remained until his death. Rankin became a full professor in 1934 and taught until his retirement in 1969. He was assistant dean of the graduate school (1929–36), acting dean (1935–36), and chairman of the Department of Political Science (1949–64). His professional and teaching specialties were American constitutional law, political institutions at the state and local levels, and, in his later years, civil liberties. At various times he was visiting professor at Alabama, Stanford, and Columbia universities, and at Wake Forest College. In 1950 Tusculum College awarded him the honorary doctor of laws degree.

Rankin was one of the founders of the Southern Political Science Association and was its president in 1931. He served for a time as book review editor of the *Journal of Politics* and on the executive council of the American Political Science Association. He participated in college basketball, tennis, and track; tennis, however, remained his athletic hobby, and in the early 1930s he won the tennis championship of Durham. At Duke he sat on the Athletic Council and was chairman of the Atlantic Coast Conference. In recognition of his contributions to collegiate athletics, the P. H. Hanes Foundation gave $25,000 in his honor to the Duke Athletic Fund.

He served on the Duke Library board and the academic council, and he headed the campus lecture committee for many years, including the centennial emphasis in 1938–39. By vote of the student body in 1969 he was named Outstanding Professor and commended for his "contributions to Duke University and to its student body, both inside and outside the classroom." An accomplished pianist, Rankin prepared more than three dozen original musical arrangements on various themes. Two of these were recorded for playing on a music box he had manufactured in Switzerland. He also collected and studied maps and worked double acrostics.

Having attracted the attention of national and state business leaders, he was appointed a member of the National Arbitration Panel in 1944. Two years later he was a guest of Princeton University for its bicentennial conference on "The Evolution of Social Institutions in America." In 1947 he was invited to formulate a new program of government for the District of Columbia, in 1949 he was project director for the Connecticut Commission on State Government, and in 1954 he headed a comprehensive state government study in South Carolina. From 1958 Rankin was a consultant to the U.S. Commission on Civil Rights, and in 1960 President Dwight D. Eisenhower appointed him one of the six members of this commission, on which he served until his death. After his death the commission named its library the Robert S. Rankin National Civil Rights Library.

By gubernatorial appointment in 1967 he served as one of six members of Governor Dan K. Moore's Local Government Study Commission. Earlier (1965) the governor had appointed him a member of the Commission on the Study of the Board of Trustees of The University of North Carolina.

Following his retirement after forty-two years of teaching at Duke, Rankin was honored by his colleagues with the publication of a festschrift, *Law and Justice: Essays in Honor of Robert S. Rankin* (1970). Between 1971 and 1976 he served on Phi Beta Kappa's panel of distinguished speakers lecturing on a wide range of related subjects at colleges and universities around the country. Under grants awarded by the National Endowment for the Humanities, he served as director of forums in the humanities in nearly thirty libraries in North Carolina.

Among Rankin's published works were *When Civil Law Fails* (1939), *Readings in American Government* (1939), *Political Science in the South* (1946), and *Government and Administration of North Carolina* (1955). He also was coauthor of *Fundamentals of American National Government* (1955), *Fundamentals of American Government: National, State, Local* (1957), *Freedom and Emergency Powers in the Cold War* (1964), and *Race and the Tobacco Industry* (1970). He was a frequent contributor to both national and state periodicals.

Rankin married Dorothy Newsom of Durham in 1933, and they were the parents of Dorothy Battle (Mrs. Robert Houston Robinson) and Robert S., Jr., both of whom became attorneys. A Presbyterian, he was buried in Maplewood Cemetery, Durham.

SEE: Carl Beck, ed., *Law and Justice: Essays in Honor of Robert S. Rankin* (1970); Duke University News Service (information file); *Durham Morning Herald*, 6 June 1976; *Nat. Cyc. Am. Biog.*, vol. 59 (1980); Raleigh *News and Observer*, 7 July 1976; U.S. Commission on Civil Rights, information release, 2 Nov. 1976; *Who Was Who in America*, vol. 7 (1981).

C. SYLVESTER GREEN

Rankin, Watson Smith *(18 Jan. 1879–8 Sept. 1970)*, physician and foundation executive, was born on a farm near Mooresville. He was the son of John Alexander and Minnie Isabella McCorkle Rankin, who had at least five sons and three daughters. Young Rankin attended the high schools of Mooresville and Statesville and for two years the North Carolina Medical College at Davidson College. After receiving his M.D. degree from the University of Maryland, he did postgraduate work at the Johns Hopkins Medical School for one year. He was a resident in obstetrics at the hospital of the University of Maryland and in pathology at the University Hospital in Baltimore.

In 1903 Rankin became a professor in the School of Medicine established at Wake Forest College that year, and from 1905 to 1909 he was dean of the school. In 1909 he became the first full-time health officer in North Carolina and served in that capacity for sixteen years. Under his administration the State Board of Health became a model for other states. Because hookworm disease and malaria were so prevalent in the state, he made special studies to determine how to eradicate them. Rankin became widely known as the buggy-riding, top-hatted inspector of privies. In 1905 he went to Panama and learned Dr. Henry Carter's methods of mosquito control; the application of those methods caused a rapid decline in the incidence of malaria in North Carolina. On receiving the annual distinguished citizenship award from the North Carolina Citizens Association in 1956, Rankin was called "an evangelist of better health." The W. S. Rankin Health Center of Charlotte and Mecklenburg County was dedicated on his eighty-first birthday (18 Jan. 1960). A ward in the Duke hospital also bears his name.

Rankin was a strong supporter of the establishment of a full-fledged medical school in the state and a crusader for the development of community hospitals. He felt that the principal way to improve health care and alleviate the shortage of doctors in North Carolina, particularly in rural areas, was to increase and improve its hospitals. Until 1924, many of the hospitals in the Carolinas had been established and maintained by surgeons. Rankin thought that the counties and the state as well as private philanthropy should contribute to their establishment and maintenance. His views on health care no doubt influenced James B. Duke to incorporate into the trust indenture of the Duke Endowment provision for the support of nonprofit hospitals in the Carolinas. After his appointment in 1925 as one of the original trustees of the Duke Endowment and director of its Hospital and Orphan sections, Rankin persuaded communities with the help of the endowment to buy private hospitals and maintain them as community responsibilities. When he retired from the directorship of the Hospital and Orphan sections in 1950, his report for the previous year showed that 130 hospitals in North Carolina and 52 in South Carolina were receiving Duke Endowment funds for operation and capital purposes. The Orphan Section was providing assistance to 40 child-caring institutions—27 in North Carolina and 13 in South Carolina.

For thirty-one years Rankin served as chairman of the Duke Endowment Trustees' Committee on Hospitals and Child Care, and he remained a trustee emeritus until he died. He was one of the first promoters of hospitalization insurance in North Carolina. His writings and addresses on medical and health subjects were numerous, and he also wrote and spoke about other subjects, particularly religion and philosophy.

Rankin was a member and an officer of a number of medical and health organizations and a trustee of the American Hospital Association (1935–39). In recognition of his contributions to health and child care, he was awarded the honorary doctor of science degree by Duke, Davidson, Wake Forest, and The University of North Carolina.

On 14 Aug. 1906 Rankin married Elva Margaret Dickson of Wake Forest, and they had one son, Jesse Dickson. Mrs. Rankin died in 1951, and in 1964 Rankin married the former Mrs. Leila Jeffries, who survived him.

Rankin was a member of Omicron Delta Kappa and Alpha Omega Alpha fraternities, and an honorary member of Phi Beta Kappa. He was a Rotarian, a Democrat, and a Baptist. His funeral was held in the Myers Park Baptist Church, of which he was a founder. He was buried in Evergreen Cemetery, Charlotte. His portrait hangs in the library of Duke University.

SEE: *Charlotte Observer*, 10 Sept. 1970; Duke Endowment, *Annual Report*, various years; Raleigh *News and Observer*, 1 Mar. 1925, 9 Sept. 1970; Watson Smith Rankin Papers (Manuscript Department, Duke University Library, Durham); *Who Was Who in America*, vol. 6 (1976).

MATTIE U. RUSSELL

Ransom, Edward [J.?] *(12 Feb. 1833–14 July 1877),* physician, farmer, and legislator, was born in Gloucester County, Va. He attended the University of Virginia and is said to have graduated from Hampden-Sydney College, although the 1867 *Catalogue, General and Annual, of Hampden Sidney College* does not list him among the graduates. In the 1850s he moved to Tyrrell County, N.C., and began farming and practicing medicine. In 1859 he married thirteen-year-old Josephine Alexander; they became the parents of five children: Caroline, Fanny, Abner, Mary, and Tammi.

Ransom was named assistant surgeon of the Thirty-second North Carolina Infantry Regiment on or about 3 Oct. 1861 but was absent with leave in November–December 1861. At the end of the war he resumed his medical practice and farming. He also was active politically from 1872 until his death five years later. In 1872 he was an elector on the Republican state ticket and in 1873–74 he served in the state senate. In 1875 he was elected as an independent from Tyrrell County to the state constitutional convention. At the outset of the 1875 convention Republicans and Democrats were deadlocked, the balance of power being held by three independents of whom Ransom was one. The Democrats nominated Ransom for president of the convention, and after thirteen ballots he broke the deadlock by voting for himself. Republicans thereafter lacked the strength to adjourn the convention, which resulted in a further loss of their power in the state. In the following year Ransom was elected to the state senate as a Democrat, serving during the 1876–77 session.

He died at his home in Columbia, Tyrrell County. His estate was sold to pay for the care of his two youngest children, Mary and Tammi.

SEE: John L. Cheney, ed., *North Carolina Government, 1585–1974* (1975); Compiled Service Records (U.S. National Archives Microfilm, North Carolina State Archives, Raleigh); *Constitutional Convention Journal* (1875); J. G. de Roulhac Hamilton, *History of North Carolina*, vol. 3 (1919), and *Reconstruction in North Carolina* (1914); Weymouth T. Jordan, comp., *North Carolina Troops, 1861–1865: A Roster*, vol. 9 (1983); John W. Moore, *Roster of North Carolina Troops in the War Between the States*, vol. 1 (1882); *North Carolina Business Directory* (1867–68, 1869); Raleigh *Register*, 17 July 1877; Tyrrell County estate papers, marriage bonds, and tax lists (North Carolina State Archives, Raleigh); John H. Wheeler, ed., *Reminiscences and Memoirs of North Carolina and Eminent North Carolinians* (1884); R. A. Shotwell and Natt Atkinson, *Legislative Record 1877* (1877).

JOSEPH EDMUND DEATON

Ransom, Matt[hew] Whitaker *(8 Oct. 1826–8 Oct. 1904),* Confederate soldier, North Carolina attorney general, and U.S. senator, was born in Warren County to Robert and Priscilla West Coffield Whitaker Ransom. He attended Warrenton Academy and was graduated from The University of North Carolina in 1847. Having studied law during his senior year, he was at once admitted to the bar and commenced practice in Warrenton. A Whig in politics, he was a presidential elector on the Scott-Graham ticket in 1852. The same year the state legislature, although under the control of the Democrats, elected the popular Ransom attorney general of North Carolina. Three years later, when the Know-Nothing party absorbed the Whigs in the state, he resigned his position and identified with the Democrats.

In the meantime, Ransom had married Martha Anne Exum of Northampton County on 19 Jan. 1853 and moved to Verona, her fine plantation on the Roanoke River. The couple had eight children, including Matthew W., Jr., Joseph E., George E., Esther, Patrick Exum, and Robert. Ransom represented Northampton County in the lower house of the state legislature from 1858 to 1861, and in the latter year he served as one of three commissioners selected by the legislature to visit the Confederate convention at Montgomery, Ala. At this time he was a strong Union man, but Abraham Lincoln's call for troops made him a secessionist. He entered the Confederate army as a private but was soon commissioned a lieutenant colonel in the First North Carolina state troops and subsequently a colonel of the Thirty-fifth North Carolina Regiment. This unit was a part of his younger brother Robert's brigade, which he later commanded. On 13 June 1863 he was promoted to the rank of brigadier general. Ransom participated in the Battles of Seven Pines, Malvern Hill, Sharpsburg, Plymouth, and Drewry's Bluff and in the siege of Petersburg. Wounded three times during the war, he surrendered his command at Appomattox.

At the close of hostilities Ransom returned to farming and the practice of law in North Carolina. In 1872 he won a seat in the U.S. Senate to succeed Zebulon B. Vance, who had been elected but denied his seat because of political disabilities. He served continuously until 1895. In Washington Ransom acquired considerable influence even though he seldom delivered formal speeches on the floor of the Senate. He was a leader in securing a peaceful settlement to the disputed presidential election of 1876. A fusion of Populists and Republicans in North Carolina brought about his defeat in 1895, but President Grover Cleveland at once appointed him minister to Mexico, a post he held for two years. Afterwards Ransom retired permanently to private life. He died on his seventy-eighth birthday and was buried on his estate, Verona.

SEE: Samuel A. Ashe, ed., *Biographical History of North Carolina*, vol. 1 (1905); *Biog. Dir. Amer. Cong.* (1961); Walter Clark, ed., *Histories of the Several Regiments and Battalions from North Carolina*, vol. 2 (1901); *DAB*, vol. 15 (1934); Raleigh *News and Observer*, 9 Oct. 1904; Ezra J. Warner, *Generals in Gray* (1959 [portrait]); *Who's Who in America, 1903–1905*.

JOHN G. BARRETT

Ransom, Robert, Jr. *(12 Feb. 1828–14 Jan. 1892)*, U.S. army officer, Confederate general, and civil engineer, was born at his family plantation, Bridle Creek, in Warren County. The son of Robert and Priscilla West Coffield Whitaker Ransom, he and his brother, Matt, were educated by private tutors and in academies in Warren and Franklin counties. Appointed to the U.S. Military Academy at West Point, Robert was graduated in 1850. As a young army officer he was assigned to Fort Leavenworth, Kans., and served in New Mexico and elsewhere in the Southwest. Along with most of the command, he contracted cholera early in his career, and for the remainder of his life he suffered a series of illnesses. His frontier duties included constructing isolated forts and scouting against hostile Indians.

In 1854 Ransom left for a year's assignment at West Point as a cavalry instructor. Afterwards he returned to Fort Leavenworth as adjutant of the newly organized First Cavalry. In Washington, D.C., in 1856, he married Mary Elizabeth (Minnie) Huntt and they returned to the Kansas frontier. Kansas was in turmoil as rival factions of proslavery and "free-staters" vied for superiority in the struggle to determine whether slavery would or would not be permitted there. The army was involved in trying to keep peace between the two groups as well as defend the region against increasingly hostile Plains Indians. The population of Kansas more than doubled in a four-month period, and no less than six governors and five acting governors exchanged offices in the course of seven years. Ransom spoke at Topeka in July 1856, when the army dismissed the Territorial Legislature and ordered several citizen militia organizations to disband. The fanatic abolitionist, John Brown, repeatedly assembled his followers as the army tried to disperse them. On one occasion Ransom personally confronted Brown with a cocked pistol and thereby ended Brown's resistance. When asked by Ransom why he had continued to cause trouble, Brown replied: "Oh, I wanted to see what stuff you fellows were made of. . . . I looked into your eye and saw 'shoot' and I was not quite ready to quit Kansas then."

During the next two years, repeated illnesses brought on through exposure and mental fatigue left Ransom physically exhausted, and he was forced to take extended sick leaves. Near the end of 1856 he contracted a serious intestinal disorder, followed by a severe case of pneumonia in 1857. In the spring of 1858 he suffered from lung hemorrhages, and in the fall of the same year he nearly died from typhoid fever. By the early part of 1859, however, he was well enough to return to duty and took up assignments at Fort Riley, Kans., and Fort Wise, Colo. He was promoted to captain in January 1861, but four months later he resigned following the secession of his native state, North Carolina, from the Union.

Back home, he was commissioned captain and ordered to organize a regiment of state troops. It was redesignated the First North Carolina Cavalry, and Ransom was promoted to colonel and made its commanding officer. He came to consider the formation, equipping, and training of this unit to be one of his "best services" of the war. General Wade Hampton later remarked that "much of the efficiency of this noble regiment [was due] to its first colonel, Robert Ransom . . . there was no finer body of men in the army of Northern Virginia." In the spring of 1862 Ransom was promoted to brigadier general for the purpose of organizing the Confederate cavalry under General Albert Sidney Johnston in the West. The fall of New Bern, however, changed these plans, and Ransom was ordered to eastern North Carolina at the head of a brigade of North Carolina infantry.

There was considerable apprehension in North Carolina over the successful coastal invasion of Federal General Ambrose Burnside's troops, and the state government competed successfully with the Confederacy for the use of its own troops in defending its own soil. The Federal troops were able to retain their control over most of the Albemarle Sound region for the duration of the war, but they were never able to muster sufficient strength to capitalize on their hold. The North Carolinians were able to turn this potentially disastrous situation into a successful holding and containment action, and Ransom considered his efforts in this affair as some of his best in "bringing order out of chaos."

By June 1862 there were more pressing needs for his services in resisting General George B. McClellan's march towards Richmond. Ransom's brigade joined Robert E. Lee's forces in the Seven Days' Battle. They fought well despite their futile piecemeal attacks against the strongly held Federal position on Malvern Hill. In September, as Lee initiated his first invasion of the North, the brigade helped General Stonewall Jackson capture Harper's Ferry and then, as part of J. G. Walker's division, stopped three Federal assaults on the bloody Sharpsburg battlefield. By December 1862 Union forces were again moving against Richmond, but this time under their new commander, Ambrose Burnside, by way of Fredericksburg, Va. The battle that took place there was a crushing defeat for the Federals, and Ransom played a major part in the Confederate success. He commanded a division that held Marye's Heights overlooking the town. Repeated Federal frontal attacks across exposed fields against the position resulted in some 9,000 Union casualties versus only about 1,500 on the Confederate side in one day's fighting. With the withdrawal of the Union Army of the Potomac, Ransom's division was once more returned to contain the Federals in North Carolina, this time in response to an enemy attack on the strategically vital Wilmington and Weldon Railroad. The Northerners pushed as far as Goldsboro but failed to capture the town, being successfully contained by the Confederates.

Ransom's success in these campaigns gained him promotion to major general in May 1863, and he was ordered to take over command of Richmond from General D. H. Hill. For two months he organized the defenses of this key city but was forced to give up his post when he had a recurrence of the ill health that had plagued him before the war. By October he had recovered sufficiently to head the Military District of Southwestern Virginia and East Tennessee, where he participated in the fighting around Knoxville and warded off Federal raids and diversionary maneuvers.

In April 1864 he was again ordered to command the defense of Richmond and was instrumental in "bottling up" Union General Benjamin F. Butler's advance up the James River at Bermuda Hundred. In June 1864, as the siege of Petersburg settled down, Ransom was assigned command of General Jubal Early's cavalry and rode out of the Shenandoah Valley to test the defenses of Washington, D.C. The U.S. capital was strong enough, but the Confederates succeeded in instilling a sense of panic among the inhabitants and the Federal government before they returned southwards. Ransom reported that he "came within 100 yards of the defense works" on the northern side of the city, closer than any other Confederate general. This action was to be Ransom's last participation in the fighting. In July 1864 he again took sick but was in charge of an investigation regarding outrages allegedly perpetrated by Confederate General John Morgan's raids in Kentucky. In November he was sent to command the forces at Charleston, S.C., but again became ill and remained on sick leave for the duration of the war.

The depressed and defeated South was not the sort of environment in which Ransom could easily adjust after some twenty years of military life under two dissimilar and competing American governments. From 1865 to 1867 he resided in Wilmington and worked as a freight company's agent and as marshal of the city. Discouraged, he turned to selling railroad supplies to rebuild the devastated southern rail system until 1875. This task completed, he settled down to a life of farming near Richmond, Va., but this interest lasted only four years. Periodically Ransom fell ill, and he frequently visited the mineral springs of western Virginia for the relief of growing rheumatism. In 1878 he became assistant to the U.S. civil engineer in New Bern and worked to improve various rivers and harbors in both Carolinas. He continued this work until his death in New Bern, where he was buried in Cedar Grove Cemetery beside his first wife, who had died in 1881.

In 1884 Ransom married his second wife, Katherine DeWitt Willcox Lumpkin, of Athens, Ga., widow of Francis G. Lumpkin. Ransom's first wife bore him nine children: Fannie Priscilla, Mary Elizabeth Huntt, Robert, Gibson Huntt, James Boisseau Jones, Matt Whitaker (daughter), Henry Huntt, George Gibson, and Seymour Herbert. His second wife gave him three more: Katherine DeWitt, Eugene Mayson, and Emily Carnes.

SEE: George W. Cullum, *Biographical Register of the Officers and Graduates of the U.S. Military Academy* (1891); Jerome Dowd, *Sketches of Prominent Living North Carolinians* (1888); Douglas S. Freeman, *Lee's Lieutenants: A Study in Command*, 3 vols. (1942–44); *New Berne Weekly Journal*, 19 May 1892; John Ransom Collection (Buffalo-Erie County Library, Buffalo, N.Y.); Matt W. Ransom Papers (Southern Historical Collection, University of North Carolina, Chapel Hill); Unfinished autobiography of Robert Ransom and Introduction by David Sweet (Southern Historical Collection, University of North Carolina, Chapel Hill); Jon L. Wakelyn, *Biographical Directory of the Confederacy* (1977).

BENJAMIN RANSOM MCBRIDE

Raper, Arthur Franklin *(8 Nov. 1899–10 Aug. 1979)*, social science analyst, was born in Davidson County, near Lexington, the third of eight children of William Franklin (Frank) and Julia S. Crouse Raper. Frank Raper was a farmer of the Carolina Piedmont and a man greatly interested in public affairs though he never ran for elective office himself. With his wife, encouragement was given to the children in their determination to secure an education; as a result, not only Arthur but also others in the family became successful professional and business leaders.

Arthur Raper received his early education at a school near home. From there he went to Churchland School in Davidson County and then to Jamestown in the adjacent county of Guilford to complete his high school studies. In 1924 he was graduated from The University of North Carolina with a B.A. degree and membership in Phi Beta Kappa; he entered the Graduate School of Vanderbilt University the same year and was awarded an M.A. degree in 1925. After a brief period of work, Raper returned to The University of North Carolina to continue graduate study in sociology. He received a Ph.D. degree in 1931, writing a dissertation entitled "Two Black Belt Counties: Changes in Rural Life since the Advent of the Boll Weevil in Greene and Macon Counties, Georgia." Raper's graduate study was directed by Howard W. Odum, a scholar who had great knowledge of, and concern for, the rural South. There can be little doubt that this association had its effect.

Raper's career was devoted largely to the study of rural life and interracial problems. Before completing graduate study he was employed by the Commission on Interracial Cooperation as research secretary with offices in Atlanta. He spent thirteen years in this position (1926–39) and during that time completed the requirements for his degree before he began teaching at Agnes Scott College, an association that lasted from 1932 to 1939. In 1939 Raper joined the staff of Gunnar Myrdal, the Swedish scholar who had been sought by the Carnegie Corporation to conduct a detailed study of the Negro in America. For two years Raper was associated with this project, during which time he wrote the basic monograph on "Race and Class Pressure," an unpublished manuscript that was deposited in the Schomburg Collection of the New York Public Library. Working with Raper and accompanying him on field trips to the Deep South was another young scholar, Ralph Bunche, who later gained distinction for his service to the United Nations. The completed Myrdal study was published in 1942 as a two-volume work under the title *An American Dilemma*.

In 1940 Raper began his long association with agencies of the federal government. From 1940 to 1952 he was employed as a social scientist by the U.S. Department of Agriculture, Bureau of Agricultural Economics, and in the years immediately following the war—1947, 1948, and 1949—he served the bureau in Japan as a social and economic consultant. Upon leaving the Bureau of Agricultural Economics in 1952, Raper spent the years 1952–54 with the Foreign Operations Administration of the Mutual Security Mission to China—actually Taiwan—and from 1955 to 1962 he was associated in various capacities with the International Cooperation Administration, working on assignments in the Middle East, North Africa, and Asia. In 1962 Raper was appointed senior adviser to the Pakistan Academy for Rural Development in East Pakistan; this work was sponsored jointly by Michigan State University and the Ford Foundation. After the completion of the program in 1964, he joined Michigan State University's Asian Studies Center and until his retirement in 1967 held the title of visiting professor of sociology.

Raper wrote, edited, or contributed to at least nineteen books, each dealing with problems of rural life, and his articles were published in scholarly journals. His best-known books were *Tragedy of Lynching* (1933), *Preface to Peasantry* (1936), *Sharecroppers All* with Ira De A. Reid (1941), and *Tenants of the Almighty* (1943). Raper's concern for racial and social justice was genuine; this is evident by the variety and nature of outside activities that laid claim to his time. He was a mediation representative for the National War Labor Board, a member of the board of the National Sharecroppers' Fund and of the Southern Regional Council, for two years executive secretary of the Council on a Christian Social Order (1938–40), and for six years (1946–52) a trustee of the Delta Cooperative Farms, Inc.

On 12 June 1929 Raper married Martha Elizabeth Jarrell, and they were the parents of four children—Charles Franklin, Harrison Crouse (Roper), Arthur Jarrell, and Margaret Raper Hummon. As for politics, Raper referred to himself as "usually a Democrat," and in religion, "at first [a] Moravian, then a Methodist by marriage." His death was apparently the result of a heart attack. Services were held in the Oakton United Methodist Church, Oakton, Va., with interment in the Oakton Cemetery.

SEE: *Contemporary Authors*, vols. 61–64 (1976); Arthur Franklin Raper Papers (Southern Historical Collection, University of North Carolina, Chapel Hill); Howard and Kenneth Raper (brothers), personal contact; *Washington Post*, 12 Aug. 1979; *Washington Star*, 13 Aug. 1979 (portrait); *Who's Who in America* (1968–69); *Winston-Salem Journal*, 13 Aug. 1979.

J. ISAAC COPELAND

Raper, Charles Lee *(10 Mar. 1870–27 Dec. 1957)*, historian, economist, and educator, was born near High Point, the son of Solomon Andrew and Luzena Hitchcoch Raper. He was graduated in 1892 with a B.A. degree from Trinity College (now Duke University) when it was located in Randolph County and served as Latin and Greek instructor at Trinity the following year. From 1894 to 1898 he taught at the Greensboro Female College. Under the direction of Professor Herbert L. Osgood, he was awarded the Ph.D. degree from Columbia University in 1902; in 1900 and 1901 he also lectured at Barnard College and Columbia.

In the latter year Raper returned to North Carolina and began a successful academic career at The University of North Carolina, serving first as associate professor of economics and history (1901–6), then professor of economics (1906–20). He also headed the economics department at one time and served as dean of the Graduate School (1909–20). In 1920 he moved to Syracuse University, serving first as professor of transportation, then as dean of business administration (1921–43), and subsequently as vice-chancellor of the university (1936–42). A noted authority on taxation and transportation, Raper was a member of the New York State Planning Council (1934–41) and administrator for the War Transportation Commission for Syracuse and Onondaga County (1942–45), formulating numerous reports on industrial trends and taxation for both the state and national governments. He was known particularly for his strong opposition to the St. Lawrence Seaway development and criticism of the Tennessee Valley Authority. Raper also served on the New York Council against Discrimination in Employment (1946–57).

An outstanding scholar and writer, he was the author of many articles and books, including *The Church and Private Schools of North Carolina* (1898); *A Study in English Colonial Government* (1904), the first definitive study of the provincial government in North Carolina; *Principles of Wealth and Welfare* (1906); and *Railway Transportation* (1912). He received honorary degrees from Lenoir-Rhyne (1917), Duke University (1939), and Syracuse University (1944).

In 1904 Raper married Henrietta Frost Williams, of Paterson, N.J., who predeceased him. Both were buried in Syracuse, N.Y. They were the parents of a daughter, Mary Lee (Mrs. Kenneth S. Graves).

SEE: *High Point Enterprise*, 16 Sept. 1928; *New York Times*, 29 Dec. 1957; Charles L. Van Noppen Papers (Manuscript Department, Duke University Library, Durham); *Who Was Who in America*, vol. 4 (1940).

HORACE W. RAPER

Raper, John Robert *(3 Oct. 1911–21 May 1974)*, botanist of international note, was born in Davidson County, near the hamlet of Welcome. He was the youngest of eight children—seven sons and one daughter—of William Franklin (Frank) and Julia S. Crouse Raper. "Mr. Frank," as the father was known to friends and neighbors, was a farmer who with the help of his sons raised tobacco and other crops; though not prosperous, he was highly respected in the community. In the last decades of his life he was not in robust health, and as the older sons left home, first to attend high school and then college, a small dairy herd replaced tobacco as the principal source of farm income. Much of the responsibility for tending the cattle fell to John during his high school years. Mrs. Raper was an efficient manager, and as the mother of a large family she still found time to devote to her children and to instill in them strong moral and spiritual values. Her husband gave firm support in the rearing of the children, who received every encouragement other than financial aid in their quest for an education.

The Rapers' home was located in the vicinity of three churches—Friedburg and Enterprise, both Moravian, and Mount Olivet, which was Methodist. The family worshiped at each, and as John Raper himself once noted, "often [at] all three on the same Sunday." Mrs. Raper taught a Sunday school class for many years, and the family's church memberships were divided between the two denominations.

It was amid such surroundings and in such a community that John Raper was reared. His formal education began in a three-room neighborhood elementary school. After completing the fourth grade he attended Arcadia School, a consolidated elementary-high school that had been recently built, largely through the efforts of Frank Raper and on land that he had donated. John entered The University of North Carolina in the fall of 1929. In high school English grammar and literature and French had been favorite subjects, with little time left for other things after farm chores were completed. But in those free hours music became his recreation and his hobby.

During the last quarter of his freshman year in Chapel Hill Raper was enrolled in "Introductory Botany," a course taught by John Couch, and it marked the beginning of his serious interest in science. This was, in fact, his first formal instruction in science, but more important it carried a spark that kindled his interest. Courses in botany and zoology taken during the sophomore year sustained and heightened this interest, and for the junior year he was offered a teaching assistantship in botany. Raper was graduated in 1933 with a bachelor of arts degree and in 1936 with a master of arts. His master's thesis, "Heterothallism and Sterility in Achyla and Observations on the Cytology of Achyla Bisexuales," bears the approval signatures of both Couch and William C. Coker.

Raper continued his graduate study at Harvard, where his mentor was Professor William Weston, and in 1939 he was awarded the doctorate and a second master's degree. He spent the academic years 1939–40 and 1940–41 as a research fellow at the California Institute of Technology. In the fall of 1941 he joined the Department of Botany at Indiana University as an instructor and remained there until 1943, when he was called to the Manhattan Project in Oak Ridge, Tenn.; he worked at Oak

Ridge for three years as a research biologist. With the end of World War II, he was invited to join the faculty of the University of Chicago as an assistant professor. From 1946 to 1954 he rose rapidly in rank to professor and then in the latter year accepted an offer to return to Harvard, where from 1970 until his death four years later Raper was chairman of the Department of Botany.

Honors and recognition came to John Raper in full measure. In 1960–61 he held both a Guggenheim Fellowship and a Fulbright Research Award; the same year he was a guest research professor at the Botanisches Institut der Universität in Köln, Germany. In 1967 he was visiting professor of genetics at the Hebrew University, Jerusalem, and with his wife (also a scientist) he had planned to spend 1974–75 as sabbatical leave at the Rijksuniversiteit te Groningen, Netherlands. Raper was a member of the American Academy of Arts and Sciences, and in 1964 he was elected to the National Academy of Science. He held membership in numerous scientific societies such as the American Society of Naturalists, the Botanical Society of America, and the Genetics Society. In 1958 he was president of the Mycological Society of America.

During the twenty years of teaching at Harvard Raper continued his research on the complicated genetics and physiology of Schizophyllum and related fungi. He taught both graduate and undergraduate courses and guided the doctoral research of a number of students. His major published work was *Genetics of Sexuality in Higher Fungi*, but in addition he was the author of over one hundred publications in related fields.

Friends knew of Raper's love for and appreciation of music, but perhaps few of those who came to know him after his student days realized the extent of his talent. As a very young boy he began to play the trumpet, due at least in part to his Moravian heritage; this is understood when one is reminded of the beautiful and remarkable brass choirs so frequently used in the worship service of Moravian congregations. He was a member of The University of North Carolina's band, symphony orchestra, and glee club, and on the professional level played with the North Carolina Symphony Orchestra. For a brief period he seriously considered music as a profession.

Raper died in Peter Bent Brigham Hospital after a brief illness. A few years earlier evidence of a heart murmur had been detected, but the cause of his final illness eluded doctors at the time. He was survived by his wife, the former Carlene Marie Allen, whom he had married on 9 Aug. 1949, by their children, Jonathan and Linda, and by William, his son by a previous marriage to Ruth Scholz. A memorial service, conducted in Harvard's Memorial Church on 30 May, was filled with the music of composers he loved—the Gabrielis, J. S. Bach, Monteverdi, and Vittoria. Perhaps John Raper is best characterized in a tribute paid by Kenneth, the brother a few years older and himself a distinguished scientist and member of the National Academy of Science, when he said, "John was withal a very generous and talented man with a complex personality—sometimes serene, often impulsive, occasionally quixotic, but never dull! He was a good man, husband and father and, fortunately, for seven of us a younger and beloved brother."

SEE: *Harvard Crimson*, 24 May 1974, *Harvard Gazette*, 24 May 1974, and Memorial Minute [of the] Faculty of Arts and Sciences, 15 Feb. 1977, as printed in *Harvard Gazette*, 29 Apr. 1977 (Harvard University Archives, Cambridge); *New York Times Biographical Edition*, 24 May 1974; Howard and Kenneth Raper (brothers), personal contact; Student records (Archives, University of North Carolina, Chapel Hill); Typescripts of the "Raper Reunion, Boothbay Harbor, Maine, 30 July–3 Aug. 1965" and "Memorial Service, 30 May 1974" (possession of Howard Raper); *Who's Who in America* (1974–75); *Yackety Yack* (1933—University of North Carolina student yearbook).

J. ISAAC COPELAND

Ravenscroft, John Stark *(17 May 1772–5 Mar. 1830)*, first bishop of the Protestant Episcopal church in North Carolina and twentieth in succession in the American episcopate, was born on his parents' plantation near Blandford, Prince George County, Va. His father, John Ravenscroft, a physician and planter, was of English and Scottish descent. His mother, Lillias Miller, was the daughter of Hugh Miller, a Scot who had settled in the same county. Dr. and Mrs. Ravenscroft were cousins, being great-grandson and granddaughter of Colonel Robert Bolling.

When John Stark was less than a year old, the family moved to Scotland, where young Ravenscroft received his early education. His father died in 1788, and the youth returned to Virginia to secure the remnants of the family property there. He entered William and Mary College, where he studied law under George Wythe and St. George Tucker. His youth, ample means, and freedom from supervision soon identified him with the undisciplined element of the college, by whom he was known as "Mad Jack" for his "vehemence of temper, speech and manner."

His marriage in 1792 to Anne Spottswood Burwell, daughter of Lewis Burwell, a young woman of beauty of person and strength of character, effectively changed the course of his life. Gambling and horse racing were laid aside, and the young Ravenscrofts settled on a plantation in Lunenburg County as respected members of the community. Ravenscroft was still indifferent to religion, however; it was not until eighteen years later that he became concerned with his soul's condition. He joined a congregation of Republican Methodists and served as their lay reader. Doubt as to the validity of this denomination's sacraments led him to the Episcopal church, and it was not long before he determined to join its clergy. Prepared by the Right Reverend Richard Channing Moore, bishop of Virginia, Ravenscroft was ordained deacon on 25 Apr. 1817 and eleven days later was made priest. He was rector of St. James's Church, Boydton, Va., from 1817 to 1823. Declining invitations to more advantageous parishes, he was about to become Bishop Moore's assistant at Monumental Memorial Church, Richmond, when the newly formed Diocese of North Carolina chose him as its first bishop. He was consecrated during the session of the General Convention in St. Paul's Church, Philadelphia, on 22 May 1823.

Having suffered financial reverses, the new bishop was obliged to augment his episcopal salary of $750 a year by becoming rector of Christ Church, Raleigh, giving six months of the year to each office. A vigilant and energetic shepherd of his flock, he traveled from end to end of his diocese, nurturing the small congregations and founding new ones. At the time of his death the number of congregations had more than doubled. During his entire ministry, he never missed a General Convention of the church nor a convention of his diocese. His constant traveling took its toll; in 1828 his health forced him to give up the Raleigh parish and take the smaller congregation at Williamsboro under his charge. In the summer of 1829, in response to "a very pressing invitation from the Episcopal Congregations in the State of Tennessee, to visit them, for the purpose of performing Episcopal duties," Ravenscroft undertook the difficult trip from his home in Williamsboro to Tennessee. On 1 July he presided over the convention of clergy and laity that organized the Diocese of Tennessee. Ravenscroft noted in his journal that he found the people of Tennessee to be "orderly and civil in their deportment, and certainly more civilized and intelligent in their appearance and conversation, than the same class of men in Virginia and North Carolina."

Speaking of Ravenscroft as a preacher, W. M. Green, one of the bishop's clergy, wrote: "As a Preacher he was justly entitled to be called *evangelical* in the proper and unabused sense of that term." Concerning Ravenscroft's churchmanship, Green said: "Bishop Ravenscroft was what the world is pleased to call a 'High-Churchman,' but was, in no sense, a Party-man." He was "fearless" in proclaiming the church's "Apostolic and authoritative character."

His wife died in 1814, and in 1818 he married Sarah Buford, of Lunenburg County, Va. Having no children of his own, he had adopted several of the young Hepburn boys, orphans of a friend in Lunenburg County. Two are mentioned in his will, and it is thought that one or more in addition were members of his household. After the second Mrs. Ravenscroft's death in 1829, the bishop determined to move to Fayetteville, but on his way there he died in Raleigh at the home of his friend Gavin Hogg. He was buried under the chancel of Christ Church.

Over six feet tall, erect, and commanding in presence, with a deep, strong voice and a stern and sometimes harsh demeanor, Ravenscroft preached a strict, unbending doctrine. He laid the foundations for a church that bore the earmarks of his work for more than a hundred years after his death. During his brief tenure, the church in North Carolina grew steadily in size and strength. Bishop Ravenscroft received S.T.D. and D.D. degrees from Columbia College, N.Y., and The University of North Carolina. A striking portrait of him, painted by Jacob Eicholtz in Philadelphia in 1829, hangs in the parlor of St. Mary's College, Raleigh.

SEE: Joseph B. Cheshire, "Bishop Ravenscroft," *Carolina Churchman* (November 1910); William M. Green, *Bishop Ravenscroft* (1870); Marshall DeLancey Haywood, *Lives of the Bishops of North Carolina* (1910); *Journals of the Diocese of North Carolina* (1823–30); *Notes on St. Mary's Paintings* (undated pamphlet), St. Mary's College, Raleigh; Rev. J. D. M. Wainwright, ed., *Sermons and Memoir of the Life of Bishop John Stark Ravenscroft* (1830); *Works of the Rt. Rev. John Stark Ravenscroft, D.D.* (1856).

JAQUELIN DRANE NASH

Ray, John Edwin *(22 Jan. 1852–17 Jan. 1918)*, educator, was born near Neuse in Wake County, the son of Joseph and Mary Justice Ray. He was graduated from Wake Forest College with an A.M. degree in 1875. For ten years he served as a teacher at the North Carolina Institute for the Blind in Raleigh. During the period 1887–94 he was superintendent of the Colorado Springs School for the Deaf and Blind, and from 1894 to 1896 he was superintendent of the Kentucky State School for the Deaf and Dumb. Returning to Raleigh in 1896, he served as superintendent of the North Carolina School for the Blind until his death twenty-one years later.

Ray was influential in persuading the state legislature to appropriate funds for the school. The culmination of his efforts was the purchase shortly before his death of an eight-acre tract west of the state prison for a new school. His concern for education extended into politics, as he worked with J. Y. Joyner, state superintendent of public instruction, to convince voters of the need for a local school tax.

Active in his church, Ray served as a deacon and a Sunday school teacher in the First Baptist Church of Raleigh. He also was corresponding secretary of the Baptist State Convention from 1877 to 1889 and a member of the board of trustees for Meredith College and the Thomasville Orphanage. He was the author of *A Trip Abroad: Sketches of Men and Manners, People and Places, in Europe* (1882) and *Our Danger Signal* (1892), which advocated prohibition.

In November 1881 he married Finie Carter of Wilson. Their children were Mrs. C. O. Abernathy, Mrs. Arthur Henderson, Hardy Murphee, Dr. Barton J., and Dr. John E.; John was killed in action in World War II. Mrs. Ray was widely known for her work with disabled veterans in North Carolina, and because of her assistance at the U.S. Veterans Hospital at Oteen near Asheville, she was referred to as "Mother Ray." An evergreen tree was planted in Capitol Square, Raleigh, in her honor. Ray died in Raleigh and was buried in Oakwood Cemetery.

SEE: George W. Paschal, *History of Wake Forest College*, vol. 2 (1943); Raleigh *News and Observer*, 18, 21 Jan. 1918; John E. Ray, *A Trip Abroad* (1882); Southern Education Board Papers, Joyner Series (North Carolina State Archives, Raleigh).

REBECCA S. MASON

Ray, John Robert *(1852–post-1891)*, labor organizer, printer, and newspaperman, a native of North Carolina, was probably born in Raleigh. Since his mother, Mrs. Rachel T. Ray, was identified in Raleigh city directories as a widow, his father may have died when the son was young. The 1870 census identifies Ray as an eighteen-year-old printer residing in the household of his mother. On 23 Oct. 1873 Ray married Lucetta J. Dollar at the residence of the Reverend D. P. Meacham, minister of the Central Methodist Church.

In Raleigh on 6 Apr. 1876 Ray began publishing a triweekly Republican newspaper, the *Constitution*. The North Carolina State Republican Convention met in Raleigh on 12 and adjourned on 17 July 1876, the day on which the *Constitution* ceased publication; therefore, it appears that Ray's venture into journalism was likely to have been at the behest of the Republican party. Various Raleigh city directories between 1875 and 1891 indicate that Ray continued to work as a printer and, in 1888 and 1891, as a compositor, while his wife was a dressmaker. For much of his working life he was employed in Raleigh by the Edwards and Broughton Company, printers and publishers, but in 1883 he was employed by Uzzell and Gatling, printers. In 1879 he was also identified as corresponding secretary of the Raleigh typographical union.

On two unspecified occasions Ray reportedly was in Massachusetts, perhaps in search of employment, but it was in 1884 after his return from Philadelphia to attend the eighth annual general assembly of the Knights of Labor that he became active as state organizer of the Noble Order of Knights of Labor in America. At the Philadelphia meeting Ray suggested that paid organizers be sent to every southern state.

The first local assembly of the Knights in North Carolina, composed of workers in a variety of occupations, was organized by Ray in Raleigh on 18 June 1884; later that year he also organized a local for blacks. A convention held on 11 Aug. 1886 formed a state assembly. By 1886 there were four assemblies in Raleigh and two years later Durham had five. Other active groups existed in Guilford County and in the towns of Asheville, Charlotte, Salisbury, Statesville, and Wilmington. Ray also went to South Carolina, the last southern state to have an assembly, and there he not only organized a local group but also left a capable member to extend the order.

In North Carolina blacks expressed dissatisfaction with their treatment as members of the Knights, and Ray took steps to meet their complaints. Efforts were made to see that job opportunities were available to both races, and Ray insisted that black organizers receive commissions equal to those paid to whites.

In Wilmington the *Daily Index* was established, apparently in 1886, as "the organ of the Knights of Labor in this state," but since no copies have survived, it is not known whether Ray played a role in its publication. By 1887 assemblies had been organized in more than half of the counties in the state, although most of them were small and ineffective.

The Raleigh assembly of which Ray was an active member agitated for a ten-hour day, participated in a national boycott, brought speakers on labor subjects to address the members, encouraged self-improvement for work advancement, visited the sick, and provided financial assistance for distressed members. It also studied proposals for and supported cooperative production; the Raleigh local had a tobacco factory and its products were sold in nearly all of the city's stores. Members were encouraged to contact their representatives in the General Assembly in support of beneficial legislation. On occasion the local assembly also sent funds to aid strikers outside the state.

During at least a part of the time while Ray was peacefully organizing labor, "roving agitators" passed through the state. Labor unrest in other parts of the nation produced claims of "anarchism," and shouts of "Vive la Commune" were heard. A bomb exploded in Haymarket Square, Chicago, on 4 May 1886, and a futile attempt was made to associate Ray with some of the events there. Investigation revealed, however, that he had been falsely accused and he was exonerated. A Durham tobacco worker, under duress, had been forced to implicate Ray. Ray had been aware of the activity in opposition to him and had warned workers to use caution in associating with outsiders.

The North Carolina General Assembly in 1887 created the Bureau of Labor Statistics. Its first annual report issued later in the year contained a number of letters concerning the state policy of leasing convicts to private businesses as laborers and construction workers. One of these, dated 25 July 1887, was written by Ray; it advocated "abolition of the penitentiary system and a return to corporal punishment for certain offences." In a well-reasoned and clearly stated argument, he proposed the use of prison labor for work on public roads and waterways and in producing the necessities of prison life. He also favored abolishing capital punishment and substituting solitary confinement. His objective, of course, was the elimination of prison labor in competition with free labor.

Leaving his wife and mother in Raleigh, Ray in August 1887 took a job for a brief time as telegraph editor of a daily newspaper in Wilmington, perhaps the *Daily Index*. Evidence of considerable labor organizing activity in Wilmington during the period 1886–88, including that among telegraph operators, suggests that Ray was hard at work in that field as well. After 1887 he appears to have ended his involvement with the Knights of Labor and to have been involved only in the typographical union, an organization dating from before the Civil War in the state.

In a letter to a national officer of the Knights, Ray in 1886 recounted some of the hardships of his work. He noted that he had "walked over a greater portion of this State" and sometimes had gone nearly two days and nights without food. He had been obliged to sleep in the woods and had had to face mobs gathered to take his life. Now, at the time he was writing, "I have not a penny in the world and no work, while my family are suffering for the necessaries of life."

By 1890 labor activity had virtually ceased in North Carolina. The American Federation of Labor had been organized in 1886, and such activity as occurred involved workers in skilled industry. Mrs. Rachel Ray died on 18 Nov. 1892. John R. Ray and his wife ceased to appear in city directories after that date, although the 1891 city directory identified him as a compositor with Edwards and Broughton. There is nothing to suggest that they had any children.

SEE: Charlotte *Home-Democrat*, 22 Oct. 1886; H. M. Douty, "Early Labor Organizations in North Carolina, 1880–1900," *South Atlantic Quarterly* 34 (1935); Jonathan Garlock, comp., *Guide to the Local Assemblies of the Knights of Labor* (1982); Harley E. Jolley, "The Labor Movement in North Carolina, 1880–1922," *North Carolina Historical Review* 30 (1953); Melton A. McLaurin, *The Knights of Labor in the South* (1978); Minute Book, Local Assembly No. 3606, Knights of Labor (North Carolina State Archives, Raleigh); North Carolina Bureau of Labor Statistics, *First Annual Report* (1887); Raleigh *Daily Sentinel*, 24 Oct. 1873; Raleigh *News and Observer*, 19 Nov. 1892; *Records of the Proceedings of the Eighth Regular Session of the General Assembly [of the Knights of Labor] Held at Philadelphia, Pa., Sept. 1–10, 1884* (1884).

WILLIAM S. POWELL

Rayner, John Baptis *(1850–14 July 1918)*, educator and politician, was born into slavery in Raleigh, the son of Kenneth Rayner, a prominent plantation owner, and Mary Ricks, a slave. With the aid of his father, Rayner pursued his education after the Civil War at St. Augustine's Episcopal School in Raleigh and later at both Shaw University and St. Augustine Collegiate Institute. Upon completing his studies, Rayner taught in rural schools near Raleigh. He was first elected to public office in Tarboro, where he served as deputy sheriff. In 1874 Rayner married Susan Clark Staten and they became the parents of two children, Mary and Ivan Edward. Following his religious conversion, Rayner worked for a time in North Carolina as a Baptist minister.

In 1881 Rayner moved his family to Robertson County, Tex., where he taught school, preached, and became associated with R. L. Smith's Farmers Improvement Society. After the death of his first wife he married Clarissa S. Clark, who bore him three additional children: Ahmed Arabi, Loris Melikoff, and Susie. By 1892 Rayner exchanged his original Republican sympathies for Populism and became a highly regarded stump speaker and organizer credited with bringing thousands of Afro-Americans into the Populist party. As a member of the party's state executive committee in 1895 and 1896, he wrote two articles for its organ, the *Southern Mercury*: "Political Imbroglio in Texas" (1, 5 Aug., 19 Sept. 1895) and "Modern Political Methods" (9 Apr., 26 June 1896). These articles represent Rayner's major published statements on Populism and Afro-American politics.

With the gradual absorption of many Texas Populists into the Democratic party after the election of 1896, Rayner also became more active in Democratic politics.

He identified himself with self-help and vocational education programs for black people in Texas. In 1902 and 1903 he helped to found the Texas Law and Order League, an organization designed to promote employment and greater conformity to law among Afro-Americans. By the fall of 1904 he had accepted a position as financial agent for the developing Conroe-Porter Industrial College of Conroe, Tex. Rayner remained in that position for two years. During this period he also began to work in the Republican party for the first time since his days in North Carolina. In August 1911 Rayner was appointed by R. L. Smith to serve as financial agent and fund-raiser for the Farmers Improvement Society School at Ladonia, Tex. Retiring in 1913, Rayner spent the last five years of his life in Calvert, Tex., writing solicited letters to the editors of several newspapers in Texas and working to a limited extent for local Republican candidates. He died in Calvert.

SEE: Jack Abramowitz, "John B. Rayner—A Grass Roots Leader," *Journal of Negro History* 36 (April 1951); Alwyn Barr, *Black Texans* (1973 [portrait]); Gregg Cantrell, *Kenneth and John B. Rayner and the Limits of Southern Dissent* (1993); Roscoe C. Martin, *The People's Party in Texas* (1933); John B. Rayner Papers (Schomburg Collection, New York Public Library, N.Y.).

WILLIAM L. ANDREWS

Rayner, Kenneth *(20 June 1808–5 Mar. 1884)*, congressman, legislator, national leader of the Whig party, and planter was born in Bertie County, the son of the Reverend Amos Rayner, a Baptist minister and a veteran of the Revolutionary War, and Hannah Williams Rayner, whose family was from Gates and Hertford counties and from whom he inherited a large plantation near Winton. Educated at the Tarboro Academy, he read law under Chief Justice Thomas Ruffin but never practiced. He entered politics and in 1835 was elected to the North Carolina Constitutional Convention. Here Rayner, the youngest delegate present, associated with Nathaniel Macon, William Gaston, David L. Swain, John M. Morehead, and other prominent leaders of the state. Rayner participated in the debate and attracted statewide attention. Despite his antislavery views he served in the state House of Commons in 1835, 1836, and 1838 and in the U.S. Congress during the period 1839–45. Returning to the General Assembly, he served in the lower house between 1845 and 1851 and in the senate in 1854–55.

While in Congress Rayner acquired a national reputation. He had entered politics as a supporter of Andrew Jackson, but he followed John C. Calhoun as an advocate of strong states' rights and throughout his congressional career was a consistent and vocal antagonist of John Quincy Adams. During his stormy congressional service, he opposed the annexation of Texas and fought the policies of both Martin Van Buren and John Tyler. A man of fiery temper, Rayner on several occasions came to blows on the floor of the House and at other times served as a second in duels between political figures of the day.

In 1848 Rayner sought an honor, which had he achieved it, would have made him president of the United States. His close personal friend, Zachary Taylor, was seeking the Whig nomination for the presidency, and it was Rayner's desire to join him on the ticket as candidate for the vice-presidency. Taylor's nomination was assured inasmuch as he had the backing of Thurlow Weed, of New York, the powerful boss of the Whig party. Rayner's opponent for the vice-presidential nomination was Millard Fillmore. The two men were close friends and agreed to submit their pretensions to a caucus of party leaders to choose between them. There Rayner lost to Fillmore by one vote. Taylor and Fillmore went on to victory. After but a year in office, Taylor died, and it is reported that Rayner was among those attending the inauguration of President Millard Fillmore on Wednesday, 10 July 1850, at noon in the hall of the House of Representatives.

Many years later when Rayner, then a poor old man and no longer a power in public affairs, was solicitor of the U.S. Treasury (1877–84) under appointment of President Ulysses S. Grant, the incumbent president, James Garfield, was urged to turn Rayner out because he had not been a Garfield supporter. Garfield refused, stating: "I won't do it. Though an old man, and out of favor with fortune he was a host in his day. He is still an able and accomplished lawyer. He fills the office admirably, and he needs the salary. He may not have many friends—but he has at least one and a mighty important friend, for it is I myself—and I am not going to turn him out. I am not going to remove from a little place in the Treasury, whose duties he fully meets, an old man who came within a single vote of filling the place I fill, and being President of the United States."

Following his failure to win the vice-presidential nomination, Rayner's political career began to decline. In 1852 he repudiated the nomination of Winfield Scott and became a leader of the new American or Know-Nothing party. Within his new political affiliation he obtained the party's agreement to defend the Union under all circumstances, a sentiment that he personally never completely abrogated.

When President Abraham Lincoln called for troops, however, Rayner's states' rights philosophy forced him to support secession, and he was a member of the Secession Convention of 1861. Rayner had married Susan Polk (1822–1909), the daughter of Colonel William Polk of Raleigh, and he remained in Raleigh during the war. He personally disliked Jefferson Davis and refused to vote for him. In 1863 he secretly joined a peace movement and the following year, as General William T. Sherman approached the city, Rayner formally surrendered North Carolina's capital to the Union army. In 1865 he endorsed Andrew Johnson's policies for the South, and in 1866 he anonymously published the first biography of the new president—a volume of 363 pages.

Rayner became a Republican. In 1869 he moved to Tennessee and from there to Mississippi, where he owned cotton plantations as he did in Arkansas. President Grant appointed him judge of the *Alabama* Claims Commission, a position he resigned in 1877 to become solicitor of the U.S. Treasury, a post he held until his death.

A number of Rayner's addresses and speeches were published. Among them was one he delivered at the convention of 1835 and another before the graduating class of the U.S. Military Academy at West Point in 1853, when he was a member of the Board of Visitors.

Rayner was buried in the Polk family plot in the Old City Cemetery, Raleigh. He and Mrs. Rayner were the parents of Sallie (1845), Henry Albert (1847), Kenneth, Jr. (1849), Fanny (1851), Susan (1853), William (1857), and Hamilton (1860). By Mary Ricks, a slave, he also was the father of John B. Rayner (1850) and apparently of Cornelia as well. There may also have been another mulatto son.

SEE: John H. Brown, ed., *Cyclopaedia of American Biographies*, vol. 6 (1903); *DAB*, vol. 15 (1928); J. G. de Roulhac Hamilton, ed., *The Papers of Thomas Ruffin*, vols. 2–4

(1918–20); *New York Times*, 6 Mar. 1884; John Nichols, *History of Hiram Lodge No. 40, Raleigh* ([1901]); Kenneth Rayner Papers (Southern Historical Collection, University of North Carolina, Chapel Hill); Raleigh *News and Observer*, 6 Mar. 1884; John H. Wheeler, *Historical Sketches of North Carolina* (1851) and ed., *Reminiscences and Memoirs of North Carolina and Eminent North Carolinians* (1884); B. B. Winborne, *Colonial and State Political History of Hertford County* (1906).

JOHN R. JORDAN, JR.

Read, Jesse *(1744–6 June 1820),* Revolutionary War officer, Baptist minister, and historian, apparently was born in Isle of Wight County, Va. His father, Harmon Read, bought land in Halifax County, N.C., and died there in 1767, bequeathing to his son the home plantation. His mother, Mary Pendry Read, died testate in 1781, and he and his brother Moses served as joint executors of her comfortable estate. The writings of Jesse Read reveal few details of his labors in the ministry and modestly fail to include any reference to his youth in Halifax County or to his military career of five years in the Continental Line.

Early in the Revolution—on 20 Oct. 1776—he entered the Sixth North Carolina Regiment with the rank of second lieutenant. He was advanced to first lieutenant on 25 Oct. 1777 and to captain on 15 Oct. 1781, serving until the cessation of hostilities. He had transferred to the Second North Carolina Regiment on 1 June 1778 and to the Third Regiment on 1 Jan. 1781. Not long after his capture at the Battle of Eutaw Springs on 8 Sept. 1781, he was exchanged and soon returned to private life. Several surviving vouchers provide details of the final settlement at Halifax of payments authorized for his military service. On 10 Nov. 1796 Read was also issued a bounty land warrant, which he later sold to Henry Wiggins.

During the remainder of his life the Reverend Mr. Read appears to have preferred that his associates remember him only for his life as a religious leader. In 1767 he first began to take a serious interest in the salvation of his soul, and about 1770 he set aside a piece of land on which he and other recent converts erected a meetinghouse near Rocky Swamp—about ten miles north of Enfield in Halifax County. In 1773 he was baptized by Elder Jeremiah Walker into the membership of the Rocky Swamp Baptist Church, which was still a branch of the Lower Fishing Creek Baptist Church.

The church was constituted with eight members on 11 July 1774 by Elders Walker, John Tanner, and Joseph Anthony. On 5 May 1775 Read was ordained to the ministry and installed as the regular pastor by Elders Anthony and Samuel Harris. He took his church into the Kehukee Association on 9 Aug. 1777, and in subsequent years he was frequently appointed a messenger to visit other associations. On 15 May 1784 he was placed on a committee of four to attempt a union between the Separate and Regular Baptists, which was finally accomplished on 10 Oct. 1789. When the United Association met at Bear Creek Church in Lenoir County on 13 Sept. 1792, he was one of three ministers "appointed a Committee to prepare a form of ceremony to solemnize the rite of matrimony."

In 1801 Elder Read assisted Elder Lemuel Burkitt in ordaining Joshua Lawrence at the Fishing Creek Baptist Church, known subsequently as Lawrence's Meeting House. (Elder Lawrence would follow them later, in both pulpit and press, as a powerful defender of the Primitive Baptist faith and practice.) On 30 Sept. 1803 Read was chosen for the first time to fill the office of moderator of the Kehukee Baptist Association, and he was elevated to that honor once again on 5 Oct. 1816.

Read gradually came to be recognized as one of the ablest ministers in the association. He also was generally esteemed for his literary talent and solid financial worth. Between 1780 and 1797 he was named executor of the wills of eight associates. Some idea of his success as a planter may be formed from his possession of over 1,400 acres and eleven slaves by 1790; the property given to his children was even more substantial. He has continued to be remembered principally because of his collaboration with Lemuel Burkitt in the writing of *A Concise History of the Kehukee Baptist Association* and its publication at Halifax in 1803. That unique work provided the foundation upon which rests the early history of the Baptists of eastern North Carolina.

The Raleigh *Register* of 16 June 1820 carried the following obituary: "DIED, At his late residence in Halifax County, on the 6th inst. in the 76th year of his age, the Rev. Jesse Read, late Pastor of the Baptist Church at Rocky Swamp Meeting House, for forty-five years. He was confined to his bed for the last six months, but with the most exemplary piety and perfect resignation to the will of his heavenly father, anxiously waiting until his change should come."

The brief holograph will of Elder Read named only two sons, Stephen, who married Doretha Eelbeck, daughter of Montfort Eelbeck of Halifax County, and Rhesa, a wealthy planter who married Fanny Carstarphen, daughter of James Carstarphen; but a daughter, Lydia, had married Henry Elisha Horn, only son of Colonel Henry Horn of Edgecombe Bounty, and had died in 1809, leaving several children. Contemporary census listings suggest the probability of two unidentified daughters, while the name of Read's wife also is unknown.

SEE: Lemuel Burkitt, *A Concise History of the Kehukee Baptist Association* (1803, 1834, 1850); Walter Clark, ed., *State Records of North Carolina*, vols. 11 (1895), 22 (1907); C. C. Cleveland, *The Great Revival in the West* (1916); Raleigh *Register*, 16 June 1820; *Roster of Soldiers from North Carolina in the American Revolution* (1932).

HUGH BUCKNER JOHNSTON

Reade, Edwin Godwin *(13 Nov. 1812–18 Oct. 1894),* jurist and Confederate senator, was born at Mount Tirzah, Person County, the son of Robert R. and Judith A. Gooch Reade. The father, a yeoman farmer, died early and the children were forced to seek work. While studying at home under his mother, Edwin worked as a farm laborer, in a tannery, and at a carriage shop. At age eighteen he entered an academy in Orange County, then one in Granville, where he served as an associate teacher. Afterwards he read law at home from books borrowed from a retired lawyer and was admitted to the bar in 1835. Reade eventually became one of the most brilliant speakers and successful lawyers of his era. He also managed a small plantation near Roxboro, owning in 1860 nineteen slaves and property valued at $50,000.

Reade was originally a Whig, but in 1855 he joined the American party because of its anti-Catholic and antiforeign positions. He was elected to the U.S. House of Representatives in 1855 but disliked the work and declined to seek reelection. During his term he witnessed Preston Brooks's savage caning of Charles Sumner; when the House voted to censure L. M. Keitt for attempting to prevent anyone from interfering in the fracas, Reade was the only Southerner voting for censure. Reade was such a strong Unionist that he was sounded out for a place in Abraham Lincoln's cabinet, but he declined the honor and proposed his friend John A. Gilmer instead. His Unionism persisted even after Lincoln's call for volunteers to force the seceded states back into the Union, and he refused to become a candidate for the May Secession Convention. In 1863 he was elected to the superior court, but before his term began, Governor Zebulon B. Vance prevailed upon him to serve the remaining months of George Davis's term as Confederate senator.

Reade took his seat on 22 Jan. 1864 and was appointed to the Committee on Finance. During his two months in the senate he made the most of his opportunity to safeguard his state against what he considered unwarranted Confederate encroachments. On 23 January, when the state's delegation had an interview with President Davis, Reade warned him to "trust North Carolina and let her alone." A week later he described to the senate the rampant dissatisfaction in his state and warned that it might undertake separate peace negotiations if the trend towards military rule continued. His voting record indicated that he opposed virtually all the emergency laws then before the senate. Reade sought reelection as a peace candidate, but he was too much of a states' rights extremist even for the North Carolina General Assembly.

In 1865 Reade was president of the Johnson Reconstruction convention, and in the same year he was elected associate justice of the state supreme court. Although he was now a Republican, both parties elected him to the same position in 1868 and continued to reelect him until 1879. Among his important decisions were ruling that homestead exemptions were valid against debts contracted before the law was adopted and that the governor rather than the legislature had the power of appointment to office. Reade retired from the bench to become president of a Raleigh bank, and his expert management rescued it from probable bankruptcy. He was grand master of Masons in the state in 1865 and 1866. He died in Raleigh and was buried in Oakwood Cemetery.

Reade was a tall, handsome man, albeit of a rather cold personality. He spoke in simple phrases with a clear voice and as a lawyer went for the jugular. His judicial opinions were brief and lucidly written. His first wife was Emily A. Moore of Person County. After she died in 1871, he married Mrs. Mary Parmele of Washington, N.C. There were no children by either marriage.

SEE: Samuel A. Ashe, ed., *Biographical History of North Carolina*, vol. 2 (1905); *DAB*, vol. 12 (1935); *Journal of the Congress of the Confederate States of America*, vol. 4 (1904); Raleigh *Standard*, various dates, 1860–65; Raleigh *News and Observer*, 19 Oct. 1894; Z. V. Walser Papers (Southern Historical Collection, University of North Carolina, Chapel Hill [portrait]); Ezra J. Warner and W. Buck Yearns, *Biographical Register of the Confederate Congress* (1975).

BUCK YEARNS

Redden, Monroe Minor *(24 Sept. 1901–16 Dec. 1987)*, congressman and attorney, was born in Hendersonville, the son of John L. and Julia Trimble Redden. Educated in the public schools of Henderson County, he was graduated from the law school of Wake Forest College and was admitted to the North Carolina bar in 1923.

Redden was elected to Congress from the Twelfth District in November 1946, when he defeated incumbent representative Zebulon Weaver on a platform that favored economy in government and reduction of taxes. Redden received the largest total vote and the largest majority of any congressional candidate in the state. Prior to his election he had been active in Democratic party politics, serving as chairman of the Henderson County Democratic Committee from 1930 to 1946 and as chairman of the North Carolina Democratic Executive Committee from 1942 to 1944. He was also a member of the State Board of Elections in 1938.

During his three terms in Congress between 1947 and 1953, Redden was on the District of Columbia Committee and was chairman of the Subcommittee on Interior and Insular Affairs. In 1950 he sponsored the amendment to the federal wage-and-hour law, which established seventy-five cents as the minimum wage for employees of firms engaged in interstate business. He resigned from Congress in 1953 to resume an active law practice with his two sons. Redden served as president of the Southern Heritage Life Insurance Company from 1956 to 1959. He had married Mary Belle Boyd in 1923, and they were the parents of two sons, Monroe M., Jr., and Robert M.

SEE: *Asheville Citizen*, 7 Feb. 1950; *Asheville Citizen-Times*, 12 Feb. 1950; *Asheville Citizen and Times*, 17 Dec. 1987; *Biographical Directory of the United States Congress* (1989); *Congressional Directory*, 82d Cong. (January 1952); *Who's Who in America* (1950).

JULIAN M. PLEASANTS

Reed, James *(d. 1777)*, Anglican clergyman and founder of the first tax-supported school in colonial North Carolina, predecessor of the celebrated New Bern Academy, was born in England. With the encouragement of Governor Arthur Dobbs, he emigrated to the province in 1753 to succeed the aged Huguenot, the Reverend John Lapierre, one of two Church of England clergymen then holding regular services in North Carolina.

Reed arrived in New Bern as Christ Church Parish was erecting its first brick church, at Middle and Pollock streets. In December 1754 he held his first service in the completed church. Clergymen of the day were notoriously underpaid, and Reed received a barely adequate annual salary of £133 proclamation money. This, with the provision of a glebe and rectory, made the living at Christ Church the best in the province. In 1759, at Dobbs's request, the Society for the Propagation of the Gospel in Foreign Parts allowed him a yearly stipend of £50 sterling.

With his marriage to Hannah Stringer, widow of Francis Stringer, and the improvement in his compensation, Reed "laid aside all thoughts of deserting my Charge or ever removing." He preached at eight chapels in Craven County and at least one in Carteret County and served for a small fee as chaplain of the Assembly. Grown deaf from malaria, he traveled as many as three weeks out of the month. He was known for his solicitude to the poor. During his rectorate, King George II gave to the parish a silver communion service by Mordecai Fox, which remains a prized possession.

Reed's dream of a well-established school was realized when he induced young Thomas Thomlinson, a native of Cumberland, to emigrate to New Bern. Thomlinson began classes on 7 Jan. 1764. In March the Assembly authorized construction of a schoolhouse and appointed Reed, the two Craven members of the Assembly, and certain borough officials among the trustees. With the arrival of William Tryon on 10 Oct. 1764 to succeed Dobbs, the school received the full support of the new governor.

With private contributions, which Reed untiringly sought from the pulpit, the schoolhouse was completed in July 1766. In the fall the Assembly created the Incorporated Society for Promoting and Establishing the Public School in New Bern and levied a penny per gallon of rum imported into the Neuse River to maintain the school and educate ten poor children to be chosen at intervals. About thirty pupils attended Thomlinson's early classes and later the number grew, with some from as far away as Wilmington. Undoubtedly Reed's personal library of 266 volumes enriched the school's resources.

Reed's pungent letters are valuable for comments on education, religion, and political events. "All America is in a most violent flame," he wrote after Parliament's punitive enactments against Massachusetts in 1774, "and every good man would forbear as much as possible adding the least Fuel to the Fire." The vestry dismissed him in 1775 for refusing to preach on a day of fasting and prayer set aside by the Continental Congress, but he was quickly reinstated and remained unmolested as a passive Loyalist. Late in 1777 he died, "weary of living," he had written, "in this land of perpetual strife and contention." There is no known portrait of Reed. He was interred in the burial ground of Christ Church, New Bern.

SEE: Walter Clark, ed., *State Records of North Carolina*, vols. 23–25 (1904–6); Archibald Henderson, *North Carolina: The Old North State and the New*, vol. 1 (1941); Elizabeth Kaye, "The Case of Thomas Thomlinson," *Historical Magazine of the Protestant Episcopal Church* 5 (1936); Alfred S. Lawrence, "Sketch of a Colonial Clergyman," *Carolina Churchman* 19 (September 1928); Lorenzo Sabine, *Biographical Sketches of Loyalists in the American Revolution*, vol. 2 (1864); William L. Saunders, ed., *Colonial Records of North Carolina*, vols. 5–7 (1887–90), 9 (1890); *Virginia Gazette*, 13 June 1771.

ALONZO THOMAS DILL

Reed, John *(6 Jan. 1757 or 1758–28 May 1845)*, gold miner, businessman, farmer, and soldier, was born in Germany, most likely in the province of Hesse-Cassel. Nothing is known of his family, childhood, or youth.

He landed at Long Island in 1778 or 1779 as a Hessian soldier hired by George III of England to squelch the rebellion of his American colonies. Precise data on Reed's service are lacking, but it is commonly agreed that he deserted his unit somewhere in South Carolina or Georgia. Like many of his fellow mercenaries, he might well have left the king's service at Charleston, been captured and whipped, and subsequently been banished from his unit. In any case, John Reed and several other Hessians made their way either singly or in groups to the rural Germanic area around Dutch Buffalo Creek in eastern Mecklenburg (now Cabarrus) County. There, in an isolated, ethnic farm community built around St. John's Lutheran Church lived numerous German farmers.

In this setting Reed was to spend his life and raise a family. He married Sarah Kizer and reared three sons and five daughters. Reed was characterized by local historians as "honest but unlearned" and "a rather primitive character, but a good liver in his way and a respected citizen." He performed his share of civic duties and became a successful farmer and small businessman.

In 1799, by which time Reed already had passed his fortieth year and acquired several hundred acres of land, the course of his life and a portion of the history of his adopted homeland were turned about by the accidental discovery of gold on his property. One Sunday his twelve-year-old son, Conrad, chose to go fishing in Little Meadow Creek on the family farm rather than attend church with his parents. Conrad retrieved a yellow object, which proved to be metallic, from the water. The wedge-shaped rock was about the size of a small flatiron and apparently weighed about seventeen pounds. No one in the immediate family could identify the stone, and it served as a doorstop in their home for three years.

In 1802 Reed took the rock to Fayetteville on a marketing trip, and a jeweler there identified the metal as gold. Still curiously unaware of its value, the farmer sold his find for what he felt to be a "big price," $3.50. The unknown merchant gladly paid him.

It was not long before Reed discovered his ignorance, and he and his family began searching in Little Meadow Creek for more gold. He early turned a profit and in 1803 expanded his operation by taking three local men—his brother-in-law Frederick Kizer, the Reverend James Love, and wealthy landowner Martin Phifer, Jr.—into partnership. After crops were planted and the stream dried up in late summer, each of the three supplied equipment and two slaves to dig for gold in the creek bed. Before the end of the season Peter, one of the slaves, unearthed a 28-pound nugget.

For the next twenty years, operations at Reed's placer mine, and increasingly at similar sites across several adjacent counties, continued on a crude, part-time basis, perhaps because mining was an unfamiliar pursuit with sporadic rewards for the simple agrarians. Reed's diggings became commonly known as the "bull of the gold mines" and continued as the principal mine in the state and nation. After gathering up obvious surface particles of gold, the workers had progressed to pits, pans, and later rockers. By 1824 haphazard digging at the spot had yielded an estimated $100,000 in gold.

Meanwhile, the decade after 1825 saw a rapid expansion of the hitherto small North Carolina mining industry. With the discovery of gold in underground veins, mining began in earnest, centered about Charlotte. Reed's mine remained, however, essentially a family operation and was to be a part of neither the most advanced technology nor, perhaps, the frenzied excitement of the time. The old German apparently preferred to continue his profitable placer operations rather than risk his capital in the uncertainty of a shift to extensive, costly vein mining. In addition, perhaps reticent about his background, he opted to retain the close-knit family pattern of the venture. Alluring nuggets of remarkable size, for which the site was famous, occasionally turned up, and before 1826 the total recorded amount of gold found there in pieces exceeding one pound reached 84 pounds.

During the 1830s work at Reed's mine finally progressed from placer mining to hard-rock underground efforts. In 1831 Isaac Craton dug the first pit on a hill above Little Meadow Creek. Although lacking technical expertise, the miners seemingly made considerable progress in excavation within a few years and sank at least four or five shafts with depths of up to 90 feet. The laborers processed the ore in rockers after extracting and crushing it.

In November 1834 one of the pits yielded a chunk of gold that weighed nearly 10 pounds when fluxed and precipitated a lengthy legal struggle among members of Reed's family. The case reached the state supreme court a decade later. Formal work at the mine was said to have ceased during the entire time because of an injunction. The dispute was over which of Reed's sons and sons-in-law owned portions of the nugget.

Shortly after the issue was settled, John Reed, who had finally become a naturalized citizen in 1842, died at age eighty-eight. His estate, including 745 acres of land and eighteen slaves, was valued a few years later at some $40,000. According to a local newspaper, the deceased immigrant had been "a good citizen, a kind parent and neighbor, and a helper of the poor."

A son-in-law and a grandson purchased the mine at the sale of Reed's estate and operated it on a marginal budget for several years. Various parties subsequently operated the mine intermittently until about 1910. The property then lay dormant until acquired as a State Historic Site by North Carolina in the 1970s.

There are no known manuscripts or portraits of Reed, whose grave remains secluded near Little Meadow Creek.

SEE: Cabarrus County Records, especially court minutes, deeds, and estates records (North Carolina State Archives, Raleigh); *Concord* (North Carolina) *Times*, 16 Apr. 1896; *DAB*, vol. 15 (1935); Richard F. Knapp, *Golden Promise in the Piedmont: The Story of John Reed's Mine* (1975); North Carolina Supreme Court Original Cases, Case 3633, *George Reid v. George Barnhart and Others* (North Carolina State Archives, Raleigh); August Partz, "Examinations and Explorations of the Gold-Bearing Belts of the Atlantic States: The Reid Mines, North Carolina," *Mining Magazine* 3 (1854); John H. Wheeler, *Historical Sketches of North Carolina* (1851).

RICHARD F. KNAPP

Reed, Walter *(13 Sept. 1851–23 Nov. 1902)*, bacteriologist, was born at Belroi, Va., the son of Lemuel Sutton and Pharaba White Reed. It is thought that he was a lineal descendant of William Reed, a colonial governor of North Carolina. Lemuel S. Reed was a Methodist clergyman and held brief pastorates at Harrellsville and Murfreesboro, N.C., in the 1850s and again at the latter town in 1874. In the intervening years, Walter Reed had graduated in 1869, at age seventeen, from the University of Virginia medical department and in 1873 from Bellevue Hospital medical college in New York. In 1874 he married Emily Blackwell Lawrence, daughter of John Vaughan Lawrence of Murfreesboro. By this time he had become an assistant surgeon in the U.S. Army medical department and would spend eighteen years at military bases around the country.

Following studies in bacteriology and pathology at Johns Hopkins Hospital in the early 1890s, Reed was promoted to major and became in 1893 curator of the army medical museum in Washington, D.C., and professor of clinic microscopy and bacteriology at the army medical school. Two years later he was appointed professor of bacteriology at what is now George Washington University Medical School. Specializing in the relatively new science of bacteriology, he became interested in a variety of diseases, including diphtheria, malaria, and typhoid fever. He was a pioneer in the advocacy of antitoxin treatment of diphtheria and federal regulation of preparation of this and other biologic remedies.

At the outbreak of the Spanish-American War in 1898, Reed was already concerned with the study of yellow fever, having in the previous year conducted an investigation to show that the specific causative agent of the disease claimed to have been found by an Italian scientist had no causal relationship to yellow fever. When yellow fever epidemics broke out in army camps at Havana and elsewhere in 1900, Reed was named to a commission of medical officers to study the cause and mode of transmission of the disease. As planning head of the commission, he became convinced that water was unimportant in transmission and began to pursue an earlier suggestion that mosquitoes might be the real agent of transmission. Experimenting with human subjects, Reed and his commission were able to establish that the mosquito *Stegomyia fasciata* (later classified *Aëdes aegypti*) was the actual carrier of yellow fever. An attack launched against the mosquito in early 1901 reduced the number of cases from 1,400 in the previous year to only 37 in that year and to 0 in Havana in 1902. With this demonstration, yellow fever was all but eliminated as a fatal disease.

Reed returned to Washington in 1901 to continue work at the army medical school and as a professor of pathology and bacteriology. He died of chronic appendicitis in Washington in late 1902. Recently he had been awarded the honorary degree of A.M. by Harvard University and the LL.D. degree by the University of Michigan, and a few days before his death he had been appointed librarian of the army medical library. He was survived by his wife and two children, Lawrence and Emily (Blossom). The army's general hospital in Washington was named in his honor.

SEE: William B. Bean, *Walter Reed: A Biography* (1982); *DAB*, vol. 15 (1935); *Dictionary of Scientific Biography*, vol. 11 (1975); T. C. Parramore, "Where Walter Reed Lived and Courted," *State* magazine 44 (January 1977).

THOMAS C. PARRAMORE

Reed, Weston Cosby *(24 Apr. 1893–30 Aug. 1970)*, Baptist minister and child care executive, was born on a farm near Sylva, in Jackson County, the fifth child of James Phillip and Marcella Farmer Reed. He attended the public schools of Jackson County and in 1914 finished Cullowhee Normal and Industrial School (now Western Carolina University). Reed received his B.A. degree from Wake Forest College in 1925 and did postgraduate work at George Peabody College (1921) and The University of North Carolina (1928). After college he served successively as president of Sylva Collegiate Institute (1925–27), principal of Cullowhee High School (1927–29), superintendent of public schools in the Sylva school district (1929–33), and superintendent at Balls Creek Consolidated School at Newton (1933–41).

Reed had been ordained by Scott's Creek Baptist Church in the Tuckaseigee Baptist Association and was called to the Maiden First Baptist Church in 1942. This was his only full pastorate and after a year and a half, he began twenty-five fruitful years in the ministry of child care with the Baptist Children's Homes of North Carolina. From 1943 to 1950, Reed served as superintendent of the Kennedy Memorial Home, Kinston. Under his leadership the work grew, services and facilities were improved, and many friends for the home were cultivated in eastern North Carolina. In 1950 he was elected general superintendent of the Baptist Homes of North Carolina and moved to Thomasville to live and work. During the next eight years he was a very effective promoter of the children's homes—raising funds far and wide and never missing an opportunity to speak out for better care for the homeless and parentless children who needed the security of Christian influences in their early lives.

After his retirement, Reed served as copastor of the Kinston First Baptist Church and as consultant for the Baptist Homes. For many years he was active in the Rotary Club in Kinston and served six years as chairman of the Lenoir County Board of Public Welfare. He was a former first vice-president of the Baptist State Convention of North Carolina and the first president of the Child Care Executives of Southern Baptists. Much of his time was spent in writing a history of the Baptist Children's Homes. This was completed by his wife after his death and published as *Love In Action: The Story of the Baptist Children's Homes of North Carolina* (1973).

Reed married Mellie Parker on 23 Dec. 1916. They had three children: Westen Ollin, Marcella (Mrs. Theodore L. Huguelet), and Mary Nell (Mrs. Charles C. Mason).

Reed died in the Kinston hospital after a heart attack. Funeral services were held in the Kinston First Baptist Church and at Sylva First Baptist Church, where he was interred in the church cemetery.

SEE: *Kinston Free Press*, 31 Aug. 1970; *North Carolina Baptist State Convention Annual, 1970* (portrait); Weston Cosby Reed Biographical Folder (Baptist Historical Collection, Wake Forest University, Winston-Salem); Alvin A. Walker, *History: First Baptist Church, Maiden, N.C.* (1966); *Who's Who in the South and Southwest* (1956).

JOHN R. WOODARD

Reed, William *(1670?–11 Dec. 1728)*, acting governor, president of the Council, Proprietor's deputy, Church of England vestryman, and Virginia–North Carolina boundary commissioner, probably came to the colony from England. William Reed was a fairly common name in North Carolina and it has not always been possible to identify him in the records. J. R. B. Hathaway states that the governor appeared in Currituck Precinct as early as 1692; one of this name was a witness in court as well as a juror on 8 Oct. 1697.

According to documents in the *Colonial Records*, one William Reed on 17 Mar. 1703 answered a suit for a debt of £17. In the same year, William Reed appeared as a juror, and on 1 Aug. 1703 he brought suit to recover money owed him. On 26 Oct. 1703 Reed petitioned the General Court that a tract of land formerly in the occupation of Captain John Gibbs be granted to him.

In July 1711 Governor Edward Hyde, the Council, and the Assembly addressed a letter to Virginia Governor Alexander Spotswood denouncing Cary's Rebellion. Reed was one of the signers, and the following year he also signed another letter from the Council and Assembly to Spotswood petitioning for help against the Tuscarora Indians. Baron Christoph von Graffenried was also one of the petitioners. The Council ordered Reed on 12 Sept. 1712 to arrest mutineers who encouraged other colonists not to join the expedition against the Indians.

In 1715 the Assembly passed an act to establish the Church of England in the colony and appointed select vestries. Colonel William Reed was named a vestryman for the Currituck Precinct parish.

Reed was first mentioned as a Proprietor's deputy and member of the Council in 1712, and he filled that position for the remainder of his life. On 30 Oct. 1718 Governor Charles Eden appointed Reed, Fred Jones, and Captain Richard Sanderson to the Virginia–North Carolina Boundary Line Commission. The location of the line between the two colonies had been in dispute for a number of years, and although the survey was begun in 1719, the final determination came only in 1729.

Following the death of Governor Charles Eden on 26 Mar. 1722, Reed helped choose Thomas Pollock as his successor on 30 March. With the election of Pollock, Reed became the ranking member of the Council in point of service. Pollock died on 30 August and on 7 September Reed was unanimously chosen "President of the Council and Commander in chief of this province till the Lords Proprietors' pleasure be further known."

William Reed was acting governor from 7 Sept. 1722 to 15 Jan. 1724, when George Burrington qualified. Reed had filled a majority of the provincial offices with general satisfaction. He was aggressive in arresting mutineers and prosecuting the Tuscarora Indian war as well as an enterprising land speculator. He purchased land from the Porteskill and Yawpim Indians and pursued lapsed land patents. Nevertheless, criticism of his administration is found in a report of the Committee of Grievances, Pasquotank Precinct, 12 Apr. 1726. It was stated that "contrary to law" Reed had pretended to assume to himself a power to appoint commissioners and assessors. He had levied a tax of five shillings per poll in 1724, and he had collected it under the pretense of building a courthouse "in some place unknown," although the justices had already arranged for such a building according to their own ideas. In 1723 Reed had named himself and others as town commissioners to enlarge the town of Carteret, recently incorporated on the northeastern side of Roanoke Island.

With the Proprietors' appointment of Burrington as governor in January 1724, Reed became president of the Council. He and others were accused of selling liquor without licenses at their homes, but the charges were apparently dropped. Reed, however, was involved in several other lawsuits. He does not appear in the records as a quarrelsome man, although he was quick to defend himself when attacked. On 31 Oct. 1724 Colonel Thomas Swann of Pasquotank accused Reed and John Norton of abusing Governor Burrington. According to John Pendleton, Reed told Swann that "he would wipe his Arse" with the governor's order. Moreover, Reed reminded Pendleton that he was not Mr. Reed but President Reed.

The militant and colorful Reed was attacked by Edmund Porter, of Chowan, who was tried for sedition in March 1727. Porter shared the same sentiments as Swann in that he thought Reed was "worthy of death." Reed was on the court that tried Porter.

In his position as senior councillor, Reed assisted in inducting Sir Richard Everard into office as the successor of Burrington on 17 July 1725. Reed's friendship with Governor Everard appears to have lasted only a short time, however, as he joined other councillors in signing an address stating that "the great Incapacity and Weakness of our present Governor, Sir Richard Everard, whose behaviour is so extraordinary that every day produces some Extravagant action." Everard was charged with numerous offenses from tyranny towards subordinates to treason against the House of Hanover.

Reed was married twice; his first wife was named Christian and his second, Jane, but the records do not reveal their maiden names. He left several sons; the oldest was Christian who married Mary Durant, a great-granddaughter of George Durant, the elder. Mary and Christian Reed had a son, William, who married Penelope Williams, also a descendant of Durant. Another son of Governor Reed was Joseph who married Elizabeth Durant, a sister of the wife of Christian. The latter couple left a large family, and among their descendants were the Peace and Kittrell families of Granville County. By his second wife, Jane, Governor Reed had a son, William, who married Elizabeth Hatch, also a descendant of Durant.

Governor Reed died at his home in Pasquotank County. His widow, Jane, sued for the return of her husband's property after she had been expelled from it. The Council also ordered that the arrears of the late president's salary be paid to his widow by the receiver general.

SEE: Samuel A. Ashe, *History of North Carolina*, vol. 1 (1908); Joseph Blount Cheshire, *Nonnulla* (1930); Walter Clark, ed., *State Records of North Carolina*, vol. 25 (1906); J. R. B. Hathaway, ed., *North Carolina Historical and Genealogical Register*, vols. 1–3 (1900–1903); Francis L.

Hawks, *History of North Carolina*, vol. 2 (1858); John W. Moore, *History of North Carolina* (1880); William L. Saunders, ed., *Colonial Records of North Carolina*, vols. 1–3 (1886); Charles L. Van Noppen Papers (Manuscript Department, Duke University Library, Durham).

VERNON O. STUMPF

Rees, Mary De Berniere Graves *(6 June 1886–28 Apr. 1950)*, portrait painter, was born in Chapel Hill, the daughter of Ralph Henry (1851–89) and Julia Charlotte Hooper Graves (1856–1944). Ralph Graves taught mathematics at The University of North Carolina from 1875 until his death; his father was a member of the class of 1836 and an educator, and an earlier ancestor on the Graves side was the first steward of the university at its opening in 1795. On her mother's side, Mary's grandfather and great-grandfather were professors at the university. William Hooper, her great-grandfather, also served as president of Wake Forest College and was buried with his mother and stepfather, Joseph Caldwell, first president of The University of North Carolina, at the foot of the Caldwell monument. An earlier William Hooper was one of the three signers of the Declaration of Independence for North Carolina.

Mary Graves Rees was the youngest of the four surviving children of Ralph and Julia Graves. Her older brothers were Ralph, a journalist in New York; Earnest, an army engineer; and Louis, editor of the *Chapel Hill Weekly*. After the early death of her husband, Julia Graves maintained a popular boardinghouse on the site of the present Carolina Inn until her children were grown. Mary spent a year at the university with the class of 1909 but left to pursue her artistic interests, studying at the Maryland Institute of Art in Baltimore, the Pennsylvania Academy of Fine Arts in Philadelphia, and with Henry McCarter and William Chase in New York.

Living in New York during World War I, she illustrated a number of war posters and drew sketches for newspapers and magazine covers such as "Slackers," which was on the front cover of the magazine section of the *New York World*. Her illustrations appeared in the New York *Evening Post*, the New York *Tribune*, the *Southern Magazine*, the *Ruralist*, *Country Life*, and others. Her major work, however, was portraiture. While maintaining a studio in New York, she painted portraits of such people as Mrs. Fred Astaire, Tony Heard, son of the editor of *Home and Field*, and E. N. Potter III, great-grandson of Bishop Potter. Some of her pastels were exhibited in the Ferargil Galleries in New York.

On 18 Sept. 1919 Mary Graves married Arthur Dougherty Rees (d. 28 Dec. 1961), playwright and teacher of history. The couple had one son, Pembroke, born in July 1920.

In 1923 Mary Graves Rees and her son returned to Chapel Hill to live with her mother on Battle Lane (later they moved to Hooper Lane). After teaching art at the university for one year, she turned first to pen-and-ink drawings (many copies of her scenes of the university are in Chapel Hill homes) and then to portraits in oil and pastel. Establishing a studio in Baby Hollow, she painted numerous children in the neighborhood, many of them children of professors; some she sold, others she displayed in her studio. Among the favorites of viewers were several oil portraits of Negro children, now in possession of her family.

Her major and best-known portraits are of Thomas Walker Bickett, governor of North Carolina; William Rufus King, a graduate of The University of North Carolina, minister to France from 1844 to 1846, elected vice-president of the United States in 1852 but died soon after taking the oath of office in Cuba (this portrait is in the American Embassy in Paris); the Reverend William Hooper (after one painted by John Singleton Copley, now in Trinity Church, Boston); Representative John Steele, in Durham Public Library; W. W. Fuller and Howard Alexander Foushee, lawyers in Durham; Edward Kidder Graham and Frank Porter Graham, presidents of The University of North Carolina, and Charles S. Mangum, Collier Cobb, Archibald Henderson, Horace Williams, Elisha Mitchell, W. D. Toy, and Kent Brown, all professors at the university; Paul Green, playwright; Gertrude Pahlow, novelist; Lamar Stringfield, musician; Cornelia Phillips Spencer, a resident of Chapel Hill who was instrumental in the reopening of the university after the Civil War; Sally Foard MacNider of Chapel Hill; and Emily Pemberton of Durham.

In 1926 the North Carolina Federation of Women's Clubs awarded Mary Graves Rees its prize for the best work by a North Carolina artist. In 1927 the Southern State Art League selected her portrait studies of Archibald Henderson and Paul Green for a traveling exhibition showing the work of representative southern artists, and in 1928 she won a silver cup for a portrait in an exhibition at the Kenilworth Art Galleries, Asheville. In 1931 she was instrumental in organizing the North Carolina Association of Professional Artists and served as the first president of this group.

Mary Graves Rees was a handsome, generous person with a quick mind and wit. Her studio was a popular gathering place in Chapel Hill. She was a very talented artist and with her portraits produced fine records of many North Carolinians and others. After a year's illness, she died suddenly in Chapel Hill and was buried in the old Chapel Hill Cemetery.

SEE: *Chapel Hill Weekly*, 17 Nov. 1944, 5 May 1950; *Charlotte Observer*, 10 May 1931; *Durham Morning Herald*, 11 June 1935, 4 Mar. 1941, 19 Mar. 1944; Ola Maie Foushee, *Art in North Carolina: Episodes and Development, 1585–1970* (1972); Harriette Hammer, *Busy North Carolina Women* (1931); Cuthbert Lee, *Portrait Register* (1968); Cornelia Spencer Love, *When Chapel Hill Was a Village* (1976); *New York Times*, 30 Apr. 1950; Raleigh *News and Observer*, 28 Apr. 1929; Rees Papers (possession of Pembroke Rees, Huntsville, Ala.).

MARTHA B. CALDWELL

Reese, Addison Hardcastle *(28 Dec. 1908–1 Sept. 1977)*, banker and civic leader, was born in Baltimore County, Md., the son of Gordon Lippincott and Edith Octavia Ford Reese. His great-grandfather, John T. Ford, was owner of Ford's Theater in Washington, D.C. His parents were divorced when he was three, and for a time he and an older brother lived with their mother. When she remarried and moved to Virginia, the two young men took an apartment in Baltimore, and the older brother cared for the younger one with occasional oversight by an aunt. After attending the public schools of Baltimore, Reese was graduated from Marston's University School in Riderwood, Md., and entered Johns Hopkins University for three years. Leaving after his junior year, he worked for a short time as a laborer in a paper mill in Ypsilanti, Mich.

Back in Baltimore in 1930, Reese became a statistician for the Franck-Rosenburg Company, a private banking firm, but it soon was liquidated. In 1931 he became a clerk in the Bank of Sparrows Point, Md., and in 1932 he was appointed an assistant national bank examiner for the Office of the Comptroller of the Currency. During the period 1933–34 he was on loan to the Reconstruction Finance Corporation, which extended credit to failing banks. In this temporary employment he had an opportunity to examine the workings of banks and to discover mistakes that managers had made. In 1936 the Federal Deposit Insurance Corporation was formed, and as a bank examiner Reese was sent to Richmond, Va., to determine which banks were qualified for the program.

In 1937, at age twenty-nine, he became the nation's youngest senior national bank examiner. In 1941 he was named director and vice-president of the Nicodemus National Bank in Hagerstown, Md., but from August 1942 until December 1945, during World War II, he worked in statistical control in the Air Force. He was discharged with the rank of major.

In 1947 Reese began a period of service as president, chief executive officer, and director of the nineteen-branch County Trust Company of Maryland in Baltimore. He moved to Charlotte, N.C., in 1951 as executive vice-president and director of the American Trust Company. In 1954 he became president and led the bank in a series of significant mergers—in 1957 with the Commercial National Bank of Charlotte, in 1959 with the First National Bank of Raleigh, and in 1960 with the Security National Bank of Greensboro—ultimately resulting in the formation of the North Carolina National Bank in 1960. Other mergers followed, including those with banks in Chapel Hill, North Wilkesboro, and Wilmington. Under his leadership banking service was expanded in various ways, including the opening of a branch in London. Reese was named board chairman of the North Carolina National Bank in 1967, serving until he retired from the bank in 1973.

A significant force in the formation of the University of North Carolina at Charlotte, Reese was a strong supporter of the school from 1956, when it was the small, two-year Charlotte College, until it became a four-year institution and eventually part of the Consolidated University of North Carolina system in 1965. The administration building on that campus now bears his name in recognition of his efforts and support. He was awarded the honorary LL.D. degree by the university in 1968. Also interested in art, Reese supported the Mint Museum of Art in Charlotte and encouraged the use of works of art in the banks under his care.

Reese served as president of the Association of Reserve City Bankers, a director of the American Bankers Association, a trustee of the foundation of full service banks, and a director and member of the Program Committee of the International Monetary Conference in 1972. He was married in 1936 to Gertrude Rasin Craig of Baltimore. They had no children. A Democrat and a member of Christ Episcopal Church, he died of cancer in Charlotte and was buried in Baltimore.

SEE: LeGette Blythe and Charles D. Brockman, *Hornet's Nest: The Story of Charlotte and Mecklenburg County* (1961); Mary Snead Boger, *Charlotte 23* (1972 [portrait]); *Charlotte News*, 27 May 1968, 1, 15 Sept. 1977; *Charlotte Observer*, 15 Feb. 7 Aug., 2–3, 16 Sept. 1977; *North Carolina Biography*, vol. 4 (1956); William S. Powell, ed., *North Carolina Lives* (1962); Raleigh *News and Observer*, 15 Nov. 1959, 18 Apr. 1973; *Who's Who in the South and Southwest, 1969–70* (1969).

STEPHEN R. PECK

Reese, Thomas *(1742–1796?)*, Presbyterian minister, educator, author, and self-taught medical practitioner, was born in Pennsylvania and during his early youth moved to Mecklenburg County, N.C., with his parents. He was the son of David and Susan Polk Reese and the grandson of the Reverend David Reese, a Presbyterian minister. His brothers were George, James, Charles, and Solomon, and his one sister was named Catherine. At the proper age, Thomas enrolled in the classical school taught by Joseph Alexander and a Mr. Benedict at the Sugar (Sugaw) Creek Presbyterian Church in Mecklenburg. Later he attended the College of New Jersey (Princeton), receiving a bachelor of arts degree in 1768, and then devoted several years to an independent study of theology. After passing the necessary trials, Reese was licensed as a Presbyterian clergyman by the Presbytery of Orange in 1773 and immediately accepted a call to the Salem Church, on Black River, Sumter District, S.C.

The young minister and his family were strong supporters of the American Revolution. His brother, George, so devoted to Thomas that he moved to Sumter District in order to live near him, became an officer in the Continental army. Unable to find a place for himself as a chaplain in the hastily organized army, and, as Tory persecutions and British atrocities made the Black River territory unsafe for Patriots, Reese prudently moved with his family to his father's home in North Carolina. In this location he preached at Sugar Creek and at Providence Presbyterian churches, while engaging in the writing and distribution of war news summaries and patriotic handbills throughout the area, where few newspapers could be found and where there was no printing press. According to William Henry Foote, Reese "used his pen for his country" and the results were particularly effective in promoting the Revolution.

At the end of the war, the clergyman returned to Black River, where he energetically endeavored to rebuild his war-torn parish. He also eloquently expressed his views on the relationship of the people to their new government in an essay entitled *Influence of Religion on Civil Society*. This treatise, favorably compared by one critic to the noted works of Bishop William Warburton and Dean William Paley, won for the author the degree of doctor of divinity from Princeton, conferred upon a Carolinian for the first time. Reese continued to write but was financially unable to publish extensively, as his literary compositions were too scholarly to enjoy a profitable sale. However, two of his homilies were included by David Austin in *The American Preacher*—the only sermons selected from a clergyman south of Virginia. According to his contemporaries, the oratorical ability of Reese, enhanced by his grace and dignity in the pulpit, greatly added to the effectiveness of his carefully composed discourses. The minister also skillfully emphasized music to an inspiring degree in his services. In fact, a controversy within the congregation over the use of hymns written by Isaac Watts as opposed to the versions of Francis Rous was one of the reasons Reese left the Salem church in 1792 and became pastor of the Carmel and Hopewell (Keowee) churches in Pendleton District, S.C.

Throughout his ministry Reese conducted a classical school for boys, and the excellent reputation enjoyed by the institution enabled his son, Edwin, to expand the enterprise into a flourishing academy at Pendleton after his father's death. The minister was also named as a trustee of Liberty Hall in North Carolina, along with David Caldwell, Samuel McCorkle, and others, which was a tribute to his ability as an educator. In addition to his duties in the pulpit and classroom, the clergyman also used his considerable store of self-acquired medical knowledge to relieve human suffering in his community, where medical doctors were often unavailable. This practice inspired his son, Elihu, to enter the medical profession.

In 1788 Reese became a charter member of the newly organized Presbytery of South Carolina and was active in its affairs until the end of his life. In this connection, he was drawn into a controversy over the moral right of professing Christians to own slaves. The minister was frankly critical of the institution, although he did not consider it anti-Christian and owned a number of slaves himself. The matter was referred to the Synod of the Carolinas for final settlement and the decision of that body was that the ownership of bondsmen was not un-Christian. When the synod met on 3 Jan. 1796 to announce its decision, it received notice of the recent death of the Reverend Thomas Reese.

In 1773 the minister married Jane Harris, daughter of Charles Harris, of Mecklenburg County. When Reese succumbed after increasingly severe attacks of hydrothorax at age fifty-four, he was survived by his wife and the following children: Edwin Tasker, Thomas Sidney, Elihu, Henry Dobson, Leah, Lydia, and Susan Polk. Ample provision for the family was made in the clergyman's will, which also specified that the money usually spent on spirituous liquors for funerals should instead be paid out of his estate to charity. Three of the sons were educated at Princeton and became professional men while the fourth was a successful planter. The children married advantageously and there are many descendants of the minister living today. Eventually, Reese's widow married a General Anderson of Pendleton. No portrait of the clergyman is known to exist.

Reese's publications include two sermons, "Death: The Christian's Gain" and "The Character of Haman," which appeared in David Austin (ed.), *The American Preacher* (4 vols., 1791–93); *Influence of Religion on Civil Society* (1788), also published serially in *The American Museum or Universal Magazine* 7 (January–June 1790), 8 (July–December 1790), and 9 (January–June 1791); and *Steadfastness in Religion Recommended and Enforced: A Sermon* (1793).

SEE: William Henry Foote, *Sketches of North Carolina: Historical and Biographical* (1846); George Howe, *History of the Presbyterian Church in South Carolina*, vol. 1 (1870); William Buell Sprague, *Annals of the American Pulpit*, vol. 3 (1858); Durward T. Stokes, "Thomas Reese in South Carolina," *South Carolina Historical Magazine* 74 (July 1973).

DURWARD T. STOKES

Register, Frank Murchison *(6 Aug. 1870–28 Sept. 1939)*, physician and public health officer, was born in Cumberland County, one of ten children of Robert and Mary McDuffie Register. Reared in Moore County, he was educated at the John E. Kelly subscription school. He then attended the medical school at Davidson, a separate institution from the college but sharing some of the same facilities and faculty. Register also took courses at Davidson College itself and is considered an alumnus of the class that matriculated in 1889. The medical school offered a two-year program in his day, but shortly after his departure it was expanded to three years and incorporated in 1893 as the North Carolina Medical College. Register then took courses at the College of Physicians and Surgeons in Baltimore (later expanded to the Medical School of the University of Maryland) and attended the Kentucky School of Medicine, Louisville, where he obtained an M.D. degree in 1893.

On returning to North Carolina, Register was involved in general practice in several locations for ten years. In 1902, however, he accepted a position as prison doctor at the Caledonia State Prison Farm, in Halifax County, where his father-in-law, James Henry Durham, had recently become superintendent of the North Carolina Lumber Company at nearby Tillery. Register remained at Caledonia for fifteen years and for a number of years also served as county coroner. In 1917 the General Assembly passed legislation permitting the flogging of prisoners with the proviso that the whipping be done in the presence of the prison doctor. Register disapproved of this form of punishment, refused to comply with the regulation, and resigned his post at Caledonia. His action attracted favorable statewide attention, but the law remained in effect until 1925.

Almost immediately, in July 1917, Register was employed as the first full-time county health officer in Northampton County, across the Roanoke River from Halifax, thus becoming one of a handful of county health officers in the entire state. In public health work he found his true calling. With a flair for innovation, Register undertook to educate the populace of the county in regard to sanitation, at the time poorly understood in rural North Carolina. So successful were his efforts that typhoid fever, which had been an annual scourge, was controlled and in the following year, not a single case was reported.

Because Register's work in Northampton County attracted statewide and even national notice, he was elected to head the Bureau of Vital Statistics of the State Board of Health and moved to Raleigh. Although he made an excellent record in this position, he was removed in 1930 after eleven years of service when the Federal Census Bureau, with which the State Board of Health cooperated, insisted that the state directors possess special training that he did not have. From Raleigh, Register moved to Wayne County, where he was public health officer for three years. In 1933 the position of superintendent of the Caswell Training School for the Feeble Minded became vacant, and he accepted the job, for which he was admirably suited in light of his patience, understanding, and kindly disposition. Here he remained until his death six years later.

Dr. Benjamin Washburn, a member of the Rockefeller Foundation when it did much to eradicate endemic diseases in the South, considered Register to have been one of the most successful health officers who took part in the early North Carolina work.

In 1890 Register married Lula Maurer of Ashland, Pa.; she died shortly after their marriage. In 1892 he married Mabel Durham of Guelph, Ontario, Canada. There were no children by either marriage, but he and his second wife adopted a son, Burton S. Sellers, of Raleigh. Active in the Presbyterian church, Dr. Register was a member of several medical societies. He died in Kinston and was buried in Montlawn Cemetery, Raleigh.

SEE: Davidson College Alumni Records (Davidson); *Journal of Southern Medicine and Surgery* 101 (December 1939); *North Carolina Biography*, vol. 3 (1928); Raleigh *News and Observer*, 8 Sept. 1933, 29 Sept. 1939; Benjamin E. Washburn, *As I Recall* (1960); Weldon, *Roanoke News*, scattered issues.

CLAIBORNE T. SMITH, JR.

Rehder, Jessie Clifford *(29 Apr. 1908–3 Feb. 1967)*, writer and teacher, was born in Wilmington, the daughter of Carl Frederick and Jessie Steward Rehder, members of the German Lutheran community. She and her three brothers were raised in that faith. Jessie Rehder was educated in the public schools of Wilmington and in 1925 entered Randolph-Macon Woman's College in Lynchburg, Va., from which she was graduated with an A.B.

degree in English. In 1931 she received a master's degree from Columbia University. She then did editorial work for the New York publishing house of Harper and Brothers. From 1932 to 1938 she worked as a copywriter for Holde and Horst, and in 1939 she was a play reader for Liebling Wood.

Jessie Rehder worked on a doctorate in education at The University of North Carolina for two years and later taught English in the Chapel Hill High School. At that time she also wrote a book review column and in 1947 was invited by Professor Clifford Lyons to join the staff of the Department of English at The University of North Carolina. She was the first woman to be granted tenure in that department.

In her high school years, Jessie was state javelin throw champion. The year that she played on the state champion girls' basketball team she won the state poetry contest.

Of her personal life, Leon Rooke, one of her students, said, "She could laugh herself into tears with one breath and leap into sorrow with the next. At center she was gently, warm, frail, but she could be tough and hard when the need was there." Of her teaching ability, the *Chapel Hill Weekly* wrote, "She was a builder of creative fires. . . . When she happened upon an embryo writer, it was like a wildcatter striking the first trace of oil. . . . Although she was an accomplished writer herself, her greatest joy seemed to come from seeing a protege's work in print."

She published widely. The most noteworthy of her works include *East Wind's Back* (1929), *Best College Verse*, ed. (1931), *Remembrance Way* (1962), *The Young Writer at Work* (1962), *The Story at Work*, ed. (an anthology), *Chapel Hill Carousel* (1967), *The Act of Writing* (1969), and *The Young Writer at Chapel Hill*, an annual magazine of student works (1962–67). An unpublished manuscript, "The Nature of Fiction," is in the North Carolina Collection, University of North Carolina, Chapel Hill.

Jessie Rehder died at her home in Chapel Hill and was buried in Oakdale Cemetery, Wilmington.

SEE: *Chapel Hill Weekly*, 8 Feb., 26 Mar. 1967; *Directory of American Scholars*, vol. 2 (1964); *Durham Morning Herald*, 26 May 1963, 26 Feb. 1967; Raleigh *News and Observer*, 22 Oct. 1933, 6 Mar. 1953.

LAWRENCE NAUMOFF

Reichel, Carl Gotthold *(14 July 1751–18 Apr. 1825)*, educator and Moravian bishop, was born in Hermsdorff, Silesia, the son of Carl Rudolph and Eleonore Sophia Reichel. His father was a Lutheran clergyman and family members had been Lutheran churchmen for four generations. Young Reichel's earliest education was at Moravian schools in Gross-Hennersdorf and Niesky. After joining the Moravian church, he received his theological degree at Barby, Saxony. He taught at Niesky in 1774 and from 1778 to 1780. In the intervening years he did educational work at Barby. At Gnadenfrei, in 1780, he married Anna Dorothea Maass, and they had seven children. From 1780 to 1784 Reichel served as secretary of the governing board of the church.

Sent to America, he was the first principal or inspector of Nazareth Hall at Nazareth, Pa. In the fall of 1785 he started teaching with eleven boys. Reichel's experience and leadership made the school such a success that students came from southern states and the West Indies. John Konkaput, a Housatonic Indian from Stockbridge, Mass., was one famous student. At this time, Reichel wrote *Geographie zum Gebranch der Schulen in den evangelischen Brudergemeinen* (2 vols., Barby, 1785). In addition, he edited *Lesebuch für Deutsche Schulkinder* (1795) by G. G. Otterbein for American use.

After seventeen years as inspector at Nazareth Hall, Reichel accepted the call to be head of the southern province of the Moravian church. In Bethlehem, Pa., Bishop John Ettwein consecrated him as bishop in 1801. Arriving in Salem to the music of trombones in 1802, Reichel assumed the duties of his office, which included being a member of Helfer Conferenz fürs Ganze. He held the usual services—among them love feasts and Easter services. But he also attempted to preach to the slaves and Indians. Simon Peter was ordained by him as the first presbyter of Wachovia. In 1803 Reichel conducted the services when the cornerstone was laid for the Salem Female Academy. At this time he was teaching singing classes for children in English and German. In 1806 his first wife died and was buried in Salem's God's Acre.

Governor Nathaniel Alexander toured Salem in 1809 as a guest of Reichel. In the same year the clergyman consecrated the new church built in Salem. During a trip to Pennsylvania he married Catharina Fetter of Lancaster at Lititz, Pa. The following year Joseph Caldwell, president of The University of North Carolina, visited Salem and Reichel. After receiving an honorary D.D. degree in 1811, Reichel presented the university with the *Periodical Accounts*, a three-volume series on Moravian missions to the Indians in the world. After accepting a call to go to Bethlehem, Pa., he visited all of the Moravian congregations in the Salem area.

Arriving in Bethlehem in 1811, he held the same position as in Salem. In 1818 he was selected to go to the General Synod at Herrnhut, Saxony. Traveling by way of New York and England, he went with his wife and two younger sons. Due to poor health, Reichel visited Niesky. In 1820 his second wife died, and five years later he died in Niesky. His heirs include William C. Reichel and Levin T. Reichel, who also were prominent in the Moravian church.

SEE: *DAB*, vol. 8 (1935); Adelaide L. Fries, ed., *Records of the Moravians in North Carolina*, vol. 6 (1947 [portrait]); Daniel L. Grant, *Alumni History of the University of North Carolina* (1924); Charles Gotthold Reichel, *Periodical Accounts* (1790); Levin T. Reichel, *A History of Nazareth Hall* (1855) and *The Moravians in North Carolina* (1857); William L. Saunders, ed., *Colonial Records of North Carolina*, vol. 5 (1890).

MICHAEL EDGAR GOINS

Reichel, William Cornelius *(9 May 1824–25 Oct. 1876)*, educator, historian, and Moravian clergyman, was born in Salem, the son of the Reverend Gotthold Benjamin and Henrietta Frederica Vierling Reichel. Reichel's ancestors were distinguished clergymen of the Lutheran church until his grandfather, the Reverend Charles Gotthold Reichel, joined the Moravians at Herrnhut, Saxony.

William Reichel received his early education at Nazareth Hall in Nazareth, Pa. He studied for the ministry in the Moravian College and Theological Seminary at Bethlehem, Pa., receiving his bachelor's degree in theology in 1844. After teaching drawing and Latin at Nazareth Hall from 1844 to 1852, he was transferred to the Boys' School at Bethlehem to perform the same duties. Four years later, in 1858, he became the professor of classical languages at the Moravian College. He served in this capacity until 1862, when he was appointed the principal of Linden Hall School for Girls at Lititz, Pa. In 1870 he retired to Bethlehem to engage in historical research. He was still able, however, to devote a few hours of each week to teaching drawing and watercolor painting in the Bethlehem Seminary for Young Ladies.

Reichel was a member of the Moravian Historical Society and of the Historical Society of Pennsylvania. Among his publications were *A History of the Rise, Progress, and Present Condition of the Bethlehem Female Seminary* (1858); *A Memorial to the Dedication of Monuments . . . to Mark the Sites of Ancient Missionary Stations in New York and Connecticut* (1860); *Historical Sketch of Nazareth Hall, from 1755 to 1869* (1869); *Memorials of the Moravian Church* (1870); *A Red Rose from the Olden Time* (1872); *The Crown Inn near Bethlehem* (1872); *The Old Sun Inn at Bethlehem* (1873); and an edition (1876), for the Historical Society of Pennsylvania, of J. G. E. Heckewelder's *History, Manners, and Customs of the Indian Nations.*

Reichel was married twice: in 1852 to Mary Jane Gray of Camden Valley, N.Y., who died at Lititz in May 1863, leaving two daughters; and on 27 Oct. 1867, to Addie Harkins, who survived him. Reichel died in Bethlehem, Pa.

SEE: *DAB*, vol 15 (1928); *Nat. Cyc. Am. Biog.*, 5 (1894); *Who Was Who in America, 1607–1896* (1967).

E. THOMAS SIMS

Reid, Christian. *See* **Tiernan, Frances Christine Fisher.**

Reid, David Settle *(19 Apr. 1813–18 June 1891)*, antebellum governor and U.S. senator, was the son of Reuben and Elizabeth Settle Reid of Rockingham County. He was the nephew of Thomas Settle, Sr., U.S. congressman and superior court judge, and a member of the Settle-Reid-Martin family, an important political dynasty in North Carolina history. A year after the birth of his eldest son, Reuben Reid purchased a farm on a major north-south state route and established a store and an ordinary. Around Reid's store grew a crossroads village that eventually became the city of Reidsville. Essentially self-educated, David Reid began to work at age twelve, clerking in a relative's store in Wentworth. By the time he was sixteen he had returned home to help his father in his store and was appointed the first postmaster of Reidsville on 24 Oct. 1829. In the next decade Reid acquired nearly 600 acres and three slaves and began producing tobacco.

A strict Jeffersonian Republican–Jacksonian Democrat, Reid began his political career in 1835, when at age twenty-two he was elected colonel of the county militia regiment and state senator. He commanded the Sixty-seventh Militia Regiment for seven years until his resignation in November 1842 as a result of his election to the U.S. House of Representatives. Reid had been in the state senate until 1840, serving on various committees and developing into a skillful legislator and party leader. In his later terms he sat on the important Education and Liberty Fund Committee that drafted the legislation that created the first state public school system.

In 1841, at the urging of Democratic leaders in his congressional district, he ran for the House of Representatives but was defeated by the veteran Whig, A. H. Shepperd. Reid spent the next year reading law, passed the bar exam, and by April 1843 began his practice. On his second try for Congress he was successful and represented the newly reapportioned Third District for two terms (1843–47) until he was gerrymandered out. In Washington he was an ardent supporter of the James K. Polk administration and its expansionist policies that led to the annexation of Texas, the war with Mexico, the Mexican cession, and the settlement of the disputed Oregon Territory. He served on the post office committee, spending much of his time on postal patronage. In Congress Reid met a freshman representative from Illinois, Stephen A. Douglas, who became his close friend, adviser, and cousin by marriage.

Under consideration by party leaders, especially the influential William W. Holden, for the gubernatorial post for several years, Reid reluctantly agreed to accept the Democratic nomination in 1848. He consented only after he was assured that he could campaign on the "free suffrage" issue, the elimination of the fifty-acre freehold qualification on the state senate electorate, which was the last property qualification in the state. Although unsuccessful in his strenuous campaign against the Whig candidate, Charles Manly, Reid polled the highest vote of any previous Democratic candidate and came within 854 votes of winning. In 1850 Reid was renominated, despite the fact that he initially declined, and this time was victorious. In addition to free suffrage, he supported improvements in the public schools, a responsible system of internal improvements, and the defense of Southern rights. Reid's 1850 victory truly wrought "a revolution in party politics" that created the Democratic ascendancy that dominated North Carolina for over 125 years.

Reid's two terms as governor were marked by progress towards passage of the free suffrage amendment, which was finally ratified in 1857; increased aid to internal improvements, particularly construction of major railroads and turnpikes; improvements in the state public school system, resulting primarily from the establishment of the Office of the Superintendent of Common Schools; and the inauguration of a major state geologic and agricultural survey. Named a trustee of The University of North Carolina in 1850, he served on the board until 1868.

In November 1854 the General Assembly elected Reid to a vacancy in the U.S. Senate; he accepted and resigned the gubernatorial post just a month before his term would end. In the Senate his committee service involved the transcontinental railroad, Indian affairs, Revolutionary claims, the District of Columbia, commerce, and the patent office. He was chairman of the patent office committee in the Thirty-fifth Congress. Normally he took little part in the floor debate, but the argument over the Kansas-Nebraska Bill was an exception. Reid joined his regional colleagues in a defense of Southern rights.

His time in Washington was curtailed by interest in a growing family and by several periods of illness, particularly a serious bout with pneumonia in 1858. On 19 Dec. 1850 Governor Reid had married his first cousin, Henrietta Williams Settle, the daughter of Thomas Settle, Sr., and the Reids had four children: David Settle, Jr. (1852–1871), Thomas Settle (b. 1854), Carrie Settle (1856–57), and Reuben David (1859–1909). Reid was held in high esteem by the general public, but ill health and his growing remoteness from the party's leadership led to his defeat for reelection to the Senate in 1858.

Reid retired to his Dan River tobacco plantation, which in 1860 consisted of 700 acres and twenty-two slaves. He took no part in the growing secession crisis, although he was a moderate spokesman for the South and a defender of the institution of slavery. He was elected by the General Assembly in January 1861 as one of five North Carolina delegates to the Washington Peace Conference, which failed to achieve a compromise. Shortly afterwards he was elected to the state constitutional convention that voted to secede from the Union on 20 May 1861, and he continued to serve in the convention in the succeeding sessions. A staunch supporter of the war effort, Reid made public statements on the war but did not serve the Confederacy in any official capacity. In the postwar years he remained in political retirement with the exception of his attendance at the 1875 constitutional convention, which he had a key role in organizing. At the height of the Ku Klux Klan activity in his county in 1870, Reid courageously joined with his Republican cousin Thomas Settle in publicly denouncing violence and intimidation. His influence was such that not long after this incident the local Klan disbanded.

After the war Reid continued his law practice in Wentworth and in 1877 established a partnership with his son Thomas. In May 1881 he was stricken with a severe stroke that left him partially paralyzed and confined to a wheelchair. After a decade of declining health he died and was buried in Reidsville. A religious man, Reid never joined a church, but his family was Baptist, and he attended Baptist churches throughout his life. Several portraits and photographs were made in his lifetime, the most notable portrait set being the William Garl Brown pair of David and Henrietta Reid that is still in the family. His son, Reuben D. Reid, also an attorney, served in the state senate in 1907–8.

A contemporary historian, John Hill Wheeler, wrote of Reid, "There are few men in the State who enjoy more of the respect, regard, and the affection of the people than Governor Reid, for unaffected simplicity of character, stern integrity, and unsullied purity of life." Reid never lost his democratic faith in the intelligence and honesty of the common man, and the citizens of North Carolina never lost their trust in his basic integrity and wisdom. He was a living example of what could be achieved by a man who was willing to work and had the ambition to succeed. Reid held most of the important political offices that his state could bestow. He always adhered to the democratic concept of a public servant and retained the public trust. Father of the modern Democratic party, he has been honored most for sponsorship of the free suffrage amendment.

SEE: Lindley S. Butler, "David S. Reid, 1813–1850: The Making of a Governor," *Journal of Rockingham County History and Genealogy* 4 (June 1979); Greenview Cemetery, Reidsville; Clarence C. Norton, *The Democratic Party in Ante-Bellum North Carolina, 1835–1861* (1930); David S. Reid Papers (North Carolina State Archives, Raleigh, and Duke University, Durham); Reid Family Papers (Eden); Paul A. Reid, *Gubernatorial Campaigns and Administrations of David S. Reid, 1848–1854* (1953); Rockingham County Deeds; Allen Trelease, *White Terror: The Ku Klux Klan Conspiracy and Southern Reconstruction* (1971); U.S. Census, 1840, 1860; John H. Wheeler, ed., *Reminiscences and Memoirs of North Carolina and Eminent North Carolinians* (1851, 1966).

LINDLEY S. BUTLER

Reid, Frank Lewis *(16 June 1851–24 Sept. 1894)*, Methodist minister and educator, was the son of Numa F., a Methodist minister, and Ann E. Wright Reid of Wentworth. His father moved frequently on his pastoral duties, but the Reid children were reared at the family home in Wentworth and educated in the local school. Frank Reid's grandfather, James Reid, was a pioneer North Carolina Methodist minister. Frank Reid entered Trinity College and was graduated in June 1870. In 1873 Trinity granted him an A.M. degree.

At age nineteen he became principal of Kernersville High School, a position he held until December 1870, when he joined the North Carolina Conference as a minister. His first pastoral charge was the Madison Circuit in Rockingham County, and in January 1874 he was appointed to Louisburg. In Louisburg he was selected president of Louisburg Female College, a Methodist-affiliated junior college, and served until ill health and a throat infection led to his resignation in June 1878 from both the pulpit and the college.

In October 1878 he became co-owner of the *Raleigh Christian Advocate*, the journal of the North Carolina Conference, and by 1884 he purchased the journal and became the sole proprietor and editor. Reid was an effective journalist and established the *Advocate* as the leading voice of Methodism in the state. His advocacy of the enlargement of the North Carolina Conference with territory in eastern North Carolina from Virginia and in western North Carolina from Tennessee contributed to the formation of the Western North Carolina Conference. In addition to his profuse writing for the *Advocate*, Reid coedited with his brother a compilation of his father's sermons entitled *Life, Sermons, and Speeches of Rev. Numa F. Reid Late of the North Carolina Conference* (1874).

In 1881 Reid became pastor of the Edenton Street Methodist Church, and by 1888 he was named presiding elder of the Raleigh District. He was a delegate to the General Conference of the Methodist Episcopal Church, South, at St. Louis in 1890 and the following year attended the Ecumenical Conference in Washington, D.C. While in Raleigh, he filled a number of civic positions, serving as director of the state penitentiary and secretary of the penitentiary board. He was a member of the city school committee, and Governor Elias Carr appointed him to the board of the North Carolina Railroad Company.

A lifelong Mason, Reid was twice chaplain of the state Grand Lodge. In 1888 he was named a trustee of Trinity College and remained on that board until his death. Reid was awarded the honorary D.D. degree by The University of North Carolina in 1890. In 1893 he was appointed president of Greensboro College, a Methodist female senior college, and began his tenure in May. He applied himself to his new position with his usual dedication but died the following year and was buried in Greensboro.

He married Minnie E. Cardwell (b. 1853) of Rockingham County on 3 June 1873, and they had four children: a son, W. Fuller, and three daughters, Minnie LeGrand, Lula McGee, and Annie Field. His brother, James W. Reid (1849–1902), was a U.S. congressman.

SEE: Lindley S. Butler, *Wright Tavern: A Courthouse Inn and Its Proprietors* (1973); Josephus Daniels, *Tar Heel Editor* (1939); *Journal of the Annual Conference of the Methodist Episcopal Church, South, 1894*; Frank Lewis Reid Papers (Manuscript Department, Duke University, Library, Durham); Samuel B. Turrentine, *A Romance of Education* (1946 [portrait]); Nathan H. Wilson, "The Reids: Eminent Itinerants Through Three Generations," *Trinity College Historical Papers* (1912).

LINDLEY S. BUTLER

Reid, James Wesley *(11 June 1849–1 Jan. 1902)*, U.S. congressman, was the son of Numa F., a Methodist minister, and Ann E. Wright Reid of Wentworth and the brother of Frank L. Reid, Methodist minister and educator. James Reid was reared in Wentworth and educated in the local academy. He attended Trinity College (1866–67), where he was an honor student, and was graduated from Emory and Henry College in 1869. He returned home to a position as a teacher and then principal of the Wentworth Male Academy. Reid studied law and was admitted to the bar in 1873, opening his practice in Wentworth with Andrew J. Boyd as a partner. Excelling in debate in college, Reid was soon in demand in both North Carolina and Virginia as a speaker at political rallies, reunions, and college commencements. Several contemporaries described his eloquent but florid speaking style, and he was known in his day as "the silver-tongued orator."

Reid married, on 19 Dec. 1872, Mary Frances Ellington (1851–1906) of Wentworth, and they had two daughters, Ann and Lucile. A Mason and an active lay member of the Methodist church, he addressed church conferences and served as a lay delegate in district and general conferences. He was appointed a lay member of the Conference Board of Missions. With his brother, Reid coedited *Life, Sermons, and Speeches of Rev. Numa F. Reid Late of the North Carolina Conference* (1874). In addition to his law practice Reid helped his grandfather, James Wright (d. 1876), run the family enterprise, Wright Tavern. Reid was responsible for extensive remodeling of the famed hostelry in the 1870s, and after the death of his grandfather the tavern became known as the Reid House. In 1880 he was an agent for Home Insurance Company.

James Reid's political career began with his election as the county treasurer in 1874, a position he held until 3 Nov. 1884, when he resigned to run for the U.S. House of Representatives. While serving as county treasurer Reid was secretary to the Rockingham County Democratic Executive Committee, and in 1884 he was elected county chairman. Reid was in the Forty-eighth and Forty-ninth Congresses from 1884 to 31 Dec. 1886, when he resigned. His most notable stand on Capitol Hill was his strong support of the Blair Education Bill, which would have provided federal aid to public education.

In the 1870s Reid amassed considerable property by borrowing heavily. Eventually overextending himself, he had to declare bankruptcy, and by 1887 his property was auctioned to cover his debts. At the same time a scandal surfaced over Reid's alleged mishandling of public funds during his term as county treasurer. Although he was exonerated by a committee appointed by the county commissioners, his political opponents continued to agitate the issue. The emerging scandal and his impending personal financial ruin caused Reid to leave his home and family and settle in Lewiston, Idaho, in 1887.

In Idaho Reid resumed the practice of law and became active in the statehood movement. He was elected to the state constitution convention and served as convention vice-president. In the convention he chaired the committee that wrote the statehood resolution. He was appointed to the board of trustees of Lewiston State Normal College in 1893 and later served on the board of regents of the University of Idaho. Reid was a delegate to the Democratic National Conventions of 1896 and 1900. He died and was buried in Lewiston.

SEE: *Biog. Dir. Am. Cong.* (1950); Lindley S. Butler, *Wright Tavern: A Courthouse Inn and Its Proprietors* (1973); *Dan Valley Echo* (Leaksville), 16 Oct. 1886; John M. Gallaway, "Rockingham County Finances: An Appeal for Justice"; Allen J. Going, "The South and the Blair Education Bill," *Mississippi Valley Historical Review* 44 (1957); Greenview Cemetery, Reidsville; James W. Reid Scrapbook, Eden; *Reidsville Times*, 11 May 1884; Rockingham County Deeds.

LINDLEY S. BUTLER

Reid, James William *(15 Sept. 1917–19 June 1972)*, broadcaster, public relations officer, sports director, banker, and mayor, was born in Asheville, the son of Bessie Perkinson and William Ernest Reid. In the early 1900s Mrs. Reid's family lived across Woodfin Street in Asheville from the W. O. Wolfe home and is portrayed in Thomas Wolfe's novel, *Look Homeward, Angel*, as the Tarkinton family.

Young Reid attended Mars Hill Junior College and was graduated from Wake Forest College in 1937 with a degree in physics. Between 1938 and 1942 he was a staff announcer for radio stations in Asheville, Wilson, Greenville, S.C., and Raleigh. During World War II he served in the Aleutian Islands with the Naval Air Force for two years and afterwards was radar officer at Adak, Kokiak, and Attu, and finally with the Bureau of Ships in Washington, D.C. He returned to radio station WPTF in Raleigh as staff announcer, sports director, and weather reporter; in 1958 he became manager of the Raleigh office of WTVD television station. From October 1960 until his death he was senior vice-president of Branch Banking and Trust Company in Raleigh. Reid also had a political career, serving on the Raleigh City Council, as mayor pro tem, and as mayor. In these municipal offices he actively supported improved race relations, library service, the construction of a new municipal building, and other causes.

It was as a radio and television personality, however, that Reid was best known. He won numerous awards, particularly in the field of sports broadcasting and for his thrice-daily weather programs. His interest in meteorology stemmed from his naval experience, and he was active in the North Carolina chapter of the American Meteorological Society, being the first nonprofessional to receive the national organization's Special Award. Reid served on countless boards, commissions, and committees at the local and state levels and rendered effective service in such diverse areas as rent control, airport development, community planning, youth fitness, and music.

Reid married Elizabeth Davis of Wadesboro and they were the parents of Michael E., Nancy K., and James W., Jr.

SEE: Documents in possession of Mrs. Elizabeth Reid Murray, Raleigh; *Raleigh Amateur Radio Society News*, Issue 33 (July 1972); Raleigh *News and Observer*, 23 June 1963, 20–21 June 1972.

WILLIAM S. POWELL

Reid, Paul Apperson *(10 Aug. 1902–13 June 1982)*, a professional educator who in a forty-three-year career served North Carolina at every level of the public education system, was born in Stokes County, the son of Margaret Apperson and William Henry Reid. Nevertheless, he consistently claimed Surry as his native county, noting that his father was only temporarily managing the Vade Mecum mineral springs at the time of his birth. Educated in the Pilot Mountain public schools, Paul Reid entered The University of North Carolina to prepare for a business career. He interrupted his studies to become a temporary teacher in a rural two-teacher Surry school. There he met his future wife Magdalene (later known in Cullowhee as Madeline) Fulk, the other teacher in the Hill's Chapel elementary school, and decided on a career in education. Subsequently, he returned to the university and was awarded a B.A. in education (1929). In 1938 he received the M.A. degree in history.

Reid's service to North Carolina public education may be summarized as follows: teacher in Pilot Mountain elementary and high schools (1923–27); business manager and assistant superintendent of schools, Roanoke Rapids (1929–35); principal of junior and senior high schools, Roanoke Rapids (1935–38); principal of Needham Broughton High School, Raleigh (1938–41); superintendent, Elizabeth City public schools (1941–44); controller, State Board of Education (1944–49); and president, Western Carolina Teachers College (now University) (August 1949–June 1968, with an interim, March 1956–August 1957, during which he returned to Raleigh to serve as assistant director of the newly formed North Carolina Board of Higher Education).

When Reid accepted the presidency of Western Carolina Teachers College in 1949, it was against the advice of some Raleigh friends who believed that the Cullowhee institution had no future and that he would fade into oblivion in the remote mountains of western North Carolina. Indeed Western Carolina, founded in 1889 as Cullowhee High School, had long struggled for survival and was still relatively small and obscure. But Reid, mindful of the efforts of his predecessors, undertook his work with skill, diplomacy, and optimism. He began to plan for an expanded curriculum and for the addition of land and buildings. In 1953 the state legislature authorized a change in function and name; Western Carolina College was authorized to offer baccalaureate degrees in the liberal arts and graduate degrees in education. Subsequently programs in business and industrial arts were developed, and in the 1960s masters' degrees in the arts and sciences were initiated. In 1967 Western Carolina became a regional university and was reorganized into several academic schools, and a faculty senate was established.

When he retired as chancellor of Western Carolina University in 1968, Reid could reflect on two decades of solid accomplishment. The board of trustees praised his "dynamic leadership, exceptional educational statesmanship and wise administrative guidance," noting the following growth during his presidency, 1949–68: student population, from 600 to 4,000; faculty, from about 50 to 240; buildings, from 12 to 36; capital investment, from $1.6 million to $26 million; and operating budget, from $500,000 to $5.5 million per year.

After Madeline Fulk Reid died in March 1955, Paul Reid was lonely, despite numerous friends in Cullowhee and the region. A year later he resigned and returned to Raleigh to become assistant director of the Board of Higher Education, a position he held for eighteen months. During this time he was awarded an honorary Litt.D. by High Point College, and a new physical education-athletic facility on the Cullowhee campus was named in his honor. In August 1957, after his marriage to Nettie Dockery Haywood of Raleigh, Reid resumed the presidency of Western Carolina College. After his retirement in 1968, he and Nettie Reid traveled extensively and divided their time between homes in Florida and at Lake Junaluska before settling in his native Pilot Mountain. But his interest in Western Carolina never flagged. In his last years the Reids gave the institution over $100,000 to support student scholarships and to provide annual awards to outstanding faculty members and administrators.

Trained in history, Reid published one book: *Gubernatorial Campaigns and Administrations of David S. Reid, 1848–1854* (1953). Reid and his subject were not related.

SEE: *Asheville Citizen*, 7 Dec. 1958, 12 June 1968; William E. Bird, *The History of Western Carolina College* (1963); *Winston-Salem Journal*, 11 Jan. 1981; Reid Personnel File, Western Carolina University; Western Carolina University Board of Trustees Resolution, 11 May 1968.

MAX R. WILLIAMS

Reilley, Charles Norwood *(2 Mar. 1925–31 Dec. 1981)*, chemist and educator, was one of the world's guiding lights of the renaissance in analytic chemistry after World War II and only the second analytic chemist in modern times elected to the National Academy of Science. He was born in Charlotte, the son of Eugene Holmes Reilley, a representative of the American Seating Company, a manufacturer of school furniture, and Marie Norwood Reilley; when he was a boy his father died from injuries received in World War I, and he was raised by his mother, a public school teacher. Charles became fascinated with radio and electrical things while he was in grammar school, and his introduction to science in high school so seized his imagination that he could never turn his eyes away again.

He was graduated from The University of North Carolina with a B.S. in chemistry in 1947, winning undergraduate awards sponsored by Alpha Chi Sigma as a sophomore, junior, and senior; and the Archibald Henderson medal in mathematics and election to Phi Beta Kappa as a junior. After college he joined the faculty at Queens College in Charlotte and for years afterwards told stories about standing in the hallway, simultaneously teaching three laboratories in three subjects and answering questions from all three rooms at the same time.

In 1949 he began graduate work at Princeton University with Professor N. H. Furman, one of the most distinguished analytic chemists of that generation. Furman's group included a number of brilliant scientists who would in the next few years create a revolution in analytic chemistry, bringing the development of analytic electronic instrumentation within the province of the analytic chemist; Reilley was a leader among this number from the beginning. He received an M.A. in 1951 and a Ph.D. in 1952, winning the national competition for the prestigious Merck Award in 1951.

Returning to his alma mater in 1951 as instructor, Reilley was promoted to assistant professor in 1953 and associate professor in 1956. In 1957, at the urging of nominators across the country, he was awarded an unsolicited and unrestricted grant from the Research Corporation to further his interests. The novelty of such an unrestricted award captured the imagination of the press; newspapers quoted spokesmen: "If Professor Reilley feels that buying a convertible automobile will further his research, he may use the money to buy the convertible automobile." He used the money in traditional ways, however.

In 1961 he became professor and won a Guggenheim Fellowship to study at Basle for the year. In due time, when the grand old man of American analytic chemistry, Izaac M. Kolthoff, retired from the University of Minnesota and colleagues there asked him to prepare a full list of persons to invite to succeed to his chair, Kolthoff replied, "There is only one: Charles Reilley." But Reilley would not be moved from Chapel Hill, either for this signal honor or for many others that were offered to him throughout his career. In 1963, at age thirty-eight, he was named Kenan Professor.

Honors continued to crowd upon him. He was invited to present distinguished lectures at Notre Dame, West Virginia, Iowa, Pittsburgh, Louisville, Colorado, Kansas, Stockholm, Virginia Polytechnic, and Cornell. The American Chemical Society honored him with its Fisher Award in Analytical Chemistry (1965), Herty Medal (1968), and Stone Award (1971). He won the ANACHEM Award in Analytical Chemistry in 1972, the Manufacturing Chemists Association College Teacher Award in 1975, and the Kolthoff Award in Analytical Chemistry in 1979. In 1977 he was elected to the National Academy of Sciences, the first analytic chemist in nineteen years and the first after Kolthoff himself.

Indeed Reilley was preeminently, after Kolthoff, the world's renaissance man of analytic chemistry. His early interests were in electrochemistry, and one of his earliest studies, setting forth the correct theoretical model of high-frequency titrimetry, set the tone for teaching the fundamentals of electrochemistry across the world for fifteen years; his concept of response function additivity stimulated an enormous amount of work by other scientists, and his theoretical and experimental studies of galvanic membrane electrodes led to a simple, inexpensive method of measuring dissolved oxygen in rivers and lakes. At the same time he developed theory and innovative methods for the study of multidentate metal complex chemistry; he developed a reagent for the titration of calcium in the presence of magnesium that is used today in many clinical laboratories, and he was responsible for articulating the nature of the "chelate effect," the exceptional stability of metal complexes in which the ligands have several sites from which electrons may be donated to the metal ion. His application of nuclear magnetic resonance spectrometry to these complexes broke ground from which sprang years of others' works on the dynamics of the formation and breaking of chemical bonds between sites in the ligand and the metal ion.

His clarity in explaining his concept of microscopic protonation equilibria guided many other workers in further development of theories of bond formation in these complexes, and his definitive work on the origins of chemical shifts in nuclear magnetic resonance spectra of metal complexes paved the way for the development of shift reagents, some of the most valuable tools of the chemist in probing the structures of these complexes in solution. His early contributions in chromatography on sequential and mixed-bed columns in gas-liquid chromatography ultimately became so pervasive in analysis that, to most workers, their origins have become lost; his thoughts about detector response provoked the development of inverse chromatography.

Reilley was one of the first to think about how computers could simplify the interpretation of analytic data, and his pioneering work on the application of pattern recognition techniques to the interpretation of mass and infrared spectra of organic compounds in order to deduce their structure was the origin of the discipline of chemometrics. His last major work was in the application of microcomputers to chemical analysis, and their impact is still to be fully felt. After the Manhattan project, analytic chemistry had lost some of its impetus and even its respectability in academic institutions; when there were chemists who would push analytic chemistry back into the dreary world of old-fashioned volumetric and gravimetric procedures and call all the rest the province of other branches of the discipline, Charles Reilley pointed out that "analytical chemistry is what analytical chemists do" and let his own creations, and what they engendered, stand as testimony to the new vibrancy of his discipline.

A teacher of prodigious vision, Reilley earned the Manufacturing Chemists Association Award not only for his profound influence in graduate education through his research, but also for his genius in revising the classical undergraduate curriculum in chemistry at Chapel Hill, so that the university was recognized in the late 1960s and 1970s as the major national innovator in chemical education. The program of instruction proved so exciting to young science students that for 80 percent of the years following its installation, Chapel Hill ranked first in the nation in the number of degrees granted to baccalaureate chemists.

As a teacher and scholar he was also sought by many chemical and instrumentation producers as a consultant and by many government agencies as a member of distinguished advisory panels. He served as coeditor of *Advances in Analytical Chemistry and Instrumentation*, as secretary-treasurer and then chairman of the Division of Analytical Chemistry of the American Chemical Society, and on the Advisory Council on College Chemistry.

Reilley never married. He was survived by his mother, whom he cared for until his sudden death in Chapel Hill; a brother, Eugene Holmes Reilley, Jr., of Atlanta; and two sisters, Miriam Reilley Bell of Wilmington and Marie Reilley Ridgeway of Tacoma, Wash.

SEE: Maurice M. Bursey, *Carolina Chemists* (1982); *Chapel Hill Newspaper*, 3 Jan. 1982; *Durham Morning Herald*, 17 Feb. 1957; T. L. Isenhour, *Analytical Chemistry* (1982); Raleigh *News and Observer*, 2 Jan. 1982.

MAURICE M. BURSEY

Reilley, Laura Holmes *(28 Nov. 1861–25 Feb. 1941)*, was best known for her work in women's clubs on the local, state, and national levels. So varied and extensive were her activities that she was the first North Carolina woman to be included in *Who's Who in America*. Born in St. Louis, Mo., to Charles Francis and Mary Linn Parry Holmes, she attended the "Mary Institute," the Women's Department of Washington University, and was graduated in 1882. Later that year, on 15 November, she married James Eugene Reilley (d. 1939), also of St. Louis. They lived in several places—St. Louis, New Mexico, Chicago, Baltimore, and Atlanta—before finally settling in Charlotte in the 1890s and had six children: Lucile R. (MacDonald), Eugene Holmes, Ruth R. (Mrs. Preston B. Wilkes, Jr.), Laura Holmes (1891–1973), who served as a hostess at the governor's mansion in Raleigh from 1944 to 1961, Alfred Shapleigh, and Maurice Eliot.

Mrs. Reilley's contributions to women's organizations, especially those concerned with politics, history, and culture, were many. Most prominent was her long association with the Charlotte Woman's Club, of which she was president from 1903 to 1908 and from 1920 to 1922 and parliamentarian from 1934 to 1938. Under her leadership a clubhouse was built and the membership raised from 200 to 600. She was elected president of the North Carolina Federation of Women's Clubs for a two-year term beginning in 1909 and was chairman of Club Institutes for the state from 1926 to 1932. In 1910 in Cincinnati, she was elected to the board of the General Federation; from 1912 to 1916 she was corresponding secretary (elected in San Francisco), and from 1916 to 1918, vice-president (elected in New York). In 1924 the General Federation made her an honorary vice-president.

In September 1920 Mrs. Reilley was one of ten delegates from the United States attending the International Council of Women in Christiana, Norway. In May 1925 she was elected chairman of hospitality for the council at its meeting in Washington, D.C. In 1939 the governor of New York invited her to be a member of the Advisory Committee for the Participation of Women at the New York World's Fair.

Her political activities were mostly in the realm of voting rights. She was a member of the advisory board of the North Carolina League of Women Voters and a delegate to the 1924 Democratic state convention in Raleigh. In addition, she was an organizer of the North Carolina Suffrage Association, a charter member and first vice-president of the Equal Suffrage League, and a representative, appointed by Governor Locke Craig, to the Southern Suffrage Conference in New Orleans in 1914. There she was elected vice-president.

While working for woman suffrage she served on Governor Thomas W. Bickett's War Savings Committee, a part of the State Council of Defense during World War I, and also was chairman of the Committee on Women's Defense Work, a committee under the Council of National Defense set up by Congress. For the YWCA she was requested to carry out an educational and financial campaign in the state districts after World War I.

Her affiliations with historical organizations were numerous. She was a regent of the Liberty Hall Chapter of the Daughters of the American Revolution for two terms (1910–12, 1926–28), corresponding secretary (1912–16), and a parliamentarian. From 1936 to 1938 she was chairman of the Mecklenburg County Committee of Colonial Dames and in 1925 had been one of a Committee of 12 to plan the 150th anniversary celebration of the Declaration of Independence. She was a charter member and for a term governor (1937–38) of the Society of Mayflower Descendants.

Her work for cultural organizations was also notable. In the fall of 1922 she helped organize a Better Films Committee of Charlotte and was its first president. She was president of the state committee and vice-president of the Southeastern Council of Better Films. She was twice president of the Charlotte Sorosis, organizer of the Charlotte branch of the Needlework Guild of America (vice-president, 1930), and a trustee of the Mint Art Museum.

Active in church affairs, Mrs. Reilley was twice president of the Ladies' Aid Society, a charter member of the Westminster Presbyterian Church, and later a charter member of the Myers Park Presbyterian Church. She was buried from Myers Park Presbyterian Church in Elmwood Cemetery.

SEE: *Charlotte News*, 25–27 Feb. 1941, 1 Mar. 1973; *Charlotte Observer*, 26 Feb. 1941 [portrait]; League of Women Voters of North Carolina, *Monthly News*, February 1924, April 1926; Charles L. Van Noppen Papers (Manuscript Department, Duke University Library, Durham); *Who's Who in the South* (1927); *Who Was Who in America*, vol. 1 (1943).

EVA MURPHY

Reilly, James *(17 Apr. 1823–5 Nov. 1894)*, soldier, was born at Athlone, County Roscommon, Ireland, the son of James and Anne Brady Reilly. At age sixteen he ran away from home and enlisted in the British army, having dreamed of being a soldier from his early boyhood. Though his mother soon secured his discharge, he joined the army again when he reached eighteen. Discontented with the service and his ill treatment, he deserted and fled to America. He lived at first with his uncle in New York, but, returning to his childhood desire to be a soldier, enlisted in the U.S. Army in New York in 1845 and was assigned to the Second Artillery Regiment. Reilly served throughout the Mexican War as a private, was wounded at Churubusco, and then was injured when his horse was shot from under him at Molino del Rey. Discharged with a surgeon's certificate of disability for the injury in 1848, he recovered sufficiently to enlist again in the Second Artillery less than two months later. Over the next few years, he rose to the rank of first sergeant of his company, serving in Virginia, South Carolina, Georgia, Florida, and Indian Territory. He wrote of his experiences in the army in the early 1850s in reminiscences published over fifty years later, after his death.

In 1857 Reilly was promoted to ordnance sergeant, a rank set aside for a few dozen noncommissioned officers who had distinguished themselves by their faithful service. Initially assigned to Fort Myers, Fla., he was transferred to Fort Johnston near the mouth of the Cape Fear River in about 1859. Ordnance Sergeant Reilly had full responsibility for the fort and the weapons and ammunition stored in its magazine since no regular army troops were stationed there. On 9 Jan. 1861 a number of local citizens of Smithville (present-day Southport) banded together and forced Reilly at Fort Johnston and Ordnance Sergeant Frederick Dardingkiller at Fort Caswell on nearby Oak Island to open their magazines and surrender their ordnance stores. Soon realizing that they did not have much popular support for their actions, the citizens returned what they had taken to the two ordnance sergeants and a crisis was averted.

When the Civil War broke out in April, Colonel John Lucas Cantwell headed a force of North Carolina troops that compelled Reilly to surrender Fort Johnston. Reilly chose to resign his warrant as an ordnance sergeant and was subsequently discharged by order of the adjutant general. His decision to join the Confederate cause clearly resulted from his having passed nearly all of his army service in the slave states. Initially he served as a drillmaster under Major William H. Whiting, but in May 1861 the North Carolina governor granted him a commission as a first lieutenant and assigned him to the First North Carolina Artillery (Tenth North Carolina Regiment). Because of his long experience in the regular army, he was advanced to the rank of captain just a month later and assumed command of the Rowan Artillery, which came to be known as Reilly's Battery. Throughout most of his more than two years' service with the battery, it was a part of General Robert E. Lee's Army of Northern Virginia.

Reilly commanded his battery with remarkable competence and reliability. Since he was unusually attentive to the maintenance of his equipment and the condition of his horses, the inspector general consistently rated his battery to be among the best in the army. The battery was also noteworthy for its performance on the battlefield. Reilly's men took part in each of the Army of Northern Virginia's major engagements from the Seven Days' Battle to Gettysburg with the exception of Chancellorsville, when the battery was temporarily in North Carolina. At various times, Generals Whiting, D. H. Hill, J. E. Johnston, and E. M. Law observed that they would rather have Reilly's Battery than any other in the Confederate army.

By mid-1863 Reilly was discouraged and angered because many less experienced artillery officers had been promoted to the rank of major. Merit had produced his commission in 1861, but the Irish-born soldier found that merit was secondary to politics and personal favoritism in his further advancement. In August 1863 he submitted his resignation, but it was not accepted. Still, his letter produced the desired effect. Governor Zebulon Vance promoted Reilly to major of North Carolina Troops in September, and, soon afterwards, President Jefferson Davis also raised him to that rank. Reilly accepted Vance's promotion and declined Davis's, thus paving the way for his return to North Carolina. In the spring of 1864 he reported to General Whiting, commander of the Department of North Carolina, and was placed in charge of an artillery battalion assigned to the Cape Fear defenses. Reilly helped to repulse the Union attack on Fort Fisher in December 1864. Fort Fisher was again attacked in January 1865 and when both its commander, Colonel William Lamb, and General Whiting were wounded, the command passed to Major Reilly. When Union forces overwhelmed the defenders, Reilly surrendered his sword to Captain E. L. Moore of Massachusetts and was taken prisoner. Nearly three decades later Moore would return the sword to him. Reillly was confined at Fort Delaware until released after taking the oath of allegiance four months after his capture.

After the war Reilly resided in Wilmington and worked as superintendent of the Wilmington and Brunswick ferry company. He spent his last years farming in Columbus County.

Reilly married Irish-born Anne Quinn in Brooklyn in 1848 shortly after he was granted a disability discharge and before he began his second term of enlistment. After her death in 1872, he married Martha E. Henry in about 1876. At the time of his death, he was survived by four children by his first wife and two by his second.

SEE: Rod Gregg, *Confederate Goliath: The Battle of Fort Fisher* (1991); D. H. Hill, Jr., *Confederate Military History of North Carolina* (1899); Lawrence Lee (Charleston, S.C.), personal contact; Louis H. Manarin, comp., *North Carolina Troops, 1861–1865: A Roster*, vol. 1 (1971); James Reilly, "An Artilleryman's Story," *Journal of the Military Service Institution of the United States* 33 (November 1903), 45 (December 1909).

DALE R. STEINHAUER

Relfe (Ralph, Relph, Rolfe), Thomas *(ca. 1645–1713 or 1714)*, jurist, legislator, provost marshal, and surveyor general, was the son of Dr. Thomas and Dorothy Relfe, who moved from Virginia to the Carolina colony about 1663. It has been suggested that Dr. Relfe may have been the son of the early Jamestown settler John Rolfe and his Indian wife, Pocahontas. The theory rests on circumstantial evidence and an assumption as to the "correct" spelling of the name Relfe (Rolfe), which has many variants in the old manuscripts. More substantial evidence would be necessary to establish the theory as fact.

On 25 Sept. 1663 Dr. Relfe was issued a patent for 750 acres of land in the Carolina colony, then called Albemarle. About that time the family moved to the grant, which was on the Pasquotank River. In addition to the parents, the family included son Thomas, then about eighteen years old, and a younger son, William. Several relatives of the Relfes moved to Albemarle about the same time, including the families of Richard Roads (Rhodes) and John and William Jennings, but the relationships are not clear. There also were other Carolina settlers named Relfe, but they appear in the records a little later and their relationship, if any, is unknown.

The sparse surviving records of Albemarle tell little about the Relfe family's early years in the colony. Dr. Relfe probably died before March 1680, when a court ordered John Jennings to return an account of the estate of a "Thos. Roelph." No later reference to the doctor has been found, nor is there information respecting his wife.

By 6 Jan. 1689/90, Thomas Relfe was a justice of Pasquotank Precinct Court, an office that he also held in 1694 and 1700. No doubt he served on the court in some or all of the intervening years, for which there are virtually no extant records of that court. By the 1690s Relfe bore the title of captain, which suggests that he was active in the militia.

About 1683 Thomas Relfe married Mary Keile (Keele), widow of Thomas Keile. Before her marriage to Keile, Mary appears to have been married to one Butler and to have had a daughter, Ann, by him. She had three children by Keile—Thomas, Sarah, and Robert—and she bore Relfe two children—Thomas and Dorothy. Relfe was guardian as well as stepfather to the Keile children. Yet another member of his household was William Roads, who also was Relfe's ward. Roads was either Relfe's nephew or his wife's.

Relfe continued to live in Pasquotank Precinct, where his parents had settled. He owned at least 600 acres of land in addition to that inherited from his father. His brother William also lived in Pasquotank and had extensive landholdings. Both Thomas and William served on the Anglican church vestry for the Pasquotank parish. They were strongly opposed to permitting Quakers to serve in governmental positions.

In 1694 the General Court appointed Thomas and William Relfe administrators of the estate of Elizabeth Roads (widow of Richard Roads) as "nearest of kin" to the orphans. In spite of their being designated "nearest of kin," a later court (in 1695) granted guardianship of two of the Roads orphans to Dorothy Jennings, wife of John Jennings, in compliance with a petition in which Dorothy identified herself as "grandmother and nearest of kin" to the orphans. The William Roads who was reared by Thomas and Mary Relfe appears to have been a third orphan of Richard and Elizabeth Roads. These and other records indicate that Thomas and William Relfe were close kin to Dorothy Jennings and to either Richard Roads or his wife Elizabeth, but they do not make the relationships clear.

Thomas Relfe was politically active much of his life. In addition to sitting on the Pasquotank court, he held offices significant to the entire colony. On 27 Sept. 1694 he took oath as provost marshal (high sheriff) for Albemarle, an office he held through December 1696. From July 1696 through March 1702/3 he served as deputy for the surveyor general. By commission dated 26 Aug. 1703 Relfe himself was appointed surveyor general, a position that he held until some date in 1705. He was a member of the Assembly in 1711 and perhaps other years. In July 1712 he became a justice of the General Court, on which he sat through August 1713.

Relfe died between 26 Oct. 1713, when he made a deposition in a lawsuit, and 10 Aug. 1714, when the governor and Council ordered payment to Mary Relfe of money due her deceased husband. In the deposition Relfe gave his age as sixty-eight. For some reason his will, made in 1704, was not probated until 1720. In the will, Relfe named as legatees his wife Mary, his son Thomas, his daughter Dorothy, and William Roads.

Mary Relfe died between 13 Jan. 1724/25, when she made her will, and 20 Aug. 1725, when her will was probated. Apparently, both of her children by Relfe and one of her sons by Keile already had died, for her legatees did not include her daughter Dorothy Relfe or her sons Thomas Relfe and Thomas Keile. Indeed, she bequeathed "the chest that was my son Thomas Relfs" to William Roads, as well as other items of substantial value, including land. Possibly the bequest of land was confirmation of a bequest by her husband, who had bequeathed a tract of land to William Roads on condition that "he stays with his aunt until he comes of age." Mary Relfe's legatees also included William Relfe's two grandchildren, Thomas and Mary Relfe, as well as her daughters Ann and Sarah, her son Robert Keile, and members of their families.

SEE: John L. Cheney, Jr., ed., *North Carolina Government, 1585–1974* (1975); J. Bryan Grimes, ed., *Abstract of North Carolina Wills* (1910); J. R. B. Hathaway, ed., *North Carolina Historical and Genealogical Register* (1900–1903); Elizabeth Vann Moore and Richard Slatten, "The Descendants of Pocahontas: An Unclosed Case," *Magazine of Virginia Genealogy* 23, no. 3 (August 1985); North Carolina State Archives, Raleigh, particularly Albemarle Book of Warrants and Surveys (1681–1706), Council Minutes, Wills, Inventories (1677–1701), Colonial Court Records (Box 192), and Wills of Thomas Keile (1682), Mary Relfe (1725), and Thomas Relfe (1704); Nell Marion Nugent, comp., *Cavaliers and Pioneers*, vol. 1 (1934); Mattie Erma Edwards Parker, ed., *North Carolina Higher-Court Records, 1670–1696* and *1697–1701* (1968, 1971); William S. Price, Jr., ed., *North Carolina Higher-Court Records, 1702–1708* (1974) and *North Carolina Higher-Court Minutes, 1709–1723* (1977); William L. Saunders, ed., *Colonial Records of North Carolina* (1886–90).

MATTIE ERMA E. PARKER

Rencher, Abraham *(16 Aug. 1798–6 July 1883)*, lawyer and legislator, son of John Grant and Ann Nelson Rencher, was born in Wake County, near Raleigh. His father, a native of Ireland, was for several years the sheriff of Wake County. Young Rencher received his preparatory education at the Reverend John Chavis's school in Raleigh and in 1822 was graduated with honors from The University of North Carolina, receiving the B.A. degree. He then studied law under Judge Frederick Nash in Hillsborough. Upon receiving his license in 1825, he began to practice law in Pittsboro, which remained his legal residence until his death.

Rencher had not been in practice long before he became active in politics. From 1829 to 1839 and from 1841 to 1843 he represented the Tenth Congressional District in Congress. During his first eight years in the House of Representatives Rencher was a Democrat and for his last four a member of the Whig party. He broke with Andrew Jackson in 1835, when the president "illegally" removed the federal government's deposits from the Bank of the United States. Rencher remarked to his constituents that Jackson "too often trampled on the forms of the Constitution when they came into conflict with his own will." Up to this time Rencher had been a strong supporter of the president's policies. He voted against the recharter of the Bank of the United States, supported Jackson in his stand against nullification, voted for the compromise tariff measure of 1833, and opposed federal participation in internal improvements. His most important committee assignments were on Ways and Means and Foreign Affairs.

Rencher did not stand for reelection in 1838 because of ill health. Two years later, however, his health was sufficiently improved for him to run successfully on the Whig ticket for the Twenty-seventh Congress. In the extra session of this Congress, called by President John Tyler to meet in late May 1841, Rencher voted for the two bills proposed by the Whigs for the establishment of a national bank that were vetoed by Tyler. He said that he voted for the bank because "I was pledged so to do and because I believed, at that time, we could not have a sound currency without the aid of such an institution." He later remarked that he "had good cause to believe that, in this opinion I was wrong."

During the Twenty-seventh Congress, Rencher voted against many of the measures advocated by the Whigs. It appears that he was never in full sympathy with Whig principles and felt that the party treated Tyler unjustly. In appraising Rencher's congressional career a contemporary wrote that "he was characterized for his punctuality and diligence—as a *working* rather than a *speaking* member. He seldom addressed the House, but when he did, it was on something of importance, and his opinions never failed to command a respectful consideration even when they failed to produce conviction."

Rencher's loyalty to Tyler was rewarded when the president appointed him chargé d'affaires to Portugal on 22 Sept. 1843. He held this post until the spring of 1847, when President James Knox Polk appointed a political friend to succeed him. In January 1846 Rencher wrote a friend that he had learned that several of Polk's supporters wanted the post and that he, Rencher, "occupied too conspicuous a position to Mr. Van Buren and his friends to escape their revenge whenever they have an opportunity to exert it." Judging from the letters written to his relatives in North Carolina, Rencher enjoyed his life in Portugal. He frequently remarked on the friendly disposition of the royal family towards him and his family.

On returning to the United States Rencher resumed the practice of law in Pittsboro and the cultivation of his farm, Green Brook, situated just outside of the town. He also took up again his interest in local and state politics, now as a Democrat. Rencher delivered one of the important speeches of the Democratic state convention of 1852. He campaigned in the state for Franklin Pierce and William Rufus King and was an elector on that ticket. In 1854 he was elected president of the state Democratic convention. Following the election of 1856, President-elect James Buchanan offered Rencher the position of secretary of the navy, which he declined. Rencher was interested in securing another appointment, that of governor of the Territory of New Mexico, and waged an aggressive campaign to obtain it. Nine North Carolina state senators sent a statement to Buchanan recommending him. In August 1857 the president appointed Rencher governor of the Territory of New Mexico. Why he was so anxious for this post is difficult to understand. It is possible that Rencher's interests in the New Mexico Mining Company, organized in 1853, may have played a role. He owned six thousand shares of stock in this company. Writing to an official of the company on 22 June 1861 complaining of his treatment, Rencher said, "I have made great sacrifices for this company in every respect. As an inducement for me to come here, they agreed to pay me a certain sum of one thousand dollars per annum, until successful, and after that, twenty-five hundred." A few days later he wrote his son John that it would be greatly to his profit if he could remain in New Mexico a few years more since "we are just now beginning to work the mines to advantage."

On 11 Nov. 1857 Rencher arrived in Santa Fe with his wife and daughters to take over his duties. In his first address to the territorial legislature he stressed the need for establishing common schools, the development of the territory's natural resources, and an ad valorem tax to provide adequate revenue. He was able to accomplish the first of these objectives when in January 1860 the legislature passed a bill providing for public education. It was not until almost the end of his administration that he was able to reduce the public debt by more than half.

Rencher had not been in New Mexico long before trouble with the Navajo Indians began. He informed the secretary of state that the military establishment and the Indian agent were responsible for initiating the disturbance by their ill-advised and hasty actions. It was not long before he was at odds with not only the military but the legislature as well. Intermittent war with the Indians continued to plague his administration for almost all of his gubernatorial career.

Although Rencher was an outspoken proslavery man, he remained loyal to the Union as long as he continued in office. When Fort Fillmore was captured by Confederate troops on 26 July 1861, Rencher issued a proclamation calling upon "all good and loyal citizens to uphold the authority of the laws and to defend the Territory against invasion and violence from whatever quarter they may come." Two months earlier he had been notified that he would not be reappointed and that his successor would take over on 1 September.

Rencher returned to his home near Pittsboro where he resided for the remainder of his life. He died in Chapel Hill while visiting his daughter and was buried in the cemetery of St. Bartholomew's Episcopal Church, Pittsboro.

Rencher married Louisa Mary Jones, daughter of Colonel Edward and Elizabeth Mallett Jones, on 29 Sept. 1836 in St. Bartholomew's parish. They had four children: John Grant, William Conway, Sarah (m. Colonel S. Latham Anderson), and Charlotte Genevieve (m. Robert Newton Winston). A portrait of Rencher hangs in the hall of the Dialectic Literary Society, Chapel Hill.

SEE: *Biog. Dir. Am. Cong.* (1961); John Howard Brown, ed., *Biographical Sketches Reprinted from The Twentieth Century Biographical Dictionary of Notable Americans* (1915); *Chatham Record*, 12 July 1883; *Congressional Globe* (24th, 25th, 27th Congresses, 1835–39, 1841–43); Wade Hadley and others, *Chatham County, 1771–1971* (1971); J. G. de Roulhac Hamilton, *Party Politics in North Carolina, 1835–1860* (1916), and ed., *Papers of William Alexander Graham*, vol. 4 (1961); Calvin Horn, "Patriot from North Carolina," *New Mexico Magazine* 36 (1958); William A. Keleher, *Turmoil in New Mexico, 1846–1868* (1952); Herbert Dale Pegg, *The Whig Party in North Carolina* (1969); *Register of Debates in Congress* (21st–23d Congresses, 1829–35); Abraham Rencher, *Circular Address . . . to His Constituents* (1843), *Circular . . . to the Freeman of the Tenth Congressional District of North Carolina* (1839), *Speech . . . Delivered in the Democratic State Convention of North Carolina* (1852), and *To the People of the Tenth Congressional District of North Carolina* (1837); Abraham Rencher Papers (Southern Historical Collection, University of North Carolina, Chapel Hill).

LAWRENCE F. LONDON

Renfrow, William Cary *(15 Mar. 1845–31 Jan. 1922)*, governor of Oklahoma Territory, was born in Smithfield, the son of Perry and Lucinda Hawkins Atkinson Rentfrow [*sic*]. After attending local schools young Renfrow volunteered for service in the Civil War, joining Company C, Fiftieth North Carolina Regiment in February 1862 and becoming a first sergeant. He afterwards transferred to Company F, Sixteenth Battalion of North Carolina Cavalry, and was paroled at Goldsboro on 13 May 1865. Before the end of 1865 he went with a friend to Russellville, Pope County, Ark., where he entered business.

By the mid-1880s Renfrow was holding office in the local government but moved to Norman, Okla., in 1889, when the Oklahoma Territory was opened to general settlement. After operating a successful livery business he became involved in banking with an associate in Oklahoma City. Renfrow was chosen as a delegate to the first Territorial Convention. On 7 May 1893 he was appointed third governor of the Oklahoma Territory by President Grover Cleveland and remained in office until 24 May 1897. During his administration the Cherokee strip was opened, and he approved and signed the act establishing the Oklahoma Historical Society. After becoming involved in the lead and zinc business in southwestern Missouri and northeastern Oklahoma, he settled at Miami, where he became owner of extensive mining properties under the firm name of Renfrow Mining and Royalty Company, of which he was president for the remainder of his life. Several years prior to his death he also became involved in the gas and oil business and spent considerable time in the Mexia area of Texas because of his investments there in the Mirindo Oil Company.

On 17 Oct. 1875 Renfrow married Jennie B. York of Judsonia, Ark., and they became the parents of W. C., Jr., and a daughter who married Fred Robertson of Houston, Tex. He was buried in the city cemetery, Russellville, Ark. Renfrow's brother, James T., was the great-grandfather of James B. Hunt, Jr., who was governor of North Carolina during the years 1977–85 and again starting in 1993.

SEE: *Chronicles of Oklahoma* 1 (June 1923); Weymouth T. Jordan, comp., *North Carolina Troops, 1861–1865: A Roster*, vol. 12 (1990); Louis H. Manarin, comp., *North Carolina Troops, 1861–1865: A Roster*, vol. 2 (1968); Dora Ann Stewart, *The Government and Development of Oklahoma Territory* (1933 [portrait]); *Who Was Who in America*, vol. 1 (1943); *Wilson Daily Times*, 14 July 1979.

WILLIAM S. POWELL

Reuter, Philip Christian Gottlieb *(5 Sept. 1717–30 Dec. 1777)*, Moravian surveyor, architect, and forester, was born in Steinbach, Germany, and lived a difficult childhood as the son of Dr. Johann Marsilius Reuter—a once-wealthy surgeon who fell to the level of a poor itinerant worker after a dream convinced him that wealth was a barrier to God's true mercy. After learning mathematics from his father and completing an unusually long apprenticeship (of five years) in surveying and mapping, P. C. G. Reuter served for a time as a royal surveyor in Germany.

Reuter joined the Lutheran church at age fourteen but seven years later (1738) became an active member of the *Unitas Fratrum* [Unity of the Brethren, or Moravian church]. He was sent by the church to America in 1756 and worked for two years doing survey and architectural tasks for the Moravians in Pennsylvania. On 21 July 1758 he entered the Moravian village of Bethabara, N.C., where he performed extensive map and survey work in a region almost uncharted prior to his arrival. Much of his work is still extant.

He divided the Moravians' *Wachau* [Wachovia] holdings into smaller tracts to be assigned to those who had financed the Moravian North Carolina colonies. Reuter completed his *Grosse Reise* [Great Map] in 1762—a leviathan document measuring seven by nine feet and depicting in astonishing detail the Piedmont region in the early 1760s. The towns of Bethania and Salem were surveyed and laid out by Reuter, who also compiled a valuable record of the flora and fauna of the region in 1764. His many other duties in Bethabara included community leadership, teaching, and church responsibilities.

In 1772 Reuter and his wife moved into their new home in Salem, a building that still stands although it is known by his wife's name. After two years of declining health, he died at age sixty and was buried in God's Acre, Salem.

Reuter married Anna Catherina Antes Kalberlahn; he was her second of four husbands as she outlived each successive one. They were wed on 18 July 1762, along with six other couples in the first Moravian marriage performed in North Carolina. The Reuters had no children but cared for a small orphaned girl for two years.

SEE: Archiv der Bruder Unitat (Library of Congress, Manuscript Division, European Photostats, Germany,

Herrnhut [untranslated and unpublished material]); Archives of the Moravian Church (Southern Province, Winston-Salem, and Northern Province, Bethlehem, Pa. [untranslated and unpublished material]); Adelaide L. Fries, *The Road to Salem* and ed., *Records of the Moravians in North Carolina*, vols. 1–4 (1922–30); Peter Hatch, "The Forester in Early Salem," in *The Three Forks of Muddy Creek*, vol. 4, ed. Frances Griffin (1977); Hunter James, "Friedberg: The Early Years," in *Three Forks*, vol. 3 (1976); Rev. Levin T. Reichel, *The Moravians in North Carolina: An Authentic History* (1857); Research Files, Old Salem, Inc., Winston-Salem.

WILLIAM HINMAN

Revels, Hiram Rhoades *(27 Sept. 1822–16 Jan. 1901)*, first black U.S. senator, Methodist minister, and educator, was born in Fayetteville of free black parents who were of mixed Croatan (Lumbee) Indian and Negro blood. At an early age he moved to Lincolnton, where for several years he served as a barber. In 1844 he entered a Quaker seminary at Liberty, Ind., for two years, where he acquired little more than an elementary education. After briefly attending a theological school in Drake County, Ohio, he completed his formal education at Knox College in Illinois. Revels was ordained a minister in the African Methodist church while in school and subsequently served religious missions to blacks in Ohio, Illinois, Indiana, Missouri, Kansas, Kentucky, and Tennessee.

When the Civil War began Revels moved to Baltimore and, in addition to his usual role as a minister, took charge of a high school for black adults. He also assisted in organizing two black regiments for service in the Union army. In 1863 he moved to St. Louis, where he established a school for freedmen and aided in the recruitment of another black regiment for Federal service. Motivated by a desire to bring religious instruction to the wretched members of his race who followed Ulysses S. Grant's army into the lower Mississippi Valley, Revels went to Mississippi in 1864 and organized several black churches and schools. Although he left the state for a brief period to do missionary work in Kentucky and Kansas, he settled permanently in Mississippi in 1866, choosing Natchez as his place of residence. In 1866 he transferred his church membership from the African Methodist church to the Methodist Episcopal Church, North, but remained a minister.

Revels's entry into Reconstruction politics occurred in 1868, when the military commander tapped him to serve on the Natchez City Council. Virtually by accident, as a compromise candidate, he secured the local Republican nomination to the state senate in 1869, which was tantamount to election in the Natchez District. His prayer opening the legislative session of 1870 made such a profound impression upon the members that they selected him to fill the short term in the U.S. Senate (reputedly the unexpired term of Jefferson Davis).

As the first black member of the Senate, where he served from February 1870 to March 1871, Revels was more of a curiosity than a mover of men or an instigator of legislation. He did advocate, however, in a speech before that august body, the passage of a measure that would permit blacks voluntarily to attend white schools in the District of Columbia. He also spoke against the readmission of Georgia to the Union until that state guaranteed the political rights of blacks. On the other hand, in another address, he called for the immediate removal of the political disabilities of former Confederates. While Congress was recessed in 1870, he made an extended tour of the Northwest, speaking optimistically about the future of his race in America. Upon the expiration of his term, he returned to Mississippi and accepted an appointment as the first president of Alcorn University, a small black college north of Natchez. He also served briefly as secretary of state ad interim of Mississippi. As a moderate he supported the James L. Alcorn wing of the state Republican party in the bitter factional fight against the Adelbert Ames Radicals.

When Ames won out and became governor in 1874, Revels was dismissed from his offices. Returning to his ministerial work, he soon joined the Methodist Episcopal Church, South. During the "Revolution of 1875," which overthrew Republican rule in the state, Revels joined in the conservative attacks on the Radical Ames administration, although he affirmed his allegiance to the Republican party. When the conservatives came to power in early 1876, he was restored to the presidency of Alcorn University, in which capacity he served ably under difficult circumstances until 1883. After his retirement he moved to Holly Springs, Miss., where he continued his religious work. He died while attending a church conference in Aberdeen. Revels married Phoebe A. Bass and was survived by two of their five daughters.

SEE: *Autobiography of John Roy Lynch* (1970); "Biographical Sketches: Hiram R. Revels," William H. McCardle Papers (Mississippi Department of Archives and History, Jackson); *DAB*, vol. 8 (1935); Jackson (Miss.) *Weekly Pilot*, 22 Jan., 21, 28 May 1870; Natchez (Miss.) *Weekly Democrat*, 22 Feb. 1871; Dunbar Rowland, *Encyclopedia of Mississippi History*, vol. 2 (1907); Samuel Denny Smith, *The Negro in Congress, 1870–1901* (1940); Washington (D.C.) *New National Era*, 1870 issues.

WILLIAM C. HARRIS

Rex, John *(11 Nov. 1771–30 Jan. 1839)*, tanner, one of six children of John and Sybilla (Sebella) Bastion Rex, was born in Germantown, Pa. Of German descent, the family was well to do; most of the male members were craftsmen and tradesmen—shipwrights, wheelwrights, blacksmiths, and merchants. Rex's father owned property in Montgomery and Philadelphia counties. Why his son John decided to leave Pennsylvania is unknown; but he evidently left with his father's blessing, because he inherited property in Pennsylvania from him in 1802. John's date of arrival in Raleigh is unknown, but he was in the newly established capital of North Carolina by July 1793, when he bought half an acre of land from Joel Lane. He opened a tannery and within a few years was able to acquire land both in Raleigh and near the city limits; he also became a planter. He bought slaves and at the time of his death owned eighteen.

Rex would not be remembered today had it not been for the terms of his will. Property in Pennsylvania known as the Broad Axe Tavern was left to a kinsman and namesake living in that state. Those of his slaves who wished to leave North Carolina were to be freed and sent to Liberia under the auspices of the American Colonization Society, and certain assets were to be sold to provide the funds needed for their transportation and settlement in Africa. Two lots southwest of Raleigh and the residue of the estate were to be used "to provide a comfortable retreat for the sick & afflicted poor belonging to the City of Raleigh, in which they may have the benefit of skillful medical aid & proper attention."

Duncan Cameron and George W. Mordecai were executors of the estate. Before the terms of the will were carried out, many lawsuits, including two cases before the North Carolina Supreme Court, had been heard and many years had passed. The American Colonization Society battled with the supreme court for years before it obtained all funds legally belonging to the freed Negroes; it was almost eighteen years to the day before the last of the money was delivered to nine people in Africa who had been slaves of John Rex. Sixteen of the eighteen slaves had actually made the trip; one declined to go, nothing is known of one, and one of those who went returned to North Carolina and was last heard of in Buffalo, N.Y. This man was Abraham, the mulatto son of John Rex by his slave Malinda. What happened to those who remained in Africa but who failed to appear when the money was distributed in two portions, one in 1856 and the remainder in 1857, is unknown.

The establishment of the hospital was also delayed for years. Trustees were appointed, but they determined to invest the $9,602 awarded the hospital by the supreme court decision and wait until the investment was sufficient for the purpose before establishing a hospital. Before they had actually begun operations, the Civil War broke out, and most of the investment was lost. The nucleus of the fund remaining after the war was reinvested; the lots left for the hospital were sold after determination by the Board of Health and subsequent judicial order of their unfitness for the designated purpose. Ultimately the trustees took over the hospital, which was operated for several years by the St. John's Guild, an Episcopal organization. Rex Hospital was formally opened in the old Charles Manly house on South Street in Raleigh in 1894. A new structure was later built on that site; in 1937 the hospital was moved to a site on St. Mary's Street and Wade Avenue, and in 1980 it moved into new facilities on Blue Ridge Road.

Though no likeness of Rex remains, David L. Swain, who was slightly acquainted with the tanner, referred to his "striking resemblance to John Quincy Adams." Swain further referred to Rex as "a grave, sedate, quiet, retiring, modest man."

Rex never married. He died in Raleigh after a month's illness. Though he was not a communicant, his funeral was held in Christ Episcopal Church, the church attended by many of those involved in the administration of his estate, including Cameron, Mordecai, Edmund B. Freeman, George E. Badger, Charles Manly, Bartholomew F. Moore, and other leaders of the bar and bench. He was buried in Raleigh's old City Cemetery.

SEE: Memory F. and Thornton W. Mitchell, "The Philanthropic Bequests of John Rex of Raleigh," *North Carolina Historical Review* 49 (pt. 1, Summer 1972; pt. 2, Autumn 1972).

MEMORY F. MITCHELL

Reynolds, Alonzo Carlton *(19 Oct. 1870–4 Oct. 1953)*, educator, was born in the Sandy Mush community of Buncombe County, the son of John Haskew and Sarah Ann Ferguson Reynolds. After attending local schools and Weaver College, he began teaching at age eighteen. In 1895 he was graduated from George Peabody College, in Nashville, Tenn., where he met his future wife, Nannie Elizabeth Woods. Between graduation and 1912 he served successively as principal of Camp Academy in Leicester, president of Rutherford College while at the same time serving as superintendent of Burke County schools, and superintendent of Buncombe County schools (1905–12).

In 1912 Reynolds became the second president of Cullowhee Normal and Industrial School (now Western Carolina University). There were shortages and difficulties for the school during World War I, but he succeeded in keeping a capable faculty and stressing the preparation of teachers for the rural areas of western North Carolina. With the physical and financial aid of students, faculty, and community and using a team of ponies and a wagon, he saw the construction of a new building for the school. While at Cullowhee he served as president of the North Carolina Education Association.

Reynolds taught at Woodfin High School in 1919–20. In the latter year he became superintendent of the Haywood County schools but returned to Woodfin in 1924 as principal. He again served as superintendent of Buncombe County schools in the period 1926–33, when he promoted the consolidation of schools and saw the erection of new and better buildings. He advocated new methods of teaching, higher teaching standards, and expansion of the curriculum. He also was one of the first superintendents in the state to begin classes for retarded children. In 1930, as president of the Buncombe County Historical Society, he encouraged the publication of the *History of Buncombe County* by F. A. Sondley.

Seeing the need for a local junior college, Reynolds led the movement that resulted in the establishment of the Buncombe County Junior College in 1927. It was the first public junior college in the United States to offer free tuition. In time this school evolved into the Biltmore Junior College, which became the nucleus of the University of North Carolina at Asheville. After leaving Biltmore Junior College in 1936, he was principal of Barnardsville High School for one year and of Oakley High School for five years prior to his retirement in 1942. He had invested fifty-three years as a teacher, principal, superintendent, and college president. A men's dormitory at Western Carolina University and a high school in Buncombe County were named for him.

Reynolds was a naturalist as well as a teacher. He knew all of the native trees, wildflowers, and birds—including the bird calls. Each summer while at Cullowhee he took his family and the summer school students on a week's camping trip to Whiteside Mountain, transporting the children and the provisions in two covered wagons. Nature study was required in the summer for prospective teachers. Fishing for mountain trout was a favored pastime, and he often took visiting school officials on trips to choice streams. He believed that physical fitness was an important part of the development of the whole person.

An active churchman, Reynolds often served on his church's administrative board and he taught Sunday school. He and his wife were the parents of nine children: Mary Woods, Sallie E., A. C., Jr., Margaret Cornelia, Alphonso Curry, Evelyn, Ruth, Elizabeth, and Thomas Davies.

SEE: W. E. Bird, *History of Western Carolina College* (1963); G. A. Diggs, Jr., *Historical Facts Concerning Buncombe County Government* (1935); Leonard P. Miller, *Education in Buncombe County, 1793–1965* (1965); Papers in the possession of his children and papers in the Pack Memorial Library, Asheville; F. A. Sondley, *A History of Buncombe County, North Carolina* (1930).

CHARLESANNA L. FOX

Reynolds, Charles Albert *(10 Nov. 1848–2 July 1936)*, lieutenant governor of North Carolina, civil engineer, tobacco manufacturer, and farmer, was born in Madison, the son of Dr. Thomas and Sarah Jane Fewel Reynolds. They were not related to the tobacco manufacturing family of R. J. Reynolds. When their son was eighteen months old the Reynolds family moved to Leaksville, where he lived until he moved to Forsyth County in 1884.

Reynolds received his early education from a tutor, Colonel John R. Winston, in Leaksville. During the period 1867–68 he attended The University of North Carolina, but because of the unsettled conditions of Reconstruction he went to Princeton, where he studied engineering from 1868 to 1870. His mother died in 1870 and he returned home without graduating from either The University of North Carolina or Princeton. When his father died in 1872, Reynolds settled the family business and started work in tobacco manufacturing.

From 1876 to 1882 Reynolds served as deputy collector for the Internal Revenue Service in Reidsville. For several years he was also a justice of the peace. When a Republican governor, Daniel L. Russell, was elected in 1897, Reynolds was elected lieutenant governor. In this position, he strongly supported The University of North Carolina at a time when it was under fire from many state legislators. In 1901, during the concern over the South Dakota bond case, Reynolds published a brief pamphlet, *"Justice" Calls for the Facts: why have the Democratic newspapers . . . become so silent about who furnished the carpet-bag bonds to Cuba?* At one point near the end of his term, Reynolds was offered the governorship in an effort by Russell and other politicians to keep the Republicans in power by placing Russell in the recently vacated chief justice's seat on the state supreme court. Reynolds felt that the whole idea of such a political trade was contemptible and unfair to the people of the state and he rejected the offer.

When his term as lieutenant governor ended, Reynolds returned to Winston where he was appointed postmaster, a post he filled until 1913. During World War I he was a member of the Exception Board for Forsyth County. Reynolds also served as chairman of the Liberty Loan Committee for the county. Always a staunch Republican, he acted as chairman of that party's state committee and later as a committeeman representing North Carolina in the Republican National Convention.

In his own work as a civil engineer, Reynolds helped to build the first hydroelectric plant on the Yadkin River—the first in North Carolina. Constructed in 1897, this plant supplied power not only for homes and factories but also for the electric streetcars operated by this newly available energy source. A few years later Reynolds also worked on a larger hydroelectric plant in Asheville.

Displeased with the condition of the roads in his county, Reynolds requested the use of convict labor to crush stone for road construction. His request was granted and he began work on the first macadamized road in the county. The project was successful and in the next few years many roads were macadamized.

Reynolds was married on 18 May 1873 to Carrie Watkins Fretwell, also of Leaksville. They had no children and in his later years they moved from Winston-Salem to Colfax, where he died. He was buried in the family plot in Leaksville (now merged with adjoining Draper and Spray and renamed Eden).

SEE: *Charlotte Observer*, 3 July 1936; Daniel L. Grant, *Alumni History of the University of North Carolina* (1924); *Greensboro Daily News*, 4 July 1936; *Winston-Salem Journal and Sentinel*, 25 Aug. 1929.

WARREN F. WEST III

Reynolds, Richard Joshua *(20 July 1850–29 July 1918)*, founder of the R. J. Reynolds Tobacco Company, was born in the shadow of Nobusiness Mountain, Patrick County, Va. His father was Hardin William Reynolds, a manufacturer of tobacco, a merchant, and a farmer all on a substantial scale; his mother was Nancy Jane Cox from a family famed in Revolutionary activities and long settled in northwestern Stokes County, N.C. Both were descended from English forebears. Reared in a comfortable home by strong and able parents, young Reynolds had ample opportunities for an education and escaped any drudgery in his early years by virtue of his father's large holding of slaves. He did begin early to work in his father's chewing tobacco factory situated in the rear of the home known as Rock Spring (a handsome but austerely plain brick mansion afterwards restored by Nancy Susan Reynolds and entered in the National Register of Historic Places) on the old Bristol-Norfolk highway. The loss of his slaves had little effect on the financial standing of Captain Hardin W. Reynolds, since he and his two oldest sons plunged into work and the tobacco factory prospered in the late 1860s and 1870s.

Reynolds attended local subscription schools and possibly received additional training from a family tutor before attending Emory and Henry College for two years (1868–70). He deserted his studies in 1870 and began working for wages in his father's factory. During the first part of 1873 he attended Bryant and Stratton Business College in Baltimore at his own expense and while there solicited orders for chewing tobacco made in his father's factory, thus becoming familiar with the nature of city trade and the methods of wholesale dealers. Young Reynolds returned to Patrick County and on 1 July 1873 entered into partnership with his father in operation of the elder Reynolds's factory at Rock Spring. For a variety of reasons, including his father's desire to admit a younger but less able son into partnership, a need to be nearer flue-cured tobacco which grew in greater quantity farther south, and the need to locate in a town with railroad connections, Reynolds on 19 Oct. 1874 purchased a one-hundred-foot lot on Depot Street from the "Congregation of the United Brethren of Salem and its Vicinity" for $388.50. Here, in present-day Winston-Salem, N.C., he built his first factory—38 by 60 feet—with railway connections to Greensboro on the main line of the Richmond and Danville railway system.

Reynolds manufactured what was known as Southern flat plug chewing tobacco—150,000 pounds the first year and something more than one million pounds by the early 1890s. This type of chewing tobacco, made from flue-cured leaf, provided a durable chew, though it did not absorb sweetening agents as readily as chewing tobacco made from Burley leaf. In the late 1880s Reynolds made a revolutionary change in his formula for producing Southern flat plug by using saccharin as his chief sweetening agent, thus producing a sweeter and more durable chew than that made of the porous Burley leaf. Seeing his opportunity, Reynolds immediately built a large, modern factory by securing credit from every possible source but chiefly from his family and from the Parletts, wholesale handlers of chewing tobacco in Baltimore. This new plant was five times larger than his business then warranted. During these months Reynolds played a forceful role in building the Roanoke and Southern Railway, which was completed in late 1891 and almost immediately taken over by the Norfolk and Western Railway, thus giving the towns of Winston and Salem shipping facilities to the east and west without dependence on the Richmond and Danville system, which in 1893 became the Southern Railway.

Within weeks of the completion of the Roanoke and Southern from Winston and Salem to Roanoke, Reynolds began his first official advertising. He was manufacturing more than five million pounds of chewing tobacco by 1898. His business had outgrown his capital, more was necessary for expansion, and James B. Duke's American Tobacco Company was beginning to undersell all manufacturers of chewing tobacco, whether flat plug or navy.

Either by force of Duke's monopoly or by Reynolds's need for capital, the R. J. Reynolds Tobacco Company became affiliated with the American Tobacco Company on 4 Apr. 1899. Reynolds resented Duke's control and, when not permitted to manufacture smoking tobacco, he began work on a formula for three brands of smoking tobacco in the hope that at least one would become successful. He held them off the market until 1907, when the U.S. government began its famous antitrust suit against the American Tobacco Company. By 1911 Prince Albert smoking tobacco had been established on a national scale; its success was also based on a radical change in formula—inclusion of both Burley and flue-cured leaf. In the same year the American Tobacco Company was dissolved, and Reynolds went on to create the Camel cigarette—a blend of flue-cured and Burley leaf with very little Turkish tobacco. It was the first truly American cigarette, which other manufacturers were forced to copy. Reynolds had the lead and for many years his company stood first in the sales of all three major tobacco products. Until 1954, no product developed by the company achieved any success except those created by Reynolds. He became an immensely wealthy man, and many who followed his plan of low salaries and investment in his company likewise became wealthy.

Reynolds was a generous and humane man who contributed freely to various projects designed to uplift the people of his area—a practice followed by his heirs with funds derived from the greatly increased sales of the Reynolds products. He enjoyed great camaraderie with his employees and went along with the notion that he had risen from poverty and ignorance—a matter that gave rise to the general belief that he was ignorant and uneducated. He was a strong Democrat, departing from support of the presidential nominees only in 1896. He considered the income tax the fairest ever devised and carried no exaggerated idea of himself.

On 27 Feb. 1905 he married Mary Katharine Smith, his distant cousin. They were the parents of four children: Richard Joshua, Jr., Mary Katharine, Nancy Susan, and Zachary Smith. He grew up a Methodist but, perhaps influenced by his wife, later became a Presbyterian. Reynolds died at his home, Reynolda, after a long illness of incurable cancer of the pancreas and was buried in the Salem Cemetery. For many years his portrait hung alone in the board room of the R. J. Reynolds Company until his successors in the early 1960s placed their own on the same walls.

SEE: Samuel A. Ashe, ed., *Biographical History of North Carolina*, vol. 3 (1906); Bristol, Va.-Tenn., *Herald Courier*, 23 May 1915; John D. Cameron, *A Sketch of Tobacco Interests in North Carolina* (1885); *Catalogue of Emory and Henry College*, 1868–69, 1869–70; Raleigh *News and Observer*, 5 Apr. 1896; *Report of the Commissioners of Corporations on the Tobacco Industry*, 3 vols. (1909–15); Hardin W. Reynolds Papers and Recollections of Abram David Reynolds (Wake Forest University Library, Winston-Salem); *Southern Tobacco Journal*, 14 Mar. 1898, 17 June 1919; *U.S. v. Am. Tob. Co. et al., Record of Testimony of Witnesses*, 5 vols. (1907); *Winston-Salem Journal*, 25 Apr. 1915, 30 July 1918.

NANNIE M. TILLEY

Reynolds, Robert Rice *(19 June 1884–13 Feb. 1963)*, U.S. senator and attorney, was born in Asheville, the son of William Taswell and Mamie Spears Reynolds. Reynolds was descended from a distinguished pioneering family. Colonel Daniel Smith, his maternal great-great-grandfather, was a hero of the Battle of Kings Mountain during the Revolutionary War and James M. Smith, Reynolds's great-grandfather, was the first white child born west of the Blue Ridge Mountains. Reynolds attended the public schools in Asheville and matriculated at Weaver College, a college preparatory school. He entered The University of North Carolina in 1902 and attended sporadically until 1907. An indifferent student, Reynolds failed to earn a degree but was active in campus activities such as football, track, wrestling, and the college newspaper. After college he worked briefly as a clerk with the *Washington Times* and published the *Asheville Magazine*. After one year of study, he was admitted to the bar and began a practice in Asheville in 1908.

A lifelong Democrat, Reynolds was elected prosecuting attorney of the Fifteenth Judicial District in his first try at public office and served from 1910 to 1914. He ran unsuccessfully for the U.S. Congress in 1914, losing to James M. Gudger. A peripatetic traveler all of his life, Reynolds announced his candidacy for lieutenant governor of North Carolina in 1924, while traveling abroad. Although he polled a large number of votes, he failed to get the nomination. He entered the race for the U.S. Senate against Senator Lee S. Overman in 1926 and once again lost in spite of an impressive vote. Encouraged by his vote in 1926, Reynolds announced his candidacy for the Senate in 1932 on a populist platform featuring the repeal of the Eighteenth Amendment (Prohibition), redistribution of the national wealth, a downward revision of federal taxes, the end to immigration to America, and vigorous enforcement of the Sherman Antitrust Act. Reynolds's most formidable opponent was the former governor and incumbent senator, Cameron Morrison.

Although most observers believed that Reynolds had no chance to win, he ran an enthusiastic race as a poor man who would serve as champion of the little people of the state against the trusts, big business, and the Republicans—the root causes of the depression according to him. Morrison gained the support of the Democratic party hierarchy and the majority of the newspapers in the state, but "Our Bob" Reynolds launched a colorful, demagogic campaign that was a prolonged vaudeville in the old political tradition of the South. Reynolds demonstrated a personal, intimate style that appealed to the voters, and he tirelessly stumped the state in an ancient Model T Ford. He abjectly described his own poverty-stricken status (an exaggeration) while chastising Morrison for his limousine, huge mansion, and immense wealth. Reynolds mimicked Morrison's pomposity and accused him of eating "Red Russian fish eggs" (caviar) instead of "good ole North Carolina hen eggs." He blamed the wealthy trusts for the depression and managed to tie Morrison to big business by emphasizing his public defense of the Duke Power Company as a "charitable institution."

Reynolds astounded the experts by leading the first primary and then won an overwhelming victory against Morrison in the runoff with 65.4 percent of the vote—the largest majority attained in a Democratic primary in North Carolina up to that time. The incredible victory was achieved by a candidate who had never won a major political office, had limited experience and resources, and was the first wet candidate for a statewide office since state Prohibition was instituted in 1908. Reynolds won because Morrison failed to take Reynolds's candidacy seriously until it was too late, and because Reynolds shrewdly parlayed the peoples' discontent with government, big business, the depression, and Prohibition into a personal attack on Morrison.

In his first term in the Senate, Reynolds served on the Committee on Territories and Insular Affairs, Banking and Currency, Military Affairs, and the District of Columbia Committee, which he later chaired. He voted for practically all of the New Deal legislation, an unusual political stance for a southern politician, and was an avid supporter of Franklin D. Roosevelt in the 1936 election campaign. From 1936 to 1944 Reynolds, along with Representative Joseph Starnes of Alabama, unsuccessfully introduced a series of bills designed to reduce immigration to the United States and to deport alien criminals. Reynolds made the reduction of immigration one of his most important political goals but had only a slight impact on immigration legislation. Senator Reynolds demonstrated a strong isolationist position on foreign affairs. He opposed America's entrance into the World Court and supported the concept of nonintervention in the affairs of foreign countries. He advocated military preparedness to create a strong fortress America capable of defending the country against all enemies.

Reynolds constantly made headlines with such antics as kissing actress Jean Harlow on the steps of the capitol and endorsing Lucky Strike cigarettes. Due to continual publicity and his support of the popular Roosevelt, Reynolds was reelected to the Senate in 1938 by a decisive margin over Frank E. Hancock, Jr., in the Democratic primary and Republican Charles Jonas in the general election. In 1939 Reynolds broke with President Roosevelt over the issues of patronage and foreign policy. He became more outspoken in his isolationism and opposed most of Roosevelt's foreign policy decisions including Lend Lease and the decision to participate in the United Nations at the end of World War II (the Connally Resolution). Also in 1939 Reynolds formed an organization called The Vindicators Association, Inc., a patriotic group dedicated to 100 percent Americanism, an end to immigration, defense against alien enemies, and keeping America out of war. In 1944 he changed the name of the Vindicators to the American Nationalist party and this organization survived until October 1945.

Because of his isolationist attitudes and some ill-considered remarks praising Nazi Germany, Reynolds was marked by the press as pro-Nazi, and this allegation followed him throughout his political career. The charge was unfounded, but the pro-Nazi allegation, his rigid isolationism, his clowning, his inattention to crucial legislation, and his failure to sponsor any meaningful legislation led to his increasing unpopularity and his decision not to stand for reelection in 1944. In 1942 Reynolds was next in seniority to succeed as chairman of the Military Affairs Committee, the committee most involved with military preparedness in the United States. After the death of Senator Morris Shepherd, the press and several key senators opposed the elevation of Reynolds as chairman because of his isolationist views, and Reynolds's critics vigorously attacked the antiquated seniority system that had thrust him into a position of power. After a protracted struggle Senator Reynolds was approved as chairman, but he exercised little real power during World War II as the key decisions were made by Roosevelt and the military establishment.

Reynolds left the Senate in January 1945 and spent most of the remainder of his life in the practice of law and in semiretirement on Reynolds Mountain near Asheville. In 1950 he emerged from retirement and announced his candidacy for the U.S. Senate seat held by Frank Porter Graham but campaigned very briefly and managed to get only 58,752 votes, which placed him third in a four-man race.

Reynolds was married five times: in 1910 to Frances Jackson—two children: Robert Rice, Jr., and Frances Jackson; in 1914 to Mary Bland—one daughter, Mary Bland; in 1921 to Denise D'Arcy; in 1931 to Eva Brady; and in 1941 to Evalyn Walsh McLean, whose mother owned the Hope Diamond—one daughter, Mamie Spears.

He was a Methodist, Moose, Elk, and a member of Beta Theta Pi and the Junior Order of United American Mechanics; he also belonged to the Asheville Country Club and the National Press Club in Washington, D.C. Reynolds was the author of *Wanderlust* and *Gypsy Trails*. He died of cancer in Asheville and was buried in Riverside Cemetery.

SEE: *Asheville Citizen*, 1930–63; *Biog. Dir. Am. Cong.* (1961); *New York Times*, 15 Feb. 1963; Julian M. Pleasants, "The Senatorial Career of Robert Rice Reynolds, 1933–1945" (Ph.D. diss., University of North Carolina, Chapel Hill, 1971); *Who Was Who in America*, vol. 4 (1968).

JULIAN M. PLEASANTS

Reynolds, William Neal *(22 Mar. 1863–10 Sept. 1951)*, tobacco manufacturer and philanthropist, was born in Critz, Patrick County, Va., the son of Hardin William and Nancy Jane Cox Reynolds and the younger brother of Richard Joshua Reynolds. (For information on the family and on the business in which both men were involved, see the sketch of Richard J. Reynolds.) In 1881 William Neal Reynolds began working with Richard J. in his plug tobacco manufacturing firm in Winston, and in 1886 they formed a partnership that also included Henry Roan, the company's bookkeeper. The R. J. Reynolds Tobacco Company was chartered as a corporation by the state of North Carolina on 11 Feb. 1890. When it became a part of the American Tobacco Company trust on 4 Apr. 1899, it received a New Jersey charter. It resumed independent operations on 1 Jan. 1912.

William Neal Reynolds served as a director of the R. J. Reynolds Tobacco Company from 12 Feb. 1890 to 14 May 1942. He also was vice-president (the first one) from the beginning of his directorship until 2 Aug. 1918, when he became president. He filled this position until 8 Apr. 1924 and was chairman of the board (again, the first one) from that date until 6 May 1931. He then was chairman of the executive committee of the board until 14 May 1942.

After attending local public schools Reynolds entered King College on the Virginia-Tennessee line in the town of Bristol. His father died shortly afterwards, and in September 1882 he transferred to Trinity College, in Durham, N.C., where he remained for two years. Having worked for several years on an irregular basis in his brother's tobacco factory, he then joined him full time. He learned the business almost from the ground up and after five or six years was in charge of buying the leaf tobacco.

Reynolds had additional business interests. He was president of the Piedmont Park Company and the Winston-Salem Hotel Company and was a director of the W. S. Judy Seed Company. In addition, he was owner of Tanglewood Farm on the Yadkin River west of Winston-Salem where he raised fine stock and was widely known as the owner of standard-bred race horses. In the racing season 1909–10 one of his horses won fifteen of the seventeen races. He trained many of his horses personally and was the first president of the Union Trotting Association. Reynolds also owned the Arrowpoint breeding farm near Lexington, Ky., and held an interest in Seminole Park near Orlando, Fla. With others involved in racing he established the Hambletonian Stakes, and in 1933 one of his horses won the Hambletonian.

Duke University was an early beneficiary of his philanthropy, but he afterwards turned his attention to North Carolina State College and still later to Wake Forest College. He was active in the creation of the Z. Smith Reynolds Foundation, named in honor of the youngest son of his brother, Richard J. The foundation was instrumental in moving Wake Forest College to Winston-Salem, where it was established on the R. J. Reynolds estate. Reynolds also erected and equipped a hospital in Winston-Salem for blacks and named it the Kate Bitting Memorial Hospital in honor of his wife. He founded the Cox School in Stokes County, N.C., as a memorial to his mother and the Hardin Reynolds School in Patrick County, Va., as a memorial to his father.

He was married in 1889 to Kate G. Bitting, but they had no children. His Tanglewood estate was left as "a public park, playground, and amusement center for the white race," but in time the city of Winston-Salem acquired it and opened it to the general public. The Z. Smith Reynolds Foundation received the remainder of his estate to benefit various charitable causes in the state. Reynolds and his wife were members of the Presbyterian church, and he was a member of the Knights of Pythias and the Benevolent and Protective Order of Elks.

SEE: *DAB*, supp. 5 (1977); Bryan Haislip, *A History of the Z. Smith Reynolds Foundation* (1967); *New York Times*, 11 Sept. 1951; *North Carolina Biography*, vol. 4 (1940 [portrait]); Raleigh *News and Observer*, 13 Sept. 1951; *Trinity Alumni Register* 1 (April 1915), 2 (April 1916); *Winston-Salem Sentinel*, 11 Sept. 1951; *Who Was Who in America*, vol. 3 (1960)

PAULINE HOWES

Rhame, Jeremiah *(ca. 1733–1805)*, colonial minister, was presumably the son of Peter Remm (Rhem, Rheam), who in 1740 received a power of attorney from the High German Church in Craven County. He afterwards settled on Catfish Creek near Latta (Dillon), S.C. Nothing is known of Jeremiah's youth, but in 1758 he bought a farm on Flat Swamp in Beaufort (now Pitt) County, and by 1761 he appears to have settled on a new patent near the north side of Little Contentnea Creek.

Having been converted to the Baptist faith in 1755, Rhame was ordained to the ministry on 20 Nov. 1758. He became the first pastor of the Red Banks Baptist Church, possibly on the same property near the Red Banks Landing on Tar River that was deeded by Archibald Parker to the Freewill Baptist Church of the same name on 1 Nov. 1834. Rhame represented his church at the Charleston Baptist Association (1760–62) and later became a charter member of the Kehukee Baptist Association at its founding on 6 Nov. 1769.

Elder Rhame continued to be active in farming and preaching in Pitt County and vicinity until his removal in 1771 to St. George's Parish in South Carolina. The last of his Pitt County property was sold in 1774. From 1778 to 1788 he served as pastor of the now-extinct Catfish Baptist Church in the Welsh Neck. He and one of his sons, Elder Bradley Rhame, helped to organize the Little Peedee Baptist Church in 1790 and brought it into the Charleston Baptist Association on 7 Nov. 1792, the same year that he himself began to serve as pastor of the Mount Pleasant (formerly Cashaway) Baptist Church.

Rhame married Elizabeth Bradley, daughter of John and Abigail Bradley of Craven County, N.C. He died testate in Sumter County, S.C., leaving five children: Abigail; Jeremiah, Jr., who served in the South Carolina militia during the Revolutionary War and later settled in Clarendon County; the Reverend Bradley, who served for many years after 1810 as the pastor of the Calvary Baptist Church; Ebenezer (b. 1760), who fought under General Francis Marion in the American Revolution and was subsequently a military pensioner; and Benoni.

SEE: Lemuel Burkitt and Jesse Read, *A Concise History of the Kehukee Baptist Association* (1850); Judith D. Ellison, comp., *Index and Abstract of Deeds of Record of Pitt County*, 2 vols. [1968]; Kehukee Baptist Association Minutes, 1769–78 (microfilm, North Carolina Collection, University of North Carolina, Chapel Hill); Frederick L. Weis, *Colonial Clergy of Virginia, North Carolina, and South Carolina* (1955).

HUGH BUCKNER JOHNSTON

Rhine, Joseph Banks *(29 Sept. 1895–20 Feb. 1980)*, psychologist, parapsychologist, and university professor, was born in Waterloo, Pa., the son of Samuel Ellis and Elizabeth Ellen Vaughan Rhine. He spent a part of his youth in Ohio, served in the Marine Corps during World War I, and entered the University of Chicago in 1919. There he was awarded the B.S. degree in botany in 1922, an M.S. degree in 1923, and the Ph.D. in 1925. During the years 1924–26 he taught botany at West Virginia University, where he became interested in extrasensory perception. The work of William McDougall in experimental psychology at Harvard University attracted him, and he studied there in 1926–27; after McDougall moved to Duke University, Rhine also went to Duke. First named a Fellow, in 1928 he became a psychology instructor and in time rose to the rank of full professor.

McDougall, Rhine, and other colleagues established the Parapsychology Laboratory at Duke and conducted experiments in telepathy, clairvoyance, psychokinesis, and precognition. After the publication in 1934 of Rhine's book, *Extra-Sensory Perception*, worldwide attention was drawn to his work. In 1940 he became director of the laboratory, and from 1964 to 1968 he was director of the Institute of Parapsychology, an independent organization that he founded in Durham. While much of Rhine's early work was rejected by scientists, a *New York Times* survey in 1980 reported that "a majority of American scientists accept at least the possibility of ESP [extra-sensory perception]."

Rhine was the author of numerous other books and articles in both scholarly journals and popular magazines. Among them were *New Frontiers of the Mind* (1937), *The Reach of the Mind* (1947), and *New World of the Mind* (1953). He was coauthor of *Extra-Sensory Perception After Sixty Years* (1940) and editor of the *Journal of Parapsychology*.

In 1920 he married Louisa Ella Weckesser, who participated with him in his research and publications. They were the parents of Robert Eldon, Sara Louise, Elizabeth Ellen, and Rosemary. He died at his home near Hillsborough and a memorial service was held in Duke Chapel.

SEE: Denis Brian, *The Enchanted Voyage: The Life of J. B. Rhine* (1982); *Charlotte Observer*, 21 Feb. 1980; *Durham Sun*, 21 Mar. 1983; Raleigh *News and Observer*, 22 July 1951, 22 Nov. 1953; *Who's Who in the South and Southwest* (1954).

WILLIAM S. POWELL

Rhodes, Elisha Averitt *(7 Feb. 1791–24 May 1858)*, county official and U.S. consul to the Republic of Texas, was born in Bertie County, probably the son of William and Elizabeth Averitt Rhodes for whom a marriage license was issued in Bertie County on 2 Oct. 1786. Nothing appears to be known of his education, but he served for a time as master in equity and was clerk of court for the county from 1819 to 1833 and in the period 1850–51.

He was U.S. consul to the Republic of Texas in Galveston from 7 July 1838 to 14 Oct. 1842. At some time prior to 29 Nov. 1838, the Department of State of the Republic of Texas issued him an exequatur (a formal document permitting him to act as a diplomatic representative). With a change in administrations in Washington, D.C., Rhodes was acting consul and then consul for a period after 1843, until Texas was annexed to the United States on 29 Dec. 1845. On 15 Dec. 1846 he signed a document as public attorney and notary public. Rhodes's correspondence dealt with Mexican military activity and the negotiations that led to the admission of Texas to the Union.

Rhodes's first wife was Ann Maria Jacocks, who died in 1826 before he moved to Texas. She was the mother of William Henry Rhodes (1822–76). Other children were James G., Mark, Thadeus, and Laura. In Houston, Tex., on 9 Apr. 1838, Rhodes married a widow, Mrs. Mary Woodman Kimball Driggs, a native of New Hampshire. They became the parents of Cullen Capehart (a name in the family of Rhodes's first wife), Edward Averitt, and Robert H. The last two sons were Confederate soldiers, Edward being the one fatally wounded at Gettysburg. The 1850 census of Bertie County also lists in Rhodes's household Mary Eliza (twenty-one) and Joanna Driggs (seventeen), daughters of Mrs. Rhodes and her first husband, Sherman Driggs, both recorded as born in New Hampshire. Family records, however, indicate that they were born in Trinidad, where Driggs was a pharmacist.

William Henry Rhodes indicated in a poem, "The Love Knot," that he had two brothers who were killed in the Civil War, one on the Confederate side and one who fought for the Union. Descendants believe this is an example of poetic license, as both brothers served in the Confederate army. William wrote a very moving poem about them. He said that one was his mother's favorite and there was a suggestion that it was the (fictitious) Union one. The Confederate lieutenant (in reality Edward A.), was killed at Gettysburg on 3 July 1864. In the poem Rhodes refers to them as Eddie (Confederate) and John (Union), who conceivably was a stepbrother. Mary Rhodes, their mother, even though a native of New Hampshire, was loyal to the South; from her home in California she organized a relief association to aid sick and suffering Confederate soldiers in Northern prisons, mortgaged her farm for this purpose, and managed to confer with both Presidents Abraham Lincoln and Jefferson Davis in this cause. She received a letter of appreciation from General Robert E. Lee for her work.

At the end of his service in Texas Rhodes returned with his family to Bertie County, where he was again clerk of court. In the same year he suffered a stroke and was left virtually helpless. The family moved to California, where Mary Rhodes ran a store, kept boarders, and farmed. Rhodes died at age sixty-seven in Stockton, Calif., where he was buried. They were members of the Episcopal church.

SEE: Sam. H. Dixon, *The Poets and Poetry of Texas* (1885); Documents in the Daughters of the Republic of Texas Library (The Alamo, San Antonio); Harry S. Driggs (South Bend, Ind.) to William S. Powell, 7 May 1990; George P. Garrison, ed., "Diplomatic Correspondence of the Republic of Texas," *Annual Report of the American Historical Association*, vol. 2, parts 1–2 (1908, 1911); M. Claire Pister, "This Is the Story of My Great Great Great Grandmother . . ." (typescript, possession of Harry S. Driggs, South Bend, Ind.); E. A. Rhodes's consular dispatches (Rosenburg Library, Galveston, Tex.); Richard W. Rhodes (Saratoga, Calif.) to William S. Powell, 18 Aug. 1992; Francis D. Winston, "William H. Rhodes: Lawyer and Writer," Raleigh *North Carolina Review*, 5 May 1912.

WILLIAM S. POWELL

Rhodes, Henry *(1715?–December 1780)*, colonial officeholder and Revolutionary leader, was the son of Henry and Mary Rhodes. In 1751 he inherited his father's "manner plantation," in Onslow County, where the county militia mustered and trained in October 1754 and perhaps at other times as well. In 1758 he was one of the executors of the will of James Gray. His earliest public service apparently was as a justice of the peace for Onslow County; commissioned by Governor Arthur Dobbs, he took the oath of office on 4 Jan. 1759 and remained a justice for the rest of his life. On 3 July 1759 he was also sworn in as sheriff of the county, a position he held longer than any other colonial sheriff in North Carolina.

Early in 1774 he was elected to represent Onslow County in the House of Commons of the colonial Assembly and attended sessions that met in New Bern on 4–7 Apr. 1775. He also served in the Second Provincial Congress, which met on 3–7 April at the same time. These were sessions of the final royal legislature and the beginning of the state government. Both bodies were composed of virtually the same men meeting in the same hall, the Congress an hour before the Assembly. Rhodes again represented his county in the Third and the Fifth Provincial Congresses (August–September 1775 and November–December 1776). It was at the last of these meetings that a constitution for the state was drawn up. The congresses took the steps necessary to form a civil government for North Carolina as well as to lay the foundations for military activity.

Although there is nothing to suggest that Rhodes engaged in active military service, he was made lieutenant colonel of the Onslow militia on 9 Sept. 1775, and his appointment was renewed on 22 Apr. 1776. Though few participants are identified in surviving records, Rhodes probably was present at the Battle of Moore's Creek Bridge with his command of minutemen. He was serving as a county justice in 1776 and 1777 when he also was a member of the county committee of safety and of the Council of Safety for the Wilmington District. Rhodes's name was mentioned for appointment to the Council of State but, instead, he was appointed treasurer of the Wilmington District. As a member of the legislature Rhodes was one of the commissioners named in 1778 to superintend the printing of bills of credit for the state. His commission was renewed in 1779 and in 1780, and he was the only member to serve all three years. The commission produced paper money for North Carolina.

Rhodes's first wife was Mary Woodhouse (d. 5 June 1769), and they were the parents of Sarah, Elizabeth, Woodhouse, Aliff, and Mary. On 15 Aug. 1770 he married Elizabeth Ward, by whom he had two more children: Henry, who died as a young man while attending school in Wilmington, and Henrietta.

Deeds indicated that Rhodes was buried in a family cemetery at Stones Creek plantation, where his father had lived and was buried in the Stone Bay area on property later occupied by Camp Lejeune. The grave was not found, however, when the site was acquired for the military base.

SEE: Joseph Parsons Brown, *The Commonwealth of Onslow: A History* (1960); John L. Cheney, Jr., ed., *North Carolina Government, 1585–1979* (1981); Walter Clark, ed., *State Records of North Carolina*, vols. 12–13, 21–24 (1895–1905); J. Bryan Grimes, ed., *Abstract of North Carolina Wills* (1910); *The Heritage of Onslow County* (1983); John T. Rhodes to William S. Powell, 12 Sept. 1992; William L. Saunders, ed., *Colonial Records of North Carolina*, vols. 8–10 (1890).

WILLIAM S. POWELL

Rhodes, James Manly *(1850–2 July 1941)*, Methodist minister, educator, and college owner and administrator, was born in Four Oaks, Johnston County, the son of Atlas J. K. and Spicey West Rhodes. He received bachelor's and master's degrees from Trinity College and in December 1875 was received into the North Carolina Conference of the Methodist Episcopal Church, South.

He served as pastor of the Fifth Street Methodist Church in Wilmington until January 1882, when he became the first principal of Central Institute in Littleton. After 1888 it was known as Littleton Female College, and in 1912 it became simply Littleton College. Except for the years 1887–88, when he was principal of the nearby Henderson Female College, Rhodes was president of Littleton College until it was destroyed by fire in January 1919. He had purchased the college property in 1889 from its stockholders and immediately began an extensive improvements program.

Rhodes was described as "a man of convictions, who felt that he had work to do." He devoted his life to the training and development of young ladies "of real refinement and culture, with those principles that enter into the formation of noble character." Though small physically, he was portrayed as "huge in determination, perseverance, [and] consecration."

About 1906 he founded Central Academy in Littleton, a military school with a farm operated by self-help students. His wife's nephew, Jesse Aiken, served as principal of the academy, which continued to function until 1919.

On 28 Nov. 1880 Rhodes married Florence Simmons (1856–88) of Virginia. After her death he married, on 27 Nov. 1889, Lula Hester (1868–1937), the daughter of the Reverend and Mrs. W. S. Hester of Oxford. She was educated in Oxford, was graduated from Greensboro Female College, studied in New York City, and was a teacher of voice at Littleton College. James and Lula Rhodes adopted a daughter, Lillian Bridgers Rhodes.

In 1923, following the destruction of Littleton College, the Rhodes moved to Florida, where he died in Bartow. During their last years the couple received financial assistance from the Littleton College Memorial Association, formed in 1927 through the efforts of Vara L. Herring of Raleigh, former treasurer of the college, and other alumnae. The purpose of the association was to keep alive the spirit and work of the former school, and the members also gave financial support to Scarrit College in Nashville, Tenn., and North Carolina Wesleyan College in Rocky Mount. A portrait of Rhodes hangs in the library of Wesleyan College.

At the time of his death Rhodes was the oldest minister in the North Carolina Annual Conference of the Methodist church. His body was returned to Littleton for burial in Sunset Hill Cemetery.

SEE: D. N. Earnhardt (Belhaven) and alumnae of Littleton College, personal contact; Nolan B. Harmon, *Encyclopedia of World Methodism* (1974); Johnston County census records and marriage bonds (North Carolina State Archives, Raleigh); Littleton College Memorial Collection (North Carolina Wesleyan College, Rocky Mount, and Manuscript Collection, Joyner Library, East Carolina University, Greenville); Ralph Hardee Rives, "Littleton Female College," *North Carolina Historical Review* 39 (July 1952).

RALPH HARDEE RIVES

Rhodes, John Melancthon *(29 Aug. 1849–20 Apr. 1921)*, textile manufacturer, temperance leader, and patron of education, was born in Gaston County, four miles north of the town of Dallas. Of German ancestry, he was the son of Caleb and Myra Hoffman Rhodes and a descendant of Frederick Rhodes (Roth), who came to America in 1752. Educated by Dr. Robert L. Abernethy at Table Rock Academy in Burke County and at Catawba College, then located at Newton, he was elected register of deeds in Gaston County for the 1878–82 term and at the same time began his lifelong support of the temperance movement in North Carolina.

In 1889 Rhodes started his career as a textile manufacturer at Kings Mountain and helped build the first cotton mill in that locality. During the ensuing years he was a leading figure in the erection of seven other textile plants at Cherryville, Rhodhiss, Lincolnton, and Kings Mountain. The town of Rhodhiss was named after John M. Rhodes and his partner, George B. Hiss. Rhodes was the mayor of Cherryville from 1894 to 1900 and promoted the establishment of the Cherryville High School. In all the communities where he resided he was a member of the Lutheran church.

Rhodes was one of the founders of Gaston Female College at Dallas in 1879 and served on the board of trustees of Lenoir Rhyne College at Hickory from 1891 to 1921. Prior to 1918 he was the largest financial supporter of the latter institution.

He married Susan Catherine Aderholdt (1847–1917) on 15 Dec. 1870 and was the father of seven children: David Polycarp, Myra Sarah Ada, Lillie Mae, Caleb Junious, Violet Almeta, Mabel Rosalee, and Georgia Agnes. After Susan's death he married Nina C. Crowell of Lincolnton on 1 Sept. 1919. There were no children of this marriage. Rhodes was buried in the old Lutheran church cemetery at Lincolnton.

SEE: F. P. Cauble, "John Melancthon Rhodes" (typescript, Lenoir Rhyne College Library, Hickory, 1975); L. M. Hoffman, *Our Kin* (1915); Lincolnton *Lincoln County News*, 21, 25 Apr. 1921; Charles L. Van Noppen Papers (Manuscript Department, Duke University Library, Durham).

FRANK P. CAUBLE

Rhodes, William Henry *(16 July 1822–14 Apr. 1876)*, pioneer writer of science fiction, poet, lawyer, and judge, was born in Windsor, Bertie County, the oldest son of Elisha Averitt Rhodes, a lawyer who also served as clerk of court and master in equity for the county and was a consular officer to the Republic of Texas, and his wife, the former Ann Maria Jacocks. His mother died when William was six. His half brother, Lieutenant Edward A. Rhodes, distinguished himself as a member of the Eleventh North Carolina Regiment at Gettysburg, where he was killed in action. (A stepbrother may have been a Union soldier, killed with William T. Sherman's troops in

Georgia; one of Rhodes's poems refers to him as John, his stepmother's favorite, but this name does not appear in a list of her children, and he may have been only a figment of the poet's imagination.)

The Rhodes family was wealthy and prominent in the community, and young Rhodes attended the Bertie Union Academy at Woodville, then under the supervision of the Reverend Andrew M. Craig. He is said to have gone to the College of New Jersey at Princeton but returned home after a very short time—perhaps even before formally enrolling—when his father was appointed U.S. consul to the Republic of Texas stationed in Galveston. Accompanying his father as secretary, young Rhodes participated in various literary and debating clubs in Galveston until 1844, when he enrolled at Harvard to study law, perhaps to please his father more than to satisfy his own interests. He spent much of his time at college reading literature.

Following his graduation in 1846, Rhodes returned to Galveston to practice law. He served one term as a probate judge before moving to New York for a short time. He then returned to his native town, Windsor. Sometime between 1847 and 1849 he married Mary Eliza Driggs, his stepsister, and they became the parents of two daughters who died young. His wife died in 1851. In Windsor and later in Galveston he practiced law until 1850 before setting out by sea for California, to which he was lured by news of the gold rush and because his father and stepmother were living there. In San Francisco he practiced law and was active with the 1856 Vigilance Committee, a body of men who attempted to keep order during a period of weak city government following the gold rush. His humor and gentle manners easily won him many friends, and for about six months in 1856 he was coeditor with Washington Bartlett (later governor of California) and Bartlett's brother of the *Daily True Californian*. On 29 Dec. 1859, in Oroville, Calif., he married Susan McDermott of Crewkerne, Somerset, England, and they became the parents of six children: Arthur Pym, William, Jr., Raleigh Elisha, John, Susan, and Mary.

While at Harvard, or perhaps even earlier, Rhodes began to write poetry and essays. Among the first to be published were some poems in the *Southern Literary Messenger*. It was at Harvard that he completed *The Indian Gallows and Other Poems*, published in book form in 1846. This narrative poem, inspired by two trees in Bertie County that had grown together some eighteen feet above ground, concerns the Tuscarora Indian tradition of their origin. Also included in the book is a poem in blank verse about Theodosia Burr, who, according to tradition, was forced by pirates to "walk the plank" off the coast of North Carolina.

Rhodes continued to write for periodicals and newspapers wherever he lived for the rest of his life. Much of his work appeared anonymously or under the pseudonym Caxton, and it has never all been collected. In San Francisco he joined the Bohemian Club, and many of his poems, composed for the monthly gathering of its members, apparently were never published. His manuscripts were lost in a fire following an earthquake some years after his death. Among the journals to which he contributed were the *Golden Era*, *Pioneer*, *Hesperian*, and *Daily True Californian*. His essays, editorial comments, and other contributions appeared in the San Francisco *Bulletin* and were picked up by other newspapers across the country.

Although his poems were most numerous, Rhodes's primary literary contribution was of the type later recognized as science fiction. At the time his pieces were written, however, they were presented as factual accounts of unusual happenings. His most noted contribution appeared in the *Sacramento Union* on 13 May 1871 and was signed only with his initials. Afterwards it was published in book form as *The Case of Summerfield*. It told of a man who discovered a substance to break down water into its component parts which would then burst into flames, and who threatened to destroy the world by setting the oceans afire unless he was paid a large amount of money. The reaction of those who read this story in 1878 has been described as similar to the reaction in New Jersey in 1938 following the radio broadcast of Orson Welles's "The War of the Worlds." Even though another newspaper had recently exposed the original story as a hoax, Rhodes followed this with a sequel, "The Summerfield Case Again." Rhodes was soon recognized as the author, and a host of admirers asked for still more stories. From time to time some of them have been reprinted and late-twentieth-century science fiction periodicals found them still to be intriguing. Others were "The Aztec Princess," "The Earth's Hot Center," "Phases in the Life of John Pollexfen," and "The Telescope Eye."

It had long been Rhodes's ambition to collect some of his writings for publication as a book, but he never seemed to find the time. This was the case in spite of the fact that his friends often commented that he devoted only about one day a week to his legal practice (thereby earning only a limited income for his family) and the remainder of his time he spent in writing. Rhodes, in fact, was said to have been supported by his father at least until he was twenty-seven and on many occasions thereafter to have spent on himself family funds entrusted to him for other purposes.

In 1876, following his death, some friends collected what they regarded as the best of his compositions and published them in a volume entitled *Caxton's Book: A Collection of Essays, Poems, Tales, and Sketches*. Royalties from its sale were added to his family's modest inheritance.

On a dark night early in April 1876 Rhodes and his wife were awakened by a burglar in their bedroom. Several children were asleep in an adjoining room. Rhodes attempted to capture the burglar, a fight ensued, members of the family rushed around terrified and screaming in the dark, and the burglar's knife slashed and cut Rhodes severely. This encounter was said to have left him "bereft of reason" and he died shortly afterwards.

SEE: Sam. H. Dixon, *The Poets of Texas* (1885 [portrait]); Harry S. Driggs (South Bend, Ind.) to William S. Powell, 7 May 1990; James D. Hart, *A Companion to California* (1978); *Nat. Cyc. Am. Biog.*, vol. 7 (1897); *National Union Catalog*, vol. 491 (1977), for a list of Rhodes's works; Richard W. Rhodes (Saratoga, Calif.) to William S. Powell, 18 Aug. 1992; [William Henry Rhodes], *Caxton's Book: A Collection of Essays, Poems, Tales, and Sketches*, ed. Daniel O'Connell (1876), and ibid., with a new introduction by Sam Moskowitz (1974); *San Francisco Chronicle*, 28 Dec. 1875; Oscar T. Shuck, *History of the Bench and Bar of California* (1901); Francis D. Winston, "William H. Rhodes: Lawyer and Writer," Raleigh *North Carolina Review*, 5 May 1912.

WILLIAM S. POWELL

Rhyne, Abel Peterson *(29 Feb. 1844–29 Oct. 1932)*, textile manufacturer, Confederate soldier, and patron of education, was born on a farm near Mount Holly in Lincoln (now Gaston) County. Of German ancestry, he was a descendant of Jacob Rhyne (Rein), who came to America in 1753, and the son of Moses H. and Margaret Hoffman Rhyne.

On 22 Mar. 1862 he enlisted in Company H, Forty-ninth North Carolina Regiment, for Confederate service and fought in fourteen engagements, including Antietam and Fredericksburg, but was never wounded. At the end of the war, however, he was at home on sick leave. He had a congenial disposition and after the war enjoyed attending many reunions of both Confederate and Union veterans.

His father was a pioneer cotton manufacturer and, along with five associates, began to operate the Woodlawn cotton factory in Gaston County in the summer of 1852. Young Rhyne purchased his father's interest in the business in 1869 and after several years, in partnership with Ambrose Costner and Daniel Efird Rhyne, his father-in-law and brother, erected a new mill near where Dutchman's Creek enters the Catawba River. The town of Mount Holly, which he named, grew up in the vicinity and he served as one of its first mayors. He eventually owned a controlling interest in a number of textile plants and was a leading figure in the rapid expansion of the textile industry in Gaston County.

Although he attended high school for only one year, he taught school for a while and in 1879 was one of the founders of Gaston Female College in Dallas. He was a member of the board of trustees of Lenoir Rhyne College at Hickory from 1895 to 1898. Both of these institutions were affiliated with the Lutheran church, of which he was a lifelong member.

He married Martha Jane Costner (1854–1939) of Lincoln County on 22 Oct. 1872 and was the father of seven children: Augusta G., Walter G., Henry A., Lily C., Susie M., Helen A., and Mary C. Rhyne was buried in the Mount Holly Cemetery.

SEE: Samuel A. Ashe, ed., *Cyclopedia of Eminent and Representative Men of the Carolinas*, vol. 2 (1892); *Charlotte Observer*, 4 Dec. 1927; L. M. Hoffman, *Our Kin* (1915); Charles L. Van Noppen Papers (Manuscript Department, Duke University Library, Durham).

FRANK P. CAUBLE

Rhyne, Daniel Efird *(8 Feb. 1852–25 Feb. 1933)*, textile manufacturer, banker, and philanthropist, was born on a farm in Gaston County near the town of Mount Holly. A son of Moses H. and Margaret Hoffman Rhyne, he was a descendant of pioneer German settlers. He received his early education in the common schools and in 1872 and 1873 attended North Carolina College, a Lutheran school at Mount Pleasant.

At age twenty-one he formed a partnership with Ambrose Costner and Abel Peterson Rhyne, his brother, and erected a cotton mill near where Dutchman's Creek enters the Catawba River. Eventually he became a large stockholder in a score of textile plants in Belmont, Cherryville, and Lincolnton and was generally regarded by his contemporaries as a genius in cotton mill management. Rhyne owned the Piedmont Wagon Company, one of the oldest industries in Catawba County, and his real estate holdings included 15,000 acres of farm and mineral land in Gaston, Lincoln, Catawba, McDowell, and Rutherford counties. At one time he had 3,000 acres under cultivation. He was president of a bank in both Lincolnton and Cherryville and was a director of two banks in Charlotte. New inventions fascinated Rhyne, and the Lincolnton *Lincoln Journal* reported in November 1899 that he was the first person in North Carolina to own an automobile.

His generous donations made possible the erection of a dozen Lutheran church buildings in Lincoln, Catawba, Gaston, Iredell, Mecklenburg, and Guilford counties, and his large benefactions to Lenoir College at Hickory resulted in the name of the institution being changed to Lenoir Rhyne College in 1923. A new college administration building, for which he supplied the funds, was also named in his honor.

In his personal appearance, Rhyne was short of stature and of stocky build. In 1887 he moved to the village of Laboratory, near Lincolnton, and resided there until his death. He never married. A baptized member of Lutheran Chapel Church in Gaston County, he was buried in the Lutheran Chapel Cemetery.

SEE: Frank P. Cauble, "Daniel Efird Rhyne" (Lenoir Rhyne College Library, Hickory, 1973); L. M. Hoffman, *Our Kin* (1915); *North Carolina Biography*, vol. 4 (1928 [portrait]).

FRANK P. CAUBLE

Rice, John Andrew *(1 Feb. 1888–17 Nov. 1968)*, educator and founder of Black Mountain College in Black Mountain, was born near Lynchburg, S.C., the son of a Methodist minister of the same name and the nephew of Senator "Cotton Ed" Smith of South Carolina. Rice attended the Webb School in Bellbuckle, Tenn., and Tulane University. In 1911 he was chosen Rhodes Scholar from Louisiana and went to Oxford University as a student of jurisprudence. On his return from Oxford in 1914, he taught at the Webb School. Rice was a graduate student in the classics at the University of Chicago in 1916–17 and served in military intelligence in 1918–19. In 1920 he was named associate professor of the classics at the University of Nebraska, eventually becoming chairman of the department. During this period he served on the American Rhodes Scholarship Committee. In 1928–29 he taught classics at New Jersey College for Women and then accepted a fellowship from the Guggenheim Foundation to study in England the works of Jonathan Swift, on which he became an authority.

Since his Oxford days Rice had been known as a sharp critic of American higher education. Because of Rice's liberal ideas about education, Hamilton Holt chose him in 1930 to be professor of classics at Rollins College, Winter Park, Fla., which the liberal Holt was promoting as the most exciting place in American higher education. But at Rollins Rice soon became involved in issues of academic freedom, and after a strenuous battle on the subject Holt dismissed him, thereby bringing down on Rollins censure from the American Association of University Professors.

As a result of this conflict, three professors and fifteen students left Rollins with Rice and looked about for a place in which to establish a new college devoted to the principles of democracy and academic freedom. They settled on the Blue Ridge Assembly of the YMCA at Black Mountain, which would be available to them from October to May at a nominal fee, and named the new institution Black Mountain College. The group conceived of the institution as having a minimum of administrative apparatus: no president, but a presiding officer to be known as the "rector" who could be recalled from the office at the will of the faculty, and no deans. There was a treasurer. Rice became rector in 1934 and remained in that office until 1938. Other faculty and more students were recruited. The curriculum was to be whatever could be offered with the faculty available. A student could elect what he pleased from what was offered, and much of the course work would take place in informal discussion groups.

In line with Rice's conviction that the whole person should be educated, art was to be made the center of the curriculum. Rice believed that art would not only educate the senses and emotions but also would teach the lesson of integrity to one's self. The doctrine of integrity was foremost in Rice's thinking. He challenged insincere and unthinking beliefs. In every situation the students must learn to think, and Black Mountain had a great variety of situations since it operated as a democratic community with many necessary services being provided by the faculty and students. Democratic discussion between faculty and students, group enactment of student rules and standards, and participation in an assortment of community enterprises, it was thought, all combined to develop a personality ready for intelligent living and public service.

The college was not, however, anti-intellectual. At one time or another it offered not only courses in the classics, history, and economics but in literature, languages, the sciences, and mathematics. Graduation was determined not by credits or years of attendance, but by readiness. Those who aspired to graduation must sometime at the end of two or three years take a general subject matter examination written by the faculty for each examination period. If the faculty found the aspirant's examination satisfactory, he was then admitted to a major of his own choosing. The term of major study was to be determined by the student's own feeling of readiness for examination—oral and written—in his subject by a specialist in the field from outside the college. Black Mountain was never certified as a degree-granting institution by the Southern Association. As a result many students dropped out to enroll elsewhere and hardly a score was ever certified for graduation.

In 1939 the college bought a property on Lake Eden west of Black Mountain village where students and faculty built a studies building that has since been a model for structures in other institutions. The college went on to have an enrollment of just over a hundred after World War II and a faculty of sixteen. Its most famous art teacher was Josef Albers, a German refugee. He and his wife, Ani, a weaver, drew many students. The result was that the college became famous as an art school, and many luminaries in the national and international art world of the fifties and sixties had been teachers or students there. After Albers left, it became prominent as a school of poetry under the American poet Charles Olson, who founded the *Black Mountain Review* and developed a number of exciting poets. For financial reasons, the college ceased to exist in 1955.

Rice left the college in 1940 after his faculty peers had charged him with self-aggrandizement and self-indulgence. Moving to South Carolina, he became a writer and in 1941 published his autobiography under the title *I Came Out of the Eighteenth Century*, the Harper 125th Anniversary Prize book. He had come to believe that he had lived too much in opposition, that there must be a world of law, but that the ideal person would arrive at truth using the Socratic method of questioning and also have that love of his fellows that inhered in the teachings of Christ. Though repelled by the self-centered and egotistic competitiveness of the professional artist, he finally felt that he had come into his true calling when he became a creative writer. Rice published short stories in *Colliers'* magazine and in the *New Yorker*. These were collected into a volume entitled *Local Color*, published in 1959. Though he had built his college on negations, it managed from his foundations to pioneer many of the freedoms that characterized the changes in conventional colleges in the 1960s.

Rice's first wife was Nell Aydelotte, whom he married in 1914 and by whom he had two children: Frank Aydelotte and Mary Rice Marshall. Following his divorce in 1942 he married Caroline Dikka Moen, by whom he had two children: Paul Nicolai and Elizabeth Rice Fenger.

SEE: Black Mountain College Papers (North Carolina State Archives, Raleigh); *DAB*, supp. 8 (1988); Theodore Dreier, "Black Mountain College" (mimeographed, 10 May 1949, North Carolina Collection, University of North Carolina, Chapel Hill); Martin Duberman, *Black Mountain: An Exploration in Community* (1972 [portrait]); John Evarts, "Black Mountain College: The Total Approach," *Form* magazine, vol. 6 (December 1967), and "Black Mountain College: The Years from 1933 to 1942" (typescript, North Carolina Collection, University of North Carolina, Chapel Hill); Raleigh *News and Observer*, 25 Oct. 1942; John A. Rice, "Black Mountain College Memoirs," in Mervin Lane, ed., *Black Mountain Sprouted Seeds* (1990), and "Fundamentalism and the Higher Learning" (reprinted from *Harper's Magazine*, May 1937, in North Carolina Collection, University of North Carolina, Chapel Hill); *Who's Who in the South and Southwest* (1961).

D. H. CORKRAN

Rice, Nathaniel *(d. 29 Jan. 1753)*, colonial official, entered North Carolina from England early in 1731. Previously (ca. 1725) he had visited and acquired property in South Carolina. Rice carried with him commissions as provincial secretary and royal councillor, much to the dismay of the new governor, George Burrington. He owed his appointments to his brother-in-law, Martin Bladen, a member of Parliament since 1715 and of the Board of Trade since 1730. Thus Rice had an independence from Burrington that most other North Carolina officials did not enjoy, and that independence generated increasing tension between the secretary and the governor.

Before 1731 ended, Rice had joined with William Smith, John Baptista Ashe, and others in firm and consistent opposition to Burrington's dealings with the two houses of the legislature. When Smith resigned from the Council in May 1731 to carry his objections about Burrington to London, Rice as next senior councillor assumed presidency of that body. From that vantage point he became the governor's chief nemesis, and the growing opposition to Burrington increasingly began to rally around Rice. The secretary led petition-writing efforts against the governor—documents that were sent to many powerful figures in London, including Burrington's patron, the Duke of Newcastle.

The tension surrounding the governor reached a high point at the legislative session in the summer of 1733. Wishing to dissolve the body but fearing some clever manipulation by Rice, Burrington on 17 July 1733 seized all of the official secretarial seals of office and dissolved the legislature the following day. When it became necessary for Burrington to go to South Carolina on business in April 1734, Rice became acting governor by virtue of his presidency of the Council. No records of Rice's activities in this period survived, but shortly after his return in September 1734, Burrington suspended Rice from office, claiming that the secretary had plotted to kill him.

With the replacement of Burrington by Gabriel Johnston in November 1734, Rice was again restored to the Council. The following year he became a member of the General Court and a justice of the peace for New Hanover County. With the passage of time he became embroiled in Lower Cape Fear politics and sided with the pro-Brunswick forces in opposing the establishment of Wilmington, which was advocated by the governor and William Smith. By 1750, however, Rice and Johnston were reconciled, having been brought together by the common and mutual attacks on them of Henry McCulloh.

When Johnston died in July 1752, Rice as senior councillor began acting as governor. He was by this time an ill, old man. He left a son named John and his wife Mary. His will refers to a niece in Hampshire, England, which may have been his birthplace.

SEE: William S. Price, Jr., "A Strange Incident in George Burrington's Royal Governorship," *North Carolina Historical Review* 51 (1974); William L. Saunders, ed., *Colonial Records of North Carolina*, vols. 3–4 (1886); Secretary of State Papers and Wills (North Carolina State Archives, Raleigh).

WILLIAM S. PRICE, JR.

Rice, Oscar Knefler *(12 Feb. 1903–7 May 1978)*, chemist and educator, was cited in an honorary Sc.D. degree, awarded posthumously by the University of North Carolina at Chapel Hill a few days after his death, as "very likely the most distinguished chemist ever to have lived in North Carolina." He was born in Chicago, Ill., the son of Oscar Guido and Thekla Knefler Rice. His father died of typhoid fever when the couple had been married only six months, and his mother never remarried but raised Oscar with the help of her sister, Amy Knefler.

Rice studied at San Diego Junior College (later San Diego State University) from 1920 to 1922, and then at the University of California at Berkeley, where he received a B.S. in 1924 and a Ph.D. in physical chemistry in 1926. After one more year at Berkeley as an associate in chemistry, he won a prestigious National Research Fellowship (later called a National Research Council Fellowship) and spent two years of it at the California Institute of Technology (1927–29) and the last at the University of Leipzig (1929–30). During the early part of his postdoctoral investigations he completed the first version of his great work on the theory of unimolecular reactions, and when he had been an instructor at Harvard for two years, he was given the second American Chemical Society Award in Pure Chemistry for it. (His good friend Linus Pauling had received the first.)

He remained at Harvard until 1935, producing brilliant theoretical and experimental studies of unimolecular reactions, predissociation, and diffuse spectra, and applying the then-new quantum mechanics to inelastic molecular collisions. This new tool and Rice's contributions on unimolecular reactions were keys to an enormous expansion in the understanding of chemical reactions; at a time when the world was sunk in depression and fear, physical chemists were filled with elation over discovery after discovery in what has been called the "glorious thirties."

Yet Rice was apparently not happy at Harvard, and after a year spent again at Berkeley, he went to The University of North Carolina in 1936 as associate professor of chemistry; he remained at the university for the rest of his life except for occasional leaves of absence. There he published his seminal textbook, *Electronic Structure and Chemical Bonding* (1940), which had begun with lectures at Harvard and was among the first to introduce students to the implications of the quantum theory for chemical bonding. Early in his Chapel Hill years Rice also produced his pioneering studies on the fundamental problem of determining intermolecular forces from the bulk properties of a substance. He was promoted to full professor in 1943. In 1946–47 he was principal chemist at the Clinton Laboratories, Oak Ridge National Laboratory. There is a story, often repeated, that the army officer in charge of the laboratory was much concerned about the productivity of this man who sat all day in an armchair thinking. At the review of what had been produced that year, the quality of Rice's work was so impressive that stuffed armchairs were recommended for every scientist whom the officer supervised. His only other extended departures from Chapel Hill were in 1968, when he was a visiting professor at the Virginia Polytechnic Institute (later the Virginia Polytechnic Institute and State University), and in 1969, when he was Seydel-Woolley Visiting Professor of Chemistry at the Georgia Institute of Technology.

Later in his career Rice turned his attention to phase transitions and critical phenomena, in which he contributed some of the fundamental concepts and laws. His series of elegant experimental studies on the aniline-cyclohexane system through the 1950s, the classic study of the critical phenomenon, were combined with a grand theory that tied together seemingly unrelated observations about different kinds of phase transitions. His second book, *Statistical Mechanics, Thermodynamics, and Kinetics* (1967), written from the viewpoint of a contributor to nearly every topic discussed, is still considered a remarkably original contribution.

Thus it is not surprising that the title of his address on receiving the American Chemical Society's Peter Debye Award in Physical Chemistry (1970) was "Secondary Variables in Critical Phenomena." Other awards included the Southern Chemist Award (1961), the North Carolina Award in Science (1966), the Florida Section Award of the American Chemical Society (1967), and the Charles H. Stone Award of the society's Carolina-Piedmont Section (1972). Rice was elected to the National Academy of Sciences in 1964 and served as chairman of the American Chemical Society's Division of Physical and Inorganic Chemistry; he sat on many scientific boards and panels and held numerous editorial offices.

Many stories grew up around him. He was famous for apparently sleeping through seminars and then asking the most penetrating questions of the speakers, and for being able to retrieve instantly whatever he needed from an office piled high with books and papers in—to others—utter disarray.

No less for his personal qualities than for his brilliant contributions to science, Oscar Rice was remembered for his tolerance, for his patience with those with whom he disagreed, and for his unwillingness to be reconciled to injustice. On receiving the Southern Chemist Award in 1961, he noted his great indebtedness to The University of North Carolina and "the atmosphere of free and open discussion . . . , the acceptance of new ideas, and the growth of a new cosmopolitanism, which now encompasses not only people of the far corners of the world, but also some Americans who until recently have been partially excluded from the world of culture through irrelevant circumstances, not connected with their own worth and value."

At Oak Ridge Oscar Rice met Hope Ernestyne Sherpy, and they were married in 1947. They adopted two daughters, Margarita and Pamela, both of whom were born in Germany and were given to the Rices on trips made there to attend scientific conferences. They were active members of the Community Church in Chapel Hill.

SEE: Maurice M. Bursey, *Carolina Chemists* (1982); *Chapel Hill Newspaper*, 8, 11 May 1978; *Journal of Statistical Physics* 21 (1979); Raleigh *News and Observer*, 8 May 1978; *University [of North Carolina] Gazette*, 28 Aug. 1981; Benjamin Widom and Rudolph A. Marcus, "Oscar Knefler Rice, February 12, 1903–May 7, 1978" (typescript [photocopy], 1987, North Carolina Collection, University of North Carolina, Chapel Hill).

MAURICE M. BURSEY

Rich, Joseph Hampton *(14 July 1874–1 Dec. 1949)*, editor and promoter, was born in Davie County, the son of Samuel Chase and Betty Carolina McMahan Rich. He was graduated from Wake Forest College in 1898. For a short time he was a Baptist preacher and schoolteacher, then acquired a small press and operated a print shop in Winston-Salem. By 1913 he was general manager of the Southern Agricultural Advertising Bureau, and in 1919 he listed himself as president of the Piedmont Printing Company. For a while he published a small weekly newspaper, the *Labor Leader*.

Rich's name is associated with highways, an interest reflected in two organizations that he formed and managed almost single-handedly. The first of these, the Boone Trail Highway and Memorial Association, he organized in North Wilkesboro on 13 Oct. 1913. Its original purpose was to promote the building of "an arterial highway to reclaim the counties of the northwestern part of the state," but this goal was soon extended to the promotion of additional routes and to the construction of markers commemorating Daniel Boone. At first he cooperated with the Daniel Boone Trail Committee of the Daughters of the American Revolution, but within a few years the flamboyant Rich took over the effort. About 1916 he went to Washington, D.C., and engaged a sculptor named Henley to prepare a model for a tablet showing Boone sitting on a boulder with his dog, rifle, and powder horn—looking westward, of course. He persuaded the navy to give him four hundred pounds of metal from the gun carriage of the USS *Maine*, a bit of which he mixed into the metal tablets cast from the model. The tablets were reproduced by the dozens. Many were placed on concrete and stone arrowheads constructed along the supposed travel routes of Daniel Boone; others were bolted to granite slabs or walls of buildings.

For more than twenty-five years Rich made his living visiting communities, stirring the imaginations of civic leaders and schoolchildren, raising funds, constructing arrowheads, conducting colorful unveiling ceremonies, and issuing carefully prepared press releases. The Boone Trail Highway and Memorial Association's *Boone Trail Herald*, published sporadically from 1924 to 1938, recorded the proliferation of the increasingly familiar arrowheads and reported on "Major" Rich's speech-making and promotional activities.

Once markers had been placed along the highways leading from the Yadkin Valley to Kentucky, Rich turned his attention to other routes. There were the "Coal-to-Cotton Highway" from West Virginia to the Carolinas, the "Detroit to St. Augustine Cross-Line," and a transcontinental "Boone Trail" from Virginia Beach to San Francisco. In placing a Boone marker at the Golden Gate, he wrote, "The spot was never reached by Boone perhaps except in his dreams but we know that he longed to reach the Pacific and asked many questions about the far famed country of California." Along all these routes he stimulated interest and financial support for the construction of markers, each dedicated with patriotic fervor. On the Georgia state capitol grounds, for instance, a torchlight ceremony "gave a fine imitation of a campfire scene with Daniel Boone as the central figure."

Having marked the South and West with scores of Boone monuments, the director of the Boone Trail Highway and Memorial Association took his movement to New England, enlisting civic clubs and schoolchildren in the construction of two Boone markers in Boston. He wrote that in one of them was "a rock from the summit of Mt. Washington where the director spent a very delightful night, seeing a glorious sunrise." He claimed to have discovered in his research that an ancient route called the Sokoki Trail from Boston to New York had been used by the Apanake Tribe a thousand years ago, and that it was the southern leg of this trail through Pennsylvania that the Boone family followed to North Carolina. Naturally, Boone arrowheads were placed along the route.

By 1930 Rich had decided to honor other white pioneers, Indians, and animals. He drew a map naming the highway from Winston-Salem to Bryson City (one route via Asheville, one via Hendersonville) the "Appalachian Indian Road and Buffalo Trail." Monuments along these routes sometimes held two metal tablets—one honoring the Indian chief, Sequoyah, the other a buffalo. In Davie County he built a monument to Nathaniel Brock; in Orange, to Thomas Burke; in Catawba, to David Crockett. In the Joppa Cemetery in Davie, he marked the graves of Daniel Boone's parents.

In 1925 Rich persuaded the General Assembly to charter the Daniel Boone High School at Deep Gap, to be used as a consolidated school under the administration of the Watauga County Board of Education for eight or nine months of the year and as a Boy Scout training camp in the summer. His plans to establish a Daniel Boone Boy Scout Camp in Yellowstone Park apparently failed.

Rich's other consuming interest was the Boys' Road Patrol, which was chartered by the General Assembly of 1915 "to look after the maintenance of the stretch of road indigenous to each member of the patrol, dragging and ditching same by the use of machinery placed in the care of the patrol by the State and county." For ten years the program was under the Department of Agriculture, but in 1925 it was transferred to the State Board of Education. It apparently was most active in the counties of Forsyth and Davie where Rich personally oversaw the work. In the days before paved roads, the patrol, with the slogan, "A Boy on Every Mile," helped keep country roads dragged and drained. A simple road drag formed the patrol's seal. With the advent of improved roads in the 1930s, the organization (in essence, Rich himself) preached traffic and pedestrian safety.

About 1934 Rich headed the American Institute of Heraldry in North Carolina, offering to research and register arms as a "token of the achievement of blood." In the following decade in Chapel Hill he built inexpensive log cabins for students at the university, and in 1945 he served on the staff of the General Assembly.

Rich married Ino Bagby and they had four children—Katherine Elizabeth, Edith Huldoh, Charles Hampton, and Samuel Frederick Chase. He died in Duke Hospital and was buried at Eaton's Church in Davie County.

J. Hampton Rich, who claimed to have placed more than 350 metal tablets throughout the country and to have addressed more than 50,000 schoolchildren on just one cross-country tour, was an enigma. Given to exaggerations, less than scholarly in his research, and not above a little chicanery, Rich was nevertheless a gentle and generous man who enjoyed the luxury of making his hobby his career. For more than two decades he stirred the interest of countless schoolchildren in what he called "pioneer lore," which formed the "mud-sill of our republic." Many of his markers may still be seen from the Atlantic to the Pacific and from Florida to Michigan and Massachusetts. In memorializing Daniel Boone, Hamp Rich probably exceeded the old pioneer in both travel and exploration.

SEE: *Greensboro Daily News*, 22 June 1976; Charles H. Rich to H. G. Jones, 28 Aug. 1978; *State* magazine, 22 Feb. 1958; Wake Forest University Alumni Files; Winston-Salem *Boone Trail Herald*, 1924–38; *Winston-Salem Journal*, 2 Dec. 1949; Winston-Salem *Twin City Sentinel*, 10 Dec. 1969.

H. G. JONES

Richardson, Edmund *(28 June 1818–11 Jan. 1886)*, the world's largest cotton planter, was born in Caswell County, the son of James and Nancy Payne Ware Richardson. Educated in local schools, he worked on the family farm and clerked in a dry goods store in Danville, Va. In 1833, when others from the county were moving to the Deep South, he settled in Brandon, Miss., and again became a clerk. In 1840 he used a moderate cash settlement and a few slaves from his father's estate, plus his own savings, to create a joint mercantile firm in the state capital, Jackson, and to establish branches in nearby communities. The firm flourished, and in 1852 he became a junior partner in a factorage company in New Orleans. He invested excess profits from his store in land and slaves, and by 1861 he owned five plantations and several hundred slaves. During the Civil War, because of the economic upheaval in the South, the factorage business was suspended and at the war's end Richardson was deeply in debt. By buying and selling cotton, however, his skill in business soon enabled him to recover. Establishing a new firm, he annually moved 100,000 bales of cotton.

His extensive operations earned for him the sobriquet "Cotton King," and he was a commissioner from the cotton-producing states at the Philadelphia Centennial of 1876 to observe the one-hundredth anniversary of the Declaration of Independence—an occasion widely ignored by Southerners who had recently lost their own struggle for independence. He also was vice-president of the Atlanta Cotton Exposition in 1881, and President Chester A. Arthur appointed him commissioner of the World's Industrial and Cotton Centennial Exposition in New Orleans in 1884. Of the latter he was president of the board of management and made the opening address. His formal report on the exposition, submitted to the president shortly before his death, stressed the significance of this undertaking for the industrial advancement of the South as well as of the nation.

In the belief that cotton mills should be operated near the source of their raw material, Richardson leased in 1868 the Mississippi state penitentiary, installed machinery, and leased convict labor, a practice common throughout the nation at that time. To employ all of the laborers available, he bought and leased additional plantations and in time raised cotton on 25,000 acres in some fifty locations in Mississippi, Louisiana, and Arkansas. On each of his plantations he kept a store and sold supplies to his employees. In productive seasons they produced 12,000 bales, worth in excess of $500,000. He soon acquired controlling interest in other cotton mills and extended his interests to include cottonseed oil and railroads. Richardson's fortune was variously estimated at between 10 and 12 million dollars.

On a buying trip for his stores in 1847, Richardson met Margaret Elizabeth Patton, of Huntsville, Ala., the sister of former governor Robert Patton, and they were married the following year. They became the parents of seven children. During his last years Richardson moved from New Orleans to Jackson, where he died.

SEE: *Appleton's Cyclopedia of American Biography*, vol. 5 (1888); *DAB*, vol. 8 (1935); John N. Ingham, ed., *Biographical Dictionary of American Business Leaders*, vol. 3 (1983); James W. Silver, "North Carolinians in Mississippi History," *North Carolina Historical Review* 22 (1945); Stephen B. Weeks Scrapbook, vol. 4 (North Carolina Collection, University of North Carolina, Chapel Hill).

WILLIAM S. POWELL

Richardson, J[acob] Henry Smith *(19 July 1885–11 Feb. 1972)*, president and chairman of the board of the Vick Chemical Company (now Richardson-Merrell, Inc.), through his sales and marketing techniques and his long-range corporate planning was responsible for much of the expansion and lasting success of this international pharmaceutical firm. The eldest child of Lunsford and Mary Lynn Smith Richardson, he was born in Greensboro in the home of his maternal grandfather, Dr. Jacob Henry Smith, a Presbyterian minister for whom he was named. His father, at that time a druggist in Selma, moved his family to Greensboro in 1890. As a boy, Smith (as his family called him) performed daily tasks assigned by his father, such as hoeing the garden and milking the family cow, and then was free to roam with his friends in the nearby Fisher woods. On Sunday the family attended morning and evening church services, and Smith was expected to memorize the catechism and Bible verses.

After attending local schools, he entered, in 1902, Davidson College, where his uncle, Dr. Henry Louis Smith, was president. During his sophomore year, Richardson persuaded his reluctant parents to let him go to the U.S. Naval Academy. He passed the competitive examination and enrolled at Annapolis in 1904, but the following year he was dismissed for various disciplinary offenses such as chewing tobacco and hazing. Not wanting to go home, he worked in New York successively as a railroad clerk, streetcar conductor, sales clerk at Gimbels and Wanamakers, and salesman for a blanket company. In 1907 he returned home to become sales manager for the Vick Family Remedies Company, which his father had started two years earlier.

Smith Richardson persuaded his father to concentrate sales efforts on the most successful and unique product of the firm, a medicated salve for colds, and to call it Vicks VapoRub to stress its unique characteristics and to distinguish it from other "salves" on merchant's shelves. Merchants, if they bought a certain quantity, were given free samples to give to selected customers on condition that they report the results. By 1910 a surplus was available for advertising and throughout the rural South signs and billboards were placed along the roads for all to see.

When VapoRub was introduced into the middle-sized cities of the North after 1912, advertising was done through the local newspapers using the same style type and copy as the news articles and positioned preceding, following, or alongside the local news. A coupon in the advertisement promised a free sample from the local druggist while the supply lasted. In New York and the larger northeastern cities with various newspapers but a concentrated population, advertising was done through signs placed on streetcars. In 1917 the company began a widespread distribution of samples on a house-to-house basis in many areas of the Northeast, and when postal regulations were changed allowing mail to be sent to rural free delivery boxes, it sent millions of samples to the vast but diffused population lying west of the Mississippi—the first distribution of samples on such a large scale. Vick was probably also the first drug company to hire a doctor to review the medical accuracy of all its advertising copy. During the influenza epidemic of 1918–19 Vick advertisements claimed no cure, only "relief to difficult breathing when used as directed."

In 1915 Richardson was made general manager of the business (now known as the Vick Chemical Company), in 1919 he became president upon the death of his father, and in 1929 he was named chairman of the board. Until his retirement in 1957, he was the dominant influence in the decisions of the company as it expanded internationally and diversified into different products and fields. By 1923 sales in America had grown to $4.5 million, and in 1924 the first attempts to open foreign markets were made in Mexico and Great Britain, with Richardson personally heading the British effort. By 1929 sales had expanded to more than 60 foreign countries and by his death to 120. In 1931 the first expansion from a one-product company started with the introduction of nose drops, cough drops, and a gargle for colds. Seeking diversification into other fields Vicks merged with Bristol-Myers, Life Savers, Sterling Products, and United Drug (Rexall) in 1930 to form Drug Inc., but the alliance did not work out and Vick was "de-merged" in 1933. During these years headquarters were moved to New York to better handle the export business and advertising. Starting in 1938 with the purchase of the William S. Merrell Company, an ethical drug company making prescription products for doctors, the company moved outside the cold medication field and in the years that followed acquired additional companies in the ethical drug, veterinary medicine, chemical, plastic packaging, and toiletry fields. To reflect this, the name of the parent company was changed to Richardson-Merrell, Inc., in 1960.

The Great Depression brought home the mortality of businesses, and Richardson in his later years devoted most of his time to long-range planning to ensure "an enduring enterprise." The key elements, he decided, were adequate capital funds, stockholder control through family solidarity, and identification and attraction of creative leaders into top management. In pursuit of the last goal, he established in 1937 the Vick School of Applied Merchandising, which provided training in marketing to men who simultaneously worked as salesmen for a two-year period. At the end of that time, the company promised that for those it hired training would be continued to prepare them for top management positions. Other programs were devised to ensure that behind each key executive was an equally talented replacement, and it was made a company policy that the president retire at age sixty, though serving as a member of the board for five more years, to make room at the top for the ambitious while providing insurance should the new executive die or not work out. In 1935 the Smith Richardson Foundation was established, the bulk of whose expenditures have gone to programs for the identification and development of innovative leaders.

In 1957, after fifty years with the Vick company, Richardson suffered a slight stroke and retired. During that half century he had seen the company grow in sales from $25,000 to nearly $95 million and by the time of his death to approximately $450 million. Richardson was the largest individual stockholder in Richardson-Merrell and held stock in several smaller family companies that had been established in the real estate, insurance, and financial investment fields. With his family he donated funds for the L. Richardson Memorial Hospital in Greensboro, and through his foundation (valued at over $90 million at the end of 1971) grants have been made to educational institutions, historic preservation projects, and other philanthropies, mostly in North Carolina and South Carolina.

Richardson married, on 16 Dec. 1914, Grace Stuart Jones, of Danville, Va., who died on 7 Feb. 1962. They had two daughters, Grace Stuart Stetson and Mary Keene Jackson Lange, and three sons, J. Henry Smith, Jr., Robert Randolph, and John Page. Forward thinking in his ideas and loving the outdoor life, he remained physically active into his eighties, riding horseback and fishing on western ranches, hunting on land he owned in South Carolina, and swimming in the waters of Long Island Sound at his home in Greens Farm, Conn. He was buried in the Green Hill Cemetery, Greensboro.

SEE: *Annals of an American Family* (no date); Ethel S. Arnett, *Greensboro, North Carolina* (1955); Laurinda Richardson Carlson, "Lunsford Richardson II (1854–1919)" (typescript, Greensboro, 1978); *Greensboro Daily News*, 11 Dec. 1960; H. Smith Richardson, *Early History and Management Philosophy of Richardson-Merrell* (privately printed, 1975); John W. Simpson, *History of the First Presbyterian Church of Greensboro, North Carolina* (privately printed, 1945); Dick Toomey, "The Cold War," *Duke Power Magazine* (Summer 1974); "Vick Manufacturing, Then and Now," *Richardson-Merrell Newsletter Supplement* (1969).

NORRIS W. PREYER

Richardson, Lunsford *(30 Dec. 1854–21 Aug. 1919)*, pharmacist and founder of the Vick Chemical Company, grew up on a plantation in Johnston County southeast of Raleigh. His father, Lunsford Richardson, Sr., died before he was two, and his mother, Laurinda Vinson, daughter of Archibald and Rutha Smith Vinson, took over the operation of the plantation and raising of the five children. Lunsford was the youngest child and his closest companions were slaves on the plantation. His two older brothers, who had joined the Confederate army, were away when, in April 1865, the home and farm were looted by passing troops from William T. Sherman's army. At age fourteen he went off to the Horner and Graves School in Oxford and then in the fall of 1872 enrolled at Davidson College. His mother died in January 1873 and Richardson, short of money, completed the four-year curriculum in three years, graduating in May 1875 as salutatorian of his class and winner of the Greek and Latin medals and the Debater's Medal of the Philanthropic Literary Society.

For four years he was principal of the Little River Academy in Lyndon, but finding prospect for economic advancement poor, he left teaching in 1880 and with his savings purchased a drugstore in Selma. Four years later he married Mary Lynn Smith, daughter of the Reverend Jacob Henry Smith, minister of the First Presbyterian Church of Greensboro. His wife's brother, Henry Louis Smith, later president of Davidson and of Washington and Lee, was best man. In 1890 Richardson moved his family to Greensboro, where, with John B. Fariss as partner, he established the Richardson-Fariss Drug Store, which became the town's largest. In 1898 he dissolved his partnership and formed the L. Richardson Drug Company, one of four wholesale drug companies in the state. Richardson had developed many pharmaceutical preparations, and his new company was formed as a means of selling them to a wider market; but he soon found that his stockholders were more interested in dividends than in using funds to promote his products. Consequently, in

1905, at age fifty, he left the wholesale business and with $8,000 capital launched the wholly owned Vick Family Remedies Company. The Vick name was used because it was short, "catchy," and easy to remember. Richardson had seen it in an advertisement for "Vicks Seeds" but may have also wanted to honor his brother-in-law, Dr. Joshua W. Vick of Selma.

His Vick Family Remedies were manufactured in the back half of a building on South Davie Street. In the front half, he had the distributorship for Pepsi Cola to provide funds while a market developed for his Vick preparations. By 1910 he was able to drop the Pepsi franchise and build a two-story brick building on Milton Street for the manufacture of his Vick products. His most successful preparation was Vicks VapoRub, a medicated salve for colds first developed in 1894. When spread on the chest, it acted like a mustard plaster and vaporization of the salve by the body's heat allowed its vapors to be inhaled, making breathing easier. Once tried, the product largely sold itself and eventually all efforts were concentrated on VapoRub alone. Aided by the distribution of free samples, it expanded into seven southeastern states and in 1913 was first introduced in the North. Sales climbed from $25,000 in 1907 to nearly $150,000 in 1913 and to over $600,000 in 1917. The great influenza epidemic of 1918–19 sent sales soaring to nearly $3 million and made Vicks a household name throughout the United States. At the beginning of 1919 the business was incorporated as the Vick Chemical Company.

Having experienced the South's poverty after the Civil War, Richardson had determined to use all of his efforts to help his state prosper once again. He dreamed of establishing a worldwide business but did not live to see this happen, for he died of pneumonia while on a trip to San Francisco—another victim of the influenza epidemic. Though the business he founded (renamed Richardson-Merrell, Inc.) has since grown manyfold and today markets thousands of different products, Richardson's original preparation, VapoRub, still remains a major company product, and millions of the little blue jars are sold annually throughout the world.

Portraits of Richardson in possession of the family show him to have been of medium build with dark brown eyes and hair. A thoughtful, kind, unselfish man, and an elder in the First Presbyterian Church of Greensboro, he took his Christian commitment seriously, always finding time to help others. Every Sunday for over twenty years he taught adult Bible classes in his church in the morning and in the Negro community in the afternoon. His special interests were the problems of the blacks, help to any who sought an education, and the benevolent causes of his church, to which he left a large portion of his Vick stock. Over twenty years after his death, during World War II, blacks in Greensboro petitioned that a Liberty ship be named for this "white friend" whose "splendid example did so much to bring about a better understanding of the races." Richardson loved poetry and found relaxation in reading Vergil in the original Latin. Surviving him were his wife and five children: J. Henry Smith, Laurinda Vinson Carlson, Mary Norris Preyer, Lunsford, and Janet Lynn Chapin Prickett. He was buried in Greensboro's Green Hill Cemetery.

SEE: References accompanying sketch of J. Henry Smith Richardson.

NORRIS W. PREYER

Richardson, Robert Payne, Jr. *(28 Mar. 1855–24 June 1922)*, tobacco manufacturer, was a native of Rockingham County and the son of Robert Payne Richardson (1820–1909) and his second wife, Mary Elizabeth Watlington. Young Richardson grew up on the family plantation at Wright's Crossroads, which is now located within Reidsville. He attended local schools in Reidsville and Wentworth and the Bingham School in Orange County in 1872. The next year he joined his father's tobacco and mercantile business as a clerk and was also involved in tobacco sales.

In 1877 he left his father's firm and founded R. P. Richardson, Jr., and Company for the purpose of manufacturing smoking tobacco. At the time, the tobacco industry in Reidsville produced chewing tobacco almost exclusively. Richardson launched a new smoking tobacco, Old North State, that soon became a leading regional brand. The success of Old North State influenced several local manufacturers to follow Richardson's lead, and by the turn of the century Reidsville was second only to Durham in the production of smoking tobacco. As early as 1890 Richardson erected a modern, commodious five-story brick structure to house his factory. Although the factory burned in 1917, it was partially rebuilt and continued to be the major family business until 1926, when it was sold to Brown and Williamson of Winston-Salem. Other family enterprises included the acquisition of 33,000 acres in Tennessee, gold mining in Montgomery County with the Rich-Cog mine and Rockingham Mining and Investment Company, and large-scale farming in Rockingham County.

Richardson was a member of the Democratic party but never sought political office. He was a charter member and elder of the First Presbyterian Church of Reidsville. On 30 Oct. 1877 he married Bettie Watt, and she had one son, Pickney Watt, before her death on 30 Aug. 1882. Richardson then married, on 20 Dec. 1892, Margaret M. Watt, and she had three children: Robert Payne III, Margaret Elizabeth, and Sarah Dillard, who died young. Richardson died in Greensboro and was buried in Greenview Cemetery, Reidsville. He was survived by his wife, who died on 14 July 1924.

Robert Payne Richardson III (12 Jan. 1897–17 Feb. 1967), his son, was graduated from Davidson College in 1918 and then served for a year in the U.S. Marine Corps. He married Lucy Irvin on 5 Nov. 1921. He assisted his father in the tobacco factory, and after it was sold he joined in 1927 the Nu-Shine Manufacturing Company, a local producer of shoe polish. He was president of Nu-Shine from 1927 to 1938, when the company was merged with American Products. In addition to his involvement in the other family businesses of land trading, timber operations, farming, and mining, Richardson directed the Belmont suburban development of Reidsville. He served on the State Board of Mental Health from 1948 to 1967.

SEE: Samuel A. Ashe, ed., *Biographical History of North Carolina*, vol. 2 (1917); Charlotte W. Cate, "Reidsville Scenes: An Interview with W. Benton Pipkin," *Journal of Rockingham County History and Genealogy* 1 (October 1976); Marion S. Huske, *The Centennial History of the First Presbyterian Church, Reidsville, N.C.* (1975) and "Robert Payne Richardson, Sr." (biographical sketch in possession of Lindley S. Butler); *North Carolina Biography*, vol. 3 (1941); *Reidsville Review*, 27 Jan. 1922; R. P. Richardson Papers, 1855–1967 (Rockingham County Historical Collection, Rockingham Community College, Wentworth); Rockingham County Death Register, 1922, 1924.

LINDLEY S. BUTLER

Richardson, Robert Vinkler *(4 Nov. 1820–5 Jan. 1870),* lawyer, Confederate officer, and civil engineer, was born in Granville County. At an early age, he and his family moved to Tennessee, settling in Hardeman County. Here young Richardson received his early education and then studied law. Admitted to the bar, he subsequently moved to Memphis and established a practice. In this station of life Richardson had occasion to associate himself, among other prominent individuals, with two future comrades in arms, Gideon J. Pillow and Nathan Bedford Forrest. Richardson's law practice soon prospered and he was able to acquire considerable wealth for his day. The 1860 census lists his real estate and personal holdings at a total value of $39,000.

At the outbreak of the Civil War, he served with General Pillow's forces in the early campaigns of the war and afterwards participated in the Battle of Shiloh on 6–7 Apr. 1862. On 6 September, however, Richardson was given approval by the War Department to organize and lead a regiment of partisan troops from counties in western Tennessee. Through great energy and exertion on his part, he was able to raise more than enough troops for this regiment, which was commissioned the First Tennessee Partisan Rangers, with Richardson elected as its colonel. The difficulty of this task can in no way be underestimated because he recruited his men from counties that had been overrun by the advancing Union forces and were under their occupation. Once the regiment was organized and trained, Richardson led it in countless partisan operations against Union field and garrison posts and communications. His men had daily skirmishes with Union forces, and it would appear that his harassment tactics caused a great deal of concern and annoyance to the Union leaders. The *Official Records* are filled with messages and dispatches between various Union district and post commanders that mention Richardson's command and the trouble it was causing them.

Several expeditions were sent to find and destroy his force and perhaps the most successful of these occurred on 9 Mar. 1863, when attacking Union forces captured and drove Richardson from his camps near Covington, Tenn. On the following day, he found that his regiment was greatly outnumbered and in danger of being crushed between two powerful Union columns, but he eluded these by dissolving his regiment into individual companies, which easily escaped and then harassed the Union forces until they returned back whence they had come. Richardson had had no formal military training in his prewar career, but apparently he had a natural flair for leadership and tactics. In the spring of 1863 there seems to have developed some sort of controversy between Confederate leaders and Richardson due to the fact that his regiment was a partisan unit rather than coming under the jurisdiction of regular Confederate service. Richardson was charged with "great oppression" and "exercising authority not intended to be given," resulting on 15 Apr. 1863 in an order for his arrest. As to the exact nature of the charges and of the proceedings, the *Official Records* contain virtually nothing, but the situation appears to have been resolved by transferring Richardson's regiment into regular Confederate service and recommissioning it as the Twelfth Tennessee Cavalry, with Richardson continuing as its colonel.

While these nebulous circumstances were transpiring, Richardson was called upon to lead a cavalry force in the unsuccessful efforts of Confederate commanders to intercept the famous raid of Colonel Benjamin H. Grierson's Union cavalry through Mississippi from 17 April to 2 May 1863. Richardson remained in the Department of Northern Mississippi, under Brigadier General J. R. Chalmers, with an enlarged command through the summer. On 2 October he was given formal command of a brigade of Tennessee cavalry, which became known as the West Tennessee Brigade. The core of this command centered around Richardson's own Twelfth Tennessee, the Thirteenth and Fourteenth Tennessee Cavalry Regiments, augmented at times by the temporary attachment of one or more other regiments or artillery batteries. Two days later, Richardson and his new brigade participated in a raid with General Chalmers on the Memphis and Charleston Railroad.

On 21 Nov. 1863 Richardson and the West Tennessee Brigade were transferred back to their native Tennessee to serve in the cavalry command led by another of Richardson's former associates, the brilliant Major General Nathan Bedford Forrest. On 3 December Richardson was appointed to the rank of brigadier general, to rank from December 1, and his brigade became the First Brigade of a division led by General Chalmers. In February 1864 he participated with Forrest in the spectacular repulse of Union General William Sooy Smith's expedition against Meridian, Miss. On 5 March his brigade, with that of Brigadier General L. S. Ross, attacked the Union garrison at Yazoo City, Miss., capturing the town with many stores and forcing the Union troops to take refuge in the strongest redoubt in the town's defenses. This gallant affair later caused Union forces to abandon the area altogether.

On 12 Mar. 1864 General Richardson was relieved of his command due to charges preferred by one of his regimental commanders, Colonel John Green, of the Twelfth Tennessee, the previous month. Once again, the *Official Records* do not disclose the nature of the offense or the proceedings that appear to have followed. It is certain, though, that because of these charges his nomination to the rank of brigadier general was returned by the Confederate Senate at the request of President Jefferson Davis on 9 Feb. 1864. These proceedings appear to have kept Richardson out of the field for some months, and during this time General Forrest, in a complete reorganization of his cavalry corps, found it necessary to dissolve the West Tennessee Brigade for administrative reasons and assign its regiments elsewhere. On 21 Oct. 1864 Richardson was ordered to return to the command of his Twelfth Tennessee Cavalry at his previous rank of colonel, serving in the brigade of Colonel Edmund Rucker, Chalmers's division of Forrest's command. In this capacity he served until the end of the war. He was surrendered and paroled with Lieutenant General Richard Taylor's army at Citronelle, Ala., on 4 May 1865.

After the war Richardson traveled abroad for a time and then returned to Memphis to take up civil engineering in levee and railroad building. Here he again had associations with his old commander, General Forrest. Later he moved his family to Hardeman County. Early in January 1870 he was engaged in the interest of a projected railroad and stopped on the night of 5 January at a tavern in Clarkton, Dunklin County, Mo. At about ten that evening he stepped out on the porch of the tavern to get a drink of water from a pail on the porch and was suddenly shot by an unknown assassin who was concealed behind a wagon in the yard. Richardson died early the next morning, and his body was returned to Memphis for burial in a family plot in Elmwood Cemetery. He and his wife, Mary E. Richardson, of Alabama, had three children: Robert, Jr., James W., and Mary.

SEE: C. A. Evans, ed., *Confederate Military History*, vols. 8, 12 (1899); Memphis *Public Ledger*, 11 Jan. 1870; Stewart Sifakis, ed., *Who Was Who in the Confederacy* (1988); U.S.

Census, 1860; *War of the Rebellion: The Official Records of the Union and Confederate Armies* (1885–1900); Ezra Warner, *Generals in Gray* (1959); Marcus J. Wright, *General Officers of the Confederate Army* (1911); Daniel J. Yanchisin (Memphis/Shelby County Public Library), correspondence.

PAUL BRANCH, JR.

Richardson, Willis *(5 Nov. 1889–8 Nov. 1977),* playwright, was born in Wilmington, the son of Willis Wilder and Agnes Ann Harper Richardson. After the riot of 1898, he moved with his parents from Wilmington to Washington, D.C. There he attended elementary schools from 1899 to 1906 and was graduated from the M Street High School in 1910. Richardson entered government service on 7 Mar. 1911 and on the fourteenth was appointed a skilled helper in the Wetting Division of the Bureau of Engraving and Printing. After receiving numerous promotions, he was appointed custodian of presses effective 17 Sept. 1936. He retired from the bureau in 1954. From 1916 to 1918 he prepared himself for playwrighting by taking correspondence courses in poetry and drama.

Richardson was the first black playwright to have a serious play produced on Broadway when *The Chip Woman's Fortune* opened at the Frazee Theatre on 15 May 1923. Earlier this play had opened in Chicago as a production of the Ethiopian Art Players (29 Jan. 1923), in Washington, D.C. (23 April), and on 7 May at the Lafayette Theater in Harlem. In the early twenties black drama groups were searching for plays by black writers, and Richardson was the first to fulfill this need with his black history plays and plays that "emphasized the physical strength, the nobility, and the courage of his heroes."

The Gilpin Players of Cleveland produced Richardson's *Compromise* at the Karamu Theater on 25 Feb. 1925, their first play by a black playwright. Reuben Silver, in his dissertation on the history of the Karamu Theater, praised Richardson for "urging the retention of the Negro heritage through the Arts." Among the other early black theater groups producing Richardson's plays were the Howard Players in Washington, D.C., and the Krigwa Players in New York.

Richardson was awarded the Amy Spingarn Prize in the drama contest conducted by *Crisis* magazine in 1925, with Eugene O'Neill as one of the judges. He won a second time in 1926 and received honorable mention in the *Opportunity* magazine drama contest in 1925. Richardson, whose play *The Idle Head* was published in *Carolina Magazine* (April 1929), was identified by the editor of this "Negro Play" number of the magazine as "the foremost playwright of the younger group." Recognized by Darwin Turner, critic of black theater, as the first significantly productive Afro-American playwright, Richardson wrote more than forty plays and edited two anthologies of plays by black writers, *Plays and Pageants from the Life of the Negro* (1930) and, with May Miller, *Negro History in Thirteen Plays* (1935).

In his plays and in the anthologies he edited, Richardson attempted to dramatize black heroes and to give a realistic view of black life. As early as 1919 in a *Crisis* magazine essay, he stated his philosophy and purpose of the plays he hoped to write: "the kind of play that shows the soul of a people." His plays reflected this philosophy throughout his writing career. Richardson was a member of the Dramatists' Guild of the Authors' League of America, the Harlem Cultural Council, and the National Association for the Advancement of Colored People.

Richardson married Mary Ellen Jones on 1 Sept. 1914, and they had three daughters: Jean Paula, Shirley Antonella, and Noel Justine. He was a Roman Catholic.

SEE: M. Marie Booth Foster, *Southern Black Creative Writers, 1829–1953* (1988); James V. Hatch, *Black Image on the American Stage* (1970); James V. Hatch and Omanii Abdullah, *Black Playwrights* (1977); Fannie E. F. Hicklin, "The American Negro Playwright" (Ph.D. diss., University of Wisconsin, 1965); Memoranda of Designations of Employees, Bureau of Engraving and Printing, Civil Archives Division, 1911–51 (Record Group 318, National Archives); Linda Metzger, *Black Writers* (1989); Bernard L. Peterson, Jr., "An Evaluation: Willis Richardson: Pioneer Playwright," *Black World* 24 (April 1975); Willis Richardson, "The Hope of a Negro Drama," *Crisis* 19 (November 1919), and interview, 1972 (audiotape in Hatch-Billops Archive, with duplicates in Cohen Library, CUNY, and in Schomburg); Theressa G. Rush, *Black American Writers, Past and Present* (1975); William F. Sherman (National Archives) to Pattie B. McIntyre, 8 Sept. 1982; Reuben Silver, "A History of the Karamu Theatre of Karamu House, 1915–1960" (Ph.D. diss., Ohio State University, 1961); Darwin T. Turner, *Black Drama in America* (1971); *Who's Who Among Black Americans* (1950); *Who's Who in Colored America* (1927–44).

PATTIE B. MCINTYRE

Ricks, (David) Peirson *(21 Aug. 1908–21 Apr. 1950),* writer, was born in Mayodan, the oldest of four children of David Absalom and Jessie Peirson Whitaker Ricks, both from Halifax County. Absalom Whitaker, Margaret Montgomery (Mrs. J. Hill Clay), and David Burton were his younger brothers and sister. When he was twelve, the family moved to Winston-Salem, where he attended public school. In 1925 he worked his way across the Atlantic to Glasgow, and during 1926–27 he attended The University of North Carolina, contributing to the literary magazine and providing cartoons for the humor publication. He dropped out of college to write a novel, but it went poorly. Off and on for more than five years, he worked in a Winston-Salem cotton mill, concurrently trying his hand at writing in various genres. At one juncture he quit the job to attend the Yale University School of Fine Arts on a scholarship, and at another to undergo surgery to correct a serious condition. A satire, *Bye-Bye Britches* (1936), was published by a vanity press with his own illustrations, but later the book embarrassed him and he attempted to round up all copies and destroy them. For four years (1936–40) he was a copywriter for a Philadelphia advertising firm, then for two more years he worked in New York in a similar capacity.

After returning to Winston-Salem and being five times rejected by the army, he was briefly employed by a technical school and then by the Office of Strategic Services in Washington, D.C. As a proofreader for the *Winston-Salem Journal*, and as an employee of several local advertising agencies, Ricks was restive. Of some fifty short stories—alternating between formula pieces for the "slicks" and more personally satisfying stories for the nonpaying little magazines—about twenty appeared in *Collier's*, *Today's Woman*, *Southwest Review*, *Story*, *Quarterly Review of Literature*, and others. His novel *The Hunter's Horn* came from Scribner's in 1947. Its central character is a seventeen-year-old boy snared in the social and economic confusion of eastern North Carolina before the turn of the century, and through him the novelist opposes the Puritan ethic of work and struggle with the survival of pagan hedonism from the Old South. The book was cordially reviewed, but its failure to sell plunged Ricks into despondency. Though he was in debt and was living with his parents, he began extensive research on a historical novel about the War of the Regulators under the working title "Eye of Darkness." His voluminous notes and cross-references became an insufferable burden, and once in a drunken malaise he seized the half-completed pages of the manuscript and "flung" them "into the air like large squares of confetti." Two months later he committed suicide.

His friend Frank Borden Hanes, over two decades after his death, wrote a moving account of Peirson Ricks and his luckless endeavors to establish himself as a writer of serious fiction. A member of the Episcopal church, Ricks was buried in Salem Cemetery.

SEE: Frank Borden Hanes, "Looking for Peirson Ricks," *North Carolina Historical Review* 51 (Spring 1974); *North Carolina Authors* (1952); Harry R. Warfel, *American Novelists of Today* (1951).

RICHARD WALSER

Ricks, Robert Henry *(4 Apr. 1839–1920)*, farmer and capitalist, was born in the Stony Creek section of Nash County, the son of David and Martha Vick Ricks. His ancestor Isaac Ricks, an early settler on the south side of the great falls of Tar River, owned much of the land where the city of Rocky Mount now stands. Robert Ricks attended the local schools until age sixteen, and when the Civil War broke out, he was working as a hired hand on the farm of a neighbor. Enlisting in the Confederate army as a private, young Ricks saw duty in Manly's Battery and in other batteries of light artillery. After the war he returned to farming in his native county. He became unusually successful, eventually farming on a large scale, and was a pioneer in introducing bright leaf tobacco culture in eastern North Carolina.

As his capital increased, Ricks branched out into business and prospered in manufacturing and banking. He became a director (1889) and then president (1899) of the Rocky Mount Mills, the second oldest cotton mill in the state. In 1894 he was named director and vice-president of the Bank of Rocky Mount and in 1902, vice-president of the Washington Cotton Mills in Virginia. In Rocky Mount he established the Ricks Hotel firm and the Thorpe and Ricks Tobacco Company and was involved in many other smaller business enterprises. For four years a member of the Nash County Board of Commissioners, he served in the state house of representatives in 1903 and the state senate in 1905. For many years Ricks was a member of the State Board of Education and of the board of directors of the state penitentiary. He was one of the first trustees of the North Carolina Agricultural and Mechanic College at Raleigh (now North Carolina State University), and Ricks Hall on the campus honors his memory.

At his own expense Ricks erected a large marble monument to the memory of the Bethel Heroes, the Nash and Edgecombe men who fought at Bethel Church, an episode in the Peninsular campaign in Virginia at the beginning of the Civil War. Of these men, Henry L. Wyatt was the first Confederate soldier to be killed in that long and bloody conflict. The monument, placed in Battle Park on the north side of the falls of the Tar River and located a hundred yards from the first post office of the then village of Rocky Mount, was unveiled on Confederate Memorial Day, 10 May 1917.

Ricks married Tempie Thorne of Nash County in 1874; they had no children. The couple resided in a large Victorian mansion that they built on her ancestral property near the village of Gold Rock, some miles northwest of Rocky Mount. Here they were buried in a marble mausoleum. At the time of his death, Ricks was one of the wealthiest men in eastern North Carolina. In his will, considered unusually enlightened for the time, he left his business partners the controlling interest in joint enterprises. The residual estate was left in trust, the annual income to be used for the education of the lineal descendants of his nieces and nephews.

SEE: Samuel A. Ashe, ed., *Biographical History of North Carolina*, vol. 5 (1906); Bugs Barringer, *A Pictorial History of Rocky Mount* (1977); Guy S. R. Concord, *The Ricks Family of America* (1908); Thomas E. Ricks, ed., *By Faith and Heritage Are We Joined: A Compilation of Nash County Historical Notes* (1976).

WILLIAM S. POWELL

Riddick, Elsie Garnett *(15 Nov. 1876–23 Dec. 1959)*, politician, suffragist, and advocate of woman's rights, was born on her father's farm six miles from Gatesville, the daughter of David Elbert and Cornelia Ann Speight Riddick. After attending the local schools, including a coeducational private academy in Gatesville until age fifteen, she entered the Normal and Industrial College for Women in Greensboro. With limited help from her family, she worked her way through college by setting tables and washing dishes. Because of her proficiency in spelling and arithmetic, she was enrolled in the business department and was graduated in 1895. Although few businesses at that time employed women as bookkeepers or secretaries, she found summer employment with the Greensboro Lumber Company. At the end of the season she returned home and was employed at the local high school in nearby Winton to teach "business subjects."

In 1897 a female stenographer with the North Carolina Agricultural Commission in Raleigh resigned after a black man was hired to distribute fertilizer tags. With the help of politicians and friends in both political parties, Elsie Riddick was named stenographer to the commission. Boardinghouses in the area refused to rent a room to a single woman who worked all day "with no one but a man," so she roomed with her uncle, Wallace C. Riddick, professor and later president of North Carolina State College. After two years she became secretary to the North Carolina Corporation Commission, a position she held for fifteen years. Her pay during these years in Raleigh was consistently $30 a month. She next became assistant executive secretary of the commission, and when she retired in 1949 as chief clerk, she concluded fifty-two years of service.

In January 1917 she attended a meeting of sixty-two women who formed the Equal Suffrage League of Raleigh. At that first assembly she was elected secretary of the league; a month later she became president and was named a delegate to a state convention meeting in Greensboro on 27 January. In March 1920 the women in Raleigh, Riddick among them, made their first move into politics. Without warning on the evening of the twenty-seventh, groups of women showed up at all the Democratic precinct meetings in the city and read statements demanding that they be allowed to participate in the gatherings. Riddick read a statement in her precinct saying that since thirty-five states had ratified the Nineteenth Amendment "and it is a certainty that we will vote in the next election . . . we have [the] right, therefore, to vote in this precinct meeting—just as any young man would who will become twenty-one years old prior to the next election." The tactics of the women succeeded.

As a reporter from the Raleigh *News and Observer* (28 Mar. 1920) declared, "The unexpectedness of the stroke gave the male Democrats no time to formulate any answer to the claims of the women to recognition." Six days later Riddick was one of the five women in Raleigh named as a delegate to the Democratic state convention.

Pleased with their success, Raleigh women tried again. In June 1920 Riddick and a small group of prominent women (including Mrs. T. W. Bickett, wife of the governor, and Dr. Delia Dixon-Carroll) consulted with some of the "leading men" of Raleigh as to the legality of going to the precincts and demanding to be registered. They hoped, if the Nineteenth Amendment passed, that women would be in a position to vote in the coming election. The amendment passed and as they had done before, the women made their plans in secret and descended on the unsuspecting registrars. Riddick later recalled: "Just as we arrived, we women stepped up. . . . We told them why we were there. They were so surprised they could not turn us down." Not long afterwards, Riddick was made chairman of her precinct, the first woman in Raleigh to hold that position. In later years she served as vice-chairman and then chairman of the Wake County Democratic Committee, secretary to the Democratic state committee, and a delegate to the Democratic National Convention in 1924.

At about the time Riddick became involved in politics, the National Business and Professional Women's Association was organized in St. Louis. North Carolina sent several women to the convention in 1919, but Riddick was not among them. The reason was that the association did not consider her a professional because she was a stenographer. Similarly, Riddick was not invited to the local organizational meetings in Raleigh, though upon application, the local organization later admitted her. Evidently, her leadership ability gained her respect and friends for, upon the resignation of the local president, she was elected to that post. At the September meeting of the state organization in Greensboro, Riddick was elected vice-president and she later succeeded to the presidency.

Throughout the 1920s she organized local associations around the state and lectured on her concern for rising young businesswomen, good government, international peace, and moral standards. In addition, she lobbied for the construction of a dormitory for women at Chapel Hill, an end to "the discrimination shown to the unaccompanied woman by the hotels," the creation of a women's bureau in the Department of Labor, and the founding of a loan fund to help young businesswomen. In response to this last concern, the Greensboro chapter of the National Business and Professional Women's Association created the Elsie Riddick Loan Fund in October 1924 to help finance business training for young women.

During this decade she served again as president of the state association and twice as vice-president of the national organization. She also was selected as one of the organizers of an association tour of six European countries. The group consisted of sixty association leaders who hoped to interest women abroad in forming similar organizations. Riddick presided at a meeting in Paris and managed to get a small organization started. She later remarked that the other countries "took lots of literature" and formed organizations later.

Despite her success as a leader in women's organizations and Democratic politics, Riddick did not advance in her business career. In 1921 she told the state convention that women should try to be more efficient and to equip themselves better for their work "and thus be in a position to demand higher things and larger rewards for their work."

Following her own advice over the next dozen years, by working quietly and efficiently as the assistant clerk of the Corporation Commission, she took on more responsibility in preparation for a better position. In late October 1933 she made her bid for that higher position. After receiving the thanks of several prominent Democratic politicians in the state for getting out the women's vote in Wake County that fall, Riddick and her friends launched a campaign directed by Lona Glidewell, superintendent of public welfare in Reidsville, to secure for her the post of chief clerk of the North Carolina Utilities Commission, which was slated to replace the old Corporation Commission. By this time Riddick was considered to be one of the best accountants in the state and an expert on North Carolina tax law. She had the backing of the club women of the state as well as some prominent Democratic politicians, including Senator Josiah Bailey. The incumbent chief clerk, R. O. Self, was said to be "no slouch of a politician" himself. Self and his friends began a letter-writing campaign of their own, which led the *Raleigh Times* to predict that the matter would have to be resolved by Governor J. C. B. Ehringhaus.

Stanley Winborne, head of the commission, told Riddick's supporters that he intended to keep Riddick in her present position. He contended that, because of the depression, the chief clerk's position had to be merged with the job of director of Truck and Bus Operations, which by law required a person experienced in these matters, which Self was. But aside from these technical requirements, Winborne implied that the job would be too much work and too difficult for Riddick: "Due to [the] lack of finances, this State had placed quite a burden on the Chief Clerk and it is a very difficult position to handle. The clerical work is a very small part of it." To Winborne, Riddick would always be a secretary and would never be capable of holding an administrative post. In late January, when it became apparent that the pressure had not been sufficient to secure the job for Riddick, her friends tried to get her salary increased. They claimed that, with the depression on, her salary was 56 percent below the 1930 rate while "others in the same department were out only forty per cent." In this effort Riddick and her friends met with some success, although they did not get her salary restored to the same rate as her coworkers.

Riddick's own words written in the September 1922 issue of *Tar Heel Banker* had come back to haunt her. She had complained then that businessmen hired many women as secretaries but trained them for higher work and required them to do that work without receiving the title or pay to which they were entitled. It was not until 1949, just three months before her retirement, that Elsie Riddick was appointed chief clerk of the Utilities Commission.

In December 1925 the state named Riddick a delegate to the Pan American Commercial Congress in New York City, and in March 1926 she was made an honorary member of the American Woman's Association, the first from North Carolina. She became president of the North Carolina League of Women Voters in 1930 and was appointed secretary to the Raleigh Civil Service Commission in 1935 and 1938. She belonged to the Daughters of the American Revolution, the Women's National Democratic Club, and the Baptist church. In 1955 she retired to Gatesville, where she spent the remainder of her life and where she was buried.

SEE: *Alumnae News*, Woman's College of the University of North Carolina, July 1927, February 1928, February, July 1931; *Busy North Carolina Women* (1931); *Monthly News*, North Carolina League of Women Voters (November 1923, February 1925, May, October, December 1930, April, May 1931, April 1932; *North Carolina Federation of Business and Professional Women's Clubs Yearbook* (1927–28); *Proceedings*, National Association of Railroad and Utilities Commissioners, 38th Annual Convention, Asheville, N.C. (1926); Raleigh *News and Observer*, 25 Dec. 1959; Elsie G. Riddick Papers (Southern Historical Collection, University of North Carolina, Chapel Hill [portrait]); *Tar Heel Banker*, September 1922, January 1924; *Tar Heel Woman*, December 1931; *Woman's Club Year Book* of Raleigh (1917–47).

WAYNE K. DURRILL

Riddick, Joseph *(d. September 1818)*, political leader, was likely born in that portion of Perquimans County that became a part of Gates County in 1779. He may have been the son of Joseph and Hannah Riddick. His surname sometimes appears in contemporary records as Reddick, perhaps suggesting its pronunciation. One Joseph Riddick was named to the committee of safety for Chowan County on 15 Oct. 1776. As early as 1797 Riddick was referred to as colonel in county records, but by 1808 he was called general.

A Jeffersonian Republican, he represented the new county of Gates in the House of Commons for four sessions between 1781 and 1785 and in the senate for twenty-seven consecutive terms between 1785 and 1811 and again in 1815 and 1817. He did not serve in the four sessions that met between 1812 and 1816, although he remained active during this period (as he had before and would continue to do until the year before his death) as a justice of the county court, executor of numerous estates, guardian of orphans, and auditor of estates for the county court. It is possible that the War of 1812, which occurred while he was not in the Assembly, may somehow have accounted for his absence from that body. Nevertheless, he sat in the North Carolina General Assembly for a total of thirty-three terms and was speaker of the senate as well for eleven terms between 1800 and 1811, failing of election to that post only in 1805.

Early in his legislative career Riddick became chairman of the finance committee and often served on the committee of claims. In 1791 he voted in favor of a loan of five thousand pounds to the trustees of The University of North Carolina. In 1805, 1807, and 1808 bills to establish a penitentiary were defeated. In 1810, when he was speaker of the senate, a similar bill, which also liberalized the code of punishment for crime, passed the house but the senate vote was tied, 30 to 30. Riddick, although personally in favor, broke the tie by voting against the bill. He explained his vote by saying that he did not want the responsibility of creating a new criminal system for the state.

He represented Gates County in the convention of 1788 in Hillsborough, which declined to ratify the U.S. Constitution as well as in the convention of 1789 at Fayetteville, which did ratify it. In both instances, Riddick supported adoption of the Constitution.

Riddick in 1789 owned 2,126 acres of land in Gates County, 189 in Tyrrell, and 640 in Cumberland. His household at the time of the 1790 census consisted of two males over age sixteen, one under that age, four females, and fifteen slaves. In 1800 there were six males, four females, and twenty-one slaves; ten years later there were five males and five females but only six slaves.

His will, dated 24 July 1818, mentions his wife Ann; sons Reuben, Isaiah, and Arthur; daughters Hannah Rogerson, Easter Billups, Avis Eason, and Mabel Hill; and grandsons Josiah, Kedar, and Nathan Riddick, Mills Hill, Langley Billups, Solomon Eason, and Jesse Rogerson.

SEE: Sandra L. Almasy, comp., *Gates County, North Carolina: Wills—Book 1, 1779–1807* (1984), *Book 2, 1807–1838* (1985); John L. Cheney, comp., *North Carolina Government, 1585–1979* (1981); Walter Clark, ed., *State Records of North Carolina*, vol. 22 (1907); R. D. W. Connor, comp., *A Documentary History of the University of North Carolina, 1776–1799*, vol. 1 (1953); Guion G. Johnson, *Ante-Bellum North Carolina* (1937); Griffith J. McRee, *Life and Correspondence of James Iredell*, vol. 2 (1858); William C. Pool, "An Economic Interpretation of the Ratification of the Federal Constitution in North Carolina," *North Carolina Historical Review* 27 (1950); Raleigh *Register*, 9 Oct. 1818; William L. Saunders, ed., *Colonial Records of North Carolina*, vol. 10 (1890).

WILLIAM S. POWELL

Riddick, Thomas Moore *(3 Jan. 1907–26 May 1975)*, consulting engineer and chemist, was born in Woodville, Perquimans County, the son of Dr. Thomas Moore and Lucy Gatling Cowper Riddick. He attended public schools in Elizabeth City before entering The University of North Carolina, from which he was graduated with a bachelor of science degree in civil engineering (1931) and a master of science degree in sanitary engineering (1932). His schooling had been interrupted while he worked for the North Carolina and Virginia highway and bridge departments.

After leaving Chapel Hill he was employed as an assistant engineer with the North Carolina State Health Department to conduct a pollution survey in connection with shellfish. In September 1932 he joined the faculty of New York University, where he remained for two years as an instructor in hydraulic and sanitary engineering. Afterwards he worked in New York City as an engineer and chemist with Nicholas Hill, Jr.

In 1936 Riddick established his own engineering and chemical consulting firm, which—except during the years between 1943 and 1945, when he served as a major in the Public Health Service in Ethiopia—he managed for the rest of his life. In one of his catalogues he noted that "our professional field is design of municipal and industrial water and waste treatment plants, pumping stations, pipelines, standpipes, elevated tanks, submarine intakes and outfalls, and like installations. We are equipped to handle work of any size, either in or out of the United States." The business included a chemical and bacteriological laboratory. His firm, Thomas M. Riddick and Associates, continued after his death to design and supervise the construction of waterworks and waste treatment plants under the leadership of Norman L. Lindsay, a business associate of nearly thirty years to whom the firm was bequeathed.

While working in Alaska, Riddick experienced a problem with coagulation. This led him to study Zeta potential, a theory of coagulation and dispersion developed in 1879 by German physicist Hermann von Helmholtz. Riddick subsequently invented the Zeta-Meter, an electronic instrument for rapidly measuring the Zeta potential, that is, the amount of the electrokinetic charge, expressed in millivolts, surrounding particulate matter suspended in liquid. By 1960 he organized Zeta-Meter, Inc., to manufacture and market the new instrument, for which he obtained a number of patents. In due time more than a thousand Zeta-Meters were in use around the world in such varied fields as atomic energy, medical research, petroleum, petrochemicals, pulp and paper, pharmaceuticals, aluminum, cosmetics, latex, asphalt, paint, and fibers, as well as in water and waste treatment plants.

In this field Riddick developed a number of innovations such as the first velocity-controlled siphons, the first floating aerators for inducing circulation in large reservoirs, and the first water treatment plant to operate solely on the basis of Zeta potential control. He had an inventive mind, frequently working for several days without sleep on a new idea. His inventiveness, not confined to his business, assisted him in creating innovations in photography and recording equipment. The author of *Control of Colloid Stability through Zeta Potential* (1968), a book offering a detailed study of Zeta potential, he also wrote a number of articles for technical journals involving sanitary engineering, chemical engineering, hematology, and cardiology. His *Heart Disease—A New Approach to Prevention and Control* (1970) discussed his findings from over fifteen years' research on blood and heart disease.

Riddick spoke at a number of scientific symposia throughout the country. In 1952, while addressing the prestigious American Philosophical Society, an organization established in the 1740s by Benjamin Franklin, he debunked the widely read *Henry Gross and His Dowsing Rod* by Kenneth Roberts.

While a student at The University of North Carolina, Riddick was a member of the Episcopal church, but at the time of his death he belonged to the Unitarian church. He was also a member of the American Society of Civil Engineers, the American Public Health Association, the Federation of Sewage Works Association, the National Society of Professional Engineers, and the American Chemical Society.

From his youth Riddick had a love for the sea, ships, and fishermen. His last boat, a 32-foot Grand Banks trawler, *KoKo III*, was a seagoing yacht built in Hong Kong. It was equipped with advanced navigational devices, some of which he developed himself. He also enjoyed collecting and retelling tales of North Carolina fishermen.

Riddick was married three times: on 16 Sept. 1933 to Regina M. V. Scanlon, on 2 Aug. 1953 to Mary Elizabeth Gould, and on 23 Feb. 1975 to Jane Lynott Carroll. He had no children. He died at Huntington, Long Island, N.Y., and at his request his ashes were spread on Long Island Sound following a funeral service at the local Unitarian Fellowship.

SEE: Alumni Files (University of North Carolina, Chapel Hill); *Nat. Cyc. Am. Biog.*, vol. 60 (1981 [portrait]).

B. W. C. ROBERTS

Riddick, Wallace Carl *(5 Aug. 1864–9 June 1942)*, educator and engineer, was born in Wake County, the son of Wiley Goodman and Anna Jones Riddick. After attending Wake Forest College for two years, he transferred to The University of North Carolina and received a B.A. degree in 1885. He then studied civil engineering at Lehigh University in Pennsylvania, receiving a C.E. degree in 1890. Riddick returned to Wake County and was a practicing civil engineer for two years. In 1892 he joined the faculty of the North Carolina College of Agriculture and Mechanic Arts (now North Carolina State University) in Raleigh as professor of mechanics and applied mathematics. He became head of the Civil Engineering Department when it was established in 1895 and remained in this post until elected vice-president of the college in 1908. Riddick continued to teach courses in civil engineering as well as act as an engineering consultant.

In 1916, when the presidency became vacant through the resignation of Dr. D. H. Hill, Riddick was selected from a long list of candidates to head the college. His administration (1916–23), which spanned the war years and the period immediately following, was marked by rapid change. When a unit of the Student Army Training Corps was established at the college in October 1918, the institution's curricula were revised to meet the military's requirements and the whole student body was organized into a military corps. Following the armistice, the unit was demobilized and a unit of the Reserve Officers Training Corps was reestablished on the campus. In 1917 the name of the college was changed to the North Carolina State College of Agriculture and Engineering. The departments of architecture, education, highway engineering, and business administration also were established during Riddick's administration. A number of improvements were made in the physical plant, and new buildings were erected for agricultural extension (Ricks Hall) and mechanical engineering (Page Hall). A fund-raising drive was initiated and construction was begun on the Memorial Tower to honor the alumni who had given their lives in World War I. A student government was formed and two publications were founded: *Alumni News* and *The Technician* (student newspaper).

Because of the increased enrollment after the war, President Riddick felt that the administrative organization of the college was inadequate and that a reorganization was essential. After discussions with the board of trustees and the U.S. commissioner of education, it was decided that a survey should be made by an expert in higher education. Dr. George F. Zook of the U.S. Bureau of Education performed the study in March 1923 and later submitted his report. Among his recommendations was that the resident teaching be organized into four main divisions: agriculture, engineering, general sciences, and social sciences and business administration, with a dean in charge of each division. The executive committee of the board of trustees recommended that the board adopt the report with modifications and proceed with the organization of separate schools. Riddick had already advised the trustees that if a School of Engineering was established, he would like to resign the presidency and become dean of engineering. At its meeting on 28 May 1923, the board adopted the general principles of organization outlined in the Zook report, accepted Riddick's resignation, and appointed him first dean of the new School of Engineering.

Riddick organized and for the next fourteen years effectively administered the largest school in the college. On retiring in 1937, he became dean emeritus of engineering and professor of hydraulics. In 1951 the Riddick Engineering Laboratories building was named in his memory.

Riddick had played football at Lehigh University and maintained a lifelong interest in athletics. In 1898 and 1899 he served as football coach at the College of Agriculture and Mechanic Arts, and for many years he was a member of the athletics council. During the 1912–13 football season the college's football stadium was named in his honor.

On 18 Oct. 1893 Riddick married Lillian Daniel. They had five children: Wallace Whitfield, Lillian Ivy (Mrs. Julian Rand), Narcissa Daniel (Mrs. William D. Dewar), Anna Ivy Jones, and Eugenia Trovers (Mrs. Frederick Steck).

Riddick was instrumental in organizing the North Carolina Society of Engineers in 1918. He received honorary LL.D. degrees from Wake Forest College and Lehigh University in 1917 and a doctor of engineering degree from

North Carolina State in 1939. He died in Baltimore, Md., and was buried in Raleigh's Oakwood Cemetery.

SEE: "Faculty and Staff News Releases and Clippings," Wallace C. Riddick (Archives, North Carolina State University, Raleigh); David A. Lockmiller, *History of the North Carolina State College, 1889–1939* (1939); *Who Was Who in America, 1943–1950*, vol. 2 (1950).

MAURICE S. TOLER

Ridley, Dan *(ca. 1744–April 1777)*, Revolutionary patriot, was probably the son of Nathaniel Ridley II of Southampton County, Va., and his wife Priscilla Applewhaite. As a young man, Ridley moved across the line from Southampton County, Va., to Hertford County, N.C., where he became active in the movement that led to the American Revolution. A member of the committee of safety for the Edenton District, he represented Hertford County in the Third, Fourth, and Fifth Provincial congresses held at Hillsborough and Halifax between August 1775 and December 1776. He was present when the Halifax Resolves were adopted and when the Declaration of Rights and the State Constitution were drawn up. He also served as paymaster for troops in his district. His promising career was cut short by his death at a young age. By his wife Martha, daughter of Timothy Thorpe, he had sons, Nathaniel and Timothy, and daughters, Margaret and Martha.

SEE: Henry W. Lewis, *Southampton Ridleys and Their Kin* (1961); William L. Saunders, ed., *Colonial Records of North Carolina*, vol. 10 (1890); Benjamin B. Winborne, *Colonial and State Political History of Hertford County* (1906).

CLAIBORNE T. SMITH, JR.

Rieusset, John *(d. 1763)*, colonial official, despite his French name immigrated to North Carolina from Dublin, Ireland, where he had been a merchant. His brother Peter had been a resident of Bath when he died in 1734 and left John all of his property in the colony. By 1740 John settled in Beaufort County, where he was a justice of the peace ten years later. In September 1750 he was removed as justice for failing to appear before the Council to answer charges of extralegal practices.

The following year, however, he was nominated to the Royal Council by Governor Gabriel Johnston. Rieusset took his seat on 2 Apr. 1753. By 1754 he had moved to the Albemarle region and was a colonel in the Perquimans County militia. During this period he purchased Hayes Plantation near Edenton and became collector of the port of Roanoke around 1755. His star continued to rise as he became chief baron of the exchequer early in 1758, but by late 1759 he had become severely ill. His attendance at Council meetings virtually ceased, and he died in the late summer or early fall of 1763. Rieusset apparently never married and left the bulk of his estate to his only brother, David, who was in Jamaica.

SEE: Chowan County Wills (North Carolina State Archives, Raleigh); William L. Saunders, ed., *Colonial Records of North Carolina*, vols. 4–6 (1886–88).

WILLIAM S. PRICE, JR.

Rights, Douglas LeTell *(11 Sept. 1891–1 Dec. 1956)*, bishop-elect of the Moravian church, historian, and author, was born in Salem, the son of George Hanes and Emma Jones Rights. George Rights was an editor for the locally published *Union Republican* newspaper. Douglas Rights was graduated in 1905 from the Salem Boys School, where his grandfather had taught, and in 1913 he received the A.B. degree from The University of North Carolina. In 1915 he was graduated from the Moravian Theological Seminary at Bethlehem, Pa. After a year of further study, the Divinity School of Harvard University granted him the bachelor of sacred theology degree in 1916.

In October 1916 Rights was ordained and called to the First Moravian Church in Greensboro and served until entering the U.S. Army as chaplain in 1918. In 1919 he became pastor of the Trinity Moravian Church, in Salem, where he remained until his death thirty-seven years later. During his tenure the church grew from about 200 to more than 850 members. In 1947 Moravian College and Theological Seminary conferred on him the honorary doctor of divinity degree. On 15 Nov. 1956 Rights was elected bishop of the Moravian church while he was in the hospital recovering from a heart attack. He died unexpectedly a few days later before he could be consecrated.

When he was a child, Douglas Rights found an arrowhead and this began his abiding interest in Indians. His very large and comprehensive personal collection of Indian artifacts, part of which was placed in the Wachovia Historical Museum in Winston-Salem and part at The University of North Carolina, plus years of study on the subject gained him an international reputation as an authority on North Carolina Indians. Several articles and two books grew out of this interest: *A Voyage Down the Yadkin-Great Peedee River* (1929) and *The American Indian in North Carolina* (1947). Another result was that he helped to organize the Archaeological Society of North Carolina and was its first president. He also served as a director of the Eastern States Archaeological Foundation.

Rights's linguistic ability led him to translate church articles and books by German and French authors. His most important undertaking in this line was editing and translating, from German script, volume 8 of *The Records of the Moravians in North Carolina*. In 1950 Rights was named archivist of the Moravian Church, Southern Province, a position he filled until his death six years later.

A deep concern with the horrors and waste of war prompted Rights, a month before his death, to suggest to the dean that Harvard Divinity School offer a course entitled "War: Its Causes, Prevention, and Cure." The dean recommended that a lectureship be established to bring outstanding world leaders to the campus who should propose ways in which Christianity could aid the cause of peace. Rights concurred and sent a check for a thousand dollars to start the fund. "The purpose of the contribution," he wrote, "is to try to provide a way of helping people to be conscious of a recurring danger and to study war as physicians do a dangerous disease." After Rights's death his family added to the endowment fund and the first Douglas L. Rights Peace Lecture was given at Harvard Divinity School on 5 May 1960.

Rights was known throughout the area for his friendliness to all people, his enthusiasm, and his twinkling dark brown eyes which attested to his delightful sense of humor. For these qualities as well as his scholarship he was in demand as a speaker. He was a member of many organizations, including the North Carolina Literary and Historical Association, and sat on the board of editors of the *North Carolina Historical Review*. He joined the local American Legion Post, which he served as chaplain and commander; the Forty and Eight; the Red Cross; and the local Kiwanis Club, of which he was a charter member.

At the time of his death he was lieutenant governor of the Piedmont Colony, Society of Mayflower Descendants in North Carolina; president of the Wachovia Historical Society; and vice-president of Old Salem, Inc., an office he had held since its organization. Rights had been the first chairman of Old Salem's committee on antiquities and archives. He was a Mason and served as grand historian of Salem Lodge.

Active in the Boy Scout movement, he received the Silver Beaver Award for approximately twenty years of service. Rights served on many provincial and interprovincial boards of the Moravian church, was a trustee of Salem College, and at one time taught history at Salem Academy and College. He wrote several hymns, perhaps the best known being "Veiled in Darkness Judah Lay," written in 1915 and included in the hymnals of several denominations. He also published two pieces for band, "Tar Heel March," based on The University of North Carolina alma mater, and "Salem Square March."

On 15 June 1920 Rights married Cecil Leona Burton, and they had five children: Burton Jones and Graham Henry (both of whom became Moravian ministers), Eleanor (Mrs. Gerald W. Roller), Douglas LeTell, who died in infancy, and George LeTell, who died in the Korean War. Rights was buried in the Moravian Graveyard, Winston-Salem. An oil portrait of him hangs in the Douglas L. Rights Memorial Chapel, Trinity Moravian Church, Winston-Salem.

SEE: Anna W. Bair, personal recollections; Daniel L. Grant, *Alumni History of the University of North Carolina* (1924); Memorial of Douglas LeTell Rights (Moravian Archives, Winston-Salem, N.C.); Raleigh *News and Observer*, 2 Dec. 1956; *Who's Who in the South and Southwest* (1952); *Winston-Salem Journal and Sentinel*, 2 Dec. 1956 and archives, Winston-Salem; Winston-Salem *Twin City Sentinel*, 1 Dec. 1956.

ANNA WITHERS BAIR

Rippy, James Fred *(27 Oct. 1892–10 Feb. 1977)*, historian and educator, was born in a log house near Nubia, in Sumner County, Tenn., the son of Robert Sidney and Mary Frances Grant Rippy. He grew up on a subsistence farm until a fire that destroyed several of their buildings forced his parents to join relatives in Richardson, Tex., in 1902. In Texas, Rippy was graduated from Richardson High School in 1907 and entered Southwestern University, Georgetown, in 1909, where he became a member of Kappa Alpha fraternity and was a champion orator and debater. Elected to Phi Beta Kappa, he was graduated in 1913 and then taught for one year at Clebarro College, a small Campbellite school in Cleburne, Tex.

In the fall of 1914 Rippy enrolled at Vanderbilt University as a graduate student in history; he stayed one year, receiving a master of arts degree. On 19 Aug. 1915 he married Mary Dozier Allen, of Nashville, Tenn., the daughter of Purdy McFerrin and Bettie Dozier Allen. For the next two years Rippy taught at the Duncan School for Boys in Nashville before accepting a Native Sons Fellowship to the University of California in 1917.

At Berkeley, Rippy studied Hispanic American history under the direction of Herbert Eugene Bolton. After his dissertation, "The Relations of the United States and Mexico, 1848–1860," was accepted for the Ph.D. degree in 1920, Rippy was named to an instructorship in Latin American history at the University of Chicago. There his excellent record of publication and effective teaching earned him rapid promotion—to assistant professor in 1923 and to associate professor the next year. In 1924 Rippy taught at the summer school of The University of North Carolina. In the spring of 1926, while a visiting professor at Stanford University, he was offered a full professorship at Duke University, which was then in the midst of its initial expansion program. Desirous of returning to his native South, Rippy accepted the appointment and assumed his duties in the fall.

In Durham his career continued to advance. He was a popular lecturer, an editor of the Duke University Press (1929–36), and a productive scholar. His publications included a biography of Joel R. Poinsett (1935) and an edition of Furnifold M. Simmons's papers and memoirs (1936). In 1935 Rippy served as a U.S. delegate to the Pan-American Conference on History and Geography. He held both Guggenheim (1927) and Carnegie (1928) fellowships. In 1933–34 he was president of the North Carolina Literary and Historical Association. He also sat on the editorial boards of the *Hispanic-American Historical Review* and the *American Historical Review*.

In 1936 Rippy returned to the University of Chicago, where he stayed until his retirement in 1958. During his distinguished career he directed over one hundred theses and dissertations in his field, and he wrote, edited, and was coauthor of over a score of major publications. In 1960 he received the William Volker Award for distinguished service as a scholar and teacher, and in 1961 Southwestern University honored him with the D.Litt. degree.

Rippy was the father of three sons: James Fred, Jr., Robert Allen, and Frazier Winston. He was a member of the San Martin Society and the Bolivarian Society of the United States. Upon retirement, Rippy and his wife returned to Durham, where they lived until poor health necessitated a move to Wilmington in 1972. Rippy, a Democrat and a Methodist, died in Wilmington and was buried in Oakdale Cemetery.

SEE: *American Authors and Books* (1972); Biographical File, Duke University Archives (Durham); Raleigh *News and Observer*, 4 July 1936; J. Fred Rippy, *Bygones I Cannot Help Recalling* (1966); *Wilmington Morning Star*, 12 Feb. 1977.

MARK C. STAUTER

Robbins, Karl *(1892–12 Mar. 1960)*, textile manufacturer and philanthropist, was born near Kiev, Russia, and in 1905 moved to New York, where his father had already been living for four years and operating a small clothing store. Clothing and fabrics interested Karl Robbins, and he began buying and selling fabrics in New England.

Robbins first purchased goods from small manufacturers of dress goods, but as he became more established in textiles he began to buy from large firms such as the Burlington Mills Corporation. By the late 1920s he was a stockholder in Burlington Mills. In 1930 he bought the Pinehurst Silk Mills, Inc., in Hemp, N.C., and began working to make his mill a leader in the production of rayon. The mill continuously expanded and improved; it was so prosperous that there was no period of unemployment, even during the worst of the Great Depression.

Recognized for his interest in his employees and the people of Hemp, Robbins made many improvements in the mill to provide more comfortable working conditions and he initiated work bonuses and low-cost insurance programs. For the town of Hemp he financed many projects, such as the building of a baseball park, a community center, tennis courts, and a playground and improvements to the local schools and churches. He was also responsible for lowering the town tax rate, paving streets and sidewalks, providing a dial telephone system, and buying a new fire truck. In 1943 the town's name was changed to Robbins in his honor.

By acquiring textile plants in Red Springs, Aberdeen, and Rocky Mount, N.C., and in Clarksville, Va., Robbins developed a textile empire. In addition, he built a large plant in Raeford that afterwards was operated by Burlington Mills. In 1954 he sold 41 percent of the common stock of Robbins Mills to J. P. Stevens and Company and retired to devote himself to philanthropy.

Robbins was generous with his wealth. He served as chairman of the Research Triangle Committee during its planning stages and donated over 4,000 acres to the state for the site of the research park. He founded a medical school at Yeshiva University in New York City and was a founder of the Federation of Jewish Philanthropies of New York and a patron of the New York University–Bellevue Medical Center. In 1951 he established the Karl Robbins Scholarship Fund at the Massachusetts Institute of Technology to further textile technology.

Although Robbins resided in Pinehurst, his permanent address was New York City. He and his wife Mary had three children: Edgar, Allan, and Anita. He died in New York City.

SEE: *Greensboro Daily News*, 14 Mar. 1960; *New York Times*, 14 Mar. 1960 (portrait); *Robbins Record*, 17 Mar. 1960; *We the People of North Carolina* 15 (October 1957).

WARREN L. BINGHAM

Robbins, Parker David *(1834–1 Nov. 1917)*, soldier, legislator, and inventor, was born in Bertie County, the son of John A. Robbins; his mother's name is unknown. A mulatto with Chowan Indian ancestors, Robbins was regarded as a free black. He had a common school education and before the Civil War acquired a 102-acre farm, in part with money earned as a carpenter and a mechanic. In 1863 he went to Norfolk, Va., and enlisted in the Union army; Robbins attained the rank of sergeant-major in the Second U.S. Colored Cavalry before his resignation in 1866 due to illness. Returning to his home in Colerain Township, Bertie County, he was one of fifteen blacks elected to the 1868 constitutional convention. He also was one of nineteen blacks elected to the 1869–70 term in the state house of representatives. The 1870 census recorded him as a 35-year-old farmer in a household consisting of 29-year-old Elizabeth, presumably his wife, whose occupation was housekeeper, and a 17-year-old mulatto female whose name is illegible in the manuscript census.

Under the national Republican administration, Robbins was named postmaster of the town of Harrellsville. While holding this position he invented and secured a patent for a new kind of cotton cultivator and a device to sharpen saws. In 1877, with the return of Democrats to power, he resigned as postmaster and soon afterwards moved to Duplin County, where he established a sawmill and a cotton gin. While there he built a steamboat, the *St. Peter*, which plied the Cape Fear River. He also built some houses in the town of Magnolia.

There is a photograph of Robbins in military uniform in the State Archives, Raleigh. The 1917 death certificate for Robbins indicates that he was married and that he was buried in his home burial ground.

SEE: Census return, 1870, Bertie County; John L. Cheney, Jr., ed., *North Carolina Government, 1585–1979* (1981); Death certificate (North Carolina State Archives, Raleigh); J. G. de Roulhac Hamilton, *Reconstruction in North Carolina* (1914); Thomas C. Parramore, *North Carolina: The History of an American State* (1983 [portrait]).

WILLIAM S. POWELL

Robbins, William McKendree *(26 Oct. 1828–3 May 1905)*, educator, lawyer, and legislator, was born in Randolph County to Ahi and Mary Brown Robbins. He received his early education at subscription schools and at a local academy before attending Randolph-Macon College, from which he was graduated in 1851. For the next two years he was professor of mathematics at Normal College (later Trinity College) near High Point.

On 7 Sept. 1854 he married Mary Montgomery of Montville, S.C. In 1855 the couple moved to Glennville, Ala., where Robbins opened a female college. He soon abandoned teaching, qualified for the Alabama bar, and started a legal practice in Selma, Ala. Robbins's young wife died in the autumn of 1858, leaving him with two small children.

In January 1861 Robbins volunteered as a private in the Marion (Ala.) Rifles. Two months later he helped organize the Fourth Alabama Regiment, in which he served as a first lieutenant in Company G. Robbins's first action in the war was with the conquering troops at the Harpers Ferry, Va., federal arsenal on 18 Apr. 1861. He served under General James Longstreet and fought in the major Virginia campaigns of the war, in Tennessee, and at Gettysburg; in 1864 he received a serious head wound at the Battle of the Wilderness. Robbins was present at the surrender at Appomattox Court House and by that time had attained the rank of major.

Robbins returned to North Carolina in December 1865 to open a law office in Salisbury. He had married his first wife's sister, Martha Montgomery, during the war.

Elected to the North Carolina Senate from Rowan and Davie counties in 1868 and 1870, Robbins supported the impeachment of Governor William W. Holden. In 1872 he was elected to the U.S. House of Representatives from the Seventh North Carolina District and soon afterwards moved his permanent residence to Statesville. He was returned to Congress in 1874 and 1876 and in his last term served on the Ways and Means Committee. An ardent conservative Democrat and prohibitionist, he was an outspoken opponent of Republicanism, Negro suffrage, and the internal revenue tax on whiskey.

Robbins failed to win renomination for the congressional seat in 1878. He received the nomination in 1880 but lost the general election to the Liberal, antiprohibition candidate, Tyre York, in a bitterly contested campaign that focused on the Prohibition issue.

In 1878 Robbins returned to Statesville, where he began a law partnership with his son-in-law, Judge Benjamin Franklin Long. In 1894 President Grover Cleveland appointed him Confederate commissioner of the Gettysburg Battle Field Commission, a post Robbins retained until his death. He was a charter member of the Southern History Association in 1896.

Characterized by a local newspaper editor as "truly a great orator," Robbins participated in congressional debates on many issues of his day. His 1898 speech at Gettysburg in defense of secession was widely praised. A lifelong Methodist, he became a Presbyterian late in life to protest the Methodist Episcopal Church, South's procurement of a congressional appropriation for war losses.

Robbins died at the home of his son Frank in Salisbury after an acute stomach illness of one month and was buried in Oakwood Cemetery, Statesville. He was survived by his daughter by his first marriage, Mary Alice (Long), and by his second wife and their three children,

Gertrude (Wood), Maude (McLaughlin), and Frank. Robbins's son Willis by his first marriage and his son Montgomery by his second marriage predeceased Robbins, as did his wards Congressman Gaston Ahi Robbins and Mamie Lafayette Robbins, the children of Robbins's brother Julius.

SEE: *Biog. Dir. Am. Cong.* (1971); *Charlotte Daily Observer*, 4 May 1905; Jerome Dowd, *Sketches of Prominent Living North Carolinians* (1888); Homer M. Keever, *Iredell, Piedmont County* (1976); *Publications of the Southern History Association* 9, no. 5 (1905); Raleigh *News and Observer*, 4–6 May 1905; William McKendree Robbins Papers (Southern Historical Collection, University of North Carolina, Chapel Hill).

BRENDA MARKS EAGLES

Roberts, Edward Gallatin *(26 Oct. 1878–25 Feb. 1931)*, attorney and public official, was born in Flat Creek, Buncombe County, the son of Mary Elizabeth Buckner and Jacob R. Roberts. He attended Weaverville College, Washington College, and King College, the latter two institutions in Tennessee. After teaching school for several years he entered Wake Forest College in 1902 to study law. Admitted to the bar in 1904, he established his practice in Asheville and was county attorney in 1911 and 1912, represented Buncombe County in the General Assembly in 1911, 1913, 1915, and 1917, and was mayor of Asheville from 1919 to 1923 and from 1927 to December 1930, when he resigned. In the General Assembly he supported the adoption of the Australian (secret) ballot and introduced a bill to secure it for his county. He also worked diligently for woman suffrage and in 1917 introduced a bill in the legislature to confer municipal suffrage on women.

Roberts also held various local posts in the Democratic party, was a popular speaker during World War I, and was active in the Presbyterian church as an elder and a teacher of the men's Bible class. He was twice elected president of the North Carolina Forestry Association. In addition, he was president of the State Municipal Association for three terms, a director of the Bank of West Asheville, and a member of the board of the Central Bank and Trust Company. Early in December 1930 the Central Bank failed with more than $4 million in city funds on deposit. Six public officials and eleven bankers were charged with conspiracy. Protesting his innocence and that of several others who had been accused, Gallatin Roberts committed suicide in an office above the bank. He left a long, moving note addressed to the people of Asheville in which he reminded them of his long years of service, concluding: "My soul is sensitive, and it has been wounded unto death. I have given my life for my city, and I am innocent. I did what I thought was right."

In 1907 Roberts married Mary Altha Sams, and they were the parents of two children, Edward Gallatin, Jr., and Margaret Evelyn.

SEE: *Asheville Citizen*, 26 Feb. 1931; John L. Cheney, Jr., ed, *North Carolina Government, 1585–1979* (1981); *North Carolina Biography*, vol. 4 (1928); Raleigh *News and Observer*, 26 Feb. 1931; A. Elizabeth Taylor, "The Woman Suffrage Movement in North Carolina," *North Carolina Historical Review* 38 (January, April 1961).

WILLIAM S. POWELL

Roberts, Elizabeth Bond *(5 June 1801–8 Nov. 1884)*, pioneer, minister of the Religious Society of Friends (Quakers), and author, was born in Surry County, the daughter of Society of Friends members Edward and Anna (Annie) Huff Bond. In December 1811, when Elizabeth was ten, the Bonds moved to the frontier as pioneers. They settled in a tent on land that they had bought on Nolan's Fork in Indiana Territory (present-day Wayne County, Ind., about midway on the eastern boundary with Ohio). (At the time the territory already had the present boundaries of the state.) The governor of the Indiana Territory, William Henry Harrison, had fought at Tippecanoe Creek against an Indian force led by Tenskwatawa, the Shawnee religious leader and warrior. Although this action eventually secured the Indian Territory for settlers, the Bonds temporarily left their property on Nolan's Fork and moved across the boundary for safety in Ohio through the summer of 1812. They then bought a small farm just back over the boundary in the Indiana Territory, where they lived for another year. When peace with the Indians was restored, the Bonds returned to their land on Nolan's Fork.

Still living in the wilderness, the family and others established a Friends Meeting at New Garden, three miles from Nolan's Fork. For about three weeks Elizabeth attended the Friends Meeting School at New Garden, to which she walked alone through the woods. This was her only formal schooling in learning how to read and write.

At New Garden Meeting Elizabeth Bond married Solomon Whitson Roberts, son of Thomas and Ann Roberts, on 5 Dec. 1816, when she was fifteen; over the years they would have thirteen children, several of whom predeceased her. Her marriage took place in the same year that Indiana was admitted to the Union. The Roberts family continued to live in Indiana near Richmond and in Pendleton, where Elizabeth and Solomon Roberts and his parents were very active in the Ministry of Friends meetings within the limits of Whitewater Monthly Meeting. They had eight acres of land in the green woods where Elizabeth Roberts says she spent "many lonesome hours; but blessed be the name of the Lord, who still dwells with me. He often allowed the light of His countenance to fall upon me." She felt that she had her first divine revelation in 1823 commanding her to speak out for the Lord. After refusing the call for about two years, she became seriously ill and almost died. At that time she "surrendered to the Lord, recovered from her sickness, and was most content." In 1827 she "spoke for the Lord but was uncomfortable; she preferred silence. She lived in poverty often but was blessed with divine visions."

All her life Elizabeth Roberts was against slavery and for the freedom of all with whom she came in contact—whites, blacks, and Indians. In addition to several of her children, she lost her husband, who died on 6 Apr. 1857 at age sixty-two. In March 1871 she was officially recognized as a minister by the Fall Creek Monthly Meeting. She then spoke willingly at meetings, traveled to visit other meetings, and helped to establish First-day Schools among Friends.

In spite of her brief formal schooling, she was the author of twelve short pieces: *Memoirs of Elizabeth Roberts*, "An Exhortation to the Youth," "How I Have Mourned for the Society of Friends," "A Prayer" (21 Apr. 1845), "Concerning the Condition of the Society of Friends," "A Letter Written to My Cousins, Jehiel and Lydia Wasson," "A Prayer" (three parts—part one, undated; part two, 28 Dec. 1845; and part three, January 1846), "A Few Lines Written for Her Children," "A Short Memorial Concerning Esther Roberts" (a daughter), "Some of the Last Expressions of Milton Roberts" (a son), "A Memorial Concerning My Dear Husband, Solomon W. Roberts," and "A Memorial Concerning Eunice Roberts" (a daughter).

In 1882 and again in 1884 Elizabeth Roberts visited one of her sons and his family in Nebraska. She became sick there in the autumn of 1884 and returned home to Indiana. She died at Fall Creek Meeting, Ind., at age eighty-three and was eulogized on 7 Mar. 1885 at the Whitewater Quarterly Meeting of Friends in Milton, Ind.

SEE: Data on Elizabeth Bond Roberts's ancestors and descendants and a diary kept by her cousin, Lydia Wasson (Lilly Library, Earlham College, Richmond, Ind.); Willard C. Heiss, *Abstracts of the Records of the Society of the Friends in Indiana* (1962); Elizabeth Bond Roberts, *Memoir of Elizabeth Roberts . . . Together With Some Other Writings and Memorials: Written by Herself* (1885); John L. Thomas and Martha M. Morris, "Memorial of Elizabeth Roberts," in *Memoir of Elizabeth Roberts* (1885); Donald E. Thompson, comp., *Indiana Authors and Their Books, 1917–1966* (1974).

DOUGLAS J. MCMILLAN

Roberts, John *(ca. 1760 or 1765–1823)*, planter, legislator, and militia officer, probably was born in the Bogue Sound area of Carteret County. His parents were William and Jemima (Jamima) Roberts, who owned a well-stocked, 400-acre plantation at the time of William's death (ca. 1786). Nothing is known about the early life and education of the son. Revolutionary War pay vouchers indicate that one John Roberts of Carteret County saw brief service in that conflict. Whether it was the subject of this sketch is unknown. In any case, by the early 1800s he had acquired an estate of more than 400 acres and owned one slave.

Roberts was elected to the House of Commons in 1804 and served twelve consecutive terms. He was chosen to represent Carteret County in the North Carolina Senate in 1816. Roberts had an undistinguished career in the house. He chaired no committees and rarely received important committee assignments; he did serve on such committees as divorce and alimony, military land warrants, privileges and elections, and claims. As a member of the senate, however, he was elected to the powerful finance committee. While in the House of Commons Roberts introduced local legislation concerning boundary lines, the county court, battalion musters, and the establishment of an academy. His fellow representative from Carteret County in 1808 and 1809 was Jacob Henry, whose eligibility was questioned during the 1809 session because of his Jewish faith. During the ensuing debates Roberts, among others, spoke in favor of Henry, who was able to retain his seat.

During the War of 1812 Roberts's voting record on military issues generally demonstrated his support for the prowar, Republican faction. Although he failed to vote on several war-related questions, he supported a resolution on Christmas Day 1812 for the governor to borrow $10,000 to procure necessary munitions of war. On the previous day he had been recommended by the Assembly and commissioned a lieutenant colonel in the Sixth Division, Second Brigade, of the North Carolina militia in Carteret County. Placed in charge of the militia at Fort Hampton, he was commander during the British alarm of 1813–14. Governor William Hawkins rewarded Roberts with a commission as assistant paymaster general for his district in May 1814. Evidence of his increasing popularity among his colleagues in Raleigh were his appointment and commission as brigadier general on 18 Dec. 1815.

With his military promotion and his election to the senate in 1816, Roberts reached the apex of his public service. His brief term in the senate was a stormy one, and his hopes of further political gain were dashed in December 1816, when the General Assembly received a petition of inquiry into his conduct as assistant paymaster during the war. Soon afterwards several petitions followed from militiamen who complained about not receiving their pay from Roberts.

A joint legislative committee found evidence of forgery and fraud and adopted a resolution requesting Governor William Miller to bring a suit against Roberts and to initiate court-martial proceedings against him. Another resolution declared him ineligible for office and vacated his seat in the senate. On 31 December Roberts reluctantly submitted his resignation as brigadier general and as a justice of the peace.

Court-martial proceedings were brought against him in 1817, but Roberts was able to secure his discharge from military arrest; he was ordered to appear at the Wake County Superior County during the spring term of 1818 to answer to the charges filed against him by the state. Governor Miller issued a writ against him and his securities on the $5,000 bond entered into by Roberts for performance of his duties as paymaster. After numerous delays the court finally decided in favor of Roberts at the spring term of 1822. But Attorney General William Drew, who represented the state, obtained an appeal to the state supreme court because a key piece of evidence had been rejected by the jury. In July 1822 the high court decided that the evidence in question, an account settled with the comptroller showing payroll information, should have been presented to the jury. Therefore, the prior judgment was reversed and a new trial was ordered for the fall term of 1822.

The case was continued from the August term because poor weather prevented the appearance of key witnesses; the sheriff of Wake County was ordered to hold Roberts in his custody until the spring term of 1823. This sudden reversal was greatly distressing to Roberts. In fact, the whole lengthy trial had been a great drain on his physical, emotional, and financial well-being. Roberts had hired some of the finest attorneys in the state for his defense including John D. DeLacy, James F. Taylor, Frederick Nash, Henry Seawell, and Thomas Ruffin. Before his trial he had owned well over 1,000 acres in Carteret County, but the mounting expenses of his litigation had caused him to mortgage much of his holdings.

Roberts, apparently a broken man, made one last attempt to get the charges dismissed. In November 1822 he submitted a lengthy petition to the General Assembly describing his poor health and the horrible living conditions in the Wake County jail. His memorial asked the Assembly to request Governor Gabriel Holmes to drop all actions against him and release him from prison. Although guilt or innocence had not been established, the General Assembly apparently believed that Roberts had suffered enough and passed a resolution granting his request; Holmes pardoned the former general on 3 December. Roberts never fully recovered from his ordeal, and court records in his home county suggested that he was dead by March 1823.

Roberts seems to have married, but the name of his spouse could not be determined. He had two daughters, Esther (m. Joseph Davis) and Vashti (Vasti) (m. Lot Holton).

Roberts held the position of justice of the peace in 1805–6 and from 1809 to 1816. He also served as an overseer of the poor at St. John's Parish in Beaufort from 1806 to 1813. In February 1813 he was appointed commissioner of wrecks for Carteret County. He had held the post of trustee of Swansboro Academy in 1810. Roberts likely died in Carteret County, but his place of burial is unknown.

SEE: Guion Griffis Johnson, *Ante-Bellum North Carolina: A Social History* (1937); *Journals of the Senate (1816–1822) and the House of Commons (1804–1822); North Carolina Reports*, vol. 9; *Raleigh Register and North Carolina Gazette*, 6 Dec. 1822; Raleigh *Star*, 4 Jan. 1810. Also North Carolina State Archives, Raleigh: Adjutant Generals' Records; Carteret County Court of Pleas and Quarter Sessions, Deeds, Estates Records, Superior Court Records, Tax Records, and Vestry Books, St. John's Parish, Beaufort; First (1790), Second (1800), Third (1810), and Fourth (1820) censuses of the United States (microfilm copies); General Assembly Session Records; Governors' Letterbooks (Hawkins, Miller, and Holmes); Military Collection, War of 1812; Supreme Court Records; Treasurers' and Comptrollers' Records; Wake County Superior Court Records.

STEPHEN E. MASSENGILL

Roberts, John Calvin *(February 1833–12 Aug. 1909)*, active Methodist Protestant layman and benefactor of Kernersville, was a member of the board of trustees of the Methodist Protestant Publishing House in Greensboro and was almost singularly responsible for the impetus given to the efforts of the Reverend J. F. McCulloch in the early twentieth century to establish a Methodist Protestant college in North Carolina. Roberts was a charter member of the Kernersville Methodist Protestant Church, organized in 1884, and took part in all its activities, serving for many years as Sunday school superintendent and class leader.

At the meeting of the North Carolina Annual Conference of the Methodist Protestant church in 1901, Roberts offered $10,000 to be used for the establishment of a denominational college in the state and a special Ways and Means Committee of nine persons was appointed. Due to the economic conditions surrounding the panic of 1907, however, efforts to establish the school were postponed. When Roberts died two years later, he left the $10,000 bequest in his will; the bequest stipulated that the funds be used by the Conference Board of Education in the building or support of a college provided that it was opened by 1920. If not, the money was to be used as a trust fund and the income applied towards educating young men for the ministry.

The cornerstone of the Administration Building at High Point College was laid on 29 June 1922, and the building was named Roberts Hall in memory of the man whose generosity began the movement that culminated in the establishment of this college. The Reverend W. F. Kennett, in a tribute prepared shortly after Roberts's death, referred to him as the "bishop of Kernersville" because of the high esteem and respect in which he was held.

SEE: J. Elwood Carroll, *History of the North Carolina Annual Conference of the Methodist Protestant Church* (1939); Greensboro, *Our Church Record*, 23 June 1898; *Journals of the North Carolina Annual Conference of the Methodist Protestant Church*, 1901, 1908–9.

RALPH HARDEE RIVES

Roberts, William Anderson *(22 May 1837–1899)*, artist, farmer, and Confederate soldier of English descent, was born in new Prospect Church three miles west of Yanceyville, the son of Elijah, a farmer, and Rebecca B. Davis Roberts. Reared in Caswell County, he knew the deprivations of rural farm life and was educated in the local schools. Early in life he manifested an interest in art, but how and from whom he received training is unknown.

At age twenty he was painting portraits on a commercial basis, the first of which was of Starling Gunn, a veteran of the American Revolution, for which he received $20. His commissions grew and the cost of individual portraits soon advanced to $35. His standard charge for groups of three was $60. During 1857 he painted 106 portraits of well-known people in his native county. In 1858 and 1859 he painted in adjoining Rockingham County, primarily in the families of Scales, Timberlake, Montgomery, Leissure, Spencer, Willard, Watkins, and Dillard.

His career interrupted by the Civil War, Roberts enlisted in Alamance County on 21 June 1861 and later in Halifax County he was assigned to the Fourteenth Regiment. On 17 Sept. 1862 he was wounded in the right hand at Sharpsburg, Md. Suffering from this injury and other disabilities, he entered the Confederate hospital at Danville, Va., on 23 Dec. 1862 because of chronic bronchitis.

Roberts participated in the Battle of Gettysburg, which he described as "commenced on July 1, 1863 and continued 3 days." Ill with jaundice, he entered Moore Hospital, Richmond, Va., on 17 Sept. 1863 but in November was transferred to the hospital at Danville with a dislocated elbow. Complications ensued because he "failed to enter at proper time." Other illnesses that plagued him while in service included chronic diarrhea, neuralgia, and "general disabilities" for some of which he also was hospitalized. Although absent from his unit on many occasions, he remained in service for the duration of the war. On 13 Jan. 1865 he was transferred to the invalid corps and finally paroled at Greensboro on 13 May.

After the war Roberts returned to his family in Caswell County, where he farmed and resumed his occupation as an itinerant painter of portraits. Between 1865 and 1868 he worked in his home county for fees of $50 for individual and $75 for full-length portraits.

From January to July 1869 he was in the Shelbyville-Louisville, Ky., area seeking commissions but found only fourteen. Returning home, he soon painted seven portraits. During the period 1870–72 he was in Virginia at Danville and Richmond, where he painted nineteen portraits. In 1872 he painted a picture of General Robert E. Lee, apparently from a photograph or another portrait, since the subject had died in 1870; his account book indicates that "no charges" were made for this one, although his customary price at the time was $80. A diligent search for this work has not been successful.

As age and infirmity had their effects on the artist, the number of his portraits declined. In 1874 he painted only the picture of Mrs. Bartlett Yancey. Between four and six each year continued through 1883, the last being that of Travis Wilson. Those of Dr. S. A. Richmond, Dr. and Mrs. A. C. Yancey, and Dr. and Mrs. L. G. Henderson were charged off to doctors' bills. Many descendants of the subjects own and prize the portraits that Roberts painted.

A deeply religious man, he carried a Bible and a copy of a *Book of Psalms, Hymns, and Spiritual Songs* during the war. His Bible was lost on 1 July 1863 at Gettysburg but later found and returned to him. It bears his marking of choice passages. A member of Prospect Church, Roberts believed in the fundamentals of Methodism. In the 1870s he strongly disagreed with the creed of the Campbellites or Disciples of Christ.

On 1 July 1859 Roberts married Mary Catherine

Watlington, and they were the parents of Annie Cutler (Mrs. William Franklin Lyon) and Mollie Belle (Mrs. Sidney Thomas Hicks). His grave, marked by a native stone, is at Prospect Church on land he gave for a congregational cemetery. A self-portrait of Roberts survives.

SEE: *American Library Association Portrait Index* (1906); Weymouth T. Jordan, comp., *North Carolina Troops, 1861–1865: A Roster*, vol. 4 (1973); Walter Clark, ed., *Histories of the Several Regiments and Battalions from North Carolina*, vol. 1 (1901); Roy Meredith, *The Face of Robert E. Lee in Life and Legend* (1947); William A. Roberts's original list of portraits, personal notes and correspondence, and Bible (possession of M. Q. Plumblee, Burlington).

M. Q. PLUMBLEE

Roberts, William Paul *(11 July 1841–27 Mar. 1910)*, Confederate soldier, legislator, and state auditor, was born in Gates County, the son of John Smith and Jane Gatling Boyt Roberts. He received little formal education other than in local schools a few months out of each year and one year at a small private school at Harrellsville. At the outbreak of the Civil War he was teaching in a small local school, and on 10 June 1861 he enlisted for the duration of the war in Company C, Nineteenth North Carolina (First Cavalry) Regiment, as orderly sergeant. Roberts quickly rose to the rank of second lieutenant on 30 September, and on 14 Mar. 1862 his regiment was present at the Battle of New Bern but was not engaged. Afterwards his company remained on detached picket duty in the district of Pamlico and participated in the attack on Washington, N.C., on 6 Sept. 1862. It then moved to Virginia and took part in General James Longstreet's Suffolk campaign, after which it rejoined its regiment and became a part of Robert E. Lee's Army of Northern Virginia, serving in the cavalry brigade of Lee's son, W. H. F. Lee.

Roberts became first lieutenant of his company to rank from 1 May 1863 and then advanced to captain, to rank from 13 Aug. 1862. He fought in the Battle of Brandy Station, the Gettysburg campaign, the "Buckland Races," and the Wilderness campaigns of 1864. Meanwhile, he was commissioned major of the Nineteenth North Carolina on 18 Feb. 1864, and later, during the initial struggles for possession of the railroads into Petersburg, Va., Roberts was commissioned colonel of the regiment on 19 August, to rank from 23 June 1864. Scarcely a week after his promotion he participated gallantly in the Battle of Reams's Station, on 25 August, where he dismounted his regiment and led it against an entrenched position of Union troops, which he captured along with numerous prisoners.

He continued to command the regiment until, in recognition of his bravery and distinctive leadership, he was commissioned brigadier general on 23 Feb. 1865 to rank from 21 February (confirmed on 23 February) and was even personally presented the gauntlets of General Robert E. Lee as a sign of the commanding general's recognition of his valor. At age twenty-three, he had the additional distinction of being the youngest commissioned general officer of the Confederacy. Roberts was given command of a small brigade of North Carolina cavalry in W. H. F. Lee's division, consisting of the Fifty-ninth North Carolina (Fourth Cavalry) and the Seventy-fifth North Carolina (Seventh Cavalry), also known as the Sixteenth North Carolina Battalion.

On 1 Apr. 1865 Roberts's new command was assigned the task of maintaining contact between the extreme right of the Confederate defense lines around Petersburg and the left flank elements of General George E. Pickett's Confederate troops holding the strategic crossroads of Five Forks, a distance of several miles in which Roberts simply did not have enough men for an adequate defense line. Powerful Union forces, which outnumbered Roberts many times over, attacked and quickly overwhelmed his thinly spread brigade in what later turned out to be a disaster to Pickett's Confederate troops at Five Forks. The remnants of Roberts's brigade participated in the retreat to Appomattox and during the surrender of Lee's army at that place Roberts's command pitifully contained only five officers and eighty-eight men who were not killed or captured in the fighting or the retreat. Roberts himself was paroled there and returned home to Gates County.

Shortly afterwards he married Eliza Roberts, daughter of Mills and Margaret Bond Roberts (of no kinship to the general), and although they had two children, both died in childhood. Later the couple adopted Mrs. Roberts's niece, Eugenia Walton. General Roberts represented Gates County in the constitutional conventions of 1868 and 1875. In 1876 he won a seat in the state legislature. Roberts was elected state auditor in 1880 and reelected in 1884; he declined a third term in the election of 1888. Afterwards, President Grover Cleveland named him consul to Victoria, British Columbia, a post he held for a number of years before returning to Gates County to once again take up farming. He died in Norfolk, Va., and was buried in Gatesville.

SEE: John L. Cheney, Jr., ed., *North Carolina Government, 1585–1974* (1974); Walter Clark, ed., *Histories of the Several Regiments and Battalions from North Carolina* (1901); William T. Cross (Gatesville, N.C.), personal contact; Clement A. Evans, ed., *Confederate Military History*, vol. 4 (1899); Louis H. Manarin, comp., *North Carolina Troops, 1861–1865: A Roster*, vol. 2 (1968); Ezra Warner, *Generals in Gray* (1959); Marcus J. Wright, *General Officers of the Confederate Army* (1911).

PAUL BRANCH

Robertson, James *(28 June 1742–1 Sept. 1814)*, pioneer, surveyor, soldier, Indian agent, political leader, and founder of Nashville, Tenn., was the son of John and Mary Gower Robertson. Born in Brunswick County, Va., he moved with his family to Wake County, N.C., in 1750 and spent his youth on a 320-acre farm, located on the south side of the Neuse River, that his father had purchased from Nathaniel Kimbrough. Although he obtained only limited formal schooling, he appears to have been at least acquainted with current political thought. Robertson was married in Wake County on 28 Oct. 1768 to Charlotte Reeves, the daughter of George and Mary Reeves; the couple had eleven children, nine of whom grew to adulthood.

While accompanying Daniel Boone on his third journey across the Blue Ridge Mountains in 1769, Robertson discovered the fertile region along the Watauga River. In 1771, after the Battle of Alamance and the defeat of the Regulators with whom he had a great deal of sympathy, Robertson led a group of sixteen families from the outskirts of present-day Raleigh across the mountains to the Watauga River Valley to settle. They were joined in route by Daniel Boone and his brother, Squire, from the Yadkin Valley, along with others from the Sandy Creek Baptist Church section of Orange (now Randolph) County, all of whom were leaving North Carolina to escape the tyranny of the Royal government. The settlement soon saw, however, the need for some sort of government; consequently, under the leadership of Robertson and John Sevier of Virginia, they drew up a government modeled after that of a typical Virginia county. The resulting Watauga Association formed a court of five men to undertake the business of government; both Robertson and Sevier were among the original members. This government was the first one free and independent of a foreign crown in North America, independent in the sense that it was organized without reference to outside authority.

During these years Robertson was very active, and not only with matters relating to the government of Watauga, although most had to do with Indian affairs. He was appointed as one of the first agents for Watauga in negotiating with the Indians on the terms of the lease for the land on which the settlement was prospering. In 1774 he participated in Lord Dunmore's War at the Battle of Point Pleasant, and in 1775 he played a vital role as negotiator in Richard Henderson's purchase of Kentucky lands from the Indians. Concurrently he held the rank of captain in defense of Watauga's settlements against the attacks of the Cherokee. Robertson was well acquainted with the Cherokee, as he lived among them for part of 1777, and was instructed by the North Carolina Assembly in 1778 to live with them in the fulfillment of his task as agent for the state, but he soon resigned this post. Meanwhile, in 1776 he had signed the petition of the Wataugans for incorporation into North Carolina.

Early in 1779 Robertson led an exploratory party of nine men overland across the Cumberland Mountains from Watauga and contemplated future settlement at French Lick, a trading post on the Cumberland River, on land purchased by the Transylvania Company. On 1 Jan. 1780 he returned with a small group of settlers and they founded what is now the city of Nashville, Tenn. In collaboration with Judge Richard Henderson, founder of the Transylvania Company, Robertson and the rest of this small settlement drew up the Cumberland Compact, signed on 1 May 1780, which set up a government for the entire western North Carolina territorial district that was patterned after the Watauga Association. Robertson was elected chairman of the twelve-man Committee of the Cumberland Association, and he exhibited a firm and wise leadership during the early, critical years of the settlement. His own lack of education fostered his interest in providing educational facilities for the settlement. When the North Carolina Assembly chartered Davidson Academy (later the University of Nashville) in 1785, Robertson became a trustee. In the same year he represented his county in the North Carolina Assembly. When difficulties in the western settlements led the frontiersmen to believe that the states were indifferent to their interests, Robertson, with others, played an active though obscure part in the Spanish Conspiracy from 1786 to 1789. He sat again in the North Carolina Assembly in 1787. During the same year he led the Coldwater expedition against the Indians.

At the organization of the Tennessee country into the territory of the United States south of the River Ohio (commonly known as the Southwest Territory) in 1790, President George Washington appointed William Blount territorial governor. Blount, on 19 Dec. 1790, commissioned Robertson justice of the peace for Davidson County as well as lieutenant colonel commandant of the Davidson County militia. Early the next year Washington appointed him one of the brigadier generals, a post he resigned after ordering the militia on the Nickajack expedition against the Indians. Only three years earlier, Robertson had aided Blount in negotiating the Holston treaty with the Cherokee.

Robertson remained active in politics. In 1796 he represented Davidson County in the constitutional convention of Tennessee, and in 1798 he entered the Tennessee Senate in place of Thomas Hardeman, who had resigned. During that year Governor John Sevier appointed him to represent Tennessee at the first Treaty of Tellico between the United States and the Cherokee. In 1807 he acted with Return J. Meigs in negotiating yet another treaty with the Cherokee. During his later years Robertson served as Indian agent to the Chickasaw, residing for some time at Chickasaw Bluffs, site of present-day Memphis, and there he died and was buried. His remains were removed in 1825 and reinterred in the old city cemetery in Nashville.

SEE: *DAB*, vol. 8 (1935); Robert M. McBride, ed., *Biographical Directory of the Tennessee General Assembly*, vol. 1 (1975); T. E. Mathews, *General James Robertson: Father of Tennessee* (1934); Raleigh *News and Observer*, 17 Nov. 1980; A. P. Whitaker, "Letters of James Robertson and Daniel Smith," *Mississippi Valley Historical Review* 12 (December 1925).

NEIL C. PENNYWITT

Robertson, Judge Buxton *(26 Oct. 1875–20 Dec. 1946)*, teacher and author, was born in Alamance County, the son of Columbus Florentine and Ledoska Coble Robertson. Graduated from The University of North Carolina in 1905, he delivered a commencement oration entitled "America as a Liberator"; he received the master of arts degree in 1931. During the early years of his career Robertson was principal and superintendent successively of schools in Graham, Reidsville, and Randleman and secretary of the North Carolina Sunday School Association. From 1911 to 1917 he was superintendent of the Alamance County schools, after which he became superintendent of the Cabarrus County schools. In retirement he lived near Burlington.

In 1918, to assist "young, inexperienced country teachers," he published *Guide-posts for the School Room, for Institutes, Normal Schools, Reading Circles and Self-instruction of Teachers*. A popular public speaker and local historian, Robertson in 1932 brought out a collection of short stores and anecdotes, *Gems of Truth in Stories of Life*, described as "for parlor, platform and pulpit." He was also the author of other professional publications in the field of education.

Robertson married Alice McPherson but they had no children. A Lutheran, he was buried in Pine Hill cemetery, Burlington.

SEE: Card catalogue, North Carolina Collection, University of North Carolina, Chapel Hill, for his publications; Daniel L. Grant, *Alumni History of the University of North Carolina* (1924); Raleigh *News and Observer*, 22 Dec. 1946.

WILLIAM S. POWELL

Robertson, Lucy Henderson Owen *(15 Sept. 1850–28 May 1930)*, educator and first woman college president in the South, was born in Warrenton, the daughter of Henry Lyne and Catherine Rebecca Watkins Owen. Her father was a merchant, moving his family in 1852 to Chapel Hill and later to Hillsborough. There young Lucy attended the Misses Nash and Kollock School for Young Ladies for seven years before entering Chowan Baptist Institute (now Chowan College) at Murfreesboro. After graduation in 1868, she returned to Hillsborough and on 1 Nov. 1869 married Dr. D. A. Robertson. The couple had two sons, Charles Henderson and David William, before Dr. Robertson's early death in 1883.

In 1872 the family moved to Greensboro, and there Mrs. Robertson began her teaching career. She served first, in 1878, as an assistant in the literary department at Greensboro Female College and by 1890 was head of the English language and literature department. In 1893 she left that post to become head of the history department at the newly formed State Normal and Industrial College for Girls (now the University of North Carolina at Greensboro). Seven years later she returned to Greensboro Female College to become lady principal and teach history. In 1902 the board of the college elected her—by unanimous vote—president of the college, thus making her the first woman college president in the southern states and the head of the second oldest state chartered college for women in the United States. She held that position until her retirement in 1913, when she was named president emerita. In 1925 a chair of religious education was established in her honor.

Beyond her achievements in education, Mrs. Robertson was active in the Women's Foreign Missionary Societies of Greensboro and the state, serving as president of the Western Conference for thirty-six years. She was also president of the United Society of Foreign and Home Missions, an ardent worker for the Woman's Christian Temperance Union, and involved in the Methodist Episcopal Church, South, the United Daughters of the Confederacy, and the Woman's Club of Greensboro.

After a long illness, she died in the infirmary of Greensboro College. She was buried in Green Hill Cemetery, Greensboro.

SEE: Samuel A. Ashe, ed., *Biographical History of North Carolina*, vol. 4 (1906); Delta Kappa Gamma Society, *Some Pioneer Women Teachers of North Carolina* (1955); *Greensboro Daily News*, 29 May 1930; Helen D. Harrison, "Noted North Carolina Women" (typescript, North Carolina Collection, University of North Carolina, Chapel Hill); *North Carolina Biography*, vol. 4 (1941).

ANNA JEANETTE BASS

Robertson, Reuben Buck *(11 June 1879–26 Dec. 1972)*, industrialist, was born in Cincinnati, Ohio, the son of Charles Dunbreck and Cynthia Buck Robertson. A Scottish immigrant, his father served as an Ohio jurist. After graduating from Cincinnati public schools, Robertson attended Yale University, receiving an A.B. degree in 1900. He then spent three years in the University of Cincinnati Law School, passed the Ohio bar, and joined his father's firm of Robertson and Buchwalter. Entrance into the paper industry in 1907 cut short his legal career. At the request of his father-in-law, Peter G. Thomson, owner of Champion Coated Paper Company of Hamilton, Ohio, Robertson journeyed to Canton, N.C., to supervise construction of the Champion Fibre pulp mills. His planned fifty-day stay turned into sixty-five years of service to the company and to western North Carolina.

After directing Champion's lumber and pulpwood operations at the Sunburst Logging Camp near Canton, he became the mill's general manager in 1912. Six years later the company promoted him to vice-president and in 1925 to president. Following the Canton mill's merger with the Hamilton plant in 1936, Robertson became executive vice-president of Champion Paper and Fibre Company. Eleven years after that, as he "climbed the industrial ladder of success," he moved into the president's office and soon graduated to chairman of the board. In 1961 he went into semiretirement as honorary chairman of the board. For sixty-five years, the lawyer-turned-papermaker developed his company into a major industry of multinational scope. The company, with the Canton branch still operating, became the Champion International Corporation.

Under Robertson's leadership, Champion perfected two technical processes of major importance to the paper industry. In 1912 plant chemists had devised a method of extracting tanning acid from chestnut logs and making bleached pulp from the spent wood. Champion was the first pulp mill in the world to make high-quality white paper from spent wood. The company built and operated the world's largest tanning extract plant at Canton. A second "Champion first" involved developing a satisfactory bleached pulp from southern pines. During the 1920s chemists in Champion's laboratories solved numerous technical problems to produce fine white paper from the plentiful pine trees. Champion used the new procedure at Canton and at its new mill in Pasadena, Tex., where the entire wood supply came from pine. Other pulp mills began to use the process and by the 1950s, one-third of all long-fiber pulp made in the United States came from yellow pine.

In addition to technical and mechanical guidance, Robertson worked to improve management-labor relations. His own brand of paternalism included concern for the welfare of workers on and off the job. He established a safety committee, a credit union, old-age bonuses, wage incentive plans, and profit-sharing programs. Champion led the pulp industry in all five areas. Robertson also demonstrated this interest in speeches to civic, business, and governmental groups and in founding and directing the Southern Industrial Relations Conference. Attended by hundreds of area and regional leaders, those yearly meetings held at Blue Ridge aimed to promote human relations in industry and business.

A third major interest lay in forest preservation. He encouraged people to consider trees as a resource that could and should be replenished. At a time when others stripped land of its timber without regard to future growth, Robertson advocated selective cutting, reforestation with nursery seedlings, and flood and fire prevention. A realization that the pulp and paper industry was a young giant whose expansion required a perpetual and dependable wood supply motivated his conservation efforts. Financial value to the company and aesthetic and environmental worth to the people of western North Carolina became apparent with the passage of time. For his pioneering role, the American Forestry Association gave Robertson its Distinguished Service Award in 1952 and its conservation award in 1954.

As a manufacturing leader, Robertson served on several government commissions and joined several business associations. He was chairman of the Wood Utilization Committee of the U.S. Department of Commerce in 1926, was one of twelve industrialists invited to Franklin Roosevelt's 1941 Labor-Industry Conference, and sat on the National War Labor Board (1942–44). He also was director of the National Association of Manufacturers and a member of its war and industrial relations committee, a graduate member of the Business Advisory Council, and president of the American Paper and Pulp Association. On the state and local levels, he presided over the North Carolina Forestry Association, held membership in the Appalachian Forestry Research Council, and served as long-term director of the Wachovia Bank and Trust Company. As a supporter of higher education, he was a trustee of Western Carolina Teachers College (chairman) and of The University of North Carolina.

During his long life, Robertson received much recognition for public service. In 1932 North Carolina State College awarded him an honorary doctorate of science for "achievements in science, in industry, and in promoting social welfare." Two decades later, the *Dixie Business* magazine named the Ohioan its Man of the South for 1950. Also in the 1950s he received the Distinguished Citizens Award from the North Carolina Citizens Association. Acknowledgement of his leadership in the pulp and paper industry came when twelve companies endowed the R. B. Robertson Chair of Forestry at North Carolina State College and when Champion employees honored their boss by establishing a scholarship fund in his name for needy area youths.

Known as a "quiet philanthropist," Robertson contributed to the Champion and Robertson YMCAs, to the Canton Public Library, to several area churches, to organized charities, and to colleges. People throughout the South benefited from his generosity.

In 1905 Robertson married Hope Thomson. They had four children, the late Laura Thomson, Reuben, Jr., Hope Robertson Norborn, and Dr. Logan Thomson. Reuben, Jr., served for three years as deputy defense secretary in the U.S. Department of Defense; he died in an automobile crash in 1960, while president of the Champion Paper Company.

Robertson was a lifelong Democrat and Presbyterian. Fraternal membership included the Masons (he reached the thirty-second degree) and Zeta Psi at Yale. Though he spent his last sixty-five years in western North Carolina, Reuben Robertson was buried at the Spring Grove Cemetery in Cincinnati, Ohio.

SEE: *Asheville Citizen*, 26, 31 Dec. 1972; *Asheville Times*, 27, 31 Dec. 1972; Canton, *Haywood Enterprise*, 28 Dec. 1972; *Proceedings of the Southern Industrial Relations Conference, 19 July 1973*; Reuben B. Robertson Papers (Southern Highlands Research Center, University of North Carolina, Asheville); *Who's Who in America* (1971).

ELAINE KAYE LANNING

Robeson, Edward John, Jr. *(9 Aug. 1890–10 Mar. 1966)*, civil engineer, shipyard executive, and congressman, was born in Waynesville to Edward John and Sarah Frances Ferguson Robeson. The family moved to Wythe County, Va., soon after his birth and to Cartersville, Ga., in 1891. Young Robeson attended the public schools of Quitman, Marietta, and Sparta, Ga., and was graduated from the University of Georgia at Athens in 1910. From 1910 to 1915 he was employed as a civil engineer successively for the Louisville and Nashville Railroad, the Sibley Land Company in Bay Minetta, Ala., and the Newport Mining Company in Ironwood, Mich.

In 1915 Robeson moved to Newport News, Va., to begin work for the Newport News Shipbuilding and Dry Dock Company. During his long career with the company he served variously as civil engineer, employment manager, personnel superintendent, personnel manager, and vice-president. He also was director and vice-president of Citizens Marine Jefferson Bank and chairman of the board of managers of Riverside Hospital, both in Newport News. In addition, he was a director of the National Association of Manufacturers (1948–59), president of the Virginia Manufacturers Association (1949–50), and president of the Society of Naval Architects and Marine Engineers (one term).

Robeson retired as vice-president and personnel manager of the Newport News Shipbuilding and Dry Dock Company on 30 Apr. 1950 in order to enter politics as a Democrat. He ran in the special election of May 1950 for the First District Virginia congressional seat vacated on the death of Schuyler Otis Bland. Robeson won the election and was reelected for four additional terms but failed to secure the nomination in 1958. While in the House Robeson was a member of the Merchant Marine Committee, Post Office Committee, and Civil Service Committee.

Robeson married Ruth Richards on 15 Aug. 1916, and they were the parents of three daughters, Mrs. J. Weaver Kirkpatrick, Mrs. Robert L. Amsler, and Martha Richards, and a son, Edward J. III. After Mrs. Robeson's death early in 1964, Robeson sold his Virginia estate in June and returned to his native Waynesville. He married Kathryn Danforth in July 1965.

After suffering a heart attack in January 1966 while visiting a daughter in Pascagoula, Miss., he was hospitalized there for several months before his death. He was buried in Greenhill Cemetery, Waynesville. Robeson had been a member of the Methodist church.

SEE: *Biog. Dir. Am. Cong.* (1961); Newport News *Daily Press*, 11 Mar. 1966; *Who's Who in the South and Southwest* (1954).

BRENDA MARKS EAGLES

Robeson, Thomas, Jr. *(11 Jan. 1740–2 May 1785)*, Revolutionary hero, legislator, and landowner, was the first son of Thomas and Sarah Singletary Robeson of Bladen County. His grandfather, Andrew Robeson, had immigrated around 1690 from Scotland to Pennsylvania, where he became a member of the Council in Philadelphia; he also served on the Council of West Jersey and as chief justice of Pennsylvania. Andrew was a graduate of Oxford and married Mary Spencer of the Stuart family. His fourth son, Thomas Robeson, Sr., left his home for North Carolina soon after his father's death in 1719. In Bladen County, on the Cape Fear River, he built a home called Walnut Grove, where his children Thomas, Jr., Peter, and Mary grew up.

Thomas Robeson, Jr., married Mary Bartram, daughter of Colonel William Bartram and niece of John Bartram, the botanist. Active politically early in the rebellion movement in the colonies, he was a member of the Third Provincial Congress, held at Hillsborough in August 1775, which appointed him colonel for the Bladen militia. He also served in the Fourth Provincial Congress that declared for independence at Halifax in April 1776, and at a November meeting in the same town he was appointed to a committee to bring the Bladen Tories to justice. In 1777 at New Bern he was a member of the first Assembly after the colony became a state.

Colonel Robeson was a Whig officer in an area where the Tories outnumbered the Whigs as much as five to one during the Revolution. The Scottish population was very large in the Cape Fear area. Some Scots appeared before the 1715 Jacobin uprising, many came after it, and many more arrived after the Battle of Culloden in 1746. Before the latter were allowed to leave Scotland, they had to take an oath that they would support the king. The oath ended with the grim declaration: "and should I break this, my solemn oath, may I be cursed in all my undertakings, family, and property; may I never see my wife, children, father, mother or other relations; may I be killed in battle as a coward and lie without Christian burial in a strange land, far from the graves of my forefathers and kindred. May all this come to me if I break my oath."

In 1775 Governor Josiah Martin fled the colony to a British ship, from whence he convinced the British that he could raise an army of three thousand in North Carolina. The call went out to the Scots who followed General Donald McDonald, who was to join British forces that would arrive at Wilmington. On the way, McDonald's forces ran into Colonels Richard Caswell and Alexander Lillington at Moore's Creek Bridge and were defeated and scattered. Thomas Robeson fought with the Whigs in this battle.

During the remainder of the war Robeson and other leaders were fighting primarily a civil war in which the area around Lumber River changed hands several times. This was one of the places in which General Francis Marion was very active, although he and Robeson did not fight in the same skirmishes.

When the Tories gained control, many of the Whig leaders escaped to friendly areas. One small group of Whigs was hiding out in Duplin County. When their numbers dwindled to only seventy, they agreed to Robeson's plan to make a do-or-die march on the Tories and British at Elizabethtown in Bladen County. Colonels John Slingsby and "Godden" [Robert Godwin?] were there with four hundred troops, and Colonel David Fanning was only four miles away with more. According to tradition, Sally Musslewhite Salter, the wife of one of the soldiers, had gone into the British camp selling eggs and was able to tell Robeson the camp's layout. On the night of 28 Sept. 1781 the small band reached a point on the Cape Fear across from Elizabethtown. A couple of hours before dawn the moon went down. One man was left with the horses. The other sixty-nine waded the river and quietly covered the ground to Elizabethtown. Their attack was sudden and furious as they charged yelling "Washington!" Colonel Robeson called out from the center of the line: "On the right! Colonel Dodd's Company! Advance! . . . On the left! Colonel Gillespie's company! Advance! . . . On the right! Colonel Dickinson's company! Advance! . . . On the left! Major Wright's company! Advance!" The main body of the small band rushed madly from one position to another, reloaded, and fired. Both Tory colonels were killed along with fifteen others. Their army was in disorderly flight, and many of them fell into a ravine still known as the Tory Hole. Soldiers who were there reported that they had been attacked by George Washington's whole army. This battle ended Tory activity in the area and gave the Whigs confidence to organize and plan attacks, but only a few skirmishes were left because the war was winding down.

Colonel Robeson was considered a fair and just man even by his enemies. After the war he and his brother, Captain Peter Robeson, offered protection to Tories who were sincere in taking the oath of loyalty to their new country. Robeson paid all his men out of his own pocket with the understanding that if they were paid by the government, the soldiers would return the money. This $80,000 was never repaid, and Robeson wrote into his will a request that no member of his family would ever try to collect it.

After the Revolution he again served in the state legislature. There, in 1786, was created a new county out of western Bladen that was to perpetuate posthumously the name of Thomas Robeson, the favorite hero of that area in which civil war raged fiercely for so many years.

SEE: Samuel A. Ashe, ed., *Biographical History of North Carolina* (1905–17); E. W. Caruthers, *Interesting Revolutionary Incidents, and Sketches of Character Chiefly in the "Old North State"* (1856) and *Revolutionary Incidents, and Sketches of Character Chiefly in the "Old North State"* (1854); R. D. W. Connor, *History of North Carolina*, vol. 1 (1919); William D. Cooke, comp., *Revolutionary History of North Carolina in Three Lectures* (1853); Betty (Mrs. Paul Vernon) Cox (Oxon Hill, Md.) to Hector MacLean (Lumberton, N.C.), 8 March 1968; Malcolm Fowler, *They Passed This Way: A Personal Narrative of Harnett County History* (1955); General Joseph Graham, "Closing Scenes of the Revolution in North Carolina from an Unpublished Manuscript," *North Carolina University Magazine* 1 (June 1852); Marshall De Lancey Haywood, comp., *Membership and Ancestral Register: North Carolina Society of Sons of the Revolution* (1898); Robert C. Lawrence, *The State of Robeson* (1939); Lawrence Lee, *The Lower Cape Fear in Colonial Days* (1965); Angus W. McLean, *Lumber River Scots and Their Descendants* (1942); Hamilton McMillan, "The Battle of Elizabethtown" (letter to the editor, *Fayetteville Observer*, 25 June 1901); Judge James C. Macrae, "The Highland Scotch Settlement in North Carolina," *North Carolina Booklet* 4 (February 1905); John W. Moore, *History of North Carolina; From the Earliest Discoveries to the Present Time* (1880); M. C. S. Noble, "The Battle of Moore's Creek Bridge, February 27, 1776," *North Carolina Booklet* 8 (March 1904); John Alexander Robeson Collection (North Carolina State Archives, Raleigh); Susan Stroud Robeson, "The Cape Fear Section during the Revolution," *Atlantic Monthly Magazine* 11 (October 1897); *Roster of Soldiers from North Carolina in the American Revolution*; Phillips Russell, *North Carolina in the Revolutionary War* (1965).

MAUD THOMAS SMITH

Robinson, Benjamin *(1843–3 Aug. 1888)*, newspaper publisher, editor, novelist, political activist, lawyer, and Confederate officer, was born in Fayetteville, the son of Dr. Benjamin (Young Ben) West (1811–85) and Joanna Huske Robinson. The family had been in Fayetteville since the arrival in 1805 of his grandfather, also Dr. Benjamin (Old Ben) West Robinson (1775–1857), a Vermont native and builder of the family home, Monticello. For a century, three generations of the family played leading roles in both medicine and public affairs in the town.

His educational record is unknown, but as he was listed as a sixteen-year-old "student" in the census of 1860, it is probable that he attended Donaldson Academy, then the major school in Fayetteville. At seventeen, Robinson (called "Benny" in a diary of a contemporary) enlisted in the Confederate army on 2 May 1861 and was named second lieutenant in Company A of the Fifth North Carolina Infantry Regiment. His military service spanned virtually all the campaigns of the Army of Northern Virginia through the Battle of Spotsylvania in May 1864.

Robinson was promoted captain of the company on 6 Mar. 1862, just prior to the Battle of Williamsburg, Va., in which he played a conspicuous role by carrying the regimental battle flag "until the staff was shot to pieces." As a result of the Battle of Chancellorsville in May 1863, he was among only four captains remaining unwounded of the regiment's field officers. The depleted regiment was badly mauled again on 1 July 1863, on the first day of the Battle of Gettysburg. Slightly wounded, he returned to duty the next day. His active service ended when he was severely wounded in the foot at Spotsylvania, Va., on 9 May 1864. He returned to Fayetteville and was assigned to the Invalid Corps. In March 1865, when General William T. Sherman's Union army approached the town, Robinson organized a "shovel corps" intending to dig ditches for Confederate troops.

He began a journalism career in June 1865, when he and his brother-in-law, James H. (Harry) Myrover, founded the *Fayetteville News*, which had both a weekly and a daily edition. In 1866 he was listed as copublisher with H. H. Smith. He then went to Wilmington to become an editor of the *Wilmington Dispatch*, founded by William Henry Bernard, who had been a wartime editor in Fayetteville. He apparently also worked on the *Wil-*

mington Star, established by Bernard in 1867. It is probable that Robinson got his earliest training as a journalist on Bernard's wartime papers in Fayetteville.

While engaged in journalism in Fayetteville and Wilmington, he also found time to write a 180-page novel, entitled *Dolores: A Tale of Disappointment and Distress*, published in the autumn of 1868. The publisher was the newly opened New York house of E. J. Hale and Sons, an enterprise of the former publisher of the *Fayetteville Observer*, which had departed the South in 1866. The work, which Hall advertised as "a southern novel," mixed scenes of life in Fayetteville, Civil War action, and a love affair linking families in Vermont and North Carolina. Using the form of letters, journals, and "conversations with the Vernon family of Rushbrook in Carolina," the book is a colorful and authentic panorama of life of its period, intriguing for its timeliness, depicting as it does the very days when it was written. Its straightforward passages of Civil War army life and battle are among the earliest of such scenes penned by a combatant who experienced it as a frontline officer.

In 1873 Robinson was back in Fayetteville, both as a journalist and with a law license. On 5 Apr. 1873 he founded *The Statesman*, a weekly newspaper. In six articles that covered an entire page, he described his conversion to the Republican party and announced his political and editorial philosophy. He called for national reconciliation and home rule. For the next five months, he carried out a vigorous editorial policy, promoting education, backing establishment of a fire company composed entirely of freed slaves, jousting with Democratic critics among his editorial peers and local politicians, and writing informative accounts of visits to Raleigh and to local cotton factories. His newspaper also carried his card as a lawyer. In September 1868 he gave up the editorship, apparently intending to make a living as a lawyer. In addition, he advertised for a "literary partnership" in polishing material for another novel. The newspaper ceased publication in 1874, leaving a unique journalistic legacy of enlightened partisanship for the GOP at a time when the Democratic party was regaining political control in North Carolina.

In 1874 he plunged into an active role in the Republican party, which fielded full tickets in local elections that year. Robinson was the party's candidate for mayor of Fayetteville. He was defeated by a single vote, 362 to 361.

After that election, Robinson virtually disappears from the public record and from the archives of his extended family. Despite the varied promise of the years of his young manhood, Robinson's life after 1874 went downhill, and details of his last years are sketchy. In censuses of 1870 and 1880, his wife and children were listed in households of first her father-in-law and then her brother. He is not listed. In 1880, with five children ranging in age from five to fourteen, she listed herself as a milliner. In 1885 the couple appears in court records disposing of his portion of his father's estate and borrowing small sums from a local developer.

When he died, Robinson was living in Fernandina, Fla. The notice of his death in the *Fayetteville Observer* by editor George Haigh said of him: "He has had many trials, and tried many vocations, but fortune seem never to smile upon his labors. The writer knew him well, his faults and foibles, and can say with truth that he was a truly brave and honest man." The place of his burial in unknown.

Robinson married Celia U. Myrover (b. Jan. 1845) on 8 Feb. 1863, while home on furlough. She was the younger sister of his journalism associate, Harry Myrover. Six children were living when the 1880 census was taken: Lewis (b. 1866), Bennie (b. 1867), Nettie (b. 1869), Huske (b. 1871), Celia (b. 1873), and Augustus (b. 1875).

SEE: Walter Clark, ed., *Histories of the Several Regiments and Battalions from North Carolina*, vol. 1 (1901); Cumberland County census, 1850, 1860, 1870, 1880; *Fayetteville News*, various issues, 1865–66; *Fayetteville Observer*, 30 Aug. 1888; Fayetteville *Statesman*, various issues, 1873–74; Weymouth T. Jordan, comp., *North Carolina Troops, 1861–1865: A Roster*, vol. 4 (1973); John A. Oates, *The Story of Fayetteville and the Upper Cape Fear* (1950); J. Roy Parker, Jr., *Cumberland County: A Brief History* (1990); Melinda Ray Diary, 1860–65 (Cumberland County Library, Fayetteville).

ROY PARKER, JR.

Robinson, Cornelius *(25 Sept. 1805–29 July 1867)*, planter, commission merchant, and Confederate congressman, was the son of Todd Robinson, a Wadesboro, Anson County, planter, and his wife, Martha Terry. His maternal grandfather was James Terry, a prominent Anson County Tory. Young Cornelius received his LL.B. from The University of North Carolina in 1824 but never practiced law.

Sometime prior to 1828 he was lured out of his native North Carolina by the booming cotton economy of the Alabama Black Belt. Settling in the central Alabama county of Lowndes, Robinson soon established himself as a planter. On 3 Jan. 1828, in Montgomery, he married Martha Owen DeJarnette, an Anson County native of Huguenot descent. Little is known about his antebellum business career except that he also had commission house interests in Mobile. Robinson served in the state militia; during the Seminole War of 1836 he was captain of Lowndes County's Benton Company, and later he rose to the rank of brigadier general.

Politically, he was a staunch Democrat who became a fierce Southern rights advocate as agitation over the issue of slavery in the territories intensified. Robinson, along with other radical Southern rights men, opposed the Compromise of 1850 because it failed to guarantee the South permanent equality with the North in the Federal system. Incensed by Third District Alabama Congressman Sampson W. Harris's support of the compromise, Robinson ran against the incumbent in the election of 1850. Harris, a bold Southern rights Democrat who suddenly found himself branded an unprincipled political opportunist by many of his former allies, won a narrow victory over Robinson and Unionist Democrat William S. Mudd.

Despite his defeat, Robinson's devotion to the Southern rights cause never faltered. Living between Montgomery and Cahaba, two urban strongholds of Southern rights extremism, he was drawn into the orbit of some of Alabama's most radical Southern rights leaders. Ultimately, he was elected to represent Lowndes at the Alabama convention of 1861 as an advocate of immediate secession.

After the Confederacy was formed, Robinson replaced John Gill Shorter in the Provisional Congress of the Confederate States when Shorter was chosen governor of Alabama. However, Robinson served in Congress for less than two months (30 Nov. 1861–24 Jan. 1862), resigning because his health prevented him from making the trip to Richmond for the next session. During the Civil War, he served briefly on General Braxton Bragg's staff before failing health again forced his resignation. Returning to his home in Lowndes County, Robinson continued his planting operations even after the Confederacy's death in

1865. He died on his plantation, outliving his beloved Confederacy by only a little more than two years.

SEE: William Brewer, *Alabama: Her History, Resources, War Record, and Public Men, 1540–1872* (1872); Thomas McAdary Owen, *History of Alabama and Dictionary of Alabama Biography*, 4 vols. (1921); J. Mills Thornton III, *Politics and Power in a Slave Society: Alabama, 1800–1860* (1978); Jon L. Wakelyn, *Biographical Dictionary of the Confederacy* (1977); Ezra J. Warner and W. Buck Yearns, *Biographical Register of the Confederate Congress* (1975).

LACY FORD

Robinson, Harold Frank *(28 Oct. 1918–3 July 1988)*, plant geneticist and university administrator, was a native of Mitchell County, the son of Fred H. and Geneva J. Robinson. As a towheaded youngster growing up in the village of Bandana, he was given the nickname "Cotton" by which he was known to friends and family throughout life. Education was important to the Robinsons, and Cotton proved to be an apt student. But there was little money; young Robinson first planned to become a Bandana merchant, continuing what had been a part-time job. In the summer after his high school graduation, he decided instead to attend Mars Hill College, a Baptist institution known for its assistance to struggling mountain families. His first tuition was paid with forty bushels of potatoes and his work in the college kitchen. He later attended North Carolina State College, where he received bachelor's (1939) and master's (1940) degrees.

Robinson's first employment, as a seed specialist with the North Carolina Crop Improvement Association, was interrupted by World War II. A line officer in the U.S. Navy from 1941 to 1945, he saw service in the war against German submarines in the Mediterranean. When the conflict ended, he was navigator of the aircraft carrier *Saginaw Bay*.

After the war Robinson joined the experimental statistics faculty at North Carolina State College, beginning a twenty-three-year stint at that institution. Having received a doctorate in genetics and plant breeding from the University of Nebraska in 1948, he rose to a full professor in 1951. His research in quantitative genetics gained international attention. In 1958 he became head of the Department of Genetics, and in 1962 he was named director of the Institute of Biological Sciences and assistant director of the Agricultural Experiment Station. From 1965 to 1968 he served as North Carolina State College's administrative dean for research. In 1964 President Lyndon B. Johnson appointed Robinson executive director of his Science Advisory Committee on the World Food Supply, a panel that produced a landmark study of food and population problems.

Robinson left North Carolina in 1968 to become deputy chancellor of the University of Georgia System, with responsibility for academic affairs. In 1971 he became provost of Purdue University, a position he held until his appointment as chancellor of Western Carolina University (WCU) three years later. Robinson considered his move to Cullowhee a homecoming, particularly since his wife, Katherine Palmer Robinson of Waynesville, had been a student there. He once stated his motives simply: "I wanted to do something for my people here in western North Carolina, and I saw WCU as an opportunity to really build an institution dedicated and committed to serving the people of the region."

The new chancellor went to Western Carolina in 1974 after the university had experienced a period of administrative instability. Morale among students, faculty, and staff was low. With characteristic energy Robinson launched a number of initiatives simultaneously, all signaling that he would be an activist chancellor. For the next ten years he worked diligently and tirelessly, while expecting the same effort by the faculty and administrative staff, to secure for Western Carolina University curricular expansion, increased state appropriations, and a broader service area. A strengthened faculty and curriculum in Cullowhee were to be the basis for regional programs.

During the decade Robinson was chancellor, Western Carolina University experienced impressive development. Undergraduate programs increased from 68 to 90 and graduate programs, from 43 to 80. Emphasis was placed on new programs in fast-growing career fields and on preprofessional programs. Two new schools—the School of Technology and Applied Science and the School of Nursing and Health Sciences—were founded to reflect this emphasis. Library holdings, housed in a modern new facility, increased from 442,301 to 1,037,070. The physical plant doubled in value to $100 million and total expenditures rose from $16.2 million to $42.7 million. Cooperative education, army ROTC, graduate programs in Asheville, and a Western Carolina Center in Cherokee all were initiatives of special interest to the chancellor. Reflecting his concern for western North Carolina, Robinson was instrumental in establishing the Center for Improving Mountain Living to promote economic development and the Mountain Heritage Center to preserve the region's history and culture. Annually the celebration of Mountain Heritage Day, replete with mountain crafts and music, drew thousands of people to the Western Carolina campus.

It would be incorrect, however, to leave the impression that Robinson's efforts were concentrated only on the mountain region. In the 1970s and 1980s Western Carolina University became involved in regional development programs in fifteen countries in Latin America, Africa, and Asia. Robinson was particularly interested in a water development–forestation project in Nepal, in university development in Swaziland, in the education of Jamaicans on their home island and in Cullowhee, and in fostering ties with China's Yunnan University. In 1981 he was appointed to a ten-person Foundation Committee to assist in establishing the Sultan Qaboos University in Oman, a venture that took him to the sultanate three times a year.

Upon his retirement in 1984, Chancellor Emeritus Robinson was appointed director of institutional research and in that capacity continued his efforts to promote regional and international development. He was instrumental in the establishment of the Joint Private and Voluntary Organizations/University Rural Development Center, the Mountain Aquaculture Center, and the North Carolina Center for the Advancement of Teaching. In addition, he was active in Western North Carolina Tomorrow and was cochairman of the I-26 Corridor Association.

Despite a busy career in academic administration, Robinson never lost interest in plant genetics and the world food supply problems. He was appointed by President Jimmy Carter to serve on the Board for International Food and Agricultural Development, and in 1978 he was named to the U.S. Department of Agriculture's Joint Council on Food and Agricultural Science. He took particular pride in a research project conducted on his Cullowhee property in which he purified Cherokee Indian corn, returning it to its original, hardy state.

Robinson and his wife Katherine had two daughters, Karen and Joanne. After a memorial service attended by Cullowhee folk and the state's political and education leaders, Robinson was buried in the Greenhill Cemetery, Waynesville.

SEE: *Asheville Citizen*, 4 July 1988; *Sylva Herald*, 7, 14 July 1988; Transcript of an interview with Chancellor and Mrs. Robinson by Curtis Wood and Tyler Blethen, 31 Mar. 1988 (Library, Western Carolina University, Cullowhee).

MAX R. WILLIAMS

Robinson, James Lowrie *(17. Sept. 1838–11 July 1887)*, legislator, lieutenant governor, and railroad champion, was born in Franklin, Macon County, the son of James, a merchant and native of Tennessee, and Matilda Lowrie Robinson, a niece of Governor David L. Swain. Robinson attended the local schools in Franklin and studied for a year at Emory and Henry College in Virginia before returning to Franklin in 1856 to begin a career as a merchant. At the outbreak of the Civil War, he enlisted as a private in Company H, Sixteenth North Carolina Regiment. Robinson soon became quartermaster sergeant and was commissioned captain of his company on 25 Apr. 1862. He served at the Battle of Seven Pines, where he was wounded, and at Second Manassas, Chantilly, and Antietam. On 12 Oct. 1864 Robinson married Alice L. Siler, by whom he became the father of three daughters and one son.

After the war he entered politics as a Democrat and soon rose to prominence as a staunch opponent of Republican Reconstruction policies. He won a seat in the state house of representatives in 1868 and was reelected three times in succession, serving as speaker during the sessions of 1872–74 and 1874–75. In 1876 and 1878 he was elected to the state senate and served as president of that body during both terms. After the election of Governor Zebulon B. Vance to the U.S. Senate in 1879 and the consequent promotion of Lieutenant Governor Thomas J. Jarvis to the governorship, Robinson became acting lieutenant governor. He won election to a full term in that office in 1880 as Jarvis's running mate, and at the expiration of his term in 1884 he was again elected to the lower house of the legislature. From 1 to 28 Sept. 1883, while Jarvis was out of the state, Robinson served as governor. He also was a trustee of The University of North Carolina from 1877 to 1886.

During his entire political career, Robinson was an ardent champion of the interests of western North Carolina and an unflagging promoter of the construction of the Western North Carolina Railroad. In 1875 he served with Governor Curtis H. Brogden and Robert F. Armfield on the commission that purchased the scandal-wracked railroad for the state. In the 1876–77 session of the legislature, Robinson was a participant in the understanding that won eastern support for the construction of the road in return for western support for the county government act, which removed the election of county commissioners and justices of the peace from the people in order to prevent blacks from winning office in the eastern counties. In 1877 Robinson was named a director of the Western North Carolina Railroad by Governor Vance, and in 1885 he sponsored the bill that provided for completion of the road to its western terminus at Murphy, in Cherokee County.

In 1885, after the inauguration of President Grover Cleveland, Robinson was rewarded for his services to the Democratic party with an appointment as special paymaster for the Bureau of Indian Affairs in order to arrange for the payment of a government annuity to the Winnebago Indians in Wisconsin. While engaged in this duty he contracted malaria and returned to North Carolina in 1887 to regain his health but instead died at his home in Franklin soon after his return.

SEE: John P. Arthur, *Western North Carolina: A History* (1914); *Asheville Citizen* (daily), 20 Aug. 1885; *Asheville Citizen* (weekly), 14 July 1887; J. S. Tomlinson, *Assembly Sketch Book: Session 1883* (1883); John H. Wheeler, ed., *Reminiscences and Memoirs of North Carolina and Eminent North Carolinians* (1884).

ALAN B. BROMBERG

Robinson, John *(8 Jan. 1768–15 Dec. 1845)*, clergyman and teacher, was born in Mecklenburg County near Charlotte, the son of David and Mary Hayes Robinson, of English and French descent. His grandfather, Andrew Robinson, settled in Lancaster County, Pa., in the early 1700s, and his father moved to North Carolina in 1750. Young Robinson's education was directed by Dr. Thomas Henderson of Charlotte and the Reverend Robert Archibald of the Poplar Tent Academy in Cabarrus County. He completed his classical education at Mount Zion College in Winnsboro, S.C., from which he received the A.B. degree. The University of North Carolina awarded him a master's degree in 1810 and a doctor of divinity degree in 1829.

On 4 Apr. 1793 he was licensed to preach by the Orange Presbytery. His first assignment was in Duplin County. In 1736 the Reverend Hugh McAden had organized a church in the Grove Pond area, but it had been without a pastor for some years. Robinson bought a home and remained there for five years. In 1800 he accepted an invitation from the Presbyterians in Fayetteville, and soon after his arrival he began to organize a church. The six elders elected were Robert Donaldson, Duncan McLeran, David Anderson, Duncan McAuslin, Archibald Campbell, and Colonel John Dickson. On 6 Sept. 1801 the ordinance of the Lord's Supper was administered for the first time in Fayetteville. "There were seventeen members, but there were one hundred and fifty who sat down to the table." In addition to his pastoral duties, Robinson was principal of the Fayetteville Academy. The combined salary for the year was one thousand dollars. He found the double duty too much for his strength, and in December 1801 he resigned.

Robinson went to Poplar Tent Church in Cabarrus County where he became pastor and teacher. In 1803 he was "induced by earnest solicitations of the citizens of Fayetteville to return," yet not until 1805 did he actually take up the pastoral duties and the classical school there. His second ministry lasted until 1808, when he resigned again for the same reason. Returning to Poplar Tent, he remained at the church until 1841, when he resigned his pastorate due to age and infirmity. For many years Robinson also was president of the board of trustees of Davidson College.

Resolutions adopted by the people of Fayetteville at the time of his death reflect the stability of the Presbyterian congregation as well as the lasting impression Robinson's labors made on the community. A tablet hangs in the vestibule of the church and his portrait is in the historical room. A marble slab erected by his pupils marks his grave in the cemetery at Poplar Tent.

On 9 Apr. 1795 Robinson married Mary Baldwin, the stepdaughter of his old teacher, Dr. Henderson. She died in 1836; four of their children, two sons and two daughters, reached maturity.

SEE: Samuel A. Ashe, ed., *Biographical History of North Carolina*, vol. 3 (1905); Kemp P. Battle, *History of the Uni-*

versity of North Carolina, vol. 1 (1907); *Cabarrus Black Boys Chapter, Daughters of the American Revolution* (1934); William Henry Foote, *Sketches of North Carolina: Historical and Biographical* (1846); William S. Harris, *Historical Sketches of Poplar Tent Church* (1901); Kate Robinson McDiarmid (North Wilkesboro), notes on the family; Harriet Sutton Rankin, *History of First Presbyterian Church, Fayetteville, North Carolina* (1928); J. K. Rouse, *Interesting Colonial Churches in North Carolina* (1961).

LUCILE MILLER JOHNSON

Robinson, Joseph Edward *(23 Sept. 1858–17 Mar. 1931)*, lawyer, newspaper editor, and civic leader, was born near White Hall (now Seven Springs) but in Lenoir County, of Irish parentage. He was the son of John, a graduate of the University of Dublin where he became a professor of mathematics and elocution, and Margaret Dillon Robinson, of County Antrim, a devout Roman Catholic who converted her Presbyterian husband to that faith. The couple, fearing that there was no more hope for Ireland, emigrated in 1847, with their two children, to Lenoir County, where John and his brother William conducted a school that they moved in 1854 to the new town of Goldsboro, where it flourished as the Wayne Institute and Normal College.

One of nine children, Joseph Edward Robinson grew up on his father's plantation, Tara (named for the ancient seat of the Irish kings), three miles west of Goldsboro at Belfast and at his father's town house in Goldsboro. He and his brothers were educated at the Wayne Institute and under private tutors, who grounded them in Latin and Greek before they studied English. Afterwards, for seven years, they had as their preceptor a Catholic priest of the Dominican Order.

In 1879 Robinson was graduated from St. Charles College, in Maryland, operated by the Sulpician Fathers, a teaching order. Rather than taking final orders for the priesthood, he studied law. In 1881 he was licensed by the North Carolina Supreme Court and began to practice at the Goldsboro bar along with Charles B. Aycock, William R. Allen, Frank A. Daniels, and, in the next few years, William T. Dortch, Jr. Their youthful friendship deepened with the years; later Governor Aycock appointed Robinson a member of his personal staff, with the rank of colonel.

Robinson won a reputation for himself in the practice of law, but in the meantime he began doing editorial work for the leading newspaper in Wayne County, a semiweekly called the *Goldsboro Messenger*. In April 1885 he joined with Charles Brantley Aycock and William Clement Munroe to establish the *Goldsboro Daily Argus* (now the *Goldsboro News-Argus*). For a time the three men were joint editors, but eventually Robinson, who had initiated the business, bought his partners' shares. Colonel Joe, as he was called, a dedicated Democrat, in contrast to his older Republican brother, Judge W. S. O'B. Robinson, developed the *Argus* with its motto "We go forward" into one of the leading Democratic papers in eastern North Carolina, and his influence frequently helped to advance Aycock's political career.

University of North Carolina professor Joseph L. Morrison, in the *Greensboro Daily News*, wrote that Robinson built his community, but as for his paper he would publish nothing to "bring a blush to a maiden's cheek, or a tear to a mother's eye." Even before the great temperance wave swept the country, Robinson came out flatly against the issuance of licenses to saloons and bars and made it plain that not one advertising line could be bought at any price in the *Argus* by any of the thirty-one saloons then operating in Goldsboro. At the time of Robinson's death, the editor of the *Greensboro Daily News* wrote:

> As a pioneer editor of the state, 43 years he devoted to his craft, and a patriotic citizen he never dodged the call to service but was always to be found in the forefront for any reform movement, for any advancement, for any undertaking which he believed would help his city, his section, or his fellow man. In his newspaper columns he ever avoided the unpleasant or the sordid. He weighted the contents of his paper in their human relationships and their human reactions. When he spoke out against individuals, it was always in the interest of a broader service and the community good. The paper which he long ran was not primarily the Argus; it was Colonel Robinson and recognized as such.

In his community Robinson was long chairman of the Wayne County Board of Education, a trustee of the Goldsboro Public Library, and a force in establishing and completing the Goldsboro Hospital, which he served for years as secretary of the board of trustees. He also inaugurated the "Empty Stocking" fund campaign at the Christmas season.

In recognition of his many services, the citizens of Goldsboro in 1927 established Robinson Park in the center of Goldsboro on South Center Street. Nine years after his death the Robinson Park Marker Unveiling Exercises were held on 9 June 1940. The inscription on the marker reads: "Dedicated in appreciative memory of Joseph E. Robinson, 1858–1931, who as devoted citizen and as editor of The Goldsboro Daily Argus for forty-four years inspired his neighbors to create a better community."

Colonel Joe was married on 15 Nov. 1893 to Ada Clingman Humphrey, a daughter of Colonel Lott W. Humphrey of Goldsboro. They left no children. He died at his home at the Hotel Goldsboro and, like so many of his brothers and sisters, was buried from St. Mary's Roman Catholic Church. Interment was in Willow Dale Cemetery.

SEE: Frank A. Daniels, *History of Wayne County* (1914?); *Goldsboro News-Argus*, 4, 7 Apr. 1935; *Greensboro Daily News*, 18 Mar. 1931; *North Carolina Biography*, vol. 6 (1919); Oliver H. Orr, Jr., *Charles Brantley Aycock* (1961).

BLACKWELL P. ROBINSON

Robinson, Leonidas Dunlap *(22 Apr. 1867–7 Nov. 1941)*, attorney and congressman, was born on the family plantation in Gulledge township, Anson County, the son of John and Araminta Robinson of English ancestry. Educated in the common schools of the county, at Anson Institute in Wadesboro, and at Carolina College in Ansonville, he studied law under Colonel Risden Tyler Bennett. A delegate to every Democratic state convention in North Carolina from 1888 to 1941, he was admitted to the bar in 1889, appointed solicitor of the Thirteenth Judicial District in 1901 by Governor Charles B. Aycock, and elected thereafter until he retired in 1910. Robinson was mayor of Wadesboro from 1890 to 1893 and served in the North Carolina House of Representatives in 1895 and 1901. He was a delegate to the Democratic National Convention of 1912, 1920, and 1924. Robinson owned and operated extensive farming interests and was one of the organizers of the North Carolina Cotton Growers Association. A Democrat, he was elected to Congress in 1916 and served until 1921.

In 1909 Robinson became president of the Bank of Wadesboro, a post he filled for thirty years. Although baptized in the Methodist faith, he is said never to have formally "joined" a church even though he contributed to the First Methodist Church in Wadesboro and to Bethel Methodist Church in the southern part of Anson County near his birthplace.

Robinson married Nettie George Dunlap on 7 Apr. 1897, and they were the parents of two sons, E. Carl and L. D., Jr. After her death in 1931, he married Mrs. Emma Hunter Craven of Warrenton. He was buried in the family plot of East View Cemetery, Wadesboro.

SEE: *Biog. Dir. Am. Cong.* (1971); John L. Cheney, Jr., ed., *North Carolina Government, 1585–1979* (1981); *North Carolina Biography*, vol. 4 (1928); *North Carolina Manual* (1919); Raleigh *News and Observer*, 8 Nov. 1941; Wadesboro *Messenger and Intelligencer*, 8 Nov. 1941.

MARY L. MEDLEY

Robinson, William Smith O'Brien *(27 Apr. 1852–17 Oct. 1927)*, judge, lawyer, and Republican leader, was born in Lenoir County near White Hall (now Seven Springs) of Irish parentage. He was the son of John, a graduate of the University of Dublin where he became a professor of mathematics and elocution, and Margaret Dillon Robinson, of County Antrim, a devout Roman Catholic who converted her Presbyterian husband to that faith. Fearing that there was no more hope for Ireland, they emigrated in 1847 with two children to Lenoir County, where John and his brother William conducted a school that they moved in 1854 to the new town of Goldsboro, where it flourished as the Wayne Institute and Normal College. John named his first son born in this county William Smith O'Brien for the Irish patriot and revolutionary.

Young Robinson grew up on his father's plantation, Tara (named for the ancient seat of the Irish kings), three miles west of Goldsboro at present Belfast (later so named by Robinson for his mother's native county seat) and at his father's town house in Goldsboro. He and his younger brother, Joseph E., were educated at their father's school and under private tutors who grounded them in Latin and Greek. Then for seven years they had as their preceptor a priest of the Dominican Order.

Robinson's first job was as a railway mail messenger between Richmond and Wilmington, after which he studied law at Chief Justice Richmond Pearson's law school at Richmond Hill in Yadkin County. After being licensed in 1876, he practiced in Danbury for a year and then returned to Goldsboro, where he practiced for nearly fifty years.

A dedicated Republican, he followed in the footsteps of his father who, with the coming of the Civil War, was a Unionist and later a Republican who vowed he would cut off his right arm before he would fight against the country to which he had pledged his allegiance. In 1880 Robinson was a presidential elector and led his ticket. From April 1882 to 1885 he was district attorney for the Eastern District of North Carolina. He also served as Republican national committeeman from North Carolina for many years and won his party's nomination for Congress in the Third Congressional District but withdrew from the campaign before the election.

In 1894 he helped engineer the fusion of the Populists and the Republicans and became the nominee of his party for judge of the superior court of the Sixth District. He defeated the Democratic incumbent, Judge William R. Allen, his close personal friend and neighbor. Robinson was the last elected Republican superior court judge in the state for many years.

At this time Josephus Daniels admitted that the Raleigh *News and Observer* was "severe on his political activities, always calling him 'Alphabet Robinson,'" which provoked the judge to refuse to speak to Daniels for some time, despite their former friendship and the intimate friendship between him and Daniels's brother, Judge Frank Daniels. Later, after cordial relations were restored, Josephus Daniels admitted that Robinson, in spite of his eccentricities, "was unlike any man I have known, with a charm that could not be resisted, even by his political foes."

In an appraisal of his eight years on the bench, in which he held court in all the districts of the state, his Democratic friend, Judge Daniels, wrote that Robinson demonstrated that he was grounded in the principles of the law and the decisions of the courts interpreting them, but that he resented the "fine spun decisions, the nice sharp quillets" employed by some judges who "beclouded their authoritative declarations of the law and obscured the gladsome light of jurisprudence." At the time of Robinson's death, the *Greensboro Daily News* wrote that he would best be remembered throughout the state for his remark that "no man should be allowed to sit on the Superior Court bench until he has served a term in the state penitentiary."

President William Howard Taft appointed him to the U.S. District Court for the Eastern District of North Carolina in 1909, but while the Senate was deliberating over his confirmation, Taft saw fit to withdraw his name and place in its stead Henry Groves Connor, a Democrat and close friend of Robinson's. Taft's decision was based on the fact that Robinson, while presiding over a murder trial in western North Carolina, had ordered the sheriff to go out and buy him a quantity of cotton. He promptly stuffed all he could get in his ears in protest against the strident and lengthy defense put up by one Elias Kope. The jolly tenant of the White House, according to the *Greensboro Daily News*, "literally laughed the Judge out of court."

Robinson married Grace Moseley of Halifax County, by whom he had three sons: William S. O'B., Jr., John Moseley, and Russell Marable. All three were graduates of The University of North Carolina and Columbia University Law School who became highly successful lawyers. His wife died in 1907, and on 26 Aug. 1914 he married Annie Williams Pierce, of Weldon, by whom he had one son, Blackwell Pierce.

Judge Robinson died at his home in Goldsboro. A devout Catholic, he was buried from St. Mary's Catholic Church, established by his and four other families, and on whose altar stood the crucifix brought over from Ireland by his father exactly eight decades previously. He was buried in Willow Dale Cemetery. His portrait hangs in the Wayne County courthouse.

SEE: Frank A. Daniels, *History of Wayne County* (1914); North Carolina Bar Association, *Reports*, vol. 30 (1928); *North Carolina Biography*, vol. 6 (1919); Oliver H. Orr, Jr., *Charles Brantley Aycock* (1961); Scrapbook of newspaper clippings, periodical articles, and obituaries (possession of Blackwell P. Robinson); Charles L. Van Noppen Papers (Manuscript Department, Duke University Library, Durham).

BLACKWELL P. ROBINSON

Rochester, Nathaniel *(21 Feb. 1752–17 May 1831)*, Revolutionary leader, merchant, and land developer, was born in Westmoreland County, Va., the son of John and Hester Thrift Rochester. His siblings were William, John, Ann, Phillis, and Esther (or Hester). The Virginia farm had been the American home of the family since 1689, when Nathaniel's forebear, Nicholas Rochester, migrated from his English home in the county of Kent. It was located near the birthplaces of both George Washington and James Monroe, and later developments in Nathaniel's career indicate a possibility that he may have been acquainted with Monroe during his boyhood.

Widowed when Nathaniel was four, his mother married Thomas Cricher, who moved the family to Granville County, N.C., in 1763. Young Rochester grew to manhood in his new home and attended the school of the Reverend Henry Pattillo, where he evidently was an apt pupil. In 1768 he obtained employment with James Monroe, a Scottish merchant in Hillsborough, the seat of Orange County, and his progress was rapid and rewarding. Within two years he was made clerk of the vestry of St. Matthew's Parish, and in 1773 he became a partner with Monroe and John Hamilton in a Hillsborough store. This venture prospered but the business was liquidated in 1775 because of problems connected with the approach of the Revolution. Rochester cast his lot with the Patriots and immediately became involved in political and military affairs.

In 1775 he was named to the Committee of Safety for Orange County and on 20 August attended the Third Provincial Congress as a borough representative of Hillsborough. He was also appointed a major in the militia, a justice of the peace, and paymaster of the battalion of minutemen in the district of Hillsborough. The following year, he was assigned the command of two companies of infantry and one of cavalry to follow Colonel James Thackston in pursuit of the Tories marching to join the British at Wilmington. En route his force captured five hundred Tories retreating from the Battle of Moore's Creek Bridge. Having no place to imprison such a number, the major paroled all except fifty officers, whom he turned over to Colonel Alexander Martin at Cross Creek.

In 1776 Rochester represented Orange County in the Fourth Provincial Congress meeting at Halifax. He was also elevated to the rank of colonel in the North Carolina Continental Line, appointed commissary general of military stores, and assigned to serve with Thomas Burke and Cornelius Harnett on the Committee of Claims and Military Accounts. Named to a commission to establish a gun factory near Hillsborough, he led a wagon train to Philadelphia to obtain iron for the enterprise. In the same year, he was rendered unfit for military duty by a serious illness and resigned his command; however, his role in politics was not affected, for in 1777 Orange County elected him as its representative in the first General Assembly of the state of North Carolina. Later that year he resigned to serve the county as clerk of court and was commissioned as a supervisor for the building of a new courthouse as well as to assist in establishing an academy in the Hillsborough area. In 1778 he resigned as clerk because the fees collected were insufficient to cover the necessary expenses of the office and entered into a mercantile venture in Hillsborough in partnership with Colonel Thomas Hart and James Brown. The business was successful and Rochester began to invest his earnings in real estate, a practice he continued throughout his life.

When the occupation of Hillsborough by the British army became a probability in 1780, the business was liquidated and Hart moved his family to Hagerstown, Md., for safety. The affluent Colonel Hart offered to back his former partner in business in Philadelphia, and the twenty-eight-year-old Rochester accepted. On his arrival in the Pennsylvania city in 1781, he was almost immediately stricken with smallpox. After a lengthy convalescence he abandoned his plans to settle in Philadelphia and joined Hart in Hagerstown, where the two became partners in a flour mill, a nail and rope factory, a bank, and a farm. Rochester lived in Maryland for thirty years; during that time he made two business trips to Hillsborough, was elected to the Maryland legislature, and served as postmaster, judge, sheriff, presidential elector, and vestryman of St. John's Protestant Episcopal Parish.

In 1788 he married Sophia Beatty and eventually became the father of twelve children: William Beatty, Nancy Barbara, John Cornelius, Sophia Eliza, Mary Eleanor, Thomas Hart, Catherine Kimball, Nathaniel Thrift, Anna Barbara, Henry Elie, Ann Cornelia, and Louisa Lucinda. There are many Rochester descendants in the United States today.

In 1810, after Hart had moved to Kentucky, Rochester closed his Maryland firm and moved to Dansville, N.Y., where he built a paper mill. Four years later, he moved to Bloomfield, N.Y., where he conducted a banking business and served again as a presidential elector. At this time he purchased a tract of one hundred acres on the Genessee River and laid it out in lots for a town that he named Rochesterville. In 1818 he established his residence in the settlement, the name of which was changed to Rochester, by which the city into which it developed is known today.

For the rest of his life, Rochester was engaged in developing the town he had created and was active in its financial and political life. He was responsible for the creation of Monroe County with his town as the county seat. In addition, he served in the New York legislature, was one of the founders of St. Luke's Protestant Episcopal Church, and amassed a comfortable fortune from his various business interests. A stalwart influential Jeffersonian Republican in politics, Rochester made his last public speech in 1828 while campaigning for John Quincy Adams and against Andrew Jackson for the presidency of the United States.

He was first buried in the Buffalo Street Cemetery in Rochester, but later his remains were transferred to the Mount Hope Cemetery in the same city. The Hagerstown Trust Company, in Hagerstown, Md., owns an excellent portrait of the colonel painted when he was a young man. The Rochester Historical Society owns a portrait of Rochester at age seventy, one of Mrs. Rochester at age thirty, and several portraits of various members of the Rochester family.

Nathaniel Rochester's greatest asset was the confidence he inspired in all who knew him, a trust he rewarded with scrupulous honesty, an industrious application of his abilities, exemplary moral conduct, and the valuable contribution of his own ingenuity. Because of this characteristic and its results, he is honored today in the four states where he resided as a Patriot, a pioneer, and a founder.

SEE: Walter Clark, ed., *State Records of North Carolina*, vols. 12–13, 19, 24 (1895–1905); Records of Orange County, N.C. (Courthouse, Hillsborough); Nathaniel Rochester, *A Brief Sketch of the Life of Nathaniel Rochester, Written by Himself for the Information of His Children*, vol. 3 (Rochester Historical Society Publication Fund Series, 1924); William L. Saunders, ed., *Colonial Records of North Carolina*, vol. 10 (1890); Durward T. Stokes, "Nathaniel Rochester in North Carolina," *North Carolina Historical Review* 38 (October 1961).

DURWARD T. STOKES

Rockwell, Elijah Frink *(6 Oct. 1809–15 Apr. 1888),* Presbyterian minister, writer, historian, teacher, and college president, was born in Lebanon, Conn., the son of Joseph and Sarah Huntington Rockwell. He received his early education in the schools of his home community, in the town of Windham, and in Bacon Academy, Colchester, Conn. In 1829 he entered Yale but because of financial difficulties was not graduated until 1834. For a time he taught school to earn sufficient funds to complete his college course. Following his graduation he taught for a year in Monson, Mass., and then went to Fayetteville, N.C., to teach in the Donaldson Academy.

In 1837, as a candidate for the ministry under the guidance of the Fayetteville Presbytery, he entered Princeton Theological Seminary. Finding the winter climate unsuitable, however, he transferred to Columbia Seminary in South Carolina. Although listed as a member of the class of 1840, he left the seminary in the spring of 1839. In June 1839 he was licensed by the Fayetteville Presbytery. After supplying the Fayetteville church for a brief time, Rockwell went to Statesville, in the fall of 1840, as supply for the Presbyterian church. Upon being called as pastor, he was ordained and installed by the presbytery of Concord on 15 Dec. 1841.

During the Concord pastorate he helped raise money for Davidson College, where in 1850 he was elected professor of chemistry and natural philosophy. In 1852 he became professor of chemistry and geology and in 1854, professor of Latin and modern history, a chair he filled until 1868. One of his students wrote: "His learning was varied, extensive, and curious; his mind a repository of unexpected and unusual knowledge. . . . He was a man of deep scriptural piety, unaffected, unobtrusive, undemonstrative." Another commented: "He was not magnetic, but an accomplished Latinist, a good teacher and a kindly man." Rockwell collected many minerals, which he gave to the college for its museum; in 1921 this collection was destroyed in a fire that devastated the main building on the campus. He also offered the first prize ever given at Davidson in 1860, and he donated one hundred dollars, the interest from it to be given in money or books to the student making the highest grades in science. While teaching he wrote innumerable articles on a variety of subjects that were published in various magazines and newspapers. His presbyterial biographer, the Reverend Jethro Rumple, D.D., said that he wrote "in all about one hundred important articles besides numerous little contributions upon current events."

In addition to his writings on theology, natural history, and linguistics, Rockwell was the author of a number of historical papers. Several of these dealt with the history of local churches, others with events that occurred during the Revolutionary War, and still others with prominent men of that period and of later years who contributed to the moral and social life of the South.

In 1868 Rockwell was elected president of the Concord Female College, where he had been one of its trustees from its beginning. He returned to Statesville to serve in this post, but the aftermath of the Civil War precluded a successful administration. Enrollment was low and money was scarce, handicaps that the new leader could not overcome. In 1870 the college was closed and a little later sold; thus, for a time, it passed out of the control of the presbytery that had founded it.

Rockwell taught briefly in the Statesville Academy for Boys but soon began supplying churches in the area. In 1871 or 1872 he left the academy and devoted his full time to preaching. He supplied Third Creek, Bethany, Bethesda, Fifth Creek, Unity, and Tabor churches. In 1882 he received the honorary doctor of divinity degree from The University of North Carolina. During the last few years of his active ministry he was stated supply of Bethany and Tabor churches. Ill health forced his retirement to his home in the Cool Springs community, near Fifth Creek Church, where he died. Funeral services were held at both the Fifth Creek and Statesville Presbyterian churches. Although his will requested that he be buried in the Bethany graveyard, his body was carried from the Statesville church to the Fourth Creek cemetery. On 31 Dec. 1888 his remains were disinterred and transferred to Oakwood Cemetery, which had recently been opened in Statesville. His final burial was in Lot 8, Section 4, which had been bought by his widow shortly after the new city cemetery became available.

Rockwell's first wife was Margaret K. McNeill, of Fayetteville, who died about 1866. His second wife was Elizabeth Holmes Browne, also a native of Fayetteville, who was living in Davidson at the time of their marriage in 1868. To this second union were born two sons, Douglass Browne, who died in infancy, and Joseph Huntington, who was given his paternal grandmother's family name. He also had an adopted son, George Rockwell McNeill, a relative of his first wife.

SEE: Iredell County records (courthouse, Statesville); *Library of Southern Literature* 15 (1907); T. W. Lingle, ed., *Alumni Catalogue of Davidson College, Davidson, N.C., 1837–1924* (1924); *Ministerial Directory of the Presbyterian Church, U.S., 1861–1941* (1942); Alfred Nevin, *Encyclopedia of the Presbyterian Church in the U.S.A.* (1884); *North Carolina Presbyterian*, 25 Apr. 1888; *North Carolina Teacher* 5 (April 1888); Presbyterian Church in the USA, Synod of North Carolina, *Minutes* (1888); William C. Rose, "E. F. Rockwell—An Uncommon Man" (typescript, North Carolina Collection, University of North Carolina, Chapel Hill); Statesville *Landmark*, 1888–89.

NEILL R. MCGEACHY

Rockwell, James Chester *(21 Jan. 1868–14 Sept. 1893),* poet, editor, and minister, whose early death at age twenty-five was believed to have deprived North Carolina of one of its most promising literary figures of the late nineteenth century, was born in Whiteville, the son of Henry Clay and Sallie J. Powell Rockwell. He attended the academy of Professor W. G. Quackenbush in Laurinburg but otherwise was self-educated from extensive reading. Regarded as a child prodigy, he had his essays and poetry published in southern and other periodicals.

His father served in the Confederate army as a captain with the Fifty-first North Carolina Regiment in the early coastal battles and later in Clingman's Brigade. When he died on 24 Feb. 1874, his son James Chester was only six. As a boy James was encouraged in his literary interests by the distinguished South Carolina poet, Paul Hamilton Hayne, of Charleston, who bought Rockwell's first poem, written at age eleven. Hayne published it in the Augusta, Ga., *Chronicle*, which he then edited, paying for it at the rate of eleven cents a line. A little later the lad startled Carolina literary circles by writing in his sixteenth year the substantial poem—of extraordinary length for a teenager—"Chrystella: The Echo of a Dream," which contained much mature thought and expression as well as passages of poetic grace. It appeared in pamphlet form in 1887. When Eugene C. Brooks published the anthology, *North Carolina Poems*, in 1912, he included a biographical sketch of Rockwell together with a selection of his poems. Four lines from Rockwell appeared as a foreword to the book:

If we have weal, if we have woe,
If we have rights, if we have wrongs,
The world must all our feelings know—
We tell our stories in our songs.

The young poet labored indefatigably with a magazine he acquired in 1885 entitled *The Belles-Lettres*, published at Raleigh, but the post–Civil War poverty of the South made a journal of pure literature, issued twice a month at one dollar a year, impractical. Editors and reviewers lauded the magazine, but it ultimately folded. Rockwell had made it the outlet for much of his own writing; still its demise did not cause him to drop his pen. He arranged for the subscriptions to be filled by another publication so that no one lost by supporting him. His poems, essays, and book reviews shortly appeared in a new journal, the *State Chronicle*, launched in Raleigh by Walter Hines Page and Edward A. Oldham. Rockwell began to win acceptance for his verse and essays in northern publications.

Grief over the loss of his favorite brother, William, who had sponsored and supported him in his education and writing efforts, caused his health to decline. He spent the summer of 1886 at Old Fort, at that time a flourishing resort at the eastern foot of the Blue Ridge. There he came under the inspiration of a militant Baptist minister, the Reverend C. M. Murchison. Rockwell had been reared a Presbyterian, but under Murchison's influence he was converted to the Baptist faith and induced to enter the ministry. He enrolled in the Southern Theological Seminary at Louisville, Ky. While engaged in studies there he went to South Carolina and at Nichols, in Marion County, he married Loula Ayres at her family home, Beachwood, on 29 Feb. 1888. There their first son, Paul Ayres, was born on 3 Feb. 1889.

Rockwell's health did not permit him to complete his studies in Louisville. Being advised to settle in the mountains, he took an assignment in 1889 at the Baptist church in Waynesville but later in the year transferred to Morristown, Tenn. He soon found the climate there to be unsuitable and accepted a call to the First Baptist Church in Newport, Tenn., where his second son, Kiffin Yates, and daughter, Agnes, were born.

Rockwell died in Newport of typhoid fever and was buried in Morristown. He was known as a preacher of great forensic power, and his first sermon in Waynesville, the Waynesville *Courier* reported, left the congregation "spellbound." He was tall, wore a black beard, and, according to former governor Ben W. Hooper of Tennessee, "looked somewhat like my conception of one of the Twelve Apostles."

SEE: *Biblical Recorder*, 17 Mar. 1915; Eugene C. Brooks, ed., *North Carolina Poems* (1912); *Library of Southern Literature* 15 (1907); *North Carolina Poetry Review* 3 (January–February 1936); "Poems," with a memoir by Paul Ayres Rockwell (copy, North Carolina Collection, University of North Carolina, Chapel Hill [1956]); Paul A. Rockwell, *Three Centuries of the Rockwell Family in America, 1630–1930* (1930). A sketch of his life by his wife is in the Weeks manuscript bibliography, North Carolina Collection.

GLENN TUCKER

Rockwell, Kiffin Yates *(20 Sept. 1892–23 Sept. 1918)*, American aviator in World War I and pioneer in aerial combat, was a charter member of the Lafayette Escadrille, an American volunteer squadron formed on 20 Apr. 1916, approximately one year before the United States entered the European conflict. He was the first American to shoot down a hostile airplane, the second American killed in aerial warfare, and probably the first American to take up the Allied cause in the war.

Born in the Appalachian mountain town of Newport, Tenn., he was the son of James Chester, a native of North Carolina, and Loula Ayres Rockwell of Marion County, S.C. Because of the father's delicate health, the family moved to the East Tennessee mountains and during his convalescence there Kiffin was born. When the child was almost a year old, James Chester was stricken in an epidemic of typhoid fever and died.

Both of young Rockwell's grandfathers had been Confederate soldiers. Though his paternal grandfather, who served with Clingman's North Carolina Brigade, died about twenty years before Kiffin's birth, his maternal grandfather, Enoch Shaw Ayres, who served from Manassas to the surrender of General Joseph E. Johnston's army near Durham, was a companion of his early years. After her husband's death, his mother spent the winters on her father's cotton plantation along the Lumber and Little Pee Dee rivers of northeastern South Carolina but returned to the Tennessee mountains for the summers. Perhaps due to the war stories told by "Marse Enoch" and the coterie of Confederate veterans who came to his home to relive their battle experiences, the family retained a strong pride in Confederate feats of arms, which sent both grandsons—Kiffin and his older brother, Paul Ayres Rockwell—into military careers.

When Kiffin Rockwell was fourteen, the family moved across the mountains to Asheville, N.C., thereafter their home. While attending Asheville High School, he so strengthened his interest in the army that he enrolled in the autumn of 1908 in Virginia Military Institute at Lexington, Va. The next year he received an appointment to the U.S. Naval Academy at Annapolis. After a session at the Werntz Preparatory School studying for the entrance examinations, he concluded that the navy would not see action in his lifetime and he was not attracted to peacetime service. His brother Paul was attending Washington and Lee University, near Lexington, which Kiffin had frequently visited and where he now matriculated. He joined the Sigma Phi Epsilon fraternity, had a happy college life, and was pointed towards a newspaper career in the university, which, under the presidency of General Robert E. Lee, conducted the nation's first school of journalism. By this time Rockwell had grown into a handsome man: six feet, four inches tall, with eyes of clear blue, he had a charming manner and was a graceful dancer. He was popular with his schoolmates but reserved with strangers; he was never the back-slapping type.

His interest in journalism was intensified by a trip he took at this time through the United States and western Canada in order to discover the locality where he would like to settle. He loved San Francisco and spent several months there, later confiding during the barracks talk in France that life in the Golden Gate city was more like that of France than any other American city he knew. For a time he conducted an advertising agency there; though only nineteen, his height and demeanor made him appear older. After returning to Asheville in late 1913, he went on to Atlanta, Ga., on 1 Jan. 1914, where his brother was engaged in newspaper work. Kiffin joined another advertising agency, enrolled in an advertising correspondence school, and was achieving success in that field when war broke out in Europe.

On 3 Aug. 1914, when Germany declared war on France and President Woodrow Wilson issued his neutrality proclamation for the United States, Kiffin Rockwell, speaking also for his brother, wrote to the French consul in New Orleans volunteering for the French army. Later, at a time when he experienced a presentiment of death, he explained in a letter to his mother: "If I die you will know that I died as every man should—in fighting for the right. I do not consider that I am fighting for France alone, but for the cause of humanity, the most noble of all causes."

Without waiting for a reply from the French consul, the Rockwell brothers left Atlanta for New York and sailed for France on 7 August, well before aerial combat had entered warfare. Kiffin, then twenty-one, had handled firearms since he was ten and sought an infantry assignment. He and Paul joined the French Foreign Legion; for the French, Kiffin's attendance at Virginia Military Institute was a strong point in his record. Both men were severely wounded. In an infantry assault at Nouville-Saint-Vaast on 9 May 1915, Kiffin received a thigh injury that ended his marching and infantry service, while Paul's wound sent him into the French Army Grand Headquarters service. On recovery, Kiffin became one of the first Americans to join the newly formed Escadrille Americaine, soon renamed, upon complaint of the American government, the Lafayette Escadrille.

Airplanes, still in their infancy, and at first used only for reconnaissance, had become machines of combat in the boundless heavens, and air superiority was soon a factor in victory. After brief training and twenty-eight days after the formation of the Lafayette Escadrille, Kiffin, who had had no previous experience in aviation, shot down—on the Alsatian front on 18 May 1916—the first enemy plane credited to this new organization of American volunteers. Thereafter he saw continual combat with a leave in Paris after four months. Meantime, Kiffin had shot down his second enemy plane and had participated in every mission of his squadron. He gloried in the melee of squadron battle. In his first combat mission upon returning to duty, he encountered a two-seater German plane, dived into a dogfight with it, and was hit in the chest with what was described as an expanding bullet that shattered and killed him. The action occurred behind the French lines in the Vsoges sector, and his riddled plane fell into a field of flowers. Rockwell was a sergeant at the time but had been recommended for a commission as second lieutenant.

His funeral was notable, attended by his squadron comrades, fifty British pilots, and numerous French pilots and mechanics; the cortege included a regiment of French territorials and a battalion of colonials. The French government awarded him numerous citations and medals, made his grave a shrine, marked the place where he fell, and placed exhibits in its aviation museum. He also was honored in numerous ways in the United States—by North Carolina and his colleges; in poetry, including memorial poems by Edgar Lee Masters and Paul Scott Mowrer; and in a substantial literature on the Lafayette Escadrille. But perhaps the greatest tribute was that spoken at his grave-side service by the French aviator, Captain Georges Thenault, commandant of the squadron: "His courage was sublime. . . . The best and bravest of us is no longer here."

The Veterans of Foreign Wars post in Newport, Tenn., and an American Legion post in Asheville, N.C., are named in his honor. His letters home have been published in English and French. He was awarded posthumously the Cross of the Legion of Honor.

SEE: *DAB*, vol. 8 (1935); Philip M. Flanner, *The Vivid Air: The Lafayette Escadrille* (1981); Edmond C. C. Genet, *An American for Lafayette* (1981); James R. McConnell, *Flying for France with the American Escadrille at Verdun* (1917); *North Carolina Booklet* 19 (April–June 1920); Kiffin Yates Rockwell, *War Letters of Kiffin Yates Rockwell: Foreign Legionnaire and Aviator, France, 1914–1916* (1925); Paul A. Rockwell, *Three Centuries of the Rockwell Family in America* (1930); Georges Thenault, *Story of the Lafayette Escadrille* (1921); Arch [Arthur G. J.] Whitehouse, *Legion of the Lafayette* (1962).

GLENN TUCKER

Rodenbough, Grace Taylor *(5 Oct. 1897–8 Jan. 1967)*, educator and legislator, was born Grace Pemberton Taylor at Danbury, Stokes County, of English ancestry. Her father was James Spotswood Taylor, a wealthy tobacco farmer, at one time the second largest grower of flue-cured tobacco in the world. Her mother was Nellie Pemberton Moon, a Quaker, whose mother, Mary Moon Meredith, had been a world renowned Quaker evangelist. Grace was raised in the small courthouse town of her birth, surrounded by a large family of brothers and sisters. Among other business enterprises, her parents owned and operated the Piedmont Springs Hotel, a mineral springs resort a few miles above Danbury, where the family spent its summers. Grace attended the public schools until 1912, when she entered Guilford College; she was graduated with an A.B. degree in 1917. For the next several years she taught in various school systems in Stokes and Rockingham counties. On 12 Nov. 1929 she married Rex Exum Stuart, and they located in Winston-Salem, where she became an instructor of history and government at Salem College. She was divorced on 24 Nov. 1936 and returned to Danbury.

Becoming active in politics, she was president of her county's Young Democrats (1936–37) and then became vice-president of the North Carolina Young Democrats (1938–39). She also began taking a leadership position in the field of education, serving as president of the Stokes County chapter of the North Carolina Education Association (NCEA) in 1939–40. During World War II she was involved with various service committees: she was president of the Stokes County Red Cross (1942–43) and county chairman of War Savings Bonds sales (1943–45). In 1943 Governor J. Melville Broughton appointed her to head the county recruiting campaign for the Women's Army Corp. In 1943 she was elected a trustee of The University of North Carolina, the first citizen of Stokes County chosen for that board; reelected three times, she held her seat until her death.

In 1945 she became executive director of the American Red Cross in Tallahassee, Fla., but returned to North Carolina in 1946 as a field representative for the Red Cross. She was married for a second time, on 4 Aug. 1947, to Stanley Leigh Rodenbough, Jr. They purchased and restored the old Covington home north of Walnut Cove. In 1948 she was appointed supervisor of schools for Stokes County. To become more qualified for this job, she entered the University of North Carolina at Greensboro and received her master's degree in education (1952).

Two of Grace's brothers, Ed and John, had served in the North Carolina legislature, and John was sheriff of Stokes County from 1928 to 1948. Active in all the campaigns involving her family, Grace had become popular throughout the county. In 1952 she decided to seek a seat in the North Carolina House of Representatives and was elected handily to the 1953 legislature, the first woman elected to any office from Stokes County. She was the only woman in that session of the legislature, the eleventh in the history of the state. Mrs. Rodenbough was reelected seven more times, and her thirteen years in office far exceeded the tenure of any other legislator from Stokes.

In Raleigh, her chief interests centered on education and agriculture. She was an early supporter of Governor William B. Umstead and her friends Luther Hodges and Terry Sanford. In the campaign of 1964 she actively supported her close friend Richardson Preyer, but when Dan K. Moore was elected, she gave her legislative endorsement to him. Thus, she usually found herself in harmony with the state executive and could be counted on for crucial support. Throughout the state she became a favorite speaker on the emerging cause of wider involvement of women in business, government, and the professions. She did not advocate major shifts in the law but did introduce legislation creating more equal opportunity and a more humane application of the law. She said, "Men have run the affairs of this world a long time. I believe we can help them run it more humanely."

In 1953 Governor Umstead appointed her as the only legislator on the Commission on Higher Education. As a direct result of the work of this group, she introduced the bill that created the State Board of Higher Education. In 1956 she was a member of the special legislative subcommittee to consider school desegregation. That year Mrs. Rodenbough also was a delegate to the Democratic National Convention in Chicago. Governor Hodges named her to the Commission to Study the Cause and Control of Cancer in North Carolina. She fought against the Speaker Ban Law, which limited speakers who could appear on the campuses of state-supported colleges, and she helped in the successful repeal of the law in the next legislature. In 1965, in her last legislative session, she was appointed chairman of a special Committee on the Status of Women, a reflection of the growing significance of female awareness. In this last session Grace also was made vice-chairman of the House Finance Committee, the first woman to hold a major finance post in the state legislature. Because of declining health she did not run for reelection in 1966.

Grace Rodenbough was on the board of governors of the Governor's School, an educational experiment she fostered in the legislature. She was a trustee of the Northwestern Regional Library, director of Carolinas United, president of the Hanging Rock Park Foundation, and a member of Delta Kappa Gamma, Daughters of the American Revolution, United Daughters of the Confederacy, North Carolina Literary and Historical Association, North Carolina Society for the Preservation of Antiquities, and American Association of University Women. She was raised both in the Quaker church of her mother and the Methodist church of her father, but after her second marriage she joined the Presbyterian church. She had no children of her own but had two stepsons, Stanley Leigh and Charles Dyson Rodenbough. Her oil portrait hangs in the South Stokes High School. She died at Baptist Hospital in Winston-Salem after an extended illness and was buried in the family plot at Danbury.

SEE: John L. Cheney, Jr., ed., *North Carolina Government, 1585–1974* (1975); Stephen E. Massengill, *Biographical Directory of the General Assembly of North Carolina, 1963–1978*, vol. 2 (1979); Grace Taylor Rodenbough, family papers and scrapbook (possession of Charles D. Rodenbough, Madison, N.C.); Cameron P. West, *A Democrat and Proud of It* (1959).

CHARLES D. RODENBOUGH

Rodman, William Blount *(29 June 1817–7 Mar. 1893)*, lawyer and jurist, was born in Washington, Beaufort County, the son of William Wanton and Polly Anne Blount Rodman. His first known ancestor was John Rodman, an Irish Quaker who died in Barbados in 1686 and whose son John, a physician, moved first to Rhode Island and then to New York City by 1698. Rodman's father, the son of John and Marcia Pell Rodman of Pelham Manor in Westchester County, N.Y., moved to North Carolina about 1810 and on 6 June 1811 married the daughter of Mary Harvey and John Gray Blount of Washington. To them were born two girls and one boy, William Blount. Orphaned at age eight, Rodman together with his sisters were reared by his maternal grandfather and his aunt, Patsey Baker Blount. Rodman was a precocious child who loved to read and study. At age seven he could scan and translate Latin. He entered The University of North Carolina at age fifteen and was graduated first in his class at nineteen, having gained reading proficiency in Latin, Greek, French, and German. Rodman developed the habit of reading omnivorously and assimilating all that he read.

Before the Civil War he was devoted mainly to the practice of law. After studying under William Gaston and being admitted to the bar in 1838, he established a lucrative practice specializing in land law in Beaufort, Pitt, Martin, and Hyde counties. In 1854 Rodman was appointed to a three-man commission to revise the North Carolina Code; this work resulted in the revision of 1855. In his pleadings he was an eloquent speaker who depended more on reason than passion to carry his argument. Because Rodman was a Democrat and his home county voted Whig, he made few ventures into politics. In 1842 he ran for the legislature and was defeated, and in 1860 he was a Breckinridge elector. When Abraham Lincoln was elected president, Rodman advocated secession.

On 1 Sept. 1858 Rodman married Camilla Holliday Croom (d. 26 May 1887), the daughter of Elizabeth Holliday and Willie Jones Croom of Greensboro, Ala. Five children survived them: William B., Jr., general counsel of the Norfolk and Southern Railroad; Lida T.; Mrs. Owen H. Guion; Dr. John C., a surgeon; and Willie Croom.

Although Rodman served the Confederacy well, the Civil War caused him great financial loss. On 21 Oct. 1861 he organized Company C, Fortieth Regiment, North Carolina Artillery, known through 1862 as "Rodman's Battery," and was commissioned a captain. Because his guns had not been mounted, his battery fought as infantry at the Battle of New Bern in March 1862. On 13 March he was promoted to major of quartermaster and assigned to Lawrence O'B. Branch's Brigade. Then on 20 Dec. 1862 President Jefferson Davis appointed him presiding judge of a military court with a rank of colonel and sent him to General Edmund Kirby Smith's corps in Virginia. When Rodman learned that General Robert E. Lee would surrender at Appomattox, he walked from Pamplin's Station, Va., to Greensboro to surrender with General Joseph E. Johnston. When the war began, Rodman had expected that Washington, his home, would fall to Union forces, so he bought a plantation near Greensboro as a haven for his family. As anticipated, his plantation just across the river from Washington was pillaged and destroyed, and over one hundred slaves were carried off and scattered. Union forces seized as abandoned property all of his furniture, household goods, stock, and farm implements and destroyed many of the plantation buildings. But Rodman returned home and managed to regain his fortune. At his death he was a leading landholder in eastern North Carolina.

Rodman is most noted for his activities during Reconstruction. He believed that because Congress and the GOP would control Reconstruction, native whites should join the Republicans in drafting a new state constitution in order to restrain their excesses. Although other political leaders in Beaufort would not follow him, he joined the Republican party and was elected a delegate to the constitutional convention of 1868. As chairman of the judiciary committee Rodman found his committee so badly divided that he had to submit the major points on the judiciary to the convention for its decision. He did not like the article as finally drafted because it provided for the popular election of judges. But the provisions in the constitution limiting county taxes and establishing a ratio between poll and property taxes were drafted by him. His conservative views distinguished him in the convention. Without actively seeking the office, Rodman was elected associate justice of the state supreme court in 1868 and served for ten years. His decisions demonstrated scholarship and erudition in the law. From 1868 to 1873 he and two other state commissioners drafted codes of civil procedure and criminal procedure and a penal code. Only the code of civil procedure, adapted from the New York code, was approved by the legislature.

He became indirectly involved with George W. Swepson but denied that this relationship affected his supreme court decisions. In August 1869 Rodman went to the Nicholas Hotel in New York City, as was his habit before the war, and met Swepson, who offered his guarantee for the margin for Rodman to purchase $100,000 of North Carolina bonds. Instead of rising, as Rodman expected, the bonds fell sharply in value and were sold at a loss.

Of medium height with a handsome face and dark hair, Rodman was noted for his modesty, courtesy, friendliness, reasonableness, indulgence of his family, and reserved nature. He died a few days after suffering a serious fall and was buried in Oakdale Cemetery, Washington.

SEE: Samuel A. Ashe, ed., *Biographical History of North Carolina*, vol. 3 (1906), and *Cyclopedia of Eminent and Representative Men of the Carolinas*, vol. 2 (1892); Clipping files (North Carolina Collection, University of North Carolina, Chapel Hill); J. G. de Roulhac Hamilton, *Reconstruction in North Carolina* (1914); Louis H. Manarin, comp., *North Carolina Troops, 1861–1865: A Roster*, vol. 1 (1966); *North Carolina Reports* 116 (1895); Otto H. Olsen, *Carpetbagger's Crusade* (1965 [portrait]); Raleigh *News and Observer*, 8 Mar. 1893; C. Wingate Reed, *Beaufort County* (1962); United Daughters of the Confederacy, North Carolina Division, Pamlico Chapter No. 43, Washington, N.C., *Confederate Reveille: Memorial Edition* (1898).

JOHN L. BELL, JR.

Rodman, William Blount, Jr. *(19 Feb. 1862–18 Oct. 1946)*, lawyer, was born in an old hotel in Tarboro whence his mother had fled from the family plantation near Washington, N.C., during the Civil War. His father was William Blount Rodman. His mother, Camilla Holliday Croom of Alabama, was the daughter of Willie Jones and Elizabeth Holliday Croom. Willie Jones Croom was the son of Richard Croom and Ann Hare, who was the granddaughter of John Haywood of North Carolina.

Rodman's early life was filled with hardship, privation, and responsibility. During the war he lived on a plantation near Greensboro, but afterwards he moved with his family to the home place near Washington. Between the ages of nine and fourteen he was sent by his father to a plantation twenty miles from home to assist the overseer in executing his father's orders. Rodman learned to direct the shipment of cotton, corn, and produce. He entered The University of North Carolina in 1878, but after two years his father called him home to superintend a plantation, despite the pleadings of his professors that he was brilliant in mathematics. Rodman studied law every spare moment while he supervised the plantation, and in September 1883 he was admitted to the bar. A few months later he entered his father's office as a junior partner. He became a practical surveyor and a good land lawyer.

Over the next twenty years Rodman centered his activities around Washington. In addition to practicing law, he enlisted in 1881 as a private in the North Carolina State Guards, where he rose to the rank of colonel before retiring in 1902. While serving in the 1890s as chairman of the Democratic district executive committee and as a member of the state executive committee, he also was mayor of Washington for three terms. In addition, he chaired the Beaufort County executive committee of his party from 1898 to 1904. In 1903 the legislature selected Rodman and two others to codify the statute laws, and their work resulted in the code of 1905. During this period he was a director of the Bank of Washington, Haven's Oil Company, and E. Peterson Company; he was also attorney for the Old Dominion Steamship Company at Washington.

In 1904 Rodman moved to Charlotte and became a corporation lawyer for the remainder of his career. Also in 1904 the Southern Railway Company appointed him division counsel, a post he held until the Norfolk and Southern named him general solicitor in 1911, when he moved to Norfolk. In 1920 the Norfolk and Southern appointed him general counsel. He also served as a director of the Norfolk and Southern, the John L. Roper Lumber Company, and the National Bank of Commerce in Norfolk. He retired in 1942 because of ill health. In 1909 he became a trustee of The University of North Carolina.

On 17 Oct. 1888 Rodman married Addie Fulford, the daughter of Nathaniel S. Fulford, a Washington businessman. They had five children, four of whom survived him: William Blount, Jr., of Washington; Nathaniel Fulford, a Norfolk doctor; Mrs. John Robinson of Charlotte; and Mrs. George H. Curtis, Jr., of Norfolk.

A tall man with a dark complexion and gray eyes, Rodman was distinguished looking and quite reserved. His hobby was flower gardening. An Episcopalian and a Democrat, he was a member of the Princess Ann, Virginia, and Chesapeake clubs of Norfolk. He was buried in Oakdale Cemetery, Washington.

SEE: Samuel A. Ashe, ed., *Biographical History of North Carolina*, vol. 3 (1906); Norfolk *Virginian-Pilot*, 19 Oct. 1946; Raleigh *News and Observer*, 19 Oct. 1946; *Who Was Who in America*, vol. 2 (1982).

JOHN L. BELL, JR.

Rogers, John Henry *(9 Oct. 1845–15 Apr. 1911)*, attorney, congressman, and judge, was born near Roxobel, Bertie County, the son of Absalom and Harriet Rice Rogers. In 1852 the family moved to Mississippi and settled near Madison Station, where young Rogers attended the common schools. During the Civil War he served in the Ninth Mississippi Volunteer Regiment, advancing in rank from private to first lieutenant. He participated in battles in Georgia and in nearly all of the battles in which the Army of Tennessee was engaged; he was wounded twice. After the war he attended Centre College, Danville, Ky., and was graduated from the law department of the University of Mississippi at Oxford in 1868. Admitted to the bar, he practiced first in Canton, Miss., and then in Fort Smith, Ark. In 1877 he was elected circuit judge; reelected the following year, he served until his resignation in May 1882. He was elected as a Democrat to the Forty-eighth Congress and was returned three times, serving from March 1883 to March 1891. In 1895 he made the commencement address at Centre College and was awarded the LL.D. degree.

In Congress, as a member of the Committee on the Judiciary, Rogers focused his attention on the court system and on the administration of the Indian Territory. Declining to be a candidate in 1890, he resumed his practice in Fort Smith. In 1892 he was a delegate to the Democratic state convention and to the Democratic National Convention in Chicago. On 27 Nov. 1896 President Grover Cleveland appointed him U.S. district judge for the Western District of Arkansas, a post he held until his death in Little Rock.

An active Mason, Rogers was also a member of the United Confederate Veterans; on 22 May 1903 at the Confederate reunion in New Orleans, he delivered an impressive address reviewing the history of the idea of secession from early New England threats through the Civil War. Coming from a federal judge and former congressman, his remarks attracted national attention when they were printed as *The South Vindicated*. The original typescript copy is in the Southern Historical Collection at the University of North Carolina at Chapel Hill. Several other of his addresses were also published, including one on John Marshall on the occasion of the one-hundredth anniversary of his accession to the chief justiceship of the United States.

Rogers married Mary Gray Dunlap in October 1873 at Danville, Ky., and they became the parents of four sons, the first of whom, Theodore, died at age two, and a daughter. His surviving children were Albert Dunlap, John H., Jr., Randolph, and Bessie (Mrs. Roy Johnston). The town of Rogers, a mountain resort in northwestern Arkansas, was named for him. He was buried in Oak Cemetery, Fort Smith.

SEE: *Biog. Dir. Am. Cong.* (1989); *Confederate Veteran*, vols. 11, 19 (June 1903, May 1911 [portrait]); *Congressional Record* (March 1883–March 1891); *Fort Smith Times Record*, 17–18, 20 Apr. 1911; John E. Tyler (Roxobel, N.C.), personal contact, January 1980; *Who Was Who in America*, vol. 1 (1943).

LINDA ANGLE MILLER

Rogers, Sion Hart *(30 Sept. 1825–14 Aug. 1874)*, lawyer, congressman, soldier, and attorney general, was born in Wake County near Raleigh. His parents were Sion, a planter whose father was the nephew of the first sheriff of Wake County, and Narcissa Gray Jeffreys Rogers. After attending the Lovejoy Academy in Raleigh, Rogers entered The University of North Carolina, where he received a B.A. degree in 1846 and an M.A. degree in 1849. He was admitted to the bar in 1848 and began his practice at the law office of U.S. Senator George E. Badger in Raleigh.

Rogers, a Whig, was nominated in 1852 for a seat in the North Carolina House of Commons, only to be defeated by Judge Romulus M. Saunders, who was able to obtain a majority of twenty-seven votes. In 1853 Rogers was again nominated by the Whig party but this time for a seat in the U.S. House of Representatives. Rogers won the election, defeating Abram W. Venable, a Democrat, by a small majority. He declined, however, to be a candidate for renomination in 1854 and returned home to be a solicitor for the Raleigh district of the superior court.

With the secession of North Carolina from the Union on 20 May 1861, Rogers, like many of North Carolina's leading citizens, offered his services to the Confederacy. On 21 May he received a commission as first lieutenant of Company K (the Raleigh Rifles) in the Fourteenth Regiment of North Carolina Troops. After resigning from this regiment on 11 Nov. 1861, he received a commission as a colonel in April 1862 and was placed in command of the Forty-seventh Regiment, North Carolina Troops, which was still in the process of organizing. Rogers and those companies of the Forty-seventh that had arrived in Raleigh were sent to eastern North Carolina, near Kinston, and placed under the overall command of Brigadier General Nathan George (Shanks) Evans. Rogers and his regiment assisted in the attempt to block Federal forces under the command of Major General John Gray Foster that were advancing up the Neuse River. The Forty-seventh Regiment remained in and around Kinston for several weeks before returning to Raleigh to complete its organization. Colonel Rogers resigned from the Confederate army on 5 Jan. 1863, after his election as attorney general of the state of North Carolina the previous December. He served in this position until the constitution of 1868 took effect.

Having become a Democrat after the war, Rogers won a seat in the Forty-second Congress (4 Mar. 1871–3 Mar. 1873). James H. Harris, his Republican opponent, contested the election and thus prevented Rogers from serving the Fourth District for the full two years; not until 23 May 1872 did he begin his duties in Congress. In his bid for reelection Rogers was defeated by William A. Smith, a Republican who won a majority of 724 votes. Rogers's most successful initiative on Capitol Hill was to secure the funds for a federal post office and courthouse building in Raleigh. The cornerstone of this structure was laid on 4 July 1874, but construction was not completed until after Rogers's death.

Rogers married Jane Frances Haywood, the daughter of U.S. Senator William H. Haywood, on 8 Mar. 1853. They had four children: William Haywood (m. Kate Avera Wilder), Allen Gray (m. Margaret Trapier), Sion Hart (m. Elizabeth Woodard), and Minnie Baker (m. Edward S. Hughes). Rogers died in Raleigh and was buried in the City Cemetery.

SEE: *Biog. Dir. Am. Cong.* (1971); John L. Cheney, Jr., ed., *North Carolina Government, 1585–1974* (1975); Walter Clark, ed., *Histories of the Several Regiments and Battalions from North Carolina*, vol. 3 (1901); Daniel L. Grant, *Alumni History of the University of North Carolina* (1924); Louis H. Manarin, comp., *North Carolina Troops, 1861–1865: A Roster*, vol. 5 (1975); U.S. Department of the Interior, *National Register of Historic Places Inventory—Nomination Form* (Rogers-Bagley-Daniels-Pegues House).

ALAN C. DOWNS

Rolfe, Thomas. *See* **Relfe, Thomas.**

Rollins, Edward Tyler, Sr. *(12 Mar. 1864–22 June 1931)*, newspaper publisher, was born at Cary, the son of Wyatt Paul and Eliza Jane Smith Rollins. His early education was meager, and his formal schooling did not extend beyond the grammar grades of Page's School. He moved to Durham about 1880 and worked first for the North Carolina Railroad and then for Blackwell Tobacco Company. In 1895 he became part owner of the *Durham Morning Herald* and for thirty-six years that paper was his life.

In October 1894 three printers, W. W. Thompson, Zeb V. Council, and one Gates had formed a partnership to publish a small daily, the *Morning Herald*. In November another Durham paper, the *Daily Globe*, suspended publication, its composing room foreman, Joe H. King, joined the partners, and the fledgling paper became the afternoon *Globe-Herald*. By January 1895 Council and Gates withdrew and Thompson and King retained ownership. Immediately, they reverted to a morning paper and restored the name, the *Morning Herald*. In February 1895 Thompson sold his half of the business to E. T. Rollins, and the partnership with King continued for twenty-four years. Rollins assumed responsibility for the business end of the operation, although he did help with gathering local news. King served as editor, makeup man, reporter, and advertising manager.

From the beginning, the King-Rollins partnership was successful. Carl C. Council became a partner with Rollins in 1918, when he purchased the interest of King. The Durham Herald Company, as it became known, bought the afternoon *Durham Sun* in 1929, and a 24-hour, seven-day-week newspaper service was provided for Durham. Rollins insisted that his paper should be profitable and should serve the community with conviction, courage, and accuracy. Fair in all his dealings, he inspired loyalty among his employees and was quick to compliment one for a job well done. He was always amenable to suggestions from them for improving the papers.

In service to the community, Rollins served on the boards of directors of several banks and building and loan associations. His advice was sought by local firms whose heads had come to know him through advertising. He was a director of the Durham Chamber of Commerce during its initial years.

His principal extracurricular obsession was economic administration of government, especially at the local level. To have a voice in that, he was a member of the Durham City Council for five years and was one of the first advocates of the council-manager form of government. In his stress on economy, he was not parsimonious, only insistent that expenditures be made on the basis of good judgment with full value for every dollar spent, a concept he used in his business. Rollins was one of the first publishers in the area to purchase a linotype machine as early as 1899.

The schools of Durham and Durham County were also among his special interests, and he was vocal in his opposition to what he labeled "slip-shod" financial administration of the schools. He insisted on the control of public expenditures "by the idea of permanent public service." His convictions were so strong that he refused in 1925 to run for reelection to the council because he opposed a proposed added countywide tax. It was said of him that "he hated hypocrisy—shunned flattery and was utterly frank. He was a man of many parts and all of them admirable and wholesome."

Rollins married Bessie Steed of Oxford on 13 June 1900, and they were the parents of four children: Elizabeth (Mrs. P. G. Wallace), Mary Webb (Mrs. W. Y. Pickell), Steed, and Edward Tyler, Jr. He died at his home in Durham and was buried in Maplewood Cemetery.

SEE: *Charlotte Observer*, 23 June 1931; *Durham Morning Herald*, 8 Apr. 1925, 23 June 1931, 6 Mar. 1949; *Durham Sun*, 1 Mar. 1949; Raleigh *News and Observer*, 23–24 June 1931 [portrait]).

C. SYLVESTER GREEN

Rondthaler, Edward *(24 July 1842–31 Jan. 1931)*, Moravian bishop, pastor, administrator, teacher, historian, editor, writer, linguist, and community leader, was born at Schoeneck, Northampton County, Pa., in the parsonage of Schoeneck Moravian Church, which his father, Edward Rondthaler, Sr., served as pastor from 1841 to 1844. His mother, the former Sarah Louisa Rice of Bethlehem, Pa., was the granddaughter of John Heckewelder, missionary to the North American Indians, whose father, George, had emigrated from Moravia to Saxony in the 1720s, and of Owen Rice, a Welshman who was minister of the Moravian church in Philadelphia. She bore three children, Edward, Jr., Mary, and Howard, and died at Nazareth, Pa., in 1854.

The first Rondthaler of record, being Protestant, was exiled from Salzburg, Austria, to Prussia around 1731. Edward Rondthaler's great-grandfather, Albert Rondthaler, was a Lutheran pastor in Pomerania. His grandfather, Emmanuel Rondthaler, was born there in 1764 but grew up in a Moravian congregation (Neusalz) in Silesia, served the Moravian church at Sarepta, Russia, for ten years, and, having been ordained at Sarepta, returned to Germany. Sent to America, he became pastor in 1808 of the Moravian church at York, Pa., and in 1819 of the Moravian church at Nazareth, where he died in 1847. His father, Edward Rondthaler, Sr., born in 1817 at York and educated at Nazareth Hall, a Moravian boys' boarding school, and Moravian Theological Seminary, then also in Nazareth, was a pastor and teacher, author and linguist, principal of Nazareth Hall, and afterwards professor in the theological seminary until his death in 1855.

Edward Rondthaler, Jr., entered Nazareth Hall in 1853 and Moravian College and Theological Seminary in 1856. At the seminary, which was relocated in Bethlehem in 1858, he studied biblical and classical languages, biblical exegesis, dogmatics, mathematics, history, and classical literature; he was graduated in 1862. Nine months of graduate study at the University of Erlangen, Germany, were followed by a walking tour of Germany, with visits to Switzerland and Italy. After teaching for a year at Nazareth Hall, he received a call to the Moravian church in Brooklyn, N.Y. Ordained a deacon at Central Church in Bethlehem in 1865, he was raised to the rank of presbyter at a synod in Bethlehem in 1868.

On 1 Oct. 1867 Rondthaler (no longer known as Jr.) was married in Bethlehem to Mary Elizabeth Jacobson, daughter of Bishop and Mrs. John Christian Jacobson. To their union, which lasted sixty-three years and four months, were born six children: Alice, on 27 July 1868, and Howard Edward, on 17 July 1871, both in Brooklyn; a second daughter, who lived only five months, in Salem; and three children who died in infancy and were buried in Bethlehem.

While pastor in Brooklyn, Rondthaler directed rebuilding of the church and parsonage, which had been destroyed by fire, and contributed to *The Independent*, a magazine of news and opinion. Called to the First Moravian Church in Philadelphia in 1874, he earnestly appealed to his congregation for its full dedication to Christ, while strengthening his own belief in the crucifixion and resurrection of Jesus Christ as the cardinal doctrines of the Christian faith.

In 1877 he became pastor of the Salem Moravian congregation, arriving on 19 October to occupy the brick parsonage on South Church Street—constructed in 1841 by his wife's father, as principal of Salem Female Academy—where he lived until his death. In addition to his pastorate at Home Moravian Church he became, in 1884, the tenth principal of Salem Female Academy; he served for four years, continuing thereafter to teach the courses in biblical literature. First elected to the Provincial Elders' Conference (governing board) of the Southern Province in 1880, he held office until 1929, serving as president from 1891. In this capacity he not only presided over the triennial synods and went as fraternal delegate to the Northern Province synods but also attended the decennial assemblies of the General Synod of the worldwide Moravian church (Unity of the Brethren) held in Herrnhut, Germany, in 1879, 1889, 1899, 1909, and 1914, with the journey in 1889 including travel to the Holy Land. As president of the Provincial Elders' Conference he was ex officio chairman of several boards, including that of Salem Academy and Salem College, and a member of the Moravian College and Theological Seminary Board of Trustees. Chairman of the Salem Boys' School Board of Directors, he also taught Bible courses at the school.

Elected bishop, Edward Rondthaler was elevated to the episcopacy of the Moravian church on 12 Apr. 1891. Only the second bishop ever consecrated in Salem, he was the senior *Episcopus Fratrum* in the world at the time of his death. After founding *The Wachovia Moravian* in 1893, he continued as the Provincial monthly's editor until his death, except for a five-year period.

In 1908 Bishop Rondthaler relinquished his duties as pastor of Home Church to devote more time to the development of the Salem congregation, of which he remained head pastor, and the Southern Province as a whole. Through 1930 he conducted the Easter Sunrise Service at the Salem Moravian graveyard and prepared the annual *memorabile* of the Salem congregation. *The Memorabilia of Fifty Years, 1877 to 1927* appeared in 1928; those of 1928, 1929, and 1930 were published in a separate volume. Aside from biblical studies, history, especially Moravian history, was Rondthaler's favorite subject; he presented before the Wachovia Historical Society papers on "The Life of Bishop August Gottlieb Spangenberg" and "The Use of the Lot in the Moravian Church." Also a linguist, he was not only fluent in English and German but also read Hebrew, Greek, and Latin. Conversant in one or more romance languages, he began to study Spanish at about age eighty.

In 1880 The University of North Carolina conferred upon him a doctor of divinity degree. So distinguished was his career of service and scholarship, and so keen his insight into local, state, national, and international affairs, that the university summoned him to Chapel Hill again in 1918 to award him a doctor of laws degree.

In 1930 the Winston-Salem Chamber of Commerce named Rondthaler the city's Outstanding Citizen and awarded him its Service Cup for "meritorious, unselfish and distinguished community service." The cup, filled with white flowers, stood beside his casket until the funeral service at Home Church on 2 Feb. 1931, the day of his burial in a reserved space in the first lot ever used in God's Acre, the Salem Moravian graveyard.

In 1913 the Rondthaler Memorial Building of Home Church was named in his honor, and in 1949 Moravian Theological Seminary established the Bishop Edward Rondthaler Chair of Practical Theology in memory of the life and work of this compassionate, learned, and saintly servant of God.

SEE: Walser H. Allen, *Recollections of Bishop Edward Rondthaler* (1966); John H. Clewell, *History of Wachovia in North Carolina* (1902); J. Taylor Hamilton and Kenneth G. Hamilton, *History of the Moravian Church: The Renewed Unitas Fratrum, 1722–1957* (1967); "Memoir of Edward Rondthaler" (Moravian Archives, Winston-Salem); *North Carolina Biography*, vol. 3 (1941); William N. Schwarze, *History of Moravian College and Theological Seminary* (1910); Edwin L. Stockton, Jr., ed., *Salem's Remembrancers* (1976); John R. Weinlick, *Twentieth-Century Moravian College—Challenge and Response* (1977); Manly Wade Wellman, *Winston-Salem in History* (1966).

WALSER H. ALLEN, JR.

Rondthaler, Howard Edward *(17 June 1871–22 Oct. 1956)*, Moravian bishop, college president, civic and cultural leader, scholar, and raconteur, was born in Brooklyn, N.Y., the son of the Reverend Edward and Mrs. Mary Elizabeth Jacobson Rondthaler. His great-grandfather, Emmanuel Rondthaler, emigrated from Germany to America, where he was pastor of two Moravian congregations in Pennsylvania. His paternal grandfather, Edward, Sr., was pastor of Moravian congregations in Maryland and Pennsylvania before becoming principal of Nazareth Hall (a Moravian boys' boarding school) and then professor at Moravian Theological Seminary. His father, Edward, was pastor of Moravian congregations in New York and Pennsylvania before moving in 1877 to Salem, where he served for varying periods as pastor of Home Church, head pastor of Salem Moravian congregation, president of the Provincial Elders' Conference of the Moravian church, Southern Province, and a bishop of the worldwide Moravian church (Unity of Brethren) until his death in 1931.

Howard Rondthaler's mother, the daughter of Bishop and Mrs. John Christian Jacobson of Bethlehem, Pa., formerly of Salem, accompanied her husband and their two children to Salem, where she died in 1934. Howard was the younger of the two children. His sister Alice, also born in Brooklyn, was three years older. A second sister, born in Salem in 1879, lived only for five months.

Howard was educated at the Salem Boys' School from 1882 to 1889. He was graduated from The University of North Carolina in 1893 with a bachelor of philosophy degree, only narrowly missing the distinction of Phi Beta Kappa. In 1892–93 he participated in the North Carolina Geological Survey. He received the bachelor of divinity degree from Moravian Theological Seminary in Bethlehem, Pa., in 1896.

On 2 July 1896 he was ordained a deacon of the Moravian church and became, under his father, an assistant pastor of Salem congregation. Put in charge of Christ Church and, at various times, the Fairview, Mayodan, and Moravia congregations, he proved himself worthy of advancement and was ordained a presbyter by his father in 1899. In 1903 he was called to Bethlehem and made resident professor at Moravian College and Theological Seminary, assigned to teach Latin, mathematics, and natural science in the college and homiletics and liturgics in the theological seminary. While in residence he earned a master of arts degree from Moravian College in 1907.

In 1909 Rondthaler was appointed president of Salem Academy and College. President Rondthaler headed the dual Moravian institution for women throughout his forty-year administration, the longest institutional presidency in American Moravian history. The Salem faculty grew from a total of 49 for the combined preparatory and collegiate departments in 1909 to a total of 45 for the college alone in 1949. In 1909 there were 109 students classified as preparatory, while 203 comprised the collegiate group; but by 1949 the college alone included 397 students. In 1909 buildings and grounds were valued at $211,000, with the endowment listed at $40,000. Persistent and fruitful effort by Rondthaler gradually increased the value of assets in both categories. Particularly noteworthy was his success in raising funds in response to challenge grants by the General Education Board and in completing in 1930 the three-building complex that provided an adjoining campus with separate facilities for the academy. Moravians and other local benefactors also contributed monies for the building of a library and other essential structures for the college. In the 1940s Mrs. Hattie M. Strong established a fund for the college and made possible the construction of another residence hall and the refectory.

While the institution was earning accreditation by the Southern Association of Colleges and Schools, its head served as president of the North Carolina College Association in 1926 and of the Southern Association of Women's Colleges in 1938. Awarded the D.D. degree by Moravian College in 1913 and the LL.D. degree by The University of North Carolina in 1931, Rondthaler was long active in civic as well as church affairs. He served as president of the Winston-Salem Salvation Army, the Winston-Salem Travelers Aid, and the North Carolina Conference for Social Services and as chairman of the North Carolina YMCA's overseas personnel committee (1917–19). During World War II he became a member of the Forsyth County Selective Service Board and after 1942 president of the North Carolina School for the Deaf (at Morganton) Board of Directors, on which he had served since 1928. He twice was district governor (North Carolina, South Carolina, and Virginia) of Rotary International and president of The University of North Carolina Alumni Association. Though offered the presidency of The University of North Carolina, he declined the prestigious post in order to honor his obligations to the Moravian church.

Rondthaler was long and closely associated with his father in the latter's pastoral and administrative labors. In later years he himself was elected a member and vice-president of the Provincial Elders' Conference of the Southern Province of the Moravian church and served with wisdom and faithfulness.

For many years he commanded a loyal and widespread following through the radio broadcast of the lessons that he taught to the Men's Bible Class of Home Church. Travel in England, Europe, Egypt, and Palestine helped to make him effective as a preacher, teacher, and public speaker. He belonged to and advocated the work of the Moravian Society for the Propagation of the Gospel. On 19 Nov. 1947 Rondthaler was elected bishop by the Synod of the Southern Province, and on 12 Jan. 1948 he was consecrated at Home Church.

Identified with various cultural and scientific groups, he held membership in the Cosmos Club, Fossils, Torch Club, Elisha Mitchell Scientific Society, Newcomen Society of Great Britain and America, and North Carolina Literary and Historical Association, of which he was president in 1915. In 1930 he was an incorporator of the Wachovia Historical Society. He also belonged to the Moravian Historical Society (in Pennsylvania) for over half a century. As a student at The University of North Carolina he had been tapped by Sigma Alpha Epsilon and the Order of the Ginghoul.

On 29 Sept. 1898 Rondthaler married Katharine Genther Boring, daughter of Edwin and Elizabeth G. Boring of Philadelphia. They had four children: Theodore E., Edward III, Elizabeth, and Jane. Howard Rondthaler died in Winston-Salem. After his triumphant funeral service at Home Church, on 24 Oct. 1956, he was buried in the Salem Moravian graveyard.

SEE: References cited for Edward Rondthaler; Jacques Cattell and E. E. Ross, *Leaders in Education* (1948); *New York Times*, 23 Oct. 1956; *Who's Who in American Education*, vol. 14 (1950); *Who Was Who in America* (1960).

WALSER H. ALLEN, JR.

Rondthaler, Theodore Edward *(5 Aug. 1899–8 Apr. 1966)*, teacher, was born at Christ Church parsonage in Salem. The first of his forebears to come to America was Emanuel Rondthaler, who was raised by a Moravian pastor in Herrnhut, Saxony; he became a Moravian missionary and was sent to Sarepta, Russia, before moving to York, Pa., in 1808. One of his three sons, Edward (1819–55), was a Moravian pastor in Nazareth. This man's son, Edward (1842–1931), served as bishop of the Southern Congregation and president of Salem College in North Carolina. The bishop's son, Howard Edward (1871–1956), the father of Theodore Edward, was a Moravian pastor who served as president of Salem College and then as bishop of the Southern Province. Theodore's mother was Katherine Boring Rondthaler, a Philadelphia Quaker. Another ancestor was the Reverend John Heckewelder, a missionary and historian among the Indians, who assisted President George Washington in preventing an Indian war in the present state of Ohio.

Rondthaler attended Moravian Preparatory School in Bethlehem, Pa., and three schools in Winston-Salem—Salem Preparatory School, Tinsley Military Institute, and Winston-Salem High School. During the summers from 1912 to 1921 he visited his aunt at Pocono Lake Preserve, Pa., where he learned rowing, swimming, and canoeing and entertained with his guitar and clarinet. At the Quaker camp of a hundred cottages, he worked delivering supplies by boat and came to appreciate the high Quaker standards and ideals.

In 1915 he entered The University of North Carolina, where his education was interrupted when he and others in his class were sent to Officers' Training School at Plattsburg, N.Y. After about six months' training at Buffalo University, he was discharged as a second lieutenant. In Chapel Hill he and others were graduated with the class of 1919 without having to make up the courses missed. While at the university he ran cross-country and was editor-in-chief of the *University of North Carolina Magazine*, secretary of Phi Beta Kappa, and a member of the student council. He also was a member of Golden Fleece, the highest honorary organization on campus.

During the year following his graduation he was an instructor at the university and began to work on a master's degree. Rondthaler then went to New York to try to decide whether he really wanted to teach; he lived in the Bowery YMCA and worked at such jobs as unloading bananas and fish. Later he was employed for about six months with National Carbide in Jersey City, until offered a position as superintendent of a department. By this time he had decided that he really wanted to become a teacher and entered Princeton University, from which he received a master's degree in 1923 with a major in English and Latin; he met his expenses by tutoring pupils at the Hunn School. Afterwards he bicycled through Europe and attended classes at the University of Munich (1923) and the University of Paris (1924).

Returning to Winston-Salem for the Christmas of 1924, he began to teach Latin at Salem College. There he fell in love with his father's secretary, Alice Billing Keeney, of Connecticut, who became his wife in 1927, and gave up his plans to study for a doctorate. From 1928 to 1945 Rondthaler was a high school teacher and the principal at a school in Clemmons near Winston-Salem. In 1945 he became treasurer of Black Mountain College, a utopian educational endeavor, and taught a variety of unusual courses such as "Extraordinary Communities" and "Conventional Punctuation." As treasurer he successfully negotiated for accreditation under the GI Bill of Rights and used his initiative to obtain buildings and equipment from the federal government.

With their own children enrolled in Reed College,

Portland, Oreg., the Rondthalers in 1948 began teaching at the school on Ocracoke Island, where they owned a home. He ceased to teach in 1962 but remained active in the community until his death.

Rondthaler, who had become a licensed land surveyor in 1956, entered this field after his retirement. He also was chairman of the Board of Mosquito Control but demoted himself to manager in order to become more involved in the actual work. For many years he taught the adult Bible class in the Methodist church and served as a lay preacher. Having been a scoutmaster in Forsyth County many years before, he also was a scoutmaster on Ocracoke Island. Music was his hobby, and he played the clarinet, oboe, bassoon, flute, Autoharp, and guitar as well as composed music. An outdoorsman, he enjoyed hiking, sailing, and swimming. On one occasion he swam across the Yadkin River at flood stage and on another he climbed the cables of Brooklyn Bridge.

The Rondthalers had two children: Howard Mayro, who was employed by the National Forest Service in Portland, Oreg., and Alice Katherine, who married Dr. George M. Woodwell, an ecologist at Woods Hole, Mass. Rondthaler died in Durham, where he and his wife had moved in October 1965 to live in the Methodist Retirement Home in anticipation of his auditing classes at the Institute of Government in Chapel Hill. He was buried in the community cemetery at Ocracoke.

SEE: Martin Duberman, *Black Mountain: An Exploration in Community* (1972); *Durham Morning Herald*, 9 Apr. 1966; *Durham Sun*, 8 Apr. 1966; Daniel L. Grant, *Alumni History of the University of North Carolina* (1924); *North Carolina Biography*, vol. 3 (1928); Raleigh *News and Observer*, 9 Apr. 1966; Alice Kenney Rondthaler, "Memoir of Theodore Rondthaler," *Ocracoke Island News*, 8 Apr. 1966.

B. W. C. ROBERTS

Root, Charles Boudinot *(31 Oct. 1818–7 May 1903)*, silversmith, businessman, and civic leader of Raleigh, was born in Montague, Mass., the son and only surviving child of Elihu Root (1767–1869), a prominent landowner, and Sophia Gunn, daughter of Samuel Gunn, Patriot soldier in the American Revolution. He was a descendant of the Englishman Thomas Root, who settled in Hartford, Conn., in 1637 and lived there until his death in 1694. Charles was educated at the academy in Greenfield, Mass. In 1835 he went to New York, but his stay was brief. Two years later he moved to Raleigh and went into business with Bernard Dupuy, a flourishing silversmith and jeweler. Both Dupuy and Root were skilled craftsmen; a sizable number of exceptionally beautiful pieces made by both survive. Examples of their work are on display in the North Carolina Museum of History. Root acquired the business from Dupuy in 1842 and operated it successfully until he sold it in 1860.

During the first years of the Civil War Root was the acting mayor of Raleigh in the absence of the elected mayor, Captain William Harrison. After the war his principal business interest was the Raleigh Gas Company, which he served as president for eighteen years. In 1884 he was elected to the post of city tax collector, a position he held for several years. At various times during the following years Root was a magistrate, a city alderman, and chairman of the board of county commissioners. His political affiliation was with the Democratic party.

In 1847 Root married Annie Freeman Gales of Raleigh, the bond being dated 10 June. She was the daughter of Weston R. Gales and the granddaughter of Joseph Gales. There were two children who reached maturity, Love Gales (Mrs. V. E. Turner of Raleigh) and Charles, also of Raleigh.

C. B. Root was greatly esteemed by his contemporaries. His funeral was conducted at Christ Church, with interment in Oakwood Cemetery, Raleigh.

SEE: Moses N. Amis, *Historical Raleigh with Sketches of Wake County and Its Important Towns* (1913); Samuel A. Ashe, *Cyclopedia of Eminent and Representative Men of the Carolinas*, vol. 2 (1892); George B. Cutten and Mary Reynolds Peacock, *Silversmiths of North Carolina, 1696–1850* (1973); ; Raleigh *News and Observer*, 8 May 1903; *Raleigh Register*, 17 Nov. 1843; Wake County Marriage Bonds.

M. R. B. PEACOCK

Rose, Paul Howard *(17 Oct. 1881–19 Jan. 1955)*, founder of the chain of Roses Stores, was born in Jackson of Scottish and English ancestry. He was the son of Thomas Bragg Rose, a cabinetmaker and wheelwright, and his wife, Andrew Etta Warrick.

Born during a period when money was scarce, Rose soon learned the necessity to work. His talent for merchandising came early. As a boy in Jackson and Seaboard, he cut lightwood splinters and bundled and sold them; his mother baked cookies for him to sell; and he concocted a drink made of vinegar and soda that sold well. Later he obtained a large wooden packing case for his first place of business and stocked it with assorted items. A friendly doctor-druggist allowed him to put the case in his drugstore each night.

His formal education was limited, but he was always determined to study and to improve his mind. While in his teens, he learned to be a telegraph operator and found work utilizing his training. Rose studied the printing trade, acquired a large foot press and cases of type, and at one time published a trade magazine. He also learned the art of sign painting. Later he attended a business school in Norfolk, Va., and soon became a stenographer for a tobacco firm. All of this stood him in good stead when he decided to go into business for himself.

After finishing his schooling Rose opened his first "real" store in Littleton. His capital was very limited and to make his store look full he ordered empty shoe boxes to fill many of the shelves. He also bought remnants of material to wrap around pieces of cardboard to give the appearance of full bolts of cloth.

Rose was a great sales promoter. In his little store, he featured candy by staging a Popular Girl Contest. As a result of this promotion, he sold a quantity of candy that was out of proportion to the size town. He also attracted the attention of the manufacturers from whom he purchased most of his candy, and they promptly summoned him to New York with an offer to represent their line in all of the southeastern states. Being a natural-born salesman he soon established a good sales record. Because he called on only one merchant in each city, he had considerable time on his hands between trains (in those days there were no automobiles for the traveling salesmen). This gave him an opportunity to approach the five-and-tens in the places he visited and discuss the problems of merchandising with the managers. During this period he conceived the idea of organizing a buying syndicate to consolidate stores' purchases in order to obtain better prices. This buying association proved to be successful and was, in effect, the forerunner of several such modern buying organizations.

Every worthwhile endeavor must have an objective, and Rose's goal was to own a chain of stores. So he decided to abandon the buying organization and his Littleton store and start a chain of stores known as the United 5 & 10¢ Stores. He and two other men formed a partnership and opened several units, one in Henderson and another in Charlotte. Competition was keen, and sales were disappointing. This prompted one of the partners to withhold the money he had agreed to put into the new venture, which left the young and struggling business without sufficient capital to survive. It was a difficult time for Rose because he found himself financially embarrassed and his business reputation and integrity at stake. Yet disappointment did not conquer his spirit of enthusiasm nor lessen his determination to own and operate a chain of stores. He believed where there is a hill, there is a valley; where there is a disappointment, there is a compensating blessing. He borrowed $500 from his brother-in-law to buy the Henderson unit of the defunct United Stores and negotiated an agreement with the creditors to pay them $50 a week until the purchase price of the store was paid in full. Thus was started in 1915 the first unit of what was destined to be the chain of Roses Stores, Inc., consisting of 250 variety and junior department stores located in eleven southeastern states, three distribution warehouses, a fixture manufacturing plant, and a fleet of trucks.

Rose was active in the Methodist church, of which he was a member. He also took a lively interest in the Rotary Club and all community projects. Though a lifelong Democrat, he had no political aspirations. He shunned publicity for himself but sought it vigorously for his stores. On 13 Sept. 1911 he married Emma Myrick of Littleton and they were the parents of four daughters: Virginia Edgerton, Jessie Myrick (m. L. H. Harvin, Jr.), Alice Warrick (m. William J. Vaughan), and Emma Thomas (m. John T. Church). Rose was buried in Henderson.

SEE: *Charlotte News*, 12 Nov. 1933; *Heritage of Vance County* (1984); *North Carolina Biography*, vol. 5 (1941); Raleigh *News and Observer*, 20 Jan. 1955; Southern Pines *Pilot*, 6 Mar. 1974.

THOMAS B. ROSE, JR.

Rosenau, Milton Joseph *(1 Jan. 1869–9 Apr. 1946)*, epidemiologist and founder of the School of Public Health at The University of North Carolina, was born in Philadelphia, Pa., the son of Matilda Blitz and Nathan Rosenau, a Jewish merchant. He attended the Philadelphia public schools before entering the University of Pennsylvania, where he received the M.D. degree in 1889. Later he studied at the Hygienic Institute in Berlin (1892–93) and at the Pathological Institute in Vienna and the Pasteur Institute in Paris (1900).

Rosenau served as assistant surgeon with the U.S. Marine Hospital Service (now the U.S. Public Health Service) in Washington, D.C. (1890–92) and as quarantine officer at San Francisco (1895–98) and in Cuba (1898). In 1899 he was appointed director of the Hygienic Laboratory (the nucleus of the National Institute of Health) of the U.S. Public Health Service, a research facility, where he produced important work on the epidemiology of diphtheria, typhoid fever, yellow fever, malaria, botulism, and the tubercle bacillus, and where his studies on milk sanitation greatly helped popularize the pasteurization process in the United States.

In 1909 Rosenau was appointed Charles Wilder professor of preventive medicine at the Harvard Medical School, where in 1913 he established and served as director of the first school of public health in the United States; from 1922 until his retirement in 1935, he was professor of epidemiology in the school. Also in 1913 Rosenau published his most important work, *Preventive Medicine and Hygiene*, which in its tenth edition remains the standard text on the subject. With his long teaching career and his influential textbook, Rosenau was so instrumental in educating health workers in the advances of microbiology and immunology that he was regarded as the father of preventive medicine in the United States.

At his retirement from Harvard in 1936, Rosenau went to Chapel Hill to establish the Division of Public Health within the School of Medicine; in 1940 it became a separate school with Rosenau as dean. The school was the result of the collaborative efforts of Dr. Charles S. Mangum, dean of the medical school, Dr. Carl V. Reynolds, state health officer, and Consolidated University president Frank Porter Graham to set up a major training and educational center for public health personnel in the Southeast. It was the eighth school of public health organized in the United States, and the only one between those at the Johns Hopkins University in Baltimore and Tulane University in New Orleans.

Securing the services of Rosenau, with his national reputation and proven administrative skills, ensured the success of the school, which immediately attracted students from across the country as well as from Central and South America. In 1936 the U.S. Public Health Service transferred its venereal disease laboratory and its training center for health personnel for the states from Delaware to Florida to the new school. The first project funded by the Z. Smith Reynolds Foundation was for a venereal disease study by the North Carolina State Board of Health, which subcontracted much of the work to the new school in 1939. Rosenau secured funding for further venereal disease research from the Rockefeller Foundation, as well as funds from the Kellog Foundation for establishing a field training program for public health workers. In 1946 he had assembled a faculty of twenty-four, the largest of the schools of public health, which offered public health courses in administration, education, nursing, sanitary engineering, nutrition, industrial hygiene, biostatistics, parasitology, and other disciplines. Rosenau saw the school move in 1939 from cramped quarters in Caldwell Hall to a new building shared with the medical school, MacNider Hall, built with federal funds largely secured by Rosenau's efforts.

At the time of his death from a heart attack, he was president-elect of the American Public Health Association; in 1935 he had received the Sedgwick Memorial Medal, the association's highest award for distinguished service in public health. In 1912 he was awarded the Gold Medal of American Medicine for service to humanity.

Rosenau was married in 1900 to Myra F. Frank of Allegheny, Pa., and they were the parents of William Frank, Milton Joseph, and Bertha Pauline. Myra Rosenau died in 1930, and Rosenau married the widow Maud Heilner Tenner in 1935. The Rosenaus lived on Laurel Hill Road in Chapel Hill where they pursued their interests in gardening; he was also an avid tennis player. When the university built a handsome new building for the School of Public Health in 1963, it was named in Rosenau's honor. Portraits of Rosenau can be found at the schools of public health at Chapel Hill and Harvard.

SEE: *Chapel Hill Weekly*, 12 Apr. 1946, 27 Mar. 1963; *Charlotte Observer*, 7 Dec. 1939; *DAB*, supp. 4 (1974); *Durham Herald-Sun*, 23 Dec. 1941; *New York Times*, 10 Apr. 1946 [portrait]; *North Carolina Medical Journal* 7 (1946); Rosenau Papers and School of Public Health Historical Papers (Southern Historical Collection, University of North Carolina, Chapel Hill); *Who Was Who in America*, vol. 2 (1951).

J. MARSHALL BULLOCK

Ross, James *(3 Sept. 1801–March 1878)*, author, teacher, and farmer, was born on a farm a few miles east of Williamston in Martin County. He was the son of Mildred Yarrell and Elder Reuben Ross, a pioneer Baptist preacher who began his ministry in Martin County and brought it to maturity and prominence in middle Tennessee and southern Kentucky. The family migrated to Tennessee in 1807 and settled near Clarksville.

Most of what is known about James Ross comes from his one book, *Life and Times of Elder Reuben Ross*. Now and again he tells of his pursuit of an education. There were then no public schools in Tennessee, and for a few years during and after the War of 1812 he occasionally attended a private school in the neighborhood of his father's farm. There he learned Latin and Greek, and to some extent mathematics. A Clarksville lawyer took an interest in him, gave him several Latin and Greek books, and communicated to the boy his own conviction that classical studies exercised and developed every faculty of the mind—memory, reason, taste, judgment, and imagination. In 1818, fearing that his father could not incur the expense of providing him the education he needed, Ross made an abortive attempt to run away from home to seek an education on his own. He was then sent to a school on the farm of Dr. Charles Meriwether at Meriville, Todd County, Ky. Meriwether was a man of extensive learning and a friend of Thomas Jefferson. Sometimes after supper he would talk to Ross about chemistry, and the boy stayed on during a holiday period to study geometry with him. Later, at a school run by John W. Tyler, Ross expressed regret at his deficiency in Greek, and Tyler, who stressed only Latin, undertook to read Greek with him, though he had discontinued his study of that language some years earlier. Thus, to a great extent Ross's education developed through a seeking out of kindred spirits.

While in his twenties, he married Mary Barker, the daughter of Charles and Barbara Barker, and they became the parents of seven children. They lived on a several-hundred-acre farm, Wheatlands, at Rossview, about eight miles northeast of Clarksville. Not content simply to farm, Ross erected a log cabin school near his house and for forty years taught Greek and Latin to the young in his farm community. (The school, converted into a home, still stands.) Perhaps by accident, he acquired his third vocation, writing. The introduction to excerpts from *Life and Times of Elder Reuben Ross*, in Stark Young's *A Southern Treasury of Literature*, states: "He was generally thought by his family to be indolent and unenterprising. Legend has it that his children suggested his writing of his father's life 'to keep Papa busy.'" Be that as it may, the book was written near the end of his life and published posthumously in 1882. He was buried in the cemetery at Meriville.

The title of the book and perhaps some of the material in the first chapters came to Ross from the Reverend J. M. Pendleton's "Funeral Discourse" for his father. Pendleton also wrote the introduction to *Life and Times*. Ross says in the dedication to his daughter, Mrs. Marion R. Dudley, that he hopes "she and others of his descendants . . . may feel an interest in the narrative." However, the book did not make an immediate imprint beyond the family. His youngest son, Dr. John Walton Ross, at one time director of the medical service of the U.S. Navy, bore the publication costs. About five hundred copies were printed, and for many years numerous copies were stacked in the attic of the family farmhouse at Wheatlands. Then all of a sudden copies of the book became almost impossible to find. In the nineteen thirties a man of letters, Allen Tate, recognizing the literary, historical, and sociological value of *Life and Times*, sought unsuccessfully to get it reprinted. It was his idea to make the book more compact by editing out some of the religious passages and chapters. Tate did persuade Stark Young to include three excerpts in *A Southern Treasury of Life and Literature* (1937) and grounded an eighteen-page story, "The Migration," on the chapters narrating the Ross family's migration from North Carolina. The book was finally reprinted in its entirety by Anne E. Alley and Ursula S. Beach in 1977.

The anonymous author of a biographical sketch of another of Ross's sons, Captain Edward Barker Ross, terms *Life and Times* "not only a faithful history" of a pioneer Baptist preacher "but also the best interpretation of the men and women of those early times which has ever been written" and adds "that in point of style and quaintness of humor it approaches that of Charles Lamb and Thackeray." Allen Tate calls the book a masterpiece.

Perhaps *Life and Times*'s greatest achievement is that it gives concrete embodiment to the frontier movement, both in the detailed story of the pioneer Baptist's preacher's experience and in its depiction of life in early North Carolina and Tennessee. Ross had an acute memory for his own firsthand experience and for the stories that others told him. The times were themselves right to sharpen memory, as he points out when recollecting the two months' migration by covered wagon from North Carolina to Tennessee. "What things I shall relate, and many besides, were themes of conversation in the family circle long years afterward, and thus became fixed in my memory." Later in the book he expresses surprise "at the distinctness with which long forgotten scenes and incidents re-appear even now when I think of those early times."

In the first hundred pages Ross gives his recollections of the Williamston and Martin County of his early childhood and the story of his father's conversion. The next fifty or so pages narrate the arduous journey across the mountains, and the balance of the book tells of life in early nineteenth-century Tennessee and of his family's personal experiences, especially his father's struggles and triumphs in the church. Incidentally, all three of the excerpts in the Stark Young book are drawn from the North Carolina period. One deals with attitudes of children towards old women and Negroes, one with scenes around the old Williamston courthouse, and the final one with the first day of the great journey.

It is the part of the book narrating the life and times in middle Tennessee that Tate felt needed editing. However, throughout *Life and Times* there is a feeling for the physical and social milieu, for the customs of the people, and for individualizing character. Ross views people both satirically and compassionately. He sees scenes with a droll eye and pokes fun at pomposity but never forgets the sadness in people's lives, particularly as they grow older: "The stress of time, on its mighty but silent current, bears away the generations of men." Finally, Ross's style—its simplicity and the soft rhythms of his sentences—is noteworthy. Undoubtedly the style owes much to his arduous classical training and to the serenity and unhurriedness with which he let scenes and incidents arise in his memory.

SEE: James Madison Pendleton, "Funeral Discourse: Life and Times of Elder Reuben Ross," *Southern Baptist Review*, September 1860; James Ross, *Life and Times of*

Elder Reuben Ross (1882 [portrait], reprinted by Anne E. Alley and Ursula S. Beach with photograph, categorized indexes, and picture of grave marker added, 1977); Allen Tate, "The Migration," *Yale Review* 24 (September 1934); Stark Young, *A Southern Treasury of Life and Literature* (1937). Some material was obtained from conversation with Allen Tate and others.

DANFORTH ROSS

Ross, John *(3 Oct. 1790–1 Aug. 1866)*, friend and leader of the Cherokee Indians, was born in Cherokee country near Lookout Mountain in an area that was relinquished by North Carolina to the federal government in the same year. He was the son of David, a Scottish Loyalist, and Mary McDonald Ross, one of whose grandparents had been a Cherokee. His earliest training was under a tutor at home, after which he studied briefly at Kingston Academy in Tennessee.

When just nineteen he was sent by the federal government on a mission to the Cherokee who had moved across the Mississippi River to the part of the Louisiana Purchase that later became Arkansas, where some Cherokee Indians had moved. As an officer with the Cherokee regiment at the Battle of Horseshoe Bend, Ross fought under Andrew Jackson. He became a member of the national council of the Cherokee in 1817 and served as its president from 1819 to 1826. Having helped draft the Cherokee constitution, he was elected assistant chief in 1827. The following year he became principal chief of the eastern band.

An active opponent of the removal of the Cherokee from the fertile land of their eastern home to a territory across the Mississippi, he was often in Washington, D.C., on their behalf. When all efforts failed and the federal government forced the Cherokee to move to what became Oklahoma, it was Ross who reluctantly led them. In 1835–37, at the time of the removal, his daughter Sophia attended the Salem Female Academy conducted by the Moravians at Wachovia. Ross was interested in the Moravian mission to the Cherokee and frequently visited Wachovia as he traveled between the Indian Territory and Washington.

In Oklahoma the eastern and western bands were united in 1839 under a constitution that Ross helped draw up, and he was chosen chief, a role he held for the remainder of his life. During the Civil War he attempted to keep the Cherokee neutral, but when he was unsuccessful they signed a treaty of alliance with the Confederacy. Some actively supported the Confederacy, but Ross's sentiments favored the North. After Federal troops invaded the Territory in 1862, he moved to Philadelphia.

Ross, whose Cherokee name was Cooweescoowe or Kooweskowe, was married in 1813 to Quatie, a Cherokee, who died on the tragic Trail of Tears en route to the Indian Territory. In 1845 he married a white woman, Mary Bryan Stapler, who died in 1865. At the time of his death Ross was in Washington to assist in drawing up a treaty for his people.

SEE: *DAB*, vol. 8 (1935); Rachel C. Eaton, *John Ross and the Cherokee Indians* (1978); R. David Edmunds, *John Ross* (1980); Adelaide L. Fries and others, eds., *Records of the Moravians*, vols. 8–11 (1954–69); Gary E. Moulton, *John Ross: Cherokee Chief* (1978) and ed., *The Papers of Chief John Ross*, 2 vols. (1985 [portrait]); Stewart Sifkas, *Who Was Who in the Civil War* (1988 [portrait]).

WILLIAM S. POWELL

Ross, Martin *(27 Nov. 1762–2 Feb. 1828)*, Baptist minister, was born in Martin County, the son of William and Mary Griffin Ross. His ancestors had emigrated from Scotland to Virginia, and his father moved from there to North Carolina. Martin had four sisters and five brothers, two of whom, Reuben and James, also became Baptist ministers. Nothing is known of his education, but biographers mention his service in the American Revolution.

In January 1782 Ross became a member of Flat Swamp Baptist Church and was baptized by John Page. Two years later the same church granted him a license to preach. In 1786 a branch of Flat Swamp church worshiping at Skewarkey Meeting House in Martin County chose Ross as its pastor. On 26 Mar. 1787 Skewarkey was constituted as a separate church, and Ross was ordained as its first pastor by Lemuel Burkett and John Page. During this pastorate he also reorganized and served as pastor of Morattock Baptist Church. Much to the regret of the Skewarkey church, he took his letter of dismissal in 1796 and moved to Yeoppim Baptist Church, ten miles west of Edenton in Chowan County. He continued in this charge until 1806, when he was called to the church at Bethel in Perquimans County, "a church which had been formed by his own hand." He served as pastor of Bethel until his death in 1828.

Ross preached widely in northeastern North Carolina and southeastern Virginia. He was a vigorous and highly respected leader, first in the Kehukee Association and then in the Chowan Association, and a staunch advocate of training for ministers and for cooperation among the churches. One biographer mentions the progressive aspects of his work as "1. An improved ministry; 2. Missions; and 3. Organized effort." He was a prime mover in organizing the General Meeting of Correspondence (1811–21), the forerunner of the Baptist State Convention, and was strongly advocating the organization of the convention at the time of his death.

He married Mrs. Deborah Clayton Moore, widow of James Moore, who died in 1796. Ross's second marriage was to Mrs. Mary Harvey, widow of Miles Harvey. She and a son both died in 1825. Ross had two other sons: Asher, who never married, and Martin, Jr., who married Eliza Townsend.

With the death of his second wife and son, Ross's health began to decline, and he was unable to do the work of corresponding with other associations in North Carolina with a view to forming a state convention. After his death he was buried near his wife on his farm near Hertford (owned by John O. White in 1931).

SEE: J. A. Easley, "Martin Ross," and Harold D. Gregory, "Reuben Ross," *Encyclopedia of Southern Baptists*, vol. 2 (1958); J. R. B. Hathaway, ed., *North Carolina Historical and Genealogical Register*, vol. 3 (July 1903); Thomas Meredith, "Memoir of Martin Ross," *Chowan Baptist Association Minutes, 1828*; G. W. Paschal, "Martin Ross," *Biblical Recorder*, 3 Dec. 1924; Raleigh *Star*, 21 Feb. 1828; Martin Ross Collection (portrait) and Skewarkey Baptist Church Minutes, vol. 1, 1786–1861 (North Carolina Baptist Historical Collection, Wake Forest University, Winston-Salem); Mrs. Watson Winslow, *History of Perquimans County* (1931).

JOHN R. WOODARD

Ross, Reuben *(9 May 1776–28 Jan. 1860)*, pioneer Baptist minister in the Cumberland settlements in Tennessee and Kentucky, was born in Martin County a few miles east of Williamston, the ninth of ten children of William and Mary Griffin Ross. Two of the sons, Martin and

James, became noteworthy Baptist ministers serving longest in Perquimans and Bertie counties. Ross family tradition says that several persons of this name emigrated from Scotland to Virginia as a group; one of the descendants of "these supposed traditional ancestors," Reuben's grandfather for whom his father was named, moved from Roanoke, Va., to Martin County, possibly with other family members, for court records show Ross property transactions there as early as 1763. Reuben's devout parents were members of the Skewarkey church, led by Regular Baptists, strong in Calvinistic doctrine. Reuben did not join the church until age twenty-six, four years after his marriage in 1798 to Mildred Yarrell, daughter of Matthew and Mary Wheatley Yarrell, who were Episcopalians; Mildred joined the Skewarkey church two years before Reuben.

Despite his belief in the Bible and Christianity in a general way, Reuben looked upon religion as suited "to those in the declining years . . . no longer able to enjoy the . . . pleasures of this world." He was fond of worldly amusements that Baptists frowned upon, but when one of his companions of a Sabbath evening spent "very wickedly" was taken ill and died suddenly, he was awakened to a sense of guilt. A rigorous period of self-examination led him into the church and soon after, into the pulpit. He sold the farm he had recently inherited from his parents and invested the proceeds in a store in Williamston, intending to support his family from its profits and to preach in his spare time. By 1806, however, he decided to emigrate to Tennessee and sold his store to pay his debts. On 6 May 1807, on the eve of his departure for the Cumberland, he was ordained by a council of three elders: his brother James, Joseph Biggs, and his pastor Luke Ward, who had baptized both Reuben and his wife.

On their eight weeks' journey Ross and his family were accompanied by other families, including that of his wife's sister Rosa, Mrs. Charles Cherry; others from both sides of the family joined them later in Tennessee. During the first year Ross taught school at Fort Royal for three months and planted a crop on a place nearer Clarksville before moving to Stewart County, where he farmed for four years. He then bought three hundred acres in Montgomery County on the Kentucky line, his home for twelve years. Ross spent the last thirty-three years of his active life (1824–57) at his farm, Cedar Hill, on the north side of Spring Creek, just a few miles north of Clarksville. Wheatlands, the home place of his son James, his biographer, is in the Rossview Community, named for James; it is six miles away but about the same distance from Clarksville and is sometimes confused with Cedar Hill.

Soon after his arrival in Montgomery County on 4 July 1807, Reuben Ross began preaching and continued as time from the support of his family permitted. In November 1809 he was chosen pastor of Spring Creek of the West Fork of the Red River, which he had helped organize the previous year; it was an outgrowth of the Red River Church near Port Royal, which Ross and his wife had joined immediately upon their arrival. Spring Creek was a part of the Red River Association, of which he was elected assistant clerk in 1810; he preached the introductory sermon in 1812, serving as moderator that year and for several years thereafter. Red River Association consisted of churches in the newly opening Middle Tennessee and adjoining Kentucky counties, served by Regular Baptist preachers as the Skewarkey church had been.

Ordained to preach and having studied progressively through the years, Ross by 1817 had become convinced that he must preach that atonement was unlimited, rather than for the elect alone. He decided to make his position known at the funeral sermon for Miss Eliza Norfleet, to be held at a place just outside Port Royal towards Nashville, where most of the area preachers and church leaders would be present. After the sermon he left immediately, knowing that his associates would need to think through and discuss with each other the message he had brought. A conference was indeed held and Elder Sugg Fort was commissioned to talk with Ross to endeavor to bring him back into the consensus; but after a long session Elder Fort was won over to Ross's philosophy. Subsequently, over a period of years, many congregational members and a few preachers also followed him, with the result that in 1825 the Bethel Association in Kentucky, made up of churches in harmony with Ross's position, was formed after a peaceful separation (in spite of sharp differences) from the Red River Association.

Ross presided over the Bethel Association as moderator for twenty-six years, a rewarding and productive period. The numerical increase of members was greater than that of any other association in Kentucky; the seven hundred members in the eight original churches—Red River, Spring Creek, and Little West Fork in Tennessee and five Kentucky churches—had been joined by five additional Kentucky churches. By the time of Ross's retirement as moderator in 1851, the number of churches had increased to sixty-two with more than seven thousand members. The first meeting of the Southern Baptist Convention after the Civil War was held, perhaps significantly, in one of the churches of the Bethel Association in Russellville, Ky.

Ross's longest pastorates were at Spring Creek (1809–37), Little West Fork (1818–60), and Bethel (1835–52). According to James Ross, his biographer, his father's "success as a preacher was more splendid than at any other period of his ministry" during the seventeen years at Bethel Church, Christian County, Ky. Reuben Ross preached over a six-county area for more than forty-two years, generally serving two or more churches simultaneously in Montgomery, Robertson, and Stewart counties in Tennessee and Todd, Logan, and Christian counties in Kentucky. Soon after 1851 he withdrew from his wide circuit because of his diminishing strength. From 1857 until his death he lived with his daughter Nancy (Mrs. John Morrison) and her family at their farm home near Pembroke, Ky., from where he could still serve as pastor of the Little West Fork Church. He was buried in Montgomery County in the family cemetery at Cedar Hill, where his wife and other family members were buried. He was survived only by his son James and daughter Nancy Morrison. Seven other children had died in childhood or very early life after their arrival in Tennessee: Mildred, age three and one-half, in 1807; four children in one month in 1815, the oldest only nine; Nancy's twin sister, age seventeen, in 1816; and Garrard, age sixteen, in 1823.

Memorial services for Elder Ross have been held periodically: in the fall of 1860 at the time of the presentation of his life-size portraits to the Bethel Association (two portraits were authorized at the last association meeting before his death, one to be placed in Bethel Female College in Hopkinsville and the other in Bethel College in Russellville; both colleges were founded by the association, actions strongly supported by Reuben Ross); in 1861 in Bethany College chapel at the time of the dedication of the portraits; in 1871 at the dedication of the monument erected at the head of his grave by the Bethel Association, which also had built a strong iron fence around the cemetery; and in 1954, at his grave, the 178th anniversary of his birth, when he was remembered as the dean of the churches of his area and the father of the Bethel Association. His wise leadership came at the same period as the so-called reformation, when Peter Cartwright and Alexander Campbell were stirring the hearts of the Cumberland country settlers and the widespread study of doctrinal principles was redefining the differences in various denominations. Two statements regarding his role and strength as a church leader are, from his coworkers, "he never lost his nerve" and from his son James in the biography, "I think he had a genius for the management of affairs of great moment in church or state, had he been called to do so."

Incidents from his life, taken from the *Life and Times of Elder Reuben Ross* by his son James, have been set out in several ways in literature and history: the Clarksville (Tennessee) sesquicentennial historical drama of 1934 shows him as the master of ceremonies, introducing the clergy of Clarksville around 1830 (in 1834 he became the first pastor of the town's First Baptist Church, organized in 1831 and formerly a branch of Reuben's Spring Creek Church); Stark Young included excerpts from *Life and Times* under the title "Pioneer Days in Tennessee" in *A Southern Treasury of Life and Literature* (1937); Allen Tate based his eighteen-page story, "The Migration," in the September 1934 *Yale Review*, at least in part, on Reuben's background, family, and early experiences; and Ross's historic 1817 funeral sermon delineating his convictions on unlimited atonement is outlined in Goodspeed's *History of Tennessee*, followed by a discussion of the widespread controversy over doctrine for a number of years.

SEE: The Reverend Dr. Samuel Baker, address at Bethel College, Louisville *Courier-Journal*, 8 May 1876; Joseph H. Borum, *Biographical Sketches of Tennessee Baptist Ministers* (1880); John Burnett, *Tennessee's Pioneer Baptist Preachers, First Series*, vol. 1 (1919 [portrait]); William Cathcart, *Baptist Encyclopedia*, rev. ed. (1883); *Encyclopedia of Southern Baptists*, vol. 2 (1958); W. W. Gardner, address at the "Memorial Service at the Grave of Elder Reuben Ross, 20 June 1871," reported by J. W. Rust in Louisville, Ky., *Western Recorder*, 1 July 1871; Goodspeed Publishing Company, *History of Tennessee* (1886); "Historical Table, 1825–1933," in *Bethel Baptist Association Minutes*, Russellville, Ky., September 1933; Maloy A. Huggins, *History of North Carolina Baptists, 1727–1932* (1967); M. Fred Kendall, "Division of Red River Association," in *History of the Tennessee Baptist Convention* (1974); James Madison Pendleton, "Funeral Discourse: Elder Reuben Ross," *Southern Baptist Review*, September 1860; Red River Baptist Church, Robertson County, Tenn., Minutes, 1791–1826 (Microfilm #379, Southeastern Baptist Seminary, Wake Forest, N.C.); James Ross, *Life and Times of Elder Reuben Ross* (1882 [portrait]); Oury Wilbur Taylor, *Early Tennessee Baptists* (1957); Arthur E. Whittle, *Through the Mist of the Years*, pt. 2, episode 1 (1934).

DANFORTH ROSS
CLARA HAMLETT ROBERTSON FLANNAGAN

Ross, Robert Alexander *(18 July 1899–15 Apr. 1973)*, nationally known obstetrician and gynecologist, professor of obstetrics at Duke University, and first chairman of the Department of Obstetrics at The University of North Carolina, was born in Morganton of Scottish ancestry. He was the son of Dr. Charles Ellis Ross, a native of the Steele Creek Community on the outskirts of Charlotte, and the former Kate Lenoir Chambers of Morganton. The Ross family and some relatives—the Griers, the Strongs, and the Harrises—were among the early settlers of that area. His maternal ancestors included the Avery, Erwin, and Chambers families, early settlers in Burke and/or adjoining counties. Among these was Waightstill Avery, an able lawyer who first lived in Mecklenburg County. All of these families were members of the Presbyterian or the Associate Reformed Presbyterian church in their respective communities.

Ross entered The University of North Carolina as a premedical student in 1916 and received the B.S. in Medicine degree in 1920; the University of Pennsylvania awarded him the M.D. degree in 1922. As a freshman in Chapel Hill and a member of the ATO fraternity, he earned the appellation, "Daddy," by which he was known to state, national, and international practitioners. The nickname had nothing to do with his professional activities. Rather, according to his university associates of the period 1916–20, it resulted from his kindness to colleagues and from his care of those who became rowdy and difficult to handle on Saturday night imbibing parties. For the remainder of his life as physician, teacher, or friend, he functioned superbly and quietly in this role.

In preparation for a career in obstetrics-gynecology, Ross was an intern and assistant resident at the Episcopal Hospital (1922–24) and a resident of the Kensington Hospital for Women (1924–26), both in Philadelphia. In 1926 he returned to North Carolina and began to practice in Durham—unquestionably the first well-qualified specialist in his field in that community and one of the earliest and best in the state. Shortly afterwards he became chief of the Obstetrical-Gynecological Service at Watts Hospital, where he did much to improve the quality of care on that service. He also was instrumental in establishing the Salvation Army Home to care for unmarried mothers and assist in their deliveries and served as a consultant obstetrician and gynecologist on the staff of the Lincoln Hospital.

In 1930, with the opening of the Duke University School of Medicine and hospital, Ross joined the faculty and the staff of the hospital and began his career as an academician. He remained at Duke, with promotions over the years from assistant professor to professor, until 1952. In 1934 he was appointed a lecturer at The University of North Carolina School of the Basic Medical Sciences and continued in that capacity until 1952.

A superb student throughout life, Ross in 1931 became a diplomat of the American Board of Obstetrics-Gynecology. Early in his career, in the search for the intellectual stimulus so important to his personal and professional life, he, together with a small group of his specialty in the South Atlantic states, provided a nucleus of men in an association that became the South Atlantic Association of Obstetricians and Gynecologists. Later he was the moving spirit in organizing the North Carolina Obstetrical-Gynecological Society. In time Ross served as president of both organizations.

In 1940 he entered the Medical Corps of the U.S. Naval Reserve as a lieutenant commander, served in the Pacific in 1944, and rose to the rank of captain before his discharge in 1946; he was also a recipient of the Purple Heart. Continuing as a representative of the commandant of the Sixth Naval District, Ross was promoted to the rank of rear admiral in the Medical Corps at the time of his retirement in 1962, one of the few reservists in his specialty to reach that rank.

In 1952 he became professor and chairman of the Department of Obstetrics and Gynecology at The University of North Carolina School of Medicine at the beginning of its expansion to a four-year school and served in that post until his retirement in 1965. Because of his distinguished record as a clinician and teacher, he soon recruited a very able faculty—both full- and part-time. Positions in his residency program were much sought after by graduates of The University of North Carolina and other schools of medicine.

Ross's many contributions were recognized by his election to prominent scientific and honorary societies. He was the first North Carolinian to receive the honor of membership in the American Association of Obstetricians and Gynecologists (president, 1960) and the American Gynecological Society. A charter member of the American Board of Obstetrics and Gynecology, he served as an associate examiner of the board from 1950 through his remaining active years. In addition, he was a member of the American College of Obstetrics and Gynecology (president, 1968–69), North Carolina Chapter of the American College of Physicians (president, 1964), Association of Professors of Gynecology and Obstetrics, Chorionepithelioma Register, Pan-American Cytological Society, Intersociety Cytology Council, South Atlantic Association of Obstetricians and Gynecologists (president, 1947), and North Carolina State Medical Society (president, 1967–68). He was an honorary member of the gynecological societies of seven states and Canada, Alpha Omega Alpha, and Sigma Xi and a faculty member of the Southern Postgraduate Seminar at Saluda, N.C. (dean of Obstetrical Section, 1954–57). He was listed in *American Men of Science* (11th ed., 1967).

He was the author of more than one hundred papers, mostly scientific articles published in journals of his specialty and of the societies of which he was a member. These also included, however, chapters in textbooks on obstetrics-gynecology as well as lectures on a variety of topics. Ross had a continuing interest in the etiology of toxemias of pregnancy, particularly the relationship of dietary factors in this disease.

His scholarly interests and activities covered many areas in addition to those of his specialty, including not only the history of obstetrics-gynecology, but also that of North Carolina, the South, and the Bible. He was a member of the Democratic party and of the Presbyterian church.

On the occasion of his retirement as chairman of the department at The University of North Carolina in 1965, former residents, faculty members, and a few selected colleagues with whom he had worked closely for many years formed the Robert A. Ross Obstetrical and Gynecological Society "not only for the promotion of scientific knowledge, but also to honor perpetually the man who had contributed so much to the education and training of all of its members. The members of the Society decided that their first project would be the establishment of a Trust Fund to endow a Professorship named for Dr. Ross." The latter objective was achieved with the establishment of the Robert A. Ross Professorship in 1971. The society contributed funds for the portrait of Ross that hangs, along with those of other department chairmen and former faculty members and deans of The University of North Carolina School of Medicine, in the Health Sciences Library. In addition, the Nick Carter Obstetrical-Gynecological Travel Club organized at Duke in honor of Dr. Bayard Carter, the first chairman of the department, presented a portrait of Ross to the Duke University Medical School. In appreciation of his outstanding contributions to medicine, the *North Carolina Medical Journal* dedicated a special issue to Ross (November 1966, vol. 27, no. 11).

In 1933 Ross married Rosalie Walters, of Orangeburg, S.C., who died in 1952. They were the parents of Robert Alexander, Jr., Charles Allen, and Rosalie Walters. Ross died at his home near Hillsborough and was buried in the family plot in the Durham cemetery.

SEE: *American Men of Science*, 11th ed. (1967); *Chapel Hill Newspaper*, 17 Apr. 1973; *North Carolina Medical Journal* 27 (November 1966); *Obstetrical-Gynecological News*, 15 Aug. 1974; Charles H. Ross (Morganton, N.C.), personal contact.

REECE BERRYHILL

Roulhac, Joseph Blount Grégoire *(13 Aug. 1795–23 Jan. 1856)*, merchant, was the first son of John G. Roulhac (Jean-Baptiste Ignace Grégoire de Roulhac de la Tronchère) and his second wife, Frances Lee Gray of Bertie County. The ancestors of his father were merchants and of the nobility. His grandfather was a distinguished lawyer and for many years mayor of the city of Limoges, France, and the family was well educated and well-to-do. His father was the sixth child of thirteen born to Joseph Grégoire de Roulhac de Thias and his wife Marie Jeanne Dumas de la Vaille and was the second of three sons of the family that settled in America between 1777 and 1793.

Psalmet Grégoire de Roulhac came to America in 1777 as an agent of a French mercantile firm, hoping to establish a house bearing his name as partner; when this venture failed, he settled near Bath, where his brother John joined him in 1783. Ten years later their younger brother, Francis Leonard Grégoire de Roulhac de Lavergne, arrived; he had spent some time working in the West Indies, had studied law, and finally turned to medicine, practicing first in Georgia and then settling in Tennessee. Having come to this country expecting that his brother was wealthy, John thought at first that he would go to sea but changed his mind when Psalmet introduced him to François-Xavier Martin, a lawyer who as a French immigrant advised John to read law. Working and studying with James Iredell, he obtained a license.

John Roulhac, who earned a reputation for integrity and honesty, became known as the "Honest Lawyer." He purchased a plantation called Fairfields, seventeen miles from Edenton in Martin County near the Washington County line. In 1788 he married Jamima Maule, the youngest sister of Psalmet's wife, and in 1789 their first son, William Maule, was born. In 1794, after the death of his first wife, John married Frances Lee Gray; their first son, Joseph Blount Grégoire, was followed by John Gray (1797), Frances Lee (1799), and Jane Margaret (1802).

As a child, Joseph was described as "vif"—animated, lively, with lots of spirit. A talented boy with an exceptionally good memory, he worked hard and did especially well in rhetoric. Graduated from The University of North Carolina in 1811 at age sixteen, he was educated for the law but never practiced. Roulhac was interested in the military and would have preferred the life of a soldier to all others, but because of the feelings of his mother did not pursue it. He also considered a career in the law but saw that kind of life centered outside or away from the home. Although single, he was a great supporter of marriage and the family and did not wish to do a great deal of traveling.

An active, industrious, and practical man, Roulhac turned to the mercantile world and followed it to his death. Fond of books, he had a knowledge of a variety of subjects; he was able to converse on almost any subject with fluency, particularly those of a practical nature. He showed shrewd judgment and keen appreciation of character. A good business man, he was very prompt and systematic, and he had a special talent for financial dealings. His credit rating was excellent, both within the state and in the northern cities where he traveled regularly to conduct his business, such as New York, Philadelphia, and Pittsburgh. For some time he served on the board of directors of the bank of North Carolina.

A particular feature of his character was the love of order. Roulhac enjoyed the highest confidence and warm, personal regard of his customers, and he was honest, fair, conscientious, and dedicated to his work. A leader in the community, he involved himself in matters of public improvement and enterprise and was a generous contributor to relieve human suffering. He had a strong attachment to the Episcopal church. Cheerful and even-tempered, he was devoted to his family and had few equals as husband and father. His highest ambition was to raise children in the observance of sound morals and to educate them for usefulness in life. The large collection of his letters reveals his deep attachment to his wife and children and to his wife's family. Roulhac also had a strong affection for the home of his early years and his own family ties. He established a correspondence with his uncle Joseph, who had gone to England because of the French Revolution and decided to remain there, and he wrote in detail about the American branch of the family. His papers show that he served as executor to various estates throughout North Carolina.

Roulhac had no interest in political conflict and was a candidate for public office only once. In 1835 he was elected to represent Bertie County at the convention to revise the state constitution.

On 24 Nov. 1836 he married, in Orange County, Catherine Ruffin, the oldest daughter of Chief Justice Thomas and Annie M. Kirkland Ruffin. The couple had four sons (Joseph Blount Grégoire, Thomas Ruffin, John, William Sterling) and three daughters (Annie Kirkland, Frances Gray, Elizabeth Ruffin); the oldest was Annie Kirkland (b. 7 Oct. 1837), and the youngest was William Sterling (b. 18 Mar. 1851).

Roulhac died suddenly at his store in Raleigh. The funeral was held in Raleigh on 27 January and the burial took place the following day in Hillsborough at the Episcopal church cemetery. He was survived by his wife, who died in Hillsborough in 1881.

SEE: Laura MacMillan, *The North Carolina Portrait Index, 1700–1860* (1963 [portrait]); Helen M. Prescott, *Genealogical Memoir of the Roulhac Family in America* (1894); Raleigh *North Carolina Star*, 30 Jan. 1856; Ruffin-Roulhac-Hamilton Papers, J. B. G. Roulhac Diary and Letters, and Manuscrit de Roulhac-Monthéley (Southern Historical Collection, University of North Carolina, Chapel Hill); *Weekly Raleigh Register*, 30 Jan. 1856.

DOROTHY H. OSBORN

Roulhac, Psalmet Grégoire de (or Roulhac de Thias, Psalmet Grégoire de) *(30 Oct. 1752–8 Oct. 1808)*, French immigrant and farmer, was born at Limoges, France, the second child and second son of Joseph Grégoire de Roulhac de Thias and his wife Marie Jeanne Dumas de la Vaille. His father came from a family of merchants and his mother, from nobility. Married in 1750, Joseph and Marie had nine sons and four daughters. Though Joseph was the second son, he inherited by right of primogeniture half of the property of his father because of the death of his older brother. The family was well-to-do and well educated. A good student and a distinguished lawyer, Joseph became regulator of the police and was for many years the mayor of Limoges. He saw that there would be advantages attached to nobility for his children, so he bought offices and thus "purchased" nobility. In France among people who pretended to any gentility a second surname was given to distinguish a man from his brothers; thus "de Thias" was added to Joseph's name as well as to Psalmet's.

Convinced that a good, solid education would make up for the small amount of property that he could leave his younger children because of the law of primogeniture, Joseph employed a well-educated tutor. Psalmet's early life was sheltered in a strict household with hours of study and play enforced, although not severely. At the usual age Psalmet went away to school, and when his collegiate training at Notre Dame de Grace ended, he entered the Congregation of the Oratoire and later became a professor of belles lettres.

As the second son, Psalmet was entitled to only a small share of the family money. With the onset of the American Revolution the mercantile class in France saw a new market, and many commercial houses in the seaports engaged in business speculation, among them a Bordeaux company with a strong credit rating, a good reputation, and ties to citizens of Limoges. Rainbau, Barmarin, and Company invited Psalmet to become its agent and partner, with a plan to form a house under the name of Roulhac, Barmarin, and Company in America. The prospect seemed advantageous to a young man with limited means, so the elder Roulhac encouraged Psalmet to accept, thinking that his success would provide opportunities for the younger brothers later on. Psalmet decided that he should investigate the situation before making a full commitment, and he arrived in Boston on 20 Apr. 1777 prepared to sign the articles of copartnership sent him from France should he deem the enterprise a reliable one. Once in America, he saw that such an act would involve him irrevocably, and he refused to sign. Many cargoes from France were consigned to him as an agent, but ships were often taken at sea by British cruisers or they put in at the first American port they could enter, leaving their cargoes in the care of undependable agents. This led to the failure of the firm, which asserted to its creditors that Roulhac as their agent had become rich. The truth was that he was reduced to beggary.

As early as February 1776 one privateer was being fitted out in each of the towns of Wilmington, New Bern, and Edenton, and later others were equipped by several merchants, North Carolina privateers, to harass British commerce and capture needed supplies. Roulhac was listed as one of the owners of the brig *Rainbeau*, and his liabilities as a result of his business connections followed him for some time.

His health impaired and the money advanced him by his father nearly gone, Roulhac purchased a small tract of poor land in Beaufort County and arranged with a Dr. Savage in Richmond to sell dry goods and groceries on commission. A party of Tories in the neighborhood, knowing that he was French with sympathies for the opposition, raided his business, bound him and his clerk, and stole all his goods, money, books, papers, and even the clothing worn by the men. The militia later recovered most of the belongings except the money. The law provided that claims made on lost certificates be processed. Roulhac went from committee to committee, all reporting in his favor, but no law required that payment be made and after ten years the claim was sold. A few days after the incident with the Tories, his younger brother John (Jean-Baptiste Ignace Grégoire de Roulhac—the sixth child of the family) arrived, having had reports that Psalmet was a wealthy man. Psalmet was surprised by the visitor; not recognizing him and having reason to look with suspicion on strangers, he ran for his gun. John had received a part of his paternal legacy and had obtained passage on a French frigate as a supernumerary midshipman. Unused to the English language and work habits, he had planned to go to sea; however, with Psalmet's help and while living with him he began to study English, then read law and obtained his license.

An enlightened, generous, and liberal man, Psalmet had more of the vivacity belonging to the French than did the other brothers who came to America (John and Francis). His difficult experiences were made more tolerable by his lightness of heart, gaiety, and cheerfulness.

On 17 July 1783 Psalmet and Anne Hare Maule were married at Smith's Point on the Pamlico River. The Maule family, which owned land and slaves, gave the Roulhacs one hundred acres. But their life provided them with little beyond the essentials, and Roulhac wrote to his mother that "necessity obliges me to content myself with very little." Frugality made it possible for them to acquire a house, which was originally an old fort on Pamlico Sound, built of bricks brought from England in 1721. Called The Hermitage, it was a few miles from the town of Bath in Beaufort County. The Roulhac home was a resort, often an asylum for unfortunate Frenchmen when they first came to America. In letters to France, John wrote of teaching Psalmet's wife, Anne, to read. Anne's brother, Moses Maule, lived with the family; he was a wealthy and hospitable man, who on his death left the greater part of his property to his sister's children.

In France Psalmet's oldest brother, Guillaume Grégoire de Roulhac de la Borie, having inherited a fortune from his father and uncle and married to a wealthy heiress, now bore the responsibility for the rest of the family. The coming of the French Revolution reduced his fortunes considerably and resulted in the temporary confinement of him and some other members of the family as prisoners. The family fortunes were restored to some extent under Napoléon I. The bulk of the Roulhac family was against the French Revolution, but Psalmet and John were great admirers in the hope that it would be better for the French nation.

According to the first U.S. Census, taken in 1790, the Roulhac household consisted of two free white males of sixteen and older, one free white male under sixteen, two free white females, and nineteen slaves. In 1793 the third brother, Francis Leonard Grégoire de Roulhac de Lavergne, the twelfth child of the family, joined Psalmet; afterwards Francis studied medicine under several physicians, practiced in Georgia, and finally settled in Tennessee. Anne Maule Roulhac died in childbirth on 23 Nov. 1794, leaving four children: Elizabeth, Joseph, Mary Jane, and John Maule. On 5 Aug. 1798 Psalmet married Elizabeth Barrow.

He became a candidate for the legislature but was defeated when the influential Blount family opposed him, largely because he was foreign, a fact that he was never able to forgive. His oldest daughter, Elizabeth, at age seventeen, married James Blount, a member of the hated family.

Never a very robust man, Roulhac was subject each fall to long attacks of fever, and these sapped his strength. He died of a violent attack of influenza during the U.S. epidemic of that year.

SEE: Walter Clark, ed., *State Records of North Carolina*, vol. 14 (1896); Charles Christopher Crittenden, *The Commerce of North Carolina, 1763–1789* (1936); Helen M. Prescott, *Genealogical Memoir of the Roulhac Family in America* (1894); Psalmet Roulhac, Extracts of Letters from Roulhac to Jolidan, 8 July 1779 (Manuscript Department, Duke University Library, Durham); Ruffin-Roulhac-Hamilton Papers and Manuscrit de Roulhac-Monthéley (Southern Historical Collection, University of North Carolina, Chapel Hill); W. Savage to Governor Richard Caswell, from Executive Letter Book, New Bern, 30 May 1779 (Confederate Memorial Library, Hillsborough); U.S. Bureau of the Census, *Heads of Families at the First Census of the U.S. Taken in the Year 1790: North Carolina* (1908).

DOROTHY H. OSBORN

Roulstone, George *(8 Oct. 1767–10 Aug. 1804)*, first printer and newspaper publisher in the Tennessee country, was born in Boston, Mass., where he received a fair education and learned the printer's trade. He possibly was the son of Mary and George Roulstone, sexton of the First Church of Boston between 1776 and 1780. In March 1786 he established the *Salem Chronicle and Essex Advertiser*, which failed in August. He then became a journeyman printer.

In 1789 he moved to Fayetteville, N.C., and worked for a newspaper until March 1791, when he and Robert Ferguson, recently of Hillsborough, N.C., were induced by William Blount, newly appointed governor of the Southwest Territory (later the state of Tennessee), to found a newspaper for Knoxville, intended to become the territorial capital. Named the *Knoxville Gazette*, the paper was first published on 5 Nov. 1791, in Rogersville, before Knoxville was established. This was two years before the first newspaper appeared in the Northwest Territory, created in 1787. Roulstone also printed the journals and the acts of the Tennessee legislature, a practice that his widow continued after his death. He printed the ordinances of the Southwest Territory in 1793 and a compilation of the acts of the General Assembly of both the territory and the state of Tennessee in 1801. Known as *Roulstone's Laws*, it has been cited by bibliographers as "the first book published" in Tennessee.

Roulstone also was elected clerk of the Council of State when the first legislature of the Southwest Territory was organized. When Blount College (now the University of Tennessee) was established in 1794, he was named a trustee in its charter. He became the state printer in 1796, and in the legislatures of 1797–98 and 1801 he was chief clerk of the senate.

On 1 May 1794 Roulstone married Elizabeth Gilliam of Knox County. Their oldest child, James G., joined his stepfather, William Moore, in publishing the Carthage *Gazette* following his return from the Creek War and the Battle of New Orleans with the rank of colonel. Among the other children were Harriet C., Charlotte M., George, Jr., and Rachel. There may have been others, but if so they were minors at the time of their father's death.

SEE: Samuel A. Ashe, ed., *Biographical History of North Carolina*, vol. 1 (1905); Douglas C. McMurtrie, *Early Printing in Tennessee* (1933); Richard D. Pierce, ed., *Records of the First Church in Boston, 1630–1868*, 3 vols. (1961); Samuel C. Williams, "George Roulstone: Father of the Tennessee Press," East Tennessee Historical Society *Publications*, nos. 17 (1945), 51 (1979).

STANLEY J. FOLMSBEE

Rountree, George *(7 July 1855–19 Feb. 1942)*, attorney and judge, was born in Kinston, the son of Robert Hart and Cynthia Biddle Loftin Rountree. As a ten-year-old boy he witnessed the Battle of Kinston shaping up as he rode his pony at Tower Hill. When shots were fired in his direction, he made a disorderly retreat. Rountree attended an excellent private school in Kinston and in 1873 entered the second-year class at Bethany College in West Virginia. He proved to be a good student and after two years entered Harvard College, from which he was graduated in 1877. Returning from Cambridge, he began to read law under the guidance of George V. Strong, of Raleigh, one of the outstanding lawyers of his day.

After receiving his license in 1878, Rountree opened an active practice in Kinston. After a short time, however, he moved to New York and joined the practice of Rountree and Company, established by his father in 1873. In 1884 he moved to Richmond, Va., and engaged in the wholesale shoe business. In time he settled in Kinston to form a law partnership with his uncle, Andrew J. Loftin.

In 1881 he married Meta Alexander Davis, the daughter of George Davis, of Wilmington, former attorney general of the Confederacy. In 1890 the Rountrees settled in Wilmington, where he continued to practice law until his death.

In 1898, with the Republican party virtually in complete control of state government, the racial situation in eastern North Carolina seemed unbearable to many whites. White supremacy clubs were organized in an effort to unify the whites. George Rountree was induced to run for the General Assembly and with the cooperation of many white Republicans, he was elected. In 1899 he served as chairman of the committee on constitutional reform that drafted and sponsored the so-called Grandfather Clause, which provided in substance that male citizens could vote if they could read and write or if their grandfather voted. Supporters maintained that the right to vote should be determined by character and intelligence. Although he was a key figure in the preparation, passage, and final ratification of the amendment, Rountree was said never to have been animated by hostility to blacks. Elected to a second term, he opposed in 1901 a constitutional amendment providing that all taxes paid by whites should be applied exclusively to the education of whites. At that session of the General Assembly he introduced legislation prepared by Dean Samuel F. Mordecai to codify and simplify the probate laws.

In 1899, in Raleigh, Rountree was one of the founders and charter members of the North Carolina Bar Association, and in 1906 he was elected president. He was a life member of the American Bar Association. In July 1913 he was appointed to the superior court bench by Governor Locke Craig, who had also been active in the Democratic campaign of 1898. After two years on the bench Rountree resigned and returned to his law practice in Wilmington. He was one of the counsel in the case of *South Dakota v. North Carolina*, which was instituted in the U.S. Supreme Court to collect some bonds issued soon after the Civil War and whose payment was contested. He devoted more than a year to preparing for the case.

Rountree possessed an outstanding legal library, which included reports of the English courts, and the study of legal principles was almost a passion with him. He often spent weeks on a single subject in striving to attain perfection. The rough-and-tumble antics sometimes seen in trial courts were distasteful to him. He was always outspoken and sometimes caustic in his remarks.

He was a member of St. James Episcopal Church in Wilmington. Bishop Thomas Wright once said that it never concerned him when Rountree looked at his watch during a sermon, but when he put the watch to his ear and shook it, he knew that it was time to end the sermon.

The Rountrees were the parents of five children: Isabel Davis (m. Van R. C. King), Robert Hart (1886–87); Cynthia Polk (m. Sidney Gardner Macmillan), Meta Davis (m. the Reverend Robert Coolidge Masterton), and George, Jr. (m. Helen E. Johnson).

SEE: Samuel A. Ashe, ed., *Biographical History of North Carolina*, vol. 8 (1906); John L. Cheney, Jr., ed., *North Carolina Government, 1585–1979* (1981); North Carolina Bar Association *Report*, vol. 8 (1906); Personal information and letters (possession of Albert W. Cowper); Raleigh *News and Observer*, 20 Feb. 1942; Charles C. Ware, *Rountree Chronicles, 1827–1840* (1947).

ALBERT W. COWPER

Rowan, Matthew (*d. April 1760*), colonial official and acting governor, of Scottish descent but born in Ireland, was the son of the Reverend John Rowan and his wife, Margaret Stewart of County Antrim, Ireland. It is not clear when Rowan arrived in North Carolina, but he first appeared in the records in 1726 as a church warden in Bath, where he was a merchant who also had an interest in shipbuilding. An affidavit of about 1729 notes that Rowan was sent to the colony (in 1724?) to build one or two ships for some persons in Dublin and that he "is now run away with one of them loaded with enumerated goods contrary to the Acts of Trade."

He relocated in the Lower Cape Fear and resided at Rowan (now called Roan) plantation, near the modern community of Northwest in Brunswick County. He resided there until his death, which occurred between the dating of his will on 18 Apr. 1760 and his failure to attend a meeting of the Council scheduled to be held four days later.

In 1742 Rowan married Elizabeth, widow of his brother Jerome. There were no children from this union, but she had four daughters (Elizabeth, Anna, Esther, and Mildred) from her previous marriage. Matthew Rowan, nevertheless, was the father of a son by Jane Stubbs of Bath. Although they were never married, Rowan did not hesitate to acknowledge his son, who was known as John Rowan. John, who was a mariner in Barbados, received a considerable portion of his father's estate.

In 1727 Matthew Rowan became a member of the Assembly, and in 1731 he was named to the Council, where he served until his death. In 1735 he was a member of the team that surveyed the boundary between the two Carolinas, and in 1737 he was appointed surveyor-general for North Carolina. In 1750–51 he served as receiver-general for the colony. Following the death of acting governor Nathaniel Rice on 29 Jan. 1753, Rowan, as president of the Council, became acting governor, serving until the arrival of Governor Arthur Dobbs at New Bern on 31 Oct. 1754. It was formally noted that Rowan's brief term as governor was agreeable to both the people and British officials. As chief executive he attempted to reorganize the colony's military force in light of the French and Indian War then under way but was unsuccessful. This failure was considered more a reflection of conditions in the colony than of Rowan's leadership.

It was also during his administration that a large new county was created on the frontier and named Rowan in his honor. Following the arrival of the new royal governor, Rowan resumed his position on the Council. It is believed that he was buried on his Brunswick County plantation, although the grave is not marked.

SEE: John L. Cheney, Jr., ed., *North Carolina Government, 1585–1979* (1981); Walter Clark, ed., *State Records of North Carolina*, vol. 22 (1907); E. Lawrence Lee, *The Lower Cape Fear in Colonial Days* (1965); New Hanover County Deeds, Book D (New Hanover County Courthouse, Wilmington); William L. Saunders, ed., *Colonial Records of North Carolina*, vols. 3, 5 (1886–87).

H. KENNETH STEPHENS

Rowe, Gilbert Theodore *(10 Sept. 1875–10 Feb. 1960),* Methodist minister, editor, and seminary professor, was born in Rowan County, the son of Joseph Columbus and Nannie Brown Rowe. He received an A.B. degree from Trinity College in 1895 and the S.T.D. from Temple University in 1905. Later Duke University awarded him two honorary degrees.

Rowe was admitted to membership in the Western North Carolina Conference of the Methodist Episcopal Church, South, in 1896. He served pastorates at Greensboro, Hendersonville, Bessemer City, Albemarle, Concord, Asheville, Charlotte, High Point, and Winston-Salem, and as presiding elder of the Greensboro District. In addition, he was professor of Greek at Hendrix College in Arkansas (1895–96), editor of the *North Carolina Christian Advocate* (1920–21), book editor of the Methodist Episcopal Church, South, and editor of the *Methodist Quarterly Review* (1921–28), and professor of Christian doctrine at Duke Divinity School (1928–46). He was the author of two books, *The Meaning of Methodism* and *Reality in Religion.*

A member of the Conference Board of Education for forty years, he also served for a long period on the General Board of Education of the Church. For many years he was a trustee of Greensboro College. Rowe was a delegate to eight General conferences, as well as to the Uniting Conference of 1939 and the Ecumenical Methodist conferences of 1921 and 1931. He was a fraternal delegate from his denomination to the 1928 General Conference of the Methodist Protestant church. At the 1930 General Conference of his own church he received ninety votes for the office of bishop.

Rowe married Pearle Bostian of Albemarle on 26 Nov. 1902, and they had two children, Theodore Bostian and Charles Gilbert. His funeral was held on 12 February in Duke Chapel, with interment in Maplewood Cemetery, Durham.

SEE: O. Lester Brown, *Gilbert T. Rowe: Churchman Extraordinary* (1971); Nolan B. Harmon, ed., *The Encyclopedia of World Methodism* (1974); *Journal of the Western North Carolina Conference of the Methodist Church* (1960).

LOUISE L. QUEEN

Rowland, Alfred II *(9 Feb. 1844–2 Aug. 1898),* lawyer and congressman, was born in Robeson County, the son of John A. and Florah A. Rowland. His mother was a native of South Carolina. In May 1861 young Rowland, then a student, enlisted in the Confederate army and was chosen lieutenant of Company D, Eighteenth Regiment, North Carolina Troops. This was an action company throughout the war, serving under Generals James H. Lane and A. P. Hill. On 12 May 1864 Rowland was taken prisoner during the Battle of Spotsylvania Court House and imprisoned at Fort Delaware until his release in June 1865.

After returning home, he read law with Giles Leitch in Lumberton and obtained his license to practice in the county court in January 1867 and in superior court in January 1868. In 1867 he was elected register of deeds, the first of many local offices that he held. He served in the General Assembly (1876–77 and 1880–81), where he was a member of the judiciary committee and the committee on the jurisdiction of magistrates. In 1884 he represented the Sixth Congressional District as a presidential elector in support of Grover Cleveland and Thomas A. Hendricks.

Running for Congress on the Democratic ticket in 1886, Rowland defeated his independent opponent by more than two-to-one. He served in the Fiftieth and Fifty-first congresses (4 Mar. 1887–3 Mar. 1891). Afterwards he retired to Lumberton to resume his law practice; he also served as master of St. Alban's Masonic Lodge. After his death in Lumberton and funeral at the Presbyterian church, of which he had been a member, he was buried in Meadowbrook Cemetery. The town of Rowland (incorporated in the year of his death) in the southeastern part of Robeson County was named in his honor.

Rowland married a Miss Blount, and they were the parents of a son, John A., and three daughters, May, Penelope, and Winifred.

SEE: *Biog. Dir. Am. Cong.* (1971); Jerome Dowd, *Sketches of Prominent Living North Carolinians* (1888); *Fayetteville Observer*, 4 Aug. 1898; Weymouth T. Jordan, Jr., comp., *North Carolina Troops, 1861–1865: A Roster*, vol. 6 (1977); Robert C. Lawrence, *The State of Robeson* (1939); *Legislative Record* (1887); Lumberton *Robesonian*, 26 Feb. 1951; Raleigh *News and Observer*, 4 Aug. 1898.

MAUD THOMAS SMITH

Royal, Benjamin Franklin *(7 Oct. 1884–26 Sept. 1971),* physician, surgeon, and founder and chief of staff of the original Morehead City Hospital, was born in Morehead City, the son of John, Jr. (a railroad conductor) and Mary Franklin Royal. His mother was the daughter of J. R. and Harriet Pigott Franklin. The Royal family traces its North Carolina ancestry to Marmaduke and Sarah Royal, who lived in the Shackleford Banks–Harkers Island District in 1800. His paternal grandparents were John (keeper of the lighthouse on Shackleford Banks) and Caledonia Moore. John inherited fifty acres of Banks land from his father, Marmaduke.

Benjamin F. Royal was graduated from The University of North Carolina in 1906 and Jefferson Medical College in Philadelphia with an M.D. degree in 1909. He interned at the Methodist Episcopal Hospital in Philadelphia, practiced six months in Shelby, N.C., and began a lifelong practice in Morehead City in 1910.

Royal soon was taking care of the personnel at the isolated Coast Guard station in the area north and southwest of Beaufort. He opened Morehead City's first hospital in 1911 with seven beds. In 1918 he founded a new hospital with twenty-six beds. When influenza raged in Morehead City as elsewhere that year, Royal and his faithful nurse, Miss Edna Broadway, saw the community through the epidemic. In 1928 the town of Morehead City took over operation of Royal's hospital.

In 1942 the Atlantic Ocean off the North Carolina coast was a war zone as the Battle of the Carolina Capes raged. Altogether some 250 American and Allied ships were sunk by German U-boats with around 3,500 men from the ships in need of Royal's medical and hospital care. Many of these were burn victims from the flaming oil from sunken ships; it is said that Royal did not lose a single one of these patients.

In addition to practicing medicine, he was a leader in state, regional, and local civic affairs. Royal was a promoter of the North Carolina State Port, a member of the North Carolina Navigation and Pilotage Commission, a trustee of The University of North Carolina School of Medicine, a member of the State Board of Medical Examiners, and vice-president and president of the North Carolina Medical Society. He formally retired from his medical practice on 10 Apr. 1962. His hobbies were ornithology and wood carving. He died in a nursing home in Durham and was buried in Bay View Cemetery, Morehead City.

Royal married Annie McTyeire Adams on 15 Oct. 1914. They were the parents of three children: Benjamin Franklin, Jr., who was killed in World War II, Florence F., and Ruth Adams.

SEE: Pat Dula Davis and Kathleen Hill Hamilton, eds., *The Heritage of Carteret County, North Carolina*, vol. 1 (1982); Daniel L. Grant, *Alumni History of the University of North Carolina* (1924); Dorothy Long, ed., *Medicine in North Carolina*, vol. 1 (1972); Morehead City *Carteret County News-Times*, 21 July 1967, 27 Sept. 1971; *A Pictorial Review of Morehead City, 1714–1981: History Through 1981* (1982); Benjamin Franklin Royal Collection (Southern Historical Collection, University of North Carolina, Chapel Hill); *Transactions of the Medical Society of the State of North Carolina* (1936).

DOUGLAS J. MCMILLAN

Royall, Kenneth Claiborne *(24 July 1894–25 May 1971)*, lawyer, secretary of war, and the first secretary of the army after President Harry S Truman's reorganization of the armed services under the Department of Defense, was born in Goldsboro, the son of George Claiborne, a manufacturer and civic leader, and Clara H. Jones Royall. Among his ancestors were Joseph Royall of Turkey Island, Va., and George Durant, a colonial governor of North Carolina.

Royall attended Goldsboro High School and then the Episcopal High School in Alexandria, Va., from which he was graduated at age fifteen. From 1910 to 1914 he studied at The University of North Carolina, where he majored in mathematics and participated in debating and athletics. Elected to Phi Beta Kappa, he received a B.A. degree in 1914. The next year he entered Harvard Law School, where he became associate editor of the *Harvard Law Review* and earned the LL.B. in 1917.

In May 1917, shortly after the United States entered World War I, Royall joined the army. After training at Fort Oglethorpe, Ga., Camp Jackson, S.C., and Fort Sill, Okla., he was commissioned a lieutenant. From August 1918 to February 1919, when he was wounded in action, he served with the Thirty-seventh Field Artillery in France.

On returning home in 1919, Royall was admitted to the North Carolina bar and began a law practice in Goldsboro. During 1929–30 he was president of the North Carolina Bar Association, and in 1937 he joined with other lawyers to form the partnership of Ehringhaus, Royall, Gosney, and Smith. By 1942 he had built a fifty-thousand-dollar-a-year law practice in Goldsboro and Raleigh and a reputation for being "one of the State's best trial lawyers." In 1927 he served as a state senator and in 1940 as a presidential elector.

On 5 June 1942, at the request of Under Secretary of War Robert Patterson, Royall rejoined the army as chief of the Army Service Forces legal section with a colonel's commission. In May 1943 he became deputy fiscal director of the Army Service Forces, and in November he was promoted to brigadier general. During 1944 and 1945 he saw duty overseas. In April 1945 he became a special assistant to Secretary of War Henry L. Stimson. In this capacity he served as a liaison with the Department of Justice in cases of fraud involving war contractors, coordinated proposals for legislative action and executive orders relating to procurement, represented the War Department at congressional hearings, and helped draft an early atomic control bill. For his "exceptionally meritorious service" he was awarded the Distinguished Service Medal in November 1945.

In October 1945 President Truman named General Royall as under secretary of war; he was confirmed by the Senate on 8 November. Although his major concern in this post was with the handling of terminations of war contracts, in January 1946, while acting secretary of war, Royall became embroiled in the administrative and morale crisis over the issue of postwar demobilization. Members of the Senate, reacting to the mass meetings and demonstrations of soldiers overseas protesting the slowness of demobilization, blamed civilian and military unrest on the War Department. But Royall held the American people to account. He warned that the current hysteria to "get the boys back home" endangered American occupation policy and, in consequence, "the victory so recently won."

Royall was a staunch defender of War Department policy, touring military installations abroad to investigate the disposition of surplus material, cemeteries (in April 1946 he sponsored a million-dollar program to provide for the return and reburial in the United States of most of the 328,000 American war dead in foreign cemeteries), and military justice systems. Nevertheless, later in 1946, Royall conducted a review of army court actions because of the feeling that under wartime conditions investigations may have been carried out too hastily and punishments inflicted with unnecessary harshness.

On 19 July 1947, only twenty-four hours after his nomination by Truman, Royall was confirmed by the Senate as secretary of war, following the resignation of Secretary Patterson. In this capacity he worked both for continued U.S. military preparedness and for U.S. trade policy for the American zones of Austria and Germany and for Japan. With the reorganization of the military bureaucracy in August 1947, Royall continued on as secretary of the army under Secretary of Defense James V. Forrestal. A strong believer in the necessity of American strength, Royall urged that the United States be prepared to use even its atomic weapon to ensure world peace. He continued to speak on industrial and trade matters as well, arguing in one appearance before Congress for the extension of the European Recovery Plan to include western Germany.

In April 1949, after several requests that he be allowed to return to private life, Royall resigned as secretary of the army and resumed the practice of law as a senior partner in the firm of Dwight, Royall, Harris, Koegel, and Kaskey in New York City and Washington, D.C. In 1958 he became head of the firm, reorganized as Royall, Koegel, and Rogers, and remained in that position until 1967, when he retired to Raleigh. He died at Watts Hospital in Durham after a brief illness.

He was a member of the American and North Carolina bar associations, the American Law Institute, Phi Beta Kappa, Delta Kappa Epsilon (honorary president, 1947), the Rotary and Goldsboro clubs in Goldsboro, the Links, Blind Brook, and Recess clubs in New York, the Chevy Chase (Md.) Club, and the Burning Tree and Army and Navy country clubs in Washington, D.C.

A lifelong Episcopalian, Royall was buried in Willow Dale Cemetery, Goldsboro. He was survived by his wife, Margaret Best Royall, whom he had married on 18 Aug. 1917; a son, Kenneth Claiborne, Jr.; a daughter, Mrs. James Evans Davis; six grandchildren: James Evans Davis, Jr., Kenneth Claiborne Royall III, Kenneth Royall Davis, George Harrison Davis, Jerry Zollicoffer Royall, and Julia Bryan Royall; and two half sisters: Mrs. Robert McDonald Moore and Mrs. Herbert Steel.

SEE: *Current Biography* (1947); *Goldsboro News-Argus*, 26 May 1971; *Nat. Cyc. Am. Biog.*, vol. 57 (1977); *Who Was Who in America*, vol. 5 (1976).

GEORGE M. CALDWELL

Royall, William *(30 July 1823–3 Jan. 1893),* Baptist minister and educator, was born in Edgefield District, S.C., the son of William and Mary Ann Riley Royall. His great-grandfather, William Royall, settled on James Island near Charleston, S.C., in the latter part of the seventeenth century on a grant of land obtained from the Crown. For a short time young Royall also lived on James Island. At age ten he was ready for high school and his parents moved to Charleston. There, under the influence of Dr. Basil Manly, Sr., Royall made a profession of religion and joined Manly's church at age eleven.

He began the study of languages under Joseph Lee and attended classes at the Furman Manual Labor and Classical Academy, in Fairfield District, S.C., where his uncle, William E. Bailey, was principal and Dr. William Hooper (later president of Wake Forest College) was head of the theology department. From this school Royall entered South Carolina College in Columbia at age fifteen. After graduation in 1841 he read law under Attorney General Henry Bailey and taught classes in Bailey's academy in the morning to support himself. As an active church member he was soon under the influence of Drs. J. L. Reynolds and Thomas Curtis, both pastors in the city. Royall decided to enter the ministry and moved to Mount Pleasant, S.C., where he was in charge of a school and studied theology under Curtis and Dr. William T. Brantly. He supplied the pulpit for Brantly on several occasions and was ordained in Charleston in 1843.

In 1844 Royall took charge of three country churches in Abbeville and Edgefield districts, S.C. He then served churches in Georgia for two years before moving to Ocala, Fla. In Florida he assisted a number of missions and remained there until 1855. His own poor health and that of his family after suffering from malaria prompted him to accept a call to become principal of the preparatory school of Furman University. This was the beginning of his great work in the field of education. "From this period he never quit the recitation-room," according to one biographer.

In 1859 Royall became professor of languages at Wake Forest College. His method was analytical, logical, and philosophical and, according to F. P. Hobgood, "created great enthusiasm in his own department" and its "stimulating and quickening influence was felt by the entire college."

After the Civil War began, Wake Forest College closed for lack of students and Royall was appointed chaplain of the Fifty-fifth Regiment of North Carolina Troops. He served from 20 May 1862 to 24 July 1863, when he resigned because of a physical disability. Taking notice of his appointment, the *Biblical Recorder* described him as a "finished scholar, an interesting preacher, and a man of industry and energy." It predicted that he would do much good in his work as chaplain.

In 1866 Royall and three other professors (including his son, William Bailey) reopened Wake Forest College and began to prepare to instruct new students. Royall organized the course work into a flexible system of schools to replace the inflexible prewar curriculum. In 1870 he resigned his professorship to become president of the Raleigh Baptist Female Seminary. Failing health caused him to withdraw from that position, but after a period of rest he accepted the presidency of Louisburg Female College.

In 1874 he moved to Texas and became president of Baylor Female College in Independence. While in Texas, Royall also taught in seminaries in Bryan and Calvert. He moved to San Antonio in 1878 and remained there until 1879, when he accepted the presidency of Jonesboro College, Tenn. During his eighteen-month stay he also served the Baptist church in Jonesboro.

In June 1880 he was elected professor of modern languages at Wake Forest College. In this post he taught French, German, and English and assisted in the School of Moral Philosophy. In 1888 the growth of the college required the establishment of a separate Chair of English, which Royall was chosen to fill. In 1889 The University of North Carolina awarded him an honorary doctor of laws degree. Earlier, in 1868, he had received an honorary doctor of divinity degree from Furman University.

While still engaged in the field of education, Royall assisted from time to time with interim pastorates in the Wake Forest Baptist Church and served several pastorates in the area around Wake Forest. He was the author of a book, *A Treatise on Latin Cases and Analysis*, published in New York in 1860. One of his sermons was published in 1866, and he wrote numerous articles, essays, and sketches for the *Wake Forest Student* magazine.

Royall was married on 12 Oct. 1843 to Elizabeth Bailey, the oldest daughter of Dr. Robert S. Bailey. She died on 24 July 1892. The couple had three sons—William Bailey and two others, and two daughters, Mary (Mrs. F. P. Hobgood) and Mrs. W. C. Powell. Royall was spending the holidays with his daughter and son-in-law in Savannah, Ga., when he died suddenly. His funeral was held in the Wake Forest Baptist Church with friends, former students, and his son giving sketches of the influence of his life on theirs. He was buried in the local cemetery.

SEE: Raleigh *Biblical Recorder*, 27 July 1892, 11, 18 Jan. 1893; William Cathcart, *The Baptist Encyclopedia*, vol. 2 (1881); Robert Norman Daniel, *Furman University: A History* (1951); Franklin P. Hobgood, "Rev. William Royall," *North Carolina Baptist Historical Papers* 1 (January 1897); John F. Lanneau, "Sketch of Professor William Royall, D.D." (portrait), *Wake Forest Student* 12 (January 1893); J. R. Link, ed., "Rev. William Royall, D.D.," *Texas Historical and Biographical Magazine* 2 (1892); G. W. Paschal, *History of Wake Forest College*, vol. 2 (1943), and "William Bailey Royall: A Biographical Sketch," *Wake Forest Student* 45 (April 1928).

JOHN R. WOODARD

Royster, Frank Sheppard, Sr. *(24 Dec. 1849–1 Mar. 1928),* industrialist and philanthropist, was born in Granville County on the farm of his father, Marcus D., near Oxford. Marcus, the son of Francis and Elizabeth Sheppard Royster, was of Scotch-Irish descent. He married Frances Young Webb, daughter of John and Margaret Howard Webb, also of Granville County. Marcus and Elizabeth spent their lives on the land they tilled for their livelihood.

Frank S. Royster, the third oldest of five children, attended Oak Hill Academy, near his father's home. At age twelve he was sent to Bethel Academy, Person County, under the care of the Reverend T. J. Horner. He remained with Horner until the end of the Civil War, when he returned home to help on the farm and in his father's store. In 1870 Royster started his business career as a clerk for O. C. Farrar in Tarboro. He later became a partner in Farrar's merchandising firm, which furnished all kinds of supplies to farmers. Royster was credited with the discovery of the remedy for cotton rust and the use of bainit, a salt imported from Germany, in the manufacture of fertilizer.

In 1881 he founded in Tarboro the firm of Royster and Strudwick to provide general supplies to farmers and to manufacture and sell fertilizer. Ten years later he established and became president of F. S. Royster and Company, in Norfolk, Va., as a wholesale dealer in flour, sugar, and provisions. The firm also began producing fertilizer on the premises rented from M and M Steamship lines.

From this humble beginning S. Royster and Company became the largest independent, closely held fertilizer firm in the country, with some twenty-five manufacturing plants in the southeastern and middle western United States. The management was continuous and successful, stemming from the business ethics and principles of its founder and his associates. Royster remained president until shortly before his death.

A leader in civic and religious affairs and an elder in the Presbyterian church, Royster gave generously to the Norfolk General Hospital, Union Theological Seminary at Richmond, Va., and countless civic causes. He was the first president of the Norfolk-Portsmouth Chamber of Commerce and a director of the Norfolk and Western Railway, Chesapeake Steamship Company, and Virginia National Bank.

He married Mary Rice Stamps of Milton on 5 Nov. 1874. The Roysters had two sons, William S. and Frank Sheppard, Jr., and two daughters, Mrs. Richard Dickson Cooke of Norfolk, Va., and Mrs. William H. White, Jr., of Charlottesville, Va.

SEE: Samuel A. Ashe, ed., *Biographical History of North Carolina*, vol. 5 (1906 [portrait]); Family Bible, letters, and papers (possession of M. D. Edmondson); Norfolk, Va., *Ledger Dispatch*, 1 Mar. 1928; Portsmouth *Star*, 2 Mar. 1928; Raleigh *News and Observer*, 2 Mar. 1928; W. J. Webb, *Our Webb Kin of Dixie: A Family History* (1940).

M. D. EDMONDSON

Royster, Fred Stovall *(31 Dec. 1908–3 June 1972)*, tobacco warehouseman, legislator, and tobacco industry promoter, was born in the community of Dabney in western Vance County. His parents were John Stovall (24 May 1869–23 Oct. 1923), a farmer, merchant, and sheriff of Vance County, and Alvada Green Royster, natives of Granville County. He was the grandson of John Henry and Esther Anne Stovall Royster, also of Granville. Two of his relatives, Beverly S. Royster and Thomas Sampson Royster, represented Granville County in the General Assembly.

Royster attended the public schools of Vance County and was graduated from Henderson High School in 1924. His family had moved into Henderson around 1922 but had retained ownership of its four-hundred-acre farm near Dabney. Royster was enrolled at Duke University in 1926 but was forced to withdraw when hail destroyed much of the family tobacco crop.

He took a position in a Henderson tobacco warehouse and was engaged in the tobacco industry for the remainder of his life. Between 1927 and 1937 Royster farmed and was employed in several tobacco warehouses, including the Young and Daniel establishment. He acquired an interest in that business in 1938 and operated various warehouses until 1957. Royster also was a fertilizer salesman for the Virginia-Carolina Chemical Corporation from 1937 to 1957.

Around 1943 Royster, along with other flue-cured auction warehousemen, had become interested in forming a trade organization to regulate and oversee the marketing of tobacco. As a result of that sentiment, the Bright Belt Warehouse Association, Inc., was formed in 1945. Royster was appointed full-time director and served in that capacity until his death. Between 1954 and 1972 the headquarters of the Bright Leaf Warehouse Association, Inc., was located at the Carolina Warehouse in Henderson. The association became the most influential warehouse organization in the United States. Its membership was composed of the majority of auction warehouses that sold flue-cured, Bright tobacco in Virginia, North Carolina, South Carolina, Georgia, and Florida.

During his term as managing director of the association Royster emerged as one of the strongest supporters of the tobacco industry. He favored flue-cured acreage-poundage control and price supports and advocated cooperation among farmers, warehousemen, buyers, the U.S. Stabilization Corporation, and the U.S. Department of Agriculture. His contributions to the industry were not confined to the trade association but covered the entire scope of tobacco programs from their operation to their defense. Royster particularly was adamant in his support of the cigarette industry during the antismoking campaigns of the 1960s.

Due to his many accomplishments in the industry, Royster was known widely as "Mr. Tobacco." He also served as president, Henderson Tobacco Board of Trade (1940–45); member, North Carolina Tobacco Advisory Council (1945–72); director, vice-president, president, and chairman of the board, Tobacco Tax Council (1949–72); and member, Council for Tobacco Research (1954–72), Tobacco Growers Information Committee (1958–72), and National Tobacco Industry Advisory Committee, U.S. Department of Agriculture (1962–72).

Royster first entered the political arena as chairman of the Vance County Board of Elections from 1934 to 1936. He then was elected to four consecutive terms as a state representative (1945–51) but failed in his bid to become speaker of the house in 1951. Royster also served two terms as state senator (1953 and 1965–66). As a legislator he not only supported tobacco legislation but also favored increased appropriations for schools and roads. He served as chairman of the house committees on roads, agriculture, and health and of the senate committee on education and agriculture. In addition, he was a member of the state Democratic executive committee and was mentioned often as a possible candidate for appointment to national office. At the state level he was director of the North Carolina Agricultural Foundation, chairman of the North Carolina Personnel Council, and chairman of the North Carolina Merit System Council. Of national importance, Royster held membership on the board of governors and administrative committee of the National Highway Users Conference.

Royster married Launah Parker of Mooresville on 4 Jan. 1942. They had no children.

Despite his time-consuming business and political activities, Royster was associated with many fraternal, civic, educational, and religious organizations. He served as director of Henderson Savings and Loan Association and was a trustee of Maria Parham Hospital in Henderson. He also was director and vice-president of the North Carolina State University Foundation and helped sponsor the Royster-Parker Scholarship Fund for High Point College, Meredith College, and Vance-Granville Technical Institute. He was director of the Vance County Chamber of Commerce from 1940 to 1948 and was a member of the Masonic order, Rotary Club, and Elks Club. A member of the Methodist church, Royster was chairman of the board of stewards and served on the committees of finance and pastor-parish relations.

He died of complications brought on by diabetes at Duke Medical Center in Durham and was buried at Elmwood Cemetery in Henderson.

SEE: John L. Cheney, Jr., ed., *North Carolina Government, 1585–1974* (1975); *Durham Morning Herald*, 4–5 June 1972; *North Carolina Manual, 1945–1953*, 1965; "Profile," *Southern Tobacco Journal*, September 1971; Raleigh *News and Observer*, 17 Dec. 1950, 21 Feb. 1960, 4 June 1972; Mrs.

Fred S. Royster, personal contact, August 1978; *Session Laws of North Carolina, 1973 General Assembly, First Session 1973*—Resolutions (1973).

STEPHEN E. MASSENGILL

Royster, Hubert Ashley *(19 Nov. 1871–7 Nov. 1959)*, physician, was born in Raleigh, the son of Dr. Wisconsin I. and Mary Finch Royster, granddaughter of Colonel R. B. Creecy, who was editor of the Elizabeth City *Economist*. Royster attended the Raleigh Male Academy and was graduated in 1891 from Wake Forest College with the A.B. degree. He received a doctor of medicine degree in 1894 from the University of Pennsylvania, alma mater of his father, and in 1894–95 was resident surgeon in Mercy Hospital, Pittsburgh. In 1896 he entered practice with his father.

In 1897 Royster became surgeon in charge of St. Agnes Hospital, which he helped found, and gynecologist at Rex Hospital, Raleigh. From 1902 to 1910 he was dean of The University of North Carolina School of Medicine, which was located in Raleigh. He is believed to have been the first physician in North Carolina to specialize in surgery; additionally, he concentrated on women's diseases. At his retirement in 1939, he was professor of surgery at Wake Forest College. Afterwards, he was honorary chief of the surgical services at Rex Hospital, chief of staff at St. Agnes Hospital, and consulting surgeon emeritus at State Hospital in Raleigh.

Royster was president of the Wake County Medical Society in 1912 and of the North Carolina Medical Society in 1922. The author of *Appendicitis* (1927) and *Medical Manners and Morals* (1937), he also wrote extensively for medical journals and served on the editorial board of the *North Carolina Medical Journal*. In 1941–42 he was president of the North Carolina Literary and Historical Association. In the Central Park Hotel Dr. Royster removed a bug from William Jennings Bryan's throat, where it had lodged during a campaign speech.

In 1901 Royster married Louise Page of Princess Ann County, Md. They were the parents of three children: Mrs. Thomas Oxnard of Savannah, Ga.; Dr. Hubert A., Jr., of Blue Hills, Maine; and Dr. Henry P. of Gladwyne, Pa. A nephew was Chauncey L. Royster of Raleigh. Louise Page Royster (5 Sept. 1873–29 Dec. 1972), a recognized gardener, died at age ninety-nine. Their home was on Beechridge Road in Raleigh. Dr. Royster and his widow were interred in the Royster family plot in Oakwood Cemetery, Raleigh. In 1962 a portrait of Royster was unveiled at Rex Hospital.

SEE: Grady L. E. Carroll, *They Lived in Raleigh*, 2 vols. (1977); Josephus Daniels, *Editor in Politics* (1941); Mary Lynch Johnson, *History of Meredith College* (1956); Dorothy Long, *Medicine in North Carolina* (1972); *North Carolina Historical Review* 20 (April 1943); Oakwood Cemetery records, Raleigh, and superintendent of Oakwood Cemetery, personal contact, 25 May 1978; Raleigh *News and Observer*, 31 Dec. 1972, 8 Aug. 1976; *Raleigh Times*, 30 Dec. 1972; Hubert A. Royster, *Appendicitis* (1927) and *Medical Manners and Morals* (1937); Charles L. Van Noppen Papers (Manuscript Department, Duke University Library, Durham).

GRADY LEE ERNEST CARROLL, SR.

Royster, James Finch *(26 June 1880–21 Mar. 1930)*, university administrator and Kenan Professor of English Philology at The University of North Carolina, was born in Raleigh, the son of Wisconsin Illinois and Mary Willis Finch Royster. The Royster family was prominent in the civic and professional life of the capital at the turn of the century, and a number of its members gained eminence in medicine, teaching, and commerce. Young "Jim," as he was affectionately called by his intimates, attended the Raleigh public schools and was graduated from Wake Forest College with an A.B. degree in 1900. At Wake Forest he had come under the influence of such teachers as Benjamin Sledd in English and William L. Poteat in the natural sciences. Among his classmates was Joseph Quincy Adams, who became a well-known Shakespearean scholar.

Already imbued with the ambition to become a teacher of English, Royster entered the University of Chicago, where he was a protégé of the famous Chaucerian scholar, John Matthews Manley, a fellow southerner. At Chicago he developed his lifelong interest in Chaucer and linguistic studies. After a brilliant career as a graduate student, including a year of study (1902–3) in the University of Berlin and interrupted by a year (1905–6) as instructor of English at the University of Colorado, he received his Ph.D. degree from the University of Chicago in 1907.

In the fall of that year Royster joined the brilliant group of young men destined to place The University of North Carolina Department of English among the leaders in the nation. Dr. Edward Kidder Graham, then head of the department, was able to bring to Chapel Hill such men as Edwin Greenlaw, Norman Foerster, James Holly Hanford, and Edwin Mims, all of whom later became influential scholars in their respective fields. President Graham later praised Royster's "virile scholarship" and "rare gifts as a teacher and executive." During his seven-year tenure on the faculty, he edited Shakespeare's *Love's Labours Lost*, saw the publication of his doctoral dissertation, "A Middle English Treatise on the Ten Commandments" (*Studies in Philology* 5 and 8), and wrote numerous popular essays on literary research, as well as several scholarly papers on philology.

In 1914 Royster joined the faculty of the University of Texas to remain for another seven years before accepting, in 1921, the Kenan Professorship of English Philology at The University of North Carolina, a post he held until his untimely death. At Texas he had continued to write, producing a three-volume series for high schools, *Good English: Oral and Written* (1922, 1927), and a freshman text, with Stith Thompson, *Guide to Composition* (1919). At Chapel Hill he was, in 1922, made dean of the College of Liberal Arts. His annual reports of the period reflect his penetrating and forward-looking views on the meaning and purpose of a liberal education. Under his direction the foundation of the major-minor system, the practice of sectionalizing students according to ability, and the introduction of the advisory system, out of which grew the General College, all had their beginnings. Sentences from his *Annual Report* for 1922–23 well express his educational philosophy: "If we are to demand of the student adherence to duty, the severe responsibility rests upon us of giving him something to which he may intelligently . . . apply himself. . . . There may be joy in the work if we are joyful over it, there may be belief in it if we severely believe in it. . . . The intangible and elusive, and therefore more precious, aim of a liberal education should be more clearly presented."

Upon the resignation in 1925 of Edwin Greenlaw as dean of the Graduate School, editor of *Studies in Philology*, and head of the Department of English, Royster was the natural choice of faculty and administration for these positions. He threw himself into the work with such abandon that his health suffered, and in 1927 he was given a leave of absence to try to regain it but the attempt was only partially successful. Under his guidance the Department of English burgeoned, adding to its illustrious faculty and increasing the number of students, both graduate and undergraduate, who flocked to the classes of such brilliant teachers as Norman Foerster, Howard Mumford Jones, and George Coffin Taylor. With his encouragement the department organized and maintained for many years the Bull's Head Bookshop (later taken over as a part of the Student Stores). Royster was also instrumental in having a dormitory set aside for graduate students. Smith Dormitory, with its spacious lounge, became during his administration a center for meetings of the Graduate Club, the Philological Club, and other societies of scholars and faculty.

As editor of *Studies in Philology*, Royster continued the high standards of his predecessor. Both the circulation and the reputation of the journal increased during his five-year administration. In his memory, a *Royster Memorial Volume* of *Studies in Philology* appeared in October 1931; it contained contributions by his friends and colleagues, and a dedication by Edwin Greenlaw, his predecessor and colleague, praising his contributions and his editorial services as well as his "rare power to transmit his enthusiasm to others."

In recognition of his qualities as scholar and administrator, Royster was invited, in 1929–30, to serve as director of the American University Union in London. He had barely started his work there when illness forced him to relinquish it. In November 1929 he returned to the United States, where a few months later his tragic death occurred while he was a patient at a Richmond, Va., sanatorium. He was buried in the Chapel Hill Cemetery on 23 Mar. 1930.

Royster's forceful mind, his effervescent wit, and his keen insight into the problems of his profession were a constant source of delight to his colleagues and students. "With him," as noted in his biography in *The Kenan Professorships* (1956), "scholarship came first, . . . good teaching was the outgrowth of scholarly activity . . . [and] he was a living example of his philosophy." Not least among his accomplishments was his development of a carefully balanced Department of English made up of brilliant individuals held together by his wise administration.

Royster married Carrie Belle Lake on 17 June 1908. They had one son, Chauncy Lake, and one daughter, Martha Ellen.

SEE: *DAB*, vol. 16 (1935); Durham *Morning Herald-Sun*, 23 Mar. 1930; A. C. Howell, *The Kenan Professorships* (1956); Raleigh *News and Observer*, 22–23 Mar. 1930; *Who Was Who in America*, vol. 1 (1981).

A. C. HOWELL

Royster, Wilbur High *(26 Feb. 1887–22 Mar. 1951)*, lawyer, merchant, and teacher, was born in Raleigh, the son of Vermont Connecticut and Hallie Lee High Royster. He attended the Morson Academy in Raleigh and was graduated from The University of North Carolina in 1907. A member of the North Carolina National Guard between 1904 and 1911, he attended the Johns Hopkins University in 1908–9 and the American School of Classical Studies in Athens, Greece, in the same year. He received the master of arts degree from Harvard University in 1911.

From 1912 to 1915 Royster was an instructor of Latin and Greek at The University of North Carolina. While there he contributed to *Studies in Philology* an article on the authorship and interpretation of a work attributed to Aeschylus. Leaving the university, he returned to Raleigh to manage the A. D. Royster Candy Company on Fayetteville Street, a popular Raleigh institution for many years, founded by his father. When the company was sold some years later, he studied law and became a member of the Wake County bar.

In 1913 Royster married Olivette Broadway, of Monroe, La., and they became the parents of three children: Vermont Connecticut II, Saravette, and Thomas Broadway, who was killed during World War II in the invasion of Tarawa. Royster, a Baptist, was buried in Oakwood Cemetery.

SEE: Daniel L. Grant, *Alumni History of the University of North Carolina* (1924); Raleigh *News and Observer*, 23 Mar. 1951; *Who's Who in the South* (1927).

WILLIAM S. POWELL

Ruark, Robert (Bobby) Chester, Jr. *(29 Dec. 1915–1 July 1965)*, columnist, satiric essayist, and novelist, was born in Wilmington, the son of Robert Chester, an accountant, and Charlotte Adkins Ruark. His paternal grandparents were Harrison Kelly (Hanson) and Carolina Ruark; his maternal grandparents were "Captain" Hawley Adkins and his wife Lottie. It was Captain Adkins who owned the house at the corner of Lord and Nash streets in Southport where Bobby spent much of his childhood and which he later bought from his grandfather's estate. Adkins also taught the boy to hunt and fish and to look skeptically at life; he was later immortalized in Ruark's autobiographical novel, *The Old Man and the Boy*. Bobby had no siblings, but his parents later adopted a younger boy, David.

A bright youth, cocky and self-assured, Ruark was admitted to The University of North Carolina at age fifteen. There he drew cartoons for the Carolina *Buccaneer* and was graduated in June 1935 with an A.B. in journalism. Recommended by Professor Oscar J. Coffin, he was taken on as a cub reporter by the Hamlet *News-Messenger*. Ruark later commented, "I was the only guy that he considered mean enough and slap-happy enough to survive in that job." He found himself writing all the local news, selling subscriptions and advertising, helping make up the paper, and delivering it from door to door. In desperation he transferred to the Sanford *Herald*, but, not thriving there either, he came close to abandoning newspaper work forever. He took an accounting job with the Works Progress Administration in Washington, D.C., but soon enlisted as an ordinary seaman in the Merchant Marine. In 1936 he quit this too for a place as copy boy on the *Washington Post*. From there he quickly moved again, to the *Star*, and, finally, to the *Washington Daily News*, where he settled down happily.

In August 1938 Ruark married Virginia Webb, an interior decorator, of Washington, D.C. Having discovered the publicity value of stone throwing, he accused Detroit's pitcher, Bobo Newsom, of being a show-off and of fighting in the Shoreham Hotel. This led to a confrontation in the Tigers's locker room that started a free-for-all, got Ruark's name onto all the sports pages in the country, and gained him additional readers.

In World War II he joined the navy as a gunnery officer, with the rank of ensign, on munitions ships in the Atlantic and Arctic; later he was press censor under Admiral Chester W. Nimitz in the Pacific. In 1945 he returned to the *Daily News*, where he established himself as a Scripps-Howard syndicated columnist and by 1950 was earning $50,000 annually. Again employing his stone-throwing technique, he gained notoriety in August 1947 by "blowing a loud whistle" on Lieutenant General John C. H. Lee (Courthouse Lee) for Lee's misuse of government materials, maltreatment of subordinates, and other alleged abuses in Leghorn, Italy. The War Department officially cleared Lee, but Ruark claimed a technical victory in that Lee, who had sometime before requested retirement, soon received orders to return to the United States.

Ruark wrote lampoons on every conceivable topic from women's dress styles and southern cooking to Broadway columnists and psychiatrists. He did not, however, become embroiled in politics. "I'm a political eunuch," he said, "and I don't evaluate myself as a heavy thinker." But he was pleased when compared with Westbrook Pegler, "the best technical writer I ever read." He began to consider his writing seriously and turned out best-selling novels at the rate of one every year or two, although, as he pointed out, the research had often taken many years. In 1947 *Grenadine Etching*, a flip, brash take-off on the historical novel, a genre he claimed was traditionally of poor quality but needed only a bawdy heroine such as Grenadine to make it a success, sold over 40,000 copies. It was followed in 1952 by *Grenadine's Spawn* in the same vein. Meanwhile, there had appeared in 1948 *I Didn't Know It Was Loaded*, a collection of forty spicy essays gathered from his syndicated columns and, the next year, *One for the Road*, further satire on the contemporary scene. He was also publishing articles regularly in the *Saturday Evening Post, Collier's, Pic, Esquire*, and *Field and Stream*.

On the advice of his physician he took a year off and went with Virginia to hunt big game in Africa. Patterning his life on that of Ernest Hemingway, whom he admired extravagantly (Ruark even called his wife "Mama"), from 1950 onwards Ruark spent a good deal of time in Africa. In 1953 he published *Horn of the Hunter*, the story of an African safari, and in 1955, his first major success as a serious novelist, *Something of Value*, based on the racial strife that led to the Mau Mau uprisings. He made well over a million dollars from the royalties on the latter book and from the movie rights sold to Metro Goldwyn Mayer. He purchased a house, his "castle in Spain," at Palamos on the Costa Brava near Barcelona and also maintained a swank penthouse in London. In 1957 Ruark returned to visit in Southport, Wilmington, Raleigh, and Chapel Hill. At The University of North Carolina he discussed plans for a scholarship trust fund to be awarded on the basis of need alone. Having been "pinched for funds" as a student in the depression years, he said that he wanted his beneficiaries "to have a good time." The scholarships would be named for the four professors "I got the most from while I was at the University"—Oscar (Skipper) Coffin, Wallace Caldwell, Penrose Harland, and Phillips Russell. "They were the best," he said, "at preparing a person's mind to receive a little knowledge in subsequent years."

About 1963 he sold his grandfather's old house in Southport because, he said, "I do not think I could ever live with all the old ghosts." After that he did not go home again. Permanently settled in Spain, he wrote five more books: *The Old Man and the Boy* (1957), *Poor No More* (1959), *The Old Man's Boy Grows Older* (1961)—all autobiographical; *Uhuru* (1962)—another study of race relations in Africa; and *The Honey Badger* (1964)—his novel defining American womanhood. By the 1960s he and Virginia were divorced, and he became engaged to Marilyn Kaytor, food editor for *Look* magazine. In the last week of June 1965, however, Ruark suffered an attack at his home on the Costa Brava. Flown to London for medical treatment, he died there of internal bleeding. Accompanied by Miss Kaytor and Alan Ritchie, Ruark's longtime friend and secretary, his remains were returned to Spain and buried in the Colina LaFosca Cemetery near his home.

Ruark was an Episcopalian and a member of Phi Kappa Sigma. In his will, dated 6 May 1965, he left bequests totaling $125,000 to Alan Ritchie and others, with the bulk of his property divided equally between Virginia Webb Ruark and Marilyn Kaytor. His Rolls Royce and extensive library went to his literary agent, Harold Matson, and his private papers including letters, portraits, and other pictures to The University of North Carolina, where they now form a part of the university's manuscript collection.

SEE: Beverly Lake Barge, "A Catalog of the Collected Papers and MSS of Robert C. Ruark" (M.A. thesis, University of North Carolina, Chapel Hill, 1969); Hardy Burt, "It's a Wonderful Life—for Ruark," *Redbook* (April 1948); Dan Carlinsky, comp., *A Century of College Humor* (1971); *International Celebrity Register* (1959); William S. Powell, ed., *North Carolina Lives* (1962); Robert C. Ruark Papers (Southern Historical Collection, University of North Carolina, Chapel Hill); *Who Was Who in America*, vol. 4 (1968).

EMMA WILLIAMS GLOVER

Ruffin, Peter Browne *(26 Jan. 1821–5 Aug. 1900)*, Hillsborough merchant, financier, and for many years treasurer of the North Carolina Railroad, was the seventh child and fourth son of Chief Justice Thomas (1787–1870) and Anne M. Kirkland Ruffin (1794–1875). He was the grandson of Sterling and Alice Roane Ruffin of Essex County, Va., and Rockingham County, N.C., and of William and Margaret Blain Scott Kirkland of Ayr Mount, near Hillsborough. Young Ruffin, named for his father's devoted friend, the Scots Highlander Peter Browne (d. 1833), a native of Knockandock in Aberdeenshire, who lived in North Carolina for more than forty years and became an influential Raleigh banker, was born at Thomas Ruffin's first home on the eastern boundary of Hillsborough, a small estate later named Burnside by the Paul C. Cameron family.

No record of Ruffin's early education appears to have been preserved, but it is possible that he may have been sent to the Warrenton Male Academy at Warrenton, which his father had attended. He enrolled as a freshman at The University of North Carolina in 1838 but remained only through the 1838–39 year. Kemp P. Battle's *History of the University of North Carolina* recounts an amusing tale of Ruffin's schoolboy nickname, noting that it was then the campus vogue to exchange a student's real name for some ludicrous one that was often extended to younger brothers: "Peter Browne Ruffin (1838–39) had a favorite anecdote in which the upsetting of a stage was the chief incident. So he was universally known as Stage Ruffin. When his brother Thomas (1844), late Judge of the Supreme Court, matriculated, he became Hack Ruffin, a hack being of inferior dignity to a stage. Even when he attained his highest eminence at the bar an old student would give him this ridiculous nickname." Battle further lists P. B. Ruffin as a nongraduate of the class of 1842. It should be noted that, in preserved letters in J. G. de Roulhac Hamilton's edited *Papers of Thomas Ruffin*, Chief Justice Thomas Ruffin usually referred to his son Peter Browne as "Browne."

Although it is almost certain that the younger Ruffin began his highly successful business career in Hillsborough with little or no actual capital in pocket, he quickly established himself in the town's mercantile affairs. On 14 Nov. 1843, at age twenty-two, he married twenty-year-old Mary Rebecca Jones (10 Nov. 1823–20 Dec. 1878), daughter of Colonel Cadwallader, Sr., and Rebecca Edwards Long Jones of West Hill, near the western boundary of Hillsborough. In a letter William A. Graham noted that "the wedding of Mr. Ruffin was a large party," attended by his [Graham's] own family "and all the world besides."

The P. B. Ruffins had eleven children, including three sets of twins: Rebecca Edwards, b. 15 Sept. 1846; Mary Browne (Min), b. 20 Sept. 1850; twins Thomas and Susan Brodnax, b. 25 Nov. 1852; Cadwallader Jones, August 1854–June 1870; Sarah (Sallie) Jones, 1 Feb. 1856–25 Apr. 1859; twins Sterling and Allen Jones, b. 27 Dec. 1857; twins Sarah (Sallie) Jones (known as Lily) and Annie Kirkland (known as Daisy), b. 22 Aug. 1860; and Joseph Roulhac, b. 1862. In addition, the Ruffins took into their home, adopted, and reared a niece, Mary Cameron Jones (b. 10 July 1843), the daughter of Dr. Pride and Mary E. Cameron Jones.

As a home for his daughter and her family, Cadwallader Jones, Sr., with the aid of builder-architect Captain John Berry, renovated and enlarged a house at 320 West King Street, "the old Davie place," former home of Jones's near relative, the turfman and horse fancier, Major Allen Jones Davie. With additional purchases the Ruffins acquired in all a small home estate of eight acres, six of which, including the house, were on the north side of West King Street, with two acres, including servants' quarters and garden, on the south side. The Ruffin family continued to own the place until 1913, when it was sold and broken up for development. The Peter Browne Ruffin house, however, still stands and has been restored.

Ruffin had very early demonstrated a distinct flair for business and finance and rapidly became a vigorous leading merchant and civic figure in the Hillsborough area. From about 1844 onwards, he consistently bought real estate, particularly the river lots and holdings of the Thomas Faucett heirs. Among other business ventures, he established a large and flourishing tannery on a two-acre tract southwest of his home and operated a sizable general store in downtown Hillsborough to the east of Court Square. Hillsborough deeds and mortgage records reveal that he was frequently named the trustee in deeds of trusts. Many years later his brother-in-law, Colonel Cadwallader Jones, Jr., observed that Ruffin had "an enviable character for integrity and honor."

In 1849 Ruffin was named one of a committee of six to tender a public homecoming dinner to Governor William A. Graham, who pleased his Hillsborough friends and neighbors with a speech and toast warmly endorsing their efforts to improve public transportation. In 1857 Ruffin was a member of the Court of Wardens of the Poor, a commission of seven prominent citizens appointed by the county justices to serve three-year terms. On 11 May he served on a committee to inspect the Poor House Building. Later he assisted in repairing the west building, and on 5 Apr. 1858 he and Dr. Pride Jones constituted a committee to examine the vouchers and expenditures of the superintendent. In 1857 Ruffin was also made a trustee of the briefly revived Episcopal Female Seminary on East Tryon Street.

Like his father-in-law, Ruffin seems never to have been attracted to political office. His prime interests were always business, industry, and finance, and in all those areas he was preeminently successful.

In the late 1840s leading Hillsborough residents made a vigorous, concerted effort to ensure that the route of the new North Carolina Railroad would be laid by Hillsborough rather than by Chapel Hill. The most powerful promoters of the Hillsborough route, who were also stockholders and generous donors to the project, included Ruffin, his father-in-law Cadwallader Jones, Sr., John W. Norwood, former Governor William A. Graham, and Paul C. Cameron, as well as Giles Mebane and other property owners along the route. The case for the Hillsborough route was immensely strengthened by Chief Engineer Walter Gwynn's report that the projected Hillsborough route was both cheaper and more efficient than the Chapel Hill one. The railroad, when completed, skirted Jones's property (later sold as the site of the new Hillsborough Military Academy) and was immediately adjacent to Ruffin's tannery, located on the northern side of the tracks near the Hillsborough depot and siding. On one occasion Ruffin mentioned a contract for some $20,000 worth of hides from his tannery. For many years he served as the highly respected treasurer of the North Carolina Railroad, eventually moving his office from Hillsborough to Company Shops (Burlington).

Mrs. Ruffin died at age fifty-six, and her husband, twenty-two years later at age seventy-nine. Both were buried in St. Matthew's Episcopal churchyard, Hillsborough, as were various members of their families. A portrait of Peter Browne Ruffin, painted in his mature years by Garl Browne, later was owned by his grandson, Peter Browne and Virginia Bellamy Ruffin of Wilmington. The portrait showed Ruffin to have been a massive, imposing man with a handsome, square bearded face and keenly penetrating eyes.

SEE: Kemp P. Battle, *History of the University of North Carolina*, vol. 1 (1907); Documentation of the Burnside estate and the Peter Brown Ruffin House and survey of St. Matthew's Episcopal Cemetery (possession of Mary Claire Engstrom, Chapel Hill); Family records of Mr. and Mrs. Peter Browne Ruffin, Wilmington; *A Genealogical History* [of the Jones family] (1900); J. G. de Roulhac Hamilton, ed., *The Papers of Thomas Ruffin*, vols. 2–4 (1918–20); J. G. de Roulhac Hamilton and Max Williams, eds., *The Papers of William A. Graham*, vols. 1–5 (1957–73); North Carolina Society of the Cincinnati, *Minutes, 1939–1963* [Minutes of 28 Apr. 1951] (no date); Ruffin family Bible (possession of Mrs. Charlotte Trant Roulhac, Mount Vernon, N.Y.).

MARY CLAIRE ENGSTROM

Ruffin, Thomas *(17 Nov. 1787–15 Jan. 1870)*, chief justice of the North Carolina Supreme Court, statesman, and agriculturist, was born at Newington, the residence of his maternal grandfather, Thomas Roane, in King and Queen County, Va. His father was Sterling Ruffin, a substantial planter of Essex County who later moved to Rockingham County, N.C. His mother was Alice Roane, whose distinguished family included Spencer Roane, chief justice of the Virginia Supreme Court.

Young Thomas attended local schools in Essex County and prepared for college at the classical academy of Marcus George in Warrenton, N.C. Among his schoolmates, who became lifelong friends, were Robert Brodnax of Rockingham County; Cadwallader Jones, then of Halifax but later of Orange; and Weldon N. Edwards of Warren. He entered the junior class of the College of New Jersey (later Princeton) and was graduated in 1805, after which he began the study of law under David Robertson, a learned Scottish lawyer of Petersburg, Va. There he was a classmate of Winfield Scott. In 1807 he followed his family to Rockingham County and completed his law studies under Archibald D. Murphey, with whom he would later be intimately connected. He was admitted to the bar in 1808 and began a practice in Hillsborough, where, on 9 Dec. 1809, he married Anne, the daughter of William Kirkland, whose handsome home, Ayr Mount, still stands east of the town.

At the Orange County bar and neighboring ones he joined a distinguished array of barristers, including Murphey, Frederick Nash, William Norwood, Duncan Cameron, Henry Seawell, and Leonard Henderson. An ardent Jeffersonian Democrat, he represented the borough of Hillsborough in the North Carolina House of Commons in 1813, 1815, and 1816. His only other purely political office was as a Crawford candidate for presidential elector in 1824.

In 1816 Ruffin was elected by the legislature as a superior court judge but resigned after two years to return to practice in order to repay a security debt contracted by Murphey. For forty-three weeks a year he almost always attended two courts a week, despite the weather and the fatiguing and hazardous traveling conditions. He served as reporter of the state supreme court in 1820 and 1821 (his reports are found in the first volume of Francis L. Hawks, *North Carolina* [Supreme Court] *Reports*) and then returned again to his legal practice, in which by 1825, according to Justice Leonard Henderson, he stood at the head of his profession. In 1825 Ruffin again accepted the appointment as judge of the superior court, but in 1828 he again resigned, this time to become president of the State Bank of North Carolina, which had become deeply in debt. After a year he effectively redeemed the institution and prepared the way to close out the remaining term of its charter in credit.

While he was so engaged, the legislature, upon the death of Chief Justice Henderson, elected him associate justice of the supreme court in 1829. In 1833 he became chief justice, a position he held until 1852, when he resigned to retire to the Hermitage, his plantation in Alamance County, which he had acquired from Murphey in satisfaction of debts. Six years later, however, by almost unanimous election of the legislature, he was returned as chief justice but resigned after one year.

Ruffin was a North Carolina delegate at the Washington Peace Conference in February 1861 in the last-ditch effort to effect a compromise between North and South. As an ardent Unionist he sought diligently and eloquently to avert war and received the only ovation save one at the nineteen-day session. After the conference's failure and President Abraham Lincoln's call for volunteers from North Carolina, Ruffin still denied the constitutional right of secession but championed a revolutionary separation from the United States. He was elected to the Secession Convention in Raleigh, on 20 May 1861, where he supported the George Badger ordinance, which based secession on the right of revolution, rather than on the right of secession, sponsored by Burton Craige. Realizing the strong opposition to the former, Ruffin proposed a compromise solution that called for immediate secession but one that set forth the reasons. After further debate Ruffin finally acceded to Craige's motion, which was unanimously adopted. Henceforth he vigorously supported the Confederate cause, heart and soul—and pocketbook. He and William A. Graham, at the request of the convention, went to Richmond and arranged with the Confederate government for the reception of state troops and volunteers into the Confederate government.

After Appomattox, Ruffin renewed his allegiance to the United States and received an individual pardon from Andrew Johnson. Though he bitterly opposed congressional Reconstruction on constitutional grounds, he also opposed the Ku Klux Klan movement; he wrote his son that the Klan was a proceeding "against Law and the Civil power of Government" that was "wrong—all wrong."

Throughout his life, Ruffin was a leading agriculturist who operated two plantations—one in Rockingham County and the other at the Hermitage in Alamance. He and the "Southern Agriculturist," Edmund Ruffin of Virginia, his kinsman whose son married Ruffin's daughter, carried on an extensive correspondence about the latest developments in scientific agriculture. As a result of his influence in extending this knowledge, he was chosen president of the State Agricultural Society (1854–60).

A devoted member of the Episcopal church, Ruffin gave the land for St. Matthew's Church, Hillsborough, on the site where Anne Kirkland had accepted his proposal of matrimony. For many years he served on the vestry and was a delegate to the triennial General Convention of the Episcopal church.

He was also a loyal friend of The University of North Carolina. His advice was frequently sought by Presidents Joseph Caldwell and David L. Swain, and he served as a trustee from 1813 to 1831 and again from 1842 to 1868, when Reconstruction terminated the old board's existence. In 1834 the university awarded him a doctor of laws degree.

Ruffin's chief contribution to his adopted state and to the nation was as a jurist, whose reputation was recognized wherever English law was known. Authorities such as Chief Justice William Howard Taft and Justice Felix Frankfurter ranked him as a pioneer in adapting the English common law to the quasi-frontier conditions in the United States, as a result of which his decisions were followed more than any others by the southern and western courts. Roscoe Pound, long dean of the Harvard Law School, rated him one of the ten foremost jurists in the United States. Ruffin's 1,453 opinions, which embrace almost every topic of civil and criminal law and equity, are noted for their force of reasoning, breadth of view, clarity, and departure from precedent if Ruffin felt it would administer justice. In *Hoke v. Henderson* (15 N.C. 1), the first case of its kind in the United States, he held that the holder of a public office had an estate in it and therefore the legislature could not divest him of it because such a procedure was an exercise of judicial power. In *Raleigh and Gaston Railroad Company v. Davis* (19 N.C. 263), he ruled that the legislature had the power to provide for condemnation of a right of way for railroad purposes without the owner's being entitled to a jury trial for assessment of damages. Perhaps his most sensational case was *State v. Mann* (13 N.C. 263), in which he handed down the stern decision that "the power of the master must be absolute to render the submission of the slave perfect" and that the master or hirer of a slave was not liable for a battery upon the slave.

After the war, Ruffin moved from the Hermitage to Hillsborough, where he died, survived by his wife and thirteen of his fourteen children. He was buried in St. Matthew's churchyard in the grounds that he had donated almost a half century before. His portrait by James Hart hangs in the law school library at The University of North Carolina.

SEE: Samuel A. Ashe, ed., *Biographical History of North Carolina*, vol. 5 (1906); *DAB*, vol. 8 (1935); J. G. de Roulhac Hamilton, ed., *The Papers of Thomas Ruffin*, vols. 2–4 (1918–20); Ruffin family Bible (possession of Mrs. Charlotte Trant Roulhac, Mount Vernon, N.Y.); Thomas Ruffin Papers (Southern Historical Collection, University of North Carolina, Chapel Hill).

BLACKWELL P. ROBINSON

Ruffin, Thomas *(9 Sept. 1820–18 Oct. 1863)*, attorney, congressman, and Confederate officer, was born in Greene County not long before his parents, Henry John Gray and Mary (Polly) Tartt Ruffin, moved to their new plantation near Louisburg in Franklin County. After attending a private academy, he received a B.A. degree from The University of North Carolina in 1841 and then studied law under George E. Badger of Raleigh before beginning his practice in the new town of Goldsboro.

Having decided to try his fortune in the Ozark region of Missouri, Ruffin became circuit attorney for the Seventh Judicial District there and attained considerable recognition in 1844–48 as a fearless upholder of law and order despite the considerable personal risk. In 1846 The University of North Carolina awarded him an M.A. degree. On 31 August he became first lieutenant of the Ozark Mountain Guards, First Infantry Regiment, which had been organized for the Santa Fe Expedition and continued to campaign in the southwest, without actually crossing the border, during the course of the Mexican War.

Returning to Goldsboro by 1850, Ruffin resumed the practice of law and became active in local Democratic affairs. The wealthy and childless Dr. Josiah O. Watson, who had married a sister of Ruffin's mother, thought so highly of him that Watson's will of 1852 enriched Ruffin with a large plantation in Johnston County and fifty-one slaves. The uncle's generosity was not misplaced, because his admired nephew served as a representative to the U.S. Congress from 4 Mar. 1853 to 3 Mar. 1861 and to the special Peace Congress of 4–27 Feb. 1861. Ruffin resigned shortly after the secession of North Carolina and represented the Second North Carolina District in the Provincial Congress of the Confederate States held at Richmond during the period 18 June–25 July 1861.

On 16 May 1861, after declining the rank of colonel of an infantry regiment, Ruffin became captain of Company H, Ninth North Carolina (First Cavalry) Regiment, Confederate States of America. He was actively engaged most of the time until captured on 29 June 1862 at Willis Church, Va., and confined briefly at Fort Warren near Boston before being exchanged at Aiken's Landing on 5 August. In a fierce cavalry charge at the Battle of Gettysburg, he received a serious saber cut on the head but shot and killed the Yankee officer who had inflicted it.

Ruffin had been elevated to the rank of major on 29 June but was promoted to lieutenant colonel on 23 July, the day after being admitted to the military hospital at Richmond. On 15 October he was "mortally wounded during a successful charge" at Auburn's Mill, near Fairfax Court House, where he fell from his horse and was captured with a minié ball in his forehead. He died unmarried in the Federal Military Hospital at Alexandria. His remains were placed in a private vault at the hospital, and all his personal effects were carefully preserved by some Southern women until they could be returned safely to his family in Franklin County.

SEE: Clement A. Evans, ed., *Confederate Military History*, vol. 4 (1899); *North Carolina Biography*, vol. 3 (1928); *A Biographical Directory of the American Congress* (1971).

HUGH BUCKNER JOHNSTON

Ruffin, Thomas, Jr. *(21 Sept. 1824–23 May 1889)*, lawyer, North Carolina Supreme Court justice, and Confederate officer, was born in Hillsborough, the fourth son of Chief Justice Thomas and Anne Kirkland Ruffin. He was the grandson of Sterling Ruffin, who had been a member of the Virginia House of Burgesses. Young Ruffin attended the academy of Samuel Smith in Rockingham County and was graduated from The University of North Carolina in 1844. He studied law for a year under his father and his brother William before moving to Morganton, where he completed preparation for the bar.

Receiving a superior court license in 1846, Ruffin settled in Yanceyville to begin his practice but in 1848 moved to Wentworth to become the partner of John H. Dillard. In 1850–51 he represented Rockingham County as a Democrat in the North Carolina House of Commons. Three years later, in 1854, he was appointed solicitor of the district, where he served until 1860.

On 20 Apr. 1861, at the beginning of the Civil War, Ruffin enlisted as a private in the Twenty-seventh Regiment but was promoted to captain of the Alamance Company of the Thirteenth Regiment on 8 May. He resigned his commission in October 1861, when urged by Governor Henry T. Clark to fill a vacant superior court judgeship. Nevertheless, he served on the court only until March 1862, when he was appointed lieutenant colonel of his regiment; later in the year he was promoted to full colonel as regimental commander. Ruffin led the Thirteenth Regiment in the Battles of Second Manassas, Sharpsburg, and South Mountain. In the last battle, in September 1862, he was severely wounded, forcing him to resign his command six months later. He soon was appointed presiding judge of General E. Kirby Smith's corps, making him one of only three North Carolinians to serve on a Confederate military court.

Ruffin remained in that post until the end of the war, when he returned to his law practice in Graham. In January 1868 he moved to Greensboro to enter into partnership with Judge John H. Dillard and John Gilmer. While there he helped to organize the first Episcopal church in Guilford County. When Ruffin's health deteriorated, he had to abandon his practice. In December 1870 he moved to Hillsborough and opened an insurance agency. With improving health he again practiced law and in 1874 ran as an independent for the judgeship in the Seventh District against the Democrat, John Kerr. In a hotly fought contest, in which Judge Kerr accused Ruffin of being a traitor to the Democratic party, Ruffin lost the election by a little over four hundred votes.

In August 1875 Ruffin entered into partnership with John W. Graham, which, with the exception of two years (1881–83) when he served on the North Carolina Supreme Court, lasted until his death. During this period Ruffin acquired a reputation as one of the state's best lawyers. In 1884 he headed the state's delegation to the Democratic National Convention. His greatest contribution to North Carolina, however, was in helping—without charge—to prepare the contract for the sale of the Western North Carolina Railroad. For this service he and George Davis were called by Governor Thomas Jarvis, "the ablest, most powerful, and most unselfish men in the state."

Ruffin married Mary Cain of Hillsborough in 1858, and they were the parents of three sons and a daughter. He was buried in the St. Matthews Episcopal churchyard, Hillsborough.

SEE: Samuel A. Ashe, ed., *Biographical History of North Carolina*, vol. 5 (1906); John L. Cheney, Jr., ed., *North Carolina Government, 1585–1979* (1981); Walter Clark, "The

History of the Superior and Supreme Courts of North Carolina," *North Carolina Booklet* 18 (October 1918); Weymouth T. Jordan, Jr., comp., *North Carolina Troops, 1861–1865: A Roster*, vols. 5 (1975), 8 (1981); North Carolina Bar Association, *Report*, vol. 13 (1913); *North Carolina Supreme Court Reports*, September Term, 1889; Raleigh *News and Observer*, 24 May 1889.

THOMAS W. AUSTIN, JR.

Ruffin, William Haywood *(8 Feb. 1899–28 Feb. 1988)*, textile manufacturing executive, was born in Louisburg, the son of William Haywood and Sally Johnson White Ruffin. He attended Porter Military Academy in Charleston, S.C., and was graduated from The University of North Carolina in 1921. During World War I he enlisted in the Students Army Training Corps and was in officer training school when the war ended. Nevertheless, he was commissioned second lieutenant in the reserve.

Ruffin's lifelong career with Erwin Mills in Durham began almost immediately after his university graduation in 1921. He spent the first few years working at various places in the mill to learn every phase of textile production, beginning with weaving. Moving into administration in 1923, he became assistant to the secretary and treasurer and worked closely with William A. Erwin, cofounder of the mills. He was promoted to secretary and assistant treasurer in 1941 and to vice-president and treasurer in 1942. In 1948 he became president and treasurer.

Even after Erwin Mills were merged with Burlington Industries, they retained their original name, and although Ruffin became a vice-president of the new firm, he continued as president and chairman of the board of directors of Erwin Mills. Based on the 1892 foundations laid by William Erwin and Benjamin N. Duke, the Erwin Mills grew to eight plants, seven in North Carolina and one in Mississippi.

Ruffin served on the board or was a director of such firms as Wachovia Bank and Trust Company, General Telephone of the South East, and the Durham and Southern Railway and was a member of the Durham board of Woodward, Baldwin, and Company of New York City. He was president of the North Carolina Cotton Manufacturers Association, the North Carolina Industrial Council, the National Association of Manufacturers (the first native southerner to hold that post), and others. A member of the Episcopal church, he also held numerous public offices at the local and state levels.

In 1929 he married Josephine Craige Klutz of Salisbury, and they became the parents of two sons and a daughter: William H., Jr., Josephine B. (Adamson), and Burton Craige, who died at age twenty-one.

SEE: *Durham Morning Herald*, 27 Sept. 1961, 1 Apr. 1962; Daniel L. Grant, *Alumni History of the University of North Carolina* (1924); *International Year Book and Statesmen's Who's Who* (1982); *Men of Achievement in the Carolinas* (1952); North Carolina Collection, University of North Carolina, Chapel Hill (Thirteen large scrapbooks of clippings, letters, etc., three binders of speeches, two reels of film, and ten albums of phonograph records of speeches); William S. Powell, ed., *North Carolina Lives* (1962); Raleigh *News and Observer*, 1 Feb. 1953, 29 Feb. 1988.

WILLIAM S. POWELL

Ruggles, Edward Wolfe *(3 Feb. 1900–25 Aug. 1982)*, educator, was born in Southern Pines, the son of Adolphus Stephens and Sarah Frances Young Ruggles. Educated in local public schools, he spent his final two years of high school at Buies Creek Academy. As a teenager he worked for the telephone company doing technical work in the office as well as on the lines. He was graduated from North Carolina State College in 1922 with a degree in electrical engineering. As a student he was enrolled in the ROTC program and upon graduation was commissioned second lieutenant in the Signal Corps Reserve. Ruggles worked briefly for the General Railway Signal Company but contracted tuberculosis in 1923 and was hospitalized for many months. In 1926 he became an instructor in the Electrical Engineering Department at State College and took graduate courses.

In 1928 he became assistant director of extension, a new form of education begun just four years earlier, and in 1934 he became director of the Extension Division at the college. Initially it consisted chiefly of a few short courses and some correspondence work, but during World War II it expanded greatly. The division offered courses at Fort Bragg and Pope Field, near Fayetteville, and at Cherry Point Marine Air Station, in Craven County, through which men in military service could earn college transfer credit. At the request of the government, more than 4,000 students received instruction in defense-related courses. Countless inspectors, supervisors, machinists, welders, and others were trained. After the war courses were offered in the field of agriculture, in truck driving, and in numerous technical subjects as the need for adult education grew. Technicians received training in machine work, radio, television, and electronics. Avocational training also was offered, and fishing courses conducted at Nags Head proved especially popular. Extension divisions in colleges and universities evolved into Continuing Education Centers, and Ruggles's thirty-one years in the program before his retirement in 1965 had much to do with the enlarged concept. More than 12,000 students had enrolled under his guidance, and the division had gained a national reputation.

In 1927 Ruggles married Anna Rose Latham of Plymouth, and they became the parents of two children: Edward L. and Mary Frances. He was an Episcopalian.

SEE: Raleigh *News and Observer*, 29 Jan. 1956, 27 Aug. 1982.

WILLIAM S. POWELL

Rumple, Jethro *(10 Mar. 1827–20 Jan. 1906)*, Presbyterian minister, historian, and "father" of the Presbyterian Home for Children, was born in Cabarrus County, the son of Mary Winecoff Rumple and David Thomas Houston. He was reared by his oldest brother and his wife, Levi and Christina Rumple. When told of the circumstances of his birth, he chose to use the Rumple name. His maternal grandfather refused to allow his mother, who was a widow, to remarry. Young Rumple received his early education in the local old field schools, then enrolled in the academy in the Poplar Tent community. He entered the sophomore class at Davidson College in 1847 and was graduated in 1850 as the second honor man; he used the inheritance from his father to finance his education.

After teaching school in North Carolina and South Carolina for several years, Rumple began the study of theology privately under the Reverend Walter W. Pharr, pastor of the Poplar Tent Presbyterian Church. In 1854 he entered Columbia Theological Seminary, where he remained for two years. On 31 July 1856 he was licensed to preach by the Presbytery of Concord and, upon receiving calls from the Providence and Sharon churches in Mecklenburg County, he was ordained and installed as their minister on 9 Jan. 1857. There he served until called to the Presbyterian church in Salisbury. Installed on 24 Nov. 1860, he spent the rest of his life in that city.

In addition to his pastoral work, Rumple was a missionary chaplain to the Army of Northern Virginia for at least a brief period during 1863–65. He served on most of the important committees of the Presbyterian Synod and the Presbytery of Concord. In 1858 he was elected a trustee of Davidson College and served until 1905, when poor health forced his resignation; for a brief period he was the board's treasurer and for twenty-seven years, its secretary. From 1863 until his death Rumple was also a member of the board of trustees of Union Theological Seminary in Virginia. In 1888, when the Synod of North Carolina began planning for an orphans' home, he was named chairman of the committee; thereafter Rumple became the leader of and chief spokesman for this project until his death. In his honor, the principle building at the home, which was built at Barium Springs, was called Rumple Hall, as was a dormitory at Davidson College. As a tribute to his work for and interest in the church at Blowing Rock, it was named Rumple Memorial Presbyterian Church. In 1882 The University of North Carolina awarded him a doctor of divinity degree.

Rumple had an abiding interest in history. The author of *A History of Rowan County Containing Sketches of Prominent Families and Distinguished Men* (1881), he wrote articles on "The History of Presbyterianism in North Carolina" that were published in the *North Carolina Presbyterian* from 1878 to 1887 and a number of his historical writings appeared in other church newspapers. He also served as one of the assistant editors of Nevin's *Encyclopedia of the Presbyterian Church* (1884), to which he contributed many articles on the church in North Carolina.

Rumple married Jane E. Wharton of Greensboro on 13 Oct. 1857. They had four children: one who died in infancy; Watson Wharton, who died at the beginning of the second term of his senior year at Davidson; James Wharton Walker, who became a lawyer and was drowned in the Shenandoah River, Va., in 1893; and Linda Lee, who married the Reverend Charles Graves Vardell, D.D., founder and first president of Flora MacDonald College in Red Springs. Rumple died in his daughter's home after more than a year of ill health. His body was interred in the Chesnut Hill cemetery, Salisbury.

SEE: Samuel A. Ashe, ed., *Biographical History of North Carolina*, vol. 3 (1906), and *Cyclopedia of Eminent and Representative Men of the Carolinas in the Nineteenth Century* (1892); Jerome Dowd, *Sketches of Prominent Living North Carolinians* (1888); Alfred Nevins, *Encyclopedia of the Presbyterian Church in the U.S.A.* (1884); Eugene C. Scott, *Ministerial Directory of the Presbyterian Church, United States, 1861–1941* (1942); Synod of North Carolina, *Minutes* (1906).

NEILL R. MCGEACHY

Runnels, Hiram George *(17 Dec. 1796–7 Dec. 1857)*, governor of Mississippi, was born in North Carolina but moved with his family first to Georgia and later, in 1810, to Mississippi. His father, Harmon Runnels, had served with the Continental army in Georgia during the American Revolution; in Mississippi, he was a member of the 1817 constitutional convention, served in the state legislature, and was one of four men officially designated to greet General Andrew Jackson in 1818 on his visit to Jackson, the capital of Mississippi.

Young Runnels's only education was that provided by Mississippi's old field schools. In 1822 the legislature elected him auditor of public accounts, and he served until 1830, when he represented Hinds County in the legislature and was instrumental in securing a branch of the U.S. Bank in the state. Runnels was an unsuccessful Democratic gubernatorial candidate in 1831 but in 1833 became the first governor elected under the new state constitution of 1832. Narrowly defeated for reelection in 1835, he was elected a state senator in 1837. As governor, Runnels was the main force behind attempts to build a new capitol, borrowing $20,000 on his own note for its construction. The year after he left office he was awarded a contract to furnish three and one-half million bricks for the unfinished building but was later discharged from the contract.

Runnels served as president of the Mississippi Union Bank from its founding in 1838 until its failure in 1841, with Runnels liable to the bank for a sum in excess of $200,000. He created a great scandal in July 1840, when he wounded a Jackson newspaper editor critical of his banking abilities in a duel and severely caned Governor Alexander G. McNutt, also a critic of Runnels, on a main street in Jackson. The next year, however, he was elected to the state legislature.

Runnels married Obedience A. Smith, a member of a prominent Hinds County family. They were the parents of two sons, Hal and Henry. In 1832 Mrs. Runnels was one of five people who organized the first Baptist church in Jackson. In 1842 Runnels moved to Texas, where he died in Houston. His nephew, Hardin R. Runnels, was the fifth governor of Texas.

SEE: J. F. H. Claiborne, *Mississippi* (1880); Rowland Dunbar, *Mississippi*, vol. 2 (1907); Mabel B. Fant and John C. Fant, *History of Mississippi* (1920); *Journal of Mississippi History* 7 (1948), 21 (1959); Robert Lowry and William H. McCardle, *A History of Mississippi* (1891); William D. McCain, *The Story of Jackson* (1953); *Nat. Cyc. Am. Biog.*, vol. 13 (1906).

J. MARSHALL BULLOCK

Rush, Christopher *(4 Feb. 1777–10 July 1873)*, second superintendent (a title later changed to bishop) of the African Methodist Episcopal Zion Church and a full-blooded African, was born a slave in Craven County. Whether he was manumitted or purchased is unknown. In 1793 he embraced Christianity.

He escaped to New York in 1798 and in 1803 joined the Zion Church, which licensed him to preach in 1815. On 30 July 1822 he and several colleagues were ordained deacons and elders in the AME Zion Church. He was consecrated bishop on 28 May 1828, and from then until 1840 he was the only episcopal leader of the denomination, successor to James Varlick (1750–1827), founder and first bishop of the church. From 1828 to 1842, the year of his retirement from active service due to feebleness and blindness, Rush was presiding officer or host bishop at the General Conference in New York and in Philadelphia. His immediate successors were William Miller (1775–1845), consecrated in 1840, and George Galbraith (1799–1853), consecrated in 1848. Denominational historians note discrepancies in the records of Rush's years of service with Bishop Varlick and in the exact dates of his blindness and death; they also omit the names of Rush's parents and possible travel and service in North Carolina. Bishop James W. Hood noted that Rush "was debarred by the prejudice of caste from collegiate training."

Rush, nevertheless, served as secretary of the General

Conference in New York in 1824, initiated foreign mission work in Canada in 1829, and assisted in the preparation of the *Discipline* of the denomination in 1820 and the *Hymn Book* in 1858. He exercised pastoral leadership in New Haven, Conn., and encouraged the organization of the Zion African Literacy Society work in local congregations to assist slaves in educating themselves. Rush ordained many church leaders and traveled through the northeastern United States, where he organized four conferences. In 1833, with the support of sixty black and white directors, he organized and served as president of the Phoenix Society in New York. Phoenix Hall, on West Broadway, became the site of educational work and antislavery activity. In many northern cities the Phoenix Society expanded and functioned as the Phoenix Moral and Reform Society.

In 1843 Rush wrote *The Short Account of the Rise and Progress of the African Methodist Episcopal Zion Church in America*, published in New York. In the 1840s he was deeded 160 acres of land by Gerrit Smith, a New York lawyer, abolitionist, and later congressman. Rush turned the property over to the trustees of Rush Academy in Essex County, N.Y.; plans for Rush University at Fayetteville, N.C., never materialized.

Rush established a friendship with Frederick Douglass, agent of the American Anti-Slavery Society, orator of national prominence, and minister in the Methodist Episcopal Church, North. Douglass became acquainted with the AME Zion Church in New Bedford, Mass., and in time Rush gave him "authority to act as an exhorter" in the church.

In November 1865 Rush, in his eighty-eighth year, was honored in "The Rush Festival" at Masonic Hall, New York City. Named in his honor are the Rush Memorial AME Zion Church in Cambridge, Mass., the Rush Temple in Jamaica, and the Rush Metropolitan AME Church in Raleigh.

Rush was described as short of stature, reserved in manner, and stern in address, with a commanding style as a preacher. He was said to have acquired a vast fund of knowledge and his counsel was sought by succeeding church authorities. Counted "one of the giants of the reform movement of the 1830's," he died in Philadelphia and was buried in the Mother Zion Church's Cypress Hill Cemetery, New York.

SEE: Gordon P. Baker, ed., *Those Incredible Methodists: A History of the Baltimore Conference of the United Methodist Church* (1972); Emory Stevens Bucks, ed., *History of American Methodism*, vols. 1–2 (1964); Nolan B. Harmon, ed., *Encyclopedia of World Methodism* (1974); James W. Hood, *One Hundred Years of the African Methodist Episcopal Zion Church* (1895 [portrait]); William S. McFeely, *Frederick Douglass* (1991); William J. Walls, *African Methodist Zion Church: Reality of the Black Church* (1971).

GRADY LEE ERNEST CARROLL

Russell, Charles Phillips *(5 Aug. 1884–20 Nov. 1974)*, teacher, author, and newspaperman, was born in Rockingham, the son of Moses H. and Lucy Plummer Phillips Russell. He was graduated in 1904 from The University of North Carolina, where he was editor of *The Tar Heel*, the student newspaper, and one of the founders of the Golden Fleece, an honorary society. After graduation he worked on the *Charlotte Observer*, *New York Times*, New York *Herald Tribune*, *Philadelphia Evening Press*, and London *Daily Express*. While in London he also handled publicity for prizefighter Jack Dempsey.

In 1931 Russell returned to Chapel Hill to teach creative writing at The University of North Carolina for the next twenty-five years, first in the English Department and then in the School of Journalism. His students included many future American authors. The *Atlantic Monthly* described his class, often held outdoors under the trees, as one of the four best in the United States. One of his writing precepts, his students often recalled, was to "Bring on the Bear" (get the action started); when he retired from teaching, his former students presented him with a huge white bearskin rug.

He also wrote a weekly book review column, "The Literary Lantern," and a column of nature notes, "Carolina Calendar." For a time he edited a local newspaper, the Chapel Hill *News Leader*.

His numerous books ranged from an early travel account of Mexico and the Yucatan, *Red Tiger* (1925), and one novel, *Fumbler* (1928), to such highly regarded biographies as *Benjamin Franklin: First Civilized American* (1926), *John Paul Jones: Man of Action* (1927), *Emerson: The Wisest American* (1929), *William the Conqueror* (1934), and *Jefferson: Champion of the Free Mind* (1956). His book about his great-aunt Cornelia Phillips Spencer, *The Woman Who Rang the Bell* (1949), received the North Carolina Mayflower Award, and in 1968 he received the North Carolina Award "for his creative work in writing and teaching others to write." Russell was the first president of the North Carolina Society of County and Local Historians and the author of a book of history, *North Carolina in the Revolutionary War* (1965). His last book was *These Old Stone Walls* (1972), a collection of stories and historical anecdotes about Chapel Hill, where he had lived and taught for many years.

In 1931 Russell married Caro Mae Green, of Chapel Hill, sister of playwright Paul Green. He was survived by two daughters, Claire Russell Shaffner of Charlotte and Avery of New York City, and one son, Leon.

SEE: Bernadette Hoyle, *Tar Heels Writers I Have Known* (1956); William S. Powell, ed., *North Carolina Lives* (1962); Raleigh *News and Observer*, 15 Mar. 1953, 23 Nov. 1974; Richard Walser, *Literary North Carolina* (1970); *Who Was Who in America*, vol. 7 (1981).

WALTER SPEARMAN

Russell, Daniel Lindsay *(7 Aug. 1845–14 May 1908)*, judge, congressman, and governor, was born at Winnabow plantation, in Brunswick County near Wilmington, the son of Daniel Lindsay and Carolina Sanders Russell. Both the Russell and Sanders families were wealthy and owned large numbers of slaves. Few people in North Carolina were such ardent Democrats or more enthusiastic about the cause of secession than the planters of the Lower Cape Fear. Yet in this respect Russell's immediate background was different. His father and his maternal grandfather, David W. Sanders, were active Whigs, and in 1860 the fifteen-year-old Russell and his father took the highly unpopular course of opposing secession.

The following spring, however, when war became a reality, young Russell, then a student at The University of North Carolina, left Chapel Hill and returned home, where he and his father each organized a Confederate company and was commissioned captain. If the two Russells had been converted to the cause of secession, neither of them showed the slightest inclination to give up his established habit of quarreling with those gentlemen who were now the chief Confederate leaders. First, the Russells objected to the nature of their military assignments and applied to have their companies transferred to combat duty with the Army of Northern Virginia. Yet each was assigned to routine garrison duties around the forts of the Lower Cape Fear.

Next, they took exception to the Confederate conscription acts, which exempted from military service large slaveholders as well as persons who could afford to hire a substitute. Both of them were comfortably exempt on either of these grounds. The younger Russell was still further exempted because he was not old enough to be in the army anyway. Nevertheless, they added their protests to the hue and cry that rose from the white poor. A colonel called them "Political Demagogues" who obstructed his efforts at a muster of conscripts, "mixing with the crowd and freely speaking of the injustices and oppression of the conscription law."

Young Russell's difficulties with the Confederacy culminated in January 1864, when he walked into the office of the chief enrolling officer and "did then and there violently assault" him. When called upon to explain the sound beating that he had given a superior officer, the eighteen-year-old captain angrily replied, "I should not have done [so] had I not been provoked by his unparalleled mendacity." Russell was saved from the consequences of his rash deed by powerful civilian friends, especially a neighboring planter, George Davis, who was Confederate attorney general, and Zebulon Vance, Whig governor of North Carolina. Vance appointed him a commissioner of Brunswick County and declared him "necessary to the civil administration of the State Government." This in effect not only removed him from the jurisdiction of the army but also put him beyond the reach of the government in Richmond.

At the time Russell was catapulted from the army into politics, a political reaction against secession and war was gaining ground in the piney woods of Brunswick County, a movement that he was not slow in turning to his own advantage. Shortly after his nineteenth birthday, Russell stood for election to the North Carolina House of Commons and won. He served until the end of the war and for more than a year afterwards. While in the legislature, he began to study law. Upon the completion of his term in 1866, he was admitted to the North Carolina bar and, at age twenty-one, began a practice in Wilmington.

With the establishment of the Republican regime in 1868, Russell announced that he would run for judge of the superior court. The *Wilmington Star* was willing to concede his ability but, in view of his youth, found preposterous "the idea of Dan Russell being a judge of anything except groundpeas or persimmon beer!" Nevertheless, he won the election and served until 1874.

Meanwhile, on 16 Aug. 1869, Russell married Sarah Amanda Sanders, a cousin from Onslow County. They made their home mostly in Wilmington, though Russell traveled a good deal on his circuit as judge as well as to his scattered family plantations, which he was attempting, with only limited success, to restore to normal production using free labor.

Russell, on the other hand, enjoyed considerably more success in politics. As he matured he was becoming an increasingly influential member of a small circle of men whom their Democratic opponents called the "Wilmington Ring." The Republican party in southeastern North Carolina was composed overwhelmingly of people who were poor, uneducated, and politically inexperienced; about 90 percent of them were black. It was easy, therefore, for the well-to-do and educated businessmen who composed the Wilmington Ring to control the party rather completely in the counties of the Cape Fear region.

The chief threat to Russell's political ambitions was the ardent racism of the Democratic party. If the Democrats could convince enough people to vote their skin color, the Republicans could not carry more than two counties in the whole Cape Fear region. In 1876 Russell was reelected to the North Carolina House of Commons from his native Brunswick County, but Brunswick had a white majority of scarcely 60 percent. If Russell were ever to rise any higher in politics, he would have to be able to carry a series of counties with large white majorities.

A lucky break occurred for Russell as a result of the depression of 1873 and the rise of the Greenback party. Thousands of desperate farmers abandoned the Democratic for the Greenback party, which put a greater stress on the alleviation of debt than on the celebration of the white skin. In 1878 he received the endorsement of both the Republican and Greenback parties and was elected to Congress. But the national Greenback party collapsed as the depression of the mid-1870s gave way to the relative prosperity of the 1880s, when white farmers could once again afford the luxury of color loyalty and racial politics. In 1880 Russell did not stand for reelection.

All doors to political advancement seemed closed to Russell. So he withdrew to Belville plantation and devoted his energies towards trying to achieve with free labor some of the prosperity that his and Sarah's families had once enjoyed from the labor of slaves. He did not succeed, though at one time he was reported to have been the largest cotton planter on the Lower Cape Fear. The soil of the area was poorly suited to cotton.

The soil was well suited for high-quality Carolina rice, but free labor balked at a return to the rice paddies. Planters complained that, with the inducements that they had to offer, free labor was far more expensive but only slightly more productive than slave labor. Even during the comparative prosperity of the 1880s, the revival of plantation production on the Lower Cape Fear was weak and full of uncertainties.

Although Russell was enjoying little success as a planter, something in the routine of life at Belville seemed to tame the fiercely rebellious spirit of his youth. As a Greenback congressman he had thundered that the restoration of control in the South by "Bourbon" Democrats was "a menace to free institutions. It means retrogression and reaction." But by the late eighties Russell was capable of making statements that one might more normally expect from a planter of the Lower Cape Fear. In an article he wrote in 1888, he reiterated that the Democrats had gained power by catering to racial antipathy and by terror, that the blacks had been "by most monstrous wrong degraded." Yet degraded they were: "The negroes of the South are largely savages. . . . They are no more fit to govern than are their brethren in African swamps."

Russell would come to regret those words as political opportunity began to beckon again. The farmers had been in economic trouble all along. But with the arrival of the depression of 1893, which affected all parts of the economy, smoldering unrest blazed into agrarian revolt. It presented Russell with his supreme opportunity to help pull down the pillars of "Bourbon" North Carolina. Yet for the rest of his life his enemies would never let him forget that he had once called his black supporters "savages."

In 1896 Russell received the Republican nomination and was elected governor of North Carolina in a three-party race that saw thousands of desperate farmers abandon the Democrats, who called themselves "the white man's party," for the Populists, who claimed to be the poor man's party. An important achievement of his administration was winning "home rule" for a series of eastern counties. A previous Democratic administration had abolished local self-government in a number of counties having Republican minorities. Local officials in these counties had been appointed by the Democratic majority in the legislature.

When Russell challenged the North Carolina retainers of the railroad titan, J. P. Morgan, he was less successful. Morgan's Southern Railroad, by means that are not entirely clear, had been able to persuade the Democratic administration of Governor Elias Carr to grant it a ninety-nine-year lease on the state-controlled North Carolina Railroad. Many people, especially Populists, but including some Bryan Democrats such as Josephus Daniels, raised the cry of scandal. Russell pledged himself to recover the railroad for the state. But in this fight he faced not only the opposition of many Democrats but also a large number of Republicans. The governor and his allies went down in defeat before the Morgan interests.

If the depression of 1893 had opened the way for Russell's return to political life, the Spanish-American War and the return of prosperity signaled his final demise. In the summer and fall of 1898 the Democrats staged the Red Shirt campaign, the most impassioned crusade for white supremacy and Democratic rule in North Carolina history. All other issues were swallowed up. The Populists and the Republicans suffered a crushing defeat.

This time, however, the Democrats had no intention of allowing Russell to return to a secure local stronghold on the Lower Cape Fear, controlled by his friends in the Wilmington Ring and supported by black majorities in New Hanover and Pender counties. Immediately after the election, the Red Shirt political crusade was transformed into a quasi-military campaign directed against the Republican-Populist municipal administration of North Carolina's principal city, Wilmington. In a proceeding that some writers have described as a "race riot," as it entailed the destruction of black lives and property, bands of armed men, led by prominent Democrats, seized control of Wilmington. The city officials were forced to resign, the Ring was broken up, and such a reign of terror was directed against the blacks that by 1900 New Hanover County had a white majority. Russell dispatched state troops to Wilmington. But, commanded by officers who were Democrats, they only served to help consolidate the new regime.

Russell's political ruin was now complete. He had suffered defeats before, but now he had no organized constituency to return home to. He considered resigning as governor. Persuaded by his friends, however, including the tobacco magnate, Benjamin N. Duke, he decided to continue in office until the end of his term in 1901.

While serving as governor, Russell had also suffered financial ruin. In part this was due to the final eclipse of the North Carolina rice industry that followed the rise of large-scale rice production on the Gulf coast, based on mechanized techniques, especially the combine harvester, which could not be used on the soft soils of the Lower Cape Fear. But Russell had also been ruined by the expenses that he had entailed as governor. He and other governors had faced an unhappy dilemma: on one hand, their salary—$3,000 a year—was comparatively low. Yet they were expected to sustain a variety of activities and maintain a grand style of living, which could not possibly be paid for out of their salary. Russell estimated that he had spent $12,000 more than he had been paid during his four years in office.

He therefore spent the seven years of life remaining to him, after his return to Belville plantation, trying to repair his financial situation. He pinned his chief hope on a scheme for speculating on repudiated North Carolina state bonds. When the Democrats had regained control of the legislature after Reconstruction, they had refused to honor at full value the bonds floated by Reconstruction legislatures on the grounds that the passage of these bond issues had been due to corrupt practices and that much of the money made from the sale of the bonds had been improperly used. Russell, and a number of other lawyers, believed that, if the validity of these bonds could be tested in the courts, the courts would reject the legislature's argument for repudiation and uphold the bonds. Nevertheless, individual bondholders considered their property virtually worthless because, according to the Eleventh Amendment of the U.S. Constitution, an individual could not sue a state.

Russell devised a scheme for virtually bypassing the limitations imposed against suing a state. He and some associates arranged for the New York owners of a certain class of North Carolina bonds—bonds that had not been totally but only partially repudiated—to give some of the bonds to the state of South Dakota. South Dakota could and did sue the state of North Carolina for the value of these bonds and won in the U.S. Supreme Court. Russell and his associates then said in effect to the North Carolina legislature: We cannot sue you, of course. But before we allow ourselves to be robbed we will donate these bonds to a state that will obtain full value for them. You will find it cheaper if you meet us in a reasonable compromise, which Governor Robert Glenn and his Democratic legislature finally felt compelled to do.

Russell's bond scheme required years of expensive litigation, and he was in failing health. He had to curtail his law practice and could not take a very active part. Shortly before his death he received about $12,000 as his share of the scheme. If this settlement gave him the satisfaction of having struck a last blow at his "Bourbon" enemies, it hardly solved his financial problems. When he died, his assets were only about $1,000 more than his debts. Sarah Sanders Russell had to spend her last years managing a small dairy farm. They had no children.

SEE: *Biog. Dir. Am. Cong.* (1950); Robert F. Durden, *Reconstruction Bonds and Twentieth-Century Politics: South Dakota versus North Carolina* (1962); Helen Grey Edmonds, *The Negro and Fusion Politics in North Carolina, 1895–1901* (1951); Governor's Papers, Daniel Lindsay Russell, 1897–1901) (North Carolina State Archives, Raleigh); Daniel Lindsay Russell Papers (Southern Historical Collection, University of North Carolina, Chapel Hill).

WILLIAM MCKEE EVANS

Russell, Elbert *(29 Aug. 1871–21 Sept. 1951)*, Quaker teacher, minister, biblical scholar, social reformer, ecumenical leader, and university administrator, was born in Friendsville, Tenn., the son of William and Eliza Sanders Russell. After his parents' death when he was seven, he lived with his grandfather, Josiah, and stepmother, Ruth Carpenter Barnett Russell, in West Newton, Ind., where he attended school for eleven years, graduating from high school in 1890. He was enrolled in Earlham College in Richmond, Ind., from 1890 to 1894, receiving an A.B. degree. Russell married Lieuetta Lilian Cox on 14 Aug. 1894, and they were the parents of two children: Josiah Cox, born on 3 Sept. 1900, and Marcia Rachel (Mrs. Luther L. Gobbel), born on 31 Mar. 1903.

Following brief periods of study at Chautauqua, N.Y., and in the Moody Bible Institute in Chicago, Russell was governor of boys and head of the Bible Department at Earlham College from 1894 to 1901. He studied in the Divinity School of the University of Chicago from 1901 to 1903 and was awarded a Ph.D. in 1919. After returning to Earlham as head of the Bible Department in 1903, he finally resigned in 1915 because of a divisive controversy over his views on modern biblical scholarship and their role in a Quaker college.

From 1915 to 1917 Russell lived in Baltimore, where he taught at Johns Hopkins, studied Semitics, and gave wide leadership to the Society of Friends as a resident minister. In 1917 he was invited to become director of the new Woolman School, founded by Quakers at Swarthmore, Pa. He continued in the post until 1926, giving much time to adult education, speaking, writing, preaching, traveling among Friends, and visiting many churches, colleges, and universities. For fifteen months during 1925–26 he studied, lectured, and represented the American Friends Service Committee in Germany and other parts of Europe. He was closely associated with both Orthodox and Hicksite Friends, Haverford and Swarthmore colleges, and the many Friends schools in the Philadelphia area.

In 1926 he was appointed professor of biblical instruction in the new School of Religion at Duke University. In 1928 he became dean, and for the next thirteen years in that position he helped to build the school into a widely recognized, accredited, and influential institution. Serving also as a minister in the new Duke Chapel, Russell became one of North Carolina's major theological spokesmen during the depression and World War II. After retiring as dean in 1941, he continued for another four years as professor, giving a total of nineteen years to Duke University and the Divinity School (1926–45). He served for the next year as professor of religion and college pastor at Guilford College, where he had also been a trustee, and taught for two terms early in 1951 at the College of the Gulf States in Mobile, Ala.

Russell was a pioneer in the teaching of modern biblical studies in America, particularly in Quaker and Methodist institutions and at summer conferences. He became an international leader in the Society of Friends, particularly in the movement towards unity, social reform, world peace, race relations, and the ecumenical movement. In conferences such as those at Stockholm and Utrecht, he presented papers and worked on many commissions representing the American Friends Service Committee, the Fellowship of Reconciliation, and the Methodist church, which led to the establishment of the World Council of Churches. During visits to Europe and Latin America, and on one trip around the world (1933–34), he carried out a variety of missions furthering the cause of theological education, church unity, and social reform.

He was among the founders of the Chapel Hill and Durham Friends Meetings and the Carolinas Institute of International Relations. An ardent Prohibitionist, he frequently supported liberal political action. Russell was a prolific writer as well as speaker. Among his best-known books are *A Book of Chapel Talk* (1935), *More Chapel Talks* (1938) (at Duke Chapel), and his definitive one-volume *A History of Quakerism* (1942), which won the Mayflower Cup for best book published in North Carolina in 1942. He was one of the principal preachers invited to Friends Meetings in Washington, D.C., during the administration of President Herbert Hoover.

In addition to his participation in the university community of Durham–Chapel Hill–Raleigh, he also enjoyed many summers of teaching at Lake Junaluska in the North Carolina mountains, not far from his birthplace, as well as many holidays at a summer home in Myrtle Beach, S.C. He spent the last five years of his life in the midst of another small new Quaker Meeting in St. Petersburg, Fla.

SEE: *Asheville Citizen*, 23 Sept. 1951; Dorothy Gilbert, *Guilford: A Quaker College* (1937); Raleigh *News and Observer*, 23 Sept. 1951; Elbert Russell, *Elbert Russell, Quaker: An Autobiography* (1956); Opal Thornburg, *Earlham: The Story of a College* (1963).

J. FLOYD MOORE

Russell, Lindsay *(18 Nov. 1870–8 Oct. 1949)*, international and corporation lawyer and advocate of improved foreign relations, was born in Wilmington, the son of Thomas B. and Fanny Bryan Havens Russell. Governor D. L. Russell was his half uncle. Russell was educated in the schools of Wilmington, attended The University of North Carolina, and received a bachelor of law degree from the University of Michigan in 1893. After practicing briefly in Detroit, he moved to New York and joined an established firm. In 1904, with two others, he formed the firm of McLaughlin, Russell, and Bullock in New York with which he remained until his final retirement in 1947; he ceased active practice in 1930 and thereafter made his home in Wilmington.

Following the panic of 1907, Russell was named receiver by federal courts of the Otto Heinze and Company, Montana copper king; of two stockbrokers, J. M. Fiske and Company and Ennis and Stoppand; as well as of other businesses. He made extensive business contracts in person in Europe and for a time early in the century was in London as counsel for the Equitable Life Assurance Company. While in London during 1902–3, he organized the Pilgrims Society with branches in London and New York. He founded the Japan Society in New York in 1907. The emperor of Japan decorated him with the Order of the Rising Sun for his successful efforts in improving relations between that country and the United States.

Russell also devoted his efforts towards improving relations between the United States and Italy during World War I, and for that he was decorated by the King of Italy. In 1918–19 he was chairman of the Council of Foreign Relations. He was one of the founders of the North Carolina Society in New York, active in reorganizing the New York Southern Society, a trustee of the Canton (China) Christian College, a member of the advisory board of St. Luke's Hospital, Tokyo, and active in conservation, the Good Roads movement, and other public causes.

He married Mary Eloise Davis of New York, and they had one child, Fanny, who married Richard S. Andrews of Wilmington. Russell was a Republican and a Presbyterian. He was buried in Oakdale Cemetery, Wilmington.

SEE: Mrs. Fanny Russell Andrews (Wilmington), personal contact; Daniel L. Grant, *Alumni History of the University of North Carolina* (1924); New York *Herald Tribune*, *New York Times*, 9 Oct. 1949; *New York Law Journal*, 18 Oct. 1949; *Wilmington Star*, 9 Oct. 1949.

WILLIAM S. POWELL

Russell, Phillips. *See* **Russell, Charles Phillips.**

Ruth, Earl Baker *(7 Feb. 1916–15 Aug. 1989)*, congressman, college professor, and governor of Samoa, was born in Spencer, the son of Earl Monroe and Marian Beatrice Baker Ruth; he spent his youth in Charlotte. In 1938 he was graduated from The University of North Carolina, where he was an all-conference basketball player and where he received the M.A. and Ph.D. degrees in 1942 and 1955, respectively. Between 1942 and 1945 he served as an ensign and then a lieutenant in the U.S. Navy. After

World War II he was mayor pro tem of Salisbury and a city councilman for three terms. A member of the Catawba College faculty for twenty-two years, he became chairman of the Department of Physical Education and dean of students.

Having found the Rowan County voter registration book closed before he chose to change his party affiliation and run for Congress, Ruth secured a landmark decision from the State Board of Elections. A signed agreement to change his registration from Democrat to Republican as soon as the books reopened was accepted, and he was permitted to file as a Republican candidate for Congress. He was elected in 1968 and reelected for two succeeding terms, serving until 1974, when he was defeated. A highly respected conservative, he served on the House appropriations, veterans affairs, education, and labor committees.

In 1975 President Gerald Ford appointed Ruth governor of American Samoa. Ruth and Ford had become acquainted when both were in Chapel Hill as young naval officers during World War II. He remained on Samoa until President Ford was defeated for reelection.

A Presbyterian, Ruth died at his home in Salisbury following a yearlong battle with cancer. He was survived by his wife, the former Jane Wiley of Charlotte, and four children: Billie Jane, Earle Wiley, Marian Ann, and Jacqueline Dell.

SEE: *Charlotte Observer*, 15 Jan. 1975; *Durham Sun*, 7 Feb. 1975; *Greensboro Daily News*, 14 Jan., 12 Feb. 1965; *North Carolina Manual* (1971); Raleigh *News and Observer*, 22 Dec. 1968, 17 Aug. 1989; *Who's Who in America, 1976–1977* (1976); *Who's Who in American Politics, 1975–77* (1975).

WILLIAM S. POWELL

Rutherford, Griffith *(ca. 1721–10 Aug. 1805)*, colonial and Revolutionary official, military officer, and land speculator, was born in Ireland, the son of John and Elizabeth Griffith Rutherford. His grandfather, the Reverend Samuel Rutherford, had been banished from Scotland to Ireland because church officials opposed his liberal Presbyterianism. What little is known about his early life was obtained from his son Henry by Lyman C. Draper. According to family tradition, both parents died at sea in 1721, and the infant Griffith was left with relatives in Pennsylvania. Although his later writings indicate that he was barely literate, Rutherford had a keen mind and very early mastered the craft of surveying. He moved first to Halifax County, N.C., and in the early 1750s settled in Rowan County. In 1754 he claimed a 656-acre tract on Grant Creek in what was known as the Irish Settlement. In the same year he married Elizabeth, the daughter of James Graham, another early landholder in the area.

There is little documentation concerning Rutherford's participation in the French and Indian War; however, he probably served with troops under the command of Colonel Hugh Waddell, as he was listed as a captain in the Rowan militia in 1760. His public life on the northwestern Carolina frontier began with his appointment as deputy to John Frohock, surveyor for Henry E. McCulloh. In 1766 Rutherford, along with Frohock, represented Rowan County in the Assembly, thus commencing a long legislative career that continued for two turbulent decades. He was also a justice of the peace and served as sheriff of Rowan County from 1767 to 1769. Although a member of the "Courthouse Ring," Rutherford was able to survive politically the upheaval associated with the Regulator movement. He did this by promoting some of the Regulator causes in the Assembly, notably advocating the creation of additional western counties. In September 1768 he participated in the council of war held at Hillsborough, which recommended that most of the Regulators be pardoned. Whether by choice or by force, Rutherford was one of the Rowan officials who agreed to return any excessive fees he may have collected as surveyor. His militia company obeyed General Waddell's orders to join the western troops in the expedition against the Regulators in May 1771. When Waddell's forces were met by a large number of Regulators near the Trading Ford on the Yadkin, Rutherford was among those who advised the general to remain encamped and to discontinue his march towards a rendezvous with Governor William Tryon. The following year, 1772, he was commissioned colonel of the Rowan County militia.

Rutherford was not among those leaders who first agitated for rebellion against Britain. The argument had been advanced that perhaps he was distrustful of the eastern Whig leadership of the movement. But by the fall of 1775, the Third Provincial Congress had appointed him to the Safety Committee of the Salisbury District and colonel of minutemen for Rowan County. Soon he was called upon to lead his men into South Carolina to aid in crushing the Scovillite Tories in the "Snow Campaign" of December 1775.

In February 1776 Rutherford led his Rowan troops east to Cross Creek in an effort to thwart Loyalist activities in the Upper Cape Fear region. Although he arrived too late to take part in the Battle of Moore's Creek Bridge, his military efforts did not go unnoticed and unrewarded. When he attended the Fourth Provincial Congress in April, he was named brigadier general of militia for the Salisbury District, an area that included the entire western frontier of the province.

Even as this appointment was being made, unrest was rampant on the western frontier as the Cherokee, bound by treaty to the British, grew wary of increased encroachments by settlers into tribal lands. By mid-July the new brigadier was gathering his forces on the headwaters of the Catawba for an invasion of the Cherokee country. The Council of Safety attempted to coordinate North Carolina's military action with similar efforts by Virginia and South Carolina. However, Rutherford, ever suspicious of the eastern-dominated council, chafed for action. On 1 September he led his force of approximately 1,700 officers and men into the Cherokee lands, falling first on the middle settlements and then on the valley towns, where he joined forces with South Carolinians led by Colonel Andrew Williamson. By late September the two armies made their way home after destroying thirty-six towns and laying waste to crops and storehouses, thus reducing the Indians to a state of near starvation as winter approached. Although the Cherokee threat was effectively neutralized by this campaign, Rutherford was ordered by the legislature to raise independent companies to range and to construct forts along the frontier. He also turned his attention to the growing menace of roving Loyalist bands in his western district.

Late in 1778 Governor Richard Caswell ordered Rutherford's troops southwards to help defend South Carolina and Georgia from the British invasion. By early January 1779 his troops were encamped near the Savannah River. The militia troops were dispirited and ill-equipped. After the defeat at Briar Creek of a North Carolina force commanded by General John Ashe, Rutherford participated in the court of inquiry against Ashe. As the period of enlistment for his men was nearing an end, Rutherford returned home by mid-April. The next year he was again ordered south, this time to aid in lifting the siege of Charleston, but the city fell before the backcountry militia arrived. The brigadier realized that a British invasion of the Salisbury District was almost a certainty, and that the invading army would in a large degree be dependent on local Loyalist support. Therefore, he set about systematically to destroy Loyalist resistance in the area. This began with the defeat of Tory partisans at the Battle of Ramsour's Mill on 20 June 1780. By mid-July he was raising forces to assist General Horatio Gates in his attempt to stop Lord Charles Cornwallis. This ended in disaster at Camden on 16 Aug. 1780. Rutherford, shot through the leg and with a saber wound to the head, was captured by the British.

After being detained at Camden he was first transported to Charleston and later taken by prison ship to St. Augustine. His exchange was arranged in June 1781. Released in Philadelphia, he reached Rowan County in August only to find that British forces had "stripped" his plantation. Immediately he resumed command of his brigade and by early October marched his troops eastwards, where on 15 October he attacked and defeated a Loyalist band at the Battle of Raft Swamp. By the end of the month he had reached Wilmington, the last major British outpost in the state. Before the battle could be joined, word arrived of the surrender at Yorktown and the city was evacuated. Upon returning to western North Carolina, Rutherford continued to harry Tory enclaves. During the fall of 1782 he assisted General Charles McDowell in his expedition against a renewed Cherokee threat. This campaign effectively ended Rutherford's military career.

Rutherford's successful military exploits enhanced his political clout. Within a month after his return from the Cherokee campaign of 1776, he attended the Fifth Provincial Congress, in November, where he served on the committee to draw up a "Bill of Rights and Form of a Constitution" for the new state. Although his role in this endeavor cannot be determined, certainly he favored the dominance of the legislative branch and other radical provisions of the constitution. Subsequently, he represented Rowan County in the state senate for the next decade.

His attempt to pass a radical confiscation act failed in 1777, but many of his demands were included in the revised act of 1779. In politics, just as on the battlefield, Rutherford was ruthless in his determination to destroy those who did not ardently embrace the Revolutionary cause. During the 1782 session he was elected to the Council of State and was appointed commissioner of confiscated property for the Salisbury District. Within a few months he had identified eighty-two parcels for confiscation. Rutherford continued to advocate more stringent laws against Loyalists as well as a twofold tax on Quakers and Moravians. This last action prompted one leading conservative to refer to him as a "blood thirsty old scoundrel." No doubt his radicalism was a primary factor in the defeat of his nomination as governor in 1783. When the Treaty of Paris was placed before the state senate in 1784, Rutherford successfully led the opposition to Article 5, which concerned the restoration of confiscated Loyalist property. The article was defeated.

When the convention was called to meet at Hillsborough in 1788 to consider the adoption of the federal Constitution, Rutherford was in attendance. Although he favored an open discussion of the document, he was unmoved by Federalist arguments and voted with the majority not to ratify. He was unsuccessful in his attempt to rally support at the convention for the selection of Fayetteville as the location of the state capital. In 1789 Rowan County did not return him as a delegate to the Fayetteville convention, which ratified the new Constitution. However, the legislature continued to elect him to the Council of State.

By the end of the war Rutherford held in excess of 2,000 acres, mostly in Rowan, with lesser tracts in Lincoln and Burke counties. He soon became caught up in speculative western land ventures. In 1783 he joined with William Blount, Richard Caswell, Joseph Martin, John Donelson, and John Sevier in a scheme to settle the area known as the "Bent of the Tennessee" or Muscle Shoals. This effort failed. Also in 1783 Rutherford was appointed by Governor Alexander Martin to survey the western lands set aside by the General Assembly to satisfy the claims of those who had served in the North Carolina Continental Line. For the performance of this duty, he received 3,000 acres of Tennessee land. It is estimated that by 1790 Rutherford owned between 12,000 and 20,000 acres west of the mountains. In 1792 he sold his home plantation on Grant Creek and at age seventy-one moved to Sumner County in the Tennessee country. It was a new frontier and Rutherford found it necessary to build a stockade around his new home to protect against Indian attacks.

William Blount prevailed upon the first session of the territorial legislature to nominate Rutherford to the legislative Council. He was duly appointed by President George Washington on 13 June 1794 and was subsequently elected president of the Council. In 1803 the state of Tennessee created Rutherford County. Earlier, in 1777, the North Carolina legislature had honored the backwoods brigadier in naming a county for him in that state.

In his eighty-fourth year the old soldier died peacefully in his sleep. According to family tradition, he was buried in a cemetery near Lagardo, Tenn. When in his prime he was described as being 5'8" in height, weighing approximately 180 pounds, and having red hair. There is no known portrait of him.

Griffith and Elizabeth Graham Rutherford were the parents of ten children: Jane (b. 1756, m. James Cathey), James (1758–8 Sept. 1781, killed at the Battle of Eutaw), Blanche (m. Francis Locke), Henry (17 Aug. 1762–20 May 1847, m. Mary Johnston), Elizabeth (m. James Wright), Alfred, Newton, Margaret (m. Elijah P. Chambers), John (13 Mar. 1774–8 Sept. 1855, m. Ann McGuire), and Griffith Weakley (1775–December 1846, m. Elizabeth Johnson).

SEE: Thomas P. Abernethy, *From Frontier to Plantation in Tennessee: A Study in Frontier Democracy* (1932); Samuel A. Ashe, ed., *Biographical History of North Carolina*, vol. 2 (1905); James S. Brawley, *The Rowan Story, 1753–1953* (1953); Robert Claude Carpenter, "Griffith Rutherford: Frontier Military and Political Leader" (M.A. thesis, Wake Forest University, 1974); John L. Cheney, Jr., ed., *North Carolina Government, 1585–1979* (1981); Walter Clark, ed., *State Records of North Carolina*, vols. 11–23 (1895–1904); Draper MSS, 28S–29S (microfilm, 1980, State Historical Society of Wisconsin); Robert L. Ganyard, "Threat from the West: North Carolina and the Cherokee, 1776–1778," *North Carolina Historical Review* 45 (January 1968); Minnie R. H. Long, *General Griffith Rutherford and Allied Families* (1942); William L. Saunders, ed., *Colonial Records of North Carolina*, vols. 7–10 (1890).

JERRY C. CASHION

Rutherfurd, John *(25 Jan. 1724–31 May 1782)*, receiver general of the quitrents and member of the Royal Council of North Carolina, was born at Bowland, Midlothian County, Scotland. He was a twentieth-generation descendant of Robertus dominus de Rodyrforde, the twelfth-century founder of the Rutherfurd family. John Rutherfurd was the eldest of seven children born to James and Isabella Simpson Rutherfurd. His brothers who survived to majority, James (1725–82) and Thomas (1734–80), followed him to America. In 1743 James conducted a mercantile business in Wilmington after which he moved his residence to Cumberland County, where he was justice of the peace and colonel of the militia. Thomas Rutherfurd, also a resident of Cumberland County, served as deputy secretary of the province in the mid-1760s and register and clerk of the Cumberland County Court in the 1770s. After his election from that county to the first four provincial congresses, he joined the Loyalists at Moore's Creek Bridge. The subsequent defeat led to the capture of Thomas Rutherfurd and confiscation of his property. He was sent to Philadelphia, paroled, exchanged, and died on board ship in 1780 in Clinton's fleet, which was returning to Charles Town.

John Rutherfurd arrived in America in 1739. He was a protégé of his cousin, James Murray, who established him in the merchandising business in the Cape Fear. Rutherfurd was barely twenty-one in 1745, when he served New Hanover County as a commissioner of the roads. By 1747 he was living in Wilmington, where he conducted the affairs of Rutherfurd and Company, dealers in lumber and merchandise. He was elected town commissioner of Wilmington from 1749 to 1751, and in the latter year the Assembly named him commissioner of the pilotage of the Cape Fear River.

In March 1750 Rutherfurd embarked for England, where he procured by assiduous personal effort, and with the assistance of Surveyor General of the Customs Robert Dinwiddie, a commission as receiver general of the quitrents for North Carolina dated 13 Nov. 1750. In 1752 the Crown appointed him to the Council of North Carolina. In 1757, however, Governor Arthur Dobbs in Council suspended Rutherfurd from his offices for the following reasons: allowing James Murray, a member of the Council and former secretary and clerk of the Crown, to issue small denomination promissory notes to be accepted by Rutherfurd for quitrent payments; disbursing quitrent moneys without the governor's consent; failing to discharge properly and diligently his duties as receiver general; and aiding Murray to form a junto in the Council and Assembly to thwart the will of the governor and Crown. Rutherfurd again journeyed to England, where he successfully defended his conduct; on 2 and 30 Apr. 1761 he received renewed commissions as receiver general and councilor respectively. By December 1761 he again enjoyed possession of those offices, which he retained until the outbreak of the Revolution.

Rutherfurd's position in the government improved upon the accession of William Tryon as governor in 1765. Tryon appointed Rutherfurd a member of the expedition to survey the Cherokee boundary line in 1767. The next year the governor elevated him to the rank of lieutenant colonel in the campaign against the Regulators and when ill relinquished command of the troops to the receiver general. Rutherfurd also served in the 1771 expedition against the Regulators, which culminated in the Battle of Alamance. In 1772 he and William Dry joined commissioners from South Carolina to survey an extension of the boundary line between the two colonies.

At the onset of the Revolution Rutherfurd gave nominal support to Governor Josiah Martin, after which he retired to his country estate, Hunthill. He remained unmolested until 1781, when upon the arrival of Lord Charles Cornwallis he announced his support for the British cause. After Cornwallis withdrew his troops, Rutherfurd fled for safety to Charles Town, S.C., leaving the bulk of his estate to Patriot confiscation. Ill health and poverty forced Rutherfurd to embark for Scotland in 1782. He died the same year in Cork, Ireland, before reaching his homeland.

In 1754 Rutherfurd married Frances Johnston, twice a widow, first of one Button and second of Governor Gabriel Johnston. In the aftermath of the settlement of the Johnston estate, Rutherfurd obtained a Royal warrant dated 5 Feb. 1761 for £12,500.8.8 sterling for the arrears of salary due to Johnston while governor of North Carolina. The warrant was made on the South Carolina quitrent fund, as similar moneys in North Carolina were insufficient. Rutherfurd experienced difficulty obtaining payment despite the best exertions of his friend and attorney in Charles Town, Henry Laurens. At the outbreak of the Revolution £2,018.19.2 remained to be paid, which sum was collected after much delay by the Rutherfurd heirs.

Rutherfurd greatly enlarged his estate in the 1750s, at which time he acquired a plantation at Rocky Point which he called Bowland. Between 1762 and 1766 he maintained a mercantile partnership with Alexander Duncan of Wilmington. Apparently Rutherfurd financed many of his transactions by a loan of £7,440 sterling obtained from John Murray of Philiphaugh in May and June 1761. Rutherfurd's delay in liquidating the debt prompted Murray to demand additional security for the loan in 1768 in the form of Rutherfurd's landholdings, a bequest of £1,000 in Duncan's will, unpaid debts owed the Duncan partnership, and twenty-two slaves. Subsequently, Rutherfurd was bankrupted and, after a decision by the Chancery Court of North Carolina on 15 Jan. 1771, presumably lost the above assets including Bowland. In desperation he prepared to leave the province and inquired of friends about possible positions in government offices in London. However, by 1775 he had executed a remarkable financial recovery, which found him in possession of a 4,000-acre estate, Hunthill, acquired from Sampson Moseley. Hunthill, located at Holly Shelter Creek about thirty miles north of Wilmington, contained 300 cleared acres, 150 slaves, 26 teams of oxen, 150 head of cattle, a gristmill, a large double sawmill, and naval stores facilities.

By temperament Rutherfurd was a genial man. Although he complained of severe deafness in 1758 and Governor Martin declared him unfit for public office by virtue of the same malady in 1774, Rutherfurd conducted private and public business with seeming ease. Nor did gout prevent him from being a charming host and traveling often in his service to the government and in a private capacity. Although Governors Dobbs and Martin accused Rutherfurd of indolence, particularly in regard to his duties as receiver general, Rutherfurd appears to have been an industrious, even tenacious, individual when the occasion demanded.

Nevertheless, Rutherfurd was a retiring, scholarly person who enjoyed the solitude of his large library. His intellectual attainments were exemplified by the publication in England in 1761 of *The Importance of the Colonies to Great Britain*. Dedicated to the Earl of Halifax (George Montague-Dunk), this was essentially a mercantilistic tract positing the argument that England should encourage colonial production of raw materials in order to stimulate English manufacturing. This policy would curtail colonial manufacturing, produce a larger colonial market for English manufactures, reduce English unemployment, and diminish English dependence on external trading markets. Rutherfurd observed significantly that to compel the colonials, intentionally or not, to resort to manufacturing would result in their eventual independence.

John and Frances Rutherfurd, who died in 1768, had three children: Frances (1756–1809), John, Jr. (1762–1813), and William Gordon (1764–1818). The children were probably born at Bowland plantation, Rocky Point, but upon the death of their mother were sent to Scotland for their education. They returned to North Carolina briefly on the eve of the Revolution. Rutherfurd subsequently entered John, Jr., in the British army and William Gordon in the navy where they both enjoyed distinguished careers. After the Revolution the children worked tirelessly to obtain restitution of their father's estate, but not until 1811 did their perseverance produce a final, and satisfactory, settlement.

SEE: Walter Clark, ed., *State Records of North Carolina*, vols. 11–25 (1895–1906); New Hanover County Records (Deeds) (North Carolina State Archives, Raleigh); William S. Powell, ed., *Correspondence of William Tryon and Other Selected Papers*, 2 vols. (1980–81); John Rutherfurd, *The Importance of the Colonies to Great Britain with Some Hints toward making Improvements to their mutual Advantage; And upon Trade in General* (1761); W. K. and A. C. Rutherford, *Genealogical History of the Rutherford Family*, vol. 1 (1969); William L. Saunders, ed., *Colonial Records of North Carolina*, vols. 5–10 (1887–90); Janet Schaw, *Journal of a Lady of Quality* (1923).

ALAN D. WATSON

Rutherfurd, William Gordon *(19 June 1764–14 Jan. 1818)*, captain in the British navy who participated in the Battle of Trafalgar in 1805, was born at Bowland plantation, Rocky Point, approximately twenty miles north of Wilmington. He was named for Lord Adam Gordon, his godfather and a British army colonel who visited North Carolina shortly after his birth. Called "Little Billie," he was the younger son and third child of Frances Button Johnston and John Rutherfurd. His mother was formerly married to Governor Gabriel Johnston of North Carolina; his father was receiver general of the quitrents for the colony and a member of the Royal Council.

Upon the death of his mother in 1768, William Rutherfurd was sent to Scotland for his education. He returned to North Carolina in 1774, but the outbreak of the Revolution forced his departure a year later. His father then placed him in a free school in England under the protection of Lord Townshend. In 1778 Rutherfurd joined the British navy as a midshipman on the *Suffolk*. Between 1783 and 1789 he served on merchant ships in the Orient. Later he rejoined the navy, eventually becoming senior frigate captain under Admiral Horatio Nelson. In 1805 Nelson made Rutherfurd captain of the new seventy-four-gun *Swiftsure*. Rutherfurd participated in the pursuit of the fleet of the French admiral Pierre de Villeneuve to the West Indies and then in the Battle of Trafalgar, in which the *Swiftsure* wrecked the French *Archille* while suffering small losses. Rutherfurd remained captain of the *Swiftsure* until 1807, when he was discharged. In the same year he became captain of the *Sea Fencibles* and remained in that post until 1810. In 1815 he was made a Companion of the Bath and in 1816, one of the four captains of Greenwich Hospital, where he died two years later.

Rutherfurd married Lilia (Lilas or Lillias), the eldest daughter of Sir George Richardson, Baronet, of London, in 1795. She died in 1831 without children. However, the couple apparently had an adopted son, John Henry Defou, known as Henry Rutherfurd. William Gordon Rutherfurd and his wife were buried at St. Margaret's Church, Westminster, London.

SEE: W. K. and A. C. Rutherford, *Genealogical History of the Rutherford Family*, vol. 1 (1969); Janet Schaw, *Journal of a Lady of Quality* (1923 [portrait]); *Winston-Salem Journal and Sentinel*, 17 Jan. 1960.

ALAN D. WATSON

Said, Omar Ibn *(1770–1864)*, a slave and Arabic scholar, was born in Futa Toro (now a part of the Republic of Senegal) of an aristocratic Moslem family. Educated in Koranic schools, he was a teacher and tradesman for about fifteen years and purportedly made a pilgrimage to Mecca during the period 1790–1805. In 1807 he was found guilty of an unspecified crime and sold by his people, the Fulas, to an American slave trader. Taken to Charleston, S.C., Omar was among the last Africans to reach the United States prior to the outlawing of the overseas slave trade at the end of 1807. After working for two years as a slave in Charleston and on a South Carolina rice plantation, he escaped in 1810 and made his way to Fayetteville, N.C., near which he was recaptured. When efforts to find his legal owner proved unavailing, he became the property of General James Owen of Bladen County. At Owen's Cape Fear River estate called Milton, Omar was taught English and converted to the Christian religion, joining the First Presbyterian Church in Fayetteville in 1820.

The Owen family, intrigued by Omar's facility with Arabic and his scholarly bent, gave him little work and permitted him ample time to study an Arabic translation of the Bible that was procured for him by General Owen. Occasional spates of journalistic interest, fanned by false reports that Omar was the son of an African king, circulated his name and circumstances widely during the antebellum era. In 1836 he moved with the Owen family to Wilmington, where he was active in the Presbyterian congregation and host to many visitors anxious to witness his unusual ability to read and write in Arabic. There are reports that he accompanied his owners to resort springs in the South and there entertained children with folk stories. An added source of public interest in the 1850s was Omar's advanced age.

During the Civil War the Owen family moved to Owen Hill, a Cape Fear farm formerly the home of General Owen's brother, Governor John Owen, where Omar died at age ninety-four. Much of the information about him is contained in a brief autobiography in Arabic that he composed in 1831. He appears to have been the only formally educated African among the slave population of North Carolina. The North Carolina Collection at the University of North Carolina at Chapel Hill has a paper with Arabic writing by Said as well as a daguerreotype of him.

SEE: Fayetteville, *North Carolina Presbyterian*, 23 July 1859; J. F. Jameson, "Autobiography of Omar ibn Said, Slave in North Carolina," *American Historical Review* 30 (July 1925); Philadelphia, *Christian Advocate*, July 1825; J. L. Wilson, *Western Africa: Its History, Condition, and Prospects* (1856).

THOMAS C. PARRAMORE

Sampson, John *(d. 1784)*, planter and colonial official, arrived in North Carolina during the 1730s from his native Ireland. He quickly obtained major landholdings in New Hanover County and purchased a residence in

Wilmington. After the formation of Duplin County from New Hanover in 1750, he became a leading planter and officeholder in the new county. In 1740 he became a justice of the peace for New Hanover County, and in 1747 the people of Wilmington elected him to its town commission. During 1749 he served as sheriff of New Hanover County, and two years later he was appointed inspector of commodities for the Cape Fear River. Sampson evidenced an interest in military affairs by commanding militia troops in combating the Spanish invasion of 1748. By 1754 he was a lieutenant colonel of the Duplin militia (the Duplin Foot), and in 1768 Governor William Tryon named him a lieutenant general at Hillsborough during the Regulator difficulties.

Sampson became involved in legislative affairs in 1747, when he was elected to the General Assembly. As an assemblyman he served on the committee on public claims and on committees to prepare bills for creating Duplin, Rowan, and Anson counties. He served in the legislature continuously until 1754, when he apparently left North Carolina and returned to Great Britain. While there he entered into an agreement with his uncle, George Vaughan, who offered to donate £1,000 annually for the support of an academy or seminary to educate Indians in North Carolina. This project was never realized.

Upon his return to North Carolina sometime prior to 1759, Sampson resumed an active public life. He became mayor and alderman of Wilmington in 1760 and a representative from Duplin County in the General Assembly in 1761. Governor Arthur Dobbs appointed him to his Council during the fall of 1761; after taking the oath of office in November, Sampson faithfully served three succeeding royal governors as councillor. In the upper house he repeatedly served on the joint committee to settle public claims. He was also appointed to committees to inspect Fort Johnston (1764), consider vestry acts (1764), select a town site at Cross Creek (Campbellton), and decide on Assembly decorum (1768). Sampson disagreed with fellow Council members on the location for a permanent capital, and, along with John Rutherford and Lewis De Rosset, he opposed a Council resolution supporting New Bern as the capital.

As difficulties with Great Britain mounted during the 1770s, Sampson found himself in the disagreeable position of opposing Governor Josiah Martin while declaring complete loyalty and fidelity to Great Britain. When Sampson split with Martin on the highly controversial court bill issue, the governor requested that Sampson, along with Rutherford, De Rosset, William Dry, and Samuel Cornell, be dismissed from the Council for failure to support him. Martin complained that Sampson was "a man of middling fortune and of good moral character, but of very shallow understanding and an implicit follower of the opinions of Mr. De Rosset on all occasions."

Despite the Revolutionary fervor of the time, Sampson remained loyal to the king and expressed to Governor Martin his "abhorance for republican principles." Even after the Royal governor was forced to flee the province and take refuge on the British warship *Cruizer*, Sampson, James Hasell, and Lewis De Rosset attended a Council meeting aboard ship in the Cape Fear River on 18 July 1775. The three-man Council, in approving actions taken by Martin, was of the opinion "that the deluded people of this Province will see their error and return to their allegiance."

Obviously, the Duplin County planter was able to reconcile himself with the Revolutionary government of North Carolina. In 1779 he was elected to the North Carolina Council of State, an honor that Sampson rejected due to his inability to serve. In a letter to Governor Richard Caswell, he explained that "it's not in my power to attend, being at present very infirm and old age creeping fast upon me."

Sampson died at Sampson Hall Plantation, Duplin County, after the death of his wife, the former Ann Walker of Wilmington. They had no children, and his grandnephew, James Sampson (son of his nephew of the same name) inherited his 1,000-acre plantation. In 1784 a new county, formed from Duplin, was named in honor of Colonel John Sampson. Sampson Hall Plantation was located near the present-day county seat of Clinton. Richard Clinton, for whom the town was named, had been an heir to a portion of the Sampson estate; he is believed to have been a natural son of Sampson.

SEE: Cora Bass, *Sampson County Yearbook, 1956–1957* (1957?) and comp., *Abstracts of Sampson County, North Carolina, Wills, 1784–1895* (1958); Walter Clark, ed., *State Records of North Carolina*, vols. 22–24 (1905–7); Donald R. Lennon and Ida Brooks Kellam, eds., *Wilmington Town Book, 1743–1778* (1973); William L. Saunders, ed., *Colonial Records of North Carolina*, vols. 4–9 (1886–90).

DONALD R. LENNON

Sampson, Oscar R. *(17 Jan. 1866–9 Jan. 1928)*, minister and educator, was born in the Deep Branch community of Robeson County, the son of William, a farmer and Baptist minister, and Mary Dial Sampson, both identified as mulattoes in the 1860 and 1870 census returns. The 1928 death certificate of Oscar Sampson, however, records his race as Indian. In 1889 he was among the earliest graduates of the Indian Normal School at Pembroke. He began teaching school in 1890 and in time became principal of the Pembroke graded school. Sampson also owned a farm and a large tract of land within the bounds of the town of Pembroke. Named to the board of trustees of Pembroke Normal School in 1896, he served until his death thirty-two years later.

Sampson was long in fellowship with the Plymouth Brethren and preached twice a month for many years. A strong supporter of the Pembroke Normal School, he was a leader among the local people who contributed to and planned its growth and expansion into Pembroke State University. The administration building, in which an oil portrait of him hangs, was named for Sampson.

In 1893 he married Susie J. Oxendine, and they became the parents of fifteen children, ten of whom survived to adulthood: Mary E., Ruth, Charity, Nettie B., James Albert, Katie Lee, John Paul, Lucy, Joseph, and Martha. He was buried in the Harpers Ferry cemetery, Robeson County.

SEE: Death certificate (North Carolina State Archives, Raleigh); *North Carolina Biography*, vol. 3 (1928); *Path Toward Freedom* (1976); Raleigh *News and Observer*, 17 Feb. 1957.

WILLIAM S. POWELL

Sandburg, Carl August *(6 Jan. 1878–22 July 1967)*, poet, journalist, biographer, and folk song recitalist, was a national celebrity long identified with the Midwest when he moved to North Carolina in 1945 after purchasing the historic Connemara Farm at Flat Rock. In 1958 the legislature made him "Honorary Ambassador" of the Old North State.

Sandburg was born in Galesburg, Ill., the second child of pious Swedish immigrants. His father, unable to write, is believed to have changed the family name from Johnson shortly after beginning work as a blacksmith's helper in the C. B. and Q. railroad shops. His mother was the former Clara Mathilda Anderson. Leaving school after the eighth grade, Sandburg held an array of humble jobs in Galesburg and then bummed his way as a hobo westward as far as Colorado, with intervals of labor in harvest fields or washing dishes in grubby restaurants. These early adventures are colorfully described in the portion of his autobiography entitled *Always the Young Strangers* (1953). In 1898 he was back in Galesburg and working as a painter's apprentice when he enlisted in the Sixth Illinois Regiment; Sandburg served briefly in Puerto Rico during the Spanish-American War.

With a veteran's privileges he entered Lombard College, a tiny Universalist school in Galesburg; flunked the examinations required for admission to West Point after being nominated by an army friend; and resumed studies at Lombard until 1902, when he left without graduating. His four years at college were crucial, for there he was stimulated by musical, forensic, and literary activities and hailed as a genius by a professor named Philip Green Wright, who introduced him to the arts and crafts movement of Ruskin, Morris, and Elbert Hubbard and encouraged his social radicalism then bordering on Syndicalist Anarchism. The professor also operated an arty press in his basement where he published four little volumes of Sandburg's juvenilia, beginning in 1904. Rudyard Kipling and standard favorites of the nineties were major influences on Sandburg's early verse, but independently he had come across Walt Whitman, whose free verse he imitated until a decade later he mastered his own version of that medium.

Another period of wandering followed departure from college; this time he went to the East to sell stereopticon pictures. With the muckraking fervor then in full swing, socialism burgeoned and new periodicals multiplied. Sandburg took to the hustings as an organizer for the Socialist party and acted as press secretary for a Socialist mayor of Milwaukee, but after his marriage on 15 June 1908 he was more the journalist than poet or politician. His wife was Lillian Steichen, a high school teacher and a Phi Beta Kappa from the University of Chicago—also an ardent Socialist. Her brother, Edward Steichen, later a famed photographer, became a potent influence on Sandburg's views of art. The Sandburgs had three children, Margaret, Janet, and Helga, the last-named also a writer. Another daughter died in infancy.

In 1912 the poet returned to journalism in Chicago, shifting from post to post with magazines and newspapers until he eventually found a niche on the *Daily News*, an afternoon paper for which he worked on and off for many years as labor reporter, movie critic, editorialist, or columnist. His divorce from the Socialist cause became greater as the party split over the entrance of the United States into World War I. Sandburg thereafter called himself an independent and in time heartily endorsed Franklin D. Roosevelt and the New Deal. Later he was on close terms with Adlai Stevenson and Presidents John F. Kennedy and Lyndon B. Johnson.

A sturdy family man, Sandburg avoided the bohemian excesses of the artistic crew active in Chicago, then in an era of remarkable crescendo, but soon was propelled into prominence by being hailed as one of the first "finds" of *Poetry: A Magazine of Verse*, whose establishment in 1912 is often regarded as a wellspring of the "New Poetry." The editors of this Chicago journal awarded him their Levinson Prize and prompted a New York publisher to bring out his *Chicago Poems* (1916), previously printed in *Poetry*, Socialist sheets, and elsewhere. Unconventional subjects, slang, "realism" of the ashcan sort laced with wistful flashes of beauty, and a kind of chanting music quickly made his free verse famous in advanced quarters and notorious in conservative purlieus where "shredded prose" was the slogan of stigma. "Chicago," "Fog," "Nocturne in a Deserted Brickyard," and other poems in the volume remain his best-known pieces. The most popular, "Fog," was an effort to emulate the Japanese *Haikku* and was written in the anteroom of a police court judge whom Sandburg was sent to interview. On the way he had stopped to look at the dense mist gathering over the Chicago harbor. Similar odd moments in the turmoil of journalism produced much of his subsequent verse. And the style remained unchanged.

Cornhuskers (1918), *Smoke and Steel* (1920), *Slabs of the Sunburned West* (1922), *Good Morning, America* (1928), and *The People, Yes* (1936) in chronology illustrate the rise and fall of the "Poetical Renaissance" in which Sandburg was a major figure. *The People, Yes* was his longest poem—teeming with proverbs, wisecracks, and other sorts of folklore picked up during his travels or sent in for his newspaper column. It is as choice a sample of affirmative Americana as the depression era produced; "it attempts to give back to the people their own lingo," as its author stated. Sandburg was scarcely a young man when he vaulted into the sky of the New Poetry, and when in 1950 his *Complete Poems* appeared, without selection or revision, there were few additions to the above-named volumes, and these were chiefly poems of occasion. Two subsequent collections appeared as *Harvest Poems: 1910–1960* (1960) and *Honey and Salt* (1963), the latter containing several pieces revealing his deep and abiding affection for his wife.

Fame as a poet with the ensuing honors and prizes cannot keep *lupus americanus* from the door, however. Sandburg continued to work for the press and in 1918 went to Scandinavia as correspondent for the Newspaper Enterprise Association; when this syndicate later fired him, he took refuge again with the *News*. In 1922 his whimsical tales for his children were revamped as *Rootabaga Stories*, to be followed by *Rootabaga Pigeons* (1923). Altogether, he put out five subsequent books for the young, including appropriate segments of his autobiography and his study of Abraham Lincoln. More remunerative were his lectures. Beginning in the 1920s, when the colleges turned to the "new" poetry, Sandburg soon was recognized as a surefire entertainer—a superb platform artist who could read his poems to perfection, reel off a "Rootabaga" yarn, provide a store of belly-shaking mirth, temper the mood with a bit of fetching philosophizing, and top off with a round of work songs, new and old, sung in a rich baritone accompanied by his guitar. His taste as a collector of songs is to be seen in his anthologies *The American Songbag* (1927) and *The New American Songbag* (1950).

Indulgence to a celebrity by his newspaper bosses and his lecture tours enabled Sandburg to cut down on hack work and to spend more time composing at a summer cottage at Tower Hill, Mich., to which he later moved from the Chicago area. As the popularity of contemporary verse faded with the public, a new rage for long-winded biographies flourished. It was such a biography that enabled Sandburg to own the summer place as a permanent home, to buy expensive animals to gratify the goat-breeding hobby of his wife, and to possess six guitars. His monumental work on Lincoln, originally conceived as another book for young people, came in two installments, *Abraham Lincoln: The Prairie Years* (1926) and *Abraham Lincoln: The War Years* (1939). This six-volume opus was so widely proclaimed that its author passed from the region of famous poets to the empyrean of movie stars. Honorary degrees now came in showers, reporters eagerly sought his views on current topics, public schools were named for him, and Democratic presidents were flattered when he wrote them letters saying that Abraham Lincoln would have approved of their actions.

In addition to broadcasts and news reports, Sandburg's offerings on the Lincoln shrine numbered a one-volume redaction of the full biography (1954), a book on Mary Lincoln, another on the photographs of the Emancipator, and a third on a noted private collection of Lincolniana. Others did most of the work on these last. In 1959 Lincoln's birthday was celebrated in Washington by a solemn gathering of Congress, the Supreme Court, the Eisenhower cabinet, and the diplomatic corps. The choice of Sandburg as chief speaker for the occasion constituted a unique honor.

During World War II he patriotically defended U.S. policies, helped with propaganda in the various news media, and even took on for a while a column for the *Chicago Daily Times*. In 1959 he went on a mission to Russia for the Department of State.

After settling in North Carolina his most extensive publications were a huge panoramic novel *Remembrance Rock* (1948) and the autobiographical *Always the Young Strangers*, one of his best books. The reaction to the novel was at best merely polite. But a first novel by a man seventy years old, planned to be a movie "spectacular" intended to arouse a sense of patriotism, can hardly be expected to lay a claim to immortality.

Of Sandburg's enormous production of labor news, miscellaneous journalism, scripts, and so forth, *You and Your Job* (1908), *The Chicago Race Riots* (1919), and *Home Front Memo* (1943) offer samplings. It was only during his last few years that he did not have a finger in some sort of project. When death came, the tributes were front-page items. After a family service at Flat Rock conducted by a Unitarian clergyman, his body was cremated and the ashes were buried at Galesburg. In a special ceremony held in Washington at the Lincoln Memorial, President Johnson spoke of him as "the echo of the people." Of all the encomia Sandburg probably would have like that one best.

In 1956 Sandburg sold his papers, proofs, and library to the University of Illinois. To date this collection lacks his own letters, a selection from which, however, was indifferently edited by Herbert Mitgang (1968).

SEE: For his early years *Always the Young Strangers* (1953), which may be checked against Karl Detzer, *Carl Sandburg* (1941); North Callahan, *Carl Sandburg: Lincoln of Our Literature* (1970), which adds certain details for the later years; for pictures *Sandburg: Photographs View Carl Sandburg* (1966), ed. Edward Steichen.

CLARENCE GOHDES

Sanderlin, George Washington *(22 Feb. 1843–6 Nov. 1899)*, Baptist minister and politician, was born in Camden County, the son of Maxcy and Martha Sanderson Sanderlin. He was one of thirteen children. After attending schools in Elizabeth City, he entered Wake Forest College in 1858 and was graduated in August 1861 because of the Civil War. Sanderlin enlisted in Company E, Thirty-third North Carolina Regiment, as a private. Promoted through the ranks to captain, he served for four years, participated in forty battles, was hospitalized once, and had one brief furlough.

At the close of the war Sanderlin settled in Elizabeth City, but feeling a call to the ministry, he entered the Southern Baptist Theological Seminary in Greenville, S.C., and was graduated with honors in 1867. In the same year he also received an M.A. degree from Wake Forest College. Sanderlin was ordained at the Wake Forest Baptist Church on 1 Mar. 1868 and immediately took charge of the Goldsboro Baptist Church, which he served until January 1871. He resigned in anticipation of a tour of Egypt and Palestine with Dr. John A. Broadus. Sanderlin missed the steamer to Rome, but while in Baltimore, Md., he preached in the Franklin Square Baptist Church and was unanimously called to the pastorate of that church later in 1871. His health began to fail and he resigned in 1876.

Retiring to Goldsboro, Sanderlin turned his attention to agriculture and wrote for various publications in that field. He became widely known, and as his health had improved, he accepted the Democratic nomination for state auditor in 1888, won the election, and assumed office in January 1889. His reputation as an able, charming speaker and active campaigner caused his name to be placed in nomination for governor of North Carolina, but Elias Carr was named. After campaigning for the Democratic ticket, Sanderlin was appointed by President Grover Cleveland as fourth auditor of the Treasury Department and he and his family moved to Washington, D.C. He resigned this position after the inauguration of President William McKinley but continued to live in Washington.

Two years of ill health followed by a serious fall led to Sanderlin's death in a sanitarium in Baltimore. His remains were sent by train to Raleigh, where they were met by a large delegation, including the governor, all state officers, and members of the Raleigh First Baptist Church and of fraternal orders to which Sanderlin had belonged, and escorted to Oakwood Cemetery for interment.

Sanderlin served as vice-president of the North Carolina Baptist Convention and as a trustee of Wake Forest College from 1869 to 1871 and from 1883 to 1892. He was a member of the Odd Fellows, Raleigh Council Royal Arcanium, No. 551, and Knights of Pythias, Oak City Lodge Knights of Honor. Both Wake Forest College and Judson College, Hendersonville, awarded him an honorary doctor of laws degree in 1891.

He married Eliza W. Wooten, the daughter of Council Wooten of Lenoir County. They had six children: Nannie Eliza Wooten, Beulah, Georgia, Pattie, Rosalie, and one other.

SEE: Samuel A. Ashe, ed., *Biographical History of North Carolina*, vol. 8 (1917 [portrait]); Judson College Records, 1859–92, and George Washington Sanderlin Biography File (Baptist Historical Collection, Wake Forest University, Winston-Salem); George W. Paschal, *History of Wake Forest College*, vol. 3 (1943); Raleigh, *Biblical Recorder*, 27 Oct. 1875, 15 Nov. 1899; Raleigh *News and Observer*, 8 Nov. 1899; John R. Sampey, *Southern Baptist Theological Seminary: The First Thirty Years, 1859–1890* (1890); Charles E. Taylor, ed., *General Catalogue of Wake Forest College, North Carolina, 1843–5–1891–2* (1892); *Wake Forest Alumni Directory* (1961).

JOHN R. WOODARD

Sanders, Daniel Jackson *(15 Feb. 1847–6 Mar. 1907)*, Presbyterian clergyman, editor, and educator, one of five children of William and Laura Sanders, was born a slave near Winnsboro, S.C. His mother was owned by the Reverend Thomas Hall, a Methodist minister, and his father was owned by Major Samuel Barkley, a Confederate officer and shoemaker. Shortly after Sanders's birth, Hall died and willed all of his property, including his slaves, to Barkley. The owners of Sanders permitted him to learn the alphabet, and at age nine he received his first instruction in the trade of shoemaking. After three years of tutelage, his master was able to collect pay for Daniel's services. By the time the Emancipation Proclamation went into effect, the boy had learned to read and spell, skills that he refined later in life.

According to his "Memoirs," in early March 1866, at about 3:00 A.M., the nineteen-year-old Sanders secretly left home in Winnsboro, taking with him only a small shoemaker's kit. His destination was Chester, S.C., where he worked at the only trade he knew, until befriended by two whites, John and William Knox, who lived near Chester. Tutored by the Knox brothers, Sanders by 1869 was ready to enter Brainerd Institute, a normal and industrial school in Chester.

Sanders was graduated after two years of study. He proved such an apt student that he was made a tutor at Brainerd in 1870. In the same year, he was licensed by the Fairfield Presbytery as a minister in the northern branch of the Presbyterian Church of the United States. In 1871 he entered Western Theological Seminary at Allegheny, Pa., where in 1874 he was graduated with honors and prizes in Hebrew and Sanskrit.

After graduation Sanders became the stated supply of the Chestnut Street Presbyterian Church in Wilmington. In 1875 he was appointed principal of that town's school for blacks. For these endeavors Lincoln University of Pennsylvania awarded him the honorary degrees of master of arts and doctor of divinity. In 1876 he resigned the positions of pastor and principal in order to go abroad to raise money for the Presbyterian Board of Missions for Freedmen. For more than a year, Sanders traveled with Scottish students in England and Scotland to raise money for the board. He returned to Wilmington with $6,120.17 committed to Biddle (now Johnson C. Smith) University, a Presbyterian institution for blacks in Charlotte. In 1878 he resumed his pastoral duties at the Chestnut Street Presbyterian Church in Wilmington, and during the same year he was named to the board of directors of Biddle University. On 1 Jan. 1879 he began to publish the *Africo-American Presbyterian*, a semimonthly religious and educational journal, which he continued to edit until his death.

On 16 Sept. 1880 Sanders married Fannie Price; they had nine children: Ruth, Irene, Alderia, Danetta, George, William, Daniel, Jr., Brooks, and one whose name is not recorded. One of his daughters, Danetta, became a professor at Hunter College in New York, and another daughter, Irene, taught music at Hampton Institute in Virginia.

Dr. and Mrs. Sanders remained in the Wilmington area until early 1891, during which time he served as pastor of the Pilgrims' Chapel and Chadbourn Presbyterian churches. At the end of the academic year 1890–91, the Reverend W. F. Johnson resigned as president of Biddle University. He was to be the last white president of that institution. Amid considerable controversy, the Board of Missions for Freedmen informed the General Assembly of the Presbyterian church that the purpose of Biddle was to create leadership qualities among blacks and that the time had come to put its teachings to the test. Accordingly, it recommended Daniel Sanders for the presidency. There was heated debate, during which three of the four white faculty members resigned and blacks were hired to replace them. After the smoke cleared, the church's ruling body (the General Assembly) agreed to the recommendation, and on 12 Oct. 1891 Sanders became the first black president of Biddle University.

Fondly called "Zeus" by his students, Sanders served as president of Biddle for seventeen years. During his administration, many firsts in the areas of education and sports were recorded. In 1892 the first black intercollegiate football game was played between Biddle and Livingstone College of Salisbury. The campus was expanded academically and physically. In 1891 fourteen students were graduated (seven in theology and seven in arts and science); that number increased threefold by 1907.

In 1905 Sanders revisited England as a delegate to the Pan-Presbyterian Alliance. The first black moderator of both the Yadkin and Cape Fear presbyteries, he also served as a stated clerk in the Atlantic and Yadkin presbyteries and the Catawba Synod.

Sanders became sick in December 1906 and died the following year. He was buried in the Ninth Street Cemetery in Charlotte, also known as Elldonwood Cemetery.

SEE: *Africo-American Presbyterian*, vol. 29 (14 Mar. 1907); Barkley Family Papers (Southern Historical Collection, University of North Carolina, Chapel Hill); *Charlotte Advertiser*, 9 Mar. 1907; *DAB*, vol. 16 (1935); *Minutes of the General Assembly of the Presbyterian Church in the U.S.A. 1891*, vol. 14 (1891); Inez M. Parker, *Biddle-Johnson C. Smith University Story* (1975); *Who Was Who in America*, vol. 1 (1942).

R. A. MASSEY, JR.

Sanderson (Saunderson), Richard *(ca. 1641–1718)*, Council member and justice, settled in the Currituck area of what is now North Carolina in 1661. According to a deposition that he made in 1711, he was born about 1641. Nothing more is known of his early life.

By 10 Nov. 1681 Sanderson had become a member of the Council of the North Carolina colony, which was then called Albemarle. He probably was also a member of the Assembly, for his seat on the Council was one filled by the Assembly, which ordinarily elected its own members to the Council seats it controlled. Sanderson sat on the Council again in 1687 and 1689.

By March 1693/94 he was serving on the Council in the reorganized government established after the ousting of Governor Seth Sothel. Sanderson appears to have remained a Council member from that time through 1712 with the exception of the years 1707–9. In the 1690s and afterwards he sat as a Lord Proprietor's deputy, and for the last portion of his tenure he was deputy of "the heirs of Seth Sothel." As deputy to Sothel's heirs he did not attend Council meetings, probably because of a question as to his legal status in that capacity, for the Proprietors did not recognize the heirs' claim to Sothel's Proprietorship and made other disposition of Sothel's share in Carolina. In January 1712/13 the Council issued an order calling attention to Sanderson's consistent absence from meetings and directing that he attend the next meeting or be suspended and replaced. Sanderson appears to have ignored the order.

As Council member he was an ex officio justice of several courts held by the Council, including the Palatine's court, the Court of Chancery, and, until 1698, the General Court. He also was an ex officio member of the upper house of the Assembly, which was composed of the Council members.

In the political struggles between Anglicans and dissenters in the early 1700s, Sanderson, an Anglican, supported the establishment of the Anglican church and the imposition of political disabilities on dissenters. He also supported his church in private life. He was on the vestry of Currituck Parish at the time it was organized and apparently continued to serve until his death. Much of the time he was senior warden. An Anglican missionary who had lived in Sanderson's home for about a year reported in 1710 that Sanderson intended to bequeath valuable properties to the Currituck Parish. If Sanderson's will contained such provisions, however, they were not executed, for the will was set aside as invalid.

Sanderson continued until his death to live in Currituck, where he had settled as a young man. He patented about 900 acres of land and acquired considerable wealth in cattle and other property. About 1700 he owned at least one vessel, the *Richard*, a shallop of four tons, which was engaged in the coastal trade. At one time he was a partner in a venture involving a large stock of cattle bought from Seth Sothel's estate, but the nature of the venture is not clear.

Sanderson was married at least twice, but the name of only his last wife is known. About 1711 he married Demaris Coleman, widow of Ellis Coleman. By this time he already had grown children.

Late in July 1718, after his death, his widow took his will to court for probate, but probate was prevented by a caveat entered by Sanderson's son Richard. Subsequently the courts held the will invalid, as the scribe, one William Alexander, testified that some provisions were not written on orders from Sanderson but at the direction of Sanderson's wife.

Sanderson had two sons and two daughters. One son, Richard, followed in his father's footsteps and served on the Council for many years. Another son, Joseph, was a member of the Assembly in 1722 and 1725 but otherwise appears not to have been active in politics. Both Richard and Joseph lived in Currituck for a time, but Richard moved to Perquimans Precinct about 1714. Richard died in 1733, survived by a son, also named Richard, and two daughters, Grace and Elizabeth. Joseph died before October 1746, survived by his wife, Julian, and seven sons: Richard, Samuel, Joshua, Thomas, William, Benjamin, and Joseph. One of Sanderson's daughters, whose name is not known, married Henry Woodhouse, by whom she had a son, Hezekiah. The other daughter, Susanna, married one Tulley and subsequently one Erwin.

Sanderson's widow, Demaris, married Thomas Swann soon after her husband's death, but she died about a year later.

SEE: John L. Cheney, Jr., ed., *North Carolina Government, 1585–1974* (1975); J. Bryan Grimes, ed., *Abstract of North Carolina Wills* (1910) and *North Carolina Wills and Inventories* (1912); J. R. B. Hathaway, ed., *North Carolina Historical and Genealogical Register* (1900–1903); Gordon C. Jones, comp., *Abstracts of Wills and Other Records, Currituck and Dare Counties, 1663–1850* (1958); North Carolina State Archives (Raleigh), various documents in Albemarle Book of Warrants and Surveys (1681–1706), Albemarle County Papers (1678–1739), British Records (photocopies and microfilm), Colonial Court Records (boxes 139, 148, 184, 189, 192), Council Minutes, Wills, Inventories (1677–1701), and North Carolina Wills; Mattie Erma Edwards Parker, ed., *North Carolina Higher-Court Records, 1670–1696* (1968) and *1697–1701* (1971); William S. Price, Jr., ed., *North Carolina Higher-Court Records, 1702–1708* (1974) and *North Carolina Higher-Court Minutes, 1709–1723* (1977); William L. Saunders, ed., *Colonial Records of North Carolina*, vols. 1–2 (1886).

MATTIE ERMA E. PARKER

Sanderson, Richard *(d. 1733)*, councilman, assemblyman, and justice, was the son of Richard Sanderson (ca. 1641–1718), a longtime member of the Council who had settled in the Currituck area in 1661. The young Sanderson no doubt grew up on his father's plantation in Currituck, where he may have been born. Neither his mother's name nor the date of his birth is known.

Sanderson's public career began before September 1694, by which time he was a justice of the Currituck Precinct Court. He appears to have remained on the court at least through February 1702/3. He held a seat in the lower house of the Assembly about 1703 and also in 1709 and 1715; in 1709 he was elected speaker.

In 1712 Sanderson was commissioned justice of the General Court, and he was recommissioned from time to time for more than a decade. He seems, however, to have attended the General Court only occasionally, for his name seldom appears as one of the justices present when the court sat.

About 1717 Sanderson was appointed to the Council, on which he was active through 1730. As councilman he sat ex officio as justice of the Court of Chancery. He also sat in the upper house of the Assembly in 1722–23, 1725, and 1727.

Apparently he was active in the militia, as he bore the title colonel in later years. His earlier title, captain, denotes his rank as master mariner, although he may also have held that appellation in the militia at some period. Like his father, he was an Anglican and served as a vestryman of Currituck Parish. He later sat on the vestry of Perquimans Parish, to which he had moved.

Sanderson lived in Currituck Precinct until 1714 or early 1715, when he moved to Little River in Perquimans Precinct. The Assembly met at his house in Little River in the fall of 1715, and the Council, Court of Chancery, and General Court met there in 1715 and 1716.

In Perquimans and elsewhere Sanderson acquired extensive landholdings. His properties included Cape Lookout and Ocracoke Island, on which he raised horses, cattle, sheep, and hogs. He also cultivated one or more plantations in Perquimans. As a young man he was a master mariner and commanded various vessels in the coastal trade, including the *Richard*, a shallop that his father owned. He later engaged in the coastal trade on his own account and traded with Bermuda and probably the West Indies. He owned three vessels: the *Seaflower*, a brigantine of forty tons' burden; the *Thomas*, a sloop of eight tons; and the *Lark*, a sloop of ten tons. At various times his son Richard served as master of these ships. Sanderson disposed of the *Thomas* during his lifetime but owned the *Seaflower* and the *Lark* at the time of his death.

He was married at least twice. The earliest marriage of which record has been found occurred about 1711, when he wed Elizabeth Mason, widow of Thomas Mason of Norfolk County, Va. About 1727 he married Ruth Minge, widow of James Minge of Perquimans and daughter of Benjamin Laker. Ruth died before 29 Jan. 1727/28, when her will was proved.

Sanderson died between 17 Aug. 1733, when he made his will, and 15 Oct. 1733, when the will was proved. He was survived by his son Richard and daughters Grace, wife of Tulle Williams, and Elizabeth, wife of Thomas Pollock, son of the former governor Thomas Pollock. Sanderson's son died before October 1737, survived by his wife Hannah and at least two children, John and Elizabeth.

SEE: John L. Cheney, Jr., ed., *North Carolina Government, 1585–1974* (1975); J. Bryan Grimes, ed., *Abstract of North Carolina Wills* (1910) and *North Carolina Wills and Inventories* (1912); J. R. B. Hathaway, ed., *North Carolina Historical and Genealogical Register* (1900–1903); Gordon C. Jones, comp., *Abstracts of Wills and Other Records, Currituck and Dare Counties, 1663–1850* (1958); North Carolina State Archives (Raleigh), various documents in Albemarle County Papers (1678–1739), Tillie Bond Collection, British Records (photocopies and microfilm), Colonial Court Records (boxes 148, 184, 192), North Carolina Wills, and Perquimans Deeds (microfilm); Mattie Erma Edwards Parker, ed., *North Carolina Higher-Court Records, 1670–1696* (1968) and *1697–1701* (1971); William S. Price, Jr., ed., *North Carolina Higher-Court Minutes, 1702–1708* (1974) and *North Carolina Higher-Court Minutes, 1709–1723* (1977); William L. Saunders, ed., *Colonial Records of North Carolina*, vols. 1–2 (1886); *Virginia Magazine of History and Biography* 4 (July 1896); Ellen Goode Winslow, *History of Perquimans County* (1931).

MATTIE ERMA E. PARKER

Sarratt, Alexander Reed, Jr. *(17 Sept. 1917–15 Mar. 1986)*, journalist, was born in Charlotte, the son of Alexander R. and Joncie Elizabeth Hutchison Sarratt. He was graduated from The University of North Carolina in 1937 with a degree in economics and membership in Phi Beta Kappa. As a senior he was managing editor of the student newspaper, the *Daily Tar Heel*.

Following his graduation, Sarratt became editor of the *Blowing Rocket* during the summer and served in turn as reporter, book editor, assistant city editor, city editor, and special writer on the *Charlotte News* until 1946. Between 1946 and 1952 he was an editorial writer with the *Baltimore Evening Sun*. He then joined the staff of the *Winston-Salem Journal* and the *Twin City Sentinel*, filling a number of posts including editorial director, executive editor, assistant to the general manager, and executive assistant to the publisher in charge of news, advertising, circulation, and promotion. In May 1960 he became executive director of the Southern Education Reporting Service in Nashville, Tenn., which, operating under a Ford Foundation grant, collected and published information on school segregation-desegregation in the South. The foundation's *Southern School News* containing factual reports was widely distributed to the regional and national press and others. Sarratt was also director of the journalism project of the Southern Regional Education Board in Atlanta. In 1973 he became executive director of the Southern Newspaper Publishers' Association, a position he held until his death.

Sarratt was the author of *The Ordeal of Desegregation: The First Decade* (1966); edited two volumes, *The Impact of the Computer on Society* (1966) and *Education for Newspaper Work* (1973); and contributed to various professional journals. In 1985 he was inducted into the North Carolina Journalism Hall of Fame.

In 1938 he married Elva Ann Ransom of Charlotte, and they became the parents of three children: Ann Ransom, Alexander Reed III, and John Lester. He was a Democrat and a member of the Presbyterian church.

SEE: *Charlotte Observer*, 17 Mar. 1986; *Durham Morning Herald*, 28 Aug. 1960; Hal May, ed., *Contemporary Authors*, vol. 118 (1986); *New York Times*, 17 Mar. 1986; William S. Powell, ed., *North Carolina Lives* (1962); Raleigh *News and Observer*, 16 Mar. 1986; *UNC Journalist* (April–May 1986).

WILLIAM S. POWELL

Satchwell, Solomon Sampson *(26 Oct. 1821–9 Nov. 1892)*, physician, was born in Beaufort County, the son of James, Sr., and Elizabeth Satchwell. He attended Wake Forest College from 1839 to 1841 and received an M.D. degree from New York University in 1850. Thereafter he practiced medicine in southeastern North Carolina until 1860, residing variously at Wilmington, Washington, and Long Branch. During 1860–61 he studied at the Sorbonne in Paris. Upon his return to North Carolina in 1861, Satchwell was made surgeon of the Twenty-fifth North Carolina Regiment and held the rank of major. In 1862 he became head surgeon of Confederate States Army General Hospital No. 2, at Wilson, where he remained until the end of the Civil War in April 1865. He then returned to private practice in Pender (until 1875, New Hanover) County, residing successively at Rocky Point and Burgaw.

Imbued with "the spirit of original thought and investigation" and the duty of the medical practitioner to communicate through appropriate channels the results of his research and practice, Satchwell early became a clinical investigator of the diseases prevalent in eastern North Carolina and, later, a promoter of a state medical journal. In 1852 he reported to the Medical Society of the State of North Carolina the results of his research on malaria, which he described as the leading cause of death in the South. Whoever should discover a means of combating malaria, he declared, would confer a greater boon on mankind than had Jenner in developing smallpox vaccination. Though he did not suspect the lowly mosquito as the culprit and subscribed to the miasmatic theory of the cause of malaria, Satchwell did recognize a positive correlation between the existence of bodies of stagnant water and the incidence of the disease. He believed therefore that proper sanitation and the practice of good personal hygiene offered possible means of limiting its spread.

Satchwell was, in fact, a pioneer in hygienic therapy—fresh air, sunshine, diet, and a minimum of drugs—and in public health. In commenting on one of the medical fads of the nineteenth century, namely attending springs and watering places as a means of treating disease, he noted that the "real instrumentality of good" in the practice was the "observance on such occasions of hygienic rules and regulations, and not the use of water." He consistently stressed the need for commonsense cleanliness in every aspect of medical practice and urged the development of a public health program in the state. Satchwell was a principal leader at every step in the creation of the State Board of Health, which he helped to organize at Greensboro on 21 May 1879. He was a member of the board from 1879 to 1884 and served as president from 1879 to 1881. In 1892 he was superintendent of public health for Pender County.

As a leading member of the Medical Society of North Carolina (organized in 1849) from 1850 until his death, Satchwell labored diligently to improve the status of the medical profession in North Carolina, serving as the society's secretary from 1854 to 1856 and as its president in 1868. He helped to promote the establishment in 1858 of the *Medical Journal of North Carolina*, which the society published until 1861, and served as associate editor in 1860 and 1861. Satchwell was a foremost leader in urging upon the legislature the authorization (1859) of the State Board of Medical Examiners, which the medical society was empowered to organize and administer. Satchwell was a member of the board from 1866 to 1872 and secretary in 1872. In 1873 he played a prominent role in the society's creation of the Board of Censors for the purpose of policing the practice of medicine in the state and adjudicating disputes arising out of practice by the society's members. This move did much to improve intraprofessional comity as well as the relationship of the medical profession with the public.

As secretary of the Board of Medical Examiners, Satchwell in 1872 presented to the medical society the credentials of Dr. Susan Dimock, the first female native of the state to receive the M.D. degree. As a young girl growing up in Washington, N.C., Dr. Dimock had once lived across the street from Satchwell, her family's doctor, and he had encouraged her interest in medicine. She was graduated from the medical school of the University of Zurich, Switzerland, in 1871 and was engaged in specialized study in Paris in 1872. Following a fierce debate on the propriety of women's entering the medical profession, the Medical Society of North Carolina admitted her to honorary membership as a compromise. Dr. Dimock never practiced medicine in North Carolina, however. She died on 8 May 1875 after a brief but busy practice in Boston, Mass., when the ship on which she was traveling to Europe was wrecked on a reef near the Scilly Isles, twenty-five miles off the coast of Cornwall, England.

Satchwell had considerable reputation as an orator, both among his colleagues and with the public. A man of exceptional cultural, practical, and intellectual attainments, he was called upon to speak before a variety of audiences on a wide range of topics, many of which had little to do with medicine. His published addresses and papers show that he possessed an excellent command of the English language.

Satchwell was married twice. His first wife, whom he wed in 1865 or earlier, died no later than 1875. By this marriage he had three sons—James M., Solomon S., and Paul D.—and one daughter—M. B. (Only her initials are given in the 1880 census.) At some time after 1 June 1880, Satchwell married a daughter of H. F. Bell, of nearby Rocky Point. She died at Burgaw on 17 Jan. 1892, leaving a young son, and was buried according to the rites of the Methodist church, of which she was a member, in the family cemetery on her father's farm. Less than ten months later Satchwell died at Burgaw of typhoid fever and was buried in Oakdale Cemetery, Wilmington.

SEE: Guion Griffis Johnson, *Ante-Bellum North Carolina: A Social History* (1937); Kinston *American Advocate*, 27 Nov. 1856; Dorothy Long, ed., *Medicine in North Carolina: Essays in the History of Medical Science and Medical Service, 1524–1960*, 2 vols. (1972 [portrait]); Ursula F. Loy and Pauline M. Worthy, eds., *Washington and the Pamlico* (1976); Ninth Census of the United States, 1880: Rocky Point Township, Pender County (microfilm, North Carolina State Archives, Raleigh); *North Carolina Medical Journal* 5 (1880); George W. Paschal, *History of Wake Forest College*, vol. 1 (1935); Raleigh *News and Observer*, 20 Jan., 10 Nov. 1892; Satchwell's works: *Address on the Welfare of the Medical Profession . . .* (1868), *Address on Immigration: Delivered Before the North Immigration Association . . .* (1869), *Influence of Material Agents in Developing Man: An Address Delivered Before the Literary Societies of Wake Forest College . . . June 1885* (1885); *Transactions of the Medical Society of North Carolina* 3 (1852), 7 (1856), 8 (1857), 9 (1858), 46 (1899), 64 (1917); Works Progress Administration, Pre–1914 Grave Index (North Carolina State Archives, Raleigh).

W. CONARD GASS

Saunders, Romulus Mitchell *(3 Mar. 1791–21 Apr. 1867)*, lawyer, legislator, congressman, and diplomat, was born near Milton, Caswell County, to William and Hannah Mitchell Saunders. His mother died while he was an infant, and Romulus was taken by his father to Sumner County, Tenn. Upon his father's death in 1803, the youngster was adopted by his uncle, James Saunders, and brought back to Caswell County. He attended Hyco and Caswell academies and in 1809 entered The University of North Carolina. The following March, however, the university's board of trustees concluded that Saunders "had fired a pistol in the College and had thrown a stone at the Faculty," and he was expelled. Nine years later he was elected to the board of trustees, where he served for forty-five years.

Following his expulsion from the university, young Saunders moved back to Tennessee and read law under Hugh Lawson White. After his admission to the bar in Nashville in 1812, he again returned to Caswell County and in 1815, at age twenty-four, was elected to the North Carolina House of Commons. The next year he served in the state senate, then returned to the house for the sessions of 1818–20; in the last two years he was elected speaker. As a member of the U.S. House of Representatives in the Seventeenth through Nineteenth congresses (1821–27), Saunders earned a reputation as an acid-tongued partisan of the states' rights faction, which supported William H. Crawford for the presidency in 1824. John Quincy Adams, the victor in the election, later said of him, "There is not a more cankered or venomous reptile in the country." Saunders, an admirer of Nathaniel Macon, was a fiscal conservative, observing that "men in power are apt to think that the peoples' money is intended to be expended in such way as their distempered fancy may support." He was, however, a supporter of internal improvements.

In 1828 he declined to run for reelection, but in the same year he accepted the position of state attorney general and held it until the post was declared vacant in 1834 because he had, since 1833, been serving a presidential appointment on the French spoliations claims commission, thus violating a state law against duel officeholding.

Saunders became a judge of the superior court in 1835 and rode the circuit until 1840, when he accepted the Democratic nomination for governor. A memorable campaign followed, featuring for the first time a statewide joint canvass by the candidates. Despite Saunders's popularity as a rough-and-tumble stump orator, he was defeated by John Motley Morehead, the Whig candidate. Saunders, by then a resident of Raleigh, ran for and was again elected to the U.S. House of Representatives, serving in the Twenty-seventh and Twenty-eighth congresses (1841–45).

During the period of Whig ascendancy in North Carolina, the Democrats divided into factions. Saunders was a leader of the more extreme states' rights faction that generally followed John C. Calhoun; another native of Caswell, Bedford Brown, who had served in the U.S. Senate (1834–40), was a leader of the more moderate faction that sought not to further inflame sectional passions. Brown had resigned in 1840 rather than follow the instructions of the Whig-controlled legislature, and when the Democrats regained control of the General Assembly in 1842, he sought to regain his seat in the Senate. Romulus Saunders stood in his way, and in a bitter contest that lasted for a month, neither Brown nor Saunders could gain a majority. Finally, both withdrew and the position went to William H. Haywood of Wake County.

Saunders, retaining his seat in the House of Representatives, now became even more outspoken against the Van Buren faction of the Democratic party to which Brown belonged. In order to block Martin Van Buren and to prevent the nomination of any candidate who opposed the annexation of Texas, Saunders in the Democratic National Convention of 1844 successfully sponsored a resolution requiring a two-thirds vote of the convention for the selection of a presidential candidate. This action effectively eliminated Van Buren, and James Knox Polk, a native of North Carolina, was nominated and subsequently elected. Perhaps in appreciation for that assistance, Polk in 1846 appointed Saunders to the post of minister plenipotentiary to Spain. A secret temporary agreement was negotiated under which Spain offered to sell Cuba to the United States, but because of premature publicity, the negotiations came to naught and Saunders resigned in 1849.

Returning to Raleigh, Saunders in 1850 was elected from Wake County to the House of Commons, where he served through 1853. He was a strong supporter of the construction of the North Carolina Railroad and the strengthening of the older lines. In 1852 he lost his bid for the U.S. Senate but was elected instead to a judgeship on the superior court, a position he held until the end of the Civil War. From 1852 to 1854 he was also a member of the North Carolina Code Commission.

Saunders married Rebecca Peine Carter on 27 Dec. 1812, and they had five children—James, Franklin, Camillus, Anne Peine, and Rebecca. After his first wife's death, he married, on 26 May 1823, Anne Heyes Johnson, the daughter of William Johnson, an associate justice of the U.S. Supreme Court, and they had at least four children—William Johnson, Margaret Madeline, Jane Claudia, and Julia A. About 1831 Saunders purchased Elmwood, a handsome residence in Raleigh built about 1813 by Chief Justice John Louis Taylor. He was living there at the time of his death and was buried in the Old City Cemetery.

Romulus Saunders was a man of considerable ability and talent, but he was rough-hewn in his appearance and speech, often intemperate in his statements, and intensely partisan in his associations. He was popular among the rank-and-file Democrats, but his inveterate pursuit of public office eventually diminished his influence among party leaders.

SEE: Samuel A. Ashe, ed., *Biographical History of North Carolina*, vol. 3 (1905); *Biog. Dir. Am. Cong.* (1961); Joseph Blount Cheshire, *Nonnulla: Memories, Stories, Traditions, More or Less Authentic* (1930); *DAB*, vol. 8 (1935); A. R. Newsome, ed., "Letters of Romulus M. Saunders to Bartlett Yancy, 1821–1828," *North Carolina Historical Review* 8 (1931); William S. Powell, *When the Past Refused to Die: A History of Caswell County, North Carolina, 1777–1977* (1977 [portrait]); James Edmonds Saunders, *Early Settlers of Alabama* (1899).

H. G. JONES

Saunders, William Laurence *(30 July 1835–2 Apr. 1891)*, lawyer, soldier, editor, state official, and amateur historian, was born in Raleigh, the son of the Reverend Joseph Hubbard and Laura J. Baker Saunders. The Episcopal minister took his family to Florida, where in 1839 he died from yellow fever. After his widow and children returned to Raleigh, William attended the Raleigh Academy and later The University of North Carolina, from which he was graduated in 1854. He then studied law under William H. Battle and Samuel F. Phillips, was admitted to the bar, and received his LL.B. degree in 1858.

Said to have been "too diffident to become a great orator," Saunders was less successful as a lawyer than as a writer for the *Salisbury Banner*, of which he and J. J. Stewart were editors and proprietors in 1861. Then, even before North Carolina seceded from the Union, the young man enlisted with the Rowan Rifle Guards. By July 1861 he was a second lieutenant in the Tenth Regiment, and by 1864 he was a colonel commanding the Forty-sixth Regiment, North Carolina Troops. He was wounded three times at the Battle of Fredericksburg in 1862 and two years later suffered a near-fatal wound at the Battle of the Wilderness when a ball entered his mouth, exited through the back of his throat, and permanently impaired his ability to speak clearly.

On 3 Feb. 1864 Saunders married Florida Cotten, the daughter of John W. Cotten of Edgecombe County. She died less than eighteen months later, only a short time after their only child was stillborn. Saunders went to live in Chapel Hill but in the next several years spent much of his time on a farm at Grimes's Landing in Pitt County. Although his throat wound prevented him from pleading before the bar, he emerged as a leader in the secret orders opposing the Union League's activities. Whether or not he was, as J. G. de Roulhac Hamilton asserted, the head of the Invisible Empire in North Carolina, his complicity was indicated by his being summoned in 1871 before the congressional Joint Select Committee to Inquire into the Condition of the Late Insurrectionary State. Face-to-face with his antagonists, he repeatedly declined to answer questions concerning his relationship with the organizations. In the same year a letter from "the brotheren" warned that "bill sanders will swing."

From 1870 to 1874 Saunders served as seasonal chief clerk of the state senate. Meanwhile, in 1872 he joined his brother-in-law, Joseph A. Engelhard, in editing the *Wilmington Journal*, a major voice of the Democratic party. When Engelhard was elected secretary of state in 1876, Saunders followed him to Raleigh and, with Peter M. Hale, established the *Observer*, characterized by Josephus Daniels as "the best daily paper North Carolina had known." In 1879, upon the death of Engelhard, the forty-four-year-old Saunders gave up his newspaper career and accepted appointment as secretary of state, winning reelection in 1880, 1884, and 1888. He also was a member of the board of trustees of The University of North Carolina from 1875 until his death, serving as its secretary-treasurer from 1877 onwards. The university granted him an honorary LL.D. degree in 1889.

In addition to his partially paralyzed throat, Saunders suffered from a more serious infirmity: a crippling case of rheumatism contracted during the war. At first he was able to get around by means of crutches and canes, but before assuming office as secretary of state he was confined to a wheelchair. The disease became progressively worse, and he was forced to spend weeks at a time at the medicinal springs then popular in the South. Despite his poor health, however, Saunders became an acknowledged spokesman for the Democratic party, editing its handbooks, preparing speeches for candidates, and devising campaign strategies. His close associate, former governor Thomas J. Jarvis, urged him to seek the Democratic nomination for governor in 1888, offering to substitute his legs and voice for Saunders's in the campaign, but Saunders refused.

His most lasting contribution was in the field of history rather than politics. Following the discovery in 1879 of a cache of colonial records in the old arsenal on Capitol Square, he prepared a report detailing the wretched condition of the manuscript records and outlining efforts of earlier historians to collect and publish them. With the support of Governor Jarvis, Saunders wrote and the General Assembly passed a resolution in 1881 authorizing the printing of "such number of volumes of suitable size, of the records, papers, documents and manuscripts as they [the trustees of the State Library] may deem proper, bearing date prior to the year 1781, belonging to the state of North Carolina." During the next two years Saunders further surveyed the records in the state offices and concluded that there existed many "gaps and chasms" that could be filled only by copies of records in England. At his request, the General Assembly in 1883 gave virtually a carte blanche for his proposals, authorizing the copying and printing of all colonial records "as may be missing from the archives in the state." Subsequently, he hired several part-time clerks to copy records in Raleigh, enlisted local historians to search for documents outside the capital city, and engaged W. Noel Sainsbury, senior clerk in the Public Record Office, to supervise a copying program in London. By 1888 Sainsbury had sent approximately 15,000 pages of transcripts of English records relating to North Carolina, comprising, except for legislative journals after 1749, the largest single portion of the collection. Unfortunately for future researchers, Saunders wrote captions on many original documents in Raleigh and sent them directly to the printer; some appear never to have been returned.

Published in 1886–90, the ten volumes of the *Colonial Records of North Carolina*, under Saunders's editorship and with his extensive "Prefatory Notes," contained 10,982 printed pages of documents from 1622 through 1776 and constituted the most monumental and significant historical enterprise in the state to that time. The editor's name has probably appeared in more footnotes than that of any other North Carolinian, and the series notably stimulated the study and writing of North Carolina history. Yet each volume of 750 copies cost the state only about $1,250 for printing and about the same amount for transcripts, excluding Saunders's own meager salary of $1,000 per year.

Shortly after the tenth volume was published, Saunders's health deteriorated further; he was generally confined to his room in Yarborough House, where he continued to receive visitors and discuss politics and history. In February 1891 the General Assembly extended the "thanks of the people of the state" to Saunders for the accomplishment of his "laborious work." A few weeks later the secretary of state died. On 3 April his body was placed aboard Colonel A. B. Andrews's private railroad car and taken to Tarboro by way of Goldsboro, Wilson, and Rocky Mount, where mourners met the train. At Tarboro he was buried near his wife and infant daughter in the Calvary Episcopal Church cemetery. His tombstone reads, in part, "For twenty years he exerted more power in North Carolina than any other man. I Decline to Answer."

SEE: Samuel A. Ashe, ed., *Biographical History of North Carolina*, vol. 4 (1906); R. A. Brock, "Colonel William L. Saunders," *North Carolina University Magazine*, n.s. 12 (1893); *DAB*, vol. 8 (1935); *Joint Select Committee to Inquire into the Conditions of the Late Insurrectionary States, Report No. 6* (1871); H. G. Jones, *For History's Sake* (1966); William Laurence Saunders Papers (North Carolina State Archives, Raleigh, and Southern Historical Collection, University of North Carolina, Chapel Hill); Secretary of State's Records (North Carolina State Archives, Raleigh); Alfred Moore Waddell, *The Life and Character of William L. Saunders . . .* (1892); Peter Michel Wilson, *Southern Exposure* (1927).

H. G. JONES

Saunders, William Oscar *(24 May 1884–25 Apr. 1940)*, newspaper editor, politician, and spokesman on state and national affairs, was born at Goodens Pond Mill in Perquimans County. He was one of six children—two sons and four daughters—of Mary Ella Byrd and John Robinson Saunders, a poor farmer. A few years after his birth the family abandoned its farm, which was overgrown with weeds, and moved to the county seat town of Hertford, where his father opened a butcher shop. Apparently John Saunders had not succeeded at farming, and in his new endeavor he struggled to provide a modest living for his family.

The key to understanding Saunders's adult behavior and thinking lies in his childhood, when he had to do without and experienced insecurity over having a father who was not a successful breadwinner. His father's weaknesses reinforced his need to assert himself, for the rest of his life W. O. Saunders always seemed to yearn for recognition and at the same time disdain wealth. The powerful were always his chief antagonists in the communities in which he published. Ministers, who he felt held too tight control over the thinking and actions of their congregations, and crooked politicians were his main targets.

Saunders's education is sketchy, but he must have read on his own to have achieved the level of competence evidenced in his editorials and other writings. He did attend the common school in the village but was never graduated. In school he often read ahead of his class; this annoyed his teachers, who viewed his actions as misbehavior rather than curiosity. There is little doubt that he was intellectually capable of attending college, but his parents could not afford to send him. By the time he had reached his teens, he had become a nonconformist—probably as a result of his frustration in not having an opportunity to further himself. Yet he was determined to succeed in life.

In an article in which he reminisces about his childhood, Saunders states that he thought of becoming an evangelist or a patent medicine faker but decided on a career in journalism because he could gain more exposure that way. On his seventeenth birthday he left Hertford to work on a daily newspaper in Norfolk, Va. Opportunities for advancement did not materialize, and he soon grew impatient; thus he resigned and returned home. When a much-publicized murder occurred in nearby Elizabeth City, the same Norfolk paper wired him to cover the ensuing trial. This constituted the first real break for him in the news business, for his factual reporting earned him the respect of court officials and the community at large. Saunders spent the next few years with newspapers in Norfolk, Elizabeth City, and Edenton, but his overzealous efforts to expose political dishonesty and his cutting social commentary resulted in several dismissals.

He then left the area to become a staff correspondent for the *Lumber Trade Journal* in New Orleans and remained until the panic of 1907 cost him his job. By now he had a wife and two children, having married in 1903 Columbia Ballance of Elizabeth City, where he brought his family following the panic and moved in with his in-laws. Saunders found a job on a city paper but lost it when he disagreed with the owner over editorial content. With the assistance of a local politician, Roscoe Turner, who hoped to gain office through Saunders's support, the editor started his own newspaper on 8 June 1908. The paper, a one-page sheet, was named *The Independent*. His courtship with the politician did not last long, for when he printed a story that was unfavorable to him, Turner withdrew his support.

Working more than sixteen hours a day, Saunders wrote hundreds of hard-hitting editorials and covered newsworthy stories that other papers passed up. He also attempted to influence the community by sponsoring discussions on a wide range of subjects. During the lifetime of *The Independent*, he spoke out against fundamentalism, anti-Semitism, and racial prejudice, to name a few, while championing birth control, clean politics, and educational improvement. Saunders is credited with being one of a handful of southern journalists during the period to view the South critically and still reside there. His coverage of the news evoked the wrath of many, some of whom sued his paper for libel. Indeed, the editor was in and out of court during the first decade of his paper's existence.

Saunders, a Democrat, twice tried his hand at elective office. The first time he ran, he lost the race for a seat in the General Assembly representing Pasquotank County, but in 1919 he was elected. In the legislature he was both unpopular and considered radical by his colleagues when he introduced bills to abolish the death penalty and to assure a standard of weights and measure for farm produce. The weights bill passed, but the measure on the death penalty failed. Uncomfortable in the political scene and aware that the prospects of reelection were unlikely, he never again ran for public office.

Saunders chose instead to work within his party and constantly supported candidates for office. As a maverick, he usually backed liberal contenders. The highlight of his involvement occurred in 1928, when he broke with the Furnifold Simmons faction of his party to support the antiprohibitionist and Catholic, Al Smith. Saunders served as a delegate to the stormy state convention and later attended the national convention, where he led his state's delegation for the New York governor. During the campaign he threw his support behind Smith and drew considerable fire from the Simmons camp.

Each chapter of his life provides exciting reading, for just four years earlier in 1924, in his own Elizabeth City, he had confronted Mordica Fowler Ham, a popular fundamentalist minister who was holding religious revivals throughout the eastern section of the state. In many ways Ham personified the fundamentalist movement. During the evangelist's seven-week campaign in the town, Saunders accused him of misrepresenting facts, which he used to expose the preacher's anti-Semitism and later to attack his fundamentalist creed. Although he succeeded in dissolving the meeting, it is questionable whether he permanently damaged Ham's career.

Unable to accept his town's support of the minister—an outsider—despite the incriminating evidence the editor felt he had presented against him, a bitter and disgusted Saunders left Elizabeth City. In New York City he became an associate editor for *Collier's* magazine. Since his first article, "The Autobiography of a Crank," appeared in the June issue of *American Magazine*, he had contributed to several magazines including *The Country Home*, *Nation's Business*, *The American*, *Woman's Home Companion*, *The Mentor*, *Farm and Fireside*, and *Collier's*. He spent nearly a year with *Collier's*, devoting most of his time to interviewing notable Americans. When homesickness overcame his bitterness and he returned to Elizabeth City and *The Independent*, Saunders had many new influential friends across the country.

Even before joining *Collier's*, Saunders had achieved a national identity. By 1927 he was recognized by John H. Casey, a University of Missouri journalism professor, as one of the top weekly newspaper editors in the country among 12,000 studied by Casey's department. Subscriptions to *The Independent* came in from all over the country as his paper's frank presentation of the news appealed to many people. One of his most often quoted columns, "The Bank Clerk and the Soda Jerker," was a masterpiece of writing intended to get across his political and social messages to an unsophisticated audience.

Among his many accomplishments Saunders is perhaps best remembered for his stroll down Fifth Avenue in New York City in pajamas to demonstrate the versatility of that garment. On a more serious side, he is credited with starting a campaign to have a monument erected at Kitty Hawk, site of man's first flight by Orville and Wilbur Wright. He originated the idea for a play to be written about the first English colony, the "Lost Colony" of 1587, on Roanoke Island. And he brought birth control advocate Margaret Sanger to Elizabeth City for a meeting, which he hailed as her first appearance in the South.

In 1937, ten years after he was named one of the country's leading editors, his paper faced serious financial trouble. Publishing a weekly as opposed to a daily entailed high overhead expenses, and through the years Saunders had emphasized literary rather than business matters. A national depression resulted in fewer advertising dollars, and most businesses preferred to spend their money at the *Daily Advance*, Saunders's competitor. A decision was made to convert to a daily schedule, but this move proved unsuccessful probably because it had come too late. The editor then decided that he should close the paper and seek another job with the hope that the paper could be revived at a later date.

The same year, 1937, he left Elizabeth City for Washington, D.C., for a new career in free-lance journalism. A year later he was running a news feature service in the capital. On his way from Elizabeth City to Norfolk, Va., his car plunged off the highway into a canal and he drowned.

SEE: *Charlotte Observer*, 26 Apr. 1940; Elizabeth City *The Independent*, 1908–37, scattered issues; Raleigh *News and Observer*, 16 Aug. 1937, 26–28 Apr. 1940; Keith Saunders, *The Independent Man* (1962 [portrait]); William O. Saunders, "The Autobiography of a Crank," *American Magazine*, January 1922.

B. CULPEPPER JENNETTE, JR.

Saunooke, Osley Bird *(19 July 1906–15 April 1965)*, chief of the Eastern Band of Cherokee Indians and world heavyweight wrestling champion, was born near Cherokee, N.C., the son of an Indian father and an English mother. He was descended from a lineage of Indian chiefs for five generations. Saunooke attended Haskell Institute in Kansas, where he played tackle on the football team. He served in the U.S. Marine Corps, drove a taxicab, and worked in the wheat fields and on the railroad in the Midwest.

During the depression he began wrestling professionally and at one time weighed in at 369 pounds. He won the heavyweight title in 1937 from Thor Johnson and held it for fourteen years. After taking part in more than five thousand matches, including seventeen main events in New York City's Madison Square Garden, he retired from the ring in 1951 and returned to Cherokee to enter business.

Saunooke served as tribal chief of the Eastern Cherokee from 1951 to 1955 and from 1959 to 1963. He also was elected vice-president of the National Congress of American Indians. Chief Saunooke is credited with developing a model Indian reservation at Cherokee, and towards this end he spent considerable time in Washington, D.C., where he promoted legislation in Congress to benefit his people. In 1935 he married Bertha Smith, and they became the parents of five children.

SEE: *Asheville Citizen*, 16 Apr. 1965; Raleigh *News and Observer*, 29 Aug. 1954, 8 Sept. 1962.

ROBERT O. CONWAY

Sauthier, Claude Joseph *(10 Nov. 1736–26 Nov. 1802)*, one of the ablest civilian and military surveyors and mapmakers of the Revolutionary period, was born in Strasbourg, Alsace, the eldest child of Joseph Philippe, a saddler, and Barbe Primat Sauthier. Sauthier presumably acquired his skill as surveyor and draftsman during the impressive survey of Alsace made (1757–59) under the direction of the academician Cassini de Thury, whose innovation of triangulation revolutionized European mapmaking. This survey was followed immediately by the careful cadastral mapping of Alsace by de Luché, Alsatian superintendent. In this Sauthier may also have taken part, as on occasion in the early 1760s he signed himself "Géographe," while mapping several towns, gardens, and battlefields situated in France and Germany. He was already an accomplished surveyor and draftsman. In 1763 he wrote a compendium on architecture with an added section on garden planning. The manuscript contains over forty expertly drawn colored architectural designs, including several for a governor's mansion and nineteen plans for ornamental gardens.

In 1767 Governor William Tryon, who began building the great governor's palace at New Bern, brought Sauthier to North Carolina. Whether or how Sauthier assisted John Hawks, the architect of the palace, in special capacities is not known; he may have designed the gardens. Tryon appointed both architects to make the fortifications protecting the palace in 1771.

From October 1768 to March 1770 Sauthier surveyed and drew the plans of Hillsborough, Bath, Brunswick, Edenton, Halifax, New Bern, Wilmington, Beaufort, Cross Creek, and Salisbury, set in their environs, with the location of public and private buildings, gardens, farms, and roads. This series of ten town plans, now in the British Library, is unsurpassed in any other colony or province for number, detail, and charm of execution. On 1 Jan. 1771 Tryon commended Sauthier to the Assembly as a "gentleman of integrity," noting his great labor in the town surveys. He also stated that Sauthier had prepared a draft of part of the maritime region of the province from drawings given by various inhabitants, complementing the map of the Granville District made by William Churton. John Collet may have incorporated Sauthier's draft in his map of North Carolina (1770). In May 1771 Sauthier accompanied Tryon to Alamance, where the Regulators were defeated; four drafts of Sauthier's plan of the battle exist.

In 1771, when Tryon was appointed governor of New York, he took Sauthier with him. For several years Sauthier made extensive surveys of the province and the city. His first map of the province, which included surveys by Bernard Ratzer, was published by Faden in 1776; his great "Chorographical Map of New York" appeared in 1779. In 1773 Tryon appointed him New York commissioner to run the boundary line between New York and Quebec. About this time he acquired 5,000 acres from Tryon "for private services" in the township of Norbury, Vt. In 1774 he accompanied Tryon to England and returned with him in 1775.

These peaceful occupations and preoccupations of Sauthier came to a sudden end. With the coming of the Revolution he became a military surveyor and draftsman. After William Howe landed his troops from Halifax on Staten Island in 1776, he ordered Sauthier to survey the island; this very map, with heavy stains on it from field use, is now at Alnwick Castle. When Earl Percy made his attack on Fort Washington, Sauthier on the day of the battle surveyed the field and made a map now in the Library of Congress; I. P. N. Stokes calls Faden's engraving of it the most accurate and probably the most beautiful map of northern New York Island. Sauthier made several other maps for Percy at this time, including a map of New York that shows the fortifications built on General George Washington's orders in the winter of 1776 to defend the city from the British and the area destroyed by the fire of September. Percy evidently thought highly of Sauthier; he took him along to Newport, R.I., and, when he returned to England in 1777, Sauthier accompanied him as his private secretary. After Percy became the second Duke of Northumberland, Sauthier made numerous estate maps, which are in Syon House, near London.

Sometime after 1788 Sauthier returned to his native Strasbourg, where he lived at 14 de la Grand' rue until his death at age sixty-six. There in the library of the Grand Séminaire, where his distinguished younger brother, John-Philippe, was professor of theology and philosophy, are Sauthier's work on architecture and some of his manuscript and printed maps on American and European subjects.

SEE: William P. Cumming, *Southeast in Early Maps* (1962) and *British Maps of Colonial America* (1974); A. T. Dill, *Governor Tryon and His Palace* (1955); William S. Powell, ed., *Correspondence of William Tryon and Other Selected Papers*, vol. 2 (1981); Public Record Office, London, A.O. 12/24; William L. Saunders, ed., *Colonial Records of North Carolina*, vol. 8 (1890); Sauthier's manuscript maps in Alnwick Castle, British Library, Library of Congress (Faden Collection), and Grand Séminaire, Strasbourg.

WILLIAM P. CUMMING

Sawyer, Lemuel *(1777–9 Jan. 1852)*, writer and politician, was born in Camden County, the youngest of nine children of Lemuel and his first wife, Mary Taylor Sawyer. The elder Sawyer, whose family connections were numerous and affluent, was active in local affairs. His son attended the country schools, then in 1793–96 Flatbush Academy on Long Island. In May 1796 he went to Philadelphia to visit his brother-in-law, Congressman Dempsey Burgess, and quickly succumbed to the elegant living and the genial social life of the city. He studied mathematics briefly at the University of Pennsylvania. The following year Sawyer was back in Camden County, where he had inherited a dilapidated farm. In 1799 he was a student at The University of North Carolina, in 1800 and 1801 he held a seat in the North Carolina House of Commons, and in 1804 he was a presidential elector, casting his vote for Thomas Jefferson and DeWitt Clinton. Also in 1804 he was admitted to the bar and set up a law office in Elizabeth City. In these years, to support his improvident ways, he began to sell his property, first the slaves, then the land.

Sawyer served eight terms in Congress (1807–13, 1817–23, and 1825–29). Twice during this period he ran unsuccessfully and once did not stand for reelection. Though he neglected his duties and often was absent from the sessions because of illness, so attractive and pleasant was his easygoing manner and so widespread and undiminished his personal popularity that he was able to defeat such formidable opponents as William H. Murfree and James Iredell. In Congress he supported the Embargo, championed Arctic exploration, and, ironically, was for rigid government economy. His favorite haunt was the reading room in the Library of Congress. From time to time he returned to North Carolina.

The first of Sawyer's three wives was Sarah Snowden, of Camden County, whom he married in 1810. She died two years later. In 1820 he married, in Washington, D.C.,

Camilla Wertz, who died in 1826. The three children of these marriages did not survive childhood. His third wife was the wealthy Mrs. Diana Rapalye Fisher, of Brooklyn, whom he married in 1828. He thereafter moved to New York State, where his liberal and spendthrift nature, extravagant style, and chronic invalidism eventually dissipated his wife's fortune and led to downright poverty. During his last two years he held a minor clerkship in Washington, where he died. Family tradition holds that he was buried in an unmarked grave beside his brother Enoch at Lambs Ferry in Camden County. In 1954 a marker was erected at the spot.

Sawyer's literary productions, like the books he chose to read, were quite diversified. First to be published was the now-lost *Journal to Lake Drummond* (ca. 1797), concerning which David L. Swain commented: "The events are without interest, the remarks puerile, and the language the most superlative bombast." Also lost are three unpublished manuscripts: "Essays Literary, Political, and Dramatic" (ca. 1805), a "Roman History" (ca. 1822), and a work on "Greek Literature" (late 1840s). His four-act comedy *Blackbeard* (1824), the first play by a native North Carolinian as well as the first to use North Carolina scenes and North Carolina characters, is a mixture of low farce and flowery melodrama. Neither of its two plots has to do with the famous pirate: instead, Sawyer deals, first, with a group of gullible rustics who in 1823 are intent on recovering Blackbeard's buried treasure and, second, with a disreputable crowd of corrupt Currituck County politicians. The play was sold by subscription to members of Congress, and so delighted was Sawyer with the financial reward that he immediately brought out another play, *The Wreck of Honor* (1824). One of its two plots follows the amorous adventures of an American in Paris, while the other, in blank verse, is a drama of seduction and murder, including a scene at the Battle of Waterloo. Neither play has ever been staged.

Quite a different sort of literary effort is *The Observatory* (1833), advocating a national observatory in Washington for the purpose of spreading scientific knowledge. In *A Biography of John Randolph of Roanoke* (1844), Sawyer's congressional colleague is portrayed as a coward, a mountebank, and a quarrelsome and egotistical numskull. Poorly organized and hastily put together, it was, according to reviewers at the time, false, scandalous, malicious, and libelous. Even so, his book on Randolph is no more scathing than the *Auto-Biography of Lemuel Sawyer* (1844), a frank disclosure of his gambling, wastefulness, dissipation, chicanery, and tawdry love affairs. This book must be one of the most self-condemning documents in all American letters. His last publication was "The Vine of North Carolina," included in *Report of the Commissioner of Patents* (1849), where Sawyer encourages the growing of scuppernongs in northeastern North Carolina to promote the commercial production of wine. Though once ascribed to him, the novel *Printz Hall* (1839) is now known not to be by Sawyer.

SEE: *Biog. Dir. Am. Cong.* (1950); *Facsimile Edition of Lemuel Sawyer's Blackbeard*, introduction (1952); Sawyer folder, Richard Walser Papers (Southern Historical Collection, University of North Carolina, Chapel Hill).

RICHARD WALSER

Sawyer, Samuel Tredwell *(1800–29 Nov. 1865)*, lawyer, congressman, editor, collector of customs, and Confederate officer, was born in Edenton, Chowan County, the oldest son of Dr. Mathias and Margaret Hosmer Blair Sawyer. He attended Edenton Academy and The University of North Carolina, and after reading law he began to practice in his hometown.

From 1829 to 1832 Sawyer represented the borough of Edenton in the General Assembly, where he was identified with the antitariff group. In both 1831 and 1832 he was an unsuccessful candidate for speaker. He was a delegate to the Philadelphia antitariff convention in 1831, a friend of John C. Calhoun, a supporter of the Barbour movement in 1832, and a staunch advocate of South Carolina during the Nullification crisis. In 1834 he represented Chowan County in the state senate and worked for a revision of the state constitution and for state support of public works. In 1835 he represented Chowan at the state constitutional convention.

An anti–Van Buren coalition including Whigs elected Sawyer to the Twenty-fifth Congress (1837–39). In Washington he quickly reacted against the positions taken by Henry Clay's followers and was soon working with the Southern Democrats. In 1838 he was defeated for reelection when the Whigs supported Kenneth Rayner of Winton. During his one term in the House, Sawyer was chairman of the Committee on Expenditures on Public Buildings.

After leaving Congress he moved to Norfolk, Va., and resumed the practice of law. During the Polk administration he founded a newspaper to support the president. The first number of the *Southern Argus and Virginian and North Carolina Advertiser*, with the motto "Southern Views and Southern Rights" on the masthead, appeared on 8 Jan. 1848. Sawyer was editor and proprietor until 1853, when he was named collector of customs for Norfolk, a position he held for five years. In 1858 he tried unsuccessfully to organize a Stephen A. Douglas paper in Norfolk. Soon afterwards he moved to Washington.

When the Civil War began, Sawyer returned to the South and in September 1861 was appointed a commissary major in the Confederate army. He was assigned to Elizabeth City with responsibility for helping to get supplies to forces defending Roanoke Island and the coastal area. This front quickly collapsed, as Roanoke Island, Elizabeth City, and Edenton all fell to Union forces in February 1862. Six months later Sawyer retired from military service.

Sawyer married Lavinia Peyton, the daughter of Francis Peyton of Alexandria, Va. They had three daughters: Fannie Lenox, Sarah Peyton, and Laura. The former congressman died in Bloomfield, N.J.

SEE: *Biog. Dir. Am. Cong.* (1971); Lester J. Cappon, *Virginia Newspapers, 1821–1935* (1936); John L. Cheney, Jr., ed., *North Carolina Government, 1584–1979* (1974); P. M. Goldman and J. S. Young, *U.S. Congressional Directory* (1971); Daniel M. McFarland, "Rip Van Winkle: Political Evolution in North Carolina, 1815–1835" (Ph.D. diss., University of Pennsylvania, 1954).

DANIEL M. MCFARLAND

Scales, Alfred Moore *(26 Nov. 1827–9 Feb. 1892)*, lawyer, legislator, congressman, soldier, governor, and banker, was born in Reidsville, Rockingham County. His parents were Robert H. Scales, whose father, Nathaniel, was a longtime representative to the North Carolina House of Commons from Rockingham County, and Jane W. Bethel Scales.

Young Scales attended the Caldwell Institute, a preparatory school for boys, in Greensboro. In 1845 he entered The University of North Carolina, where he studied law but never completed work for a degree. (The university awarded him an honorary LL.D. in 1889.) After leaving school Scales read law under Judge William H. Battle and was admitted to the bar in 1852. In the same year he was solicitor for Rockingham County. After serving in the House of Commons in 1852 and 1856–57, Scales, a Democrat, was elected to the Thirty-fifth Congress (4 Mar. 1857–3 Mar. 1859). Following this term in office Scales represented North Carolina as a presidential elector on the Democratic ticket of John C. Breckinridge and Joseph Lane.

With the secession of North Carolina from the Union on 20 May 1861, Scales volunteered for Confederate military service. Enlisting as a private in Company H (the Rockingham Guards), Thirteenth Regiment of North Carolina Troops, on 30 Apr. 1861, he was elected captain of the company on the same date. On 12 Oct. 1861 he was promoted to colonel of the Thirteenth Regiment, succeeding fellow North Carolinian William Dorsey Pender of Edgecombe County. Scales commanded the regiment at Yorktown, Williamsburg, the Seven Days' battles, and Fredericksburg. During the action at Chancellorsville, Va., on 1–3 May 1863, he was wounded in the thigh. While convalescing at home, he was appointed brigadier general on 13 June.

Scales's brigade (consisting of the Thirteenth, Sixteenth, Twenty-second, Thirty-fourth, and Thirty-eighth North Carolina Troops) was assigned to Pender's division in Ambrose Powell Hill's Third Corps of the Army of Northern Virginia. At the Battle of Gettysburg on 1–3 July 1863, the brigade participated in the action of all three days. Scales himself was wounded by a shell fragment during an engagement on 1 July near Seminary Ridge in which every field officer in the brigade except one was disabled. After making a complete recovery he commanded the brigade at the Battles of the Wilderness and Spotsylvania and at the siege of Petersburg but was home on sick furlough during the retreat to Appomattox Court House and the surrender of the army.

After the war Scales resumed his law practice in Greensboro. He was elected to the North Carolina House of Representatives in 1866 and served until 1869. In 1874 he was elected as a Democrat from the Sixth District to the Forty-fourth Congress and was subsequently returned to the four succeeding congresses, remaining on Capitol Hill until 1884. In Congress Scales served as chairman of the Committee on Indian Affairs and participated in the exposure of fraud in the Indian Bureau. In 1884 he was nominated for the governorship and ran against the antiprohibitionist platform of Republican Tyre York of Wilkes County. After defeating his opponent by a majority of 20,000 votes, Scales resigned his seat in the House of Representatives on 30 Dec. 1884.

Scales served a rather uneventful quadrennium as governor from 21 Jan. 1885 to 17 Jan. 1889. However, he did make an effort to call attention to the poor condition of transportation facilities in the state, especially railroads and public highways. He also pushed for more and better schools and suggested that the federal government use surplus funds to aid state education.

During the remaining years of his life, Scales lived in Greensboro where he was the president of Piedmont Bank. He served as an elder in the First Presbyterian Church of Greensboro and as moderator of the Synod of North Carolina, the first layman in the state to hold that office.

Scales married Kate B., the daughter of Colonel Archibald Henderson, whose father was Chief Justice Leonard Henderson of present-day Vance County. Their only child, Kate Lewis Scales, was adopted. Scales died in Greensboro and was buried in Green Hill Cemetery.

SEE: *Biog. Dir. Am. Cong.* (1971); Mark M. Boatner III, *The Civil War Dictionary* (1959); John L. Cheney, Jr., ed., *North Carolina Government, 1585–1974* (1975); Walter Clark, ed., *Histories of the Several Regiments and Battalions from North Carolina*, vol. 3 (1901); R. D. W. Connor, *Address on Alfred Moore Scales Given in the Hall of the House of Representatives* (1907); Graham, *Alamance Gleaner*, 3 July 1884; Daniel L. Grant, *Alumni History of the University of North Carolina* (1924); Louis H. Manarin, comp., *North Carolina Troops, 1861–1865: A Roster*, vol. 5 (1975); Ezra J. Warner, *Generals in Gray* (1959).

ALAN C. DOWNS

Scales, Archibald Henderson *(14 Apr. 1868–16 Feb. 1952)*, U.S. naval officer, the son of Junius Irving and Euphemia Hamilton Henderson Scales, was born in Greensboro. He was the nephew of Governor Alfred Moore Scales and the great-grandson of Chief Justice Leonard Henderson. After attending the public schools of Greensboro, he received an appointment to the U.S. Naval Academy, from which he was graduated in 1887. He was commissioned an ensign in the navy in 1889.

Scales first saw action at sea in 1895 in an engagement off Amoy during the upheavals in China. As head of a fire-rescue party, he directed the saving of the German steamer *Tai Chiong*, which was loaded with kerosene. The high degree of cleanliness that he later maintained on his ships is believed to have stemmed from this experience. For his service in the Spanish-American War he earned the Sampson Medal.

By 1906 Scales had risen in rank to command the USS *Severn* and then the USS *Columbia*. In 1907, as a lieutenant commander on the USS *Missouri*, he was chosen to go on the around-the-world cruise by a major portion of the Atlantic Fleet. This tour lasted until February 1909. Afterwards he served as chief of the Bureau of Equipment in the Navy Hydrographic Office in Washington, D.C. In 1910 he was transferred to the command of the USS *Hertford*, *Olympia*, and other ships assigned to the Naval Academy, a post he filled until 1912 when he took command of the USS *Prairie*. In July 1913 he assumed command of the Receiving Ship at Norfolk and the Naval Training Station at St. Helena, Va., during which he attained the rank of captain.

In that rank he commanded the USS *Delaware* from May 1916 to November 1918 and saw action in the North Sea as part of the British Grand Fleet during World War I. For this service he was awarded the Distinguished Service Medal and was decorated Commander of the Order of Leopold (Belgium).

After the war and until February 1919 Scales commanded the Great Lakes Training Station, where he was elevated to the post of superintendent of the Naval Academy. The temporary rank of rear admiral was granted him at this time but made permanent in June 1921. During his tenure at the Naval Academy, Scales effectively handled a hazing scandal, potentially a source of embarrassment, for which he was commended. In 1921, wishing to return to sea, he accepted the command of Battleship Division Five (the name was changed to Battleship Division One, Scouting Fleet, in 1922), after which he commanded the Fourth Naval District from Philadelphia from 1923 until his retirement in 1926. He retired to Greensboro and lived at Hamilton Lakes.

Scales was appointed by Governor J. C. B. Ehringhaus

to serve as a delegate to the Transylvania Celebration in Boonesborough, Ky., in October 1935. After a long illness, Scales died at the U.S. Naval Hospital in Bethesda, Md., and was buried in the Naval Academy Cemetery in Annapolis.

An Episcopalian, he married Harriet Pierce Graham, the daughter of General William Montrose Graham. Their children were Harriet Graham (Mrs. A. G. Cook), Aroostine Henderson (Mrs. F. L. Riddle), and Effie Irving (Mrs. A. L. Thompson).

SEE: Thomas G. Frothingham, *Naval History of the World War* (1926); *Greensboro Daily News*, 20 Feb. 1952; *North Carolina Biography*, vol. 3 (1929); Archibald Henderson Scales Papers (Southern Historical Collection, University of North Carolina, Chapel Hill); *Who Was Who in America*, vol. 3 (1961).

ROGER N. KIRKMAN

Scales, Hamilton *(20 Jan. 1821–7 Sept. 1890)*, tobacco manufacturer and warehouseman, was the son of James and his second wife, Elizabeth Deatherage Scales. Young Scales's mother died in 1824, and thirteen years later his father married Charlotte Dalton. By his three wives James Scales was the father of eight children, all born in Rockingham County.

Little is known of Hamilton Scales's personal life. In 1850 he was still living in western Rockingham County with his brother Peter. The census for that year records his occupation as trader, and he possibly was associated with Peter, whose occupation was listed as tobacconist.

On 12 Aug. 1851 Scales married, in the Madison Presbyterian Church, Elizabeth Wall McAdoo, a widow. They were the parents of two children, Marvin and Raleigh. Raleigh was born on 1 Aug. 1853, and his mother died on 13 November.

Following his wife's death Scales moved to Stokes County, where, on 10 June 1861, he was commissioned captain of Company H ("The Stokes Boys"), Twenty-second Regiment of North Carolina Troops. After a brief period he was forced to resign because of ill health, but he soon became a major in the Battalion of Home Guards.

In 1870 he moved to Forsyth County and began to manufacture plug tobacco in a converted carriage house on Liberty Street in Winston. At the time there were no sales warehouses in the town, and he obtained his tobacco by buying directly from local and regional farmers. In 1873, in order to ensure a more convenient supply of tobacco for his factory, Scales established the Piedmont Warehouse, the first tobacco warehouse in Winston. His business associate in this venture was S. M. Hobson.

Scales enlarged his manufacturing operation in 1875 by building a two-and-a-half-story factory and including both a cooling room and a dry house. In 1876 his warehouse was taken over by M. W. Norfleet. The principal brands of plug tobacco made at Scales's factory were Aleck Stephens, No. 1, Bob Toombs, and Piedmont. By 1888 he was producing others named Ida Bryan, Spanker, and Rabbit Gum. In January 1890 he sold his factory to N. S. and T. J. Wilson and apparently left the business entirely.

Scales became a member of the Winston Lodge of Freemasons on 8 Apr. 1876 and was associated with the Presbyterian church most of life, probably through the influence of his stepmother, Charlotte. He died in Winston and was buried in the Salem cemetery.

SEE: Fambrough Brownlee, *Winston-Salem: A Pictorial History* (1977); John D. Cameron, *Sketch of Tobacco Interests in North Carolina* (1881); Graham, *People's Press*, 11 Sept. 1890; Nannie Mae Tilley, *The Bright Tobacco Industry, 1860–1919* (1948); Manly W. Wellman and Larry T. Tise, *Industry and Commerce, 1776–1896* (1976); Winston, *Piedmont Advertiser*, 23 Jan. 1890; Winston, *Union Republican*, 23 Jan., 11 Sept. 1890.

LINDA MYLAN

Scarborough, John Catre *(22 Sept. 1841–26 Dec. 1917)*, educator and educational administrator, was the eighth of ten children of Daniel and Cynthia Horton Scarborough, whose farm was located about fifteen miles east of Raleigh, Wake County, on the east side of Buffalo Creek. His paternal great-grandfather, Samuel, of English descent, had moved to Wake from Dinwiddie County, Va., in the mid-eighteenth century and served in the Revolutionary army. His maternal great-grandfather, Amos Horton, of Scottish descent, also was a soldier in the Revolution.

Prepared for college in a public school near his home and in the Buffalo Academy, young Scarborough deferred his further education with the outbreak of the Civil War. On 16 Apr. 1861 he volunteered in the company of Captain William Henry Harrison, known as the "Raleigh Rifles," which became Company K of the Fourth North Carolina Volunteer Regiment (later the Fourteenth Regiment, North Carolina Troops). Subsequently he was transferred to Company I, First Regiment, North Carolina Troops, where he remained until the end of the war, surrendering with the troops at Appomattox.

After the war Scarborough worked on his father's farm prior to enrolling in Wake Forest College in January 1866. Upon his graduation in June 1869, he was employed by the college as a tutor in Latin and mathematics—a position he retained until 1871. During the same two-year period he taught Latin in a school for young ladies that was operated by Mrs. James Simpson Purefoy of Wake Forest.

Except for the period he was commissioner of labor and printing for the state of North Carolina (15 Feb. 1889–20 Dec. 1892), Scarborough devoted the rest of his life to education and educational administration. During his varied career he served as principal of Selma Classical and Mathematical School, Johnston County (1871–76), state superintendent of public instruction (1877–85 and 1893–97), teacher at Thomasville Female College (1888–89), president of Chowan Baptist Female Institute (1897–1909), and superintendent of Hertford County Schools (1910–15). He spent his brief years of retirement in his home adjacent to the campus of Chowan College, Murfreesboro.

Apart from his role as classroom teacher, Scarborough's major contributions to public and private education in North Carolina are demonstrated by his work during the three terms he served as superintendent of public instruction and during his twelve-year tenure as president of Chowan Baptist Female Institute. Many of his recommendations to improve the public schools in North Carolina are reflected in the progressive measures enacted by the General Assembly in 1881 and 1885. Conversely, he considered his efforts to make further reforms to have been thwarted by the General Assembly of 1883 and by the ill-fated "school law" of 1879. In the latter instance, progressive legislation had passed both the house and the senate, only to be declared void when the speakers of those bodies failed to sign the measures before the legislature adjourned. Scarborough always believed that an opponent of the bill had deliberately removed it from the bundle of measures to be signed, "replacing" it after adjournment.

Scarborough's administration as president of Chowan Baptist Female Institute was marked by considerable improvements to the physical plant and by a general upgrading of the curriculum. Existing dormitory and classroom space nearly doubled with the erection of a four-story east wing to the major college edifice in 1905–6. Moreover, Scarborough used his experience as superintendent of public instruction to good advantage in modifying and refining the curriculum of an institution where many of the students were preparing to be public school teachers. He reduced the teaching load of faculty members and sought to standardize certain basic minimum requirements for the successful completion of the school's varied courses of study. By 1905–6 he had outlined and introduced a solid academic program, successful completion of which would justify the awarding of a baccalaureate degree, which replaced the "diplomas of proficiency" that previously had been granted to graduates of the institute's collegiate department.

A Democrat and a devout Baptist, Scarborough sat on one or more administrative boards and agencies of the Baptist State Convention of North Carolina each year from 1876 to 1917. He was elected vice-president of the convention on four occasions (1881, 1889, 1891, and 1896) and served three consecutive one-year terms as president (1882–84). He took a particular interest in the affairs of the Thomasville Baptist Orphanage, which he helped to establish and on whose board of trustees he served for twenty years (1897–1917), and in his alma mater, Wake Forest College, where he served as a trustee for forty-four years (1873–1917).

On 12 Jan. 1876 Scarborough married Julia Vass Moore of Johnston County. They had five children: Anna Lyndall and Mamie Leone, who both died in infancy, Hartwell Vick, Anna Royster (m. Frank Lawrence), and Julia Catre (m. Russell Cobb Nicholson). He was buried in Selma.

SEE: Samuel A. Ashe, ed., *Cyclopedia of Eminent and Representative Men of the Carolinas*, vol. 2 (1892); "John Catre Scarborough," in *State School Facts*, February 1947; Minutes, Chowan College Board of Trustees, 1897–1909; M. C. S. Noble, *A History of the Public Schools of North Carolina* (1930).

R. HARGUS TAYLOR

Scarborough, Macrora *(1693–1752)*, colonial official, sprang from the Quaker Scarboroughs of Pasquotank Precinct, although there is no indication that Macrora was a practicing Friend as an adult. He was appointed a justice of the peace for Pasquotank in April 1724 and served as one of the precinct's assemblymen in 1725–26. Subsequent terms in the lower house in 1731, 1739–40, and 1743–45 were served from Perquimans.

Shortly after George Burrington became royal governor early in 1731, Scarborough became associated with him. The governor commended Scarborough to the Board of Trade for appointment to the Royal Council as early as 1731. In October 1732 Burrington placed him on the General Court, where Scarborough worked with Chief Justice William Little to protect the governor's interests. With his government collapsing around him, Burrington made an emergency appointment of Scarborough to the Council in September 1734, but it was voided two months later with the arrival of Gabriel Johnston as North Carolina's new royal governor.

Scarborough was named treasurer for Perquimans County in 1739 and held the office for five years. Around 1740 he married a widow named Elizabeth Reed. At his death early in 1752, he had three sons and a daughter: Benjamin, Macrora, William, and Elizabeth. After 1745 he withdrew from political life and tended to his several plantations in Pasquotank and Perquimans counties.

SEE: William L. Saunders, ed., *Colonial Records of North Carolina*, vols. 2–4 (1886); J. Bryan Grimes, ed., *North Carolina Wills and Inventories* (1912).

WILLIAM S. PRICE

Schaub, Ira Obed *(28 Sept. 1880–13 Sept. 1971)*, educator and agricultural extension leader, was born at King in Stokes County. He was the fourth of five sons of William Henry and Mary Laura Grabs Schaub, Moravians whose forebears settled in Stokes (now Forsyth) County in 1756. His father was a farmer and miller. Ira Obed Schaub received his early education at Pinnacle Academy near his home and in 1896 enrolled at the North Carolina College of Agriculture and Mechanic Arts (North Carolina State University), where he received a B.S. degree in agriculture in 1900. After three years of graduate work in chemistry at Johns Hopkins University, he accepted a position as assistant chemist with the Illinois Agricultural Experiment Station. In January 1905 Schaub moved to Iowa State College to become an assistant professor of soils. He returned to North Carolina in March 1909 as an agronomist with the North Carolina Agricultural Experiment Station.

While Schaub was on the faculty at Iowa State, he met Maud Kennedy, the daughter of an Iowa farm family. They were married on 27 July 1910 and became the parents of two children, Maud Kennedy and Ira Obed, Jr.

In July 1909 the North Carolina College of Agriculture and Mechanic Arts became the first land-grant school in the nation to sign an agreement stating that the college would cooperate in the sponsorship of "Farmers' Boys Clubs." Schaub was appointed to lead the new program, which was the beginning of 4-H Club work in North Carolina. He left North Carolina in 1914 to take a position as superintendent of farm demonstration work with the Frisco Railroad. This was followed by six years as southern field (extension) agent for the U.S. Department of Agriculture. Schaub returned to North Carolina State College in 1924 to become the first full-time director of the Agricultural Extension Service, a post he held until his retirement in 1950. He also served as dean of the School of Agriculture from 1925 to 1945 and acting director of the Agricultural Experiment Station from 1937 to 1940.

Active during his retirement years, Schaub wrote histories of the Agricultural Extension Service and the Experiment Station and helped to organize records and materials for a university archives. He received a number of scholastic and professional honors during his lifetime, including an honorary doctorate from Clemson College in 1937. His alma mater, North Carolina State University, gave him an honorary doctorate in 1951 and named its new food science building for him in 1969.

Schaub remained in remarkably good health until about three years before his death, which occurred in Raleigh just two weeks before his ninety-first birthday. He was buried in the Mount Pleasant Methodist Church Cemetery at King.

SEE: David A. Lockmiller, *History of the North Carolina State College, 1889–1939* (1939); Office of Information Services, "Faculty and Staff News Releases and Clippings,

Ira Obed Schaub," and Ira Obed Schaub Papers (Archives, North Carolina State University, Raleigh); *State College Record* 25 (May 1926); *Who Was Who in America*, vol. 5 (1969–73).

MAURICE S. TOLER

Schaw, Janet *(b. ca. 1740)*, traveler and diarist, was born in Lauriston, a suburb of Edinburgh, Scotland. Little is known about her personal life. The editors of her journal conjecture that at the time of her voyage to America, she was about thirty-five or forty years old. Her father, Gideon Schaw, married Anne Rutherfurd on 23 Jan. 1723; she bore him six children. As early as 1726 Gideon and Anne were living at Lauriston Yards on a fourteen-acre farm, which at that time was outside the city limits of Edinburgh. Because Gideon held positions in other areas of Scotland from 1730 to 1751, no records of Janet's birth or baptism can be found. But it is believed that she spent many years in Lauriston, and that she was living there at the time of her father's death in 1772.

On 25 Oct. 1774 Miss Schaw and her brother Alexander, along with Fanny, an attractive girl of eighteen or nineteen, John, Jr., a lad of eleven, and William Gordon, who were the three children of John Rutherfurd, a prominent resident of North Carolina who had sent his children to Scotland for their education in 1767, all sailed aboard the *Jamaica Packet*, bound for the West Indies and North Carolina. Also on board were Mrs. Mary Miller (Janet's maid) and Robert (Alexander's East Indian manservant). On the same day that she sailed, Miss Schaw began her journal.

First sailing to the West Indies, the Schaw entourage stopped by the islands of St. Christopher and Antigua, where they were entertained by some of the first families of the islands. Alexander had received an appointment in the customs office of St. Christopher, but he obtained a leave from that position. From there they sailed to North Carolina.

Apparently Janet Schaw intended to return with her brother to St. Christopher after leaving the children with their father in North Carolina, although it is unlikely that she expected to remain in the islands any length of time. Landing first in Brunswick, she stayed in that town from 14 Feb. to 17 Mar. 1775. From there she went to Schawfield, the plantation of her elder brother Robert, which was located on the northwestern branch of the Cape Fear River, a few miles above Wilmington. She then journeyed to Wilmington and then to Point Pleasant, the plantation of Colonel James Innes, which was located on the northeastern branch of the river. Janet spent the remainder of her time in North Carolina visiting the last three places named.

On 6 or 7 July her brother Alexander returned to England, having been persuaded by Governor Josiah Martin to carry his dispatches and inform Lord Dartmouth of the situation in North Carolina. Because of the worsening situation in the colony, Miss Schaw, Fanny, and the Rutherfurd boys went aboard the *Cruizer*, a British warship stationed in the Cape Fear. From there they boarded the *George* to cross the Atlantic. On 4 Dec. 1775 the party arrived in Portugal, where Janet remained until at least the middle of January 1776. Then she and the boys returned to Scotland aboard the *George*. There is no record of Miss Schaw's life after her return, other than that in 1778 she was living in "New Town," in the northern section of Edinburgh.

Janet Schaw was a most remarkable woman, and her *Journal of a Lady of Quality* gives an excellent Loyalist viewpoint of North Carolina just prior to the outbreak of the Revolution. The North Carolina Collection at the University of North Carolina at Chapel Hill has a contemporary manuscript copy of her journal.

SEE: Evangeline Andrews and Charles McLean Andrews, eds., *Journal of a Lady of Quality; Being a Narrative of a Journey from Scotland to the West Indies, North Carolina, and Portugal, in the Years 1774 to 1776* (1923).

HUGH F. RANKIN

Schenck, Carl Alwin *(25 Mar. 1868–15 May 1955)*, forester, was born in Darmstadt, Germany, the son of Carl Jacob and Olga Cornelia Alewyn Schenck. His grandfather was chief of forestry in Hesse. His cousin, George Merck, was the U.S. representative of the chemical firm, E. Merck of Darmstadt, whose son, George W. Merck, became president of the vast Merck Pharmaceutical Company.

At eighteen Schenck was graduated from the Institute of Technology in Darmstadt. He then studied botany at Darmstadt before enrolling at the University of Tübingen School of Forestry, where his work was interrupted by a severe lung infection. After his recovery in 1888 he entered the forest school of the University of Giessen; at Giessen he first passed the law examinations and remained to receive a doctor of philosophy degree summa cum laude in 1895. From 1889 to 1895 Schenck also served as assistant and secretary to Sir Dietrich Brandis, a former inspector general of forestry in India, who instructed candidates for the Indian Forest Service during their required year's tour with German supervisors of forestry. It was Brandis who recommended Schenck, through Gifford Pinchot, to George W. Vanderbilt for the position of forester at his Biltmore Estate in Asheville.

On 3 Apr. 1895, when Schenck arrived in the United States to become the forester for the Biltmore Estate, he became the third scientifically trained forester in the country (the other two were Gifford Pinchot and Bernhard Eduard Fernow). From 1895 to 1909, when his employment with Vanderbilt ended, Schenck developed a working plan for the Pisgah Forest and managed Pisgah's 100,000 acres, setting up logging and lumbering operations, road systems, and firebreaks. Schenck was successful in getting laws favorable to forestry passed in the North Carolina legislature. He also established practical scientific forestry on the 7,500-acre Biltmore Estate. This work became known as the first private forestry practiced in America.

In the early fall of 1898 Schenck opened, with the permission of George Vanderbilt, the first school of scientific forestry in the United States. A few weeks later the New York State College of Forestry was begun at Cornell University, and Yale University's Forest School was created in 1900. The Biltmore Forest School provided a one-year course with lectures and textbooks on silviculture, logging, lumbering, timber cruising, forest protection, and forestry management, provided mainly by Schenck. Students observed and participated in all types of forestry and lumbering operations. Visiting specialists from American and European universities were among the lecturers at Schenck's school, which ultimately produced four hundred alumni.

In the summer of 1909 George Vanderbilt asked for Schenck's resignation as a result of a disagreement between Schenck and C. D. Beadle, chief of the landscape department and of the Biltmore Nurseries. Beadle accused Schenck of an untruth and in the ensuing fracas filed a complaint against him for assault and battery. Schenck's friends and acquaintances came to his defense and a justice of the peace in Asheville only fined him one dollar. However, the affair received much publicity and apparently led to unpleasant meetings with Vanderbilt.

Although forced to resign as forester at the Biltmore Estate, Schenck continued his school with the help of American lumbermen, his cousin George W. Merck, and his European professional and family ties. From 1909 to 1914 he secured six working fields for the forestry students, ranging from Oregon to Darmstadt, Germany, with two fields in North Carolina. Headquarters for the school during this period were at Sunburst on land owned by the Champion Fibre Company at the invitation of its manager, Reuben B. Robertson. Because of decreasing enrollments (down to twenty by the end of 1913), Schenck disbanded the Biltmore Forest School in the fall of 1913 and returned to his native Darmstadt. From there he wrote in the January 1914 issue of the monthly newsletter, *Biltmore Doings*, his reasons for leaving (reprinted in his *The Biltmore Story* [1955]) and sent it to his former students. The Biltmore Forest School and its director made a lasting impression on the alumni, many of whom continued their relationship with Schenck through correspondence and visits until his death.

After returning to Germany, Schenck was drafted into the German army and served until he was wounded in Poland in December 1914. He returned to his summer home in Lindenfels im Odenwald to recuperate and never returned to the army. In 1916, while working with the barley program in Brussels, Schenck met Herbert Hoover. He later was chief of a child feeding program operated by American Quakers in Frankfurt.

Schenck refused an appointment as chief of forestry in Hesse in 1923 in order to be free to accept lectureships in the United States and conduct summer groups of American and English forestry students through Germany, Switzerland, and France for the Oxford University professors of forestry. During World War II he led a retired life at Lindenfels im Odenwald. It was here that a U.S. army officer and graduate of Cornell School of Forestry, Abraham George, saw him and wrote to Professor C. H. Guise of Cornell that Schenck had not been molested by the Nazis during the war. When the American Military Government was established in West Germany in 1945, Schenck was made chief of forestry in Hesse.

In connection with his work at Biltmore and with his forestry school, Schenck was active in national forestry and lumbering societies and organizations. He was one of the first eight members elected to the Society of American Foresters and served as a director of the Hardwood Lumber Manufacturers Association of the USA. He often spoke at forestry congresses in the United States and Canada. When he came to America in 1951 on a trip sponsored by the American Forestry Association, a plaque was erected in his honor at the site of the Biltmore Forest School near Pisgah. Other dedications during the visit included a redwood grove near Orrick, Calif., a working circle of a 200,000-acre tree farm at Coos Bay, Oreg., and a long leaf pine plantation near Aiken, S.C.

In 1952 Schenck received an honorary doctor of forest science degree from North Carolina State University. After his death the Carl Alwin Schenck Memorial Forest, a 250-acre pine forest four miles west of Raleigh, was dedicated on 26 Apr. 1957. Other memorials established at North Carolina State University are the Carl Alwin Schenck Distinguished Professorship of Forest Management and four scholarships endowed by Biltmore Forest School alumni.

In 1896 Schenck married Adele Andrewna Bopp, daughter of Heinrich and Maria Bopp of Darmstadt. They had no children. According to *Wer ist's* (1935), he was married a second time in 1932, to Marie Louise Faber, widow of Hermann Kulenkampff-Post. When Schenck died, a memorial service was held in his native Germany, but at his request his ashes were strewn over the Carl Alwin Schenck Forest west of Raleigh.

He was the author of numerous publications, papers, and articles, some of which are listed in the bibliography of *The Biltmore Story*. There has been no extensive biographical study of Schenck, but the following sources contain substantial material about him.

SEE: Biltmore Forest School—Carl Alwin Schenck Collection of papers (North Carolina State University Library, Raleigh), described in *Listing of Biltmore Room Collections, North Carolina State University* (July 1975); Collier Cobb, *The Forests of North Carolina* (1912, reprinted from *North Carolina Booklet*); Richard C. Davis, comp., *North American Forest History: A Guide to Archives and Manuscripts in the United States and Canada* (1977), describing a number of collections of papers with correspondence and information on Schenck; Gifford Pinchot Papers (Manuscript Division, Library of Congress, Washington, D.C.); Carl A. Schenck, *The Biltmore Story* (1955) (later published as *The Birth of Forestry in America: Biltmore Forest School* [1974]), and ed., *The Biltmore Immortals*, 2 vols. (1953–57); Carl Alwin Schenck Papers (Forest History Society, Santa Cruz, Calif.); *Wer ist's* (1909, 1935); *Who's Who in America* (1916–17, 1934–35).

PATTIE BARTEE MCINTYRE

Schenck, David *(24 Mar. 1835–26 Aug. 1902)*, lawyer, judge, public servant, and author, was born to David Warlick and Susan Bevins Schenck in Lincolnton. His father, a surgeon, was the son of the founder of the earliest cotton mill in the South. David Schenck was educated in local schools, including Chief Justice Richmond Pearson's famous "Richmond Hill" law school. He began a practice in Dallas, Gaston County, in 1857. Shortly after moving to Dallas he was appointed county solicitor. Also while living there he met and married Sallie Wilfong Ramseur.

In 1860 the Schencks returned to Lincolnton, where he was promptly made solicitor for Lincoln County and then elected as the youngest delegate to the Secession Convention. When war came in 1861, he served as Confederate States receiver, in which capacity he collected large sums of money for the Confederacy. In the immediate postwar period he took an active role in public life, serving as alderman and mayor; in the life of his church, as a Presbyterian elder; and in educational matters, as a trustee of Davidson College and an enthusiastic supporter of better public schools. These services were recognized when, in 1874, he was nominated by the Democratic party and elected as judge for the Ninth Judicial District. The courts had come into public disrepute during the early Reconstruction period, and Judge Schenck performed notable service in restoring confidence in the sanctity of the law. His most notable cases involved the conflict of authority between the state courts and the federal courts. Not surprisingly, Schenck vigorously defended the state's right of jurisdiction. The University of North Carolina recognized his legal services in 1880, when it awarded him an honorary LL.D.

The next year he resigned from the bench to accept a position as general council with the prosperous Richmond and Danville Railroad (later Southern Railway). Since the Railroad's main offices were in Greensboro, Schenck moved his family to that community. Despite an offer of appointment to the North Carolina Supreme Court, he was firm in his decision to remain in private practice. In Greensboro Schenck continued to evince interest in those areas of public life where he had distinguished himself previously. As a town commissioner he vigorously pushed for modernization of community facilities like paved streets and sidewalks, electric lights, and better schools. Schools were one of his foremost interests, so it was personally gratifying when he dedicated the town's first brick schoolhouse in 1887.

His most significant personal project, after 1886, was saving the Guilford Battle Ground. It was largely through his efforts that a company was formed to raise money and arouse public interest in rescuing the battle site from oblivion and decay. It was also through his support, physical and financial, that land was purchased, money was appropriated by the state legislature for maintenance, and monuments and other markers were erected. His energy and foresight were rewarded in 1917, when the Guilford Battlefield was incorporated into the National Park Service.

Schenck's interest in history did not end with Guilford. In 1889 he published his study, *North Carolina, 1780–81*. This book was the first comprehensive attempt to put the Revolutionary War campaigns of Nathanael Greene and Lord Charles Cornwallis into perspective. Although the text is now dated, it still contains valuable information for students of the Revolutionary period.

The last years of his life were marked by debilitating illness, but he still found time to devote to his practice, his family, and his extensive interests. When Schenck died, numerous newspapers around the state carried obituaries praising him as an erudite, energetic, and multifaceted public figure.

SEE: Bettie D. Caldwell, comp., *Founders and Builders of Greensboro, 1808–1908* (1925); Jerome Dowd, *Sketches of Prominent Living North Carolinians* (1888); *History of North Carolina Family and Personal History* (1956); *Western North Carolina: Historical and Biographical* (1890); John H. Wheeler, ed., *Reminiscences and Memoirs of North Carolina and Eminent North Carolinians* (1884).

JAMES R. LEUTZE

Schenck, Michael *(15 Feb. 1771–6 Mar. 1849)*, merchant and cotton manufacturer, was born in Lancaster County, Pa., of Swiss ancestry. His father was also named Michael. Around 1790 young Schenck moved to Lincolnton and established himself as a merchant. He purchased items for his store in his native Pennsylvania and paid for the goods with cattle that were driven north from Lincolnton. In Pennsylvania Schenck had been a member of the Mennonite church. He joined the Dutch Lutheran church in Lincolnton but later grew dissatisfied with some of its tenets and became a Methodist. Schenck was an early member of Lincolnton's first Methodist congregation, organized in 1824. His enthusiasm for Methodism was conveyed to his children, for his four daughters all married Methodist ministers.

The chronology of Schenck's career as a merchant is uncertain. It is known that he established a second store at Sherrills Ford in present-day Catawba County, and he was a partner in the firm of McBee, Reinhardt, and Schenck, from which he retired in 1821. In 1813 Schenck was one of the first southern merchants to enter the cotton textile industry. By 1860 some of the most important southern cotton manufacturers were former merchants who, like Schenck, sought other outlets for investing their capital. Schenck's first mill, a small structure by later standards, was built at McDaniel's Spring, about two miles from Lincolnton. He ordered the spinning machinery from Providence, R.I. The gears and shafting were manufactured locally by two skilled ironworkers, Schenck's brother-in-law Absalom Warlick and Michael Beam. A flood destroyed the dam of the first mill, and Schenck moved downstream on Mill Branch to rebuild.

In 1819 Schenck, Dr. James Bivings, and John Hoke, another Pennsylvanian who moved to Lincolnton in 1797 and became a prosperous merchant, purchased new machinery and constructed a mill about two miles south of Lincolnton on the south fork of the Catawba River. Called the Lincoln Cotton Factory, it was one of the most successful factories in antebellum North Carolina. By 1840 the production of coarse yarn was valued at $21,373 annually. As was common at many of the early mills, the proprietors operated several small industries, including an ax factory. Schenck and Bivings sold their interest in the company to John Hoke in 1835, and Schenck retired. The Lincoln Cotton Factory operated until 1863, when it burned.

Schenck married Barbara Warlick on 11 May 1801. They had seven children: Henry (b. 1 July 1802), Elizabeth (b. 30 July 1804), John (b. 7 June 1807), David Warlick (b. 3 Feb. 1809), Catherine (b. 18 Jan. 1811), Lavinia (b. 17 Apr. 1813), and Barbara (b. 11 Aug. 1815). Schenck's wife died on 23 Aug. 1815. Michael Schenck was first buried beside her in the Emanuel Church Cemetery, Lincolnton, but in 1885 their remains were moved to the Methodist Cemetery.

SEE: David Schenck, *Historical Sketch of the Schenck and Bevens Families* (1884); William Sherrill, *Annals of Lincoln County, North Carolina* (reprint, 1967); Diffee W. Standard and Richard Griffin, "The Cotton Textile Industry in Ante-Bellum North Carolina," pt. 1, *North Carolina Historical Review* 34 (January 1957).

A. H. STOKES, JR.

Schloss, Simeon Archibald *(10 Oct. 1865–22 Dec. 1913)*, predominant figure in theatrical management in North Carolina in the late nineteenth and early twentieth centuries, was born in Lynchburg, Va., one of four children of Marx (1817–94) and Mary Burrows Schloss (1835–1903). His father, who had emigrated from Bavaria about 1840, was a hotelkeeper by trade (he managed hotels in Raleigh, Salisbury, and Wilmington, among others) and served in the Quartermaster Corps of the Confederate army. The other Schloss children were Nathan (1855–1914), Jeanette (1858–1929), and Joseph (1869–1921).

S. A. Schloss began his career as a clerk in his father's hotel in Wilmington. By 1888 he was an auctioneer and commission merchant, and later that year he opened a crockery and glassware business in partnership with his brother-in-law, Aaron A. Nathan, who later figured in the development of Wrightsville Beach. Schloss was also employed by J. M. Cronly as assistant manager of the Wilmington Opera House (better known as Thalian Hall). In 1895, after a stint as a cornetist with Barlow, Dolson, and Powers' Minstrels, a national touring company, Schloss signed a lease with the city of Wilmington and became manager of the Opera House in his own right.

In the 1890s the process of booking acts for local theaters was a haphazard affair. During the summer, theater managers from all over the country would converge on New York's Union Square, then the center for theater business, and attempt to line up their seasons by contacting agents for individual attractions, often accosting them on the street. Once the agent and the manager came to terms, there was nothing to prevent an agent from reneging on an agreement to play a particular theater if a better offer came along from another manager. But there was also nothing to prevent a manager from double-booking two attractions for the same play date to prevent having a hole in his schedule if one company did not show up. Once a production company was out on the road, the results of these slipshod arrangements could be disastrous, particularly if a producer decided to cut his losses and fold the company before it returned to New York. (The practice of leaving actors stranded on the road became one of the major reasons for the founding of Actors' Equity Association.)

It was ostensibly to correct these abuses, but mainly to ensure profitability for all concerned, that in 1896 five theater owners and booking agents formed a trust, the Theatrical Syndicate, that came to be known by the names of its two most prominent members, Marc Klaw and Abraham L. Erlanger. The Syndicate began by controlling a significant number of theaters throughout the country and within a very short time controlled nearly all the major theaters on major transportation routes. The effects of the Syndicate are still being debated: on the one hand, formation of the Syndicate standardized financing, touring, contracts, and promotion; on the other, independent theaters could not get the best attractions (which usually belonged to the Syndicate) and independent attractions could not get booked into the best theaters (which were usually controlled by the Syndicate).

S. A. Schloss became the Syndicate's main representative in North Carolina. Operating from his home base in Wilmington, and with the clout of the Syndicate behind him, he developed a chain of theaters that brought theatrical attractions of every type to nearly every part of the state. In 1898 he leased the Academy of Music in Raleigh, and in 1901 he secured the lease for the Grand Opera House in Greensboro, located in the new City Hall. In 1902 he was outbid for the lease on the Wilmington Opera House by James H. and Robert H. Cowan (who also held the lease on New Bern's Masonic Opera House) but regained it by merging his growing operations with theirs in 1905. Other theaters followed: Charlotte's Academy of Music in 1903; the Elks' Auditorium in Winston-Salem in 1905; Asheville's Grand Opera House by 1906; the Monroe Opera House by 1907; the Tarboro Opera House, the Messenger Opera House in Goldsboro, and Wilson's Lyceum Theater by 1909; and the Asheville Auditorium in 1910. At its greatest extent, the Schloss Theaters Circuit controlled fourteen theaters in North Carolina, Virginia, and Tennessee; at the time of his death, it controlled theaters in Asheville, Charlotte, Concord, Goldsboro, Raleigh, Wilmington, and Winston-Salem; also in Danville, Va., and Chester, S.C.

With the booking arrangements for these theaters all handled by Schloss and his local managers (his nephew Marx S. Nathan in Charlotte and Greensboro, the Cowan Brothers in Wilmington, J. S. Upchurch in Raleigh, among others), theater programming became more consistent. Audiences in Tarboro or Monroe could see the same attractions for the same prices as the audiences in Raleigh or Charlotte, because major attractions would be more likely to play a smaller venue if they were also booked into the larger towns. This did not mean that they consistently got the best: though major stars of the day like Richard Mansfield, Otis Skinner, De Wolf Hopper, and others long forgotten did play North Carolina towns during the era of the opera house, most of the programming that Schloss and his fellow managers brought in was typical of that found in other theaters across the country. ("Opera house," of course, was a euphemism: despite the popularity of individual attractions, there was still a general antitheatrical prejudice. The term *opera house* gave a patina of respectability to attending entertainments that might have been suspect. Very little grand opera made its way into any but the halls in the largest towns.)

The fare was a steady diet of melodrama, light comedies, and minstrel shows, occasionally spiced by something more substantial like Shakespeare or concerts by soloists and groups ranging from the New York Philharmonic to John Philip Sousa's band. Most people did not mind how bland most of it was; the goal was entertainment, not an aesthetic or moral uplift. One of the last mentions of Schloss in the *New York Dramatic Mirror* was a note from the paper's Greensboro correspondent on 20 Mar. 1912: "The theatregoers of the city of Greensboro certainly cannot complain of the class of attractions here this season; Mr. Schloss appears to know just what the people want."

In addition to his theatrical activities, Schloss owned and operated a music store as well as the bill-posting company that was a forerunner of the modern outdoor advertising industry. The company was operated by his son as Outdoor Advertising of Charlotte. Schloss's widow ran his theater enterprises after his death but finally sold them to S. A. Lynch of Asheville in 1915. By then the great days of touring theater were over, and movies had become the country's chief form of popular entertainment.

Schloss married Miriam (Mamie) Bear (20 Aug. 1872–23 Oct. 1927) of Wilmington on 23 Feb. 1897. They had four children: Florette (b. 1898), S. A., Jr. (1899–1900), a second S. A., Jr., known as "Happy" (1902–69), and Mary (b. 1904).

Schloss died in Wilmington after suffering a stroke. Perhaps in an oblique comment on the breadth of his interests, his death certificate lists his occupation as "Capitalist." He was buried with his wife, two sons, parents, and many other family members in Wilmington's Oakdale Cemetery.

SEE: Julius Cahn, ed., *Julius Cahn's Official Theatrical Guide*, 15 vols. (1896–1910); Julius Cahn and R. Victor Leighton, eds., *The Cahn-Leighton Official Theatrical Guide*, vols. 16–17 (1912–13); *Charlotte Observer*, 3 Feb. 1969; Monroe Lippman, "The Effect of the Theatrical Syndicate on Theatrical Art in America," *Quarterly Journal of Speech* 26 (1940); *New York Dramatic Mirror*, "Correspondence" column (1879–1913); Donald J. Rulfs, "The Era of the Opera House in Piedmont North Carolina," *North Carolina Historical Review* 35 (1958), "The Professional Theater in Wilmington, 1870–1900," *North Carolina Historical Review* 28 (1951), and "The Professional Theater in Wilmington, 1900–1930," *North Carolina Historical Review* 36 (1959); Milo L. Smith, "The Klaw-Erlanger Myth," *Players* 44 (1959); Jerry Stagg, *The Brothers Shubert* (1968); Steve Travis, "The Rise and Fall of the Theatrical Syndicate," *Educational Theatre Journal* 10 (1958); Isabel Williams, "Thalian Hall," Notebook, 4 vols. (New Hanover Public Library, Wilmington); *Wilmington Morning Star*, 20 Oct. 1894 [Marx Schloss obituary], 23 Dec. 1913 [S. A. Schloss obituary], 27 Feb. 1920 [Aaron A. Nathan obituary], 3 Feb. 1969 [S. A. Schloss, Jr., obituary].

PAUL F. WILSON

Schober. *See* **Shober.**

Schonwald, Johann (or John, Janos, James) Tossy *(23 Nov. 1801–29 Aug. 1882)*, physician, was born near Budapest, Hungary, reputedly of "a noble family of pure

Magyar stock," although there now appears to be no trace of such a family. His obituary noted that he was a surgeon in the Austrian army before immigrating to America in 1836. He first settled in New York City but afterwards resided in Baltimore, Md., before finally moving to Wilmington, N.C., in 1840. Descendants relate two traditional accounts as to why he left home. One says that his parents died while he was in the army and his older brothers defrauded him of his portion of the inheritance. He deserted the family and took as his surname Schonwald, the name of the estate in northern Hungary; as a youth he probably was known as Janos Tossy.

According to the second story, on one occasion he and a fellow officer went to the La Scala theater in Milan, Italy. Both officers had had too much wine and when an attractive lady occupied a box across the theater from them, Tossy (or Schonwald) stood up and rudely gazed at her. She happened to be a friend of the other officer, and Schonwald's action provoked a fight in which he was stabbed in the throat. Schonwald killed his fellow officer and fled in disgrace, having been disowned by his family. A granddaughter of Dr. Schonwald remembered that he wore a silver tube in his throat and spoke in a high-pitched voice.

Although the name Tossy can be found around Budapest, and an estate named Schonwald was known in the early nineteenth century, research in Budapest in 1981 disclosed no documentary sources to support the traditions concerning his military service.

It is related that Schonwald, homesick for contact with his countrymen, went to Wilmington when he heard that a disabled ship with a Hungarian crew and captain had put into port. There was sickness aboard and no one in the town could communicate with the crew. Since he spoke English, French, German, and Italian as well as Hungarian, he was soon happily settled in Wilmington as the port doctor. In the absence of quarantine laws, it was the doctor's custom to meet incoming ships and clear them for entry. As an army surgeon, he understood the treatment of various fevers and put this knowledge to good use in treating sailors suffering from the epidemics of fevers that raged in those days.

On 31 Dec. 1849 Schonwald married Catharine Joyner, of Myrtle Grove, who was of Scotch-Irish descent. They were the parents of John Tossy, Alice, Carolina (Carrie), Fanny Cornelia, and twins, Jackson and Lee, born in 1864. The infant Lee died and Jackson was given his name, becoming Jackson Lee Schonwald. There are numerous descendants of these children, with the name John occurring for several generations; three of them are physicians.

In 1851 Schonwald published a 250-page book, *The Child. A Treatise on the Diagnosis and Treatment of the Diseases of Children, According to the Simple Laws of Nature, Without Medicaments*. Printed in Philadelphia, it was dedicated to the wife of the governor, Mrs. David S. (Henrietta W.) Reid. A copy specially bound in purple velvet with brass trim for Mrs. Reid is in the North Carolina Collection in Chapel Hill. Following the author's name on the title page is his degree: "Dr. M. from Hungary, Practical Physician and Accoucheur, Member of the Botanical Faculty of the Hydro-therapeutical Institute of Vienna." Schonwald was buried in the Joyner family cemetery at Myrtle Grove.

SEE: *The Bookmark*, Friends of the University of North Carolina Library, no. 24 (December 1955); Endra Ferenczy (Budapest) to William S. Powell, 27 Oct., 13 Nov. 1981; Kiss Jenö (Budapest) to William S. Powell, 19 Nov. 1981; New Hanover County Wills (North Carolina State Archives, Raleigh); William S. Powell, comp., "James T. Schonwald, 1801–1882, Wilmington Physician" (manuscript in North Carolina Collection, University of North Carolina Library, Chapel Hill, including letters from descendants and others); J. T. Schonwald, *The Child* (1851 [portrait]); *Wilmington Chronicle*, 11 July 1849; *Wilmington Daily Review*, 30 Aug. 1882; *Wilmington Morning Star*, 30 Aug. 1882; *Wilmington Weekly Chronicle*, 7 Jan. 1850; *Wilmington Weekly Star*, 1 Sept. 1882.

WILLIAM S. POWELL

Schumacher, Francis Xavier *(14 Mar. 1892–3 June 1967)*, pioneer in the field of forestry mensuration, was born in Dayton, Ohio, the son of Joseph and Julia Lavender Schumacher. He attended Emanuel's Parochial School prior to entering St. Mary's College (which became the University of Dayton) in 1909–10 for one year of study in philosophy. Afterwards he took a six months' business course at Miami Commercial College and then worked as a bookkeeper for a Dayton wholesaler until 1912. In the 1912–13 school year he studied forestry at the University of Michigan.

In Saskatchewan and Alberta, Canada, he spent two years ranching, homesteading, railroad surveying, and logging that involved topping towering Douglas firs. He next worked briefly for the National Cash Register Company before entering the U.S. Army in 1916. Schumacher served as a company commander of infantry in the Meuse-Argonne, Saint-Mihiel, and Ypres-Lyn offensives before being wounded by gunshot in the left foot. He received the Distinguished Service Cross, the Belgium Croiz du Guerre, and the Purple Heart. Discharged in 1919 with the rank of captain, he reentered the University of Michigan where he received a bachelor of science degree in forestry in 1921. With no doctoral program in forestry available, after considering a doctorate in philosophy, he decided to pursue his studies in forestry independently. For several months he served as a ranger with the U.S. Forest Service in Salmon, Idaho. In the fall of 1921 he became an instructor at the University of California and also served as a research assistant to Professor Donald Bruce on projects in forest mensuration.

In 1925 Schumacher was placed in charge of the work in forest mensuration both in the School of Forestry and in the Agricultural Experiment Station at the University of California. Three years later he became a professor and conducted the first university course in the United States—and perhaps the first in the world—that introduced the use of a statistical method as a research tool in forestry. Soon afterwards a number of other universities adopted similar courses. In 1930 he accepted the position of silviculturist and chief of forest measurements with the U.S. Forest Service. In this capacity Schumacher conducted research projects in forest mensuration and, as a faculty member of the U.S. Department of Agriculture Graduate School in Washington, D.C., trained government foresters in statistical methods for forestry research. In 1935 he was promoted to the position of senior silviculturist. In the same year he collaborated with Donald Bruce on a college textbook, *Forest Mensuration*, which became widely used and had several English editions as well as a French one.

In 1937 he became a professor of forestry at Duke University. While at Duke he trained foresters from many parts of the world in forestry biometrics. Before joining the faculty of Duke, Schumacher had considerable experience in forestry research and had published articles as well as the textbook with Bruce. From 1937 to 1946 he served as an associate editor of the *Journal of Forestry*, and in 1942 he collaborated with R. A. Chapman on a forestry textbook, *Sampling Methods in Forestry and Range Management*.

After his retirement from Duke in 1961, Schumacher served as professor emeritus of forestry until his death. When he retired, the School of Forestry alumni created the F. X. Schumacher Forest Biometrics Library. In 1961 he became a special consultant with T. S. Coile, Inc., forest land consultants of Durham. In 1963 he served as a visiting professor at the University of Stellenbosch in the Union of South Africa.

Schumacher, known as "Schu," was elected a Fellow in such professional societies as the American Association for the Advancement of Science (1942), the American Statistical Association (1957), and the Society of American Foresters (1959). He held membership in the Biometrical Society; Xi Sigma Pi, an honorary forestry association; Phi Sigma, a national honorary biological society; and Sigma Xi, a national scientific society.

In 1958 he was a recipient of the Achievement Award for Outstanding Contributions to the Profession of Forestry, conferred by the Appalachian Section of the Society of American Foresters. In 1959 North Carolina State College gave him an honorary doctor of science degree. And in the same year he was presented an award for "Outstanding Achievement in Biological Research Contributing to the Advancement of Forestry" by the Society of American Foresters. He was the fourth American to be so honored for his pioneering efforts in the application of biometrics to the study of forestry.

He married Muriel McBride on 16 Sept. 1931 in the Church of the Peoples, a mission church on the East Side of New York City that was demolished when the United Nations building was erected. Their two children were Sally Ann and Donald Francis Xavier.

Schumacher's hobbies included fishing, painting, and studying and visiting the Civil War battlegrounds. He died at Duke University Medical Center at age seventy-five and was buried in the National Cemetery, Raleigh.

SEE: Duke University News Service, "Francis X. Schumacher—Biographical Sketch" (n.d.); Duke University School of Forestry, *Alumni Newsletter*, September 1959; *Durham Morning Herald*, 9 Dec. 1936, 7 Feb., 19 Nov. 1959, 4–6 June 1967; *Durham Sun*, 1 Nov. 1937, 25 May 1959, 10 June, 5–6 Aug. 1961.

B. W. C. ROBERTS

Schumann, Marguerite Ellen *(19 May 1923–14 Mar. 1986)*, author, was born at Sturgeon Bay, Wis., the daughter of the Reverend Frederick and Adelia Schumann. In her senior year at Lawrence College in Appleton, Wis., she became the first female president of the student body. Graduated with a degree in music, she was an assistant in the college publicity office for a brief time before becoming supervisor of vocal music in the schools of Portage, Wis. Returning to Lawrence College, she was director of publicity and publications from 1945 to 1968. Her history of Lawrence College, *Creation of a Campus*, was published in 1957.

When Douglas M. Knight, president of Lawrence, became president of Duke University, Marguerite Schumann joined his staff in Durham as assistant to the president for publications and research. On leaving Lawrence she was awarded an honorary master of arts degree, the first time an honorary degree had been bestowed upon someone who was not retired. In 1969 she was employed by The University of North Carolina as publications officer for the Carolina Population Center, and in 1973 she became the first editor of the *University Gazette*, a post she held until February 1982. In 1978 she also became the editor of the National Humanities Center's *Newsletter* in the Research Triangle.

She was the author of *The First State University: A Walking Guide* (1972, 1985), *Bricks and People: A Walking Guide to the University of North Carolina at Greensboro* (1973), *Strolling at State: A Walking Guide to North Carolina State University* (1973), *Stones, Bricks, and Faces: A Walking Guide to Duke University* (1976), *The Living Land: An Outdoor Guide to North Carolina* (1977), and *Tar Heel Sights: Guide to North Carolina's Heritage* (1983). She also was editor of *Grand Old Ladies: North Carolina Architecture during the Victorian Era* (1984) and coauthor of *Bull Durham and Beyond: A Touring Guide to City and County* (1976).

SEE: Appleton (Wis.) *Post-Crescent*, 20 Feb. 1953, 14 Mar. 1986; *Durham Morning Herald*, 19 Sept. 1982; *In Remembrance of Marguerite Schumann, 1923–1986* (1986); Lawrence College, *Alumni Magazine* (Summer 1968); National Humanities Center, *Newsletter* (Spring 1968); Raleigh *Spectator*, 19 Mar. 1981.

WILLIAM S. POWELL

Schweinitz, Emil Alexander de *(18 Jan. 1864–15 Feb. 1904)*, biochemist, author, and educator, was born in the Moravian town of Salem, the sixth child and only son of Bishop Emil Adolphus and Sophia Hermann de Schweinitz. His ancestors on both sides were among the early founders and spiritual leaders of the Moravian Church in America. His grandfather, Lewis David von Schweinitz, was a clergyman and noted botanist. His father was administrator of the church's southern province and head of Salem Academy.

Emil Alexander began his formal education at the Moravian school in Salem. In 1877 he entered the Nazareth Hall Military Academy, a boarding school in Nazareth, Pa., where he was graduated at the head of the class within a year. From there he went to the Moravian College at Bethlehem, Pa., and took courses in classical studies. In August 1881 he transferred to The University of North Carolina, graduating in June 1882. That summer Schweinitz took courses in chemistry and mineralogy at the University of Virginia, and in September he reentered The University of North Carolina, from which he received a Ph.D. in 1885. During his last year in Chapel Hill he was an assistant professor of natural history. After earning his doctorate Schweinitz went abroad for additional study at the Universities of Berlin and Göttingen; he received a second Ph.D. at Göttingen in 1886.

Returning to the United States in late 1886, Schweinitz took a teaching position with Tufts College, near Boston, but left within a year to teach at the Agricultural and Mechanical College of Kentucky. In August 1887, at a professional convention in New York City, he met Dr. W. H. Wiley, head of the Bureau of Chemistry in the U.S. Department of Agriculture. Wiley, impressed with Schweinitz's credentials, secured him a job as a minor assistant in the Bureau of Chemistry. In April 1890 Schweinitz transferred to the Bureau of Animal Husbandry, where he remained until his death. In 1896, when a Biochemic Division was formed within the bureau, he was chosen as its first head.

Schweinitz specialized in the study of disease-producing bacteria, their formation, and methods of immunization against them. His attention was particularly directed towards hog cholera and tuberculosis, and he discovered the technique of injecting cows with human tuberculosis germs to give them immunity. During his career he published sixty-four scientific articles in three languages and represented the United States at a series of international medical congresses.

His service to the Department of Agriculture represented only one-half of his career. In 1892 he joined the faculty of the Medical College of Columbian (now George Washington) University as professor of chemistry and toxicology. Five years later he was elected dean of the Medical College. Under his direction the Medical School underwent tremendous growth over the next seven years, adding a University Hospital and all new medical school buildings. In recognition of his service, the university awarded him an honorary doctorate of medicine in 1898.

SEE: Samuel A. Ashe, ed., *Biographical History of North Carolina*, vol. 3 (1905 [portrait]); Columbian University, *In Memory of Emil Alexander de Schweinitz* (1904); *DAB*, vol. 8, pt. 2 (1937).

MARION M. EDMONDS

Schweinitz, Lewis David von *(13 Feb. 1780–8 Feb. 1834)*, Moravian clergyman and internationally respected botanist, was born in Bethlehem, Pa. His parents, Hans Christian Alexander and Dorothea Elizabeth von Watteville von Schweinitz, went to Bethlehem when Hans was assigned to be the first administrator of the Moravian Church in America. Lewis attended Nazareth Hall, a Moravian School for Boys in Nazareth, Pa., until his father was recalled to Europe in 1798. Lewis, then eighteen, accompanied his parents and entered the Moravian Theological Seminary, at Niesky in Lusatia, where he studied theology and botany. One of his teachers inspired him to work intensively on the topic of fungi, and together they published a treatise on fungi in 1805. In 1807 von Schweinitz began to teach at the Boys' Boarding School in Niesky. He was soon appointed superintendent of the Single Brethren in Gnadenberg, Silesia, and a year later he was transferred to the same position in Gnaden, Saxony.

He must have impressed the Moravian Elders with his supervisory abilities, because in 1812 he was called to be administrator of the entire Moravian Southern Province in America. His diary of the trip from Herrnhut, Germany, to Salem, N.C., via Bethlehem, Pa., is in the archives of the Moravian Church in America, Southern Province, Winston-Salem. It was a long journey filled with obstacles and tragedy, but in November 1812 von Schweinitz and his wife arrived safely in Salem.

Upon his arrival he was made a member of the Helpers' Conference and saw to all the business affairs of Salem and the other towns in the Southern Province. Often he assisted in church services and festival days for the various choirs within the congregation. He was a comfort to everyone, especially the widows of Salem, and he served as their curator beginning in 1813.

When it came time to elect a representative to the General Synod in Herrnhut, Germany, to be held in 1818, von Schweinitz was the overwhelming choice. In September 1817 he and his family left Salem for Philadelphia and from there sailed for Germany in November. They were away for sixteen months, returning to Salem in 1819, when the General Assembly of North Carolina elected him as a trustee of The University of North Carolina. In 1821 he accepted the call to serve as head pastor for the congregation in Bethlehem, Pa., and returned to the place of his birth. From there he attended the General Synod of 1825 in Herrnhut. At that session he was made senior civilis, overseer of the material interests of the Church in America. Afterwards he returned to Bethlehem, where he died nine years later.

Today von Schweinitz is best remembered for the contribution he made to the study of botany in America. He continued his early interest in the study of fungi and published a number of works on that and other previously unidentified plant species native to America. In his last published paper, "Synopsis of the American Fungi" (1831), he listed more than 1,200 fungi that he had discovered and named along with over 3,000 already known species. He corresponded with botanists in Europe and America and enjoyed an excellent reputation throughout the scientific world. In 1817 the University of Kiel, in Denmark, conferred on him an honorary doctor of philosophy degree in abstentia. He was also a member of the Lineian Society of Paris and the Academy of Natural Sciences in Philadelphia.

Many of von Schweinitz's manuscripts, letters, sketches, and important herbaria are now owned by the Academy of Natural Sciences in Philadelphia. Other papers relating to his administration in Salem and his work in botany as well as a portrait of him are in the Moravian archives in Winston-Salem.

Schweinitz married Louisa Amelia LeDoux in 1812 before leaving Herrnhut. Their first child, Edward William, was born in Salem and died in infancy. Four more boys—Emil Adolphus, Robert William, Edmund Alexander, and Bernard Eugene—all became ministers and educators in the Moravian church.

SEE: Ann L. Flora Bynum, "Father of American Mycology," *Three Forks of Muddy Creek*, vol. 2 (1975); John Henry Clewell, *History of Wachovia in North Carolina* (1902); Adelaide L. Fries, ed., *Records of the Moravians in North Carolina*, vol. 7 (1947); Levin T. Reichel, *Moravians of North Carolina: An Authentic History* (1857).

ROSAMOND C. SMITH

Schweinitz, Robert William de *(20 Sept. 1819–29 Oct. 1901)*, Moravian minister and educator, was born in Salem, the son of the Reverend Lewis David and Louisa Amelia von Schweinitz. Though the father used the German form "von," his sons, including Robert, adopted the Latinized scholarly form "de." Robert was a great-great-grandson of Count Nicholas von Zinzendorf and the brother of Emil Adolphus de Schweinitz, principal of Salem Female Academy (1848–53).

In 1821 the family moved to Bethlehem, Pa., where Robert received his education. He entered Nazareth Hall in 1830 and was graduated from Moravian College and Theological Seminary in 1839. After teaching at Nazareth Hall for several years, Schweinitz traveled to Europe, where he met Marie Louise von Tschirschky; they were married in Herrnhut, Saxony, in 1846. The couple had six children: Helen Louise, Louis Alexander, Clara Amelia, Lucy Bertha, Robert Edmund, and Paul Robert.

Following his return to Bethlehem, Schweinitz was ordained deacon on 24 Oct. 1847. He was elevated to the post of professor at the Theological Seminary and subsequently appointed pastor of the Moravian congregations in Graceham, Md., and, later, Lancaster, Pa.

When Emil Adolphus, Robert's brother, was promoted from his position as principal of Salem Female Academy in 1853, Robert was appointed to replace him. Robert immediately determined to replace the academy's aging Gemein Haus and in 1854, with plans drawn up by Schweinitz and Francis L. Fries, the cornerstone of the new Main House was laid on the site of the demolished Gemein Haus. Later improvements to the campus included the construction of a new chapel. During this time, on 13 May 1856, Schweinitz was ordained a presbyter.

Under Robert's leadership, the academy grew swiftly. In 1857, 152 new names were added to the roster, for a total of 370 students in the following year. The onset of the Civil War provided added impetus to this growth, which Adelaide L. Fries has attributed to the idea of protecting young ladies in a peaceful Moravian town. Even the end of hostilities had no effect on this growth, for in 1866 another 152 new names were added to the roll.

In May 1866 Schweinitz left his post to become principal of Nazareth Hall. This position was short-lived, however. In 1867 he was elected president of the Society of the United Brethren for Propagating the Gospel among the Heathen, which he led until 1878. In 1881 he became treasurer of the society and served until 1899. From 1885 to 1890 Schweinitz made numerous trips to Washington, D.C., to negotiate with the government on Moravian missions to the Eskimos in Alaska. This was in conjunction with his post as mission agent of the Moravian Church in America, in which capacity he served from 1885 to 1898. Failing health resulting from Bright's Disease and increasing blindness, which ultimately became total, finally forced his retirement. He died at Bethlehem and was buried in the Old Moravian Cemetery.

SEE: John Henry Clewell, *History of Wachovia in North Carolina* (1902); Adelaide L. Fries, *Historical Sketch of the Salem Female Academy* (1902); Fries and others, eds., *Records of the Moravians in North Carolina*, vols. 10–11 (1960, 1969), and *Forsyth: The History of a County on the March* (1976); Augustus Schultze, *Guide to the Old Moravian Cemetery of Bethlehem, Pennsylvania, 1742–1910* (1912); Dorothea de Schweinitz, *Summary History of the Schweinitz Family, 1350–1975* (1974); "Rev. R. W. de-Schweinitz Dead," undated clipping (Moravian Archives, Winston-Salem).

ROGER KIRKMAN

Scott, Andrew *(d. 1767)*, physician and natural scientist, left Prince Georges County, Md., and settled in North Carolina about 1753. While practicing in Maryland, Dr. Scott on at least one occasion sent a collection of thirty-six indigenous plants of that colony to Dr. Richard Middleton Massey, an English botanist. Massey eventually gave these specimens to Dr. Hans Sloan, the great Irish naturalist, and they became a part of the collections that formed the beginnings of the British Museum. Scott's specimens are still among the museum's holdings. In 1739 Scott wrote to Sloan offering some seeds and seeking his influence with Lord Baltimore in securing an appointment as sheriff of Prince Georges County, but nothing seems to have come of it. Lord Petre was another of Scott's British correspondents and received seeds from him.

In or about 1753 Scott moved to Bath and practiced medicine there for a time before settling permanently at New Bern in 1757. An Anglican layman and justice of the peace, he was evidently New Bern's foremost physician during the decade of his residence there. He was a personal friend of Samuel Johnston, Sr., father of the future governor of the same name, and attended the elder Johnston at his deathbed in the fall of 1757. He also appears to have pioneered in the use of smallpox vaccine, an effort that earned him a court appearance and was apparently the only occasion in the history of the colony when a physician experimented with this controversial procedure.

An inventory of Scott's estate in 1767 lists among other items in his library one entitled "Vegetable Kingdom MS by A. Scott (1 Vol.)." This was evidently a herbal compiled by the doctor and indicates that he had continued to pursue his naturalistic investigations as a resident of North Carolina. The manuscript, along with the doctor's other personal belongings, appears to have been sent to his brother George in Maryland by executors of the estate.

SEE: W. H. Brown, ed., *Archives of Maryland: Proceedings of the Council of Maryland, 1732–1753* (1908); Craven County Miscellaneous Estate Papers (North Carolina State Archives, Raleigh); J. E. Dandy, ed., *The Sloane Herbarium* (1958); Dorothy Long, "Smallpox in North Carolina," *North Carolina Medical Journal* 16 (October 1955); Andrew Scott to Samuel Johnston, 28 Oct. 1757 (Hayes Collection, Southern Historical Collection, University of North Carolina, Chapel Hill).

T. C. PARRAMORE

Scott, Armond Wendell *(1873–18 Sept. 1960)*, lawyer and municipal judge, was a native of Wilmington and the second of six sons born to Benjamin and Athalea Harris Scott. The elder Scott ran a livery stable and a general store at Sixth and Walnut streets, purchasing many of his supplies from ships tied up at the wharves. Apparently, when Armond Scott was around twenty he founded the *Record*, a small newspaper dedicated to black interests. He worked his way through Biddle (later Johnson C. Smith) University and in a similar fashion attended Shaw University, from which he received a law degree in March 1898. He passed the bar exam and was the only black in the class.

Scott then returned to Wilmington and began to practice law. Early in November 1898 a simmering conflict between Democrats and "radical Republican whites and blacks" came to a boil on the morning of the tenth, when a race riot erupted and the *Daily Record* building was burned to the ground. For some time prior to this, the *Daily Record* and the Raleigh *News and Observer* had been exchanging editorials inflammatory in nature, and the Democratic supporters claimed that Scott was responsible for the *Record*'s views. Years later, however, some Wilmington whites disputed the accusation, saying that Scott had sold his interest to Alex Manly and was only his assistant at the time.

In any case, young Scott, knowing that the opposition had demanded he leave town, decided to accept an offer from a brother-in-law, Dr. Tom Mask, to go to Rose Hill, a railroad stop about twenty miles away, in Mask's buggy. On reaching Washington, D.C., with some savings, Scott rented an upper-floor room at Fifth and D Street, N.W., for $3.00 a week, sleeping on the couch at night, and again began the practice of law. However, because his clients were too poor and too few and his money was exhausted, he turned to more lucrative jobs, such as elevator operator, Pullman porter, and bellhop, the last at a fashionable hotel in Saratoga Springs, N.Y. At this nadir of his career, when years of study seemed wasted, fortune smiled unexpectedly. He was instructed to take a jug of ice water to a certain room, where he was suddenly confronted by the chief justice of the North Carolina Supreme Court (most likely William Faircloth), who had admitted him to the bar.

The justice thundered, "Is this what we gave you a license to practice law for? . . . I don't care if you have had bad luck. Go back and start again!" Smarting from the accusation, Scott returned to Washington, reopened an office, and was eventually able to establish a successful practice, most of it in criminal law. In 1935, when Scott was sixty-two, President Franklin D. Roosevelt managed to get Scott's nomination to the Washington, D.C., municipal court approved, but only after a great hue and cry about FDR employing the "spoils system," a claim based on the fact that Scott's predecessor, James Cobb, had been a Republican. In spite of this inauspicious beginning, Judge Scott was now launched on a long career aptly described as "colorful."

It was said that his bench served as both a pulpit and a stage. He thrived on crowded courtrooms. "Where's the audience?" he was likely to ask if benches happened to be largely empty. His own experiences had made him considerate of the poor. To counsel the sinful, forgive the penitent, and sympathize with the unfortunate became one of his dictums. He often used another dictum, "He that knoweth the reason of the law, knoweth the law," to explain to the accused why he or she was in court. It was said of Judge Scott that he dispensed a brand of justice "flavored with philosophy and the tolerance that comes to men who have studied the passing parade."

On the other hand, he was aroused to fury by witnesses who perjured themselves on the stand. Also vexing were lawyers who avoided courts where only the poor could be found, thus making it difficult for the bench to see that the accused had legal representation. He chided his fellow judges who gave convicted bootleggers nominal fines and began handing such lawbreakers jail sentences right and left. When, on one occasion, a child had to testify and obviously did not know the meaning of truth, Judge Scott said angrily, "It's incredible! This child has never been to Sunday School. We talk of juvenile delinquents when the real trouble is adult delinquents."

When Scott's term expired in 1953, President Dwight D. Eisenhower chose not to name a successor for two and one-half years so that Scott could qualify for the twenty-year retirement pension. Even then he existed in a state of semiretirement, serving as a judge for three months a year. "It's better to wear out than rust out," he would say. At a dinner in October 1956, when Scott was eighty-three, he was honored by friends of the bench, bar, and the community. In 1958 one of his dreams was realized when action was taken to treat alcoholics as people needing medical attention, rather than just handing them another jail term. For years these inebriates had hung around the courthouse steps, waiting their turn to face "The Dean," as he was known to them. He died two years later at age eighty-seven and was buried in Lincoln Cemetery.

Scott was married twice, first to Effie Harris, of Washington, D.C., who left a son, Armond Wendell II, and then to Annie Cotton of Alabama. He was a member of St. Luke's Episcopal Church and an Elk, holding the post of grand ruler during the governorship of Al Smith, whom he backed for the presidency. The judge left behind an unfinished autobiographical sketch, *Up from Hell*, telling the story of his life from youth in Wilmington to old age in Washington, D.C.

SEE: Andrew J. Howell, *The Book of Wilmington* (1930); Louis T. Moore Collection (Wilmington Public Library); Alfred Scott (nephew, Winston-Salem), personal contact; Shaw University records (Raleigh); *Washington Post* and *Washington Star*, 19 Sept. 1960; *Wilmington Record*, 1895; *Wilmington Daily Record*, 1897–98.

JOHN MACFIE

Scott, George Randolph *(23 Jan. 1898–2 Mar. 1987)*, motion picture actor, was born in Orange, Va., the only one of his seven brothers and sisters not born in Charlotte, N.C., the family's home. He was the son of North Carolinians, Lucy Crane and George Grant Scott. (Some biographical sources refer to him as Randolph Crane and the year of his birth as 1903, but neither of these is confirmed by contemporary records.) Although Scott later said that he had had no acting ambitions as a youth, he did take part in plays produced in Charlotte under the direction of the United Daughters of the Confederacy, the Junior League, and other organizations. In the early months of 1918, during World War I, he served briefly with the Fourth Division.

He attended Woodberry Forest preparatory school, enrolled at Georgia Tech in 1919 but remained only a short time, and entered The University of North Carolina in the spring quarter of 1920. As a special student in commerce, he remained for two quarters before returning home to Charlotte, where he was recorded as a member of his parents' household until 1930. He worked as an accountant in his father's accounting firm, rose to auditor, and then became office manager. In 1921 he became a charter member of the Charlotte Civitan Club. While vacationing in California with a hometown friend in 1929, he reportedly met Howard Hughes on a golf course and, without even the formality of a screen test, was offered a role as an extra in a picture, *The Far Call*, that Hughes was filming.

His friend returned to Charlotte, but Randolph Scott remained in California and enrolled in the Pasadena Community Playhouse, a dramatic training school. During the next eight months he appeared in a series of plays under the direction of Gilmore Brown and won the lead in *Under a Virginia Moon* at the Hollywood Vine Street Theater. His performance resulted in an offer of a movie contract, but he declined it in favor of additional experience. Another play, *The Broken Wing*, brought him a contract with Paramount. He had minor parts in several motion pictures made in 1931, including *Sky Bride*, his first picture; *Women Men Marry*; and *The Lone Cowboy*. Two more were filmed in 1932 and three in 1933. Scott was making a name for himself in westerns, but in 1935 he began to break out of that mold. He had nonsinging parts in several musicals and then appeared in assorted roles in such films as *So Red the Rose*, *Follow the Fleet*, *Go West, Young Man*, *The Last of the Mohicans*, and, with Shirley Temple, *Rebecca of Sunnybrook Farm*.

War films occupied him in the 1940s during World War II, while in the late 1940s he made several "quickie" westerns. It was in this decade that Scott formed his own production company, Ranown, making it possible for him to determine the kind of pictures in which he would appear. As a result, in the 1950s he played in a series of westerns described as relating "violence and betrayal to moral dilemma."

Badman's Territory, made in 1946, was his first big box office success. During the forties and fifties some of his pictures were *Belle of the Yukon*, *Abilene Town*, *Albuquerque*, *Santa Fe*, *The Bounty Hunter*, *Decision at Sundown*, and *Westbound*. His last film, *Ride the High Country*, made in 1962, was accounted his best. Altogether he appeared in ninety-six motion pictures.

A modest man, Scott was never ostentatious, yet he always dressed well. He disliked publicity and he was offended by screen sex. On occasion he returned to North Carolina to visit his family and always seemed comfortable in that setting. Many people in the state long had pleasant memories of backyard picnics when he was in town. In later years his father worked in the state auditor's office in Raleigh and delighted in introducing young female employees to his movie star son.

From his first appearance in Hollywood, Randolph Scott was known as a man of integrity and high principle. Recognized as a "Southern gentleman," he was said to have been the only movie actor accepted for membership in the Los Angeles Country Club. Early in his career he began investing in real estate, and in later years he was regarded as a multimillionaire and one of Hollywood's wealthiest stars.

In 1936 Scott married Mrs. Marion du Pont Somerville, an heiress of the du Pont fortune. Social and business affairs kept her in the East for long periods, however, and in 1944 they were amicably divorced. Soon afterwards he married Marie Patricia Stillman of New York, and they adopted two children: Christopher and Sandra. Scott's family belonged to St. Peter's Episcopal Church in Charlotte and at his burial in Elmwood Cemetery there, the private service was conducted by the rector and by the Reverend Billy Graham, a longtime friend of Scott's.

SEE: Alumni Files, University of North Carolina, Chapel Hill; Liz-Anne Bawden, ed., *The Oxford Companion to Film* (1976); Chapel Hill *Daily Tar Heel*, 7 Oct. 1936; *Chapel Hill Newspaper*, 3 Mar. 1987 (portrait); *Charlotte City Directory*, 1921–30; *Charlotte Observer*, 10 Nov. 1935, 5 Mar. 1987; Daniel L. Grant, *Alumni History of the University of North Carolina* (1924); *Los Angeles Times*, 3 Mar. 1987; *New York Times*, 4 Mar. 1944, 3 Mar. 1987 (portrait); David Ragan, comp., *Who's Who in Hollywood, 1900–1976* (1976); Raleigh *News and Observer*, 13–14 Nov. 1935, 3 Mar. 1987; Raleigh *Spectator*, 21 Apr. 1983, 4–10 June 1987; Terry Ramsaye, *International Motion Picture Almanac, 1939–40* (1939); David Thomson, *A Biographical Dictionary of Film* (1981); *Washington Post*, 3 Mar. 1987; *Winston-Salem Journal*, 3 Mar. 1987.

WILLIAM S. POWELL

Scott, Hugh Reid *(9 Jan. 1855–2 Nov. 1947)*, attorney and banker, was born in rural Rockingham County, the son of William and Rhoda Reid Scott. His father, a planter and merchant, was a member of the Court of Pleas and Quarter Sessions; his mother was the sister of Governor David S. Reid. Young Scott attended a local old-field school and the Reidsville Academy, where he was taught by Frank P. Hobgood. After a busy student career that included debating and other activities, he was graduated from Wake Forest College in 1875. He then studied law under Chief Justice Richmond Pearson at Richmond Hill, Yadkin County, and received a license to practice in 1877.

Scott established a practice in Wentworth and remained there for seven years before moving to Reidsville, where he spent the rest of his life. He was elected to two successive terms (1881–85) in the North Carolina Senate. Although he had no banking experience, he was chosen in 1895 to organize the Citizens' Bank of Reidsville, which prospered under his leadership. Returning full-time to his law practice in 1909, he continued serving as legal counsel to businesses and businessmen. His banking and legal services were predicated on what he termed a policy of "Safety first, and as far as consistent with safety, profits." He also held extensive property and farming interests.

A man of wide reading interests, Scott owned what was considered to be one of the best legal libraries in his part of the state. In addition, he collected books, pamphlets, periodicals, and newspapers concerning North Carolina and North Carolinians. In 1946 his law library was presented to the courthouse of Rockingham County, whereas many of his personal papers and much of his North Carolina material were later given to the University of North Carolina at Chapel Hill.

When he was fifty-three Scott married Flossie Brewer, and they were the parents of one child, Cecilia (Mrs. William Hester). He was buried in Greenview Cemetery, Reidsville.

SEE: Samuel A. Ashe, ed., *Biographical History of North Carolina*, vol. 1 (1905); *Greensboro Daily News*, 24 Jan. 1960; *North Carolina Biography*, vol. 6 (1919), vol. 4 (1941); *Prominent People of North Carolina* (1906); Raleigh *News and Observer*, 3 Nov. 1947; John S. Tomlinson, *Assembly Sketch Book* (1883); *Who's Who in the South* (1927).

C. SYLVESTER GREEN

Scott, James Edwin *(1 Aug. 1859–24 Aug. 1888)*, merchant and tobacco manufacturer, was born in Alamance County, the son of Robert W. Scott. He attended the Bingham School when it was under the direction of Major Robert Bingham and studied at The University of North Carolina during the period 1877–78. He was close to his brother, Robert W., and the two joined in several business ventures.

Scott briefly attended a business college in Poughkeepsie, N.Y., before opening a general store in Mebansville (after 1883, Mebane). Because of the number of merchants already there, however, he became a salesman of fertilizer to farmers living along the Haw River. After several unwise business investments, Scott left Mebansville for Philadelphia in 1880 and established a tobacco business. On 8 June 1881 he returned to North Carolina and founded a new tobacco firm that proved to be successful. His brother Robert, owner of the Alamance Stock Farm, at Melville, where he bred cows, horses, and sheep, and his friend, Joseph A. Tate, a dealer in leaf tobacco in Hickory, became minor partners in the business. They formed Scott Bros. Merchants and Scott and Company, Manufacturers of Tobacco, with primary operations centered in Mebansville.

To establish agents and buyer for his product, James E. Scott traveled to Chicago, Indianapolis, St. Louis, Cincinnati, Louisville, Memphis, Nashville, Vicksburg, Birmingham, New Orleans, Mobile, Montgomery, Atlanta, Buffalo, Toledo, Cleveland, Grand Rapids, Milwaukee, La Salle, Davenport, Burlington, Bloomington, and Springfield. He developed a strong market in those cities.

Scott was innovative in packaging his product. He sold tobacco in paper pouches that advertised his firm's name. With the purchase of a pound of "processed" tobacco, his customers received a free handmade pouch. Scott's wife and her friends in Mebansville made the pouches, so the cost of production was countered by the savings on the paper pouches.

The business grew slowly but steadily and produced such chewing tobacco brands as Alamance, Beauty Bright, Carolina, Della, Honest Sam, Josie, Mattie May, Melville Chief, Robina, and Rob Roy. Smoking tobacco brands were Old Bill and Tried and True.

On 15 Sept. 1885 Scott married Mary Belle, daughter of Dr. Benjamin Franklin and Frances Lavina Mebane of Mebane. They were the parents of a daughter, Margaret Graham, who married John Rumple Ross. After suffering poor health and an extended illness, Scott died at age twenty-nine.

SEE: Elizabeth Scott Carrington, *Historical Sketch of Hawfields Presbyterian Church* (no date); Daniel L. Grant,

Alumni History of the University of North Carolina (1924); Mebane Family Papers (Southern Historical Collection, University of North Carolina, Chapel Hill).

F. CRAIG WILLIS

Scott, Levi M. *(8 June 1827–27 Nov. 1911)*, lawyer, teacher, postmaster, and state representative, was born in Rockingham County, the son of John D. and Jane McLean Scott. While Scott was still an infant, his parents moved back to their original home in Guilford County. His father's family, which had emigrated from Pennsylvania, was of Irish descent; his mother's family was Scottish. John D. Scott was a farmer and a colonel in the North Carolina militia cavalry, a commission he held until the outbreak of the Civil War. Levi had two brothers, Allen H. and William Lafayette, an alumnus of The University of North Carolina.

Levi Scott attended schools in Guilford County and in 1845 entered Greensboro High School, where he excelled in debate and served as president of the Hermean Literary Society. In 1847 he transferred to Alamance Academy, a classical school opened by his instructor, Dr. Eli W. Caruthers. In 1849 Scott obtained a teaching position at Greensboro High, where he remained until appointed postmaster of Greensboro in 1851. During the same period he began studying law under John A. Gilmer and received his license to practice in state superior courts in 1852. He resigned as postmaster in 1853 after his election as clerk of the superior court in Guilford County, an office he held until 1856, when elected to the North Carolina House of Representatives as a Whig. He served in the legislature for one term.

In 1858 Scott was elected solicitor of Guilford County for a four-year term. He was reelected in 1862 and also appointed receiver of sequestered property by the Confederate government. In the post of receiver, which he held until the end of the war, his duties involved collecting all debts owed to Northern creditors from Southern debtors for the benefit of the Confederate states. Also during the war the law offices of Levi and his brother, William L., who maintained a joint practice, were used temporarily by Governor Zebulon B. Vance while he was avoiding the chaotic conditions of Raleigh. Thus, it was in Scott's office that Vance wrote his surrender proclamation when the war ended.

Scott also served as a commissioner, striving to establish the railroad from Greensboro to Danville, Va. Seen as a war measure, the railroad was chartered on 8 Feb. 1862, despite the state's resistance to internal improvements leading out of the state. From 1885 to 1889 Scott served on the board of directors of the State Penitentiary. Long active in the Independent Order of Odd Fellows, he served as grand master of the state in 1866.

In 1861 Scott married Mary Eliza Weatherly, the daughter of Andrew Weatherly, mayor of Greensboro, and they had two children. He died in Greensboro at age eighty-five.

SEE: Samuel Ashe, ed., *Biographical History of North Carolina*, vol. 2 (1906 [portrait]), and *Cyclopedia of Eminent and Representative Men of the Carolinas*, vol. 2 (1892); Thomas W. Davis, ed., *Proceedings of the North Carolina Bar Association*, vol. 15 (1913); J. G. de Roulhac Hamilton, ed., *The Papers of William A. Graham*, vol. 4 (1961); Earl A. Weatherly, *The First Hundred Years of Historic Guilford* (1972).

ANNA JEANETTE BASS

Scott, Ralph Henderson *(12 Dec. 1903–2 Apr. 1989)*, dairyman, political leader, and legislator, was born near Haw River in Alamance County, the son of Robert Walter and Elizabeth Jessie Hughes Scott. His brother, William Kerr Scott, and his nephew, Robert S. Scott, were governors of North Carolina during the years 1949–53 and 1969–73, respectively. A 1924 graduate of North Carolina State College, he owned and was president of Melville Dairy, Inc., a milk distributor in Burlington.

A Democrat, Scott served consecutive terms in the North Carolina House of Representatives between 1951 and 1956 and between 1961 and 1980; serving one term in the senate, he was president pro tem in 1963. He was a member of such committees as Agriculture, Propositions and Grievances, Rules, Higher Education, Finance, Education, and Appropriations. At various times he held a seat on the Advisory Budget Commission and on the North Carolina Department of Human Resources' Council on Developmental Disabilities. In the General Assembly in 1953, Scott introduced the bill that created the State Milk Commission and he was vocal in his opposition to the Speaker Ban bill. He was a member of or served in advisory and official capacities numerous organizations, among which were those concerned with education, retarded citizens, agriculture, senior citizens, and health care.

As a relative of two governors, Scott worked effectively between the legislative and executive branches during their incumbency. He played significant behind-the-scenes roles in the resolution of a strike by food workers at the University of North Carolina in Chapel Hill and in questions concerning the creation of a medical school at East Carolina University in Greenville. He was awarded an honorary doctorate by Elon College and received the North Carolina Award in 1981.

Scott married Hazeleene Tate of Alamance County in 1925, and they were the parents of a daughter, Marian, and two sons, Ralph H., Jr., and William Clevenger. Scott was a Presbyterian and an active member of the Hawfields Church.

SEE: *Charlotte Observer*, 4–5 Apr. 1989; John L. Cheney, Jr., ed., *North Carolina Government, 1585–1979* (1981); *Durham Morning Herald*, 15 Apr. 1973, 13 Dec. 1975; Gayle Lane Fitzgerald, *Remembering a Champion* (1988 [portrait]); Stephen E. Massengill, *Biographical Directory of the General Assembly of North Carolina, 1963–1978*, vol. 2 (1979); *North Carolina Award, 1981* (1981); *North Carolina Manual* (1971); Raleigh *News and Observer*, 8 May 1956, 7 Jan. 1979; Southern Pines *The Pilot*, 10 Apr. 1989; Jean Speck, *The Gentleman from Haw River* (1990 [portrait]).

WILLIAM S. POWELL

Scott, Ralph James *(15 Oct. 1905–5 Aug. 1983)*, congressman, state legislator, and district attorney, was born on a farm in southeastern Surry County's Shoals Township, the son of Samuel Martin and Daisy Murphy (Cook) Scott. His four brothers were Arthur, Adam, Robert, and Paul Scott, and his half brother was Wallace Scott. At age nine, he moved with his family to Pinnacle in southwestern Stokes County, where he was graduated from high school in 1925. Scott chose to remain at Pinnacle High School for another year to play basketball and baseball, two sports in which he possessed exceptional talents. He then enrolled at Wake Forest College and studied law. Due to the lack of funds, he had to work his way through two years of undergraduate study and two years and one summer of law school before receiving an LL.B. degree and admission to the state bar in 1930.

In September 1930 Scott began practicing in Danbury with John D. Humphreys, but their partnership was short-lived. Three months later, Humphreys, who had been elected a superior court judge in November, died unexpectedly. Scott continued to operate the law office, which was situated in a two-room wooden building across the street from the Stokes County Courthouse. With his wife, the former Verna Denny of Pilot Mountain, whom he married on 30 Nov. 1929, Scott raised two daughters; Patricia Ann (Mrs. William F. Southern of Walnut Cove) and Nancy Ellen (Mrs. Grady C. Shumate of Winston-Salem).

In 1934 Scott began a long political career with his election as chairman of the Stokes County Democratic Executive Committee, a position he held until filing for his first congressional race in 1956. Meanwhile, he won a seat in the North Carolina House of Representatives in 1936 and served in that year's special session, as well as in the regular and special sessions of 1937. Instead of seeking reelection in 1938, Scott opted to run for the district attorney's seat in the Twenty-first Judicial District, which comprised Surry, Stokes, Rockingham, and Caswell counties. Elected, he held the position until 1956, after winning reelection four times and facing opposition only once, in 1950. During his eighteen-year tenure as district attorney, Scott never missed a court date, nor was he ever late for work.

With two years remaining in his fifth term, Scott decided to seek the Democratic nomination for the seat of the Fifth Congressional District, which at that time represented Caswell, Forsyth, Granville, Person, Rockingham, Stokes, Surry, and Wilkes counties. He was elected to the Eighty-fifth Congress after defeating four-term incumbent Thurmond Chatham, who had refused to sign the Southern Manifesto. Scott's congressional career endured until 1967, when he chose not to seek a sixth term and returned to Danbury, despite pressure to run again. After each term, Scott had wanted to leave Washington, but his friends and political aides always coaxed him into seeking reelection. Scott, a political conservative, often claimed that his thinking did not correspond with "the trends of the time" and because of this, he felt that he was not accomplishing much as a legislator.

After returning to Danbury, Scott worked as an assistant district attorney for the Seventeenth Judicial District, which served Surry, Stokes, Rockingham, and Caswell counties. He also was active as a Mason, Shriner, Moose, Elk, and member of the Pinnacle Baptist Church. Fearful that Stokes County officials might move the county seat, Scott donated most of the land for a new government center in Danbury. His benevolence paid off and the county seat remained intact.

After suffering a stroke in 1979, he decided to retire in October 1980. But Scott could not stay away completely. In 1981 he served as temporary district attorney for several weeks. At age seventy-seven he died at Forsyth Memorial Hospital after suffering another stroke and a series of heart attacks. He was buried in the Pinnacle Baptist Church cemetery.

SEE: *Biog. Dir. Am. Cong.* (1962); *Greensboro News and Record*, 6 Aug. 1983; *North Carolina Manual* (1965); William S. Powell, ed., *North Carolina Lives* (1961); Raleigh *News and Observer*, 17 June 1956, 8 May 1963, 2 Sept. 1965; *Winston-Salem Journal*, 6 Sept. 1979, 12 Feb., 28 Sept. 1980, 6 Aug. 1983.

BENJAMIN A. JOLLY

Scott, Randolph. *See* **Scott, George Randolph.**

Scott, Thomas Fielding *(12 Mar. 1807–14 July 1867)*, Episcopal bishop, was born in the community of Scotts in west central Iredell County, the son of James and Rebekkah Worke Scott. Sometime in his youth he was a blacksmith and after a day of hard work he would gather lightwood knots to provide illumination for reading in the evening. This, he later said, was the means of his earliest education. As a young man he moved to Georgia and in 1829 was graduated from Franklin College in Athens (now the University of Georgia), from which he also received an honorary doctor of divinity degree in 1853. He was a large man, over 6 feet tall and weighed around 250 pounds.

Scott was licensed as a Presbyterian to preach in 1830 and served a number of rural churches in small towns in Georgia and Tennessee. After meeting Bishop James H. Otey and the Reverend Leonidas Polk, he "made a thorough study of the Scriptural and historical claims of the Episcopacy" and reached "the firm and unalterable conclusion that the doctrine was true." Having become concerned over the splits in the Presbyterian church, he became an Episcopalian in 1842. The following year he was ordained deacon in St. Paul's Church, Augusta, Ga. Advanced to the priesthood in Christ Church, Macon, in 1844, he served churches in Marietta and Columbus. In 1852 at Macon, Ga., at the Seventh Annual Fair of the Southern Cotton and Agricultural Society, he was awarded a silver pitcher for the best acceptable essay on "The Management and Treatment of Slaves."

The General Convention of the Episcopal Church in 1853 elected Scott missionary bishop of the Territory of Oregon, with jurisdiction in the Territory of Washington—a region that also included the later state of Idaho and portions of western Montana and western Wyoming. He was consecrated in Christ Church, Savannah, on 8 Jan. 1854. Bishop Scott was counted a good scholar and an effective preacher. In his own words he was "conservative and catholic," yet an acquaintance from his early days in Oregon recalled that he never wore vestments but instead "officiated in a citizen's suit."

Sailing south and crossing the Isthmus of Panama, the new bishop and his wife reached Oregon on 22 April. He made his headquarters at Portland and served his vast territory during the period 1854–66; at times he also administered the Diocese of California. It was reported that he traveled by canoe, stagecoach, horseback, or foot. Sometimes his route lay through uncharted country, through Indian territory, and in places where food and lodging were scarce. In spite of these apparent difficulties, Scott set about laying broad plans for the growth of the Episcopal church in the Northwest. One of the stations in his territory was five hundred miles from his home, yet after just a little over two years two schools were operating and in 1861 publication of the *Oregon Churchman* was begun.

The labors of Bishop Scott, so far removed from other churchmen, served as an inspiration for the whole country. His magnificent work was well known and appreciated, and in spite of extreme handicaps he laid secure foundations which were necessary for the achievements of those who followed him. It has been said that his "vision was greater than his opportunity," and he was considered "an authentic martyr of the American Church."

In 1830, while living in Georgia, he married Evelyn Appleby, whose ill health in 1866 prompted the bishop to offer his resignation. En route to the General Convention of 1867 by sea and again crossing Panama, Scott became ill and on 11 July was taken from the ship to a hospital in New York where he died three days later of "Panama fever." He was buried in Trinity churchyard in the cemetery beside the Chapel of the Intercession at 155th Street and Broadway. Bishop and Mrs. Scott had no children.

SEE: Thomas E. Jessett, "Bishop Scott and the Episcopal Church in Washington," *Pacific Northwest Quarterly* 38 (January 1947), and "Thomas Fielding Scott: Bishop of Oregon," *Oregon Historical Quarterly* 55 (March 1954); *Journal of the . . . Protestant Episcopal Church in a General Convention . . . 1853* (1854); Mildred J. Miller, ed., *The Heritage of Iredell County* (1980); *North Carolina Churchman* 44 (May 1955 [portrait]); *Oregon Churchman* 3 (September 1911), 5 (December 1913); Thomas F. Scott Papers (Archives of the Episcopal Church, Austin, Tex.); Statesville, N.C., *Landmark,* 6 Sept. 1875; *Who Was Who in America: Historical Volume, 1607–1896* (1967).

WILLIAM S. POWELL

Scott, William Kerr *(17 Apr. 1896–16 Apr. 1958)*, U.S. senator, North Carolina governor, and agricultural leader, was born at Haw River in Alamance County. He was the sixth of eleven children of Robert Walter and Elizabeth Josephine Hughes Scott. A farmer by profession, his father served in the North Carolina General Assembly and was a member of the State Board of Agriculture and a trustee of North Carolina State College. His mother died when Kerr (pronounced kär) was eighteen.

Scott attended Alamance County public schools, graduating from Hawfields High School in 1913. Four years later he received a B.S. degree in agriculture from North Carolina State College, where he excelled in track and debating.

Following a brief stint as emergency food production agent for the U.S. Department of Agriculture, he enlisted as a private in the U.S. Army Field Artillery. Shortly after receiving his army discharge, Scott purchased 224 acres of land near his birthplace and began a lifelong career as a farmer. In 1920 he was elected master of the North Carolina State Grange. As master, he supported rural electrification during the early days of the Great Depression. From 1934 to 1936 he served as regional director for the Farm Debt Adjustment Program, Resettlement Administration.

Scott first ran for public office in 1936, when he waged a successful campaign for the post of North Carolina commissioner of agriculture, defeating incumbent William A. Graham. Serving for three terms, he led a successful effort to rid the state of Bang's disease, an ailment afflicting cattle. In 1938 the *Progressive Farmer*, a leading farm journal, named Scott Man of the Year, citing his attempts to revitalize the State Department of Agriculture.

By 1948, when Scott resigned as commissioner of agriculture to seek the state's highest office, he had established a broad base of support among Tar Heel farmers. Placing second in a field of six candidates in the May Democratic primary, he requested a runoff against state treasurer Charles M. Johnson. Scott's advocacy of improved roads and his plea for ending the state's "deficit in services" resulted in his victory over Johnson in the 26 June runoff primary. In the November general election he easily defeated Republican candidate George M. Pritchard of Asheville, thus becoming the first farmer to be elected governor in the twentieth century.

In his 6 Jan. 1949 inaugural address, Scott assigned top priority to road construction and improvement and public school construction. His effective leadership was a major factor in voter approval of a $200 million bond issue for construction of a secondary road system and a $25 million bond issue for expansion of public schools in a 4 June 1949 referendum. Both bond issues were major projects in Scott's "Go Forward" program, much of which was enacted into law by the 1949 General Assembly.

Scott's energetic leadership was directly responsible for expansion of electric and telephone service in the state's rural areas. During his term as governor 21,000 miles of power lines were strung to homes occupied by almost 150,000 people.

At a time when racial segregation was firmly embedded in the state's social fabric, Governor Scott appointed the first black to serve on the State Board of Education and ordered elimination of salary discrimination against staff members at the mental hospital for blacks in Goldsboro. Moreover, recognizing the need to utilize the latent talents of North Carolina women, he appointed more women to state boards and commissions than any of his predecessors. Particularly significant was his selection of Miss Susie Sharp of Rockingham County as the first female superior court judge in the state's history.

Progressive measures proposed by Scott during his term included lowering the minimum voting age to eighteen, stricter enforcement of existing liquor laws and a statewide referendum on the question of liquor sales, stream pollution control, minimum wage legislation, and reinstatement of the 1947 motor vehicle inspection law repealed by the 1949 General Assembly.

When Senator J. Melville Broughton died in 1949, Scott appointed Consolidated University of North Carolina president Frank P. Graham to complete his unexpired term. Graham's defeat in his bid for a full Senate term in the 1950 Democratic primary diminished Scott's prestige and strengthened anti-Scott forces in the 1951 General Assembly.

When his gubernatorial term ended in January 1953, Scott returned to his Alamance farm; however, his retirement from public life lasted only a few months. A triumph over Wilmington attorney Alton Lennon in the 29 May 1954 Democratic primary assured Scott a seat in the U.S. Senate the following January. As a freshman senator, Scott spent the majority of his time listening and learning. On those few occasions when he did speak on the Senate floor, his remarks were invariably succinct. He served as a member of three Senate committees—Agriculture, Interior and Insular Affairs, and Public Works. On the latter committee he played a major role in the framing and enactment of legislation providing for financing the interstate highway network, then in its formative stage. Development of water resources and a more prosperous farm economy were goals he strove to achieve during his senatorial career.

His rural background, coupled with his daily custom of wearing a rose in his coat lapel, led one observer to describe Scott as "a jet-propelled plowboy with a rose in his lapel." During his entire public career "the Squire of Haw River," as he was affectionately called, played the political game to the hilt to accomplish goals he considered worthwhile. He knew how to trade a vote, honor a pledge, do a favor, and demand one in return, always with the public well-being as his ultimate objective.

Throughout his life Scott was a champion of the average man or, in his phrase, "the branchhead boys." Both as a governor and as a senator, his philosophy and programs reflected his years on country back roads with rural people. He felt equally at home making a college commencement address or milking a cow.

Scott suffered a heart attack early in April 1958 and was admitted to Alamance General Hospital, in Burlington, where he died. He was buried in the cemetery of the Hawfields Presbyterian Church near the graves of his parents and grandparents.

On 2 July 1919 Scott married Mary Elizabeth White, a

childhood friend whom he called "Miss Mary" throughout his life. They had two sons, Robert and Osborne, and a daughter, Mary Kerr. Both Scott and his wife were active members of the Hawfields Presbyterian Church. Even during Scott's term as governor, they seldom missed Sunday morning worship services in their home church.

SEE: *Biog. Dir. Am. Cong.* (1971); John L. Cheney, Jr., comp., *North Carolina Government, 1585–1979* (1981); John W. Coon, "Kerr Scott, The Go Forward Governor: His Origins, His Programs, and the North Carolina General Assembly" (master's thesis, University of North Carolina, Chapel Hill, 1968); *Durham Morning Herald*, 17 Apr. 1958; *Memorial Services Held in the Senate and House of Representatives of the United States for William Kerr Scott* (1958); *New York Times*, 17 Apr. 1958; *Public Addresses, Letters, and Papers of William Kerr Scott, Governor of North Carolina, 1949–53* (1957); Raleigh *News and Observer*, 17 Apr. 1958.

A. W. STEWART

Scruggs, Lawson Andrew *(15 Jan. 1857–1914)*, physician, pharmacist, and one of the first three black doctors licensed by the state of North Carolina, was born to slave parents in Bedford County, Va. His early education was a scant few months in the common schools of his Virginia neighborhood immediately after the Civil War. While engaged in farming during the day, he studied at night to acquire a rudimentary education, continuing these efforts when later employed in construction work for the Atlantic and Mississippi Railroad and for the Western Union Telegraph Company. In October 1877 he enrolled at the Richmond Institute, a Baptist Home Mission Society school, and in May 1882 he was graduated second in his class. A book Scruggs published in 1893 was dedicated in part to "Charles J. Pickford, the author's early friend and benefactor." An introductory sketch of Scruggs's own life to that date was written by another benefactor and teacher at Richmond, Mrs. Josephine Turpin Washington.

Entering Shaw University in Raleigh in the fall of 1882, Scruggs completed the literary course as valedictorian of his graduating class. While working towards his A.B. degree he simultaneously pursued medical courses in the Leonard Medical School at Shaw. The faculty was composed of white physicians practicing in Raleigh. One of the six recipients of M.D. degrees in Leonard's first graduating class in 1886, Scruggs was again valedictorian and received the class prize in surgery. In the same year three of the graduates (including Scruggs) took their examinations before the State Board of Medical Examiners, becoming the first black doctors licensed by the state.

Also in the year of his graduation and licensing, Scruggs was appointed resident physician at Leonard Hospital as well as lecturer in physiology, hygiene, and chemistry in the college department at Shaw, the first black to hold these positions. Four years later, in March 1890, he resigned to devote full time to private practice. Soon, however, he accepted appointment as visiting physician and lecturer in physiology and hygiene at St. Augustine's Normal and Collegiate Institute (now St. Augustine's College). Again, he was the first black to occupy these chairs. When in October 1886 St. Agnes Hospital for Negroes opened in a building adjacent to St. Augustine's, Scruggs was its first attending physician and lecturer.

In 1887 he was one of the four cofounders of the Old North State Medical, Dental, and Pharmaceutical Society. Later a Raleigh chapter of the state organization was named the L. A. Scruggs Medical Society.

As a result of Scruggs's work in the 1890s, Raleigh's health superintendent, Dr. James McKee, attributed to Scruggs "very much of the credit for the remarkable reduction of the death rate of the colored people in this community." In the early 1900s Scruggs left Raleigh to run a hospital in the Southern Pines–Pinehurst area of Moore County, returning to Raleigh about 1913, only a few months before his death.

Meanwhile, when Shaw University instituted the Leonard School of Pharmacy in 1891, Scruggs was designated a registered pharmacist and was licensed by the State Board of Pharmacy. For a time he was the pharmacist at the Capital City Pharmacy, at 403 Fayetteville Street, owned by two Negro brothers, J. H. and Thomas H. Love, Jr. The pharmacy was later known as Love's Drug Store.

Scruggs was also active in civic and literary pursuits. As president of the Hesperian Literary and Social Club of Raleigh, he established a reading room and library in the 1890s. For several years he was North Carolina correspondent for the *National Baptist*, published in Philadelphia. Among his published articles was a response to a piece by Thomas Nelson Page appearing in the *North American Review* that was considered derogatory to blacks. In 1893 Scruggs edited a volume entitled *Women of Distinction: Remarkable in Works and Invincible in Character*, to which some fifteen writers contributed biographical sketches. It was dedicated in part to his first wife, who had died during preparation of the manuscript and whose biography is included among its sketches. Affiliated with the Grand Foundation, United Order of True Reformers, he was medical director of its Raleigh division.

Politically Scruggs was a Republican. In an address to the Republican State Convention in Raleigh in 1896, he opposed a racially inflammatory speech by Daniel L. Russell, who became the party's successful gubernatorial candidate. Later, after the Democrats returned to office, a Negro State Council adopted a resolution urging blacks to emigrate from the state in case the Democrats made their stay in North Carolina "intolerable." Scruggs, believing the wording to be too strong and counterproductive, resigned from the council when it refused to modify the resolution.

Widowed twice, Scruggs was married three times. He met his first wife, Lucie Johnson (14 Oct. 1864–28 Nov. 1892), while both were students at Shaw University. They were married on 22 Feb. 1888 in New York, where she and her sister taught at a school for young girls, both black and white, and where she was correspondent for the *Richmond Planet* and other journals. They had two children, a son Leonard and a daughter Goldie. While in New York Lucie Scruggs wrote an elementary school textbook, *Grammar-Land*, and a drama, *Farmer Fox*, later performed in Raleigh. She was the organizer and first president of the Ladies' Pansy Literary Club at the Second (Blount Street) Baptist Church, Raleigh. Some years after her death, Scruggs married his second wife Clara (ca. 1875–11 Jan. 1903). The couple lived at 21 East Worth Street, where the doctor also maintained his office until he relocated in Pinehurst. His third marriage, to Phoebe B. Turner (born ca. 1857), took place at her home in Raleigh on 7 Sept. 1905. Surviving him by many years, his widow continued to live in Raleigh until the late 1930s. His daughter married and moved to St. Louis, where several grandchildren were living in the 1970s.

SEE: Wilmoth Carter, *Shaw's Universe* (1973); W. Montague Cobb, "Saint Agnes Hospital, Raleigh, North Carolina, 1896–1961," *Journal of the National Medical Association*, September 1961; Josephus Daniels, *Editor in Politics* (1941); J. Bustee Davis, ed., "The Negro in Medicine," Old North State Medical, Dental, and Pharmaceutical Society, Golden Anniversary Program (1937); Helen G. Edmonds, *The Negro and Fusion Politics in North Carolina, 1894–1901* (1951); Frank Emory, ed., *Paths Toward Freedom* (1976); Cecil D. Halliburton, *A History of St. Augustine's College, 1867–1937* (1937); Charles N. Hunter, biographical sketch of L. A. Scruggs (ca. 1895), in Charles N. Hunter Papers (Manuscript Department, Duke University Library, Durham); Dorothy L. Long, ed., *Medicine in North Carolina*, vol. 1 (1972); W. H. Quick, *Negro Stars in All Ages of the World* (2d ed., 1898); Raleigh City Directories, 1896–1940; Register of Deaths in the City of Raleigh, vol. 1, July 1887–1903 (microfilm, North Carolina State Archives, Raleigh); Elizabeth D. Reid, guest ed., "Black Studies," *Raleigh* magazine, vol. 3 (December 1971); Lawson Andrew Scruggs, *Women of Distinction: Remarkable in Works and Invincible in Character* (1893); Wake County Health Department, Register of Practicing Physicians, vol. 1 (microfilm, North Carolina State Archives, Raleigh); Wake Deed Books (Wake Courthouse, Raleigh).

ELIZABETH REID MURRAY

Scurlock, Mial *(25 May 1803–6 Mar. 1836)*, defender of the Alamo, was born in Chatham County, the second oldest of five children of Joseph and Martha Jones Glosglow Scurlock. The other children—in order of birth—were Joseph, Eliza, William, and Timothy. In 1826 the Scurlock family moved to Tennessee and later to Mississippi. In 1834 Mial and his brother William, with their slaves, migrated to Texas. They entered the territory at Gaines Ferry at the Sabine River Crossing on the Old San Antonio Road. Subsequently they settled in San Augustine. On 17 Oct. 1835 both men joined the Texas army as privates.

Mial and William Scurlock took part in the siege of San Antonio de Béxar, which lasted from 5 to 12 Dec. 1835. After General Martin Perfecto de Cós's forces were defeated, Mial remained in San Antonio, while his brother joined a detachment of troops destined for Matamoros. Mial was still in San Antonio in February 1836, when the forces of Cós's brother-in-law, General Antonio López de Santa Anna, reached the town. Mial joined the other Texans in San Antonio in defending the Alamo. He died when the Alamo fell on 6 March.

SEE: Alamo records (Daughters of the Republic of Texas Library, San Antonio); Sheppard Family Bible (Sheppard Memorial Library, Greenville, N.C.); W. P. Webb, ed., *The Handbook of Texas*, vol. 2 (1952); Amelia W. Williams, "A Critical Study of the Siege of the Alamo and the Personnel of Its Defenders," *Southwestern Historical Quarterly* 37 (1933–34).

R. H. DETRICK

Scurlock, William *(22 Oct. 1807–31 Jan. 1885)*, Texas military officer, was born in Chatham County, the fourth of five children born to Joseph and Martha Jones Glosglow Scurlock. In 1826 his family migrated to Tennessee and later to Mississippi. In 1834 William and his brother Mial moved to Texas, entering the territory by way of Gaines Ferry which was situated in the northeastern portion of Texas on the Sabine River. William settled in San Augustine. On 17 Oct. 1835 he enlisted as a private in a Texas military unit commanded by Henry W. Augustine. At this time the unit was en route to the Mexican-held town of San Antonio de Béxar.

On 26 November Augustine's contingent came under the command of James Bowie and participated in an attack on a Mexican foraging party that was returning to San Antonio. The engagement, known as the Grass Fight, cost the Mexicans fifty men. In January 1836 Scurlock joined a force, commanded by Dr. James Grant, that was on its way to participate in the Matamoros campaign. Grant's unit, consisting of twenty-three Americans and three Mexicans, was surprised and attacked by a superior Mexican force on 2 March. In the ensuing engagement of Aqua Dulce Creek, the Mexicans triumphed. Only six Americans escaped. One was William Scurlock, who fled to Goliad and joined Colonel James W. Fannin's force.

Promoted to captain, he fought in the Battle of Colete, which began on 19 Mar. 1836. For a second time Scurlock found himself facing a superior Mexican force. On 20 March, after suffering six killed and sixty wounded, the Texans surrendered. His captors detailed Scurlock to tend the Texas wounded, and the assignment probably saved his life. Most of the other prisoners were taken to Goliad and executed on 27 March.

Scurlock escaped from his Mexican captors in May and returned to San Augustine, where he became a captain in the San Augustine volunteers. He served with the unit from 4 July to 4 Oct. 1836.

About the time he left the Texas army, Scurlock married Frances Thompson and moved to Red River County, Tex. In 1839 and 1840 he represented the county in the Texas legislature, and at the end of his term he returned to San Augustine. He was a member of the Texas Veterans Association.

SEE: Alamo records (Daughters of the Republic of Texas Library, San Antonio); *Biographical Directory of Texas Conventions and Congresses* (1941); Herbert Davenport, "Men of Goliad," *Southwestern Historical Quarterly* 42 (1939–40); W. P. Webb, ed., *The Handbook of Texas*, vol. 2 (1952).

R. H. DETRICK

Seabrook, James Ward *(6 Nov. 1886–26 Mar. 1974)*, educator, college president, leader in race relations, and public servant, was born in Sumter, S.C., the son of Lucy Hadden and Morris James Seabrook. He attended Johnson C. Smith University in Charlotte, from which he received a bachelor of arts degree in 1909. Having decided to devote his life to the education and uplift of southern blacks, Seabrook began his teaching career immediately, joining the faculty of the Slater State Normal School, in Winston-Salem, where he taught for three years. In 1912 he left Slater for Kittrell College, near Henderson, where he taught for one year before accepting an invitation to join the faculty of his alma mater. Seabrook remained at Johnson C. Smith for nine years.

In 1922 he accepted an offer to become dean of the Fayetteville State Normal School, the institution he would serve for the bulk of his active years. He remained dean until 1933, with leaves of absence to earn a master's degree from Columbia University in 1925 and to study at the University of Chicago in 1928. In 1933 Seabrook succeeded Dr. E. E. Smith as president of the newly reorganized Fayetteville State Teachers College, a position he held for twenty-three years. Under his leadership Fayetteville State experienced impressive growth, both in the expansion of its physical plant and in an increase in faculty and student populations. President Seabrook became known as an effective advocate for his school, especially in biennial appearances before the powerful

Advisory Budget Committee of the North Carolina legislature. Following his retirement from Fayetteville State in 1956, he served for one year as president of Johnson C. Smith University.

In addition to his educational activities, Seabrook became a community and state leader in various social welfare endeavors. Long active in the North Carolina Commission for Interracial Cooperation, he served as vice-president of that organization from 1934 to 1942. From 1932 to 1935 he was a member of the Advisory Committee of the U.S. Office of Education, and in 1932 he was a member of the Survey Commission of Methodist Colleges for Negroes. Locally, Seabrook was a member of the Fayetteville Parks and Recreation Commission (1948–49) and an influential participant on the hospital building committee of Cumberland County. A veteran of World War I, he was active in the American Legion and was a member of the Army Advisory Committee to the Third Army, organized in 1951 to assist in the racial integration of the armed forces.

In 1971 he was appointed to the North Carolina Employment Security Commission, the first Negro so named. He had also served as president of the North Carolina Teachers Association (1940–41), as associate editor of the *Journal of Negro Education*, and as a lifelong member of the National Education Association of the United States; he also participated in the Society for the Advancement of Education.

In 1954 Seabrook served briefly on the Pearsall Committee, a group appointed by Governor Luther Hodges to survey the implications for North Carolina of the 1954 Supreme Court decision outlawing racial segregation in the public schools. On leaving that committee, he presented a strong statement advocating that North Carolina obey the court's mandate.

A lifelong Presbyterian and a Democrat, Seabrook was twice married. His first wife, Mayme Louise Worsham, died fifteen months after their marriage, on 12 Dec. 1926. With his second wife, Mae Louise Hatchette Seabrook, whom he married on 29 Sept. 1928, he had one daughter, Mae Louise. Seabrook remained active well into his eighties, continuing to serve as a trustee of the Central North Carolina Orphanage and of Johnson C. Smith University. He died in Fayetteville and was buried in Rockfish Memorial Park.

SEE: *Fayetteville Observer*, 27 Mar. 1974; *Greensboro Daily News*, 27 July 1961; Raleigh *News and Observer*, 28 May 1953, 28 Mar. 1974; *Who Was Who in the South and Southwest* (1959).

A. M. BURNS III

Seaton, William Winston *(11 Jan. 1785–16 June 1866)*, journalist, was born in King William County, Va., at Chelsea, the family home, which at that time contained ancestral portraits and memorabilia. He was one of four sons and three daughters of Augustine and Mary Winston Seaton, married in 1776; the grandson of George and Elizabeth Hill Seaton, married in 1734; and the great-grandson of Henry and Elizabeth Todd Seaton. Mary was the daughter of Samuel Winston of Louisa County, Va., of the family of Winstons of English ancestry, prominent and distinguished for both the leadership of the men and the graciousness of the women. Dolley Payne Todd Madison and Patrick Henry were of this line. Members of the family went to North Carolina, where they were outstanding citizens. Elizabeth, wife of George, was the daughter of Leonard Hill, of King William County. Elizabeth Todd, wife of Henry, was the daughter of "a gentleman of standing" in Gloucester County, Va. Henry Seaton, the eldest son of John, arrived in the colony of Virginia in 1690 with other Scottish Loyalists.

As a young boy William was under the training of tutors in the home. He early developed the love of reading, which was nurtured by the books in his father's fine library. He became interested in the sport of hunting and maintained his enthusiasm for it all his life. As a grown man he owned a farm and a shooting box in Prince George County, Va., and liked to "bag a dozen woodcock" when he was advanced in age. He entered a Richmond, Va., academy kept by Ogilvie, the Earl of Finlater, a Scotsman.

The death of his father occurred suddenly at this time and William, at age eighteen, began what proved to be his lifelong career, that of political journalism. For a short period he was assistant editor of the Richmond *Virginia Patriot*. He went from there to Petersburg, Va., where he was editor of the *Republican*. In the spring of 1807 he accepted the offer to become editor of the *North Carolina Journal* in Halifax, described as the "seat of elegance, wealth, and refinement." Seeking a larger sphere, he moved in 1809 to Raleigh, the "young capital," with a "society refined, intelligent, simple in manners, unaffected in worth." He became associated with Joseph Gales of the Raleigh *Register*. In 1799 Gales and his wife, Winifred Marshall Gales, had moved from Philadelphia, Pa., to Raleigh, established in 1792 as the state capital. Seaton paid a visit to his uncle, Joseph Winston, at his estate in Stokes County and wrote in a letter that he enjoyed the "full view" of the mountains from there. He was a lifetime lover of nature. On 30 Mar. 1809 he married the Gales's daughter, Sarah Weston.

In October 1812 the Seatons moved to Washington, D.C., where William joined his brother-in-law, Joseph Gales, Jr., on the *National Intelligencer*. In 1810 Gales had become sole proprietor of the paper formerly owned by Samuel Harrison Smith, who, in turn, had bought the senior Gales's paper in Philadelphia and, on moving to Washington with the government, had rechristened it. In Washington the Seatons enjoyed the esteem and respect of the prominent people of the city. Interesting letters of their life there are quoted in the Seaton biographical sketch by his daughter Josephine. Among them is one telling of the second Madison inauguration. Henry E. Davis gives a good description of their elegant home on E Street, North, built in 1823, where Mrs. Seaton was a charming hostess.

An active public servant, Seaton served as alderman (1819–31); mayor (1840–50), persistently pursuing the cause of public education during his terms; one of the founders of the Washington Monument Society; and treasurer of the board of regents of the Smithsonian Institution from the first meeting in 1846 until his death and on the first building committee. For many years he was an executive member of the American Colonization Society. He freed his own slaves. He enrolled in the Virginia militia and saw service at the Battle of Bladensburg in the War of 1812. He was a Unitarian, a Free Mason, and a Whig.

Seaton always conducted himself with candor and fairness. He wrote, "We established and have always conducted the *Intelligencer* as an organ of public intelligence and general discussion. We have never lent it to personal predilections or antipathies." His editorials were short and dignified, but it was his shorthand reports of Senate debates that proved to be his best work. The Congress authorized publication of his reports for the Senate, those of Joseph Gales, Jr., for the House, and those of earlier reporters for both House and Senate.

They were published by Gales and Seaton in forty-two volumes from 1834 to 1856 as *The Debates and Proceedings in the Congress of the United States*, more popularly known as *The Annals of Congress*.

In 1838 Seaton traveled to Canada. In 1855 he went to Europe for three months and called that trip a "steeple chase." In 1859 the Seatons celebrated their golden wedding anniversary. When Joseph Gales, Jr., died in 1860, James C. Welling became associated with Seaton on the paper. On Christmas Day in 1863 Sarah Gales Seaton was buried after an illness of ten days. The *National Intelligencer* of 31 Dec. 1864 announced Seaton's retirement.

Family records list eleven children for the Seatons: Augustine Fitzwhylson, Julia, Altona, Gales, William Henry, Ann Eliza, Josephine, Caroline, Virginia, Malcolm, and Arthur. The oldest, a West Point graduate, died when his health failed during an expedition against the Indians on the plains of the Ozarks in 1835. A son, aged six, died in 1827 in a riding accident. Josephine survived her parents and published the biographical sketch. Caroline married Francis Schroeder.

In 1974 the National Portrait Gallery of the Smithsonian Institution acquired a portrait of William Winston Seaton. Since it was painted in 1822, it had been in the possession of the family, coming to the present generation through the line of Caroline Seaton Schroeder. It is an oil on paper, mounted on panel, attributed to Joseph Wood (ca. 1778–1830), eight and three-fourths inches by six and one-half inches. The pose is knee-length and bears out the description of him as "tall, vigorous, handsome." A woodcut reproduced in *Harper's* also shows him as a very handsome man. Clark shows two likenesses: a portrait of G. P. A. Healy and a Mathew Brady photograph.

SEE: *Appleton's Cyclopedia of American Biography*, vol. 5 (1887); *Atlantic Monthly*, October 1860, July 1871; Catalogue of American Portraits, National Portrait Gallery Files; Allen C. Clark, "William Winston Seaton and His Mayoralty," Records of the *Columbia Historical Society*, vol. 29–30; Henry E. Davis, "The Seaton Mansion," *Records of the Columbia Historical Society*, vol. 29–30; *DAB*, vol. 8 (1963); Harold D. Eberlein and Cortland Van D. Hubbard, *Historic Houses of George-Town and Washington City* (1958); *Harper's Weekly*, 16 Jan. 1858; Frederick L. Harvey, *Monograph of the Washington National Monument Dedicatory Ceremonies* (1885); Blackwell P. Robinson, ed., *The North Carolina Guide* (1955); Josephine Seaton, *William Winston Seaton of the "National Intelligencer": A Biographical Sketch* (1871); Oren Andrew Seaton, ed., *The Seaton Family* (1906).

CAROLINE HOLMES BIVINS

Seawell, Benjamin *(1741–16 July 1821)*, Revolutionary Patriot and legislator, was born in St. Andrew's Parish, Brunswick County, Va., the son of Benjamin and Lucy Hicks Seawell. In 1770 the elder Seawell and his family moved to Bute County, N.C., some thirty miles south of their former home, where he died in 1778. His will, probated in November 1778, mentioned his wife Lucy; sons Joseph, Thomas, and Benjamin; married daughters Mary Hill, Sally King, Elizabeth Mabry; and unmarried daughters Nancy, Rebecca, and Mildred. His sons Benjamin and Joseph and his son-in-law Green Hill were named executors. In addition to the usual bequests of land and slaves, the will referred to a bookcase and a colt by the racehorse Mark Anthony.

Young Benjamin Seawell was an early member of the Bute County Safety Committee in 1775. Though he had been a resident of the county for only a few years, he was elected a delegate to the Provincial Congress held in Halifax in November 1776. In 1777 he represented Bute in the senate, and on 19 November he introduced a bill to divide the county. No action was taken until 1779, when Bute was finally divided into the counties of Warren and Franklin. Because Seawell's lands fell in the latter county, the act of the legislature establishing Franklin directed that the first court be held at Seawell's residence. He represented Franklin in the senate in 1779. In May of that year the Assembly appointed him as one of the commissioners to determine a suitable place for the capital in Johnston, Wake, or Chatham County. Seawell was a member of the Council of State for North Carolina in 1781–82 and 1795.

Serving in the militia as lieutenant, captain, and colonel, he saw active duty in the closing years of the Revolution when the scene of conflict shifted to the southern colonies. Several letters from Colonel Seawell concerning the performance of his duties have been preserved in the state records. In a letter of 2 Oct. 1780 to General Horatio Gates, General Jethro Sumner referred to Seawell as "a diligent good officer of the line he fills." The march of Lord Cornwallis northwards through the state in the spring of 1781 incited uprisings among the local Tories, and Seawell wrote from his home county on 13 May 1781 that "our situation at present is not very comfortable. Not a man of any rank or distinction or scarcely any man of property has lain in his house since the British passed through Nash County."

Sometime before his death, Seawell moved to Tennessee and died near Lebanon in Wilson County. He was buried at McMurray Place in Horn Springs. In 1927 a monument was erected to his memory in Lebanon. In addition, his name is inscribed on a monument on the grounds of the capitol in Nashville erected to the memory of the Revolutionary officers who died in Tennessee.

Seawell married first, in 1768, Mary Booker. After her death in 1786, he married Susan Brown, the widow of Thomas Tullocks. He was the father of sons William, Benjamin, Joseph, and John, and daughters Elizabeth and Margaret.

SEE: John Bennett Boddie, *Seventeenth-Century Isle of Wight County, Virginia* (1938); Walter Clark, ed., *State Records of North Carolina*, vols. 12, 14–15, 17, 20, 24 (1895–1905); Fitzhugh Lee Morris, comp., *Lineage Book, North Carolina Society Sons of the American Revolution* (1951); Raleigh *Register*, 24 Aug. 1821; Ben Lee Seawell, *Genealogy of Col. Benjamin Seawell and Lucy Hicks* (1935).

CLAIBORNE T. SMITH, JR.

Seawell, Henry *(23 Dec. 1774–6 Oct. 1835)*, lawyer, legislator, attorney general, and judge, was born in that portion of Franklin County that was then Bute County. The son of Joseph and Martha Macon Seawell, he was principally of English ancestry. His father, a landowner and planter, was the son of Benjamin Seawell and the brother of Colonel Benjamin Seawell of the American Revolution. His mother was the daughter of Gideon and Priscilla Jones Macon and the sister of Nathaniel Macon, North Carolina statesman. Although his formal education was limited, young Seawell prepared himself for the law profession, was awarded his law license, which is dated at Hillsborough 10 Apr. 1797, and at about that time began practicing in Raleigh. He was the first lawyer to offer his services in the new capital city.

Early in his career he became interested in public office, and he represented Wake County in the 1799 session of the General Assembly. Seawell served six terms in the house during the years 1799–1802, 1810, and 1812. For eight sessions, 1821 to 1826 and in 1831–32, he was a state senator from Wake. In 1803 he became attorney general of North Carolina, an office that he held until 1808. He was appointed judge of the superior court in July 1811 and served until the end of that year; reappointed in 1813, he maintained his seat until his resignation in 1819, following the General Assembly's failure to appoint him a member of the newly created supreme court. He began a third term on the superior court bench in 1832 and presided until his death.

In 1823 Seawell represented the United States as arbitrator on a commission to settle claims and legal controversies with Great Britain arising from the conditions of the Treaty of Ghent. His able performance during this assignment was highly praised by Secretary of the Commission Charles Manly (later governor of North Carolina). It was principally through Seawell's efforts and influence that the capital remained in Raleigh following the destruction of the capitol building by fire in 1831. At the time Fayetteville made a vigorous and almost successful bid to have the seat of government moved to that city. After much political maneuvering and delay, Seawell won legislative approval of a bill that appropriated $50,000 to rebuild the capitol on the original site in Raleigh. Then he and the other four members of the building commission in a bold move spent the entire appropriation on the building foundation. Additional appropriations were eventually made in order to produce the architectural classic that still stands. In 1835 Seawell was a delegate from Wake County in the state constitutional convention, where he took a prominent part in the considerations and actions of that body. He was unsuccessful, however, in his opposition to the disfranchisement of the free Negro and to the proposal for biennial (instead of annual) meetings of the General Assembly.

In politics he was identified with the Republican party of that day (later known as the Democratic-Republican party and finally as the Democratic party). In a letter of introduction from Nathaniel Macon to Thomas Jefferson, Seawell was characterized as "A worthy man of the old Republican school in politics." In middle or late life he was described as handsome, possessing a ruddy complexion and white hair; an existing portrait indicates the same physical features. In professional life, he demonstrated outstanding legal abilities, with a keen interest in public and political issues.

On 17 Apr. 1800 he married Grizelle Hinton, the daughter of Major John Hinton and the granddaughter of Colonel John Hinton. They had nine children: John Hinton, Joseph James, Leonard Henderson, William, Pherabe Smith, Henry, Jr., Robert Williams, Richard Bullock, and Martha Macon. Henry Seawell died at his home in Raleigh. He was buried in the family cemetery which was then adjacent to his home (now on Hill Street in northeastern Raleigh), but his grave and the others in this cemetery (including the markers) were moved in 1977 to Oakwood Cemetery, Raleigh.

SEE: Samuel A. Ashe, ed., *Biographical History of North Carolina*, vol. 2 (1905); Kemp P. Battle, *Early History of Raleigh* (1893); J. G. de R. Hamilton, ed., *Papers of Thomas Ruffin*, vol. 1 (1918); Thomas Jefferson Papers (letter from Nathaniel Macon, 7 Jan. 1826) (Library of Congress, Washington, D.C.); Ellen Mordecai, *Gleanings from Long Ago* (1933); *Raleigh: Capital of North Carolina* (1942); Raleigh *Register*, 22 Apr. 1800, 13 Oct. 1835; Henry T. Shanks, ed., *Papers of Willie P. Mangum*, vol. 1 (1957).

HENRY SEAWELL

Seawell, Herbert Floyd *(8 Aug. 1869–15 Feb. 1949)*, lawyer and public official, was born in Wallace, Duplin County, the son of Dr. Virgil Newton and Ella Croom Seawell. His father was a native of Moore County, but after receiving an M.D. degree from the University of Maryland, he began his career as a medical practitioner in Bladen. His maternal grandmother, a Moore of the old Brunswick community, was a descendant of Alfred Moore, for whom Moore County was named.

Young Seawell attended the graded school at Goldsboro, Clement High School, Wallace, and Wakefield School. After a written examination he received a North Carolina state certificate and for a year taught school at Clarksville, Va. During this period he was also reading law under Dr. John Manning and James E. Sheppard. He entered Wake Forest College for special courses in 1890 and was graduated from the law school of The University of North Carolina in 1892. In the latter year the supreme court granted him a license to practice. He opened his law office in Carthage and from that town entered on his long and successful career as a lawyer.

At the Market House in Fayetteville in 1894, Seawell was nominated by the Republican-Populist party for solicitor of the Seventh District, which at the time included the counties of Cumberland, Richmond, Anson, Bladen, Robeson, Columbus, Moore, and Brunswick. Elected, he served in that position for four years.

In 1898 he received the Republican-Populist nomination for judge of the superior court but lost at the polls. Two years later he was the Republican nominee for lieutenant governor but again did not win. In 1904 he declined to be his district's Republican candidate for the U.S. Congress. In 1907 Judge Jeter C. Pritchard appointed him a special master for some cases involving intricate law knowledge and research. Pritchard was so impressed with his work that he recommended Seawell to President Theodore Roosevelt as a promising jurist. Upon the death of Judge Thomas Richard Purnell, U.S. district judge for eastern North Carolina, Roosevelt, at the close of his administration in 1909, appointed Seawell to fill that judgeship. But the senate, embroiled at the time in partisan politics, dallied and, though no complaint was filed against Seawell, did not act on the nomination. Finally, leading partisans persuaded the incoming president, William Howard Taft, to appoint a Democrat. However, on 1 Mar. 1910, though Seawell did not apply for the position, President Taft appointed him U.S. attorney for the Eastern District of North Carolina, a post that Seawell served with distinction from 1910 to 1914.

In 1928 the Republican party nominated him for governor of the state. Although he received more votes than any Republican at the time, he did not win the election. In 1929 President Herbert Hoover appointed him to the U.S. Board of Tax Appeals (now the U.S. Tax Court). Judge Seawell's record on the tax board, where he served from 1929 to 1936, was reported by the national press as unique: "Of the many cases decided by Judge Seawell over the six years, sixteen were appealed to the United States Supreme Court. In passing on these appeals, the Supreme Court, as shown by their reports and opinions, found no error in any case and confirmed each of Judge Seawell's decisions."

He held office in the North Carolina Bar Association, American Bar Association, and American Law Institute. He was a Republican, a Mason, a member of Kiwanis, and a deacon and trustee of the present Baptist church in Carthage. In the forefront of progress in the county, Seawell served as chairman of the local school board, aided in the formation of the Pinehurst Forum, and, having built a store-office building on Courthouse Square in

Carthage, constructed the first concrete sidewalk in the town. When the old elm trees on the courthouse lawn were destroyed shortly after the erection of the present courthouse, he petitioned the county commissioners for permission to plant four white oaks on the grounds: two on either side of the east and west entrances. Seawell personally selected the trees from his own farmlands and had them planted in the fall of 1927. They are now taller than the three-story courthouse and have a pleasing complementary spread. In 1964 a bronze plaque commemorating Seawell's gift was placed on a side wall of the courthouse, at the east entrance.

On 30 July 1895 Seawell married Ella McNeill, the daughter of Colonel Alexander Hamilton and Margaret Currie McNeill. They had three children: Ella Meade, Herbert Floyd, Jr., and Henry.

SEE: *The State* magazine, 12 July 1941; *Wake Forest Student* 30 (February 1911); *Who's Who in America* (1936); *Who's Who in Jurisprudence* (1925).

K. S. MELVIN

Seawell, Herbert Floyd, Jr. (Chub) *(5 Nov. 1904–30 Sept. 1983)*, attorney, after-dinner speaker, editorial writer, and religious lay leader, was born in Carthage, the son of Herbert Floyd, Sr., and Ella McNeill Seawell. A graduate of Wake Forest College and of the Wake Forest law school, he joined his father's law firm upon graduation but had to wait until he was twenty-one to receive his license to practice. In 1926 he was an unsuccessful Republican candidate for solicitor in Moore County. From 1927 to 1941 he was U.S. referee in bankruptcy, and in 1928 he worked for his father's gubernatorial campaign. Active in town affairs, he served as town attorney in the period 1935–40.

Seawell treated friend and foe with a jolly form of respect, playfully calling them "Cousin," followed by a long string of colorful adjectives before saying their name. He was well known throughout the state because of his nonstop stream of letters to newspaper editors and a busy schedule of after-dinner speeches. Perhaps because of his appearance he was nicknamed "Chub" and seldom referred to by his given name. In editorials and speeches he combined his flair for humor and right-wing criticisms. During World War II, while running for the state senate, Seawell advised citzens: "Don't talk around strangers, there is a government agent in every crowd and before you know it you may be off to jail for violating some New Deal rule you didn't know existed." He described himself as a local Will Rogers or Mark Twain style humorist. As a lawyer he thrived on captivating juries. He would appear in court wearing sneakers and a cap that proclaimed " Jesus is Lord,~" then would preach to the jury, punctuating his points by yelling every fifteen to twenty minutes. He won most of his cases.

In 1952 as the Republican nominee for governor against William B. Umstead, Seawell advocated "Ike in the driver's seat and me in the rumble seat." He attacked the notion that North Carolina was a progressive state, pointing to glaring social problems that he said the Democratic party virtually ignored. Calling himself a "consecrated layman" of the Baptist church, he also spoke out in favor of Prohibition. Despite "campaigning as though he could win," Seawell attracted just over a third of the vote, although that was more than the past three Republicans had received. Proud of his efforts, he was deeply angered when his party rejected him for the patronage position of U.S. district attorney for the Piedmont. Consequently he captured headlines by publicly lambasting the GOP for its "fascist rule" and "carpetbagger" politics, then quit the party.

Seawell published two books, *Sir Walter Raleigh: The Earl of Chatham* (1959) and *Satire in Solid Skitches* (1974). Both consisted of folksy essays with pearls of Chub's wisdom and sketches (or "skitches," as he termed them) of local leaders. References to state leaders such as Governor Daniel K. Moore—"Dan Klan Speaker Ban Moore"—inevitably were branded with Seawell's distinctive style. His colorful phraseology caught the eye of Jesse Helms, who invited him to fill in for him on radio station WRAL when the editorialist went on vacation. His comments, however, increasingly took on the cast of racial diatribes, and on occasion Helms had to rein in Chub.

In the early 1970s Seawell joined the right-wing American party and in 1976 ran for governor on that ticket. He devoted the final years of his life to the Gospel Chapel Mission (of which he was president in 1952) in Carthage and to conservative politics.

In 1926 Seawell marrried Jane Bloxham, and they were the parents of a daughter, Betty Jane (Mrs. Paul E. Freed). Following the death of his first wife, he married Mrs. Harriett McGraw.

SEE: *Charlotte Observer*, 1 Oct. 1983; *Durham Morning Herald*, 2 Dec. 1975; *Greensboro Daily News*, 20 June 1952, 29 Dec. 1974 (portrait); William S. Powell, ed., *North Carolina Lives* (1962); Herbert Floyd Seawell Papers (Manuscript Department, East Carolina University Library, Greenville); Southern Pines *The Pilot*, 3 Dec. 1975, 5 Oct. 1983; *Who's Who in the South and Southwest* (1963); *Winston-Salem Journal*, 25 Oct. 1976.

JONATHAN HOUGHTON

Seeley, Walter James *(30 Nov. 1894–29 July 1974)*, electrical engineer and engineering educator, was born at Hazelton, Pa., the son of Frank Wesley and Mame Seaborne Seeley. In 1913 he was graduated from the Polytechnic Institute of Brooklyn, where he received a degree in electrical engineering in 1917. He earned a master's degree in physics from the University of Pennsylvania in 1924 and spent the next two years at Columbia University for special study in engineering. Beginning as an instructor in electrical engineering at the University of Pennsylvania in 1919, he was promoted to a full professor in 1929 and to chairman of the department in 1935. In 1953 he became dean of the College of Engineering at Duke University in Durham and one of the original group of fourteen faculty members named to a James B. Duke Professorship.

Following his graduation from the Polytechnic Institute, Seeley was commissioned an ensign in the U.S. Navy and worked on antisubmarine devices from 1917 to 1919. For six months he also served at the Navy Radio School at Harvard University. Throughout his teaching career he frequently served as a consultant to municipalities, public utility agencies, and private companies. Among them were Trenton, N.J., for street lighting design; Cheltin Electric Company, Frankford Machine Company, and Gardner and Hepburn, all of Philadelphia, for design of radio equipment; and American Telephone and Telegraph Company, Duke Power Company, Fairchild Airplane and Engine Company, and others for various consultations.

During World War II he was stationed intermittently (June 1941–September 1944) at the U.S. Naval Ordnance Laboratory in Washington, D.C. He also assisted in the organization of the Technical Reserve and was a consultant on the staff of the technical director until 1946.

Professionally, he was a member of the American Institute of Electrical Engineers (chairman, North Carolina Section, 1936–37), Institute of Radio Engineers, American Society for Engineering Education, National Society of Professional Engineers, Professional Engineers of North Carolina, Naval Ordnance Technical Reserve (first president), and others. By gubernatorial appointment he was a member of the North Carolina State Board of Registration for Professional Engineers and Land Surveyors.

As a resident of Durham he was active with the chamber of commerce, served on a working committee of the Research Triangle Park, and was a trustee of Durham Technical Institute. As a member of the Duke Memorial Methodist Church, he taught a Bible class in the Sunday school and served several terms on the official board of the church.

He contributed to such professional publications as *Radiofax* (editor, 1925–31), *Journal of the American Institute of Electrical Engineers*, *Journal of Engineering Education*, *The Mathematics Teacher*, and *Electric Light and Power*. Among his books were *Manual of Direct Current and Alternating Current Circuit Experiments* (1932), *Impedence Computing Tables* (1936), and *Introduction to the Operational Calculus* (1941).

In 1920 Seeley married Emetta Susan Weed, and they became the parents of three children: Carolyn Ada (Mrs. H. A. Scott, Jr.), Mary Elizabeth (Mrs. James R. Hill, Jr.), and Naomi Ruth (Mrs. B. A. Ross). He was buried in Maplewood Cemetery, Durham.

SEE: Data files, Office of Information Services, Duke University, Durham; *Durham Sun*, 30 July 1974; *Who Was Who in America*, vol. 6 (1976).

C. SYLVESTER GREEN

Seely, Fred Loring *(22 Dec. 1871–14 Mar. 1942)*, pharmaceutical manufacturer, newspaperman, architect, and developer, was born in Fort Monmouth, N.J., the son of Colonel Uriah, a Union officer disabled by wounds at the Battle of Shiloh, and Nancy Hopping Seely. Having to support and help educate his brothers and sister, young Seely received only a public school education. At age eighteen he was hired by Parke-Davis and Company of Detroit as one of eight employees making up the first formal pharmaceutical firm in the country. He developed a machine to make pills or tablets and another to count and package them. While in Detroit Seely shared a loft over a boardinghouse stable with Henry Ford.

In 1897 Seely joined E. W. Grove in St. Louis as secretary-treasurer of Grove's pharmaceutical manufacturing company. One of this firm's leading products was Dr. Grove's Tasteless Chill Tonic, made from the bark of the cinchona tree from Peru to treat malaria. Due to poor health, Seely resigned and traveled. When political unrest in Peru threatened the source of quinine, an ingredient of the chill tonic, Seely moved thousands of young cinchona trees to Java, making that country the world's largest producer of quinine.

Returning to the United States, Seely in 1905 bought two Atlanta newspapers, *The Georgian* and the *Atlanta News*. John Temple Graves was his editor, and Grantland Rice and Bill Nye were staff members. Seely was one of the few newspapermen who supported Admiral Robert E. Peary's claim to have been the first to reach the North Pole in 1909. He also waged a campaign to establish Prohibition and to eliminate the convict lease system in Georgia. Under this system, private individuals could lease convicts for fifty cents a day without being subject to supervision from state penal authorities. Opposition arose from businessmen who benefited from this system; they ceased to advertise in his papers, and his life was threatened. Seely sold the papers to William Randolph Hearst, but his campaigns to end the practice and to establish Prohibition succeeded.

With only an eighth-grade education, Seely followed a lifelong ambition and entered the School of Architecture at Princeton University. In Princeton he lived next door to Professor Woodrow Wilson and they became lifelong friends. Seely, in fact, became a campaign manager for Wilson in his bid for president of the United States. Seely remained at Princeton only long enough to gain the information he felt necessary for an undertaking he had in mind. In the early stages of World War I President Wilson prevailed upon him to take charge of the Ford-financed peace mission to Norway aboard the SS *Oskar II*. Lay and clerical persons of stature met with the leaders of Great Britain and Germany in Norway in an unsuccessful effort to end the war.

Some time earlier, E. W. Grove had been sent to Asheville suffering from a pulmonary complication. Asheville, a center for the treatment of tuberculosis, had a number of sanatoriums. Recognizing the potential of the region for development as a tourist attraction, Grove sent for Seely. Together, they located and bought thousands of acres of land for hotel and residential development.

Moving to Asheville in 1912, Seely supervised the building of, and later operated, the Grove Park Inn, which, when it opened, was described as the finest resort in the world. It was completed in eleven months with 700 men and 400 mules working 24 hours a day in shifts. The developers also laid out a model city in the heart of Asheville, having spent weeks in Washington to secure authorization for a new Asheville Post Office to serve as a nucleus for this innovative plan. The old Battery Park Hotel was torn down, the mountaintop on which it stood was leveled, and a new Battery Park Hotel and shops were erected.

In 1916 Seely purchased the Biltmore Industries from Mrs. George W. Vanderbilt and in English cottage-type buildings expanded the operation where local artisans made and sold pottery, wove cloth, and produced other crafts. As far as possible, he employed the deaf and dumb in these industries; he was particularly interested in their welfare as he had a sister and a brother who were so afflicted.

Seely was convinced that if Asheville were to flourish, it must have a balanced economy with industry as well as tourism. To that effect, he spent months in Holland and ultimately persuaded Dr. Van Vlissingen, an old friend from his days in Java, to move his huge Enka Rayon Plant from Arnhem to Asheville. Seely was the only non-Dutch member of the Enka board of directors.

Like Grove, his friend, benefactor, and father-in-law, Seely contributed generously but anonymously to numerous causes. He provided surgery and hospital treatment for children, particularly clubfooted mountain children, and as a member of the Masonic order, he donated clothing for children in the Masonic Orphanage at Oxford, N.C.

In 1898 Seely married Evelyn Grove, the daughter of E. W. Grove, and they were the parents of Gertrude (Mrs. John Eller, Sr.), Fred L., Jr., John, and Louise. His home, Overlook on a mountain above Asheville, was a Gothic castlelike building to which he frequently made additions. It housed his large collection of manuscripts of the great composers and authors of history and his collection of early printing, including the works of Gutenberg and Caxton. He was a member of the Sons of the American Revolution and the Society of the Cincinnati. Seely was decorated by the pre-Hitler German Republic for finding and reburying the bodies of twelve crewmen of a German U-Boat who had died in the Veteran's Hospital near Asheville in 1918. A handsome monument was erected at the site. At the time of his death Seely directed operations of the Battery Park Hotel, owned by his wife. An active Episcopalian, he was buried in the churchyard of Calvary Church, Arden.

SEE: *Charlotte Observer*, 15 Mar. 1942; *Greensboro Daily News*, 20 Apr. 1934; *Nat. Cyc. Am. Biog.*, vol. 32 (1945); *New York Times*, 15 Mar. 1942; *Wachovia* 22 (1929); *Who Was Who in America*, vol. 2 (1950).

FRED L. SEELY, JR.

Sellers, Isaiah *(5 Oct. 1803–6 Mar. 1864)*, Mississippi River pilot, was born in Iredell County but for unknown reasons departed for the West as a young man. Sometime during the early 1820s he reached the Mississippi River, where he established his fortune and reputation. Sellers received his river baptismal by working on keel boats on the Ohio River–to–New Orleans run. By February 1825, however, he had shipped on board a steamboat, the *Rambler* out of Florence, Ala., and acquired the skills of a riverboat pilot. He next served on the *General Carroll*, operating between Nashville and New Orleans. On the *General Carroll* Sellers replaced the unreliable practice of shouted commands for soundings with the bell-tap, a system that improved river safety by ensuring that crewmen would hear the pilot's command to "heave the load." As steamboats increased in size, the practice of bell-tapping, generally ascribed to Sellers, became standard. After a brief tenure on the *President* in 1827, Sellers commenced his career in the upriver St. Louis trade as pilot of the *Jubilee*. In 1836 he helped construct and piloted the 400-ton steamboat *Prairie* out of Pittsburgh. The *Prairie* earned the distinction of being the first steamboat with a stateroom cabin to touch at St. Louis.

From the mid-1830s until his death, Sellers traded between his adopted home of St. Louis and New Orleans. One contemporary account credits him with 460 round-trip runs. Remarkably, Sellers "never sank a steamboat" or experienced a serious accident as a riverboat pilot. During a time when steamboats regularly foundered on snags and rocks in the river and suffered collisions and boiler explosions, his safety record was unsurpassed. The *Aleck Scott*, a vessel he partly owned and piloted for many years, became the favorite of both the commercial and traveling public. Sellers's success largely owed to his mastery of navigational skills, his long acquaintance with the river's patterns, his habit of recording river information in his diary for reference, and, doubtless, his legendary gift of memory. More important, he persisted in his experiments to increase river safety. In 1857, for example, he regularized the signals for meeting steamboats and so avoid collisions. In his emphasis on river safety, however, he did not sacrifice speed. In 1844, during the maiden season of the wooden sidewheeler *J. M. White, II*, he and copilot Nathan Way accomplished a record run of less than four days from New Orleans to St. Louis. This mark stood for a quarter of a century.

"Strictly a gentleman of the old school," Sellers maintained a staid, almost "stately," deportment that belied his good humor and fondness for company. He frequently entertained passengers with "rehearsals of his experiences as a boatman" and the history of the river. At least one contemporary found his reminiscences "amusing and instructive." Certainly, he did not lack for friends. But his sober bearing and lapses into self-inflating ramblings on the exploits of the rivermen exposed him to ridicule. Another river pilot, Samuel Langhorne Clemens, once subjected Sellers to a cruel burlesque as "Sergeant Fathom" (1859); later, in his *Life on the Mississippi* (1883), he devoted a chapter to limning an amusing, although inaccurate and sometimes farfetched, vignette of the benevolent "patriarch" of the rivermen. Clemens's attention to Sellers led him to insist that he adopted his pseudonym Mark Twain from Sellers, who, according to Clemens, contributed articles under that signature to New Orleans newspapers. Serious students of American literature dismiss this story as another of Clemens's fabrications. No articles signed Mark Twain appeared in any New Orleans newspapers for the period, and the few entries Sellers did publish under his own name consisted of bland, "rather routine river data" for the enlightenment of other pilots. Sellers evidenced no literary pretensions or aspirations. Indeed, his contemporaries knew him as a man of only "limited education" at best, and Sellers's manuscript logbook, since destroyed by fire, apparently revealed a tortured prose and wretched spelling, which raises the question of his capacity to write essays for newspaper publication. It is small wonder that editors of the papers that received his river intelligence labored hard to hammer his scribblings into a form intelligible to readers. Still, the Clemens account, which enjoys wide popular acceptance, when mixed with Sellers's real accomplishments, continues to assure Sellers's place as a folk hero along the Mississippi River.

After a "short illness," probably pneumonia, Sellers died. Before his death he had commissioned a bust, cut in sandstone, which today stands over his grave in the Bellefontaine Cemetery, St. Louis. He was survived by a nephew, for his wife Amanda, about whom nothing is known, died without issue twenty years earlier.

SEE: Ivan Benson, *Mark Twain's Western Years* (1938); Guy B. Cardwell, "Samuel Clemens' Magical Pseudonym," *New England Quarterly* 48 (June 1975); *DAB*, vol. 16 (1935); John F. Darby, *Personal Recollections* (1880); Ivan Fatout, "Mark Twain's Nom de Plume," *American Literature* 24 (March 1962); E. W. Gould, *Fifty Years on the Mississippi* (1889); Ernest E. Leisy, "Mark Twain and Isaiah Sellers," *American Literature* 13 (January 1942); Albert B. Paine, *Mark Twain: A Biography*, 3 vols. (1912); St. Louis *Daily Evening Gazette*, 9 May 1844, *Daily Missouri Gazette*, 10–11 Mar. 1864, *Missouri Republican*, 10, 17 Mar. 1864.

RANDALL M. MILLER

Selwyn, George Augustus *(11 Aug. 1719–25 Jan. 1791)*, landowner, was born on his family's county estate near Maston in the Cotswold Hills overlooking the Severn Valley in England. His father, Colonel John Selwyn, a man of education, ability, extensive influence, and ample means, was well known in the courts of the Georges; Selwyn also served as a member of Parliament for Gloucester (1734–47) as well as the treasurer of Queen Caroline's pensions. George's mother, Mary, the daughter of General Sir Anthony Farrington of Kent, has been described as a woman of unusual beauty, vivacity, and wit. She was a Woman of the Bed Chamber of Queen Caroline. After his father and an older brother died in 1751, George inherited large tracts of land in Piedmont North Carolina that the Crown had granted to his father in 1737.

George Selwyn's early education was at Eton College and continued at Hart College, Oxford. In 1745 he was forced to withdraw from Oxford without a degree to escape expulsion for using a chalice as a drinking cup at a student's party. Two years later, however, he entered Parliament where he remained until 1780. As a member of Parliament, Selwyn was silent and inactive, showing no serious interest in affairs of state. In general, he never exerted himself over either his business or his land interests, delegating this to agents.

The town of Charlotte, N.C., was being established on a small part of Selwyn's land about the time he inherited it. The whole tract was known as "The Selwyn Grant." He appointed Henry E. McCulloh, Abraham Alexander, Thomas Polk, and John Frohock as trustees and directors of the new town. Frohock, Alexander, and Polk were also commissioners to hold land in trust for the county of Mecklenburg on which to erect a courthouse, prison, and stocks. Because the land was a grant from the king, they felt obliged to settle one person to every 200 acres. McCulloh saw that the interest of his employer, Selwyn, would be advanced by locating the county seat on his lands, so Charlotte was formally made the county seat by act of Assembly in 1766. In 1767 Selwyn had his Carolina land surveyed by McCulloh as his agent, and it was found that the tract contained over 200,000 acres.

Even though he never visited his vast possessions in America, Selwyn showed a great deal of interest, as reflected in his correspondence and through his agent's activities. He also kept abreast of the movements of the British general, Lord Charles Cornwallis, through the Carolinas during the American Revolution.

In England Selwyn's reputation rested on his unusual wit and humor, which he was believed to have inherited from his mother. An early member of the leading London clubs, he was widely known and frequently quoted. He was on friendly terms with statesmen, politicians, and literary men, as well as with the court circle.

Nevertheless, Selwyn evidently lived a lonely personal life; he never married and had no near relatives in his last years. He adopted a girl named Maria Fagniani because of his fondness for children—a trait that he generously demonstrated frequently over a long period of time. There was a dispute between the Duke of Queensbury and Selwyn over the paternity of the girl, and both left large sums to her at their deaths, but recent studies suggest that Selwyn was not her father.

In his later years, which he spent in London, Selwyn suffered from gout and dropsy. He died at his home in St. James's. There is a portrait of him at Castle Howard painted by his friend Sir Joshua Reynolds showing Selwyn with Frederick, fifth earl of Carlisle, and with his beloved dog, Raton. Selwyn is depicted as a handsome man with a periwig and dressed in the elegant and expensive style of the day—a velvet suit, silk hose, lace frills, and a fine stack buckle.

SEE: *DNB*, vol. 17 (1882); Fanning-McCulloh Papers (Southern Historical Collection, University of North Carolina, Chapel Hill); S. Parnell Kerr, *George Selwyn and the Wits* (1909 [portraits]); *North Carolina Booklet* 16 (July 1916); William S. Powell, ed., *The Correspondence of William Tryon and Other Selected Papers*, vol. 1 (1980); E. S. Roscoe and Helen Clergue, eds., *George Selwyn: His Letters and His Life* (1899 [portraits]); William L. Saunders, ed., *Colonial Records of North Carolina*, vols. 5–7 (1887–90); Oscar Sherwin, *A Gentleman of Wit and Fashion: The Extraordinary Life and Times of George Selwyn* (1963 [portrait]).

GAYLE E. CALDER

Sequoyah *(1770?–August 1843)*, inventor of Cherokee syllabary, was born in the Indian town of Taskigi, Tenn., then western North Carolina. His father probably was Nathaniel Gist, a trader who abandoned his mother, a woman of mixed Indian blood, before the birth of the child. He grew to manhood ignorant of the Indian language and engaged in hunting and fur trading until crippled by an accident. Increased contacts with white people led him to ponder over their "talking leaves," and he resolved to master the secret and apply it to the benefit of the Indians. By 1821, despite ridicule, he had completed a table of eighty-five or eighty-six syllables in the Cherokee language.

A council of chiefs approved his work, and thousands of Indians learned to read and write. In 1822 he visited the western Cherokee, gave them his syllabary, and made his home with them. His invention stimulated the printing of books and a newspaper, *Cherokee Phoenix*, in the Indian language. Sequoyah was active in the political life of the tribe and in 1828 visited Washington, D.C., as an envoy. In 1841 the Cherokee National Council voted him an allowance and two years later an annuity of $300, which was continued to his widow. Early in 1843 he began a journey in search of a band of Cherokee said to have moved to the region west of the Mississippi, and he died in Mexico in the fall of that year. According to one account, he had five wives and twenty or more children. His is commemorated by a California redwood tree called Sequoyah and a statue in Washington, D.C.

SEE: *DAB*, vol. 16 (1935); Grant Foreman, *Sequoyah* (1938); *Greensboro Daily News*, 25 Dec. 1938; *Los Tulares* (Quarterly Bulletin, Tulare County, California Historical Society), no. 19 (June 1954).

STANLEY J. FOLMSBEE

Settle, Thomas *(9 Mar. 1789–5 Aug. 1857)*, congressman and superior court judge, was the son of David and Rhoda Mullins Settle of Rockingham County and a member of one of the most important political dynasties in North Carolina history. He was the father of Thomas Settle, Jr., legislator, supreme court justice, and a founder of the North Carolina Republican party; the uncle and father-in-law of David S. Reid, senator and governor; and the uncle by marriage of Stephen A. Douglas, of Illinois, the prominent senator and presidential candidate in 1860.

Settle was educated by tutors, read law, and was admitted to the bar in 1816. In the same year he was elected to the North Carolina House of Commons, where he served on the committees of propositions and grievances and privileges and elections. The next year he defeated Bartlett Yancey for a seat in the U.S. House of Representatives and won another term, serving in the Fifteenth and Sixteenth congresses (1817–21). Declining to run again, probably because he had recently married, he returned to his law practice. Settle ran for the House of Commons again in 1826 and in the two succeeding sessions. He was an active member of the General Assembly in both committee work and floor debate. For two sessions he served on a conference committee, the committee of propositions and grievances, and a select committee on the wool tariff. When Speaker of the House James Iredell won the governorship, Settle was elected speaker on 6 Dec. 1827 to succeed him.

He served as speaker of the house throughout the 1828 legislative session. In this assembly Robert Potter sponsored resolutions to investigate mismanagement of banks in the state and to prosecute the banks in order to cancel their charters. Some banks were indeed poorly managed, but Potter's resolutions threatened the whole banking structure of North Carolina. The House of Commons vote was a tie, and Speaker Settle cast the deciding vote against the resolution to prosecute the banks. After this session he did not seek reelection.

On 24 Dec. 1832 the legislature voted to send Settle to the state superior court. After serving ably on the bench for twenty-two years, he resigned on 1 Aug. 1854 because of declining health. In his day he was one of the most highly respected superior court judges in the state. A contemporary and early biographer, John H. Wheeler, wrote that Settle was "distinguished for his ability as a statesman and as a judge, and esteemed for his virtues, learning, and deportment." After the founding of the Whig party in the 1830s, Settle was considered one of its leading members. In 1836 he was nominated for a seat in the U.S. Senate but was defeated in the legislature by one vote. Settle became a trustee of The University of North Carolina in 1826 and remained on the board until his death in 1857. An active Baptist, he was a member of the Hogan's Creek Church and was moderator of the Beulah Association for a number of years. He served as a trustee of Wake Forest College. In his lifetime he accumulated several thousand acres of land, incorporating several large plantations. In 1850 he owned thirty slaves.

On 21 Sept. 1820 Settle married Henrietta Williams Graves (1799–1886), of Caswell County, the daughter of Azariah and Elizabeth Williams Graves and the sister of Calvin Graves, a state legislator. Thomas and Henrietta Settle had four daughters and two sons: Henrietta Williams and Caroline L., twins born on 7 Oct. 1824 (Henrietta married Governor David S. Reid, and Caroline married the governor's brother, Hugh K. Reid); Thomas, Jr., born 23 Jan. 1831; Fannie K., born 10 Nov. 1833 (married first J. W. Covington and then, after his death, Oliver H. Dockery; David A., born 7 Nov. 1839 (remained unmarried); and Elizabeth, born in 1842 and died young. Thomas and Henrietta Settle died in Rockingham County and were buried in the family cemetery near Reidsville. Photographs of the Settles are in possession of the family.

SEE: Kemp P. Battle, *Sketches of the University of North Carolina* (1889); *Biog. Dir. Am. Cong.* (1950); *Journals of the Senate and House of Commons of the General Assembly of the State of North Carolina* (1816, 1826–28); John W. Moore, "Early Baptist Laymen in North Carolina" (a scrapbook of *Biblical Recorder* clippings in the North Carolina Collection, University of North Carolina, Chapel Hill); William R. Reece, *The Settle-Suttle Family* (1974); Rockingham County Deeds and Wills; Richard R. Saunders, *Open Doors and Closed Windows* (1948); Settle Family Cemetery, Rockingham County; U.S. Census, 1850; John H. Wheeler, ed., *Reminiscences and Memoirs of North Carolina and Eminent North Carolinians* (reprint, 1966).

LINDLEY S. BUTLER

Settle, Thomas, Jr. *(23 Jan. 1831–1 Dec. 1888),* state supreme court justice and a founder of the North Carolina Republican party, was the son of Thomas and Henrietta Graves Settle of Rockingham County. His father was a speaker of the House of Commons, congressman, and superior court judge. Thomas Settle, Jr., was educated by private tutors and attended The University of North Carolina, where he was graduated with an A.B. degree in 1850. He then became the private secretary of the recently elected Democratic governor, David S. Reid, who was Settle's brother-in-law and first cousin. After a year on the governor's staff, Settle studied law with state supreme court justice Richmond M. Pearson, a former colleague of his father's on the superior court bench. In 1854 Settle began practicing law in his native county.

Although his father was a leading Whig, Settle, probably influenced by Governor Reid, chose the Democratic party and was elected to the House of Commons in 1854. Reelected in two succeeding terms, he became speaker of the house in the 1858–59 session. In the presidential election of 1856 he was a Democratic elector for James Buchanan, and in 1860 he supported his cousin by marriage, Stephen A. Douglas. Settle was appointed to the board of trustees of The University of North Carolina in 1856 and served until 1874. In November 1860 he was elected solicitor of the Fourth Judicial Circuit.

Although he opposed secession, when North Carolina left the Union, Settle volunteered for the army and was commissioned a captain in the Third North Carolina Regiment. After a year's service he returned to his position as solicitor and remained in that office throughout the war. In the postwar era Settle became one of the most prominent political leaders in the state. He was a delegate to the constitutional convention of 1865–66, which sought to meet the conditions of presidential Reconstruction so that the state could rejoin the Union. In this convention Settle was chairman of committees that prepared resolutions abolishing slavery and repudiating the state's war debt. He won a seat in the state senate in the fall of 1865, and when the assembly met in November, he was elected speaker of the senate. A supporter of William W. Holden for governor, Settle gradually became identified with the radical congressional Reconstruction program and urged the early adoption of the Fourteenth Amendment. As an heir of the prewar plantation elite, he was nevertheless a strong Unionist and would not compromise with the secession-tainted Democratic-Conservatives. Consequently, he was drawn into the Republican fold and became one of the founding leaders of the state Republican party in the spring of 1867.

In April 1868 Settle was elected an associate justice of the state supreme court. He resigned on 24 Mar. 1871 to accept an appointment as the U.S. minister to Peru. After he had spent a year in Lima, illness forced his resignation from the diplomatic service on 20 Feb. 1872. Upon his return to North Carolina, he was appointed on 20 June by Governor Todd Caldwell to a vacancy on the supreme court bench. An associate justice for four years, Settle resigned on 13 July 1876 to accept the Republican nomination for governor. In 1872 he presided over the Republican National Convention and was nominated that fall as the Republican candidate for the U.S. House of Representatives from his district. He narrowly lost the election to Democrat James M. Leach by 268 votes of some 21,000 cast. In 1876 Settle was opposed in the gubernatorial race by Zebulon B. Vance, Civil War governor and the most popular politician in the state. The 1876 canvass, which centered on a colorful series of joint debates, is considered one of the most important elections in North Carolina history and is known as "The Battle of the Giants." Settle's defeat officially ended Reconstruction and relegated the Republican party to a permanent minority, a position that has been overcome only twice in the last century. In January 1877 Settle was appointed a U.S. district court judge in Florida. He served on the federal bench until his death eleven years later.

Settle possessed a superb physique, a charming personality, and a superior intellect. A contemporary, H. S. Pearson, wrote of Settle that "his career bears no inconsiderable resemblance to that of the second Fox. Like him, the major part of his life was passed in opposition to the prevailing current of opinion; he had the same constitutional intrepidity, the same dauntless defiance when pressed, the same capacity to attach friends, the same enjoyment of the good things of the earthly life."

Although not a student of the technicalities of the law, Settle had, according to Judge R. P. Dick, "in a high degree the genius of common sense and seemed to have an intuitive knowledge of the eternal principles of reason, justice, and truth." He was considered a fair and impartial judge.

As a gift from his father, Settle received the Mulberry Island Plantation of over one thousand acres on the Dan River and constructed a home there in 1860. That year he owned twenty-nine slaves. In 1859 he had married Mary Glen (d. 4 Mar. 1895), the daughter of Tyre Glen of Yadkin County. The couple had nine children: Henrietta, Mary, Thomas III, Douglas, Elizabeth, Caroline, David, Florida, and Julia. The Settles moved to Greensboro in 1870, during the turbulent Reconstruction years, and retained their residence there even after he had been appointed to the federal bench in Florida. They were members of the Baptist church in Greensboro. A portrait of Thomas Settle is in the state Supreme Court Collection in Raleigh. He died and was buried in Greensboro.

Thomas Settle III (10 Mar. 1865–20 Jan. 1919) was born in Rockingham County, educated at Georgetown College in Washington, D.C., passed the bar in 1885, and began practicing law in Wentworth. He was solicitor of the Seventh Judicial District (1886–94), a Republican congressman for two terms (1893–97), and an unsuccessful candidate for governor in 1912. He later resided in Asheville but was buried in Wilmington, the home of his wife, Eliza Potter.

SEE: Kemp P. Battle, *Sketches of the University of North Carolina* (1889); *Biog. Dir. Am. Cong.* (1950); William P. Bynum, Jr., "Thomas Settle," *Literary and Historical Activities in North Carolina* (1907); *DAB*, vol. 8 (1935); J. G. de Roulhac Hamilton, *Reconstruction in North Carolina* (1914); *Journals of the Senate and House of Commons of the General Assembly of the State of North Carolina* (1860, 1865); William R. Reece, *The Settle-Suttle Family* (1974); John H. Wheeler, *Reminiscences and Memoirs of North Carolina and Eminent North Carolinians* (1884).

LINDLEY S. BUTLER

Sevier, John *(23 Sept. 1745–24 Sept. 1815)*, Indian fighter, land speculator, Revolutionary soldier, and statesman, was born near the present town of New Market, Va., the son of Valentine and Joanna Goade Sevier. Religious persecution drove the Xavier family, as the Seviers were known then, from France to England, and by 1740 Valentine and his brother William had arrived in America. Valentine, settling in the Shenandoah Valley in modern Rockingham County, Va., soon married and became a prosperous farmer, trader, merchant, and tavern owner.

The oldest of seven children, John Sevier received little formal education (he studied briefly in Fredericksburg and at Staunton Academy), but even as a youngster he demonstrated qualities of maturity, perseverance, affability, and good judgment, which in adult life made him a leader among the frontier people. At age sixteen he married Sarah Hawkins and settled in the vicinity of his birth where he farmed, dealt in furs, speculated in land, and ran a tavern. By 1773 he had received a commission in the Virginia militia, but in that year he moved with his immediate family to the Watauga region of North Carolina (then the western frontier of the state but now in Tennessee) and settled on the Holston River.

Sevier became a commissioner of the Watauga Association, a homespun government developed by the frontiersmen, and in that capacity was among those who petitioned North Carolina officials for recognition of Watauga. When officials created the Washington District (soon to become Washington County) from the Watauga settlement, Sevier was a delegate to the Provincial Congress in Halifax. Soon appointed a lieutenant colonel in the state militia, he became known for his prowess as an Indian fighter. As one writer has indicated, he was "a scourge of the Cherokees" as he drove the natives from the Watauga area.

Sevier's reputation as a leader and a soldier was greatly enhanced in 1780, when the Revolutionary War reached into the frontier and he, with other colonials, repelled the British at King's Mountain. Major Patrick Ferguson, the British officer assigned to protect the left flank of Lord Cornwallis's troops, had been annoyed by the presence of armed frontiersmen and determined to "march over the mountains" and "lay their country waste with fire and sword." Sevier and others got together a group of frontiersmen and, armed with rifles, went to meet him; they encountered Ferguson's army of more than one thousand men at King's Mountain just over the border in South Carolina. Effectively camouflaged, they killed and wounded more than one-third of the troops and made prisoners of the others. The victory, a turning point in the Revolution in the South, brought widespread recognition to Sevier and gave great impetus to his political and military career, which would continue for thirty-five years.

Several months before King's Mountain Sevier had moved his family southwards from the Holston settlements to land on the Nolichucky River. There he built a comfortable home, established a plantation that he called Plum Grove, served as clerk of the county court of Washington County, and became one of the West's foremost land speculators. It was because of his residence on the Nolichucky River that he acquired the name of "Chucky Jack."

Talk about western statehood began even before the war ended, and frontiersmen listened with considerable interest to plans developed by Thomas Jefferson for more than a dozen new states in the transmontane country. It was a spirit of independence and desire for recognition that brought about in 1784 the "State of Franklin," with Sevier as governor. In defiance of North Carolina, frontier leaders formed a government and petitioned Congress to create Franklin as the fourteenth state of the new Union. National authorities did not wish to defy a sovereign state, however, and within a few years the statehood movement collapsed. Sevier was arrested and charged with treason but was never tried.

In the same year that Franklin collapsed (1788), Sevier was elected to the North Carolina Senate and participated in the passage of a resolution pardoning him for his association with the rebellious Franklinites. He represented Greene County in the convention in which North Carolina voted to ratify the new federal Constitution. In 1790 he was elected to Congress.

After one term in the House Sevier returned home to participate in the affairs of the newly created Southwest Territory, which eventually would become the state of Tennessee. He probably was the choice of a majority of the backwoodsmen for governor of the territory, but that appointment was given to his friend, William Blount, who immediately appointed Sevier as one of the two brigadier generals. Sevier played a prominent role in the civil as well as military affairs of the territory. In December 1793 freemen possessing a freehold of at least fifty acres elected a territorial house of representatives consisting of thirteen members, who, in turn, selected a group of ten men from whom President George Washington appointed five to serve as a "council," or upper house. Sevier was one of the five appointed; his selection, Blount wrote, was "considered by the people at large a thing certain."

The territorial government continued to function until 1796, when Tennessee was admitted as the sixteenth state. In the selection of officials, voters elected Sevier as governor. The state constitution provided that the first governor should hold office until the fourth Tuesday in September 1797, that the term should be two years, and that an incumbent should "not be eligible more than six years in any term of eight." Sevier was reelected in 1797 and again in 1799.

Constitutionally barred from seeking the governorship in 1801, Sevier plunged into land speculation, farming, and military activity for a year or two but then returned to the hustings in 1803 and defeated incumbent governor Archibald Roane. He was reelected in 1805 and 1807 with little if any opposition and thus served for six terms as governor of Tennessee.

Sevier was faced with the usual problems of establishing a government in the rapidly growing frontier state, more than two-thirds of which was under Indian control when he became chief executive. The population of the state grew from approximately 85,000 to more than 250,000 while he was governor, and frontier towns such as Knoxville, Nashville, Jonesboro, Greeneville, Kingston, and Clarksville became commercial and trade centers. Land prices fluctuated, and Montgomery Bell began to development iron and soon became one of the greatest producers in the West.

After Sevier's term expired in 1809, the frontier leader was elected for one term to the state senate and then to the twelfth, thirteenth, and fourteenth sessions of Congress. Early in 1815, while still in Congress, he was appointed to a commission to survey the boundary provisions after a treaty was executed with the Creek Indians in the territory that soon became the state of Alabama. He died while fulfilling that obligation and was buried with honors by federal troops on the east bank of the Tallapoosa River near Fort Decatur. In 1887 his body was exhumed and reinterred on the court square in Knoxville. His monument over his grave in Knoxville summarizes his career: "John Sevier, Pioneer, soldier, statesman, and one of the founders of the Republic; Governor of the State of Franklin; six times Governor of Tennessee; four times elected to Congress; a typical pioneer, who conquered the wilderness and fashioned the State; a projector and hero of King's Mountain; fought thirty-five battles, won thirty-five victories; his Indian war cry 'Here they are! Come on boys!'"

SEE: John H. DeWitt, ed., "Journal of John Sevier," *Tennessee Historical Magazine* 5 (1919), 6 (1920); Carl Driver, *John Sevier: Pioneer of the Old Southwest* (1932); Cora Bales Sevier and Nancy C. Madden, *Sevier Family History, With the Collected Letters of General John Sevier . . .* (1961); Samuel C. Williams, *History of the Lost State of Franklin* (1924).

ROBERT E. CORLEW

Seymour, Augustus Sherrill *(30 Nov. 1836–19 Feb. 1897)*, federal judge, state judge, and legislator, the scion of a distinguished family including Governor Horatio Seymour, was born at Ithaca, N.Y., the son of Mary Sherrill and Hezekiah C. Seymour, state engineer of New York in 1850, prominent contractor, builder of railroads, and chief engineer of the New York, Lake Erie, and Western railroad. Following graduation from Hamilton College in 1856, he took law courses there, was admitted the next year to the bar, and began to practice in New York City. In 1864 he moved to New Bern and was admitted to the North Carolina bar in 1866 at the first term of the superior court after the Civil War.

Although Seymour was a carpetbagger in the South amid difficult times, his marked ability, honest and sympathetic character, and considerate and kindly personality endeared him to the New Bernians who returned home after the war. During corruptible eras his reputation remained untarnished. A staunch Republican, Seymour became city attorney and chairman of the judiciary committee in 1867. In May 1868 he was elected to the North Carolina House of Representatives for its extra session during 1 July–24 August. That fall he was appointed judge of the Craven County criminal court but resigned and went back to the state house for its regular session from 16 Nov. to 12 Apr. 1869. Elected a state senator in 1872, he became an influential member of the judiciary committee and the special committee on constitutional amendments.

Named a judge of the superior courts in 1874, Seymour served ably during the term ending in 1882. His sense of justice tempered with mercy made him so universally admired that his appointment as judge of the U.S. District Court by President Chester A. Arthur in 1882 met with general approval. He held the post until his death. He was a Presbyterian, Mason, and member of several collegiate societies. Both his alma mater and The University of North Carolina conferred upon him the LL.D. degree. His writings included *Seymour's Sixth and Seventh Digests of North Carolina Reports*.

On news of his death, the state supreme court adjourned in his memory. The Raleigh *News and Observer* commented: "From the day of his elevation to the bench, Judge Seymour eschewed politics, and grew to be a learned, upright and just judge, esteemed by the bar of all shades of political opinion. He was a man of scholarly tastes, had traveled extensively, and was one of the most accomplished men in the state." The *New Bern Weekly Journal* wrote: "He was regarded by his profession as one of the most learned and impartial judges on the bench. Socially Judge Seymour was held in high esteem, especially in this his own city. His manner was always courteous, and he was interested in everything going on. His loss will be very keenly felt by the entire community."

In 1863 Seymour married Nancy O. Barton (26 July 1838–26 Nov. 1905), the daughter of the Reverend John Barton, Presbyterian minister of Clinton, N.Y. She was active in civic and cultural affairs at New Bern, serving for a time as president of the Silver Cross chapter of the International Order of King's Daughters and Sons and then as chairman of its local circulating library. On 15 Feb. 1902 a meeting to consider the purchase of more books for the library was held at her fine frame home, which her husband had built on East Front and Short streets (now moved back to the south side of Change Street). This library, the first permanent one in New Bern, was the forerunner of the current New Bern–Craven County public library, one of the oldest in the state.

Both Judge and Mrs. Seymour were buried in Cedar Grove cemetery, New Bern. Surviving them were a daughter, Mrs. Cornelia Walsh, and a son, John Barton.

SEE: Samuel A. Ashe, ed., *Cyclopedia of Eminent and Representative Men of the Carolinas*, vol. 2 (1892) Gertrude S. Carraway, "History of the New Bern Library," in New Bern *Sun-Journal*, March 1937; Crockette W. Hewlett, *The United States Judges of North Carolina* (1978 [portrait]); Frank Nash, "Augustus Sherrill Seymour," in Charles L. Van Noppen Papers (Manuscript Department, Duke University Library, Durham); Tombstone inscriptions, Cedar Grove cemetery, New Bern.

GERTRUDE S. CARRAWAY

Shackelford, John Williams *(16 Nov. 1844–18 Jan. 1883)*, congressman, state legislator, Confederate officer, attorney, merchant, and farmer, was born at Richlands, the only child of Dr. John and Indiana Ambrose Humphrey Shackelford. Reared by his maternal grandfather, Colonel William A. Humphrey, Shackelford attended the Richlands Academy. He entered college but left at age seventeen to enter the Confederate army. From the rank of private in Company H of the Third North Carolina Regiment, he rose to the rank of lieutenant in the Thirty-fifth Regiment of North Carolina Volunteers and was taken prisoner near Greenville. In August 1865 he returned home, where on 19 Sept. 1865 he married Mary Catherine Wallace of Richlands.

A Democrat, Shackelford represented Onslow County in the North Carolina House of Representatives from 1872 to 1878 and in the North Carolina Senate from 1879 to 1880. In 1880 he was elected a representative to the Forty-seventh Congress and served from 4 Mar. 1881 until his death in Washington, D.C. In the state legislature Shackelford served on the Committee on Banks and Currency, the Committee on Fish and Fisheries, and as chairman of the Committee on Engrossed Bills. In the Congress he was a member of the Committee on Public Land Claims.

On the local level Shackelford served twice as a magistrate, farmed, and engaged in various mercantile ventures. He had a cotton gin in 1879, and he was a partner in Harget and Steed (1881) and in Harget, Taylor, and Company (1882). Though he had no children of his own, he raised a girl named Fannie Heath, whose indigent father gave her to the Shackelfords at age two and a half. The foster parents renamed her Katie Williams Shackelford.

Shackelford was a member of the Methodist Episcopal Church, South. He was interred in the Wallace family cemetery at Richlands. A photograph of him can be found in the Tucker Littleton Collection at the North Carolina State Archives, Raleigh.

SEE: *Biog. Dir. Am. Cong.* (1971); J. Parsons Brown, *The Commonwealth of Onslow: A History* (1960); John L. Cheney, Jr., ed., *North Carolina Government, 1585–1979* (1981); *Kinston Journal*, 8 May 1879; *Memorial Address, Life and Character of John Williams Shackelford* (1883 [portrait]).

TUCKER REED LITTLETON

Shaffner, Henry Fries *(19 Sept. 1867–3 Dec. 1941)*, banker, industrialist, and civic and church leader, was born in Salem, the son of Dr. John Francis and Caroline Louisa Fries Shaffner. He was educated in the Boys' School of the Moravian church and at The University of North Carolina, from which he was graduated in 1887 with a Ph.B. degree. His marriage to Agnes G. Siewers, which took place on 21 Nov. 1901, produced five children: Henry Siewers, who died in infancy, Eleanor Caroline (Mrs. R. E. Guthrie), Anna Pauline (Mrs. R. S. Slye), Emil Nathaniel, and Louis DeSchweinitz.

For several years following college Shaffner worked in his father's drug business, operated the pottery that had been established by his grandfather, and was involved in the tobacco business. In 1893 he and his uncle, Colonel F. H. Fries, organized the Wachovia Loan and Trust Company. Shaffner served as its secretary and treasurer until 1911, when the company was merged with the Wachovia National Bank to form the Wachovia Bank and Trust Company. He was vice-president of Wachovia Bank and Trust Company in Winston-Salem from 1911 to 1931 and chairman of its board of directors from 1931 to 1941. He was also president of Winston-Salem Building and Loan Association, president of Briggs-Shaffner Company, and a director of Oakdale Cotton Mills.

Shaffner was for ten years a commissioner of the town of Salem and was a member of the first board of aldermen of the consolidated towns of Winston and Salem. For several years he was secretary and treasurer of the Salem Water Supply Company. A lifelong member of the Moravian church, he served as president of its Central Board of Trustees and as a member of the Financial Board of the Southern Province of the Moravian church. He was a member of Sigma Alpha Epsilon fraternity, the Democratic party, the Twin City Club, and the Forsyth Country Club. Shaffner was buried in Salem Cemetery.

SEE: Adelaide L. Fries and others, eds., *Forsyth: The History of a County on the March* (1976); Daniel L. Grant, *Alumni History of the University of North Carolina* (1924); *North Carolina Biography*, vol. 4 (1928); *Who Was Who in America*, vol. 2 (1950).

PHILIP A. WALKER

Shaffner, John Francis *(14 July 1838–18 Sept. 1908)*, Civil War surgeon and leader in civic, business, and medical affairs, was born in Salem, the son of Henry and Lavinia Hauser Shaffner. Baptized and confirmed in the Moravian church, he was affiliated with the Salem congregation for the remainder of his life. Shaffner was educated in the Moravian schools of Salem, by private tutors (most notably, William Meinung), and at The University of North Carolina. He attended Jefferson Medical College, in Philadelphia, from which he was graduated on 14 Mar. 1860.

His private medical practice, which he had begun in Salem, was interrupted in 1861 when he volunteered as a private in Company A (later Company D), under Captain A. H. Belo, Twenty-first Regiment, North Carolina Troops. For a time he was an assistant surgeon with the Seventh, Twenty-first, and Thirty-third regiments. Promoted to surgeon in the Confederate army in March 1862, he served in the field with the Fourth and Thirty-third regiments and as brigade surgeon of Lawrence O'B. Branch's and Stephen D. Ramseur's brigades until the surrender of General Robert E. Lee's army at Appomattox Court House, Va., on 9 Apr. 1865. A chronicler of the Fourth Regiment wrote: "Chief Surgeon J. F. Shaffner was a man of splendid ability; a man of education and fine attainments, and always faithful to the important tasks committed to him." And in the chronicle of the Thirty-third Regiment it was written: "Our surgeons, Doctors J. F. Shaffner and John A. Vigal, were the kindest and best of men. They were ideal surgeons—capable, honest, firm, sympathetic, self-sacrificing, courageous and unremitting in their attentions to the sick and wounded, oftentimes exposing themselves to imminent peril in the discharge of their official duties. By such unflinching heroism and devotion to duty they won the gratitude of the entire command."

In a letter dated 27 May 1862, Shaffner wrote an enlightening comment about his own situation: "Surgeons are in ever-growing danger of becoming too abstract—of losing sympathy with passing emotions and sufferings, and particularly with those shared by numbers. The danger is, lest we forget, we too are mortal, . . . because now, at present, we do not feel the pains, the agonies, of the poor sufferers in our charge."

Shaffner's wartime experiences included his capture by enemy troops while attending the wounded of his regiment who had necessarily been left behind. His friendships formed in the army remained strong for the remainder of his life, and for years he maintained an active interest in the affairs of the Confederate veterans, himself a charter member of the Norfleet Camp, United Confederate Veterans.

On 16 Feb. 1865 he married Caroline Louisa Fries, a native of Salem and the daughter of Francis and Lisetta Vogler Fries. The couple had five children: Henry, William, Caroline, John F., Jr., and one who died in infancy.

After the war Shaffner resumed his medical practice in Salem and in 1867 established a drugstore. He was a member of the North Carolina Medical Society and for four years was one of the seven members constituting the Medical Examining Board for the state of North Carolina. In 1872 he represented the North Carolina Medical Society at a meeting of the American Medical Association; he served as orator of the state society in 1877 and as its president in 1880.

From 1878 to 1884 he was first commissioner and then mayor of the town of Salem. He took an active part in the organization of the North Western North Carolina Railroad, of which he was elected a director in 1870. Shaffner was the first president of the Salem Water Supply Company, which later was transferred to the town of Salem, and a founding member, vice-president, and director of the Winston-Salem Building and Loan Association. He served as a board member of the Salem Boys' School for several terms, was a trustee of the Salem congregation from 1878 to 1890, and was a member of the financial board of the Southern Province for several years.

Shaffner was buried in Salem Cemetery. The concluding prayer at the funeral service was offered by his lifelong friend and chaplain of the United Confederate Veterans, Dr. H. A. Brown.

SEE: *Burial Service: John Francis Shaffner, M.D.* (1908); Adelaide L. Fries and others, eds., *Forsyth: The History of a County on the March* (1976); Daniel L. Grant, *Alumni History of the University of North Carolina* (1924); *North Carolina Biography*, vol. 4 (1928).

PHILIP A. WALKER

Shanks, Henry Thomas *(7 Feb. 1896–16 Dec. 1959)*, historian, author, and teacher, was born in Vance County, the son of Henry Taylor and Maude Jenkins Shanks. He was educated at Buies Creek Academy and at Wake Forest College, where he received a bachelor of arts degree in 1918 and a master of arts degree in 1920. During World War I (1917–18) he served in the U.S. Navy. After attending Columbia University in the summer of 1921, he entered the University of Chicago and, working under William E. Dodd, earned a master of arts degree in history in 1923. He received a Ph.D. from The University of North Carolina in 1929.

Shanks began his teaching career at South Georgia State Woman's College, Valdosta, where he was professor of history and political science from 1920 to 1922. From 1923 to 1929 he was an instructor in history at The University of North Carolina; he also taught at East Carolina Teachers' College (summer 1923) and Wake Forest College (summer 1927). In 1930 he joined the faculty of Birmingham-Southern College, Alabama, where he taught history for thirty years, fifteen of which he held the position of dean. In the summer of 1930 and 1931 he taught at West Virginia University, and in the summers of 1934, 1935, 1937, and 1939 he taught at Emory University. In 1958 he retired as dean at Birmingham-Southern and returned to full-time teaching as head of the Department of History. "Modest but strongly principled, genial but exacting in standards," scholarly and dedicated, Shanks inspired students to strive to attain his level of academic quality. Some of these were not young college students, for Shanks directed many night study groups, especially in Civil War history.

His dissertation, *The Secession Movement in Virginia, 1847–1861*, was published in 1934. In 1935–36 he received a grant-in-aid from the Social Science Research Council and a General Education Board Fellowship while working on the papers of Willie Person Mangum. Selected to edit the Mangum papers, he spent several years on the project; the first volume was published in 1950 and the fifth and last, in 1956. He also was the author of numerous articles and book reviews in scholarly and church journals.

Shanks was an elder in the Independent Presbyterian Church in Birmingham. He was a member of Phi Beta Kappa, Omicron Delta Kappa, and Phi Gamma Mu honorary fraternities and of Pi Kappa Alpha social fraternity. In addition, he was a member of the Alabama Historical Association, American Historical Association, Southern Historical Association, North Carolina Literary and Historical Association, and Association of Alabama Administrators (president, 1956–57). He served on the board of editors, *Journal of Southern History*, 1946–50; on the Alabama Historical Association Council, from 1947; and on the advisory committee, Carraway Methodist School of Nursing, from 1955. He read papers and presided over meetings in the Alabama, North Carolina, and Southern historical associations.

On 31 Aug. 1929 he married Anne Graham, and they had one son, Alexander Graham. Henry Shanks was buried in Chapel Hill. The Henry Shanks Memorial Collection in American History at the M. Paul Phillips Library of Birmingham-Southern College was established in commemoration of his three decades of unstinting service to the school.

SEE: *Birmingham News*, 2 July 1943, 12 Nov. 1955, 16 Dec. 1969; Birmingham *Post-Herald*, 17 Dec. 1959; Birmingham-Southern College, "Campus and Community," *Bulletin* 53 (January 1960), and materials on file in the office of the president; *Chapel Hill Weekly*, 23 Dec. 1959; Raleigh *News and Observer*, 18 Dec. 1959; *Who Was Who in America*, vol. 31 (1960–61).

MAUD THOMAS SMITH

Sharp, Hunter *(5 Oct. 1861–17 Dec. 1923)*, diplomat, was born at Harrellsville in Hertford County, the son of Colonel Starkey and Jane Lewis Sharp. The Sharps were large landowners and active in local affairs. After being prepared for college at Harrellsville, young Sharp entered Trinity College, Durham, in September 1876. Two years later he transferred to The University of North Carolina, where he remained from 1879 to 1881. He concluded his studies at the University of Maryland during 1881–82. Sharp had originally intended to become a surgeon but abandoned the idea and returned to Harrellsville.

Shortly afterwards he accompanied his sister Frances to Japan to join her husband, Thomas R. Jernigan, who was American consul at Kobe. In 1886 Sharp was appointed marshal and vice-consul for Osaka and Hioga and thus began a diplomatic career that lasted for thirty-seven years. From 1900 to 1902 he was vice-consul and later deputy consul and interpreter at the same post. In 1902 he was transferred to Kobe as vice-consul.

Sharp and his wife built a home in Kobe. He led an active social life and was fond of rowing and sulky racing. In addition, he became known in diplomatic circles as an inveterate collector of fine china. In fact, his dinner guests invariably lifted their plates to read the makers' names.

Sharp was legislated out of office by the election of President William H. Taft. Furthermore, he learned that the U.S. government intended to close the American consulate at Kobe. After traveling to Washington, D.C., Sharp was granted an interview with the president. Taft was so impressed with Sharp's arguments that he not only decided to retain the consulate in Kobe but also instructed him to return to that city as the U.S. consul (1905).

In 1908 Sharp was sent to Russia as consul general in order to transfer the consulate from St. Petersburg to Moscow. Once this was accomplished, he began collecting rugs. However, because he suffered with pneumonia and hardening of the arteries—a consequence of the harsh climate—he was allowed to leave after only ten months in Moscow.

The following year he was transferred to France and became consul at Lyons (1909–11). Despite a pleasant eighteen months there, Sharp wished his children to be educated in an English-speaking country and applied for the position of American consul at Belfast, Ireland. His request was granted, and for the next nine and one-half years (1911–20) he was stationed in Belfast. During World War I Sharp found his work especially demanding. Whenever an American ship was sunk by the Germans, it was his responsibility to do everything possible for the survivors. With a small staff to aid him, he often worked far into the night. Meanwhile, his wife headed the American Red Cross for Northern Ireland.

In 1920 Sharp was appointed consul at Edinburgh and the family moved to Scotland. After he died three years later in the Scottish capital, his remains were returned to North Carolina and interred in the family cemetery at Harrellsville.

On 27 June 1900, in Swarthmore, Pa., Sharp married May Adelaide Suydam. They were the parents of three children: Myra Adelaide, Dorothy Katherine, and Hubbard.

SEE: Daniel L. Grant, *Alumni History of the University of North Carolina* (1924); Miss Katherine Sharp (New York, N.Y.), personal contact, 1975; *Trinity Alumni Register* 2 (April 1916); *Who Was Who in America*, vol. 1 (1981).

JAMES ELLIOTT MOORE

Sharp, Jacob Hunter *(6 Feb. 1833–16 Sept. 1907)*, lawyer, Confederate officer, legislator, and newspaper editor, was born in Hertford County and at an early age moved with his family to Pickens County, Ala. Not long after arriving in that state, however, the family moved again and settled in Columbus, Miss. Both his father, Mississippi state senator Elisha Hunter Sharp, and his mother, Sallie Carter Sharp, were North Carolinians.

Sharp attended the University of Alabama from 1850 to 1851, studied law, and was admitted to the bar in Lowndes County, Miss., sometime before the Civil War began. He and his older brother, Thomas L. Sharp, became partners in a law practice in Columbus.

When the Confederate States government was established, Sharp and his brother enlisted as privates in the Tombigbee Rangers. Jacob soon was chosen to be captain of his company, which was part of the battalion commanded by Colonel A. K. Blythe. After Blythe's death at the Battle of Shiloh, Sharp was elevated to colonel of the reorganized unit, which became the Forty-fourth Mississippi Infantry.

Sharp was commended frequently by superior officers for bravery and gallantry in action. Among the battles in which he was engaged in Georgia, Tennessee, and North Carolina were Shiloh, Murfreesboro, Chickamauga, Jonesboro, Franklin, Nashville, Atlanta, and Bentonville. When the commander of the Forty-fourth Division was killed, Sharp was promoted temporarily to the rank of brigadier general and received his commission on 28 July 1864. He surrendered his command at Greensboro in April 1865.

After the war Sharp returned to Columbus and entered into a law practice with J. E. Leigh and later with W. W. Humphries. He was elected to the state legislature in 1886, 1888, 1890, 1892, 1900, and 1902 and served as speaker of the house during the session of 1886–88. In 1903 he made an unsuccessful bid for the office of state treasurer.

Sharp was active in Reconstruction politics, and in 1879 he became owner and editor of the *Columbus Independent*. He participated in white supremacy movements and was made head of the Ku Klux Klan in Lowndes County. After several years of failing health, Sharp died in Columbus and was buried in Friendship Cemetery. His portrait, showing him in military uniform, hangs in the Mississippi Hall of Fame. He was married to Sallie Harris, the daughter of a Mississippi judge with whom he read law. They had one son, T. H.

SEE: R. W. Banks, *Famous Mississippians* (1918); *Columbus Independent*, 16 Sept. 1907; *Mississippi Official and Statistical Register* (1908); Dunbar Rowland, *Encyclopedia of Mississippi History* (1907), and *Military History of Mississippi, 1803–1898* (1928); Ezra J. Warner, *Generals in Gray* (1959); Benjamin B. Winborne, *Colonial and State Political History of Hertford County, North Carolina* (1906).

GARY TERPENING

Sharpe, William (Lawyer Billy) *(13 Dec. 1742–6 July 1818)*, lawyer, surveyor, land speculator, militia officer, and local and state political leader, was born near Rock Church in Cecil County, Md., the son of Thomas, Jr. (1718–85), and Elizabeth Sharp. His parents used the form Sharp, but he spelled it Sharpe. His grandfather, Thomas Sharp, Sr., had migrated from Scotland to Cecil County. William received a good education and read law. Although the exact date of his arrival in North Carolina is uncertain, evidence indicates that he joined a large group of Marylanders who moved into the southern Piedmont between the Catawba and Yadkin rivers. He was admitted to the bar in Mecklenburg County in 1763.

On 31 May 1768 Sharpe married Catherine Reese, the daughter of David Reese, a justice of the Mecklenburg County Court and an early supporter of the American cause. Land records indicate that in late 1768 or early 1769 Sharpe moved from Mecklenburg to western Rowan (now Iredell) County.

Like his father-in-law, Sharpe early became involved in Revolutionary activities. He was a member of the Rowan County Committee of Safety from 1774 to 1776 (appointed 23 Sept. 1774) and served as secretary. The minutes of the committee, now lost, were preserved by the Sharpe family and published in John H. Wheeler's *Historical*

Sketches of North Carolina (1851). Along with Griffith Rutherford and William Kenyon, Sharpe represented Rowan County at the Second Provincial Congress, held in New Bern (3–7 Apr. 1775), where he signed a pledge to support the Continental Association. One of seven delegates from Rowan County in attendance at the Third Provincial Congress at Hillsborough (20 Aug.–10 Sept. 1775), he subscribed to an oath of allegiance to George III while denying the right of the British government to tax the colonies. The following year he and Hezekiah Alexander of Mecklenburg County represented the Salisbury District on the Provincial Council of Safety (5 June–25 Oct. 1776). It was the Council of Safety that exercised the executive functions of the Revolutionary government prior to the drafting of a state constitution in December 1776. While Sharpe was serving on the Council of Safety, he accompanied North Carolina militia troops commanded by Brigadier General Griffith Rutherford on a successful campaign against the Cherokee Middle and Valley settlements.

At the Fifth Provincial Congress, held in Hillsborough (12 Nov.–23 Dec. 1776), Sharpe, again a delegate from Rowan County, was placed on several committees, the most noteworthy being a committee to draft a bill of rights and constitution for the new state of North Carolina. He, Waightstill Avery, Robert Lanier, and Joseph Winston were appointed to negotiate a treaty with the Overhill Cherokee. By the Treaty of Long Island of Holston (July 1777), the Overhill Cherokee ceded claims to tribal lands east of the Blue Ridge as well as a corridor from the Watauga settlements to North Carolina. Cherokee hostages were sent to Sharpe's home to ensure compliance.

Sharpe was first elected a delegate to the Continental Congress on 4 Feb. 1779; he was reelected on 30 Apr. 1780 and 12 July 1781. After attending sessions during 15 Apr.–8 Dec. 1779 and 4 Oct. 1780–1 Oct. 1781, he resigned from the Congress, which he called a "house of bondage," on 20 Dec. 1781. While a delegate he opposed the wholesale cession of western lands and advocated increased Continental support of the war in the South. When the British army under Lord Charles Cornwallis invaded the backcountry, Sharpe proposed that the Americans launch an attack from the sea in order to force a British withdrawal from the interior.

When he resigned his seat in Congress, Sharpe informed Governor Alexander Martin that this action was caused by the "derranged condition of my estate." However, this did not prevent him from serving the following year, 1782, in the North Carolina House of Commons. At this session he served as spokesman for the committee that found the western land claims of the Transylvania Company illegal. He also was an unsuccessful candidate for the offices of governor and comptroller. Again in the house the following year, he was disappointed in his bid for a seat on the Council of State. Serving in the 1784 House of Commons, Sharpe supported the repeal of the Tennessee Cession, as well as legislation against former Tories. It was at this session that he introduced an unsuccessful bill for "Establishing the North Carolina University." A similar bill introduced by William R. Davie was passed in 1789. After 1784 Sharpe held no elected office, although there was an attempt to return him to Congress in 1786. Evidence seems to indicate that his health declined. He was unable to attend the laying of the cornerstone of The University of North Carolina in 1793. In commenting on his "ambitious friend, Billy Sharpe," Davie noted: "He was ever eager to serve, but being no Verulam, seems better suited to make a treaty with the savages in the Western Woods than to set afoot a seminary of learning."

Sharpe held extensive lands in western North Carolina and Tennessee. He was listed as owning eight slaves in the 1790 census. He died at his home north of Statesville and was interred nearby in the Snow Creek Burying Ground. Catherine Reese Sharpe survived her husband. The couple had twelve children: Matilda Sharpe Erwin (b. 4 Mar. 1769), Ruth Reese Sharpe Caldwell (b. 3 Mar. 1770), Thomas Reese (b. 18 May 1771), Abner (b. 1 Oct. 1772); Betsy Sharpe Starke (b. 22 Jan. 1774), David (b. 11 Feb. 1775), Elam (b. 3 Jan. 1777), Marcus (b. 22 Feb. 1778), Cynthia Sharpe McGuire (b. 18 Nov. 1780), Elvira Sharpe Caldwell (b. 20 July 1782), Edwin (b. 1 Dec. 1783), and Carlos B. (b. 15 Feb. 1786).

SEE: *Biog. Dir. Am. Cong.* (1971); John L. Cheney, Jr., ed., *North Carolina Government, 1585–1974* (1975); Walter Clark, ed., *State Records of North Carolina*, vols. 11–24 (1895–1905); *The Heritage of Iredell County* (1980); Homer M. Keever, *Iredell, Piedmont County* (1976); William L. Saunders, ed., *Colonial Records of North Carolina*, vols. 9–10 (1890); Paul H. Smith, ed., *Letters of Delegates to Congress, 1774–1789*, vols. 12–18 (1985–91); *Who Was Who in America: Historical Volume* (1967).

JERRY C. CASHION

Sharpe, William (Bill) Pleasants *(13 Aug. 1903–6 Jan. 1970)*, press agent, journalist, author, magazine editor, and publisher, was born near Madison in rural Rockingham County, the son of William Pleasants and Minnie Isabelle Anderson Sharp. His mother was the daughter of a Confederate army veteran, and his father was an uncle of Susie Sharp, chief justice of the North Carolina Supreme Court.

Young Bill, who spelled his name Sharpe, was one of three sons and three daughters. When his family moved to New Orleans, he remained in Winston-Salem to complete the requirements for a diploma from Reynolds High School, class of 1921. He earned his expenses through such work as editing the school paper and reporting sports events for the *Winston-Salem Journal-Sentinel*. His energy and intelligence so impressed attorney Fred Parrish that he prevailed in seeking an appointment for Sharpe to the U.S. Military Academy at West Point. Already enamored of newspapering, Sharpe declined the appointment in favor of the job that led to a lifetime of writing and publishing.

After brief stints with the *Johnstonian* at Selma and the New Orleans *Times-Picayune*, he returned in 1926 to Winston-Salem, where he remained with the *Journal and Sentinel* for eleven years, reaching the rank of managing editor. In 1939–41 he would return once more to Winston-Salem to publish and edit his own nondaily, *Thursday*.

In Selma, while deciding not to purchase the paper there, he met Sallie Herring, the oldest of six daughters and two sons of William Abia of Lenoir County and Emma Gertrude Hardy Herring of Beaufort County. Bill and Sallie were married on 11 May 1926 in Raleigh. The couple had four daughters: Betty Lou (Mrs. Ed Burt Bruton), Polly Ann (Mrs. Homer Lee Jenkins), Susan Herring (Mrs. Wayne Perry Zarr), and Sallie (Mrs. Andrew Matthew McCauley, Jr.).

In 1937 Governor Clyde Roark Hoey appointed Sharpe to head the new Division of Advertising and News of the North Carolina Department of Conservation and Development. Breaking new ground beyond any the state had tried in travel promotion, Sharpe devised an operation that became a national model. War curbed travel and interrupted the fledgling campaign. Sharpe, ineligible for military duty, became the first director of the North Carolina Office of War Information, an arm of the federal organization; later he was public relations director of a Fairchild Aircraft plant in Burlington that was developing a new aircraft for wartime use.

At war's end he returned to promoting state vacation and scenic attractions with a zest that multiplied visiting tourist trade. In the summer of 1949 he became director of publicity for the Carolina Power and Light Company and two years later purchased *The State* magazine from Carl Goerch. For the next nineteen years he crisscrossed North Carolina to interview Tar Heel characters and to continue promoting travel into the state after his own fashion in his own publication.

Sharpe had served as the state's top publicist under four governors—Hoey, J. Melville Broughton, Gregg Cherry, and W. Kerr Scott—and his energy and initiative had won nationwide respect of competing press agents who flattered him by copying his methods to counter his competition for tourists. He played promotion straight. Once, when Madison Avenue types asked him to have tobacco festival queens vestooned with leaves of tobacco, squirted with champagne, and pushed into a pool for publicity pictures, his response was "go to hell!" Travel editors respected him and accepted his invitation to return as "Honorary Tar Heels," a group that he formed to cement and sustain friendships.

Of his magazine he once wrote: "One of the purposes of *The State* might be expressed this way: So that North Carolinians might better appreciate and enjoy their environment by becoming better acquainted with it." Towards that goal he also published several books: *Tar on My Heels: A Press Agent's Note Book*, illustrated by photographer John Hemmer (1946); *North Carolina Counties* (1948); and *A New Geography of North Carolina* (4 vols.; 1954, 1958, 1961, and 1965). Profusely illustrated, the new geography presented profiles containing anecdotes, folklore, and legends of each of the state's one hundred counties. It found its way into most public schools and libraries and went into subsequent reprints. Academic regard for the four-volume geography was expressed thus by Hugh T. Lefler, University of North Carolina professor of history: "All those who teach and write about North Carolina will find it an indispensable book." In 1962 the work won Sharpe the Mayflower Cup, North Carolina's highest literary award.

Accentuating the positive, Sharpe inventoried the good things about the state, captioning a 112-page edition (his largest) as *The State*'s "What's Right About North Carolina Edition." The Travel Council of North Carolina gave him the Parker Award for his "outstanding contribution to the promotion and development of North Carolina's travel industry."

Following his unexpected death, fellow editors across the region showered their accolades. *The State*, which had saluted him as North Carolinian of 1948 long before he ever dreamed of owning that magazine, featured him as North Carolinian of 1969 with cover pictures. Typical of tributes was WRAL-TV's "Viewpoint" editorial by Jesse Helms (later a U.S. senator) saying Sharpe "so loved North Carolina that he became at once her press agent, her historian—and her conscience."

A Presbyterian, he was buried at Raleigh Memorial Park.

SEE: *Asheville Citizen*, 26 July 1951; Raleigh *News and Observer*, 10 June 1949, 6 July 1952, 7–8 Jan. 1970; Bill Sharpe, *Tar on My Heels* (1946); *The State* magazine, 1951–70, esp. 15 Jan. 1970; WRAL-TV *Viewpoint*, no. 2250 (12 Jan. 1970).

JACK RILEY

Shaw, Henry Marchmore *(20 Nov. 1819–1 Feb. 1864)*, physician, congressman, and Confederate army officer, was born in Newport, R.I. His parents were John Allen and Betty Marchmore Shaw, both of Scotch-Irish descent. The Shaw family moved to North Carolina after suffering severe financial losses. Young Shaw was fortunate to have a benefactor, Dr. G. C. Marchant, who allowed Shaw to study in his office and later financed his medical education at the University of Pennsylvania, where Shaw received his M.D. and two certificates of surgery in 1838. After graduation Shaw began a practice in Indiantown, Currituck County.

He also became active in politics. In 1851 he was elected as a Democrat to the state senate; his opponent was John Bernard. In 1853 Shaw defeated Colonel David Outlaw for the seat from the First Congressional District. Shaw's opponent in 1855 was Robert Treat Paine, who defeated Shaw. However, Shaw was reelected to the Thirty-fifth Congress in 1857 and served his final term.

Shaw represented Currituck County at the Secession Convention of 1861, where he strongly favored North Carolina's secession from the Union. He felt so intensely that he resigned from the convention and joined the Confederate army. On 16 May 1861 he was appointed colonel of the Eighth Regiment, North Carolina Troops.

Organized at Camp Macon in Warren County on 14 Sept. 1861, the Eighth Regiment was first ordered to Roanoke Island, where Shaw assumed command. On 8 Feb. 1862 the regiment was captured by a Federal expeditionary group commanded by General A. E. Burnside. The prisoners were taken to Elizabeth City and paroled on 21 February. But it was not until 10 Nov. 1862 that Shaw was exchanged at Aiken's Landing, James River, Va.

Near Raleigh, at Camp Mangum, the Eighth Regiment reorganized in September 1862. Shaw reassumed command after his exchange, and the regiment was attached to General Thomas L. Clingman's brigade. Shaw was present or accounted for until the skirmish at Batchelder Creek, near New Bern, where he was killed. The regiment had been ordered to New Bern from South Carolina to aid General Robert F. Hoke's brigade. After Shaw's death, Lieutenant Colonel J. M. Whitson assumed command of the regiment.

On 2 Apr. 1836 Shaw married Mary Riddick Trotman of Camden County. The couple had three children: William B., Henry M., and Mary T. Colonel Shaw was buried at Shawboro in Currituck County.

SEE: *Biog. Dir. Am. Cong.* (1971); D. H. Hill, Jr., *Confederate Military History*, vol. 4 (1899); James Sprunt Historical Monographs, no. 1 (1900); Weymouth T. Jordan, Jr., comp., *North Carolina Troops, 1861–1865: A Roster*, vol. 4 (1973).

ELLEN TAYLOR COOK

Shaw, Herbert Bell *(9 Feb. 1908–3 Jan. 1980)*, bishop of the African Methodist Episcopal Zion Church, was born in Wilmington, the son of John Henry and Lummie Virginia Hodges Shaw. He was named for the Reverend Herbert Bell, pioneer Zion minister in the Cape Fear Conference of the church. Shaw was educated in the public schools of Wilmington; St. Emma's Preparatory School, Castle Rock, Va.; Fisk University, Nashville, Tenn., from which he received the A.B. degree; and Howard University School of Religion, where he earned a master's degree. He was awarded an honorary doctor of divinity degree from Livingstone College, Salisbury.

Converted to the Christian faith at St. Luke's AME Zion Church, Wilmington, in 1920, he preached his trial sermon on 12 July 1927 and was ordained deacon the following year. In 1930 he was ordained an elder. He served several churches in North Carolina as well as in Washington, D.C. From 1937 to 1943 he was presiding elder of the Wilmington District of the Cape Fear Conference. Still residing in Wilmington, Shaw headed the denomination's pension plan from 1944 to 1952. In May 1952 he was consecrated bishop and assigned to supervise churches in the two Carolinas and in the Bahamas. Becoming ever more active in the AME Zion church, Shaw organized overseas conferences in 1968, 1972, and 1976 in Jamaica, London, and Trinidad-Tobago, respectively. He was elevated to the post of bishop of the First Episcopal District, which included such widely scattered areas as New England, New York, Cape Fear, many islands of the Caribbean, and the London-Birmingham conferences in England.

Shaw was second vice-president of the National Council of Christ in the USA and chairman of the board of trustees of Livingstone College, Salisbury. He was a member of the General Commission of the Army and Navy Chaplains, the presidium of the World Methodist Council (1971–76), the World Council of Churches, the board of directors of the Community Boys Club of America and of the 4-H Club Foundation of America, and other boards and bodies. He also helped to prepare a hymnal for his denomination. Between 1951 and 1971 he was a delegate to five World Methodist Conferences and served as an officer at several of them. In 1962 he was a special guest of the Russian Orthodox Church. At the bicentennial celebration of Methodism in North Carolina in 1972, he was the principal speaker.

In September 1931 Shaw married Mary Ardelle Stokes, and they became the parents of a son, John Herbert, and a daughter, Marie. He died at a meeting of the board of bishops at Indianapolis, Ind., and his funeral was held at the mother church of AME Zion Church in New York City with burial in Wilmington.

SEE: Nolan B. Harmon, ed., *Encyclopedia of World Methodism*, vol. 2 (1974); *North Carolina Christian Advocate* 118 (8 Feb. 1973); Raleigh *News and Observer* and *Raleigh Times*, 4, 9 Jan. 1980; *Who's Who Among Black Americans*, vol. 1 (1976); Ethel L. Williams, ed., *Biographical Directory of Negro Ministers* (1975); *World Parish* 17 (December 1977).

GRADY L. E. CARROLL

Shaw, John Gilbert *(14 Jan. 1858–21 July 1932)*, lawyer and congressman, was born in Cumberland County, the son of Catherine Gillis and Colonel Duncan Shaw, a farmer. His Scottish grandfather, Gilbert Shaw, arrived in North Carolina in 1796. John G. Shaw attended the common schools and briefly operated his own turpentine business. From his youth he was "financially independent," owing to ownership of a thousand-acre plantation west of Fayetteville, which had a sawmill, gristmill, and cotton gin.

After studying the law in 1887, Shaw was admitted to the Fayetteville bar. He was almost immediately elected to the North Carolina legislature as a Democrat. One of the youngest members of the house, Shaw served on the Committee on Penal Institutions during his single term. He was Cumberland County attorney from 1890 to 1894 and a Cleveland presidential elector in 1892. In 1894 "The Plough Boy of Cumberland," as he was called in the local newspaper, was nominated for the U.S. Congress from the Third District. One of only two Democratic congressional candidates to survive the landslide Fusion election of that year, he defeated Populist Cyrus Thompson and Republican Oscar J. Spears. The campaign was very heated and twice Shaw's speaker's platform was torn down by political opponents. He failed to win reelection in 1896. In 1920 Shaw attempted a comeback in the Sixth Congressional District but lost the race.

Shaw played a key role in the location of Camp (now Fort) Bragg military base near Fayetteville. In 1918 Major General William J. Snow, the artillery chief for the army, sent Colonel E. P. King to the eastern United States to find a site for an artillery encampment. While in Fayetteville, King encountered Shaw, who gave him an extensive tour of a possible site west of the city. King was impressed and gave Snow a positive report. Shaw later performed much of the legal work required for the establishment of the camp, named in honor of the Confederate general Braxton Bragg.

Interested in local history and preservation throughout his life, Shaw was active in preserving the Scottish heritage of the Upper Cape Fear as well as in Civil War activities. The story on "The Oldest Road in Cumberland" appearing in John A. Oates's *Story of Fayetteville* was written by Shaw. Despite his historical and political undertakings, he was best known as a lawyer. After serving briefly as county attorney, he spent most of his legal career as a defense attorney. Shaw was proud that in no capital case that he argued was a defendant ever given a death sentence. On Law Day 1963 a portrait honoring his legal accomplishments was unveiled in the Cumberland County Superior Court.

In 1893 Shaw married Elizabeth Avery McPherson, the daughter of Captain John A. McPherson. They had four children: Gilbert and Duncan, both lawyers; John Alexander, a physician; and Sarah McNeill. Shaw, a Presbyterian, was a founder of the Highland Presbyterian Church. After several years of illness, he died in Fayetteville and was buried at the McPherson's Cemetery in Seventy-first Township.

SEE: *Biographical Directory of the United States Congress, 1774–1989* (1989); "Census of Cumberland County: Free Schedule," 1860 (microfilm, North Carolina Collection, University of North Carolina, Chapel Hill); John L. Cheney, Jr., ed., *North Carolina Government, 1558–1979* (1981); *Fayetteville Observer*, 11 Oct. 1894, 18 Nov. 1919, 22–23 July 1932, 29 April 1963; *Legislative Biographical Sketch Book: Session 1887* (1887); *North Carolina Biography*, vol. 5 (1919); John A. Oates, *The Story of Fayetteville and the Upper Cape Fear* (1950); Raleigh *News and Observer*, 23 July 1932.

RONNIE W. FAULKNER

Shaw, Ruth Faison *(1887–3 Dec. 1969)*, teacher, artist, lecturer, and originator of finger painting, was born in Kenansville, the daughter of the Reverend William M., a Presbyterian minister, and Alberta Faison Shaw. She was related to the Hicks, Thomson, Moore, Ivey, and Bannerman families.

After attending elementary school in Cabarrus County and the James Sprunt Institute in Kenansville, she entered the Peabody Institute of Music in Baltimore. She taught elementary school in Transylvania County and music in Kenansville and Wilmington. During World War I she did YMCA work in France. In Italy from 1922 to 1932, she directed the Shaw School in Rome for English-speaking boys and girls. While there, she discovered the art of finger painting and also devised a formula for making finger paint.

In 1932 Miss Shaw taught for a time at the University of Paris and then set up a finger painting studio in New York and later at Cape Cod, where she taught finger painting. During World War II she entertained servicemen with finger painting demonstrations, and for two years she worked with mental patients at the Menninger Psychiatric Clinic in Topeka, Kans. She was the author of *Finger Painting: A Perfect Medium for Self-Expression* (1934).

In 1959 Miss Shaw moved to Chapel Hill and was employed as a consultant in the Department of Psychiatry, where she remained until her death. She lectured and gave finger painting demonstrations to groups in person as well as on television. She was buried in Oakdale Cemetery, Wilmington. Her large collection of finger paintings was given to the University of North Carolina at Chapel Hill.

SEE: *American Magazine*, no. 122 (1947 [portrait]); Chapel Hill, *Living*, 29 Apr. 1979; *Chapel Hill Weekly*, 24 Apr. 1977; Crockette W. Hewlett, *Two Centuries of Art in New Hanover County* (1976); *Holland's The Magazine of the South* 59 (February 1940); Clinton, *The Sampsonian*, 12 Sept. 1968, 24 Sept. 1971; *Scholarship* 27 (25 Jan. 1936).

CLAUDE HUNTER MOORE

Shearer, John Bunyan *(19 July 1832–14 June 1919)*, educator and minister, was of Dutch, English, and Welsh ancestry. The first of seven children born to Ruth Akers Webber and John Akers Shearer in Appomattox County, Va., he received the usual farm training provided the sons of farmers. In addition, from ages six to seventeen he spent every year except one at Union Academy in his native county. His study of Latin and Greek led to his employment as an assistant instructor of these subjects in Union Academy. At eighteen he entered Hampden-Sydney College, in Virginia, where he was graduated with honors and an A.B. degree in 1851. That fall he embarked on a three-year theological course at the University of Virginia and earned an M.A. degree in 1854. He helped finance his education by offering his services as a tutor, teaching school, and preaching during his stay at the university.

Four years before completing his education, Shearer married Lizzie Gessner at Hampden-Sydney. To him she was a major source of inspiration. In 1858 he finished the theological program at Union Seminary in Hampden-Sydney. Licensed to preach by the Roanoke Presbytery on 17 Apr. 1857, he successively became the pastor of churches in Bethlehem and Concord, a church in Chapel Hill, and the Orange Presbytery. Since the Civil War had left the university in Chapel Hill disorganized, Shearer became pastor of Spring Hill Church, in Halifax County, Va., where he could teach as well as preach.

In May 1870 he took charge of Stewart College in Clarksville, Tenn., and later was made president by the board of trustees. Shearer and one of the institution's chief trustees, the Honorable D. N. Kennedy, became close friends and together were responsible for the founding of Southwestern Presbyterian University in Clarksville (now Memphis). Shearer received a D.D. degree from the McCown School in 1872 and an LL.D. from Southwestern Presbyterian in 1889.

As president of Southwestern Presbyterian University, Shearer organized a faculty and gained support that led to the enrollment of 150 students. At the peak of his accomplishments, however, his health began to fail; indeed, the years 1878–79 were almost totally lost to him because of ill health. Shearer withdrew as head of the university and nominated the Reverend John W. Waddell as chancellor. Still unable to leave the field of education completely, he began to provide biblical instruction in English, Greek, and Hebrew.

Shearer spent nine years laying the foundations and building the walls of the institution and another nine in the classroom teaching. In 1888, after recovering his health, he accepted the presidency of Davidson College, in North Carolina, a position he held for thirteen years. Once more he resigned because of poor health, but he continued to teach his favorite subjects—biblical instruction and philosophy. After the death of Shearer's wife Lizzie in January 1903, the Reverend M. E. Sentelle, D.D., was elected adjunct professor of biblical instruction and professor of philosophy to succeed Shearer.

As a result of Shearer's ministering and teaching, Bethlehem and Concord churches at Hampden-Sydney, Va., and Spring Hill Church at Halifax County, Va., became self-sustaining. The effectiveness of his teaching is demonstrated by the large number of pupils who passed under his tutelage.

Shearer was the author of a three-volume *Bible Course Syllabus* (1895–96), *Modern Mysticism* (1905), *Sermon on the Mount* (1906), *Studies in the Life of Christ* (1907), *The Scriptures: Fundamental Facts and Features* (1908), *Selected Old Testament Studies* (1909), *Hebrew Institutions: Social and Civil* (1910), *Selected Old Testament Studies* (1911), and *One Hundred Brief Bible Studies* (1912). He died at his home in Davidson.

SEE: Samuel A. Ashe, ed., *Biographical History of North Carolina*, vol. 8 (1917); *Presbyterian Church in the United States, Synod of North Carolina Minutes, 1849–1972* (1919); Rev. E. C. Scott, *Ministerial Directory of the Presbyterian Church, United States, 1861–1941* (1942); *Who Was Who in America*, vol. 1 (1981).

IRENE CALDWELL

Shelby, Evan *(1719–4 Dec. 1794)*, frontiersman, trader, and militia officer, was born in Tregaron, Wales, the son of Evan, Sr., a merchant and farmer, and Catherine Daviess Shelby. The family emigrated to America in 1735, settling first in Pennsylvania and then in Maryland. One sister, Eleanor, moved to Mecklenburg County and married John Polk, who was of the family that afterwards produced James K. Polk, eleventh president of the United States.

Evan Shelby became a trapper and farmer, living on a plantation called the Mountain of Wales near Frederick, Md. When the French and Indian War broke out, he was commissioned a captain in the provincial army and served as a scout in the ill-fated Braddock campaign. He later was in charge of surveying and laying out the Forbes Road, or Pennsylvania Road, and was in the advance detachment at the fall of Fort Duquesne.

After the war Shelby continued his farming operations and began a fur trading company in the Northwest. The outbreak of Pontiac's Rebellion caused him severe losses that resulted in the forced sale of his Maryland lands. In 1771 he migrated to the Holston River area in the Virginia–North Carolina backcountry. There he built a fort and a store, one of only two on the frontier, on the site of what later would be Bristol, Tenn.-Va. The store became an important supply center for pioneers making their way along the Wilderness Trail into the trans-Appalachian region.

In 1774, when hostilities broke out between Virginia and the Ohio Indians, Shelby was appointed a captain in the local company of militia and led his force to the place where the Kanawha River empties into the Ohio River. There he became the leading participant in the Battle of Point Pleasant, the only battle of Lord Dunmore's War, which quieted the Indians in the Ohio Valley for several years.

Active in politics, he was a leader of the Fincastle County settlers who in January 1775 signed the "Fincastle Resolves," which gave their approval to the actions of the Continental Congress. He later served on a Committee of Safety to carry out the boycott of British goods. At the outbreak of the Revolution he wanted to join his friend, George Washington, in Massachusetts but was persuaded by Governor Patrick Henry to take charge of the defense of Virginia's frontier. He was promoted to the rank of major in 1776 and led a contingent of militiamen in fights against the Cherokees in the Tennessee Valley. In 1777 he was appointed a colonel and led his troops against the Chickamauga tribe, destroying for a time Indian power in the Virginia–North Carolina backcountry.

In the fall of 1779 a line was surveyed between Virginia and North Carolina, and most of the Shelby land was found to be in North Carolina. Therefore, he resigned his commission in the Virginia militia but remained active in frontier defense.

Following the Revolution Shelby opposed the abortive attempt to form the state of Franklin. Though he favored statehood for North Carolina's western counties, he opposed the manner in which it was carried out. North Carolina, in an attempt to conciliate the secessionists, formed a new military district called Washington, and Shelby was made brigadier general of the area in 1787. When John Sevier left the governor's position, the state of Franklin elected Shelby to succeed him, but he declined. He also resigned his post as military commander of the area, feeling that he had failed in pacifying the opposing groups, and retired from public life.

Shelby was married twice: in 1745 to Letitia Cox, who died in 1777, and in 1787 to Isabella Eliot. By his first wife he had five sons—John, Isaac, who led the mountain men at Kings Mountain and became the first and sixth governor of Kentucky, James, Evan, and Moses—and three daughters—Rachel, Susannah, and Catherine. By his second wife he had one son, James, and two daughters, Letitia and Eleanor. He died at his home and was buried in the city cemetery in Bristol, Tenn. No known portraits exist, but he was reputed to be dark, fairly tall for the day, and serious of demeanor. He was raised in the Anglican faith but attended the Presbyterian church.

SEE: Thomas P. Abernethy, *From Frontier to Plantation in Tennessee* (1932); James G. M. Ramsey, *Annals of Tennessee to the End of the Eighteenth Century* (1853); Shelby Family Papers (Library of Congress, Washington, D.C.); Shelby and Hart Family Papers (Southern Historical Collection, University of North Carolina, Chapel Hill); Sylvia Wrobel and George Grider, *Isaac Shelby: Kentucky's First Governor and Hero of Three Wars* (1974).

PAUL W. BEASLEY

Shelby, Isaac *(11 Dec. 1750–18 Jul. 1826)*, frontiersman, soldier, and twice governor of Kentucky, was born in Frederick (now Washington) County, Md., the third child and second son of Evan and Letitia Cox Shelby. His father was a native of Tregaron, Cardiganshire, Wales, who had immigrated to America with his father's family about 1734, when he was sixteen. It is believed that the Shelby clan originated in Yorkshire, England, and originally bore the name Seby. In America the Shelbys, who had been members of the Church of England in Wales, became Presbyterians, the denomination of which Isaac was a member. Isaac early learned the use of arms and became accustomed to the rigors of frontier life. He received a fair English education, worked on his father's plantation, occasionally surveyed land, and at age eighteen became a deputy sheriff. About 1773 the Shelbys moved to the Holston region in what is now upper East Tennessee but was then considered a part of Fincastle County, Va. There Isaac fed and cared for herds of cattle in the extensive range that then characterized that area of the country.

At age twenty-three Shelby took part in his first major military engagement, the Battle of Point Pleasant, fought at the mouth of the Kanawha River, which was the culmination of the brief Lord Dunmore's War, in which Virginia frontiersmen defeated the Northwestern Indians. He served as a lieutenant in the Fincastle company of his father, who was in overall command of the Virginia troops at the end of the battle, his superiors having all been killed in the fierce fighting.

Young Shelby was left as second in command of the garrison of Fort Blair, which was erected on the site of the battle. There he remained until Lord Dunmore discontinued the garrison in July 1775 for fear that it would prove useful to the American rebels. Immediately thereafter Shelby went to Kentucky, where he surveyed lands for the Transylvania Company. The following year he returned to Kentucky to survey and improve lands for himself and to perfect military surveys earlier selected and entered by his father. During his absence from home in 1776, the Virginia committee of public safety appointed him captain of a company of minutemen. From 1777 until well into 1779 Shelby was largely occupied in securing—sometimes at his own expense—supplies for the Continental army and for various expeditions by Virginia troops.

In spring 1779 Shelby was elected to represent Washington County in the Virginia Assembly. The following autumn he was commissioned a major in the escort guard to the commissioners for extending westward the boundary between Virginia and North Carolina. As a result of this extension his home was found to be in North Carolina rather than Virginia. Shortly afterwards he was appointed a colonel in the militia of Sullivan County, which had been created in order to provide local government for the inhabitants of the new territory acquired by North Carolina in the recent boundary survey.

In the summer of 1780 Shelby was in Kentucky locating and securing the lands he had marked out and improved for himself four years earlier, when he received news of the fall of Charleston (12 May 1780) to the British. Hurrying home he arrived in Sullivan County in July and found a message from General Charles McDowell requesting his aid in resisting the British, who had already overrun Georgia and South Carolina and were then at the borders of North Carolina. Shelby assembled the militiamen of his county, asked them to volunteer their services for a short period, and marched with three hundred men to McDowell's camp near the Cherokee Ford in South Carolina. During the next three weeks Shelby and his men contributed importantly to three American victories over British and Tory forces.

News of the American defeat at Camden (16 Aug. 1780) halted operations by McDowell and Shelby, but

Shelby proposed to fellow westerners that they cooperate in attacking the force of Provincials and Tories under British Major Patrick Ferguson operating in the South Carolina uplands. The result was the Battle of Kings Mountain (7 Oct. 1780), a decisive American victory in which Ferguson met his death. Shelby has been given credit for the scheme of attack that led to another important American victory at Cowpens (17 Jan. 1781).

In October 1781, in response to a request for aid from General Nathanael Greene, Shelby raised a force of four hundred riflemen and accompanied by two hundred more under Colonel John Sevier went off to join Greene in the South Carolina low country, where Greene planned to use them in blocking a possible return to Charleston of Lord Cornwallis's army. However, when this danger was removed by Cornwallis's surrender (18 Oct. 1781) at Yorktown, Shelby's force was sent to join the command of General Francis Marion on the Pee Dee. In joint operation with Colonel Hezekiah Maham of South Carolina, Shelby captured a strong British post at Fair Lawn, near Monck's Corner, S.C., on 27 Nov. 1781. Having been elected to the North Carolina legislature in the meanwhile, Shelby obtained a leave of absence and attended the legislative sessions in December 1781. Reelected to the legislature in 1782, he attended its sessions at Hillsborough in April.

In early 1783 Shelby served as one of three commissioners appointed to supervise the laying off of the land south of the Cumberland River in Middle Tennessee that had been allotted to the officers and men of the North Carolina line and to settle the preemption claims on the Cumberland. Once he had completed this service, Shelby returned to Kentucky the following April and established himself on his new plantation near Boonesboro, where for the next six years he devoted himself to his favorite occupation, the cultivation of the soil and the raising of livestock.

Shelby became a trustee of Transylvania Seminary (later Transylvania University) in 1783. He was chairman of the convention of military officers that met at Danville on 7–8 Nov. 1783 to consider an expedition against the Indians and to discuss a possible separation from Virginia. He founded the Kentucky Society for the Promotion of Useful Knowledge, organized at Danville on 1 Dec. 1787. In January 1791 he was appointed a member of the Board of War for the District of Kentucky, which was created by Congress and authorized to provide for the defense of frontier settlements and to conduct punitive raids against the Indians. For several years he was sheriff of Lincoln County. He served in the early conventions that met at Danville for the purpose of securing independent statehood for Kentucky and in the convention of 2–19 Apr. 1792 that drafted the first Kentucky constitution.

In May 1792 Shelby was chosen governor for four years by the electors to whom the constitution of 1792 entrusted the selection of the chief magistrate. He was inaugurated at Lexington on 4 June but soon moved to Frankfort, the newly chosen state capital. As first governor of the Commonwealth he confronted numerous problems in establishing the infant government on a sound basis. He nevertheless gave strong support to the operations of General Anthony Wayne against the Northwestern Indians, who constituted the principal threat to the fledgling state. During Shelby's administration Kentuckians were also greatly perturbed by the possibility that Spain would close the lower Mississippi to American commerce. This concern was fertile soil for speculative ventures and conspiracies designed to take Kentucky out of the Union. Shelby's firm and moderate policy, which nevertheless came under criticism then and later, frustrated all conspiracies and held Kentucky firmly in the Union. He declined reelection in 1796 and retired to his home in Lincoln County.

The outbreak of the War of 1812 brought a renewal of the threat from the Northwestern Indians, who had kept Kentucky in a constant state of apprehension during Shelby's governorship (1792–96). With an overwhelming demand for Shelby's return to office, he was elected by popular vote in August 1812. As governor Shelby cooperated wholeheartedly with the national government in the prosecution of the war. In 1813 he personally raised, organized, and led four thousand Kentucky volunteers to join the army under the command of General William Henry Harrison in the Northwest in an invasion of Canada. This invasion culminated in the decisive defeat of the British and their Indian allies in the Battle of the Thames (5 Oct. 1813).

In 1816 Shelby again retired from the governorship. The following year President James Monroe asked him to be the secretary of war, but he declined on the basis of age. In 1818 Shelby performed his last public service when he went with Andrew Jackson to arrange a treaty with the Chickasaw Indians by which they ceded to the United States their lands west of the Tennessee River. Shelby served as president of the first Kentucky Agricultural Society, organized at Lexington in 1818. He was chairman of the first board of trustees of Centre College, founded at Danville in 1819.

On 19 Apr. 1783 he married, at Boonesboro, Susannah Hart, the second daughter of Captain Nathaniel Hart, one of the earliest settlers of Kentucky. By her he had eleven children. Shelby's daughter Sarah married Ephraim McDowell, the surgeon who at Danville on Christmas Day 1809 performed the first successful ovariotomy.

Shelby was a large man, six feet tall, sturdy, and well proportioned, with strongly marked features and a florid complexion. He could endure long hours of work, physical hardship, and great fatigue. Dignified and impressive in bearing, he was nevertheless affable and winning. A good soldier and able politician, he possessed great executive ability. In 1820 he suffered a paralytic stroke that deprived him of the use of his right arm and lamed him in his right leg. However, his mind remained clear until his death of apoplexy six and a half years later. He was buried on his estate, Traveler's Rest, in Lincoln County. The Commonwealth of Kentucky erected a monument over his grave in 1827. In 1952, 126 years after his death, Kentucky accepted the Shelby family cemetery at Traveler's Rest as a state shrine. Counties and towns in nine states are named in Shelby's honor.

SEE: John R. Alden, *The American Revolution, 1775–1783* (1954); Paul W. Beasley, "The Life and Times of Isaac Shelby, 1750–1826" (dissertation, University of Kentucky, 1968); F. F. Beirne, *The War of 1812* (1944); Thomas D. Clark, *A History of Kentucky* (1954); Harry L. Coles, *The War of 1812* (1965); Lyman C. Draper, *King's Mountain and Its Heroes* (1881, 1971); G. W. Griffin, *Memoirs of Colonel Charles S. Todd* (1873); Glenn Tucker, *Poltroons and Patriots*, 2 vols. (1954); Christopher Ward, *The War of the Revolution*, vol. 2 (1952); Sylvia Wrobel and George Grider, *Isaac Shelby: Kentucky's First Governor and Hero of Three Wars* (1974).

W. CONARD GASS

Shepard, Charles Biddle *(5 Dec. 1807–24 Oct. 1843)*, state legislator and congressman, was the son of William and Mary Williams Blount Shepard of New Bern. An older brother, William Biddle, was a congressman and state senator from Pasquotank County. Charles Shepard was named for his uncle, Captain Charles Biddle of Philadelphia, who on 25 Nov. 1778 at Beaufort had married Hannah Shepard, the daughter of merchant Jacob Shepard. Among the Biddles' children were Commodore James Biddle, U.S. Navy, and Nicholas Biddle (1786–1844), president of the U.S. Bank. After studying at private schools in his native New Bern, Charles Shepard was graduated from The University of North Carolina in 1827. The next year he was admitted to the bar and began practicing law in New Bern.

In 1831, when Charles George Spaight, the youngest of the three sons of Governor Richard Dobbs Spaight, Sr., died before taking his seat in the North Carolina House of Commons, Shepard was named to fill the vacancy; he subsequently won reelection. As a Democrat he served in Congress from 4 Mar. 1837 to 3 Mar. 1841, then resumed the practice of law in New Bern until his death. Following the funeral from Christ Episcopal Church, his remains were interred in Cedar Grove Cemetery, New Bern.

On 20 Dec. 1830 he married Lydia G. Jones, of New Bern, the daughter of Frederick Jones. She died on 24 Nov. 1833, leaving a son. On 24 Mar. 1840 he married Mary Spaight Donnell (28 Sept. 1817–30 Apr. 1883), the daughter of Judge John Robert (1789–1864) and Margaret Elizabeth Spaight Donnell (1800–1831) and the granddaughter of Governor Richard Dobbs Spaight, Sr.

One of their daughters, Mary Spaight Shepard (18 Mar. 1843–1 Jan. 1892), married James Augustus Bryan (13 Sept. 1839–30 Jan. 1923) of New Bern; they were the parents of Colonel Charles Shepard Bryan (1865–1956). The other Shepard daughter, Margaret Donnell Shepard, married Samuel Steward Nelson. All were buried in Cedar Grove Cemetery, New Bern.

SEE: *Biog. Dir. Am. Cong.* (1971); John L. Cheney, Jr., ed., *North Carolina Government, 1585–1979* (1981); Christ Church records, Craven County records (New Bern); Raleigh *Register*, 31 Oct. 1843; Tombstone inscriptions, Cedar Grove Cemetery, New Bern; John H. Wheeler, *Historical Sketches of North Carolina* (1851); *Who Was Who in America: Historical Edition, 1607–1896* (1967).

GERTRUDE S. CARRAWAY

Shepard, James Biddle *(14 Nov. 1815–17 June 1871)*, lawyer, legislator, and poet, was born in New Bern, the son of William Biddle and Mary Blount Shepard of Elmwood, Pasquotank County. He was related to the Biddle and Pettigrew families. After attending the New Bern Academy, he entered The University of North Carolina and was graduated with first distinction in his class; he received a bachelor's degree in 1834 and a master's degree in 1838. With his widowed mother he moved to Raleigh in 1838. He studied law with John H. Bryan of New Bern, and as soon as he was licensed he began a practice that lasted until about 1846.

Shepard was appointed U.S. district attorney in 1839 but soon resigned as he did not find the position to his liking—it was reported that he was "too wealthy to undergo the drudgery of the bar." He represented Wake County in the North Carolina Senate in the session of 1842–43 and in the House of Commons in 1844–45. The nominee of the Democratic party for governor in 1846, he was defeated by the Whig nominee, William A. Graham.

A noted orator, Shepard saw several of his speeches published in pamphlet form. Among the latter were *An Address Delivered Before the Citizens, Mechanics, and Guards of the City of Raleigh, July 4, 1839*; *Speech Delivered at the Great Republican Meeting, in the County of Granville, in the Presidential Canvass of 1840*; *An Address Delivered Before the Two Literary Societies of Wake Forest College, June 17, 1841*; *Introductory Lecture, Read Before the Raleigh Mechanics Association, at the Opening of Their Course, July 12, 1841*; and *An Address Delivered Before the Two Literary Societies of the University of North Carolina, in Gerard [sic] Hall, June 5, 1844*. His long poem, "Carolina," was published in the second volume of *Wood-Notes; or, Carolina Carols* (1854), compiled by Mary Bayard Clarke. "The Change," "An Evening Reflection," and "Grave of Macon, By Roanoke" were included in Hight C. Moore, ed., *Select Poetry of North Carolina* (1894). "The Pilot," about Pilot Mountain, and "Roanoke," about the river, were included in the anthology, *North Carolina Poems* (1912), prepared by Eugene C. Brooks.

Shepard married Frances Teach Donnell of New Bern, but she died soon after the birth of their only child, John Robert Donnell, on 8 May 1845. He spent the last fifteen years of his life in travel, often in the Holy Land, Egypt, Greece, and various parts of Europe, sometimes in the company of John C. Breckinridge of Kentucky, and often lived in Paris, where his son also resided. Shepard was buried in the eastern end of the old City Cemetery in Raleigh to which the remains of members of his family from eastern North Carolina had recently been brought.

SEE: Eugene C. Brooks, *North Carolina Poems* (1912); John L. Cheney, Jr., ed., *North Carolina Government, 1585–1979* (1981); Daniel L. Grant, *Alumni History of the University of North Carolina* (1924); J. G. de Roulhac Hamilton, ed., *Papers of William Alexander Graham*, vol. 2 (1959); Raleigh *Sentinel*, 19–20 June 1871; Mary L. Thornton, comp., *A Bibliography of North Carolina, 1589–1956* (1958).

WILLIAM S. POWELL

Shepard, James Edward *(3 Nov. 1875–6 Oct. 1947)*, college president, was the oldest of twelve children born in Raleigh to the Reverend Augustus and Hattie Whitted Shepard. He attended the public schools of Raleigh before entering Shaw University, where he received a degree in pharmacy in 1894. After working for one year in Danville, Va., Shepard opened a pharmacy in Durham. In 1898 he moved to Washington, D.C., and became comparer of deeds in the recorder's office. He returned to Raleigh to work from 1899 to 1905 as deputy collector of internal revenue for the federal government. From 1905 to 1909 he was a field superintendent of the International Sunday School Board for work among Negroes.

In 1910 Shepard founded the National Religious Training School and Chatauqua in Durham. He served as the school's president and devoted most of his energies to its development. Though it had ten buildings and more than one hundred students by 1912, the school faced continual financial difficulties, so Shepard traveled widely soliciting funds. To satisfy its creditors in 1915 the facilities were auctioned off, but a personal donation from Mrs. Russell Sage of New York enabled the school to repurchase its property. The reorganized school became the National Training School and in 1923 the Durham State Normal School when the state assumed control. Under Shepard's continuing leadership the school in 1925 survived a major fire and became the North Carolina College for Negroes, the first state-supported liberal arts college for blacks in the nation. The General Assembly changed the name to the North Carolina College at Durham in 1947 and to North Carolina Central University in 1969.

Often compared to Booker T. Washington, Shepard rejected both confrontation and legislation to better race relations. He favored conciliation at the conference table and argued that "we cannot legislate hate out of the world or love into it." Shepard's approach won praise from the General Assembly in 1948: "this native born North Carolinian labored . . . with wisdom and foresight for the lasting betterment of his race and his state, not through agitation or ill-conceived demands, but through the advocacy of a practical, well considered and constant program of racial progress." More radical blacks, however, found Shepard's approach "disgusting uncletommism." One northern black critic charged that he "speaks not for the New Negro but for his little band of bandana wearers and them alone." Shepard articulated his views on racial affairs in a series of statewide radio broadcasts in the 1930s and 1940s and in speeches and writings for national audiences in which he supported and defended the progress of North Carolina.

A Republican in national politics, Shepard supported Democrats locally. He effectively presented his college's case before the state legislature. One political commentator declared in 1948, "He was regarded by many legislators the best politician ever to come before them. He probably got a larger percentage of his requests than anybody did and he generally aimed high." In 1945 the High Point *Enterprise* called him one of the state's ten more valuable citizens.

Shepard was a member of the Baptist church, a grand master of the Prince Hall Free and Accepted Masons of North Carolina, a grand patron of the Eastern Star, and a secretary of finances for the Knights of Pythias. He was president of the North Carolina Colored Teachers Association, the International Sunday School Convention, and the State Industrial Association of North Carolina; a trustee of Lincoln Hospital and Oxford Colored Orphanage; a director of Mechanics and Farmers Bank; and a member of the North Carolina Agricultural Society. Shepard received honorary degrees from Muskingham College (1912), Selma University (1913), Howard University (1925), and Shaw University (1945). He was the only black speaker at the World Sunday School Convention held in Rome in 1910.

On 7 Nov. 1895 Shepard married Mrs. Annie Day Robinson. They had two daughters, Annie Day and Marjorie. He died at his home in Durham of a cerebral hemorrhage and was buried in Beechwood Cemetery. The library at North Carolina College was named for Shepard in 1951, and a statue of him stands on the campus. The James E. Shepard Foundation was established to provide scholarships for worthy black students.

SEE: *Carolina Times*, 11 Oct. 1947; *Durham Morning Herald*, 18 Feb. 1944, 7 Oct. 1947; *Greensboro Daily News*, 9 Oct. 1947, 31 Dec. 1948; High Point *Enterprise*, 9 July 1945; *Peoples Voice*, 26 Feb. 1944; Raleigh *News and Observer*, 7 Oct. 1947, 3 Nov. 1950; Elizabeth Irene Seay, "A History of the North Carolina College for Negroes" (M.A. thesis, Duke University, 1941); James E. Shepard Papers (North Carolina Central University Library, Durham); *Who's Who in Colored America*, 6th ed. (1941–44);

CHARLES W. EAGLES

Shepard, William Biddle *(14 May 1799–20 June 1852)*, lawyer, congressman, and state senator, was born in New Bern, the third of ten children of William and Mary Williams Blount Shepard. His father, a wealthy landowner, was a noted public speaker who owned large tracts of land. William B. Shepard's younger brother, Charles, was also a member of Congress.

Shepard attended preparatory schools in New Bern before entering The University of North Carolina in 1813. Having inherited his father's talent for public speaking, he was encouraged by fellow students to make a speech on the war between the United States and Great Britain and, more specifically, to denounce a member of the university faculty, a British subject who expressed his English sentiments with a bit more freedom than the students liked. Shepard delivered his speech (including statements that the president had directed him not to include) before a large number of receptive students who cheered him on. He was the hero of the day, and word of his action spread throughout the state. Nevertheless, because trustees' regulations prohibited students from making political speeches, Shepard and several other students who had supported him were obliged to withdraw.

Shepard continued his studies at the University of Pennsylvania, from which he was graduated; afterwards he studied law in New Bern, where he was admitted to the bar. His first law practice was in Camden County, where he owned extensive land, but he later moved to Elizabeth City and remained there for the rest of his life.

In 1829 Shepard was elected to the U.S. House of Representatives as a Republican. Although one of the youngest members when he took the oath, he quickly established himself as a fearless, earnest, and able congressman. He began his career in Washington during the administration of President Andrew Jackson and in the midst of a stormy dispute between Jackson and the U.S. Bank. Shepard sided with the bank against Jackson, and it was over this issue that his speeches gained him the most notice as a congressman. Although opponents of the bank suggested that Shepard's stand was due to kinship ties (Nicholas Biddle was his first cousin as well as president of the bank), their allegation was never substantiated.

In other congressional action, Shepard was instrumental in procuring appropriations for the opening of Roanoke Inlet and devoted much of his time to that project. His efforts in that area were considered critical in opening access to the Albemarle section of the state.

Shepard retired from Congress voluntarily in 1837. Returning to Elizabeth City, he was appointed president of the branch of the state bank there. He also was a member of the North Carolina Senate from 1838 to 1840 and from 1848 to 1850. As a senator he became popular for his firm stand on states' rights.

At the urging of his friends Shepard became a candidate for the U.S. Senate in 1844, but he lost to George E. Badger by a very slim margin. He then retired from public life until his return to the state senate in 1848. In the interim he continued to discharge his duties as president of the branch bank and to pursue literary interests. For his knowledge of the English classics and sixteenth- and seventeenth-century writers, he came to be regarded as one of the state's most scholarly men.

Shepard was married twice and had one child by each wife. In 1834 he married Charlotte Cazenove, of Alexandria, Va., who died a year later leaving a daughter, Gertrude. In 1843 he married Annie Daves Collins of an influential Edenton family. They were the parents of William Biddle.

From 1838 until his death Shepard was a member of

the board of trustees of The University of North Carolina. He was buried in St. Paul's Churchyard, Edenton.

SEE: Samuel A. Ashe, ed., *Biographical History of North Carolina*, vol. 7 (1908); Kemp P. Battle, *History of the University of North Carolina*, vol. 1 (1907); Daniel L. Grant, *Alumni History of the University of North Carolina* (1924); John H. Wheeler, ed., *Reminiscences and Memoirs of North Carolina and Eminent North Carolinians* (1884); *Who Was Who in America: Historical Edition, 1607–1896* (1967).

MARJO E. RANKIN

Shepherd, Henry Elliot *(17 Jan. 1844–29 May 1929)*, college president, author, and lecturer, was born in Fayetteville, the son of Jesse George and Catherine Isabella Dobbin Shepherd. His mother was a sister of James C. Dobbin, secretary of the navy. Young Shepherd was educated locally at Donaldson Academy, studied briefly at Davidson College until poor health forced his withdrawal, attended the North Carolina Military Institute in Charlotte for eighteen months, and then was at the University of Virginia until he entered the Confederate army in 1861. Commissioned a lieutenant at age seventeen, he trained recruits for a time before entering the Forty-third Regiment, North Carolina Troops. He was captured at Gettysburg and held as a prisoner until the end of the war.

Returning to Fayetteville as a battle-scarred veteran of twenty-one, Shepherd taught briefly at an academy in Louisburg, but in 1868 he began teaching in City College, Baltimore. In 1875 he became superintendent of the Baltimore public schools, and after seven years he was named president of the College of Charleston in South Carolina. Under his administration the years between 1882 and 1897 saw what came to be regarded as "the renaissance of the College of Charleston." During his summer vacations, Shepherd taught in colleges and universities in Vermont, Massachusetts, New York, and North Carolina.

Leaving Charleston in 1897, Shepherd settled in Baltimore to spend the remainder of his life in literary and historical research and in writing and lecturing. He was the author of *History of the English Language, Life of Robert Edward Lee, Narrative of Prison Life at Baltimore and Johnson's Island, Ohio, An Historical Reader for the Use of Classes in Academies, High Schools, and Grammar Schools, Historical Readings for the Use of Teachers' Reading Circles*, and *A Commentary Upon Tennyson's In Memoriam*. The latter was prepared with the assistance of Alfred, Lord Tennyson, himself. In addition, he edited a history of Baltimore, prepared a study of Edgar Allan Poe, and contributed multiple entries to the *New English Dictionary* published by the Oxford University Press. His articles appeared in scholarly, popular, and religious journals throughout the United States and in Great Britain. Shepherd once estimated that he had published over eight hundred articles. He was an active member of many professional and scholarly organizations.

There is no record that Shepherd ever received an earned degree, but Lafayette College in Easton, Pa., awarded him an honorary master's degree, and Davidson College and The University of North Carolina in 1883 each granted him honorary doctor of laws degrees. An ardent Presbyterian churchman, he often spoke at church gatherings. He was a Democrat but apparently took no part in political activities, and he is not known to have had any interest in sports.

On 25 June 1867 he married Kate MacGregor Goodridge of Norfolk, Va. They became the parents of two sons and one daughter. Shepherd died and was buried in Baltimore.

SEE: Samuel A. Ashe, ed., *Biographical History of North Carolina*, vol. 6 (1907); *Baltimore Sun*, 30 May 1929; *Charlotte Observer*, 26 Feb. 1928; Davidson College alumni records (Davidson, N.C.); *Nat. Cyc. Am. Biog.*, vol. 33 (1947); Raleigh *News and Observer*, 17 Jan. 1926.

C. SYLVESTER GREEN

Shepherd, James Edward *(26 July 1847–7 Feb. 1910)*, jurist, was born at Mintonville, near Suffolk, Va., the son of Thomas S. Shepherd. Orphaned at age ten, he was placed under the care of his brother, William S. Shepherd, and attended school in Murfreesboro, N.C. In 1861, although only fourteen, he attached himself to the Sixteenth Virginia Regiment and served as a "marker" for the regiment. Later he became a military telegraph operator and served in West Virginia and in Wilson, N.C.

In 1867 and 1868 Shepherd studied law at The University of North Carolina. After being licensed in 1868, he practiced first in Wilson and then in Washington, N.C. He served as a member of the constitutional convention of 1875 and the next year became chairman of the Inferior Court of Beaufort County. Between 1882 and 1888 he was a superior court judge. Elected to the North Carolina Supreme Court in 1888, Shepherd was appointed chief justice in 1892 following the death of the incumbent, Augustus S. Merrimon. He served in that position until 1895, when he was defeated for reelection. The University of North Carolina, where he taught law for eight summer terms, awarded him an honorary LL.D. degree in 1889.

In 1871 Shepherd married Elizabeth Bowen Brown of Washington, Beaufort County. They resided in Raleigh after he became a member of the supreme court. An Episcopalian, a Democrat, and a Freemason, he was buried in Oakwood Cemetery, Raleigh. His portrait hangs in the North Carolina Supreme Court.

SEE: Samuel A. Ashe, ed., *Biographical History of North Carolina*, vol. 6 (1907); Kemp P. Battle, *History of the University of North Carolina*, vol. 2 (1912); Josephus Daniels, *Editor in Politics* (1941); Daniel L. Grant, *Alumni History of the University of North Carolina* (1924); North Carolina Bar Association, *Proceedings*, vol. 12 (1910); Stephen B. Weeks Scrapbook, vols. 1–2 (North Carolina Collection, University of North Carolina, Chapel Hill).

GRADY L. E. CARROLL

Shepherd, Lilla (May) Vass *(23 Sept. 1881–30 Dec. 1953)*, poet, was born in Raleigh, the youngest child of Lillias Margaret McDaniel and William Worrell Vass. She had a brother William Worrell, Jr., a sister Eleanor Margaret, and a half brother Samuel Nathaniel. Her father, an affluent railroad executive, was of Huguenot descent. After attending St. Mary's School in Raleigh and Mary Baldwin College in Virginia, she spent the rest of her life in Raleigh, where she married, on 11 Oct. 1900, Sylvester Brown Shepherd, an attorney. Their four children were Lillias McDaniel (Williamson), James Edward, Sylvester Brown, Jr., and William Vass.

Mrs. Shepherd was active in welfare projects and participated in the work of the Church of the Good Shephard (Episcopal). Her first poem, written about 1911 to her sister Eleanor, evinced a quality sustained throughout the next forty-one years and over eight hundred poems. Not until the early 1920s did she agree to having them published, and then only in the Raleigh dailies, the *North Carolina Churchman*, and other newspapers and religious publications. The brief lyrics, addressed to family and friends or celebrating Episcopal feast days, were often mystic condensations like those of Emily Dickinson, to whom she has been compared. Sometimes she had poems privately printed to pass out to acquaintances, and at Christmas there was always a seasonal verse on her greeting cards.

After her death, Eleanor M. Vass and W. Vass Shepherd asked Lodwick Hartley, Edwin McNeill Poteat, and Richard Walser to make selections for a book. *The Old Ever New* (1956) was never on sale and received a limited distribution. Typescripts of her unpublished poems are in the North Carolina Collection, University of North Carolina, Chapel Hill.

SEE: Samuel A. Ashe, ed., *Biographical History of North Carolina*, vol. 6 (1907); Raleigh *News and Observer*, 31 Dec. 1953, 14 Jan. 1954, 13 Feb. 1972; Lilla Vass Shepherd, personal contact, 1947.

RICHARD WALSER

Sheppard, Abraham *(fl. 1759–90)*, sheriff, legislator, and soldier. The first documentary evidence of Sheppard's private and public life is the notice of his appointment as a justice of the peace at the time of the formation of Dobbs County in 1759. He owned property along the Contentnea Creek. Sheppard was an associate of Richard Caswell, later governor, joining with him in 1767 to bring about a division of Dobbs and the establishment of Kinston as the county seat, finally accomplished in 1779.

A report filed by the colonial Assembly for taxes due to the colony from sheriffs for the years 1759–70 suggests that Sheppard and three other Dobbs County sheriffs "play into each others hands" with the result that the county's arrears were the second largest in the colony. In March 1773 Sheppard's tax collections were in arrears of £1888 14s 8d, a figure considerably larger than from any other sheriff in North Carolina. This suggests that he was either guilty of inefficient tax collection, poor record keeping, corruption, or a combination of these problems. Subsequent records written by Sheppard while acting as a military commander substantiate this judgment.

Sheppard served in the assemblies of 1760 and 1769, the Third, Fourth, and Fifth Provincial congresses in 1775 and 1776, and the House of Commons in 1779 and 1780. He completed his legislative career as a member of the Council of State in 1784. From 1783 to 1790 he served as chairman of the Court of Pleas and Quarter Sessions for Dobbs County.

A letter written by Richard Caswell indicates that Sheppard served with him as a militia commander at the Battle of Alamance in 1771 and at the Battle of Moore's Creek Bridge on 27 Feb. 1776. In December 1776 Sheppard was appointed colonel of the First Battalion of the state militia and joined the defense of Charlestown, S.C., which was threatened by a British invasion. In April 1777 he wrote from South Carolina pleading to be "rescued from the most miserable part of God's creation—both men and lands." At the instruction of the Continental Congress, North Carolina created nine Continental regiments in 1775. On order of Governor Richard Caswell, while Sheppard was still in South Carolina, the North Carolina legislature established, without the authorization of the Continental Congress, a tenth regiment. The governor pressured the Congress to accept this latest unit, to be commanded by Colonel Sheppard, and it was made a part of the Continental line on 12 June 1777.

The conditions of appointment and acceptance of Sheppard's command in April 1777 were that he would recruit a minimum of three hundred men and move them northwards to join George Washington's Grand Army by 1 June 1777. Through the efforts of the governor, Sheppard received special aids and privileges to assist his recruiting efforts that were denied to the commanding officers of the earlier created North Carolina Continental regiments. From June 1777 to January 1778 the Tenth North Carolina Regiment remained in the state while the governor and the Continental Congress pleaded with Sheppard to move his troops northwards. The colonel complained with some validity of a lack of supplies, arrears in soldiers' pay, and the difficulty of recruiting. But these were problems common to all commanders during those years.

In December 1777 committees of both houses of the legislature found Sheppard's reasons for delay "frivolous and insufficient." These findings were reached after the colonel's son Benjamin, paymaster for the regiment, was declared to have been suspected of counterfeiting while with the militia in 1776 and was placed under a £1000 bond. At the same time the regiment's quartermaster, Alexander Outlaw, failed to appear in court in Halifax on charges of corruption.

By February 1778 Sheppard was moving his greatly understrength regiment northwards at the rate of a mile per day. While doing so, he lost a deserter per mile, an average of one per day. In mid-March the regiment reached Georgetown, Md., the location of a smallpox inoculation camp, where it was delayed by an outbreak of the measles.

Scanty records suggest that the small remnants of the Tenth Regiment arrived at Valley Forge in mid-May 1778. Losses had reduced all North Carolina regiments to skeleton strength, and the Third through Tenth were added to the First or Second regiments. Colonel Sheppard resigned his commission in the Continental army on 1 June 1778.

Little evidence survives of Sheppard's personal life. He had at least two sons, Benjamin and Captain Abram.

SEE: Fred A. Berg, *Encyclopedia of Continental Army Units* (1972); John L. Cheney, Jr., ed., *North Carolina Government, 1585–1974* (1975); Walter Clark, ed., *State Records of North Carolina*, vols. 11–13, 16, 22 (1896–1907); Talmage Johnson and Charles R. Holloman, *The Story of Kinston and Lenoir County* (1954); Military Collections (North Carolina State Archives, Raleigh); Hugh F. Rankin, *North Carolina Continentals* (1971); Phillips Russell, *North Carolina in the Revolutionary War* (1965); William L. Saunders, ed., *Colonial Records of North Carolina*, vols. 8–10 (1890).

WILLIAM F. HOHENWARTER

Sheppard, Muriel S. Earley *(6 Oct. 1898–6 Feb. 1951)*, writer, was born in Andover, N.Y., the daughter of Florence Eliza Stephens and Crayton I. Earley. In December 1909, when she was eleven, her father had a local printer issue a small volume of poems by her entitled *Little Poems by a Little Girl*. In 1920 she was graduated from Alfred University magna cum laude and on 21 December married civil engineer Mark Sheppard III. Their only child, Mark Earley, born on 15 July 1927, became an anesthesiologist. Muriel Sheppard was a Unitarian and a Democrat.

Moving to North Carolina in the 1920s, she became a feature writer for the Asheville newspapers and established her home in the nearby Blue Ridge Mountains. In 1935 her major work, *Cabins in the Laurel*, was published by The University of North Carolina Press. It was an account of the Toe River Valley in western North Carolina, including much on the history, traditions, and way of life of the people there. The book was copiously illustrated with photographs by Mrs. Bayard Wootten of Chapel Hill. Well received and favorably reviewed, it remained in print for many years and was most recently reissued in 1991. Muriel Sheppard continued to write feature articles for the Asheville papers and for the *Pittsburgh Press*. She also wrote magazine articles for a variety of publications ranging from *American Home* to the *South Atlantic Quarterly*.

Her last book was published by The University of North Carolina Press in 1947. Entitled *Cloud by Day: The Story of Coal and Coke and People*, it was an account of life among the coal miners of western Pennsylvania. She died at her home in Barrackville, W.Va., and was buried in Hillside Cemetery, Andover, N.Y.

SEE: Kaliopy Hames (Andover Historic Preservation Corporation) to William S. Powell, 6, 13 May 1991; *North Carolina Authors* (1952); *Publishers' Weekly* 159 (24 Feb. 1951); *Saturday Review of Literature* 11 (30 Mar. 1935).

ELMER D. JOHNSON

Shepperd, Augustine Henry *(24 Feb. 1792–11 July 1864)*, lawyer and congressman, was born at Rockford, a village on the Yadkin and the seat of Surry County until 1851. His parents were Jacob and Pamela Shepperd. In early life he practiced law in his hometown and represented his county in the lower house of the Assembly from 1822 to 1826. He was a presidential elector for the People's ticket of Andrew Jackson and John C. Calhoun in 1824.

Shepperd began his congressional career in March 1827, when he defeated Bedford Brown for the seat vacated by Romulus Saunders. Though elected as a Jackson man, his political course in time took him into the ranks of the Whigs. He opposed nullification, supported Jackson's Force Bill, and championed the national bank. In 1836 he pledged to support the choice of the electorate of his state should the presidential contest be decided in the House of Representatives, but he clearly preferred someone other than Martin Van Buren. For five terms Shepperd was reelected without serious competition until Democrat John Hill defeated him in 1839. Two years later Shepperd regained his seat by defeating David S. Reid, of Wentworth, the future Democratic governor and U.S. senator. Reid held the seat from 1843 to 1847. Shepperd then returned to serve two final terms from 1847 to 1851.

During his eighteen years in Congress Shepperd held several important committee assignments, and he gained some prominence as one of the leading southern Whigs. He was a presidential elector on the Whig ticket in 1844, and he played a role in getting President Millard Fillmore to appoint William A. Graham as secretary of the navy in 1850.

In October 1842 Shepperd bought forty-one acres from the Moravians. On this land, located within the bounds of modern Winston-Salem, the Shepperds built a home that they called Good Spring. Augustine had married a Miss Turner during his first term in Congress. They had at least seven children. Samuel Turner Shepperd was a graduate of West Point in 1854 and died the following year while on frontier duty in Kansas. William Henry was next. Francis E., the third son, was a graduate of the U.S. Naval Academy at Annapolis and later served in the Confederate navy. Hamilton saw service in the Confederate army, and Jacob was killed at Fredericksburg in 1862. Mary Frances married William Dorsey Pender just before the Civil War; her famous husband was fatally wounded at Gettysburg. Pamela Martha married William S. Mallory in 1867.

After retiring from Congress in 1851, Shepperd returned to Forsyth County and resumed the practice of law. He died there and was buried in Salem Cemetery.

SEE: *Biog. Dir. Am. Cong.* (1971); Adelaide L. Fries and others, *Forsyth: A County on the March* (1949); J. G. de Roulhac Hamilton, ed., *Papers of William Alexander Graham*, vol. 3 (1960); W. W. Hassler, ed., *The General to His Lady: Civil War Letters of W. D. Pender* (1962); H. D. Pegg, "The Whig Party in North Carolina, 1834–1861" (dissertation, University of North Carolina, Chapel Hill, 1932); A. H. Shepperd Papers (Southern Historical Collection, University of North Carolina, Chapel Hill).

DANIEL M. MCFARLAND

Sheridan, Louis *(ca. 1793–1844)*, farmer, free black merchant, and Liberian official, was probably the Louis Sheridan mentioned in the 1800 will of Joseph R. Gautier (d. 15 May 1807), Elizabethtown merchant, as the son of Nancy Sheridan, "my emancipated black woman" to whom he left "my plantation at the Marsh." Louis obtained a good education and engaged in extensive mercantile operations. Although he was a mulatto with a fair complexion, he was recorded as white in the Bladen County censuses for 1810, 1820, and 1830. He was aided in business by John Owen, former governor, and other white men of the Lower Cape Fear who gave him letters of introduction. Sheridan made business trips to nearby Wilmington as well as to Philadelphia, New York, and elsewhere, sometimes making purchases of goods valued in excess of $12,000. As a young man he preached for a brief time and also subscribed to and served as an agent for two black newspapers.

Sheridan occupied one of the best houses in Elizabethtown, and his household in 1829 was composed of himself, aged twenty-six, eight male and four female slaves, and three free blacks. In 1830 the household consisted of twenty-three persons including sixteen slaves, five free blacks, one of whom is said to have been his mother, and two white males under the age of thirty, who may have been clerks in his store since many of his customers were white. As a slave owner, Sheridan had the reputation of being "a severe master."

Although he had friends of both races, Sheridan had difficulty in finding his place in society. Until the liberties of free blacks in America began to be restricted following a slave insurrection in Virginia in 1831, he opposed the colonization of blacks in Africa. Legislative action and changes in the North Carolina Constitution in 1835, however, led him to yield to the suggestion of agents of the American Colonization Society that he move to Africa. They observed that "[f]or energy of mind, firmness of purpose and a variety of practical knowledge, Sheridan has no superior."

In 1836 Sheridan decided that he and "39 other persons of my family" would begin plans to move. He freed his own slaves in 1837 and sailed for Liberia two days before Christmas, taking with him between $15,000 to $20,000, a large quantity of lumber, and thirty tons of merchandise to be sold there. He had refused to take a ship from Norfolk and agreed to sail only when a ship was made available in Wilmington. He also insisted that ample good food and drinking water be provided for the voyage as well as comfortable accommodations for his family.

After arriving in Liberia Sheridan was unhappy with the provisions made for his people, and he expressed his displeasure to the chief administrator. He quickly gained the reputation of a troublemaker, especially after he tried in vain to get some of the colonists to petition backers in the United States for a change in the rules. Nevertheless, Sheridan acquired a long-term lease for six hundred acres and was authorized to establish a new settlement. Under his leadership land was cleared, and corn, sugarcane, and coffee trees were planted; he also experimented with other produce such as corn, rice, and sweet potatoes and with cattle. He soon was at odds with some of the white administrators and corresponded with Americans who had abandoned the idea of colonization and joined the abolitionist movement. He spoke out against inefficiency and bemoaned the fact that Liberia was so dependent on supplies from the United States. And even though he employed some native labor, he complained of the "barbarous natives."

One of his critical letters, published in William Lloyd Garrison's *Liberator*, was used by abolitionists in their opposition to colonization. Because of this as well as his conflict with local officials, Sheridan was not chosen to fill an important vacancy in the government, and he became even more dissatisfied. He once considered returning to North Carolina but lacked the necessary resources.

Liberia became a commonwealth in 1839, and with the arrival of a new governor, Sheridan's position improved. He was made official storekeeper and general agent for a portion of the country. During a native uprising he successfully organized military defenses and fed the populace. Afterwards he worked to earn the goodwill of native chieftains, negotiated treaties, and enlarged the boundaries of the commonwealth. At the death of the governor, however, Sheridan was displeased with the choice of a successor, and he frequently voiced his objections to conditions. Towards the end of 1843 he became ill and he died the next year, so unappreciated that the journals that had praised him highly a few years before did not even report his death.

SEE: Bladen County census returns, 1810, 1820, 1830; Wanda S. Campbell, *Abstracts of the Wills of Bladen County, North Carolina, 1734–1900* (1962); Willard B. Gatewood, "'To Be Truly Free': Louis Sheridan and the Colonization of Liberia," *Civil War History* 29 (December 1983); *Paths Toward Freedom: A Biographical History of Blacks and Indians* (1976).

WILLIAM S. POWELL

Sherrill, Miles Osborne *(26 July 1841–8 Apr. 1919)*, Confederate soldier and state librarian, was born at Sherrills Ford, Catawba County, the son of Hiram and Sarah Osborne Sherrill. On 27 Apr. 1861 he joined the Catawba County troops in anticipation of secession. Mustered in as a corporal, he was promoted to first sergeant in May 1863. In May 1864 he was wounded in the right leg and captured at Spotsylvania Court House, Va. After the amputation of his leg he was sent to Federal hospitals until October, when he was confined to the Old Capitol Prison in Washington, D.C. In December 1864 he was transferred to a prison in Elmira, N.Y., and held until his transfer to Cox's Wharf on the James River in Virginia for exchange.

With his return to civilian status in Catawba County, Sherrill became clerk of the superior court. He also represented his county in the General Assembly, serving in the house in 1883 and the senate in 1885 and 1893.

Sherrill's most significant contribution to North Carolina was as state librarian between 1899 and 1916. His administration of the library was an enlightened one. Suggestions and recommendations by him, some realized during his period of service, resulted in significant improvements. In 1900 he modified the system of classifying and cataloguing books, using the Dewey decimal system and by placing cards in a catalogue recording author, title, subjects, place and date of publication, and the location of each book in the library.

His biennial reports recorded progress in the publication of the colonial and state records under the editorship of Chief Justice Walter Clark. Sherrill lamented the lack of appreciation by North Carolinians of the publications of the state. He commented that the northern and western states showed more interest in their regimental histories of the Civil War than North Carolinians did. These, he said, contained records of the "greatest citizen soldiery the world has ever witnessed."

An interesting acquisition was recorded in the librarian's reports of 1906 and 1914. This was the private library of James Hassel, a North Carolina colonial official, which consisted of about 420 volumes. Located by Colonel Fred A. Olds in an abandoned house near Wilmington, the library apparently had been neglected for a century or more, and Lieutenant Commander Edwin A. Anderson authorized it to be transferred to the State Library. Hassel's bookplate was in many of the volumes together with autographs of former owners going back to the time of Christopher Gale, who died in 1735. One of the books had been published in 1695.

It was Sherrill who suggested the appointment of a state archivist or historian "whose duty it shall be to take charge of all the old wills, petitions, and letters now on file in the capitol which had been accumulating more than one hundred years and that same be arranged and properly labelled and that a proper place be provided for them where they can be 'come-at-able' when needed." He recognized the efforts of R. D. W. Connor and the North Carolina Historical Commission, assisted by Secretary of State Bryan Grimes, in preserving the sources of the state's history.

Sherrill consistently pointed out the need for larger and more adequate space for the library. In 1912 legislation was passed providing an appropriation and naming a commission or committee to investigate the possibilities for new quarters. In 1914 the pleas of the librarian were partially answered when the library moved into "handsome new quarters" in the state Administration Building. Located on the first floor, the library acquired new fixtures and equipment.

Sherrill married Sarah H. Bost in 1867, and they became the parents of seven children: Dr. J. Garland of Louisville, Ky., Mrs. S. L. Alderman of Greensboro, C. O. of Washington, D.C., E. G. of Greensboro, G. M. of Chicago, Russell G. of Raleigh, and Mary of Greensboro. Sherrill, a member of the Methodist Episcopal Church, South, was buried in Greensboro.

SEE: Biennial Reports of the State Librarian, 1900–1914; *Greensboro Daily News*, 9 Apr. 1919; Weymouth T. Jordan, Jr., comp., *North Carolina Troops, 1861–1865: A Roster*, vol. 5 (1975); *North Carolina Christian Advocate*, 17 Apr. 1919.

BETH G. CRABTREE

Sherwood, Francis Webber *(9 Feb. 1890–13 Feb. 1963)*, agricultural scientist and college professor, was born in Raleigh, the son of Francis Webber and Mary Bates Sherwood. His ancestors can be traced to the Mayflower (John Howland) and to the Bates family of Virginia. His mother was a teacher and principal in the Raleigh public schools for nearly half a century. Sherwood-Bates elementary school was named for her and for her sister, Grace Bates.

Young Sherwood attended the Raleigh public schools and North Carolina State College (now North Carolina State University), where he received a B.S. degree in chemistry in 1909 and an M.S. degree in 1911. In the meantime he had already begun his career as an analytic chemist at the North Carolina Agricultural Experiment Station. He began doctoral work at Cornell University but was forced to drop out for financial reasons and take a job as a research chemist with the Federal Dyestuff and Chemical Corporation during 1916–17 and with the DuPont Chemical Corporation in 1919. During World War I he worked for the Chemical Warfare Service of the U.S. Army. Sherwood returned to State College as a research professor in 1919 and was able to complete his work at Cornell, receiving the Ph.D. degree in 1921. He remained at North Carolina State College until his retirement in 1956, when he became professor emeritus in animal nutrition.

Sherwood was identified with several phases of southern life: agriculture, through his contribution to basic knowledge in feeding cattle and swine; economy, through the increase in profitable production of better livestock through improved feeding practices; and education, through his years of inspiration at State College. He made research contributions on practically every agricultural product of economic importance to the South. Sherwood was one of the earliest biochemists in the nation to use statistical experiment design in his work. He was known especially for his nutritional research on cottonseed meal as animal feed, peanut feeding in pork production, and the relationship between soil fertility and the nutritive value of forage. He published numerous papers in scientific and technical journals.

In recognition of his service to the profession of chemistry in the South, he received the fourth Southern Chemist Award of the American Chemical Society in 1953. He was a Fellow in the American Association for the Advancement of Science, a life member of the Academy of Science in North Carolina, chairman of the North Carolina section of the American Chemical Society and a member of the society for over fifty years, and a member of Sigma Xi, Gamma Alpha, and Alpha Chi Sigma fraternities. He was president of the Raleigh Natural History Club and a member of the Raleigh Executive Club. Sherwood, a Democrat, served as deacon and treasurer of the First Presbyterian Church.

In 1918 he married Amelia Tate Stockard, the daughter of Lula Tate and Henry Jerome Stockard. The couple had two children, Mary Bates and Francis Webber, Jr. Sherwood died in Raleigh and was buried in Oakwood Cemetery. There is a portrait of him in Polk Hall on the North Carolina State University campus.

SEE: *American Men of Science*, vol. 30 (1961); *Chemical and Engineering News* 31 (14 Dec. 1953); *Extension Farm News* 39 (December 1953 [portrait]); *Greensboro Daily News*, 4 Dec. 1953; William S. Powell, ed., *North Carolina Lives* (1962); Raleigh *News and Observer*, 30 Nov. 1953, 14 Feb. 1963; *Southern Chemist* 13 (December 1953).

MARY BATES SHERWOOD

Shipp, Albert Micajah *(15 June 1819–27 June 1887)*, Methodist minister, university professor, college president, seminary dean, and church historian, was born in Stokes County, the son of John and Elizabeth Oglesby Shipp. He received an A.B. degree from The University of North Carolina in 1840. Later he was awarded an LL.D. from the university and a D.D. from Randolph-Macon College.

Shipp was licensed to preach in December 1840 and admitted to the South Carolina Conference of the Methodist Episcopal Church in 1841. He served pastorates in the Cokesbury Circuit, Charleston, Santee Circuit, Cheraw, and Fayetteville and for one year was presiding elder of the Lincolnton District. In 1848, when a throat infection left his voice too weak to pursue a pulpit ministry, he was named president of Greensboro Female College. In 1849 he became professor of history at The University of North Carolina, where he remained for nine years.

In 1858 Shipp was appointed president of Wofford College in Spartanburg, S.C., and remained in that post for sixteen years. From 1875 to 1885 he held the chair of exegetical theology at Vanderbilt University in Nashville, Tenn., three years of the time serving as dean of the theological department and vice-chancellor of the university. In 1885 he was at his own request superannuated by the South Carolina Conference.

Shipp was elected a delegate from the South Carolina Conference to each quadrennial General Conference of the Methodist Episcopal Church, South, from 1848 to 1886. His most notable literary achievement was *The History of Methodism in South Carolina*, requested by the conference in 1876 and finally published in 1883.

He married Mary Gillespie of Rose Hill Plantation in Marlboro County, S.C., and they reared a large family. Shipp died in Cleveland Springs, N.C., where he had gone for his health. He was buried in Gillespie Cemetery near Wallace, S.C.

SEE: *DAB*, vol. 17 (1935); Daniel L. Grant, *Alumni History of the University of North Carolina* (1924); Nolan B. Harmon, *Encyclopedia of World Methodism* (1974); *Minutes of the South Carolina Conference, M. E. Church, South* (1887); D. D. Wallace, *Wofford College* (1951).

LOUISE L. QUEEN

Shipp, Bartlett *(8 Mar. 1786–26 May 1869)*, lawyer and legislator, was born in that part of Surry County that became Stokes County in 1789 near the future site of Danbury, the son of Thomas and Hannah Joyce Shipp. The elder Shipp, a Virginian, was a veteran of the American Revolution; he was at Yorktown in 1781 but soon moved to Surry County. Largely self-educated, Bartlett Shipp taught school in his youth. During the War of 1812 he volunteered for service and became a private with the Stokes County regiment. After studying law under Joseph Wilson, Shipp practiced briefly in Wilkes County.

In 1818, about the time of his marriage to Susan, the daughter of Peter Forney of Lincoln County, he moved to Lincoln County. Shipp represented that county in the House of Commons for the terms 1824–25, 1826–27, 1828–29, 1829–30, and 1830–31, and in the Senate during 1834–35. In the house he served for a time on the Committee on Education and in 1830 supported a bill to prevent the teaching of slaves to read and write, but the measure was defeated. Although an unsuccessful candidate for Congress in 1831, he represented Lincoln County at the constitutional convention in 1835. In 1852, with F. M. Reinhardt, he bought an interest in the former Rehoboth forge near his home when it was known as the Reinhardt furnace.

Shipp and his wife were the parents of a son, William M., who became a jurist in Charlotte, and two daughters, Eliza (m. William Preston Bynum) and Susan (m. V. C. Johnson). He was buried in the Episcopal churchyard in Lincolnton.

SEE: Charlotte *Western Democrat*, 1 June 1869; John L. Cheney, Jr., ed., *North Carolina Government, 1585–1974* (1975); Charles L. Coon, *The Beginnings of Public Education in North Carolina*, vol. 1 (1908); Raleigh *Daily Sentinel*, 4 June 1869; William L. Sherrill, *Annals of Lincoln County, North Carolina* (1937); John H. Wheeler, ed., *Reminiscences and Memoirs of North Carolina and Eminent North Carolinians* (1884).

ROSAMOND PUTZEL

Shipp, Catherine (Kate) Cameron *(18 Mar. 1859–16 Nov. 1932)*, teacher and administrator, was born in Hendersonville, the daughter of William Marcus and Catherine Cameron Shipp. After attending the preparatory school in Lincolnton operated by Miss Mary Wood Alexander and St. Mary's School in Raleigh, she pursued further studies at Harvard and at Cambridge University, England.

For over forty years Kate Shipp was an educator in North Carolina. She taught in the public schools of Charlotte and Raleigh, at St. Mary's School (now St. Mary's College), and at the Charlotte Female Institute (now Queens College), and she operated two private schools. During the late 1880s, she taught mathematics at the Charlotte Female Institute, where she also was associate principal. She returned to St. Mary's to teach from 1894 to 1897. It was her custom to chaperone small groups of students to Europe during the summer.

By 1898 Kate Shipp and her sister, Mrs. Anna Shipp McBee, had opened in Lincolnton a school to prepare boys and girls for college. This school, which they named the Mary Wood School to honor their former teacher, operated successfully for about four years. Miss Shipp closed it in order to study in England (1902–4). She returned to St. Mary's with a teacher's diploma from Cambridge and taught mathematics and English literature (1904–6).

In 1907 Miss Shipp established in Lincolnton her Fassifern School "to prepare girls for the best colleges, or to be self-supporting, and to help them become lovers of the best in literature, music, and art." The catalogue plainly stated, "This is not a school for the idle and would-be fashionable young lady." Situated in a large house overlooking the South Fork River, the school was described as a Christian home giving individual attention and emphasizing religious and physical training and ladylike behavior as well as scholarship. Miss Shipp was assisted by Mrs. McBee and a strong faculty. By 1914 Fassifern was overcrowded despite an addition, and Miss Shipp accepted the offer of financial backing from a Hendersonville group that wanted the prestigious school in its community. Located in that salubrious climate on a spacious and well-equipped campus, the school prospered. By 1923 the student body numbered over one hundred from ten states. After the death of Mrs. McBee (25 Dec. 1924), Kate Shipp sold Fassifern School to the Reverend Joseph R. Sevier, D.D., and retired to Lincolnton.

The more than two hundred graduates of Fassifern organized the Kate Shipp Alumnae Association and held annual reunions with their former headmistress. Kate Shipp was an excellent teacher—demanding but fair and possessed of a sense of humor. A large and imposing woman, she inevitably was called "the Ship of State" by her pupils. Her qualities of leadership—a forceful personality, a highly trained intellect, discriminating judgment, and business ability—prompted a leading lawyer to remark that she would have made a great governor of her native state.

Kate Shipp died in Lincolnton and was buried in the family plot at St. Luke's Episcopal Church. She had been a devout and active Episcopalian.

SEE: Nardi Reeder Campion, *Look To This Day! The Lively Education of a Great Woman Doctor: Connie Guion, M.D.* (1965); Catalogues of Charlotte Female Institute, Fassifern School, and St. Mary's School; Delta Kappa Gamma Society, *Some Pioneer Women Teachers of North Carolina* (1955); *Lincoln County News*, 17 Nov. 1932; *St. Mary's Muse*, October 1907; W. L. Sherrill, *Annals of Lincoln County, North Carolina* (1937).

MARTHA S. STOOPS

Shipp, Margaret Busbee *(9 Nov. 1871–11 Mar. 1936)*, magazine writer, was born in Raleigh. Her father was Fabius H. Busbee, a Confederate veteran, University of North Carolina graduate, and prominent lawyer. His father was Perrin Busbee, a member of the Dialectic Society while at The University of North Carolina and a reporter of the North Carolina Supreme Court at his death in 1853. Her mother was Annie McKesson, the daughter of Margaret McDowell McKesson, "a brilliant wit," and William F. McKesson, a well-to-do trader and contractor of Morganton.

Margaret Busbee attended St. Mary's School in Raleigh, where she soon displayed some talent in writing when the senior class magazine, *The Muse*, printed an article she had written when only ten. On 17 Jan. 1894 she married Lieutenant William Ewen Shipp, a graduate of West Point who had seen service against Geronimo while with the Tenth Cavalry; when they met, he was inspector of state troops in Raleigh. The Shipps soon moved to Winston, where he was commandant of cadets at the Davis Military School and where their two sons, William E., Jr., and Fabius B., were born.

At the outbreak of the Spanish-American War, Lieutenant Shipp's regiment embarked for Cuba. On 1 July 1898 he was killed at the Battle of San Juan Hill, where he was in charge of black troops. Of that day Colonel Theodore Roosevelt remarked, "It was Shipp who brought me word to advance with my regiment. . . . He had been riding to and fro with absolute coolness and fearlessness, paying no more heed of bullets than if they were hail stones."

To augment her limited military pension the young widow, with two small sons to raise, now turned her thoughts to writing for the national magazines, "a more difficult feat than to scale the walls of a fortified city," a friend observed. Nevertheless, by background she was not entirely unprepared to cope with the matter of expression. From a highly literate father she had inherited a remarkable memory and while still a child was given to rattling off quotations from Shakespeare; later she recited pages from Elizabeth Barrett Browning. Though something of an infant prodigy, she was described as having "refreshing naivete, remarkable precocity and quiet self confidence." Further, apparently prior to her husband's death she had had material accepted by the *Charlotte Observer* and possibly by other North Carolina periodicals. This local popularity depended upon emphasis on the local scene, vignettes of life in and of her native state, with a good ear for dialect, dialogue, and background.

Her first story to be accepted by a national magazine, *Ainslee's*, appeared in January 1899. By 1903 she was published in *Collier's*, *Everybody's*, and *Munsey's* and in 1910 by the prestigious *Saturday Evening Post*.

In 1923 Archibald Henderson, writing for *The Southern Literary Magazine*, stated, "Today I dare say, Margaret

Busbee Shipp is the most admired, the best loved woman in North Carolina. This enviable distinction is regarded by those who know her well as the most natural thing in the world. She has always appeared to be the incarnation of romance. . . I will say she writes most diverting love stories, full of whimsicality, sentiment, and feminine contrariety; [and] charming stories of children straight from life."

Her works appeared in numerous magazines. Titles of her stories with exact dates of the magazines can be found in a typed bibliography in the North Carolina Collection, University of North Carolina at Chapel Hill. Although most of the periodicals to which she contributed published several of her works, *Munsey's*, a popular family magazine, printed at least thirty-six between 1903 and 1926, the date the bibliography was prepared. Others for which she wrote were *American, Blue Book, Century, Cosmopolitan, Designer, Green Book, Maclean's of Canada, National, Pearson's, Red Book, Rotarian, Smith's, The Smart Set, Southern Review, Watson's, Woman's Home Companion*, and *Youth's Companion*.

Margaret Shipp died in Rome at age sixty-five and was buried next to her husband at St. Luke's Episcopal Church cemetery in Lincolnton. She was survived by her oldest son, William E. Neither son left issue.

SEE: Jerome Dowd, *Sketches of Prominent Living North Carolinians* (1888); Adelaide L. Fries and others, *Forsyth: The History of a County on the March* (1976); Edward W. Phifer, *Burke: The History of a North Carolina County* (1982); *North Carolina Journal of Education* 3 (1900); *Raleigh Daily News*, 17 Oct. 1874; Raleigh *News and Observer*, 15 Mar. 1936; *Southern Literary Magazine* 1 (September 1923).

JOHN MACFIE

Shipp, William (Willie) Ewen *(23 Aug. 1861–1 July 1898)*, army officer, was born in Asheville, the son of Judge William Marcus and Catherine (Kate) Cameron Shipp. The family moved to Lincolnton in 1862. His mother died when Willie was four, and he spent his youth in Lincolnton and Charlotte under the care of his grandmother, Mrs. Bartlett Shipp. He received his earliest education from Miss Mary Wood Alexander and the Reverend W. R. Wetmore, noted teachers of the day. In 1874 the family moved to Charlotte, where he attended the Carolina Military Institute, benefiting from the example of its commandant, Colonel John P. Thomas. Fond of sports and exercise, young Shipp was described by his contemporaries as being "of fine physique, of admirable morals, of marked mental ability, with studious habits."

A brilliant examination in 1879 in competition with forty contestants won him an appointment by Congressman Walter L. Steele to the U.S. Military Academy at West Point. Eleventh in a class of fifty-two, he was graduated in 1883, the first southerner to do so since the Civil War. At his own request he was assigned to the Tenth Cavalry, a unit composed of black soldiers. As a second lieutenant he joined his unit on the western frontier and saw hard service in the Indian campaigns, for which he received a commendation for gallantry in the uprising headed by Geronimo. Shipp was promoted to first lieutenant in 1889. Because of a sprained ankle he was disabled for active service and was assigned to the Davis Military Institute at Winston, N.C., as professor of military tactics and special instructor of the North Carolina State Guard. Having recovered, he joined his regiment in August 1897 at Assiniboine, Montana, and accompanied it to Chickamauga and afterwards to Florida.

At the beginning of the Spanish-American War he was offered assignments that would have kept him out of Cuba, but he requested active service and thus was attached to General William R. Shafter's army of invasion. Made brigade quartermaster, he volunteered once again and met his death in the charge on San Juan Hill. He had been sent by General Leonard Wood to deliver an order to advance to Colonel Theodore Roosevelt. After his return, Shipp had rejoined his own regiment and was leading his Troop F when he was killed.

Shipp married Margaret Busbee of Raleigh in 1894, and they were the parents of two sons, William Ewen, Jr., and Fabius Busbee. A member of the Episcopal church, he was buried beside his mother in St. Luke's churchyard at Lincolnton. His military funeral, with the assistance of Confederate veterans and the Lee Rifles from Charlotte, was attended by three thousand people.

In Charlotte the children of the school that Shipp had attended began a campaign to raise funds for a monument to him. Subsequently a fifteen-ton granite obelisk, thirty feet tall, was dedicated in front of the former U.S. Mint both to honor Shipp and to commemorate the military reinstatement of the Southern states after the Civil War.

SEE: *Charlotte Daily Observer*, 20, 25–26 Aug., 4, 8 [portrait] Sep. 1898; *Military Collector and Historian* 9 (Summer 1957 [portrait]); *The New South* 1 (February 1899 [portrait]); *North Carolina Journal of Education* 3 (April–May 1900); Raleigh *News and Observer*, 11 Nov. 1934; Blackwell P. Robinson, ed., *The North Carolina Guide* (1955); *The William E. Shipp Memorial, at the Slater College and State Normal School* (1898? [portrait]).

WILLIAM S. POWELL

Shipp, William Ewen, Jr. *(9 Nov. 1894–2 Nov. 1961)*, army officer and diplomatic military attaché, was born in Winston, the son of William E. and Margaret Busbee Shipp. A 1916 graduate of the U.S. Military Academy at West Point, he ranked 54 in a class of 125. Commissioned upon graduation, he participated first in the Mexican Border Service in New Mexico. During World War I he held a temporary commission as major of cavalry, and in 1918 he was an instructor in modern languages at the Military Academy. Returning to the grade of captain, he was commanding officer of troops on transport ships to Europe. He served in Germany, Belgium, and France, part of the time with the American Graves Registration Service. Following a number of assignments in the United States and graduation from several service schools, he was executive officer of the 463d Field Artillery Battalion in Charlotte.

In 1927, having recently served in the military intelligence division of the War Department in Washington, D.C., Shipp became assistant military attaché at the American Embassy in Rome, where he remained until 1930. From 1932 to 1936 he was military attaché to the Baltic States and to Finland. Between 1938 and 1941 he served in the Eastern European Intelligence section and was promoted to lieutenant colonel. There followed a year with the American Legation in Lisbon, Portugal. He was named attaché to Yugoslavia and later to Iran, but both assignments were canceled due to the war. Promoted to colonel in 1942, he was attaché at Quito, Ecuador, for a year and a half before being transferred to Asunción, Paraguay. Returning to the United States, he was with the War Department General Staff in Washington for three years and in 1944 became assistant chief of staff, G-2, in the Panama Canal Department. He served in Baghdad, Iraq, from 1947 to 1950.

Shipp received a decoration for service on the Mexican Border and was honored with the following orders: Crown of Italy; Vasco Núñez de Balboa (Panama); Chevalier of the White Rose (Finland); Abdon Calderón, First Class (Ecuador); and the Gold Medal, Military Circle of the Army (Ecuador). After retiring from the army on 31 Aug. 1954 as a colonel, he lived in Front Royal, Va. He died in Winchester, Va., after he was thrown from a horse while on a hunting trip. Shipp was buried in the National Cemetery, Alexandria, Va. He never married.

SEE: *Biographical Register of the Officers and Graduates of the U.S. Military Academy*, vol. 6-B (1920), supp. 7 (1940?), 9 (1950); Raleigh *News and Observer*, 20 June 1944, 4 Nov. 1961.

WILLIAM S. POWELL

Shipp, William Marcus *(9 Nov. 1819–28 June 1890)*, lawyer, judge, and attorney general, was born in Lincoln County. His father, Bartlett Shipp, an able lawyer "traveling on horseback hundreds of miles" as he followed the circuit court, was born in Stokes County in 1786 and is said to have been the first person of that name to settle in Lincoln. He served in the War of 1812 and was twice elected a member of the North Carolina House of Commons. William's mother was Susan Forney, the daughter of "General" Peter Forney, of Huguenot stock, who saw action with the rangers operating in the western part of the state in the Revolutionary War. British general Lord Charles Cornwallis is said to have occupied the Forney log cabin for three days during these skirmishes.

William M. Shipp attended the Pleasant Retreat Institute in Lincolnton, a school for boys, and then entered The University of North Carolina; during his graduation in 1840, he delivered the salutatory address in Latin. His cousin, Albert Micajah Shipp, was the valedictorian. Both young men were great-grandsons of Josiah and Nancy Cox Shipp of Lunenburg County, Va., and grandsons of Thomas and Hannah Joyce Shipp of Surry County, N.C. As a private in the Revolution, Thomas saw action in North Carolina.

After reading law in Morganton, Shipp received his license in 1842 and settled in Rutherfordton, then a leading town in the western part of the state. He represented Rutherford County in the House of Commons during 1854–55. In 1857 he bought the house of Judge John Baxter in Hendersonville and soon built up a large law practice there. Shipp was a delegate to the constitutional convention of 1861–62, and in the latter year he was elected to the senate.

During this period he enlisted in the Confederate army and was made captain of Company I, Sixteenth Regiment, which served with the Army of Northern Virginia. Its marchings ranged from the cold mists of Valley Mountain in the west to the tidal waters of Yorktown, Va., and included numerous frays and some major battles such as those at Harpers Ferry, W.Va., and Mechanicsville, Va. On 16 Dec. 1862, after over a year of service, Shipp resigned to accept a superior court judgeship back home and held that post until 1868, when he was defeated by George W. Logan.

Shipp then moved to Charlotte to practice law. However, the clarion call to arms soon sounded with the coming election of 1870, an era of rebellion against Reconstruction, "the time of the carpetbagger and the scalawag." Feelings ran high. The Democrats nominated Shipp, a former "staunch Whig," who was regarded as "a man of ability and good record," for attorney general. His opponent was Samuel F. Phillips of Orange County. Shipp won in a close race and was said to have been the only man on the ticket to be elected.

He was soon appointed chairman of a three-man committee to investigate charges of fraud, corruption, and "general official venality." This involved the Cape Fear Navigation Company, which operated between Wilmington and Fayetteville and was in a sad state of physical neglect; the missing Penitentiary Bonds and other vanished records; and various western railroads, such as the Wilmington, Charlotte and Rutherford line, where excessive fees and discounts had increased the cost 23 percent in ten months. It was claimed that bonds had been given to legislators to influence their votes.

Possibly the inquiry had made Shipp unpopular in some circles, but on the other hand the Republicans gained in the election of 1872 and Shipp was defeated by Tazewell Hargrove. Shipp then applied for payment of $4,700 in fees not collected when he was a judge from 1862 to 1865 under the "Provisional Government." Hargrove rejected the claim, labeling it the "Back Salary Grab," and said the money should have been collected at the time. But Shipp's talents were not entirely overlooked. In 1881 Governor Thomas Jarvis appointed him judge of the Ninth Judicial District of the superior courts, a position he held until his death.

Jerome Dowd remarked that "Judge Shipp was one of the best informed lawyers in the State. He had a markedly legal mind, reasoned closely and as a jurist was eminent. He had no superior on the bench." Shipp was fond of reading history and the standard literature of the time. Like his lawyer father, he was quick-witted and full of humor and repartee. His sayings were a byword among lawyers over much of the state.

Shipp was married twice. In 1851 he wed Catherine Cameron, the daughter of John A. Cameron. Their four children were Anna, who married Dr. Sumner McBee; Catherine, who founded Fassifern, a well-known school for young ladies at Lincolnton, which later moved to Hendersonville; William Ewen, the husband of Margaret Busbee and a graduate of West Point, who was killed at the Battle of San Juan Hill during the Spanish-American War; and Bartlett, a University of North Carolina graduate who practiced law in Charlotte and Washington State, then returned to Lincolnton and married Prue Crouse.

The first Mrs. Shipp died in 1866, and in 1872 Shipp married Margaret Iredell, the daughter of Governor James Iredell. Their only child was Mary Preston of Raleigh. Shipp, a member of St. Peter's Episcopal Church in Charlotte, was buried in Elmwood Cemetery. Other close relatives were interred at St. Luke's Episcopal churchyard in Lincolnton.

SEE: Samuel A. Ashe, ed., *Biographical History of North Carolina*, vol. 5 (1906); *Charlotte Chronicle*, 1 July 1890; Jerome Dowd, *Sketches of Prominent Living North Carolinians* (1888); Daniel L. Grant, *Alumni History of the University of North Carolina* (1924); Clarence W. Griffin, *History of Old Tryon and Rutherford Counties, 1730–1937* (1937); J. G. de Roulhac Hamilton, *Reconstruction in North Carolina* (1914); *North Carolina Fraud Commission Report* (1872); William L. Sherrill, *Annals of Lincoln County* (1937 [portrait]).

JOHN MACFIE

Shober, Emanuel *(13 Feb. 1789–14 June 1846)*, Moravian church official and state senator, was born in Salem, the third child of Gottlieb and Magdalena Transou Shober. He attended the Salem church school and studied law under Archibald D. Murphey of Hillsborough. After receiving his license to practice, he made his home in Germantown for a short time before moving to Salem, where in 1815 he was one of three Moravians to be made agents for a bank.

Elected to the state senate in 1819, Shober served on a committee for education and helped to secure passage of "An Act making the affirmation of Moravians and Menonists evidence in criminal cases as well as in civil controversies in this state." He represented Stokes County as a senator in the general assemblies of 1819–20, 1822, 1824–25, 1827–28, and 1828–29. In 1835 he was elected as an independent to the constitutional convention held in Raleigh. There Shober took a leading part in promoting more liberal constitutional amendment procedures. In opposing the Meares report, he warned that to "adopt a plan by which it shall be necessary that two-thirds or three-fifths of the legislature shall pass upon the subject [of amending the constitution] no amendments to the Constitution would ever be made." In this regard he voted with the rest of the western delegates.

As an advocate for the Moravian church, Shober was ever ready to promote its interest and to serve in its cause. He was a member of the congregational council from 1820 until his death and played a key role in the formation of the law revising the fire code and in the establishment of a fire company in Salem in 1842. He served as captain of the Salem Light Infantry, and during the alarm over a slave revolt near Wilmington in September 1831, he was ordered to be prepared to move his unit to Montgomery County "where a Negro insurrection is in progress." The report of an uprising in the gold mine regions was greatly exaggerated, and the Salem company did not report to Montgomery County. In the same year, however, Shober went to West Point, N.Y., in order to attend the examination of the cadets and possibly to learn more about military affairs in case a real insurrection should occur.

On 8 Jan. 1833 Shober became postmaster at Salem, taking over the job from his father, who with another son, had been in charge since the position was established in 1792. Shober was retained as postmaster until his death.

On 30 Mar. 1826 he married Anna Hanes, the daughter of Philip Hanes of Hope Congregation, Davidson County. They were the parents of eight children: Charles Eugene, Francis Edwin, Louisa Maria, Adelaide Matilda, Beatus who died in infancy, Mary Ann who died at age two, Susan Regina who died in infancy, and Nathanael Augustin who died in infancy. Emanuel and his wife Anna were buried in the Salem graveyard.

SEE: Harold J. Counihan, "The North Carolina Constitutional Convention of 1835," *North Carolina Historical Review* 46 (October 1969); *Laws of North Carolina, 1819*, chap. 33; Adelaide L. Fries and Douglas L. Rights, ed., *Records of the Moravians in North Carolina*, vols. 7–8 (1947, 1954); Minnie J. Smith, ed., *Records of the Moravians in North Carolina*, vol. 9 (1964); R. H. Taylor, "Slave Conspiracies in North Carolina," *North Carolina Historical Review* 5 (1928).

JAMES S. BRAWLEY

Shober, Francis Edwin *(12 Mar. 1831–29 May 1896)*, lawyer and congressman, was born in Salem, the son of Emanuel and Anna Hanes Schober and the grandson of Gottlieb Schober. After attending the Moravian schools in Salem and in Bethlehem, Pa., he was graduated from The University of North Carolina in 1851. He then studied law and was admitted to the bar in 1853. Moving to Salisbury in 1854, he began practicing law.

Although a Democrat before the Civil War, he opposed secession. In 1862 he won a seat in the House of Commons as a Conservative, his first political office. He was reelected in 1864. Shober was a trustee of The University of North Carolina from 1862 until the Republicans took over the state in 1868.

In 1865, after the war, Rowan County sent him to the state senate. Also in 1865 provisional governor William W. Holden appointed him to the Salisbury Board of Commissioners as well as a justice of the Rowan County Court. But Shober soon broke with Holden, aligning himself with the Democrats and Governor Jonathan Worth. In 1868 Worth named Shober a director of the Western North Carolina Railroad. In the same year Shober was elected as a Democrat to the Forty-first Congress from North Carolina's Sixth Congressional District. However, the election was contested by his Republican opponent, Nathaniel Boyden. Boyden accused the Democrats of having ballot boxes at the polls that were not clearly marked, of intimidating and threatening Republican voters, and of circulating a forged document—purporting to come from the chairman of the National Republican Executive Committee—that was antiblack in tone so that the freedmen would not vote for Boyden. In April 1870 the House of Representatives reported that although there was probably some minor intimidation and fraud, there was not enough to change the election results. In addition, it found no evidence that Shober had anything to do with these activities. Over a year after his election, Shober was finally seated in the House. He was reelected to the same seat in 1870.

In Congress Shober supported the concept of states' rights and southern autonomy from federal control. For example, in 1871 he spoke against a bill on the enforcement of the Fourteenth Amendment as one that would increase the power of the central government and completely annihilate the sovereignty of the states. He maintained that the Democratic party in the South recognized and protected the rights of blacks as citizens, including their right to vote and that, therefore, such a bill was unnecessary.

In 1872 Shober did not seek reelection to Congress but instead returned to his law practice in Salisbury. Still active in Democratic state and national politics, however, he served as a delegate to the North Carolina Constitutional Convention of 1875, a county judge from 1877 to 1878, chief clerk of the U.S. Senate during the Forty-fifth Congress, acting secretary of the Senate during the Forty-seventh Congress, delegate to the National Democratic conventions of 1880 and 1884, and a member of the North Carolina Senate in 1887.

Besides his law practice and political activities, Shober engaged in manufacturing after the Civil War. Along with G. A. Bingham, he established one of the largest mercantile firms in Rowan County—Bingham and Company—which made boots, shoes, caps, and wood and willow ware.

Shober married Anna May Wheat, the daughter of the Reverend Dr. John Thomas Wheat, a North Carolina religious and literary leader. They had two sons, Francis Emanuel and Charles E., and three daughters, Anna May, Selina R., and Frances W. Shober died at his home in Salisbury and was buried in the old English cemetery; later his remains were moved to Chestnut Hill Cemetery.

SEE: *Biog. Dir. Am. Cong.* (1950); James S. Brawley, *The Rowan Story* (1953); John H. Wheeler, ed., *Reminiscences and Memoirs of North Carolina and Eminent North Carolini-*

ans (1884); Wheat-Shober Papers (Southern Historical Collection, University of North Carolina, Chapel Hill); *Who Was Who in America: Historical Volume, 1607–1896* (1967). For documents on the contested congressional election of 1868, see the North Carolina Collection, University of North Carolina, Chapel Hill.

ROBERTA SUE ALEXANDER

Shober, Francis Emanuel *(24 Oct. 1860–7 Oct. 1919)*, minister, journalist, and congressman, was born in Salisbury, the son of Francis Edwin, a lawyer and congressman, and May Wheat Shober, the daughter of the Reverend John Thomas Wheat. He studied in select schools and was graduated from St. Stephen's College at Annandale, Dutchess County, N.Y., with A.B. (1880) and M.A (1883) degrees. He studied theology at Berkeley School, Middleton, Conn., and in 1884 was ordained a deacon at St. Luke's Episcopal Church, Salisbury, by the Right Reverend Theodore Benedict Lyman, bishop of North Carolina.

On 17 Apr. 1882 he married Helen Lloyd Aspinwall of Barryton-On-Hudson, N.Y., where Shober was priest-in-charge at St. John's Episcopal Church. He served this parish from 1880 to 1891, when he left the priesthood for uncertain reasons. An item in the local Salisbury newspaper tersely reported on 30 June 1892 that "the case of the Rev. Francis E. Shober is creating a sensation in Barryton, N.Y." It was during this crisis that he was divorced.

Shober then became a reporter for the *News-Press* in Poughkeepsie, N.Y., and editor of the *Rockaway Journal* at Far Rockaway, N.Y. He later moved to New York City and joined the editorial staff of the *New York World*, a position he held for twelve years, the last six of which he was in charge of the Harlem branch. In 1902 he was nominated to represent the Democrats of the Seventeenth Congressional District and won in a traditionally Republican district. After serving in the Fifty-eighth Congress (4 Mar. 1903–3 Mar. 1905), he was an unsuccessful candidate for renomination in 1904.

On 24 Feb. 1898 Shober was initiated into the Alma Lodge No. 728, Free and Accepted Masons; he was elected senior warden in 1901 and master in 1902 and 1903. In 1907–8 he served as deputy tax appraiser for the state of New York. Resuming newspaper work, he became editor of the *New York American*, where he remained until his death in New York City. Shober was buried in Worcester Cemetery, Danbury, Fairfield County, Conn.

SEE: *Biog. Dir. Am. Cong.* (1928); Family papers (possession of James Shober Brawley, Salisbury); *History of Alma Lodge No. 728, F. and A.M., 1874–1904* (1904); Salisbury *Carolina Watchman*, 29 May 1884, 30 June 1892; Salisbury *Truth-Index*, 7 Nov. 1902.

JAMES S. BRAWLEY

Shober, Gottlieb *(1 Nov. 1756–29 June 1838)*, industrial and business pioneer, lawyer, state senator, postmaster, and church official, was born in Bethlehem, Pa., the son of Andreas and Hedwig Schubert Schober. His grandfather, Johannes Joubert, lived in France, then moved to Germany where his name became Schober. In Silesia, Johannes was associated with the Unitas Fratum. Andreas Schober also became active in the church, and after his marriage in 1743 to Hedwig Regina Schubert at Marienborn, the couple immigrated to Bethlehem, Pa., an established Moravian settlement, where Gottlieb was born.

Young Shober received his early education at Nazareth Hall in Bethlehem and at age thirteen was sent with a group of boys to the Moravian settlement of Bethabara, N.C., with a letter of instruction from his parents that he be taught a suitable trade. In his first winter in Wachovia, he was apprenticed to a leather maker in the newly established town of Salem, where he began to demonstrate his opposition to church control over the secular affairs of the community. While working in the leather store he accepted outside work, thereby drawing church disfavor. In 1779 Shober was appointed instructor in the Salem school, a position he held for three years. In 1782 he became an assistant in the Salem store and sold leather breeches that he made. As assistant, he made frequent trips to Charleston, S.C., to trade for articles not produced in Salem.

In 1785 Shober left the leather store to learn the trade of a tinsmith, and in 1786 he opened a tinware shop in Salem. In 1787 he added house painting to his services, and in 1789 the Aeltesten Conferenz (the group that oversaw the religious affairs of the congregation) gave him permission to erect and operate a paper mill. He hired Christian Stauber and sent him to Ephrata, Pa., to learn papermaking. Shober went to Raleigh and obtained a loan from the state for £300 without interest for three years to build the mill. In 1791, when the mill began operating, he made Stauber a partner, but in 1793 the partnership was dissolved. The mill, the first of its kind in North Carolina, was located west of Salem on Peter's Creek near where it crosses Academy Street. The superior quality of his product is evident by the fact that one of his customers, the editor of a Salisbury paper, apologized in November 1826 for the inferior quality of the newsprint "last week and this week as the regular supply was exhausted." Shober purchased the land on which the mill was located in 1824 (before this date the church owned all the land in Salem) and continued to run the mill until 1836, when it was sold to Charles Blum. The mill operated until 1874, when it burned. In 1884 another paper mill was erected on the site of Shober's mill.

For some years Shober studied law on his own, and in 1794 he was admitted to the bar in Stokes and Rowan counties. As the only lawyer among the Moravians, he handled their legal affairs and was appointed Salem's justice of the peace in 1802. His principal role as a lawyer, however, dealt with the Wilkes County land question. In 1769 the Moravians thought that they had secured the deed to two tracts in Wilkes County along the Yadkin River known as the Mulberry Fields and therefore sold it to Hugh Montgomery of Salisbury. However, due to the land confiscation acts passed during the Revolution, some of the land titles acquired from Englishmen were invalid. Litigation of this sort was vexing indeed. Over a ten-year period Shober made frequent appearances in superior courts at Morganton, Statesville, and Raleigh to obtain for the Moravians a clear title to the land. The suit was presented in the state supreme court for the seventh and last time in 1828, but its final disposition was not effected until 1856.

While Shober was serving as counsel in the land case, his friends urged him to run for the General Assembly. After obtaining tacit permission from the church, he ran for the state senate and was elected in 1805 and again in 1808. In the senate, his efforts on behalf of the land suit did not put an end to the legal controversy. Shober did, however, continue to fight for title until 1810, when he resigned from the case.

His work within the Moravian church was rewarded in 1800, when he was named a member of the Helfer Conferenz, a group no longer in existence, which oversaw the religious and secular affairs of the community. Shober, who had learned to play the organ at age fourteen, became one of the church organists for the Salem congregation. In May 1799 he was appointed one of three musicians to direct the music of Salem following the departure of Frederick Peter. He served in this capacity until his resignation in 1802. During this period the church also named him overseer of the beggars who went to Salem.

Shober became a land speculator in 1795, when he purchased through state grants a 40,000-acre tract in Surry County, 14,800 acres in Stokes County, and at least 5,000 acres in Yadkin County along Deep Creek. These purchases totaled more than 100,000 acres and were for pure speculation. Shober failed to realize any profit in the venture and was forced to sell off as much as he could; the remaining acreage he gave to the Gettysburg Seminary and to his son Emanuel. Other land that he purchased included 1,133 acres, acquired in 1813, which he later gave to his son Nathaniel and on which the present town of Kernersville is located. He also owned land in Maryland that he had obtained from the Nanticoke Indians and that he devised to Emanuel "if it can be recovered."

When a post office was established in Salem in 1792, Gottlieb Shober was selected as the first postmaster and served until his son Nathaniel assumed the position in 1805 by appointment of the postmaster general. Shober took over again in 1810 and served until 8 Jan. 1833, when his son Emanuel became postmaster. In this way Shober, with his two sons, kept the postmastership in the family for fifty-two years, except for a three-year period when it was filled by Christopher Reich. Shober's house was used as the first post office.

When only seventeen Shober had felt the call to serve as a minister. However, as the Moravian church then decided such questions by lot, and the lot went against him, he turned his attention to other fields. Shober later wrote that he "was always anxious to live a life devoted to the Lord and I knew that He often made Himself manifect to me." At the mature age of fifty-five his interest in the ministry was rekindled when he journeyed to South Carolina with his friend, the Reverend Charles Storch, a Lutheran minister from Rowan County. The following year he determined to obey the impulse that had followed him from his youth, and on 21 Oct. 1810, during the eighth annual convention of the North Carolina Synod, he was ordained a Lutheran clergyman at Organ Church, Rowan County. His action did not preclude his membership in and support of the Moravian church, for he was permitted to retain his home in Salem, to attend the services, and after a period to play the organ at services. For the Lutherans he served as supply minister to small churches in present Davie, Davidson, and Forsyth counties. A historian writing of Shober's work observed that "the congregations in Forsyth County near Salem were greatly built up by the efficient labors of the first pastor, the Rev. Gottlieb Shober."

His greatest influence within that church came from his position of leadership in the Lutheran hierarchy. He was the synod's secretary for eight one-year terms (1810–20), its first treasurer (1812–31), and president for nine terms (1821–31). In 1817 he was asked as secretary to prepare a book containing a history of the Reformation together with Martin Luther's writings and an explanation of what they meant. The manuscript was read and approved by the synod, which promptly ordered that 1,500 copies be published. Popularly known by the short title *Luther*, it became a source of rupture in the synod that convened in Lincolnton in 1822. Feelings ran high for and against Shober, causing one group under David Hinkle to separate and subsequently form the Tennessee Synod. The two groups remained apart for a century before the fracture was finally healed and the two were rejoined. Into this controversial book on Luther, Shober injected his own ideas for the growth of the church universal. He believed in cooperating with other groups and denominations even though this might call for compromise on the questions of doctrine within the Lutheran church. Shober worked untiringly, often unwisely, for a united Lutheran church and a united Protestantism in America. Hinkle, on the other hand, was equally unyielding in his opposition to any change in the doctrinal position of the early reformers of the church.

Pursuing his idea for an ecumenical movement, Shober along with two other ministers presented a "Plan of Union" at the meetings of the Lutheran Synod and the Episcopal Convention in 1821. The plan called for delegates of the two churches to attend the yearly meetings of the other. Both Episcopalians and Lutherans implemented the proposal, but after 1823 nothing more appears concerning the fraternal relations of the two ecclesiastical bodies. Through his work in helping to organize a general synod of the Lutheran church, he was named by that body to a committee to prepare a hymn book and to translate Luther's catechism. He was also appointed a director of the Gettysburg Seminary, an institution he helped to form and to which he gave funds obtained from land sales in North Carolina.

Shober was instrumental in establishing one of the first, if not the first, Sunday schools in North Carolina. On 1 Sept. 1816 he conducted the first such school at Hopewell Church, four miles from Salem, for twenty-five children and young adults. He proceeded to establish such schools in other churches under his charge, and his influence extended to other denominations. In 1828 he helped to form a Stokes County Sunday School Union and served for four years as its first president. In his will he devised to each Sunday school in "existence at my decease" ten dollars each for "increasing their reading libraries."

On 17 Dec. 1782 he married Maria Magdalena Transou, the daughter of Philip and Magdalena Gantor Transou, and they became the parents of seven children: Nathaniel, Johanna Sophia, Emanuel, Anna Pauline, Hedwig Elizabeth, Benjamin, and Maria Theresa. Mrs. Shober died on 13 June 1835, three years before her husband. Maria and Gottlieb Shober were buried in the Moravian Cemetery, Salem.

SEE: G. B. Bernheim, *History of the German Settlements and of the Lutheran Church in North and South Carolina* (1872); Adelaide L. Fries and others, eds., *Records of the Moravians in North Carolina*, vols. 2–8 (1925–54); *Life Sketches of Lutheran Ministers, North Carolina and Tennessee Synod, 1773–1966* (1966); Salisbury *Carolina Watchman*, 7 May 1847, 15 May 1884; Salisbury *Western Carolinian*, 12 June 1821, 30 Sept. 1823, 24 Jan. 1826, 27 June 1835, 6 July 1838; Gottlieb Shober Autobiography (Moravian Archives, Old Salem, Winston-Salem); Jerry L. Surratt, *Gottlieb Schober of Salem* (1983).

JAMES S. BRAWLEY

Shober, James Francis *(23 Aug. 1853–6 Jan. 1889)*, first known black physician with a medical degree to practice in North Carolina, was born in or near the Moravian town of Salem. He apparently was the son of Betsy Ann Waugh (1835–59), an eighteen-year-old mulatto slave. Circumstantial evidence suggests that she was the daughter of John H. Schulz, a white resident of the town, and that her son was fathered by twenty-two-year-old Francis Edwin Shober, an 1851 graduate of The University of North Carolina and recently admitted to the bar. Betsy Ann Waugh later married a slave named David Shober (1822–67), who was owned by a relative of Francis Edwin Shober.

James Francis Shober was graduated from Lincoln University in Oxford, Pa., in 1875 with a grade average of 95.5 and then entered the Howard University School of Medicine in Washington, D.C. One of forty-eight graduates in the class of 1878, he returned to practice in Wilmington, the largest town in North Carolina. His college and medical school expenses are believed to have been paid by members of the Shober family, perhaps by his natural father.

As the sole black physician in a city with 10,504 blacks, Dr. Shober undoubtedly was quite busy. He was well-liked and highly respected and served as an elder in the Presbyterian church. On 28 June 1881 he married Anna Maria Taylor, and they became the parents of two daughters, Mary Louise and Emily Lillian. Only thirty-six when he died, he was buried in Pine Forest Cemetery, Wilmington.

SEE: Hubert A. Eaton, *Every Man Should Try* (1984); Medical Society of New Hanover, Brunswick, and Pender Counties, *The Lonely Road: A History of the Physicks and Physicians of the Lower Cape Fear, 1735–1976* (1977?); Memoirs of Betsy Ann (1859), David Shober (1867) (Moravian Archives, Winston-Salem); Daniel Smith, ed., *Howard University Medical Department: A Historical, Biographical, and Statistical Souvenir* (1900 [portrait]); Wilmington *Daily Review* (7 Jan. 1889), *Journal* (11 Feb. 1982), *Messenger* (8 Jan. 1889), and *Star-News* (14 Feb. 1982).

WILLIAM S. POWELL

Shore, Clarence Albert *(26 Nov. 1873–10 Feb. 1933)*, physician and public health official, was born in Salem, the son of Henry Washington and Lavinia Ellen Boyer Shore. Widely known in medical circles throughout the United States, he was a recognized authority on the treatment of hydrophobia. Shore earned B.S. (1901) and M.S. (1902) degrees from The University of North Carolina, where he subsequently established a reputation as an outstanding instructor in biology.

In 1907 he received the M.D. degree from Johns Hopkins University. Several months later he became director of the North Carolina State Laboratory of Hygiene, in Raleigh, a post that he held for twenty-five years. Through his work, the laboratory established a national reputation; he was especially interested in the control of waterborne fever diseases.

In 1927 Shore was one of two delegates selected by the U.S. Public Health Service to represent the United States at an international conference on rabies at the Pasteur Institute in Paris. Two years later he was awarded an honorary doctor of laws degree by The University of North Carolina. Shore was a member of the American Medical Association, American Public Health Association, Society of American Bacteriologists, North Carolina Academy of Science, Phi Beta Kappa, Sigma Xi, Sigma Alpha Epsilon, and Nu Sigma Nu. At the time of his death he was president of the Tri-State Medical Association, an organization of physicians from North Carolina, South Carolina, and Virginia. He was a member of the Moravian church.

A tribute to his work, published in the *Bulletin* of the State Board of Health, reads as follows: "His continuous official service has already been longer than that of any other staff official ever connected with the North Carolina State Board of Health. His work in production and distribution of biologicals has saved many lives. In establishing competent diagnostic facilities through the laboratory, he has not only saved many lives but has prevented much human suffering. Twenty-five years is a long time to stick to a public job through all the vicissitudes of conflicting political, professional, and commercial interests. But Dr. Shore has never been too weary to patiently assist any physician, health officer or individual citizen who has appealed to him in any problem affecting the public health."

On 27 May 1914 Shore married Ellen Dortch of Goldsboro and Raleigh. He died in Raleigh and was buried in Oakwood Cemetery.

SEE: *Charlotte Observer*, 10 Feb. 1933; *North Carolina Biography*, vol. 4 (1919); North Carolina Medical Society, *Transactions, 1933* (1933); Raleigh *News and Observer*, 8 Nov. 1923, 10 Feb. 1933; *Who Was Who in America*, vol. 1 (1942).

ELLEN DORTCH SHORE

Shore, Ernest Grady *(24 Mar. 1891–24 Sept. 1980)*, baseball player and law enforcement officer, was born in East Bend, one of four children of Henry and Eugenia Poindexter Shore. Longtime Yadkin County farmers, the Shores traced their ancestry to Friedrich Schorr, who migrated to America from Switzerland in 1750. Young Shore was educated locally and was graduated from East Bend High School.

From 1909 to 1914 he attended Guilford College, where he was a standout pitcher on the college baseball team. Shore also played professionally during the summer, a fairly common occurrence during that period. He pitched briefly for the National League's New York Giants in 1912 and for minor league teams in Utica, New York, and Greensboro in 1913.

After graduating from Guilford, Shore joined the Baltimore Orioles of the minor International League. Later that summer his contract was sold by the financially troubled Baltimore team to the Boston Red Sox of the American League. At the same time the Red Sox also acquired journeyman catcher Ben Egan and a raw but talented young pitcher named George Herman (Babe) Ruth. At the time Shore was one of only a handful of college-educated major leaguers. Although Ruth was temporarily sent back to the minors, Shore, a tall, hard-throwing right-hander, became an immediate star. His first season he won 10 games, lost 4, and compiled the American League's fourth best earned run average.

The next year he won 18 and lost 8 as the Red Sox won the American League pennant. His winning percentage and earned run average were third best in the league. Shore pitched well in the World Series against Philadelphia that year, losing the opener 3 to 1 and winning the fourth game 2 to 1. The Red Sox won the series 4 games to 1. The Red Sox repeated as American League pennant winners and World Series champions in 1916. Shore won 15 and lost 10 in the regular season before starring in the Series. He won twice against the Brooklyn Dodgers, the opener and the final fifth game, and gave up only three earned runs in 17⅔ innings.

Boston and Shore slumped slightly in 1917. Hampered by a sore arm Shore won 13 and lost 10 in 1917, as Boston fell to second place. On 23 June Shore pitched an unusual, well-known, and somewhat controversial perfect game against the Washington Senators. Boston starter Babe Ruth, not yet a famous outfielder, walked the lead-off batter and was ejected from the game for arguing with the umpire. Shore came on in relief, the base runner was thrown out attempting to steal, and Shore retired the remaining 26 batters in order. After some debate by baseball officials Shore was credited with a rare perfect game.

After the 1917 season Shore joined the U.S. Navy, where he achieved the rank of ensign. His absence from the 1918 season due to his military service and his still sore arm combined to curtail his postwar effectiveness and shorten his career. Shore was traded by the Red Sox to the New York Yankees after the 1918 season. In 1919 he won only 5 games and lost 8. He finished his major league career with the Yankees in 1920, winning 2 and losing 2 before being released. He finished up the season in the California League, pitching for Vernon and San Francisco. Unable to pitch effectively due to his arm injury, Shore retired after the 1920 season. He ended his big-league career with a record of 63 wins, against only 42 losses, and a superb earned run average of 2.45.

After retiring from baseball Shore returned to Winston-Salem, where he sold cars and later insurance. In 1936 he was elected sheriff of Forsyth County as a Democrat. He held this position until his retirement in 1970. Shore gained a reputation as an innovative administrator, who oversaw expansion of the sheriff's department from six men to seventy men.

Shore married Lucile Harrelson on 24 Nov. 1926. They had three children: Jan, Earnest, Jr., and Julia. Shore was buried at the Forsyth Memorial Park. The baseball park in Winston-Salem was named after Shore, a member of the North Carolina Sports Hall of Fame.

SEE: Herb Appenzoller, *Pride in the Past: Guilford College Athletics, 1837–1987* (1987); Frances Casstevens, ed., *The Heritage of Yadkin County* (1981); Gene Karst and Martin Jones, Jr., *Who's Who in Professional Baseball* (1973); Joseph L. Reichler, ed., *Baseball Encyclopedia* (1985); Shore file of clippings (North Carolina Collection, University of North Carolina, Chapel Hill); Shore file, *The Sporting News* (St. Louis, Mo.); *Winston-Salem Journal*, 25–27 Sept. 1980.

JIM L. SUMNER

Shotwell, Randolph Abbott *(14 Dec. 1844–31 July 1884)*, Confederate soldier, newspaperman, state legislator, and author, was born in West Liberty, Va., the eldest of three sons of the Reverend Nathan, a Presbyterian minister, and Martha Ann Abbott Shotwell. His mother was a native of Massachusetts and of a prominent family. A precocious youth, young Shotwell at age thirteen entered Tuscarora Academy, in Mifflin, Pa., where he remained until 1860, when he enrolled at Media College, Media, Pa.

With the beginning of the Civil War Shotwell left school and returned to Virginia to enlist in the Eighth Virginia Regiment. Under the command of Colonel Eppa Hunton, the unit participated in seventeen battles. Shotwell led the sharpshooters of the regiment in Pickett's Charge at Gettysburg and was promoted to lieutenant for his gallant conduct. He was captured in 1864 and confined as a prisoner for the remainder of the war—first at Point Lookout and then at Fort Delaware.

In 1865 Shotwell went to North Carolina, where his father had become pastor of a church at Rutherfordton in 1858. He soon moved to New Bern and with Stephen D. Pool established the *Journal of Commerce*, an unsuccessful newspaper. Falling victim to malaria, Shotwell returned to Rutherfordton and, at his father's urging, studied law for a brief time. His primary interests, however, were public affairs and writing; he ran unsuccessfully to become a delegate to the 1868 constitutional convention. In February 1868 he acquired the Rutherford *Star*, which he renamed *The Vindicator*. Conservative and Democratic, the newspaper reflected Shotwell's views and it attracted attention, although, like the New Bern paper, it proved to be financially unsound. Denouncing the Radicals with enthusiasm and effect, he became the target of Radicals in Cleveland and Rutherford counties. In 1869 he established the *Citizen* in Asheville but it, too, failed. The twenty-five-year-old Shotwell once more returned to his father's home and resumed the reading of law.

His political activities soon embroiled him with the Ku Klux Klan. Though never a member, he acted as a moderating force in an effort to modify the outrages being committed. His involvement with the Klan, however, provided his Radical enemies with an excuse, and he was arrested on 5 July 1871. Brought to trial in the senate chamber in Raleigh before a partisan judge and a carefully selected jury, Shotwell was convicted and sentenced to six years' confinement at Albany, N.Y., and fined $5,000. Offered an immediate pardon if he implicated leading Democratic politicians, Shotwell refused and was sent to the federal penitentiary. In late 1872 President Ulysses S. Grant granted him an unconditional pardon.

Returning to North Carolina, Shotwell continued his newspaper career for the remainder of his life. He edited the *Southern Home* with D. H. Hill until he bought the *Farmer and Mechanic* in 1876. In July 1885 he consolidated the latter paper and the *State Chronicle*. During this period he represented Mecklenburg County for one term in the state legislature and ran unsuccessfully for the Democratic nomination for state auditor in 1884. A gifted editor and a staunch Conservative, Shotwell accepted the position of state librarian but he died suddenly soon afterwards.

Shotwell never married. He was buried in the Confederate section of Oakwood Cemetery, Raleigh.

SEE: Samuel A. Ashe, ed., *Cyclopedia of Eminent and Representative Men of the Carolinas*, vol. 2 (1892); J. G. de Roulhac Hamilton, ed., *Papers of Randolph Abbot Shotwell*, 3 vols. (1929); John H. Wheeler, ed., *Reminiscences and Memoirs of North Carolina and Eminent North Carolinians* (1884).

JEFFRY D. WERT

Shuford, Alonzo Craig *(1 Mar. 1858–8 Feb. 1933)*, farmer, Populist leader, congressman, and promoter of farmers' organizations, was born on a farm near Newton in Catawba County, the son of George Philip and Eliza Baker Shuford. Of German ancestry, he was a descendant of John Shuford, who settled in Catawba about 1760.

Shuford was educated in the common schools and attended Catawba College, then located at Newton. Afterwards he engaged in farming and cattle raising and was a part owner of the Startown Nursery Company, which sold fruit trees throughout the Carolinas and Virginia. In the 1890s he was a lecturer and officer of the Farmers' Alliance, and between 1905 and 1925 he was an organizer for the Farmers' Union.

An unsuccessful Populist candidate for Congress in 1892, Shuford was elected on the Populist ticket to the Fifty-fourth and Fifty-fifth congresses (4 Mar. 1895–3 Mar. 1899). Generally regarded as an excellent speaker and a fearless debater, he advocated rural free delivery, consolidated schools, farm credit, and better roads; he supported the establishment of the Normal and Industrial College at Greensboro, from which his three daughters were graduated. In 1924 he served as a presidential elector on the Progressive ticket of Robert M. LaFollette and

Burton K. Wheeler. Shuford retired from business in 1928 and thereafter made his home in Chapel Hill.

He married Willie Ellen Lowe of Catawba County on 21 Nov. 1882. The couple had seven children, but only Anne Lee, Malinda, and Sarah reached maturity. Shuford was buried in the Chapel Hill Cemetery.

SEE: *Biog. Dir. Am. Cong.* (1950); Albert Keiser, Jr. (Hickory, N.C.), personal contact; Charles L. Van Noppen Papers (Manuscript Department, Duke University Library, Durham); *Who's Who in America*, vol. 4 (1968).

FRANK P. CAUBLE

Shuford, George Adams *(5 Sept. 1895–8 Dec. 1962)*, lawyer, congressman, and judge, was born in Asheville, the son of George A. and Julia E. Dean Shuford. A student at The University of North Carolina from 1913 to 1915, he received a law degree from the University of Georgia in 1917 and in the same year was licensed to practice in Georgia. Following officer's training camp, he was commissioned a second lieutenant in the 119th Infantry, 30th Division, and saw service in France. He was released in 1919 with the rank of first lieutenant.

Licensed in North Carolina in 1920, Shuford opened a law practice in Asheville. He represented Buncombe County in the General Assembly sessions of 1945 and 1947. In the fall of 1947 he was appointed a superior court judge and served until July 1949. Elected to Congress in 1952, he remained on Capitol Hill until January 1959. In Congress he served on committees concerned with veterans' affairs, the Department of the Interior, the Great Smoky Mountains National Park, the Blue Ridge Parkway, and the Cherokee Indians. Following the Democratic primary, which he won in May 1958, Shuford withdrew as a candidate for a fourth term because of a stroke suffered six days before the primary. There was considerable concern among journalists that the seriousness of the congressman's condition had not been promptly revealed. After completing his term in Congress, he resumed a restricted law practice in Asheville.

Shuford was married in 1932 to Daphne Brown of Asheville, and they were the parents of Sydney Herbert, Elizabeth Dean, and Fuller Adams. He died at his home, and funeral services were conducted at Trinity Episcopal Church, where he had been a member and former warden and vestryman.

SEE: *Asheville Citizen-Times*, 20 Jan. 1953, 9 Dec. 1962; *Biog. Dir. Am. Cong.* (1961); Daniel L. Grant, *Alumni History of the University of North Carolina* (1924); *North Carolina Manual* (1963); William S. Powell, ed., *North Carolina Lives* (1962); Raleigh *News and Observer*, 17 Oct. 1947, 13, 28 July 1958; Washington, D.C., *Evening Star*, 20 Dec. 1952.

WILLIAM S. POWELL

Siamese twins. *See* **Bunker, Eng and Chang.**

Sibley, John *(19 May 1757–8 Apr. 1837)*, physician, Indian agent, politician, and planter, was born at Sutton, Mass., the son of Timothy and Anne Waite Sibley. After studying medicine with Dr. John Wilson of Hopkinton, he served with the Continental troops in the Revolution as surgeon's mate. Settling at Great Barrington, Dr. Sibley in 1780 married Elizabeth Hopkins. Around 1784 he moved his family to Fayetteville, N.C., where he became an influential citizen as postmaster; editor of the *Fayetteville Gazette*, founded by him and Caleb D. Howard in 1789; and political figure. Sibley and Howard also served for some time as public printers for the state of North Carolina. Sibley's first wife died in 1790, and in 1791 he married Mrs. Mary White Winslow. His sons George C. and Samuel H. were born of the first union.

In the summer of 1802 Sibley was called on business to Natchez, Miss., and received from the Spanish government permission to travel extensively in the lower Mississippi region. He kept careful journals of his observations among the Indians of the region, notes on their languages, data on natural history, geography, and so on. By the end of 1803 extracts and reports from his travels had begun to reach the North Carolina Medical Society and various newspapers. By this time he had also become the object of interest of the U.S. government, which was anxious for any reliable information it could obtain on the territory that was being ceded by Spain to this country in the Louisiana Purchase. Sibley became acquainted with W. C. C. Claiborne, later governor of the Orleans Territory and, through him, with President Thomas Jefferson. By a letter of March 1804 he offered his services to Jefferson and was appointed surgeon to the U.S. troops at Natchitoches. In the following year he was named Indian agent for the Orleans Territory and in that capacity visited most of the tribes in what is now Louisiana. He made extensive reports to Claiborne and Jefferson, compiling a vocabulary of the Caddo Indian tongue and two notable sketches of the ethnology and geography of the Red River and contiguous regions.

It seems evident that Sibley did not enjoy good relations with his second wife, who remained in Fayetteville until her death in 1811. She was the mother of Ann Eliza, a celebrated beauty who married U.S. Senator Josiah Stoddard Johnston of Louisiana and, after his death, a prominent Philadelphia attorney, Henry Duckworth Gilpin. Following the death of his second wife, Sibley in 1813 married Eudalie Malique of Louisiana. He lost his position as Indian agent for political reasons in 1814 but afterwards was a parish judge, served several terms in the Louisiana legislature, participated as a militia officer in Colonel James Long's raid on Texas in 1819, and became a member of the supreme council governing the military post at Macogdoches. Subsequently he retired to his plantation at Grande Ecore and concerned himself with the manufacture of salt, the planting of cotton, and other enterprises. He was survived at his death by children of all three of his marriages.

SEE: *DAB*, vol. 17 (1935); Raleigh, *The Observer*, 14, 19, 21–22, 24 Apr. 1877; *Raleigh Register and North Carolina Gazette*, 2 Jan., 31 Dec. 1804; John Sibley, *A Report from Natchitoches in 1807* (1922).

T. C. PARRAMORE

Sidbury, James Buren *(2 Mar. 1886–7 Jan. 1967)*, physician and pioneer in the establishment of pediatrics as a separate medical specialty, was a native of Holly Ridge and the son of Verlinza and Frances Williams Sidbury. After obtaining an A.B. degree from Trinity College, Durham (1908) and A.M. and M.D. degrees from the College of Physicians and Surgeons at Columbia University (1912), he served internships at Roosevelt Hospital in New York City in 1914 and New York Foundling Hospital in 1915. In the latter year he began practicing medicine in Wilmington, where he remained until his death.

On 6 June 1920 Sidbury established Babies Hospital at Wrightsville Sound to provide the most advanced pediatric care to the children of the area and to those of the summer visitors. The original hospital was destroyed by fire in 1927 and the present one built the next year. At first the hospital was open only for the summer months, but in 1939 it began operating during the entire year. Following World War II it was accredited to train pediatric residents. An affiliated nurses' training school was opened in 1942, and Sidbury donated the home for the nurses. The Babies Hospital Research Center was established in 1961. Sidbury is credited with introducing new methods of infant feeding, immunizations, and pediatric management, and with educating the public and the profession in many principles of pediatrics. The Babies Hospital closed in 1978, as there were more general hospitals able to care for babies and children.

In 1965 the J. Buren Sidbury Chair of Pediatrics at Duke University was created from an endowment given by Sidbury and set up by Duke trustees as a tribute to him. He served as a trustee at Duke (1947–63) and as president of the American Pediatric Society, Medical Society Foundation of North Carolina, North Carolina Medical Society, New Hanover County Medical Society, and North Carolina Pediatric Society. Sidbury was a Fellow of the American College of Surgeons and a member of the American Academy of Pediatricians. For many years he was a member of the Rotary Club in Wilmington.

On 1 Jan. 1916 he married Willie W. Daniel (19 June 1889–23 Oct. 1948), the daughter of the Reverend William Wellington and Alice Rowena Aull Daniel. Her father, an attorney and a Methodist minister in South Carolina, became president of Columbia College in that state. Willie Sidbury had attended Columbia College and Columbia University in New York City. Active in local and state affairs, she was a member of Sorosis and president of the North Carolina Association of Parents and Teachers, the North Carolina Garden Clubs, and the North Carolina Medical Auxiliary. During World War II she was in charge of Red Cross volunteer work for the local chapter. After her death Dr. Sidbury gave the chancel window in Grace Methodist Church in memory of her many years of faithful service to that church.

Sidbury and his wife had three children: Billie (Mrs. Robert A. Little), Rowena (Mrs. Ivan Lenart), and James Buren, Jr. (m. Alice Lucas Rayle). Both Rowena and James became pediatricians. Dr. Sidbury, Jr., for a number of years was professor of pediatrics and director of the Clinical Research Unit at Duke University before serving as scientific director of the National Institute of Child Health and Human Development, Bethesda, Md.

The Sidburys lived at 15 North Fifth Street beside the First Baptist Church. Sidbury gave the home to the church, and it was used as a Sunday school. Portraits of him—both painted by William C. Fields—are located at Babies Hospital and in Duke Medical Center. James and Willie Sidbury were buried in Oakdale Cemetery, Wilmington.

SEE: Dorothy Long, ed., *Medicine in North Carolina*, vol. 1 (1972); *Who Was Who in America*, vol. 4 (1968); *Who's Important in Medicine*, 3d ed. (1961); *Wilmington Morning Star*, 5 Dec. 1961, 14 May, 20 June 1967, 6 June 1970; *Wilmington Star-News*, 24 Oct. 1948, 7 Jan. 1967.

IDA B. KELLAM
L. H. MCEACHERN

Siewers, Nathaniel Shober *(15 Nov. 1845–12 Jan. 1901)*, physician and lay officer of the Protestant Moravian church, was born in Salem, the son of John Daniel and Rebecca Shober Siewers. His grandparents, Henry Frederick and Dorothea Wrang Siewers, traveled as Moravian missionaries in 1797 from Herrnhut, Germany, to the Danish West Indies. Nathaniel Siewers attended the Salem Boys School and Nazareth Hall, Nazareth, Pa. On 1 Nov. 1863 he went to Orange County, Va., to enlist in the Confederate army. As a private in the First Battalion, Company B, North Carolina Sharpshooters, he was detailed "as a musician" in the Twenty-first Regiment Band. His battalion joined in Robert E. Lee's surrender at Appomattox Court House on 9 Apr. 1865.

In 1865, after "reading" medicine with Dr. Theodore F. Keehln, Siewers entered the Medical School of the University of Pennsylvania. He was graduated in 1867. Eager to obtain additional training in the European clinics, he studied at the medical centers of the Universities of Berlin, Prague, and Vienna. From Vienna in October 1868 he wrote: "There is, to my mind, no profession outside of the ministry, the conscientious pursuit of which carries with it greater blessing than does that of medicine." In this spirit of dedication and with a keen awareness of his responsibility, he extended his medical study abroad through the second year to take advantage of the specialized departments of medicine then being established in Europe.

In 1869 Siewers returned to Salem to practice medicine. On 5 Oct. 1875 he married Eleanor Elizabeth de Schweinitz, the daughter of Bishop Emil de Schweinitz, a lineal descendant of Count Nicholas Louis von Zinzendorf, benefactor and "father" of the Renewed Moravian church in Herrnhut, Germany. Dr. and Mrs. Siewers had seven children—Pauline, Charles Shober, Agnes Gertrude, Ralph de Schweinitz, Ruth Eleanor, Walter Ledoux, and Grace Louise. In 1893, near the gate to what was once Cedar Avenue in Salem, Siewers built the stately gray-stone Cedarhyrst for both a residence and an office.

Siewers considered medicine to be "standing at the portals" of its potentiality; he predicted organ transplants in human beings. He was considered an excellent surgeon and is believed to have been the first in the area to perform an appendectomy. In addition, he was one of the promoters and builders of the Roanoke and Southern Railroad and among the organizers of the Wachovia Loan and Trust Company.

Bishop Edward Rondthaler characterized him as "quiet but earnest and deeply interested in the work of his church." Siewers served on the board of elders and the board of trustees of the Home Moravian Church. In 1890 he was elected a provincial elder, the first layman to fill such an office in the Moravian Unity. His last honor was that of being chosen to represent the Southern Moravian Unity at its worldwide synod in Herrnhut, Germany, in 1899, but ill health prevented him from attending. After a long illness, Siewers died at age fifty-six. He was buried in God's Acre, the Moravian graveyard, in Salem. In the University of Pennsylvania Register was this tribute: "His energy and faithfulness in his profession was [*sic*] exemplary, while his skill as a physician placed him in the front ranks as a practitioner in the South, and his practice for many years was large and covered a wide area of the country."

SEE: Louis H. Manarin, comp., *North Carolina Troops, 1861–1865: A Roster*, vol. 3 (1971); Dorothy R. Nifong, *Brethren With Stethoscopes* (1965); *North Carolina Biography*, vol. 4 (1919); Edwin Rondthaler, "Memoir of Nathaniel Shober Siewers, M.D.," 1901 (Moravian Archives, Winston-Salem); Nathaniel Shober Siewers, "Letters to His Father, 1858–1869" (typescript copy made in 1960, possession of his family.

MARJORIE SIEWERS STEPHENSON

Sikes, Enoch Walter *(19 May 1868–8 Jan. 1941)*, college president, was born in Union County, the son of John C. and Jane Austin Sikes. He attended Wake Forest College, where he played football, was an orator and a debater, and received an M.A. degree in 1891. Instead of becoming a lawyer as had been his earlier intention, he accepted an appointment as director of physical culture at Wake Forest. Sikes spent the summer at Harvard University and began teaching in the fall of 1891. Continuing his education at Johns Hopkins University, he received a doctor of philosophy degree in 1897. He returned to Wake Forest College as assistant professor of history and political science. In 1910 he was drafted to run for the North Carolina legislature as senator from Wake County but had no further political aspirations after serving the one term as senator. In 1915–16 he was dean of Wake Forest College.

In 1916 Sikes was chosen president of Coker College for Women at Hartsville, S.C. With this post he began a close connection with the state of South Carolina, where he spent over half of his lifework in education. In July 1925 he became president of Clemson College, and for fifteen years, until July 1940, he shaped the educational policies of South Carolina's Agricultural and Mechanical College. His term saw increased enrollment, the addition of new buildings and equipment, and the remodeling of older facilities. Sikes remained president for two years after the official retirement age of seventy but asked to be relieved of the responsibility. After that request was accepted, he was asked to stay on at the institution in order to direct South Carolina historical research and to serve the public with his brilliant oratory.

Sikes was a frequent lecturer and wrote several articles for the *Wake Forest Student* and Clemson College publications. He was the author of four books: *The Transition of North Carolina from Colony to Commonwealth* (1898), *The Confederate States Congress* (1905), *The Growth of the Nation, 1837 to 1860 . . .* (1905), and a *Supplement to Reinsch's Civil Government for the State of North Carolina* (1916). Many of his addresses to Clemson College students were published. Sikes served as governor of the Carolinas Kiwanis District in 1925.

He married Ruth Wingate, the daughter of Washington Manly Wingate, former president of Wake Forest College. They had one son, Walter Wingate, and one daughter, Ruth Janet. Sikes died suddenly of a heart attack. He was given a military funeral and buried on Cemetery Hill on the Clemson College campus.

SEE: Charlotte, *Beasley's Farm and Home Weekly*, 16 Jan. 1941; Enoch Walter Sikes Biography File (North Carolina Baptist Historical Collection, Wake Forest University, Winston-Salem [portrait]); Columbia (S.C.) *The Star*, 9–10 Jan. 1941; Charles E. Taylor, ed., *The General Catalogue of Wake Forest College, 1834–5–1891–2* (1892); Wake Forest Alumni Directory (1961); *Who Was Who in America* (1943).

JOHN R. WOODARD

Siler, Jacob *(1 June 1795–21 or 25 Apr. 1871)*, western North Carolina pioneer, state legislator, and Cherokee Indian agent, was born in South Carolina's Pendleton district, of German and Irish ancestry. His grandfather, Plikard Dederic Siler, emigrated to America from Weimar, Germany, and eventually settled near present-day Siler City in Chatham County. Jacob's father, Weimar, fought in the French and Indian War as a boy and married Margaret Rafferty on 12 Mar. 1786, when he returned from service in the American Revolution. One of nine children, Jacob joined the army as a young man but never saw active duty.

In 1817 he left his family in Buncombe County and, with William Britton, headed west to explore land along the Upper Little Tennessee River that had been acquired from the Cherokee a few years earlier. Siler and Britton inadvertently crossed over the boundary line set by the treaty and so returned to settle in what is now Macon County. From a Cherokee chief named Balltown George, they bought land for twenty-five cents an acre and set up a store, stocking it with provisions from their two pack horses.

Siler's brothers and parents soon joined him in Macon County. Siler's Bald in the Great Smoky Mountains is named for Jacob's brother Jesse, and Siler's Bald in the Nantahala Range is named for his brother William. Albert Mountain, also in the Nantahalas, is named for William's son.

Jacob Siler was appointed a magistrate for the newly formed Macon County in 1828, as he held the same position in Haywood County, from which Macon was formed. He and Colonel Joseph Cathey of Haywood County were appointed to establish the line between the two counties. Siler was then made county surveyor, a position he held until 1835, when he resigned to represent Macon County in the North Carolina legislature. In 1839–40 he served as a Cherokee Indian agent for the state.

Jacob was an active member of Mount Zion Methodist Church in Macon County. He was married twice: first, on 8 Feb. 1822 to Matilda Swain, sister of David L. Swain, later governor of North Carolina. Jacob and Matilda had five children. After her death on 5 Nov. 1858, Jacob married Mary Thornton Highsmith on 18 Dec. 1864 and had two more children.

SEE: Alberta Brewer and Carson Brewer, *Valley So Wild: A Folk History* (1975); Mrs. Vernon Bryson, *Macon County, North Carolina* (1972); Leona Bryson Porter, *The Family of Weimar Siler, 1755–1831* (1951 [portrait]); *The Siler Family* (1906).

MARYANN SLOAN-FARMER

Sill, James Burges *(2 Apr. 1871–18 Nov. 1958)*, Episcopal priest, was born in New York but grew to love the land and people of western North Carolina. From a family of divines, his father, Thomas Henry, served a Manhattan parish for forty years, and his brother, F. H. Sill, was a member of the Order of the Holy Cross and founded the Kent School in Connecticut. His mother was Jane Burges Miller. James Sill entered the priesthood after graduation from Columbia University (1892) and General Theological Seminary in New York (1897). After spending his early ministry in New York City, he was called in 1911 to North Carolina, where he remained for the rest of his life. He served churches in Rutherfordton, Fletcher, Shelby, and Asheville.

When he retired in 1944, Sill had the longest record of service of any priest in the diocese. At the time of his arrival in North Carolina, the Episcopal church in the mountains was a missionary church; after it became a self-supporting diocese in 1922, Sill became its historiographer and recorded the early struggling years of the church in the region. He prepared parish histories and collected biographical information on church leaders, which appeared in a series of columns printed in the diocesan paper. After his formal retirement, he collected and expanded these vignettes and published them as *Historical Sketches of Churches in the Diocese of Western*

North Carolina. Each entry of a parish or person was about two pages long and focused on the early days of the Episcopal church in the area. Sill provided vivid accounts of Episcopal clergymen who were said to have braved mobs of Baptists at Beaver Creek or who forded frigid mountain streams to serve their followers.

Described as a rugged man, Sill never learned to drive a car and walked from Tryon to Asheville, even in winter weather, rather than bother a friend to drive him. While serving parishes at Craggy or Chunn's Cove, he spent his days walking to and from parishioners' homes. Sill was regarded as a model for pioneer clergymen who served in frontier regions. He died in Tryon at age eighty-seven.

SEE: *Asheville Citizen-Times*, 19 Nov. 1958; J. B. Sill, *Historical Sketches* (1955); *Stowe's Clerical Directory of the Protestant Episcopal Church* (1953).

WILLIAM F. W. MASSENGALE

Silver, Frances [Frankie] *(d. 12 July 1833)*, who was tried, convicted, and executed for the murder of her husband, Charles, was the first woman to be hanged in North Carolina. Official records of Burke County Superior Court also show her given name as Frankey and Frankie and her surname as Silvers. Whereas court records report her maiden name as Stuart, other sources use Stewart. Her parents were Isaiah and Barbara Stuart.

Frankie Silver was executed for committing one of the most brutal murders in the history of North Carolina. In the presence of her year-old daughter, Nancy, she decapitated her husband and burned his remains in the fireplace of their home near the present community of Kona in Mitchell (then Burke) County. She attempted to conceal her deed by reporting that Charles was lost on a hunting trip. When search parties failed to find any trace of him, a more intense search was conducted in and around the Silvers' home. Jack Collis, a neighbor, noticed pieces of bone in the fireplace ashes; he also commented that the ashes were very greasy. Other evidence was found in the house to suggest that Frankie had killed Charles, and she was arrested on 10 Jan. 1832.

On 30 Mar. 1832, after two days of testimony at her trial in Morganton, she was found guilty and sentenced to be executed at the June session of court the same year. An appeal to the state supreme court was heard during the summer and denied. The case was sent back to the Burke County Superior Court so that a new execution date could be set. For some unknown reason the judge failed to appear in September, and court was adjourned until March 1833.

One year after her trial, Frankie's execution date was set for 28 June 1833. By this time she had been confined for fourteen months. With the aid of her father and uncle, ten days before her scheduled appointment with the hangman, Frankie Silver escaped from jail. Within hours, however, she was found and returned to custody. Again, the execution was inexplicably delayed but finally reset and actually carried out on 12 July 1833.

Numerous legends, romantic stories, and songs have evolved out of the few facts known of these events. No reason for the murder was ever given during the trial, and most of the evidence against the defendant was circumstantial. She never made a public confession of the crime. Legend reports that she sang a self-composed song on the scaffold in which she confessed. Eyewitness reports, however, contradict this claim. Many said that Charles Silver had badly mistreated his wife, but under the laws of the time she was prohibited from testifying against him.

Frankie was buried by her father approximately nine miles west of Morganton. It is interesting to note that other members of the Stuart family met violent deaths. Isaiah was killed when a limb from a tree he was cutting hit him on the head; Barbara died from a snakebite; and one of Frankie's brothers, Blackston, was hanged for stealing a horse in Kentucky.

SEE: Clifton K. Avery, ed., *Official Court Record of the Trial: Conviction and Execution of Francis [sic] Silver, First Woman Hanged in North Carolina* (1953); Olive Woolley Burt, ed., *American Murder Ballads and Their Stories* (1958); S. J. Ervin, Jr., "Frankie Silver," *Morganton News-Herald*, 3 Apr. 1924, 27 Mar. 1964, 29 Jan., 13 Feb., 28 Mar. 1968; *Lenoir Topic*, 24 Mar., 5 May 1886; Maxine McCall, *They Won't Hang a Woman* (1972); Silas McDowell Papers (Southern Historical Collection, University of North Carolina, Chapel Hill); Edward W. Phifer, *Burke: The History of a North Carolina County* (1977); Muriel E. Sheppard, *Cabins in the Laurel* (1935); James A. Turpin, *The Serpent Slips into a Modern Eden* (1923).

RICHARD S. SPELL

Simmons, Furnifold McLendel *(20 Jan. 1854–30 Apr. 1940)*, U.S. senator, was born at his father's plantation near Pollocksville in Jones County, the son of Furnifold Green, Jr., and Mary McLendel Jerman Simmons. He attended Wake Forest College (1868–70), was graduated from Trinity College in 1873, read law, and was admitted to the bar in 1875. Later he received honorary LL.D. degrees from Trinity (1901) and The University of North Carolina (1915).

After practicing law briefly in Jones County and in New Bern, Simmons joined a firm in Goldsboro. Several years later he returned to New Bern, which remained his home base for the remainder of his life. He was elected to the U.S. House of Representatives in 1886 but was defeated for reelection by a black Republican; in 1890 he failed to win the nomination because of the opposition of the Farmers' Alliance. In 1892 he was appointed chairman of the Democratic State Committee, and he put together a successful campaign based on county organizations that were to support him for many years. As a reward for his services, President Grover Cleveland appointed him collector of internal revenue for the Eastern District of North Carolina, a post he held until 1897.

The Democratic party chairman resigned in 1894, and within the next four years the Republicans and Populists gained control of the state legislature, won the governorship, and put a Populist and Republican in the U.S. Senate. In 1898 Simmons reluctantly accepted the party chairmanship once more and served until 1907. In the election of 1898, he sent speakers throughout the state, promised legislative favors to businessmen and religious denominations, and deluged voters with broadsides. He especially appealed to "men of Anglo-Saxon blood" to prevent "negro domination." After a campaign marked by corruption and violence, Democrats won control of the state legislature. Future control, however, was in doubt as long as black people could vote, so Simmons, in spite of campaign pledges, prepared a disfranchising amendment to the state constitution that was approved by the voters in the gubernatorial election of 1900. In 1900, too, Democratic voters nominated Simmons over Julian S. Carr in a special Democratic primary for U.S. senator, and then the Democratic state legislature elected him senator over the Populist incumbent, Marion Butler.

While in Washington, Simmons retained his interest in state politics, and a legend concerning the existence and power of a "Simmons machine" developed. This legend was largely the result of a skillful distribution of national patronage and of the influence exerted by his "friends" and his secretaries, A. D. Watts and Frank Hampton, in the selection of North Carolina governors. Simmons's friends backed Charles B. Aycock for governor in 1900, Locke Craig in 1912, Cameron Morrison in 1920, and Angus W. McLean in 1924. Simmons rarely became involved in state legislation, although he claimed considerable responsibility for the success of a campaign for state Prohibition. He collaborated in writing the Watts (1903) and Ward (1905) bills, which prohibited the liquor traffic everywhere except in large towns, and helped work out the strategy for a successful statewide Prohibition referendum in 1908.

Except in 1930 when he was defeated, Simmons's reelection to the Senate was threatened only in 1912, when three popular candidates, former governor Aycock, former governor William W. Kitchin, and Judge Walter Clark ran against him in the primary.

From the point of view of North Carolina, Simmons made his greatest contribution as a senator on the Committee on Commerce, of which he was a member from 1905 until he left the Senate. Year after year he wangled appropriations for the maintenance and development of the rivers and harbors of his state and with John H. Small and Lindsay Warren, congressmen from Washington, N.C., won support for building the Intracoastal Waterway from Boston to Wilmington.

Nationally his greatest influence was exerted as chairman from 1913 to 1919 of the Senate Committee on Finance. He guided through the Senate the Underwood Simmons Tariff and war revenue bills calling for unprecedented bond issues and taxes on incomes, corporations, and excess profits. In the League of Nations debate, he recognized the political impossibility of obtaining approval of the league without reservations and vainly attempted to work out an acceptable compromise between President Woodrow Wilson and the "Irreconcilables."

After the election of 1918, the Republicans organized the Senate and Simmons lost his chairmanship, but as ranking Democrat on the finance committee, he continued to be one of the most influential members through the 1920s. As the election of 1928 approached, Simmons's prestige was high, and his reelection was expected in 1930. In fact, however, he was not safe politically. He was showing his age of seventy-four years, he was not in good health, and young politicians such as O. Max Gardner and Josiah W. Bailey, defeated candidates for governor in 1920 and 1924 respectively, were not satisfied with his leadership.

Then came the nomination of Alfred E. Smith for the presidency. Simmons had supported William G. McAdoo in a bitter nominating battle against Smith in 1924, and in 1928, after McAdoo withdrew, he had attempted to win support for Cordell Hull. Although Simmons was not alienated by Smith's Catholicism as a religious faith, Catholicism, combined with Smith's opposition to Prohibition, his support of immigration, his membership in Tammany Hall, and his apparent tolerance of racial equality, symbolized for Simmons a change in the nature of leadership of the Democratic party that he could not tolerate. Thus he gave inspiration to the anti-Smith Democrats and personally refused to vote for his party's presidential candidate. The anti-Smith Democrats together with North Carolina Republicans carried the state for Herbert Hoover.

Through the years Simmons had made few political speeches, relying on his friends to carry on for him. Young potential political leaders now did not know him, while old friends were either dead or losing interest. Some of Simmons's positions had lost him support—his stand on labor during the strikes of 1929 and 1930, his opposition to private ownership of the Wilson dam at Muscle Shoals, and others. Carrying only 16 out of 100 counties, he was defeated by Josiah W. Bailey.

Simmons was a professional politician of the late nineteenth and early twentieth centuries. In the Senate he frequently let local interests take precedence over national interests, and he lacked a consistent worldview; he did not understand the complexities of such a limited problem as alcohol or of such a fundamental one as that of the city; he believed in white supremacy and saw no incongruity in having second-class citizens in a democracy; he accepted a political philosophy of rewards and punishments and the electioneering trickery of less-than-fastidious friends. At the same time, his legislative record was impressive: waterways, roads, forest reserves, tariffs, taxes, the postal system, and agriculture all benefited from his effectiveness as a legislator.

In 1875 Simmons married Eliza Hill Humphrey, who died in 1883 leaving him with three children, Mary Rebecca, Eliza Humphrey, and James Humphrey. In 1886 he married Belle Gibbs, and they were the parents of two daughters, Ella and Isabelle. Simmons's parents were Baptist, but in the late 1920s, apparently persuaded by his wife, he joined the Episcopal church. He died at New Bern and was buried in Cedar Grove Cemetery.

SEE: *Biog. Dir. Am. Cong.* (1961); W. J. Cash, "Jehovah of the Tar Heels," *American Mercury* 17 (1929); S. C. Deskins, "The Presidential Election of 1928 in North Carolina" (Ph.D. diss., University of North Carolina, 1944); Helen Edmonds, *The Negro and Fusion Politics in North Carolina* (1951); *Nat. Cyc. Am. Biog.*, vol. 35 (1949); Elmer L. Puryear, *Democratic Party Dissension in North Carolina, 1928–1936* (1962); J. Fred Rippy, ed., *F. M. Simmons, Statesman of the New South: Memoirs and Addresses* (1936); Furnifold M. Simmons (as told to Carl Goerch), "Senator Simmons' Own Story," *The State* magazine, 25 Nov. 1933; Richard L. Watson, Jr., "A Political Leader Bolts: F. M. Simmons in the Presidential Election of 1928," *North Carolina Historical Review (NCHR)* 37 (October 1960), "A Southern Democratic Primary: Simmons vs. Bailey in 1930," *NCHR* 42 (Winter 1965), and "Furnifold M. Simmons: 'Jehovah of the Tar Heels'?" *NCHR* 44 (Spring 1967); D. J. Whitener, *Prohibition in North Carolina* (1946).

RICHARD L. WATSON, JR.

Simmons, James Frederick *(19 Dec. 1826–19 Dec. 1905)*, poet, newspaperman, and judge, was born in Halifax, the son of James (1800–1891) and Susan Gary Simmons. His mother died when he was an infant and he was raised by an aunt, Polly Gary. He probably was educated in a local academy before joining relatives in the summer of 1843 in Grenada, Miss., where he remained for four years working as a store clerk. Simmons began writing poetry, some of which was published in a local newspaper. In the summer of 1847 he returned to North Carolina to manage property inherited from his maternal grandfather, John Gary, and it probably was during this period that he read law. On 15 Mar. 1848 he married, at Woodland in Northampton County, Elizabeth Dorothy Crump, a niece of the Reverend Hezekiah G. Leigh, one of the founders of Randolph-Macon College.

At the time of the 1850 census, when he was twenty-three, Simmons was editor of the *Weldon Herald*, of which no copy survives. He had been editor since at least May 1848, when he wrote to William Henry Haywood about being a proxy to the Philadelphia convention. This newspaper venture was not successful, and he became depot agent for the Wilmington and Weldon Railroad. With resources from his own legacy and an inheritance of his wife's, Simmons purchased a large flour mill in Weldon. This proved to be a profitable undertaking, and he sold it before returning to Mississippi. He bought a plantation in Panola County for ten thousand dollars and invested several thousand more in slaves to operate it. Here his family lived from 1860 until a few years after the Civil War. At least one of his children, Florence, had been born in North Carolina and was one year old at the time of the 1850 census. In time he and his wife had five additional children.

Early in 1862 Simmons returned to North Carolina and in spite of growing deafness served in the rank of major as quartermaster in Matthew W. Ranson's Brigade. Because of poor health he had returned to Mississippi by early 1864 and still with the rank of major was serving as paymaster with troops there; on 21 March he was commended "for gallantry and efficiency on the field." In mid-May 1865 at Memphis, Tenn., when he was paroled, it was noted that he had been president of the Electoral College in 1861 and was a lawyer by occupation.

Simmons returned to Panola County and resumed the practice of law. In 1867 he built a new home in Sardis, the county seat, and became an important force in the development of the town. In 1870 he was appointed chancellor (judge) of the Tenth District, a position he held until 1874. Previously he had been referred to as Major Simmons, but henceforth he was addressed as Judge Simmons. For a number of years Simmons had also edited the *Panola Star*, but in 1880 he bought the Henderson, Ky., *Reporter*, which he edited for five years before he moved it to Sardis and established the *Southern Reporter*. He remained senior editor of the latter paper for the remainder of his life.

Simmons continued to write, contributing to various newspapers and periodicals. He once mentioned that he did not have copies of much of what he had written. *Godey's Lady's Book* for November 1850 published an account by him of a Revolutionary War heroine from Halifax County, and the issues of *Graham's Magazine* for February and June 1853 each contained poems by him. Eight more poems were included in Mary Bayard Clarke's anthology of North Carolina poetry, *Wood-Notes*, published in 1854. Two volumes of his collected verse were issued by the commercial publisher, J. B. Lippincott and Company of Philadelphia. *The Welded Link, and Other Poems*, in 1881, contained 82 poems, and *Rural Lyrics, Elegies, and Other Short Poems*, in 1885, contained 104. The preface to the first was dated at Sardis, Miss., while the second was at Cozy Nook, Henderson, Ky. In the latter he commented that he had intended to complete one or two narrative poems but that other duties and the lack of time prevented him from doing so.

Simmons enjoyed traveling with his family and often also took friends along. His thirteen-room home, which he called Malvern Villa, surrounded by formal gardens and a landscaped park, was often the scene of elaborate parties. His health began to fail about ten years before his death at age seventy-nine, but he remained busy with his accustomed activities.

SEE: Walter Clark, ed., *Histories of the Several Regiments and Battalions from North Carolina*, vol. 4 (1901); [Mary Bayard Clarke], *Wood-Notes; or, Carolina Carols*, vol. 2 (1854); Ernestine Clayton Deavours, *The Mississippi Poets* (1922); Elizabeth M. Hutchison, "Judge J. F. Simmons: Lawyer, Soldier, Editor, Poet" (typescript, North Carolina Collection, University of North Carolina, Chapel Hill, 1943); James B. Lloyd, ed., *Lives of Mississippi Authors, 1817–1967* (1981); *Official Records of the Rebellion*, ser. 1, vol. 32, pt. 1, and vol. 52, pt. 2.

WILLIAM S. POWELL

Simmons, James Stevens *(7 June 1890–31 July 1954)*, physician, army officer, and university professor, was born in Newton, the son of James Curtley and Angie Mary Stevens Simmons. The family moved to Graham when he was four, and he considered that his home until 1916. Graduated from Davidson College in 1911, he studied medicine at The University of North Carolina for two years and then entered the School of Medicine at the University of Pennsylvania, from which he received the M.D. degree in 1915. For the next year he was chief resident at the University Hospital, and as World War I approached, he was commissioned first lieutenant in the Army Medical Corps Reserve. He studied military preventive medicine at the Army Medical School and received a regular army commission and an assignment on the Mexican border as director of laboratories. His next assignment took him to New Haven, Conn., where he organized and commanded Overseas Laboratory No. 6 at the Yale Army Laboratory School.

After the war Simmons directed various army laboratories both at home and abroad and made especially significant contributions to the knowledge of dengue fever and malaria in the Philippines and the Canal Zone. His findings were published in journals, and his book, *Laboratory Methods of the U.S. Army*, went through six editions between 1935 and 1956. In his article, "Can We Stop an Invasion by Disease?," published in the *Saturday Evening Post* for 1 Dec. 1945, he anticipated the use of DDT in "beating typhus and malaria in vermin infested areas throughout the world."

During World War II Simmons organized and directed a preventive medicine service to protect the health of military personnel around the world as well as civilians working in defense industries. It was said that this was "the greatest campaign of preventive medicine in history."

Having filled countless posts and served on innumerable commissions, made important contributions in such areas as preventive medicine, epidemiology, bacteriology, tropical medicine, and other fields, Simmons earned promotions through the ranks and was commissioned brigadier general in 1943. He received a large number of awards and medals and held high office in many professional organizations. Among his honorary degrees were those awarded by The University of North Carolina, Davidson College, Duke University, the University of Pennsylvania, and Harvard.

On retiring in 1946 at the end of World War II, Simmons was named dean of the Harvard School of Public Health. Under his direction it was reorganized and given an equal status with other schools in the university. From time to time he also lectured at Yale and George Washington universities and at the University of Michigan.

Simmons married Blanche Scott, who had grown up with him as a neighbor across the street in Graham. They were the parents of a daughter, Frances (Mrs. David M. McConnell). General Simmons died of a heart attack in Hartford, Conn., while he and Mrs. Simmons were returning home from a visit to their daughter in Chapel Hill. He was buried in Arlington National Cemetery.

SEE: Daniel L. Grant, *Alumni History of the University of North Carolina* (1924); *Harvard Alumni Bulletin*, 24 Feb.

1951; *New York Times*, 2 Aug. 1954; *North Carolina Biography*, vol. 4 (1956 [portrait]); Raleigh *News and Observer*, 23 May, 13 Oct. 1943, 14 Jan. 1945; *Who Was Who in America*, vol. 3 (1966).

WILLIAM S. POWELL

Simpson, Francis Lucas *(6 June 1789–22 July 1873)*, militia general and state legislator, was the son of Moses and Mary Lucas Garrett Simpson of Guilford County. His parents, who were originally from Fairfax County, Va., moved to northern Guilford County by 1799 and settled on the Haw River. Francis Simpson married his cousin, Priscilla Simpson (1795–1865), on 16 Dec. 1815, and they had seven children: Mary, Nathaniel Henry, Sanford Monroe, Elizabeth, Jane, Emmaline, and Joseph Hawkins, who became a physician. Simpson served as a private in the Guilford County militia and eventually became the colonel in command of the Guilford regiment. By 1851 he had been elected major general of the Ninth Division. In both Guilford and Rockingham counties, he served as a county justice.

A Democrat, Simpson had a long and useful career in the North Carolina General Assembly. He represented Guilford County for six terms in the House of Commons (1825–30 and 1836–37). After moving to Rockingham County, he was in the House of Commons for one term (1858–59) and in the state senate for two terms (1860–64). In the legislature he served on a variety of committees, including those on privileges and elections, agriculture, propositions and grievances, rules, and corporations. During the Civil War he sat on the important joint legislative committee on military affairs. Normally he took little part in the floor activity of the Assembly, but in the session of 1858, with the support of John M. Morehead, he sponsored the effort to charter the Danville-to-Greensboro railroad connection. Opposed by senators desiring the rail line in their own districts, Simpson only partially succeeded by securing a charter in February 1859 to the Dan River and Coalfields Railroad from Danville to Leaksville. This important transportation link was not completed until military requirements forced the Confederate government to build the Piedmont Railroad, which was finished in 1864.

In 1851 Simpson purchased High Rock plantation in Rockingham County, just over the county line from his family seat on the Haw River. In 1860 he owned nearly five hundred acres and had accumulated twenty-eight slaves. He continued to live at High Rock until his death and was buried at the family cemetery in Guilford County. Primitive portraits of Francis and Priscilla Simpson are in possession of the family.

SEE: Cecil K. Brown, "A History of the Piedmont Railroad Company," *North Carolina Historical Review* 3 (April 1926); John L. Cheney, Jr., ed., *North Carolina Government, 1585–1974* (1975); *Journals of the Senate and House of Commons of the General Assembly of the State of North Carolina* (1858–64); *Muster Roll of the Soldiers of the War of 1812* (1851); John Nichols, *Directory of the General Assembly of the State of North Carolina, for the Session Commencing Nov. 19, 1860* (1860); David S. Reid Papers, Rockingham County Deeds and Court Minutes (North Carolina State Archives, Raleigh); U.S. Census, 1860.

LINDLEY S. BUTLER

Simpson, Herbert Woodley *(19 Jan. 1870–21 Oct. 1945)*, architect, was born in New Bern, the son of John Archibald, a builder and undertaker, and Mary Elizabeth Higgins Simpson. No information has been discovered about Simpson's early education, but it is assumed that he attended the New Bern Academy. In August 1888 he was accepted for a year of study with W. Claude Frederick, an architect in Baltimore. Simpson studied with Frederick from October 1888 to October 1889 and received a recommendation from him in March 1890.

The first evidence of Simpson's architectural practice appeared in 1896, when he advertised "plans prepared on short notice." It is likely that before that time, he assisted his father in the construction and undertaking business. One of his first commissions (1896) was to prepare plans for the rectory of St. Paul's Roman Catholic Church. Fortunately for the young architect, New Bern was experiencing a building boom. The economic stimulation of the town was largely a result of the lumber industry, which produced magnates desirous of building the most impressive residences and commercial structures that money could buy. Simpson is credited with the design of almost every important structure built in New Bern in the first two decades of the twentieth century. A versatile designer, he excelled in the Queen Anne and neoclassical revival styles and often combined the two. The profession of architecture in the United States was still rather new, and few architects were available to eastern North Carolinians in the early twentieth century. Consequently, Simpson produced designs for buildings in other eastern North Carolina towns as well. A list of Simpson-designed buildings, organized by town, can be found in the North Carolina State Archives.

On 21 Apr. 1897, shortly after entering his profession, Simpson married Nettie Tolson. They had two children, John Arch (14 Jan. 1898–January 1968) and Helen Elizabeth (22 Feb. 1900–May 1968). His American Institute of Architects, North Carolina Chapter, registration was dated September 1913. He was also a member of the Methodist church and of the Masonic order.

Simpson left New Bern in 1914 and took up residence in Norfolk, Va., where he continued his architectural practice until his death. Despite the move, he still designed buildings for North Carolina clients. In the 1920s John Arch joined his father's firm, Herbert W. Simpson and Son, and together they designed buildings until Herbert's death in 1945. Most of the structures fashioned by the two Simpsons were built in the Norfolk area.

Herbert Woodley Simpson was buried in Cedar Grove Cemetery, New Bern. A photographic portrait of him exists in the Herbert Woodley Simpson Collection, North Carolina State Archives.

SEE: St. Paul's Catholic Church records (New Bern); Herbert Woodley Simpson Collection (North Carolina State Archives, Raleigh); Charlotte E. (Mrs. John Arch) Simpson (West Pittstown, Pa.), personal contact, 30 Nov. 1971–15 Sept. 1975 (correspondence), May 1972 (interview); Simpson Scrapbook (possession of Shirley Tucker Beckton, New Bern).

JANET K. SEAPKER

Simpson, John *(8 Mar. 1728–1 Mar. 1788)*, Revolutionary leader, was born in Boston, the son of John and Mary Randall Simpson. Shortly after 1750 he moved to Beaufort County, N.C., with a group of New Englanders. In 1757 he was commissioned lieutenant by Governor Arthur Dobbs in Captain John Hardee's militia company, and in 1760 he was elected one of Beaufort County's representatives in the Assembly. Having introduced the bill to create a new county to be named Pitt, he was appointed one of the commissioners to set it up. The county seat was established at Hardee's Chapel a few miles southeast of the present city of Greenville. Following the creation of Pitt County, Simpson was elected to represent it in the colonial Assembly for three consecutive sessions between 1764 and 1769 and for three more between 1773 and 1775.

During that time, when the Regulator uprising took place, Simpson was colonel of the Pitt County militia. Governor William Tryon called on him to provide troops for the protection of the Assembly against threats by the Regulators. Although Simpson was not present at the Battle of Alamance in 1771, some of the troops from his regiment participated.

On the eve of the American Revolution, between 1774 and 1776, Simpson represented his county in the first four Provincial Congresses. As a member of the colonial Assembly in 1774, he was also a delegate to the First Provincial Congress, both bodies being composed of virtually the same men and meeting in the same hall. Simpson was one of those whom royal governor Josiah Martin condemned for their Revolutionary activity. In addition, he was named to the Council of Safety in 1776 and served two terms on the Council of State in 1778 and 1779. He represented Pitt County in four sessions of the General Assembly, serving in the House of Commons in 1778 and 1782–83 and in the senate in 1780–81 and 1786–87.

During much of the Revolutionary period Simpson was a justice of the Court of Pleas and Quarter Sessions. In 1780 he was promoted to the rank of brigadier general, but there is nothing to suggest that he saw active military service.

In 1758 Simpson married Elizabeth, the daughter of John Hardee, and they became the parents of nine children: Mary Randall, Susannah, Elizabeth, Samuel, Alice, John Hardee, Ann, Joseph, and Sarah. Susannah married Lawrence O'Bryan, Ann married John Eason, and Sarah married Dr. Joseph Brickell. The others never married. Simpson was buried in Pitt County on the south side of the Tar River at the old Hardee place, five miles south of Greenville.

SEE: Samuel A. Ashe, ed., *Biographical History of North Carolina,* vol. 4 (1905); John L. Cheney, Jr., ed., *North Carolina Government, 1585–1979* (1981); Walter Clark, ed., *State Records of North Carolina,* vols. 11–13, 16–19, 22 (1895–1907); Marshall DeLancey Haywood, *Builders of the Old North State* (1968); Henry T. King, *Sketches of Pitt County* (1911); William S. Powell, ed., *The Correspondence of William Tryon and Other Selected Papers,* vol. 2 (1981); William L. Saunders, ed., *Colonial Records of North Carolina,* vols. 6, 8–10 (1888–90).

ARMISTEAD J. MAUPIN

Simpson, William *(21 May 1839–23 June 1905),* pharmacist and teacher, was born in New York City, the son of James and Ann Cannon Simpson, both born near Glasgow, Scotland, who had immigrated to the United States in 1837. The family moved to Richmond, Va., in 1844 and later to North Carolina, where the elder Simpson established a bakery first in Warrenton but afterwards in Raleigh. William attended school in Richmond and after moving to Warrenton, he studied pharmacy with a local druggist. At age seventeen, because of the illness of his father, he became the manager of his father's bakery while studying pharmacy in the evening under a local pharmacist named Ferguson. In 1856 he worked for a drug firm in Richmond, but after a year or so he was employed by Meade and Baker, manufacturing pharmacists in New York. He returned to Raleigh in 1860.

At the outbreak of the Civil War Simpson volunteered for service, and after brief duty with a Virginia regiment he was assigned as a pharmacist to the military hospitals in Raleigh. After the war he became a partner in the firm of Doepp and Jones, Raleigh druggists, and by 1870 had acquired the company. He continued the business until a short while before his death, earning a reputation for his professional service to the community. Simpson was particularly noted for providing medicines to the poor without charge. He patented several medicines and about 1876 published a pamphlet, entitled *Make Your Own Fertilizer,* in which he instructed farmers how to make fertilizer with ingredients that cost about $10 per ton but provided the nutrients found in commercial brands that cost up to $50. He was one of the judges to award the pharmacy prizes at the Chicago World's Fair of 1893.

In 1880 Simpson was one of the founders of the North Carolina Pharmaceutical Association, and in 1882 he served as president. For a great many years he taught pharmacy, particularly to his own clerks so that they might pass the examination of the State Board of Pharmacy, but because the demand was so great he accepted students from around the state. In 1893 he also became dean of the Leonard School of Pharmacy at Shaw University.

A member and secretary of the newly organized Board of Pharmacy in the state, he was also secretary-treasurer of the board from 1881 to 1902 and one of the examiners until his death. In addition, he was a member of the American Pharmaceutical Association and president in 1894.

In 1860 Simpson married Anne Cannon Shanks, of Richmond, whose family had arrived from Scotland at the same time as his. They were the parents of eight children, only two of whom survived: Jane (Mrs. Charles McKimmon) and Thomas Skinner. William Simpson died in Raleigh. He had been an active Mason, and his funeral was held at the First Baptist Church with Masonic honors.

SEE: J. G. Beard, "William Simpson," *Journal of the American Pharmaceutical Association* 12 (May 1923); *Nat. Cyc. Am. Biog.*, vol. 24 (1935); Raleigh *News and Observer,* 24–25 June 1905 [portrait], 19 Dec. 1926; *We the People of North Carolina* 6 (February 1949).

WILLIAM S. POWELL

Sims, George *(1728–1808),* schoolmaster and Regulator spokesman, thrust himself into the limelight with a timely appeal to the agitated people of western North Carolina and then just as suddenly disappeared from the public view. Born to George, a Brunswick County, Va., planter, and Martha Sims, he moved with his brothers to the Nutbush section of north-central Granville (now Vance) County before 1750. About 1758 Sims wed a Miss Bullock, thereby linking himself to such Granville luminaries as Len Henley Bullock, a future member of the Transylvania Company. Supporting his family, which eventually included eight sons and four daughters, as a schoolmaster and small farmer, Sims used what spare time he had to read widely.

Sims's increasing familiarity with legal theory and his growing dissatisfaction with local government bore fruit in 1765. On 6 June he drafted "An Address to the People of Granville County." Finding a responsive audience among those who would soon inaugurate the Regulator movement, the paper slowly achieved currency throughout the western half of the province. At the August 1767 session of the Orange County Court, for example, it attracted considerable attention. Herman Husband quoted large blocks of the essay in both of his pamphlets justifying the Regulation and as such parts of Sims's work were published in New England and elsewhere.

Probably intending to advance the maverick political career of Thomas Person, to whom the document was dedicated, as well as his own, Sims produced a competent exposition of the public ills of the area and a viable outline for action. Unlike the Regulators who followed him, he had not lost faith in local government in general, but only in certain officials, particularly Clerk of Court Samuel Benton. He emphasized this in the best-known passage from the document: "Well, Gentlemen, it is not our mode, or form of Government, nor yet the body of our laws, that we are quarreling with, but with the malpractices of the Officers of our County Court, and the abuses which we suffer by those empowered to manage our public affairs." Sims accused Benton of perverting the just aims of government by making exorbitant demands of the people and seizing their property to settle them. He pledged to pay no more fees to Benton until the official produced a body of law that authorized them and implored his audience to do likewise.

Recommending circumspection, Sims demonstrated his careful consideration of the situation and his familiarity with the Whig thought so influential in Revolutionary America: "And first, let us be careful to keep sober, that we do nothing rashly; but act with deliberation. Secondly, Let us do nothing against the Known and established laws of our land, that we may not appear as a faction endeavoring to subvert the laws. . . . But, let us appear what we really are, To wit, free subjects by birth, endeavoring to recover our native right according to law. . . . Thirdly, let us behave ourselves with circumspection to the Worshipful Court. . . . Let us deliver them a remonstrance."

Besides its influence on the burgeoning dissatisfaction in the backcountry that culminated in the Regulation, Sims's address draws, according to James P. Whittenburg, its significance in comparison to similar documents from three further factors: (1) Sims asserted that Benton deprived his constituents of their constitutional rights, (2) Sims cited common law as the protector of those rights, and (3) his argument introduced the appeal to legal theory into the Regulation.

Sims's bold statements of course upset the county officialdom. Benton caused him to be arrested for libel on 7 Aug. 1765. According to Herman Husband, a verdict had not been reached five years later. The plaintiff's case was no doubt aided by the defendant's ill-advised implication that Benton had been a criminal before he took office. This reaction, as well as the increasingly violent nature of the Regulation, discouraged Sims from further protest. He apparently failed to serve in the American Revolution, but in 1777 he finally gained public office as constable from St. David's District in the southwestern corner of the newly formed Caswell County.

When Sims relocated to that place is uncertain, but by the mid-1780s he was one of the more substantial members of the community, owning, in addition to six slaves, 1,138 acres. Of this, 1,038 acres had been granted to Sims by the state, and he sold these tracts for £338 North Carolina currency in 1789. His household during this period was large, consisting of five white males and seven white women as well as the blacks. In his later years Sims's land and slaveholdings fluctuated only moderately. Three years before his death at age eighty, he owned five blacks and 336 acres.

George Sims, a distant forebearer of the Duke family of Durham, achieved rapid notoriety because his views suited a certain place and time. When he failed to follow up his brief fame and the temper of the people changed, he returned as readily to obscurity. Sims's role in publicizing the backcountry grievances, however, cannot be ignored.

SEE: William K. Boyd, ed., *Some Eighteenth-Century Tracts Concerning North Carolina* (1927); Archibald Henderson, "The Origins of the Regulation in North Carolina," *American Historical Review* 21 (1916); Jane Morris, *Adam Symes and His Descendants* (1938); James F. Whittenburg, "Backwood Revolutionaries: Social Context and Constitutional Theories of the North Carolina Regulators, 1765–1771" (Ph.D. diss., University of Georgia, 1974).

ARTHUR C. MENIUS

Sims, Leonard Henly *(6 Feb. 1807–28 Feb. 1886)*, congressman and farmer, was born in Burke County, the son of Dr. Swepson and Jane Meriwether Lewis Sims. The younger Sims, who received a limited amount of schooling, moved to Rutherford County, Tenn., in 1830 and became a farmer. He was also a member of the Tennessee State House of Representatives for two terms.

In 1839 he moved to Springfield, Green County, Mo., and continued his agricultural pursuits. From 1842 to 1846 he was a member of the Missouri State House of Representatives. Elected as a Democrat to the U.S. House of Representatives from Missouri, Sims served in the Twenty-ninth Congress from 4 Mar. 1845 to 3 Mar. 1847. In the latter year he returned to Rutherford County, Tenn., to continue farming, and in 1848 he was a presidential elector for Tennessee on the Democratic ticket of Lewis Cass and William Orlando Butler.

In 1859 Sims relocated to Independence County, Ark., where he settled on a farm near Batesville and engaged in cotton planting and farming. He also served in the Arkansas State Senate during 1866–70 and 1874–78.

On 8 Dec. 1824 Sims married Louisa Batey. They had eleven children. He died on his plantation near Batesville, Ark., and was buried in the family graveyard.

SEE: *Biog. Dir. Am. Cong.* (1950); *Biog. Dir. Tenn. General Assembly* (1975); *Who Was Who in America, 1607–1896.*

E. THOMAS SIMS

Sims, Marian *(16 Oct. 1899–9 July 1961)*, writer, was born in Dalton, Ga., the daughter of Julian and Grace Gardner McCamy. She was educated in the Dalton public schools and was graduated in 1920 from Agnes Scott College with a major in history and a minor in English. After teaching French and history in the Dalton High School for four years, she became "chief copy writer for a direct-mail advertising firm." In 1927 she married Frank Knight Sims, Jr., a somewhat younger Dalton friend with whom she had grown up. Her brother, Robert G. McCamy, was married to Sims's sister.

After a year in Greensboro, where she began to write, Marian Sims and her husband moved to Charlotte in 1930. Including her first short story in *Collier's* (23 Dec. 1933), she sold, during the next two decades, forty stories to such magazines as *Saturday Evening Post, Ladies' Home Journal, McCall's, Liberty, Pictorial Review, Good Housekeeping,* and *Woman's Home Companion.* Though an expert in the elusive and often frustrating technique so essential to the writing of short stories for the popular slick magazines, she eventually "discovered that my kind of short story was largely a mechanical trick and that the novel would permit more depth and latitude." Her seven novels explored the upper- and middle-class urban South, its politics, its social conflicts, and the personal crises of its people against a background of golf clubs, bridge parties, and summer resorts—a segment bypassed by most southern writers of fiction.

Morning Star (1934) narrates a young woman's reaction to small-town conventions and stodginess. In *The World with a Fence* (1936), a Georgia schoolteacher leaves the small town for Atlanta to preserve her integrity. *Call It Freedom* (1937) delineates the problems of a divorced woman in Hanover (Charlotte). The epistolary *Memo to Timothy Sheldon* (1938) centers on an attractive woman married to one man but in love with another. *The City on a Hill* (1940), her most remembered work, exposes political skullduggery in Medbury (Charlotte), its chief character closely resembling Mrs. Sims's husband, judge of the Charlotte Recorder's Court. *Beyond Surrender* (1942) is a historical novel of Reconstruction in South Carolina. In *Storm before Daybreak* (1946), a returning war veteran becomes involved with his brother's wife.

Mrs. Sims held a fellowship in 1940 at the Bread Loaf Writers' School and Conference in Vermont. During World War II, while her husband was overseas, she lived in Atlanta. In 1949 she wrote the words for Lamar Stringfield's cantata *Peace*. Mrs. Sims, who had been a Presbyterian and a Democrat, was buried in the Sharon Memorial Mausoleum, Charlotte. A collection of her manuscripts and copies of her magazine short stories are located in the library of the University of North Carolina at Charlotte.

SEE: *North Carolina Authors: A Selective Handbook* (1952); *North Carolina Fiction* (1958); Marian Sims, "Writer's Recollections," *Agnes Scott Alumnae Quarterly* (Spring 1948); Vertical file in Public Library of Charlotte and Mecklenburg County; Harry R. Warfel, *American Novelists Today* (1951).

RICHARD WALSER

Singleton, Spyers *(d. 31 Oct. 1814)*, legislator and businessman of Craven County, was the son of Samuel (will dated 4 Dec. 1762) and Hannah Singleton (b. ca. 1728) of Dobbs County. He had one sister, Martha, who married Benjamin Caswell.

In 1775 Singleton was one of seven representatives of Dobbs County to the Provincial Congress at Hillsborough; Richard Caswell, later governor, also represented Dobbs. Singleton was then a merchant in partnership with Benjamin Caswell, Richard's brother, on Contentnea Creek near Haw Landing, between the present towns of Hookerton and Snow Hill. In the following year Singleton was appointed one of fifteen "justices for keeping the peace" in Dobbs County. He served as captain of a troop of light horse cavalry in the New Bern District Brigade of Minutemen under Colonel Richard Caswell at the Battle of Moore's Creek Bridge (27 Feb. 1776) and in the expeditions to Moore's Creek and in the defense of Wilmington.

After 1776, references in the *Colonial* and *State Records* place Singleton in Beaufort in 1777 and in New Bern in 1779. By this time he had married Elizabeth Blackledge (marriage bond 30 Dec. 1775), the daughter of Richard and Ann Blackledge, of Craven County, and apparently had moved his residence to that area. He was owner of the armed merchant ship *Cornelia* (Charles Biddle, captain), fitted out in New Bern in 1778. In the 1790 census he was listed in the Newbern District of Craven County, with a household of eight persons and eighteen slaves. His final residence was listed, in the disposal of his property after his death, as Brices Creek near New Bern.

In 1783 Singleton was one of five commissioners for the port of Beaufort, and in 1784 he was appointed a trustee and a director of New Bern Academy. By 1784 he was also part of the commercial firm of Enoch Ward, Spyers Singleton, Christopher Neale and Company, which was named in a bill permitting a canal to be dug from Clubfoot Creek to Harlowe Creek. However the canal was not approved until 1795, under Governor Richard Dobbs Spaight.

In October 1784 Singleton represented New Bern in the House of Commons. In December 1785 he was one of two nominees for councillor of state and was also appointed one of five commissioners for improving coastal navigation. In 1786 he was one of five lottery managers directed to raise money for the construction of a "house for the poor" in New Bern. Again nominated for councillor of state in December 1786, he was one of four nominees elected in January 1787. On 30 Nov. 1787 Singleton petitioned the house to require the "Public Treasurer to pay off . . . a certain warrant" issued to General Nathanael Greene for the purchase of commissary goods; his petition was granted.

In the same year Singleton was the defendant in a noted court case, *Bayard v. Singleton*, by which he retained some property acquired in 1784 for £2,160 formerly belonging to Loyalist Samuel Cornell. This case was the first in which a court declared an act of a legislature unconstitutional.

In 1793 the General Assembly appointed him as one of the seven men on the Governor's Council. Thomas Blount, in a letter to his brother, John Gray Blount, in July 1798, recommended Singleton for tax commissioner, and in August he was appointed a commissioner of one of seven divisions for "the valuation of lands and houses and for the enumeration of slaves."

In 1800 Singleton was one of five commissioners of navigation, who, among other duties, inspected incoming passengers for contagious diseases. In the census of that year he was listed as having a household of seven persons and four slaves.

On 11 Dec. 1804 Singleton's wife died in New Bern. At his death almost ten years later, he was described as "an old and respectable inhabitant of This [Craven] County." He was buried in Cedar Grove Cemetery.

SEE: Annie Burns Bell, *North Carolina Genealogical Records* (1943); Walter Clark, ed., *State Records of North Carolina*, vols. 11, 14, 17–20, 23–24 (1895–1905); Robert O. DeMond, *The Loyalists in North Carolina during the Revolution* (1940); *First Census of the United States, 1790* (1908); J. Bryan Grimes, ed., *North Carolina Wills and Inventories* (1912) and *Abstract of North Carolina Wills* (1910); Quinton Holton, "History of the Case of *Bayard v. Singleton*" (M.A. thesis, University of North Carolina, 1948); Talmage C. Johnson and Charles R. Holloman, *The Story of Kinston and Lenoir County* (1954); Jean B. Kell and Thomas A. Williams, eds., *North Carolina's Coastal Carteret County during the American Revolution* (1975); William H. Masterson, ed., *The John Gray Blount Papers*, vol. 3 (1965); Elizabeth Moore, *Records of Craven County* (1960); John Wheeler Moore, *History of North Carolina*, vol. 1 (1880); New Bern *Carolina Federal Republican*, 5, 12, 19 Nov. 1814; *Newbern Gazette*, 26 Jan. 1799, 15 Aug. 1800; New Bern *North Carolina Minerva and Fayetteville Advertiser*, 11 Aug. 1798; Raleigh *Register*, 31 Dec. 1804, 18 Nov. 1814; William L. Saunders, ed., *Colonial Records of North Carolina*, vol. 10 (1890); Superior Court Records, Newbern District, and "Superior Court Minutes, Craven County, 1787–1794" (North Carolina State Archives, Raleigh); U.S. Census Office, *Population Schedules of the Second Census of the United States, 1800, North Carolina*, "Craven County" (1961).

EVA MURPHY

Sink, H[arvey] Hoyle *(20 Dec. 1888–25 Feb. 1968)*, jurist, was born in the Tyro community, Davidson County, a son of Thomas Franklin and Martha Anne Lanning Sink. The Sink (Zink or Zinck) family emigrated from Germany to Pennsylvania about 1728 and thence to North Carolina in the 1750s. Both the Sinks and the Lannings were farmers. H. Hoyle Sink's grandfather, John Lanning, enlisted in the Confederate army at the outbreak of the Civil War.

Sink disliked his first name, never used it, and members of the family helped him conceal it. He finished public school and attended Reeds High School in Davidson County for five months before becoming a fruit tree salesman. In 1907 he obtained a teacher's certificate and while teaching studied at night to gain admission to Bridgewater, Va., College. After graduation from Bridgewater in 1910, he was for the next two years principal of Hamburg School, Mount Jackson, Va., the first consolidated school in Virginia.

Appointed a lecturer on current topics to officers of the Imperial Japanese Navy, Sink spent two years in Japan. With the outbreak of World War I in 1914 he went to Amoy, China, where he lectured in the Tung Win Institute. After a few months President Woodrow Wilson appointed him vice-consul in charge of the U.S. Consulate in Amoy; at that time he was the youngest officer in charge of a comparable consulate in the American Diplomatic Service. When the United States entered the war, he resigned and returned home to enter the officers' training corps but was rejected twice because of poor eyesight. Determined to serve, however, he studied law at Wake Forest College for sixty days and obtained his license on 29 Jan. 1918. He then was admitted as a private into the legal department of the army but later was commissioned second lieutenant in the chemical warfare division; he was not called for overseas duty.

After the war Sink began to practice law in Lexington and in 1925, with the creation of the office of commissioner of pardons, Governor Angus W. McLean named him to that position as well as executive counsel to the governor. In 1927 the governor appointed him a special superior court judge, and he moved his family to Charlotte. By appointment, election, and reelection he served on the superior court bench until he retired in 1954, living at different times in Asheville and Greensboro as well as in Charlotte. Even after retirement he frequently served on an emergency basis until shortly before his death. His record reveals that he held court for a longer period than any other superior court judge in the history of the state.

During his nearly fifty years on the bench, Sink presided over countless civil and criminal cases that greatly varied in scope. He was considered to be a stern judge, tough on jurors, lawyers, and prisoners, but fair and consistent. His mastery of law, understanding of human nature, and fidelity to justice in the discharge of his duty all combined to make his decisions almost unassailable. At one time during the depression thirty-nine cases involving bank litigation were pending in the North Carolina Supreme Court on appeal from trials held by Sink; of that number, only one was reversed by the supreme court.

Judge Sink was outspoken in his opinions. Although he had drafted the bill creating the parole board, he was sharply critical of its actions in later years. He said that "the Parole Board just assumes it has the sworn duty to reduce every sentence given by the trial judge. And it's an insult." In 1940 he initiated a work-release program for convicts in Mecklenburg County, but later he said, "Others have elaborated on it, and others, like the Parole Board have overdone it."

Sink was a charter member of the American Legion, a Democrat, and a Lutheran. He was especially interested in farming and maintained oversight of the Sink farm on which he was reared and which he owned after his parents' death. On 17 June 1920 in Salisbury, Sink married Kathleen Heilig. They had a daughter, Harriet (Mrs. Wilson Brown Prophet, Jr.). The judge died in Greensboro and was buried in Chestnut Hill Cemetery, Salisbury.

SEE: Family records (possession of Harriet Sink Prophet, South Norwalk, Conn.); *Heritage of Davidson County* (1982); Lexington *Dispatch*, 26 Feb. 1968; *Nat. Cyc. Am. Biog.*, vol. 54 (1973); Raleigh *News and Observer*, 2 Feb. 1964, 26 Feb. 1968.

M. JEWELL SINK

Sitgreaves, John *(1757–4 Mar. 1802)*, congressman, legislator, and federal judge, was born in England, the son of Thomas, a native of Philadelphia and a resident of New Bern, N.C., and Mrs. John Cady Bryan Sitgreaves. Thomas was a coroner, marshal of the court of admiralty for the port of Beaufort, member of the Anglican church, and supporter of the American cause during the Revolution.

It has been said that young Sitgreaves studied at Eton College in England, but his name does not appear in Richard Arthur Austen-Leigh's *Eton College Register, 1753–1790* (1921). He went to New Bern, studied law, and began to practice. On 16 Apr. 1776 he was appointed second lieutenant in the New Bern militia. In 1779 he served on a board of auditors for public and private accounts and claims. At the 1780 Battle of Camden he was aide to Major General Richard Caswell. On returning home he became a commissioner for the sale of confiscated property in the New Bern district. He was assistant clerk of the two sessions of the first state senate in 1777 and clerk of its three sessions in 1778–79 and its two in 1779, but he declined the post in 1781.

As clerk he ordered the preparation of a map of New Bern. Dated 11 Feb. 1779, it was certified by Allen Jones, speaker of the senate, and Thomas Benbury, speaker of the house. This map was "one of the two plans to which the Act passed at the General Assembly held at Halifax Town in January 1779 entitled an Act for the Regulation of the Town of New Bern" refers.

Elected to represent the borough town of New Bern in the first session of the 1784 House of Commons, Sitgreaves was named by that body to the board of trustees of the reorganized New Bern Academy and acted as its secretary. During 1784 and 1785 he attended the Continental Congress. At one of its last meetings in November 1785 he was absent while, by special appointment, holding a term of federal court at Williamsburg, Va.

Again the delegate from New Bern to the state legislature in 1786, 1787, and 1788, he served as speaker during the last two years. At the 1788 state constitutional convention he unsuccessfully supported ratification of the federal Constitution.

In New Bern he was noted for his hospitality. William Penn Attmore, a Philadelphia merchant who was in the town to collect debts and who was married to Sitgreaves's sister, Sarah, drew in his journal a diagram showing the seating of guests and the arrangement of food at a dinner in the Sitgreaves home. The last royal governor, Josiah Martin, is said to have taken temporary refuge in a house on a Sitgreaves lot at Broad and Burn streets prior to fleeing the city in May 1775.

In 1789 Sitgreaves was appointed as one of the first trustees for the proposed University of North Carolina. After the admission of North Carolina into the Union on 21 Nov. 1789, a U.S. district court was established at New Bern and Sitgreaves became its attorney. On 20 Dec. 1790, following the death in mid-October of Judge John Stokes, he was appointed by President George Washington, upon recommendation of U.S. Senator Benjamin Hawkins and others, as the district judge of North Carolina, a position he held until his death.

When the president visited New Bern in April 1791, Sitgreaves and Mayor Joseph Leech headed a civic delegation welcoming Washington. After using a room in the former governor's palace as his last office in New Bern, Sitgreaves moved to Halifax, where he died and was buried. The epitaph on the monument over his grave records that he had spent "a life of honor and integrity in the service of his country." From his portrait, an etching was made by Albert Rosenthal of Philadelphia.

Sitgreaves married Mrs. Martha Jones Green (d. 1822), the daughter of General Allen Jones of Northampton County and the widow of James W. Green. Surviving him were a son, John (1799–1868), who married Anne Love, and a daughter, Amaryllis, who married Frederick Lafayette Jones Pride.

Amaryllis Sitgreaves Pride was the namesake of her aunt, Amaryllis Sitgreaves, wife of George Ellis, who represented New Bern in the 1800 and 1801 House of Commons. Arete Ellis, their daughter, a home missionary and teacher at New Bern's free trade school for orphan girls (one of the first schools of its type in the country), is memorialized by large twin stained glass windows in Christ Episcopal Church, New Bern.

SEE: Samuel A. Ashe, ed., *Biographical History of North Carolina*, vol. 2 (1905); William Attmore, *Journal of a Tour to North Carolina* (1787); *Biog. Dir. Am. Cong.* (1971); John L. Cheney, Jr., ed., *North Carolina Government, 1585–1979* (1981); Walter Clark, ed., *State Records of North Carolina*, vols. 12–13 (1896); R. D. W. Connor, *A Documentary History of the University of North Carolina, 1776–1799*, 2 vols. (1953); Marshall DeLancey Haywood, *Builders of the Old North State* (1968); William L. Saunders, ed., *Colonial Records of North Carolina*, vols. 9–10 (1890).

GERTRUDE S. CARRAWAY

Skiles, William West *(12 Oct. 1807–8 Dec. 1862)*, Episcopal missionary and teacher, was born in Hertford, Perquimans County. Following a few years of formal schooling in the local schools, he worked as a mechanic and later as overseer of a group of lumber mills in the vicinity of Plymouth.

In 1844 Skiles left eastern North Carolina to settle in the newly formed community of Valle Crucis, Watauga County, where Levi Silliman Ives, bishop of the Diocese of North Carolina, was in the process of developing a center for missionary work, a classical and agricultural school for boys, and a theological school. During the next year a chapel, schoolhouse, and dormitory were built as well as a sawmill and a blacksmith shop. A farm and a dairy were maintained to help support the community.

On his arrival, Skiles was placed in charge of all agricultural activities. It was not long before the duties of storekeeper, teacher, treasurer, postmaster, and general superintendent were also assigned to him. Skiles had been at Valle Crucis for only a year when he decided to study for the ministry in the recently established theological school. He was admitted as a candidate, since the General Convention of the Episcopal church had recently enacted a canon that permitted persons without a classical education to become candidates for the diaconate. In consequence of his energetic, methodical, and patient character, he was able to add theological studies to his other responsibilities. Skiles had begun to take part in the mission at Valle Crucis when he was appointed warden upon the death of the church's rector in 1846. He prepared the report of the mission's work for the diocesan convention of 1847.

In the summer of 1847 Skiles completed his theological studies, and on 1 August he was ordained a deacon by Bishop Ives in the church at Valle Crucis. Shortly after his ordination he joined the Order of the Holy Cross, which Ives had established at Valle Crucis a few months earlier. The devotional, charitable, and disciplinary nature of the order strongly appealed to him; it undoubtedly influenced his ministry, although it existed there for only two years.

Skiles entered on his vocation as missionary and teacher with vigor and enthusiasm. He visited the mission stations in the neighborhood of Valle Crucis and assisted in the services held there. In addition, he continued as general superintendent of all physical aspects of the Valle Crucis community. This work was increasingly difficult because of the lack of financial support from the outside. By 1852, when Ives resigned as bishop of the Diocese of North Carolina, all of the educational work at Valle Crucis was terminated. At this time Skiles was the only member of the original community left there. He continued to live at Valle Crucis in one of the abandoned buildings until 1855, when he moved to the home of his friend, George N. Evans, at Lower Watauga.

With the closing of the Valle Crucis enterprise, Skiles was able to devote all of his time to missionary work in the mountain region. From the diocese he received an annual stipend of $100, which was later increased to $150. His principal work comprised mission stations in the counties of Ashe, Watauga, Mitchell, and Yancey with occasional visits to Burke, Caldwell, and Wilkes. On two occasions he visited Tennessee to hold services near Elizabethton. For a few years Skiles taught gratis a four-month day school for the children in the Valle Crucis neighborhood but had to give it up because of the increasing demands of his missionary work. In 1859 he reported that he had held services in sixteen places and had traveled more than a thousand miles on horseback. In the communities without a church building, services were conducted in private homes.

Many members of Skiles's widely scattered congregations depended on him for more than spiritual guidance. Because there were few doctors in the area, he acquired medical texts on the most common diseases of the region in order to give his parishioners some assistance and much comfort. He frequently served as a "public scrivener and legal advisor." His counsel was sought in settling differences between neighbors, in business matters, and on methods of farming. Of Skiles's work a contemporary wrote: "The people among whom he labored, not only Episcopalians, but of all Denominations, felt for him a deep attachment."

One of Skiles's missionary projects closest to his heart was the construction of a church at Lower Watauga, about six miles from Valle Crucis, where his congregation had grown too large to meet in one of the local homes. In the fall of 1859 he began building a church with funds, materials, and labor contributed by his congregation and himself. The church, a frame Gothic building with stained glass windows, named St. John the Baptist, was completed a year later at a cost of $700, of which Skiles donated more than a third. Bishop Thomas Atkinson consecrated the church on 22 Aug. 1862. Only a few months after the consecration of the church, which, in the bishop's words, was "a touching and appropriate memorial of that man of God," Skiles died at the home of a friend on the Linville River. He was buried in the churchyard of St. John the Baptist.

In a tribute to Skiles, Bishop Atkinson declared that he was "a true Missionary, humble, patient, laborious and affectionate,—not despising the day of small things, and still less despising any human soul, however rude and ignorant and sin-stained that soul might be. Long will the dwellers in the valleys and forest of that wild mountain region miss their faithful Pastor."

SEE: Joseph Blount Cheshire, ed., *Sketches of Church History in North Carolina* (1892); *The Church Intelligencer* (Raleigh), 16 Jan. 1863; Susan Fenimore Cooper, *William West Skiles* (1890); Marshall DeLancey Haywood, *Lives of the Bishops of North Carolina* (1910); *Journals of the Diocese of North Carolina*, 1844–63; James B. Sill, *Historical Sketches of Churches in the Diocese of Western North Carolina* (1955).

LAWRENCE F. LONDON

Skinner, Harry *(25 May 1855–19 May 1929)*, lawyer, Populist leader, writer, and businessman, was born in Perquimans County, the son of James C. and Elmira Ward Skinner. His ancestors had been active in the political affairs of North Carolina for three generations. He attended Hertford Academy before studying law at the University of Kentucky, from which he was graduated in 1874. Licensed to practice in 1876, he became a partner of Louis Charles Latham in Greenville and, in time, with others. From 1879 to 1886 he was aide-de-camp to Governor Thomas J. Jarvis, and it was from this service that he acquired the title of colonel.

A student of political economy, Skinner's greatest contribution was in the field of economic thought. His ideas on money and banking led him to publish an article on "A Productive Land Basis for Our National Bank Issue" in the Greenville *Eastern Reflector* and the Raleigh *News and Observer* in 1887. Skinner proposed that productive land rather than U.S. bonds serve as the basis for the issuance of bank notes. He pointed out that the retirement of bonds led to a contracted currency and that the existing system enriched northeastern bondholders and impoverished southern and western producers. In 1888 he published in the *Reflector* and the *Progressive Farmer* an article entitled, "The Hope of the South," which gained nationwide attention when it appeared in *Frank Leslie's Illustrated Newspaper* on 30 Nov. 1889. In it he proposed to extend to raw cotton the same rate of protection (47 percent) that was extended to manufactured cotton and thus raise the price of cotton to fourteen cents per pound. The plan involved the creation of government warehouses where producers could store their cotton in exchange for legal tender warehouse or cotton certificates. There is evidence to support the claim that Skinner was the father of the subtreasury scheme advocated by the Southern Alliance (National Farmers' Alliance and Industrial Union).

As a lawyer Skinner was ineligible for membership in the alliance, but he supported the farmers' movement. In January 1887 he represented Pitt County in the agricultural convention held in Raleigh that established the Farmers' Association, a short-lived organization absorbed in 1888 by the North Carolina Farmers' State Alliance. Always concerned about the problem of farm credit, he introduced a resolution to induce the General Assembly to provide financial relief for farmers. In 1890 Skinner was elected to the state house of representatives by a decisive majority, having waged his campaign on the subtreasury plan. In the legislature he advocated reduction of the interest rate to 6 percent and introduced a bill to prevent the sale of land under mortgage that did not bring 50 percent of its tax value. Among other legislation, Skinner introduced measures to establish an orphan's court and to name a committee to codify the laws of incorporation. He fought for the establishment of the Industrial Training School for Girls at Greensboro and for a railroad commission.

Although he was a staunch Democrat, in 1892 he joined the People's party. Nominated for governor by the third party, he agreed to accept only on condition that he would withdraw if his candidacy posed a threat to white supremacy. The Populist convention instead nominated Wyatt P. Exum. Skinner was then offered but declined the nomination for Congress, but in 1894 he relented and was elected—and reelected two years later. On Capitol Hill he was active on behalf of internal improvements, an industrialized South, and a protective tariff. He favored bimetallism and introduced a bill to issue bimetallic certificates that would be redeemed one-half in gold and one-half in silver at the ratio of 16 to 1. He proposed to cut official salaries by 33⅓ percent in order to reduce the government deficit. And he introduced a bill to stabilize the price of cotton. His ideas, far in advance of his time, were embodied in the Federal Reserve Banking Act and the Federal Farm Loan Bank Act passed during Woodrow Wilson's administration and subsequently in New Deal farm legislation in the 1930s.

Skinner became a powerful figure in the North Carolina People's party and challenged Marion Butler for party control. Early in 1897 he broke with the Butler wing of the party and voted for the reelection of U.S. Senator Jeter C. Pritchard, a Republican. Skinner was defeated for reelection in 1898, when Populism was on the wane. He later joined the Republican party.

Continuing his public service, Skinner was appointed U.S. district attorney for the Eastern District of North Carolina in 1901 and filled the position for eight years. Active again in the legal profession, he served as president of the North Carolina Bar Association in 1915–16 and as vice-president of the American Bar Association for North Carolina for two years. In his address before the state bar association in 1915, he asserted that law should be the instrument of justice and human progress.

An advocate of education, Skinner served on the board of trustees of The University of North Carolina from 1898 to 1902. He was a Mason and a member of the Episcopal church. In 1878 he married Lottie Montiero, of Richmond, Va., who died ten years later. Of the six children born to them, two died in infancy and a third, Harry, Jr., was killed in an automobile accident in 1909. He was survived by three daughters: Ella Montiero (Mrs. A. M. Mosely), Lottie (Mrs. H. D. Bateman), and Winifred. In 1895 he married Ella Montiero, who bore a son, Francis Xavier; the son, who reached manhood, died before his father. Skinner was buried in Cherry Hill Cemetery, Greenville.

SEE: Samuel A. Ashe, ed., *Cyclopedia of Eminent and Representative Men of the Carolinas*, vol. 2 (1892 [portrait]); *Biog. Dir. Am. Cong.* (1971); Marion Butler Papers and Thomas Settle Papers (Southern Historical Collection, University of North Carolina, Chapel Hill); Elias Carr Papers and Harry W. Whedbee Papers (Manuscript Collection, East Carolina University Library, Greenville); Henry T. King, *Sketches of Pitt County, 1704–1910* (1911 [portrait]); Philip R. Muller, "New South Populism: North Carolina, 1884–1900" (Ph.D. diss., University of North Carolina, 1971); *North Carolina Biography*, vol. 4 (1919); Raleigh *News and Observer*, 22 Apr. 1892, 20 May 1929; Raleigh *State Chronicle*, 14 Jan. 1891.

LALA CARR STEELMAN

Skinner, John *(7 Oct. 1760–31 Dec. 1819)*, first U.S. marshal for the district of North Carolina and the state's chief enumerator for the 1790 federal census, was born in Perquimans County to Joshua and Sarah Creecy Skinner. Members of the Skinner family were among the earliest settlers of the county, established in 1688. John Skinner's great-grandfather Richard moved south from Isle of Wight County, Va., prior to 1701.

Young Skinner apparently acquired his early education around tours of duty in the North Carolina Continental Line. He represented Perquimans in the state senate in 1784 and in the House of Commons in 1785, 1786, and 1787. In his first year of public service he was nominated, though never seated, as one of eight delegates to represent the state in the Continental Congress. In 1788 and 1789 he served on the Council of State under Governor Samuel Johnston. In the legislature Skinner supported acts to improve navigation in Albemarle Sound and advocated equitable rates of taxation. He was consistently a champion of the Federalist cause, and at Hillsborough in 1788 and Fayetteville in 1789 he represented Perquimans in conventions called to consider ratification of the U.S. Constitution.

On 8 June 1790 the U.S. Senate confirmed President George Washington's appointment of Skinner as the first federal marshal for the district of North Carolina. The primary responsibilities of the marshal were to attend to the federal courts and to execute all lawful precepts issued to them under authority of the U.S. government. One of his first duties was to oversee the taking of the first federal census in 1790. During his four-year term he also supervised the public auction of seized lands and impounded goods. In August 1794 he was succeeded by Michael Payne of Edenton.

In late 1794 and again in 1797 the citizens of Perquimans County returned Skinner to the General Assembly. He is believed to have built his Perquimans seat, Ashland, sometime after 1775; however, he may have acquired it through his second or third wife, both daughters of wealthy landowners in the area. Ashland, located on the Perquimans River in the Harveys Neck section and one of the finest homes in northeastern North Carolina, was destroyed by fire in 1952. In 1790 he owned 850 acres and 38 slaves in Perquimans County. At some time after 1797 Skinner moved to Chowan County, where he built an estate known as Montpelier on Albemarle Sound, three miles outside Edenton. Although Montpelier was somewhat smaller than Ashland, he owned 31 slaves in 1810. Aside from his involvement in the tobacco trade, Skinner and his brother, Joshua, owned a mill and bake house at the mouth of the Perquimans River. In 1789 they sought to retain John Gray Blount as an agent for their bread and flour in the town of Washington. John Skinner also owned a fishery in Chowan.

Skinner and his first wife, Mary Creecy, were married in 1780 and had a son, Lemuel. Skinner married Sarah Harvey, daughter of Thomas and Mary Harvey, in 1786; they had two sons, Thomas and John, both of whom died in infancy. Sarah Skinner died in August 1789, and ten months later Skinner married Anna Harvey, daughter of John and Sarah Harvey. They had eight children: William, Harriet, Joseph, John, Sarah, Henry, Alexander, and Mary. Anna was remarried in 1820 to Thomas Billings.

John Skinner's religious affiliation and burial place are unknown. However, his father, who had been a Quaker, and his mother Sarah, who had been a Methodist, are both said to have become Baptists after marriage and to have been buried in a Baptist cemetery in Perquimans. John Skinner, described by the *Edenton Gazette* as "an opulent and very respectable inhabitant of this county," died at Montpelier after "a long indisposition." According to the terms of his will, his wife Anna received the house with provision that it pass to their son, John. Sons Joseph and Henry received other tracts, and the slaves were equally divided among all the heirs.

SEE: John L. Cheney, Jr., ed., *North Carolina Government, 1585–1979* (1981); Chowan County Wills and Old Albemarle County (Perquimans District) Births, Marriages, and Flesh Marks (North Carolina State Archives, Raleigh); Walter Clark, ed., *State Records of North Carolina*, vols. 17–22 (1898–1907); *Edenton Gazette*, 4 Jan. 1820; *State Gazette of North Carolina*, various issues; Dru Haley and Raymond A. Winslow, Jr., *Historical Architecture of Perquimans County* (1982); Alice B. Keith, ed., *John Gray Blount Papers*, vol. 1 (1952); Price-Strother map (1808); Cynthia W. Rummel and Doris S. Wahl, comps., *The Skinner Kinsmen* (1958); Ellen G. Winslow, *History of Perquimans County* (1937).

MICHAEL HILL

Skinner, Joseph Blount *(18 Jan. 1781–22 Dec. 1851)*, lawyer, legislator, planter, and pioneer in the fishing industry, was born at Harveys Neck, Perquimans County, the eldest of thirteen children of Joshua and Martha Ann Blount Skinner. His father, of Quaker parentage, was a successful planter. His mother was a descendant of James Blount, the first of the name to settle in North Carolina. The Reverend Thomas H. Skinner, founder of Union Seminary in New York City, was a younger brother.

Skinner received his early instruction from tutors and local schools. In 1794 he entered Princeton University, where his performance was creditable; he stood well in his studies and in his teachers' esteem. He contracted certain debts, however, which were considered excessive by his strict and pious father, and after three years was called home to work on the family farm. Young Skinner performed his duties cheerfully and after two years was allowed by his father to begin the study of law under the tutelage of Governor Samuel Johnston. He lived at Hayes, the governor's home near Edenton, for two years, at that time the regular term of preparatory study, and in 1801 was admitted to the practice of law.

His endowments of application, independence of thought, and ability to judge men's characters stood him well in his new profession. He built up a successful and lucrative practice in Chowan and the neighboring counties. In 1804 Skinner represented Perquimans County in the House of Commons. He represented Edenton in that body in 1807, 1814, and 1815. In 1832 he was elected by the legislature to a seat on the Council of State but resigned in 1833. In 1833–34 he was a senator from Chowan. In 1814 Skinner had distinguished himself by his successful defense of the state bank. In 1835 he was a prominent member of the state convention for amending the constitution.

A recurrent chronic fever, probably malaria, forced his retirement from active practice of law in 1824. A second career, farming, engaged his energetic nature. His plantation, Beechwood, near Edenton became a model to his neighbors, and he an instructor, in scientific methods of farming. His greatest contribution to his part of the state, however, was in the fishing industry. Previously, herring and shad fishing had been confined to the shores of the rivers and creeks by individuals who set their own relatively short nets in these more protected tributaries of Albemarle Sound. Skinner envisioned the use of great nets set in the sound itself, and in the face of his neighbors' derision he experimented with nets of unprecedented length, hauled by teams of horses and mules harnessed to giant windlasses, and manned by teams of fifty or more slaves. His successful experiments are considered the beginning of the valuable herring and shad fishing industry, a chief source of prosperity to the Albemarle region. Chief Justice Frederick Nash and Governor James Iredell both gave him credit for this contribution in their obituary notices at his death.

Skinner counted among his friends some of the most eminent men of the state. Chief Justice Nash, who was his college mate at Princeton, Judge William Gaston, Governor Iredell, and Governor Samuel Johnston all enjoyed his unusual and forthright nature. Something of a character, he was the subject of many humorous anecdotes that give the picture of a complex but able man. He became an active Episcopalian and liberally supported that church's work.

On 16 Nov. 1804 he married Maria Louisa Lowther, the daughter of Tristrim and Penelope Dawson Lowther and the great-granddaughter of Governor Gabriel Johnston. They had three children, of whom two grew to maturity: Major Tristrim Lowther, a Confederate soldier who was killed at the Battle of Mechanicsville in 1862, and Penelope, who married Dr. Thomas Warren of Edenton. Two portraits of Skinner, painted in 1825 and 1837 by Thomas Sully, are owned by his descendants.

Increasing ill health and grief over the death of his wife marred his later years. He died in Edenton and was buried in St. Paul's churchyard.

SEE: John L. Cheney, Jr., ed., *North Carolina Government, 1585–1974* (1975); Chowan County Marriage Bonds (North Carolina State Archives, Raleigh); Richard Benbury Creecy, *Grandfather's Tales of North Carolina History* (1901); Thomas C. Parramore, *Cradle of the Colony* (1967); Thomas H. Skinner, *A Sketch of the Life and Character of the Late Joseph Blount Skinner* (1853); Skinner Family Papers (Southern Historical Collection, University of North Carolina); John H. Wheeler, ed., *Reminiscences and Memoirs of North Carolina and Eminent North Carolinians* (1884).

JAQUELIN DRANE NASH

Skinner, Thomas Gregory *(23 Jan. 1842–21 Dec. 1907)*, congressman and lawyer, was born in Perquimans County near Hertford, the son of James Costen and Elmira Ward Skinner. His father was a planter and served in the General Assembly. Skinner was educated at Belvidere Academy, Kellog School in Sunbury, and Horner Military School in Oxford. He entered The University of North Carolina in 1858 but withdrew in May 1861 to enlist in the Orange Light Infantry, a part of D. H. Hill's First Regiment of North Carolina Volunteers. He served in a number of units and attained the rank of sergeant.

After the war Skinner returned to Hertford and in 1868 obtained a license to practice law. Following the death of Walter F. Pool, he was elected on 20 Nov. 1883 to represent the First District in the Forty-eighth Congress. Reelected twice, he also served in the Forty-ninth (1885–87) and Fifty-first (1887–91) congresses. In 1899 he represented his state district in the North Carolina Senate.

Skinner held extensive land in the northeastern section of the state including that on which was located the Newbold-White House, perhaps the oldest surviving house in North Carolina. He was married three times: to Penelope Tucker in 1872, to Martha Tucker in 1880, and to Jessie Pailin in 1884. His children were Nellie, Fannie, James Costen, Thomas Gregory, Jr., and William Pailin. He was the half brother of Harry Skinner, another congressman from the First District. A Democrat, a Mason, and a member of the Episcopal church, he was buried in Holy Trinity churchyard, Hertford.

SEE: *Biog. Dir. Am. Cong.* (1971); Jerome Dowd, *Sketches of Prominent Living North Carolinians* (1888); Daniel L. Grant, *Alumni History of the University of North Carolina* (1924); *Year Book, Pasquotank Historical Society*, vol. 1 (1954–55).

DOUGLAS M. RENEGAR

Skinner, Thomas Harvey *(7 Mar. 1791–1 Feb. 1871)*, Presbyterian clergyman and founder of Union Theological Seminary, was born at Harveys Neck, Perquimans County, the seventh of thirteen children. His father, Joshua, was a Quaker, while his mother, Martha Ann Blount Skinner, from a prominent Chowan County family, was an Episcopalian. After their marriage they became Baptists.

Skinner's education was begun under tutors on his father's plantation, with his brothers and sisters. He later attended Edenton Academy and entered the junior class at the College of New Jersey in 1807. After he was graduated second in his class, he went to live with the family of an older brother, Joseph Blount Skinner, to study law under his brother's direction.

Due to the coincidence of the arrival of a gifted itinerant missionary just after the death by drowning of Skinner's beloved younger brother, the young man underwent a strong spiritual transformation. He returned to college, joined the Presbyterian church, and began his studies in theology. He also studied under Henry Kollock in Savannah, Ga., and John McDowell in Elizabethtown, N.J.

Licensed to preach by the presbytery at Morristown on 16 Dec. 1812, he soon was invited to be copastor of a church in Philadelphia. Less than three years later, however, the presbytery dismissed him from this first charge because of a youthful zeal that overstepped the bounds of prudence. (He later described his preaching as "Positive, unpliable, authoritative, heedless of its bearing on my position.")

In December 1816 he was called to another Philadelphia church, a seemingly backward step in his career, but some seventy parishioners from his first charge chose to follow him there. Due to his and their combined efforts, a new church was built. In 1823 Williams College awarded him the doctor of divinity degree. Skinner soon became known as an outstanding preacher. In 1828 he was called to a church in Boston. Finding the climate too rigorous for his increasingly poor health, he returned to his former charge in Philadelphia. In 1832 he was appointed to the chair of sacred theology at the Theological Seminary at Andover.

The year 1835 was an important one in Skinner's life: he became pastor of the Mercer Street church in New York—a new church where he remained for thirteen years. It was also in 1835 that he met with a group of interested persons to discuss the founding of a seminary in New York. He was named to the board of directors of the proposed institution and held that seat for the rest of his life.

In 1842 he was appointed to the chair of sacred rhetoric at the new Union Theological Seminary, the first to hold that post. His $2,000 salary was subscribed by three loyal members of his congregation. In 1848 he resigned as pastor of the Mercer Street church to become the seminary's Davenport Professor of Sacred Rhetoric, Pastoral Theology, and Church Government, a position in which he remained active until his death. Through his and his former parishioners' influence, the new seminary flourished. In 1848 Skinner was also one of the cofounders of the Evangelical Alliance.

His career spanned a period of unrest in the Presbyterian church, and he belonged to a group that became known as the New School. He was considered to be an eloquent preacher, a dedicated and able teacher, and one of the foremost sacred orators of his day. A contemporary called him "that Chesterfield of a teacher, old Dr. Skinner, so sweet in his exterior and a St. John at his soul."

He was twice married. His first wife, Emily Montgomery, bore him four children: Maria, Thomas Harvey, Jr., Caroline, and Martha Ann. By his second marriage to Frances Davenport, he was the father of Helen, James D., Frances, and Mary D. His son Thomas became professor of polemic and didactic theology at McCormick Theological Seminary, Chicago, in 1881; by his gifts and zeal he enlarged the seminary plant and built the Church of the Covenant.

Four portraits of Skinner are known to have been painted: an oil by S. F. B. Morse in the Museum of Fine Arts, Boston; another oil attributed to Morse at the Presbyterian Historical Society, Philadelphia; a miniature by Daniel Dickinson, owned by a descendant; and an oil painted by Thomas Sully, present location unknown.

Following his death at age eighty, Skinner's funeral was held at the Church of the Covenant, his own students acting as pallbearers. He was buried in the Marble Cemetery, Second Street, New York.

Skinner was the author of *Aids to Preaching and Hearing* (1839); *Religion of the Bible* (1839); *Hints to Christians* (1841); *Religious Liberty: A Discourse* (1841); and *Discussions in Theology* (1868). In addition, he translated and edited a number of works, published religious tracts and occasional sermons, and contributed to the leading church periodicals of his day.

SEE: *DAB*, vol. 9 (1936); *Nat. Cyc. Am. Biog.*, vol. 7 (1897); George L. Prentiss, *A Discourse in Memory of Thomas Harvey Skinner* (1871) and *Union Theological Seminary in the City of New York . . . Its First Fifty Years* (1889).

JAQUELIN DRANE NASH

Skinner, William *(25 Dec. 1728–29–26 Jan. 1798)*, colonial official and planter, was born at Berkeley in Perquimans County, the son of Richard (ca. 1690–1752) and Sarah Creecy Skinner, who were married about 1714. William Skinner represented Perquimans in the Assembly in 1761 and 1762, the Provincial Congress in 1775 and 1776, the North Carolina Senate in 1777 and 1785, and the constitutional convention of 1788. He served as judge of the Admiralty Court from an unknown date until his resignation on 24 Sept. 1789. From 1777 to 1779 he was treasurer for the Northern District and from 1779 to 1784 for the Edenton District. He also served as a commissioner to settle the accounts of North Carolina with the general government and as commissioner of loans for the United States in North Carolina.

After serving as lieutenant colonel of the North Carolina militia for Perquimans, he was elected brigadier general of the North Carolina militia for the District of Edenton on 20 Dec. 1777. On 10 May 1779, before the General Assembly in session at Smithfield in Johnston County, he resigned his commission with this statement: "As my experience in military matters is very small, my continuing in that office might, perhaps, be a public injury, as well as fatal to those whose lives might in a manner depend on my conduct. For these reasons I take the liberty at this time of resigning that appointment which I heretofore with reluctance accepted."

Skinner also served as commissioner or "Director" of the town of Hertford (tradition says that he helped lay out the town), as clerk of court (was serving in 1754), and as sheriff of Perquimans County (was serving in 1759).

He was married first, on 28 May 1752, to Mrs. Sarah Gale Corprew (2 Aug. 1729–29 Mar. 1795), widow of Thomas Corprew. She was the daughter of Miles Gale and the granddaughter of Christopher Gale and Mrs. Sarah Laker Harvey, widow of Governor Thomas Harvey. To this union were born four children: William Gale (died young), Penelope (m. first Joseph Creecy and second Lemuel Creecy), Elizabeth (m. Josiah Cotton), and Lavinia (m. John Harvey). Skinner's second wife was Mrs. Dorothy Black McDonald, widow of William McDonald and daughter of Samuel and Frances Glass Black, widow of James Glass. They had two children: William (b. ca. 1796) and Caroline (b. ca. 1797). After his death, Dorothy Skinner married John Mushrow Roberts.

Skinner owned several farms and in the 1790 census listed forty-seven slaves in his possession. Prior to his second marriage at age sixty-seven, the principal part of his estate was conveyed by deed to his daughters. He was buried in the Yeopim section of Perquimans County on a farm four or five miles from the town of Hertford where a marble slab marks his grave.

SEE: Samuel A. Ashe, ed., *Biographical History of North Carolina*, vol. 5 (1906); John L. Cheney, Jr., ed., *North Carolina Government, 1585–1974* (1975); William W. Hinshaw, ed., *Encyclopedia of American Quaker Genealogy*, vol. 1 (1969); Edgar Perry Maupin, *The Skinner Family of North Carolina* (no date, mimeographed copy in State Library, Raleigh); Perquimans County records (North Carolina State Archives, Raleigh).

SUE DOSSETT SKINNER

Slade, Abisha *(15 Sept. 1799–1870?)*, tobacco farmer and local politician, was born in Caswell County, the son of Ezekiel, a planter of northern Caswell County, and Mary Hubbard Slade. Reared in a comfortably situated family of large landholdings, he wrote well and stood high in his county, serving as clerk of the court for Caswell from 1840 to 1852. He also carried on extensive farming operations and owned considerable property in Yanceyville, the seat of Caswell County.

Slade's claim to fame lay in the development of a sure formula for the production of flue-cured tobacco—the basic step in the production of a type of leaf that began the great revolution in the tobacco industry and laid the foundation for such fortunes as those of Richard J. Reynolds, Julian S. Carr, the Dukes, and others.

By 1839 it had long been known that a sandy loam soil occasionally produced a bright yellow leaf of tobacco. In that year, largely by accident, Slade began efforts to make production of such leaf a certainty. On a rainy night in 1839 his slave Stephen fell asleep while he was supposed to be watching a barn of curing leaf tobacco. Waking suddenly and finding that the small open fires in the barn had almost died down, Stephen seized charred butts of logs from the adjacent blacksmith shop and placed them on the dying fires. This sudden application of drying heat drove the moisture from the curing leaves and a beautiful unsplotched yellow leaf resulted. Abisha Slade, not understanding the exact cause of this amazing curing, began experimentation that by 1856 resulted in a sure formula for producing cured yellow leaf. In Lynchburg, Va., he sold his crop of that year for an unusually large sum, which attracted newspaper comment in and far beyond the Old Bright Tobacco Belt. Though Slade's curings were made with charcoal, it was not long before wood-curing flues were evolved for the application of a drying heat at the critical juncture of curing. Thus tobacco grown in sandy loam and cured by Slade's formula, first called bright leaf, eventually became known as flue-cured tobacco—the major type produced in the United States.

Slade was known far and wide among tobacco growers of the Virginia-Carolina area. He was an enthusiastic man who actually traversed the tobacco belt to explain the details of his curing formula. Cramming his overcoat pockets with samples of his bright leaf for use in teaching farmers to produce the same type, Slade traveled over much of the area of North Carolina and Virginia known now as the Old Bright Belt. Major Robert Lipscomb Ragland of Halifax County, Va., who followed Slade as the expert grower of bright leaf, saw the "first sample of fine gold leaf" in the hands of Captain Abisha Slade at an agricultural meeting at Cluster Springs, Va., on 6 Sept. 1856. Slade had gone there "by solicitation and appointment" to teach the farmers "the new process of curing yellow tobacco."

Ruined by the Civil War, Slade naturally lost his slaves and later all of his property. Though he was the progenitor of several tobacco fortunes, he died in poverty. He was married three times: on 25 Jan. 1826 to Mary K. Harrison, on 23 Apr. 1846 to Mary Graves, and later to Sarah Taylor. He had at least three children, one named Mary Jane by his first wife and another, Pauline Williams, by his third wife. Slade was buried in a cemetery on Rattlesnake Creek near Blanch, in northern Caswell County. His grave is unmarked and for many years his name was badly garbled in the various accounts of his accomplishments.

SEE: Bible of Ezekiel Slade (possession of Mrs. Florine Slade Daily in 1937); *Branson's North Carolina Business Directory, 1867–68, 1869*; Caswell County records (North Carolina State Archives, Raleigh); Mrs. Florine Slade Daily (Blanch, N.C.), personal contact, 2 June 1937; Danville *Pittsylvania Tribune*, 26 Mar. 1886; Lynchburg *Daily Virginian*, 12 Feb. 1857; *Milton Chronicle*, 12 Feb. 1857; Raleigh *Arator*, March 1857; Richmond *Southern Planter and Farmer*, May 1876; Anderson Slade (son of slave Stephen, Blanch, N.C.), personal contact, 2 June 1937; Pauline Williams Slade (daughter of Abisha Slade, Danville, Va.), personal contact, 26 June 1937; Winston *Progressive Farmer*, 14 Apr. 1886; Winston-Salem *Southern Tobacco Journal*, 15 June 1920, 25 Sept. 1930.

NANNIE M. TILLEY

Slade, Alfred M. *(1799–25 Nov. 1840)*, legislator and diplomat, was the son of Jeremiah and Janet Bog Slade. Jeremiah Slade was a commissioner of Indian Affairs with the War Department in 1803 to deal with Indians in Bertie County. He also served over a dozen terms in the General Assembly and was a trustee of The University of North Carolina (1808–24). Alfred Slade grew up in Martin County and attended The University of North Carolina for a portion of one term in 1815–16. He was expelled for six months after he and some other students caused a disruption in Stewards Hall in support of a student who had disregarded President Robert Chapman's censorship of the student's speech. Slade did not return despite the fact that his father was a trustee, an avid supporter of the university, and a friend of its founder, William R. Davie.

Like his father, the younger Slade represented Martin County in the House of Commons (1822, 1834, and 1835) and held other local offices. He also was an active member of the Masonic order.

In 1838 Slade was appointed American consul to Buenos Aires. After a 63-day passage out of New York, he and his family arrived at Montevideo, where they learned that the French fleet had imposed a blockade of Buenos Aires. Proceeding by a different route, Slade arrived in Buenos Aires only to find the French blockade still in effect. In the absence of a chargé d'affaires, he assumed the duties of that office and immediately he set about aiding stranded American citizens and seamen, some of whom were in prison and in danger of being sold to anyone who paid their prison fee. Such financial assistance as Slade rendered came from his own personal resources. He died at age forty-one while still in Buenos Aires. An attempt two years later by his widow to be reimbursed for his expenditures was not successful. The Committee on Foreign Affairs of the U.S. House of Representatives refused to consider Slade's efforts on behalf of American citizens as sanctioned by the U.S. government.

Slade was accompanied to Buenos Aires by his wife, Elizabeth (Eliza) A. Sutton Slade, and their daughter, whose name is unknown.

SEE: Kemp P. Battle, *History of the University of North Carolina*, vol. 1 (1907); John L. Cheney, Jr., ed., *North Carolina Government, 1585–1979* (1981); Faculty minutes, 1816 (University Archives, University of North Carolina, Chapel Hill); Daniel L. Grant, *Alumni History of the University of North Carolina* (1924); *House Report 958*, 27th Cong., 2d sess. (1842); Shelby Jean Nelson Hughes, *Martin County Heritage* (1980); Francis M. Manning and W. H. Booker, *Martin County History*, vol. 1 (1977).

TIMOTHY L. HOWERTON

Slane, Willis Howard, Jr. *(21 Apr. 1921–8 Sept. 1965)*, aviator and businessman, was born in High Point, the eldest son of Willis Howard and Meredith Clark Slane. His primary education included studies at Raymond Riredon School in Highland, N.Y., and McCallie School for Boys in Chattanooga, Tenn.

In his youth Slane was profoundly influenced by meeting Colonel Charles Lindbergh, who gave a speech in Winston-Salem, and became intensely interested in flying. He attended Riverside Military Academy in Gainesville, Ga., and Parks Air College (now part of St. Louis University) in East St. Louis, Ill., and received a private pilot's license after training in 1940. This experience saw practical use during World War II; at twenty-one, Slane was the Army Air Corps's youngest civilian instructor. In February 1943 he entered the Air Corps as a second lieutenant, flying in the Foreign and Domestic Ferry Service and Military Air Transport Service. Later he flew the Burma Hump while carrying cargo to China. He left the service at the end of the war with the rank of first lieutenant.

After entering the family business, Slane Hosiery Mills, in 1945, Slane became president in 1954. In 1956 he was elected chairman of the National Association of Hosiery Manufacturers. Though he presided over the Guilford County Pilots Association and the Hatteras Marlin Club, his main concern remained in hosiery manufacture until an encounter with a small fiberglass runabout sparked his interest in a project to construct a large fiberglass cruiser, then thought impossible. Collecting local investors, Slane incorporated Hatteras Yacht in 1959 and was elected chairman. High Point was selected for building because of the availability of skilled furniture craftsmen, in spite of its distance from the ocean. The first yacht, at forty-one feet by far the largest fiberglass-hull boat ever attempted, was launched on 22 Mar. 1960. A photograph illustrating the fact that one of the early yachts survived 1961's Hurricane Carla in Galveston, Tex., established graphically the sound judgment of constructing in fiberglass, which revolutionized the industry.

Slane continued to introduce even larger craft as advances in technique permitted but died suddenly of a heart attack. Survivors included his wife, Doris Stroupe Slane, and three sons, Willis Howard III, Thomas Vance, and Robert Clark. He was buried in the Slane vault of the mausoleum at Guilford Memorial Park between Greensboro and High Point.

SEE: *Hatteras World*, Summer 1980; *High Point Enterprise*, 11 Mar. 1962; *Miami Herald*, 3 Mar. 1940; *Motor Boating*, June 1962; Slane family papers (possession of Mrs. Willis H. Slane, Sr., High Point).

STACY N. KIRKMAN

Sledd, Benjamin Franklin *(24 Aug. 1864–4 Jan. 1940)*, educator and poet, was born in Bedford County, Va., the son of William Edgar and Arabella Hobson Sledd. Members of both the Hobson and Sledd families had fought in all the wars of the nation beginning with the American Revolution. Sledd was later characterized as a "Virginia Gentleman" of the highest class. He never forgot his plantation upbringing, and his early formative years were frequently the sources for his later poems and verses. At the old field schools, he studied Holmes's readers and Sanford's arithmetics. Sledd learned at an early age to appreciate literature in any form. He was delighted when his teacher and pastor drove up in a gig from Lynchburg, Va., with new books that he had not read. All of Sledd's family were "High Church Episcopalians," but as a youth he began to attend the Hunting Creek Baptist Church near his home and was baptized into its membership by William E. Hatcher.

After Sledd had absorbed all that the old field schools and the neighborhood instructors had to offer, he "gave up the struggle with sassafras bushes, and crabgrass, worn-out soils and hopeless Negro labor, sold a big slice of my world of useless land for the princely sum of three hundred dollars; and one fine September morning [in 1881] with books and clothing packed in a pair of saddlebags, rode away on old Frank (nomen carum et venerabile) across the counties to Washington and Lee University" in Lexington, Va. An excellent student, especially in Latin and Greek, French and German, history, and English, he was graduated with an M.A. degree in June 1886. One of his professors influenced him to enter Johns Hopkins University in the fall of 1886 as a graduate student of the Teutonic languages. Sledd in his zeal overtaxed his eyes and for two months had to stay in a dark room and use his sight sparingly. He did not complete his work for a Ph.D. For a short time he was master of Charlotte Hall, a school in southern Maryland. It was during his fear of possible blindness and the aftermath beside the wintry storm-tossed Chesapeake that he began to seriously compose his poems and verse.

In August 1888 the board of trustees of Wake Forest College elected Sledd to the chair of modern languages. At this time he was barely twenty-four. From September 1888 to June 1894 the young professor taught classes in French and German and sometimes elementary Italian. He developed the course to consist of two years of work in each language, five recitations a week for the first year and three the second year. As a teacher he inspired many future newspaper reporters, journalists, poets, and educators in the language field. His students called him "Old Slick."

Sledd was in his fifth year as professor of modern languages when, on the sudden death of William Royall, he was transferred to the English department. He was formally elected professor of English and department head in June 1894. Sledd extended the English program from two to three years and required all students to begin with the first year, which stressed composition and included the foremost works of English novelists, essayists, poets, and historians. Many years later, his course load was lightened by additional faculty members, and he concentrated on his course in Anglo-Saxon and other special courses in English and American literature. After fifty years in the classroom, he retired in 1938 as professor emeritus.

Despite a demanding teaching schedule, Sledd found time to write poetry. The first volume, *From Cliff and Scaur*, was published in 1897. Five years later *The Watchers on the Hearth* appeared and in 1908, *Margaret and Miriam*. He edited *La Princess de Clives* (1896) and *Milton's Minor Poems* (1908) and published numerous poems in the nation's leading magazines and newspapers. In addition, Sledd conducted critical studies of the poetry of others and published reviews in periodicals in the United States and England. The *Wake Forest Student* contains many poems, verses, sketches, essays, and writings of Sledd and his students. A posthumous volume of his unpublished writings was edited and published as *A Young Man's Vision, an Old Man's Dream* (1957).

In an autobiographical letter in 1929, Sledd wrote: "My work in literature has not set the world on fire, although I am proud of it in a modest way." Regarding his first two volumes of poetry, he wrote that they "were kindly treated by the critics and brought me some reputation and less money."

In 1889 he married Neda Purefoy, the granddaughter of James Simpson Purefoy, one of the founders of Wake Forest College. They had five daughters, Erma, Miriam, Margaret, Gladys, Elva Douglas, and one son, Arthur Purefoy.

Sledd died of a heart attack in his home at Wake Forest. Funeral services were held on 5 Jan. 1940 at the Wake Forest Baptist Church by the Reverends John Allen Easley and Willis Richard Cullom. He was buried in the cemetery at Wake Forest.

SEE: Buies Creek *Creek Pebbles*, 4 Apr. 1936 [portrait]; Oral History Office Records (Wake Forest Archives, Wake Forest University, Winston-Salem); George W. Paschal, "Dr. Benjamin Sledd," *Wake Forest Student*, pt. 1 (February 1940 [portrait]) and pt. 2 (March 1940); Raleigh

News and Observer, 5 Jan. 1940; Benjamin Franklin Sledd Papers (Baptist Historical Collection, Wake Forest University, Winston-Salem); *Wake Forest Alumni Directory* (1961).

JOHN R. WOODARD

Slingsby, John *(d. 29? Aug. 1781)*, Loyalist officer, was a native of England and at his death was reported to have been heir to "the Beverly Farm . . . a fine estate some twelve miles from London." Many members of the Slingsby family lived in Yorkshire, however. One Henry Slingsby held 12,500 acres in the area of present Stanly County, N.C., as one of the Huey/Crymble Associates' 1.2 million–acre speculation surveyed in 1744. Scottish port records indicate that John Slingsby, master of *The Caesar*, bound for Brunswick, sailed from Glasgow during the midsummer term 1770. With stores in Wilmington and Cross Creek, the firm of John Slingsby and Company engaged in extensive trade.

When steps were taken to halt trade between England and the colonies, Slingsby demonstrated an extreme willingness to cooperate. Large shipments of goods for his stores in Wilmington and in Cross Creek arrived at Wilmington on 10 Dec. 1774. The former was valued in excess of £1,923 and the latter at £1,018. He promptly turned this stock over to the Committee of Safety for sale to the highest bidder. Slingsby himself thereupon entered bids that were slightly higher than the appraised values. He also reported that a shipment of gunpowder had not been put aboard in Glasgow, the port of origin.

In February 1775 additional goods belonging to Slingsby were sold and on 7 March he was paid for fifty pounds of gunpowder. Still he seems to have been ambivalent about supporting the Revolutionary cause. On that same day, 7 March, he was one of eight merchants, a planter, and two tailors who declined to sign the Continental Association. Nevertheless, on 13 March he had a change of heart and signed. On 25 Oct. 1775 the Safety Committee of Wilmington appointed him one of seven members of the Committee of Secrecy and Correspondence. On 20 November he was one of several men named to see to the protection of the channel of the Cape Fear River, and as a member of the Wilmington Safety Committee he attended eleven meetings between 25 Oct. 1775 and 5 Feb. 1776. On 18 April, however, he and nine other prominent men of the region were "permitted" to withdraw from the Provincial Congress.

Apparently there is nothing to suggest what role Slingsby played in the Revolutionary War until the British under Major James H. Craig occupied Wilmington on 1 Feb. 1781. He was then appointed a colonel in the Kings Militia—a term they preferred to Tories—and placed in command of the Loyalists in Bladen and Brunswick counties. On 14 August he and two other officers led a raid on Cross Creek. About a week later, with some three hundred men, he appeared unexpectedly in Elizabethtown. He had with him a number of "paroled rebels" but was told by Loyalist leader Edmund Fanning that it was "imprudent and unsafe" to hold them. Under cover of darkness early the next morning the rebels, who had concealed some arms, fired on the Loyalist camp, mortally wounded Slingsby, and fled into the woods. The Loyalists lost eighteen killed, wounded, or captured, and the local militia seized a large quantity of supplies and ammunition.

Slingsby married Arabellah McNeill McAllister, the daughter of Donald Taynish McNeill, and they had a son and two daughters, only one of whom, Annie Jean, survived her parents. Peter Duboise, a New York Loyalist who also was in North Carolina for a time, was Slingsby's brother-in-law. Annie Jean Slingsby married the Reverend William Bingham, founder of the noted Bingham School in Alamance County.

Slingsby's death was deeply mourned by both sides in the struggle. He was cited for his kindness, his good character, and especially for the severe penalties he imposed on troops under his jurisdiction for warring on unarmed men, women, and children. He was praised for his devotion to the cause in which he believed, and his widow and children were afterwards treated with great respect.

SEE: Lindley S. Butler, ed., *The Narrative of Col. David Fanning* (1981); Robert O. DeMond, *The Loyalists in North Carolina during the Revolution* (1940); Griffith J. McRee, *Life and Correspondence of James Iredell*, vol. 1 (1857); William S. Powell, ed., *The Correspondence of William Tryon and Other Selected Papers*, vol. 1 (1980); Lorenzo Sabine, *Biographical Sketches of Loyalists in the American Revolution*, vol. 2 (1864); John H. Wheeler, *Historical Sketches of North Carolina* (1851).

WILLIAM S. POWELL

Sloan, Samuel *(7 Mar. 1815–19 July 1884)*, architect and publisher, was born in Honeybrook Township, Chester County, Pa., the son of William and Mary Kirkwood Sloan. After completing apprenticeship as a carpenter in nearby Lancaster County in 1833, he worked as a builder in Philadelphia until 1849. By 1850 he was listing himself as architect, and within a decade he achieved a national reputation as a designer of both public and private institutional buildings. These included a variety of schools, churches, halls for fraternal orders, and courthouses, mainly in the Philadelphia area but frequently in the South.

His wider fame came as a collaborator of Dr. Thomas S. Kirkbride, an expert in the treatment of the mentally ill. Together they pioneered the Kirkbride System, which became the American standard for design and organization of hospitals for the insane. These buildings embodied innovative features such as fire-resistant construction, hardware and plumbing arrangements taking into account the condition of the inmates, and floor plans expressing Kirkbride's belief that the hospital staff should be dispersed among the patients.

Also in the 1850s Sloan designed at least twenty commercial structures, all in Philadelphia, and dozens of residences—many of them terrace houses and villas in the newly developed suburbs in the city's western and northern reaches. In North Carolina in 1859, he designed Baptist and Presbyterian churches built in Wilmington; the former was still standing in 1993. More important for the development of American domestic architecture was Sloan's promotion of himself and his ideas in pattern books aimed at the general public: *The Model Architect* (1851), *The Carpenter's New Guide* (16th ed., 1854), *City and Suburban Architecture* (1859), *Sloan's Constructive Architecture* (1859), *Sloan's Homestead Architecture* (1861), and *American Houses: A Variety of Designs for Rural Buildings* (1861). Also, from 1852 to about 1859 Sloan supplied many house plans in *Godey's Lady's Book.*

Although it is impossible to estimate the number and geographic location of houses inspired by these books, their impact was considerable. In them the architect discussed site selection, architectural styles, the "embellishment of grounds," furniture, and costs. The types ranged from "workingmen's model cottages" (at $300) to an "Oriental Villa" ($40,000)—the latter the famed uncompleted house for North Carolinian Haller Nutt in Natchez, Miss. (1855–62). If the ornament and styles—Gothic, Italianate, "Mansardic"—were much like those of his mid-Victorian contemporaries, Sloan's plans were often pragmatic and highly functional. But his *Architectural Review and American Builders' Journal* (1868–70), the first American periodical of its kind, was for professionals, who gave it little financial support.

During his final years Sloan spent much time in North Carolina, where he had a number of important commissions: in Wilmington, the Bank of New Hanover (1873); in Morganton, the Western State Asylum for the Insane (1875–84); and in Raleigh, the State Exposition Building (1883), the Governor's Mansion (1883–84), and additions to the State Hospital for the Insane. He designed a new jail (1882) and courthouse (1883) for Craven County. In 1883 he apparently was busy in Raleigh with additions to St. Mary's College and Peace Institute and with some rebuilding at St. Augustine's College. In the same year he also designed the second New Bern Academy. In Chapel Hill for The University of North Carolina he designed an auditorium that came to be called Memorial Hall, and with the support of alumni a commons hall and ballroom just off the campus (where dances could be held without offending certain segments of society).

Sloan's wife was Mary Pennell, of Philadelphia. They had one son, Ellwood Pennell, and perhaps a daughter who was with Sloan when he died in Raleigh from heat prostration following excessive exposure to the summer sun. After his temporary interment in Raleigh, it is believed that he was buried in Philadelphia.

SEE: *American Architect and Building News* 16 (2 Aug. 1884); Harold N. Cooledge, *Samuel Sloan: Architect of Philadelphia* (1986); Addison Hutton Papers (Athenaeum of Philadelphia).

HARRY SCHALCK

Slocum (or Slockum, Slocombe, Slokum), Anthony *(ca. 1592–ca. 1689)*, Council member, Assembly member, judge, and leader in Culpeper's Rebellion, was born in England, probably in Somersetshire, where members of the Slocum family were numerous in the sixteenth and seventeenth centuries. A deposition that he made about 1682 indicates that he was born about 1592.

Slocum came to America before 1637, arriving in New England, where he remained for thirty years or more. He is thought to have lived at Plymouth for a time and probably to have gone from there to Dorchester. In 1637 he was one of a group of forty-six colonists who purchased a tract of land that two years later was incorporated as the town of Taunton in what is now Massachusetts. He moved to Taunton soon after the purchase.

Slocum is thought to have married before leaving England. His wife appears to have been the sister of another "first purchaser" of Taunton, William Harvey. Two other relatives, Giles and Edward Slocum, arrived in New England about the same time as Anthony. Genealogists have disagreed as to whether they were Anthony's sons, his brothers, or more distant relatives. Edward, like Anthony, settled at Taunton, but Giles made his home in an area that became Portsmouth, R.I.

Slocum lived in Taunton about twenty-five years. He held no high office there but performed such civic duties as jury service and overseeing road maintenance. In 1652 he subscribed to stock in a company formed to establish a local ironworks. The foundry was established and operated several years by the company, which later leased it. In a list of Taunton residents dated 28 Dec. 1659, Slocum is recorded as holding fifty-three acres of land and heading a household of six.

Genealogists have speculated as to the identity of the members of the 1659 household. Some have considered Edward Slocum a member, believing him to have been Anthony's son, but Edward appears to have died or left Taunton about 1647. Slocum's daughter, Winifred(?), her husband, John (?) Gilbert, and one or two Gilbert children also have been counted as members of the household, but that supposition probably is erroneous also. John Gilbert, of Taunton, who probably was the husband of Slocum's daughter, died about 1657, leaving four sons. Although the daughter and her sons could have been living with her parents in 1659, the household would have numbered more than the reported six if that were so. Slocum had only one son who is so identified in Taunton records. That son, John, became lost in some woods and died in 1652, when he was nine years old. Slocum, however, had other sons, who appear not to have come to the attention of family historians. At least two sons accompanied him to North Carolina and are mentioned in records of that colony—John, namesake of the child lost in the woods, and Joseph. North Carolina records also mention a Josyas Slocum, who probably was Anthony's son, although he is not so identified in surviving records. It is likely, therefore, that the Slocum household in 1659 included John, Joseph, Josyas, and a fourth child whose name is not known, or perhaps a servant.

The last date on which Slocum is mentioned as a resident of Taunton is 3 June 1662. Soon afterwards he sold his interest in the town and moved to the area that in 1664 was incorporated as the town of Dartmouth. He was accompanied in that move by one Ralph Russell, who previously had been employed in the operation of the Taunton ironworks.

All of Slocum's children and grandchildren appear to have moved to Dartmouth with him. In an undated fragment of a letter that he wrote in Dartmouth to his brother-in-law William Harvey, who had remained in Taunton, Slocum sent greetings from "myself wife and sons and daughter Gilbert who hath four sons." He also wrote, "My sons are all married." The Slocum and Russell families are said to have been the first settlers of Dartmouth, but nothing is known of their stay there, for early records of the town have not survived.

It is known, however, that Slocum remained in Dartmouth less than a decade, for he moved to the North Carolina colony, then called Albemarle, before September 1670. Although he was nearly eighty upon his arrival, he achieved prominence in Albemarle and apparently was more active in public affairs than at any other time of his life.

Slocum arrived in Albemarle in a period marked by bitter factional rivalry, which culminated in late 1677 in the uprising called Culpeper's Rebellion. Despite his being a newcomer, Slocum affiliated with a faction supported chiefly by the early settlers, who previously had controlled the government, or largely so, but whose dominance was then being challenged by a competing faction. Slocum's participation in the struggle appears to have begun in 1677, when one Thomas Miller, a leader of the challengers, seized power as acting governor, claiming legal authority on questionable grounds.

Slocum, who had settled in Chowan Precinct, was elected burgess from Chowan and served in an Assembly called and held by Miller in the fall of 1677. In early December, however, he was among the leaders of the uprising in which Miller and his chief supporters were seized and imprisoned. In a new election called by the "rebels" and held after Miller's imprisonment, Slocum again was elected to the Assembly. He apparently was a member of the "rebel assembly" until the Proprietors restored de jure government in the summer of 1679.

Slocum was yet more prominent in the government established in 1679, as he was a Council member serving as a Proprietor's deputy. He sat on the Council in August 1679, when the new government, headed by John Harvey as acting governor, appears to have begun operation. He remained a Council member at least through November 1684, serving under John Jenkins, acting governor after Harvey's death, and subsequently under Governor Seth Sothel.

As a Council member Slocum was ex officio justice of several courts, including the General Court and the Palatine's court. In his capacity as magistrate he conducted marriage ceremonies. Among the couples that he married were Thomas Harvey, who later became deputy governor of the colony, and Joanna Jenkins, widow of John Jenkins.

It is not known whether Thomas Harvey and John Harvey of Albemarle were related to Slocum's wife and her brother, William Harvey of Taunton, Mass. Such a connection, if it existed, would help account for Slocum's move to Albemarle and his rapid rise to prominence there. No relationship, however, is indicated by the available records except the sharing of the Harvey name.

Slocum may have remained on the Council, at least nominally, until the banishment of Governor Sothel in 1689. He probably took no part in the revolt against Sothel, for his long life was then drawing to a close. He made his will on 26 Nov. 1688, but he may have lived as long as a year afterwards, for the will was not proved until 7 Jan. 1689/90. It is possible, however, that probate was delayed by disruptions attending the banishment of Sothel.

Slocum held at least six hundred acres of land, for which he received a patent in 1684. The land was in Chowan Precinct on Mattacomack Creek and Mirey Swamp. In the same year his sons John and Joseph patented adjoining tracts of four hundred and two hundred acres respectively.

Genealogists of the Slocum family have thought that Anthony was a Quaker, basing that belief on circumstantial evidence, particularly the fact that Anthony's relative, Giles Slocum of Portsmouth, R.I., was an early Quaker convert. Anthony's name, however, does not appear in the records of North Carolina Quakers, nor does the name of any member of his family. Moreover, his participation in Culpeper's Rebellion and in the "rebel" government that resulted was inconsistent with Quaker religious beliefs and with the political position held by Albemarle Quakers.

Only two of Anthony's children, his daughter and his son John, are known to have left descendants. Although Joseph Slocum is believed to have married Ann Blount, daughter of James Blount, and to have had a daughter, Ann, it appears that Joseph, his wife, and their child died before November 1688, for none of the three is mentioned in Anthony's will. Josyas Slocum, who probably was Anthony's son, is not mentioned in surviving records after 1683. The few references to him do not mention a wife or child.

John Slocum apparently was the only son living when Anthony made his will. His wife, Elizabeth, appears to have been the sister of William Munday of Albemarle. John probably was the father of all four of the Slocum grandsons to whom Anthony made bequests—John, Samuel, Josias, and Joseph. Although Anthony wrote in Dartmouth that all his sons were then married, no other information has been found respecting marriages of the sons before they moved to Albemarle.

Slocum also made bequests to his Gilbert grandchildren—John, Thomas, Joseph, and Sarah. It is likely that Sarah was a great-granddaughter, probably the daughter of Anthony's grandson Giles Gilbert, who is not mentioned in Anthony's will and presumably had died. The Gilbert grandsons and their mother appear to have remained in Dartmouth when Anthony moved to Albemarle.

Slocum's son John died about 1696, and John's widow, Elizabeth, married Richard Smith. She and her sons, who were then minors, moved with Smith to the county of Bath. The sons remained in that section when they were grown, settling in the Pamlico and Neuse areas.

SEE: J. Bryan Grimes, ed., *Abstract of North Carolina Wills* (1910); J. R. B. Hathaway, ed., *North Carolina Historical and Genealogical Register*, vol. 1 (1900); Margaret M. Hofmann, comp., *Chowan Precinct, North Carolina . . . Abstracts of Deed Books* (1972); *New England Historical and Genealogical Register*, vols. 5, 34, 38, 70; North Carolina Land Grants, vol. 1 (Land Grant Office, Secretary of State, Raleigh); North Carolina State Archives, Raleigh: various papers, particularly Albemarle Book of Warrants and Surveys (1681–1706), Council Minutes, Wills, Inventories (1677–1701), and Wills of James Blount (9 July 1683), William Munday (3 Dec. 1688), and Anthony Slockum (26 Nov. 1688); Mattie Erma E. Parker, ed., *North Carolina Higher-Court Records, 1670–1696* and *1697–1701* (1968, 1971); Charles Henry Pope, comp., *The Pioneers of Massachusetts . . .* (1900); William L. Saunders, ed., *Colonial Records of North Carolina*, vol. 1 (1886); Charles Elihu Slocum, *A Short History of the Slocums in America* (1882).

MATTIE ERMA E. PARKER

Slocumb, Jesse *(20 Aug. 1780–20 Dec. 1820)*, congressman, was born near the site of the future town of Dudley in southern Wayne County, the son of Ezekiel and Mary (Polly) Hooks Slocumb. He received a modest education locally and began farming, but in 1804, at the time of his marriage to Hannah G. Green, daughter of Colonel Joseph Green of Wayne County, he was described as a merchant in Wilmington. For a time he was a member of the Wayne County Court of Pleas and Quarter Sessions and was register of deeds for the county from 1802 to 1808. In 1810 he completed a questionnaire on his native county in response to a letter from Thomas Henderson, editor of the Raleigh *Star*. It survives in Henderson's letter book at the North Carolina State Archives as an interesting and detailed report on the history of the county as well as on the contemporary scene. In 1810 Slocumb was an incorporator of Waynesborough Academy, and three years later he was one of the founders of the Wayne County Free School. It probably was as a farmer that he earned a livelihood for his family—his plantation was named Shelburne—and at his death he bequeathed five slaves as well as farm equipment to his wife.

A Federalist, Slocumb served in the Fourteenth and the Fifteenth Congress—from December 1815 until his death five years later. As a candidate for Congress in 1819, he made no promises but said instead that if he were elected he would do "what shall appear to me the best interest of our country." His uncle, Charles Hooks, also served in the Fifteenth Congress as well as in several later ones. It was reported that Slocumb was ill when he arrived in Washington for the second session of the Fifteenth Congress beginning on 13 Nov. 1820; he died of pleurisy just over five weeks later and was buried in the Congressional Cemetery in Washington. He was survived by his wife and four children: Julia, Harriet, John, and Junius. In addition, his ward, Nancy Sasser, lived with the family for a number of years.

SEE: *Biog. Dir. Am. Cong.* (1961); John L. Cheney, Jr., ed., *North Carolina Government, 1585–1979* (1981); Nobel E. Cunningham, Jr., ed., *Circular Letters of Congressmen to Their Constituents, 1789–1829*, vol. 3 (1978); Mary D. Johnstone, ed., *The Heritage of Wayne County, North Carolina* (1982); Raleigh *Minerva*, 19 Nov. 1804; Raleigh *Register*, 19 Nov. 1804, 29 Dec. 1820; Washington, D.C., *National Intelligencer*, 29 Dec. 1820; Wayne County Wills (North Carolina State Archives, Raleigh).

JONI ELISA WILSON

Sloop, Mary T. Martin *(9 Mar. 1873–13 Jan. 1962)*, physician, educator, and reformer, was born in Davidson, where her father, William Joseph Martin, was a professor of geology and chemistry at Davidson College. Her mother was Letitia Coddington Costin Martin. Mary Martin was graduated from Statesville Female College for Women in 1891 and continued her education as Davidson College's only coed. Determined to become a medical missionary in Africa, she fought to become the first female admitted to the North Carolina Medical College in Davidson. Because she was not allowed to study anatomy there, she transferred to the Woman's Medical College of Pennsylvania at Philadelphia and earned her degree in 1906. While serving a one-year internship in Boston, she learned that she would not be accepted for foreign service by the Presbyterian Mission Board because single white women were no longer being sent to Africa and because she was considered too old (at thirty-three) for mission work in China.

Martin became the resident physician for Agnes Scott College in Decatur, Ga. A year later, in July 1908, she married Dr. Eustace H. Sloop, a surgeon she had met over a decade earlier when he was an undergraduate at Davidson. He too was interested in mission work, and they decided that their ambitions for service of that type could be fulfilled in the mountains of North Carolina. After their wedding at her family's summer home at Blowing Rock and a horseback honeymoon through the Blue Ridge Mountains, the two doctors established a joint practice at Plumtree in Avery County. Three years later they moved to nearby Crossnore, a more accessible locale in the Linville Valley, where they spent the rest of their lives. Of their intentions, she later wrote: "We figured we were both pretty good doctors, we were both as tough as pine knots, and we could take a lot of licks. We could return them, too, in terms of healthy swings at disease and poor diet habits, poverty through lack of opportunity, illiteracy, superstition, and all the other ills" that held back "these fine mountain people."

Eustace Sloop devoted the bulk of his time to the medical needs of the mountain people, providing most with the first health care they had ever received. His efforts later led to the establishment of the Crossnore Hospital, which was for a long time the only medical facility serving a four-county area. Mary Sloop responded more to the dearth of educational opportunities in the region and undertook what became a forty-year crusade to offer adequate schooling for mountain children. She was particularly appalled at the number of child brides, who married and became mothers in their early teens, and worked vigorously to provide them with what she saw as the only preventative for such early marriages, a high school education. From contributions across the country she organized the collection and sale of great quantities of used clothing. The proceeds from that effort, along with financial assistance from the Daughters of the American Revolution, supplied the funds to establish and then to expand the Crossnore School. During the 1920s and 1930s a one-room schoolhouse in use for only four and a half months a year grew into a complex of twenty buildings and over 250 acres; it provided a nine-month, eleven-grade education by trained teachers, with special emphasis on home economics, vocational training, and Bible study. As a boarding school for orphans and other mountain children who lived too far from a good school, the Crossnore School came to be largely self-supportive through an adjoining working farm and through a weaving program for the students. Under Mary Sloop's guidance, the weaving sequence revived what had almost become a lost art among mountain craftsmen.

In addition to her efforts in getting a state law raising the compulsory age for school attendance to sixteen, Mrs. Sloop pressured the legislature and the governor to provide paved roads, modern agricultural assistance and training, and more effective law enforcement against moonshiners for Avery and adjoining counties. The Sloop's two children, Emma Sloop Fink and William L., became a doctor and a dentist, respectively, and returned to Crossnore to work with their father and to administer his hospital.

Dr. Mary Sloop achieved nationwide attention in 1951 when she was named America's Mother of the Year. In 1953 she published her popular autobiography, *Miracle in the Hills*, written in collaboration with Legette Blythe. She was ninety years old when she died in Crossnore, a year after her husband's death in February 1961.

SEE: *American Women: The Standard Biographical Dictionary of Notable Women*, vol. 3 (1939); *Asheville Citizen*, 28 Apr. 1951; Mary T. Martin Sloop with Legette Blythe, *Miracle in the Hills* (1953); Raleigh *News and Observer*, 28 Apr. 1951.

JOHN C. INSCOE

Slump, John Martin *(d. May 1803)*, schoolmaster, printer, and newspaper publisher, was of German descent but of uncertain family background. His surname may originally have been spelled Schlump or Schlumpf, but it does not appear in either form in the 1790 census returns for North Carolina, South Carolina, Virginia, or Pennsylvania. His first known residence was in Cabarrus County, N.C., where he taught a German school in 1792. In the late 1790s he worked in Salisbury at an English and German print shop owned by Michael Braun, who purchased his printing equipment for £60 from Benjamin Shue of Shenandoah County, Va., in 1794. Because an entry in the *Records of the Moravians in North Carolina* for 23 Jan. 1797 notes that a "book printery" was being operated in Salisbury, the Braun print shop evidently had opened as early as 1796. Slump, Benjamin Shue, and Francis Coupee all worked in this establishment, and the weekly *North Carolina Mercury and Salisbury Advertiser*, the first newspaper published in Piedmont North Carolina, was established there in Spring 1798.

Slump was familiar with German, English, and Latin and helped publish a number of eighteenth-century imprints. In 1797 he and Coupee printed a thirty-page collection of the words of German hymns, *Sammlung von er-*

baulichen Gesängen, zum Gebrauch bey dem öffentlichen Gottesdienste, für die Deutschen Gemeinen in Nord-Carolina. This hymnal, the first publication printed in German in North Carolina, sold for one shilling and was widely used in the German Reformed and Lutheran churches. As a German schoolmaster, Slump fully appreciated the need for a German hymnal among these people. The Salisbury print shop produced a number of German items, including some German hymns for the Moravians at Salem in March and at Christmas 1798. Francis Coupee printed a German ode for the Salem Moravians as late as 1809.

In 1797 and 1798 Slump published several sermons for Samuel Eusebius McCorkle, a noted Presbyterian minister and teacher in Rowan County, and even after Slump moved to Lincolnton, around 1800, McCorkle again made use of his services. Slump printed his own English translation of a German address on George Washington, delivered at a church in Lincolnton on 22 Feb. 1800, by Andrew Loretz, a German Reformed minister. He apparently printed this address in English because of the limited market for German publications in the Lincolnton area, but it seems likely that he published a North Carolina almanac for 1801 in German.

It has been conjectured that it was Slump who published the newspaper that François A. Michaux, a French botanist, said was being printed in Lincolnton in October 1802. Slump was then living in Camden, S.C., however, where in May 1802 he established the *Carolina Journal* or the *Camden Advertiser*, the first newspaper published in Camden. This was his most successful printing venture, and it enabled him to demonstrate his ability as a printer and publisher. A copy dated 19 Oct. 1802 (vol. 1, no. 21), the only issue known to have survived, contains a statement in Latin in which Slump promised to print all the news, mingling the amusing and useful for the entertainment and instruction of the reader. An item about a Camden wedding revealed his sense of humor, and an eagle displayed on the front page was an expression of his patriotism. He continued to publish this paper until his death, which occurred before 25 May 1803, when Catharina Theresa Slump asked to be appointed administratrix of the estate of John Martin Slump, deceased. After his death, the *Carolina Journal* was almost immediately succeeded by the *Camden Intelligencer*, which appeared on 5 June 1803, with John B. Hood as editor.

SEE: James S. Brawley (Salisbury), personal contact; Clarence S. Brigham, *History and Bibliography of American Newspapers, 1690–1820*, vol. 2 (1947); Christopher L. Dolmetsch, *The German Press of the Shenandoah Valley* (1984); Adelaide L. Fries, ed., *Records of the Moravians in North Carolina*, vol. 6 (1943); T. J. Kirkland and R. M. Kennedy, *Historic Camden*, pt. 2 (1926); Rowan and Kershaw County records (courthouses, Salisbury, N.C., and Camden, S.C.); William L. Saunders, ed., *Colonial Records of North Carolina*, vol. 8 (1890).

FRANK P. CAUBLE

Small, Edward Featherston *(26 Jan. 1844–6 June 1924)*, Confederate soldier, photographer, and salesman, was born near Washington, Beaufort County, the son of Henry H. and Margaret Hill Small. He was a cousin of Congressman John H. Small. His boyhood was spent on his father's farm three miles west of Washington near the Pamlico River. In 1853 the family moved to Trinity, Randolph County, where the father worked on the construction of a substantial brick building for Trinity College and operated a carriage to transport students from the railroad at High Point to the college. In 1859 another move took the Smalls a few miles west of Thomasville to a small farm operated with the help of slave labor. Edward, however, remained at Trinity and attended college until he enlisted in Confederate service in September 1861.

Mustered in as a corporal, he was discharged on 1 Jan. 1862 following an injury during artillery drill. He reenlisted in August and saw action in eastern North Carolina as well as at Seven Pines and the Wilderness in Virginia. He also participated in the battles of New Bern, Kinston, Fort Fisher, and Bentonville. Stationed at Fort Fisher when it fell in January 1865, he happened to be on detail to escort artillery and officers' horses a few miles north of the bastion to safety. Small then made his way to Wilmington and later to Goldsboro, where he became an aide to General Joseph E. Johnston, whom he served until honorably discharged on 5 May.

During the course of the war his mother had died, his only brother had succumbed to battle wounds, and the family farm had been devastated. Small found employment as a salesman for a Thomasville shoe manufacturer and was so successful that he was employed by a Durham snuff company. Here he sold more products than the company could supply and was placed on temporary "vacation" until the backlog of orders could be filled.

About 1868 Small began a second career as an itinerant photographer. He may have learned the art from photographer David Clark of High Point. From the late 1860s to the mid-1870s Small traveled as a commercial photographer through the eastern and Piedmont sections of the state and operated temporary studios in High Point, Greensboro, Winston, Durham, Goldsboro, Clinton, and Kenansville. As he gained experience he became a talented artist. Early in 1876 he opened in Durham what he intended to be a permanent gallery and soon was described as "the busiest man in town."

In the early 1880s Small and his family resided in Lexington, where he practiced his profession, but in March 1882 his fourteen-year career in photography virtually ended when W. Duke, Sons, and Company of Durham hired him as a tobacco salesman on commission. He first came in contact with the Dukes when he was hired to take a picture of their factory in Durham for use on their business letterhead. The firm was then an emerging giant in the field of tobacco manufacturing, and Small's initial territory consisted of the two Carolinas. There was little demand for cigarettes there, but Small soon was able to extend his region to include Georgia, Tennessee, Missouri, Ohio, Indiana, and Michigan.

His selling talent, coupled with unique advertising gimmicks, significantly increased the trade of Duke products, and he became one of the firm's most successful drummers. He captured the market in Atlanta beginning in March 1884 with the cooperation of one Madame Rhea, a popular French actress who was performing there. Small asked her permission to have a life-size lithograph of herself mounted on canvas with a package of Duke cigarettes in her hand and "Atlanta's Favorites" printed below. When the picture turned up in stores around the city as well as in advertisements in the *Atlanta Constitution*, sales of the cigarettes greatly increased.

As Small moved on to other states, the home office in Durham supplied him with additional advertising devices such as playing cards, picture cards, posters, and photographs. In St. Louis he employed a charming saleslady to sell Duke cigarettes, and he acquired a roller-skating team known as the Cross Cut Polo Club of Durham, N.C. Roller skating was very popular at the time, and Small arranged matches between his club and home squads in Ohio, Indiana, and Michigan. Contests were widely promoted as battles between the North and the South. Male spectators at the arenas were given free samples of "Cross Cut" cigarettes, while female onlookers received small photograph cards.

Small remained with the Duke firm until 1888. The maverick and sometimes insubordinate salesman was not always on the best of terms with James B. Duke. He sometimes irritated company officials by entering markets without their permission, and he made numerous visits to his family in Atlanta at company expense. Duke wanted to transfer Small to Cincinnati, but he refused to go and as a result resigned in anger. Almost immediately Small was hired by a Duke rival, but in 1890 Duke acquired that firm and Small left.

During the 1890s Small worked for different firms in Atlanta and finally managed an apple orchard of several thousand acres. This gave him an opportunity to enjoy two of his avocations—horses and astronomy. In 1907 *Collier's Weekly* magazine published his article, "True Story of the Creation of the Trust."

On 22 Dec. 1870, in Smithfield, N.C., Small married Julia Johnson Telfair, the daughter of Dr. Alexander F. and Julia Boone Telfair, whom he had met while passing through the area after the Battle of Bentonville. They became the parents of eight children: Robert Telfair, Alexander Telfair, Ida Marie, Margaret Hill, Everard Hall, Lillian Gertrude, Oscar D., and Bessie Duke.

In September 1922 Small became a resident of the Confederate Soldiers Home in Atlanta. While attending a reunion of Confederate veterans in Memphis, he died as a result of injuries sustained from a fall on the pavement; he was buried in Marietta, Ga. One photograph of him as a young man survives in the Manuscript Department of Duke University.

SEE: *Atlanta City Directory* (1891–93, 1923–24); Census of the United States and of North Carolina, 1850–80 (microfilm copies, North Carolina State Archives, Raleigh), Census of Georgia, 1900 (microfilm copy, Georgia State Archives, Atlanta); Confederate Soldiers Home Records, Register of Inmates (microfilm copy, Georgia State Archives, Atlanta); Davidson County Estates and Tax Records, Johnston County Marriage Register (North Carolina State Archives, Raleigh); Robert F. Durden, *The Dukes of Durham* (1975); Franklin M. Garrett, ed., *Atlanta and Environs: A Chronicle of Its People and Events, Family and Personal History*, vol. 2 (1954); Louis H. Manarin, comp., *North Carolina Troops, 1861–1865: A Roster*, vol. 1 (1966); Stephen E. Massengill, "Washington Duke and Sons: Builders of a Tobacco-Manufacturing Dynasty in Durham, North Carolina, 1865–1890" (master's thesis, North Carolina State University, Raleigh, 1976); Edward Featherston Small Papers (Manuscript Department, Duke University Library, Durham); John K. Winkler, *Tobacco Tycoon: The Story of James Buchanan Duke* (1942).

STEPHEN E. MASSENGILL

Small, Henry. *See* **Ellenwood, Henry Small.**

Small, John Humphrey *(29 Aug. 1858–13 July 1946)*, congressman and father of the Atlantic Intracoastal Waterway, was born in Washington, Beaufort County, the son of John H. and Sally A. Sanderson Small. Small's parents, who had migrated from Pasquotank County in 1835, were prominent planters in Beaufort. Small attended the Washington schools and Trinity College (now Duke University). At the end of his junior year at Trinity, he studied law in the offices of Charles F. Warren and Judge William B. Rodman; he was admitted to the bar in 1881.

Small began his political career early, having been appointed reading clerk of the state senate only days after his admission to the bar. Between 1881 and 1885 he served as county superintendent of public instruction in Beaufort and as solicitor of the inferior court. In 1883 he became proprietor and editor of the North Carolina *State Press*, which he renamed the *Washington Gazette*. Under Small, the *Gazette* became the leading organ of the state Democratic party. In addition, he was a member of the Washington City Council (1887–90), attorney of the Beaufort County Board of Commissioners (1888–96), mayor of Washington (1889–90), a delegate to the Democratic state conventions (1889–1920), and presidential elector on the Democratic ticket of William Jennings Bryan and Arthur Sewall (1896). Small was elected as a Democrat to the Fifty-sixth Congress; reelected to the House of Representatives ten times, he served from 4 Mar. 1899 to 3 Mar. 1921.

In Congress Small was an outspoken party leader on issues such as Prohibition, woman suffrage, education, and agricultural problems. But his major interest involved increasing waterborne transportation along the Atlantic coast. Small felt that such a waterway not only would serve the transportation needs of the general public but also would provide added commerce and trade routes for the coastal regions of the eastern seaboard. He envisioned a series of interconnecting canals extending from Boston to Key West, Fla., a distance of three thousand miles.

His early attempts to obtain funding for his project ended in failure, for the Republican opposition continually defeated his proposals. Yet with the outbreak of World War I both parties began to reconsider the idea. However, the waterway was now seen as a possible defense measure and not as a new mode of commerce and transportation. In 1917, when he was named head of the House Committee on Rivers and Harbors, Small publicly stressed the defense issue but privately pushed the economic advantages. That year he proposed many new bills for the waterway, all of which passed.

With the the Atlantic Intracoastal Waterway thus assured, Small declined to be a candidate for renomination in 1920 and joined the legal staff of the Securities and Exchange Commission in Washington, D.C., where he remained until 1931. During this period he witnessed the completion of many sections of the waterway, including the Norfolk-Beaufort segment, which was finished in 1921.

On 11 June 1890 Small married Isabella C. Wharton, the daughter of Colonel R. W. Wharton. John and Isabella had one daughter, May Belle. Small was a member of the National Rivers and Harbors Congress and of the Atlantic Deeper Waterway Association. Affiliated with the Methodist Episcopal Church, South, he was buried in the Oakdale Cemetery, Washington, N.C.

SEE: Samuel A. Ashe, *Cyclopedia of Eminent and Representative Men of the Carolinas*, vol. 2 (1892); *Biog. Dir. Am. Cong.* (1961); *Prominent People of North Carolina* (1906); John Humphrey Small Papers, 2 July 1910–29 March 1940 (Manuscript Department, Duke University Library, Durham); J. H. Small Papers, May 1903–15 Apr. 1921 (Southern Historical Collection, University of North Carolina, Chapel Hill); Phyllis A. Watson, "John Humphrey Small and the Development of the Atlantic Intracoastal Waterway, 1899–1921" (M.A. thesis, East Carolina University, Greenville, 1971).

RICHARD V. SPELL

Smathers, George Henry *(29 Jan. 1854–9 June 1950)*, Asheville attorney and expert on land titles in western North Carolina, was born in Turnpike, Buncombe County, one of thirteen children of John Charles and Lucilla E. Smathers. He was educated by a private schoolteacher, Mary Ann Hutsell, and at the Montford Academy on the present William Randolph School site in Asheville, Sand Hill Academy near what is now Enka, and Pleasant Hill School House near Turnpike. Smathers worked for his father's various businesses in Turnpike, Clyde, and Waynesville before attending the law school of Dick and Dillard in Greensboro in 1880; he was admitted to the bar in 1881.

Smathers practiced law for sixty years—first in Waynesville, then in Asheville as land title counsel for the Champion Paper and Fibre Company—until past the age of ninety. Active in civic and political affairs, he was mayor of Waynesville in 1886. In 1896 he was elected state senator from the district then comprised of Haywood, Buncombe, and Madison counties and became chairman of the judiciary committee. In 1899 he participated in a convention held at the Battery Park Hotel in Asheville that grew into the movement to establish the Great Smoky Mountains National Park.

While in the state senate, Smathers and Representative J. W. Ferguson of Haywood secured a tax to help maintain the public roads of Haywood, previously maintained entirely by public labor. This was the General Assembly's first act levying a tax for roads west of the Blue Ridge.

In 1899, at the request of the Eastern Band of Cherokee Indians, Smathers was appointed special assistant U.S. attorney to clear up titles to Cherokee lands and to evict trespassers. Fourteen years of intensive investigation followed, resulting in the landmark cases *Eastern Band of Cherokee Indians v. William H. Thomas et al.* and *United States v. William H. Thomas et al.* Title was perfected in the Indians to the Qualla Indian Boundary, comprising some 77,000 acres in Jackson and Swain counties, and to 68 tracts in Jackson, Swain, Cherokee, and Graham counties. As a result of this work Smathers became an expert in land titles and land litigation and after 1903 confined his practice to that specialty. He did title work for the R. Y. McAden estate, the Haywood Lumber and Mining Company, and the William H. Ritter Lumber Company in addition to the Champion Paper and Fibre Company. In 1938, at age eighty-four, he published *The History of Land Titles in Western North Carolina*, the definitive work on the subject; it also contains valuable information on the family and generational history of the region. During 1938 he also served as president of the Buncombe County Bar Association.

Smathers married Daisy Rice Glaze of Montgomery, Ala., on 6 Jan. 1892. They had one daughter, Ellen Rice Wiley. He was buried at Waynesville.

SEE: *Asheville Citizen-Times*, 3 Apr., 28 June, 3 July 1938, 28 Jan. 1947, 10–11 June, 2 July 1950; George H. Smathers, *The History of Land Titles in Western North Carolina* (1938).

SARAH R. SHABER

Smathers, William Howell *(7 Jan. 1891–24 Sept. 1955)*, attorney, jurist, and U.S. senator, was born in Waynesville, the youngest son of Benjamin Franklin and Laura Howell Smathers. He attended local schools, Washington and Lee University, and The University of North Carolina, from which he was graduated in 1910. He was admitted to the bar in the latter year. In 1911 he "went north" to join his brother, Frank, in Atlantic City, N.J., in the practice of law with the firm of Endicott and Endicott. In spite of his many years in New Jersey, Smathers never lost his southern accent and always said he had a "hankerin" to return to North Carolina, which he finally did when he retired in 1951.

Although a Democrat in heavily Republican territory, he filled a succession of political posts in New Jersey, earning a reputation as an upsetter. In 1913 he became a supreme court commissioner, and in 1922, at age thirty-one, he was named a common pleas judge, the youngest man up to that time named to the bench. Smathers, who had a reputation as a severe judge, started a road gang system in Atlantic County to make prisoners earn money to be forwarded to their dependents. Tough on racketeers, he received many death threats and habitually carried a pistol. In 1930 the Kiwanis Club of Atlantic City, recognizing him as the city's "Most Useful Citizen," presented him with its Good Deeds Award for his outstanding services on the bench.

In August 1934 Smathers was appointed first assistant attorney general of New Jersey. While in that post he assisted in the Dorrance tax appeal case, various railroad tax appeals, and other tax cases that meant millions of dollars to the citizens of the state. The following autumn he was elected to the New Jersey Senate, the first Democrat to hold that office for Atlantic County in more than sixty years. He was then selected by Jersey City's former mayor, Frank Hague, to run for the U.S. Senate. Smathers was elected in the Roosevelt landslide of 1936, joining his nephew, Democrat George Smathers, then the junior senator from Florida. While in the Senate he was mentioned either as a possible vice-presidential candidate in 1942 or as a New Jersey gubernatorial candidate. Neither option materialized.

In 1939 Smathers introduced a bill to ease immigration restrictions for elderly political and religious refugees. He endorsed the Zionist cause in Palestine. In 1941 his resolution to admit Cuba as a state was repudiated by the Cuban government. He served on the Senate Banking and Currency Committee and was instrumental in establishing a fifth judgeship for the New Jersey Federal District Court. Smathers was defeated for reelection in 1942 by Republican Albert W. Hawkes. He practiced law in Atlantic City until his retirement and return to North Carolina. An ardent sportsman, he was particularly fond of hunting and fishing, and he raised champion English setters.

In 1916 Smathers married Syd Brady of Atlantic City. They had five children: Jane, Barbara, Polly, Joseph, and Benjamin Franklin. They were divorced in 1934. In 1938 he married Mary J. Folley of Winter Haven, Fla., and they had three children: James Folley, Fairfax Virginia, and William Howell, Jr. Smathers died in Asheville and was buried in Green Hill Cemetery, Waynesville.

SEE: *Asheville Citizen-Times*, 19 May 1935, 4, 29 Nov. 1936, 15 Feb. 1939, 4 Dec. 1940, 28 Aug. 1951, 24–25 Sept. 1955; *Biog. Dir. Am. Cong.* (1971); *National Public Affairs*, November 1942; *New York Times*, 25 Sept. 1955; *Raleigh News and Observer*, 25 Sept. 1955; *Winston-Salem Journal-Sentinel*, 25 Aug. 1951.

SARAH R. SHABER

Smedes, Aldert *(20 Apr. 1810–25 Apr. 1877)*, Episcopal clergyman, was the founder and for thirty-five years rector of St. Mary's School (now St. Mary's College), Raleigh. The eldest of twelve children, he was born in New York City, the son of Abraham Kiersted, who was from an old Knickerbocker family, and Elizabeth Sebor Isaacs

Smedes, who was of English ancestry. A brother, William Crosby Smedes, attorney and railroad president, was a member of Mississippi's Secession Convention. Another brother, the Reverend John Esten Cooke Smedes, D.D., was president (1872–84) of St. Augustine Normal School and Collegiate Institute (now St. Augustine's College), Raleigh.

Aldert Smedes entered Columbia College at age thirteen but moved with his family to Lexington, Ky., and completed his degree at Transylvania University. He also read law and was admitted to the Kentucky bar. In 1832 he was graduated from the General Theological Seminary and ordained deacon; he was ordained priest in 1834. He served Christ Church in New York City (1832–36) as assistant to Dr. Thomas Lyell.

In 1833 Smedes married Lyell's daughter, Sarah Pierce (1813–87). Of their six sons, Aldert, Lyell, Bennett, Charles Graham, Abraham Kiersted, and George Mancious, only Bennett survived both parents. Their daughters were Elizabeth Sebor (m. Moreau P. Leake), Annie Beach (m. Charles Root), and Sarah Lyell (m. William A. Erwin).

From 1836 to 1839 Smedes served as rector of St. George's Church in Schenectady, N.Y. Despite the fact that a chronic throat ailment necessitated his spending about a year of this time resting and traveling in Europe and the Holy Land, Smedes's pastorate resulted in an enlarged membership and a building program. Reluctantly, in the spring of 1839 he resigned and returned to New York City, where he and his widowed mother ran a private school for girls.

On 12 May 1842 Smedes opened St. Mary's School in Raleigh. This school for girls was a private venture under the patronage of the Right Reverend Levi Silliman Ives, D.D., bishop of North Carolina, who had asked Duncan Cameron to buy the campus of the defunct diocesan school for boys, the Episcopal School of North Carolina, and to lease the property to Smedes. These private arrangements continued through two generations of both families, but Episcopalians regarded St. Mary's as their diocesan school almost from its founding. The school became the embodiment of Aldert Smedes's conviction that society could be transformed through the influence of educated Christian women, and he gathered a competent and exceptionally dedicated faculty. Some 1,900 young women were educated under Smedes's rectorship. Although the school did not then grant diplomas, it followed a rigorous curriculum that produced many teachers. In addition, St. Mary's became the cultural center of antebellum Raleigh. Smedes opened Trinity, a classical school for boys, near Raleigh in 1847, but it existed for only about five years. The University of North Carolina recognized his contribution by awarding Smedes a doctor of divinity degree in 1854.

Although Smedes was not an ardent secessionist, he cast his lot with the South and his school did not close during the Civil War. It served as a refuge for many, including Mrs. Jefferson Davis and her children in the summer of 1862. Classes met as usual during the last weeks of April 1865, when Federal troops were encamped in the St. Mary's Grove. An astute businessman, Smedes weathered Reconstruction. He provided many scholarships from personal funds accumulated from investments in the North before the war, so that more southern young women could be educated during those depressed years.

An active churchman, Smedes served his diocese as a member of the standing committee for many years. He was a trustee of the General Theological Seminary, the University of the South, and St. Augustine's. The Right Reverend Thomas Atkinson, D.D., bishop of North Carolina, said of Smedes that he "accomplished more for the advancement of his diocese and for the promotion of the best interests of society in its limits than any man who ever lived in it." Despite declining health, Smedes continued his arduous duties at St. Mary's until his death there. He was buried in Oakwood Cemetery, Raleigh.

Portraits of Aldert and Sarah Smedes are in the possession of Mrs. Hargrove Bellamy, Wilmington, N.C.; copies are owned by St. Mary's College.

SEE: Helen Beach, *Descendants of Jacob Sebor, 1709–1793, of Middletown, Conn.* (1923); Willis T. Hanson, Jr., *A History of St. George's Church, Schenectady*, vol. 1 (1919); Marshall DeLancey Haywood, *Lives of the Bishops of North Carolina* (1910); *Journal, Diocese of North Carolina*, 1842, 1851–54, 1877; Raleigh *Observer*, 26 Apr., 3 May 1877; Raleigh *Register*, 12 May 1842; *St. Mary's Muse*, April 1906; Katherine Batts Salley, ed., *Life at Saint Mary's* (1942).

MARTHA S. STOOPS

Smedes, Bennett *(7 Aug. 1837–22 Feb. 1899)*, Episcopal clergyman and second rector of St. Mary's School, Raleigh, was born in New York. The son of Aldert and Sarah Lyell Smedes, he moved with the family to North Carolina in 1842, when his father founded St. Mary's School. He was educated in Raleigh at Lovejoy's Academy and Trinity School and at the College of Saint James in Maryland. Young Smedes was graduated from the General Theological Seminary in 1860 and ordained deacon in July of that year. He served for two years as assistant to Dr. A. C. Coxe at Grace Church, Baltimore.

Wishing to return to the Confederacy, Smedes managed to get to Raleigh in the summer of 1863 and immediately enlisted; he was assigned as chaplain to North Carolina's Fifth Regiment. On 26 July he was ordained priest by the Right Reverend Thomas Atkinson, D.D., bishop of North Carolina, despite the fact that the bishop of Maryland had refused to give Letters Dismissory. Because of his own poor health and his father's desperate need for his assistance, Smedes resigned his commission in April 1864 and returned to St. Mary's, where he spent the remainder of his life. A gentle, unassuming, and scholarly man, he taught science, logic, and Bible and assisted his father in his duties as pastor and administrator until the death in 1877 of the elder Smedes.

When no one else could be found to take over the institution, Bennett Smedes, although he preferred the roles of teacher and preacher, assumed full responsibility for the school in order "to save St. Mary's for the Church." Continuing the school's traditional emphasis on Christian responsibility and academic excellence, he strengthened the faculty, improved the facilities, and reorganized the curriculum to prepare young women for the best colleges.

In 1877 Smedes married Henrietta Harvey (1849–1929), the granddaughter of Governor Matthew Harvey of New Hampshire. The couple had four daughters: Eliza Sebor, who died during childhood, Margaret Harvey (m. John I. Rose), Mary Sherwood (m. James M. Poyner), and Helen Lyell (m. Albert W. Latta).

By 1897 Smedes felt that, having spent his inheritance and his physical strength to keep the school open, he could no longer carry the sole responsibility for St. Mary's. The Episcopal church accepted his proposal that the North Carolina dioceses buy the campus from the Cameron family. The act of incorporation vested control in a board of trustees, and in 1899 the charter was amended to involve the South Carolina dioceses. Smedes remained as rector.

Bennett Smedes served his diocese as a faithful member of important committees including the standing committee and as a trustee of St. Augustine's Normal School and Collegiate Institute (now St. Augustine's College). Generous in his support of public causes, he was even more liberal in his private charities. In 1894 The University of North Carolina awarded him a doctor of divinity degree.

Smedes died at St. Mary's. The circumstances of his death from pneumonia were typical of his unselfish devotion to others, for he had walked several miles in a driving snowstorm to collect the mail so that his young charges would not be disappointed. He was buried in Oakwood Cemetery, Raleigh. The Right Reverend Joseph Blount Cheshire, D.D., bishop of North Carolina, wrote of Smedes, "If men are to be estimated by the purity and simplicity of their Christian character and by the value of their life work to the Church and to the community, few names deserve to stand higher." Portraits of Smedes are owned by St. Mary's College and by James M. Poyner, Raleigh.

SEE: Helen Beach, *Descendants of Jacob Sebor, 1709–1793, of Middletown, Conn.* (1923); Joseph Blount Cheshire, Jr., "In Memoriam," *St. Mary's Muse*, June 1899; Marshall DeLancey Haywood, *Lives of the Bishops of North Carolina* (1910); *Journal, Diocese of North Carolina*, 1877, 1896–99; Raleigh *Morning Post*, 23 Feb. 1899; Raleigh *News and Observer*, 23–24 Feb. 1899; Katherine Batts Salley, ed., *Life at Saint Mary's* (1942); U.S. National Archives, Compiled Service Records of North Carolina Infantry, Fifth Regiment.

MARTHA S. STOOPS

Smethurst, Frank Austin *(30 Oct. 1891–18 Sept. 1941)*, newspaper reporter, columnist, and editor, was born in Raleigh, the son of William Sidney and Martha Yearby Smethurst. His paternal grandfather was Sidney Smethurst, of Lancashire, England, who moved to Raleigh in the late 1850s. Sidney Smethurst owned and operated a foundry and, while disavowing any sympathy for slavery, used his ironworks to make weapons for the Confederacy. In retaliation, Union forces confiscated his business at the end of the war, and he became a machinist and master mechanic.

Frank Smethurst attended the public schools of Raleigh, where he was president of the literary society and senior class poet. He won a scholarship to Wake Forest College, achieved an outstanding record, and was assistant to the head of the English department. Nevertheless, near graduation in 1912 he was expelled for misconduct when he participated in an escapade prior to the spring dance that involved festooning campus trees with ribbons of toilet tissue. Unwittingly he and his confederates introduced a prank popularized generations later by exuberant students who called it "rolling" trees and who were seldom if ever reprimanded for the frolic. Years later, after he had become one of the state's foremost journalists, the college relented and awarded him a bachelor's degree.

After leaving Wake Forest, Smethurst worked briefly for the *Charlotte News* before joining the Raleigh *News and Observer*, to which he devoted the remainder of his life. He rose from reporter to city editor to managing editor, a post he held for seventeen years. For a long time he also wrote a column-length daily commentary, "In My Opinion," for the editorial page. This he used to accentuate the positive, to share the poignancy of both public joy and pathos, to heighten what little humor coursed through the wire service, and—more frequently than his competitors cared to admit—to focus on incipient news developments far earlier than other daily recorders recognized them as newsworthy. His commentaries on the controversial, particularly in politics, objectively and carefully presented opposing viewpoints that often exasperated both sides.

His columns frequently were reprinted and mimicked by other writers across the nation and led to his nomination in 1934 for a Pulitzer Prize. In a commentary captioned "Ella May Wiggins Doesn't Count," he decried the cavalier attitude of certain public officials towards a fatality growing out of textile strikes in the late 1920s. His nomination was endorsed by Haywood Broun, who editorialized on 1 Nov. 1929 that Smethurst's editorial "proves that the South is not the great desert pictured by Mr. Mencken."

After publisher Josephus Daniels accepted appointment as ambassador to Mexico in 1933, responsibility for the editorial management of the *News and Observer* was vested in Smethurst. Despite a deepening depression, he managed to increase circulation by tailoring successive editions each day to feature local news of special interest to the specific geographic areas in which the varying editions were distributed. Such specialized, localized news coverage was achieved by developing an extensive fraternity of regional correspondents reporting to the state editor.

While competitors struggled simply to survive the depression of the 1930s, Smethurst was laying the foundation for the most lucrative daily newspaper in the region. His unremitting demand for accuracy and excellence of writing style challenged and attracted ambitious young staffers who later distinguished themselves on many publications of national stature. Young writers whom he trained included E. Clifton Daniel and Marjorie Hunter, both later to rank high with the *New York Times*; Jonathan Daniels, son of the publisher; James Daniel, later of the *Reader's Digest* staff; Simmons Fentress, of *Time, Inc.*; and Herbert E. O'Keefe, Charles F. Parker, Alonzo T. Dill, and J. G. de Roulhac Hamilton, Jr.

Though regarded as a raconteur of rare wit and warm conviviality, he preferred the role of recorder to that of the limelight. He declined all overtures for public office except one appeal in 1933 to serve as a public representative on the Veterans Administration economic review board.

In 1919 he married Margarette Lee Wood, a native of Danville, Va., and for a number of years woman's editor and author of a provocative daily column for the *News and Observer*. They were the parents of two sons, only one of whom, Wood, lived to maturity. In spite of deteriorating health, Frank Smethurst assembled a special staff and shared long hours of publishing the most voluminous *News and Observer* to that date, the 240-page seventy-fifth anniversary edition of 18 May 1940. A Baptist and a Democrat, he was buried in Oakwood Cemetery, Raleigh.

SEE: Raleigh *News and Observer*, 1914–41, esp. 25 Oct., 1 Nov. 1929, 17 Jan. 1937, 18 May 1940, 19 Sept., 9 Dec. 1941, 28 June 1960; Wood Smethurst Papers (Emory University, Atlanta, Ga.).

JACK RILEY

Smith, Ashbel *(13 Aug. 1805–21 Jan. 1886)*, Salisbury physician and Texas political leader, was born in Hartford, Conn., the son of Phoebe Adams and Moses Smith, Jr. He had a half brother, Curtis, and three siblings, Henry Grattan, Caroline, and George Alfred. Ashbel Smith grew up in New England and was graduated with honors from Yale University in 1824. Afterwards he was induced by Charles Fisher of Salisbury to teach in the Salisbury Academy for a salary of $300 the first year plus his traveling expenses and board. His knowledge of the classics gained for him a wide reputation, and his Fourth of July oration in 1825 was published in Salisbury and Hartford newspapers, which both praised his erudition.

During his first eighteen months in Salisbury, Smith formed many lifelong friends, among them Burton Craige, John Beard, J. J. Bruner, James Huie, and Jefferson Jones, but it was Charles Fisher who had the greatest influence on his life. Fisher was not only Smith's closest friend but his political mentor as well. Under Fisher's guidance, Smith began to read law but gave it up in 1826 to return north to study medicine at Yale. He took back with him two Salisbury boys, Archibald Henderson and Warren Huie, whom he tutored for Yale.

After obtaining a medical degree in 1828, Smith practiced in Salisbury for three years. In 1831 he left for Paris, France, for additional study. There he met and enjoyed many leisure hours with the Marquis de Lafayette, Samuel Morse, and James Fenimore Cooper. After working during an epidemic of Asiatic cholera, he published in New York in 1832 a brochure entitled *The Cholera Spasmodica As Observed in Paris in 1832*.

In June 1832 the *Western Carolinian* of Salisbury, N.C., announced that Dr. Ashbel Smith would resume the practice of medicine at his old office on Main Street. In 1833 Smith was visited by Henry Barnard, a New Englander, who reported that the physician "has quite a very large practice, which brings him in 1500 to 2000 [dollars] a year, and he is growing every day into public confidence. I have no hesitation to say, that he is better read in his profession than ⅔ of the Doctors of our country." Barnard added that "His conversation is a perpetual feast. He is a splendid scholar—spent a year in Paris and has read the great books of life and human nature with a keen eye. He understands woman thoroughly." With his knowledge of "woman," Smith had a romance with Mary Louisa Phifer of Cabarrus County and was a close friend of Warren Huie's sister, Antoinette. He was also appointed a magistrate for Rowan County and in that capacity frequently performed marriage ceremonies. In 1835–36 he was part owner with Joseph W. Hampton of the *Western Carolinian*. Under Smith and Hampton, the newspaper continued to be a democratic organ and a "good Jackson paper."

The allure of Texas drew the young doctor at the end of 1836, and the next year he was appointed surgeon general of the Texas army. Later he served with distinction in the Mexican War. Following the peace he settled on his plantation, Evergreen, on Galveston Bay. In 1851 Smith was appointed commissioner for the United States to the London Industrial Exposition, where he acted as a juror. He served in the Texas legislature in 1855, 1866, and 1878. During the Civil War he joined the Confederate army, becoming captain of the Bayland Guards and later colonel of the Second Texas Infantry. He was seriously wounded in the Battle of Shiloh, fought all through the siege of Vicksburg, and commanded the defense of Galveston. After the surrender, as a commissioner to New Orleans, he participated in drawing up the terms of surrender of the district.

In his later years his chief labor was the writing of several historical and scientific treatises, including a paper on yellow fever. As president of the first board of regents of the University of Texas, Smith was instrumental in selecting the institution's first faculty. He also helped establish Texas A&M College, Prairie View, Sam Houston State University, Stuart Female Seminary at Austin, and Galveston Medical School, as well as public schools at Evergreen and throughout the state. He served as a juror at the Philadelphia Centennial in 1876 and as honorary commissioner from Texas to the International Industrial Exposition at Paris in 1878.

Smith never married. He died in his eighty-first year at his home near Galveston. His body was taken to the capitol at Austin, where it lay in state before burial in the state cemetery.

SEE: Henry Barnard, "The South Atlantic States in 1833 as Seen by a New Englander," *Maryland Historical Magazine* 13 (September 1918); *Confederate Veteran* 27 (December 1919); Guion Griffis Johnson, *Ante-Bellum North Carolina: A Social History* (1937); Salisbury *Carolina Watchman*, 28 Jan., 4 Feb. 1886; Salisbury *Western Carolinian*, 12 July 1825, 5 Aug. 1828, 25 June 1832, 7 Mar. 1835, 2 Feb. 1838; Elizabeth Silverthorne (Temple, Tex.), personal contact.

JAMES S. BRAWLEY

Smith, Benjamin *(10 Jan. 1756–26 Jan. 1826)*, governor, lawyer, benefactor of The University of North Carolina, and planter, was the son of Thomas of South Carolina and Sarah Moore Smith, daughter of "King Roger" Moore, builder of Orton plantation house. There is some question as to whether he was born in 1756 or 1757 and whether he died on 26 January or 3 February. He was a descendant of Thomas Smith, a planter, merchant, surgeon, and governor of Carolina (1693–94). Benjamin was admitted to the Middle Temple on 12 May 1774.

At age twenty-one Smith served as aide-de-camp to General George Washington in the retreat from Long Island on 29–30 August 1776. On 3 Feb. 1779 he served with William Moultrie in driving the British from Port Royal Island (Beaufort), thereby deferring the British invasion of South Carolina. Smith was elected to the Continental Congress on 11 May 1784, but there is no record that he ever attended. Between 1784 and 1816 he served three terms in the House of Commons and eighteen in the senate; he was speaker of the senate for five terms (1795–99). A member of the constitutional convention of 1788, he cooperated with James Iredell in an unsuccessful attempt to secure adoption of the federal Constitution; he was also a member of the convention of 1789, which approved the Constitution.

When The University of North Carolina was chartered in 1789, Smith gave 20,000 acres of Tennessee land that he had received for service during the Revolution and also served on the board of trustees (1789–1824). In 1792 he gave land adjacent to Fort Johnston at the mouth of the Cape Fear River for the town of Smithville (now Southport). In 1807 Smith served as adjutant general of North Carolina under a new law that revised the militia laws of the state.

In his own right by inheritance, Benjamin Smith, a militia major general, was a wealthy man. At the time the federal census was taken in 1790, he owned 221 slaves. He married Sarah, the daughter and sole heir of Colonel William Dry, colonial collector of the port of Wilmington and a descendant of Admiral Robert Blake, supporter of Oliver Cromwell. The Smiths adopted two children, were generous with their wealth to the less fortunate, and promoted educational projects. Their generosity resulted in their ultimate impoverishment, however, when Smith became security for the bond of one Colonel Reed, collector of the port of Wilmington, who defaulted. Smith's entire wealth and that of his wife was drained off to meet this heavy obligation with the result that both died in poverty.

Smith was grand master of Masons in North Carolina in 1808–10 and governor of the state in 1810–11. Though of a benevolent nature and well educated, he had an irascible disposition, was quick to anger, and chose to settle disputes by duel. His more frequent opponents were blood kin or political antagonists, and he was twice wounded in these encounters. Contrary to some accounts, he did not die in prison in Smithville but in his dilapidated home nearby; the residence had so deteriorated that it offered little protection in inclement weather. There in 1821 his wife died, and there five years later "during unprecedented torrential rains and gale winds" so did the general. The attending physician was Dr. George Campbell Clitherall, surgeon of the garrison at Fort Johnston.

Earlier biographers have stated that either St. James's churchyard in Wilmington or St. Phillips in Brunswick (where Mrs. Smith was buried) was the place of his interment. But according to Eliza Clitherall, daughter of neighbor John Burgwin, "Burial should have been beside his wife, but . . . by dawn Jan. 27th decomposition had taken place and it was necessary interment should be performed as speedily as possible." Because of the stormy weather, transportation by land or water to Brunswick was impossible, "So . . . the remains were carried to the Smithville burying ground and there deposited."

Dr. Clitherall and two witnesses he called in found no will among the general's effects. Smith's creditors clamored for the proceeds of his few remaining possessions, which were auctioned at a sheriff's sale in Smithville in March 1826.

SEE: Samuel A. Ashe, ed., *Biographical History of North Carolina*, vol. 2 (1905); Kemp P. Battle, ed., "Letters and Documents Relating to the Early History of the Lower Cape Fear," James Sprunt Historical Monographs, no. 4 (1904); John L. Cheney, Jr., ed., *North Carolina Government, 1585–1979* (1981); Walter Clark, ed., *State Records of North Carolina*, vols. 16–19, 22, 24 (1899–1905); Eliza Clitherall Diary (Southern Historical Collection, University of North Carolina, Chapel Hill); E. Alfred Jones, *American Members of the Inns of Court* (1924); Donald R. Lennon, "The Political Views and Public Activities of Benjamin Smith of Brunswick County (1783–1816)," (master's thesis, East Carolina University, 1961); *Presentation of Portrait of Governor Benjamin Smith to the State of North Carolina* [address by Collier Cobb] (1911); Raleigh *Register*, 17 Feb. 1826; James Sprunt, *Chronicles of the Cape Fear* (1916); *University of North Carolina Magazine* 1 (February 1882).

DOROTHY FREMONT GRANT

Smith, Betty *(15 Dec. 1896–17 Jan. 1972)*, playwright and novelist, born in the Williamsburg section of Brooklyn, N.Y., was apparently named Elizabeth Lillian Wehner, though some say "Sophie." She used "Elizabeth Lillian" from earliest childhood, and her mother's pet name for her was "Littie." Later, when she needed a birth certificate to quality for social security, the only one that fit the circumstances of her birth was for a Sophie Whener. She was able to have the certificate changed legally to Elizabeth Wehner, or so she said. She was the oldest child of John Casper (1894–1915) and Catherine Hummel Wehner (1876–1966), both born in Brooklyn. All four grandparents—Regina and John Casper Wehner, Sr., and Mary and Thomas Hummel—were born in Germany. Apocryphal accounts of Betty Smith's "Irish ancestry" have arisen from the fact that after her father's death, her mother married an Irishman, Michael Keogh, a widower with young children. Betty's sister Regina (Mrs. William Hall) and a brother William, both Wehners, took the name Keogh, though Betty, being older, never did. "Williamsburg was a poor and sordid neighborhood," she wrote, "but picturesque . . . with children of Irish, German, Italian, and Jewish immigrants. We all fought to retain our own . . . speech patterns. . . . A cohesive Brooklyn accent resulted." Later, beneath the southern modulations her voice acquired, "Brooklynese" still emerged sporadically.

Petite, with chestnut hair and clear light blue eyes, she married, on 18 Oct. 1919, George Howard Edward Smith, a University of Michigan law student. They had two children: Nancy Jean (married D. F. Pfeiffer) and Mary Elizabeth (married first Walter Carroll; second, Thomas MacCaulty).

Early jobs interfered with schooling, and Betty advanced only through the eighth grade. In Ann Arbor she completed the equivalent of high school but was never awarded a diploma, nor did she earn a college degree. Admitted to the University of Michigan as a special student, she took every writing and journalism course. As part of class work, she wrote weekly articles for the Detroit *Free Press*. Her work also appeared in the New York *Herald Tribune*, the *Chicago Tribune*, and *The Chatelaine*, a Canadian magazine, and she published two plays. Given a "special dispensation" to compete, she won the Avery Hopwood Award in playwriting in June 1931 worth $1,000 and obligating its recipient to continue work in the drama. To fulfill this requirement, she was admitted by George Pierce Baker to take the three-year course in Yale Drama School without being a degree candidate. She and Elia Kazan were among thirteen known as "Baker's Dozen." Afterwards, she got a job with the Federal Theater and was sent with Robert Finch and others to Chapel Hill to work with Frederick H. Koch of the Carolina Playmakers.

In 1937 she coedited, with Koch and Finch, *Plays for Schools and Little Theatres* and wrote a one-act play catalogue. Having her two children with her and being estranged from her husband (from whom she was divorced in 1939), she stayed on when the federal project expired. Through the good offices of friends she was granted a Rockefeller fellowship in 1939 and the same year won first prize in a contest sponsored by the Berkley Players. She helped Koch compile *American Folk Plays*, attended his classes, and, in his absence, took over the classes for him. Betty Smith also published seventy-two one-act plays, sold for anything from $10 to $50 apiece "for bread and butter." When radio was set up at The University of North Carolina, she wrote radio plays with Earl Wynn and acted in them and in Playmaker productions. In 1940 she won the Dramatic Guild Award of $1,000. She edited *Twenty-five Plays for All-Girl Casts* (1942) and *Twenty Prize-Winning Plays* (1943).

Much of her fiction began life as a play. At Yale she had written a three-act drama, "You Promised Me," based on memories of life in Brooklyn. Now, in a one-room house—all she could afford—on North Street in Chapel Hill, she began to turn this material into a novel. Her house had a chimney in the center. Rising about five-thirty, wrapping an old blanket around her, with her back against the chimney wall to keep warm, she wrote *A Tree Grows in Brooklyn*. Two weeks after publication by

Harper on 17 Aug. 1943, it sold over 150,000 copies and ultimately over six million. In the end, the novel grossed her about $1 million. Twentieth-Century Fox paid $50,000 for movie rights; the movie was directed by her old friend, Elia Kazan. On 22 Apr. 1951 the musical based on *Tree* opened in New York. The movie won three Academy awards; the musical ran for over a year. The novel was made into a radio serial, appeared later on TV as a "late show," and was the basis for a comic strip in some two hundred papers. It was published in Braille, translated into twenty-two foreign languages, and rewritten in France as a child's book. Banned as "obscene" in Liberty, Ohio, in 1964, it was reinstated, Betty declared, "after I went out to Ohio."

With part of her money, she set up a fund at The University of North Carolina for annual playwriting awards. She also bought "the old Mangum house" at the corner of Rosemary and Hillsborough streets, two Cadillacs, and a cottage at Nags Head, though a few years later a hurricane washed away the cottage and all its furnishings. Three days before the publication of *Tree* she had married Joseph Piper Jones. They were divorced in December 1951. Shortly thereafter, she married Robert Voris Finch. He died on 4 Feb. 1959, and she never married again.

In 1948 her second novel appeared. *Tomorrow Will Be Better*, the locale also Brooklyn, did not do so well financially as *Tree*, though it too was a Book Club selection (as were all her novels) and eventually came out in paperback as well. Betty had articles and stories published in *Vogue*, *Mademoiselle*, *Good Housekeeping*, *Harper's*, *Life*, and *Collier's* and book reviews in the *New York Times*. In 1958 her third novel, *Maggie Now*, was published, followed by *Joy in the Morning* in 1963. In this final novel she shifted to memories of her first marriage and years at the University of Michigan, and here she again hit her stride. Royalties from *Joy* in 1964 amounted to $50,000 at the same time that those from *Tree* were still about $6,000 annually. Metro Goldwyn Mayer bought movie rights for $150,000.

Betty Smith was a member of the Authors' League, Dramatists Guild, American Federation of Radio, PEN, Pen and Brush, Matrix, and Theta Sigma Phi. Awards included *Mademoiselle* magazine's Woman of the Year; the Associated Press's Outstanding Woman of the Year in Literature; Oscar, awarded by Youth United, Inc.; Certificate of Merit from the New York Museum of Science and Industry "for accurate portrayal of contemporary American life in novels"; Carolina Dramatic Association Award; and Playmakers' Alumnae Award. Her portrait hangs in the Yale Drama School Hall of Fame. She was a Democrat and a Roman Catholic.

After she had been moved to a Shelton, Conn., convalescent home following pneumonia, she died in her sleep. A funeral mass was celebrated in St. Thomas More Church, Chapel Hill, with burial in the Chapel Hill Memorial Cemetery.

SEE: *International Celebrity Register* (1959); Orville Prescott, *In My Opinion: An Inquiry into the Contemporary Novel* (1952); Raleigh *News and Observer*, 18 Jan. 1972; Betty Smith Papers (Southern Historical Collection, University of North Carolina, Chapel Hill); Walter Spearman, *North Carolina Writers* (1949); *Who's Who in America* (1947); *Who's Who of American Women* (1959).

ERMA WILLIAMS GLOVER

Smith, Charles Alphonso *(28 May 1864–13 June 1924)*, author and educator, was born in Greensboro, the third son of Dr. Jacob Henry, a Presbyterian minister, and his second wife, Mary Kelly Watson Smith, the daughter of Judge Egbert Reid Watson of Charlottesville, Va. Named for two brothers of his father who died in the Civil War, he signed his name C. Alphonso Smith but was called Phon by his family and friends. One of his closest boyhood friends was William Sydney Porter, better known as O. Henry, who was a member with him in a Serenading Society. In 1880 Smith went to Davidson College, which his two older brothers were already attending; he, like them, at the end of four years was graduated Phi Beta Kappa. He was extremely popular with his fellow students, who carried him on their shoulders in triumph at commencement when it was announced that he had won two medals. From 1884 to 1889 he taught school in the three small towns of Sanford, Selma, and Princeton, taking one year off to earn an A.M. degree from Davidson in 1887. He entered Johns Hopkins University in 1889 and received his Ph.D. four years later. His published dissertation, *The Order of Words in Anglo-Saxon Prose* (1893), was dedicated to his father, "whose sympathy and scholarship" were both an inspiration and a goal.

In 1893 Smith was appointed professor of English at Louisiana State University, where he remained for the next nine years except for a sabbatical taken abroad in 1900–1901. In 1902 he became head of the department of English at The University of North Carolina, and the following year he was made the first dean of its graduate school. To encourage graduate scholarship at the university, he founded and edited *Studies in Philology*. On 15 Nov. 1905, he married Susan McGee Heck, the daughter of Colonel Jonathan Heck of Raleigh; they had two sons and one daughter. By 1909, when the University of Virginia appointed him its first Edgar Allan Poe Professor of English, he had acquired an international reputation. The following year (1910–11) he was invited to be Theodore Roosevelt Exchange Professor at the University of Berlin. In 1917 Smith became head of the department of English at the U.S. Naval Academy, the first civilian to hold such a post. He was the recipient of LL.D. degrees from the Universities of Mississippi and North Carolina, and the L.H.D. degree from the University of Cincinnati.

Tall, balding, with a reddish-brown mustache, Smith was an outstanding teacher, and many of his students became heads of America's foremost English departments. F. Stringfellow Barr, a former student, called him "essentially dramatic" and said that he inspired students through the force of his personality, communicating to them his own love of literature and research. These same traits made him a successful lecturer. Before leaving Louisiana he was asked to give a farewell address to the state legislature, and Dr. Archibald Henderson, a colleague at The University of North Carolina, called him "the best lecturer on literature I ever heard." Throughout his life he was in demand at universities, seminaries, and chautauquas in all parts of the country. People were introduced to literature, not only through his teaching and lecturing, but also through his best-selling book, *What Can Literature Do For Me?* (1913), which sold over 100,000 copies and showed his craftsmanship in the use of the striking, telling phrase.

Smith was a prolific scholar; a bibliography of his books and articles runs to more than one hundred titles. He was associate editor of the ten-volume *World's Orators* (1901) and of the twenty-seven-volume *Library of Southern Literature* (1907 [portrait in vol. 24]), as well as the author of numerous philological works on grammar and syntax. But he is best known as an authority on the American short story and as a folklorist. He had lectured on the short story in Germany and published many books and articles on it in America. The most important was *O. Henry Biography* (1916), the first major study of his boyhood friend, which President Theodore Roosevelt declared to be "almost as good as O. Henry, himself."

The most lasting contribution of C. Alphonso Smith may have been as a pioneer collector and popularizer of the oral prose, verse, and songs of the South. His love of people, his musical ability (he relaxed by playing the banjo, composing music, and singing), and his training in philology ideally suited him for this role. He was the founder of the Virginia Folklore Society in 1913 and was one of the first to see the importance of collecting the music as well as the words of ballads to determine the earliest version. His interest in folklore went back many years to when he had been associate literary editor of the *Library of Southern Literature* and personally responsible for volume 24, entitled *Miscellanea*. It contained, not the acknowledged belle lettres, but rather the vernacular literature of the South drawn from tombstone epitaphs, sermons, ballads, spirituals, banquet toasts, rural humor, and so forth—sources and categories usually ignored by academic scholars. At a time when the genteel tradition ruled academic circles and German historical and philological methodology reinforced an underlying belief in Anglo-Saxon superiority, this unorthodox interest in the literature of blacks and poor whites must have shocked many of his colleagues. But Smith, believing in "the glory of the commonplace," felt that without turning to such sources, the history of the nation's literature could not be adequately written. "Dixie" and "The Star Spangled Banner" were important, he said, not for the greatness of their poetry, but for what they told of the nation's culture and values.

His teaching position at the U.S. Naval Academy appealed to Smith because he envisioned that the young officers would be ambassadors to the world of the democratic values he believed in and saw reflected in the literature of the American people. Stricken suddenly by "a complication of organic trouble," he sent word to the saddened cadets preparing to leave on their annual summer cruise, "Tell the boys that I have started on a great adventure; I greet the unknown with a cheer." In accordance with his wish, a spiritual was sung at the funeral. He was buried in Greensboro's Green Hill Cemetery. A memorial plaque at Annapolis, inscribed with words from one of his books, describes the impact he had on his generation: "What he received as mist, he returned as rain."

SEE: *Annals of An American Family*, [1953] (copy, North Carolina Collection, University of North Carolina, Chapel Hill); Ethel S. Arnett, *Greensboro, North Carolina* (1955); Davidsonian Collection (Davidson College Library, Davidson, N.C.); *DAB*, vol. 17 (1935); *Greensboro Daily News*, 14 June 1924, 20 Nov. 1927; [Henry Smith Richardson], Susan H. Smith, comp., *Southern Literary Studies* (1927); *Who's Who in America* (1924).

NORRIS W. PREYER

Smith, Charles Aurelius *(22 Jan. 1861–31 March 1916)*, merchant, banker, and governor of South Carolina, was born in Hertford County, N.C., the son of Joseph H. Smith, a farmer, and Eva J. Reddick. He was educated in the common schools before attending Reynoldson School in Gates County to prepare for college. He entered Wake Forest College in 1879 and was graduated with honors in 1882.

In order to pay off his considerable college debt, the young man accepted a teaching post in the schools of Timmonsville, S.C. He soon left teaching to found and manage Charles A. Smith Company, a mercantile business, and became co-owner of Smith-Williams Company of Lake City. Smith served as president of three banks: Citizens Bank of Timmonsville, Bank of Lynchburg, and Peoples' Bank of Lamar. He was president of Timmonsville Oil Company.

Smith's dramatic business success led to his inevitable rise in the ranks of the local Democratic party. Chosen mayor of Timmonsville in 1903, he served in that position until his election to the South Carolina House of Representatives in 1910. He was lieutenant governor from 1911 to 1915. When Cole Blease resigned from the governorship on 14 Jan. 1915, Smith served the remaining five days of Blease's term.

Politically Smith was a conservative best known for his moral rectitude and strong support of Prohibition. This was perhaps reflected in his lifelong dedication to the Baptist faith. He served as president of the South Carolina Baptist Convention (1903–7), vice-president of the Southern Baptist Convention (1905–6), and moderator of the Welsh Neck Baptist Association (1902–12). A deacon for twenty-seven years, he was likewise a member of the executive committee of the education board of the South Carolina Baptist Convention.

Smith's charitable and educational activities were many. His favorite charity was the Connie Maxwell Orphanage at Greenwood, S.C., to which he gave generously and for which he served as a trustee from 1900 until his death. He also served as a trustee of Coker College in Hartsville and of Greenville Women's College, as well as chairman of the board of trustees of Furman University (1909–16).

Smith married Fannie L. Byrd of Timmonsville on 3 Jan. 1884. The couple had eight children: Eva E. (Mrs. Henry P. Lane), Charles Ray, Charles Lucien, Hugh P., Claire (Mrs. J. T. Lucius), Fannie Byrd (Mrs. Francis D. Pepper), Donald F., and Edwin B. Smith, a robust and impressive man, stood at six-feet-five and weighed 220 pounds. A Mason and a member of the Knights of Pythias, he died at Johns Hopkins Hospital in Baltimore, Md., at age fifty-five.

SEE: Roy Glasham, *American Governors and Gubernatorial Elections* (1975); J. C. Hemphill, *Men of Mark of South Carolina*, vol. 3 (1908); Ernest M. Lander, Jr., *History of South Carolina* (1960); *Nat. Cyc. Am. Biog.*, vol. 19 (1926); William S. Powell, *The North Carolina Gazetteer* (1968); C. Ray Smith, "Charles Aurelius Smith: Operation Baptist Biography Data Form," no date (Baptist Historical Collection, Furman University Library, Greenville, S.C.); Yates Snowden and H. G. Cutler, *History of South Carolina*, vol. 5 (1920); Robert Sobel and John Raimo, eds., *Biographical Directory of the Governors of the United States*, vol. 4 (1978).

RONNIE W. FAULKNER

Smith, Charles Lee *(29 Aug. 1865–14 July 1951)*, professor, university president, publisher, and bibliophile, was born at his family's country home, Wilton, in Granville County. His father, Louis Turner Smith, had been a Confederate surgeon and after the war a physician and surgeon in Durham. The family had moved to North Carolina from Gloucester County, Va., about the beginning of the nineteenth century. His mother was Nannie Green Howell, also of a Virginia family that settled in Granville County about the same time.

At age ten Charles Lee attended the Buchanan School in Durham and also studied under Charles D. McIver. In

1882 he entered Wake Forest College, from which he was graduated two years later. After teaching for two years at the Raleigh Male Academy, he became associate editor of the *Biblical Recorder*. In January 1886 he entered Johns Hopkins University, where he was a fellow in history and political science and an instructor and lecturer in sociology. He spent part of 1888 as a student at the University of Halle, Germany, and received a Ph.D. degree from Johns Hopkins in 1889. While a student he was secretary of the Baltimore Charity Organization Society and the National Conference of Charities and Corrections. The year 1888 also saw the publication of his *History of Education in North Carolina*.

Smith held the chair of history and political science at William Jewell College, Liberty, Mo., from January 1891 through the academic year 1904–5. In 1905 he became president of Mercer University, Macon, Ga., but left after one year to return to Raleigh, where he became a member of the Edwards and Broughton Printing Company. In 1910 Smith and Needham B. Broughton acquired C. B. Edwards's interest in the firm; after Broughton died in 1914, Smith purchased his stock and became president.

In 1889 in High Point he married Sallie Lindsay Jones, the daughter of Dr. William Oliver and Elizabeth Clay Lindsay Jones. They had three sons, Noell Lindsay, William Oliver, and Charles Lee, Jr., and a daughter, Katherine Clark (Mrs. Joseph H. Hardison). Mrs. Smith died in 1931, and in 1934 he married Celeste Henkel of Statesville. Following her death the next year, he married Cora Antoinette Vaughn of Franklin, Va., in 1937.

With all three of his sons and his son-in-law serving as executives of the publishing firm, Smith found time for numerous trips abroad—fifteen to Europe and three each to Asia and Africa—largely in search of rare books. On an around-the-world cruise in 1924, he visited national leaders and published a personal interview with Mahatma Gandhi in India. He won the confidence of librarians, book dealers, and private collectors who sent him advance copies of catalogues and early information on the availability of rare volumes—several from libraries of such notables as Thomas Carlyle and John Ruskin. He housed them in his home among such art objects as a Madonna by Titian. His library eventually exceeded 7,000 volumes, many unique or nearly so.

In 1941 Smith gave his library to Wake Forest College, which in 1906 had conferred on him the honorary LL.D. degree. When college officials went to his home for a formal presentation, Smith spoke of the books as his "cherished companions." He also said: "Beginning with an incunabulum published seven years before Columbus discovered America, you will find on these shelves volumes printed by the master makers of books, illustrated by famous artists, bound by great binders and carrying dates from the fifteenth century to the present time. A large number have the bookplates of distinguished men, and many are first editions inscribed by authors."

He asked that the collection be kept intact as a separate unit of the college library. His brother, Oscar Turner Smith, at his death in 1945, left a trust to Wake Forest College for acquiring rare books to be housed alongside Charles Lee's collection as a memorial to their parents. So long as he lived, Smith was to choose the books bought by the trust.

Smith was a University of North Carolina trustee from 1911 to 1932 and served on the executive and building committees. He was a charter member of the Raleigh History Club, a group of eighteen men who gathered monthly for the presentation of scholarly papers. A member of the First Baptist Church, Smith was buried in Oakwood Cemetery, Raleigh.

SEE: Grady L. E. Carroll, *They Lived in Raleigh*, vol. 2 (1977); Edgar Estes Folk, *A Catalogue of the Library of Charles Lee Smith* (1950); *Quarterly Bulletin of Mercer University*, ser. 1 (December 1905); Raleigh *News and Observer*, 1 Oct. 1938, 17 Mar. 1940, 16 July 1951; *Raleigh Times*, 15 July 1924; *Who Was Who in America*, vol. 3 (1960);

JACK RILEY

Smith, Claiborne Thweatt *(13 Nov. 1893–28 Nov. 1989)*, physician, was born in Scotland Neck, the son of William Edward, a Confederate veteran, and Virginia Peterson Cocke Smith, a native of Prince George County, Va. He was named for two maternal relatives, John James Thweatt and John Herbert Claiborne, both physicians in Petersburg, Va. After attending local schools, Smith entered Warrenton High School, a boarding school from which he was graduated in 1911. He received a B.A. degree from The University of North Carolina in 1915 after having also completed the first year of the two-year medical course. On finishing the second year of medical school, he entered the medical school of the University of Pennsylvania. After his graduation in 1918, he joined the medical corps of the U.S. Naval Reserve. Having served his internship at the Episcopal Hospital in Philadelphia, he resigned from the navy at the close of World War I.

In 1919 Smith joined the staff of the Boice-Willis clinic and the Park View Hospital in Rocky Mount, the nearest large town to his old Halifax County home. Changes in medical practice came quickly, and he took postgraduate courses at Harvard to study the new technique of electrocardiography and a course at the Tulane Medical School to study infectious diseases. As a young physician he developed an excellent reputation as a diagnostician.

Elected to the American College of Physicians in 1929 and made an honorary member of the American Society of Internal Medicine in 1955, he frequently contributed articles to many medical journals. Smith served as president of the Nash-Edgecombe Medical Society, which he had worked to create from two independent organizations for more effective performance. He also was president of a district of the state medical society. In 1955 The University of North Carolina presented him a distinguished service award for ten years of service on the committee to establish a teaching hospital and four-year medical school on the campus. At the beginning of World War II Smith was named to the state selective service appeal board, on which he served for twenty-five years. He taught in the Park View Hospital school of nursing and arranged, through the Battle Foundation of Rocky Mount, for the creation of a loan fund for the training of student nurses there.

Smith rendered community service in Rocky Mount in a variety of positions, among which were bank director, library trustee, and vestryman and senior warden of the Church of the Good Shepherd. In later years he initiated the restoration of Old Trinity Episcopal Church, near Scotland Neck, for which he was given an award of merit by the Historical Preservation Society of North Carolina.

Shortly before his retirement, Smith addressed the local medical society on his sixty years as a physician. His recollections of personal experiences and of his association with physicians who demonstrated the wisdom and understanding of the time-honored practitioner were favorably received. His reminiscences of a time of rapid advances in science were also well understood by the younger physicians in his audience.

In 1923 Smith married Bertha Sears Albertson of Scotland Neck, and they became the parents of Claiborne T.,

Jr., Maybelle Albertson (Mrs. Falke Bailey Chipley, Jr.), and Elizabeth Herbert (Mrs. John Milton Miller, Jr.). A portrait of Smith by Sara Blakeslee of Greenville is in the possession of descendants. He was buried in Trinity Cemetery, Scotland Neck.

SEE: Emily Battle and John R. Chambliss (Rocky Mount), personal contact; John Herbert Claiborne, *Seventy-Five Years in Old Virginia* (1904); *Nashville Graphic*, 19 Aug. 1976; Claiborne T. Smith, Jr., *Smith of Scotland Neck: Planters on the Roanoke* (1976); Rocky Mount *Evening Telegram*, various issues; Trinity Church parish records, Scotland Neck.

LAWRENCE F. LONDON

Smith, Conaro Drayton *(1 Apr. 1813–30 Jan. 1894)*, clergyman, geologist, and author, was born in Buncombe County, the son of Samuel and Mary Jarrett Smith. The family moved in 1820 to land the elder Smith bought that year when some Cherokee land was sold. It had been the site of the Indians' Tessentee town and later fell in Macon County when that county was formed in 1828. There C. D. Smith attended local subscription schools. In 1832 the young man returned to Buncombe County to live on Caney River and work as a clerk for Smith and McElroy, general merchants and ginseng collectors. When Yancey County was formed in 1833, it included the site of the Smith and McElroy store. John W. McElroy became clerk of court and made C. D. Smith his deputy.

In 1836 a camp meeting was held at the Caney River Camp Ground at which Smith was converted and joined the Methodist church. The following June he was licensed to preach. His first appointment was in LaFayette, Ga., which belonged to the Holston Methodist Conference. Subsequent appointments took him to the Lebanon Circuit (1838–39); Holston College, New Market, Tenn. (1839–40), as agent; Wytheville, Va., circuit (1840–41 and 1844–45); Jonesboro, Tenn., Circuit (1841–42); Emory and Henry College (1842–44), as agent; Athens Station, Tenn. (1845–46); Rogersville, Tenn., Circuit (1846–47); and the Rogersville (1849–50) and Greeneville districts (1850–51), as presiding elder. Hiwassee College in Tennessee awarded Smith an honorary doctor of divinity degree.

Poor health obliged him to retire from the active ministry. After his formal retirement, Smith became an agent for the American Colonization Society, a position in which he was able to send two emancipated black families to Liberia. He was a delegate from Macon County to the Secession Convention of 1861–62 and represented the county in the state senate from 1862 to 1864. He must have returned to the pulpit from time to time as opportunities arose, for his *Semi-Centennial Sermon, Delivered . . . Before the Holston Conference, M.E. Church, South At Its Session in Asheville, N.C., October, 1888* was published in the latter year.

Long interested in geology and mineralogy, Smith had been making discoveries and reporting observations in those fields. As a result of this work he served as assistant state geologist under Ebenezer Emmons and was a coworker with W. C. Kerr. Appendix D of Kerr's *Report of the Geological Survey of North Carolina* (1875) contains two contributions by Smith: "Corundum and Its Associated Rocks" (5 pages) and "Essay on the Geology of Western North Carolina" (22 pages). The *Smithsonian Institution Report* for 1876 contained a piece by Smith on "Ancient Mica Mines in North Carolina." He once possessed a remarkable collection of mineral specimens gathered over nearly a lifetime that he delighted in showing, but their eventual fate is unknown. He was also the author of *A Brief History of Macon County, North Carolina*, published in 1891, and he wrote a number of biographical sketches for the *Holston Methodist*.

In 1847 near Knoxville, Tenn., Smith married Margaret R., the daughter of Captain Marcus D. Bearden. They became the parents of eight children, but only five—Frank T., C. C., Emma, Conaro, and Marcus—survived childhood. While crossing Nantahala Mountain between Hayesville in Clay County and Macon County to gather timber and mineral specimens for display at the Chicago World's Fair, Smith suffered a serious injury. In dismounting from his horse, his foot slipped on a damp, mossy root dislocating his thigh bone, and he lay on the damp ground for eighteen hours before being found. Badly crippled and in great pain, he died about a year later.

SEE: John P. Arthur, *Western North Carolina: A History, 1730–1913* (1914); *Asheville Daily Citizen*, 30 Jan. 1894; John L. Cheney, Jr., ed., *North Carolina Government, 1585–1979* (1981); R. N. Price, *Holston Methodism*, vol. 4 (1912 [portrait]).

WILLIAM S. POWELL

Smith, Egbert Watson *(15 Jan. 1862–25 Aug. 1944)*, minister, author, and head of Foreign Missions for the Presbyterian Church of the United States, was born in Greensboro, the son of Dr. Jacob Henry, minister of the First Presbyterian Church, by his second wife, Mary Kelly Watson Smith, the daughter of Judge Egbert Reid Watson of Charlottesville, Va., for whom he was named. After attending school in Greensboro, Egbert Smith entered Davidson College in 1878 and was graduated in 1882 as valedictorian of his class. He taught school for a year in York, S.C., then entered Union Theological Seminary in Virginia to prepare for the ministry. Upon completion of his three-year course in 1886, he was called to be associate pastor at the First Presbyterian Church in Greensboro, serving as superintendent of Sunday school and responsible for mission work. The Westminister Presbyterian Church was organized as a consequence of his efforts, and in October 1887 Smith was called to be its minister.

In 1891 he was placed in charge of all evangelical work for the Synod of North Carolina, and during 1892–93 he served as superintendent of Home Missions for the Synod of Mississippi. In both these posts he demonstrated his organizational ability and skill in presenting a cause. On 15 Apr. 1894 he married Mary Black Wallace, the daughter of Judge Jesse George Wallace of Franklin, Tenn. They had two sons and two daughters: Margaret Heiskell, Egbert Watson, Jessie Wallace, and Marion Wallace. Also in 1894 Davidson College awarded Smith the doctor of divinity degree.

He returned to Greensboro's First Presbyterian Church in December 1893 to assist his aging father as copastor and remained as minister after his father death's in November 1897. The aristocratic appearance of Egbert Smith, with mustache, goatee, and pince-nez, was not indicative of the warm and sparkling personality within. His congregation spoke of his eloquent preaching and loving ministry. "From teaching a blind member to use a typewriter in order to earn a living to ministering to . . . souls in distress, he was indeed the `Father of his people,'" said Elder John W. Simpson. The local newspaper described him "astride his bike calling on communicants, the tails of his frock coat flying in the wind." During the twelve years of his pastorate, the church's membership increased to over nine hundred, and a new Sunday school building was erected with a skating rink in the basement. Under his leadership the church involved itself in home mission work, helping to establish three churches in the city and giving financial support to three others in the state. In January 1906 Smith became minister of the Second Presbyterian Church of Louisville, Ky., which under him became one of the strongest in the assembly.

In 1911 Smith left the pastorate to become executive secretary of Foreign Missions for the Presbyterian Church of the United States, headquartered in Nashville, Tenn. Seeking to place its operations on a more systematic basis, he wrote manuals for the guidance of missionaries and devised means of achieving a more dependable annual income for their work. He believed in the ordination of native people as ministers so that missionaries could move on to new fields. In 1927 the Presbyterian Church of the United States joined with fifteen other denominations to establish the United Church in China—an attempt to place Christianity above denominational barriers. By that date the Southern Presbyterian church was supporting 338 ministers, doctors, nurses, teachers, and others in the mission field.

During those years Smith wrote numerous books, most of which, like *The Desire of All Nations* (1928), were designed to stimulate interest in and support for mission activities. His first book, *The Creed of Presbyterians* (1901, rev. ed. 1941), written for lay people, went through numerous printings and had the largest circulation of any book on that subject. Significantly, it minimized those aspects that set Presbyterianism apart, stressing, rather, that the creed, in its essentials, was one upon which most Protestants could agree. And Smith urged his readers to do their "best to further that growing sense of the unity of all believers in Christ." In *Paul's Way in Christ* (1942), he described the techniques that made Paul an effective preacher. Many of those traits applied to Smith's own preaching and writing: his prose was clear and easily understood, he illustrated his points with interesting stories, he set a target or goal, he was earnest, and he stressed *now* as the time to act.

In 1932, at age seventy, Smith retired as executive secretary of Foreign Missions, but the church, unwilling to dispense with his services, appointed him to the newly created post of field secretary. Until his death from a heart attack twelve years later, he continued to travel, write, and speak in support of foreign missions. He was buried in Greensboro's Green Hill Cemetery. For thirty-three years he had been the strongest advocate of foreign missions in the Presbyterian Church of the United States and perhaps in America.

SEE: *Annals of an American Family*, [1953] (copy, North Carolina Collection, University of North Carolina, Chapel Hill); Ethel S. Arnett, *Greensboro, North Carolina* (1955); Davidsonian Collection (Davidson College Library, Davidson, N.C.); *Greensboro Daily News*, 12 Nov. 1905, 26 Aug. 1944; *New York Times*, 27 Aug. 1944; Raleigh *News and Observer*, 27 Aug. 1944; [Henry Smith Richardson], Eugene C. Scott, ed., *Ministerial Directory of the Presbyterian Church, U.S., 1861–1951* (1950); John W. Simpson, *History of the First Presbyterian Church of Greensboro, N.C.* (1945).

NORRIS W. PREYER

Smith, Ezekiel Ezra *(23 May 1852–6 Dec. 1933)*, educator and diplomat, the son of free blacks Alexander and Caroline Smith, was born in Duplin County on the farm where his father was working as a laborer. His mother's family had been free for many generations, but his father was the first of his family to be emancipated. Because of laws prohibiting the teaching of blacks, the young boy received no formal education, but he did learn from his white playmates. After the Civil War he attended a school in Wilmington conducted at night by the Freedmen's Bureau, but he worked in naval stores during the day. In 1869 he moved to Wayne County, where he attended the equivalent of high school while also becoming a teacher himself. After four years of preparation, he enrolled in Shaw University and received a bachelor's degree in 1878.

Accepting a position as principal of a black grade school in Goldsboro, young Smith began a lifelong friendship with Dr. Edwin A. Alderman, principal of one of the white schools there. In 1883 he was selected to succeed Charles W. Chestnut as head of the Fayetteville State Normal School, then only five years old, which met in a small four-room building and faced financial difficulties. Smith is credited with saving the school, now Fayetteville State University. Also an ordained Baptist minister, he was pastor of the First Baptist Church in Fayetteville for six years. He served as president of the State Baptist Convention and was a member of the executive board of the Lott Carey Foreign Missions Convention.

The fact that Smith had been a member of the Democratic party since the early 1870s is assumed to be the reason he won legislative support for his school. His political orientation also resulted in his appointment by Democratic president Grover Cleveland as resident minister and general consul to the Republic of Liberia in 1888. In that post he was able to restore more cordial relations between Liberia and the United States.

With a change in the national administration, Smith returned home and earned a doctorate from Shaw University. He spent one year as principal of a high school in Asheville before returning to the Fayetteville institution that he had previously led. With a new campus and new buildings came better support and development into a degree-granting college. He remained the head of that institution for the remainder of his life, spending a total of forty-two years there except for an occasional leave of absence. He was president of the State Teachers' Association in 1906.

A man of many talents, Smith was appointed a major in the Home Guard in 1880 and was adjutant with the rank of captain in the Third North Carolina Regiment in 1898; though recruited for service in the Spanish-American War, he was never called up. In 1881 he organized and operated the *Carolina Enterprise*, the first newspaper in the state for blacks. Later he was editor of the *Banner Enterprise* and the *Baptist Sentinel*.

Smith married Willie A. Burnett on 17 Nov. 1875, and they were the parents of one son, E. E., Jr., who became a physician in Newport News, Va. His wife died in 1907, and the following year he married Nannie Louise Goode. He was buried in Brookside Cemetery, Fayetteville.

SEE: Arthur B. Caldwell, *History of the American Negro and His Institutions*, vol. 4, North Carolina ed. (1921 [portrait]); *Fayetteville Observer*, 7 Dec. 1933; Charles H. Hamlin, *Ninety Bits of North Carolina Biography* (1946); Nathan C. Newbold, *Five North Carolina Negro Educators* (1939 [portrait]); *Paths Toward Freedom* (1976); *Who Was Who in America*, vol. 3 (1960).

MARTIN REIDINGER

Smith, Henry Louis *(30 July 1859–27 Feb. 1951)*, physicist and college president, was born in Greensboro, the eldest son of Dr. Jacob Henry, a Presbyterian minister, and his second wife, Mary Kelly Watson Smith, the daughter of Judge Egbert Reid Watson of Charlottesville, Va. Smith attended Greensboro's Presbyterian High School, run by his uncle, Samuel Cunningham Smith, until 1877, when he entered Davidson College; he was graduated with honors in 1881. For the next five years he was principal of the Selma Academy, where he first demonstrated his teaching and promotional abilities by quadrupling the school's enrollment and constructing a new building for classes.

Called by Davidson College to be professor of natural science (physics and astronomy), he obtained a one year's leave of absence to do graduate work at the University of Virginia, from which he received an M.A. degree in 1887 before commencing his teaching in the fall. He returned to Virginia for the 1889–90 academic year and earned his Ph.D. in physics. On 4 Aug. 1896 Smith married Julia Lorraine DuPuy, the daughter of Dr. John James DuPuy, a Davidson physician; they had eight children.

Smith's scientific knowledge twice had international consequences. Learning of Wilhelm Röntgen's experiments with X-rays, Smith shot a bullet into the hand of a cadaver and developed one of the earliest X-ray pictures in America; it was published in the *Charlotte Observer* on 27 Feb. 1896. Shortly afterwards he used the X-ray to locate a thimble lodged in a young girl's throat, making possible its surgical removal. This was the first clinical application of the X-ray, and news of the event was spread around the world.

Near the end of World War I a prize was offered for a means of informing the German people of President Woodrow Wilson's peace plans. Smith proposed attaching Wilson's message to small gas-filled balloons to be released in France, where the prevailing winds and the timed release of gas would carry them to Germany. Adopting the idea, the Allies released millions of these balloons, and most German soldiers who surrendered carried Wilson's message with them. The president later credited Smith with substantially shortening the war.

A student described Henry Louis Smith as a "brilliant, enthusiastic teacher," but it was as an administrator that he was most celebrated. He was named vice-president of Davidson College in 1896 and elected president in 1901. Davidson had languished in the forty years since the Civil War, but Smith, with his active mind and boundless energy, initiated and carried through so many projects that the students nicknamed him "Project." During his thirteen years as president, he more than tripled the college's enrollment, producing corresponding increases in faculty, plant, and endowment. In 1912 he left to become president of Virginia's Washington and Lee University, from which his father had graduated, and his efforts met with similar success there. Its larger student body doubled in size along with faculty, plant, and endowment. A fine speaker, Smith traveled widely promoting his institution and seeking funding from every possible source.

He lived at a time when liberal arts colleges, stressing classical education and pedagogical drill, were being challenged by land grant, vocationally oriented universities and by the high standards of the new graduate schools following the German university model. Smith argued that the liberal arts curriculum should prepare its students for the professional and business world they would be entering, and at Washington and Lee University he succeeded in establishing a School of Journalism. Both at Davidson and at Washington and Lee he worked hard to upgrade intellectual standards and admission requirements, believing that it was dishonest for a school that claimed to be Christian to do shoddy work. At the same time, he felt that a sound body was necessary for a sound mind and established facilities for recreation and exercise—one of his projects at Davidson was a lake to provide water sports for the students.

A Presbyterian elder and the son of a minister, he was not disturbed by the Darwinian controversy and made it clear to students that there was no necessary conflict between science and religion. He saw the individual as an "immortal being allied with God himself" and felt the role of a Christian liberal arts institution was to mold its students into effective leaders. In speeches and pamphlets he exhorted his students to develop their intellectual, physical, and moral capacities to the fullest in order to fulfill this role, but his own example probably had the greatest effect. He proved that the small liberal arts institution could adapt and play a meaningful role in American higher education.

In 1929, at age seventy, Smith retired and moved to Greensboro. Participating in the religious and civic life of the city, he remained intellectually and physically active until shortly before his death. He served as an elder and Bible class teacher in the church where his father and brother had formerly preached and was in great demand as a public speaker at colleges, civic clubs, and other groups. In 1947 he published *This Troubled Century*, a collection of essays and speeches. Though the century was troubled with wars and other problems, Smith remained ever optimistic and forward-looking, for he believed that the universe was controlled by a beneficent, loving God. His youthful zest and excitement about the future were reflected in a local newspaper column he wrote on "Science and Our World." In it he discussed new scientific developments and how they could transform the future for the better.

A gentle man who always appealed to the best in others, Smith was nevertheless a tireless fighter for social justice, attacking wrongs with the same drive that helped him succeed as a college president. After his death at age ninety-one, Greensboro named its first public housing project for him—both to honor him and because he had been the key figure in persuading the city council to provide decent housing for the poor. He was buried in Forest Lawn cemetery.

Smith was a member of Phi Beta Kappa and Omicron Delta Kappa honorary societies and held honorary LL.D. degrees from The University of North Carolina and Davidson College. His unpublished papers and correspondence are at the Washington and Lee University Library, Lexington, Va. Pamphlets and newspaper clippings by and about him are in the Davidson College Library.

SEE: *Christian Observer*, 4 Apr. 1951; *The Circle of Omicron Delta Kappa* (Summer 1951); Ollinger Crenshaw, *General Lee's College: The Rise and Growth of Washington and Lee University* (1969); *DAB*, supp. 5 (1977); *Greensboro Record*, 27–28 Feb. 1951; *Greensboro Daily News*, 28 Feb. 1951; John W. Simpson, *History of the First Presbyterian Church of Greensboro, N.C.* (1945).

NORRIS W. PREYER

Smith, Hildreth Hosea *(17 Feb. 1820–14 Sept. 1908)*, educator and journalist, was born in Deerfield, N.H., the son of William True, a farmer, and Martha Ambrose Smith. He was the father of Senator Hoke Smith of Georgia. His ancestors included the Reverend Henry Smith, a seventeenth-century Puritan missionary in Connecticut, and he himself was a first cousin on his mother's side of Mary Baker Eddy, founder of the Church of Christ, Scientist. Smith attended Foxcroft Academy in Maine and Bowdoin College, where he was graduated near the top of his class in 1842. Afterwards he taught school briefly in Bucksport, Maine, then returned to Bowdoin and received a master of arts degree in 1845. He next proceeded to Washington, D.C., where he read law and was licensed to practice, but failing eyesight soon forced him to retire from the bar.

For a time he apparently wandered, traveling briefly to the California gold fields and teaching for a year in Lancaster, Pa. In 1851 he was appointed professor of mathematics, natural sciences, and modern languages at newly founded Catawba College in Newton, N.C. Smith seems to have impressed Catawba's students and trustees from the start; appointed president of the college in 1853, he is generally credited with setting the school on a firm academic foundation.

In December 1856 Smith was elected professor of modern languages at The University of North Carolina, a chair he held until the coming of President Solomon Pool's Reconstruction administration in 1868. He offered courses in French, German, Spanish, and Italian, reportedly demonstrating a high proficiency in all of these languages, as well as in mathematics and astronomy. Although described as a gentle man, he was nicknamed "Old Tige" by his students, partly because of his great physical strength and partly because of his courage, displayed in fighting a sensational house fire off campus.

After leaving Chapel Hill in August 1868, Smith for several years operated a small academy in Lincolnton. During 1871 he moved to Atlanta, Ga., to become principal of the Luckie Street Grammar School. In 1873, at the request of the Peabody Fund, he took over the organization of the Shelbyville, Tenn., public schools, with such "marked" success that in 1877 he was called upon to organize a similar system in Houston, Tex. In September 1879 Smith was elected principal of Sam Houston State Normal College at Huntsville, Tex. The next year he received an honorary doctor of letters degree from Baylor University.

Smith returned to Atlanta about 1882 and served as principal of Girls' High School. In 1888 he resigned to become literary editor of the *Atlanta Journal*, in which his son Hoke had recently acquired a controlling share. Retiring in 1893 due to ill health, he resided in Atlanta until his death.

In addition to articles for the *Journal*, Smith wrote *The Robertsonian System of French, with Rules of Pronunciation, and a Full Vocabulary* (1858). On 19 May 1853 he married Mary Brent Hoke, a sister of Robert F. Hoke, the Confederate major general. Besides [Michael] Hoke Smith (2 Sept. 1855–27 Nov. 1931), the couple had three other children: Frances (Fanny, b. 1854), Lizzie (b. 1861), and Burton (b. 1864), a prominent Atlanta attorney and a partner in his brother's firm.

SEE: Kemp P. Battle, *History of the University of North Carolina*, vol. 1 (1907); Dewey W. Grantham, *Hoke Smith and the Politics of the New South* (1958); Jacob C. Leonard, *History of Catawba College* (1927 [portrait]); *Proceedings of the Trustees of the Peabody Educational Fund from Their Origin on the Eighth of February, 1867*, 2 vols. (1875, 1916); Hoke Smith Collection (University of Georgia Library, Athens).

BENNETT L. STEELMAN

Smith, H[ilrie] Shelton *(8 May 1893–8 Jan. 1987)*, teacher and author, was born in McLeansville, the son of Henry Brooks and Lula Jane Wyrick Smith. In 1915, while enrolled at Elon College, he was ordained to the ministry in the First Congregational Christian Church in Durham; he was graduated from Elon in 1917. During World War I he served in France as a chaplain with the rank of first lieutenant. Continuing his interrupted studies at Yale University, he first received a B.D. degree and then in 1923 a Ph.D. Later he was granted honorary degrees from Defiance College in Ohio (D.D., 1926) and Elon (Litt.D., 1940). Between 1923 and 1928 he was director of leadership education for the International Council of Religious Education. He then became associate professor of religious education at the Teachers College of Columbia University (1928–29) and at Yale (1929–31).

Smith joined the Duke University faculty in 1931 to establish a religious education program. There for a time he taught Christian ethics, the philosophy of religious education, and American religious thought. In 1945 he became James B. Duke Professor of American Religious Thought. At various times during his career he also lectured at the Pacific School of Religion, the Washington Cathedral, Hebrew Union College, the Austin Presbyterian Theological Seminary, the Princeton Theological Seminary, and elsewhere. A popular lecturer, he spoke to the American Society of Church History, the American Theological Association, the International Council on Religious Education, and other organizations. Among Smith's books were *Faith and Nurture* (1941), *Changing Conceptions of Original Sin* (1955), and *In His Image, But . . . Racism in Southern Religion, 1780–1910* (1972). He was coauthor of *American Christianity: An Historical Interpretation with Representative Documents* in two volumes (1960).

Under Smith's leadership, the study of American Christianity became a recognized field for investigation and study. He also supported local ecumenical activity and for this purpose was active in the creation of the North Carolina Council of Churches, of which he was the first president. At Duke he directed the program for graduate studies in religion from 1935 to 1962; its offerings leading to a doctorate was the first in a southern university.

In 1918 he married Alma Bowden, and they were the parents of a son, Richard Bowden. In Durham he was a member of the Pilgrim United Church of Christ.

SEE: *Directory of American Scholars*, vol. 4, *Philosophy, Religion, and Law* (1964); *Durham Morning Herald*, 31 Jan. 1963, 10 Jan. 1987; *Durham Sun*, 9 Jan. 1987; *Greensboro News and Record*, 19 Jan. 1987; Stuart C. Henry, *A Miscellany of American Christianity: Essays in Honor of H. Shelton Smith* (1963); Samuel S. Hill, ed., *Encyclopedia of Religion in the South* (1984); *Who's Who in the South and Southwest* (1952).

WILLIAM S. POWELL

Smith, Hoke. *See* **Smith, [Michael] Hoke.**

Smith, Isaac Hughes *(5 May 1852?–6 July 1915)*, black legislator, realtor, and philanthropist, was born in the Craven County area, the son of Thomas and Harriet Smith, both natives of North Carolina. Little is known about his early life, and whether or not he was born into slavery is an open question. It is known, however, that he was educated by a white family and later attended St. Augustine's College in Raleigh.

Deed records indicate that Smith began buying and

selling property in Craven County in the early 1870s. As he grew older the volume of his real estate business increased, and eventually he became a large property owner in New Bern. While acquiring his landholdings, Smith taught school in the Craven County area. In 1880 he was teaching and residing in New Bern with a black schoolteacher and former Episcopal clergyman named Alexander Bass.

When Smith became more prominent in his real estate venture, he quit teaching and entered the banking profession. He operated a money-lending and insurance agency located on Middle Street in New Bern to complement his growing realty and rental operation. A section of New Bern in which Smith owned many stores and homes was named Smithtown in his honor.

After achieving a high degree of success in business, Smith in the late 1890s decided to shift his efforts to politics. He became active in the Republican party and claimed to be one of the first men in the United States to propose William McKinley for president. Smith donated large sums of money to the Republican cause and supported Daniel Russell for governor.

In 1898 he was elected to represent Craven County in the state house of representatives. During the 1899–1900 session of the General Assembly, Smith was outspoken on many issues. Early in the session he denounced Republicans for expelling him from a caucus. Believing he deserved better treatment, he reminded his fellow legislators that Governor Russell owed his election to blacks. Smith introduced a resolution that would ask each congressman and senator from North Carolina to support the passage of a law that would restore to blacks funds they had lost about 1875 with the failure of the Freedman's Saving and Trust Company. He also proposed bills to equalize the pay of state witnesses, sheriffs, and clerks and to establish compulsory education for children between six and eleven in Craven County. Smith initiated several other resolutions, including a request that at least one black trustee be chosen for black institutions and a plea that the black race be heard by the Committee on Constitutional Amendments.

After serving one term in the General Assembly, Smith again turned his attention to business interests in Craven County. At the time of his death he had accumulated an estate purportedly worth about $150,000 and was described as the wealthiest black man in eastern North Carolina.

Smith left a rather detailed will, which was probated on 9 July 1915. In this document he appointed an executor and trustee to continue to operate his business after his death. Smith provided well for his family and gave five hundred dollars to Shaw University and to the National Religious Training Schools in Durham and Raleigh. He also donated one thousand dollars for black churches in New Bern and designated an identical amount for the Masonic order and Odd Fellows organizations.

Smith married Visey Dudley in Craven County on 24 Dec. 1875, and they had one son, Livingston. On 30 June 1898 he was married a second time, to Carrie Marie Rhone (1872–1962). They had five children: Isaac Hughes, Jr. (1899–1953), Harriet, Henrietta (b. 2 Jan. 1904), and two who died in infancy. Isaac married Annie Day Shepard, the daughter of James E. Shepard, founder of the National Religious Training School and Chatauqua, the forerunner of North Carolina Central University.

Smith held membership in the Knights of Pythias, served as grand orator of the Negro Masons of North Carolina, and was an active member of the Episcopal church. He died of diabetes at his home on Johnson Street in New Bern and was buried at Greenwood Cemetery.

SEE: *Baltimore Sun*, 10 Jan. 1899; John L. Cheney, Jr., ed., *North Carolina Government, 1585–1974* (1975); Census of 1880 and 1900, Deed, Estate, Marriage, and Will Records of Craven County, and North Carolina State Board of Health, Bureau of Vital Statistics (North Carolina State Archives, Raleigh); Annie Day Donaldson (granddaughter), personal contact, 23 Sept. 1980; *House Journal, 1899*; *Kinston Free Press*, 7 July 1915; Raleigh *News and Observer*, 24 Aug. 1899 (portrait), 12 July 1915; Isaac H. Smith, "How Long Shall the Present State of Affairs Exist?" (broadside), 1899 (North Carolina Collection, University of North Carolina, Chapel Hill); Mrs. Henrietta Walters (daughter), personal contact, 23 Sept. 1980; William Farrior Ward, personal contact, 22 Sept. 1980.

STEPHEN E. MASSENGILL

Smith, Jacob Henry *(13 Aug. 1820–22 Nov. 1897)*, Presbyterian minister, was born in Lexington, Va., the eldest son of Samuel Runckle and Margaret Fuller Smith, daughter of Jacob Fuller. His father was of German ancestry and may have been a cabinetmaker; his mother's forebears were of Scotch-Irish, French, and German lineage. Smith attended Washington College (now Washington and Lee University) and was graduated with distinction in 1843. Deciding to enter the ministry, he spent the next three years at Union Theological Seminary, where a fellow classmate described him as a methodical, disciplined student whose preparations were uniformly perfect, but who was, at the same time, vigorous and "of a cordial and joyous temperament."

Smith finished his seminary studies in August 1846 and the following month began his ministry at Pittsylvania Court House, Va. On 15 Mar. 1848 he married Catherine Malvina Miller, the daughter of Thomas Miller of Powhatan County. Two years later he became principal of the Samuel Davies Institute in Halifax County, Va., where he also taught Latin and Greek. While there he received calls from churches in Chicago, Richmond, Petersburg, Danville, Greensboro, and Charlottesville, but only after the death of his wife in June 1854 did he leave the institute to accept the call of the Charlottesville church. In Charlottesville Smith oversaw the construction of a new church building and helped organize a Literary-Theological Club, one of whose members was Judge Egbert Richard Watson. On 8 Jan. 1857 the thirty-seven-year-old Smith married Watson's twenty-year-old red-haired daughter, Mary Kelly Watson. Smith already had a six-year-old son from his first marriage, and from this second marriage were born five sons and three daughters; however, one son and one daughter died in early childhood.

In 1859 a second call was made to Smith by the First Presbyterian Church of Greensboro, and this time he accepted, arriving in April to take up his new duties. When the Civil War broke out, he served as a visiting chaplain to Confederate troops at Wilmington and in Virginia, and in March 1865 the church was turned into a hospital to care for the wounded from the Battle of Bentonville.

The ties between minister and congregation were close; Smith wrote in 1865 that the membership's "love and liberality have relieved me during these times from scarcity and from worldly anxiety." From small beginnings, he built his church into one of the largest and most influential in the synod. In 1877 he reported to the presbytery that 407 members had joined the church since his arrival and that 200 were enrolled in the Sabbath School.

Two churches were formed from the First Presbyterian—in 1868 its 139 black members established St. James Presbyterian Church, and in 1887, in response to an appeal for a church in South Greensboro, 80 members formed the Westminister Presbyterian Church. But the First Presbyterian was still too small for its membership, and in 1889 plans were made for a new building that was completed in 1892.

During these years Smith played an active role in the courts and General Assembly of the Presbyterian church and served on the board of trustees of Davidson College and Union Theological Institute. He was awarded honorary doctor of divinity degrees by Hampden-Sydney College (1872) and The University of North Carolina (1877).

Smith was an outstanding preacher with a rich, full voice. At a time when revivals were a regular part of the church year, he was in great demand throughout North Carolina and Virginia. Governor Alfred M. Scales was so impressed that he offered to pay Smith's salary for him to be a full-time evangelist, but his congregation (and probably Smith himself) would not allow it. Smith did not use "hellfire and damnation" preaching but, instead, relied on scholarly, intellectual persuasion and an appeal to the consciences of individuals to transform themselves into the persons God would have them be. This reflected the affection, warmth, and joyous nature of Smith's own personality. He was a sprightly conversationalist with a good sense of humor who remained young in spirit.

By selling off tracts of his land, Smith was able to send all his children to college. His five sons became outstanding in their own right, three as ministers and two as educators; all reflected the intellect and spirit of their parents. In 1893 Smith's son Egbert was called to be copastor of First Presbyterian in order to relieve his aging father of some of his duties. Four years later Smith died at age seventy-seven after thirty-eight years of service to his congregation and city. The citizens of Greensboro, by public subscription, raised funds for a tall granite monument that stands over his grave in the city's Green Hill Cemetery. Smith's notes and some sermons are in the archives of the First Presbyterian Church.

SEE: Bettie D. Caldwell, ed., *Founders and Builders of Greensboro* (1925); *Heritage 150: First Presbyterian Church of Greensboro* (1974); *In Memorium: Rev. J. Henry Smith, D.D.* (1898); John W. Simpson, *History of the First Presbyterian Church of Greensboro, N.C.* (1945); Susie M. H. Smith, *The Love That Never Failed* (1928).

NORRIS W. PREYER

Smith, James Strudwick *(8 Sept. 1787–7 Dec. 1852)*, physician and politician, was born in Orange County of unknown parentage; he may have been the illegitimate son of William F. Strudwick, for whom the court issued bastardy charges in 1788, omitting the name of the female involved. The Strudwicks were near neighbors of the Reuben Smith family of the Hawfields. James Strudwick Smith's many-faceted career brought him both fortune and misfortune. He studied medicine with Dr. James Webb of Hillsborough in 1810 and then, with the help of friends, completed two courses of study at the University of Pennsylvania in the winters of 1810–11 and 1811–12 but left without pursuing a degree because of insufficient funds. Later, when the state of North Carolina contemplated reestablishing a medical society, Smith, hoping to be made president, applied for his diploma and paid the necessary fee. His degree was granted on 26 June 1821, and his diploma was dated 1822.

Though apparently a sound and successful physician, he was not content to devote himself entirely to his profession. He wished, perhaps, for greater fortune than that could yield him. Throughout his life he engaged in a variety of business partnerships, starting in 1815 with a relation of his wife when he established the firm of James S. Smith and Company, probably a short-lived merchandising business. His next venture was with Dr. Thomas Jefferson Faddis. They started another general store in Hillsborough in 1819, but their account books show that in 1824 the partnership became entirely medical; their later accounts were only for medical services and drugs.

During the same period of the early 1820s, Smith was a partner of Josiah Turner in a copper shop, though he soon sold his share of the business. His largest venture was with Thomas D. Crain in the operation of mills, distilleries, and tanyard of which Smith became sole owner in 1836.

During these years Smith was investing heavily in land. He had received from his father-in-law large tracts in Chatham County, but in addition he bought land in Orange County, lots and houses in Hillsborough for his dwelling, office, and business operations, and over 7,000 acres in Illinois that had been granted to soldiers as bounty land. Like many other ambitious men of his day Smith overextended himself, and in 1845 he went bankrupt and was divested of all his property except what he had been able to transfer to his wife and children, to the chagrin of his creditors.

Ill health had interrupted his medical career in the late 1830s, for the newspaper in 1840 stated that he was resuming his practice but could not take night calls because of failing eyesight. His son Francis, by then associated with him, would take those calls. Again in 1845 he announced that he was going to devote himself entirely to his practice, an ironic notice considering the forfeiture at just that time of all his other interests. It was probably at this time, too, that he moved from Hillsborough to the Smith Level Road house outside Chapel Hill (still standing in 1978) where all his family members were to live out their lives.

By this time, Smith could no longer command support in his political career. He had early entered public service as a town trustee and justice of the peace in 1811. Then followed election as a Democratic Republican to represent the Hillsborough district in both the Fifteenth and Sixteenth congresses (4 Mar. 1817–3 Mar. 1821), in which he conscientiously served the farming interests of his constituents by advocating the repeal of various internal duties and opposing the tax on bar iron and distilleries. Smith tried to reform the presidential electoral procedure by giving the common man a larger share in the process. Despite his effectiveness as a worker and speaker, he was defeated in his bid for a third term.

He did succeed, however, in winning that same year Hillsborough's seat in the state legislature, a franchise he would later oppose successfully as a delegate to the 1835 constitutional convention, which eliminated borough representation. In his last two races, running on the Whig ticket for the Senate in 1832 and the House of Representatives in 1841, Smith was defeated.

Cultural and social organizations also interested Smith. He was a vice-president of the Hillsborough Literary Association to promote "social intercourse and mutual improvement," the first of its kind in the state, and a trustee of the Female Academy run by the Reverend William M. Green.

Smith joined the Eagle Lodge of the Masonic order in 1819 and quickly rose to the top, a pattern typical of all his other endeavors. He was appointed to a committee to plan a building for his lodge in 1821 and laid the cornerstone of the new building as grand master of the order in North Carolina in 1822. The only known portrait of Smith hangs in this building in Hillsborough; a copy hangs in the grand lodge.

The construction of the Masonic lodge was not Smith's only connection with a historic building. In 1844 he sat on a committee that determined the location and plan of the new Orange County Courthouse in Hillsborough. John Berry's famous building was the result, and Smith was deputy grand master for its dedication ceremonies.

Smith was elected a trustee of The University of North Carolina in 1821 and a member of its board of visitors in 1827. As a trustee he suggested that a physician be employed and paid for by fees collected from the students; he offered himself for this post. This kind of self-promotion seems to have been typical of the man and accounts for much of his unpopularity with his colleagues. His energy and talent put him quickly at the top of whatever field he entered, but his brash ambition always brought him dislike and loss of favor. Willie P. Mangum referred to him as the "puffing" doctor, and Dr. Webb, when asked to give a deposition in a lawsuit involving Smith, was forced to admit that he would not trust him when Smith's interest was at stake. Another of his contemporaries wrote, "Can't we keep the man of many pursuits at home? . . . He is a perfect Proteus, always varying." These are probably just accusations, but even his critics would probably have acknowledged the large role he played in his time and place, a force always to reckon with if never really to admire or respect.

From his marriage with Delia Jones (bond dated 18 Oct. 1813), the daughter of Francis and Mary Page Jones of Chatham County, Smith had three children: Mary Ruffin (1814–85), Francis Jones (1816–77), and James Sidney (1819–67). All were unmarried and left no legitimate descendants, but by both sons through a favorite slave of the Smith family named Harriot there were numerous progeny including Dr. Pauli Murray, a lawyer and activist for blacks' and woman's rights.

SEE: Kemp P. Battle, *History of the University of North Carolina*, vol. 1 (1907); *Biog. Dir. Am. Cong.* (1961); Cameron Family Papers (Southern Historical Collection, University of North Carolina, Chapel Hill); Day Book, 1819–26, of Drs. James S. Smith and Thos. J. Faddis (Manuscript Department, Duke University Library, Durham); J. G. de Roulhac Hamilton, ed., *Papers of Thomas Ruffin*, 4 vols. (1920); *Hillsborough Recorder*, 12 Nov. 1840, 12 Sept. 1844, 21 Aug., 6 Nov. 1845, 15 Dec. 1852, 22 Nov. 1854; William H. Hoyt, ed., *Papers of Archibald D. Murphey*, 2 vols. (1914); Hugh T. Lefler and Paul Wager, eds., *Orange County, 1752–1952* (1953); Pauli Murray, *Proud Shoes* (1956); Orange County Court Minutes, 1811 (North Carolina State Archives, Raleigh); Orange County Deed Books (Orange County Courthouse, Hillsborough); James S. Smith Account Books, Mary Ruffin Smith Papers, and James Webb Papers (Southern Historical Collection, University of North Carolina, Chapel Hill); William R. Smith, "Brief Sketch of Past Grand Master J. Strudwick Smith," *Orphan's Friend and Masonic Journal* 59 (15 June 1934); John H. Wheeler, *Historical Sketches of North Carolina* (1851).

JEAN B. ANDERSON

Smith, John Baptist *(19 Sept. 1843–31 May 1923)*, Confederate army signal officer and inventor of a forerunner of naval blinker signaling, was born at Hycotee in Caswell County, the fifth child of Richard Ivy (an 1820 graduate of The University of North Carolina) and Mary Amis Goodwin Smith. His great-grandfather, Colonel Samuel Smith (1729–1800), served in the French and Indian War and for his service received a grant of three thousand acres in Granville County. He fought under General James Wolfe at Quebec and later named his home Abram's Plain after the 1759 battle in which Wolfe was killed.

One of the early volunteers, John Baptist Smith left Hampden-Sydney College on 15 Apr. 1861 to enlist, at age seventeen, in the "Milton Blues," which became Company C, Thirteenth Regiment, North Carolina Troops. He rose to the rank of sergeant in Company C and, on moving to Virginia, was detailed, along with his brother, William Goodwin Smith, for training and service in a signaling system devised by Captain James F. Milligan. By order of the secretary of war on 6 Mar. 1862, all soldiers serving in that capacity were transferred into a unit called the Independent Signal Corps (ISC; in contrast to the regular Signal Corps), commanded by Captain (later Major) Milligan. Although transferred against his wishes, Smith and his brother William (who joined him in October 1863) found some compensation in learning that they were part of a handpicked group, one that included in its ranks the Lanier brothers, Sidney (the poet) and Clifford, J. Hoge Tyler (a postwar governor of Virginia), and George T. Goetchins (a postwar Presbyterian leader in North Carolina). The ISC operated a series of signal and observation posts along the James and Appomattox rivers, with headquarters at Norfolk and later at Petersburg. His signal duties made Smith an eyewitness to the historic *Monitor* and *Virginia* (*Merrimac*) encounter.

With the expansion of the ISC early in 1863, Smith was transferred to its new Second Company as first sergeant. By then he had already established a reputation for one so young. In July 1862 he had been ordered to assist in the organization of a signal system in the Cape Fear area, where, serving under Colonel William Lamb as signal officer at Fort Fisher, he was confronted with the special problems of signaling with blockade-runners. The Confederate signal system (invented in the decade before the war and patterned after that of Albert J. Myer of the U.S. Army) depended on a flag by day and torches by night, waved to the left or right in a prearranged code. Especially for night signals, the torches made an awkward arrangement in the wind and spray aboard ship. Smith devised a method of signaling in which the operator could sit between two lanterns, one red, one white, exposing them by sliding doors to represent the left-right waves of flag or torch on land. Furthermore, the Smith method had the decided advantage of being directional: it could be flashed towards land without fear of being seen by the Union blockaders. A special board convened to examine his proposal was enthusiastic. It was adopted and placed in use on all blockade-runners.

Smith's system of signaling, which he referred to as "flash lights," was the prototype for blinker signals, which became standard in navies the world over. A variation called Ardois, using four double lanterns arranged vertically, each of which could be made to show white or red, operated by a typewriter-type keyboard, was in use by the U.S. Navy and Coast Guard over fifty years later, eventually giving way to more rapid types of Morse code blinkers.

As a reward for his invention, Smith was offered a chance to serve on a blockade-runner. He chose the *Ad-Vance* out of Wilmington, of which he was signal officer from May 1863 to February 1864, when he returned to the ISC as second lieutenant of the Second Company to command a station at Hardy's Bluff on the James. In June 1864 he was placed in charge of the lines from General Robert E. Lee's headquarters in Petersburg, and his men represented the last organized body to evacuate that city the following April. He commanded the Second Company at Appomattox.

Four years to the day after volunteering for service, Smith returned to Hycotee. He farmed there and on some land of his own on the North Hyco Creek. On 23 Apr. 1872 he married Sabra Annie Long (1844–1938) of Randolph County in a ceremony at the Presbyterian Church in Concord. They lived at Crescent Farm on the North Hyco, where he raised tobacco, ran Hyco Mill, and kept a small general store and post office, later named Osmond after a son. Smith was baptized in Red House Presbyterian Church and became an elder, as were his father, his brother William, a son, and a grandson. Smith and his wife had nine children: Richard Ivy, William Osmond, Helen Long Wooding, Maggie Barringer, Francis Patillo, Lilly Webb, Robert Kennon, Edwin Comer, and Mary Amis Goodwin Griffith.

Around 1888–90 the Smiths moved to Rosedale Farm near Guilford so that their children could receive a better education. There Smith was active in the Guilford County Camp, United Confederate Veterans, and began to record his wartime experiences, originally for his children and friends; they were later published in *The Guilford Collegian* and other papers. He shared some of his adventures with James Sprunt, chronicler of the Cape Fear. In 1891, as a member of the Red House Alliance of Caswell County, Smith served as alliance lecturer of the Fifth Congressional District.

Around 1912 the couple moved to Sutherlin, Va., and built a house beside that of their daughter, Helen Wooding, where they celebrated their golden anniversary in 1922. Smith, who served as an elder in Mercy Seat Presbyterian Church, died in Sutherlin at age seventy-nine. He was described as "a lifelong Democrat, but not an overly zealous one." Twelve years before his death he received a letter from his wartime commander, Colonel William Lamb, of Fort Fisher, recalling his service and his invention, known only to a few. He was buried at Red House Church in Caswell County.

SEE: Caswell County Historical Association, *Heritage of Caswell County, North Carolina* (1985); William S. Powell, *When the Past Refused to Die: A History of Caswell County, 1777–1977* (1977); *Proceedings of the Fifth Annual Session of the North Carolina Farmers State Alliance* (1891); John Baptist Smith, typescripts (possession of his granddaughter, Mrs. Mary Ivy Smith Storey); Washington, N.C., *Daily News*, 29 May 1974.

DAVID WINFRED GADDY

Smith, Joshua G. *(1808–6 Mar. 1836)*, was born in North Carolina but moved to Bastrop, Tex., as a young man. He enlisted in the Texas army as a private and, in early 1836, accompanied a segment of the army to San Antonio de Béxar. Smith died during the defense of The Alamo. As a result of his sacrifice, his descendants received land grants in the Montgomery and Shelby land districts of Texas.

SEE: San Felipe de Austin, *Telegraph and Texas Register*, 24 Mar. 1836; Amelia W. Williams, "A Critical Study of the Siege of The Alamo and the Personnel of Its Defenders," *Southwestern Historical Quarterly* 37 (1933–34).

R. H. DETRICK

Smith, Michael *(1698–ca. 1771)*, preacher and poet, was born in County Meath, Ireland, the son of the Reverend Robert Smith. Educated at Trinity College, Dublin, he was ordained an Anglican priest by the bishop of London in 1747 and served five years as curate at Hertfordshire.

As a missionary of the Society for the Propagation of the Gospel in Foreign Parts (SPG), Smith settled in South Carolina in 1752. In the following year, during his ministry to Prince Frederick's Parish and Prince George's Parish, his wife and three of his eight children died, and from about this time rumors began to spread about his disreputable character. On 2 May 1756 the church officers of Prince Frederick's Parish wrote to the SPG charging Smith with a number of atrocities, including living with a woman whom he had not married according to law, incurring large debts, gaming, and neglecting his parish duties and his family.

Between 1753 and 1756 Smith traveled frequently and acquired for himself a good reputation in North Carolina. When the doors of the churches in Georgetown County were closed to him in 1756, he left South Carolina and began to minister to the parish of St. James in Wilmington. He was an active and apparently popular preacher throughout the coastal region, in Cape Fear, and in New Hanover, Brunswick, and Johnston counties. In 1756, in New Bern, James Davis printed a sermon Smith had preached the previous year while still officially engaged by his South Carolina parishes. *Sermon, Preached in Christ-Church in Newbern, in North-Carolina . . . Before the Ancient and Honourable Society of Free and Accepted Masons*, though it is a standard exercise on the theme of brotherly love, typical of eighteenth-century sermons preached before such audiences, is nevertheless one of the few Anglican sermons surviving from colonial North Carolina and is a good example of the plain-style discourse. On 6 Oct. 1756 Smith preached again in New Bern, this time before the governor and both houses of the Assembly. The following day the lower house resolved to thank him and to ask for a copy of his sermon to be printed. (If the sermon was printed, it is no longer extant.)

Among his regular congregations, Smith had some difficulty competing with the persistent Anabaptists, dissenters, and other "enthusiastical sects," but in a 1758 letter to the SPG secretary, he reported some progress for the established church. In the 26 Apr.–3 May 1760 issue of the *South Carolina Gazette*, there appeared an extravagantly patriotic poem, "On the Reduction of Guadaloupe by the Reverend Mr. Smith of Cape Fear," the earliest evidence that Smith was a poet of some talent. The 165 lines of handsomely crafted heroic couplets, replete with classical and biblical allusions, lavishly praise William Pitt and the British military.

But just as Smith was establishing himself as an author and preacher of merit in North Carolina, his bad reputation caught up with him. Acting on the complaints from his South Carolina parishioners, the SPG relieved him of his duties in 1759. His parishioners in North Carolina sent several letters defending his character and ability to the SPG. Each noted the difficulties under which he worked—the number of places he had to travel, his small salary, his large family, and the popular prejudice against the established church. When Smith went to England to defend himself, the SPG refused to grant him a hearing. He was not restored to his mission, but he did return to North Carolina. By 1762 he had been made a chaplain on a British warship.

Later Smith returned to England and became vicar of South Mimms in Hertfordshire. He found a patron in the Earl of Hillsborough and published two books.

Twelve Sermons, Preached upon Several Occasions (1770) is a collection of straightforward doctrinal sermons and moral lessons composed for a colonial audience. *Christianity Unmasqued; or, Unavoidable Ignorance Preferable to Corrupt Christianity: A Poem: In Twenty-one Cantos* (1771) is Smith's greatest achievement as an author. The dedicatory preface to Hillsborough contains a lengthy analysis of the SPG's failures in the colonies, and the poem itself is remarkable for the wit and versatility displayed by the author. It is a long verse essay in Hudibrastic and heroic couplets blending satiric, discursive, and heroic verse in a unique way. In the poem Smith viciously attacks the "corrupt" opponents of Anglicanism (Catholics, dissenters, "enthusiasts," and Deists) and holds up the Church of England as the most rational and least corrupt of God's instruments. *Christianity Unmasqued* is Smith's last extant work. Nothing is known of his death.

SEE: Smith's own books cited above; Hennig Cohen, *The South Carolina Gazette, 1732–1775* (1953); Richard Beale Davis, *Intellectual Life in the Colonial South, 1585–1763* (1978); David T. Morgan, "Scandal in Carolina: The Story of a Capricious Missionary," *North Carolina Historical Review* 47 (1970); C. F. Pascoe, *Two Hundred Years of the S.P.G.* (1901); William L. Saunders, ed., *Colonial Records of North Carolina*, vols. 5–6 (1887–88); Frederick Lewis Weis, *The Colonial Clergy of Virginia, North Carolina, and South Carolina* (1955).

M. JIMMIE KILLINGSWORTH

Smith, [Michael] Hoke *(2 Sept. 1855–27 Nov. 1931)*, secretary of the interior, governor of Georgia, and U.S. senator, was born on the Catawba College campus then located in Newton, the son of Hildreth Hosea of Deerfield, N.H., and Mary Brent Hoke Smith of Lincolnton, N.C. His father had been a lawyer in Washington, D.C., but failing eyesight led him to accept a professorship in science and languages at Catawba in 1851. Six years later the family moved to Chapel Hill, where the elder Smith joined the faculty of The University of North Carolina. There and in Lincolnton Hoke Smith grew up, and as an adult he returned frequently for vacations. He was educated by his father, and after the family moved to Atlanta in 1872, he began to study law.

Licensed in 1873, he soon enjoyed a lucrative practice, arguing cases against corporations, particularly railroads, and becoming an outspoken foe of big business. He entered local politics and in 1887 acquired the controlling interest in the *Atlanta Journal*, which for many years served as his political platform. The paper called for tariff reform, criticized corporation-dominated state politics, demanded a good roads program, and campaigned against lynching, the convict-lease system, and saloons. Although Smith sold his shares in the *Journal* in 1900, it continued to back him politically for many years. A vigorous supporter of Grover Cleveland in the 1892 presidential campaign, he was rewarded with appointment as secretary of the interior.

As secretary he was praised as a fair and effective administrator who corrected many problems in the department. Nevertheless, he basically acquiesced in the long-accepted practice of individual exploitation of the environment for private gain. His Indian policy continued that of the first Cleveland administration—breaking down tribal organization while individualizing and integrating Indians into society at large. Although unsuccessful, it fitted well with a related policy of opening the Indian Territory to white settlement. Although he set aside thirteen forest reserves, his conservation record proved meager.

Smith resigned from the cabinet in 1896 and returned to his law practice in Atlanta, where he helped build the Piedmont Hotel and the Fulton National Bank. As president of the Atlanta Board of Education, he introduced vocational training in the public schools. In 1906 he won the gubernatorial election on a reform platform that also proposed the disfranchisement of blacks and thereby won the crucial support of Populist party leader Tom Watson.

In his first term (1907–9), Smith strengthened the railroad commission, reformed the election system, established juvenile courts, abolished the convict-lease system, increased appropriations for education, and enlarged the state's corporate regulatory powers. A constitutional amendment disfranchising blacks was passed and ratified. Although not reelected in 1908, he was successful in 1910 and began his second term as governor in July 1911. A few days after his inauguration, he was elected by the legislature to fill an empty Senate seat. Ignoring a storm of criticism, however, he remained at the governor's post for four months in order to push through his reform program: an antilobbying bill, establishment of a Department of Commerce and Labor, modernizing and improving the school system, and several agricultural education measures.

As a U.S. senator from 1911 to 1921, Smith was recognized as a leader who became an administration spokesman. A skillful parliamentarian and compromiser, he helped smooth differences over the new income tax and the Federal Reserve Bill. As chairman of the Committee on Education and Labor, he guided through Congress several important measures, including the Smith-Lever Agriculture Extension Act of 1914 and the Smith-Hughes Vocational Education Act of 1917. He supported the Federal Farm Loan Act of 1916, as well as other legislation to help cotton farmers. He opposed the Federal Child Labor Bill on the basis that it was unconstitutional (the U.S. Supreme Court later found it so) and opposed woman suffrage and national Prohibition. Always sympathetic to labor, he voted for the Adamson Eight-Hour Act. As a member of the Judiciary Committee he fought the appointment to the Supreme Court of the liberal Louis Brandeis, but after pressure from the administration and Georgia labor and a personal interview with the appointee, Smith voted for confirmation.

His position on the European war, which made him unpopular with the administration and eventually with Georgia voters as well, paved the way for the end of his political career. Taking a strictly economic stand, he vigorously protested British seizure of exports to Germany and Austria and demanded that arms sales to Britain be prohibited in retaliation. He halfheartedly supported preparedness and in 1917 reluctantly voted for war against Germany. Smith exasperated many of his followers by first criticizing measures granting extraordinary war powers to the president, then ultimately voting for such measures. When the armistice came, he called for a quick return to "normalcy" and an end to government controls.

In the 1920 senatorial primary campaign, the League of Nations was a key issue; Smith favored it but with certain reservations. Tom Watson, who opposed the league, defeated Smith. Smith remained in Washington until 1925 lobbying for various interests and arguing alien property claims, but then he returned to Atlanta.

On 19 Dec. 1883 he married Marion McHenry (Birdie) Cobb of Athens, Ga., the daughter of Thomas R. R. Cobb, a lawyer and former Confederate general. They had two sons, Marion and Hildreth (the latter died in infancy), and three daughters, Mary Brent, Lucy, and Callie. His wife died in 1919, and on 27 Aug. 1924 he married Mazie Crawford of Cordele, Ga. His funeral was held at Atlanta's North Avenue Presbyterian Church where he had been a charter member and elder, and he was buried in nearby Oakland Cemetery.

SEE: *Biog. Dir. Am. Cong.* (1971); *DAB*, vol. 9 (1936); Dewey W. Grantham, Jr., *Hoke Smith and the Politics of the New South* (1958); John Chalmers Vinson, "Hoke Smith," in Horace Montgomery, ed., *Georgians in Profile* (1958); *Who Was Who in America, 1897–1942* (1942).

RICHARD N. SHELDON

Smith, Michael John *(30 Apr. 1945–28 Jan. 1986)*, naval officer, test pilot, and astronaut, was born in Beaufort, the son of Robert Lewis and Lucille S. Smith. He was graduated from Carteret County High School, where he played baseball, basketball, and football, was voted the most outstanding student, and was president of the student council. Smith grew up on a chicken farm across the road from the local airport and spent much of his childhood watching airplanes, making models, and finally taking flying lessons. He received a student pilot license at age sixteen and flew an airplane before he was licensed to drive an automobile. In June 1963 he entered the U.S. Naval Academy. Following graduation in 1967, when he ranked 108 in a class of 893, he entered the Naval Postgraduate School in Monterey, Calif., and earned a master's degree. Afterwards he had flight training at Pensacola, Fla., and advanced jet flight training at Kingsville, Tex. During the Vietnam War he flew navy attack planes from the aircraft carrier *Kitty Hawk*.

Returning to the United States he was stationed at the Patuxent River Naval Air Test Center, in Maryland, where he was involved with guidance systems for cruise missiles and also taught. "By then," the *New York Times* observed, "he had learned the code of the warrior, stoically accepting risks that would overwhelm others." Promoted to lieutenant commander in 1977, Smith was assigned to the Naval Air Station at Oceana, Va., where he was in charge of maintenance and operations with an attack squadron. Three years later he was tapped by the National Aeronautics and Space Administration for astronaut training. He had already been selected to command an A-6 squadron and found it difficult to leave the navy for so different an assignment. An opportunity to spend more time with his family was one factor that persuaded him to accept the new challenge.

Smith underwent a five-year period of instruction, during which he was promoted to full commander and was trained in numerous technical projects including flight operations and night landings. The anticipated call came in 1985 when he was named pilot of the ill-fated *Challenger*, which exploded moments after lift-off from Cape Canaveral, Fla., on 28 Jan. 1986. All seven astronauts aboard were killed.

Among his military honors were the Navy Distinguished Flying Cross, three Air medals, thirteen Strike Flight Air medals, and the Vietnamese Cross of Gallantry with Silver Star.

Smith married Jane Anne Jarrell of Charlotte ten days after his graduation from the Naval Academy. She recalled that when he asked her to marry him, he said that he was "planning to be a Navy pilot, a test pilot, a Blue Angel and an astronaut, and wanted to know if I'd have a problem with any of that." She replied, "No problem." In relating this later she added, "And that started it all." They were the parents of three children: Scott, Alison, and Erin, each born in a different state.

SEE: *Charlotte Observer*, 18 June 1967; *New York Times*, 29 Jan., 11 Feb. 1986; Raleigh *News and Observer*, 29 Jan., 3 Feb. 1986.

WILLIAM S. POWELL

Smith, Nimrod Jarrett *(3 Jan. 1837–1893)*, principal chief of the Eastern Band of Cherokee Indians from 1880 to 1891, was born near Murphy. His mother was Cherokee and his father was a white man who acted as translator for the Reverend Evan Jones, a Baptist missionary at Valley Town before the removal of 1838–39. Smith acquired an adequate but probably informal education and married a white woman by whom he had several children. At age twenty-five, he enlisted in one of the Cherokee companies of the Confederate Legion organized by William Holland Thomas, a white trader among the Cherokee, and served as first sergeant of Company B, Sixty-ninth North Carolina Infantry, until the close of the Civil War.

In 1868 Smith was clerk to the council that drafted the first Eastern Cherokee constitution. He came to be highly respected as a public servant, and when Principal Chief Lloyd Welch died in office in 1880, the Eastern Cherokee elected Smith to complete the unexpired term. James Mooney, a late nineteenth-century anthropologist, met Smith while he was serving in this office; he described him as "a splendid specimen of physical manhood, being six foot four inches in height and built in proportion, erect in figure, with flowing black hair curling down over his shoulders, a deep musical voice, and a kindly spirit and natural dignity."

When Smith became principal chief, the Cherokee were without an agent, their education had been neglected, and their legal position was far from definite. On 31 May 1881 Smith signed a contract with Indiana Quakers for the establishment and maintenance of schools that were to be supported by the annual interest of the trust fund held by the U.S. government for the North Carolina Cherokee and by contributions from the Western Yearly Meeting of the Society of Friends. With some initial aid from the North Carolina Meeting, the Indiana Quakers led by Thomas Brown began work immediately, and by the end of 1881 they had established a small training school in Cherokee and day schools in other settlements. In 1882 Congress appropriated funds for the establishment of an agency in Cherokee and for conducting a census that was completed in 1884.

As principal chief Smith devoted most of his time to the Eastern Cherokee's legal battles. Hoping to gain access to the annuities and other trust funds held by the U.S. government for the Western (Oklahoma) Cherokee, the Eastern Cherokee filed suit in the court of claims against the United States and the Cherokee Nation West in 1883. Two years later the court handed down a decision adverse to the Eastern Cherokee, and the U.S. Supreme Court upheld the decision in 1886. The courts ruled that the Eastern Cherokee had dissolved their connection with the Cherokee Nation by their refusal to move west. The decision deprived them not only of the trust and annuity funds but also of their tribal status and consequently left them in an extremely ambiguous legal position. Furthermore, the Eastern Cherokee had aroused hostility among neighboring whites in the 1880s by switching their loyalty from the Democratic to the Republican party, an act that made their position even more precarious.

In an effort to protect the Cherokee, Chief Smith employed attorney Fred Fisher of Bryson City to draw up an act of incorporation (such as businesses used) for the Eastern Cherokee Indians. The act was ratified in March 1889 and a state charter was issued providing that "the North Carolina or Eastern Cherokee Indians, resident or domiciled in the counties of Jackson, Swain, Graham, and Cherokee, be and at the same time are hereby created and constituted a body politic and corporate under the name, style, and title of the Eastern Band of Cherokee Indians, with all the rights, franchises, privileges, and powers incident and belonging to corporations under the laws of the state of North Carolina." Thus the North Carolina Cherokee became a corporation and adopted corporate procedures and regulations as their legal system.

With the legal position of the Cherokee clarified and their position secured, Chief Smith retired in 1891. He died two years later on Qualla Boundary.

SEE: Fred Bauer, *Land of the North Carolina Cherokees* (1970); James Mooney, *Myths of the Cherokee*, 19th Annual Report, Bureau of American Ethnology (1897–98); Sharlotte Neely, "The Quaker Era in Cherokee Indian Education," *Appalachian Journal* 2 (1975).

THEDA PERDUE

Smith, Orren Randolph *(18 Dec. 1827–3 Mar. 1913)*, soldier, son of Louis Farrar and Olive Huff Sims Smith, was born near Manson in Warren County but moved to Louisburg as a teenager. On 1 Oct. 1846 he enlisted as a private in Company H of the First Regiment of Foot Volunteers, commanded by Captain George E. B. Singletary. The unit was called into service against the Mexicans on 19 Jan. 1847 and landed at Port Isabel, Tex., on 28 March.

Discharged on 7 Aug. 1848, Smith studied engineering in New York before moving to Warren, Ohio, to live with his uncle. Residing near Fort Leavenworth, Kans., in 1857, he joined the troops commanded by Colonel Albert Sidney Johnston sent to Utah to suppress the Mormons. Afterwards he returned to Louisburg, where he was living at the outbreak of the Civil War. On 1 June 1861 he enlisted in Company B of the Second Battalion of North Carolina Troops, commanded by Colonel Wharton Jackson Green. After injuring his right arm while on leave, he was appointed quartermaster, with the rank of major, at Marion, S.C., where he remained until the end of the war. Smith then worked as a building contractor and mover, with his business centered in Raleigh.

He married Mary Elizabeth G. H. McCampbell on 10 June 1863. They had one daughter, Jessica Randolph. At the time of his death, Smith was living in Henderson. He was buried in Elmwood Cemetery.

Orren Randolph Smith is noted chiefly for claiming to have designed the Stars and Bars, the first flag of the Confederate States of America. In his later years he stated that he had created the flag in response to solicitations made in February 1861 by the Provisional Congress of the Confederate States meeting in Montgomery, Ala. Catherine Rebecca Murphy (later Mrs. W. B. Winborne) of Louisburg sewed a flag according to Smith's specifications, and, as Smith related, it was sent to Montgomery on 12 Feb. 1861. However, it is unlikely that Smith's flag was in fact the Stars and Bars, for the Committee on the Flag and Seal rejected all of the "immense" number of designs sent for consideration. Though no definite proof has been discovered, it is more likely that Nicola Marschall, an artist on the faculty of Marion Female Seminary in Marion, Ala., submitted the favored design at the request of Alabama Governor Andrew Barry Moore.

Smith was honored on numerous occasions. The United Confederate Veterans in 1915 and the North Carolina General Assembly in 1917 recognized him as the designer of the first Confederate flag. Such recognition was chiefly the result of a lengthy campaign by Jessica Randolph Smith, who referred to herself as "Dad's Daughter." Several monuments, including one placed in front of the Franklin County Courthouse in September 1923 by the North Carolina Division of the United Daughters of the Confederacy, commemorate his efforts. On 3 Aug. 1927 the North Carolina Division of the United Confederate Veterans presented a portrait of Smith to the North Carolina Historical Commission.

SEE: Alabama State Department of Archives and History, *Alabama Legislature Declares Nicola Marschall Designer First Confederate Flag, Stars and Bars* (no date); *Birmingham News*, 25 Feb. 1935; David Eggenberger, *Flags of the U.S.A.* (1964); *Fayetteville Observer*, 12 Oct. 1926; *Franklin Times*, 15 Sept. 1916; Peleg D. Harrison, *The Stars and Stripes and Other American Flags* (1914); Johnstone Jones, *Roster of North Carolina Troops in the War With Mexico* (1887); *Journal of the Congress of the Confederate States of America, 1861–1865*, vol. 1 (1904); *Laws of North Carolina, 1917*, Public Resolution 21; Mrs. J. Boyd Massenburg Papers and Thomas Merritt Pittman Papers (Southern Historical Collection, University of North Carolina, Chapel Hill); Jessica Randolph Smith Papers (North Carolina State Archives, Raleigh); *The Stars and Bars: Speech by Major Orren Randolph Smith: Report of "Stars and Bars" Committee, Confederate Southern Memorial Association, Richmond, 1915 . . .* (no date); United Confederate Veterans, *Report of the Stars and Bars Committee, United Confederate Veterans, Richmond Reunion, June 1 to 3, 1915* (no date).

MAURY YORK

Smith, Owen Lun West *(18 May 1851–5 Jan 1926)*, U.S. minister to Liberia and Methodist leader, was born in Giddensville, Sampson County, the son of Ollen and Maria Hicks Smith, both of African descent. As a youth he served as a personal servant in the Confederate army and was present at the Battle of Bentonville in March 1865. Afterwards he followed the Union army across North Carolina and finally to Washington, D.C., where he is said to have been in the parade and review marking the end of the war. Making his way back home, he was sent by his mother to a school in New Bern taught by an African Methodist Episcopal Zion minister. After a time he moved to Pitt County to work on a carpetbagger's farm, where, on a part time basis, he also attended school under a northern teacher.

In May 1870 he set out for New Orleans but in South Carolina was engaged as a schoolteacher and for a time was a justice of the peace. Enrolled in the University of South Carolina, he studied law for about two years, but after 1877 blacks were no longer admitted. He was licensed, however, and practiced law briefly. Returning to North Carolina, he "engaged in politics" and taught school until 19 Oct. 1880, when he was "converted" at a camp meeting. Smith was licensed as a local preacher in the African Methodist Episcopal Zion Church on 3 Feb. 1881 and ordained a deacon in April. At various times he served circuits in Stantonsburg, Magnolia, Elizabethtown, Ingold, and Kinston and in Cumberland County. In November 1883 he was ordained an elder. Settling in Wilson in 1885, he became pastor of St. John's Church. An active financier, organizer, and church builder, he also served as the private secretary of his bishop for a number of years, secretary of the Sunday School Convention of the conference, and corresponding editor of the *Star of Zion*. He was elected presiding elder in January 1890 and reelected until 1894.

On 14 Jan. 1898 President William McKinley named Smith to the first of two terms as U.S. minister resident and consul general in Liberia, a post he filled until 23 May 1902. Also in 1898 Livingstone College in Salisbury awarded him an honorary D.D. degree. While en route to Liberia he spent some time in London, Oxford, and elsewhere in England.

Smith's first wife, Lucy Ann Jackson, whom he married on 9 Apr. 1878, was fatally shot by a deranged relative on 6 July 1891. They had no children. At Beaufort on 29 Jan. 1892 he married Adora Estelle Oden (1870–1906); their three children died young. In Liberia the Smiths adopted Carrie Emma Johnson, but she died at age seventeen while a student at Slater Normal School in Winston preparing to return to Africa as a missionary. Smith's third wife, whom he married in 1909, was Cynthia Ann King Isler, a widow with four children. He was buried in the private cemetery of Mount Hebron Masonic Lodge at Wilson.

SEE: Applications and Recommendations for Public Office, 1897–1904, 1906–24 (Record Group 59, National Archives and Records Service, Washington, D.C.); *Biographical Sketch of Rev. Owen L. W. Smith, D.D., U.S. Minister to Liberia* (no date [portrait]); J. W. Hood, *One Hundred Years of the African Methodist Episcopal Zion Church* (1895); *Nat. Cyc. Am. Biog.* (1910); *New Berne District, North Carolina Conference, African Methodist Episcopal Zion Church* (1893) (broadside, North Carolina Collection, University of North Carolina, Chapel Hill); *Who Was Who in America*, vol. 4 (1968).

HUGH BUCKNER JOHNSTON
BRENDA MARKS EAGLES

Smith, Peter Evans *(20 Jan. 1829–14 Oct. 1905)*, inventor, the eldest son of William R., Jr., and Susan Evans Smith, was born at the Edgecombe plantation of his maternal grandfather, Peter Evans. He received his early education at the Vine Hill Academy in Scotland Neck and was prepared for college at the Bingham School. Smith was graduated from The University of North Carolina in 1851. In 1852 he married Rebecca Norfleet Hill of Scotland Neck, and his father gave him a plantation on the Roanoke to farm. Possessing a natural mechanical bent, he was never fond of farming, and the outbreak of the Civil War a few years later gave him his opportunity.

Early in the war Smith was a quartermaster officer in the Confederate army, on detached duty because of premature deafness. In 1863 the Confederate government conceived the idea of building a gunboat on the Roanoke River to aid in the recapture of Plymouth at the river's mouth. Gilbert Elliott, then only nineteen, secured the contract and arranged the financing. The plans were drawn up by John L. Porter, of Norfolk, a famous naval architect, and the responsibility for the construction was assigned to Peter Smith. The site for construction of the gunboat was in a gut in the river's edge on his father's Edwards Ferry plantation. Working against incredible odds and using only the resources available in the neighborhood, the boat was finished in a year's time. One problem encountered was in attaching the iron plates of the superstructure to the wooden hull. The drills then available took twenty minutes to bore through the armor, which was an inch and a quarter thick. Smith invented the now familiar twist drill that only took four minutes.

The *Albemarle*, as the ram was christened, had a brief period of glory in the spring of 1864, when she sank several Federal warships in Albemarle Sound and enabled the Confederate army under Robert F. Hoke to recapture Plymouth. She was torpedoed by a young Federal naval officer, Lieutenant William B. Cushing, while tied up at the wharf at Plymouth. A *New York Times* article of 7 June 1936 on Cushing described the *Albemarle* at the time of her destruction as "the most powerful warship in the world." She was the only ironclad when all the other ships were still of wood.

With the end of the war Smith turned his inventive talents to peaceful pursuits. In 1871 he invented a cotton planter that was superseded by later models because, in his design, the seed had to be wet. A sulky plow followed in 1871. His most significant invention was a buoy lighted by electricity. Patented in the United States and England, these buoys were used to light New York harbor six years before the patent expired. As Smith had been paid nothing for the use of his patent, he brought suit against the government in federal court. The case reached the Supreme Court with a verdict in the government's favor. His later inventions were a spark arrester for the smokestack of the wood-burning locomotives, then in use, patented in 1885; a self-coupling device for railroad coaches; and a form of railroad switch.

As Scotland Neck was twenty miles from the nearest railroad, he offered his services free of charge to the Wilmington and Weldon to survey a road from Halifax as an incentive to the company to build a branch line. The line was completed in 1880. The railroad later hired Smith to carry the line from Scotland Neck to Kinston, Washington, N.C., and other eastern points.

He died at his home in Scotland Neck. By his wife Rebecca, the daughter of Whitmel John Hill of Scotland Neck, he had three daughters who reached maturity: Lena, Rebecca, and Nan.

SEE: William C. Allen, *History of Halifax County* (1918); Kemp P. Battle, *History of the University of North Carolina*, vol. 1 (1907); Stuart H. Hill Notebooks (North Carolina Collection, University of North Carolina, Chapel Hill); Patent Office Records (National Archives, Washington, D.C.); Peter Evans Smith Papers and William Ruffin Smith Papers (Southern Historical Collection, University of North Carolina, Chapel Hill).

CLAIBORNE T. SMITH, JR.

Smith, Richard Henry *(10 May 1812–2 Mar. 1893)*, planter and legislator, was born in Scotland Neck, the son of William Ruffin and Sarah Walton Norfleet Smith. His great-grandfather, Nicholas Smith, was one of the early settlers of the region, having come from Surry County, Va., in 1723. Smith's education was begun at the local Vine Hill Academy, and in 1824 he was sent to Hyde Park in western Halifax County for three years. Following a session at Oxford Academy in Granville County, he entered The University of North Carolina and was graduated in 1832. The next year in Warrenton to read law, he met and married Sally Hall, the daughter of Judge John Hall. Abandoning the study of law, he returned home to Woodstock, several miles north of Scotland Neck, and became a planter. By the Civil War he had accumulated a large fortune and 10,000 acres of land.

In 1848 Smith was elected to the General Assembly as a Whig but was defeated in 1850 because of having voted for the North Carolina Railroad to which rural eastern counties were opposed. Elected again in 1852, he served a single term. In 1861 he was a delegate from Halifax County to the secession convention that met in Raleigh on 20 May. He was also a delegate to the constitutional convention that met in four sessions in 1861–62. For many years he was a member of the Court of Pleas and Quarter Sessions for the county, and at the close of the Civil War he was chairman of the court. He was removed from the latter position in 1865 by General E. R. S. Canby, the commanding officer of the Federal forces of occupation in the district.

Always interested in whatever advanced the farming interests of the state, Smith was one of the founders of the North Carolina Agricultural Society and served as an officer. For many years he also was a director of the asylum for the insane at Raleigh and at one time served as chairman of the directors. One of the founders of Trinity Episcopal Parish in Scotland Neck in 1833, he was senior warden for forty years. He was a delegate to the diocesan convention of the church for fifty-nine years and a lay delegate to the General Convention of the national church for twenty-five years. Smith was present at the 1865 convention in Philadelphia, which succeeded in reconciling the divisions in the church caused by the Civil War. In 1882 he published a pamphlet, *The Organization of the Protestant Episcopal Church of the Confederate States, A.D. 1861, and Its Reunion with the Protestant Episcopal Church in the U.S.A., A.D. 1865*, recording the events.

Hall and his wife were the parents of eight children who reached maturity: Mary Weldon, Norfleet Saunders, Richard Henry, Jr., Alexander Hall, Ann Eliza, Weldon Hall, Isaac Hall, and Sally. Jacques Busbee of Raleigh painted a portrait of Smith late in life. He was buried in the family plot in Trinity Cemetery.

SEE: William C. Allen, *History of Halifax County* (1918); John L. Cheney, Jr., ed., *North Carolina Government, 1585–1979* (1981); *Journal of the Seventy-seventh Annual Convention of the Diocese of North Carolina* (1893); John W. Moore, *History of North Carolina*, 2 vols. (1880); Wills and Deeds of Halifax County (North Carolina State Archives, Raleigh).

CLAIBORNE T. SMITH, JR.

Smith, Robert Hardy *(21 Oct. 1813–13 Mar. 1878)*, lawyer, member of the Provisional Congress of the Confederacy, and a colonel in the Confederate army, was born at Edenton. He was the son of Robert Hardy, Jr. (1780–1841) of Edenton and Elizabeth Gregory Smith (1786–1856) of Hertford, Perquimans County, and the grandson of Joseph of London, England, and Elizabeth Hardy Smith. Both sides of the family supported independence during the American Revolution.

After receiving a strong foundation in classical education, he attended West Point in the fall of 1831. Because of a deficiency in mathematics, he was obliged to leave in January 1832 and found himself on his own because of his father's financial reverses. For a time he taught young students and studied medicine at Norfolk, Va., then moved on to teach on a plantation in his home county, and finally decided to seek his fortune in the Southwest.

In the Alabama counties of Dallas and Sumter he continued to teach and began studying law. In 1835 Smith was admitted to the bar and set up practice in Livingston, Sumter County, where he was associated with William B. Ochiltree (b. Cumberland County, N.C.) and later with Colonel William M. Inge (b. Granville County, N.C.). His considerable gifts as a lawyer soon elevated him to a position of leadership in his profession and in politics. In 1849 he was elected to the lower house of the state legislature and quickly rose to the top ranks of the Whig party. Two years later he reluctantly ran for the state senate but lost by one vote to John A. Winston, a future governor. Returning to his chosen profession, he moved to a challenging and thriving practice at Mobile in 1853. When John A. Campbell, leader of the Mobile bar, was elevated to the U.S. Supreme Court, he selected Smith to take over his firm. During the decade of the 1850s Smith's character and abilities grew, his reputation as a learned lawyer flourished, he practiced his profession before the highest courts in Alabama and Washington, D.C., and he retained an active interest in the politics of his day.

In 1860 he considered himself a Union man, a conservative, and still a Whig by conviction. Smith had opposed the secession movement in Alabama for years and in the national election supported John Bell and Edward Everett. After Abraham Lincoln's election he accepted an appointment by Governor Andrew B. Moore as commissioner to his native state. On 20 Dec. 1860 he addressed the legislature at Raleigh on the subject of cooperation in the event of secession. He reported on his mission to the Alabama Convention at Montgomery and then returned to Mobile to await what he believed to be the coming revolution.

When his state seceded on 11 January, he loyally accepted the decision. Soon afterwards the Alabama convention passed over the avid secessionist William Lowndes Yancey and elected Smith as a delegate-at-large to the Montgomery convention. Alexander H. Stephens of Georgia, vice-president of the Confederacy, believed him to be the most able member of a very capable Alabama delegation. His contributions to the establishment of the Confederate government were significant indeed. The U.S. Constitution and its history were of special interest to Smith and made him a natural choice for membership on the drafting committees of both Confederate constitutions. His voice engendered respect during the convention debates, as did his origination of such reforms as the item veto and his important contribution to the final style and arrangements of the two documents.

The Confederacy had no *Federalist Papers* and no James Madison, Alexander Hamilton, or John Jay because the exigencies of time insisted that the drafting and ratification process be done quickly. There were many spokesmen for the new permanent constitution, but none spoke with greater insight, perception, or wisdom than did Robert Hardy Smith at Mobile on 30 Mar. 1861. His words were published as *An Address to the Citizens of Alabama on the Constitution and Laws of the Confederate States of America*.

After concluding his service in the Provisional Congress he returned to Mobile. In 1862 he organized the Thirty-sixth Alabama Infantry and was elected colonel. His unit was assigned to defend the district of the Gulf, which included South Alabama and West Florida. Before the year ended he was forced to resign his commission because of ill health. During the remaining years of the Confederacy he served briefly as president of the district military court, which he caused to be abolished for constitutional reasons. He also reestablished his law practice at Mobile.

During the postwar period, with his energy restored, his legal career flourished again, and he was engaged in a number of important cases of state and national significance. A portrait of this time preserved the image of a someone who had dedicated his life to the precepts of honor, duty, and virtue. A man of medium stature with slightly rounded shoulders, he had a pleasant face with strikingly deep hazel eyes and an iron gray beard. He died at Mobile. The church of his youth, the Episcopal church, ministered to him during his last days and laid him to rest in Magnolia Cemetery.

Smith was married three times: first, on 12 Jan. 1839, to Evalina Belmont, who died on 4 Dec. 1843; second, on 25 Nov. 1845 to Emily Stuart, who died on 24 Oct. 1846 (both were sisters of Colonel William M. Inge); and third, to Helen Hord, daughter of Thomas Hord Herndon of Greene County, Ala. He was survived by his wife Helen, five sons, and four daughters. Sons Richard Inge, an officer in the Confederate army, Robert Hardy, and Gregory Little were distinguished members of the Mobile bar. Hardy B. Smith, of Mobile, Ala., became the owner of Smith's portrait as a young man and daguerreotype in later life.

SEE: Ruth Royer Smith Bruckmann (great-granddaughter of Robert Hardy Smith), personal contact, 1977; Stephens Croom, "Robert Hardy Smith," *Southern Law Journal* (January 1879), reprinted in Mobile *Daily Register*, 23 Mar. 1879; *DAB*, vol. 17 (1935); William Garrett, *Reminiscences of Public Men in Alabama for Thirty Years* (1872); George B. Inge, *The Herndon and Inge Families* (1977); Mobile *Daily Register* (obituary), 15 Mar. 1878; *Nat. Cyc. Am. Biog.*, vol. 8 (1924); Thomas M. Owen, *Hist. of Ala. and Dict. of Ala. Biog.*, vol. 4 (1921); Robert Hardy Smith Papers (Southern Historical Collection, University of North Carolina, Chapel Hill); Alexander Hamilton Stephens Papers (microfilm, Southern Historical Collection); Ezra J. Warner and W. Buck Yearns, *Biographical Register of the Confederate Congress* (1977).

CHARLES R. LEE, JR.

Smith, Samuel *(3 Dec. 1729–6 Oct. 1800)*, Revolutionary officer, legislator, and local official, was born in South Farnham Parish, Essex County, Va., a younger son of Samuel (d. 1739) and Ann Amiss Smith (d. 1753). He was reared in the Anglican faith by a strong-willed mother, who assumed control of the family after the death of the father. The Smiths were descendants of Alexander Smith, who had emigrated from Scotland to Middlesex County, Va., during the Cromwellian period.

In May 1761 Samuel Smith married Mary Webb. Described as a local belle of the same parish as he, she was born in 1740 and died in Granville County, N.C., in 1827. After their wedding they went to live on Cock Quarter, a 357-acre tract that Smith had purchased from John Armistead in February 1760. Before leaving for North Carolina, they had been attracted to the persuasive ministry of Samuel Davies, a Presbyterian clergyman, and under his guidance embraced Presbyterianism. The Smiths, consisting of two adults and three infants, moved to their new North Carolina home sometime in 1766. Samuel bought a small tract of land in northern Granville County on Grassy Creek but soon added other tracts adjacent to his farm. He named his home Abram's Plains for the site of the English victory over the French at Quebec in 1759. His major crop was tobacco.

Active in local politics, Smith was commissioned a justice of the peace by Governor William Tryon. With the approach of the American Revolution, Thomas Person nominated him for a place on the Committee of Safety for the Hillsborough District. Early in 1778 Smith took the loyal census for his home district. Although there were men in his district who refused to take the oath of allegiance to the new state, there were no reprisals against them.

In 1775 Smith was made first major in the Granville Regiment of the Hillsborough Brigade of the militia, and by May 1778 he had risen to the rank of colonel. On 30 June 1779 he was reported as commanding 16 companies consisting of 16 captains, 10 lieutenants, 10 ensigns, and 854 rank and file. Smith's letter of resignation to Governor Thomas Burke on 1 Oct. 1779 contains hints of a strong difference of opinion between the two men. In the same year Smith took advantage of a recent provision by the General Assembly permitting easy acquisition of land. He sold his holdings in Virginia and bought land in North Carolina. By 1783 he held 3,703 acres in Granville County. After the war, with land speculation rampant, he acquired still more as well as two lots in the new town of Williamsboro. He also became a trustee of the academy in the town. For many years he was a justice of the county, he was the census taker, and was once elected sheriff.

He died at his home and was buried in the Smith-Davis cemetery in Sassafras Fork Township, Granville County. He and his wife were the parents of six sons (Samuel, James Webb, John, William, Maurice, and Alexander) and four daughters (Mary, Elizabeth, Jenny Murphey, and Anne). A miniature portrait of him was painted about 1760–61, and both he and his wife posed for silhouettes in their old age.

SEE: Walter Clark, ed., *State Records of North Carolina*, vols. 12–13 (1895–96); S. S. Downey Collection (Manuscript Department, Duke University Library, Durham); William L. Saunders, ed., *Colonial Records of North Carolina*, vol. 9 (1890); Jonathan K. Smith, *On This Rock . . . The Chronicle of a Southern Family* (1968); William Smith Collection (North Carolina State Archives, Raleigh).

VERNON O. STUMPF

Smith, William *(d. July 1743)*, chief justice and councilman, was an Englishman who (according to Stephen B. Weeks) was educated at Middle Temple, one of the Inns of Court. With the support of John Scrope, secretary of the treasury, he was nominated as chief justice of the North Carolina General Court and president of the Council by Martin Bladen in 1730. Despite the opposition of George Burrington to the nomination and his direct appeals to the duke of Newcastle to prevent Smith's appointment, the new royal governor could not overcome the wishes of men so powerful as Scrope and Bladen. Smith entered North Carolina and assumed his offices early in 1731. Soon other offices began accruing to him; he became provincial treasurer in April and chief baron of the exchequer in May 1732.

In May 1731 Burrington moved to undercut Smith by insisting that his fellow justices on the General Court were associates rather than assistants, therefore peers of the chief justice rather than subordinates. Smith was enraged by this ploy and resigned from the Council in disgust on 20 May in order to return to England and air his complaints against the governor. Burrington then sent a letter to the Board of Trade complaining that Smith had disgraced himself as a "sot" and "perfidious scoundrel."

Smith returned to North Carolina in July 1733 and though without official position entered into the growing political agitation against the governor. When Gabriel Johnston replaced Burrington late in 1734, Smith was restored to his earlier offices. In subsequent years Smith proved to be the governor's closest and most influential ally. Indeed, the two men became close personal friends as well. At his death Smith left the bulk of his estate to Johnston.

During 1735–36 the chief justice worked closely with

the governor to build up the town of Newton (later Wilmington) at the expense of Brunswick. This effort was viewed by the Moore and Swann families as a direct challenge to their dominance of the Lower Cape Fear region. Hostilities continued to grow until 1739, when Smith as chief justice ruled that quitrents could be demanded in specie. The decision was an enormously unpopular one in a colony where "hard" money was scarce, and the Moores and Swanns saw their chance. In the General Assembly that convened in January 1740, they led a movement to impeach Smith. With a vote on the question set for 13 February, Johnston and Smith worked hard to garner support and defeated the measure by six votes.

Just five days later the governor moved to retaliate and sent a measure to the General Assembly calling for the incorporation of Wilmington. It was clear that the vote would be close only in the upper house. On 19 February Smith noted in the minutes of the Council that by virtue of an act passed in 1711 the president of that body could vote twice in case of a tie. The very next day when the upper house deadlocked 4 to 4 on the Wilmington bill, Smith voted a second time as president to break the tie. The Moores, the Swanns, and their allies were furious, but their protests were ignored as the measure sailed through the lower house.

Smith now stood as the most powerful political figure in the colony, second only to the governor himself. To demonstrate his strength, he called for a vote of confidence in both houses during the August 1740 session of the legislature (after some libelous handbills had been circulated about him in Edenton) and received sizable vote margins.

During 1741 Smith went to England on business and upon his return took an increasingly less active role in politics. He died in the summer of 1743 without family.

SEE: William L. Saunders, ed., *Colonial Records of North Carolina*, vols. 3–4 (1886); William S. Price, Jr., "A Strange Incident in George Burrington's Royal Governorship," *North Carolina Historical Review* 51 (1974); Charles L. Van Noppen Papers (Manuscript Department, Duke University Library, Durham).

WILLIAM S. PRICE, JR.

Smith, William Alexander *(9 Jan. 1828–16 May 1888)*, farmer, railroad president, legislator, and congressman, was born in Warren County, the son of Bannister R. and Mary Smith. He attended an old field school until he was fourteen, when he became a day laborer on the Raleigh and Gaston Railroad. After working on the railroad for two years, he left the state for brief stays in Alabama, Texas, and Shreveport, La. Returning to North Carolina, he engaged in farming and married Polly Ann MacCauley. They had three children: Claude W., Roger A., and Sarah F., who married William H. Green of Richmond, Va.

In 1861 Smith was elected by Johnston County as a Union man to the secession convention. He opposed secession and voted against it. In 1864 he won a seat in the North Carolina House of Commons. When Governor William Woods Holden called the constitutional convention of 1865, Smith was again elected to serve his county. With the advent of congressional Reconstruction, he joined the Republican party. In 1868 Holden appointed him president of the North Carolina Railroad, headquartered in Alamance County.

As railroad president, Smith supported efforts to expand the company's service to the state by advocating the merger of several small railroad lines into one major company. The General Assembly opposed these efforts. When the state's Democrats met in convention in 1868, Smith refused to give reduced rail rates to them but did grant a 50 percent reduction for the Republicans that year. The North Carolina Railroad was again used for political purposes when the legislature of 1869 investigated charges of fraud in the state government. Governor Holden and Smith spirited a key witness, George W. Swepson, out of town on a special midnight train to prevent his appearance before the special inquiry committee. In 1871 the railroad was leased to the Richmond and Danville Railroad.

While living in Alamance County, Smith was elected to the state senate in 1870, but the election was contested. The General Assembly decided to allow Smith to be seated but called for an investigation. It later declared his seat vacant because Alamance County was considered in a state of insurrection due to Governor Holden's order for state troops to occupy the county after the murder of Wyatt Outlaw, a black man, by members of the Ku Klux Klan. In a new election, a Democrat was voted into office.

In March 1870 Smith purchased the Raleigh *Standard* from M. S. Littlefield. The paper was the state's major Republican organ, with editorial leadership in the hands of Joseph W. Holden, the governor's son and former proprietor of the *Standard*. The following September Smith sold the paper, reportedly saying, "I stopped printing the *Standard* because you can't print a paper for a party that can't read."

In 1872 he was elected as a Republican to represent the Fourth District in the U.S. House of Representatives, where he served on the Committee of Public Expenditures. Smith declined to run for reelection in 1874. He was appointed U.S. court receiver of the Western North Carolina Railroad Company, of which he later became president. The Republican party nominated him for lieutenant governor in 1876, but he was defeated along with Judge Thomas Settle, the gubernatorial candidate that year.

In 1876 Smith retired to his farm at Princeton in Johnston County. A lifelong Methodist, he died of stomach cancer at the home of his son-in-law, Captain William H. Green, in Richmond, Va. He was buried in Hollywood Cemetery, Richmond. His wife, who died in 1892, was interred in Selma, Johnston County.

SEE: *Biog. Dir. Am. Cong.* (1971); Cecil K. Brown, *A State Movement in Railroad Development* (1928); John L. Cheney, Jr., ed., *North Carolina Government, 1581–1975* (1975); Jonathan Daniels, *Prince of Carpetbaggers* (1958); J. G. de Roulhac Hamilton, *Reconstruction in North Carolina* (1914); Johnston County Estate Records (North Carolina State Archives, Raleigh); North Carolina *Senate Journal* (1871); Raleigh *Daily Standard*, 3 Oct. 1865, 4 Jan. 1869, March–September 1870; Raleigh *News and Observer*, 17 May 1888; Raleigh *Register*, 27 Sept., 1 Nov. 1877; Stephen B. Weeks Scrapbook, vol. 3 (North Carolina Collection, University of North Carolina, Chapel Hill); John H. Wheeler, ed., *Reminiscences and Memoirs of North Carolina and Eminent North Carolinians* (1884); *Who Was Who in America*, historical vol. (1963).

CAROL DALTON DEATON

Smith, William Alexander *(11 Jan. 1843–16 Apr. 1934)*, businessman, farmer, and local historian, was born in Anson County, the son of William Gaston Smith (1802–79), a planter, miller, merchant, magistrate, militia officer, chairman of the trustees of the Carolina Female

College, and leader of the local Methodist church. His mother was Eliza Sydnor Nelme of Anson County whose niece, Mary Ann Nelme Crump, was the mother of Mayor Edward Hull Crump of Memphis, Tenn.

Smith was born on the Nelme plantation near Ansonville, but his family soon moved to that town where his father built a handsome residence, the Oaks. He was educated in local schools and at Davidson College, from which he was graduated in 1865. His student life was interrupted by the Civil War. Joining the Anson Guards (Company C, Fourteenth Regiment, North Carolina Infantry) in 1861, he served until 1862, when, as a member of the color guard, he was severely wounded at Malvern Hill, injuries that required him to use crutches for the rest of his life.

Although the family fortune was depleted by the Civil War, Smith was able to launch a career in business by becoming a partner in a general store at Ansonville in 1866. Eventually he became sole proprietor and continued the store until 1886, a subsequent short-lived partnership proving unprofitable. The success of this store provided capital on which he based his later ventures.

As Smith's mercantile interest waned, he moved into the cotton textile manufacturing business, which occupied him for the next twenty years. The Yadkin Falls Manufacturing Company, located at Milledgeville in adjacent Montgomery County, was incorporated in 1883 and operated until it went into receivership in about 1896. Yadkin Falls Mill was succeeded by the Eldorado Cotton Mills in 1897. Smith was president of both companies. Eldorado, a supplier of goods to the Tucker and Carter Rope Company at New London in Stanly County, was absorbed by that firm in 1905. Two prominent individuals associated with Smith in these textile ventures were Senator Lee Slater Overman and the Reverend Francis Johnstone Murdoch, an Episcopal clergyman who was also a textile executive. After leaving textile management Smith maintained his interest in the industry with considerable investments in mills in North Carolina and South Carolina.

After retiring from cotton milling in 1905, he continued his business career primarily as an investor. Banking, commercial finance, textiles, insurance, real estate, tobacco, furniture, transportation, patent medicines, electric power, the telephone, and the mining of gold, copper, and mica all were included in his portfolio. His awareness of the potential of telephone communications and electric power is evidenced by his organization of the Pee Dee News–Transit Company and by his participation in the incorporation of the Yadkin Falls Electric Company in 1901. Another North Carolina manufactory in which he invested in the 1920s was the Edwards Railway Motor Car Company of Sanford, producer of gasoline-powered railroad passenger cars that were sold throughout North America and South America. At the close of Smith's career in the depression year of 1933, his investments were valued at $180,000.

At a time when banking was a limited institution in rural North Carolina, Smith served as a source of credit for the community. His financial records indicate that this activity extended from at least 1875 until the 1930s. Maintaining an office at Ansonville, he styled himself variously as banker, purchasing agent, capitalist, broker, and supplier. As banks developed, he invested in them, notably in the American Trust Company of Charlotte. Its president, George Stephens, assisted Smith for many years with banking, real estate, and other investments. Stephens headed the Stephens Company, which developed the Myers Park residential area in Charlotte, a project in which Smith invested. In addition, Smith directed the Carolina Construction Company from about 1904 to 1908, though it does not appear to have been a substantial operation.

Also active in agriculture, Smith operated a farm of 1,500 acres. Tenants worked on his estate, as was characteristic of the period. His reputation as a farmer was sufficient to warrant appointment by the governor as a delegate to the Farmers' National Congress held at Sioux Falls, S.Dak.

Smith, like his father, supported education. For many years he was a trustee of the University of the South at Sewanee, and during 1906–10 he sponsored Nona Institute at Ansonville. The Episcopal Diocese of North Carolina was residuary legatee of his will, the bequest being for the establishment of an institution, probably a school, near Ansonville. Smith chronicled the history of the Carolina Female College in *Old Carolina College*, a pamphlet published in 1923.

As a prominent layman of the Protestant Episcopal church, he regularly attended diocesan conventions and was a member of the Executive Missionary Committee. He also had the honor of being a lay delegate to the Pan Anglican Congress at London in 1908. Bishop Joseph Blount Cheshire was a friend for many years. Smith served as a member of the board of managers of the Thompson Orphanage from its inception. On the local scene he was the patron of All Soul's Church, Ansonville.

Smith's interests extended well beyond Anson County. He participated in the movement for good roads in the state and encouraged public libraries. His travels encompassed Europe, Asia, the United States, Canada, and Central America. He was a Mason and a member of the Church Historical Society and the North Carolina Literary and Historical Association.

An abiding affection for the Confederacy remained with Smith throughout his life. He was a member of the United Confederate Veterans and commander of the North Carolina Division for many years. He described an episode at the beginning of the Civil War in his pamphlet, *First Secession Flag: The Raising and Taking Down of the Flag at Ansonville in February 1861* (1917). After considerable research he wrote the history of his military unit in a lengthy book, *The Anson Guards, Company C, Fourteenth Regiment, North Carolina Volunteers, 1861–1865* (1914). During the last years of his life, Confederate veterans assembled each spring at his home.

Smith married Mary Jane Bennett of Anson County on 23 Dec. 1869. She was educated at Carolina Female College, Salem Academy, and St. Mary's at Raleigh. They had one son who died while an infant and two daughters, Etta (1870–87) and Nona (1872–77). Mrs. Smith died on 20 June 1914. Two years later Smith married Nancy Jane Flake, who survived him. Two of his writings concerned the family. He was coauthor with William Thomas Smith of *Family Tree Book, Genealogical and Biographical, Listing the Relatives of General William Alexander Smith and of W. Thomas Smith . . .* (1922). The pamphlet, *John Washington Bennett: Famous North Carolinian* (1917), concerns Mary Jane Smith's brother, who was a physician. She was honored in an anonymous pamphlet, *Memorials: Mrs. William A. Smith: The Good Samaritan and Heroine* (1914), which Smith probably wrote.

Smith died at his home, the Oaks, in Ansonville and was buried in the family plot in Westview Cemetery, Wadesboro. He was survived by his second wife and a foster son, Bennett Dunlap Nelme, a distant relation who was a nephew of his first wife.

SEE: Samuel A. Ashe, ed., *Biographical History of North Carolina*, vol. 6 (1907 [portrait]); Thomas W. Lingle, *Alum-*

ni Catalogue of Davidson College, Davidson, N.C., 1837–1924 (1924); Raleigh *News and Observer*, 17–18 Apr. 1934; William Alexander Smith Papers, 1765–1949 (Manuscript Department, Duke University Library, Durham); Wadesboro *Messenger and Intelligencer* (16, 26 Apr. 1934).

WILLIAM R. ERWIN, JR.

Smith, William Cunningham *(19 Apr. 1871–17 Dec. 1943)*, educator and author, was born in Greensboro, the son of Samuel Cunningham and Margaret Ella Cunningham Smith. As an undergraduate at The University of North Carolina he was assistant librarian (1894–96) and was graduated in 1896; he did summer graduate study at Harvard and the University of Wisconsin. At The University of North Carolina he was an instructor in history (1896–97) and English (1897–1900). In 1900 he joined the faculty of the North Carolina College for Women in Greensboro, where he was professor of history (1900–1903) and English (1903–38) and head of the English Department from 1904 until his retirement in 1938. He also served as dean of the College of Liberal Arts for eighteen years (1920–38). In 1920 The University of North Carolina granted him the honorary Litt.D. degree.

As chairman of chapel, he conducted devotional services when chapel attendance was a daily requirement. He also was an extension lecturer and spoke to student groups across the state on Robert Browning and on Bible literature. He taught a large men's Bible class at the First Presbyterian Church and was the author of *Bible Study* (1915). Smith spoke frequently before Bible classes, institutes, Christian associations, and other religious organizations. He wrote a number of biographical sketches for Samuel A. Ashe's *Biographical History of North Carolina* and was the author of historical articles published by the North Carolina Historical Commission. His *Charles Duncan McIver* appeared in 1907 and *Studies in American Authors* was published in 1913. He also contributed to the *Library of Southern Literature*.

Smith married Gertrude Allen of Greensboro on 12 Aug. 1897, and they became the parents of four daughters and a son. He was a Democrat, a member of the Presbyterian church, the Rotary Club, and other organizations.

SEE: Daniel L. Grant, *Alumni History of the University of North Carolina* (1924); Lucian L. Knight, comp., *Biographical Dictionary of Southern Authors* (1929); Raleigh *News and Observer*, 18 Dec. 1943; *Who Was Who in America*, vol. 2 (1950).

WILLIAM S. POWELL

Smith, William Nathan Harrell *(24 Sept. 1812–14 Nov. 1889)*, congressman and judge, was the son of Dr. William Lay and Ann Harrell Smith of Murfreesboro. Dr. Smith died in the first year of his son's life, but Mrs. Smith proved to be "a mother of more than ordinary intellect, great fondness for reading, [and] uncommon mental aptitude." After elementary schooling at Hertford Academy in Murfreesboro, Smith, with the support of his father's relatives in New England, attended preparatory schools at Kingston, R.I., and Colchester, Conn. In 1830 he enrolled at Yale College; becoming a convert to Congregationalism, he considered the study of theology until persuaded by an uncle to take up law instead. Elected to Phi Beta Kappa, Smith was graduated from Yale in 1834, studied law there, and in 1836 was admitted to the bar in North Carolina. He lived briefly in Texas but had returned to his hometown by the time of his marriage to Mary Olivia Wise of Murfreesboro in January 1839. They became the parents of three sons: James Murdoch (died at age eleven), William W., and Edward.

Smith's initial political campaign was for the North Carolina House of Commons in 1840, when he was elected as a Whig. He served in the state senate in 1848 and was elected solicitor for Hertford County in the following year, a post he retained until 1857. With a reputation as an able and effective attorney, he was the Whig candidate for Congress in 1857; though he lost the race, he reduced the Democratic majority in his district. Following another term in the House of Commons, he won election to the U.S. House of Representatives in 1859. During his term in Washington Smith, in spite of his freshman status, won a balloting for Speaker of the House after a protracted conflict. The House clerk, a Republican, noting that Smith's majority was one vote, approached two Pennsylvania Republicans who had failed to cast their ballots and explained the significance of their position. The two men, E. Joy Morris and Winter Davis, went to Smith with a proposal that they would vote for him if he would pledge his support for a protectionist Ways and Means Committee. A protectionist himself, Smith responded that he would make no pledges and should have the speakership unfettered or not at all. The two men then had their votes recorded against Smith, and he lost the contest.

Failing in efforts to avert secession, Smith sought and won election in July 1861 to the Confederate Congress, where he served throughout the Civil War. He was at home in Murfreesboro when the town was occupied by Federal cavalry in July 1863 but found refuge in the countryside until the enemy troops withdrew a few days later. Returning to the House of Commons in 1865, Smith supported liberal legislation for freedmen and was active in behalf of Andrew Johnson's policy of Reconstruction. He was a delegate to the National Union Convention in 1866 and a leader in organizing the Conservative party in opposition to the Radicals.

After serving as a delegate to the Democratic National Convention in 1868, Smith left politics and opened a law practice in Norfolk, Va. From there he moved to Raleigh in 1872. As counsel for Governor William Woods Holden in the impeachment trial of 1871, he argued impressively for the governor's acquittal. In 1878 he was named chief justice of the state supreme court, a post he retained until his death eleven years later. Thoroughly competent and morally above reproach, a prudent jurist, and an effective speaker, though less than brilliant, Smith has been said to have carried with him through life a strong Puritan influence acquired from his New England education. He was an active Presbyterian.

SEE: Samuel A. Ashe, ed., *Biographical History of North Carolina*, vol. 7 (1908 [portrait]); *DAB*, vol. 17 (1935); R. C. Lawrence, "Chief Justice W. N. H. Smith," *The State* magazine, 19 Feb. 1944; Petersburg, Va., *Daily Express*, 24 Aug. 1859; Edward C. Smith Papers (Manuscript Department, Duke University Library, Durham).

T. C. PARRAMORE

Smith, William Ruffin *(26 July 1779–22 June 1845)*, planter, was born in Halifax County, the youngest son of Arthur and Anne Ruffin Smith. He was the father of Richard Henry Smith and the grandfather of Peter Evans Smith. Inheriting a small farm from his father, William R. Smith became a successful farmer and by the time of his death had accumulated a large estate in land and slaves. Prominent on a local level, he at times served as a justice of the county court, a trustee of the Vine Hill Academy, and an original member of Trinity Church, Scotland Neck. In his lifetime, the Roanoke River valley in North Carolina was the horse breeding center of the nation. Smith was an active member of the Greenwood Jockey Club and owned and bred the horses Collector, Jack, and Sir Harry, and the mare, Roxanna, got by the famous Sir Archie. He died and was buried in Old Trinity Cemetery, Scotland Neck.

About 1801 he married Sarah (Sally) Walton Norfleet, one of the four daughters of James Norfleet of Gates County. They were the parents of four sons, William, Richard, James, and Robert Arthur, and two daughters, Sarah and Elizabeth. Sarah married James L. G. Baker, the son of Dr. Simmons Baker. Elizabeth and Robert Arthur never married.

In 1834 William R. Smith bought a house in Scotland Neck with notable architectural features that had been built by Lewis Bond in 1808. After his death, his widow Sally continued to reside there for many years. Known as Sally Billy to distinguish her from other women with the same first name in the family connection and neighborhood, her home was referred to locally as the Sally Billy house. In 1972 Charles Herbert Hale of Scotland Neck, who then owned the property, donated the house to the Historic Halifax Restoration Association. The building, retaining the name of the Sally Billy or William Ruffin Smith House, was moved to the town of Halifax in 1975 and restored by the state as part of the Halifax Historic Site. The North Carolina Daughters of the American Revolution, under the leadership of their state regent, Mrs. John B. Macleod of Chapel Hill, took over the furnishing of the dwelling as the project for the bicentennial year.

SEE: Jerry Cross, "Historical Research Report for the Sally-Billy House, June 1974" (North Carolina State Archives, Raleigh); C. T. Smith, Jr., *Smith of Scotland Neck* (1976); William Ruffin Smith Papers (Southern Historical Collection, University of North Carolina, Chapel Hill).

CLAIBORNE T. SMITH, JR.

Smith, Willis *(19 Dec. 1887–26 June 1953)*, lawyer and U.S. senator, was born in Norfolk, Va., the son of Willis and Mary Shaw Creecy Smith. Two years later, when his father died, his mother moved to Elizabeth City and operated a small private school. Smith attended the Atlantic Collegiate Institute in Elizabeth City and was graduated in 1910 from Trinity College (now Duke University) in Durham. In 1912 he completed the course of study at Trinity's law school and was admitted to the bar in Pasquotank County. It was in Raleigh, however, that he practiced law, first in partnership with John W. Hinsdale, then with William B. Duncan (1915–18), Raymond C. Maxwell (1922–24), and W. T. Joyner (1926–32). After 1932 his partners were Oscar Leach and John H. Anderson, Jr., in the firm of Smith, Leach, and Anderson. His practice involved civil, corporate, industrial, and insurance law.

From 1915 to 1920 Smith was inheritance tax attorney for North Carolina, with service in the U.S. Army at Fort Monroe, Va., in 1918. A successful candidate for the North Carolina House of Representatives in 1927, he was reelected for the 1929 and 1931 sessions and served as speaker of the house in 1931. He did not seek public office again until 1950 but was chairman of the state Democratic convention in 1940 and a delegate to the Democratic National Convention in 1944.

In 1950 Smith was a candidate for the office of U.S. senator, opposing Frank Porter Graham. Graham, former president of The University of North Carolina, had been appointed to the Senate in 1949 upon the death of J. Melville Broughton. He led the voting in the first primary, but Smith called for and won a second primary. As the Democratic nominee, Smith was elected to the Senate in November 1950 and took office on 27 November. The primary had been one of the most bitter in the state's history. Graham was accused of favoring the Fair Employment Practice Commission, which, it was said, would require the hiring of Negroes. He was attacked as a supporter of socialism and as an opponent of segregation. A novel based on the campaign, *The Kingpin* by Tom Wicker, was published in 1953.

Smith, a Methodist, was a member of the Kiwanis Club and the American Legion. Within the American Bar Association, he served on the general council (1935–36), on the board of governors (1941–44), and as president (1945–46). He was a member of the North Carolina State Bar Association (president, 1941–42), American Judicature Society, and International Association of Insurance Counsel (president, 1941–43). Named to the board of trustees of Duke University in 1929, he was elected chairman of the board in 1946. In 1933 he served on a committee that prepared rules of practice for the federal courts in North Carolina. In 1946 he represented the United States as an observer at the Nürnberg war trials, and in 1947 he was appointed to the President's Amnesty Board. He was a delegate from the United States to the Interparliamentary Union in Istanbul, Turkey, in 1951 and chairman of the American delegation to the Interparliamentary Union in Bern, Switzerland, in 1952.

In 1919 Smith married Anna Lee, daughter of William Thomas and Margaret Rhinehart Lee of Waynesville. They had four children: Willis, Jr.; Lee Creecy; Anna Lee, who married James K. Dorsett; and Alton Battle. Willis Smith died at the naval hospital in Bethesda, Md., and was buried in Oakwood Cemetery, Raleigh.

SEE: *Biog. Dir. Am. Cong.* (1961); *Duke Alumni Register* 39 (1953 [portrait]); *North Carolina Biography*, vol. 3 (1956), vol. 5 (1941 [portrait]); Raleigh *News and Observer*, 27 June 1953; Willis Smith Papers (Manuscript Department, Duke University Library, Durham); *Who's Who in America* (1930–53).

ROBERT L. BYRD

Smithwick (or Smethwick, Smithwike), Edward *(ca. 1649–1716)*, Council member, Assembly member, and justice, was probably born in Virginia. His parents were Hugh, who migrated to Virginia before May 1642, and Elizabeth Smithwick. In 1659 Hugh and Elizabeth moved to the Albemarle area, then a virtually unsettled part of Virginia but soon to be granted to the Lords Proprietors of Carolina and to become the nucleus of a new colony. The family then included four children—Edward, Hugh, Ralph, and Elizabeth.

Little is known of the Smithwicks' early years in Albemarle. In 1669 Hugh patented 370 acres of land under the recently established government of the North Carolina colony, then called Albemarle. He died before November 1679, and his widow married one Ward, apparently Rice Ward. Three of the Smithwick children may have died young, as no mention has been found of Hugh, Ralph, or Elizabeth as adults, but a son John, born after the family moved to Albemarle, lived to adulthood.

By March 1679/80 Edward Smithwick was married and was living in Chowan Precinct, where his family originally had settled. In the early 1680s his house was the meeting place of the precinct court and the county court.

Nothing is known of Edward's political activities before 1680, if there were any, and little is known of those during the eighties. It is evident, however, that he resisted the abuses and frauds perpetrated by Robert Holden, secretary and customs collector, who gained ascendancy over the colony in 1680 and dominated it for about two years. Smithwick was one of several colonists who were arbitrarily arrested and imprisoned on Holden's order, and later he was one of the adverse witnesses at Holden's trial.

Smithwick did not make a career of politics in any period, but he served briefly in several public offices in the 1690s and later. In July 1690 he was a member of the Council, which under the leadership of Thomas Jarvis was then attempting to restore order following the ousting of Governor Seth Sothel and the accompanying disorders. Smithwick remained on the Council at least through February 1690/91. During that period he made official trips to Virginia, apparently to consult Philip Ludwell, then governor of Albemarle, who was living in Virginia.

About 1703 Smithwick was a member of the Assembly for at least one term; he was again a member in 1711 and 1712. He was a justice of Chowan Precinct Court from 1699 to 1701 and probably longer. In 1712 he was appointed by the Council to a special court to hear an appeal from the court of admiralty.

A loyal Anglican, Smithwick served on the vestry of St. Paul's Parish from December 1701, when the parish was organized, until January 1714/15, when he resigned because of poor health. He was a warden for several terms, and for a number of years he was custodian of the Chowan set of standards for weights and measures, which was provided by the vestry. He donated the land and the plank for the first church building erected in the parish and contributed to funds for a minister's salary and other purposes.

Smithwick, who was about ten years old when his family settled in Chowan, lived in that precinct for the rest of his life. No doubt he, like most other colonists, was a planter. He acquired extensive landholdings and appears to have speculated in land. At his death he owned several thousand acres, of which 3,420 acres were sold by his executors. He gave his two older sons, Edward and John, about 800 acres apiece during his lifetime, and no doubt comparable amounts were reserved by the executors for the two younger sons.

Smithwick was married four times. His first wife, Lydia, died before 29 Mar. 1680, by which time he had remarried. His second wife, Elizabeth, was living as late as 31 July 1688. At some date before 1 Dec. 1702 he married his third wife, Africa. By 27 Oct. 1703 Africa had died, and Smithwick had married Sarah Gillam, widow of Thomas Gillam and previously widow of William Woollard.

Smithwick's will, dated 21 Jan. 1715/16, was proved the following October in Chowan Precinct Court. In it he referred to his "beloved wife," presumably Sarah; sons Edward, John, Edmond, and Samuel; daughter Sarah; and grandchildren Africa Smith and Edward, John, Martin, and Sarah Griffen.

SEE: John L. Cheney, Jr., ed., *North Carolina Government, 1585–1974* (1975); J. Bryan Grimes, ed., *Abstract of North Carolina Wills* (1910); J. R. B. Hathaway, ed., *North Carolina Historical and Genealogical Register*, vol. 1 (1900); Margaret M. Hofmann, comp., *Chowan Precinct . . . Abstracts of Deed Books* (1972); North Carolina State Archives (Raleigh), particularly Albemarle Book of Warrants and Surveys (1681–1706), Albemarle County Papers (1678–1714), Chowan County Court Minutes (1715–19), Chowan County Deeds (1715–19), Chowan County Miscellaneous Papers (1685–1738), Colonial Court Records (boxes 188–89, 192), Council Minutes, Wills, Inventories (1677–1701), Will of Edward Smithwick (1716); Nell Marion Nugent, comp., *Cavaliers and Pioneers*, vol. 1 (1936); Mattie Erma E. Parker, ed., *North Carolina Higher-Court Records, 1670–1696* and *1697–1701* (1968, 1971); William S. Price, Jr., ed., *North Carolina Higher-Court Records, 1702–1708* and *North Carolina Higher-Court Minutes, 1709–1723* (1974, 1977); William L. Saunders, ed., *Colonial Records of North Carolina*, vols. 1–2 (1886).

MATTIE ERMA E. PARKER

Smylie, James *(ca. 1780–1853)*, clergyman, church organizer, and controversialist, was born in the Guilford County area of Scots-Irish parentage. Little is known about his early life other than the fact that he attended David Caldwell's Log College. In 1804 he was licensed for the ministry by the Orange Presbytery. Ordained by that presbytery two years later, he was promptly sent, probably at his own request, as a missionary from the Synod of North Carolina to the Mississippi Territory.

Upon his arrival, Smylie organized in the town of Washington, Adams County, the first Presbyterian church in what later became the state of Mississippi. At the same time he opened a classical school, modeled on that of David Caldwell, which was said to be the first institution of learning in Mississippi. In 1811 Smylie took up permanent residence in Amite County, Miss., and there established another church called Pine Ridge from which he operated for the remainder of his career. At the time of his move to Amite, Smylie also became a landholding planter and began developing a plantation that would make him modestly wealthy. Although he continued to preach at neighboring churches until his death, he apparently did not continue long in the active pastoral ministry after moving to Amite. In his later years he spent increasingly large portions of his time instructing his and his neighbors' slaves both in Scriptures and in the Westminster catechism. He was married three times and had one child in each marriage. Although he is known to have maintained a detailed diary throughout his career, the document has not yet become available in a public repository.

Smylie is known chiefly for two major contributions, both accomplished after his removal to Mississippi. The first was to establish Presbyterianism formally in Mississippi. In addition to forming the first church in the territory, Smylie, operating from Pine Ridge, initiated steps to organize the first presbytery for Mississippi. In 1814 he personally persuaded the membership of the West Tennessee Presbytery to petition the Synod of Kentucky to create a presbytery in Mississippi. The following year the Synod of Kentucky meeting at Danville acted affirmatively, enabling Smylie to call the first meeting of the Mississippi Presbytery on 15 Mar. 1816. Smylie was promptly elected state clerk of the presbytery, a post that he held for much of the remainder of his life.

In his post as stated clerk, Smylie was the recipient of a celebrated letter in the early history of attempts to abolish slavery. On 28 Nov. 1835 the Presbytery of Chillicothe, Ohio, adopted a set of resolutions condemning slavery as "a heinous sin and scandal" and demanding that all churches find slaveholders "guilty of a great sin . . . to be dealt with, as for other scandalous crimes." The resolutions were sent to Smylie with the request that the

Presbytery of Mississippi endorse them and adopt them as basic tenets of the church in Mississippi. Smylie, already a slaveholder himself and ever eager to uphold the rights of slaveholders, responded to the letter with a scathing condemnation of the clergy and members of the Chillicothe Presbytery. He then proceeded to expand his views in a lengthy document that was published in 1836 under the title *A Review of a Letter from the Presbytery of Chillicothe, to the Presbytery of Mississippi on the Subject of Slavery*. Although the small volume was not, as some have claimed, the first defense of slavery written by a southerner, it was among the first to respond formally to the appearance of radical abolitionism and was, at the time, the most extended defense of slavery prepared by a southerner. Because Smylie's defense rested largely on scriptural and religious arguments, its publication and wide distribution throughout America made it a crucial document in the development of proslavery attitudes in the South.

SEE: Biographical Files, Historical Foundation of the Presbyterian and Reformed Churches (Montreat, N.C.); Montgomery Family Papers (Mississippi Department of Archives and History, Jackson); Alfred Nevin, *Encyclopedia of the Presbyterian Church in the United States of America* (1884); *The Presbyterian*, 18 Feb. 1854; *Southwestern Presbyterian*, 23 Feb. 1871.

LARRY E. TISE

Smyth, George Washington *(16 May 1803–21 Feb. 1866)*, surveyor, jurist, and congressman, was born in North Carolina, the son of Samuel Smyth, a German-born millwright, and a Scots-Irish mother. His father owned a gristmill on Little Swift Creek in Craven County a few years before the American Revolution, and that is probably where young Smyth was born. When George was three, the family moved to Fayetteville, Tenn., and later to Alabama. While in Tennessee he received some elementary education in Maury County. On 20 Jan. 1830, against the wishes of his family, he left for Texas, arriving at Nacogdoches on 14 February. He served for a time as a schoolteacher, then became surveyor at Bevil's Settlement near present Jasper. He continued as surveyor until 1834, when he was elected a land commissioner.

In 1835 Smyth was appointed first judge of the town of Bevil by the Provisional Government of the Republic of Texas. He was a signer of the Texas Declaration of Independence and on 1 Feb. 1836 was elected a delegate to the constitutional convention. He was also a signer of the Texas Constitution. With the establishment of the Republic of Texas, he was appointed to survey its boundary with the United States, a task that occupied him until June 1841.

A delegate to the state constitutional convention in 1845, Smyth afterwards was commissioner of the General Land Office from 1848 to 1857. Elected to Congress, he served a single term (1853–55) and was not a candidate for reelection. Although he opposed secession, his son enlisted in the Confederate army with his father's approval. Smyth died in Austin while attending the convention to form a new state constitution after the Civil War. He was buried in the state cemetery in Austin. In 1936 the state erected a marker at the site of his home ten miles southwest of Jasper. Smyth's grandchildren gave his papers to the University of Texas Library in the early 1930s.

In April 1834 Smyth married Frances M. Grigsby, and they were the parents of seven children: Sarah (Mrs. J. T. Armstrong), Susan (Mrs. Samuel S. Adams), Matilda (Mrs. R. T. Armstrong), George W., Jr., Francis, Emily (Mrs. W. Hansford Smith), and J. G.

SEE: "Autobiography of George W. Smyth," *Southwestern Historical Quarterly* 36 (January 1933); *Biog. Dir. Am. Cong.* (1989); Louis Wiltz Kemp, *Signers of the Texas Declaration of Independence* (1944); Alan D. Watson, *A History of New Bern and Craven County* (1987); Walter P. Webb, ed., *Handbook of Texas*, vol. 2 (1952).

JOSEPH L. PRICE, JR.

Snavely, Carl Gray *(31 July 1894–12 July 1975)*, college football coach, was born in Omaha, Nebr., the son of Charles, a Methodist minister, and Bessie Boggs Snavely. He was raised in Pennsylvania and attended Lebanon Valley College, where he played baseball, football, and basketball. He was graduated in 1915. From 1915 to 1926 he coached football at a number of high schools and prep schools in Pennsylvania and Ohio. Snavely gained national attention for his success at Pennsylvania's Bellefonte Academy. He also played two years of minor league baseball. In 1927 he was hired from Bellefonte to become head football coach at Bucknell University, in Lewisburg, Pa., where he compiled a record of 42 wins, 16 losses, and 8 ties in seven seasons.

In 1934 Snavely became head football coach at The University of North Carolina. His first team in Chapel Hill won 7 games, against only 1 loss and 1 tie. This team featured George Barclay, the school's first football All-American. The next year the university team won its first eight games and was being touted as a Rose Bowl possibility before a season ending upset loss to Duke University. Despite these successes Snavely did not see eye-to-eye with university president Frank Porter Graham, a persistent critic of big-time college football, whose abortive Graham Plan would have deemphasized the sport at the university and in the remainder of the Southern Conference. Snavely abruptly left North Carolina in April 1936 to become head coach at Cornell University.

Snavely stayed at Cornell for nine seasons. His 1939 team was undefeated in eight games. The coach gained favorable national attention in the 1940 Cornell-Dartmouth game when a referee's mistake allowed Cornell to score the winning touchdown on a fifth down play. After confirming the mistake on film, Snavely forfeited the game to Dartmouth. He ended his tenure at Cornell with three Ivy League championships and a record of 46 wins, 26 losses, and 3 ties.

In 1945 Snavely returned to Chapel Hill after having been assured that his program would have the full support of the administration. His 1945 team won half of its ten games. Snavely's glory years at Chapel Hill were from 1946 to 1949. Bolstered by returning GI's, most notably All-American back Charlie Justice, The University of North Carolina spent those four years among the nation's elite. The 1946 team won 8, lost 1, and tied 1 in the regular season before losing 20–10 to the University of Georgia in the Sugar Bowl, North Carolina's first bowl game. Snavely's 1947 team won 8 and lost 2 and did not play in a bowl game. The 1948 team won 9 with only a single tie. The Tar Heels then lost to the University of Oklahoma 14–6 in the Sugar Bowl. The 1949 team earned North Carolina's third bowl visit in four years, a 27–13 Cotton Bowl defeat to Rice University, which followed a 7-win, 3-loss season. In this four-year period The University of North Carolina won two Southern Conference championships, in 1946 and 1949, and finished in second place the other two years. It was ranked in the final Associated Press Poll Top Ten in 1946, 1947, and 1948, reaching a peak ranking of number three in 1948. Charlie Justice finished second in the voting for the prestigious Heisman Trophy, awarded to the nation's top player, in 1948 and 1949, and was awarded the Walter Camp Trophy as national player of the year in 1948.

Snavely was unable to maintain the program at this high level. A series of disputes, ranging from the size of the school's recruiting budget to his inability to successfully switch from the outmoded single-wing formation to the split T, handicapped the program and again alienated Snavely from the school and its supporters. After losing seasons in 1950, 1951, and 1952 he left North Carolina. Despite the dismal last three seasons, he departed with a University of North Carolina record of 59 wins, 35 losses, and 5 ties.

He finished his coaching career at small Washington University in St. Louis, where he became an increasingly vocal critic of big-time college football, and retired from coaching in 1958. With a record at four colleges of 180 wins, 96 losses, and 16 ties, he was named to the National Football Foundation Hall of Fame in 1965.

Snavely had a reputation as a hard-working, stern, no-nonsense perfectionist. He was especially well regarded as a teacher of the single wing, the most common offensive formation until after World War II. He was an active member of the American Football Coaches Association and served as its president in 1952. An enthusiastic amateur photographer, Snavely was a pioneer in the use of game films as a teaching aid. He was also an avid golfer.

Snavely married Bernice Clara Richardson in 1915. Their son, Carl Gray, Jr., a navy pilot, was killed in action in World War II. In 1944 they adopted an infant son, Carl Gray III. Coach Snavely died in Kirkwood, Mo., two years after the death of his wife.

SEE: Tim Cohane, *Great College Football Coaches of the Twenties and Thirties* (1973); *Durham Morning Herald*, 13 July 1975; Ronald L. Mendell and Timothy B. Phares, *Who's Who in Football* (1974); *New York Times*, 14 July 1975; David L. Porter, *Biographical Directory of American Sports* (1987); Raleigh *News and Observer*, 24 July 1950; Ken Rappoport, *Tar Heel: North Carolina Football* (1976); Richard Stone, "The Graham Plan of 1935: An Aborted Crusade to De-Emphasize College Athletics," *North Carolina Historical Review* 64 (July 1987); University of North Carolina, Sports Information Department: Snavely file.

JIM L. SUMNER

Snell, John Leslie, Jr. *(2 June 1923–27 May 1972)*, historian, academic administrator, and defender of academic freedom, was born at Plymouth in Washington County. The son of John Leslie and Lessie Ann McLamb Snell, he grew up in Columbia, Tyrrell County, and was valedictorian in the Columbia High School class of 1940. Snell enrolled at The University of North Carolina in September 1940 but left to join the U.S. Army Air Corps in December 1942. A bomber pilot in the European theater of operations, he flew over thirty combat missions and won the Air Medal, Distinguished Flying Cross, and five battle stars. In December 1943 he married Maxine Pybas; they later had three children, Marcia Ruth, Leslie Ann, and John McCullough.

Snell returned to Chapel Hill in 1945 and quickly completed three degrees: a B.A. in history (1946), an M.A. (1947), and a Ph.D. (1950). Working principally with Professor Carl H. Pegg, he wrote his dissertation on "The German Socialists and Wilson's Peace Policy, 1914–1918." From this research a series of articles appeared in the early 1950s that quickly stamped him as a rising American historian of Germany and of international affairs.

Although Snell taught while a graduate student as a part-time instructor, his professional academic career began at the University of Wichita in 1949. Two years there were followed by two research years made possible by grants from the American Council of Learned Societies. In 1953 he became an assistant professor at Tulane University, where his rise was meteoric. In three years he became an associate professor, in six a professor, and a decade after his arrival dean of the Graduate School of Arts and Sciences, a position he held until 1966. The years at Tulane saw a steady stream of published works, including *Wartime Origins of the East-West Dilemma over Germany* (1959) and *Illusion and Necessity: The Diplomacy of Global War, 1939–1945* (1963) (later translated into German), the editorship of two sets of text anthologies and of a scholarly work, and repeated professional appearances.

Two studies brought particular note to Snell. In *The Meaning of Yalta* (1956), which he edited, Snell and his fellow contributors challenged right-wing allegations that President Franklin D. Roosevelt "sold out" to the Russians at the Yalta conference. The sober, meticulous use of recently published diplomatic documents not only removed many illusions about the conference, but also facilitated a clearer understanding of the origins of the Cold War. Indeed, Snell's contribution on the side of moderation renders this work and his other articles on the Cold War of continuing historiographical importance. But these views on Yalta and the Cold War frequently brought Snell into conflict with both right- and left-wing political groups; his moderation and willingness to speak frankly were symbolic both of his professional integrity and personal courage, especially in the emotion-laden South of the late 1950s and early 1960s.

The second volume was *The Education of Historians in the United States* with E. Dexter Perkins (1962). Serving as executive director for the American Historical Association's study of the graduate history departments in the United States, Snell came into contact with most of the leading academic historians in the two-year investigation of graduate education in history. From this study came a set of recommendations for the restructuring and acceleration of graduate education. In it he also stressed a part of his continuing professional concern: the improvement of the quality of preparation for teaching given graduate students. Work on this project was followed by nearly continuous activity in the American Historical Association, culminating with his election to the governing council in 1965. At the same time he helped to found the European history section of the Southern Historical Association and served as its chairman in 1966.

Also in 1966 Snell moved, as professor of history, to the University of Pennsylvania. In two years there he edited two further sets of readings and continued research on a major study of the origins of democracy in Germany. In 1968 he returned to Chapel Hill as University Distinguished Professor of History. During the next four years he attracted numerous graduate students for whom he was a demanding but concerned mentor. He also continued his work in the professional associations, including attendance at the International Congress of Historical Sciences in Moscow in 1970, and his research on German history.

Never hesitant to speak his mind on professional or public issues, Snell played an important, calming influence during the campus unrest at Chapel Hill. An opponent of the war in Vietnam, Snell—ever mindful of the politicization of the German universities before and during Hitler's regime—argued forcefully that academic freedom required that a university not take institutional positions on public issues. In May 1970, in a momentous faculty debate over a resolution to establish a political action committee, Snell argued that "To commit a university to a partisan political stand is to invite those who ultimately control our universities to re-make them in whatever political image they may desire." This incisive intervention helped to defeat the resolution. In doing so Snell fused the European and American traditions of faculty control and free speech; his standing as an internationally known scholar, teacher, and former administrator ensured that his remarks would be heeded. It was possibly his most significant contribution to his beloved alma mater while a faculty member.

In the spring of 1972 Snell was suddenly stricken, anew, with cancer. Yet until the end he continued to meet his classes, to grade papers, and to read—his devotion to students, duty, and scholarship undiminished. At his death at age forty-eight he left the first volume of his major study on German democracy nearly finished. It was completed by Hans Schmitt (a former colleague from Tulane) and published as *The Democratic Movement in Germany, 1789–1914* (1976). This posthumous work reflects Snell's encyclopedic knowledge of sources, his demand for perfection, and his brilliant ability to synthesize and generalize. It traces the halting and often tragic drive towards democracy in Germany, its frustrations, its limited successes, and yet its beaconlike appeal to many Germans before and after 1914. The study will stand as a major contribution to German history since 1789.

A member of the American Historical Association, the Southern Historical Association, and the Methodist church, Snell was a Democrat. At his death a memorial service was held in the University Methodist Church in Chapel Hill. Later the Southern Historical Association established the Snell prize for the best seminar paper in European history; and the Department of History at Chapel Hill, the annual Snell lecture on European history.

SEE: Departmental Records, Department of History (University of North Carolina, Chapel Hill); Faculty memorial by Carl H. Pegg, Faculty Council Minutes, 12 Dec. 1972 (University of North Carolina, Chapel Hill); Snell Papers (Southern Historical Collection, University of North Carolina, Chapel Hill).

SAMUEL R. WILLIAMSON, JR.

Snoden, Thomas *(d. ca. March 1714)*, attorney and colonial official, first appears in the records of North Carolina in November 1693 as a minor. He had been apprenticed to one Thomas Hassold by his stepfather, Edmond Pirkins, and was to remain an apprentice until Pirkins returned for him or until he reached the age of twenty-one.

How Snoden rose from those humble beginnings to become a reasonably well-educated attorney is not known, but he began arguing cases before the General Court in July 1702 and practiced law until his death. A young man of obvious talents (court minutes surviving in his hand are the best written of the period), Snoden rose quickly in North Carolina government. From service as clerk of the General Court and Court of Chancery (as well as the General Assembly in 1703) during March 1703–July 1705, Snoden went on to become attorney general from July 1705 to 1708. In 1712 he represented Perquimans Precinct in the lower house and was chosen speaker of the Assembly by his peers.

Snoden was scheduled for appointment as a justice of the General Court when he died suddenly early in 1714. He left a wife Constance and son Thomas.

SEE: J. R. B. Hathaway, ed., *North Carolina Historical and Genealogical Register*, 3 vols. (1900–1903); William S. Price, Jr., ed., *North Carolina Higher-Court Records, 1702–1708* (1974) and *North Carolina Higher-Court Minutes, 1709–1723* (1977).

WILLIAM S. PRICE, JR.

Snow, Ernest Ansel *(4 Oct. 1850–20 Mar. 1922)*, lumberman and furniture manufacturer, was born in Ferrisburg, Vt., the son of William Henry and Lydia Jane Cramer Snow. He moved to North Carolina with his family in 1867. At Cornell University he took the mechanical arts course and became a salesman for his father's lumber business. He also helped his father establish a spoke and handle factory in 1871, and beginning in 1874 he worked for seven years as a contractor in High Point. In 1881 the family formed the Snow Lumber Company, and late in the decade Ernest was working as a salesman of lumber to furniture manufacturers in Baltimore.

It occurred to Snow that the manufacturing ought to take place nearer the source of raw materials, and, returning to High Point, he enlisted the support of John H. Tate and Thomas F. Wrenn in February 1889 to form the High Point Furniture Company. It was an immediate success, and in 1893 Snow sold his interests and joined five other partners in establishing the Eagle Furniture Company, all the while continuing his lumber business. By 1919 he was president of the Shipman Organ Company and of the Southern Chair Company, vice-president of the North Carolina Wheel Company, and secretary-treasurer of the Snow Lumber Company.

In 1876 Snow married Naomi Alice English, the daughter of a High Point merchant, and they became the parents of seven daughters and four sons, the first of whom, a son, died as an infant: Mabel Jane (1877), Bertha Augusta (1879), William Ernest (1881), Helen May (1883), Winifred Alice (1886), Josie Elfleda (1888), Ruby Constance (1890), Roy Ansel (1892), Rodney English (1894), and Dorothy Dewey (1898). He was a Mason and an elder in the Presbyterian church.

SEE: *Greensboro Daily News*, 21 Mar. 1922; *High Point Enterprise*, 16 Oct. 1988 (portrait); *High Point, North Carolina, City Directory, 1919* (1918); Holt McPherson, *High Pointers of High Point* (1975); *Prominent People of North Carolina* (1906); David N. Thomas, "Early History of the North Carolina Furniture Industry, 1880–1921" (Ph.D. diss., University of North Carolina, 1964).

WILLIAM S. POWELL

Snow, William Henry *(18 Sept. 1825–18 Nov. 1902)*, lumberman and furniture manufacturer, was born at Montpelier, Washington County, Vt., the son of William and Emily Haynes Snow. His father, a farmer and stock raiser, disappeared on a stock drive to New York State, presumably robbed and murdered. Left an orphan at a young age and raised by relatives, he began work in a woolen mill. In 1849 he married Lydia Jane Cramer (1830–1902), and they became the parents of two children. In 1851 they moved to Lowell, Mass., an industrial center. Before the end of the year he was engaged by the British government to install a telegraph line in Australia from Melbourne to Sydney—the first south of the equator. After five years there he returned to Lowell, having visited several South American countries en route home, where he opened a packing house and operated a provisions store.

Early in 1861 Snow set out for California, but in Chicago he learned of the eruption of the Civil War and returned to Lowell. There he recruited a company that was mustered into the Eighth Massachusetts Heavy Artillery. Commissioned captain, he commanded the company throughout the war, serving near the end of the conflict in North Carolina.

Back in Lowell he discovered that his wife was suffering from tuberculosis, and physicians advised that they move to a more healthy climate. Remembering pleasant weather in North Carolina, Snow moved his family to Greensboro, where his wife's health was restored. It has been said that sawmill owners in the vicinity of Archdale, from which finished lumber was usually available, refused to sell the Yankee newcomers lumber for their new home. Snow turned to the Guilford County forests, from which he cut his own timber.

In these new surroundings he was alert for an opportunity to establish himself in a business when he further recognized the potentials offered by the abundant hardwoods, such as hickory, dogwood, and persimmon trees, that grew there. He opened a factory in Greensboro to produce spokes for wheels and handles for mallets used in quarries; hickory proved to be an excellent wood for that purpose. In 1871, probably because his factory in Greensboro burned, he moved to High Point on the North Carolina Railroad and reestablished his business. From the abundant dogwood and persimmon trees, even harder than hickory, he began also to manufacture shuttle blocks for use in textile mills. He was able to meet the growing demand for all of these items and soon was recognized by mill owners as the leading source in the nation for excellent shuttle blocks and bobbins. To increase production, Snow brought to North Carolina the first Blanchard lathe and the first band saw to be used in the state. His successful operation of his Snow Lumber Company, which sold good quality lumber up and down the East Coast, attracted wide attention and led to the development of an extensive lumber industry throughout the South.

Snow also purchased land and began growing tobacco; in time he devised improved methods of curing tobacco. Instead of curing whole stalks, he cured individual leaves strung on wire. He also erected smaller barns and modified the heating method through controlled roof ventilation—a device that he patented. He taught others how to follow this new system and is said to have published folders or pamphlets explaining it. In addition, he was the original promoter of the Asheboro Railroad and invested large sums of his own money towards its construction. For thirty years Snow was regarded as the leading spokesman for the industrial development of High Point and served seven terms as mayor. For a time he also was postmaster. His son, Ernest Ansel, who had emigrated from Vermont with him, was a salesman for lumber produced by his father's sawmill and in time became president of the Snow Lumber Company as well as a leader in the development of the area's furniture industry. By 1887 High Point was considered to be the "most important manufacturing town on the North Carolina Railroad."

Snow's daughter, Bertha Emily, married Jonathan Elwood Cox in 1878, and shortly afterwards Cox joined Snow in the production of shuttle blocks and bobbins. In time Snow withdrew from the business in favor of his son-in-law, and it became the J. Elwood Cox Manufacturing Company; after forty years Cox turned it over to his nephew, Joseph D. Cox. A Presbyterian and a prewar Whig, Snow afterwards became a Republican.

SEE: George S. Bradshaw, *Biography of Captain William Henry Snow* (reprinted from *High Point News*, 24 Mar. 1921); *Greensboro Patriot*, 26 Nov. 1902; *High Point Enterprise*, 16 Oct. 1988; *North Carolina Biography*, vols. 3 (1928), 6 (1919); David N. Thomas, "Early History of the North Carolina Furniture Industry, 1880–1921" (Ph.D. diss., University of North Carolina, 1964) and "Getting Started in High Point," *Forest History* 11 (July 1967).

HOLT MCPHERSON

Snowden, Thomas. *See* **Snoden, Thomas.**

Sojourner, William. *See* **Surginer, William.**

Sondley, Forster Alexander *(13 Aug. 1857–17 Apr. 1931)*, attorney and scholar, was born at Montrealla, his maternal grandfather's home in Alexander, a community ten miles north of Asheville. As an adult he most often referred to himself as F. A. Sondley; others, however, generally used Foster, as did Wofford College in Spartanburg, S.C., which he entered as a sophomore in 1873. He was the only child of Richard Sondley, of a prominent family of Columbia, S.C. His mother, Harriet Alexander Ray, had borne five children by a previous marriage before being widowed; Forster/Foster was her last child. Members of her family were pioneers in the region around Asheville where Sondley grew up. Educated in the various schools in and around Asheville, he was graduated from Wofford in 1876 and returned to Asheville to spend the rest of his life. He studied law and was admitted to the bar by the North Carolina Supreme Court in 1879; he also was licensed to practice before the U.S. Supreme Court.

His knowledge of North Carolina law, history, and geography, coupled with a characteristic courtesy in court towards legal opponents, earned him a reputation as the ablest civil lawyer in the western part of the state. In 1905, at the peak of his career, he went into semiretirement in order to devote more time to his varied interests, especially the study of history. By 1911 he had moved into Finis Viae, a palatial home on Haw Creek near Asheville, which he had built earlier. A collector of wide and varied tastes, he accumulated firearms, Indian relics, minerals, gemstones, antique furniture, porcelains, Confederate mementos, and other items. He is chiefly remembered for his personal library of approximately 30,000 volumes containing hundreds of rare works on southern and state history and on natural history. The city of Asheville acquired the library by bequest at his death, and parts of it still form the nucleus of the Sondley Reference Library in Asheville's Pack Memorial Library.

Deeply interested in the state's history, he was a member of the first North Carolina Historical Commission, established in 1903, and he fostered the organization of the Buncombe County Historical Society. His writings on state and local history were vigorous and accurate, and at his death he was a recognized authority on North Carolina history.

Sondley was an individual of retiring habits and a curious combination of characteristics. His writings betray a provincialism unusual in such a widely read man. An ardent Carolinian, a defender of the Confederacy, he yet showed a great tolerance towards controversial subjects and possessed a wide knowledge of the world. Strong of will and opinionated, he would also listen patiently in discussion or debate. Although reclusive by nature, he still had many friends, and his hospitality and generosity were well known in the region.

In appearance he was tall and erect, with a direct, piercing gaze. Portraits are located in the Buncombe County Courthouse and the Pack Memorial Library in Asheville. Never married, he died in his home near Asheville and was buried near his boyhood home in Alexander.

Among his more important published works are *Asheville and Buncombe County* (1922), *History of Buncombe County, North Carolina*, 2 vols., (1930), and *My Ancestry* (1930 [portrait]). Many of the rare books in his collection at the Pack Memorial Library were listed and described in *Leaves from the Sondley*, vols. 1–2 (1945–52).

SEE: *Asheville Citizen*, 18 Apr. 1931; *Asheville Citizen-Times*, 19 Apr. 1931; "Foster A. Sondley: Attorney, Scholar, and Bibliophile," *North Carolina Libraries* 30 (Summer–Fall 1972); James D. Lee, "Foster Sondley: Attorney, Scholar, Bibliophile" (typescript, North Carolina Collection, University of North Carolina, Chapel Hill); Vertical files and Sondley Papers in the Asheville-Buncombe Library System.

JAMES DANIEL LEE

Sorsby, Nicholas Turner *(20 June 1818–27 Feb. 1868)*, physician, surgeon, and agriculturalist, the son of Rebecca Williams and Alexander Sorsby, was born in Nash County. After the death of his father, while Nicholas was still an infant, the family moved to Alabama, where Mrs. Sorsby married E. D. Whitehead. Referred to as "Major E.D.W." at one time by Sorsby, Whitehead was listed as the young man's guardian when he entered the University of Virginia in 1835 from his home in Havanna, Ala. Having remained away for the term 1838–39, Sorsby was graduated in 1840 from the university's School of Moral Philosophy. The next year he received a medical degree from the University of Pennsylvania and then spent four years studying in Paris.

For some years Sorsby was a physician and planter in Greene County, Ala., where his address in 1857 was Forkland. He married Ann Hill, and they were the parents of a daughter, Eugenia. In 1856 he became the guardian of Catherine R., Amanda A., Nicholas C., and Virginia H., minor heirs of his brother, Alexander W., of Autauga County, Ala.

Dr. Sorsby was the author of "Indian Millet, or Dourah Corn," published in the U.S. Patent Office report, *Report of the Commissioner of Patents for the Year 1854: Agriculture* (1855). His prize-winning essay, "On Horizontal Plowing and Hill-Side Ditching," which appeared as a 35-page article in *Transactions of the North-Carolina State Agricultural Society, for 1857* (1858), is a detailed description of antebellum farming and contains a plea for better maintenance of the fertility of the soil. He was awarded a silver pitcher for this essay at the North Carolina State Fair. It was also published as a pamphlet in Mobile, Ala., in 1860. During the Civil War Sorsby served as a surgeon in the Confederate army. He was buried in Eutaw, Ala. In 1902 his daughter in Montgomery gave a photograph of the portrait she owned to the state archives.

SEE: Archives, University of Virginia and University of Pennsylvania; Family correspondence (Alabama Department of Archives and History, Montgomery); Greensboro *Alabama Beacon*, 7 Mar. 1868; J. M. Watson, *Abstracts of Early Records of Nash County, North Carolina* (1963); Probate Minutes, 1856, Autauga County (Prattville, Ala.).

DOROTHY LONG

Sothel (or Sothell), Anna Willix Riscoe Blount *(d. 1695)*, wife of Governor Seth Sothel, was the daughter of Belshazzar Willix of Exeter, N.H., and his wife Anna. Her father, described as "a man of more than ordinary education," was born in 1595 in Alford, Lincolnshire, England, the son of Belshazzar Willix, a man of substantial means, and his wife Anne. The younger Belshazzar migrated to New England at an unknown date and by 1640 was living with his wife and children in Exeter, where he owned a small tract of land.

In 1648 Anna's mother was waylaid, robbed, and murdered on the road from Dover to Exeter. She left three daughters: Hazelelponi, the eldest, then about twelve, Anna, and Susannah. Soon after the mother's death the family moved to Salisbury, Mass., where the father married Mary Hauxworth, a widow. Following his death in about March 1650/51, two of the children, presumably the younger two, were boarded for a time with a neighbor, Robert Tuck. Their stepmother, who became mentally ill, may already have been too sick to care for them. Within a few years all three sisters became servants. Hazelelponi served in a home in Weymouth, Anna became a servant in the residence of the Reverend Timothy Dalton in Hampton, and Susannah took service in a house nearby.

Anna remained in the Dalton home until 1666, by which time both Dalton and his widow had died. She then went to Boston and lived for a time in the home of Hazelelponi, who had married one John Gee. Soon Anna married and went with her husband, Robert Riscoe, to the northern Carolina colony, then called Albemarle, where the couple was living by September 1670.

Riscoe, a mariner, was master and part owner of the *Good Hope*, a brigantine of ten tons that traded between Albemarle and New England. He seems also to have sailed to England and Ireland on occasion. In 1673 he was sued in Rhode Island by Thomas Miller, a prominent Albemarle settler and later acting governor, who charged Riscoe with breach of covenant because Riscoe had landed him in New England after agreeing to take him to Ireland. The court ruled in Riscoe's favor, as the *Good Hope* had been damaged during the voyage from Albemarle and was not in condition for a crossing to Europe.

By 13 June 1683 Riscoe had died and Anna had remarried. Her second husband was James Blount, who like Anna was recently widowed. Blount was a prosperous planter of Chowan Precinct and a member of the Albemarle Council. He died in the spring or summer of 1686, leaving Anna a substantial estate for her lifetime, with right to dispose of sixty pounds by will. At some subsequent date she married the governor of Albemarle, Seth Sothel, who was one of the Lords Proprietors of Carolina. Sothel, like Blount, lived in Chowan Precinct.

Anna's marriage to Sothel included the turbulent period of the Albemarle colonists' revolt against the governor, which ended with the trial and banishment of Sothel by the Assembly. It also included the period in which Sothel was governor of South Carolina, where he went after his banishment from Albemarle and assumed the governorship by virtue of his status as a Proprietor. At least nominally, Anna was first lady for a time in each of the Carolina colonies, although it is not certain that she actively filled the role in South Carolina. Presumably she accompanied Sothel into exile, but she appears to have been in Albemarle at least briefly while Sothel was in South Carolina.

Although Sothel's banishment from Albemarle was only for one year, it is not certain that he and Anna ever again lived in the colony. Their home plantation in Chowan appears to have been leased before Sothel went to South Carolina and to have remained in the possession of others after his return. There is evidence that the couple was living in Virginia at the time of Sothel's death, but it is not conclusive.

Sothel died before 3 Feb. 1693/94, when his will was proved. He bequeathed most of his land and practically all of his movable property to Anna. The next fall Anna married John Lear of Nansemond County, Va. Lear, who had emigrated from England about the middle of the century, was a member of the Virginia Council and a man of substantial means. Like Anna, he had been married and widowed three times.

Anna's marriage to Lear was brief, for she died before May 1695. Lear was dead by the following December. There is no evidence that Anna had children by any of her husbands, although she acquired stepchildren through her marriages to Blount and Lear. Her will has not survived, but she appears to have bequeathed much of her estate to her sisters.

At the time of Anna's death, Hazelelponi was living in Ipswich, Mass., the widow of her second husband, Obadiah Wood. Susannah and her husband, Francis Jones, were then living in Portsmouth, N.H. In May 1695 the three appointed Hazelelponi's son-in-law, Thomas Pickering, to go to Albemarle as their attorney and represent their interests in Anna's estate. Although there was extensive litigation over the property, Pickering appears to have established the sisters' right to at least 12,000 acres, including the Sothel's home plantation on Salmon Creek. In 1697 Hazelelponi, Susannah, and Francis sold their interest in the estate to Pickering.

SEE: J. Bryan Grimes, ed., *Abstract of North Carolina Wills* (1910) and *North Carolina Wills and Inventories* (1912); *New England Historical and Genealogical Register*, vols. 50 (1896), 68 (1914), 78 (1924); North Carolina State Archives (Raleigh), various documents, especially *Miller v. Riscoe* Papers in the Private Collections and the wills of James Blount (9 July 1685), Seth Sothel (25 Jan. 1689/90), and Edward Waad (9 Aug. 1691); Sybil Noyes et al., comps., *Genealogical Dictionary of Maine and New Hampshire* (1928); Mattie Erma E. Parker, ed., *North Carolina Higher-Court Records, 1670–1696* and *1697–1701* (1968, 1971); Clayton Torrence, ed., *Winston of Virginia and Allied Families* (1927); *Virginia Magazine of History and Biography*, vol. 17.

MATTIE ERMA E. PARKER

Sothel (or Sothell, Southwell), Seth *(d. 1693 or 1694)*, Proprietor of Carolina and governor of North Carolina and South Carolina, is first mentioned in extant records in a letter of June 1675 written by Lord Shaftesbury, one of the Carolina Proprietors, to the governor and Council of South Carolina. In the letter, which pertained to plans Sothel had for establishing a settlement in South Carolina, Sothel was described as "a person of considerable estate in England." Nothing is known of his earlier life.

The plan discussed in Shaftesbury's letter was never executed, probably because Sothel found a more promising opportunity in North Carolina. About October 1677 he became one of the Lords Proprietors of the province by purchasing the Proprietorship originally held by Edward Hyde, earl of Clarendon, but then owned by Henry, second earl of Clarendon. About a year after the purchase, arrangements were made for Sothel to go as governor to the northern Carolina colony, then called Albemarle. On the way to Albemarle, however, he was captured by pirates and held in Algiers for ransom.

By September 1681 the pirates had released Sothel, and he was again preparing to go to Albemarle as governor. To that end his fellow Proprietors issued a notice to the two Carolina colonies informing them of Sothel's purchase of the Clarendon share in Carolina, reminding them of a provision in the Fundamental Constitutions of Carolina under which the eldest Proprietor residing in the province was to be governor and ordering them to obey Sothel as governor unless an older Proprietor should arrive. The fact that Sothel had a legal right to the governorship under the Fundamental Constitutions, and did not hold office merely through favor of the other Proprietors, no doubt influenced his conduct in office. In effect, it placed Sothel beyond the control of the other Proprietors, making it possible for him to govern without regard for the rights of either the colonists or his fellow Proprietors.

By February 1682/83 Sothel was officiating as governor of Albemarle. Before the end of the year a flow of complaints against him had reached London, making it evident to his fellow Proprietors that he was far from being the "sober discreet gentleman" they had judged him to be. On 14 Dec. 1683 the Proprietary board ordered that a letter be written reprimanding Sothel for failure to follow the instructions he had been given and directing that he provide information on a number of matters. In a letter executing that order the Proprietors complained that Sothel, contrary to their instructions, had named to the Council men who had been prominent in the recent disorders in the colony, that he had ignored their directive to set up a special court to try actions rising from the disorders, that he had not organized a county court as instructed and as required by the Fundamental Constitutions, that he had not allowed the secretary of the colony to have the perquisites of his office but had pocketed them himself, and that he had taken from Colonel Philip Ludwell of Virginia a plantation owned by Ludwell's wife. They directed that Sothel send them the names of the persons he had appointed to the Council, that he inform them of the amount of quitrents he had collected and his disposition of the receipts, and that he give account of his handling of the other matters on which there were complaints. They further directed that he consult the Proprietor John Archdale, who had recently settled in Albemarle, concerning appointments and other matters.

On one point the Proprietors appear to have been misinformed. A county court conforming in large part to the provisions of the Fundamental Constitutions had been in operation since the spring of 1683. Sothel dominated it, however, and used it to provide color of legality for unlawful acts that he committed.

John Archdale may have had a moderating influence on Sothel for a time, but the years he was in the colony were not free from Sothel's oppression. Sothel, however, was in England for several months in 1685 and 1686, during which Archdale served as governor, giving the colonists a period of relief. Whatever influence Archdale had, it ended about 1686, when he returned to England.

Sothel appears to have been moved largely by avarice and to have recognized no deterrent to satisfying his greed. He took what he wanted, whether it was a plantation, a pewter plate, or a piece of lace. He stole from both the rich and powerful and the poor and helpless. On pretext that the land had escheated, he had the Council issue to him a patent for a plantation of 4,000 acres belonging to the wife of Colonel Philip Ludwell, a member of the Virginia Council, who had married the widow of Sir William Berkeley, one of the original Carolina Proprietors. Charging that George Durant, an early settler and influential leader in Albemarle, had committed "an Infammous Libell," Sothel confiscated and appropriated to himself Durant's plantation of 2,000 acres. Pretending that two traders from Barbados were pirates, although their papers were in good order, he confiscated their goods and threw them in prison, where one of them died. He refused to permit the dead trader's will to be probated, taking his property for himself, and when the executor, the prominent Thomas Pollock, undertook to go to London to complain, Sothel threw him in prison. Entrusted with delivery of a box sent to an Albemarle woman by her brother in London, Sothel stole from the box several yards of lace, some cloth, and two guineas. When confronted by the woman's attorney, he admitted the theft and displayed some of the lace sewed to "headlinnen" by his wife, nevertheless refusing to compensate the intended recipient. He kept for himself some pewter plates belonging to the estate of a colonist and forced an orphaned boy, who was under age, to sign a deed conveying to him the boy's plantation. Those who protested against such acts were put in jail and held for long periods without trial, while common criminals escaped punishment by bribing the governor.

The endurance of the Albemarle inhabitants reached an end in the summer of 1689. About August the colonists rose against Sothel and imprisoned him. They intended to send him to England for trial, but at Sothel's entreaty he was tried by the Albemarle Assembly instead. Finding him guilty of numerous charges, the Assembly banished him from Albemarle for a year and required him to renounce holding office in the colony forever.

News of the events in Albemarle reached London by late fall. On 2 Dec. 1689 the London Proprietors wrote to Sothel expressing hope that the allegations against him were false and that he would be cleared by an investigation they intended to make, but informing him that they were suspending him from the governorship pending such clearance. Three days later they commissioned Colonel Philip Ludwell of Virginia to be governor in Sothel's place.

The Assembly's banishment of Sothel did not take effect immediately. He remained in Albemarle at least through January 1689/90, when he made his will, recorded the deed he had forced George Durant to give him, and no doubt attended to other matters. By summer, however, he arrived in South Carolina, which he had chosen for refuge during his banishment. By 5 Oct. 1690 he had exercised his prerogative under the Fundamental Constitutions and assumed the governorship of the South Carolina colony.

Sothel did not obtain the South Carolina office easily, for the governor, James Colleton, disputed his claim. Supported by a faction that opposed Colleton, however, he took over the office without bloodshed. Almost immediately Sothel displayed the indifference for the rights of his fellow Proprietors that he had demonstrated in Albemarle. Despite instructions from the London Proprietors directing local officials not to hold a parliament until so instructed by them, Sothel called a parliament, which met in December. At his instigation the parliament banished Colleton from the colony and barred him and four others from again holding office. At Sothel's direction, the records and seal of the colony were forcibly taken from the secretary, who was removed from office and imprisoned, although he had been directly appointed by the London Proprietors. Likewise, Council members and lesser officials who had been appointed by the London Proprietors were removed from office and replaced by Sothel's supporters. In effect, Sothel overturned the government authorized by the Proprietary board and set up one controlled by himself alone.

Sothel lost little time before beginning to enrich himself. In February 1690/91 he issued survey warrants for two tracts of land of 12,000 acres each for which he secured patents. He reopened the trade with pirates and personally traded with them. He made changes in the regulations of the Indian trade, changes that are believed to have been directed towards establishing for himself a monopoly of the profitable interior trade, although that was not actually accomplished.

By spring the London Proprietors had learned of Sothel's seizure of the government and his subsequent actions. On 12 May 1691 they wrote reprimanding him for removing their appointees from office, for failing to govern according to their instructions, and for making appointments without their consent. They ordered him to restore the secretary and others he had removed and permit them to perform their duties in peace. They again insisted that he answer to them on the charges brought against him by the Albemarle colonists, which they enumerated, demanding that he go to England at once and answer. Later that month they formally dissented to the act banishing James Colleton, and the following September they informed South Carolina officials of their dissent to all acts passed by the parliament Sothel had called.

Sothel appears to have paid no more attention to the Proprietors remonstrances than he had paid to similar communications while he was in Albemarle. In November 1691 the Proprietors undertook to solve their problem by suspending the Fundamental Constitutions, thereby removing the legal basis for Sothel's claim to office. They also formally suspended Sothel from the governorship and appointed Philip Ludwell, who had succeeded Sothel in Albemarle, to serve as governor of the entire province of Carolina. In a proclamation dated 8 Nov. 1691 they announced their actions to the inhabitants of Carolina.

Ludwell reached South Carolina the following spring and on 13 May 1692 delivered to Sothel a letter from the Proprietors and other documents informing him of his suspension from office. Sothel, however, refused to accept the actions as valid and disputed Ludwell's right to the governorship. Although he appears not to have resorted to bloodshed in his efforts to retain office, Sothel continued for a year or more to claim the governorship. On 11 May 1693 the Proprietors issued a second proclamation announcing their removal of Sothel from office and their suspension of the Fundamental Constitutions. In it they warned the inhabitants not to obey Sothel as governor of Carolina or any part of it.

Sothel no doubt remained in South Carolina until some date after issuance of the Proprietors' proclamation of May 1693, but there are few traces of him in surviving documents after the spring of 1692. There is evidence that he was in Albemarle in November 1693, but he was then in the home of another colonist and may not have been living in Albemarle. His home plantation, which was in Chowan Precinct, appears to have been leased at that time, and there is no contemporary evidence that Sothel lived there after his stay in South Carolina. On the other hand, there is evidence, though not conclusive, that he was a resident of Virginia at the time of his death and that he died and was buried in that colony. His death occurred between an unknown date in November 1693, when he was said to have been at the home of John Porter in Albemarle, and 3 Feb. 1693/94, when his will was proved.

Sothel left no children. He bequeathed most of his Albemarle estate to his wife, Anna, whom he named executrix. Anna, who was the daughter of Belshazzar and Anna Willix of New Hampshire, had been married twice before her marriage to Sothel—first to Robert Riscoe, a master mariner, and second to James Blount, a member of the Albemarle Council. Her marriage to Sothel took place at some date after July 1686, when she probated Blount's will. Sothel also had been married before. In his will he identified an Albemarle inhabitant, Edward Foster, as his father-in-law and bequeathed to Foster a plantation and some cattle. After Sothel's death, Anna married John Lear of Nansemond County, Va., a member of the Virginia Council. She died before May 1695.

Sothel's Albemarle estate was the subject of extensive litigation, in large part because of the irregularities by which much of it had been acquired. Settling the estate was further complicated by Anna's death, which was soon followed by the death of John Lear. The estate eventually was settled by Lear's executors, Lewis Burwell and Thomas Godwin of Virginia.

The ownership of Sothel's share in Carolina also was disputed. Sothel's heirs in England claimed title to the share and sold it to James Bertie early in the eighteenth century. Meanwhile, the surviving Proprietors also claimed the share on the ground that Sothel had left no children, which they claimed caused the share to revert to them under an agreement among the Proprietors. In 1697 they assigned the share to Thomas Amy, who gave it to his daughter Ann and her husband, Nicholas Trott. In 1720 the conflicting claims led to a lawsuit, which resulted in a court order for sale of the share. To establish his title, James Bertie, who had bought the share once, bought it again.

SEE: Samuel A. Ashe, ed., *Biographical History of North Carolina*, vol. 2 (1905); R. D. W. Connor, *History of North Carolina: The Colonial and Revolutionary Periods, 1584–1783* (1919); J. Bryan Grimes, ed., *Abstract of North Carolina Wills* (1910) and *North Carolina Wills and Inventories* (1912); North Carolina State Archives (Raleigh), various documents, especially British Records (photocopies from British Public Record Office, London), and wills of Richard Humphries (7 Oct. 1688) and Seth Sothel (25 Jan. 1689); Mattie Erma E. Parker, ed., *North Carolina Higher-Court Records, 1670–1696* and *1697–1701* (1968, 1971); William S. Powell, *The Proprietors of Carolina* (1963); Hugh F. Rankin, *Upheaval in Albemarle: The Story of Culpeper's Rebellion, 1675–1689* (1962); W. Noel Sainsbury, ed., *Calendar of State Papers, Colonial Series, America and West Indies*, vols. 9–15 (1893–1904); Alexander S. Salley, Jr., ed., *Commissions and Instructions from the Lords Proprietors of Carolina to Public Officials of South Carolina, 1685–1715* (1916) and *Warrants for Lands in South Carolina, 1672–1711* (1910); William L. Saunders, ed., *Colonial Records of North Carolina*, vol. 1 (1886); Eugene M. Sirmans, Jr., *Colonial South Carolina: A Political History, 1663–1763* (1966); Henry A. M. Smith, *The Baronies of South Carolina* (1931); *South Carolina Historical and Genealogical Magazine*, vols. 8 (1907), 13 (1912), 33 (1932).

MATTIE ERMA E. PARKER

Southgate, James Haywood *(12 July 1859–29 Sept. 1916)*, businessman and vice-presidential candidate, was born in Norfolk, Va., but lived in several localities before his parents settled in Durham, N.C. His father, James Southgate, was a native of King and Queen County, Va., and his mother, Delia Haywood Wynne, was from Louisburg, N.C. They both began their careers as teachers and school administrators, but James Southgate eventually turned to business and presumably his wife gave up pedagogy as well. Around the beginning of 1872 he became a life and fire insurance agent and opened an office in Hillsborough; in 1876 he moved his agency to Durham.

Young Southgate was the eldest of three daughters and three sons; only he among the sons survived infancy. After attending several schools, he entered The University of North Carolina for two years. He wished to become a physician, but after joining his father in the insurance business he decided to make that his career. The firm continued for at least a century under the name of J. Southgate and Son, Inc. On 6 Dec. 1882 Southgate married Kate Shepherd Fuller, the daughter of Bartholomew Fuller, a Durham lawyer. Only two of their four children survived infancy, and five years after Southgate's wife died in 1893, his young daughter died. His one surviving child, Thomas Fuller, went into business with his father and managed the agency after his death.

Southgate, a man of massive build, has been described by historian John Spencer Bassett, who knew him well, as a person of striking appearance, magnetic and commanding personality, and excellent voice. He also credited him with breadth of mind, a level head in crises, and balanced judgment. The success of Southgate's business and his extensive participation in other activities indicate that he was a person of prodigious industry with an intense interest in the welfare of others. For twenty-five years he held an official position in the Methodist Episcopal Church, South, and he was active in the YMCA and the North Carolina Sunday School Association. In 1895 he was appointed to the board of trustees of Trinity College, the Methodist institution that had recently been moved from Randolph County to Durham; he became chairman of the board in 1897 and held that position until his death nineteen years later. He also served as president or a board member of a number of local organizations committed to the betterment of Durham. For two terms he was president of the National Association of Insurance Agents.

Possessed of a genial personality and superior oratorical talent, Southgate became widely known as a public speaker. No doubt these assets contributed to his receiving the National party's nomination for vice-president in 1896. The National party was a faction that had bolted from the Prohibition party during its national convention in 1896 after a split developed over the platform; it opposed making Prohibition the sole issue in the campaign and broadened its platform to include more than a dozen other issues. Southgate's running mate for president was Charles E. Bentley of Nebraska. They polled fewer than 14,000 votes out of nearly 14,000,000 cast for candidates representing seven different political parties. Southgate had left the Democratic party in his mid-twenties for the Prohibitionists.

At age fifty-seven Southgate died at his country home, Southgate Cabin, of what his physician diagnosed as apoplexy. His body lay in state on Trinity College campus before it was interred in Maplewood Cemetery, Durham. In his eulogy of Southgate, Bishop John C. Kilgo, formerly president of Trinity College, said that for more than twenty years they had had the "most intimate friendship of soul and oneness of labors." As a tribute to Southgate, a strong advocate of the education of women, funds were raised for the James H. Southgate Memorial

Building. This dormitory for women became the nucleus of the Woman's College of Duke University. Southgate's portrait was hung in the William R. Perkins Library among those of other trustees of Trinity and Duke.

SEE: Samuel A. Ashe, ed., *Biographical History of North Carolina*, vol. 2 (1905); *Durham Morning Herald*, 30 Sept. 1916; James Carlisle Kilgo Papers (Duke University Archives, Durham); Thomas Hudson McKee, *The National Conventions and Platforms of All Political Parties, 1789–1900: Convention, Popular, and Electoral Vote* (1900); Southgate-Jones Family Papers (Manuscript Department, Duke University Library, Durham); *Trinity Alumni Register*, vols. 2 (1916–17), 3 (1917–18), 5 (1919–20), 12 (1926).

MATTIE U. RUSSELL

Spach, William Elias *(24 Apr. 1830–21 Feb. 1891)*, wagon maker, was born on his father's farm at Waughtown in Stokes (now Forsyth) County. The son of Christian and Nancy Swaim Spach, he was a fourth-generation descendant of Adam Spach, the pioneer settler in the 1753 wilderness of Piedmont North Carolina. His German forefather established the Friedberg Moravian community and constructed the well-known Rock House, which provided protection for his family and neighbors during the Indian uprisings of the Shawnee and Cherokee tribes. During the Revolutionary War Adam Spach served as a supplier and freighter for General Daniel Morgan's and General Nathanael Greene's southern command of the Continental army.

Young Spach learned the trade of carriage making in the shops of John Vaughters, a native of North Carolina and one of the first wagon manufacturers in the state, and John P. Nissen, the son of Tycho Nissen. He married Mary Ann Vaughters, the daughter of his teacher, and at age twenty-four established his own shop in Waughtown. In 1854 in a 16-by-24-foot shed he started making wagons with limited capital and little equipment. Spach did all of the work himself, and having learned his trade from two of the finest wagon makers in the South, he improved on their product and soon won success and a reputation for his high-quality vehicles. The W. E. Spach wagon was known for its sturdiness and durability, and there was no scarcity of buyers for the vehicles that came from his shop.

During the first three years of the Civil War he produced wagons and caissons for the Confederacy. In 1864, however, when iron and other supplies became unobtainable, he and his brother Bennett went to Rockingham County, Va., and enlisted in Company B, First Battalion, North Carolina Sharpshooters (formerly Company B, Twenty-first Regiment). It is not known in what engagement Spach was captured, but the Federal provost marshal records show that he took the oath of allegiance to the United States at Washington, D.C., on 27 Feb. 1865 and was provided with transportation to Hope, Ind. That small Moravian community in southern Indiana had been founded by settlers from Friedberg, N.C., and he went there to be among his kin and friends. With the cessation of hostilities he returned home and resumed wagon making. Business prospered, and he took in his sons and taught them the trade.

Spach was married four times and had nineteen children, but it was to his oldest child, John Christian—born in the year he opened his shop—that he turned over his business in 1886, when he retired to his farm at age fifty-six. When John C. took over the plant, it employed a dozen men and produced about three wagons a day. In 1894 he took in as a partner his brother Samuel L., and they erected a large brick factory of Swedish design on five acres purchased in Waughtown. Subsequently they acquired surrounding land until the Spach Brothers Wagon Works occupied an eleven-acre site. Here they erected commodious brick and frame buildings, equipped them with machinery, and put up a flour mill. Production grew to ten wagons per day. The generator in the boiler room furnished most of the power used in the adjoining section of the town of Salem. These enterprises were operated jointly by the brothers for twenty years. In January 1914, when the partnership was dissolved, Samuel took the flour mill and John the wagon manufacturing business. William M., John's son who had joined the firm in 1910, became president of the J. C. Spach Wagon Works in 1914. It was John Christian's hope that the company would always retain the Spach name; therefore, when the company was incorporated to manufacture furniture in March 1925, it kept the designation J. C. Spach Wagon Works, Inc., even though it was selling furniture. In 1928 it ceased to make wagons. Nevertheless, Spach wagons continued to be used in southern Virginia and in western and Piedmont North Carolina for many years.

William E. Spach died on his farm at age sixty-two and was buried in Waughtown Cemetery beside three of his wives: Mary Ann Vaughters, Leanna Reich, and Louisea Lienbach. His fourth wife, Cenith Davis, was buried at Saints' Delight Primitive Baptist Church, Kernersville, of which Spach was a lifelong member.

SEE: *North Carolina Biography*, vols. 4 (1919), 4 (1928); Union Primitive Baptist Association records (Baptist Collection, Wake Forest University, Winston-Salem); Winston, *Union Republican*, 26 Feb. 1891.

JOHN THOM SPACH

Spaight, Richard *(1730–March? 1763)*, colonial secretary, councilman, and clerk of the Assembly, was born in Carrickfurgus, Ireland, the son of George and Margaret Dobbs Spaight, who were married on 7 July 1729. His paternal grandparents were James and Mary Tomkins Spaight of Carrickfurgus; his maternal grandparents were Richard Dobbs and a second wife, Margaret Clugston, of Belfast.

Accompanying his uncle, royal governor Arthur Dobbs, to North Carolina, Spaight arrived in New Bern in 1754. From 14 Dec. 1754 and for almost a year he was paymaster for the North Carolina regiment in the ill-fated expedition against the French and Indians on the Ohio River. In October 1755 Governor Dobbs appointed him secretary and clerk of the Crown for the province. Occasionally Spaight acted as Dobbs's secretary.

Commissioned in 1757 as a member of the governor's Council, he died before qualifying. He was named to a 1758 committee "to erect a city" and build public structures at Tower Hill as the provincial capital. In 1759 he was appointed to a committee to finish the courthouse at New Bern, but two years later that act was repealed and he was named to a smaller committee of three members for that purpose. He was also a justice of the peace.

In 1756 he married Elizabeth Wilson, the daughter of Colonel William and Mary Vail Jones Wilson. Colonel Wilson built two fine brick dwellings: Bellair, a few miles northwest of New Bern, the only country mansion of the kind still standing in the region; and Cleremont, on Brice's Creek, across the Trent River from the town. Cleremont was destroyed by Federal troops during the Civil War.

Mary Wilson, his wife's mother, was the daughter of

Jeremiah and Mary Lillington Vail and the granddaughter of Major Alexander Lillington. At the time of her marriage to Colonel Wilson, she was the widow of Frederick Jones. After Wilson's death she married Roger Moore of Orton Plantation. Her three husbands were said to have been chosen respectively for love, money, and prestige. Madam Moore (1705–64), as she was called, often went to New Bern from Cleremont in an elegant boat with three liveried oarsmen. Her stall in Christ Church was twice as large as the others. Presidents George Washington and James Monroe, as well as other distinguished visitors, are reported to have worshipped in it. Some of the gold of the regal socialite is reputed to be still buried at Cleremont. A nearby street is named Madam Moore's Lane.

To her daughter Elizabeth and Richard Spaight was born Richard Dobbs Spaight (1758–1802), who was governor of North Carolina for three one-year terms, 1792 to 1795. A grandson, Richard Dobbs, Jr. (1796–1850), was governor for one year, 1835–36.

Of Richard Spaight, the Reverend John McDowell, Anglican missionary at Brunswick, wrote on 26 Mar. 1763 to the secretary of the Society for the Propagation of the Gospel in London: "Mr. Spaight, one of the King's Council & your late secretary is lately dead, he came over with his excellency and was a very sprightly gay young man."

Spaight left considerable property. Governor Dobbs and Frederick Gregg qualified as guardians of his young son, Richard Dobbs. Spaight, his wife, his mother-in-law, and his grandson were among the eleven persons buried in the Spaight cemetery at Cleremont.

SEE: Alexander B. Andrews, "Richard Dobbs Spaight," *North Carolina Historical Review* 1 (1924); Marshall DeLancey Haywood, *Governor William Tryon and His Administration in the Province of North Carolina* (1903); William L. Saunders, ed., *Colonial Records of North Carolina*, vols. 5–6 (1887–88); Alan D. Watson, *Richard Dobbs Spaight* [1987].

GERTRUDE S. CARRAWAY

Spaight, Richard Dobbs *(25 Mar. 1758–6 Sept. 1802)*, governor, congressman, and signer of the federal Constitution, was born in New Bern to Richard and Elizabeth Wilson Spaight. He was the great-great nephew of royal governor Arthur Dobbs. At the death of young Spaight's father in 1763, Governor Dobbs and Frederick Gregg were appointed his guardians. His widowed mother married Thomas Clifford Howe but did not live long. At age nine the orphaned lad was sent to Great Britain for his education, probably under the care of Dobbs relatives. After attending schools in Ireland and the University of Glasgow in Scotland, he returned home in 1778 to begin a varied public career. Within little more than a year, he presented a certificate of election to the House of Commons from the borough town of New Bern, but the election was ruled illegal because of alleged irregularities at the polls.

As aide to Major General Richard Caswell, commander of the state militia, he participated in the ill-fated Battle of Camden. Although he was made first major of the militia in 1781 and later promoted to lieutenant colonel as commandant of artillery, he resigned his military commission in 1789; by then, his chief interest was politics. His support of American forces continued throughout the War of Independence. When General Nathanael Greene was in New Bern near the end of the conflict, Spaight is said to have pledged his personal assets and influence, so greatly encouraging the Patriot leader that the scene of their conference under an ancient cypress tree in his yard on the Neuse River was visited in reverence by President George Washington in 1791.

From 1781 to 1783 Spaight represented New Bern in the General Assembly, and from 1783 to 1785 he served in the Continental Congress, where he was a member of the Committee of the States as well as of a committee to draft a temporary government for the western territory. Resigning from the Congress and declining to accept reappointment, he represented Craven County in 1785 in the House of Commons and was elected speaker.

For the next two years he remained in the house, where, as usual, his opinion was often sought on different matters and he served on a number of committees. When the Assembly examined the conduct of state judges in early January 1787, he sat on the investigating committee and was selected as chairman of the whole.

In March the Assembly elected him a delegate to the federal constitutional convention. It is said that it was Spaight who proposed that U.S. senators be elected by the legislatures of the states and that the presidential term of office be seven years. He was in favor of reconsidering the decision once arrived at to choose the president by electors appointed by the state legislatures, and he objected to requiring more than a majority to pass a navigation act.

Having signed the Constitution, he spoke eleven times, arguing strongly though in vain on its behalf at the 1788 state convention in Hillsborough. Publication of the debates, however, helped secure ratification of the document the next year at Fayetteville.

In 1789 Spaight was nominated for the U.S. Senate, but his name was withdrawn. In failing health from overwork and disease, his public life was interrupted for almost four years. He traveled through America and to the West Indies, seeking rest, relaxation, and a cure. Shortly after returning home in better health, he was elected to the Assembly from New Bern in 1792, but his seat was vacated upon his election as governor. After his inauguration on 14 Dec. 1792 in Tryon Palace at New Bern, then serving as the state capital, he was twice reelected.

The last Assembly meeting in his native city was called by him for July 1794, and that December he was chief executive at the first Assembly to convene in Raleigh. During his three gubernatorial terms, lasting until 19 Nov. 1795, he was an administrator of "dignity, fidelity and moderation." In 1793 and 1796 he was a presidential elector.

As a representative in the U.S. Congress from 10 Dec. 1798 to 3 Mar. 1801, he was distinguished for his "clarity of thought and power of speech," even though he was not a lawyer. Although sometimes voting independently on measures, he belonged to the so-called Republican party and followed the Jeffersonian school of politics. Deciding not to stand for reelection, he went instead to the state senate and was succeeded in Congress by his younger political opponent, John Stanly of New Bern.

Filing for another Senate term in 1802, he became involved in a bitter controversy with Stanly, aged twenty-eight, a Federalist. Following charges and countercharges during the heated campaign, Spaight won the Senate election on 13 August, but the political rivalry lingered on, as evidenced by voluminous correspondence and print. When Spaight publicly called Stanly "both a liar and a scoundrel," adding, "I shall always hold myself in readiness to give him satisfaction," Stanly challenged him to a duel.

The pistol duel took place on Sunday afternoon, 5 Sept. 1802, in New Bern. Dr. Edward Pasteur was Spaight's second and Edward Graham was Stanly's. On the fourth round Spaight was wounded in his right side.

He wavered and fell; in twenty-three hours he was dead. The body was interred in the family cemetery on Cleremont plantation. Stanly left the city and kept out of sight until the tide of feeling against him had subsided. He wrote to Governor Benjamin Williams summarizing the circumstances leading to the duel and justifying his actions. William Gaston interceded on his behalf and was instrumental in persuading the governor to grant him a pardon.

Besides his numerous political offices, Spaight had prominent roles in educational, civic, and religious affairs. In 1784 he was one of nine men on the board of the reorganized New Bern Academy. The next year he was appointed an original trustee of the Kinston Academy. He was among five managers of a 1787 lottery to obtain funds for a poorhouse. A vestryman of Christ Episcopal Church, he was named churchwarden in 1789 to accept donations for the church. In that year he was commissioned as one of the trustees to establish The University of North Carolina, and he continued as a university trustee until his death.

Owning much property, he supervised his farming operations. Once he advertised for an "overseer that understands the cultivation of Rice." In a letter written to him (now in the possession of the Tryon Palace Commission at New Bern), George Washington thanked him for a gift of "Pease" and said that they would be planted at Mount Vernon.

Spaight's will, dated 9 Aug. 1802, less than a month before his duel, provided that his estate be divided among "my beloved wife, Mary Jones Spaight, and my four children." The widow survived him for almost eight years. They had been married on 25 Sept. 1788, at New Bern, in spite of the fact that their fathers reportedly were not on friendly terms because of a land dispute.

An account of the nuptials published in the *Columbian Magazine* of Philadelphia observed in reference to the bride: "A young lady whose amiable character and beautiful person, added to an extensive fortune, promise much felicity to this worthy pair." Mrs. Spaight, the daughter of Colonel Joseph and Mary Jones Leech of New Bern, is said to have led the first minuet with President Washington at the 1791 Palace ball in New Bern and to have been the first lady at a University of North Carolina commencement—in 1795, while her husband was governor.

From three sons and one daughter there were descendants only of the daughter, Margaret Elizabeth (1800–3 Sept. 1831), who married John Robert Donnell. Their son, Richard Spaight Donnell, represented Craven County in Congress (1848–49) and Beaufort County in the General Assembly (1860–65), where he served as speaker of the house in 1864–65.

SEE: Alexander B. Andrews, "Richard Dobbs Spaight," *North Carolina Historical Review* 1 (1924); Samuel A. Ashe, ed., *Biographical History of North Carolina*, vol. 4 (1906); *Biog. Dir. Am. Cong.* (1971); John L. Cheney, Jr., ed., *North Carolina Government, 1585–1979* (1981); *DAB*, vol. 9 (1964); Henry A. Grady, "The Two Spaights" (typescript, North Carolina Collection, University of North Carolina, Chapel Hill, 1923); R. D. Spaight and John Stanly correspondence prior to their 1802 duel (New-York Historical Society Library, New York); Alan D. Watson, *Richard Dobbs Spaight* [1987]; John H. Wheeler, *Sketch of the Life of Richard Dobbs Spaight of North Carolina* (1880); John D. Whitford, Historical Notes (typescript, New Bern–Craven County Library, New Bern).

GERTRUDE S. CARRAWAY

Spaight, Richard Dobbs, Jr. *(1796–17 Nov. 1850)*, congressman and governor, was the son of Richard Dobbs, Sr., and Mary Jones Leech Spaight, of New Bern. He attended the New Bern Academy under the Reverend Thomas F. Irving and was graduated with high honors in 1813 from The University of North Carolina. Admitted to the bar in 1818, he began to practice law in New Bern and represented Craven County in the House of Commons in 1819 and in the senate in 1820–22. He served in the U.S. Congress in 1823–25 but was defeated for reelection. Returning to the state senate, he served for eleven years until he became governor (1835–36). At the state constitutional convention of 1835 he was chairman of the rules committee.

Nominated on the Democratic ticket for a second gubernatorial term, he lost to the Whig candidate, Edward Bishop Dudley, in the first direct vote of the populace for governor under the new state constitution. He may not have been reelected as a result of his opposition to internal improvements because of competition among various projects.

Retiring from politics, Spaight returned to New Bern, where he engaged chiefly in agricultural pursuits and the management of his extensive properties. In 1842 he was named a councillor of state but declined to accept. He carried on a leisurely law practice, largely for charity. According to Stephen F. Miller in *Recollections of New Bern Fifty Years Ago*, Spaight attended courts in Craven and Jones counties, but "I never heard of his appearing in a case. He was very rich and very diffident and was not destitute of fair abilities. . . . His object in associating with the lawyers from county to county was no doubt to enjoy their society, and to improve his mind by legal discussions which constantly took place in his presence."

Spaight never married. He was an active Mason and a member of Christ Episcopal Church. He was buried in the family cemetery at Cleremont plantation.

SEE: Samuel A. Ashe, ed., *Biographical History of North Carolina*, vol. 4 (1906); Gertrude S. Carraway, *Crown of Life* (1940) and *Years of Light* (1944); John L. Cheney, Jr., ed., *North Carolina Government, 1585–1979* (1981); Henry A. Grady, "The Two Spaights" (typescript, North Carolina Collection, University of North Carolina, Chapel Hill, 1923); [Stephen F. Miller], *Recollections of New Bern Fifty Years Ago* (1874); New Bern, *Eastern Carolina Republican*, 27 Nov. 1850;

GERTRUDE S. CARRAWAY

Spangenberg, Augustus Gottlieb *(15 July 1704–18 Sept. 1792)*, bishop of the Moravian church, was born in Germany, the youngest of four sons of George and Elizabeth Nesen Spangenberg. His father was a Lutheran pastor. Augustus entered the university at Jena in 1722, and having been orphaned in 1714, he became a foster son in the home of Professor Johannes Franz Buddeus. Under the influence of Buddeus, Spangenberg changed his course of study from law to theology, was awarded an M.A. degree in 1726, and received an appointment as an assistant in theology at the university. About this time he became acquainted with Count Nicolaus Ludwig von Zinzendorf and the Moravians at Herrnhut and was much impressed with their missionary zeal. He was persuaded by the king of Prussia to take the chair of religious education at the University of Halle, but his adherence to the Moravians resulted in the loss of that position, and he went to Herrnhut to become Zinzendorf's assistant.

Spangenberg was responsible for carrying out Zinzendorf's plans for a mission in Surinam, and in 1735 he left for America to organize Moravian work in Georgia. In 1739 he made arrangements for the Georgia group to move to a site in Pennsylvania that he thought suitable for a mission center, and then he returned to Germany. Consecrated bishop at Herrnhaag in 1744, he sailed at once for America to become overseer of the Moravian settlement at Bethlehem, Pa. Internal politics caused the loss of his influence, and he was replaced by Bishop John Nitschmann. Spangenberg returned to London and engaged in writing defenses of Zinzendorf. Once the upheaval over pietism had settled down, he was again sent to Bethlehem, where he found the colony in a sad state.

After a short visit to London, he returned to America to organize new work in North Carolina on land that Lord Granville had offered to Zinzendorf. Spangenberg and a survey party left Edenton in August 1752 and completed their search the following January, having chosen a location in the Yadkin Valley. In May 1753 Spangenberg reported to Zinzendorf in London and recommended that the property be purchased. Terms were negotiated with Lord Granville's agent, the title was vested in trust for the church, and purchase money was subscribed largely among members and friends in England. Governor Arthur Dobbs of North Carolina recognized Wachovia as a special Moravian district, known as Dobbs Parish. The name of Wachovia was given by Spangenberg after Austrian lands belonging to the Zinzendorf family.

In 1762 the new organization was complete, and Spangenberg, in poor health, returned to Herrnhut, where he remained for the rest of his life. All Christian groups in Europe recognized him as the leader of missionary work.

On 5 Mar. 1740, in Württemberg, Spangenberg married Mrs. Eva Maria Zielgelbauer Immig. She died in 1751, and on 19 May 1754 he married Mrs. Mary Elizabeth Jaehne Miksch. His second wife died at Bethlehem in March 1759. There were no surviving children from either marriage.

Spangenberg retired in 1790. He died in Berthelsdorf and was buried at Herrnhut.

SEE: *DAB*, vol. 17 (1935); Adelaide L. Fries, ed., *Records of the Moravians in North Carolina*, vols. 1–6 (1922–43); Taylor Hamilton and Kenneth G. Hamilton, *History of the Moravian Church* (1967).

LOUISE L. QUEEN

Sparrow, Patrick Jones *(1802–10 Nov. 1867)*, Presbyterian minister and educator, was born in Lincoln County. At an early age he worked to support himself and his widowed mother, reportedly a "very bright woman," and distinguished himself as a precocious student. Impressed with his ability, friends and neighbors shared and discussed books with him and eventually sent him to Bethel Academy, in South Carolina, where he studied under the Reverend Samuel Williamson.

After his formal education, he continued studying languages and in 1826 secured a license to preach at Long Creek Church in Cleveland County. About 1828 he was appointed pastor of Lincoln Presbyterian Church; in 1831, of Unity Church; and in 1834, of Salisbury Church. He also became coprincipal of the Salisbury Male Academy.

In 1834 Sparrow was appointed a financial agent for a college proposed by the Concord and Bethel presbyteries. He traveled as far as Pittsburgh, Pa., to raise funds, a journey memorialized in his fragmentary "Itinerarium," now in the Davidson College archives. The fund-raising efforts proving successful in 1837 when Davidson College was organized, he was elected to the first professorship of ancient languages as well as to the original board of trustees. Two of his extant works from this period, *The Inaugural Address of Rev. P. J. Sparrow, A.M., 2 August 1837* (1838) and *The Duty of Educated Young Men of this Country* (1839), exemplify his knowledge of classics and his power as a rhetorician.

Although in 1837 he had declined an "urgent" call from the Sixth Church in Philadelphia, in the summer of 1840 he accepted the pastorate of Hanover Church, Prince Edward County, Va. About 1841 he received a doctor of divinity degree from Hampden-Sydney College. Several years later, on 1 May 1845, he was elected to the eighth presidency of Hampden-Sydney and was inaugurated on 12 November. Continued in this office for two years, he resigned on 21 Sept. 1847.

In 1847 Sparrow moved to Tuscaloosa Presbytery, Ala., and became principal of the Presbyterian High School in Eutaw. The following year he preached at Burton's Hill Church, and in 1850 he became a teacher in Newbern, Ala. Soon afterwards he began preaching at Marion, Ala., and served as a missionary in the South Alabama Presbytery.

In 1853 he settled in Pensacola, Fla., where he became the second pastor of the First Presbyterian Church, served Bagdad and Milton churches, and worked at founding a church at Warrington. Early in 1862, having lost his belongings to the invading Northern army, he was evacuated by Confederate troops. Destitute and in ill health, he settled in Cahaba, Ala.

Sparrow was married three times: first, in 1826 to Mary Thomas (1806–46); second, to Mary (1834–50); and third, in 1857 to Mary J. Douglas of Talladega, Ala., who survived him. Children of the first marriage included Thomas E. (ca. 1826–55), James W. (1834–56), and Robert H. M. (1841–59). A son of the third marriage was John Alan Simpson (1858–1924), editor of the *Birmingham [Alabama] Daily Ledger*. Sparrow died of tuberculosis in Cahaba, Ala., where he was buried.

SEE: *History of First Presbyterian Church of Pensacola, Florida, 1837–1940* (1940); *The Record of the Hampden-Sydney Alumni Association* (October 1956 [portrait]); Cornelia Rebekah Shaw, *Davidson College: Intimate Facts* (1923); Joseph M. Wilson, *The Presbyterian Historical Almanac for 1868*, vol. 10 (1868).

W. KEATS SPARROW

Sparrow, Thomas, II *(19 Apr. 1783–30 Sept. 1852)*, shipbuilder, was born at Smith's Creek, Craven County, the son of Thomas, I (1751–1822), and his first wife, Theresa (Rhesa) Delamar Sparrow. Sparrow's career in building commercial sailing vessels helps to illuminate an important but relatively unexamined early North Carolina coastal industry.

Sparrow had much in his background to lead him to shipbuilding. In the 1700s his grandfather Smith Sparrow and his great-uncle Peter Sparrow had both been shipwrights in Norfolk, Va., where his own father and his uncle Francis had lived and worked before moving to Craven County. And in his own era, many of his Craven County kinsmen—including Henry Sparrow, Joseph B. Sparrow, Samuel Sparrow, and Smith Sparrow—were shipwrights, too, not to mention his many other relatives—including Captain Robert Sparrow of New Bern and Captain William Sparrow of Smith's Creek—who were mariners. These facts suggest that the maritime industry tended to be a family business passed on from one generation to another.

Quite likely Sparrow learned the craft of building

ships from his father while still a boy at Smith's Creek. But by the time he was an adult, he was situated in New Bern and being assigned young men as apprentices "to learn," as the court minutes say, "the art and mystery of shipcarpentering." Among those bound to him for this purpose were Green Copes, John Copes, Elisha Fulshire, and Martin Howard, as well as his kinsman David I. Sparrow.

In late 1828 Sparrow issued a public announcement that suggests the progressiveness and scope of his operations. The notice says that he had built a marine railway or "inclined plane" at his place of business near Union Point, the convergence of the Neuse and Trent rivers at New Bern. This railway could handle any vessels traveling the waters of the area, and in August of that year the 120-ton schooner *Proxy* could be seen making use of the new facility. In building his marine railway, Sparrow followed the plan of that at Hallet's Cove, Long Island, N.Y., and boasted that "its advantages over the common mode of careening are generally understood and admitted." Not only did his business reflect the latest technology, but it also involved servicing older vessels as well as building new ones.

Within a few years, Sparrow's business had grown so that he took on a partner, James Howard, and the firm assumed the new name of Sparrow and Howard Shipbuilders. A representative contract dated 5 Oct. 1832 shows the firm building a vessel for Thomas and Monza L. Jarkind. The vessel was to have a 60-foot keel and a 22-foot beam, with prime live oak, red cedar, white oak, and prime pitch pine as the chief materials. The firm promised the completed vessel, "in a good and workmanlike manner," in nine or ten months. The new owners "agree[d] to pay the aforesaid Sparrow & Howard twenty-five dollars per ton for the . . . vessel, one-half at the time of delivery and the other half in a note payable six months after the delivery of the vessel."

The names of early nineteenth-century vessels in the *General Index to Savannah [Ga.] Newspapers* suggest that many may have been built by Craven County firms such as Sparrow and Howard. Among those listed, for example, are the master ship *Craven*, the schooner *Sparrow*, and the sloop *Sparrow*.

The partnership with Howard lasted for only a short time, the dissolution taking place in 1836. But Sparrow, by then in his fifties, continued to prosper with his progressive and well-situated maritime industry. The profits from his scale of shipbuilding were ample, providing a grand style of life for him and his family. The business afforded not only an education at fine schools for his children, but also a mansion for them to live in.

Around 1840 he ostensibly used the master craftsmen employed by his company to build a three-and-a-half story, 4,000-square foot home with several dependencies at 222 East Front Street (Lot 6), adjacent to his shipyard and overlooking both the Neuse and Trent rivers. This carpenter's version of the Greek Revival style is a brick side-hall house, similar to many in Charleston and to several others in New Bern; the robust quality of the Greek Revival elements inside—including mantelpieces, moldings, and doors—are said to have been "unrivaled" in New Bern. This massive landmark, sold by Sparrow's heirs in February 1859, was mythologized by generations who passed it on their way to the coast as "Blackbeard's House" and was thought to have a secret escape tunnel leading to the Neuse River. In the late twentieth century it was renovated under the supervision of the New Bern Preservation Foundation.

Sparrow dedicated much of his time to community activities, serving in such capacities as justice of the peace for Craven County and later as town commissioner for New Bern. He was also an active member of St. John's Masonic Lodge, a director of the New Bern Marine and Fire Insurance Company, and a member of the Presbyterian church. In 1827 he served on the Committee of Correspondence supporting the election of Andrew Jackson as president.

Sparrow married a distant cousin, Jane Jennette Sparrow (b. 3 Oct. 1788 at Mattamuskeet; d. 24 May 1856 at New Bern), the daughter of Paul and Ann Jennette Sparrow. Thomas and Jane Sparrow were survived by six children: Ann (b. 22 Sept. 1811); Stephen D. (b. 25 July 1814); Lucinda (b. June 1817); Thomas, III (b. 2 Oct. 1819); William Tucker (b. 21 Aug. 1825); and Mary Eliza (b. 1 Oct. 1827).

SEE: Murtie June Clark, *Colonial Soldiers of the South, 1732–1774* (1983); Craven County Court Minutes, 1788–1832; *Federal Republican* (New Bern), 20 Sept. 1817; Jennette Papers and Thomas Sparrow Papers (Manuscript Collection, East Carolina University); Alexander Justice Papers, 1750–1925 (Southern Historical Collection, University of North Carolina, Chapel Hill); *New Bern Daily Progress*, 15 Feb. 1859; *New Bernian*, 5 Oct. 1852; *New Bern Sentinel*, 17 May 1823, 17 Mar. 1827, 1 Dec. 1827, 17 May 1828, 11 Jan. 1837; *New Bern Spectator*, 22 May 1830; *Sun-Journal Sentinel* (New Bern), 30 Dec. 1981; H. Braughn Taylor, ed., *Guide to Historic New Bern, North Carolina* (1974).

W. KEATS SPARROW

Sparrow, Thomas, III *(2 Oct. 1819–14 Jan. 1884)*, Confederate officer, lawyer, and legislator, was born in New Bern. His parents were Thomas, II, a shipbuilder, and Jane Jennette Sparrow, the daughter of Paul (12 Mar. 1743–21 Oct. 1798) and Ann Jennette Sparrow (22 Feb. 1753–16 Dec. 1809). From 1836 to 1839 young Sparrow attended Caldwell Institute in Greensboro. In October 1839 he entered the sophomore class at Princeton and in 1842 was graduated as valedictorian. He then read law under Judge William Gaston in New Bern and was licensed to practice; from Princeton he received the customary M.A. degree.

In 1847, the year he was licensed to practice before the superior court, Sparrow settled in Washington, N.C., where he formed a partnership with another New Bern native and fellow Whig, Edward Stanly. In 1853 he wrote the well-known history of a dramatic criminal trial, *North Carolina v. the Reverend George Washington Carrawan*. He served as chairman of the Eighth Congressional District Whig Committee and in 1856–57 as a representative in the General Assembly. He was also a ruling elder of the Presbyterian church.

In 1859 Sparrow moved his family to Arcola, Ill., but around the outbreak of the Civil War, he moved them back to Washington. There in April 1861 he raised a company of Beaufort County volunteers, the Washington Grays, for which he served as captain.

While at Portsmouth Island waiting for transportation to northern Virginia, Sparrow and his company were called to assist in the defense of Fort Hatteras, where in August 1861, after a bombardment of some 3,000 shells, they were surrendered with the garrison to Union forces. He and his troops were held as prisoners of war at Fort Columbus, Governor's Island, N.Y., and at Fort Warren, Boston Harbor, Mass., until February 1862, when they were exchanged and paroled to North Carolina. Sparrow was then ordered to Fort Fisher, where he assisted in building forts along the Cape Fear River. He was promoted to major of the Tenth Regiment of North Carolina Artillery and, among other duties, commanded the city garrison of Wilmington.

At home on sick leave when the war ended, Sparrow refused to surrender and paddled twenty miles in a small boat in order to escape with his sword. So adamant were his loyalties to the Confederacy that for several years after the war, according to one writer, "he led a laborious life as a farmer, rather than take the oath of allegiance."

Afterwards, in partnership with James Edward Shepherd, who was later a supreme court justice, Sparrow resumed his law practice in Washington and during the sessions of 1870–72 and 1879–80 served as a conservative Democrat in the General Assembly. On 15 Dec. 1870, as chairman of the House Judiciary Committee, he was manager for the house in the impeachment of Governor William W. Holden. He was also active in establishing Confederate veterans' organizations.

On 7 May 1844 Sparrow married Ann Mariah Blackwell, the daughter of John Blackwell of New Bern. They had six children: George Atmore, Annie Blackwell, Margaret Justice, Elizabeth, Caroline, and John Blackwell. Sparrow, his wife, and some of his descendants were buried in Oakdale Cemetery, Washington.

SEE: "The Washington Grays," *Carolina and the Southern Cross* 1 (October 1913 [portrait]); Clement A. Evans, ed., *Confederate Military History*, vol. 4 (1899); Ursula F. Loy and Pauline M. Worthy, eds., *Washington and the Pamlico* (1976); Jennette Papers and Thomas Sparrow Papers (Manuscript Collection, East Carolina University Greenville); Alexander Justice Papers and Thomas Sparrow Papers, 1835–71 (Southern Historical Collection, University of North Carolina, Chapel Hill); M. G. Smith and E. M. B. Hoyt, *The Confederate Reveille* (1898 [portrait]).

W. KEATS SPARROW

Spaugh, Herbert *(30 Sept. 1896–22 Nov. 1978)*, Moravian bishop, author, musician, and newspaper columnist, was born in Salem, the son of Rufus A. and Anna Louise Hege Spaugh. In 1918, during World War I, he served in the army at Fort Jackson, S.C. A graduate of Moravian College and the Moravian Theological Seminary, he earned an M.A. degree from Davidson College, which also awarded him an honorary doctor of divinity degree. He received an honorary LL.D. degree from Moravian College.

For a short period Spaugh engaged in furniture manufacturing, but in 1924 he became pastor of a Moravian church in Charlotte. He was consecrated a bishop in 1959. Beginning in 1933 he contributed a column, "Everyday Counselor," to newspapers in Charlotte and Winston-Salem; it was syndicated in thirty newspapers elsewhere in the South. He was the author of three books: *Pathway to Contentment* (1946), *Everyday Counsel for Everyday Living* (1951), and *Pathway to a Happy Marriage* (1953).

Bishop Spaugh organized the state's first Alcoholics Anonymous group, served as a trustee of Salem College and of Moravian College in Pennsylvania, was chaplain of Civitan International and the American Legion, and was an active member of the North Carolina Council of Churches, the National Conference of Christians and Jews, the North Carolina State School Board Association, and the American Guild of Organists. He also built pipe organs and served as organist and choir director for churches in Winston-Salem and Bethlehem, Pa., and organized and directed the Charlotte Boy Scout Band, which evolved into the Charlotte public school system's music program. He himself played the French horn in the Charlotte Symphony.

In 1920 he married Ida Brown Efird. They became the parents of three children: Earle Frederick, Herbert, Jr., and Carolyn (Mrs. Robert Farmer, Jr.).

SEE: *Charlotte Observer*, 23 Nov. 1978; Barbara Harding, *The Boy, the Man, and the Bishop* (1970); William S. Powell, ed., *North Carolina Lives* (1962); Raleigh *News and Observer*, 16, 28 Dec. 1959.

WILLIAM S. POWELL

Spaulding, Asa Timothy *(22 July 1902–4 Sept. 1990)*, insurance company executive, was born in Columbus County, the son of Armstead and Annie Belle Lowery Spaulding. He attended the National Training School of Howard University, was graduated magna cum laude from New York University in 1930, and received an M.A. degree from the University of Michigan in 1932. Having joined the North Carolina Mutual Life Insurance Company in Durham in 1924, Spaulding served as an actuary from 1933 to 1958, but at different periods he was assistant secretary of the company, 1935 to 1948; a director beginning in 1938; and president from 1959 until his retirement in 1968. In addition, he held related positions with the Winston Mutual Life Insurance Company, the Dunbar Life Insurance Company, the Mutual Savings and Loan Association, and Realty Services, Inc.; he was a director of the Mechanics and Farmers Bank.

At various times Spaulding produced a weekly television program, "Your Community," and was program adviser for the Durham Broadcasting Enterprises. In 1956 he was a member of the U.S. delegation to the inaugural of the president of Liberia and of the national delegation to the UNESCO General Conference in New Delhi, India. He served as vice-chairman of the North Carolina advisory committee to the Commission on Civil Rights (1959–64) and as a member of the steering committee of the Urban Coalition, of the national advisory council of the Airline Passengers Association (beginning 1972), and of the President's Commission on Income Maintenance Programs (1968–70); he was active in numerous other state and national bodies.

Following his retirement in 1968 as president of the world's largest black-owned insurance company, Spaulding established a consulting firm that advised numerous businesses across the nation. In 1971 he delivered the annual Business Leadership Lecture at the University of Michigan Graduate School of Business Administration, which was published as *Opening Pandora's Box: A Management Dilemma*. During his career he contributed to *Best's Insurance News*, *Black Business Digest*, and the *Christian Science Monitor*.

Spaulding received numerous awards including honorary degrees from Shaw University, North Carolina College, Morgan State College, The University of North Carolina, Duke University, St. Andrews Presbyterian College, and Howard University. A Baptist, he married Elna Bridgeforth in 1933, and they were the parents of three sons and a daughter: Asa Timothy, Patricia Ann (Mrs. Oscar J. Moore), Aaron Lowery, and Kenneth Bridgeforth.

SEE: *Ebony Success Library*, vol. 1 (1973); Raleigh *News and Observer*, 6, 9 Sept. 1990; Asa T. Spaulding, *A Brief History of the Civil Rights Movement Since 1900* (1969); Walter Weare, "Charles Clinton Spaulding: Middle-Class Leadership in the Age of Segregation," in John Hope

Franklin and August Meier, eds., *Black Leaders of the Twentieth Century* (1982); *Who's Who in America* (1980).

WILLIAM S. POWELL

Spaulding, Charles Clinton *(1 Aug. 1874–1 Aug. 1952)*, black businessman and community leader, was born in Columbus County to parents descended from a long-standing community of free Negro landholders in the area. A family oral tradition holds that his great-grandfather, an emancipated house servant from Wilmington, migrated west in the early 1800s to Columbus County, where he joined an insular community of free Negro-Indian farmers. Both of his parents, Benjamin McIver and Margaret Moore Spaulding, were third-generation members of this distinctive settlement.

In 1894 Spaulding left the family farm for Durham, where he finished high school and worked at a succession of "Negro jobs"—dishwasher, waiter, bellhop, and office boy. In 1898 he became the manager of an all-black cooperative grocery store; his success in that post won him a managerial position in another black business, the North Carolina Mutual Life Insurance Company. Founded in 1898, North Carolina Mutual was on the brink of failure when Spaulding became general manager in 1900. By 1910 the company boasted of being "the world's largest Negro business," and Spaulding and two of the original founders, John Merrick and Dr. Aaron M. Moore (Spaulding's uncle), were heralded in the Afro-American community as the "Triumvirate," the epitome of Booker T. Washington's "black captains of industry." Durham, in turn, became known as the "capital of the black middle class."

In 1923 Spaulding succeeded Moore as president of North Carolina Mutual, and from that time until his death he enjoyed an international reputation as America's leading black businessman. He directed not only North Carolina Mutual but also an extended family of financial institutions, including Mechanics and Farmers Bank, Bankers Fire Insurance Company, and Mutual Savings and Loan Association. Out of such business leadership, Spaulding emerged as the patriarch of black Durham, with social and political influence extending throughout the southern region and beyond. As trustee of the John F. Slater Fund, North Carolina College, Shaw University, and Howard University, he played a significant formal role in black higher education. Informally he played a larger role, functioning as a New South broker for philanthropy and employment in black institutions. A letter from him, as from Booker T. Washington a generation earlier, carried decisive influence. As a successful business executive, he appeared to the white world of philanthropy and power as something of a brother under the skin, less the self-interested supplicant than the dispassionate statesman offering moderate advice on racial uplift. He regularly appeared before the North Carolina legislature on behalf of North Carolina College, and behind the scenes he labored to correct the inequities of the Jim Crow system, sometimes holding the fear of integration as a hostage to ransom a greater share of public funding for black institutions.

In politics and race relations, then, as in philanthropy and education, Spaulding's formal actions often masked the underlying process of Negro politics in the New South. He served as a functionary in the Democratic party, especially during the New Deal when his recommendations influenced President Franklin D. Roosevelt's appointments to the "black cabinet," and when as president of the Urban League's National Emergency Advisory Council he became the official interpreter of the National Recovery Administration to the black community. Later in life he would decline appointments to the Fair Employment Practices Committee and as minister to Liberia. But it was at a less visible level, in his home state and in Durham, where as secretary of the North Carolina Commission on Interracial Cooperation and, more important, as chairman of the Durham Committee on Negro Affairs (DCNA), that he charted the passage between two eras of southern politics and race relations, the passage between classic paternalism dating back to slavery and direct politics looking ahead to the civil rights movement. Spaulding preserved the benefits of white patron–black client relationships at the same time he directed the DCNA towards a suffrage movement designed to replace those whimsical relationships. For whites his dexterous disavowal of "social equality" promised social control; cloaked in this context, the work of his more radical colleagues in the DCNA brought about black reenfranchisement twenty years ahead of comparable southern cities.

Spaulding represented the last of a generation that hearkened back to the age of Booker T. Washington, and his skilled absorption of the politics to his left is perhaps a test case for what the Tuskegeean himself might have done. He spent his final years remaining active in the Baptist church, accepting honors, and giving speeches, his pioneering in black business long behind him and his transitional role in southern politics nearly completed. His three sons, Charles Clinton, Jr., John, and Booker, and his daughter Margaret, all children from his first marriage to Fannie Jones Spaulding, resided in Durham. His first wife died in 1919; his second wife, Charlotte Garner Spaulding, survived until 1971.

SEE: William Jesse Kennedy, Jr., *The North Carolina Mutual Story: A Symbol of Progress, 1898–1970* (1970); Charles Clinton Spaulding Papers (North Carolina Mutual Life Insurance Company, Durham); Walter B. Weare, *Black Business in the New South: A Social History of the North Carolina Mutual Insurance Company* (1973), particularly for the citation of primary sources on C. C. Spaulding.

WALTER B. WEARE

Speight, Francis Wayland *(11 Sept. 1896–14 Nov. 1989)*, artist and teacher, was born at Sharrock plantation in Bertie County, the son of Thomas Trotman and Margaret Otelia Sharrock Speight. Although he had not completed requirements for high school graduation, he attended Wake Forest College from 1915 to 1917 and took art lessons on Saturdays under Ida Poteat at Meredith College. During World War I he was drafted and served for three months, and in 1919 and 1920 he studied art in Washington, D.C., part of the time at the Corcoran School of Art. In the fall of 1920 Speight entered the Pennsylvania Academy of Fine Arts, where he studied, painted, and taught part-time for more than forty years. His decision to attend the academy was influenced by an exhibition of paintings by the noted American impressionist and academy faculty member, Daniel Garber, under whom Speight studied.

In 1923 and 1925 he was awarded Cresson Traveling scholarships for summer travel and study in Europe, and in 1935 he joined the faculty at the Pennsylvania Academy. He shared a studio with Walter Gardner at 722 Sansom Street. On leaves of absence Speight taught at a number of places including The University of North Carolina, Shrivenham American University in England, Lehigh University, and DePauw University.

Although many of his earliest works reflect the landscapes of his boyhood, with Garber's encouragement in the 1920s he began painting the hilly working-class neighborhoods of Manayunk, an older industrial suburb of Philadelphia whose colorful stone and stone-stucco houses dotted the hillsides along the Schuylkill River. Although scenes of houses, factories, canals, and the river at Manayunk dominated his work from the 1920s until 1961, he occasionally painted other landscapes in eastern Pennsylvania and in Piedmont and eastern North Carolina. In the 1930s he painted a mural for the post office in Statesville depicting the Battle of Kings Mountain. In the summer of 1934 at The University of North Carolina he taught a six-weeks' art class. It was so well received that university officials soon established a permanent art curriculum.

From 1961 until his retirement in 1975, Speight held an appointment as artist-in-residence and professor of art at East Carolina University in Greenville. During this period he painted many scenes from his childhood in Bertie County as well as in Halifax, Pitt, Forsyth, and other counties. His landscapes captured with lyrical grace the cloud-dappled skies of Pennsylvania and the looming pines of eastern North Carolina. His style, which remained virtually unchanged throughout his long career, blended a concern for fleeting effects of light and atmosphere with a love for nature's contours and colors. Although abstract art flourished during his lifetime, he once implied his independence from abstractionists by saying that his work did not need an arrow on the back indicating which end was up.

Speight earned many honors for his work, including the Gold Medal of Honor from the Pennsylvania Academy of Fine Arts (1926), Hallgarten Prize from the National Academy of Design in New York (1930), Owens Award from the state of Pennsylvania (1961), North Carolina Medal for achievement in the fine arts (1964), Morrison Award from the Roanoke Island Historical Association (1973), and O. Max Gardner Award from The University of North Carolina (1976). He received honorary doctorates from Wake Forest University (1962) and Holy Cross College (1964) and was elected a member of the National Academy of Design in 1940 and to life membership in the National Institute of Arts and Letters in 1960. In 1961 he was the first North Carolina artist to be honored with an exhibition of his works in the newly opened North Carolina Museum of Art in Raleigh.

His paintings are owned by museums in North Carolina and by the Metropolitan Museum of Art in New York, the Boston Museum of Fine Arts, the Philadelphia Museum of Art, and museums in other cities in the United States and in Canada.

In 1936 Speight married Sarah Jane Blakeslee, a student at the Pennsylvania Academy of Fine Arts who worked as a portrait and landscape painter. They were the parents of a son and a daughter, Thomas B. and Elisabeth S. He was buried in Greenwood Cemetery, Greenville.

SEE: Elizabeth H. Copeland, *Chronicles of Pitt County, North Carolina* (1982); John D. Ebbs, *The Nomination of Francis Speight for the Oliver Max Gardner Award* (1975); Ola Maie Foushee, *Art in North Carolina: Episodes and Developments, 1585–1970* (1972); *Francis Speight: A Retrospective* (Washington, D.C., 1986, with biographical and critical sketches by David Sellin); "Francis Speight: A Retrospective," 9 Feb.–11 Mar. 1988, Greenville Museum of Art (1988 [portrait]); Dorothy Grafly, "Francis Speight," *Magazine of Art* 31 (May 1938); Greenville, *The East Carolinian*, 28 Nov. 1989; *Manayunk and Other Places: Paintings and Drawings by Francis Speight: A Retrospective Exhibition Organized by the Pennsylvania State University* (1974); Randolph Osman, *Francis Speight: Selections from His Works Since 1961: A Traveling Exhibition Organized by the Gray Art Gallery at East Carolina University* (1984 [portrait]); H. C. Pitz, "Francis Speight: Painter of the Schuylkill Valley," *American Artist* 24 (April 1960); Raleigh *News and Observer*, 21 Apr. 1985, 15 Nov. 1989; Maury York to William S. Powell, 10 Apr. 1991.

W. KEATS SPARROW

Speight, Richard Harrison *(5 Jan. 1847–1 Sept. 1920)*, physician, planter, and state senator, was born in rural Edgecombe County, the son of John Francis and Emma Lewis Speight. His father was an ordained minister of the Methodist Protestant church and a prosperous farmer. Young Speight attended a neighborhood school until, at age seventeen, he volunteered as a corporal in Company K, Seventy-first North Carolina Regiment, for service in the Civil War. He participated in a number of skirmishes as well as in the Battles of South West Creek near Kinston and Bentonville near Goldsboro. In early 1865 he contracted typhoid fever and was sent home.

In the closing months of the war and for a year afterwards he completed his preparatory education and in the fall of 1866 entered The University of North Carolina, where he pursued a premedical course. Admitted to the University of Maryland School of Medicine, he was graduated in 1870 after two years of study.

Speight established a practice in Edgecombe County, where he also became a successful planter. He served three terms as president of the county medical society and one as vice-president of the State Medical Society. On his farms, which extended across county lines, he produced huge crops of peanuts, tobacco, corn, and cotton as well as grains for livestock and produce for his family and tenants. Concerned about the welfare of farmers, he served as vice-president of the State Farmers' Alliance and as a delegate to several meetings of the National Farmers' Congress. He was the principal founder and president of a large cotton seed oil mill.

In addition, he served several terms in the North Carolina Senate. As a physician as well as a humanitarian, Speight was concerned about the welfare of the insane and served as chairman of a legislative committee on insane asylums. Under the leadership of this committee, the insanity laws of the state were revised and updated. Two governors appointed him to the governing board of the North Carolina Insane Asylum, but he declined a second term when he was in the senate. As a legislator Speight sponsored the bill to place a statue of Civil War governor Zebulon B. Vance on the capitol grounds. Returning home, he continued his medical practice until age sixty-eight and his farming until his death at seventy-three.

Speight married Margaret Powell of Edgecombe County, and they were the parents of a dozen children: Robert P., Henry L., Fannie W., Mary P., Richard H., Jr., Jesse P., George W., Joseph P., Seth E., Frank J., James Ambler, and Elias Carr. After the death of his wife in 1894, Speight married Margaret Whitefield. A member of the Methodist Protestant church, he was buried in the family cemetery on his farm.

SEE: Samuel A. Ashe, ed., *Biographical History of North Carolina*, vol. 4 (1906); Daniel L. Grant, *Alumni History of the University of North Carolina* (1924); Medical Society of the State of North Carolina, *Transactions* (1920); *North Carolina Medical Journal* 3 (1941); *Prominent People of North Carolina* (1906).

C. SYLVESTER GREEN

Spelman, John *(1821–4 Apr. 1889)*, printer and newspaper editor, was born in England. Nothing appears to be recorded concerning his origin or education, but a number of Spelman men, all from the county of Norfolk, attended Cambridge University in the seventeenth and eighteenth centuries. He moved to North Carolina to become foreman of the printing office at the state school for the deaf, dumb, and blind and was living in Raleigh by August 1854, when he applied to the Wake County Court for U.S. citizenship. His earliest known employment was as a reporter for William W. Holden, publisher of the *North Carolina Standard*. The Raleigh Board of Commissioners in 1857 for the first time extended the town's limits following the taking of a special local census. Spelman was engaged to analyze the census, and his summary appeared in the *Standard*. In 1858 he became captain of one of the capital city's two volunteer fire companies. In that position he took steps to ensure an adequate source of water for fighting fires and was a member of a committee that conferred with a local engineer about repairing the fire engine.

In November 1859 it was reported that the Salisbury *Banner*, a weekly that he soon converted to a semiweekly, had been "transferred" to Spelman, who was described as "an accomplished writer and superior printer." By then he was well known in journalistic circles, as the *Wilmington Journal* of 18 Nov. 1859 confirmed this appraisal of him. It anticipated the success of his undertaking, since Spelman had been a "faithful and talented reporter of the Raleigh *Standard* for years past." As editor of the *Banner* he strongly opposed ad valorem taxation, which he associated with antislavery and pro-Union sentiment. On 1 June 1860 he also began publication of a Democratic campaign weekly in Salisbury, *The Little Adder*. It attacked the Know-Nothings and ad valorem taxation while supporting John W. Ellis for governor and John C. Breckinridge and Joseph Lane for president and vice-president, respectively. This paper appeared only during the period 1 June–27 July.

On 15 Mar. 1860 in Petersburg, Va., Spelman married Mollie Lea. The census of that year for Rowan County recorded them as residents of a hotel in Salisbury. A daughter, born on 21 Mar. 1861, died the same day and was buried in the Old English Cemetery, Salisbury. They may have intended to remain in Salisbury only briefly, because in March 1860 Spelman founded the *Weekly State Journal* in Raleigh as a continuation of the *Democratic Press*; his connection with the *Journal* lasted at least until 1882, but for some of the time others were associated with him in its operation. During the Civil War his paper served as the voice of the Confederate administration, and he printed some state currency on his press. In the later Prohibition campaign, Spelman's paper was a strong anti-Prohibition voice. For a few weeks in 1872 he also published *The Blasting Powder*, described as being "for Democrats and Conservatives, a weekly campaign paper for the people." At times during the Civil War the *Journal* appeared in weekly, semiweekly, and daily editions, and for a while it was published in Goldsboro. In March 1865, with the approach of the Federal army, a few people fled Goldsboro; among them was Spelman, editor of the *Goldsboro State Journal*. A Northern writer described him as a "little, dirty, nasty, howling, snarling, hypocritical, demagogical secesh" who had contributed to the war. By fleeing, a later historian wrote, he probably "saved his skin."

Soon after becoming governor in 1859, John W. Ellis of Salisbury named Spelman the state printer. In 1860 Spelman bought the Adams Power Press, which had formerly belonged to the North Carolina Institution for the Education of the Deaf and Dumb and Blind. Richard H. Whitaker was involved with him in this undertaking. With the aid of the governor, $3,500 was secured to acquire the press, but the total amount had not been repaid in March 1865, when the press was destroyed. After W. W. Holden's newspaper and printing office were demolished by Confederate soldiers from Georgia, Holden supporters—unhappy over Holden's support of Reconstruction—destroyed Spelman's press and his newspaper, the *State Journal*, in retaliation.

On 3 Apr. 1866 Spelman began publishing the *Daily Newbern Commercial* as a general newspaper but with emphasis on business. In time a weekly edition also appeared. As editor, Spelman followed a very close line between supporting the Reconstruction government and undertaking to justify the actions of North Carolinians during the years 1861–65. He endorsed the program of President Andrew Johnson for presidential Reconstruction, publicized actions taken by Congress of which he disapproved, and reported news of the late leaders of the Confederacy. A poem by an unidentified Englishman, "A Reply to the Conquered Banner," published in the issue of 16 Apr. 1866, surely brought comfort to many of its readers.

While continuing his *State Journal*, Spelman once more undertook to publish a new campaign paper. In June and July 1872 he produced *Blasting-Powder for Democrats and Conservatives*. Subtitled *A Weekly Campaign Paper for the People*, it supported Augustus S. Merrimon in his contest for governor against Republican Tod R. Caldwell.

The 1870 census recorded Spelman and his wife, Mary, who must have been called Mollie, as living in the home of one Francis Miller in Raleigh—apparently a boardinghouse. No children were listed. Following a period of declining health, Spelman died at age sixty-eight; after funeral services at the Church of the Good Shepherd, Raleigh, he was buried in Oakwood Cemetery. For a number of years after his death Mary Spelman, a native of North Carolina, was a matron at the St. Luke's Home for women in Raleigh.

SEE: *Branson and Farrar's North Carolina Business Directory of 1866–67*; Beth G. Crabtree and James W. Patton, eds., *Journal of a Secesh Lady* (1979); *Criswell's Currency Series*, vol. 1 (1964); *Daily Newbern Commercial*, 3 Apr. 1866; Elizabeth Reid Murray to William S. Powell, 22 Apr. 1983; *Raleigh, N.C., City Directory, 1889–1900*; Raleigh *News and Observer*, 5 Apr. 1889; Raleigh *Register*, 7 Mar. 1860; Raleigh *State Chronicle*, 12 Apr. 1889; Mary Wescott and Allene Ramage, comps., *A Checklist of United States Newspapers . . .*, pt. 4 (1936); R. H. Whitaker, *Whitaker's Reminiscences: Incidents and Anecdotes* (1905); *Wilmington Journal*, 18 Nov. 1859.

WILLIAM S. POWELL

Spence, Bessie Octavia Whitted *(26 Jan. 1885–7 Oct. 1973)*, educator and lay churchwoman, the daughter of Julius Monroe and Ella Frances Howerton Whitted, was born in Durham. She attended the public schools of Durham and was graduated from Trinity College in 1906. Between her graduation and 1913 she taught in the Durham public schools, but during the period 1906–8 she was enrolled in the graduate school of Trinity College and was awarded a master of arts degree in 1908.

Following her marriage in October 1913 to Hersey Everett Spence, she moved to Sanford, where he was pastor of a Methodist church for three years. In 1916 her husband's assignment took them back to Durham, and in 1918 he joined the Trinity College faculty. She soon returned to public school work, serving as dean of girls at Durham High School. Mrs. Spence enrolled at the University of Chicago for the session 1928–29 and earned a bachelor of divinity degree from Duke University in 1929. In subsequent years she did further work at Chicago, Northwestern University, and Columbia University.

In the fall of 1929 Bessie Spence began a career as teacher of biblical literature in the Woman's College of Duke University and in time became the first woman to receive full tenure on the Duke faculty. After forty-four years in the classroom, twenty-one of them at Duke, she retired in 1950 as assistant professor emeritus. A Sunday school teacher for more than thirty-five years, she also spent time counseling students and offering them guidance and assistance in their work.

Bessie Spence served on many academic committees and engaged in public service in the community. She was a popular speaker before religious and literary groups, a talented pianist, and an artist. The Spences had no children, but their home was the meeting place of countless student groups.

When their home in Hope Valley burned in 1962, they gave the site to Duke University; income from the property became the nucleus of an endowment for the Hersey E. and Bessie Spence Chair of Christian Education. She was buried in Maplewood Cemetery, Durham, beside her husband, who had died one week earlier.

SEE: *Duke Alumni Register*, September 1974; *Program and Recommendations for the 1974 North Carolina Conference of the United Methodist Church, June 3–6, 1974; Durham Morning Herald*, 8 Oct. 1973; Information Sheet, Office of Information Service, Duke University.

C. SYLVESTER GREEN

Spence, Hersey Everett *(12 June 1882–30 Sept. 1973)*, Methodist clergyman, teacher, and author, was born at South Mills in Camden County, the son of Joseph Newton and Lucy Indiana Howell Spence. He received his undergraduate degree from Trinity College in 1907 and a master of arts degree in 1908; in the summer of 1911 he did graduate study at Columbia University. While teaching at Duke University in its early years, he enrolled in the School of Religion and was awarded a bachelor of divinity degree in 1927; he also studied in the graduate school at the University of Chicago in 1927–28. Later he was granted honorary doctorates by Asbury College and High Point College.

Ordained a Methodist deacon in 1908 and an elder in 1910, Spence served pastorates in Raleigh, Durham, and Sanford between 1907 and 1916. In the period 1908–13 he was also assistant professor of English literature at Trinity College. He was executive secretary of the Sunday School Board of the North Carolina Conference of the Methodist Episcopal Church, South, from 1916 to 1918, when he became professor of biblical literature and religious education at Trinity College. In 1925 he was appointed professor of religious education in the newly organized School of Religion in Duke University, a position he filled with distinction until his retirement in 1952 at age seventy.

Spence was chairman of the Sunday school board of the North Carolina Conference (1918–31) and chairman of the board of education (1933–43). In addition, he was dean of the North Carolina [Methodist] Pastors' School (1918–27, 1946–52) and dean of the North Carolina Rural Church Institute. Continually in demand as a pulpit supply, he spoke almost every Sunday during his active years at some local church of many denominations, and at church conferences, assemblies, and study classes both in churches and on college campuses.

He was a Mason and a member of the Odd Fellows organization, the Knights of Pythias, and the Modern Woodmen of the World. Though a registered Democrat, he took no active part in politics. He was the first recipient of the Algernon Sydney Sullivan Award at Duke for distinguished service to the university.

Spence was a prolific writer, and his first published volume was a book of poems, *Reveries in Rhyme* (1913). As a student of religious drama, he produced many original plays and pageants: *Ruth* (1924), *When Cross Roads Meet Again* (1934), *Marching Men of Methodism* (1934), *Old Testament Dramas* (1935), and others. Among his other publications were *A Guide to Bible Study* (1922, 1926), *The Bishops' Crusade* (1937), *Holidays and Holy Days* (1946), *I Remember* (1954), and *Mcbride: A Mother in Methodism* (1957). He wrote many of his poems to memorialize special occasions.

In the classroom Professor Spence was a personable and popular teacher. He enjoyed a pleasant sense of humor, had an uncanny memory for people and incidents, and knew how to inspire his students to do original research and make practical applications of their findings. His home was a frequent gathering place for the members of his classes. He was especially cordial to candidates for the ministry in all denominations and emphasized the mission of religious education in building a complete program in the local church.

In October 1913 he married Bessie Octavia Whitted of Durham. They had no children. After their home burned, they gave the site to Duke University to begin a fund to endow a professorship in the School of Religion. He died at age ninety-one and was buried in Maplewood Cemetery, Durham.

SEE: Information Sheet, Office of Information Services, Duke University; *Who's Who in American Education*, vol. 5 (1933); *Who's Who in the Clergy*, vol. 1 (1935).

C. SYLVESTER GREEN

Spencer, Cornelia Phillips *(20 Mar. 1825–11 Mar. 1908)*, author and friend of education, although during a long life was closely identified with North Carolina and was the author of its first school history, was not born in the state but in Harlem, then a part of New York where her father conducted a boys' school. She was the youngest of three children: Charles became professor of mathematics and engineering at The University of North Carolina, and Samuel Field was U.S. solicitor general under President Ulysses S. Grant.

Her father, James Phillips, an Englishman, migrated to America in the late eighteenth century and took his family in 1826 to Chapel Hill, where for many years he occupied the chair of mathematics and wrote two textbooks. Her mother, who was Judith Vermeule, belonged to an old Dutch family living in the Raritan valley of New Jersey. Cornelia had no formal schooling and drew her education from wide reading, an interest in people, and contact with personages such as David Lowry Swain, former governor of North Carolina and president of the university during Cornelia's formative years.

In 1851, at age twenty-six, Cornelia met twenty-two-year-old James Munroe Spencer, a law student from Alabama, and they were married in 1855. The couple lived in Alabama, where their only child, Julia James, was born in 1859. Magnus, as her husband was called, was not strong, and his health declined until his death in 1861. In the next year Cornelia returned to her father's home in

Chapel Hill. By then the Civil War was in progress, and she could scarcely maintain her occupation of tutoring young people due to the feverish interest in the conflict. On Easter Sunday 1865 Chapel Hill was occupied by Federal cavalry whose commander, Brigadier General Smith Atkins, married Eleanor Swain, daughter of the university president, in an August 1865 ceremony attended by Cornelia. To relieve her frequent depression during this period, Cornelia began collecting material for *The Last Ninety Days of the War in North Carolina*, a project suggested by Governor Zebulon B. Vance. In 1868 this book was published by Charles F. Deems, editor of *The Watchman* in New York.

Finding that writing relieved her depression due to her fear for the impoverished university, she began composing articles for various publications, including the *North Carolina Presbyterian* and the Raleigh *Sentinel* in which her series of "Pen and Ink Sketches of The University of North Carolina" appeared in 1869. She also wrote a number of biographies for Samuel A. Ashe's *Biographical History of North Carolina*. Her pieces appeared in the *University of North Carolina Magazine* in every decade from 1853 to 1900. This work early proved that she had gifts as a historian. In 1870 the university, which had been steadily losing students, was closed and its faculty was dispersed.

To Cornelia this represented a challenge, and she rose to meet it. Day after day she wrote letters to the leading men of the state propounding one question: Are you going to allow the university, one of the state's chief assets, to remain closed? No definite answer came until 20 Mar 1875, which happened to be Cornelia's fiftieth birthday. A telegram from Raleigh announced that the legislature had passed a bill allowing the university to reorganize and assuring it of some financial support. For the reopening, on 15 Sept. 1875, Cornelia wrote a triumphant hymn. She also seized the rope to the campus bell, which she rang in joy. During this time she assisted the North Carolina Geological Survey by making maps and diagrams, preparing computations, and arranging, labeling, and cataloguing cabinets of specimens.

In 1879 she was editor of the *Chapel Hill Ledger*, a newspaper. The extra leisure now available to her she used in the research and writing of her second book, *First Steps in North Carolina History*, published in 1888 with subsequent editions in 1889, 1890, 1891, and 1892. She was also interested in the environment, especially trees and wildflowers, and she was active in protecting Battle Park from development. Cornelia painted china as gifts for friends and helped other widows and harried mothers with their household chores. In 1894 she went to live with her daughter, Mrs. James Lee Love, the wife of a Harvard instructor, and this closed her life in North Carolina. In 1895 the university awarded her the honorary LL.D. degree.

SEE: Samuel A. Ashe, ed., *Biographical History of North Carolina*, vol. 3 (1906 [portrait]); Kemp P. Battle, *History of the University of North Carolina*, 2 vols. (1907–12); Hope S. Chamberlain, *Old Days in Chapel Hill* (1926); Raleigh *News and Observer*, 27 Apr. 1902, 24 Nov. 1904, 28 June 1908, 3 Feb. 1927; Cornelia Phillips Spencer, *The Last Ninety Days of the War in North Carolina* (1866) and *Selected Papers*, edited with an introduction by Louis R. Wilson (1953).

PHILLIPS RUSSELL

Spencer, Samuel *(21 Jan. 1734–20 Mar. 1793)*, member of the colonial Assembly, trustee of The University of North Carolina, and justice of the superior court, was born in East Haddam, Conn. He was the oldest of nine children born to Samuel and Jerusha Brainerd Spencer, both of whom were descendants of highly respected New England families. Young Spencer was graduated from the College of New Jersey (Princeton) in 1759. The exact date of his arrival in North Carolina would be difficult to establish, but undoubtedly it was only a few years after his graduation, for by 1765 he was a resident of Anson County, and on 16 Oct. 1765 he was appointed clerk of court.

From the time of his arrival Spencer was active in governmental affairs. He represented Anson County in the colonial Assembly from 1766 to 1768 and was a member of the Provincial Council from 1774 to 1776. When the Provincial congresses met at New Bern, Hillsborough, and Halifax in 1774, 1775, and 1776 he again represented Anson, and at the conventions of 1788 and 1789—meeting in Hillsborough and Fayetteville to ratify the U.S. Constitution—he was a delegate. In 1777 he was one of the three members elected as the first justices of the superior court and served in this capacity from 1778 until his death.

Spencer held the rank of colonel in the militia. At the time of the Regulator uprising in 1768 he was fortunate in that open conflict in Anson County was avoided when the protesters dispersed. However, at the Battle of Alamance in 1771 Spencer was in the field as a supporter of the royal government, but his loyalty dissolved as relations with the mother country became more strained. When the Provincial Congress met in Halifax (4 Apr.–14 May 1776), he was appointed to the committee charged with writing "a temporary Civil Constitution," but the writing, completion, and acceptance of the document was not accomplished until months later at the fifth session of the congress (12 Nov.–23 Dec. 1776), also at Halifax. Because Spencer was not a representative at this congress, the contribution he made can be only a matter of conjecture.

As a delegate to the Hillsborough convention (21 July–2 Aug. 1788), Spencer was a major participant. With him as anti-federalists were Willie Jones, Timothy Bloodworth, David Caldwell, Thomas Person, and Griffith Rutherford, but he was the leader and ablest debater. Spencer's name appears frequently in the records of the debates, where his comments are both candid and temperate. Though favoring a stronger union, he looked with distrust upon a powerful central government. Above all, his concern was with the absence of a Bill of Rights, and his vote was one of the 184 cast against adoption. More than a year later, at the convention in Fayetteville (7–23 Nov. 1789), he was one of the minority of seventy-seven who cast their vote against North Carolina's adoption of the federal Constitution. Surely, though, he received satisfaction from his appointment to a committee charged with drafting proposals for a Bill of Rights for the new Constitution.

A conscientious and able judge, Spencer was a participant in one of the superior court's significant decisions. Mrs. Elizabeth Cornell Bayard brought proceedings for recovery of property willed to her by her father, a Tory merchant, that had been confiscated and sold to Spyers Singleton. The confiscation acts of 1777 and 1779 had made it impossible for Tories to recover lost property, and an act of 1785 had prohibited the courts from hearing cases involving such losses. Despite these laws, and the fact that she was no longer a resident of North Carolina, Mrs. Bayard decided to enter suit. Both she and the defendant were represented by well-known lawyers; those employed by Singleton argued that since Mrs. Bayard and her father were British subjects, the case should be dismissed. But the superior court justices—Spencer, Samuel Ashe, and John Williams—rejected this argument, and cited Article 14 of the Bill of Rights in the North Carolina Constitution by which a trial by jury was guaranteed. When the case went to the jury in 1787, the verdict was for the defendant, but of substantially more significance than the verdict was the action of the justices in declaring unconstitutional the act of the Assembly. This was the first reported case under a written constitution in which a justice, or justices, took such action; John Marshall's decision, *Marbury v. Madison*, now regarded as very much a part of American law, was not rendered until 1803.

Criticism of the justices was vocal, not only for their ruling in *Bayard v. Singleton*, but for other decisions and acts as well. There was talk of impeachment, some lawyers were determined to "write the judges off the bench," and the General Assembly authorized "an enquiry into the present state of the administration of Justice in the Superior Courts." But, exercising better judgment, members of the legislature silenced the criticism and voted to express appreciation to the justices "for their long and faithful service."

Among the federalists there remained those who had little regard for Spencer, and even a generation later Griffith McRee wrote, "He certainly was not below mediocrity, even in his profession, but [he] was not qualified by learning or dignity of manners for the office conferred upon him." But Spencer's alma mater held him in sufficient regard to confer an honorary doctorate of laws upon him in 1784, and in 1789 he became a trustee of the newly established University of North Carolina.

Justice Spencer was a man of substantial means. His home was located on Smith's Creek, where it flows into the Pee Dee River, only a few miles from Wadesboro, and his landholdings in Anson, Bladen, Tryon, Mecklenburg, and Rutherford counties were in excess of 5,000 acres. The census of 1790 reports him to have been the holder of eighteen slaves.

In 1776 Spencer married Phillipa Pegues, usually referred to by her pet name, Sybil, a South Carolinian of Huguenot descent; her family home was near the boundary line of the two Carolinas. The Spencers were the parents of at least four children—Mary Pegues, who married Isaac Jackson; Claudius, who died while quite young; a son, William Samuel; and a second daughter who is said to have been named Anne.

Spencer has in so many respects been forgotten. It remained for Albert Coates, in his *Three North Carolinians Who Have Stood Up to Be Counted for the Bill of Rights*, to remind North Carolinians of the greatness of this man and of their indebtedness to him.

Spencer's death came as the result of an unusual accident. It is reported that he had not been well and between court sessions was resting at his home. While sitting on the porch, with a red cap on his head, he became sleepy and began to nod; a large turkey gobbler apparently regarded the moving cap as a challenge and attacked. The justice was thrown from his chair and suffered numerous scratches from which erysipelas developed.

The accounts of Samuel Spencer's life are at times conflicting. The date of his birth was 1734, not 1738 as in some cases reported; the *Genealogy of the Brainerd-Brainard Family* . . . establishes beyond doubt the earlier date. And the Calvin Spencer, mentioned as the brother moving with him from Connecticut, was evidently a half brother who would have been at least fifteen years younger and who settled in Chesterfield County, S.C. The reports of Spencer's landholdings and the number of slaves he held have also varied, but the figures used in this sketch have been taken from the records of the Land Grant Office in the North Carolina Department of the Secretary of State, deed records located in the North Carolina State Archives, and the U.S. Census of 1790. The date reported for Spencer's death has also varied, but the minutes of the board of trustees of The University of North Carolina and the Charleston *State Gazette of South Carolina* of 22 May 1793 support the date used. The disagreement as to the year of his death can be attributed only to an error in copying; the variance as to the month is due to the fact that ultimo, or "ult." as abbreviated, was overlooked by some writers.

SEE: Lucy Abigail Brainard, *Genealogy of the Brainerd-Brainard Family in America* . . . , vol. 2 (1908); Charleston *State Gazette of South Carolina*, 22 May 1793; John L. Cheney, Jr., ed., *North Carolina Government, 1585–1974* (1975); Walter Clark, ed., *State Records of North Carolina*, vols. 16, 18, 22 (1900, 1907); Albert Coates, *Three North Carolinians Who Have Stood Up to Be Counted for the Bill of Rights* (1973); "Deed Records" (North Carolina State Archives, Raleigh); Jonathan Elliot, ed., *The Debates in the Several State Conventions on the Adoption of the Federal Constitution*, vol. 4 (1836); Marshall DeLancey Haywood, "Samuel Spencer," Charles Leonard Van Noppen Biographical Sketches (Manuscript Department, Duke University Library, Durham); Quinton Holton, "*History of the Case of Bayard v. Singleton*" (M.A. thesis, University of North Carolina, 1948); "Land Grants" (Land Grants Office, North Carolina Department of the Secretary of State, Raleigh); James McLachlan, ed., *Princetonians, 1748–1768: A Biographical Dictionary* (1976); Griffith J. McRee, *Life and Correspondence of James Iredell*, vol. 1 (1857); Mary L. Medley, *History of Anson County, 1750–1976* (1976); Henry W. Rigby, comp., "Descendants of William Spencer of Montgomery, N.C." (mimeographed, 1977, North Carolina State Archives); William L. Saunders, ed., *Colonial Records of North Carolina*, vol. 10 (1890); Lucy Irby Trenholme, *The Ratification of the Federal Constitution in North Carolina* (1967).

J. ISAAC COPELAND
JERRY C. CASHION

Spicer, John *(d. March 1789)*, port inspector, legislator, judge of the Admiralty Court, militia paymaster during the Revolutionary War, and member of the Council of State, probably settled in North Carolina with his brother James before 1766. The penchant of the family to use the name John makes it difficult to sort out the events that should be attributed to this particular man, but the account below is that best supported by facts available in contemporary public records.

By 1767 John Spicer was named inspector for New Topsail, replacing James Spicer. John held the position through 1773 and perhaps as late as 1775. The name appears in the deed books as early as 3 June 1754, when he bought land on the main branch of Queens Creek. In a 1768 purchase he is listed as "mariner." John Spicer, Jr., first appears in the records as a testator to a 16 Feb. 1770 deed to land that John Spicer bought. John Spicer frequently held his land for only a few years before reselling it.

Spicer began his legislative career by representing Onslow County in the third General Assembly under Governor Josiah Martin beginning on 4 Dec. 1773 at New Bern. In 1775 and 1776 he represented the county in the last three Provincial congresses. The assemblies of 1777, 1781, 1783, and 1785 also included him. He was elected by the legislature to one-year terms on the Council of State in 1780 and 1785. Service for an undetermined period following election by the Assembly to the post of judge of the Admiralty Court for the port of Brunswick in 1783 led to his resignation from the senate. In 1774 he sided with the majority in opposing proposed bills that would have decreased the power of the courts and the fees for the chief justice of the superior court. In November 1776 he was a member of the committee of the Fifth Provincial Congress that prepared the declaration of rights and the constitution for the government of North Carolina.

In December 1776 Spicer was named paymaster of the Second Battalion of the Continental troops raised in the state and about the same time was appointed a justice of the peace for Onslow County. The returns from the county show that in 1777 both Captain John Spicer and Lieutenant John Spicer, Jr., held commissions. In December 1777 he voted with the majority in favor of confiscating property of persons deemed inimical to the United States. In 1780 he was appointed one of the money inspectors for Onslow County, a move made necessary because of the ease with which the paper money might be counterfeited. On taking his seat in the senate on 26 June 1781, he was referred to as "Colonel John Spicer," yet two days later the journal refers to "Colonel Williams, Mr. Spicer, & General Butler." In 1780 a ship belonging to John Spicer was sent with relief supplies for Americans held prisoner by the British in Charleston, S.C. There the ship was seized despite its letter of truce signed by the British commandant in Charleston.

In his later years in the senate Spicer voted with the majority to issue £100,000 in paper currency, voted against changing from 19 Apr. 1775 to 4 July 1776 the date after which people who opposed the state could not hold state office, voted with the majority against a bill to incorporate the Protestant Episcopal Church of Wilmington, and voted with the majority in defeating an amendment to the money bill to change from 50 shillings maximum payment per hundred weight for tobacco for public use to the current price.

In January 1781 Cornelius Harnett was trying to escape from the British in Wilmington when he suffered an attack of gout and took refuge in Spicer's Onslow County home. There the British found Harnett and forced him to walk towards Wilmington until he collapsed. He was then thrown across his horse and carried into Wilmington, where he soon died.

The May 1786 census taken by John Spicer, Jr., lists the elder Spicer in a household consisting of two white males between the ages of twenty-one and sixty and one older than sixty, three white females, and twenty-four blacks. The younger Spicer's household consisted of one white male between twenty-one and sixty, three younger than twenty-one, three white females, and a dozen blacks.

Spicer's will was written on 2 Feb. 1789 and probated in April. It mentions his wife Catherine, sons John and Elisha, and daughter Cate.

SEE: Joseph Parsons Brown, *The Commonwealth of Onslow: A History* (1960); Annie Walker Burns, *North Carolina Pension Abstracts of the Revolution* (no date); John B. Davis, ed., *Onslow County Court of Pleas and Quarter Sessions—Abstract of Minutes, 1779–1782* (1989); Zae Hargett Gwynn, comp., *Abstracts of the Records of Onslow County, North Carolina, 1734–1850* (1961); *The Heritage of Onslow County* (1983); Leora H. McEachern and Isabel M. Williams, eds., *Wilmington-New Hanover Safety Committee Minutes, 1774–1776* (1974); *Roster of Soldiers from North Carolina in the American Revolution* (1932); Alexander M. Walker, comp., *New Hanover County Court Minutes, Part 1–4, 1738–1810* (1958–62).

WILLIAM S. SMITH, JR.

Spilman, Bernard Washington *(22 Jan. 1871–26 Mar. 1950)*, Baptist clergyman and denominational Sunday school executive, was the fourth of five children born to Bushrod Washington and Helva Roxanna Barham Spilman, of Weldon. Of German ancestry, the elder Spilman had become a fairly prosperous merchant and farmer after moving to Weldon from his native Westmoreland County, Va.

Spilman was given instruction in the homes of various local teachers, at the Garysburg Academy, and in a public school in Wilson prior to his matriculation in the Horner School at Henderson in 1884. Two years later he transferred to the Littleton High School, a private institution operated by Professor LeRoy W. Bagley. He enrolled at Wake Forest College in the fall of 1887 and received a B.S. degree in 1891. He was awarded honorary doctor of divinity degrees by Stetson University (1911), Baylor University (1920), and Wake Forest (1921).

Upon his graduation from Wake Forest, Spilman assumed the pastoral care of the Smyrna, Davis, and Woodville churches in Carteret County, supplementing his meager salary by teaching school. By late summer of 1892 he had saved enough money to begin theological studies at the Southern Baptist Theological Seminary in Louisville, Ky. However, he was unable to complete the two-year course because of illness, which necessitated his missing final examinations and his return to Weldon in the summer of 1894. Thereafter, he supplied churches in Smyrna and New Bern before assuming the pastoral care of First Baptist Church, Kinston, on 1 Jan. 1895.

Spilman remained with the Kinston church for only fifteen months before entering upon the occupation that would engage his time, talents, and energies for the next forty-five years. In early 1896 he was elected the first Sunday school missionary for the Baptist State Convention of North Carolina—a position that found him visiting churches and associational meetings throughout the state in behalf of his ultimate goal of a "well-equipped, well-organized Sunday School, open fifty-two Sundays a year, in every church in every community in North Carolina."

The thoroughness of his work, together with his readiness to utilize innovative methods, attracted the attention of the Sunday School Board of the Southern Baptist Convention. In June 1901 Spilman was named field secretary of the board—a post that he filled until his retirement in 1940. By the end of his first year with the board, he had designed a four-point plan of action, the objectives of which were to guide his ministry throughout his remaining career. The objectives envisioned the appointment of Sunday school promotional secretaries within each of the affiliated Baptist State conventions; employment of additional staff personnel to assist with the work of the Sunday School Board, especially with the travel involved in the successful promotion of Sunday School work; development of a comprehensive teacher training program for Sunday school workers; and the establishment of a series of state Sunday school assemblies—similar to the chautauquas that he had helped sponsor in North Carolina—headed by a general southwide assembly that would serve the entire denomination. Later he was given the special assignment of encouraging the teaching of religion in southern colleges and universities.

By the time he left the Sunday School Board, Spilman

had witnessed significant progress towards the realization of his goals. He had initiated the first Sunday school training course for the denomination with his *Normal Studies for Sunday School Workers*, published in 1902. Moreover, he was primarily responsible for the founding of the Ridgecrest Baptist Assembly (now Ridgecrest Baptist Conference Center) in 1907, serving successively as manager, general secretary, and president of the assembly's board of directors until 1933. In addition, he was an early and staunch supporter of the Baptist Student Movement throughout colleges and universities in the South.

A popular lecturer to church, civic, and student groups, Spilman was also a prolific writer. Besides serving as lesson writer for various periodicals published by the Sunday School Board, he wrote numerous articles and pamphlets—many of which first appeared in the denominational press. Among the books of which he was author or coauthor were *Convention Normal Manual for Sunday-School Workers* (1909); *The New Convention Normal Manual* (1913); *A Study in Religious Pedagogy, Based on Our Lord's Interview with the Woman of Samaria* (1920); *The Sunday School Manual* (1923); *The Mill's Home: A History of the Baptist Orphanage Movement in North Carolina* (1932); and *Yesterday Greets Tomorrow* (no date).

Spilman married Agnes Mozelle Pollock of Kinston on 24 Jan. 1900, and they had two children: Raymond Pollock, who died in infancy, and Agnes, who died at birth. Mrs. Spilman died on 16 Nov. 1928. On 12 Aug. 1939 Spilman married Esther Harrell Ward of Kinston.

A portrait of Spilman hangs in Pritchell Hall, the administrative building of the Ridgecrest Baptist Conference Center, Ridgecrest. His remains were interred beside those of his first wife in Maplewood Cemetery, Kinston.

SEE: William J. Fallis, "Spilman, Bernard Washington," *Encyclopedia of Southern Baptists*, vol. 2 (1958); C. Sylvester Green, *B. W. Spilman—The Sunday School Man* (1953); Malcolm L. Melville, *Spilman Papers* (1965); Edward C. Starr, ed., *A Baptist Bibliography*, vol. 22 (1975).

R. HARGUS TAYLOR

Spilman, John Barham *(6 Aug. 1868–25 Dec. 1935)*, business educator and college administrator, was born in Weldon, the son of Bushrod Washington and Helva Roxanna Barham Spilman. His father, a native of Westmoreland County, Va., was a merchant whose ancestral line has been traced to twelfth-century England. An uncle, Thomas Madison Spilman, was a noted commission merchant in Washington, D.C., in the last half of the 1800s. His brother, the Reverend B. W. Spilman, was a renowned clergyman and Sunday school pioneer in the first half of the twentieth century.

John Spilman attended elementary and secondary schools in Weldon and Garysburg and was graduated from Horner Military Academy, Henderson, in 1886. That fall he entered Wake Forest College, from which he was graduated with a bachelor of science degree in 1890. His college days were marked by many campus activities, principal of which was his membership in the literary society, where he distinguished himself as a debater and declaimer. In his second year he won a gold pin (first prize) for his declamation, "Israel's Political Redeemer."

For the ten years following his graduation from Wake Forest, Spilman lived in several states and held a variety of jobs. He went first to Tyler, Tex., and completed a course at Draughon's Business College, receiving a certificate in business administration. For two years (1891–93) he taught school in Starrville, Tex., and then went to Oakwood, Tex., where for two more years (1894–96) he was manager and bookkeeper of a drugstore owned and operated by Dr. E. P. Murdock. Early in 1897 he returned to North Carolina and taught during the spring semester at Southport Collegiate Institute. At some time during the year he taught two terms at Glen Alpine School, Burke County, and one term at the Raleigh Male Academy. Spilman then taught in Smyrna (1897–98) and Beaufort (1898–99), before becoming superintendent of schools in Beaufort (1899–1901). Subsequently, he was superintendent of schools in Lexington (1902–4) and business manager of Draughon's Business colleges (1904–12), with headquarters in Nashville, Tenn.

In September 1912 he went to Greenville to be the first business manager and treasurer of East Carolina Teachers' College (now East Carolina University) and served with distinction until his death. On his arrival, the college was in its fifth session, and it fell to Spilman to plan and supervise construction of the campus through its formative years. Many new buildings and student service facilities were added. The day-to-day operation of the school within the limits of the state budgetary funds was his sole responsibility. They were twenty-four years (1912–35) of stringency that demanded careful attention to fiscal matters, but officials at East Carolina praised Spilman's business acumen and his intelligent, cooperative handling of the institution's business affairs. In representing the college, he always enjoyed a cordial relationship with the state legislature and state officials.

The Administration Building on the campus was named for Spilman (15 May 1966), and an oil portrait painted by Georgia Pearsall Hearne was hung in the first floor corridor of the building. Early in 1936 East Carolina president Dr. L. R. Meadows told the campus assembly that his longtime associate had been "a sympathetic man of understanding . . . an excellent story teller . . . capable . . . lovable . . . a thorough gentleman." Both the faculty and the student body published resolutions of respect and appreciation. The college annual, *Tecoan*, had been dedicated to him in 1932. He was also elected to the East Carolina chapter of Kappa Alpha fraternity (educational).

Spilman's community involvement was limited because of his close attention to detail at East Carolina. But while in Lexington he had been especially active in Masonry, serving as master of the lodge, which later hung an oil portrait of him in its convocation hall. In Greenville he concerned himself with helping staff and faculty obtain residences. Much of the area in and around the campus was procured, with no personal profit, to be available to those who wished to build their own homes.

On 22 Dec. 1917 he married Johnetta Webb, a native of Chowan County and a teacher in the Greenville public schools. They had three children: John Barham, Jr., Frances Webb (Mrs. Hugo Facci), and Bernard Webb, who died in service in 1942 during World War II. A member of Memorial Baptist Church, Greenville, Spilman was buried in Greenwood Cemetery.

SEE: Data file, East Carolina University Library (Greenville); Mrs. J. B. Spilman, Sr. (Greenville), personal contact; Raleigh *News and Observer*, 28 Dec. 1935.

C. SYLVESTER GREEN

Spoon, William Luther, Jr. *(18 Mar. 1862–29 Aug. 1942)*, engineer, inventor, and farmer, was born near Kimesville, Alamance County, the only son of George Monroe and Nancy Stafford Shoffner Spoon. He attended the public schools of Alamance County, Oakdale Academy, and the Friendship School in Coble Township, Alamance County. Spoon entered Graham Normal College (later Elon College) at Graham in 1880 and studied at The University of North Carolina from 1887 to 1891, graduating with bachelor degrees in science and engineering.

In the years immediately following his graduation from the university, Spoon worked as a civil engineer in private practice, served briefly on the staff of the North Carolina Geological Survey, produced a widely acclaimed map of Alamance County, taught school, and held the office of county engineer for Alamance. In 1902 he became a special agent for the Office of Public Roads, U.S. Department of Agriculture, serving until 1909, when he went on leave to become, first, highway engineer with the North Carolina Geological Survey and then, from 1911 to 1913, highway engineer for Forsyth County. In 1913 Spoon returned to his position in the Office of Public Roads, where he worked until 1920. After leaving government service he joined C. F. Lewis to form the engineering firm of Spoon and Lewis, which remained in business until 1939.

An early and forceful advocate of improving public roads, Spoon spent a large part of his professional career as a road builder. At a time when individual farms, small communities, and even whole counties could be isolated for weeks because of impassable roads, and travel by railroad was awkward and time consuming, he was one of a small but articulate group of scientists, engineers, and interested citizens who argued that a relatively small investment in the construction and maintenance of highways would bring a large return in prosperity and public welfare. As a government engineer he traveled extensively in the South, Southwest, and Midwest demonstrating road-building techniques and encouraging the organization of county highway departments.

Spoon, who was particularly interested in rural areas, became an expert in the construction and maintenance of sand clay roads—inexpensive and durable, they were well suited to rural needs and resources. His publication for the Department of Agriculture, *Sand Clay and Burnt Clay Roads* (1907), remained a standard work for years and helped earn him the title, "the father of the sand clay road." He wrote that a sense of the importance of his work to future generations sustained him through many setbacks and frustrations. Although his contribution was largely forgotten, he had the satisfaction of seeing his early efforts evolve into the modern American highway system.

Also a farmer and a land developer, Spoon obtained patents on a number of agricultural and household inventions, including a water cooler, a cotton press, a cotton picker, and a coat donner (to enable a handicapped person to slip into a coat).

In 1897 he married Susan Addeline Vernon Neville (24 Apr. 1868–6 Nov. 1936), the granddaughter of North Carolina congressman Richard Stanford. They were the parents of two children, William Mozart, who died in childhood, and Nancy Miriam. The couple also raised and educated several children of relatives. In 1940 Spoon married Ruth Baldwin, and they were the parents of a daughter, Willie Ruth.

Spoon's funeral was held at Frieden Lutheran Church and he was buried in the Mount Pleasant Methodist Church cemetery, both at Kimesville.

SEE: Graham, *Alamance Gleaner*, 3 Sept. 1942; Daniel L. Grant, *Alumni History of the University of North Carolina* (1924); John William Leonard, *Who's Who in Engineering: A Biographical Dictionary of Contemporaries, 1922–1923* (1922); William Luther Spoon Papers (Southern Historical Collection, University of North Carolina, Chapel Hill).

HARRY W. MCKOWN, JR.

Spruill, Frank (Franklin) Shepherd *(9 Dec. 1862–28 June 1937)*, lawyer and congressman, was born in Martin County, the son of William E., a Confederate soldier, and Harriet Arrington Spruill. Soon after his birth, and while the Civil War was still raging, the family moved from Martin County to a safer, less exposed area of Halifax County. Spruill began his education at the Bingham School at Mebane and then went on to The University of North Carolina, where he studied law and was editor of the *University Magazine*.

In February 1884 he was admitted to the bar. He practiced at Henderson for a year before moving to Louisburg, where he became the partner of Joseph J. Davis. Davis was already highly respected in Franklin County, and this association gave Spruill an advantage in his practice.

Early on Spruill took an active part in many political affairs, including support for the concerns of farmers (he mortgaged his own home to raise money for the farmers' movement); support for Grover Cleveland for president, as a delegate to the Democratic National Convention in St. Louis; and support for the free coinage of silver in a 16-to-1 ratio to gold. In 1892 he campaigned for the election of Elias Carr as governor. Spruill himself was elected to the North Carolina legislature in 1893; in Raleigh he served on the Judiciary Committee and as chairman of the Committee on Railroads and Railroad Commissioners.

Although appointed by Governor Carr to be director of the state prison, Spruill declined to serve. Instead, he became director of the North Carolina Railroad. While he was in this post the Southern Railroad Company obtained a ninety-nine-year lease on the North Carolina Railroad, despite his objections. In 1897 Spruill became assistant U.S. district attorney for eastern North Carolina.

In 1904 Spruill was again nominated to the state House of Representatives, but when also selected as a presidential elector in the same year, he decided to devote all his time to that activity and withdrew his candidacy for the house. It was during the campaign of 1904 that Spruill earned a reputation as an accomplished speaker; his speeches were "pronounced by competent judges to be among the very best types of forensic eloquence ever heard in the State."

In 1907 he moved to Rocky Mount and continued to practice law. He gained still more recognition for his involvement as one of several attorneys for the plaintiff in *Wells Whitehead Tobacco Company v. the American Tobacco Company*, a suit involving the Sherman Antitrust Act. Spruill was also division counsel for the Atlantic Coast Line Railroad for nearly thirty years.

At The University of North Carolina Spruill had been a member of Alpha Tau Omega fraternity and of the Philanthropic Society. He later became a trustee of the university. A member of the Episcopal church, he married Alice Capehart Winston of Bertie. The Spruills had three children: Alice, Martha, and Frank. Spruill died of heart trouble at his home in Rocky Mount and was buried at Pineview Cemetery.

SEE: Samuel A. Ashe, ed., *Biographical History of North Carolina*, vol. 2 (1905); *Charlotte Observer*, 29 June 1937; Daniel L. Grant, *Alumni History of the University of North*

Carolina (1924); *North Carolina Biography*, vol. 5; Robert Watson Winston, *Memorial Address* (29 Mar. 1938).

MICHAEL KEITH TAYLOR

Sprunt, James *(9 June 1846–9 July 1924)*, exporter, Cape Fear historian, and philanthropist, arrived in Wilmington in 1854 from his native Glasgow, Scotland, with his parents, Alexander and Jane Dalziel Sprunt. She was the daughter of John and Margaret Tannahill Dalziel. Alexander's brother, James Menzies Sprunt, had emigrated from Scotland in 1852 intending to go to Boston but was diverted to Wilmington when the ship developed engine trouble. James went on to Duplin County, where he occupied a pulpit on Sunday and taught school on weekdays. From Duplin County he wrote his brother Alexander, still in Scotland, suggesting that he, too, migrate to North Carolina. The name of the James Sprunt Institute (now the James Sprunt Technical Institute) in Kenansville memorializes this antebellum teacher.

Alexander and Jane Sprunt settled first in Kenansville, but after two years they moved to Wilmington and established their permanent home at Ninth and Princess streets. The education of their son James, begun in Glasgow, continued at Kenansville and Mr. Jewett's school in Wilmington until the beginning of the Civil War, when Alexander Sprunt was captured while running the Federal blockade. At age fourteen the son left school to assume family responsibilities. He also studied navigation at night and after three years secured the purser's berth on the blockade-runners *North Heath* and *Lilian*. In Nassau he purchased sugar which he sold in Wilmington and acquired cotton. After the war his cotton was sold in England as the first transaction of the exporting firm of Alexander Sprunt and Son.

Sprunt's early enterprise was interrupted when he was captured and imprisoned at Fort Macon and afterwards at Fortress Monroe. He made a daring escape, however, and returned to Wilmington by way of Boston, Halifax (Nova Scotia), and Cape Canaveral, Fla., surviving shipwreck en route. He then became purser of the blockade-runner *Susan Beirne* until the fall of Fort Fisher on 15 Jan. 1865.

Thereafter he joined his father in the exportation of cotton and naval stores. More than fifty agencies were established overseas in England, Holland, Belgium, France, Germany, Russia, Switzerland, and Italy. When his father died in 1884, James succeeded him as British vice-consul. For five years (1907–12) he was also Imperial German Counsel. He served both posts with distinction and received special recognition from each government. Nevertheless, records in the files of the British Foreign Office suggest that he was sacked for allegedly selling cotton to the Germans after World War I had broken out.

Sprunt exerted himself in Wilmington for the improvement of river and harbor conditions, was active in the North Carolina Literary and Historical Association and the North Carolina Folklore Society, and served on the board of trustees of The University of North Carolina and of Davidson College. Aside from his extensive philanthropies, he is perhaps best remembered as Wilmington's most dedicated citizen for the preservation of the historical facts and legends of the Cape Fear region. Among his best-known works are *Information and Statistics Respecting Wilmington, North Carolina* (1883), *Tales and Traditions of the Lower Cape Fear, 1661–1896* (1896), *A Colonial Apparition* (1898), *Chronicles of the Cape Fear River* (1914, 1916), *Derelicts* (1920), and "Tales of the Cape Fear Blockade," *North Carolina Booklet* 1 (1902). In 1900 he established a fund at The University of North Carolina for the publication of historical monographs, known after 1910 as the James Sprunt Historical Publications. The university awarded Sprunt an honorary LL.D. degree in 1915.

He was thirty-seven when he married Luola, the daughter of Kenneth McKenzie Murchison, on 27 Nov. 1883. Their two daughters, Kate and Marion, died in childhood of scarlet fever; their son, James Laurence (b. 4 July 1886), died in Wilmington on 19 June 1973. In memory of his daughter Marion, James Sprunt built the Marion Sprunt Hospital for women and children.

The Sprunts' Wilmington home was the Governor Edward B. Dudley mansion, built in 1830 at the southeastern corner of Front and Nun streets. He bought Orton Plantation on the west bank of the Cape Fear River, fifteen miles south of Wilmington, from the estate of his father-in-law as a gift for his wife. He added the wings and restored the old house built in 1725 by "King" Roger Moore and later owned by Governor Benjamin Smith. Sprunt developed the gardens and built the small chapel overlooking the river.

He also gave liberally to the Presbyterian church, building several churches including, with his brother William H., the Church of the Covenant at Fifteenth and Market streets in Wilmington in memory of their parents. Sprunt supported a mission, a hospital, and two schools in Kiangyin, China. He also established a loan fund at Davidson College and a lectureship at Union Theological Seminary, Richmond, Va.

A year before his marriage an accident with a runaway horse cost James Sprunt the loss of a leg. This event aroused his profound sympathy for the suffering and the crippled and prompted his benefactions to hospitals especially for deformed and crippled children. From the mill section of Wilmington he sent all such children to Baltimore for orthopedic treatment. He also gave generously to orphanages. His private benefactions were legion. Sprunt was buried in Oakdale Cemetery, Wilmington.

SEE: Robert Cain (Raleigh) to William S. Powell, 20 Feb. 1986; *DAB*, vol. 9 (1936); John Hall (Wilmington, Sprunt's nephew), personal contact; J. G. de Roulhac Hamilton, "James Sprunt," *Literary and Historical Activity in North Carolina* (1907); *James Sprunt: A Tribute from the City of Wilmington* (1925); *Library of Southern Literature*, vol. 15 (1910); *New York Times*, 11 July 1924; Raleigh *News and Observer*, 10 July 1924 [portrait]; Alexander Sprunt and Company Papers (Manuscript Department, Duke University Library, Durham); Wilmington *Morning Star*, 10 July 1924.

DOROTHY FREMONT GRANT

Sprunt, James Menzies *(14 Jan 1818–6 Dec. 1884)*, educator, Presbyterian minister, and Confederate chaplain, was born in Perth, Scotland, the son of Laurence and Christina Sprunt. He was educated in Edinburgh.

In 1835 he left Scotland for the West Indies, where he worked as an accountant for a mercantile firm owned by his brother Alexander. When the company went bankrupt in 1839, Sprunt sailed for New York with the hope of finding a teaching position. On the way his ship was damaged in a storm, forcing it to make port in Wilmington, N.C. There he saw an advertisement for a teaching job in Duplin County. In January 1840 he arrived in Hallsville, Duplin County, where he taught school for the next five years before moving briefly to Richlands in Onslow County. In 1845 he became principal of the Grove Academy in Kenansville and remained there until 1860.

About the time he settled in Kenansville, Sprunt became interested in the ministry. He was licensed by the Fayetteville Presbytery in 1849 and was ordained pastor of Grove Presbyterian Church at Kenansville in May 1851. Soon afterwards he also served Mount Zion Church near Charity and Union Church between Bowdens and Warsaw.

In 1860 Sprunt was chosen principal of the Kenansville Female Institute, where he served until June 1861, when he was appointed chaplain of the Twentieth North Carolina Regiment. He served with the regiment in northern Virginia until 17 July 1863, when he was obliged to resign because of dysentery. Returning home, he served the pastorates of Grove, Mount Zion, and Union churches for the remainder of his life. In addition, he was county register of deeds from 1865 to 1879 as well as stated clerk of the Wilmington Presbytery from 1872 to 1884.

In his later life Sprunt became interested in gardening and botany; he sold some of his plants to the national botanical gardens in Washington, D.C. Several years after the death of his wife, he died at his home in Kenansville following a yearlong illness and was buried in the Hall Cemetery, Hallsville. He had four daughters and two sons, N. H. and J. E.

SEE: *Goldsboro News Argus*, 21 Dec. 1972; *James Menzies Sprunt* (1885); Weymouth T. Jordan, ed., *North Carolina Troops, 1861–1865: A Roster*, vol. 6 (1977); F. W. and Pearl C. McGowen, eds., *Flashes of Duplin's History* (1971); *Minutes of the Synod of North Carolina, 1884* (1885); Alfred Nevin, ed., *Encyclopedia of the Presbyterian Church* (1884); E. C. Scott, comp., *Ministerial Directory of the Presbyterian Church, U.S., 1861–1942* (1942).

PEARL CANADY MCGOWEN

Stacy, Walter Parker *(26 Dec. 1884–13 Sept. 1951)*, lawyer, legislator, arbitrator, and chief justice of the North Carolina Supreme Court, was born in Ansonville, Anson County. The son of Lucius Edney and Rosa Johnson Stacy, he was one of twelve children; his father was a minister in the Western North Carolina Conference of the Methodist church. Young Stacy attended Morven High School, Weaverville College, and The University of North Carolina, where he received a B.A. degree in 1908. At the university he distinguished himself as a debater, won the Willie P. Mangum medal for oratory, and was tapped for the Golden Fleece. In 1909 he accepted an assistantship in history at Chapel Hill, read law, and was admitted to the bar.

After briefly serving as principal of one of Raleigh's graded schools, Stacy entered law practice with Graham Kenan in Wilmington. There he was active in community affairs, serving as president of the YMCA and county attorney in 1914–15. In 1915 the New Hanover County voters sent him to the North Carolina General Assembly, where, among other concerns, he worked for the establishment of the statewide primary and fought for the creation of the fisheries commission. His abilities in the legislature won him an appointment to the North Carolina Superior Court when he was only thirty-one.

Four years later Stacy was elected an associate justice of the North Carolina Supreme Court. During the next four years the entire membership of the court changed, and by 1925 Stacy was the senior member of the court. During the summers, while the court was in recess, he was a lecturer at The University of North Carolina Law School; in 1923 the university awarded him an honorary LL.D. As a result of his growing prominence in the law, he was tendered the deanship of the law school in 1923 but declined the post. In 1925, on the resignation of Chief Justice William Alexander Hoke, Governor Angus W. McLean called upon Stacy—as the senior associate justice on the court—to replace him. In 1926 he was elected to an eight-year term as chief justice. Reelected in 1934, 1942, and 1950, he retained the post until his death. His tenure as chief justice was the longest in the history of the North Carolina Supreme Court.

While on the supreme court Stacy wrote 1,500 opinions. Although he has been described as a conservative, his judicial philosophy can be characterized more accurately as one of judicial restraint, one that required a great sense of judicial tolerance. He was unwilling to use his position to frustrate the popular will as expressed by the legislature or to substitute his view of wisdom for that expressed by the representatives of the democratic majority. To him, the "voice of the people" was "the voice of finality." With the growth of the state as a regulator of modern life, Stacy agreed that, so long as proper standards were provided by the legislature, state agencies must be allowed to use their own judgment without judicial interference. Where the legislature made no change in the law, he resisted effecting change through judicial interpretation. At times he seemed to elevate the technical aspects of the law to the highest constitutional position. Because the state retained much of the criminal common law, Stacy gave full and sweeping range to that which remained in effect, as his opinion in *State v. Beal* so clearly illustrates.

Chief Justice Stacy developed a national reputation as an arbitrator of industrial disputes. He received his first appointment in 1927, when President Calvin Coolidge named him as a neutral member of an emergency arbitration board charged with settling a wage controversy between the Brotherhood of Locomotive Engineers and several southeastern railroads. The board was created under authority of the Railway Labor Act of 1926, and during the next eight years three presidents selected Stacy to serve on six additional panels to resolve railway disputes.

During the Great Depression he expanded his service as an arbitrator to include disputes other than railway controversies. Acting in 1934 under authority of the National Industrial Relations Act, Franklin Roosevelt appointed Stacy to a labor relations board for the iron and steel industries. This board, a forerunner of the National Labor Relations Board, was charged not only with serving as a board of voluntary arbitration but also with mediating disputed issues and conducting elections to determine the agency to represent labor in collective bargaining. Several months later, Roosevelt tapped Stacy to head another such board to bring peace to the textile industry following a bitter national strike. In 1938 the president again designated Stacy as chairman of a fact-finding board to avert a threatened nationwide railroad strike.

As America moved towards war, Stacy continued to serve on national labor relations boards. During the war he was a member of the National Defense Mediation Board and the War Labor Board. After the conflict Harry Truman selected him for a fact-finding panel to resolve a General Motors–United Automobile Workers dispute and designated him as chairman of the National Labor-Management Conference, which was charged with developing plans for converting wartime industries to peacetime production. Although considered to be a conservative, Stacy often sided with labor in disputes with management. During a controversy in the shipbuilding industry, he resisted management pressure to weaken the union and steadfastly maintained the union shop. In another controversy he refused to sanction management efforts to reduce the wages of railway workers.

Stacy remained active in state Democratic politics while on the supreme court. Although he received support for challenging Furnifold M. Simmons in the 1930 North Carolina Democratic primary to determine the candidate in the U.S. Senate race, Stacy refused to run but supported Josiah W. Bailey against Simmons. Shortly afterwards, Stacy was advanced as the Democratic alternative to Republican John J. Parker for a vacancy on the U.S. Supreme Court. President Herbert Hoover, however, nominated Judge Parker. When the Senate rejected Parker, state Democratic leaders unsuccessfully promoted Stacy for the post. Over the next eight years Stacy was mentioned for each vacancy that occurred on the court, although his support seems to have remained local.

In 1926 and 1927 Stacy lectured at the Northwestern University School of Law. He married Maud DeGan Graff of New York; after her death in 1933, he never remarried. In 1931–32 he was chairman of the North Carolina Constitutional Commission, which proposed a redraft of the state constitution. Later in life ill health curtailed his activities, but it did not interfere with the new duties conferred on him by constitutional amendment in 1950 as administrator of all North Carolina courts. A Methodist, Stacy died in Raleigh and was buried in the Mary Love Cemetery at Hamlet.

SEE: *Current Biography, 1946* (1947); William A. Devin, "Chief Justice Walter Parker Stacy," *North Carolina Law Review* 30 (1951); Dillard S. Gardner, "Chief Justice Walter P. Stacy," *North Carolina Law Review* 30 (1952); Archibald Henderson, *North Carolina: The Old North State and the New*, vol. 2 (1941); *New York Times*, *North Carolina Law Review*, and Raleigh *News and Observer*, selected issues; *North Carolina Biography*, vol. 6 (1919); *North Carolina Manual* (1951); *North Carolina Reports*, selected cases; Elmer L. Puryear, *Democratic Party Dissension in North Carolina, 1928–1936* (1962); Walter Parker Stacy, "The Lawyer, His Client, and His Adversary," *North Carolina Law Review* 4 (1925), "Remarks on Opening of the Judicial Conference in the Supreme Court Room in Raleigh on June 25, 1925," *North Carolina Law Review* 4 (1925), and "Chief Justice Hoke: Patriot and Greathearted Fighter for the Right," *North Carolina Law Review* 3 (1925); Richard L. Watson, Jr., "A Southern Democratic Primary: Simmons vs. Bailey in 1930," *North Carolina Historical Review* 42 (1965).

FRED D. RAGAN

Stafford, Lillian Exum Clement *(12 Mar. 1894–21 Feb. 1925)*, legislator and attorney, was born near Black Mountain in Buncombe County, the sixth child of George Washington and Sara Elizabeth Burnett Clement. Young Exum Clement received her formal education in Black Mountain until the family moved to Biltmore, where her father was working on the constructiion of Biltmore House. There she attended the private school of All Souls' Parish, the Normal and Collegiate Institute, and Asheville Business College. She then worked as office deputy in the Buncombe County sheriff's office and in her spare time studied law under James Jefferson Britt and Robert G. Goldstein. In 1916 she passed the state bar exam, winning a prize for one of the highest grades.

Miss Clement began practicing law in Asheville in 1917 and in the next four years became known as a capable criminal lawyer. During World War I she served as chief clerk of the Buncombe County draft board.

"Brother Exum," nominated by males before women were enfranchised, was the Buncombe County Democratic candidate to the state legislature in 1920. Based on her ability, dedication, and other qualifications, she was elected by a landslide (10,368 to 41), becoming North Carolina's first female legislator. An active representative, she introduced about seventeen bills, most of which passed. These included a measure prohibiting railroads from hiring illiterates for certain positions, one providing for the secret ballot, the "pure milk bill" requiring tuberculin testing of dairy herds, and a bill reducing the time of abandonment necessary for divorce. Miss Clement was especially interested in getting the state to assume control of the Lindly Training School for unwed mothers and delinquent girls, located near Asheville.

In 1921, at St. James's Episcopal Church in Hendersonville, Exum Clement married E. Eller Stafford, a staff writer and telegraph editor of the *Asheville Citizen*. They became the parents of a daughter, Nancy. After her marriage Mrs. Stafford was never again a candidate for public office, though she returned to Raleigh for a special legislative session in 1921. Governor Cameron Morrison appointed her a director of the state hospital at Morganton, a position she held until her death.

She was one of the founders of the Asheville Business and Professional Women's Club and was active in the United Daughters of the Confederacy. In addition, she enjoyed hiking in the mountains and knew a great deal about plants and animals of her region.

In January 1921 "Brother Exum" told a Raleigh *News and Observer* reporter: "I am by nature a very timid woman and very conservative too, but I am firm in my convictions. I want to blaze a trail for other women." A member of All Souls' Episcopal Church, Asheville, Mrs. Stafford died of pneumonia at age thirty-one and was buried in Riverside Cemetery.

SEE: *Asheville Citizen*, 22–23 Feb. 1925; *Asheville Citizen-Times*, 8 May 1960; Death Certificate (North Carolina State Archives, Raleigh); "First Female Legislator Had Influence," *Hickory Daily Record*, 15 May 1980; *North Carolina Manual* (1921); Raleigh *News and Observer*, 6 Jan. 1921, 22 Feb. 1925; *The State* magazine, 27 Jan. 1951.

ALICE R. COTTEN

Stagg, James Edward *(27 June 1860–10 Sept. 1915)*, businessman, was born in Company Shops, a village on the North Carolina Railroad that became Burlington. His father, Francis Asbury Stagg, was for many years secretary-treasurer of that railroad. Sarah Anne Durham Stagg, his mother, was the sister of Dr. Bartlett Durham, for whom the town of Durham was named. Young Stagg attended an academy in Burlington and Guilford College.

After leaving college he became a telegraph operator in High Point. There he was discovered by Colonel Alexander B. Andrews, a railroad president of Raleigh, who employed him as his private secretary. Twelve years later he joined a partnership to quarry granite at Greystone in Vance County. In 1893 he returned to secretarial work as the executive secretary of Benjamin N. Duke. When Duke built the Cape Fear and Northern Railway in 1898 to haul freight, he turned the management of it over to Stagg, naming him vice-president and general manager. Later the road was reorganized as the Durham and Southern Railway Company, with a capitalization of a million dollars. By 1906 it was extended until it reached approximately sixty miles from Durham to the Seaboard Air Line at Apex and the Atlantic Coast Line at Dunn. Under Stagg's management, the road proved to be a profitable investment as well as important to the development of that section of the state.

Stagg's success in business led to his election to directorships of cotton mills in Durham and Morganton and to the board of the Fidelity Bank in Durham. In 1907 he was appointed to the board of trustees of Trinity College, and from then until his death he remained a trustee and a member of the board's executive committee. From its inception he was a trustee of Watts Hospital in Durham, and for many years he was a steward and trustee of the Duke Memorial Methodist Church.

On 15 Dec. 1897 Stagg married his employer's niece, Mary Washington Lyon, the daughter of Robert and Mary Duke Lyon and the granddaughter of Washington Duke. They had three children: Sarah Elizabeth, James Edward, and Mary Washington. A genial but unostentatious man, Stagg was known for his generosity. He died at his home, Greystone, in Durham after a two-year illness, survived by his widow, his three children, and a brother, W. L. Stagg. He was buried in Maplewood Cemetery, Durham.

SEE: Samuel A. Ashe, ed., *Biographical History of North Carolina*, vol. 8 (1917 [portrait]); Robert F. Durden, *The Dukes of Durham, 1865–1929* (1975); *Durham Morning Herald*, 11 Sept. 1915.

MATTIE U. RUSSELL

Stallings, Laurence Tucker *(25 Nov. 1894–29 Feb. 1968)*, U.S. Marine, columnist, playwright, novelist, and chronicler, was born in Macon, Ga., of a southern family known for its long line of Baptist ministers and its Confederate dead. His father, Larkin Tucker, son of the Reverend Jesse Stallings of Stallings, S.C., was, at the time of Laurence's birth, a teller for the First National Bank of Macon, but about 1911 he became treasurer of a wholesale drug company and moved his family to Atlanta, Ga. Laurence's mother, Aurora, was the daughter of Dothan, Ala., surgeon Dr. George Washington Brooks. A brother, George Brooks Stallings, and a sister, Ruth (Mrs. Preston Witherspoon), completed the household.

Laurence, the youngest, grew up romanticizing war as "a diet of shining swords" and beckoning "plumes" (phrases from his novel *Plumes*). Graduated from Gresham High School, Macon, in 1911, he worked for the Royal Insurance Company of Atlanta, then left in the fall of 1912 for Wake Forest College, where he was aided financially by the Reverend John E. White, a Baptist minister friend of his father. A handsome youth over six feet tall, Stallings played football, which he loved and described in *Plumes* as "a savage pleasure . . . a struggle for survival"; majored in classical studies and biology; and wrote for college publications, serving in his senior year as editor of the literary magazine, *The Old Gold and Black*. At Wake Forest he met Helen Poteat, who later became his first wife; she was the daughter of Dr. William Louis Poteat, college president and professor of biology. Poteat's successful efforts to defeat legislation prohibiting the teaching of evolution in North Carolina schools were labeled "Poteatism" by Stallings in an article he later wrote for the *New York World* and "Bibbism" in *Plumes* after his fictional character, Dr. John Milton Bibb.

In 1915 Stallings went to Atlanta as a reporter for the *Journal* but returned to Wake Forest for the awarding of his A.B. at commencement, 1916. During this time he served with his father's old unit of the Georgia National Guard, but on 29 May 1917 he joined the U.S. Marine Corps Reserve and was assigned to active duty on 25 July. On 9 October he accepted a second lieutenant's commission in the regular Marine Corps and sailed with the Second Division in 1918 in time to be part of the heavy action at Chateau-Thierry. He escaped injury until 26 June, the last day of the Battle of Belleau Wood, when he led an assault on a machine gun nest; his right kneecap was ripped off, but he threw his hand grenade anyway, thereby wiping out the entire nest. For this he won the Croix de Guerre and a Silver Star and suffered a lifetime of pain, anguish, and, finally, the amputation of both legs (the first in 1922 and the second, after injuries from falls, in 1963). Stallings returned home a captain in 1919; in and out of hospitals, he was out in March 1919 to marry Helen. He was retired on 28 June 1920 and settled in Washington, D.C., where he did free-lance reporting for the *New York Times*. In 1922 he received an M.Sc. degree from Georgetown University.

While recuperating from the leg amputation, he began *Plumes*, an autobiographical novel, thought by some to have been a source for William Faulkner's *Sartoris*. After a trip to Europe with his wife, he returned to New York, joined the staff of the *World*, and, with George S. Kaufman, Robert Benchley, Dorothy Parker, and others, formed the Algonquin Round Table. *Plumes* was published in 1924, the year that saw the production of the stage hit, *What Price Glory?*, which Stallings coauthored with Maxwell Anderson. The success of that play furthered the collaboration, which resulted the next year in New York productions of *First Flight* and *The Buccaneer*.

Famous overnight, Stallings was taken to Hollywood by Irving Thalberg, introduced to King Vidor, and pressured by Vidor into writing the script for *The Big Parade*, a movie that made Vidor famous as director, won stardom for John Gilbert, and helped establish Metro Goldwyn Mayer (MGM) financially. By 1926 Stallings "retired" with his wife to Forest Home, the estate near Blanch, N.C., that Helen's father had given them. There Stallings gathered an extensive library of impressive facsimiles and the complete works of his favorite authors: Shakespeare, G. B. Shaw, Balzac, and Joseph Conrad. In 1928 his daughter Silvia was born and in 1932, Diana. Restless, he acquired an apartment in New York. There he worked with Oscar Hammerstein II on the musical, *Rainbow*, produced in 1928 and filmed in 1930 as *Song of the West*. He also began writing for the *New York Sun* and published about four hundred long literary articles, mostly reviews. Meeting Ernest Hemingway, he adapted *A Farewell to Arms* for the stage and, in 1932, for the screen. In 1933 *The First World War: A Photographic History*, for which he wrote the introduction, captions, and notes, was published with great success by Simon and Schuster, but only after Lincoln Schuster had pressured Stallings to do the work just as King Vidor had done earlier. (The book was reissued in 1963.) In 1934 Stallings became editor of Fox Movietonews; in 1935, literary editor of the *American Mercury*; and in 1936, associate editor of *American Mercury*, of which "The Library" section reflects his knowledge of books and history. From 1924 to 1933 he also wrote a number of short stories, six of which were published in such magazines as *Saturday Evening Post*, *Collier's*, and *Cosmopolitan*.

In 1935 he led a news and newsreel expedition, sponsored by Fox and the North American Newspaper Alliance, to Ethiopia to cover the anticipated Italian invasion. He was back in the United States by February 1936, when he obtained a divorce from his by-now-estranged wife Helen. Beginning a "second life," he married on 19 Mar. 1937 Louise St. Leger Vance, his secretary at Fox, by whom he had a son, Laurence, Jr. (1939), and his last child, Sally (1941). He gave up his extensive library and home in North Carolina, signed a new contract with

MGM, and moved to Santa Barbara, Calif., never to return to the South.

In 1942 Stallings did go back to Washington, D.C., as marine officer, chief of the Interview Section, on the staff of General Henry H. Arnold. Retired in 1943 with the rank of lieutenant colonel, he moved back to California, this time to Whittier. He wrote one play, *The Streets Are Guarded*, which folded after only twenty-four performances in 1944; published numerous articles; and expanded one article, "The War to End War," into *The Doughboys* (1963), an account of the American Expeditionary Force from June 1917 to 11 Nov. 1918.

On 24 June 1964 Stallings was honored for his service to his country by the presentation of a silver plaque and other mementos brought to his home by Major General Raymond Kier, fleet marine commander, with a full complement of officers and men forming an honor guard. Four years later, after a short illness, Stallings died of a heart attack at his home in the Pacific Palisades. He was buried in Rosecrans Veteran's cemetery, Point Loma, Calif.

SEE: Joan T. Brittain, *Laurence Stallings* (1975); Margaret Case Harriman, *The Vicious Circle: The Story of the Algonquin Round Table* (1951); Harlan Hatcher, *Creating the Modern American Novel* (1935); Joseph Wood Krutch, *The American Drama Since 1918* (1939); *New York Times*, 29 Feb. 1968; King Vidor, *A Tree Is a Tree* (1952); "War: Capt. Stallings Heads Fox-NANA Ethiopian Expedition," *Newsweek*, 17 Aug. 1935 (portrait); Mark L. Watson, "They Were There, Lafayette," *Saturday Review* (6 July 1963).

ERMA WILLIAMS GLOVER

Stanback, Thomas Melville *(8 Sept. 1884–21 June 1982)*, pharmacist, was born in Byhalia, Miss., the son of Charles and Della Ingram Stanback. His parents had moved from Richmond County, N.C., a few years before his birth and returned when he was two years old. He attended Trinity High School in Durham and was graduated in 1905 from the University College of Medicine in Richmond, Va., with a degree in pharmacy.

After working successively in drugstores at Mount Gilead, Durham, and Thomasville, he settled in 1911 at Spencer, where he managed the Rowan Drug Company. He bought shares in the company and in time became owner. In 1910 he had developed a headache powder that he first sold from the Thomasville drugstore. Concluding that manufacturing the powder in quantity and marketing it was too difficult for one man, he formed a partnership with his brother, Fred J., in 1924. Thereafter Fred Stanback called on drugstores to sell the remedy and Thomas remained at home to attend to the manufacturing. This venture proved successful, and soon Stanback Headache Powders were being widely sold. The business grew and in 1932 moved from Spencer to larger quarters in nearby Salisbury. Additional products, including a lip balm and breath freshener, were manufactured, but headache powders, sold largely throughout the South, were the mainstays of the firm, which remained family owned and operated.

Stanback supported many local projects including a hospital and library, the YMCA, an art gallery, a community theater, and a symphony orchestra. He also provided loan funds for local and regional colleges.

In 1916 he married Ada May Middleton, of Warsaw, N.C., who had been teaching in Spencer. They became the parents of two sons, Thomas Melville, Jr., and William Charles. A member of the Methodist church, he was buried in Rowan Memorial Park, Salisbury.

SEE: Biography files, Rowan Public Library, Salisbury, N.C.; Raleigh *News and Observer*, 22 June 1982; Winnie Ingram Richter, ed., *The Heritage of Montgomery County, North Carolina* (1981); *Salisbury Post*, 9 Jan. 1955, 20 Jan. 1959, 28 May 1961, 15 Feb., 15 Sept. 1974, 21 June 1982, 4 Aug. 1991; "The Story Behind the Business," [1946] (typescript, North Carolina Collection, University of North Carolina, Chapel Hill); Heath Thomas, "The Stanback Story," Salisbury, *Snappy Speaks* 2 (August 1951).

WILLIAM S. POWELL

Stanford, Charles Whitson, Jr. *(13 Sept. 1924–19 May 1990)*, museum director, was born in Durham, the son of Charles Whitson and Mary McIver Stanford. He was graduated from The University of North Carolina in 1947, did postgraduate work at Columbia University (1948–49) and Princeton University (1949–53), and served as curatorial assistant at Colonial Williamsburg, Inc., in 1955–56. From 1958 to 1970 he was curator of education at the North Carolina Museum of Art. The museum was then located near the state capitol, and Stanford inaugurated tours for teenagers, senior citizens, newcomers, and working people on lunch breaks.

Stanford conceived of and established the Mary Duke Biddle Gallery for the Blind, the first museum sculpture gallery for the blind. He was commended for having "discovered that touching an object, holding it in one's hand, feeling its texture, studying its proportion and examining its physical features produced a sensation of beauty that thrilled the mind and soul of the blind." The reception this gallery received led many other galleries across the United States to follow his example. He frequently lectured on art history on television and radio and in 1968 was one of two Americans invited to address the Soviet Committee of the International Council of Museums in Leningrad and Moscow.

In 1968 Stanford received the North Carolina Award in Fine Arts, and in 1969 he became director of the North Carolina Museum of Art. He also was a member of the executive committee of the North Carolina Symphony, the North Carolina Art Society, and the humanities division of the North Carolina Department of Public Instruction; he served on the advisory board of North Carolina Educational Television. He was the author of *Masterpieces in the North Carolina Museum of Art* (1966, 1972) and *Art for Humanity's Sake: The Story of the Mary Duke Biddle Gallery for the Blind* (1976).

Stanford, who never married, was a member of the Presbyterian church. In 1971, while traveling in Greece as a member of the art museum building commission, he fell and broke his leg. It never healed properly, and he was able to function as museum director infrequently thereafter. He retired soon afterwards to his home near Chapel Hill.

SEE: Raleigh *News and Observer*, 23 May 1990; *Who's Who in the South and Southwest* (1975).

WILLIAM S. POWELL

Stanford, Richard *(2 Mar. 1767–9 Apr. 1816)*, congressman and teacher, was born in Dorchester County, Md., near Vienna, the son of Richard Stanford, whose father had arrived in Maryland from Scotland in 1633. He moved to the Hawfields district of Orange County, N.C., in 1789 and opened an academy in September 1790. Among his pupils was Thomas Hart Benton. Elected as a Republican to the Fifth Congress in 1797, Stanford served ten terms and died in office. A Jeffersonian Republican before it became fashionable, he later cooled towards Thomas Jefferson and joined the circle of "Quid" Republicans arrayed around Nathaniel Macon of North Carolina and John Randolph of Virginia. In a district that included much of the state's Piedmont population, he survived several vigorous attempts to unseat him. At one point he had served longer in Congress than any member of the House of Representatives. He did not, however, exert wide personal influence, being especially in the shadow of Macon. He was periodically a member of the important claims committee and in the Tenth Congress sat on the new post office and post roads committee.

In 1810 he advocated war with Great Britain but then switched to become an ardent antiwar Republican, along with a North Carolina colleague, William Kennedy. In 1808 the state's leading Federalist, Duncan Cameron, had opposed him, but Stanford won by a "huge majority." Jeffersonians grew bitter in 1812 because of his antiwar stand and ran James Mebane against him, but Stanford again won handily. In 1814, however, Roger Tillman came within 103 votes of unseating him.

During sessions of Congress, Stanford was well received in the tiny social life of Washington and in the older community in Georgetown. He lodged in the increasingly popular Crawford Hotel in Georgetown along with Thomas M. Randolph of Virginia, William Gaston of North Carolina, and a geographically mixed group of House and Senate members. He died there of erysipelas and was buried in the new Congressional Cemetery.

While living in the Hawfields district, Stanford met and married Jeanette, the daughter of Alexander Mebane, Jr. They were the parents of at least two daughters: Ariana, who married Elijah Graves of Granville County, and Mary Mebane, who married Andrew Stith of Virginia. Following the death of his wife, Stanford married Mary (Polly) Moore in 1803; she was the daughter of General Stephen Moore. By his second wife Stanford was the father of Lawrence and Adeline.

SEE: *Biog. Dir. Am. Cong.* (1971); John L. Cheney, Jr., ed., *North Carolina Government, 1585–1974* (1965); Noble E. Cunningham, Jr., ed., *Circular Letters of Congressmen to Their Constituents, 1789–1829*, vols. 1–2 (1978); *Greensboro Daily News*, 13 July 1941; William S. Hoffmann, *Andrew Jackson and North Carolina Politics* (1958); Hugh T. Lefler and Paul Wager, eds., *Orange County, 1752–1952* (1953); Raleigh *Register*, 26 Sept. 1803, 19 Apr. 1816; Richard Stanford Papers (Southern Historical Collection, University of North Carolina, Chapel Hill); Herbert S. Turner, *Church in the Old Fields* (1962).

ROY PARKER, JR.

Stanley, Edwin Monroe *(9 Mar. 1909–23 Dec. 1971)*, lawyer, chief judge of the U.S. Middle District Court, and religious, educational, and civic leader, was born in Kernersville. Of English-German ancestry, he was the youngest son of John Brantson and Nettie Louise Atkins Stanley. Young Stanley received his secondary education in the Kernersville schools and earned an LL.B. degree at Wake Forest in 1931. He passed the state bar examination before his twenty-first birthday but could not practice until afterwards. In 1964 Wake Forest University awarded him an honorary LL.D. degree.

Stanley opened a law office in Greensboro in 1931 and engaged in private practice until 1954. Between 1951 and 1954 he was judge of the Greensboro juvenile court. Appointed U.S. attorney in the Middle District of North Carolina in 1954, he served until 1957. In that position he was prosecutor in the widely publicized Junius Scales case, in which the avowed Communist was sentenced to a six-year prison term for violating provisions of the Smith Act. Later the U.S. Supreme Court threw out the sentence and ordered a new trial. Stanley could not participate in the second trial, but Scales received the same sentence that he had in the first.

On 23 Oct. 1957 President Dwight D. Eisenhower appointed Stanley a judge of the U.S. Middle District Court. Succeeding retiring Johnson J. Hayes, he began serving in a recess appointment on 1 November. In February 1957 his nomination was approved by the Senate Judiciary Subcommittee—no doubt in part because of the commendation he received from the chairman, Democratic senator Sam J. Ervin of North Carolina. At that time Ervin said, "I've never seen so many Democrats travel such a long distance to make sure a Republican was placed in a high position." He also told a Republican member of the committee, "Everything I know about Ed Stanley is good except that he belongs to your party instead of mine." Approval by the full judicial committee and Senate followed, and Stanley became judge in 1957. He was elevated to chief judge in 1961.

During his years as a federal judge he made a name for himself as "a peacemaker in school desegregation suits," praised by black and white, Democratic and Republican leaders. On 27 Dec. 1971 a *Greensboro Daily News* editorial declared: "If a single man was responsible for the relative peacefulness of school integration in the Middle District of North Carolina, many would single out Ed Stanley." With one exception—the Winston-Salem case, which was handled by Judge Eugene Gordon—Stanley heard all the public school desegregation suits brought to the court in the Middle District from the time of his appointment until his death. These suits involved schools in Albemarle, Durham, Greensboro, High Point, Lexington, Reidsville, and Salisbury. In all desegregation cases he brought the litigants together at the beginning; as a consequence, he was never forced to draw zone boundaries for school attendance.

When an integration suit was filed, Judge Stanley invariably followed this procedure: first, he set a date for a pretrial conference and presided over that conference with both sides present; second, after areas of agreement and disagreement had been determined, he directed lawyers for both sides to get together outside of court, draw up points on which they agreed, and report their conclusions to him; third, he instructed the school board to draw up a plan in accordance with the areas of agreement and to provide the court and plaintiffs' lawyers with copies of the plan; and finally he held what he termed a "final pre-trial conference" to bring the two sides into agreement. This mode of action avoided trials and appeals, kept the case within his jurisdiction, and eliminated many of the difficulties that beset school integration elsewhere. Many other U.S. courts adopted his procedure.

Committees on which he worked included the Judicial Conference Committee on Trial Practice and Technique (1960–68), Judicial Conference of the U.S. Committee on Court Administration (1969–70), and Judicial Conference on Salaries (1971). In 1968 he became a member of the Advisory Committee on Innovation and Development of the Federal Judicial Center. He was a member of the American, North Carolina, and Greensboro bar associations.

On 30 June 1933 Stanley married Lottie Belle Myers of Monroe; they became the parents of twins, Susanne (Mrs. Hoke Smith Carlan, Jr.) and Robert Myers. Also in 1933 he joined the First Baptist Church, Greensboro, where he served on the Board of Deacons (1953–58); though reelected for a four-year term, he had to resign because of other obligations. Stanley was active in Sunday school, teaching a class of young men in 1937–38 and later serving as associate superintendent of one of the departments. Interested in politics while in private practice, he was state president of the Young Republicans Club for two terms in the 1940s. At Wake Forest University he was a member of the board of trustees (1954–58, 1970–71) and chairman of the law school's board of visitors (1968).

In his civic life he was president of the first golf tournament in Greensboro in 1930. He served as president of the Greensboro Junior Chamber of Commerce in 1938 and was awarded the Distinguished Service Key for his work with the Jaycees. He joined the Greensboro Civitan Club in 1941 and served as president in 1948. From 1945 to 1951 he was a member of the Greensboro Housing Authority.

On 22 Dec. 1971 Stanley handed down his final desegregation decision in a case involving Greensboro public schools. The next night he died suddenly of a heart attack. He was buried in Forest Lawn Cemetery, Greensboro. After his death a trust fund was set up at Wake Forest University Law School in his memory. His portrait, by Joseph Wallace King, presented by the lawyers in the Middle District of North Carolina to the U.S. Middle District Court, was unveiled in the federal courtroom in Greensboro on 13 June 1975. Copies of all his decisions may be found in the office of the clerk of the U.S. Middle District Court.

SEE: *Durham Morning Herald*, 25 Dec. 1971; *Durham Sun*, 24 Dec. 1971; *Greensboro Daily News*, 24–25, 27 Dec. 1971, 14 June 1975; William S. Powell, ed., *North Carolina Lives* (1962); Raleigh *News and Observer*, 25 Dec. 1971; Stanley family members, personal contact; *Who's Who in Government* (1972).

ESTHER EVANS

Stanley, Sara Griffith. *See* **Woodward, Sara Griffith Stanley.**

Stanly, Edward *(10 Jan. 1810–12 July 1872)*, congressman and Union military governor of North Carolina, was born in New Bern, the son of Elizabeth Franks, of Jones County, and John Stanly. His father was twice elected to Congress as a Federalist, was frequently a borough representative to the North Carolina House of Commons, and served as speaker. Edward Stanly attended the New Bern Academy and at sixteen was sent to The University of North Carolina, but his father's illness interrupted his studies after one term. In May 1827 he enrolled in the American Literary, Scientific, and Military Academy, then at Middletown, Conn. Graduating in 1829, he studied law, was admitted to the North Carolina bar in 1832, and began a practice in Washington, N.C.

In 1837 Stanly was elected to Congress as a Whig after two older men had declined the nomination. His irritable temper and sarcastic tongue soon made him a well-known Whig partisan; John Quincy Adams called him "the terror of the Lucifer [Democratic] party." Twice reelected to Congress, he engaged in several personal encounters on the floor of the House and narrowly avoided a duel with Henry A. Wise of Virginia in 1842. In 1851 he fought a bloodless duel with Samuel W. Inge of Alabama. Defeated for reelection in 1843, in part because of his vote for the Whig tariff of 1842, he was prominently mentioned for the Whig gubernatorial nomination in 1844. However, it was said that he was "too young, rash and indiscreet," and the nomination went to William A. Graham. Stanly was elected to the House of Commons from Beaufort County in 1844 and reelected in 1846. At both sessions he was speaker and won the respect of the Democrats by his impartial conduct in the chair. In 1847 the legislature elected him attorney general of the state, but he resigned the following year and returned to the House of Commons. He was again passed over by the Whigs for governor in 1848, when Charles Manly won the nomination.

Narrowly elected to the House of Representatives in 1849, Stanly was one of the few southern Whigs to follow President Zachary Taylor's lead during the congressional debates over the Compromise of 1850. After Taylor's death in July 1850, Stanly cordially supported the compromise measures. In 1851 he stumped his district denouncing the secession doctrine and was reelected by an increased majority. He exerted influence with northern Whigs in Congress because of his strong Unionism and devotion to the Whig party.

The election of 1852 sounded the death knell of the Whigs in North Carolina, and Stanly did not seek reelection the following year. Instead, he moved to California and established a successful law practice in San Francisco. He was an active layman in the Episcopal church. In 1857 he accepted the Republican nomination for governor of California, although he had not joined the party and disagreed with its position on slavery in the territories. He was heavily defeated by the Democratic candidate, John Weller.

Stanly opposed the Secessionists in California in 1861 and spoke out eloquently on behalf of the Union. Convinced in his own mind that North Carolina had been tricked into secession, he offered to return to the state as a peace emissary. President Abraham Lincoln responded by appointing him military governor of North Carolina with the duty of promoting Unionist sentiment in the state. Soon after his arrival in New Bern on 26 May 1862, he learned that he faced an impossible task. Shut up within the Union lines, he could get no hearing from those who regarded him as a traitor and renegade to his native state, while his refusal to countenance Negro schools at New Bern aroused the antagonism of Northern abolitionists. He resigned his office on 15 Jan. 1863 after Lincoln had issued his final Emancipation Proclamation. Stanly warned the president that it would do "infinite mischief" and crush any hope of realizing peace by conciliatory measures. Lincoln named no successor, and presidential reconstruction was abandoned in North Carolina for the rest of the war.

After the Civil War Stanly supported President Andrew Johnson in his struggle with the Radical Republicans in Congress, and in 1868 he canvassed California on behalf of the national Democratic ticket. But he never ceased to lament the Whig party's demise and always considered himself an "inveterate old line Whig." He died in San Francisco and was buried in Mountain View Cemetery, Oakland.

Stanly was married twice: on 24 Apr. 1832 to Julia Jones, of Hyde County, who died in December 1854, and on 10 May 1859 to Cornelia Baldwin, of Staunton, Va., the sister of lawyer-author Joseph Glover Baldwin. There were no children by either marriage. There is a photograph of Stanly by Mathew Brady in the Brady-Handy Collection, Library of Congress.

SEE: Samuel A. Ashe, ed., *Biographical History of North Carolina*, vol. 5 (1906); *Biog. Dir. Am. Cong.* (1971); Norman D. Brown, *Edward Stanly: Whiggery's Tarheel "Conqueror"* (1974) and "Edward Stanly: First Republican

Candidate for Governor of California," *California Historical Society Quarterly* 47 (September 1968); *DAB*, vol. 9 (1936); *A Military Governor Among Abolitionists: A Letter from Edward Stanly to Charles Sumner* (1865); San Francisco, *Daily Alta California*, 13 July 1872.

NORMAN D. BROWN

Stanly, Fabius Maximus *(15 Dec. 1815–5 Dec. 1882)*, U.S. naval officer, was born in New Bern, the son of John, a Federalist congressman, and Elizabeth Franks Stanly. He entered the navy as a midshipman candidate on 20 Dec. 1831 and served until 1843 in the Mediterranean, Home, West Indian, Pacific, and Brazilian squadrons. Passed midshipman on 15 June 1837, he was commissioned a lieutenant on 8 Sept. 1841. Stanly performed special service in 1844–45 on board the steamer *Princeton*, and in 1846 he was ordered to the frigate *Congress* of the Pacific Squadron.

During the Mexican War he took part in the capture of San Francisco (9 July 1846) and commanded the blockhouse guarding the town. He was present at the capture of Guaymas in the state of Sonora (20 Oct. 1847) and assisted at the capture of Mazatlán in the state of Sinaloa (11 Nov. 1847). Stanly commanded an outpost at Mazatlán and had frequent skirmishes with an "active enemy," in one of which he received a lance wound in the breast. On 20 Nov. 1847 Captain Elie A. F. La Vallette, the military governor of Mazatlán, sent Lieutenant George L. Selden and Stanly with ninety-four seamen to clear the road to San Sebastián. Encountering the Mexicans near the village of Urias, about ten miles from Mazatlán, Selden's men threw them into confusion. According to Stanly, this battle was "the hardest fought and the bloodiest made by sailors during the war." In his gun crew only one man out of sixteen escaped injury.

Returning to Guaymas, Stanly on 30 Jan. 1848 led one of three groups of seamen and marines from the sloop of war *Dale* in a surprise descent on the village of Cochori, about eight miles east of Guaymas; the defenders were routed. On 13 February he led twenty-one marines and seamen to break up what was left of the Mexican barracks at Bocachicacampo. Under the pressure of the attack, the Mexicans, numbering about twenty or thirty, fled, abandoning most of their arms and equipment. Stanly received a "contusion" on the leg as a bush broke the ball's force. A week later he returned with a landing party from the schooner *Libertad* and demolished the barracks. The last fighting in the area of Guaymas took place on 9 Apr. 1848, when Stanly and a detachment of thirty men landed at the estuary of the Soldado River and marched inland for twelve miles to spike three guns. On their way back to the boats they briefly skirmished with some Mexicans and claimed to have killed one and badly wounded three others; two Americans were slightly injured. Stanly received the thanks of two secretaries of the navy for his service in the Mexican War. In 1848–50 he served in the Pacific Squadron.

In February 1851 Stanly was tried before a general court martial in Washington, D.C., for publicly posting his superior officer, Commander Zachariah F. Johnston, as a coward. Johnston had agreed to fight a duel and then declined to do so. Stanly was found guilty and was sentenced to be dismissed from the navy. However, a majority of the court recommended executive clemency, and President Millard Fillmore reduced his sentence to twelve months' suspension from service and pay in consideration of his "good character."

After returning to active service, Stanly commanded the store ship *Warren* (1852–53), a store ship at San Francisco (1855), the Mare Island Navy Yard, Calif. (1856), and the store ship *Supply* in the Paraguay expedition (1858–59). In 1860 he commanded the steamer *Wyandotte* at Key West, Fla., and cooperated with Captain of Engineers Montgomery Meigs to prevent the capture of Fort Taylor by the Secessionists. The James Buchanan administration relieved him from command for his excessive zeal and sent him to the receiving ship *Independence* at Mare Island Navy Yard. On 19 May 1861 he was promoted to commander, and in 1862–64 he was placed in charge of the steamer *Narragansett* of the Pacific Squadron, guarding mail steamers between San Francisco and Panama. He received the State Department's thanks for his diplomatic services on the Mexican coast. In 1864 he was on ordnance duty with the Mississippi Squadron.

Early in 1865 Stanly joined the South Atlantic Blockading Squadron of Admiral John A. Dahlgren off Charleston, S.C., as commander of the side-wheel steamer *State of Georgia*. From 12 to 17 February he commanded a naval flotilla that cooperated with a land force under Brigadier General Edward E. Potter in the Bull's Bay expedition. The little settlement of Andersonville, about fourteen miles from Charleston, was occupied. In his report, Stanly stated: "General [Quincy] Gillmore had paid us a special visit on the 17th, assuring us that Charleston would surrender on our obtaining a firm foothold here. I have no doubt but that our doing so added much to the fear caused by General [William T.] Sherman, which has caused the abandonment of Charleston on the 18th."

After the capture of Charleston, Admiral Dahlgren planned to occupy Georgetown as the best means of opening communication with Sherman, who was marching from Columbia towards the North Carolina line. Impressed with the "energy and vigor" Stanly had displayed in the Bull's Bay expedition, Dahlgren selected him to lead a force of marines and seamen up the Santee River to operate against the rear of the battery defending Georgetown, while the navy attacked in front. However, as Stanly was starting, word arrived that the Confederates had abandoned the town and battery (23 Feb. 1865).

Commissioned as captain on 25 July 1866, Stanly commanded the *Tuscarora* in the South Pacific Squadron during 1866–67. He was promoted to commodore on 1 July 1870 and to rear admiral on 12 Feb. 1874. On 4 June 1874, he was, at his own request, placed on the retired list. He died of heart disease at his Washington, D.C., residence and was buried in Oak Hill Cemetery. Stanly was married twice: to a Miss Love and to Cornelia Carr. A destroyer, completed at the Charleston Navy Yard in 1942, was named the USS *Stanly* in his honor.

SEE: *Appleton's Cyclopedia of American Biography*, vol. 5 (1891); Karl Jack Bauer, *Surfboats and Horse Marines: U.S. Naval Operations in the Mexican War, 1846–1848* (1969); Edward W. Callahan, *List of Officers of the Navy of the United States and of the Marine Corps from 1775 to 1900* (1901); *Court-Martial—Fabius Stanly* (32d Cong., 2d sess., H. Rept. Ex. Doc. 69); Lewis R. Hamersly, *The Records of Living Officers of the U.S. Navy and Marine Corps* (1870); *Nat. Cyc. Am. Biog.*, vol. 4 (1897); *New York Times*, 7 Dec. 1882; *Reports and Dispatches Exhibiting the Operations of the United States Naval Forces during the War with Mexico* (30th Cong., 2d sess., H. Rept. Ex. Doc. 1); *War of the Rebellion: Official Records (Navy)*, ser. 1, vols. 1–4, 11, 16, 25–26; *Washington Post*, 6 Dec. 1882.

NORMAN D. BROWN

Stanly, John *(9 Apr. 1774–2 Aug. 1833)*, Federalist congressman and legislator, was born in New Bern. His father, John Wright Stanly, was the most famous shipowner in North Carolina during the American Revolution; his mother was Ann Cogdell, the daughter of Richard Cogdell of New Bern. His father and mother died in 1789, and this double calamity interrupted his studies with private tutors, studies that were never regularly resumed. The six orphaned children of John and Ann Stanly were left in greatly reduced circumstances, and John became a clerk for his father's partner, Thomas Turner.

In 1795, at age twenty-one, he began a brief career as a merchant in New Bern. That year he married Elizabeth Franks, who inherited from her father large estates in Jones County. Association with prominent New Bern lawyers, particularly Benjamin Woods and Thomas Badger, and an appointment as a district court clerk and master of equity, led him to study law without regular instruction; in 1799, "after a mysterious disappearance of a few days from the town," he returned with a license to practice. Endowed with both mental and personal gifts, Stanly soon attained prominence in his profession and became perhaps the most accomplished orator in the state. In the courtroom his quick perception, retentive memory, keen wit, and bitter invective made him a formidable antagonist. He was equally at home in private conversation.

Stanly devoted the best of his energies and much of his life to politics. William Gaston, one of his closest friends, later testified that "public interests seemed to afford to his ardent mind that peculiar excitement in which he delighted, and to give it that full employment without which it was ill at ease." Entering public life in 1798 as an "uncompromising Federalist," Stanly succeeded Edward Graham as New Bern's representative in the North Carolina House of Commons and was reelected the following year. In 1800, despite the general enthusiasm for Thomas Jefferson, the Federalists elected four congressmen, including Stanly—then but twenty-six—who defeated the ailing incumbent Richard Dobbs Spaight in the New Bern district. On 5 Sept. 1802 Stanly mortally wounded Spaight in a duel growing out of their continuing political quarrel and forced by Spaight. The widow's kinsmen threatened criminal proceedings against Stanly, but on his petition, Governor Benjamin Williams pardoned him.

A candidate in 1803 for reelection to the House of Representatives, Stanly was defeated by William Blackledge as the Republicans made a clean sweep of the congressional races. In 1808, however, the Federalists capitalized on popular discontent against Jefferson's embargo and captured three House seats, with Stanly winning over Blackledge. In the Eleventh Congress he was an outspoken opponent of the Madison administration and the so-called *War* men who were advocating the strongest retaliatory measures against Great Britain for violations of American neutral rights. North Carolina Federalists took great pride in Stanly, pointing out that northern papers praised him and printed his speeches while generally ignoring his Republican colleagues. Despite this praise he was not a candidate for reelection in 1810, and Blackledge was again returned to Congress, defeating William Gaston. Stanly remained an unreconstructed Federalist of the Washington-Marshall stamp to the end of his life. As he declared proudly in the House of Commons in 1824, when the Federalist party in the South was just a memory: "For myself, I thank God, I can say I am still a Federalist. I never have, and I never will put on the turban and turn turk, for any share of the plunder."

North Carolina Federalists were critical of "Mr. Madison's War," as they termed the War of 1812, but unlike their dissatisfied party brethren in New England, they considered disunion a greater curse than the evils of Republican rule. As Stanly wrote Gaston when word of the Hartford Convention reached New Bern, "The severance of the Union is an evil of such magnitude, that I cannot apprehend any man of standing & influence will meet the responsibility of recommending such a resort—weighty as are the evils & curses of Madison's administration, those of disunion would be so much more awful, that I will not yet believe that the patriots of New England contemplate any such resort." Yet despite their loyalty to the Union, the North Carolina Federalists shared some of the odium that fell on the New England Federalists in their twilight years as a consequence of the Hartford Convention. No talented Federalist in the state could aspire to either the governorship or the U.S. Senate, and few were elected to the House of Representatives. Unquestioned devotion to Jeffersonian principles was the sine qua non of political advancement.

Although Stanly's Federalism thus barred him from the highest political offices, he remained a power in state affairs. New Bern sent him to the House of Commons in 1798–99, 1812–15, 1817–19, and 1823–27, and in 1821 he was one of the Craven County members of the house. Possessing "an eye like Mars, to threaten and command," he "held a rod pickled in . . . Sarcasm" over the western members. After Republican proscription of Federalists had eased, he was elected speaker in 1825 and 1826 and won high praise for his performance. On 4 Dec. 1825 David F. Caldwell, a member from Salisbury, wrote Willie P. Mangum: "Mr. Stanly whom I fear you are not partial to presides over us with impartiality, dignity & ability. He certainly gives a dignity to the deliberations of the commons, & preserves a degree of decorum which I have never witnessed."

On 16 Jan. 1827 Stanly suffered a paralytic stroke while speaking in the committee of the whole. He remained in critical condition for weeks, and friends feared for his sanity. His health improved somewhat in the summer of 1827, and he gave limited support to Andrew Jackson in the election of 1828. In 1824 he had endorsed the People's ticket while stating a preference for John C. Calhoun or John Quincy Adams. Stephen F. Miller, during a visit to New Bern from Georgia in 1829, found his "noble features" distorted by his affliction. "He tried to converse in his former commanding way, but failed." His friends, as a complimentary gesture, placed his name before the General Assembly in 1828 as a candidate for governor; Stanly received twenty-one votes on the first ballot, but his name was withdrawn on the second ballot.

During his long illness debts accumulated, reportedly because his sons were improvident. Creditors pressed claims, and only Gaston's intervention saved the Stanly mansion from sale. Mrs. Stanly had to advertise for boarders. The end finally came on 2 Aug. 1833 (not 1834 as usually stated), when he was fifty-nine. He was buried in the Episcopal cemetery in New Bern. "He was indeed a great man," Gaston wrote later, "distinguished pre-eminently for acuteness of intellect, rapidity of conception, a bold and splendid eloquence. How unfortunate it has been for his family that he lived so much for others and so little for himself." Stanly County, formed in 1841 from Montgomery, was named in his honor.

John and Elizabeth Stanly had fourteen children, five of whom died young. There were eight living sons: John (idiotic from birth), Alfred, Frank, Edward, Alexander Hamilton, Fabius Maximus, Marcus Cicero, and James Green. Elizabeth Mary, the only daughter to reach adulthood, married Captain Walker Keith Armistead, a West Point graduate, against her father's wishes. A son, Lewis Addison Armistead, born to the couple in New Bern on 18 Feb. 1817, fell at Gettysburg on 3 July 1863 while leading the remnants of Pickett's division into the Union lines on Cemetery Ridge. A portrait of Stanly—an oil on canvas (28 by 23) by an unidentified artist—was owned by John Gilliam Wood of Hayes, Edenton.

SEE: *Biog. Dir. Am. Cong., 1774–1971* (1743 [1971]); Norman D. Brown, *Edward Stanly: Whiggery's Tarheel "Conqueror"* (1974); William Gaston's obituary of John Stanly, signed "A," in New Bern *Spectator and Literary Journal*, 9 Aug. 1833; Stephen F. Miller, "Recollections of Newbern Fifty Years Ago," *Our Living and Our Dead*, vol. 1 (1874); John Stanly letters (William Gaston Papers, Southern Historical Collection, University of North Carolina, Chapel Hill); John D. Whitford, "The Home Story of a Walking Stick" (typed copy, John D. Whitford Collection, North Carolina State Archives, Raleigh).

NORMAN D. BROWN

Stanly, John Wright *(18 Dec. 1742–1 June 1789)*, merchant and Revolutionary Patriot, maintained a fleet of trading and privateering vessels that brought in supplies vital to North Carolina's wartime strength. A native of Charles City County, Va., he arrived in New Bern in 1772, in time to become an early member of the town's Committee of Safety and to be among the first to send raiders from that port.

Stanly began life as the oldest son of Dancey, a lawyer and small planter, and his wife, Elizabeth Wright Stanley, of Isle of Wight County. Despite their modest circumstances, the Stanleys had a proud tradition of direct descent from an earl of Derby. Dancey died when John had barely reached the age of fifteen, and Elizabeth promptly remarried. The boy left home to apprentice himself to a Scottish trader in Petersburg from whom he learned the intricacies and disadvantages of colonial commerce under the British mercantile system. The deaths of both his mentor and his mother within two years left him desolate. He worked in Williamsburg (probably as a clerk) until he was twenty-one and could claim his inheritance. Just prior to that time he got into serious trouble leading to an accusation of counterfeiting. His innocence was established before he could come to trial, but his experience in the Williamsburg jail impelled him to leave Virginia as soon as he had sold his property and had a small capital in hand.

Having some acquaintance with Kingston merchants, he began trading in Jamaica, where he had an initial success. This attracted the attention of a Philadelphia merchant, Jonathan Cowpland, who brought a ship regularly to Kingston. He persuaded Stanly (who had dropped the *e* from his name) to enter into a partnership and then attempted to take over the entire operation. Cowpland accused Stanly of defrauding him and, to blacken the Virginian's name, bruited it about that Stanly had been tried for counterfeiting. But too many people in Jamaica stood ready to defend the young man, so Cowpland took him by force to Philadelphia, where Stanly spent a year in debtors' prison. He managed, finally, to prove that he was the injured party, with Cowpland in his debt, and could once more make a fresh start.

This time he chose Charleston as his base of operations and sailed for that city. A storm off Cape Hatteras brought him to New Bern, instead. Acquaintance with, courtship of, and marriage to Ann Cogdell kept him there. Her father, Richard Cogdell, an ardent Whig, brought Stanly into the group pressing for revolt against the repressive measures of Lord North's government. Risking prosecution as traitors, they did all in their power to induce others to rebel, and Stanly was among the most persuasive.

By the time hostilities broke out, he was ready to send out vessels to harass British shipping and to bring in the sinews of war lacking to the Americans. The most famous of his early privateers, the *Sturdy Beggar*, despoiled numerous English merchantmen. Stanly worked particularly hard during the bitter winter of 1777–78 to get supplies to the men at Valley Forge, and later his *General Nash* took prizes, after the Battle of Camden, which helped to replace material lost by General Horatio Gates's forces. Far more numerous than those successes were the losses he suffered—privateers reckoned on the capture or wreck of four vessels to the return of one. Stanly managed, however, to make enough money to give substantial financial aid to General Nathanael Greene in 1780, when Greene marched south with a token army and no funds for its equipment.

As the conflict drew nearer to New Bern, Stanly prepared to shift his operations to Philadelphia and took his family there. Before he could get settled, he learned of the capture of St. Eustatius by the British, which meant the loss of fourteen Stanly vessels loading at Oranjestad, Netherlands Antilles. Then came news that a Tory privateer from New York had seized the brig bringing part of the family's possessions to Philadelphia. Worse trouble followed: in that summer of 1781 Tory raiders and British troops entered New Bern and burned all of Stanly's warehouses as well as dismantling his vessels at anchor. In spite of these setbacks, he invested in eleven Philadelphia privateers that sailed within the year, helping to keep British ships occupied on patrol instead of attacking American ports.

Stanly returned to New Bern with his family in 1782 and at war's end started a coastwide shipping operation that he later reduced, as he found the distillery business more profitable. He had two tremendous satisfactions: appointment as judge of the Admiralty Court of Beaufort and completion of the handsome house in New Bern that still remains as a memorial to him. But enjoyment of both title and house lasted for only a few short years. He succumbed to yellow fever in June 1789—just a month before his wife. They left six living children (three had died in infancy) of whom the eldest, John, became a member of Congress and a leader of the North Carolina bar.

SEE: G. W. Allen, *State Navies and Privateers in the Revolution* (1913); Amelia County, Va., Wills and Deeds (Courthouse, Amelia); Charles Biddle, *Autobiography, 1745–1821* (1883); Gertrude S. Carraway, *The Stanly (Stanley) Family and the Historic John Wright Stanly House* (1969); Walter Clark, ed., *State Records of North Carolina*, vols. 11, 13–15, 17–18, 24 (1895–1905); Craven County, N.C., Wills and Deeds (Courthouse, New Bern); Alonzo T. Dill, "Eighteenth-Century New Bern," *North Carolina Historical Review* 22 (1945); Edenton, *State Gazette of North Carolina*, 18 June 1789; *Naval Documents of the American Revolution*, vol. 4 (1969); *Naval Records of the American Revolution, 1775–1788* (1906); William L. Saunders, ed., *Colonial Records of North Carolina*, vols. 9–10 (1890); John D. Whitford, "Notes on John Wright Stanly of North Carolina," *Publications of the Southern Historical Association* 4 (November 1900); Williamsburg, *Virginia Gazette*, 6 Apr. 1776.

MARY S. HESSEL

Starke, Lucien Douglas *(9 Feb. 1826–21 Feb. 1902)*, newspaper editor and Confederate officer, was born at Pleasant Level near Cold Harbor, Hanover County, Va., the son of Colonel Bowling and Eliza G. New Starke. His mother was the daughter of Congressman Anthony New, a colonel in the American Revolution. As a child Starke was aware of the turmoil of the Nat Turner insurrection and later of the John Brown raid at Harpers Ferry; he wrote about both in his autobiography and diary. He attended school in Richmond and on his own initiative was apprenticed in 1841 for five years to the *Richmond Enquirer*, an organ of the Democratic party. In 1847 he moved to Norfolk and became foreman of the *Norfolk Argus*, but in 1850 he went to Elizabeth City, N.C., where, on 6 August, he established the *Democratic Pioneer*.

Clearly public spirited, Starke saw a local need for fire protection and in 1850 organized the Albemarle Engine Company for that purpose. His newspaper strongly supported the Democratic party and opposed Stephen D. Pool's Whig newspaper, the *Old North State*. On one occasion Starke attacked Pool with a cane, knocking him down. They exchanged "several blows" and Starke challenged Pool to a duel, but because of Pool's heavy indebtedness to creditors and the fact that he had a wife and six children, he rejected the encounter. In 1852 Starke was a delegate to the Democratic National Convention, which nominated Franklin Pierce as its candidate for president and North Carolina–born William Rufus King for vice-president.

While editing his newspaper, Starke read law under William F. Martin and was licensed to practice by the North Carolina Supreme Court in 1858. In 1859 he disposed of his newspaper interests in favor of the law. President Pierce named him collector of the port of Elizabeth City and President James Buchanan renewed the appointment, but Starke resigned on the election of Abraham Lincoln to the presidency.

A vocal Secessionist, Starke anticipated military action. As colonel of the Third North Carolina Militia, he was ordered by Governor John W. Ellis to Cape Hatteras on the eve of the Civil War to take charge of troops to be sent there; he remained until further steps were taken to organize North Carolina troops. Entering active service on 17 July 1861, he was promptly placed in charge of the construction of a battery on Cobb's Point on the Pasquotank River for the defense of Elizabeth City. The local militia was called out and manned the battery under Starke's command. On 16 May 1862, with the rank of captain, he became assistant commissary of subsistence in the Seventeenth Regiment of North Carolina Troops, of which his former law instructor, William F. Martin, was colonel. Starke saw action at Wilmington, Kinston, New Bern, and various other points in eastern North Carolina, as well as with the regiment at Drewry's Bluff, Second Cold Harbor, Petersburg, and Bermuda Hundred in Virginia. He also served briefly as temporary acting adjutant general of General James J. Pettigrew's brigade but declined a permanent appointment to that post.

His bravery in action was often the subject of comment. In February 1864, while serving as acting brigade inspector, he was cited for his work with a select group of men in bridging the White Oak River in a single night. On another occasion, when he ordered his supply wagons to the rear and remained in the front to participate in the fight, he was described as the "fighting commissary."

On 8 Jan. 1855 Starke married Elizabeth Ferebee Marchant of Indiantown, Currituck County, and they were the parents of Eliza New, Emily Daugé, Elizabeth Marchant, Marian McMorine, and Gideon Marchant. During the war, when much of the coastal region of North Carolina was occupied by the enemy, Mrs. Starke and the children took refuge at Kittrell Springs in Granville County and in Franklinton in Franklin County. She died on 18 Apr. 1863, and on 8 Jan. 1868 he married Tabitha L. Pippen of Tarboro, Edgecombe County; they were the parents of Lucien D., Tabitha Pippen, Mary Mayo, Virginia Lee, and William Wallace. Starke recorded in his autobiography that he married his second wife on the anniversary of his first marriage because of his devotion to his first wife, nor did it escape notice that the first child of each marriage was born nine months and a few days after the wedding.

At the end of the war Starke, finding both his home in Elizabeth City and the residence at Indiantown occupied by Union forces, was obliged to live with relatives until the end of 1865. On Christmas Day 1867 he and his children moved to Norfolk, Va., where he established a law practice and in time was joined by two of his sons. He served in the Virginia legislature for two terms (1875–76 and 1876–77) and was president of the Landmark Publishing Company, publisher of the *Norfolk Landmark*. His funeral was held at St. Luke's Episcopal Church, Norfolk.

SEE: Walter Clark, ed., *History of the Several Regiments and Battalions from North Carolina*, vols. 1, 4 (1901); William A. Griffin, *Ante-Bellum Elizabeth City: The History of a Canal Town* (1970); Weymouth T. Jordan, comp., *North Carolina Troops, 1861–1865: A Roster*, vol. 6 (1977); *Norfolk Landmark*, 22 Feb., 4 Mar. 1902; *Norfolk Public Ledger*, 23–24 Feb. 1902; *Official Records of the War of the Rebellion*, ser. 1, vol. 23 (1889); Starke-Marchant-Martin Papers (Southern Historical Collection, University of North Carolina, Chapel Hill); John H. Wheeler, ed., *Reminiscences and Memoirs of North Carolina and Eminent North Carolinians* (1884).

WILLIAM S. POWELL

Starkey, Edward *(d. 18 Oct. 1789)*, assemblyman, councillor of state, justice of the peace, and merchant, was the son of Peter and Sarah Starkey and a native of the White Oak River area of Onslow County. He was thus a member of colonial Onslow's wealthiest and most distinguished family and a nephew of Colonel John Starkey, the Southern District treasurer. Like his uncle, Edward served as the executor of numerous wills and as a justice of the peace for Onslow County. In 1773 he entered the House of Commons as the representative of Onslow. In 1775–76 he was one of Onslow's delegates to the Second, Third, and Fifth Provincial congresses and served in the Assembly from Onslow during the years 1779–81, 1783–84, and 1787. Elected to the first Council of State in 1776, he rendered important service in that capacity during the Revolutionary War years of 1777–79. In 1779 and again in 1784 Starkey was unsuccessfully nominated for delegate to Congress. In 1783 he was unanimously elected speaker of the House of Commons. He ended his political career as a delegate to the North Carolina Constitutional Convention of 1788.

On the local level, Starkey was associated during the Revolution with the court of admiralty at Bogue (now Swansboro). In 1779 he was nominated for treasurer of the Wilmington District, and in 1783 he was one of the incorporators and trustees of the Innes Academy at Wilmington. Also in 1783 he was named a trustee of the school at "the Rich Lands of New River." Starkey served during part of the Revolution as one of the commissioners for the Wilmington District, and in 1784, as a prominent Swansboro merchant (importer-exporter), he was appointed to the commission for the navigation of Bogue Inlet.

In the Assembly Starkey was deeply involved in the Patriot cause as a member of the committee to ascertain the needs of the army, the committee to consider sending aid to South Carolina, and numerous committees of lesser importance associated with the Revolution. He was one of the committee of three appointed to superintend the outfitting of North Carolina's war vessels. In addition, he served on the committees of privileges and elections, propositions and grievances, claims, public accounts, ways and means; the committees to review the treasurer's accounts, to consider bills of public utility, and to set proper allowances; and several committees to prepare specific legislation. Starkey also introduced the bill to continue the executive powers of the government of the independent state. One reference implies that he served for a time as state auditor and resigned from that position in 1780.

Onslow County records reveal that Edward Starkey was the brother of Peter, Jr., William, John, Jr., Mary Eaves, Anna Wallace, and Elizabeth Haslin. He had a daughter, Sarah Dudley. In 1766, following his father's death, Starkey appeared in court to choose his guardian—evidence that he was not then twenty-one. However, his appointment to the grand jury in January 1769 implies that by that time he had reached his twenty-first birthday. Thus Starkey was born between 1745 and 1748. He is presumed to have been buried in the Starkey family cemetery at the Bluff, four miles above Swansboro on the White Oak River.

SEE: J. Parsons Brown, *The Commonwealth of Onslow: A History* (1960); Walter Clark, ed., *State Records of North Carolina*, vols. 13–14, 16–17, 19, 22 (1896–1907); Onslow County Estates Records (North Carolina State Archives, Raleigh); William L. Saunders, ed., *Colonial Records of North Carolina*, vols. 9–10 (1890).

TUCKER REED LITTLETON

Starkey, John *(ca. 1697–1765)*, assemblyman, Southern District treasurer, public school advocate, militia colonel, justice of the peace, attorney, coroner, and county treasurer, first appeared in the White Oak River area in 1723 and received his first land grant there in 1730. His parentage and early years remain obscure. Eventually acquiring vast holdings of land, Starkey appears in the early records as a planter, accountant, and attorney, serving as the executor or coexecutor to numerous wills in the counties of Onslow, Carteret, Craven, and even one in Hyde. Though he remained a bachelor all his life, he was often named a guardian of orphans.

Starkey's political career began in 1734, when he was appointed one of the justices of the peace for Onslow Precinct and elected to the House of Commons, though not seated in that term of the Assembly. He was again elected to represent Onslow in the Assembly in 1739 and held that office until his death. Almost from the moment of his appearance in the House of Commons, Starkey began to assume a position of leadership; he was described as a "commanding personality." Serving on most of the important committees in the colonial Assembly, he introduced some of the most valuable legislation to be presented. His legislative career has been described as enlightened, independent, and advanced. In 1739 he joined the effort to impeach the corrupt Chief Justice William Smith. Starkey's committee memberships included the committees on propositions and grievances (1746); correspondence (1748); public claims (1749), for which he appears to have served as chairman until his death; and revision of the laws (1749); and the committee to direct the colonial agent (1758). He usually served as moderator whenever the Assembly resolved itself into a committee of the whole.

Following the Spanish Alarm of 1748, Starkey was made overseer for the construction of the Bear Inlet fort, and in 1749 he was one of the commissioners appointed to issue paper money. In 1750 the colonial Assembly elected him Southern District treasurer, its most influential office, and kept him there until his death.

Many of Starkey's legislative bills were strongly humanitarian in nature. In 1749 he introduced a measure for the relief of the poor, a bill to improve the quality of justice in the courts and for establishing courts of justice, as well as the first bill in North Carolina's history to provide for a free public school. In 1756 he was coauthor with Cornelius Harnett of legislation to prevent the unlawful killing of slaves. It was also Starkey who introduced the bill to provide the initial postal route and service from Suffolk, Va., to Charleston, S.C., thus linking communications from Boston to Charleston.

Concomitant with his career in the Assembly, Starkey dominated the political and cultural life of Onslow County, where he served as a justice of the peace from 1734 to 1765. From the 1740s to 1765 he appears to have served as chairman of the Onslow Court of Pleas and Quarter Sessions. He is listed in the county records as holding various local offices, including coroner (1741), church warden (1743), commissioner of the town of Johnston (1744), colonel of the Onslow militia (1754), and treasurer of Onslow County (1759).

It was as Southern District treasurer that Starkey rendered his most valuable and far-reaching service; he used the influence of that office to oppose every royal encroachment on the rights of the people and to advance the cause of liberty. Starkey refused to be called the treasurer for the Crown and regularly referred to his position as "Public Treasurer." With Samuel Swann, John Ashe, and George Moore, he formed a junta that exerted a controlling influence over the Assembly and essentially the political life of the colony. Despite his wealth and station, Starkey refused to wear the silver shoe buckles and powdered wig that distinguished a gentleman of means. His plainness of dress and humble demeanor were especially offensive to Governor Arthur Dobbs, who mentioned Starkey's considerable fortune and unusual popularity and called him "the most designing man in the whole province." Dobbs complained about the rising tide of republicanism in the colonies, observing that republicanism nowhere had a stronger hold than in North Carolina largely due to the influence of John Starkey, whom Dobbs called the foremost republican of all. As treasurer, Starkey was known for his integrity, financial responsibility, and balanced frugality, a quality associated with his frequent opposition to new taxes.

As a person, Starkey was described by both friend and foe as a man of unimpeachable character, punctuality, and good fortune, much liked and esteemed by the populace, having won their confidence by his capabilities and diligence. One historian wrote that in his lifetime Starkey was "the most powerful figure in the province of North Carolina." Though death removed Starkey from the scene before the Revolution was fully born, something of his impact on the direction of liberty may be estimated by the fact that many of the younger men with whom he had been most intimately associated in politics and whom he had influenced later emerged as the leaders of the Revolution in North Carolina, among them Cornelius Harnett, Samuel Johnston, William Cray, and Edward Starkey.

Starkey's only known immediate relatives were his older brother Peter and his sister, Phoebe Warburton. Starkey's year of birth is conjectured as 1697 from a deposition made on 31 Mar. 1733 in which he stated that he was "aged 36 years." His death appears to have occurred in March or April 1765, for he was present when the Onslow Court adjourned on 12 March and his death was announced to the colonial Assembly when it convened on 3 May. A member of the Church of England, Starkey is reported by tradition to have conducted religious services on his lawn on occasion because no chapel or minister of the Anglican faith was located in his area of Onslow. He was buried in the Starkey family cemetery at the Bluff, about four miles up White Oak River from Swansboro.

SEE: J. Parsons Brown, *The Commonwealth of Onslow: A History* (1960); Walter Clark, ed., *State Records of North Carolina*, vols. 23–25 (1904–6); William L. Saunders, ed., *Colonial Records of North Carolina*, vols. 4–8 (1886–90).

TUCKER REED LITTLETON

Staton, Adolphus *(28 Aug. 1879–5 June 1964)*, naval officer, was the younger brother of Henry and the son of Dr. Lycurgus Lafayette and Kate Baker Staton. The scion of a prominent family in Tarboro, he attended the Virginia Military Institute, The University of North Carolina, and the U.S. Naval Academy, from which he was graduated in 1902. In 1917 he was granted a law degree from George Washington University, where he was president of his class. Staton first saw action in Mexico during the Dolphin Incident (1914), when he distinguished himself as a member of the assault force of marines and seamen who secured the port of Vera Cruz. For his gallantry he was awarded the Medal of Honor.

When the United States entered World War I, Staton was attached to the judge advocate general's office. In January 1917 he requested sea duty in a war zone. Accordingly, he was assigned as navigator aboard the USS *Oklahoma* and was soon given command of the USS *Dubuque*. On 1 Jan. 1918 he moved to the army transport *Calameres* as senior naval officer. After a year he was made chief executive officer aboard the USS *Mount Vernon*. He was serving in that capacity when the ship was heavily damaged by torpedoes two hundred miles off Brest, France. Staton, through his quick and heroic actions, enabled the *Mount Vernon* to return to port under her own power. He received the Navy Cross for his conspicuous bravery during the incident.

After the war he returned to the judge advocate general's office and in June 1921 began duty at the Naval War College. Upon completion in May 1922 he was made assistant judge advocate general. Staton remained on shore duty until 1924, when he was ordered to Chefoo, China, aboard the USS *Argonne*. While en route, however, he received orders to proceed to Shanghai to take command of the USS *Asheville*. In the Far East Station he was charged with safeguarding U.S. lives and property, suppressing rebel activities around Chinese ports served by American ships, and protecting the American legation in Peking. The diligence with which he pursued his duties was rewarded in September 1925, when he was placed in command of the USS *Black Hawk*, a substantially larger ship.

On 17 Mar. 1926 Staton was instructed to return to Washington, D.C., as chief of the Bureau of Navigation. He remained in that position until 1929, when he again was called to sea duty as commander of destroyer squadron eleven. In April 1931 he was transferred to destroyer squadron four, where he served as commander until granted permission to attend the Army War College in August. He next was assigned to naval intelligence in Washington, only to be recalled to sea duty in December 1933 as commander of the USS *Nevada*. In January 1935 he became an instructor in the Command and General Staff School at Fort Levenworth, Kans.

Staton retired from the navy in 1937 but was recalled to active duty during World War II. Assigned to the staff of the undersecretary of the navy, he headed a board administering the removal of subversives who were radio operators on American ships. He left the navy at the end of World War II with the rank of rear admiral.

In his last years Staton was engaged in the real estate business in Chevy Chase, Md. He was active in the Boys' Club and the Boy Scouts in the greater Washington area. In 1917 he had married Edith Blair of Baltimore. They had one daughter, Sally. He was buried in Arlington National Cemetery.

SEE: Daniel L. Grant, *Alumni History of the University of North Carolina* (1924); Dudley W. Know, *A History of the U.S. Navy* (1948); Adolphus Staton Papers (Southern Historical Collection, University of North Carolina, Chapel Hill).

JORDAN BELL

Staton, Lycurgus Lafayette *(1 Feb. 1849–1 July 1921)*, physician and businessman, was born in Edgecombe County, the son of Henry Lafayette and Margaret Batts Staton. He attended the local public schools, Wilkinson's Male Academy in Tarboro, Horner School in Oxford, and Virginia Military Institute. In 1869 Staton began to study medicine under a preceptor, Dr. J. W. Jones of Tarboro; later he attended the College of Physicians and Surgeons of New York and then the University Medical College of New York, from which he received an M.D. degree in 1870. After practicing for a while in New York, he continued his profession in Tarboro, where he also established a drug business under the name of Staton and Zoeller. His partner, the chemist Edward V. Zoeller, was in charge of the work.

Staton was especially interested in surgery and in the 1880s reported a number of his cases in the *North Carolina Medical Journal*. One of his articles describes the restoration of a hand that had been separated from the arm; another is on "Gastrotomy or Gastrostomy." In his "Textbook on Surgery" he described an unusual operation for that time: surgery on a child whose esophagus had been destroyed by swallowing lye. Also interested in public health, Staton served as the health officer of Edgecombe County for twelve years. He was one of the founders of the Pittman Sanatorium, where he became a visiting physician, and was active in the state and county medical societies.

In addition to practicing medicine, Staton was a successful businessman. He organized the Shiloh Mills, the Tar River Steamboat Company, and the Tar River Oil Company. He also reorganized and was a director of the Pamlico Insurance and Banking Company and was president of the Tar River Cotton Factory. Further, he owned several large cotton plantations and was interested in the improvement of farming methods.

In 1871 he married Katherine E. Baker of Tarboro. They had three children—Henry, who became a lawyer and practiced in New York City; Adolphus, who became a naval officer; and Sallie Baker, who was graduated from Vassar College in 1897.

SEE: Samuel A. Ashe, ed., *Biographical History of North Carolina*, vol. 7 (1908 [portrait]); *Prominent People of North Carolina* (1906); John Staton, *Staton History* (1906).

DOROTHY LONG

Stearns, Shubal, Jr. *(28 Jan. 1706–20 Nov. 1771)*, Baptist leader, was born in Boston, the son of Shubal and Rebecca Larriford (Sanford?) Stearns. In his youth he moved with his parents to Connecticut and joined the Congregational church at Tolland. Little is known of his early years, but it is apparent from the few extant records that he belonged to a family of solid citizens. His father was one of the town proprietors of Tolland in 1716, the "proprietor clark" in 1722 and 1724, and a selectman in 1724.

Much more is known of young Stearns and his activities after 1745. Stirred deeply by George Whitefield's preaching in that year, he, along with other advocates of the Great Awakening, left the Congregational fold and formed a "Separate" church. For six years this church grew steadily under Stearns's leadership, but the Connecticut Separates and their leader encountered some serious obstacles. Stearns became deeply involved in a crusade to secure the Connecticut General Assembly's recognition of the Separate churches' right to exist, but petitions of 1746 and 1748 were "resolved in the negative" in both houses. In turning down the petition of 1748 the Assembly insinuated that Stearns and the other 324 people who had signed it were revolutionaries, although the document plainly denied that the signers had any intention of promoting revolution. The petition did, however, assert for every Christian an "unalienable Right, in matters of ye worship of God, to Judge for himself as his Conciance Receives the Rule from God." All they wanted, claimed the petitioners, was the religious toleration guaranteed them in the Toleration Act, which Parliament had passed in the reign of William and Mary.

As if trouble with the provincial legislature were not enough, the Separates began to quarrel among themselves in 1751. The major issue was infant baptism. Stearns, coaxed by the New Light Baptist preacher Wait Palmer, renounced infant baptism and was himself baptized by Palmer. On 20 May 1751 he was ordained to the Baptist ministry. Meanwhile, he had organized a Separate Baptist church and served as its minister until 1754, when he became convinced that God wanted him to move "far to the westward, to execute a great and extensive work." Taking a few of his church members with him, he left Connecticut and moved to the backcountry of Virginia. There he "joined companies" with other Baptists led by Daniel Marshall, who was married to Martha Stearns, Shubal's sister. When it became apparent that the opportunities for Separate Baptist evangelism were too limited in the sparsely settled Virginia hinterland, the combined parties of Stearns and Marshall moved two hundred miles south to Sandy Creek in what was then Guilford County, N.C. There, Stearns had heard, were people eager to hear preaching. Shortly after their arrival at Sandy Creek in November 1755, the Separate Baptists established Sandy Creek Baptist Church. From this base of operations the Separate Baptists, making emotional appeals for people to be saved and preaching a diluted Calvinistic theology, formed churches throughout North Carolina and then fanned out into Virginia, South Carolina, and Georgia. Led by Stearns, seven of the Separate churches in North Carolina and Virginia organized the Sandy Creek Baptist Association about 1760. As new churches were constituted, the association grew larger. The Sandy Creek church itself grew from 16 to 606 members in less than fifteen years.

The militant evangelism of the Separate Baptists, which Shubal Stearns launched in 1755, suffered two blows in 1771. In May of that year Governor William Tryon crushed the North Carolina Regulators, many of whom seem to have been Baptists. From the Sandy Creek area there ensued an exodus that drastically depleted the membership of the Sandy Creek Baptist Church. Later in the year Shubal Stearns died. The Separate Baptists would recover from the Regulator disturbance, the death of Stearns, and even the disrupting effects of the coming Revolutionary War, but the movement they had begun was clearly in disarray by the end of 1771. Not until the late eighteenth and nineteenth centuries would the seeds sown by Stearns and his followers yield their greatest harvests.

On 6 Mar. 1726 Stearns married Sarah Johnson (Johnstone?) of Lexington, Mass. According to the early Baptist historian Morgan Edwards, Stearns "left no issue." He was buried at Sandy Creek.

SEE: David Benedict, *A General History of the Baptist Denomination in America and Other Parts of the World*, 2 vols. (1813); J. R. Cole, *History of Tolland County, Connecticut* (1888); Ecclesiastical Records, vols. 2, 10, and Towns and Land Records, vol. 5 (Archives, History, and Genealogy Unit, Connecticut State Library, Hartford); Morgan Edwards, "Material Towards a History of the Baptists in the Provinces of Maryland, Virginia, North Carolina, South Carolina, and Georgia" (original manuscript in the Furman University Library, Greenville, S.C.); Clarence C. Goen, *Revivalism and Separtism in New England, 1740–1800* (1962); David T. Morgan, "The Great Awakening in North Carolina, 1740–1775: The Baptist Phase," *North Carolina Historical Review* 45 (July 1968); George W. Paschal, *A History of North Carolina Baptists*, 2 vols. (1930, 1950); Robert B. Semple, *A History of the Rise and Progress of the Baptists in Virginia* (1810); Loren P. Waldo, *The Early History of Tolland: An Address Delivered Before the Tolland County Historical Society* (1861).

DAVID T. MORGAN

Stedman, Andrew Jackson *(20 Apr. 1828–7 May 1884)*, journalist, lawyer, minister, and Confederate officer, was born in Gatesville, the fifth son of William Winship (1798–1836) and Rebecca Walton Stedman (1794–1873) of Chatham and Gates counties. His father, a large planter, merchant, and state legislator, was of an old Connecticut family that had settled in North Carolina in the 1780s.

Jack Stedman, as he was familiarly known, probably attended local schools or academies before qualifying to practice law, although no record of his education seems to exist. His name does not appear in the alumni lists of The University of North Carolina, yet secondary sources credit him with "degrees" from the university. He served as a presidential elector in 1848 in the Taylor-Fillmore balloting. In January 1858 he published in Salem, N.C., the initial issue of *Stedman's Salem Magazine*, a literary magazine intended for circulation throughout the South. Because of problems with the printer—poor correction of proof, failure to meet a deadline, and the use of unsuitable paper—Stedman moved his enterprise to Raleigh where Vol. I, No. 1, of *Stedman's Magazine* appeared in May 1858. Contributions to both numbers were from writers in various southern states. This, too, was the only issue offered. Stedman cited as reasons for the magazine's failure the unsettled times and the lack of paying subscribers. Nevertheless, both issues contained a variety of material by well-known contemporary writers. Several chapters of a novel that he included appeared later when the author's work was published under a New York imprint. An interest in journalism seems to have been characteristic of the family. Relatives were founders of the *Southern Literary Messenger* and the *Wilmington Star*.

On 5 Feb. 1855 Stedman married Susan Catherine (Kathleen) Staples (1836–97), the daughter of Colonel

John C. Staples of Stonewall, Patrick County, Va. They became the parents of Mary Walton, who died in infancy; William Winship (1858–1900), an editor and publisher; Malvern Vance (1863–1951); and Sallie Rebecca Roberta (b. 1871), who married Henry Lee Mylton.

Stedman enlisted on 18 Mar. 1862 in the Chatham Cossacks of Pittsboro, a unit that became Company B, Forty-ninth Regiment, North Carolina Troops. Soon elected third sergeant, he was severely wounded at Malvern Hill on 1 July 1862, and, although named to the Roll of Honor for his bravery under fire, he was unable to return to the field. Through the intervention of Governor Zebulon Vance, Stedman on 13 Oct. 1862 was appointed first lieutenant in the newly formed Confederate States Army Signal Corps. Ordered in November to report to General Howell Cobb in southwestern Georgia, Stedman served as chief signal officer to Cobb, Joseph Finegan, William Montgomery Gardner, and James Patton Anderson, successive commanders of the military districts of East and Middle Florida. With his headquarters at Quincy, near Tallahassee, Stedman was responsible for lines of signal posts and observation points, which transmitted messages by flag, torch, and telegraph. He was paroled in May 1865, a month after Appomattox, as part of the general surrender of troops.

After the war Stedman practiced law and with his family lived for a time in Pittsboro, then settled in Danbury. There, beginning on 3 June 1870, he published a weekly newspaper, *The Old Constitution*, and served as solicitor of the Fifth North Carolina District. He was the author of a forty-page pamphlet, *Murder & Mystery: History of the Life and Death of John W. Stephens, State Senator of North Carolina, From Caswell County*. Printed in Greensboro in 1870, this is considered to be an unbiased, well-written account of a murder that remained unsolved until 1935, after the death of the last member of the Ku Klux Klan responsible for it. In 1873, after moving to Taylorsville (now Stuart), Va., Stedman edited and published *The Voice of the People*, the first newspaper in Patrick County, his wife's home.

In Taylorsville he became an ordained Baptist minister about 1874 and preached regularly in the local church. He also participated in local civic organizations and was a Master Mason. In Virginia he continued to practice law, serving as commonwealth attorney, and engaged in agriculture and horticulture. His wife's ancestor, Colonel William Martin, had planted the famous "Old Hardy Apple Tree" in Patrick County in 1790, and her family was interested in growing root stock from this tree. Stedman and a son, Malvern Vance, planted over 150,000 apple trees in the county and established the area's apple industry.

An industrious man of many talents, "Colonel" Stedman, as most knew him in later life, was considered to have deep convictions in politics, religion, and agriculture, and he was a polished speaker. The town of Stedman in Patrick County was named for him. He died in Taylorsville (Stuart) and was buried there.

SEE: David W. Gaddy, "Confederate States Army Signal Corps Insigne," *Military Collector and Historian* (Summer 1973); Weymouth T. Jordan, Jr., comp., *North Carolina Troops, 1861–1865: A Roster*, vol. 12 (1990); Salem, *People's Press*, 15 May 1884; Melvin Lee Steadman, Jr., "Our Family-Stedman, Steadman, Steedman" (manuscript, possession of M. L. Steadman, Virginia Beach, Va.); *Stedman's Magazine* 1 (May 1858); *Stedman's Salem Magazine* 1 (January 1858) (North Carolina Collection, University of North Carolina); *Virginia Biography*, vol. 6 (1924).

DAVID WINIFRED GADDY

Stedman, Charles Manly *(29 Jan. 1841–23 Sept. 1930)*, Confederate officer, lawyer, and congressman, was born in Pittsboro, the son of Nathan A. and Euphania W. Stedman. His father, a merchant, served in the state legislature and as state comptroller. Young Stedman attended the Pittsboro Academy—then taught by the Reverend Daniel McGilvery, later a missionary to Siam—and the Donaldson Academy in Fayetteville, where his family moved in 1853. Entering The University of North Carolina in 1857, he made an exceptional record as a scholar during four years of study. He was awarded first distinction in every course he took and was graduated with highest honors in 1861, shortly after the Civil War began.

Stedman enrolled in the Fayetteville Independent Light Infantry as a private and served with that company in the First North Carolina Regiment at Big Bethel (10 June 1861). When the Forty-fourth North Carolina Regiment was organized, he was elected lieutenant of Company E, composed of Chatham County men. In time promoted to regimental major, Stedman, a gallant and skilled soldier, fought with the Army of Northern Virginia in every major campaign, sustaining wounds in the Wilderness campaign, at Spotsylvania Court House, and on the Squirrel Level Road near Petersburg. Nevertheless, he was one of twelve North Carolinians who had fought at Bethel and surrendered at Appomattox.

After the war Stedman returned to Chatham County, where he taught school while reading law with Robert Strange and John Manning. In 1866 he married Catherine de Rosset Wright of Wilmington, a daughter of Joshua G. Wright. Shortly afterwards, having been admitted to the bar, he established a legal practice in Wilmington. He was immediately successful and enjoyed a large clientele. A staunch Democrat, he was a delegate to the Democratic National Convention in 1880. Four years later he was elected lieutenant governor of North Carolina. Stedman presided over the state senate with dignity and fairness. In 1888 and again in 1904 he was a strong contender for the Democratic gubernatorial nomination. Both times he was defeated but, without rancor, worked for the election of his former opponent.

From 1891 to 1898 Stedman practiced in Asheville; in 1898 he moved to Greensboro. His concern for public institutions was manifest in various ways. He was director of the Guilford Battle Ground Company (1898–1917), a trustee of The University of North Carolina (1899–1915), president of the North Carolina Bar Association (1900–1901), and director and president of the North Carolina Railroad Company (1909–10). In 1910 he was elected to the U.S. House of Representatives as a member of the Sixty-second Congress. He was reelected nine times and served until his death. Though attentive to his duties, he played an insubstantial role in the legislative process. On his death at age ninety, Representative Stedman was the last surviving Confederate veteran in Congress.

Of a tall, courtly presence, Stedman was the epitome of the southern gentleman and was widely popular among his colleagues. He was characterized as belonging to the "so-called Southern aristocracy" and as "a Chesterfield in manners."

Stedman was survived by a daughter, Mrs. Katherine Stedman Palmer. He was interred in Cross Creek Cemetery, Fayetteville.

SEE: Samuel A. Ashe, ed., *Biographical History of North Carolina*, vol. 3 (1906); *Biog. Dir. Am. Cong.* (1971); *Congressional Record*, 62d–71st Cong.; Daniel L. Grant, *Alumni History of the University of North Carolina* (1924); Raleigh *News and Observer*, 9 Mar. 1888, 24 Sept. 1930, 23 Sept. 1962.

MAX R. WILLIAMS

Steel, Elizabeth Maxwell *(1733–22 Nov. 1790)*, Salisbury innkeeper, Revolutionary Patriot, and the subject of legend, was born in western Rowan County. The Maxwell family was of Scotch-Irish origins and emigrated from Pennsylvania to the Carolina frontier in 1733. Elizabeth's first husband, Robert Gillespie, was scalped by Cherokees following a siege of Fort Dobbs and died in 1760. Their daughter, Margaret, married the Presbyterian preacher and teacher, Samuel Eusebius McCorkle.

After the death of her second husband, William Steel, in 1774, Elizabeth continued to operate an ordinary in Salisbury, engaged in local real estate speculation, and managed, despite a lack of formal education, to accumulate a modest estate. In addition, she provided more than adequate parental care for her son, the Federalist statesman John Steele.

During the Revolution Elizabeth was an ardent Whig Patriot. This is largely reflected in letters written to her brother-in-law, Ephraim Steel, a resident of Carlisle, Pa. Other correspondence, as well as the opinions of her contemporaries and descendants, indicates that she was a strong-willed, self-sufficient woman of unusual capabilities. According to legend and a number of unverified secondary sources, the "Widow Steel" provided lodging and a gift of three bags of specie to a despondent General Nathanael Greene during the 1780–81 Cornwallis campaign in western North Carolina. But whether or not this incident actually occurred, it is evident that Elizabeth Maxwell Steel was largely responsible for the acquired values and character of her son John.

SEE: James S. Brawley, *The Rowan Story* (1953); Archibald Henderson, "Elizabeth Maxwell Steele: Patriot," *North Carolina Booklet* 12 (October 1912), and *The Old North State and the New*, 2 vols. (1941); Archibald Henderson Papers, John Steele Henderson Papers, James M. McCorkle Papers, and Ephraim Steele Papers (Southern Historical Collection, University of North Carolina, Chapel Hill); Lou Rogers, *Tar Heel Woman* (1949); Jethro Rumple, *A History of Rowan County, North Carolina* (1929); Wills of William Steel (1774) and Elizabeth Steel (ca. 1789) (Rowan County Wills, Carolina State Archives, Raleigh).

WILLIAM S. WEST

Steele, James Columbus *(10 July 1839–13 July 1921)*, inventor and industrialist, was born near Elmwood, Iredell County, the son of John Mitchell and Elizabeth Derinda Bell Steele. He was the great-great-grandson of Ninian Steele, a captain in the Continental army who served with distinction during the Revolutionary War. James C. Steele attended Ebenezer Academy at Bethany Church and subsequently studied under James H. Foote, J. H. Hill, and H. J. Grimes in Taylorsville. His father was a farmer and noted cabinetmaker, and so James received early training as a carpenter and cabinetmaker, a trade he plied before the Civil War.

On 7 June 1861 Steele enlisted in Company C, Fourth North Carolina Infantry. The next month he was assigned to the regimental band, in which he remained, with only forty days' absence, throughout the conflict. He frequently served as courier and litter bearer, and though he did not carry weapons, he was exposed to all the hazards of the battlefield at Seven Pines, Antietam, and Gettysburg. Steele also ran messages pertaining to the surrender at Appomattox. He preserved his recollections in his book, *Sketches of the Civil War* (1919).

After the war Steele operated various sawmills and at least two small and elementary brick factories in the Statesville area. On 19 Oct. 1871 he married Eudora Velinda Montgomery, the daughter of William Thomas and Elizabeth Crawford Montgomery, of Cool Spring Township.

Being mechanically inclined, Steele endeavored to become a manufacturer of brick plant equipment. In the aftermath of the Civil War he perceived that such equipment had to be rugged, as well as unusually simple and durable; yet to be effective it must also multiply the effort of hand labor. Moreover, it had to be suitable for an area lacking both trained technicians and money for capital investment. Responding to these strict criteria, Steele in 1887 invented and in 1889 patented a light hand-operated brick truck that enabled one man to move brick more quickly and safely over rough yard terrain from sites of fabrication, drying, and firing than three men could do previously. Accordingly, in 1889 Steele formed with his eldest son, Clarence Montgomery, the New South Brick Machine Company to manufacture and sell the improved brick truck; he soon established a vigorous market in the eastern half of the United States.

Between 1889 and 1900 Steele's business flourished as three other sons—Henry Oscar, Alexis Preston, and Flake Futhey—entered the firm and expanded its operations to the manufacture of other clay-working equipment. By 1896 New South was marketing various items of brick plant equipment as well as the brick truck. In 1900 the firm was renamed J. C. Steele and Sons, a name retained throughout the years.

Although Steele retired in 1902, he remained an adviser to the firm until his death. Thereafter he turned his energies to public service. For many years he won election to the Statesville Board of Aldermen and served for two terms as mayor (1903–7). He also was an elder of the First Presbyterian Church of Statesville and for several years sat on the board of regents of the Presbyterian Orphans' Home at Barium Springs. He was buried in Oakwood Cemetery, Statesville.

SEE: *Captain Ninian Steele and His Descendants* (1901); Weymouth T. Jordan, Jr., comp., *North Carolina Troops, 1861–1865: A Roster*, vol. 4 (1973); "North Carolina" (Limited Supplement), *The American Historical Society* (1927); *Statesville Landmark*, 22 May 1890; Steele family records (possession of A. P. Steele, Statesville).

JOHN MACNICHOLAS

Steele, John *(16 Nov. 1764–14 Aug. 1815)*, planter, Federalist legislator, and comptroller of the U.S. Treasury, was born in Salisbury of Scots-Irish ancestry. His father, William Steel, a merchant, innkeeper, and local real estate speculator, died when John was nine years old. Thus his mother, Elizabeth Maxwell Steel, was the major parental influence. The "Widow Steel" was the owner/operator of an ordinary, the mother-in-law of the Presbyterian divine Samuel E. McCorkle, an ardent Whig Patriot, and the subject of Revolutionary-era legend.

Though exposed to a classical education at the English School in Salisbury and the Reverend James Hall's Clio's Nursery near present Statesville, Steele spent most of his youth in mercantile activities. On 9 Feb. 1783 he married Mary (Dolly) Nessfield of Cross Creek (Fayetteville), the stepdaughter of Robert Cochran, a prominent merchant. This union produced three surviving daughters: Ann, Margaret, and Elizabeth.

Beginning in May 1784, when he was chosen assessor for the Salisbury District, Steele periodically held local offices, including justice of the Rowan County Court. Following election to the North Carolina House of Commons in November 1787, he was selected to represent the borough of Salisbury as a Federalist member of both the Hillsborough and Fayetteville ratification conventions and gained recognition as a perceptive advocate of the new U.S. Constitution. According to James Iredell, leader of the Federalist faction in North Carolina, he was "laborous, clear sighted and serviceable by his knowledge of men." At both conventions Steele's comments on the proposed federal court system constituted an early recognition of judicial review as a check on the legislature. To this was added a strong defense of the new government's taxing power. In later years he would alter his position and views on both issues and, essentially, support the more "Republican" position.

Reelected to the House of Commons in 1788, Steele successfully initiated a motion calling for the partition of an Iredell County out of Rowan. He was also appointed a special commissioner to treat with the Indian tribes in the western part of the state and to secure new boundary agreements. In 1790, and again in 1792, he defeated the ardent Anti-Federalist Joseph McDowell for the Yadkin Division seat in the First and Second U.S. congresses. In that office he spoke out for the extension of post offices and roads to interior North Carolina; favored limitations on federal spending; opposed Alexander Hamilton's plans of assumption and funding and the "odious" whiskey tax; favored creation of the U.S. Bank; chaired the house committee to report on amendments to the Constitution proposed by Congress; and expressed disapproval of an increase in the size of the house, Quaker antislavery petitions, expansion of the free list to include cotton, and the Giles resolutions recommending the censure of Hamilton. Influenced in part by his experience as chairman of a house committee charged with investigating the St. Clair expedition, he played a major role in defending the militia concept and criticizing a standing army accompanied by excessive executive authority.

Though support of the militia was good republican doctrine, his comment that whites were often the aggressor on the frontier may have damaged his popularity with residents of western North Carolina and land speculators. In December 1792 he was defeated by Alexander Martin in a General Assembly vote for the U.S. Senate and returned to the House of Commons in 1793, 1794, and 1795 as a representative from the borough of Salisbury. An energetic legislator, he served on a number of committees including Finance, was nominated for speaker, and was appointed a major general in the state militia, a post he held until 1796. He supported George Washington's neutrality proclamation and court reform legislation and opposed a tax penalty for Quakers, Moravians, and members of other religious sects not serving in the militia. When offered five shares of stock for legislative assistance rendered the Catawba Navigation Company, Steele refused this gratuity on the stated grounds that discharge of a public duty did not allow "private recompense." In 1795, as a result of resurgent antifederalism in North Carolina and Republican control of the legislature, he was again defeated for a seat in the U.S. Senate—this time by Timothy Bloodworth. Throughout his career Steele never lost a popular election, but as party factionalism developed he was increasingly identified with a declining Federalist minority that received few favors from a Republican leadership.

On 1 July 1796 Steele was appointed comptroller of the U.S. Treasury by President Washington—probably on the recommendation of Hamilton. He continued to serve in this important post after the election of Thomas Jefferson to the presidency and was, until his resignation in September 1802, the highest ranking "Federalist" in the Jefferson administration. As a moderate and independent-minded "friend of government," Steele developed and maintained cordial and unique political associations, often across party lines, with many national leaders and intimate friendships of long standing with individuals of such diverse and opposing views as Nathanael Macon and William R. Davie.

Following his departure from the comptroller's office and the national political scene, Steele chose to devote attention to his Lombardy and Lethe plantations, local civic affairs, and county court service. After election to the House of Commons in 1806, he was identified with opposition to court reform legislation calculated to diminish the political influence of court towns and boroughs. An outspoken critic of embargo and war initiatives, he also joined in unsuccessful efforts to create an antiwar coalition of Quid Republicans and Federalists. Appointed a North Carolina boundary commissioner in 1805 and 1807, he helped to settle serious dividing line disputes with both South Carolina and Georgia.

From 1808 to 1811 Steele was an agent for the Bank of Cape Fear and the first representative of a chartered bank in western North Carolina. As a cotton planter he had suffered financially from the embargo and nonintercourse policies of the national administration. In 1811 he again represented Salisbury in the Commons, was elected speaker when William Hawkins was elevated to governor, and led a faction in the house that opposed electoral law changes that were calculated to secure Republican party control of the state's entire electoral vote in presidential elections. Until its repeal in 1813, the Electoral Law of 1811, which Steele described as an "aristocratical bias," was the most controversial question in North Carolina politics and aroused Steele as no other issue since the embargo. Defeated for speaker in 1812, he joined William Gaston, John Stanly, William Barry Grove, and Archibald Henderson as unsuccessful electoral candidates. From 1812 to 1815 he served as a trustee of The University of North Carolina. Returned to the Commons in 1813, he supported the war effort but opposed the censure of Senator David Stone as an antiwar Republican.

Steele's death in Salisbury, shortly after his reelection to the Commons, removed a respected advocate of political moderation from the North Carolina scene and contributed to the demise of the Federalist party. According to David L. Swain, first Whig governor of North Carolina and a president of the university, "North Carolina has produced few individuals whose public careers offer more interesting topics for history and biography." Representative of a third political force during the Federalist and Jeffersonian eras, Steele rejected the extremes of both high Hamiltonian federalism and Republican particularism. By resisting factionalism and adhering to the essential republican principles of his day, he enjoyed a modicum of reputation, alleviated his state's extremist propensities, and helped cultivate a moderate Federalist sympathy in North Carolina. The only existing portrait of Steele, painted by the miniaturist James Peale in 1797, shows a pleasant and rather handsome countenance.

SEE: Kemp P. Battle, "Letters of Nathaniel Macon, John Steele, and William Barry Grove, with Sketches and Notes," *James Sprunt Historical Monographs*, no. 3 (July 1902); James S. Brawley, *The Rowan Story* (1953); Archibald Henderson Papers, John Steele Henderson Papers, and Ephraim Steele Papers (Southern Historical Collection, University of North Carolina, Chapel Hill); Archibald Henderson, "John Steele," *North Carolina Booklet* 18 (January, April 1919), and *The Old North State and the New*, 2 vols. (1941); Henry M. Wagstaff, ed., *The Papers of John Steele*, 2 vols. (1924); William S. West, "John Steele and North Carolina Federalism, 1787–1803" (master's thesis, University of North Carolina, 1967) and "John Steele: Portrait of a Moderate Southern Federalist" (Ph.D. diss., University of North Carolina, 1971).

WILLIAM S. WEST

Steele, John Hardy *(4 Jan. 1789–3 July 1865)*, designer and builder of textile machinery, was the first man to weave cotton cloth by waterpower in New Hampshire. He served his adopted state as governor for two terms and in 1833 was a member of a committee that established the first free public library supported by taxation in the United States.

He was the baseborn son of Elizabeth Taylor and John Steele, a brick mason who immigrated to Salisbury, N.C., from Ireland. (The 1790 census suggests that he was married and had several children as well as sixteen slaves.) Although John Steele was compelled by the court to pay Elizabeth Taylor for the support of their illegitimate child, John Hardy Steele was probably raised by his grandfather, Absalom Taylor, the father of Elizabeth. He acquired the rudiments of education under teacher Edmund Burton at the little school located in front of the Old English Cemetery in Salisbury but probably gained most of his taste for learning in the law office of Archibald Henderson, whose extensive library provided him with a variety of books. Apprenticed at age fourteen to the cabinetmaker's trade, he became a journeyman in Salisbury before moving to Fayetteville when he was about twenty-two.

In Fayetteville he so impressed his employer, Nathaniel Morison, a native of Peterborough, N.H., that when Morison returned to New Hampshire, he took Steele with him. Morison used the young man's natural mechanical skill to help him in the manufacture of spinning mules and looms in Peterborough. In the new mill that Morison and others were building, Steele was put to work with Nathaniel Holmes, Jr., a competent machinist only a year or two older than Steele, to make the spinning equipment. Upon completion of the mill, Steele, whose ability as a designer and builder of textile machinery was now recognized, was placed in charge of converting an old factory from a spinning mill to one that could also weave the yarn into cloth. When this mill was put into operation in May 1818, he became the first man in New Hampshire to weave cotton cloth by waterpower.

By 1824 it was apparent that other localities in the town promised waterpower on a much greater scale. He therefore joined others in organizing the Union Manufacturing Company to develop the falls on Nubanusit Brook in West Peterborough, a place often known as Steele's Village. Steele managed this mill for the next twenty-one years, acquiring a reputation for the high quality of the sheetings, skirtings, and fine yarn produced. The mill continued to produce cloth until 1947. Steele also is remembered for the quality of the workers' houses that he erected near his mill. Copying the southern style that he remembered from his childhood, he built houses with external chimneys and fireplaces at each end. They were laid out to follow the course of the stream.

Steele was a Democrat in a town that was a Whig stronghold, yet because of his personal popularity and integrity he was elected to the state legislature in 1829. Having little taste for politics, he declined reelection. His role in the legislature was so impressive, however, that in 1831 he was nominated for a seat in the state senate, an opportunity that he also rejected. Nevertheless, in 1840 and 1841 he was elected counsellor for the old Hillsborough district. Well known in the state, he was elected governor in 1843 without effort or desire on his part and reelected for a second term the following year. Steele now regarded his political career closed and retired to his farm near Peterborough to practice skillful and scientific husbandry. Yet in 1850 when a convention was called to revise the state constitution, he became a member and served on the judiciary committee.

Steele never forgot that he was a native of North Carolina, that he had grown up in Salisbury where he had made many friends. In 1838 he noted that "with the lapse of time, my anxiety once more to revisit my native land increased," and with a friend he took the stage to visit Salisbury. Some years after his journey, he wrote to Thomas B. Long, a Salisbury friend, in tender terms of his old hometown. Steele observed that "while life lasts and reason holds her empire over my mind, I shall never forget our meeting at your uncle's [Richard Long, who operated the Mansion Hotel in Salisbury] in 1838."

He recalled that it had been thirty years since he had left Salisbury, and "when I entered the bar room I took a hasty survey of the many faces there assembled. My heart sank within me, for when I left Salisbury, there was not a man, woman, or child that I did not know. There was a room full of men, not one of them known to me or I to them. A stranger in my native place." However, he continued, he later encountered his old friends, Dr. Alexander Long and Mr. and Mrs. John Beard, whom he had known as a boy. He attended the Presbyterian Meeting House, built in 1825, and thought that the courthouse, "which when erected [1800] was the largest and most imposing building" he had ever seen, now "was not an object of admiration."

John Hardy Steele was married twice. His first wife, whom he wed on 5 Nov. 1816, was the daughter of John and Jane Moore. She died on 30 July 1831. His second wife, Nancy Moore, whom he married on 8 Jan. 1833, was the sister of his first wife. Surviving her husband for nearly five years, she died on 26 Feb. 1870.

SEE: James S. Brawley, "Salisbury Orphan Becomes N.H. Governor," *Salisbury Post*, 8 Oct. 1967; Archibald Henderson, "Native Tar Heel Was Twice Governor of New Hampshire," *Charlotte Observer*, 15 Apr. 1929; Rowan County Court Minutes, 7, 12 Feb. 1791 (North Carolina State Archives, Raleigh); Robert Sobel and John Raimo, *Governors of the United States*, vol. 3 (1978); John Hardy Steele to Thomas B. Long, 27 Oct. 1852 (possession of Mrs. Seth Murdoch, Salisbury).

JAMES S. BRAWLEY

Steele, Walter Leak *(18 Apr. 1823–16 Oct. 1891)*, lawyer, politician, and businessman, was born at Steeles Mill (now Littles Mill) near Rockingham, the son of Thomas and Judith Moseley Leak Cole Steele. He began his higher education at the preparatory school of the Reverend Solomon Lea in Boydton, Va., then enrolled at Randolph-Macon College, where he remained only a few months. After attending freshman classes at Wake Forest College for a time, he returned to Richmond County and entered a school in Wadesboro taught by the Reverend John Burke. In January 1840 he was a student at The University of North Carolina but in September the faculty prevented him from continuing. Dr. Elisha Mitchell interceded, however, and Steele reentered as a freshman in 1841. At Chapel Hill he subsequently earned A.B. (1844) and A.M. (1847) degrees.

On 27 June 1844 he married Harriet Ann Crawford, the daughter of Thomas Crawford of Paris, Tenn. They had seven children: Alice, James Crawford, an infant daughter, Lula, Walter Leak, Jr., Hallie, and Judith.

After studying law (though he did not obtain a license), Steele won election to the state House of Commons in a bitterly fought contest; he served in 1846, 1848, 1850, and 1854. In 1852 and 1858 he was a member of the state senate. In 1854 he introduced a bill to incorporate the Wilmington and Charlotte Railroad Company, amended to extend the line to Rutherfordton. Afterwards he was elected to the company's board of directors. Though Steele began his political career as a Whig, he switched to the Democratic party in 1856 but that year was defeated at the polls.

In 1860 he was a delegate to the Democratic National conventions in Charleston and Baltimore. With the success of the Republican ticket, however, Steele became involved in the secession movement. At the state convention of 1861 he served as secretary and signed the ordinance of secession. He then offered to raise a company of cavalry, but was turned down; he finally became a private in the state troops, though he never saw action. After the death of his wife in 1863, he married Mary J. Little, the daughter of his cousin Thomas Little. Their children were William Little, George Spencer, Robert Thomas Stephen, Samuel Spencer, Mary Little, and Anna Leak.

At the end of the Civil War, Steele's former connection with the Secessionists precluded his political activity for a short time, but he was vocal in his opposition to the Reconstruction acts. When Reconstruction ended, he reentered the political arena as a presidential elector for the Tilden (Democratic) ticket. From 1877 to 1881 he served two terms in the U.S. House of Representatives. Declining to seek reelection in 1880, he returned to his home in Richmond County and in 1882 succeeded his brother as president of the Pee Dee Manufacturing Company, a textile mill that eventually housed Rockingham Industries. He remained in that post until his death.

In 1852 Steele was appointed a trustee of The University of North Carolina; he also presided over the alumni association. In recognition of over thirty years' service to the university, he received an honorary LL.D. degree in 1891. He often contributed articles on various subjects to magazines, but particularly to hunting journals as he was an avid hunter. Steele was also a noted chess player, eulogized as the best in the state. However, he was best known for his ability as a speaker, a talent he had sharpened in college as a member of the Dialectic Society, one of the two debating societies at the university. A popular commencement speaker, he gave addresses at Greensboro, Mount Pleasant, Randolph-Macon, and The University of North Carolina, among other institutions. On the latter occasion he was notified of his appointment in another's absence only two days beforehand but prepared the obligatory long oration without apparent difficulty. Steele also was involved in financial affairs and served on the board of directors of the state penitentiary, to which he was appointed without his knowledge.

In 1891 Steele traveled to Baltimore to undergo surgery, from which he did not recover. He was buried in the Leak family cemetery near Rockingham.

SEE: *Biog. Dir. Am. Cong.* (1961); Beatrice Mackey Doughtie, *McDonald, Kimball, Wade, Leak* (1971); Jerome Dowd, *Sketches of Prominent Living North Carolinians* (1888); Daniel L. Grant, *Alumni History of the University of North Carolina* (1924); James E. Huneycutt and Ida C. Huneycutt, *History of Richmond County* (1976); John Gilchrist McCormick, "Personnel of the Convention of 1861," *James Sprunt Historical Monographs*, no. 1 (1900); Raleigh *Register*, 9 July 1844; David S. Reid Papers (North Carolina State Archives, Raleigh); Walter Leak Steele Papers (Southern Historical Collection, University of North Carolina, Chapel Hill); John H. Wheeler, ed., *Reminiscences and Memoirs of North Carolina and Eminent North Carolinians* (1884).

ROGER N. KIRKMAN

Steele, Wilbur Daniel *(17 Mar. 1886–26 May 1970)*, writer, was born in Greensboro, the third of four children (Arthur, Beulah, Wilbur Daniel, and Muriel) of Rose Wood and Wilbur Fletcher Steele, both of New England ancestry. His father, a clergyman and then principal of Bennett Seminary, a Methodist Episcopal school for Negro girls, took the family to Germany in 1889 for additional study, and there the boy attended kindergarten. In 1892 Steele's father joined the faculty of the University of Denver, where his son was a student from 1903 to 1907, majoring in history and economics, with heavy participation in athletics and fraternity affairs. Thinking he wished to become a painter, young Steele enrolled at the Boston Museum School of Fine Arts and went on a sketching trip to Italy, but an interest in writing gradually thwarted his plans for a career as an artist.

His first short story was published in 1910. During the summer of 1913 in Provincetown, Mass., he shared quarters with Sinclair Lewis. There he was a close friend of Eugene O'Neill, and the two of them were among the original playwrights for the Provincetown Players. Meanwhile, encouraged by his success as a writer of short stories, he married the painter Margaret Thurston, by whom he had two sons, Thurston and Peter.

A consummate professional writer as well as a rigid technician, Steele met the demand of his market by submitting short stories to both women's slick magazines and the literary journals, then turned to novels and plays when the time seemed propitious. Though he always returned to his base on the Massachusetts coast, a wanderlust took him to Ireland, England, France, Switzerland, Tunisia, the Caribbean, and South America, providing the tall, bespectacled writer with a wide variety of settings for stories. His first novel was published in 1914 and his first collection of short stories in 1918. Between 1916 and 1933 he won numerous O. Henry awards and citations in the annual *Best Short Stories*, edited by Edward J. O'Brien.

After two winters in Charleston, S.C., Steele returned in late 1929 to North Carolina and rented the Greenlaw House (729 Franklin Street) in Chapel Hill, where he enjoyed the friendship of Paul Green and the university community. He wrote in the morning, played golf after lunch, and attended the movies (he had never seen a bad one, he said) or "partied" in the evening. For "The Man without a God," a two-part story whose central character was based partially on Paul Green, the *Ladies' Home Journal* paid him the unprecedented sum of $10,000. It was only after the death of his wife in 1931 that Steele decided he could no longer remain in the village. Twice during his four years in the Carolinas he returned for short visits to Greensboro. In 1932 he married in London a family friend, the writer Norma Mitchell, then lived at her home in Hamburg, Conn. In 1956 he moved to nearby Old Lyme, where he died fourteen years later.

Like O. Henry, also born in Greensboro, Steele often provided for his stories an unexpected but logical ending. In addition to "Light" and "A Way with Women," two of his most highly acclaimed stories also have North Carolina settings: "How Beautiful with Shoes" and "Man and Boy," whose earlier titles were "Town Drunk" and

"The Man without a God." By 1955 he had published seven volumes of short stories, ten novels, and three books of plays. Martin Bucco's authoritative critical biography (1972) indicates that a number of unpublished stories and plays are among the Steele Papers at the Stanford University Library. A portrait of him used in promotion was painted by W. Langdon Kihn.

SEE: Martin Bucco, *Wilbur Daniel Steele* (1972); *North Carolina Authors* (1952); *Publishers' Weekly*, 20 June 1970; Richard Walser, ed., *North Carolina in the Short Story* (1948); Harry R. Warfel, *American Novelists of Today* (1951).

RICHARD WALSER

Steiner, Abraham Gottlieb *(27 Apr. 1758–22 May 1833)*, Moravian clergyman, Native American missionary, and school inspector, was born and raised in Bethlehem, Pa., the son of Abraham Gottlieb and Salome Borstler Steiner. He was educated at the Moravian school of Nazareth Hall, where he later taught for a few years. In 1788 he was called to Hope, N.J., to run the church store, and the next year he was needed in Bethabara, N.C., to tend the store and tavern. When it became necessary for the community to register another justice of the peace under North Carolina law, Steiner assumed that position as well.

It was as a missionary among Native Americans that Steiner made his most significant contribution to the congregation of North Carolina. In 1799 the Helfer Conferenz, which supervised Moravian affairs worldwide, instructed the Salem congregation to establish a mission for the education of the Cherokee Indians in the area. Missionary work was a major concern of the Moravians, and Steiner had long been interested in the progress of the Indian mission on the Muskingum River, in Ohio, which had been founded by the Moravians from Bethlehem. He had visited that mission and was well qualified to help establish a similar outpost in the South.

Responding enthusiastically to the missionary call, Steiner and another Moravian brother left Salem in 1800 bound for Knoxville, Tenn., to begin planning a settlement and school in an Indian village. After lengthy negotiations with the Indian chiefs and with the U.S. government officials for Indian affairs, it was decided that the mission would be located at Spring Place, Ga., nearly four hundred miles from Salem. Although Steiner never lived at the mission on a full-time basis, he made frequent trips there over the next five years. He was responsible for much of the planning and for overseeing the building of a school at Spring Place. When conflict arose between the Indians and the missionaries, Steiner negotiated with them and made settlements that were fair to both sides.

By 1803 the mission at Spring Place was going well enough for the Moravians to consider starting another one. Steiner met with Colonel Benjamin Hawkins, federal agent for the Creek Nation, to discuss the possibility of opening more missions like the one at Spring Place in other locations. Hawkins was very receptive to the Moravians' proposals and promised to help in any way that he could. Plans progressed too slowly for Steiner to have a hand in the actual establishment of more missions, and he was forced to abandon his visits to the Indian villages when he became weak from fevers sustained during the trips to the unaccustomed climate.

When he returned to Salem in 1803, he was ordained a deacon in the church and sent to Hope as the minister for that small congregation. In 1806 he was asked to return to Salem to become inspector of the girls' school. At that time, by virtue of his new position, he was made a member of the Helfer's Conferenz in Salem. In 1809 he and his wife also became members of the Elder's Conference in Salem. Poor health forced Steiner's retirement as inspector in 1816. His resignation was accepted regretfully because he was so well liked by the students and the community as a whole. He did remain active in the affairs of the congregation by occasionally filling in as school inspector, traveling to Pennsylvania on congregation business, and making brief inspection trips to the missions. From 1820 to 1822 he took on the job of inspector for the boys' school but again had to retire due to failing health. While in the latter position he served for a year as Pfleger (warden) of the choir of single brothers.

In 1822 a Negro congregation was organized, and Steiner was asked to serve as its minister; he accepted and for ten years held one service each month. In 1826 and again in 1830 he was elected to the Aufseher Collegium in charge of the material and financial affairs in Salem. His many years of public service ended in 1832, when, after returning from a visit to Bethlehem, Pa., his health worsened and he died.

Steiner's first wife, Christina Fischer, whom he married in 1789, died in childbirth the following year. In 1791 he married Catherine Sehner, who bore him four children: Maria, Sarah, Carl Abraham, and Elizabeth.

SEE: Adelaide L. Fries, ed., *Records of the Moravians in North Carolina*, vols. 5–8 (1941–54); Edmund Schwarze, *History of the Moravian Missions among Southern Indian Tribes of the United States* (1923).

ROSAMOND C. SMITH

Stem, Thaddeus Garland, Jr. *(24 Jan. 1916–22 June 1980)*, poet, essayist, newspaper columnist, and short-story writer, the son of Thaddeus G., attorney at law, and Hallie Mayes Stem, was born in his parents' home at 104 East Front Street, Oxford. He lived all his life and died at the same address. Interment was in Elmwood Cemetery, Oxford. He had one older brother, John Mayes. Never called Thaddeus but always Thad, he had been well christened "Junior." After his father's death in 1959, he reminisced: "My father was the most wonderful man I ever knew . . . the kindest, gentlest. He couldn't stand for anybody to make a child unhappy. . . . We were very close. Maybe too close. He had an office up the street and when he had an idea he'd come down to see me [in Thad, Jr.'s, one-room writer's office in an old buggy factory] and when I had an idea, I'd go up to see him." Upon further study, other parallels and parental influences become clear.

After playing football, basketball, and baseball at Oxford High, Thad, Jr., was sent in 1933 to Darlington School in Rome, Ga., to prepare him for Duke, where his father (an alumnus of Trinity Park School, Trinity College, and Trinity Law School) was by then a trustee. Entering Duke as a freshman in September 1934, Stem was more interested in social life than in scholarship. He "wrote a lot of junk," but no poetry, and left in the spring of 1938 with too few credits for a degree. This ended his formal education. Back at home that fall he "did a lot of fox hunting" and "ran around a lot." A big man with a small-boy grin and a puckish twinkle in his eye, he had been troubled by a bronchial condition and decided to spend the winter of 1938 in Florida. There he worked for a West Palm Beach newspaper. Returning home the following summer, he took a job selling life insurance and worked seasonally on the Oxford tobacco market until the outbreak of World War II delivered him from this effort. He served in the army throughout the war and afterwards worked as veterans' service officer for Granville County.

About 1943 or 1944 he began writing poems for the love of expressing himself in this medium, and in 1945 he sent some of them to *Lyric* magazine in Roanoke, Va. They were returned by editor Leigh B. Hanes, who suggested that Stem rework and resubmit them. Having done so, Thad was rewarded by the publication of nine of the poems in one issue of *Lyric* that year. He continued to work at his verses, sometimes writing as many as two or three in one day, then going for several weeks without completing anything. In 1947 this more-or-less unfocused activity was forced into more positive channels by his marriage on 21 November to Marguerite Dety Laughridge Anderson, of Marion, widow and mother of a three-year-old son, William Eugene Anderson. "I suddenly realized I had to get serious," he later said. Soon he was turning out some 15,000 words a week of publishable material—newspaper articles, essays, poems, and short fictional pieces.

Appearing in 1949 was his first book, *Picture Poems;* and in 1953, *The Jackknife Horse*, another book of poems, which won the Roanoke-Chowan Award in 1954. By 1960 he had two other books to his credit. *The Perennial Almanac* (1959) was a collection from his contributions to that date to the Raleigh *News and Observer*, and *The Animal Fair* (1960) was a series of sketches or informal essays in which he molded small-town vernacular into a poetic medium. He had also sold, he estimated at the time, about 8,000 short "pieces"—mostly to in-state newspapers, especially the *News and Observer* and *The Pilot* (Southern Pines)—and was doing a weekly column that developed over the years into an informal daily editorial on a variety of subjects.

Stepping up this already vigorous pace, he published before 1978 eleven more books: *P.T.A. Impact: Fifty Years in North Carolina, 1919–1969* (1969); *Senator Sam Ervin's Best Stories*, which he and Alan Butler did jointly in 1973; *The Tar Heel Press* (1973), a history of journalism in the state for the one-hundredth anniversary of the North Carolina Press Association; a foray into the area of semantics, *Ransacking Words and Customs from A to Izzard* (1977), which gives hard-to-come-by information, curious and fascinating, on the origin of many common English words and phrases; two more collections of poems and essays, *Penny Whistles and Wild Plums* (1962) and *Spur Line* (1966); two books of essays, *Light and Rest* (1964) and *Entries from Oxford* (1971); a volume of short stories, *A Flagstone Walk* (1968); one of poetry, *Journey Proud* (1970); and one of all three genres—essays, fiction, and poetry, *Thad Stem's First Reader* (1976).

When, in 1978, he learned that because of kidney failure he would need to undergo weekly dialysis at Duke Medical Center for the rest of his life, he recovered from his "initial period of hopeless despair" by a valiant turning anew to his study and writing. "When I'm writing, I don't think about dialysis," he said, and, "All my life I've believed that the chief importance of learning is that ultimately one is naked save for it. . . . Old age, adversity, disease, all come. Friends die, money goes, . . . but learning is always the seed corn to grow another crop." During the next few months he wrote six articles for *The State* magazine, three short stories, hundreds of editorials for the *News and Observer*, and his last published book, *Thad Stem's Ark* (1979), a collection of essays with a few poems and one story. In all, he estimated that he had published at least 75,000 words in the period after 1978.

A seventeenth volume, in progress at the time of his death, was to have been a history of Johnston County. The manuscript may now be seen at the Johnston County Library in Smithfield.

Stem's hobbies included all spectator sports, taking part in political campaigns, walking in the woods, and reading. Favorite authors were Twain, Cather, Glasgow, Whitman, Wolfe, and Frost. He belonged to Sigma Nu, to the Democratic party, of which he was for several years Granville County chairman, to the American Legion, and to the Methodist church. Long a member of the Granville County Library Board, he also served for six years as chairman of the State Library Commission and was chosen to help draft the National Library Construction bill. He was in demand as a speaker and appeared often before civic organizations, book clubs, and writers' groups. Once called the "last great poet of small town America," he was a past chairman of the North Carolina Writers' Conference, which honored him at its annual meeting at Raleigh in July 1979 with a testimonial dinner. Besides the Roanoke-Chowan Award, he had received the Edward Arnold Young Cup for Poetry and the North Carolina Award in Literature. He was chairman of the North Carolina Arts Council and a member of the Mark Twain Society; shortly before his death he became a member of the North Caroliniana Society.

His only children were his stepson, Bill Anderson, and Bill's son, William Thaddeus. (The Andersons' daughter was born after Stem's death.) But all children loved him, just as they had loved his father. Late in his life the young people at Oxford designated him "Our man for all seasons." Most fitting, then, was the scholarship fund for Granville County schools, established after his death in his memory, providing annually a $1,000 stipend to the graduating senior demonstrating the greatest creativity in one of the arts. The first award was made in the spring of 1981. An oil portrait of Stem hangs in the Granville County Library.

SEE: *Contemporary Authors*, vols. 97–101 (1981); Bernadette Hoyle, *Tar Heel Writers I Know* (1956); *International Who's Who of Writers and Authors* (1981); *North Carolina Authors: A Selective Handbook* (1952); Scrapbooks of newspaper clippings on North Carolina books and authors and clipping files (North Carolina Collection, University of North Carolina, Chapel Hill); Thaddeus Garland Stem, Jr., Papers (Manuscript Department, Duke University Library, Durham).

ERMA WILLIAMS GLOVER

Stephen, Walter Benjamin *(3 Oct. 1876–31 Dec. 1961)*, master contemporary artistic potter who discovered new glazes and techniques for producing some of the finest art pottery in America, was born in Clinton, Iowa, the son of Andrew and Nellie C. Randall Stephen. Walter's Scottish-born father was a construction worker, a rock mason, and a well digger. In 1891 the family moved to Chadron, Nebr., where they lived in a sod house. Young Stephen attended a sod school until, he once said, "[I] was so mean that my Dad took me out of school and put me to work." This ended his formal education.

In 1896, when he was nearly twenty, the family moved to Shelby County, Tenn., near Memphis, where he and his father engaged in building and masonry work. Meanwhile his parents, especially his mother, who was artistically inclined, had become interested in making pottery and experimenting with different colors and kinds of clay they found when digging a well. They soon attracted attention with the cameo pottery they were able to produce, and they entered the art as a business with enough success to make a living at it.

During their early years in Tennessee the Stephens' pottery was named "Nonconnah" for the small river that flows around Memphis. For well over a dozen years Walter and his mother, with the aid of his father, operated the plant. After the aging couple died in 1910, he sold the home place to a friend of the family and took any kind of work that would earn him a living. He visited several sections of the country examining the clays and feldspar in search of better and purer materials with potentials for pottery. He also sought someone who would back him financially in his efforts to produce a line of superior art pottery. C. P. Ryman of Skyland in Buncombe County, N.C., agreed to form a partnership and to sponsor and finance the work to build a kiln and a shop. Ryman was familiar with the type of cameo pottery that Walter Stephen and his mother had been producing in Tennessee, but he believed that the variety of clays and of such varied colors, together with the superior qualities of feldspar so abundant in the mountain region, would enable them to turn out a much better product. And so it proved.

From 1913 to 1916 Ryman and Stephen operated the pottery with fair success, but at the end of this period they dissolved their partnership. Stephen withdrew to set up a pottery of his own, as well as to wait out the unfavorable conditions created by the beginning of World War I. In 1914 he married Mrs. Nancy Teresa Lee Case, a widow and a native of Skyland.

During the war Stephen abandoned pottery briefly to work in the aluminum plant at Badin. His return to the mountains of North Carolina marked the start of the Pisgah Forest Pottery on Avery's Creek along the French Broad River near Asheville. It was here that he resumed the production of fine artistic pottery with superior clays and glazes.

One of Stephen's special interests in the Pisgah Forest Pottery was to discover new and hitherto unknown glazes and colors, particularly in the crystalline glazes, several of which he was able to produce in his new shop. He constantly experimented and made new observations, and he carefully recorded the numerous formulas that he developed for different effects and results under different temperatures. He was scientific in his work and a master of exact methods and techniques.

It was the distinct cameolike decorative work that earned Stephen his place among ceramic artists. This consists of early pioneer scenes in raised porcelain on the pottery body. His work was compared to the famed Wedgwood, but Stephen's cameo was done by hand whereas the Wedgwood decoration is produced in molds. Further, Wedgwood is decorated with scenes from mythology, while the cameo depicts scenes from early American life, such as square dancers or covered wagons.

Using a whiteware body made up of ball clay, kaolin, feldspar, and quartz, Stephen employed a large repertory of bright glazes, including turquoise, aubergine, rose pink, and jade green. He also developed a crystalline glaze that formed surface designs like snowflakes. The ability to produce this effect lay partly in mixing the different glazes in the right proportion and partly in the firing in the kiln, as Stephen explained to those who visited the shop.

His distinct contribution was that he turned out pottery with unique porcelain scenes of early America in various colors and shapes for upwards of sixty-five years. At age eighty-five, a short time before his death, he was still experimenting and polishing his skills, "trying to improve on the excellent." His work has been displayed in the Smithsonian Institution and the North Carolina Museum of Art. While Dwight D. Eisenhower was president, a piece was given to Mrs. Eisenhower.

Stephen died in an Asheville hospital after an illness of two weeks and was buried in the New Salem cemetery at Skyland. After his death, the Pisgah Forest Pottery continued under the direction of Mrs. Roy Case (his daughter-in-law), her son Thomas Case, and Grady Ledbetter.

SEE: *Asheville Citizen-Times*, 5 July 1953, 1 Jan. 1962; Allen H. Eaton, *Handicrafts of the Southern Highlands* (1937); Artus Monroe Moser, personal recollections and observations during 1914–16, when he was employed in the pottery at Skyland, and during the intervening years to 1962; Marcia Ray, "Pisgah Forest Pottery, "*Spinning Wheel*, January–February 1971.

ARTUS MONROE MOSER

Stephens, George *(8 Apr. 1873–1 Apr. 1946)*, civic and business leader, was born in Guilford County, the only child of Addison H., a Confederate veteran, and Lydia Lambeth Stephens. After attending Oak Ridge Institute, he was graduated from The University of North Carolina in 1896. As an outstanding athlete who had taken a course at the Springfield College of Physical Education, he was able to earn his way through college as a physical education instructor. In 1903 the university annual was dedicated to Stephens in recognition of his contributions as a devoted alumnus. In the same year he was appointed a trustee, and in 1937 he was elected president of the Alumni Association. As a trustee until his death, he served on many important committees, including search committees for the selection of a new president and building committees during a period of rapid physical expansion.

After graduation Stephens settled in Charlotte and helped to organize an insurance company. In 1901 he established the Southern States Trust Company (later the American Trust Company and still later the North Carolina National Bank), of which he became president in 1902. While continuing his banking career, he entered the field of real estate development in 1909 with the opening of Kanuga Club, near Hendersonville, as a summer resort. This was a private club of limited membership, consisting of a group of cottages built around a central clubhouse where members could live or simply have their meals. Through central management of the facility, services and maintenance could be provided at cost. The club was discontinued in 1916 after severe flood damage and became an Episcopal conference center.

In 1912 he formed the Stephens Company to develop Myers Park in Charlotte as a residential area on 1,100 acres that he had bought from his father-in-law, John Springs Myers. Both Kanuga Club and Myers Park showed his great love of natural beauty by the efforts he made to preserve and enhance it. Stephens also appreciated the importance of planning, as indicated when he obtained the services of a professional city planner—one of the first in the country. His concern for conservation and for making areas available for the enjoyment of natural beauty, as well as for recreation, was shown by his organization of the Charlotte Park and Tree Commission and by his role as one of the leaders who acquired land for Independence Park in Charlotte. Many years later he was part of a group that helped persuade the federal government to locate the Blue Ridge Parkway in the western part of the state.

Stephens was a director of the Charlotte YMCA for

many years and of the North Carolina and South Carolina Interstate Committee of that organization. He also was one of the organizers of the club that later became the Charlotte Country Club. During World War I he helped to influence the location of Camp Greene near Charlotte, and he was chairman of the Liberty Loan bond campaigns during and after the war. From 1912 to 1916 he was part owner and publisher of the *Charlotte Observer*.

In 1919 Stephens moved to Asheville, where he became copublisher of the *Asheville Citizen*, which he owned with Charles A. Webb until 1930. In addition, he bought Biltmore Village from the George Vanderbilt estate for resale to individual purchasers. In 1939 he became president of the Beverly Hills Company for the development of a large suburban tract. Stephens was the first chairman of the Asheville City Planning Commission.

He was a member of the Episcopal church and of the Democratic party. In 1943 a group of Charlotte friends commissioned a portrait to be painted as part of the permanent collection of the Mint Museum. On the frame is the inscription: "Portrait of George Stephens, first in the building of modern Charlotte."

On his death in Asheville, he was survived by his widow, Sophie Convere Myers Stephens, of Charlotte, whom he had married on 9 Dec. 1902. He also left two children, George Myers and Sophie Stephens Martin, and seven grandchildren. He was buried at Calvary Episcopal Church in Fletcher.

SEE: *Asheville Citizen-Times*, 16 Dec. 1943, 2 Apr. 1946; *Chapel Hill Weekly*, 5 Apr. 1946; *Charlotte Observer*, 15 Dec. 1943; *North Carolina Biography*, vol. 4 (1928); *Who Was Who in America*, vol. 2 (1950).

SOPHIE S. MARTIN

Stephens, George Myers *(19 July 1904–20 Dec. 1978)*, author, publisher, conservationist, and civic leader, was born in Charlotte, the son of George and Sophie Myers Stephens. His father, one of the most effective business and civic leaders of the state, planned and developed Myers Park in Charlotte and the Episcopal conference center, Kanuga, near Hendersonville. The elder Stephens was at different times half owner of the *Charlotte Observer* and the *Asheville Citizen*, a longtime trustee of The University of North Carolina, and influential in bringing the Blue Ridge Parkway to the state.

After graduation from the Asheville School for Boys (1922) and The University of North Carolina (1926), George Myers Stephens developed and expanded his father's interests in his own way. In his senior year at Chapel Hill the yearbook *Yackety Yack* described him as "the best exemplification of things that really count." He served the university as a trustee from 1946 to 1964 and was awarded an honorary LL.D. degree in 1946.

After college Stephens took a job appraising timber in Swain and Haywood counties. His rich knowledge of this area, which became a part of the Great Smoky Mountains National Park, enabled him to write the authoritative guidebook to the park. His experience in the outdoors led him to become an organizer in planning, conservation, and recreation. In 1946 he helped create the Western North Carolina Associated Communities in eleven counties to encourage voluntary local support for the completion of the Blue Ridge Parkway, the formation of a Western North Carolina Tourist Association, the founding of the Cherokee Historical Association, and similar cooperative projects. As a conservator of mountain lore and history as well as of land and communities, Stephens was active in the formation of the Western North Carolina Historical Association and the Cherokee Historical Association. The Indian museum in Cherokee benefited from his time and energy as well.

In 1928 he joined his father's newspaper in Asheville. During his four-year association with the *Citizen* he used the paper to promote rural electrification, and in 1930 he was appointed to the North Carolina Rural Electrification Authority. As a result of his interest in rural mountain counties, he became editor of the *Farmers' Federation News* in 1932. The Farmers' Federation, begun in the 1920s by James G. K. McClure, Jr., undertook to organize buying and agricultural training among mountain farmers in a Christian cooperative. Stephens remained with the *Federation News* until 1936, when he left to form his own publishing company in Asheville.

The Stephens Press issued "a steady stream of books, maps, and other publications about North Carolina and particularly about the mountains of Western North Carolina." Stephens, who also encouraged libraries and reading, was president of the Friends of the Library of the university library in Chapel Hill as well as a permanent trustee of the Asheville-Biltmore Library system. His unique combination of scholar, civic leader, and naturalist was also exemplified in his service as chairman of the board of the North Carolina Botanical Garden, which had been established at Chapel Hill for the study and conservation of North Carolina's native plants.

In 1929 Stephens married Eleanor Waddell. They were the parents of two sons, George M., Jr., and Hugh W., and a daughter, Eleanor (Mrs. David A. Johnson).

SEE: *Asheville Citizen-Times*, 21–22 Dec. 1978; *Chapel Hill Weekly*, June 1964.

WILLIAM F. W. MASSENGALE

Stephens, John Walter *(14 Oct. 1834–21 May 1870)*, Republican state senator from Caswell County assassinated by the Ku Klux Klan, was born near Bruce's Crossroads, Guilford County, the son of Absalom and Letitia Stephens. As a child he moved to Wentworth and later to Leaksville, Rockingham County, where his father, a tailor, died about 1848. John received only the most rudimentary education and went into the harness-making business in Wentworth. In 1857 he married Nannie E. Walters (or Nancy Waters); she died two years later, leaving an infant daughter. In 1860 he married Martha Frances Groom, of Wentworth, who also gave birth to a daughter. An active Methodist, Stephens was an agent for the American Bible and Tract Society for a year or so. Then he became a tobacco trader, moving to Yorkville (now York), S.C.

When the Civil War broke out, Stephens went to Greensboro and for a time served as a press agent commandeering horses for the Confederate army. He avoided military service until near the end of the war, by which time he had returned to Wentworth and resumed the tobacco trade. Following his army service he got into a quarrel with a neighbor over two of the latter's chickens, which had strayed onto his property. After spending a night in jail for killing the chickens, Stephens retaliated by caning the neighbor and then shooting two bystanders who tried to interfere. Thus originated the slurring political epithet, "Chicken" Stephens, by which Democrats referred to him in later years.

In 1866 Stephens moved to Yanceyville, Caswell County, where he continued in the tobacco business. Subsequently he served as an agent of the Freedmen's Bureau and became an active member of the Union League and the Republican party. In these capacities he associated frequently and freely with local blacks, who outnumbered whites in Caswell, and they accorded him a position of political leadership. As a result he was elected to the state senate in 1868 over Bedford Brown, a former U.S. senator and an elder statesman. Stephens came to be hated by the white community as a racial and political renegade, and no accusations of incendiarism or perfidy were too extravagant to win credence. He was socially ostracized and expelled from the Methodist church. As a result of repeated threats, he insured his life, fortified his house, and took to carrying three pistols on his person.

In truth, Stephens threw his influence on the side of political and racial moderation. He consistently advised blacks against physical retaliation following white terrorist attacks. In May 1870, while observing a Democratic county convention at the courthouse, he was lured to his death by Frank Wiley, a former Democratic sheriff whom Stephens was urging to accept the Republican nomination for reelection. By prearrangement with other waiting Klansmen, Wiley persuaded Stephens to leave the courtroom and accompany him downstairs to a small room, where the others quickly overpowered and stabbed him to death, leaving the body on a woodpile to be discovered the next day. The details of the murder were not revealed for sixty-five years, but Klan involvement was suspected from the outset. It was in response to this crime that Governor William W. Holden called out the militia under Colonel George W. Kirk, leading in turn to Holden's impeachment and removal from office by a Democratic legislature.

SEE: Samuel A. Ashe, ed., *Biographical History of North Carolina*, vol. 4 (1906); Luther M. Carlton, "The Assassination of John Walter Stephens," Trinity College Historical Society, *Annual Publication of Historical Papers, 1898*, vol. 2; Otto H. Olson, "The Ku Klux Klan: A Study in Reconstruction Politics and Propaganda," *North Carolina Historical Review* 39 (1962); Andrew J. Stedman, *Murder and Mystery: History of the Life and Death of John W. Stephens* (1870).

ALLEN W. TRELEASE

Stephens (Stevens), Samuel *(ca. 1629–70)*, governor of Albemarle County, was born in Virginia, the son of Richard (ca. 1600–ca. 1636) and Elizabeth Piersey Stephens (b. 1610). In records of the Virginia Company of London, his father is referred to as "Mr. Rich: Stephens of London painter stainer," a short way of saying that Stephens was a member of the City of London Livery Company of Painters. London Painter Stainer was one of the organizations that had subscribed to the Virginia Company. Perhaps because of his membership in it, Richard Stephens was assigned one "share" of land in Virginia at a meeting of the council of the Virginia Company held in London in March 1622/23. In early July he signed an agreement to go to Virginia as a settler and take with him supplies to the value of £300, which he later agreed to increase by £30. The promised supplies, contained in twenty-one hogsheads, were put on board the ship *George* by 31 July 1623, and soon afterwards Stephens, with two servants, sailed on the *George* for Virginia. By the end of 1623 Richard Stephens had acquired a house and lot in Jamestown and had been granted additional land for a garden. In March 1623/24 he was a member of the House of Burgesses, and by 1630 he was a member of the Virginia Council, on which he apparently remained for the rest of his life.

Samuel Stephens's mother, Elizabeth, was the daughter of the wealthy Abraham Piersey and his wife Elizabeth Draper, the daughter of Vincent Draper of London. In 1616 Piersey, who appears to have been recently widowed, migrated to Virginia, leaving in England his two small daughters, Elizabeth and Mary. In Virginia, Piersey operated a mercantile business as factor for English merchants. He soon became prominent politically. By 1618 he was cape merchant, or treasurer, for the colony, in 1622 he was burgess, and by 1624 he was a Council member, a position that he held until his death. In 1623 he brought his daughters to Virginia. He died in October 1628, leaving an estate considered the largest then known in Virginia.

Richard Stephens and Elizabeth Piersey appear to have married about the time of Abraham Piersey's death. Samuel was the elder of their two children; their younger son, William, was born about 1631. Richard died about 1636, apparently in the summer of that year. By 1638 Elizabeth had married Sir John Harvey, then governor of Virginia.

Nothing is known of Samuel Stephens's early life. In 1652 he married Frances Culpeper, the daughter of Thomas Culpeper of Feckenham, Worcestershire, England, and his wife Katherine St. Leger, whose father was Sir Warham St. Leger of Ulcombe, County Kent. Frances is believed to have migrated to Virginia with her parents about 1650. Shortly before his marriage, Stephens executed documents that provided that a plantation known as Bolthorpe, consisting of 1,350 acres on Warwick River, was to become the property of Frances at his death.

On 9 Oct. 1662 the Council of Virginia appointed Stephens, then called captain, to be "commander of the southern plantation," with authority to appoint a sheriff. The "southern plantation" was the newly begun settlement in the Albemarle area, which then was part of Virginia but soon would be included in a grant from the Crown to the Lords Proprietors of Carolina. Presumably Stephens, as commander, governed the Albemarle settlement until late 1664, by which time the Lords Proprietors had possession of the area and had appointed their own governor, William Drummond. No record, however, has survived regarding Stephens's activities as commander.

On 8 Oct. 1667 the Lords Proprietors appointed Stephens to succeed Drummond as governor of Albemarle. Stephens took office at some subsequent date and governed the colony until his death. In that period or earlier he acquired about five thousand acres of land in Albemarle, including Roanoke Island.

Few records of his administration have survived, but those few make it evident that the period was a difficult one for him and for the colony at large. Conditions in Albemarle were bad when Stephens took office, and they grew worse. The Proprietors, during Drummond's administration, had promulgated land policies that were so restrictive that many colonists considered them ruinous. The widespread discouragement resulting from the Proprietors' policies was increased by hardships caused by natural disasters. Two months before Stephens's appointment, a hurricane had devastated the colony, destroying most of the crops and many buildings. The next year's crops were killed by a three-months' drought and a month of excessive rain that followed the drought. The next year, 1669, crops and buildings again were destroyed by a hurricane. The frustration and despair of the colonists were aggravated by diseases that killed cattle and hogs in large numbers and by illnesses, apparently epidemic, that incapacitated the people for long periods.

The spirits of the colonists were lifted briefly in 1668, when the Proprietors, in response to an earlier petition, ostensibly liberalized their land policies, sending to Stephens a document called by the colonists the "Great Deed of Grant," which authorized Stephens to grant land on the liberal terms in effect in Virginia. Hope soon fell, however, for the Proprietors, in a letter to Stephens, directed him to have the Assembly enact legislation imposing many of the restrictions that the Great Deed purported to remove, in effect nullifying most of the concessions that appeared to have been made in the Great Deed of Grant. Despite what must have been bitter opposition, Stephens succeeded in getting the Assembly to enact most of the legislation that the Proprietors demanded.

No doubt animosities aroused by enactment of the new laws were a significant factor in the political situation that existed during much of Stephens's administration. The colony became divided into factions, torn with dissension, and filled with hostility towards Stephens, who was subjected to insolence and abuse. Some colonists were reported to have drawn their swords against him. Although Stephens met such actions with mildness and apparently did not have the offenders punished, the hostility towards him continued until his death, which occurred in late February or early March 1669/70.

Despite the hostility that Stephens aroused in Albemarle, he appears to have had many virtues. Sir William Berkeley, then governor of Virginia and one of the Proprietors of Carolina, described him as a man of courage and great integrity who loved the Albemarle colony and had many personal traits that usually arouse love and admiration. Admitting that Stephens lacked "that fullness of understanding" that men reared in Europe gained from early experience in handling important affairs, Berkeley felt that Stephens's personal virtues offset that lack. According to Berkeley, it was Stephens's mildness alone that had prevented those threatening him with swords from suffering capital punishment.

Stephens had no children. Soon after his death a Virginia court put his widow, Frances, in possession of Bolthorpe, as provided in his marriage settlement. For unknown reasons, Stephens's will was judged invalid when presented for probate in Virginia, and his estate in that colony was administered under common law, with Frances as administratrix. The portion of the estate that was in Albemarle was administered by John Culpeper, who appears to have been Frances's brother.

In June 1670 Frances married Sir William Berkeley. At Berkeley's death she inherited his Proprietorship in Carolina but sold it in the 1680s. About 1680 she married Philip Ludwell, a member of the Virginia Council, who in 1689 was appointed governor of Albemarle. Frances, however, did not officiate a second time as first lady of Albemarle, for Ludwell retained residence in Virginia, going to Albemarle only at intervals. She died about 1691.

SEE: Albemarle Book of Warrants and Surveys, 1681–1706 (North Carolina State Archives, Raleigh); James Branch Cabell, *The Majors and Their Marriages* (1915); Fairfax Harrison, *The Proprietors of the Northern Neck: Chapters of Culpeper Genealogy* (1926); William Waller Hening, ed., *Laws of Virginia* (1823); John C. Hotten, ed., *Our Early Emigrant Ancestors* (1962); Annie L. Jester and Martha W. Hiden, comps., *Adventurers of Purse and Person, Virginia, 1607–1625* (1956); Susan M. Kingsbury, ed., *Records of the Virginia Company of London* (1906–35); E. R. McIlwaine, ed., *Minutes of the Virginia Council and General Court* (1924); Nell Marion Nugent, comp., *Cavaliers and Pioneers*, vol. 1 (1934); Mattie Erma E. Parker, ed., *North Carolina Higher-Court Records, 1670–1696* (1968); William S. Powell, ed., *Y^e^ Countie of Albemarle in Carolina: A Collection of Documents, 1664–1675* (1958); William L. Saunders, ed., *Colonial Records of North Carolina*, vols. 1, 3–5 (1886–87); William G. Stanard and Mary N. Stanard, comps., *The Colonial Virginia Register* (1902); *The Virginia Magazine of History and Biography*, vol. 7 (April 1900), vol. 8 (January 1901), vol. 25 (January 1917).

MATTIE ERMA E. PARKER

Stephenson, Gilbert Thomas *(17 Dec. 1884–9 June 1972)*, lawyer, banker, author, educator, and farmer, was born at Warren Place near Pendleton, Northampton County, the only child of Susan Anna Fleetwood and James Henry Stephenson. His forebears were large plantation owners in the community. He was graduated from Severn High School in 1899 and at age fourteen entered Wake Forest College, where he earned an A.B. degree in 1902 and an M.A. degree in 1904. From Harvard University he received an M.A. degree in 1906 and an LL.B. degree in 1910. Wake Forest, on whose board of trustees he served for twenty-one years, three years as president of the board, awarded him an honorary doctor of civil law degree in 1955.

Admitted to the bar in 1910, Stephenson began the practice of law in Winston-Salem. He was city solicitor, judge of the municipal court, and chairman of the Forsyth County Democratic Executive Committee. During World War I he was chairman of the state war bond campaign.

Turning to banking as a career in 1919, he joined Wachovia Bank and Trust Company in Winston-Salem as secretary, then rose to assistant trust officer and associate trust officer; he was a director of the bank from 1922 to 1929. In 1922 he was transferred to Raleigh to head the bank's new office. In 1929 he was named vice-president in charge of the trust department of Equitable Trust Company in Wilmington, Del., where he lived until his retirement in 1950. From 1937 to 1950 he devoted full time to trust scholarship as director of the trust research department of the Stonier Graduate School of Banking of the American Bankers Association and also served as a faculty member of Stonier and other banking schools. He was president of the trust division of the American Bankers Association in 1930 and 1931.

Upon returning to Warren Place in 1950, Stephenson continued to write and lecture on trust subjects and was a director of Planters National Bank in Rocky Mount and of Virginia National Bank in Boykins, Va. He spent much of his retirement in farming, managing the total plantation land of 4,341 acres. Continuing his strong interest in church and civic affairs, he helped to establish the Roanoke-Chowan Foundation and was active in the Robert Chapel Baptist Church. In Winston-Salem, Raleigh, and Wilmington, he had participated fully in the church and civic life. In Wilmington he was president of the Rotary Club. Active in the North Carolina Bankers Association and its trust programs, he also was involved in establishing the trust program at Campbell College, where the trust library was named in his honor and his portrait was hung.

A prolific writer, Stephenson was the author of twenty-five books, principally on trusts, including *Estates and Trusts*. He and his wife wrote about their life and retirement in *We Came Home to Warren Place*. His extensive research, writing, and lecturing and his pioneer work in trust education earned for him the national honorary title of Dean of Trust Business.

On 19 Dec. 1912 he married Grace Morris White. They

had two sons, Thomas Wilson of Wilmington, Del., and James Henry of Baltimore, five grandchildren, and six great-grandchildren. Following several months of critical illness, he died at age eighty-seven at Warren Place and was buried on the plantation in the family cemetery. Campbell University and the North Carolina Bankers Association have photographs of Stephenson.

SEE: Campbell College, *Prospect*, June 1972; T. Harry Gatton, personal contact with Stephenson and his family; Raleigh *News and Observer*, 10 June 1972; Mary C. Smith (Washington, D.C., a former secretary of Stephenson), personal contact; Gilbert T. Stephenson, *We Came Home to Warren Place* (1958); *Tarheel Banker*, June, July 1972; *Who Was Who in America*, vol. 5 (1973).

T. HARRY GATTON

Stephenson, William Hermas *(12 May 1897–5 Jan. 1986)*, manufacturer of life-saving and safety equipment, was born in Raleigh, the son of Charles Henry and Annie Evelena Jones Stephenson. He was graduated from The University of North Carolina in 1918 with a degree in electrical engineering and membership in Phi Beta Kappa. After serving as a lieutenant in the navy during World War I, he attended Harvard Law School and in 1922 received LL.B. and S.J.D. degrees from the University of Texas. He was promptly admitted to the state bar there, in New York the following year, and in California in 1924. From 1922 to 1928 he practiced in Dallas. In 1929 he founded in Mina, Nev., the American Mines and Metals Corporation, which he operated until 1934.

Between 1935 and 1940 Stephenson developed for the American Medical Association the first automatic resuscitator. In 1946 he founded the Stephenson Corporation, in Red Bank, N.J., which became the largest manufacturer of resuscitators and oxygen-breathing equipment in the world. Among his other products were the Drunkometer, the Breathalizer to test for drunken driving offenses, and radar equipment to detect automobile speeding violations. In addition, he was vice-president of Life Support Systems, Inc., and other firms. With his cousin, Katherine Buford Peeples, he cofounded the Austro-American International Conservatory of Music at Mondsee, Austria, and served as executive vice-president. He also established the Institute for World Affairs, Mondsee, Austria, in 1934, and was cofounder of the International Rescue and First Aid Association in 1948.

Stephenson was active in the Presbyterian church and was a member of the New Jersey Council on Historic Sites. In 1942 he married Esther C. Myers, who died in 1959; they were the parents of Dorothy Esther and William Hermas. His second wife was Irene W. Stephan.

SEE: Daniel L. Grant, *Alumni History of the University of North Carolina* (1924); Raleigh *News and Observer*, 8 Jan. 1986; *Who's Who in the East, 1979–1980* (1979).

WILLIAM S. POWELL

Steppe, Clarence Maddrey *(5 May 1913–25 May 1991)*, landscape nurseryman, was born at Dana in eastern Henderson County, the son of Norman Fanning and Annie Laurie Fordham Steppe. Known throughout life as "Kit," he was graduated at age fourteen from Marion High School in McDowell County, where his father was superintendent of schools for fifty years. He then entered Lenoir-Rhyne College. After graduation in 1931, he earned a diploma from the American Landscape School (1933) and attended Wake Forest College for a short time. Between 1934 and 1938 he worked for the National Park Service on projects in the Great Smoky Mountains National Park, on Mount Mitchell, and at Mount Vernon.

From 1941 to 1946, during World War II, Steppe served with the U.S. Army Corps of Engineers and with the navy. For a part of the time he was engaged in projects at the new Supreme Court building on Constitution Avenue in Washington, D.C., and on assignment to the navy he directed the first drilling for oil on the north slope northeast of Point Barrow, Alaska. He also worked for a year (1945–46) on the Manhattan Project and received a presidential citation for outstanding scientific achievement. From the University of Tennessee he held B.S. degrees in civil engineering and nuclear engineering (both awarded in 1945) and one in political science (1946). In 1946 Steppe was a graduate student in history at The University of North Carolina. Between 1946 and 1951 he was with the Division of State Parks in the North Carolina Department of Conservation and Development. He served a term as president of the Navy League of the United States and remained active in the Naval Reserve until 1964.

In 1951 Steppe founded Wayside Nurseries on U.S. 64 east of Raleigh, and in time he received fifteen national awards for landscape engineering from the American Association of Nurserymen. He held a patent for the Pink Sachet, a flowering dogwood tree. Among his noted commissions were those at the North Carolina Farm Bureau headquarters near Raleigh and at Balentine's Cafeteria and Confederate House in Cameron Village and Quail Corners Shopping Center, both in Raleigh. He also landscaped portions of the Research Triangle Park. He considered his best work to have been at the Cherry Hill Mall in Haddonfield, N.J., but he was equally as pleased with the campus of St. Andrews Presbyterian College in Laurinburg, the Charlottetown Mall in Charlotte, and the grounds of the Reynolds Tobacco Company in Winston-Salem. In 1977 he was named honorary lieutenant governor of North Carolina and was recognized as layman of the year by the North Carolina Baptist Men. In 1983 he sold his business in Raleigh and retired.

Steppe was married first to Muriel Alma Spurr, and they were the parents of William Norman and Elizabeth Maddrey. Following a divorce, he married Helen Marie Allred; their children were James Fordham, Rebecca Joy, and David Lewis. Divorced again, he took a third wife, Muriel Wunder Fiscus; his fourth wife was Gilda Marini Brackett. There were no children of the last two marriages.

Because of poor health, Steppe left Raleigh in December 1988 to live with his daughter, Maddrey, in Groton, Conn. Although he was a Baptist, had served as a deacon, and had taught Sunday school for many years, his fourth wife was a Roman Catholic who lived in Watertown, Mass. At his death special arrangements were made for his funeral to be conducted by a priest of her church and for a military burial service by the U.S. Navy; he was buried in her family lot at St. Patrick Cemetery, Watertown.

SEE: *Boston Globe*, 27 May 1991; Raleigh *News and Observer*, 1 July 1973, 26 May 1991; Rebecca Joy Steppe, "My Father: Clarence Maddrey Steppe" (typescript, possession of the author, Knightdale, N.C.).

WILLIAM S. POWELL

Sterling, Richard *(1812–3 Oct. 1883)*, educator, publisher, and mayor, was born in County Down, Ireland. When he was twelve, his parents immigrated to the

United States and settled in Newburgh, N.Y. He received an A.M. degree from Princeton University in 1835 and for the next thirteen years taught school in Fredericksburg and Richmond, Va. In Fredericksburg he married Marion L. Howison, the daughter of Samuel Howison. Their children were Samuel Graham (d. 1852), Helen Mary (d. 1855), and R. O. Sterling.

After teaching natural philosophy and chemistry at Hampden-Sydney College (1848–51), Sterling moved to Greensboro, N.C., to become the principal of the Edgeworth Female Seminary. While serving in that position from 1851 to 1864, when the school was closed because of the Civil War, he was also the professor of belles lettres and physical science. According to the Greensboro *Times* of 2 Apr. 1869, "Professor Sterling is a ripe scholar and enjoys an enviable reputation as an instructor—the best testimonial of which is the fact that during the whole of his charge of Edgeworth the school was always filled with scholars and was considered inferior to no institution in the south."

In addition to his teaching duties, Sterling was active in civic and business affairs. In 1852 he was one of the founders of the Greensboro Mutual Life Insurance and Trust Company. During the wartime administration of Governor Zebulon B. Vance, he served on the State Literary Board, which worked to establish public schools. In 1864 he was elected mayor of Greensboro, a post he held until Colonel William L. Scott, a former Edgeworth Female Seminary teacher (1852–54), took over as military mayor in 1865.

When the Civil War started in 1861, Sterling and J. D. Campbell, a teacher at the Edgeworth Female Seminary, wrote a series of textbooks entitled *Our Own First Reader, Our Own Second Reader, Our Own Third Reader, Our Own Fourth Reader, Our Own Fifth Reader, Our Own Primer*, and *Our Own Spelling Book*. With James W. Albright, Sterling and Campbell formed the publishing firm of Sterling, Campbell, and Albright, Book Publishers and Printers. They sent J. J. Ayers, a Frenchman, to Liverpool, England, to obtain stereotypes, which were brought to North Carolina on the *Advance*, a Confederate blockade-runner. Using paper from the Salem and Wake Forest mills, they published the *Our Own Series* as well as other southern textbooks and printed information for nearby county governments. All of the books were copyrighted by the Confederate States of America and used throughout the South. When the Civil War ended, the publishing firm was closed by the federal government because the textbooks offered a "Bible View of Slavery," which explained biblical teachings in support of slavery. In 1866 Sterling and his son opened the publishing business and bookstore of R. Sterling and Son.

While living in Greensboro, Sterling was an active member of the First Presbyterian Church. He served as an elder of the church (1863–68) and as a delegate to the Orange Presbytery (1863) in Milton. In 1865 the First Presbyterian Church opened a Sabbath School for freedmen, and Sterling was appointed to find teachers for the school. During 1867 he was the superintendent of the Sabbath School for former slaves.

Early in 1868 he became the head of the Shelbyville Female College in Shelbyville, Ky. Two years later he moved to Paris, Tenn., where he was principal of a female seminary for three years. In 1873 he opened a boarding school in Evansville, Ind. Returning to North Carolina in 1875, he was principal of the Episcopal Boys School in Mocksville. In June 1881 he became the superintendent of the Davie County schools and served until November 1882. Sterling was buried in the Mocksville First Presbyterian Church cemetery.

SEE: James W. Albright, *Greensboro, 1808–1904* (1904); *Appleton's Cyclopedia of American Biography*, vol. 5 (1888); *A Bill to Incorporate the Greensboro Mutual Life Insurance and Trust Company* (1852); Edgeworth Female Seminary ledgers, 1851–64 (Greensboro Historical Museum); *General Catalogue of Princeton University* (1908); *Greensboro Daily News*, 23 Jan. 1943; *Greensboro Patriot*, 15, 29 May 1852; *Greensboro Times*, 2 Apr., 5 Nov. 1868; John W. Simpson, *History of the First Presbyterian Church of Greensboro, N.C.* (1945); Richard Sterling and J. D. Campbell, *Our Own Fifth Reader* (1862) and *Our Own Spelling Book* (1862); James W. Wall, *History of Davie County* (1969) and *A History of the First Presbyterian Church of Mocksville* (1963).

CAROL E. DALTON

Sternberger, Bertha Strauss *(27 Oct. 1878–17 Feb. 1928)*, civic leader and philanthropist, was born in Mayesville, S.C., on the the large cotton plantation of her parents, Mr. and Mrs. Alfred A. Strauss. Her earliest schooling was in Sumter, and she was graduated from Winthrop College in Rock Hill. On 25 Apr. 1900 she married Emanuel Sternberger, a rural merchant in South Carolina. He was a friend of Moses and Ceasar Cone, who welcomed Sternberger into their recently established manufacturing business in Greensboro, N.C. The three men began to produce Canton flannel, which Sternberger had recommended as a desirable product, and they soon gained a wide reputation because of it.

When Bertha Sternberger was stricken with bulbar paralysis, her throat became so constricted that she had to be fed through a tube and her weight fell to a mere seventy-five pounds. Some fifty physicians were consulted, among them Dr. S. Weir Mitchell of Philadelphia. He told her about a park and playground program that was being established in Philadelphia and supported by the sale of special stamps. She was interested but was too ill to help. Instead, she went to Germany to seek treatment from specialists. Finally, after eight years of suffering, she began a slow recovery. During this time the people of Greensboro had expressed their concern in many ways, and with her recovery she began to think of ways to thank them.

Remembering Dr. Mitchell's account of Philadelphia's park and playground program, she proposed that a similar program be organized in Greensboro. She was rebuffed by city officials until 1910, when a small facility was opened. Nearby residents objected to the noise of the children, however, and it was closed. This effort attracted support from city authorities, parent-teacher associations, and private donors, and in 1918 a playground director for recreational programs was hired but discharged after a year for lack of funds. But the experience demonstrated the value of parks and playgrounds, and soon afterwards they were firmly established. Half a century later Greensboro had a dozen active centers.

Bertha Sternberger also was interested in public education, and from 1921 to 1927 she was the first woman to serve on the city board of education. In the face of considerable opposition, she succeeded in gaining approval for the acquisition of a large tract of land for a cluster of schools—afterwards the site of Brooks Elementary, Kiser Junior High, and Grimsley Senior High schools. In addition, she urged an improved course of study, and it was largely through her interest and support that a high school orchestra was organized.

After the death of her husband in 1924, Mrs. Sternberger and her two daughters, Blanche and Emelia, established the Emanuel Sternberger Education Fund from which loans were made without interest for the educational expenses of students, without regard to their age, creed, color, or sex. Large sums of money were made available, and some recipients later made significant contributions to the state and nation. Mrs. Sternberger also gave generously of her intellectual and financial resources to the Travelers Aid Society, the Children's Home Society of North Carolina, the Crippled Children's Commission, the League of Women Voters, the American Red Cross, and the center of her religious activities, Temple Emanuel.

Bertha Sternberger believed in the value of human dignity, and she encouraged everyone she knew to do their best—both for themselves and for others. Her greatest gift, according to associates, was her ability to bring out the best in others. In her fiftieth year, at the height of her usefulness, she contracted sleeping sickness and died. Her remains were deposited in a family mausoleum in Forest Lawn cemetery, Greensboro.

SEE: Family records (possession of Mr. and Mrs. Edward B. Benjamin, New Orleans, La.); Files of the director, Emanuel Sternberger Educational Fund (Jefferson Building, Greensboro); *Greensboro Daily News*, 18 Feb. 1928, 19 Feb. 1960, 5 Sept. 1963; Greensboro Public Library files; Miscellaneous articles on deposit at Temple Emanual synagogue, Greensboro.

ETHEL STEPHENS ARNETT

Steuart, Andrew *(fl. 1764–69)*, Wilmington printer and journalist, was born in Belfast, Ireland, where he learned the printing trade from James MacGee. In 1758 he went to Philadelphia and established a printing shop and bookstore at Laetitia Court. Later he moved to the Bible-in-Heart in Second Street between Market and Arch streets. After accumulating land and other property in Philadelphia, Steuart opened a second shop in Lancaster, Pa., in 1761. He achieved some notoriety in 1762 when he printed Francis Hopkinson's "Science, A Poem" without his permission. Steuart said he did it to promote good poetry and not for his own gain, and Hopkinson did not complain or seek redress. When Steuart immigrated to North Carolina, he took only part of his printing equipment, and he maintained ownership of his shops in Philadelphia and Lancaster.

Arriving in Wilmington on 24 June 1764, he soon became the center of a controversy between Governor Arthur Dobbs and the Assembly over the division of power. There had been some dissatisfaction with James Davis's performance as public printer, and on 5 Mar. 1764 Dobbs recommended that the Assembly find a new printer—one who would be more concerned with serving the state than with making a profit. On 8 March the Assembly named a committee to seek a printer willing to work for £200 per year. Dobbs apparently lured Steuart to Wilmington with the promise of being named public printer.

At the time the Governor's Council was sitting as the upper house of the Assembly, and in mid-November 1764 the Council defeated a bill to reappoint James Davis. Almost immediately the Council, as the advisory body to the governor, approved Dobbs's nomination of Steuart as the public printer. On 21 November Dobbs notified the Assembly that he had appointed Andrew Steuart "printer to his Majesty . . . from the 24th day of June." Furthermore, he told the Assembly that it was honor-bound to pay Steuart an adequate salary.

The Assembly reacted angrily on 24 November. Believing that it should have taken action on the defeated Council bill—the one reappointing Davis—the Assembly charged that Dobbs had acted in a "most extraordinary and unparliamentary manner" and that he had rendered the upper house "useless or a mere property of his Excellency." Furthermore, the appointment was "of an unusual nature truly unknown either to our Laws or Constitution" and "a most extensive stretch of power" that would call for new offices and new fees to support it. After venting its anger, the Assembly refused to create the position of "His Majesty's Printer." (Some accounts have suggested that the Assembly rejected Steuart's appointment because of his title as "His Majesty's Printer," but the Assembly's journal indicates that the major reason for the rejection of Steuart was Dobbs's misuse of the Council.)

Dobbs responded two days later, saying that the Assembly did have the power to appoint someone to print its votes and resolutions, but it was "his Majesty's undoubted prerogative to nominate and appoint a printer to Publish his Proclamations." Dobbs reaffirmed his appointment of Steuart and asked the Assembly to raise the money to pay him. He told the assemblymen that he was going back to England for a year for health reasons; while there, he wanted to present the colonial legislators in the most favorable light, so he hoped that they would comply with his request.

On the same day, 26 November, the Assembly responded by sending a resolution to the Council reaffirming the Davis appointment. The members agreed that Dobbs could appoint his own printer but made it clear that he had to pay him as well. Then, in a spirit of magnanimity, the Assembly granted Steuart £100 for his travels expenses to North Carolina. Nevertheless, Steuart remained and apparently did some government printing, although Davis continued as the official public printer. As early as 27 Oct. 1764, a motion was made in the Assembly to deliver a record of the proceedings to Steuart to be printed and delivered to each member, but the journal does not report the fate of the motion. On 11 Jan. 1765 Steuart placed a notice in James Davis's *North Carolina Magazine* to advertise the sale of the laws of the Assembly. On 1 Dec. 1766, in response to the Council's request to pay Steuart for some printing, the Assembly claimed that the commission he acted under was "unknown to the Laws and Constitution of Our Country" and his salary was not definite. It does not appear that the Assembly refused to pay him but only wanted proof of his work and submission of a legal claim.

Meanwhile, Steuart had established the *North Carolina Gazette and Weekly Post Boy* in Wilmington in September or October 1764. The colony's second newspaper, it would keep Steuart in the center of a public controversy for the next two years. The 20 Nov. 1765 issue described the angry reactions of Wilmington citizens to the Stamp Act. An evening of parades and bonfires was climaxed with the forced resignation of the town's appointed stamp distributor, who was then paraded around the town on an uplifted chair. The mob went to Steuart's house and demanded to know whether he planned to continue to print his newspaper. Steuart, who had suspended publication for several weeks because of illness, told the crowd he could not publish because he did not have any stamped paper. The crowd told Steuart that if he did not print his newspaper without the stamps, he would receive the same treatment as the stamp distributors. Steuart capitulated: "That rather run the Hazard of Life, being maimed, or having his Printing-Office destroyed, he would comply with their request." For his own protection, however, he had witnesses affirm that he was doing so under threat. The margin of that issue bore a skull-and-crossbones imprint with the words: "This is the place to affix the STAMP."

The Stamp Act caused Steuart further problems. When the citizens of Wilmington maintained their steadfast defiance, Governor William Tryon's forces seized ships coming into the port and would not allow vessels to leave unless their cargo had stamps. In retaliation, the people refused to provide supplies for the king's ships. In the middle of this standoff Steuart published a letter in his 12 Feb. 1766 issue, signed by a "Philanthropos" from Cross Creek, that urged the people to seize the ships and to open the port for shipping again. In a preface to the letter, Steuart described his "very disagreeable situation" over printing the letter. "At the earnest desire, or rather stern command of the people, he [the printer] has endeavored with great difficulty, to carry on a Newspaper, well knowing, that that Province that is deprived of the liberty of the Press, is deprived of one of the darling Privileges, which they, as Englishmen, boast of. What part is he now to act?—Continue to keep his Press open and free, and be in danger of corporal punishment, or bloque it up and run the risk of having his brains knocked out? Sad alternative.—One thing he has long ago resolved on, viz: That as he looks upon himself to be a free-born subject, no man shall ever horse whip him, if it is in his power to prevent it; and whenever any such threats are made towards him, he'll take care to be on his guard." On 26 February Tryon presented the Council with a copy of Steuart's 12 February issue, which contained "such inflammatory Expressions That His Excellency declared his intentions of suspending him, And accordingly delivered His letter for that purpose to the Secretary." It is not known whether this was a suspension from publishing the newspaper or from the printing Steuart was doing for the governor.

Steuart also had other problems with the citizens of Wilmington that eventually caused his demise as newspaper publisher. When he began his newspaper, he was apparently encouraged by town leaders, perhaps because of their desire for an advertising medium in that port. He soon lost their confidence, however, beginning with his alleged opening and publishing of the letters of a prominent citizen. At any rate, the newspaper ceased publication in 1767 for lack of support.

Isaiah Thomas might very well have settled in North Carolina had it not been for Steuart's high demands for the purchase of his printing equipment. Thomas was working in Charleston, S.C., and heard that Steuart wanted to sell his equipment and move back to Philadelphia. Realizing that the supply of printing equipment and type was extremely limited, Steuart originally asked Thomas three times the cost of a new press. He lowered his demand to twice the original cost, but when he saw that Thomas could raise that much money, he threw in a slave and her child in addition to the equipment. Thomas agreed to that, but Steuart countered with the inclusion of his household furniture. Thomas finally refused, and by the time Steuart reduced his demands to the earlier terms, Thomas had departed. (Thomas made one more attempt to locate in Wilmington. After Adam Boyd acquired Steuart's equipment, Thomas tried unsuccessfully to get Boyd to take him on as a partner. In 1770 Thomas returned to Boston to a distinguished career as journalist and newspaper historian.)

Sometime in 1769 Steuart was drowned while bathing in the Cape Fear River near his home in Wilmington. It was probably before October, since Adam Boyd purchased his equipment and began to publish his *Cape Fear Mercury* on 13 Oct. 1769.

SEE: Douglas C. McMurtrie, *A History of Printing in the United States* (1936); William L. Saunders, *Colonial Records of North Carolina*, vols. 6–7 (1888–90); Isaiah Thomas, *The History of Printing in America* (1874); Stephen B. Weeks, *The Press of North Carolina in the Eighteenth Century* (1891).

THOMAS A. BOWERS

Stevens, Henry Leonidas, Jr. *(27 Jan. 1896–5 Aug. 1971)*, jurist, Veterans' leader, and soldier, was born in Warsaw, Duplin County, of Scots-Irish ancestry. The son of Fannie Walker and Henry Leonidas Stevens, an attorney and banker, he was a descendant of a long line of military men. His maternal great-great-grandfather, William Walker, was an officer in the American Revolution and a grandfather was a veteran of thirty-two battles during the Civil War.

Stevens attended the local schools in Warsaw and was graduated from Porter Military Academy in Charleston, S.C., in June 1913. He immediately began a course of study at The University of North Carolina, which was interrupted by his enlistment in the army in April 1917. After training at Fort Oglethorpe, Ga., he was commissioned a second lieutenant in Company B, 318th Machine Gun Battalion, 81st, or "Wildcat," Division. He served overseas during the campaigns at Meuse-Argonne and St. Die (Vosges Mountains). Thereafter he remained active in the Army Reserve, rising to the rank of lieutenant colonel.

After the war he entered The University of North Carolina Law School but transferred to Harvard University to complete his studies. He then returned to Warsaw in January 1921 and began to practice law in the firm of Beasly and Stevens at Kenansville.

In June 1928, upon its organization, Stevens was named judge of the general court of Duplin County; he served until more pressing duties forced him to resign in 1931. By appointment of the Board of County Commissioners, he was county attorney from 1936 to 1938. In January 1939, following a bitter campaign, he was sworn in as resident judge of the Sixth Judicial District. Following reelection to two more eight-year terms, he retired on 31 Dec. 1962. Governor Terry Sanford appointed him an emergency judge of the North Carolina Superior Court for life, effective 1 Jan. 1963. Known throughout his judicial career as a workhorse, Stevens once held forty-eight weeks of court in one year and fifty weeks of court in another.

In Warsaw he organized and was elected commander of the Charles R. Gavin American Legion Post. Stevens established the Veterans' Day parade. He also served as commander of the district organization and in 1925 was elected state commander after a heated contest. Under his leadership, the highest membership to date was achieved. In addition, the legion completed its quota for the National Five Million Dollar Legion Endowment Fund and cleared the state department of all debts, turning over to his successor a cash balance of $2,500. In September 1931, at the American Legion's national convention in Detroit, Mich., he was elected national commander by acclamation after an incomplete roll call showed him to be far ahead of the sixteen opposing candidates. During this period he began many new programs to benefit veterans. As a result of his employment program, over one million jobs were found for deserving veterans—this during the Great Depression years of 1932–33. Stevens was the youngest man, the first southerner, and from the most humble beginnings of any man elected national commander up to that time.

Among his many honors and awards he counted the

Legion of Honor of France, the Greek Decoration, the World War I Victory Medal, the Cross of Military Service, the North Carolina World War I Victory Medal, the Verdun Medal (for the defense of Verdun, France), the American Legion Bronze Medallion for fifty years' service, and the American Legion Citation of Appreciation. In 1932 President Herbert Hoover appointed him to deliver to the French government a panoramic painting of the funeral cortege of Marshal Ferdinand Foch, supreme Allied commander during World War I. Judge Stevens presented the gift to the president of France after giving an address in French at the Palace of Versailles. During his life he was the personal guest of Albert I of Belgium, the prince of Wales and later king of England, President Aristide Briand of France, and Presidents Herbert C. Hoover and Franklin D. Roosevelt of the United States.

In 1922 he married Mildred Beasley, the daughter of Bertha Johnson and Luther Addison Beasley, his well-known and highly respected law partner. They had one son, Henry Leonidas III.

While at the university in Chapel Hill, Stevens was a member of the Philanthropic Society, the YMCA, the Athletic Association, the Dramatic Association, and other organizations. (As national commander of the American Legion, he performed in a film and received an offer of a contract to make movies.) He was a brother of Kappa Sigma fraternity, served as chief commencement marshal during his junior year, and was the leader of the fall German Club dance during his senior year. In addition, he was a member of Phi Delta Phi legal fraternity, the Golden Fleece honor society at the university, the Junior order, the Masonic order, and the North Carolina Society of the Cincinnati.

Stevens was a ruling elder in the Warsaw Presbyterian Church and in 1948 served as president of The University of North Carolina's General Alumni Association. He was the first North Carolinian to appear on the cover of *Time* magazine. Stevens was buried in Devotional Gardens Cemetery, four miles east of Warsaw on North Carolina highways 24 and 50.

SEE: *American Legion Monthly*, February 1932; *Annuarie de la Noblesse de France et d'Europe*, vol. 89 (1960); Faison and Pearl McGowan, *Flashes of Duplin's History and Government* (1972); Robert V. Parker, "The Bonus March of 1932," *North Carolina Historical Review* 51 (Winter 1974); Henry L. Stevens, Jr., scrapbooks (microfilm, North Carolina State Archives, Raleigh); Mildred B. Stevens, personal contact; *Yackety Yack* (1913–17).

CHARLES M. INGRAM

Stevenson, (Little Gabriel) William *(1725–1809)*, the original ancestor of an American family that produced two vice-presidents of the United States and a nominee for the office of president, was born in Antrim County, province of Ulster, Ireland. His father, Robert, had migrated to Ireland from Scotland in the early 1700s. William's education consisted of a seven-year apprenticeship to a tailor, which prevented him from leaving for America with his widowed mother and siblings in the early 1740s. Once he had completed the apprenticeship, he joined the family in present Washington County, Pa., in 1748.

William had changed the spelling of the family name from Stephenson to Stevenson by about 1780. He was the ancestor of Vice-presidents Adlai Stevenson I (1892–96) and Alban Barkley (1948–52). Adlai Stevenson I was the grandfather of the late Adlai E. Stevenson II, who was the governor of Illinois, a Democratic nominee for the office of president of the United States (1952 and 1956), and later ambassador to the United Nations. Governor Stevenson was the father of Adlai E. Stevenson III, a U.S. senator from Illinois. There is reason to believe that William Stevenson's nephew, George Stephenson, was the Englishman, George Stephenson (1781–1848), who contributed much to the success of the steam locomotive. On a few occasions the American Stevensons claimed that George Stephenson was "some of our people."

William Stevenson married Mary McLelland, also a Scots-Irish immigrant, in the early 1750s, and moved from Pennsylvania to Rowan County in 1762. He received a grant of 369 acres from Earl Granville in present-day Iredell County. Best remembered in his community for being a devout Christian of the Presbyterian faith, he was among the first board of elders elected to the Fourth Creek Presbyterian Church (now the First Presbyterian Church of Statesville). In prayer he impressed others with his fervor and, like the Angel Gabriel, appeared to be speaking directly to God. This boldness accounts for his receiving the title of Little Gabriel, by which he was widely remembered. A great-grandson, Adlai E. Stevenson I, who visited Statesville one hundred years later (1876), declared in a letter to his mother that the expression "Little Gabriel" was well known because "they talk about 'Little Gabriel' as familiarly in Statesville as if they had seen him day before yesterday." Perhaps the most notable instance of his power of prayer came when he prayed that the "deaf and dumb" spirit would depart from his beloved paster, the Reverend Dr. James Hall, so that Hall could again be able to "hear the promises of the Word and preach the gospel to this dying people." Following Elder Stevenson's prayer, which "touched many hearts," Hall resumed his preaching.

In 1896 Stevenson was described as a man of "low stature" whose character exhibited a "quiet self assured manner." He spoke with a "soft, clear, far-carrying voice" according to great-grandson Andrew P. McCormick, who was then a district federal judge in Texas. McCormick said that his great-grandfather prospered in "his basket and store." Over the years Stevenson increased his landholdings to nearly 3,400 acres, which included part of the land on which the modern city of Statesville is located. He acquired slaves but apparently did not aspire to hold public office.

William and Mary Stevenson had twelve children, most of whom settled in Iredell County. They included Thomas, John, William, Mary, James, Joseph, Mary, Robert, Moses, Jane, Nancy, and Elizabeth. The two Marys died in infancy, and Thomas was killed in the Revolutionary War while a soldier in the Continental army. The third son, William, participated in the Battles of Cowan's Ford and Guilford Court House. Their fourth son, James, was the ancestor of the three descendants who later bore the name of Adlai Ewing Stevenson. The youngest daughter, Elizabeth, was the ancestor of Vice-President Alban Barkley.

William Stevenson died during the spring of 1809 and was buried in the Fourth Creek Burying Ground, Statesville.

SEE: Family letters, notes, and genealogical tables (possession of Miss Mabel Stevenson and Tom Stevenson, Stony Point, N.C.); Samuel Harris Stevenson and others, *A History and Genealogical Record of the Stevenson Family from 1748 to 1926* (1926).

LOUIS A. BROWN

Stevenson, William Francis *(23 Nov. 1861–12 Feb. 1942)*, lawyer and congressman, was born at Loray, the son of Elizabeth McFarlan and William Sidney Stevenson. He was graduated from Davidson College in 1885 and was awarded an LL.B. degree in 1921. In 1887 he was admitted to the bar in South Carolina. A South Carolina legislator from 1896 to 1902, he served as speaker of the house from 1900 to 1902. Stevenson was general counsel for the State Dispensary Commission as well as a member of the Chesterfield County Democratic committee (1888–1914), of which he was chairman from 1896 to 1902. Frequently referred to as "the most colorful figure in South Carolina politics," he acquired the nickname "Seaboard Bill" because for many years he was counsel for the Seaboard Air Line Railroad.

Elected to the U.S. House of Representatives from the Fifth District of South Carolina in 1916, Stevenson held the seat until 1932. He was appointed to the Federal Home Loan Bank Board in 1933 and served as chairman during the period 6 March–12 November 1933; he retired from the board in 1939.

Stevenson was an elder of the Presbyterian church. He was largely responsible for the publication of the second edition of a family genealogy in 1926. Although married three times, he had no children. He married first Mary Elizabeth Prince in 1888. Two years after her death in 1924, he married Clara Malloy Finney, who died in the early 1930s. On 24 June 1936 he married Ruth Culberson, who survived him. He was buried at Cheraw, S.C., where he had moved as a young man when he became head of the Cheraw Academy.

SEE: *Biog. Dir. Am. Cong.* (1989); Family letters, notes, and genealogical tables (possession of Miss Mabel Stevenson and Tom Stevenson, Stony Point, N.C.); J. C. Hemphill, *Men of Mark in South Carolina*, vol. 3 (1908); *Washington Evening Star*, 13 Feb. 1942; *Who Was Who in America* (1950).

LOUIS A. BROWN

Stewart, Alexander *(1723–71)*, Anglican clergyman, was born at Lisburn, County Antrim, Ireland, the son of Charles Stewart. He matriculated at the University of Dublin on 4 Oct. 1739 and was graduated with a B.A. degree in 1744. Soon afterwards he received an M.A. degree and entered the Anglican priesthood. There is no record of his activities in Ireland prior to his leaving for North Carolina.

He arrived in the colony in 1753 to serve as chaplain to his relative, Governor Arthur Dobbs, also a native of County Antrim. Stewart had expected to be assigned to Christ Church Parish, New Bern, but finding that post already occupied by the Reverend James Reed, he accepted the vacant parish of St. Thomas in the town of Bath, Beaufort County. He began his tenure on 1 Oct. 1753 and resided at Bath until his death. In 1754 he was appointed missionary from the Society for the Propagation of the Gospel in Foreign Parts to St. Thomas Parish with the salary of £50 a year. Stewart also held services in Hyde County and in Pitt after that county was formed from Beaufort in 1761. At one time he had thirteen chapels under his care in addition to the parish church of St. Thomas.

Stewart also was appointed agent and superintendent for North Carolina for the society called "Dr. Bray's Associates." This Church of England group, dedicated to the spiritual welfare and education of the Indians and Negroes in the colonies, had been organized in 1723 by the Reverend Thomas Bray, the same clergyman who in 1701 had founded the Society for the Propagation of the Gospel and had sent three libraries to North Carolina—one to St. Thomas Parish—as a part of the society's work. Stewart paid visits to the remnants of the "Attamuskeet," Hatteras, and Roanoke tribes in Hyde County and held services among them. In 1763 he established a school in the county for their benefit, undoubtedly with funds provided by the Bray group.

When Stewart arrived in Bath, the brick church, still standing, had been finished. A glebe of three hundred acres adjoining the town had been granted to the parish in 1706, but no dwelling had ever been built. Under his direction a glebe house and appropriate outbuildings were erected and finished by the spring of 1763, the first such glebe residence, as he wrote his superiors in London, that had ever been built in North Carolina.

During Stewart's ministry the Baptist faith began to spread in North Carolina. Concerned by his flock's "falling off from the Church," he attempted to counter this influence by baptizing by immersion himself on occasion and by writing a small pamphlet, *The Validity of Infant Baptism*, published by James Davis in New Bern in 1758. The only known copy of this work, by "A. Stewart, A.M. Minister of Beaufort County, North Carolina," is in the library of Harvard University.

Like many settlers who were not native to the climate, Stewart's health began to fail after ten years in the province. He spent much of the year 1766 on crutches and, when traveling to New Bern on business, had to be carried in a horse litter. He visited Portsmouth Island in the hope that bathing in the sea water would relieve his lameness. For that year, the vestry of St. Thomas refused to pay his salary because he had been unable to officiate. In 1767 he moved from the glebe house to a nearby plantation on Durham's Creek south of the Pamlico River, thinking that this location would be healthier. Later in the year he paid a short visit to England. Stewart died in the spring of 1771, leaving, as the Reverend James Reed informed the London authorities, a widow, four children, and his affairs in great confusion.

Despite the illness towards the end of his life, Stewart was more effective than the average Anglican clergyman in colonial North Carolina, although not on the level of his contemporary, the Reverend Clement Hall. Unlike most ministers, he had some means of his own; he began to acquire property in Beaufort County soon after his arrival and contributed £60 of his own funds to the construction of the glebe house in Bath. It is to Stewart's credit that two of his parishioners became clergymen. In 1769 he recommended his lay reader of twelve years, Peter Blinn, for holy orders. Blinn, who had represented Bath in the Assembly in 1767, was ordained in England, but there is no record that he ever officiated in North Carolina. Nathaniel Blount, a native of Beaufort County, was ordained two years after Stewart's death and thereafter, until his own death in 1816, ministered to the Episcopal church in what had been the colonial parish of St. Thomas.

Alexander Stewart is said to have married five times. His first wife and their sons, Alexander and Charles, died soon after arriving in Bath. In 1755 he married Elizabeth, the daughter of Benjamin Peyton and the widow of John Peyton Porter of The Garrison, Beaufort County. It is not known when she died. By 1763 Stewart had married Sarah Pilkington, the widow of Michael Coutanche. On the decease of Sarah he married Penelope Johnston Dawson, widow of John Dawson. The widow he left behind was a Miss Hobbs. The record of Stewart's children is unclear as no will has been found. In 1760 he spoke of two unnamed sons being educated in Ireland. By his second wife he had a daughter Rosa, who married John Kewell and went to England to live. A daughter of this marriage, Anna Maria Kewell, returned to Beaufort County, where she married John Gallegher of Washington and left descendants. The deeds and estate records of Beaufort and Pitt counties indicate that Stewart had four other children: Alexander, second of the name, James, William Samuel, and a daughter who married Jordan Shepherd of Pitt County and had three daughters.

SEE: George D. Burtchaeli and Thomas U. Sadleir, eds., *Alumni Dublinenses* (1935); Joseph B. Cheshire, "The Church of the Province of North Carolina," in *Sketches of Church History* (1892); Desmond Clarke, *Arthur Dobbs, Esquire, 1689–1765* (1957); Deeds of Beaufort and Pitt Counties (North Carolina State Archives, Raleigh); Marshall D. Haywood, *Lives of the Bishops of North Carolina* (1910); Herbert R. Paschal, Jr., *A History of Colonial Bath* (1955); C. Wingate Reed, *Beaufort County* (1962); Blackwell P. Robinson, ed., *The North Carolina Guide* (1955); William L. Saunders, ed., *Colonial Records of North Carolina*, vols. 5–9 (1887–90).

CLAIBORNE T. SMITH, JR.

Stewart, Alexander *(9 Dec. 1725–30 July 1772)*, public official and perhaps a poet, was born in Scotland but was clerk of court in Beaufort County, N.C., by 1751. He may have been the Stewart who represented one of the borough towns in the Assembly in 1746, although his given name and the town are not cited in the records. It was he, however, who represented Pitt County in 1771. In April 1758 Alexander Stewart, Robert Palmer, and Francis Corbin were surety for five hundred pounds that Palmer would faithfully execute the duties as receiver of powder and lead in the port of Bath. Stewart was witness to many wills and land grants in Pitt County beginning in 1761, the year after Pitt was formed from Beaufort. He himself had grants in 1768 for a total of 300 acres and an additional grant for 320 acres on 13 Mar. 1772, shortly before his death. The fact that he acquired land just four months before his death suggests that his death was unexpected.

Stewart's wife was named Elizabeth. Their daughter died in 1760 at the age of nine months, but a son, John, born in 1766, lived to the age of thirty-six. There may have been other children. They were all buried in the cemetery at Yankee Hall near Pactolus in Pitt County, but some of the markers are broken too badly to be read. Stewart's body was placed in a brick vault with a stone slab bearing the following inscription:

Here Lies Interred the Body of
COL. ALEXANDER STEWART
Born in Scotland ye 9th of December 1725
Died ye 30th of July 1772

1
Oh Have I Sat With Secret Sighs
To View my Flesh Decay
Then Groaned Aloud With Frightened Eyes
To See the Tottering Clay.

2
But I Forbid My Sorrows Now
Nor Dare the Flesh Complain.
Diseases Have their Pleasure Too
The Joy Overcomes the Pain.

3
My Cheerful Soul, Now all the day
Sits Wafting Here and Sings,
Looks Through the Ruins of Her Day
And Practices Her Wings.

4
Had But the Prison Walls Been Strong
And Been Without a Flaw
In Darkness She had Dwelt too Long
And Less of Glory Saw.

5
But How the Everlasting Hills
Thro' every Chink Appear
And Something of the Joy she Feels
While She's a Prisoner Here.

6
Oh May These Walls Stand Tottering Still
The Breaches Never Close
If I Must Here in Darkness Dwell
And All This Glory Lose.

7
Or Rather Let the Breach Decay
The Ruins Wider Grow
Till Glad to the Enlarged Way
I strock my Pinions Through.

Because attempts to trace the origin of these verses have been unsuccessful, it is believed that they may have been written by Stewart.

SEE: John L. Cheney, Jr., ed., *North Carolina Government, 1581–1979* (1981); John G. Duncan, *Pitt County Potpourri* (1966); Judith DuPree Ellison, comp., *Index and Abstracts of Deeds of Pitt County, North Carolina*, vol. 1, 1761–85 (1968); J. Bryan Grimes, ed., *Abstract of North Carolina Wills* (1910); J. R. B. Hathaway, ed., *North Carolina Historical and Genealogical Register*, vol. 1 (January 1900); Jeannette Cox St. Amand, comp., *Pitt County Gravestone Records*, vol. 3 (1960); William L. Saunders, ed., *Colonial Records of North Carolina*, vol. 5 (1887).

WILLIAM S. POWELL

Stewart, George Alton *(29 May 1897–25 Dec. 1929)*, pioneer aviator, was born in Buies Creek, Harnett County, the son of George Washington and Sally Jackson Stewart. He was educated in the schools of Buies Creek and at Coats High School. As an automobile mechanic in Coats, he became interested in the airplanes that flew over from Pope Field at Fort Bragg. When a military pilot made a forced landing in a cotton field near Stewart's shop, the young mechanic was able to make the repairs necessary to get the plane in the air again. Making friends with the pilot, he was invited to visit the airfield and there his interest in flying was encouraged. He bought an army surplus *Flying Jenny* in a crate and assembled it, and under the direction of his new friends at Pope Field he became an aviators' mechanic. Lieutenants Russell G. McDonald and Edmund P. Gaines, military pilots, taught him to fly.

On 17 May 1924, after just six hours of training, he flew solo; soon afterwards he acquired a wrecked plane that he repaired. Licensed in 1926, Alton Stewart was referred to in contemporary newspapers as the first North Carolinian to receive a civilian pilot's license. The Aviation Department of the Department of Commerce, created in 1924, licensed civilian aviators. Early records of licenses granted, however, were destroyed a number of years ago when they were deemed to have no further value, so the fact of his priority probably can never be officially established.

Stewart was instrumental in the creation in 1926 of the first flying field in Raleigh, where he moved the following year. He became the chief pilot of Carolina Airways, Inc., with headquarters in Raleigh, and also offered flying lessons. Because of his acclaimed record for skill and safety, he was frequently called upon to transport state officials on business. *News and Observer* reporter Ben Dixon McNeill engaged Stewart to fly him on assignments, and the newspaper printed McNeill's early aerial photographs taken from Stewart's plane. Stewart participated in air races and won numerous cups, citations, and other awards. He appeared at fairs around the state to take passengers on short flights and occasionally was engaged to fly businessmen on cross-country trips. Even before moving to Raleigh he began publishing *The Air News* as a supplement to the *Dunn Dispatch* to publicize civilian flying. The first plane known to have landed on Roanoke Island was piloted by Stewart, an accomplishment in which he took considerable pride. One of his passengers at that time had witnessed the Wright brothers' first flight. In 1928 Stewart assisted the Prudential Insurance Company of America with its investigation of aeronautical hazards for insurance purposes.

In 1916 he married Reva Mae Jones, and they became the parents of Luther Harold, Geraldine Gretchen, and David Wallace. At age thirty-two Stewart was killed in a plane crash at Dunn when flying with two passengers, one of whom was a student pilot. He was buried in the municipal cemetery at Coats.

SEE: *Dunn Dispatch*, 14 Mar. 1969; *Goldsboro News-Argus*, 16 June 1968; *Historical Raleigh* 1 (October 1968); Raleigh *News and Observer*, 6 June 1927, 9 Dec. 1928, 27 Dec. 1929, 18 May 1940, 17 June 1968; Stewart's log book and other papers (possession of his daughter, Mrs. H. C. Glenn III, Eufaula, Ala.).

WILLIAM S. POWELL

Stewart, George Marshall *(3 Oct. 1855–6 Nov. 1930)*, farmer, merchant, mill owner, banker, real estate developer, and a founder of Wingate College and of the town of Wingate, was born in New Salem Township, Union County, the son of Coleman and Jane Ross Stewart. His paternal and maternal ancestors were early settlers in the county, and his father served for four years in the Confederate army. With only limited formal education, the young man became a farmer but soon began to buy and sell real estate and developed an acumen for business.

In 1890 he moved to Ames Turnout and purchased a tract of land near the railroad from the Reverend A. C. Davis. Eager to develop a community, he urged his brother-in-law, William M. Perry, who possessed mechanical skills, to join with him in establishing milling and mercantile enterprises. Perry, who wished to provide educational opportunities for his nine children, originally had planned to move to Marshville, where an academy already existed, but he agreed to become Stewart's partner provided that they would build a school in the community. In 1895 the Union Baptist Association was searching for a site on which to construct a school. The association considered three sites but selected the one that was more centrally located, was situated near the railroad, and had two other advantages: Stewart offered to give ten acres of land with a spring on it, and Perry volunteered to saw the lumber for the school at his mill, without charge, from logs provided by people in the community. The school opened in the fall of 1896 and was named Wingate in honor of a former president of Wake Forest College. A town grew up around the school, as Stewart perhaps had envisioned, and in 1901 it was incorporated and its name was changed from Ames to Wingate.

Stewart and Perry operated a corn and flour mill, a lumber mill, a cotton gin, and a general merchandise store. In 1909, with others, they founded the State Bank of Wingate, which despite its limited resources survived the economic crash of 1929.

Stewart remained a staunch supporter of the Wingate school, contributing money as well as land. In 1898 he sold the institution an additional twenty-six acres for $208, and in 1918 he was instrumental in providing a new women's dormitory, which bears his name. He served on the board of trustees for many years and was chairman of the board at the time of his death.

A developer by nature and talent, Stewart owned stock in a bank in Mount Croghan, S.C., and in cotton mills in Monroe, as well as property in Lee County. In 1924, sensing greater opportunity in the burgeoning city of Charlotte, he sold most of his interests in Wingate and Union County and bought land for development on the outskirts of Charlotte. He died at his home in Charlotte after a brief illness and was buried in the Wingate cemetery.

In 1876 he married Mary Ellen Perry, the daughter of Jeremiah and Elizabeth Griffin Perry and the sister of his business partner, William Marion Perry. From 1896 to 1924 Stewart and Perry lived across from each other on Elm Street, which they had laid out when the school was built at the opposite end of the street. Stewart and his wife had no children but adopted Perry's youngest daughter, Martha, in 1888 after the death of her mother. Stewart was a member of Meadow Branch Baptist Church and a Democrat.

SEE: *Bransons North Carolina Business Directory* (1896); Hubert I. Hester, *The Wingate Story* (1972); *Monroe Inquirer*, 1 Feb. 1912; Perry family Bible, newspaper obituary, and other records (in possession of Percival Perry).

PERCIVAL PERRY

Stewart, James *(11 Nov. 1775–29 Dec. 1821)*, farmer, merchant, state legislator, and congressman, was born in Scotland, where he had a "liberal" education. Immigrating to the New World, he settled with other Scots near what came to be called the community of Stewartsville in Richmond (now Scotland) County. Stewart, who became a prominent farmer and merchant, served in the North Carolina House of Commons in the sessions of 1798 and 1799 and in the North Carolina Senate in 1802–4 and 1813–15. From 5 Jan. 1818 to 3 Mar. 1819, as a Democrat, he filled the vacancy in Congress left by the resignation of Alexander McMillan.

The census of 1820 indicated that he was engaged in "commerce" and that his household consisted of himself and four females aged ten, sixteen, twenty-six, and forty-five. His will, dated ten days before his death, left his home, farm, and other property to his wife, Margaret, during her lifetime and afterwards to his son, John. He also left his son twenty-five volumes of "British poets," his "congressional books," a silver watch, a number of slaves, and goods that appear to have been the stock in his store, as well as slaves to his wife during her lifetime. Nineteen slaves were mentioned by name. In addition to land in North Carolina, he bequeathed 1,000 acres in South Carolina and 160 acres in Illinois (which had been admitted to the Union only three years previously). He also mentioned his daughters—Ann McInnis, Margaret McQueen, Mary, and Penelope. He was buried in the Old Stewartsville Cemetery near Laurinburg.

SEE: *Biog. Dir. Am. Cong.* (1989); John L. Cheney, ed., *North Carolina Government, 1585–1979* (1981); Richmond

County Wills (North Carolina State Archives, Raleigh); *Who Was Who in America*, historical vol. (1967).

WILLIAM S. POWELL

Stewart, James Alexander *(13 Feb. 1910–11 July 1975)*, missionary, evangelist, and author, was born in Glasgow, Scotland, the third of six children. His parents were John and Agnes Jamieson Stewart, both of whom had moved from Northern Ireland to Scotland, where they met and married. Following his youthful conversion, he began preaching publicly at age fourteen and became an effective worker for the London Open-Air Mission in its evangelistic efforts along the border between England and Scotland.

After founding the Border Movement in 1928, he was fully engaged in the evangelism of the Scottish border and areas throughout England until 1933. In 1934 he began his evangelistic career on the continent of Europe, starting in Latvia, where he was associated with Pastor William Fetler (Basil Malof). Stewart carried his mission work to Poland and Estonia in 1935 and to Czechoslovakia in 1936–46. While working in Czechoslovakia he occasionally made missionary trips to Hungary during 1937–38. On one of his visits to Hungary, he married on 23 May 1938 Ruth Mahan, a Southern Baptist missionary, who from that time on became his faithful companion and colleague in his evangelistic efforts. Also in 1938 he visited the United States for the first time and organized the European Evangelistic Crusade, locating its American headquarters in Seattle, Wash.

From 1938 to 1947 the European Evangelistic Crusade sponsored an aggressive campaign throughout Poland, Austria, Greece, Hungary, Yugoslavia, Czechoslovakia, Finland, Estonia, Latvia, Carpatho-Ruthenia, and Germany. Again in 1939 his work in Czechoslovakia was interrupted by missionary activities in Poland and Ruthenia. In 1939–40 he made frequent trips to Yugoslavia, Hungary, Bulgaria, Rumania, and Bessarabia. Similar endeavors characterized the work of the European Evangelistic Crusade until almost the moment that World War II erupted.

In 1943 the European crusade moved its headquarters to Buffalo, N.Y., which served as Stewart's base of operations until the end of the war. In 1945 he bought the home in Asheville, N.C., which later became his headquarters and legal address. As soon as the war was over, he sought to return to postwar Europe, and in 1945–46 he was back in Czechoslovakia to complete ten years of ministry, which had had its longest interruption during the war. Stewart had the distinction of being the first preacher from the Free World to go behind the iron curtain. From 1945 to 1950 he organized relief work for the war-torn countries of Europe, and in 1947, when the work was most intense, he made additional missionary journeys to Norway, France, and Switzerland.

In July 1948 North Carolina became Stewart's official residence. In 1949–59 he launched a program of radio evangelism to Europe over Radio Luxembourg. Scandinavia beckoned in 1953, and from there he traveled to Norway and Denmark. In 1954, when the world evangelist became a U.S. citizen (19 May), he began an evangelistic outreach to his native Scotland. In 1958 he returned to the Scottish and English borders of his youth and organized a new program for the evangelization of that area. Years of missionary work had brought him into contact with many leaders of the Western world, and by the time he resigned from the European Evangelistic Crusade in December 1952, he had preached in Morocco, Israel, Mexico, the United States, and every country in Europe except Albania.

His last efforts were channeled through Gospel Projects, Inc., which he founded in 1957 as a vehicle for raising funds to support missionary projects worldwide and for distributing Christian literature to missionary workers and native pastors around the globe. Through the organization's publishing arm, called Revival Literature, numerous works, written or edited by Stewart, were offered for sale in the United States and distributed free to missions. Stewart directed Gospel Projects until his death. Also in 1957 Stewart took over the work of the Russian Bible Society—at the request of its founder, Basil Malof—and became international president. While performing these duties, Stewart briefly served as pastor of a Baptist church in Spartanburg, S.C.

Stewart, who devoted most of his later years to writing, was the author of more than fifty books and pamphlets, edited the works of several older Christian authors, and saw many of his publications translated into several foreign languages. His first book, *The Phenomena of Pentecost*, was written in Swansboro in 1960. Among his most widely read volumes were *Evangelism Without Apology*, *Heaven's Throne Gift*, *I Must Tell*, and *Come, O Breath*. In addition, he wrote biographies of William Chalmers Burns, Robert Murray M'Cheyne, Charles Haddon Spurgeon, and Basil Malof.

In June 1960 Bob Jones University awarded him an honorary doctor of divinity degree. From 1970 to 1975 Stewart was plagued by ill health; he died at his home in Asheville. He was the father of three children: Sheila, James, and Sharon.

SEE: *Asheville Citizen*, 12 July 1975; James A. Stewart, *I Must Tell* (no date); Ruth Stewart, *James Stewart: Missionary* (1977).

TUCKER REED LITTLETON

Stick, Frank Leonard *(10 Feb. 1884–12 Nov. 1966)*, artist, author, conservationist, and developer, was born in Huron, S.Dak., the son of David L., a banker and merchant, and Lydia Jane Marcellus Stick. He attended public schools in Huron and later in Oglesby, Ill., where the family moved in 1899, and as a teenager he was expected to do his share of the work in the family store. But young Stick was much more interested in the outdoors than in the confinement of the mercantile business and spent as much of his time as possible hunting, fishing, and camping. Always a keen observer of detail in the things he saw around him, and inquisitive by nature, he began making sketches of the animals and birds he saw in the woods around Oglesby, thus demonstrating at an early age an exceptional natural talent for painting.

Encouraged by his parents in his pursuit of a career as an artist, he moved to Chicago in his late teens in order to secure some basic instruction in painting and sold his first illustration to *Sports Afield* magazine when he was nineteen. Later he received a coveted invitation to study in Wilmington, Del., under the famed illustrator Howard Pyle, sharing one of Pyle's studios with N. C. Wyeth. During this period he developed specialized techniques in the field of outdoor illustration, and for the next quarter of a century his paintings appeared regularly in the *Saturday Evening Post*, *Ladies Home Journal*, *Country Gentleman*, *St. Nicholas*, *Field and Stream*, and other periodicals, including numerous covers for *Outdoor Life*. In addition, he painted many calendars, almost invariably scenes of hunting, fishing, and canoeing. Many people knew him best for his paintings of dogs, and over a period of more than a decade he produced dozens of illustrations for the popular short stories of Albert Payson Terhune.

Stick was both an avid conservationist and a hunter, and an irony of his attitudes and of his artwork was that at the same time as he was illustrating shooting scenes for the calendars of major manufacturers of arms and ammunition, he was also turning out widely used paintings, without pay, for the Anti-Vivisection League of America.

He wrote numerous articles on the outdoors for national magazines, served for a brief time as editor of *Field and Stream*, and was coauthor, with Van Campen Heilner, of an early book on surf fishing, *The Call of the Surf*, which he also illustrated. With other Howard Pyle students he established an informal artists' colony in Interlaken, on the New Jersey coast. Stick was elected the first mayor of the borough of Interlaken in 1922.

An avid fisherman, he was a close friend and frequent fishing companion of Zayne Grey and illustrated some of Grey's books. One of their trips together in the mid-1920s was to the Outer Banks of North Carolina in quest of channel bass, and Stick was so impressed with the area that he began acquiring extensive Outer Banks property holdings. In 1929, having tired of producing a steady flow of illustrations-on-order for magazine and calendar publication, he moved his family to Skyco, on Roanoke Island, put aside his brushes and paints, and for fifteen years concentrated on making a living from house construction, real estate, and other activities entirely unrelated to his profession as an artist. At the same time he worked for the orderly development of the Outer Banks as well as the preservation of its natural resources.

In 1933 Stick conceived and for nearly two decades promoted the establishment of a national park on the Outer Banks, and as secretary of the Cape Hatteras National Seashore Commission he secured donations of extensive landholdings that formed the nucleus for the nation's first national seashore recreational area. An integral part of his plan for a national seashore park on the coast was the stabilization of the fragile sandbanks, and towards this end he designed and supervised the construction and installation of the first sand fences erected on the barren beach and the planting of beach grasses and other vegetation. By the late 1930s more than 4,000 men, including members of the Civilian Conservation Corps, transient laborers, and local WPA work forces were engaged in this work along the Outer Banks.

In the early 1940s his interest again turned to art. Having worked previously only in oils, he began experimenting with other mediums, including sculpture and watercolors. A self-trained ichthyologist, he was called on frequently by local commercial fishermen to identify unusual species, and he began making watercolor sketches of these as he identified them. This led to a major project, which occupied much of his time for more than a decade, in which he planned to produce a series of accurate and lifelike watercolors of East Coast fish. When the work was completed in the mid-1950s, he had produced paintings of nearly three hundred fish, but his plan to put these in book form during his lifetime did not materialize.

In 1947 he began the development of the community of Southern Shores near Kitty Hawk, dividing his work load between real estate and construction activities and painting in his studio there. During the winter months he headed south, spending considerable time on the Florida Keys, on the Isle of Pines, and in the Virgin Islands. In the 1950s Stick was instrumental in the establishment of the Virgin Islands National Park.

During the last ten years of his life he worked extensively in watercolor. More than seventy-five of these paintings, mostly seascapes, are preserved at the Outer Banks History Center in Manteo, along with approximately fifty line illustrations that appeared in two books written by his son, *Graveyard of the Atlantic* and *The Outer Banks of North Carolina*.

In 1908 Stick married Ada Maud Hayes, of Wilmington, Del., an artists' model. They had two children, Charlotte Stick McMullan (1909–69) and David.

SEE: *The Art of Frank Stick* (1974); Marion Brown, "The Stick Team," *The State* magazine, 4 Oct. 1952; Manteo, *Coastland Times*, 18 Nov. 1966; Raleigh *News and Observer*, 13 Nov. 1966.

DAVID STICK

Stirewalt, Jacob *(17 Aug. 1805–21 Aug. 1869)*, Lutheran clergyman, was born near Salisbury, the second son and third and youngest child of John and Mary Elizabeth Rendleman Stirewalt. He was the grandson of Joannes Stirewalt, who emigrated from Germany in 1749 and built the pipe organ from which Organ (Zion) Church, Rowan County, gained its name. His father was a prosperous Rowan County farmer and a prominent member of Organ Church, where the infant Jacob was baptized on 3 Nov. 1805. Carefully reared and educated by his Lutheran parents, he "acquired that firmness of Christian character and those habits of persevering and systematic labor which marked his entire life." As a young man he tried his hand at farming and also taught school, but influenced by various members of the Henkel family, he resolved to enter the ministry and was licensed to preach by the Evangelical Lutheran Tennessee Synod in 1837. He preached his first sermon in Mount Calvary Church, Page County, Va., and was ordained by the Tennessee Synod in Salem Church, Lincoln County, N.C., in 1838.

From the day of his ordination, Stirewalt played an active role in synod affairs. He often preached at synod convocations and was elected treasurer of the synod in 1853 and reelected in 1859. At the same session at which he was ordained, Stirewalt, Ambrose Henkel, and Jacob Killian were asked to prepare a "Liturgy" for use in the churches. The synod approved their work at the session of 1839 and published the Liturgy in 1840. In 1848 the synod directed Stirewalt and several others to respond to certain "erroneous statements in regard to our body" that were made by Dr. Ernst L. Hazelius in his *History of the American Lutheran Church*. The committee asked the editors of the *Lutheran Standard* and the *Lutheran Observer* to publish corrections of these "errors." Five years later Stirewalt and others urged the synod to decline an invitation to unite with the General Synod of the Evangelical Lutheran Church of the United States which had been extended by the Pennsylvania Synod. An orthodox or confessional Lutheran, Stirewalt disapproved of the "American" Lutheranism of the General Synod. His colleagues shared his view and officially rejected the offer on the grounds that "under existing circumstances" such a union was not possible.

In the course of his ministry Stirewalt served many churches, chiefly in Page, Rockingham, and Shenandoah counties, Va., including Mount Calvary Church, Page County (1837–60); Rader's Church and Timberline Parish, Rockingham County (1837–39 and 1858–69); Soloman's Church, Forestville, Shenandoah County (1845–69); and St. Paul's, Jerome (Orkney Springs Parish), Shenandoah County (1837–67). "In the 32 years of his ministry," his obituary recounts, "he preached 3132 sermons, of which 560 were funeral discourses; he confirmed 708 persons, and baptized 1259, and united in marriage 171 couples." A biographer described him as "energetic by nature, of a nervous temperament, and zealous in the advancement of everything in which he was interested." In addition to the Liturgy, Stirewalt translated Luther's "Large Catechism" for the first English edition of the *Christian Book of Concord; or, Symbolical Books of the Evangelical Lutheran Church* (1851, rev. ed., 1854) and was the author of *Grades in the Ministry*, published posthumously in 1881. Both works were printed by the Henkel family press at New Market, Shenandoah County, Va.

Stirewalt married Henrietta Henkel at New Market, Va., on 8 Jan. 1833. They had six sons and four daughters. Seven children survived their father, and two sons, John Nathaniel and Jerome Paul, became Lutheran ministers. Stirewalt died at his home in New Market at the age of sixty-four years and four days and was buried at Emmanuel Church, New Market. An engraving of him appears in J. C. Jensson's *American Lutheran Biographies*, and an illustration of the home in which he was reared can be found in T. T. Waterman's *The Early Architecture of North Carolina*.

SEE: Charles L. Coon Papers (Manuscript Department, Duke University Library, Durham); William E. Eisenberg, *The Lutheran Church in Virginia, 1717–1962* (1967); Evangelical Lutheran Tennessee Synod, *Minutes* (1837–69); Socrates Henkel, *History of the Evangelical Lutheran Tennessee Synod* (1890); J. C. Jensson, *American Lutheran Biographies* (1890); *Life Sketches of Lutheran Ministers: North Carolina and Tennessee Synods, 1773–1965* (1966); Ronald W. Miller, letters to Gary G. Roth; Jacob L. Morgan and others, eds., *History of the Lutheran Church in North Carolina* (1953); M. L. Stirewalt, "Memorandum Books of 100 Years Ago Record Interesting Facts About Trips from Here to Virginia," *Salisbury Evening Post*, 24 June 1934.

GARY G. ROTH

Stockard, Henry Jerome *(15 Sept. 1858–5 Sept. 1914)*, poet and educator, was born in Chatham County. His ancestors emigrated from Scotland to Pennsylvania and moved to Chatham County between 1750 and 1760. His grandfather, John Stockard, was a captain in the War of 1812 and represented Chatham County in the North Carolina legislature sixteen times. Young Stockard was the son of James Gibbs, a farmer and lumberman, and Mary Johnson Stockard. After the Civil War the family moved to Alamance County, where John Stockard died in 1870, leaving his wife with ten sons. Henry Jerome, the ninth son, was twelve at the time. He always gave credit to his mother for what he was able to achieve.

Stockard attended Graham High School and took special courses at The University of North Carolina, where he was encouraged and influenced by Dr. Thomas Hume. After receiving an A.M. degree from Elon College in 1889, he taught in Alamance County before becoming the principal of Graham High School and then the superintendent of Alamance County Schools. In 1892–93 he returned to the university as assistant professor of English. From Chapel Hill he went to Fredericksburg, Va., where he taught English and political science at Fredericksburg College. In 1900 he moved back to North Carolina to teach Latin at Peace Institute in Raleigh, then served as president of Peace from 1907 to 1912. Preferring the classroom to administrative duties, Stockard resumed his position as professor of Latin until his death two years later. In 1914 Wake Forest awarded him an Litt.D. degree in recognition of his literary work.

In 1886 Stockard won a poetry contest sponsored by the *North Carolina Teacher*, and from this beginning he went on to acquire fame for his poetry, especially his sonnets. He became the unofficial poet laureat of North Carolina, and his work was published in such national magazines as *Harper's*, *Scribner's*, *Century*, *Atlantic Monthly*, and *Youth's Companion*. His poems also appear in *Library of Southern Literature* (vol. 11), *Songs of the South*, Edmund C. Stedman's *American Anthology*, and Richard Walser's *North Carolina Poetry*. Stockard himself published two volumes: *Fugitive Lines* (1897) and *A Study of Southern Poetry* (1911), an anthology used as a text. In 1939, twenty-five years after his death, another volume, *Poems*, was published. He was often called on to write poems for special memorial occasions. These included "The Last Charge at Appomattox," written for the unveiling of the North Carolina monument at Appomattox, and "Stanzas," for the unveiling of the monument to the women of the Confederacy on Capitol Square in Raleigh.

In 1878 Stockard married Sallie Holleman, of Morrisville. Before her death in 1888, they had four children: Lelia, Leon, Albert, and Elsie. In 1890 he married Margaret Lula Tate, of Graham, who died in 1936. Stockard and his second wife had six children: Amelia, Henry Jerome, Lula, James, Armstrong, and Hubert.

Stockard was a Democrat, an elder in the Presbyterian church, and one of the founders of the North Carolina Literary and Historical Association. He died at his home in Raleigh and was buried in Oakwood Cemetery. A portrait of him—a gift of the Stockard family—is at Peace College.

SEE: Samuel A. Ashe, ed., *Biographical History of North Carolina*, vol. 5 (1905); R. D. W. Connor, *North Carolina: Rebuilding an Ancient Commonwealth*, vol. 2 (1929); *North Carolina Literary and Historical Association Proceedings* (1914); *North Carolina Poetry Review* 2 (May–June 1935); *North Carolina Teacher* 7 (February 1890); *State Normal Magazine* 15 (January 1911); *Trinity Archive* 9 (March 1896).

MARY BATES SHERWOOD

Stockard, Sallie Walker *(4 Oct. 1869–6 Aug. 1963)*, teacher, author, and the first woman to receive a degree from The University of North Carolina, was born near Saxapahaw, Alamance County, the daughter of John Williamson and Margaret Ann Albright Stockard. In 1897 the university trustees passed an ordinance admitting women to postgraduate courses. Already a graduate of Guilford College, Sallie Stockard enrolled and received an undergraduate degree in 1898 and a master's degree in 1900. Her graduate thesis, a history of Alamance County, was published in the latter year. Her graduate diploma is now in the North Carolina Collection at the university.

She continued her education at Clark University in 1902–3 and afterwards at the University of Texas, at the University of Oklahoma, and finally, in 1923–24, at Teachers College of Columbia University, from which she received a second master's degree. She taught at schools in Texas, New Mexico, and Oklahoma.

In 1900 she published *The Lily of the Valley*, described as a dramatic arrangement of the Song of Solomon. County history seems to have been of particular interest to her, and in addition to the history of her native county published in 1900, her *History of Guilford County* appeared in 1902. After moving to Arkansas, she published *The History of Lawrence, Jackson, Independence, and Stone Counties of the Third Judicial District of Arkansas* in 1904.

She married P. Magness, and they were the parents of a son, Scott A., and a daughter who became Mrs. Wendell Kilmer. She lived in Orlando, Fla., for a time but then moved to West Hempstead, N.Y., to live with her daughter. An Episcopalian, she died in a nursing home on Long Island, N.Y.

SEE: Kemp P. Battle, *History of the University of North Carolina*, vol. 2 (1912); Daniel L. Grant, *Alumni History of the University of North Carolina* (1924); *Library of Southern Literature*, vol. 15 (1910); *New York Times*, 8 Aug. 1963; Sallie W. Stockard, *Lily of the Valley*, (1901 [portrait]); *University of North Carolina Alumni Review* 52 (January 1964).

WILLIAM S. POWELL

Stockton, Richard Gordon *(12 Feb. 1892–12 Dec. 1960)*, lawyer and bank executive, was born in Winston-Salem, the son of Madison Doughty and Martha Vaughn Stockton. He was graduated from Winston-Salem High School in 1907 and received a bachelor of arts degree from The University of North Carolina in 1911. After studying law at Columbia University for one year, he was admitted to the Forsyth County Bar in 1913. Stockton practiced law from 1913 to 1922 and taught at The University of North Carolina during the summers of 1914, 1915, and 1916.

When President Woodrow Wilson ran for a second term in 1916, Stockton served as chairman of the Forsyth County Democratic Committee. He enlisted as a private in the U.S. Army on 13 June 1917 and was discharged as a first lieutenant on 4 Apr. 1919 after serving in the Judge Advocate General's Office.

Stockton began his banking career in 1922, when he was appointed assistant trust officer and secretary of the Wachovia Bank and Trust Company in Winston-Salem. He became vice-president and associate trust officer in 1930, trust officer in 1936, vice-president and senior trust officer in 1941, director in 1942 (a position he held until his death), senior vice-president and senior trust officer in 1946, acting president in 1949, and chairman of the board in 1951. He was chairman of the executive committee from 1956 until his retirement in 1958)

He served as a trustee of the Greensboro College for Women; president of the Methodist Children's Home, Inc., from 1941 until his death; and president of the North Carolina Foundation of Church-Related Colleges from 1956 to 1960, when he became chairman of the foundation's advisory board. During 1953 he was state treasurer of the Crusade for Freedom and president of the Carolinas United Red Feather Services.

Stockton was also state chairman of the Boys' Clubs of America, president of the YMCA, chairman of the board of trustees and managers of the Forsyth County Tuberculosis Hospital, president of the North Carolina Citizens Association, and board chairman for the Foundation for Education in Economics of the American Bankers Association. During World War II he served on the home front as general chairman of the United War Chest Campaign (1943) and chairman of the Red Cross Fund Campaign (1944). After the war he was chairman of the advisory board of the Salvation Army and served on the State Education Commission. He was a member of the Winston-Salem Chamber of Commerce (president, 1920–22), the American Bankers Association (president, Trust Division), the American Bar Association, the North Carolina Bar Association, Beta Theta Pi, and Knights Templar.

Over the years Stockton was active in the Democratic party as well as in the Winston-Salem Rotary Club, the Kiwanis Club, the Forsyth Country Club, the Twin City Club, and the Old Town Club. A member of the Centenary Methodist Church, he served as chairman of the board of stewards.

He married Hortense Haughton Jones of Asheville on 13 Oct. 1917, and they had two daughters, Sarah Elizabeth Stockton Hill and Jean Stockton Rhodes. Stockton died at age sixty-eight and was buried in Salem Cemetery, Winston-Salem. A portrait is available at the *Winston-Salem Journal-Sentinel*.

SEE: *Who's Who in America* (1962–63); *Who's Who in Commerce and Industry*, 10th international ed. (1957); *Who's Who in the South* (1927); *Who's Who in the South and Southwest* (1950–52); *Winston-Salem Journal*, 12 Jan. 1958, 15 Sept. 1960; *Winston-Salem Sentinel*, 19 Mar. 1941, 12 Jan. 1958, 12–13 Dec. 1960.

SHELDA M. WILLS

Stoga, John Astooga *(d. 15 Sept. 1862)*, popular Cherokee leader from that part of Jackson County in southwestern North Carolina that became Swain County in 1871, was the grandson of Junaluska. His name was said to mean "standing in the doorway," suggesting that he was regarded as a door or shelter. The name also has appeared as Astoogatogeh and without the given name, John. As a Christian, Stoga was instrumental in persuading the American Bible Society to translate the New Testament into the Cherokee language. It was published in 1857.

On 9 Apr. 1862 he was commissioned second lieutenant in Company A of Captain William H. Thomas's legion of Cherokee troops, the Sixty-ninth Regiment of North Carolina Troops (also designated as the Seventh Regiment of Cavalry). In the late summer of 1862 several companies of the regiment were ordered to Powell's Valley between Jacksboro and Cumberland Gap in East Tennessee, where Federal activity threatened to cut Confederate lines of communication. At Baptist Gap, Lieutenant Stoga, described as "a splendid specimen of Indian manhood and warrior," led his men in an attack on a Federal position, but he was fatally shot. A contemporary reported that the lieutenant's men were "furious at his death and before they could be restrained, they scalped several of the Federal wounded and dead." The arrival of reinforcements, however, brought victory for the Cherokee warriors.

SEE: Walter Clark, ed., *Histories of the Several Regiments and Battalions from North Carolina*, vol. 3 (1901); Vernon H. Crow, *Storm in the Mountains* (1982); James Mooney, *Myths of the Cherokee* (1902); John Wheeler Moore, comp., *North Carolina Troops in the War between the States*, vol. 4 (1882); *National Union Catalog*, vol. 55 (1980); P. Marion Simms, *The Bible in America* (1936).

WILLIAM S. POWELL

Stokes, John *(20 Mar. 1756–12 Oct. 1790)*, Revolutionary patriot, surveyor, lawyer, and first federal district judge appointed for North Carolina, was the son of David and Sarah Montfort Stokes. Born in Lunenburg County, Va., located about thirty miles southwest of Petersburg, he spent his early years in Virginia and perhaps in Halifax, N.C., the home of his mother's family.

At the outbreak of the Revolutionary War Stokes was commissioned an ensign in the Sixth Virginia Continental Regiment on 16 Feb. 1776. In the same year he was promoted to second lieutenant (July) and then to first lieutenant (18 December). On 20 Feb. 1778 he rose to the rank of captain. His active military career came to an end on 29 May 1780 in The Waxhaws on the border between North Carolina and South Carolina. Here, under the command of Colonel Abraham Buford, the American forces were cut to pieces, and Captain Stokes was severely wounded in many places; his hand was completely severed by a British saber. One biographer of Andrew Jackson states that Jackson's mother nursed Stokes and other wounded Americans after the battle. On 29 May 1780—the day of that engagement—Stokes was appointed a captain in the First Rowan Artillery, but there is no record of his participation in any further battles.

After the war Stokes settled in Halifax County, where his brother Montfort, his sister, Mrs. Benjamin McCulloch, and his first cousins, Mrs. Willie Jones and Mrs. Benjamin Ashe, also lived. It was in Halifax that Stokes probably received his law license, for on 4 May 1784 he presented to the Rowan County court his license to practice as an attorney. The same day the Rowan court appointed him to act as attorney for the state during that term of court in place of Spruce Macay, who was ill. Although he owned no property in Rowan County, Stokes remained there during the years 1784 and 1785, when he taught law to his brother, Montfort, and to the young Andrew Jackson. Spruce Macay, who had taken Jackson under his wing in 1784, advised him to read under Stokes, whose law library "exceeded any other in that region."

In 1786 Stokes moved to Montgomery County, which he represented as a state senator in 1786–87. During 1786 his name was not carried in the Rowan court minutes, but in August 1787 he again appears in the records taking an active part in the legal and military affairs of Rowan County. Also in 1787 the state appointed him lieutenant colonel of the Salisbury District.

On 8 May 1788 Stokes married Elizabeth (Betsy) Pearson, the daughter of Richmond Pearson, and in November of that year Pearson gave Stokes 698 acres of land in the Forks of the Yadkin River on Anthony's Creek. Soon afterwards Stokes built his home near present Cooleemee, Davie County.

In 1789 he was named one of the original trustees of The University of North Carolina and was elected, together with Matthew Locke, a representative in the House of Commons. Also that year he was elected a delegate to the constitutional convention at Fayetteville as a Federalist. Because of his loyalty to the Federalist cause, he was named by President George Washington on 3 Aug. 1790 as the first federal judge for the district of North Carolina, William R. Davie having declined the appointment. After holding his first court in New Bern, Stokes died of "pleurisy of the brain" in Fayetteville on his return trip home. He was buried there with Masonic honors. He was the father of one child, Richmond Pearson. His father-in-law was named administrator of his estate under bond of 2,000 pounds, which suggests the extent of Stokes's wealth. Stokes County, created in 1789, was named in his honor.

SEE: Samuel A. Ashe, ed., *Biographical History of North Carolina*, vol. 7 (1908); John L. Cheney, Jr., ed., *North Carolina Government, 1585–1974* (1975); Walter Clark, ed., *State Records of North Carolina*, vols. 16, 18 (1899, 1901); William O. Foster, "The Career of Montfort Stokes in North Carolina," *North Carolina Historical Review* 26 (1939); Thomas Felix Hickerson, *Happy Valley* (1940); Don Higginbotham, ed., *The Papers of James Iredell*, vol. 2 (1976); Alice B. Keith, ed., *The John Gray Blount Papers*, vol. 2 (1959); Blackwell P. Robinson, *William R. Davie* (1957); Rowan County Court Minutes, Deeds, and Marriage Bonds (Courthouse, Salisbury); Jethro Rumple, *History of Rowan County* (1929); Salisbury, *Western Carolinian*, 19 Dec. 1826.

JAMES S. BRAWLEY

Stokes, Montfort *(12 Mar. 1762–4 Nov. 1842)*, Revolutionary veteran, U.S. senator, governor, and Indian commissioner, was born in Lunenburg County, Va., the eleventh child of David and Sarah Montfort Stokes of Halifax County, N.C. At an early age Montfort Stokes went to sea. When the Revolution began, he enlisted in the Continental navy, was soon captured by the British, and remained a prisoner in New York for some time.

After the war Stokes settled in Salisbury, where he read law under the direction of an older brother, John. From 1786 to 1790 Montfort was assistant clerk of the state senate. In 1790 he became clerk of the senate, a position he held for eighteen years. The Assembly offered him a seat in the U.S. Senate in 1804, but he declined the post for family reasons. In 1804 and 1812 he was a presidential elector, and from 1805 to 1838 he was a trustee of The University of North Carolina. The Assembly also gave him a commission as major general of state militia in 1804, and he held this rank at the beginning of the War of 1812. During this period Stokes was active in Masonic affairs, serving as deputy grand master for North Carolina from 1802 to 1807. He was a member of the North Carolina–South Carolina boundary commission in 1807.

When James Turner resigned from the U.S. Senate in November 1816, the Assembly appointed Stokes to complete Turner's term and then reappointed him for a full term. Serving from December 1816 to March 1823, he sat on the District of Columbia and Militia committees and was chairman of the Post Office and Post Roads committee. At first identified with the Crawford faction in Washington, he supported John C. Calhoun for a while and then became an ardent Jackson partisan. He broke with Senator Nathaniel Macon over the Missouri Compromise, and in 1820 he wrote Governor John Branch that he would join any constitutional movement to abolish slavery. In 1823 the Assembly replaced Stokes with Branch in Washington.

Returning to North Carolina, Stokes continued to be active in politics. He was chairman of a reform convention in Raleigh in 1823 and a Jackson presidential elector in 1824 and 1828. In 1824 he was nominated for governor in the Assembly but was defeated by Hutchins G. Burton. From Wilkes County he was elected to the state senate in 1826 and to the House of Commons in 1829 and 1830. In 1828 he was nominated again for the U.S. Senate and for governor but was not selected. His name was also placed in nomination for the U.S. Senate seat in 1829 and 1830 without success. In the latter year he was president of the board of visitors of the U.S. Military Academy at West Point.

Stokes was finally elected governor in December 1830. As candidate of the western forces in the Assembly, he defeated Richard Dobbs Spaight, Jr., by a vote of 98–83. The Spaight forces failed to block his reelection in 1831, and he served as chief executive of North Carolina until 6 Dec. 1832. His administration is remembered because of the burning of the state capitol, the repercussions to the Nat Turner Revolt in Virginia, the breakup in Andrew Jackson's cabinet, Jackson's Indian policy, the Nullification controversy, and the growing tensions between the eastern and western sections of the state over constitutional reform.

President Jackson appointed Stokes a commissioner of Indian affairs in 1832, and Stokes resigned the governorship to accept Jackson's offer. By February 1833 the former governor had established himself at Fort Gibson in Indian Territory. In 1837 he was agent to the Cherokees, but in 1841 John Tyler and the Whigs refused to renew that commission and Stokes became a subagent to the

Seneca, Shawnee, and Quapaws. He died and was buried at Fort Gibson in modern Oklahoma.

Stokes by blood, marriage, and friendship was connected with many prominent persons. His brother John, for whom Stokes County was named, was a Revolutionary hero who became North Carolina's first federal judge. Montfort's only daughter by his first wife married William B. Lewis, Jackson's lieutenant in Tennessee. Willie Jones and James Wellborn, both powerful political figures in North Carolina, were connected to Stokes by marriage. Stokes was an inveterate politician, but his love of gambling and his dangerous temper frequently got him into trouble. He was once wounded in a duel with Jesse A. Pearson of Rowan.

Stokes was married twice. His first wife was Mary, the daughter of Henry Irwin. His second marriage was to Rachel, the daughter of Hugh Montgomery. Rachel inherited property in Wilkes County, and the Stokes family moved to Wilkesboro about 1810. There were five sons and five daughters by the second marriage. One son, Montfort Sidney Stokes, fought in the War with Mexico and died defending the Confederacy in the Civil War. The homesite at Wilkesboro is indicated by a North Carolina historical marker.

SEE: *Biog. Dir. Am. Cong.* (1971); *DAB*, vol. 18 (1936); W. O. Foster, "The Career of Montfort Stokes in North Carolina," *North Carolina Historical Review* 16 (July 1939); Little Rock, *Arkansas State Gazette*, 7 Dec. 1842.

DANIEL M. MCFARLAND

Stokes, Montfort Sidney *(6 Oct. 1810–8 July 1862)*, military officer, was born at Morne Rouge, the Wilkes County home of his parents, Montfort and Rachel Montgomery Stokes. He was a grandson of Hugh Montgomery, who served under royal governor William Tryon in suppressing the Regulators. The elder Montfort Stokes was a major general in the War of 1812, governor of North Carolina (1830–32), and a U.S. senator. Sid, as the younger Stokes was called, was appointed a midshipman on 12 May 1829 and received his initial training at the Navy Yard in Norfolk and at the Norfolk School. During his training he also served on the frigate *Brandywine*, initially in the Mediterranean. On 15 Sept. 1835 it was noted in his record that he was "warranted as passed midshipman" from 3 July. At various times from 1834 to 1836 he was reported on leave of absence, usually in three-month spans but once for six months, although no reason was given.

In 1837 Stokes was awaiting orders for active service. From St. Petersburg, Russia, on 10 Aug. 1837 he wrote a long letter to his childhood friend, James Gwyn, recounting some of his naval experiences. He had recently been in England and Denmark and described in considerable detail his impressions of Russia. He also reported a recent visit by the Russian emperor to his ship. Czar Nicholas I, who spoke excellent English, was disguised as an ordinary sailor, as he wanted to see the American ship and not be given a royal reception. His disguise, however, was quickly discovered but not revealed to the guest until his tour of the ship was over. Thereupon he was most properly welcomed aboard.

On 20 Mar. 1837 Stokes received orders for service on the razee *Independence* off the coast of Brazil, but on 6 Apr. 1838 he was granted permission to return to the United States at his own expense. On 7 Dec. 1838 he was reported "Destined for the West Indies" for service on the frigate *Macedonian*. Writing from Raleigh on 24 December, however, he "reluctantly" asked for a twelve-month furlough. The request was denied, and he resigned effective 6 Feb. 1839.

After resigning from the Navy, he returned to Wilkes County and engaged in farming. On 10 Apr. 1847 the First Regiment of North Carolina Foot Volunteers was called into federal service at the beginning of the War with Mexico, and Stokes was commissioned major of the regiment. He served in Mexico, where he was highly regarded by his men not only for his excellent leadership but also for his consideration of them under adverse conditions; after the war they had a handsome sword made for him and engraved: "Presented to Major M. S. Stokes, of the N.C. Vol. by the non-commissioned officers and privates under his command in Mexico" and "Major M. S. Stokes, the Soldier's Friend." The sword is now in the North Carolina Museum of History in Raleigh.

After the war he settled in Wilkes County, where he raised cattle that he drove to market in Philadelphia. The General Assembly named him to the Council of State for the years 1850–51. Stokes was a friend of President Franklin Pierce and visited him in the White House. He also was an interesting lecturer and often visited community schools to talk with young people about his wide-ranging experiences.

At the beginning of the Civil War, Stokes volunteered for service with the Wilkes Valley Guards and was chosen first lieutenant. His unit, sent to Warrenton for its initial training, was designated Company B, First Regiment. A soldier from Mississippi, who was already at the camp when the North Carolina troops arrived, commented that Stokes was "a splendid officer, well prepared to drill in regimental or brigade maneuvers." With the formal organization of the regiment, Stokes was appointed colonel on 15 May 1861. His earliest active service was in Virginia until he was called back to help defend Goldsboro. After returning to Virginia and participating in action there, he was severely wounded in an engagement at Elyson's Mill on 26 June 1862. When offered something for the pain, Stokes declined and directed that it be given to wounded soldiers instead. Eleven days later he died in a Richmond hospital. His body was taken home by his body servant, Isaiah, and buried in the family cemetery in front of his home on the banks of the Yadkin River.

In 1858 Stokes married Sarah E. (Sallie) Triplett of Wilkes County. They were the parents of a son, Laurence Crane, who became a physician but died while still a young man, and a daughter who married Charles Hunt. Mrs. Stokes died a few months before her husband of typhoid fever contracted at Goldsboro when she visited him there.

SEE: *Carolina and the Southern Cross* 1 (August 1913); John L. Cheney, Jr., ed., *North Carolina Government, 1585–1979* (1981); Walter Clark, ed., *Histories of the Several Regiments and Battalions from North Carolina*, vols. 1 (portrait), 5 (1901); Alice S. Creighton (Nimitz Library, United States Naval Academy, Annapolis, Md.) to William S. Powell, 29 Aug. 1991, with information from the *Navy Register* and the *Abstracts of Service Records of Naval Officers*; Johnson J. Hayes, *The Land of Wilkes* (1962); T. Felix Hickerson, *Echoes of Happy Valley* (1962) and *Happy Valley: History and Genealogy* (1940); William S. Hoffmann, *North Carolina in the Mexican War, 1846–1848* (1959); Louis H. Manarin, comp., *North Carolina Troops, 1861–1865: A Roster*, vol. 3 (1971); *Roster of North Carolina Troops in the War with Mexico* (1887); John H. Wheeler, ed., *Reminiscences and Memoirs of North Carolina and Eminent North Carolinians* (1884).

WILLIAM S. POWELL

Stokes, William Brickley *(9 Sept. 1814–4 Mar. 1897)*, Tennessee political leader, was a native of Chatham County, the son of Sylvanus and Mary Christian Stokes. In 1818 Sylvanus, who owned extensive property in Tennessee, mounted an expedition to move his family west of the Blue Ridge. Tragedy struck, however, as Stokes was killed when his team bolted and ran away. His family settled in Smith County, Tenn., where William B. Stokes received a common school education. Later he became a DeKalb County planter and breeder of blooded horses. Ariel, his great stakes racer, won frequently and was a serious rival of Andrew Jackson's Truxton.

A Union Whig by predilection, Stokes was a member of the lower house of the Tennessee Assembly (1849–53) and of the state senate (1855–57) as a Know-Nothing after the demise of the national Whig party. Elected to the U.S. House of Representatives in 1858, he represented his district from 1859 to 1861. A staunch Unionist, he entered Federal service as a major of cavalry when the Civil War erupted. Subsequently, he was elected colonel of the Fifth Tennessee Cavalry (also known as the Middle Tennessee Cavalry). After the Battle of Murfreesboro, which secured Middle Tennessee for the United States, Stokes's regiment was garrisoned at Sparta. He was brevetted brigadier and major general before accepting an honorable discharge on 10 Mar. 1865.

Despite his military career, Stokes never abandoned politics. In 1864 he was a Lincoln-Johnson elector. He supported the wartime reconstruction of Tennessee and later became a Radical Republican noted for organizing black support for reunion on congressional terms. And he was a member of the U.S. House of Representatives in the Thirty-ninth, Fortieth, and Forty-first congresses (1866–71). In 1867 he was admitted to the Tennessee bar, established a legal practice in Alexandria, and unsuccessfully contested Parson Brownlow for a seat in the U.S. Senate. Two years later he was a candidate in a controversial gubernatorial race. The Radical Republicans split, with the extremists supporting Stokes and the moderates backing DeWitt C. Senter, a Brownlow associate. In a campaign that focused on the issue of universal suffrage for Confederate veterans, both candidates were motivated by ambition and personal animus. Stokes initially opposed enfranchisement but eventually became its advocate. Senter won by a substantial majority—slightly better than two to one. Defeated in 1870 as a candidate for a seat in the Forty-second Congress, Stokes claimed fraud but could offer no proof. In 1871 he was appointed Tennessee supervisor of the internal revenue system. This was his last public function, but he continued his legal practice until his death. He was active in the affairs of Post No. 16, Grand Army of the Republic, and the Free and Accepted Masons.

On 19 Jan. 1832 Stokes married Paralee A. Overall, the daughter of Abraham and Hannah Leath Overall. They had nine children: Melissa J., Hannah Leath, Harriet A., Paralee Frances, William Jordan, Sarah E., Sylvanus, Nora, and Charlie. Upon his death Stokes was interred in East View Cemetery, Alexandria, Tenn.

SEE: *Biog. Dir. Am. Cong.* (1986); S. J. Folmsbee, *History of Tennessee*, 2 vols. (1960); R. M. McBridge, ed., *Biographical Directory of the Tennessee General Assembly*, vol. 1 (1975); James W. Patton, *Unionism and Reconstruction in Tennessee* (1934).

MAX R. WILLIAMS

Stone, Barton Warren *(24 Dec. 1772–9 Nov. 1844)*, evangelist and author, was born near Port Tobacco, Md., the son of John and Mary Warren Stone and a descendant of the first Protestant governor of Maryland. When Stone was quite young, the family moved to Pittsylvania County, Va., just across the North Carolina state line, where he spent his youth not far from Danville. Intending to become a lawyer, he entered the academy conducted in Guilford County, N.C., by the Reverend David Caldwell. Although he had grown up in the Anglican church, Stone was swayed by the preaching of the Reverend James McGready in North Carolina and there became a candidate for the ministry in the Orange Presbytery in 1793. Not completely satisfied with the theology to which he was exposed, he went to his brother's home in Oglethorpe County, Ga., and obtained a teaching position in a Methodist school in the adjacent county of Wilkes. He returned to North Carolina in 1796, was licensed by the Orange Presbytery, and then took charge of several congregations in Tennessee and Kentucky. Despite his reservations with respect to the Confession, he accepted ordination "so far as I can see it consistent with the word of God." He still felt uneasy with some aspects of Calvinism, however.

The Great Revival of the early nineteenth century brought his objections into focus, and with four other ministers he withdrew from the Orange Presbytery and formed a new Presbyterian Synod. Within a year, convinced that there was no scriptural authority for synods, they dissolved the organization in June 1804 and for a time were referred to as "Stoneites." Other groups separated from the Methodist Episcopal church. Baptist congregations soon joined them, and they came to be called Christians with no creed except the Bible. Stone spent the remainder of his life organizing new congregations in Ohio, Kentucky, and Tennessee; he also sometimes taught school and in 1826 established a periodical, the *Christian Messenger*.

Along the way Stone made the acquaintance of Alexander Campbell, leader of a group known as the Disciples of Christ. The two men led their followers into a cooperative relationship, and at a conference in Lexington, Ky., on 1 Jan. 1832, the Christians and the Disciples agreed to act as a unit. A Disciple became coeditor of the *Messenger*. Although he never gave up the title Christian, Stone considered the union to be "the noblest act of my life." He was the author of a number of published letters, addresses, tracts, and books and wrote part two of the *Apology of the Springfield Presbytery* (1803), which has been cited as the first declaration of religious freedom in the Western Hemisphere. He also composed a hymn, "The Lord Is the Fountain of Goodness and Love."

In 1801 Stone married Elizabeth Campbell, who died in 1810; by her he had five children. In 1811 he married her cousin, Celia Wilson Bowen, and soon afterwards settled in Lexington, Ky. They were the parents of six children. In 1834 he moved to Jacksonville, Ill., and extended his work into Missouri. While on a preaching tour, Stone died at the home of his son-in-law, Captain S. A. Bowen, in Hannibal, Mo., and was buried in the cemetery at Cane Ridge, Ky.

SEE: *Appleton's Cyclopedia of American Biography*, vol. 5 (1888); *DAB*, vol. 9 (1936); Samuel S. Hill, ed., *Encyclopedia of Religion in the South* (1984); Wheeler Preston, *American Biographies* (1940); C. C. Ware, *Barton Warren Stone: Pathfinder of Christian Unity* (1932?); David N. Williams, "The Theology of the Great Revival in the West As Seen Through the Life and Thought of Barton Warren Stone" (Ph.D. diss., Vanderbilt University, 1979).

WILLIAM S. POWELL

Stone, Charles H. *(19 June 1877–20 Oct. 1963)*, chemist and pioneer southern dyestuff manufacturer, was born in Stokes County, the son of Thomas J. and Charlotte Venable Stone. He attended the Boonville Academy in Yadkin County and as a young man taught school. In 1904 he became associated with Farben-Fabriken, a German dye manufacturer and importer. During World War I supplies of dyestuffs from Germany were cut off, and Americans were forced to develop their own products for the first time. Stone's thirteen years' experience with dye manufacture proved critically important in the South for the continued availability of dyes. He remained extremely active in this development, eventually moving to Charlotte in 1923 with the Grasselli Dyestuff Company. In 1926 he was general manager of the General Dyestuff Company in Charlotte, where in 1928 he finally established his own dyestuff manufacturing company. Stone's firm was purchased by the American Cyanamid Company in 1937.

Active in many civic and professional groups, Stone in 1929 initiated and led the movement for the city manager form of government in Charlotte. In 1943 he led the movement for the establishment of the Carolina-Piedmont Section of the American Chemical Society. He served as president (1939) and district governor (1944) of the Rotary Club, president of the Charlotte Community Chest (1940–41), and chairman of the Charlotte Parks and Recreation Commission (1941–47). He left a bequest for the establishment of the Charles H. Stone Scholarship Fund (later the Charles H. Stone Award of the American Chemical Society) and for the Charles H. Stone professorships of chemistry at the University of North Carolina at Charlotte.

Stone was a member of Myers Park Methodist Church. He and his wife, Clara Kouns McKay Stone, had no children.

SEE: *Charlotte Observer*, 21 Oct. 1963, 5–6 Jan. 1986.

MAURICE M. BURSEY

Stone, David *(17 Feb. 1770–7 Oct. 1818)*, governor, congressman, senator, legislator, and justice, was born in Bertie County of English ancestry. He was the son of Zedekiah and Elizabeth Shivers (or Shriver) Hobson Stone. His father, who moved to North Carolina from Massachusetts before 1769, was active in commercial, agricultural, and political ventures during the American Revolution. David Stone was graduated with first honors from the College of New Jersey (now Princeton University) in 1788. He studied law under William R. Davie and was admitted to the bar in 1791.

As a Federalist he was elected to represent Bertie County in the 1789 convention at Fayetteville, which ratified the U.S. Constitution on behalf of North Carolina. The following year he was elected to his first term in the North Carolina House of Commons. Serving until 1795, he displayed an interest in internal improvements and advocated improved education. On leaving the house, he was a superior court justice from 1795 to 1798. In 1798 Stone won a seat in the U.S. House of Representatives and there was appointed to the first standing committee on Ways and Means. At the same time he made his first crucial political decision when he switched from the Federalist to the Republican party and supported Thomas Jefferson for president in 1800. Elected to the U.S. Senate in 1800, he upheld the Republican party except for his votes opposing the Embargo Acts. After completing his term in the Senate, he returned to the North Carolina Superior Court for two more years (1806–8).

The General Assembly elected Stone governor in 1808 and 1809. In that office he recommended legislation to improve higher and lower educational facilities, to nurture infant industries, and to increase the salaries of judges. Negotiations on the boundary dispute between North Carolina and South Carolina, the controversy over the Granville claims, the establishment of a state bank, and military matters were significant issues during his two terms as governor.

Controversy began to surround him after his election to the House of Commons in 1811. Stone supported legislation to improve navigation of the state's rivers and led the floor fight to repeal the Electoral Act of 1803, which provided for the election of presidential electors by the district system. The Electoral Act of 1811 required that electors be chosen by the General Assembly. The repeal of the act of 1803 was bitterly contested, and Stone sponsored a new act in 1812 that called for the election of the electors by the voters of North Carolina.

The second crucial phase of his political life began with his election to the U.S. Senate in 1812. Stone refused to support the War of 1812, the embargo, the direct tax, diplomatic appointments, or the curtailment of the illegal shipping trade. As a result of his opposition to war policies, he was censured by the North Carolina General Assembly. The legislature complained that he would not follow its instructions and accused him of going against the will of the majority of the state's citizens. Opposed to the instruction of senators by the state legislature, he resigned from the Senate in 1814, convinced that his judgment must be his guide.

After his resignation he resumed his legal career and developed plantations in Wake and Bertie counties. His interest in internal improvements was heightened with his election as president of the Neuse River Navigation Company in May 1818. He died suddenly at Restdale plantation, where he was buried near the Neuse River, six miles east of Raleigh.

Stone married Hannah Turner on 13 Mar. 1793. Of their eleven children, five died in infancy. Five girls, Rebecca, Hannah, Elisabeth, Sarah, Anne, and one son, David Williamson, survived. Hannah Stone died in April 1816. In June 1817 Stone married Sarah Dashiell, a resident of Washington, D.C.; she died in July 1838. A portrait of Stone from the North Carolina Museum of History, Raleigh, hangs in the house at Hope Plantation, Bertie County, one of his homes.

SEE: *Annals of the Congress of the United States*, vols. 9, 12–15 (1851); Samuel A. Ashe, ed., *Biographical History of North Carolina*, vol. 4 (1906); Bertie County Records and David Stone Papers (North Carolina State Archives, Raleigh); Delbert H. Gilpatrick, *Jeffersonian Democracy in North Carolina* (1931); Ernest Haywood Collection (Southern Historical Collection, University of North Carolina, Chapel Hill); Governor David Stone Letter Book and Legislative Papers (North Carolina State Archives, Raleigh); *Raleigh Register and North Carolina Gazette*, 9 Oct. 1818; Wake County Record Book 15, Wills, Inventories, and Settlements of Estates (North Carolina State Archives, Raleigh).

MELONIE JOHNSON TAYLOR

Storch, Carl August Gottlieb *(16 June 1764–29 Mar. 1831)*, the third Lutheran minister to serve in North Carolina, was the son of Georg Friedrich Storch, a German merchant, and the former Miss von Asseburg. Carl A. G. Storch was born in Helmstedt in the duchy of Braunschweig, Germany. Confirmed in the Lutheran church in

1779, he spent three years in high school and the next three years as a student of theological sciences at Helmstedt University. In 1785 he became a tutor of a rich nobleman; later he taught the children of a rich Bremen merchant.

Early in 1788 the Reverend Abbot Verthusen, director of the Helmstedt Mission Society, called Storch to become a pastor in North Carolina. In May, after he had been examined and ordained, the young man began his journey to America. Two months later he arrived in Baltimore. He sailed to Charleston, S.C., then joined the Reverend Adolph Nussman, a pioneer Lutheran minister who lived on Buffalo Creek in Rowan County, N.C. Following a short illness after his exhausting journey to North Carolina, he assumed his duties as pastor of Salisbury Church, Organ Church, and Peintkirche (or Pine Church). By November he was established and residing in Salisbury. He performed his ministerial duties at the three churches from 1789 to 1803.

On 2 May 1803 Storch attended a special conference at Salisbury, where plans for a North Carolina Synod were discussed. On 17 October he was present at the first North Carolina Lutheran Synod meeting at Lincolnton, where a constitution was adopted. Storch and the Reverend Johann Gottfried Arends led in the establishment of the synod. During those early years Storch exercised leadership, serving as synod president during the period 1805–11, 1813, and 1816–20. Known for his liberal attitudes towards other religious groups, he encouraged the members of the North Carolina church to cooperate with other Lutheran synods and with other denominations. Cooperation was extended to the South Carolina Lutheran Synod, and under Storch's direction, the North Carolina Synod considered uniting with the Lutheran General Synod of Pennsylvania. The North Carolina Synod requested that the Moravians properly instruct Lutheran children around Salem. Storch also helped the Protestant Episcopal church organize itself in North Carolina. He and four other Lutheran ministers even signed a certificate of ordination for Robert Johnstone Miller into that church. Miller, in turn, assisted in Lutheran affairs and attended sessions of the North Carolina Synod.

Amid the move towards cooperation in the 1810s, controversy erupted. While Storch was president, a conservative reaction emerged against interdenominational cooperation and against unification with the General Synod. The primary dispute concerned the fact that David Henkel, after a four-year wait, was refused ordination. Henkel was the leader of the splinter group and became the symbol for its opposition. On 29 May 1820 President Storch presided at the annual North Carolina Lutheran Convention in Lincolnton; Henkel and his supporters attended, and the issues were debated. Storch opened the meeting with a "fervent prayer" to "establish peace and harmony among us." He suggested that both sides forget their differences and admit their mistakes. However, his conciliatory tone was abandoned by the convention. After angry debate, the synod refused to ordain Henkel, and Henkel and his followers left the North Carolina Synod and in July established the Tennessee Synod.

Following the synod break, Storch never again accepted the presidency even though he was twice reelected. Poor health, which had plagued him earlier, dominated the rest of his life. He was afflicted with an "incurable disease of the eyes" and suffered "fits of depression and melancholy." These disorders often interfered with his regular ministry, which ended in 1825, and caused his complete retirement in 1828. Storch spent his last few years on his farm near Salisbury. He died after an extended illness and was buried in the Organ Lutheran Church Cemetery.

Contemporaries characterized Storch as a devoted and well-educated preacher. His sermons were simple but relevant; he cared little for worldly affairs. Proficient in Hebrew, Greek, and Latin, he spoke five or six languages. Physically, he was tall with irregular features and a massive head. His diary, which is entirely in German, meticulously lists the hundreds of persons he baptized, buried, and confirmed and the payment he received for each service.

In addition to being a pastor, Storch was the local banker and librarian, and he taught school in Salisbury. He was an early adherent of the temperance movement. But his periods of depression and his slowness in social discourse limited his effectiveness. Indeed, the Tennessee Synod split occurred despite his attempts to avert it. According to one observer, he was unable to cope with the split.

On 14 Jan. 1790 Storch married Christine Bahrt (Beard), the daughter of Johann Ludwig Bahrt of Salisbury. Of their eleven children, only Anna and Theophilus survived infancy. The Reverend Theophilus Storch, D.D., was a leader of the Virginia Lutheran Synod and later became president of Newberry College in South Carolina.

SEE: Gotthardt B. Berhheim, *History of the German Settlements and of the Lutheran Church in North and South Carolina* (1872); *Evangelical Review* 8 (1856–57); John G. Morris, *The Stork Family in the Lutheran Church* (1886); F. W. E. Peschau, trans., *Minutes of the Evangelical Lutheran Synod of North Carolina, 1803–1857* (1894); Joseph Stewart, trans. and ed., "Extract from a Letter by Pastor Storch in North Carolina, Dated Salisbury, January 20–February 15, 1796," *North Carolina Historical Review* 20 (1943).

ROBERT C. CARPENTER

Stradley, Thomas *(15 Mar. 1798–2 May 1891)*, Baptist clergyman, was born in Woolwich, England, the sixth child of John, a junior constructor of carriages at the Royal Arsenal in Woolwich, and Sarah Wheeler Stradley. At age fourteen he was apprenticed to a blacksmith in the Royal Arsenal. He married Mary Frances Diblin in 1819. With his wife and five children, Thomas left England for the United States, arriving in Charleston, S.C., in 1828. He settled in Asheville, N.C., where his brother Peter had located in 1823, and established a blacksmith's shop near the later site of the Battery Park Hotel. In 1829 Thomas joined Peter and eleven others in the constitution of a Baptist church. After the new church was admitted to the twenty-three-year-old French Broad Association in 1830, Thomas was ordained to the ministry and immediately became active in the association. He later played a prominent role in the Salem Association, formed in 1838, until his retirement in 1875.

Stradley was the first mountain minister to attend the newly established North Carolina Baptist Convention when that body held its third annual session in 1833. He was one of the original agents of the *Biblical Recorder*, the journal of the Baptist Convention, and continued that association for several decades. When the convention divided the state into missionary districts, he was entrusted with the Eleventh District, one of two covering western North Carolina. He also was one of forty members of the board of trustees named in the charter of 1833 granted to Wake Forest Institute. Stradley remained on the board—the sole representative of mountain Baptists—until July 1835, when his resignation was announced.

When difficulty of travel resulted in the organization of the Western North Carolina Baptist Convention in 1845 as an auxiliary of the state convention, Stradley began to play a vital role in that convention. In 1857 he was elected president and served three terms. During his presidency the Western North Carolina Convention became an independent body, voted to establish a Baptist Female College, and took charge of the Taylorsville Institute. In 1859 he was named to the board of trustees of the Female College. From 1852 until at least 1871, after which there is a gap in the records, he was one of six men who seemed preeminent in the life of the Western North Carolina Convention.

From 1829 to 1875 Stradley was pastor of the First Baptist Church of Asheville. He built a new church, seating 450, and to pay for it mortgaged his own property and traveled to New York and Boston after the Civil War to raise funds. Throughout his ministry he was a stout champion of education, temperance, Sunday schools, and missions. He also served temporarily as pastor of numerous other churches and traveled widely in behalf of Baptist causes.

Stradley was the father of thirteen children, one of whom, the Reverend J. A. Stradley, became a well-known Baptist minister. He was buried in the Beaverdam Baptist Church cemetery, Buncombe County.

SEE: *Biblical Recorder*, 1834–91, 1 July 1891; Minutes of the First Baptist Church of Asheville (1829–81), of the French Broad Baptist Association, of the North Carolina Baptist Convention, and of the Western North Carolina Baptist Convention (Baptist Collection, Wake Forest University Library, Winston-Salem); Stradley family papers (possession of Mrs. G. W. Stradley, Asheville); *Wake Forest Student* 26 (September 1906); Wake Forest University, Minutes of the Board of Trustees (University Library, Winston-Salem).

RICHARD C. BARNETT

Strange, Robert, Jr. *(20 Sept. 1796–20 Feb. 1854),* lawyer, judge, author, and U.S. senator, was born in Manchester, Va., the son of James Strange, a native of Glasgow, Scotland, who with his wife settled in Petersburg in 1783. The elder Strange was trained as a physician but gave up his practice to become a merchant. In Virginia young Robert attended schools in Lunenburg and Rockbridge counties and at New Oxford Academy. In 1811 he was at Hampden-Sydney College but the next year entered Washington College. In 1815 the family moved to Fayetteville, N.C., where Strange studied law and was admitted to the bar. He was elected borough representative from Fayetteville to the General Assembly in 1821 and while still a member in 1826 was elected a judge of the North Carolina Superior Court, where he served for ten years.

In 1831 Willie P. Mangum won a seat in the U.S. Senate, but as a Whig he was in conflict with the Democratic majority in the North Carolina legislature. He was instructed by the House of Commons to vote against his own wishes, and in 1836 he resigned. Judge Strange was elected on 5 Dec. 1836 to complete the term and was reelected in 1837.

In 1838 Strange and Senator Bedford Brown, the state's other senator, voted for Thomas Hart Benton's resolution to remove the censure of President Andrew Jackson from the journals of the Senate. After this action, the Assembly passed a resolution taking a stand against the Jackson administration and instructing the senators to follow more closely the wishes of the voting majority in the state. Both senators resigned their seats in 1840, and Strange was replaced by William A. Graham.

Strange resumed his law practice in Fayetteville and in Wilmington. Some of his extended remarks appear in *The Trial of Ann K. Simpson*, a noted murder case in western North Carolina.

In addition to his legislative career at both the state and the national levels, Strange was a director of the Bank of Cape Fear from 1818 until his death. He also was the twelfth grand master of the North Carolina Masons in 1823–24.

While he was a senator, Strange wrote the first novel with a setting in the state by a native of North Carolina: *Eoneguski, or, The Cherokee Chief: A Tale of Past Wars, by an American*. Published anonymously in 1839, the book was critical of the treatment of Indians by whites although it quickly was out of print. Because actual people and events were readily identified by many readers, it received some adverse criticism in North Carolina. In 1960 a facsimile edition appeared with an explanatory foreword by Richard Walser.

Strange often expressed regret that he had not been able to enjoy a literary career. Two poems by him appeared in *The Rainbow*, published in New York in 1847, while ten were included in Mary Bayard Clarke's anthology, *Wood-Notes*, published in 1854. A number of his addresses, speeches, and biographical writings also appeared in print; many of them can be found in the North Carolina Collection in Chapel Hill.

In 1817 Strange married Jane Kirkland, the sister-in-law of Judge Thomas Ruffin. They were the parents of six children: James, Margaret, Alexander, John, French, and Robert. After Mrs. Strange's death, he married a Mrs. Nelson; there were no children of the second marriage. He was buried in the family cemetery at his plantation, Myrtle Hill, then near Fayetteville but now within the city limits.

SEE: *Biographical Sketches of Distinguished American Lawyers* (1852?); John L. Cheney, Jr., ed., *North Carolina Government, 1585–1979* (1981); A. J. Morrison, *College of Hampden-Sidney, Dictionary of Biography, 1776–1825* (1921); *North Carolina Authors: A Selective Handbook* (1952); *Orphan's Friend and Masonic Journal*, 1 Aug. 1939; Richard Walser, "Senator Strange's Indian Novel," *North Carolina Historical Review* 26 (January 1949).

JOHN L. MYERS

Strange, Robert *(27 July 1823–24 Jan. 1877),* army officer and lawyer, was born in Fayetteville, the son of Judge Robert and Jane Kirkland Strange. After graduation from The University of North Carolina in 1841, he read law, was admitted to the bar, and moved to Wilmington. He was solicitor of the Wilmington District for two terms—the first by appointment of Judge Romulus Saunders and the second by election. For a number of years he was a director of the Bank of Cape Fear.

Strange served as a major in the War with Mexico, and between 1849 and 1852 he was a paymaster in the U.S. Army in Washington, D.C. At some time prior to 29 July 1852 he was promoted to colonel. He represented New Hanover County in the North Carolina House of Commons in 1852. As the Civil War approached, he was an aide to Governor John W. Ellis. Strange was a member from New Hanover County of the 1861–62 Secession Convention and of the Constitutional Convention for the same period.

At the beginning of the war he became aide to General Braxton Bragg, a post he filled faithfully throughout the conflict with the title of major. In the early months of the war he also was a member of the Wilmington Committee of Safety, created to secure the support of both the state and the Confederate governments in obtaining troops and supplies to protect southeastern North Carolina from Federal invasion. As late as March 1862 delegations from the committee went to Raleigh and Richmond in a vain attempt to secure protection for coastal North Carolina. Referred to as major, he was called upon several times to survey and make reports on railroads and bridges in southeastern North Carolina, and on one occasion he inspected and reported on the railroads from Richmond to Wilmington for the Confederate government. He was an unsuccessful candidate for the Confederate Congress in 1863.

By his first wife, Sarah Caroline Wright, who died on 6 Apr. 1866, Strange was the father of three sons—Thomas Wright, Robert, and Joseph Huske. His second wife was Mrs. Bettie Andrews Lane, of Henderson, by whom he had two daughters—Caroline Wright and Jane Hawkins. Strange collapsed and died in court while representing a client. An Episcopalian, he was buried in Oakdale Cemetery, Wilmington.

SEE: John L. Cheney, Jr., *North Carolina Government, 1585–1979* (1981); Daniel L. Grant, *Alumni History of the University of North Carolina* (1924); Robert Strange, Jr., Papers (Southern Historical Collection, University of North Carolina, Chapel Hill); *War of the Rebellion . . . Official Records*, vols. 9, 36, 47 (1883, 1891, 1895); John H. Wheeler, ed., *Reminiscences and Memoirs of North Carolina and Eminent North Carolinians* (1884); *Wilmington Daily Journal*, 25–26 Jan. 1877; *Wilmington Morning Star*, 25 Jan. 1877.

WILLIAM S. POWELL

Strange, Robert *(6 Dec. 1857–23 Aug. 1914)*, Episcopal bishop, was the grandson of Judge Robert Strange, a U.S. senator from North Carolina, and the son of Colonel Robert Strange, an army officer and attorney of Wilmington, and his wife Caroline, the daughter of Thomas Henry Wright. He was baptized in St. James's Church, Wilmington, by the Reverend Dr. Robert B. Drane and educated in the schools of Wilmington, at Horner and Grimes Military Academy, Hillsborough, and at The University of North Carolina, from which he received a B.A. degree in 1879. He was prepared by the Reverend Robert B. Sutton, D.D., of Pittsboro for his confirmation on 20 Nov. 1877 in the Chapel of the Cross by Bishop Thomas Atkinson. For a short time Strange tutored the children of Mrs. Edmund Ruffin, Jr., of Hanover County, Va. Admitted as a candidate for Holy Orders in 1880, he studied at the Berkeley Divinity School in Connecticut and was ordained deacon by Bishop Alfred Watson in April 1884.

After serving as a missioner among the Negroes of Brunswick County, Va., in response to an appeal by Mrs. Pattie Buford, and traveling in Europe, Strange returned to North Carolina and was advanced to the priesthood by Bishop Theodore Lyman on 15 Nov. 1885. He was successively rector of the Church of the Good Shepherd, Raleigh (1885–87), St. James's Church, Wilmington (1887–1900), and St. Paul's Church, Richmond, Va. (1900–1904). Elected bishop coadjutor of East Carolina on 26 May 1904 and consecrated on 1 November in St. James's Church, he became the diocesan in April 1905 on the death of Bishop Watson.

Building on the sound foundation laid by his predecessor and preserving traditions of which he was a product, Bishop Strange ably led the diocese to an awareness of changing times and opportunities for the Episcopal church at home and abroad. He was a member of his church's Joint Commission on Social Service, of the American Red Cross, and of the University Peace and International Arbitration movements. His administration was characterized by his efforts to reduce sectarianism; support education, with a special interest in The University of North Carolina, which awarded him an honorary D.D. degree in 1894; strengthen the missionary program of the diocese; enhance the status of the work among Negroes, including appointment of a black archdeacon in 1909; and stimulate the spiritual resources and social responsibility of clergy and laity. Eloquently by word and deed he set forth the high principles that motivated his life.

Despite periods of rest and recreational travel, the bishop's health became impaired in carrying out the demands of his active mind and dedicated spirit. In November 1913 he turned over the ecclesiastical authority to the standing committee. Death came for him the following August, and he was buried beneath the chancel of St. James's Church. A portrait of Bishop Strange, painted by Mrs. Helen McMillan Lane, was presented to the parish house of St. James's by her aunt, Mrs. William Latimer, in 1945.

Surviving Strange were his wife, Elizabeth Stone Buford, whom he married on 29 Sept. 1886, a son Robert, and a daughter Helen. Mrs. Strange was the daughter of Judge Francis E. and Pattie Buford, the granddaughter of Governor David Stone.

SEE: Lawrence F. Brewster, *A Short History of the Diocese of East Carolina, 1883–1972* (1975); Gertrude Carraway, *Crown of Life* (1940); Joseph Blount Cheshire, "Robert Strange" (typescript), and Diary of Bishop Strange for 1907 (manuscript) (Diocesan House Library, Kinston); *Journals of the Diocese of East Carolina* (1883–1914); *The Mission Herald*, 1894–1914; *One Hundredth Anniversary Commemorating the Building of St. James Church, Wilmington, N.C.* (1939).

LAWRENCE F. BREWSTER

Strayhorn, William (Billy) Thomas *(29 Nov. 1915–31 May 1967)*, African American jazz musician, came from families (Strayhorns, Youngs, and Craigs) established in Hillsborough for generations; there seems to be some evidence of West Indian strains in his ancestry. The second son of Hillsborough natives James Nathaniel and Lillian Morgot Young Strayhorn, William (named for a Durham uncle) was born in Dayton, Ohio, but spent many months in his childhood at the Hillsborough home of his Strayhorn grandparents, Jobe, employed at the local mill as an office clerk and still remembered for his fine penmanship and manners, and Lizzie, whose flower garden where the child played is said to have furnished imagery for his later lyrics. This grandmother, Strayhorn told an interviewer, was the primary influence during his first ten years, and her house his first real home. There his musical precocity surfaced very early when, as a preschooler, he learned to play hymns on her piano and to pick out any Victrola record requested. His first year of school was in a Hillsborough building later destroyed, with all its records, by fire.

His education continued in Pittsburgh, where his family settled and his father entered the construction business. Aware of the boy's gifts, the parents provided him with private music lessons and sent him to the Pittsburgh Musical Institute, where he studied classical music. At Westinghouse High School, he played in the school band and attended the classes of the same teacher who had instructed jazz pianists Mary Lou Williams and Errol Garner.

By Strayhorn's own account, a Pittsburgh performance by the band of the well-established jazz musician Duke Ellington dazzled and inspired the eighteen-year-old boy, then employed as a soda fountain clerk. He formed a trio that played daily on a city radio station, and he composed three songs with lyrics: "My Little Brown Book," "Something to Live For," and "Life Is Lonely," later famous under the title "Lush Life" and judged by a jazz authority in 1968 as a sophisticated work that alone qualified its writer for a place in an exclusive hall of fame.

When Ellington returned to Pittsburgh four years later, a friend persuaded Strayhorn to seek an audition at which he played these compositions. Impressed, Ellington took "Something to Live For" and recorded it three months later; the resulting praise prompted him to send for Strayhorn, who joined him in New Jersey as a promising protégé with a vague appointment to write lyrics for Ellington's songs. By the end of the year, Strayhorn was scoring most of Ellington's small band dates and beginning to arrange and compose for the full band. His lifelong collaboration with Ellington had begun.

Described by a historian as "without parallel in the history of jazz and possibly of all music," this remarkable partnership between Ellington the famous and flamboyant cosmopolite and Strayhorn the modest provincial sixteen years his junior merged the gifts of both into what appeared to many observers to be one creative musical organism. They composed together so spontaneously and interdependently—sometimes even by long-distance telephone—that it was said, "Neither was sure at times who contributed what to a finished piece." Many of Strayhorn's compositions were attributed to Ellington, partly because his fame ensured an audience and sales and partly because neither man genuinely cared so long as the music was written, performed, and heard as widely as possible. In time, even their piano playing was indistinguishable except to experts, a phenomenon that puzzled the partners, who considered their styles distinctly different. Strayhorn maintained that Ellington's real instrument was his band, through which he melded the many instrumentalists (including an extraordinary number of top-ranking performers) into a varying whole that produced what was called the unmistakable "Ellington sound." Strayhorn and Ellington wrote for this instrument as its components changed when musicians joined the band and left it. Strayhorn is credited with discovering Jimmy Blanton, who revolutionized the role of the bass. In addition to composing music and lyrics, Strayhorn did arrangements and orchestration for the band and sometimes substituted for Ellington at piano. His marked indifference to attention, publicity, status, credits, and money in a profession in which such goals are avidly pursued made it notoriously difficult to lure him to recording studios or concert stages for star performances, with the result that recordings of these rare events are now treasured by collectors.

In his first two years with Ellington, Strayhorn composed "Day Dream," "Like a Ship in the Night," "Savoy Street," "You Can Count on Me," "Minuet in Blue," "Passion Flower," "Raincheck," and "Chelsea Bridge," inspired by Whistler's painting of Battersea Bridge but misnamed by the composer in a confused moment at a recording studio. To this period belongs his most popular work, "Take the A-Train," which he termed a set of directions on how to take this Eighth Avenue express from 59th Street in Manhattan to 125th Street in Harlem, at that time a yeasty African American cultural mix of musicians, writers, entertainers, and sports champions. Ellington, who had got his start there, adopted this as his theme song. (Later, Strayhorn's "Lotus Blossom" became the band's sign-off song.) Strayhorn also during this apprenticeship wrote the lyrics for "I'm Checkin' Out," "Lonely Co-ed," "Tonk," and "Your Love Has Faded"; did the arrangement of "Flamingo"; played piano for recordings; and conducted a series of small band dates.

The vicissitudes of World War II affected the band adversely at first but indirectly brought it its first Carnegie Hall concert in 1943, when Strayhorn's "Johnny Come Lately" and "Dirge," said to resemble Milhaud and Stravinsky, were performed. At the next Carnegie concert, in 1944, Strayhorn's "Strange Feeling," from *Perfume Suite*, was presented, and in 1946, the Strayhorn-Ellington *Deep South Suite*, of which only one piece has survived. *Esquire* magazine gave Strayhorn its Silver Award for arranger that year, and in the same capacity he won the poll conducted by the jazz periodical *Down Beat*.

Strayhorn went to Europe for the first time in 1950, when the band had a French tour. His work received admiring attention, and after that he visited Paris as often as possible, becoming fluent in French and something of a cult figure. In Chicago his "Violet Blue" was featured at a band performance at the Civic Opera House and also in New York at a benefit concert for the NAACP at the Metropolitan Opera House, along with "Take the A-Train."

Mixed reviews met the work *A Drum Is a Woman*, with music, lyrics, and arrangement done by Strayhorn and Ellington in 1956, but their most ambitious undertaking was a decided critical success in 1957: the *Shakespearean Suite*, also entitled *Such Sweet Thunder* (from *Midsummer Night's Dream*), composed for the Shakespeare Festival at Stratford, Ontario. Both men read the plays in toto, discussed them with experts, and devoted serious attention to their selection of themes, producing a total of twelve compositions with such titles as "Sonnet in Search of a Moor," "Sonnet to Hank Cinq," and "Star-Crossed Lovers." Conservatives who complained of levity were told that this suite, like the plays, threaded tragedy with comedy.

"Toot Suite" and "Portrait of Ella Fitzgerald" followed, and then another European tour, to France and to the Leeds Festival in England. There the musicians met Queen Elizabeth II, and Prince Philip, at the first performance, mentioned his regret at having missed their rendition of his favorite, "Take the A-Train." Strayhorn and Ellington later wrote *The Queen's Suite*, of which Strayhorn alone composed the section "Northern Lights," intended to convey majesty; the single recording pressed was presented to the queen.

Strayhorn wrote "Multi-Colored Blues" for the recording *Newport 1958*, and much of *Suite Thursday*, commissioned by the Monterey (Calif.) Jazz Festival to be based on John Steinbeck's novel *Cannery Row*. The British periodical *Melody Maker* chose Strayhorn's arrangement of Tchaikovsky's *Nutcracker Suite* as its jazz LP record of the year 1960. The partners' *Peer Gynt Suite* appeared in 1962, and in 1963 Strayhorn supervised the performance and played piano at the presentation of Ellington's *My People* during the Century of Negro Progress Exposition in Chicago. That autumn the band set off for the Middle East on a tour sponsored by the U.S. Department of State, according to its then current policy of sending American musicians abroad as universally understood messengers of the national culture. Given VIP status, they were entertained by American diplomats at high-level social affairs attended by the royalty, diplomatic corps, and artists of the host countries. Concerts were given in Damascus, Jordan, Jerusalem, Kabul, and New Delhi, where

Strayhorn, his patience frayed by the attempts of reporters to bait the band members about the racial situation in America, sharply reminded them that the subject at hand was music. When Ellington fell ill, Strayhorn took over the piano playing at concerts in Hyderabad, Bangalore, Bombay, and Madras, where his skill evoked an enthusiastic review in the *Indian Express*. The tour continued to Dacca, Lahore, and Karachi, where Strayhorn ventured off to see the Taj Mahal; and to Teheran, Isfahan, Abadan, Kuwait, Baghdad, Beirut, and Ankara, where the news of President John F. Kennedy's death abruptly terminated the tour.

A Japanese tour in 1964 completed Strayhorn's experience of Asia. The result was the Strayhorn-Ellington *Far East Suite*, of which "Agra," celebrating the Taj Mahal, is Strayhorn's. A Caribbean tour prompted the *Virgin Island Suite* by both men.

Now known to be gravely ill, Strayhorn allowed himself to be coaxed onstage at the Pittsburgh Jazz festival in 1965 to play a piano version of "Take the A-Train." The New York chapter of the Duke Ellington Jazz Society presented him to a packed audience at the New School auditorium, where he played a selection of eighteen of his pieces and then, with some other band members, representative joint works of the partners.

His last composition, "Blood Count," written while he was hospitalized for cancer of the esophagus and presented at Ellington's 1967 Carnegie Hall concert, was finished not long before he died. A private family funeral at St. Peter's Lutheran Church in New York preceded a large one given by Ellington and attended by friends and colleagues in musical, theatrical, and film circles. The body was cremated and the ashes scattered, as Strayhorn's will directed, on the Hudson River by the Copasetics Club, a charity organization founded by Billy (Bojangles) Robinson for show business members who donated their services for the benefit of African American children in the South. Strayhorn was its second president, and after his death the club honored him by refusing to have another with that title; its chairman is called vice-president.

Nicknamed "Willie" and "Swee'pea" (for the baby in the cartoon strip *Popeye* because of Strayhorn's small five-foot-three-inch stature), he is credited by Lena Horne, his close friend, with contributing greatly to her musical education, particularly in regard to classical music, during their many hours together. He cited as his reasons for never marrying both his frenetic activities as a jazz musician traveling to concerts, dances, theaters, clubs, and recording studios on three continents, and his impulsive mode of life, incompatible with domestic order. Coteries of admirers formed in Paris, Helsinki, Stockholm, and London. Influenced by Ravel, Stravinsky, Debussy, and Rimsky-Korsakov, his work was more celebrated in Europe, where jazz was taken seriously as an art form, than in America. His music has been called "sheer and shimmering in quality," "gentle, reflective melodies in minor moods" and "pastel colors."

In 1968 the Ellington band recorded a Strayhorn album, *And His Mother Called Him Bill*, consisting of eleven Strayhorn compositions and, at the end, an unscheduled and spontaneous solo by Ellington at piano of "Lotus Blossom," the sign-off song, which an alert studio technician fortunately caught. This final tribute was acclaimed by jazz critics, an unsentimental lot, as both impeccable and moving.

Strayhorn has been termed an éminence grise, a genius, a legend, one of the nation's top composers and arrangers, and the most revered figure in jazz. Even if the puffery is discounted, his prestige not only remains but also continues to grow in the present jazz revival. The fame he never sought has increased since his death.

SEE: "Adieu à Billy," *Jazz Magazine* 144 (1967); Ole Just Astrup, "Strayhorn," *Orkester Journalen* 41 (1973); Whitney Balliett, *Such Sweet Thunder* (1966); Jean Pierre Binchet and Philippe Carles, "Billy Strayhorn," *Jazz Magazine* 134 (1966); Richard O. Boyer, "The Hot Bach," *New Yorker*, July 1944; Claude Carrière, "Lush Life: Billy Strayhorn," *Jazz Hot* 289 (1972); William Coss, "Ellington & Strayhorn, Inc.," *Down Beat* 29 (1962); Stanley Dance, "Lightly and Politely," *Jazz Journal* 18 (1965), and *The World of Duke Ellington* (1970); Duke Ellington, "Eulogy for Sweet Pea," *Down Beat* 34 (1967) and Edward Kennedy Ellington, *Music Is My Mistress* (1973); Leonard Feather, "The Duke's Progress," *Down Beat* 29 (1962), "Strayhorn: A Place in the Hall of Fame," *Melody Maker* 43 (1968), "Strayhorn: Genius in the Shadow of Duke," *Melody Maker* 42 (1967), and "Weely," *Down Beat* 34 (1967); Max Jones, "*Nutcracker Suite*: Jazz LP of 1960," *Melody Maker* 36 (1961); Burt Korall, "Strayhorn and the Duke," *Saturday Review* 50 (1967); Gordon Parks, "Jazz," *Esquire* 84 (1975); Billy Strayhorn, "The Ellington Effect," *Down Beat* 19 (1952), and "Just Follow Rimsky-Korsakoff's Advice," *Melody Maker* 38 (1963); Barry Ulanov, *Duke Ellington* (1946).

Valuable information was also generously supplied by Mr. and Mrs. James N. Strayhorn, Jr., and Mr. John Strayhorn, all of Pittsburgh; Mrs. Georgia Strayhorn Conaway, of Long Island; and relatives and friends of the family in Hillsborough. The research was undertaken at the instigation of the Hillsborough Historical Society, which produced a program on Strayhorn's life and work in October 1974.

MARY PETTIS SANFORD

Street, James Howell *(15 Oct. 1903–28 Sept. 1954)*, author, journalist, and onetime Baptist minister, was born in the little sawmill village of Lumberton, Miss. His father was John Camillus Street, a lawyer of Irish Catholic descent later to become a judge. His mother was William Thompson Scott Street, a Scots-Irish Calvinist, whose father was so disappointed at not having a son that he passed on to his daughter his own name, as well as the attendant confusion resulting from a girl with a boy's name. Of his ancestry Street once said: "We have melted enough to have everything in us, except Chinese—and I could do with some of that."

When Street was nine, his family moved to Laurel, Miss. His early part-time jobs were concerned with newspapers—selling Sunday editions at first, and then at age fourteen going to work for the *Laurel Daily Leader*, where he was a printer's devil, general "handy boy," and reporter, if writing personal items on "who was in town and why" on Saturdays could be classed as reporting. Of those boyhood years he later said: "In those days boys worked. It was the age of idolatry of thrift. Somehow, it was believed that work was the sacred thing. A boy must work. Nonsense. It was a silly era. It's better for boys to play. They'll work soon enough."

After attending Laurel High School for three years he was enrolled at Massey School in Pulaski, Tenn., but he soon ran away, bumming around the country, working at odd jobs, and traveling as far as Honolulu. At age eighteen he was back in Mississippi holding down his first full-time job, as a reporter for the *Hattiesburg American*.

In 1923 he married Lucy Nash O'Briant of Hattiesburg and left newspaper work to become what one biographer described as the youngest ordained Baptist minister in the United States. In rebuttal to speculation that he had left the Catholic church for some psychological reason, Street later said: "Hell, I did it because I fell in love, and the girl's daddy was a Baptist preacher and I wanted to impress her."

In order to be better prepared for the ministry he attended Southwestern Theological Seminary in Fort Worth, Tex., and Howard College in Birmingham, Ala., but did not complete his studies at either. After three years as a minister in St. Charles, Mo., in Lucedale, Miss., and in Boyles, Ala., he gave up the ministry, despite being a very popular preacher, because he was concerned that he had "neither the emotional, intellectual, nor spiritual equipment for this work."

After brief stints as a press agent for politicians, and as an advertising salesman, forest guide, and swimming instructor, he became a full-time newspaperman, serving as news editor of the *Pensacola Journal*, as assistant state editor of the *Arkansas Gazette*, and as a correspondent for the Associated Press. While in the Atlanta division office of the Associated Press in 1932, he wrote a five-hundred-word story about the demise of the Panama Limited, a crack Chicago to New Orleans train, which had passed through his hometown when he was a boy. The story received honorable mention for the Pulitzer Prize awards that year and was so favorably received by his superiors that he was transferred to New York and given an assignment as a special feature writer.

Later he joined the Hearst *New York American*, working on a wide variety of assignments. On occasion, while covering major stories, he found that he had excess time on his hands, and during such a twenty-eight-day period while covering the Lindbergh kidnapping trial he wrote his first book, *Look Away! A Dixie Notebook*. Concerning its reception Street later said: "I wrote my first book, *Look Away!*, and that's exactly what the public did." The following year, 1937, he left the Hearst organization and became assistant literary editor of the *World-Telegram*. While there he wrote a satire on doctors called "I've Never Lost A Father Yet," which has been republished many times, for which he received thirty-five dollars, a by-line, and no copyright.

A few months later, in need of cash, he wrote his first short story and sold it under the title "Nothing Sacred" to *Cosmopolitan* magazine for $450. Subsequently the story was made into a moving picture starring Carole Lombard and Frederic March, and with the $2,500 Street received for the movie rights he embarked on a career as a free-lance writer. From late 1937 until 1940 he turned out a number of articles and short stories for such magazines as the *Saturday Evening Post* and *Collier's*, including one of his more famous stories, "The Biscuit Eater," and a second book, *Oh, Promised Land*. Except for a brief stint in Hollywood his base of operations during this period was Old Lyme, Conn., but in 1940 he moved to Natchez, Miss., and then in 1941 back again to New York, where he remained until 1945, when he took up permanent residence in Chapel Hill.

By the time he became a Tar Heel seven of Street's books had been published, three of them, *Oh, Promised Land* (1940), *Tap Roots* (1942), and *By Valor and Arms* (1944) in the popular Dabney series. The others were *Look Away!* (1936); *The Biscuit Eater* (1941), an adaptation into a novel of his famous short story; *In My Father's House* (1941), the book Street considered his best; and a compilation of his *Short Stories* (1945). His eighth and most successful book, *The Gauntlet* (1945), was published soon after he moved to North Carolina.

For Street a literary dry spell followed his move to Chapel Hill, but in 1949 he collaborated with James Saxon Childers on a novel, *Tomorrow We Reap*. In the next four years he turned out at least one short story and two articles annually for national magazines and six books: *Mingo Dabney* (1950), the last of the Dabney series, *The High Calling* (1951), *The Velvet Doublet* (1953), *The Civil War* (1953), *Good-Bye, My Lady* (1954), and *The Revolutionary War* (1954).

Three of Street's novels and four of his short stories were bought by motion picture companies, and he wrote three other original scripts for the movies. His first short story, "Nothing Sacred," was not only made into a moving picture of the same name but also later was used as the basis for a broadway musical comedy, *Hazel Flagg*, and a second moving picture, *Living It Up*. Nine of his books were book club selections, and one, *The Gauntlet*, sold more than a million copies. On a worldwide basis his most popular book was *The Biscuit Eater*, which was translated into twenty-seven languages.

On 28 Sept. 1954, after presenting awards at an Associated Press broadcasters' meeting in Chapel Hill, he collapsed with a heart attack and died a few minutes after being taken to the North Carolina Memorial Hospital.

Three other books were published posthumously: *James Street's South* (1955), a collection of articles on the South compiled and edited by his son, James, Jr.; *Captain Little Ax* (1956), based on five of his short stories that had appeared in *Collier's* and rewritten "according to Street's own plan" by Don Tracy; and *Pride and Possession* (1960), in which Tracy combined two of Street's earlier short stories.

James and Lucy Street were the parents of three children, James, Jr., John, and Lucy Ann.

SEE: Clipping files (North Carolina Collection, University of North Carolina, Chapel Hill); Josephine Frazier, "James Street: Southern Storyteller," *Southeastern Librarian* 12 (Spring 1962); Bernadette Hoyle, *Tar Heel Writers I Know* (1956); *North Carolina Authors: A Selective Handbook* (1952); Richard Walser, *Young Readers' Picturebook of Tar Heel Authors* (1975).

DAVID STICK

Stringfield, Lamar *(10 Oct. 1897–21 Jan. 1959)*, composer, conductor, and flutist, was born near Raleigh, the son of the Reverend Oliver Larkin and Ellie Beckwith Stringfield. He was the sixth of seven children. In 1902 the family moved to western North Carolina, and as a lad Lamar grew up among the mountains, which he came to love and which later had a significant influence on his musical career. His father served short terms as pastor of churches in Barnardsville, Burnsville, and Asheville before establishing a permanent home for the family in Mars Hill, where a son and a daughter were already employed as teachers at Mars Hill College. Lamar, with his family, joined the Baptist church in that community.

As was true of all the Stringfield children, Lamar received his early education at home, taught by his mother and his older sisters. He was enrolled for three semesters in the academy program at Mars Hill College, but his attendance was irregular and the college seems to have had a very limited effect on his intellectual development. Far more important was the influence of a family in which study and music were a natural part of each day's activities. His oldest sister gave him his first formal music lessons when he was six. Within a few years he had not only acquired a good foundation in the piano but had also begun to experiment with other instruments, especially the cornet. While the family lived for a few months at the Baptist Assembly in Ridgecrest, he became interested in the banjo. Day after day he "picked" with local people as they sat around the railway station and heard some of the folk tunes that would inspire compositions of his own. It is probable that he first learned the ballad of John Henry from railroad workers in Ridgecrest.

World War I interrupted his sporadic studies at Mars Hill College and opened an exciting career in music. In 1916 he joined the army, serving first on the Mexican border and then in France as a member of the band with the 105th Engineers, 30th Division. The band members, who doubled as litter bearers, were assigned to the medical corps and given the task of bringing the wounded from front-line positions to first-aid stations before they were sent on to hospitals. The group also served in Belgium and finally on the Hindenburg Line.

When Stringfield joined the army, he was playing the cornet, but he soon discarded that instrument for the flute and began taking lessons with Harold Clark, a member of the Tennessee contingent from Knoxville. At the same time he began to study music theory with the bandmaster, Joseph DeNardo. From the beginning Lamar showed considerable promise as a flutist, and after the armistice was signed and the band pulled back for reorganization, he was selected as one of five men to study in Paris with some of the best instructors in France.

Discharged from the army in April 1919, Stringfield returned home to devote his life to music. He resumed his studies in theory with DeNardo, who had moved to Asheville, and enrolled for flute lessons with Emil Medicus, another teacher in Asheville. During this time he also began composing in earnest. In 1919 he wrote "Lost" for piano, and the next year he composed "In Lindy's Cabin" for violin and piano, "Polka Dot Polka" for cornet, and three other short pieces.

In 1920 he decided to move to New York, where he would have better opportunities for study and for performing. Entering the Institute of Musical Art (later the Julliard School of Music), he studied flute with George Barrere, composition with Percy Goetschius, Franklin Robinson, and George Wedge, and conducting with Chalmers Clifton and Henry Hadley. As a student he won his first cash prize for his "Indian Legend," a symphonic poem based on folk materials and Cherokee Indian themes. Another of his student compositions, "Mountain Sketches" (1923), written for flute, violoncello, and piano, was first performed at the institute. In 1924 he was graduated with an artist's diploma in flute playing.

Stringfield remained in New York, conducting and performing as a flutist. He served as guest director for the Baltimore Symphony, the New York Civic Orchestra, the Philadelphia Civic Orchestra, and some fifteen other organizations. As a flutist he played for two seasons with the Chamber Music Art Society and for three seasons with the New York Chamber Music Society. During the 1927–28 season he served as one of the conductors of the National Opera Association in Washington, D.C. For his orchestral playing and conducting he was awarded a certificate by the American Orchestral Society. Meanwhile, this was one of his most productive periods in composing. In 1928 his "From the Southern Mountains" won the Pulitzer Prize for Composition.

The year 1928 was pivotal in Stringfield's life. Not only did it bring him one of the highest awards for composing, but it was also the year in which he turned from a concentration in music making to an emphasis on establishing musical organizations and on implementing private financial plans. In 1930 he returned to North Carolina, where he spent the rest of his life, except for short summer tours as a lecturer at the Julliard School of Music and one summer at Claremont College in California. Establishing his residence in Chapel Hill, he immediately began to sell his ideas for a program in folk music to the Department of Music at The University of North Carolina. The outcome was the creation of the Institute of Folk Music, with Stringfield as its research associate. It was the institute's purpose, as he saw it, to utilize old folk tunes in such a way as to preserve them for future generations. Out of its work and its concerts came the idea for organizing a state symphony orchestra. During the summer of 1927 Stringfield had already set up and directed the Asheville Symphony Society.

The North Carolina Symphony Society was formed in March 1932, and through its efforts a symphony orchestra was established. On 7 Apr. 1934 Stringfield left the Institute of Folk Music in order to devote full time as director of the new orchestra. No substantial funds had been committed to the project, but on 4 May the Federal Relief Administration of North Carolina granted $45,000 for its support for a period of thirty-six weeks. During the summer and fall the orchestra gave seventeen concerts throughout the state, and the foundation was laid for a good musical organization. Statewide acceptance of the project was demonstrated when, after federal funds were no longer available and it became evident that the orchestra could not sustain itself, the North Carolina legislature appropriated funds for its support and thus created the first state-supported symphony orchestra in the United States.

Meanwhile, in October 1935 Stringfield was appointed regional director of the Federal Music Project under the Works Progress Administration and found it necessary to give up his work with the symphony. His new assignment was to promote the establishment of a number of orchestras in seven southern states, using the North Carolina plan as a model. The idea of amateur orchestras greatly appealed to Stringfield, and he set himself the tasks of organizing a Southern Symphony Orchestra and of establishing a Society of American Symphony Orchestras to sponsor a system of orchestras nationwide. As he envisioned it, the Southern Symphony would provide concerts for more than four million people who lived in small towns or rural areas and had little or no opportunity to hear good musicians perform. It also would encourage young musicians and provide a vehicle for the presentation of American compositions. Stringfield visited major cities in the South and conferred with many groups, but he did not succeed in selling his plans for a Southern Symphony. Though the Society of American Symphony Orchestras was organized in July 1940, his plans for both a Southern Symphony and a national network of orchestras were given up when the United States entered World War II in December 1941.

The period after 1935 was less productive for Stringfield than earlier years. His work with the Federal Music Project consumed much of his time without providing compensatory satisfaction in the fulfillment of his cherished dreams, and marital difficulties added to the disappointments experienced in his work. He and his wife, Caroline Crawford, whom he had married on 1 May 1927, were divorced in July 1938; they had one child, Meredith. Afterwards Stringfield returned to New York as associate conductor at Radio City Music Hall for one season, but his earlier creativity seems to have escaped him. World War II added one more dimension to his personal frustrations.

When the United States entered the war, Stringfield became so emotionally involved that he had little time for music. Rejected by the armed forces because of age, he sought other means by which he could contribute to the war effort. For this reason the musician undertook research on the feasibility of using overtones in the treatment of shell-shock patients and of piping music into clubs and dining halls for the mental relaxation of service members. Although interested, the Federal Security Agency was unwilling, or unable, to invest any money in the project. His second effort on behalf of the nation was more fruitful. In October 1942 he took a job with the Vaught-Sikorsky Aircraft Corporation and spent two years working in an airplane factory, first on the assembly line and then as inspector of engines.

After the war Stringfield became involved in a variety of musical projects, among them the writing of music for a number of outdoor dramas (in 1937 he had composed the music for Paul Green's play, *The Lost Colony*). In the late forties he worked with LeGette Blythe on his *Shout Freedom*, a play commissioned by the Mecklenburg Historical Society, and in 1952 he wrote the music for Hubert Hayes's *Thunderland*, which ran for two seasons in Asheville. He also resumed his interest in conducting, and during the 1946–47 season, he commuted from Asheville to Knoxville, Tenn., to serve as conductor of the city's symphony orchestra. He turned down a three-year contract with that orchestra because of the stipulation that he establish permanent residence in Knoxville and accepted a position with the Charlotte Symphony instead. In January 1947 Stringfield was asked to serve on the National Board of Directors of the National Society of Music and Art, and in April he was elected regional consultant of the National Association for American Composers and Conductors. In December 1949 he accepted a commission to write the music for *Peace*, a Christmas contata based on a poem by Marian Sims. The composition was first presented at the New York Avenue Presbyterian Church in Washington, D.C., on 18 December.

Two other projects engaged Stringfield during the forties and fifties. For several years he had wished to make a more nearly perfect flute. After studying acoustics with a physics professor at Case Institute of Technology in California and then working with casting and making molds, he set up a woodwind repair shop in Charlotte and set about constructing his new, improved flute. He modeled the flute after one made by Louis Lot in Paris about eighty years earlier, using white gold for the tubing and springs. He also patented an invention that eliminated the use of screws to hold the pads in the key cups. A Stringfield Design Flute was built, but the detailed work necessary to duplicate his model made it unattractive to commercial producers. His second project, that of establishing a business to prepare plates for engraving music and of teaching the art of engraving to his most talented students, also failed and left him heavily in debt.

The financial failure of these projects was only one of several disappointments marring Stringfield's last years. In 1951 he began work on his last major composition, a musical folk drama called *Carolina Charcoal*. He spent four years on it, hoping for a good reception on Broadway and then success in Hollywood. Neither goal was realized. The play premiered at the Barter Theater in Abingdon, Va., and ran for three showings in Charlotte, but he found no backers in New York and Hollywood turned him down. His efforts to make "Daniel Boone," a song from *Thunderland*, a best-seller and a financial asset also failed. His performing honorariums helped with expenses, but he was plagued by debts. Attempts to secure a teaching position, first at Mars Hill College and then with the state school system, did not succeed because he had neither a traditional college degree nor the professional training needed to teach. Faced with financial disaster, he tried to keep a full recital schedule but repeated illness made that difficult.

As his health deteriorated during the fifties, Stringfield returned to Asheville to be near his family. Attacks of sinusitis, repeated operations for a hernia condition, a broken leg, and other physical problems, as well as extreme sensitivity to the effects of alcohol, left him a broken man. At age sixty-two he died in the hospital of lung congestion. He was buried in Riverside Cemetery, Asheville.

Stringfield left some 400 compositions, 150 published and about 250 unpublished. Most of his larger works were for symphony orchestra and chamber music, but his collection also included an opera, integral music for stage plays and radio, and smaller pieces for voice and instrumentals. Most of his compositions and other materials are at the University of North Carolina at Chapel Hill.

SEE: *Asheville Citizen*, 18 Dec. 1949, 19 Feb. 1950, 25 May, 4 Aug. 1952, 7 Aug. 1953, 23–24 Jan., 1 Feb. 1959, 22 Oct., 2 Nov. 1967; *Chapel Hill Weekly*, 5 Nov. 1967; *Charlotte Observer*, 1 Mar. 1950, 21 Aug. 1951, 2 Apr., 8 May, 31 July, 23 Oct. 1955, 15 Oct. 1967; *The Flutist* 9 (February 1928); Knoxville, Tenn., *News Sentinel*, 23 Jan. 1959; Mrs. Bernice Stringfield McKay (Mars Hill, N.C.), personal contact, 4 Oct., 9 Nov. 1970, and handbills and programs in her possession; Douglas R. Nelson, "The Life and Works of Lamar Stringfield, 1897–1959" (Ph.D. diss., University of North Carolina at Chapel Hill, 1971); Lamar Stringfield, *America and Her Music*, University of North Carolina Extension Bulletin 10 (March 1931).

EVELYN UNDERWOOD

Stronach, William *(3 Nov. 1803–9 May 1857)*, state capitol stonemason, marble carver, Raleigh businessman, and founder of the family in North Carolina, was born at Stroneveagh (meaning "the place of the Stronachs") in Moray County (Elginshire), Scotland, the son of Ann Barron and Thomas Stronach. According to the minister of his home parish, Rafford, his parents "were respectable and bestowed upon him the ordinary advantages of education," and their son grown to manhood "conducted himself with undeviating propriety—so far as known to us—and creditably supported himself by his industry." Soon after the date of the foregoing letter of recommendation (20 Feb. 1833), young Stronach immigrated to America by way of Leith (now part of Edinburgh). By 1834 he was among those stonecutters brought "from the North" by the architects of the state capitol to construct that building. His name appears on the "List of stonecutters employed at the Capitol" in the 4 Dec. 1834 report of the superintending commissioners; his pay was two dollars a day. The following August, indicating his intention of settling permanently in North Carolina, he applied to the Wake County Court of Pleas and Quarter Sessions for U.S. citizenship.

Prior to completion of the capitol in 1840, Stronach had opened his own "marble-yard" at his home, 554 East Hargett Street, opposite the southeastern corner of Raleigh's City Cemetery. Among the tombstones he is known to have made is that of John Rex. He carved tombstones and offered "all kinds of granite work, . . . plaistering and mason work of all kinds" and eventually "hearth[stones], paint-stones, slabs for Soda Founts, Baker's Slabs, and Nova Scotia grindstones"—all indicated in his local newspaper advertisements. The state employed him for "putting up Gothic Mantle Pieces in the Library" of the capitol and repairing other mantelpieces in the new building. In 1847 he won another state contract to construct, with Raleigh foundryman Silas Burns, the stone coping for the iron fence surrounding Union Square, which they completed in November 1848 and which was fifty years later (1898) removed to enclose City Cemetery.

In September 1836 Stronach married Sarah Eubanks Moody Savage (ca. 1814–18 Feb. 1866), a widow from Richmond, Va. The couple had four sons and two daughters. Three of the sons became well-known local business and civic leaders. William Carter (1 Nov. 1844–3 Mar. 1901) and Alexander B[arron] (29 Aug. 1847–2 June 1910), after serving in the Confederate army, opened the W. C. and A. B. Stronach grocery firm. They operated as many as three stores at one time but later formed separate businesses, including a cotton brokerage and commission houses. W. C. was an organizer of the North Carolina Confederate Veterans' ("Old Soldiers") Home in Raleigh, which he served as executive director, succeeded by A. B. He also built a large warehouse at 319–323 South Wilmington Street; designed as a tobacco salesroom, it was also utilized for inaugurations, balls, and other state and community activities. An incorporator and eventually president of the Raleigh Savings Bank, W. C. was a Raleigh alderman from 1872 to 1876, serving once as mayor pro tempore, and from 1892 to 1896 he was chairman of the Wake County Board of County Commissioners. He was also a director of the Atlantic and North Carolina and the Seaboard Air-Line railroads, of Oakwood Cemetery Association, and of Peace Institute.

For the W. C. Stronach family, Thomas Briggs in the 1870s built the home known as Willowbrook or "Geranium Valley" at the northwestern corner of North Boundary and Bloodworth streets (601 North Bloodworth Street), still the residence of descendants a hundred years later. A. B. served one term (1905–7) in the North Carolina House of Representatives. Frank Stronach (4 Feb. 1851–8 Apr. 1934), who had an auction business and also dealt in wagons, buggies, and furniture, was elected to successive terms on the Raleigh Board of Aldermen, serving from 1891 to 1897. The eldest son, George Thomas (1842–10 Jan. 1887), served in the Confederate army, then became a cotton factor as well as a wholesale and retail grocer.

William Stronach, patriarch of the Raleigh family, was a member and elder of Raleigh's First Presbyterian Church. One of the organizers of a local chapter of the national temperance society, he served as its first vice-president in 1845. His strict family rules, as remembered by his son and namesake, were cited by a grandson, Alexander: "Sunday was one continuous session of Sunday school, church and religious instruction; no amusements, no reading of secular books or papers—a day to meditate upon your misdeeds, to fear Hell and perhaps to question the happiness of a Presbyterian Heaven 'where congregations ne'er break up and Sabbaths have no end.'" Even on Saturdays, "before there was any hunting or fishing or playing, a portion of the Shorter Catechism had to be memorized and recited" to the boys' father. A tribute of respect inserted in the *North Carolina Standard* by fellow members of the Sons of Temperance after his death noted that "he always had a word of counsel, admonition or reproof to administer in behalf of Temperance, and never let an opportunity escape unimproved for inculcating its sublime precepts." Politically, he was a Whig.

Stronach's death followed a lengthy illness. Buried in Raleigh City Cemetery, his body was later moved to Oakwood Cemetery, as was that of his widow, who survived him by nine years.

SEE: Willis G. Briggs, "Ante-Bellum Homes of City," Raleigh *News and Observer*, 26 Apr. 1942; Grady L. E. Carroll, *They Lived in Raleigh*, 2 vols. (1977); John L. Cheney, Jr., ed., *North Carolina Government, 1585–1974* (1975); Mary Lee McMillan, "Old Raleigh Home Has Silent History," *Raleigh Times*, 3 Mar. 1966; Memory F. Mitchell and Thornton W. Mitchell, "The Philanthropic Bequests of John Rex of Raleigh," *North Carolina Historical Review* 49 (Summer 1972); North Carolina Comptroller's Report [1840–41], May 1841; *North Carolina Laws, 1846–1847*, Resolutions; Raleigh Board of Aldermen, Minutes, 4 Feb. 1898; Raleigh City Directories; Raleigh *Constitutionalist*, 3 Sept. 1833; Raleigh *Daily Sentinel*, 20 Feb. 1866, 14 Jan., 23 July 1873; Raleigh *News and Observer*, 8 Jan. 1960; Raleigh *North Carolina Standard*, 13, 20 May 1857; Raleigh *Register* (weekly), 13 Sept. 1835, 4 June 1838, (semiweekly), 13 Feb. 1843, 7 Nov. 1845, 4 May 1847, 18 Nov. 1848, 5 Jan. 1853, 1 Nov. 1854, 9 Jan. 1856; Report of Com[m]issioners Appointed to Superintend the Re-building of the State Capitol, 4 Dec. 1834, in Legislative Documents, 1834 (North Carolina State Archives, Raleigh); Alexander Stronach, *The "Geranium Valley" Stronachs* (1956); Wake County Board of County Commissioners, Minutes, 1892–96; Wake County Court Minutes, Aug. 1835; Wake County Deed Book 12 and Marriage Bonds; R. H. Whitaker, *Incidents and Anecdotes* (1905).

ELIZABETH REID MURRAY

Strong, George Vaughan *(7 May 1827–10 Oct. 1897)*, judge and legislator, was born near Clinton in Sampson County, the son of Dr. Salmon and Eliza Sampson Strong. The family of Dr. Strong had moved to North Carolina from Bolton, Conn. Eliza was the daughter of Michael Sampson and of the family of John Sampson, for whom the county was named. In the eighteenth century John Sampson was given a large tract of land in North Carolina by his uncle, George Vaughan of Dublin, Ireland. George Vaughan Strong was named for that connection. As a boy he lived for some time with his uncle, Dr. Fred Hill, at Hill's estate, Orton, on the Cape Fear River below Wilmington. The doctor later became his guardian. Strong was prepared for college at Lovejoy Academy in Raleigh and then entered The University of North Carolina, where he was graduated with honors in 1845. In 1847 a New York publisher issued his *Francis Herbert, A Romance of the Revolution, and Other Poems*, a juvenile production dedicated to a university classmate, Jesse P. Smith. Several of the poems related to the Lower Cape Fear, while one commemorated the death of his classmate, John W. Burton, of Halifax, the son of Governor Hutchins G. Burton. Later in life Judge Strong tried to suppress this work as being inconsistent with his career.

For a while Strong taught in Wilmington before moving to Goldsboro, where he continued to teach until he acquired the *Goldsboro Telegraph*. He studied law, was licensed, and became a partner of William T. Dortch in Goldsboro.

Strong represented Wayne County in the Secession Convention of 1861. He raised a company of volunteer soldiers for the Confederacy but did not serve himself, as he was appointed Confederate States district attorney. He was also a member of the 1861–62 constitutional convention. During his residence in Goldsboro he was for many years vestryman and senior warden of St. Stephen's Episcopal Church. Strong moved to Raleigh in 1871 and joined the practice of former governor Thomas Bragg and W. N. H. Smith under the firm name of Bragg, Smith, and Strong. In 1874 he was elected to represent Wake County in the General Assembly. In the important session of the Assembly in 1875, Strong was a leader in reopening the university, which had been closed since 1868. It was reported that on this occasion he "made one of the most eloquent of his many eloquent speeches during a long and successful career at the bar."

He was elected judge of the criminal court of Wake County in 1876 and filled the post with distinction for many years. Also in 1876 Strong was one of the incorporators of the Historical Society of North Carolina. From 1877 to 1889 he was a trustee of The University of North Carolina, which awarded him an LL.D. degree in 1889. In his *History of the University of North Carolina*, President Kemp P. Battle cited Strong as "an excellent lawyer and judge, distinguishing himself in procuring the revival of the University."

An oval portrait of Strong painted by William Garl Browne is in the possession of his great-grandson, George V. Strong IV of Philadelphia. According to tradition, it was painted while the artist was living at the Strong home in Goldsboro during the Civil War.

Strong married Anna Eliza, the daughter of Robert Cowan of Wilmington and his wife Sarah, the daughter of Governor David Stone. They had nine children, seven of whom reached maturity. Of the sons, George married Sally Smith and Robert Cowan married Daisy Horner. The daughters of Judge Strong were Mrs. William Hicks, Mrs. Weston Gales, Mrs. Norwood Giles, Mrs. John Calvert, and Mrs. John H. Kornealy. He was buried in Oakwood Cemetery, Raleigh.

SEE: Kemp P. Battle, *History of the University of North Carolina*, 2 vols. (1907–12); John L. Cheney, Jr., ed., *North Carolina Government, 1585–1979* (1981); Frank A. Daniels, *Address on Presentation of a Portrait of the Late George Vaughan Strong to the Supreme Court of North Carolina. . . 18 May 1934* (no date); Daniel L. Grant, *Alumni History of the University of North Carolina* (1924); *Library of Southern Literature*, vol. 15 (1907); William M. Robinson, Jr., "Admiralty in 1861: The Confederate States District Court for the Division of Pamlico of the District of North Carolina," *North Carolina Historical Review* 17 (April 1940).

CLAIBORNE T. SMITH, JR.

Strother, John *(d. 19 Aug. 1815)*, land agent and topographic surveyor, was born in Culpeper County, Va., the son of George and Mary Kennerly Strother. He is usually confused with his cousin-german of the same name, a trustee of the Baptist church on Cain Creek, Orange County, N.C., and sometimes confused with his second cousin, John Strother, who, like the surveyor, was in the Creek War but whose army career ended in 1815 following the mutinous conduct of soldiers under his command. When George Strother died in 1767, he left provision for the education of his children. His elder son, John, was taught the surveyor's business. Sometime after 1785 young Strother left Culpeper County, Va., for Wilkes County, Ga., presumably drawn there as a surveyor by Georgia's intended opening of the Indian lands lying on its northern and northwestern frontiers. There he met Zachariah Cox, of Georgia, an indefatigable land speculator, and fell in with Cox's scheme to secure a large tract of land at Muscle Shoals in the bend of the Tennessee River.

The Muscle Shoals lands were a lodestone to draw the eyes of the covetous, for here the produce of the western country, shipped down the Tennessee River, which held the territory in its embrace, could be gathered and transported a short distance to the Alabama River for shipment to Mobile and the Gulf. The shoals lay well within Indian country, the ultimate jurisdiction over the region in which they were situated being claimed simultaneously by Georgia and South Carolina under their charters, Great Britain through conquest, and Spain through occupation. By the convention of Beaufort, April 1787, South Carolina recognized the superior claim of Georgia to jurisdiction over the territory lying between Fort Prince George and the Mississippi. Georgia, in turn, disdained the pretensions of Great Britain and ignored the claims of Spain. Land speculators welcomed the convention and formed companies to engross as much of the Indian lands as they could persuade Georgia to let them have.

Zachariah Cox and John Strother, with Thomas Gilbert and a small number of associates, organized the Tennessee Company and successfully negotiated a purchase from the Georgia Assembly in 1789 of 3.5 million acres on Muscle Shoals for the sum of $46,785. (Two other companies, the Virginia Company and the South Carolina Company, purchased grants of 7 million acres and 5 million acres respectively.) Cox, Strother, and Gilbert moved their operation from Georgia into Tennessee Territory in 1790. In September of that year they advertised bounties of 500 acres per family and 250 acres for single men willing to embark with their fleet downriver to Muscle Shoals on 10 Jan. 1791. The company opened a land office at the confluence of the Holston and French Broad rivers (to be moved to Muscle Shoals after embarkation), with a promise to give undoubted fee simple title to lands laid out under authority of the land office.

Despite a proclamation by President George Washington forbidding this projected expedition into Indian lands protected by treaty from incursions by white settlers, the promoters went on with their plans. Their small party of seventeen descended the Tennessee to the bend early in 1791 and built a blockhouse and defense works on an island in Muscle Shoals. In the interim Governor William Blount of Tennessee Territory had sent to the Indians word of the Cox expedition. Chief Glass of the Cherokee suddenly materialized at the shoals with a group of warriors from the Lower Cherokee Towns and uttered words that caused Cox and his party to abandon the place. The Indians then burned the blockhouse. This put an end to the immediate hopes of the Tennessee Company.

Prevented by the Indians from surveying, subdividing, and selling the land to settlers, Cox, Strother, and Gilbert were unable to raise the full purchase price of the original grant. Consequently the 1789 sale fell through. Cox, in whom the lust for land was deeply seated, persisted in his efforts to secure a defensible title to the land. In 1795, when the notorious Yazoo Land Act was pushed through the Georgia Assembly, he secured a fresh grant of the Muscle Shoals land for the Tennessee Company at a cost of $60,000. It is not clear that Strother remained a member of the company at this time, but investors speculating in other of the 1795 Yazoo lands included William Blount, David Allison, and Judge James Wilson, all of whose careers were to influence the course of Strother's life.

The Muscle Shoals venture brought Strother under the eye of Governor William Blount, who had himself attempted to procure the same land earlier. When Blount (and his associates) negotiated to purchase by "Indian title" the property in the bend of the Tennessee River in 1784 and 1785, there can be little doubt that he acted both for himself and for his brothers Thomas and John Gray. In the early 1790s John Gray Blount began speculating in North Carolina lands in earnest. He acquired land for himself and associates in a multitude of entries in various eastern counties and in Buncombe totaling more than three million acres. These entries were surveyed individually by the county surveyors and their deputies. Some of the larger entries were for huge tracts that embraced earlier grants to landowners or their predecessors. Blount found that to dispose of his speculation lands to advantage he needed surveyors who were capable of joining these multitudes of surveys into general plans delineating the whole and the watercourses that drained them, or of laying out the great tracts in a manner that showed in correct detail the property lines of those who owned land within the tract under earlier patents of title. For this purpose he employed two men: Jonathan Price, of Pasquotank County, who had an established claim to the skills of a topographic surveyor, and John Strother, who probably was introduced to John Gray Blount by Governor William Blount. Strother was characterized by a friendly address and a prudent discretion, and his involvement in the Muscle Shoals venture of the Tennessee Company must have convinced Governor Blount of Strother's intrepidity.

The year in which Strother met John Gray Blount, or how early he was employed by Blount, is unknown. By the beginning of 1795 Strother was in southeastern North Carolina making a comprehensive plan of all of Blount's surveys, totaling more than 850,000 acres in Robeson, Bladen, Cumberland, and Richmond counties. It was probably at this time that Strother met Jonathan Price, who was surveying Blount's land in Holly Shelter and Whiteoak Pocosin in New Hanover and Onslow counties; by August 1795 Price and Strother were jointly surveying the huge tracts in Carteret County owned by Blount's partner, David Allison. Three years earlier Price had entered into an agreement with Nathaniel Christmas of Orange County to produce a map of North Carolina. Towards this end he and Christmas had borrowed £290 from the state on a three-year loan. They completed a manuscript draft of their map in 1795. Their work, however, must not have answered expectations, for it is not mentioned after an unsuccessful attempt to find subscribers to underwrite the cost of publication.

Price abandoned the first version of his map after Strother agreed to join his considerable talents to those of Price in preparing a superior map of the state and in making a fresh survey of the coast. Early in September 1795 Price borrowed from the state another £300, which presumably was for the purpose of producing the new version of the state map. If so, he and Strother had reached an accord by that date. On 7 Mar. 1796 the two surveyors copyrighted their projected survey of the coast from Cape Henry to Cape Roman and their intended map of the state by entering their titles in the U.S. Circuit Court for the District of North Carolina. By December of that year Price and Strother had expended over $3,000 but had completed draft surveys of only about two-thirds of the counties. Consequently they petitioned the Assembly for another loan and were allowed £500.

John Gray Blount encouraged Price and Strother in their work by allowing them to use his own surveys and plans and, apparently, assisted in their surveys of the various counties. For example, in the spring of 1797 Strother completed surveying Wake, Cumberland, Richmond, Anson, Montgomery, Rowan, Cabarrus, Mecklenburg, Lincoln, Rutherford, Burke, and Iredell counties, the southwestern part of Wilkes, and part of Buncombe. Most of this work appears to have been done by Strother while en route to Buncombe County on Blount's business. (The single surviving example of Strother's county surveys is the one for Robeson County located in the John Gray Blount Papers in the North Carolina State Archives.) Strother's surveys in the spring of 1797 brought the map so near to completion that Price announced forthcoming publication in an advertisement opening subscriptions to the map in June of that year. By mid-1798 Strother had completed all his county surveys, enabling Price to finish a version of their map in a manuscript that was exhibited to the General Assembly with a request for a further loan in aid of publication in December 1798. The Assembly refused the loan. Despite this setback, Price pushed on with the remainder of his work and in the spring of 1799 completed his survey of roads in the counties lying in the northeastern sector of the state from the fall line to Pasquotank County. This finally brought the work to an end. After that the matter was out of Strother's hands, as Price attended to the details of publication.

In May 1797 John Gray Blount gave Price a hint to proceed with publication of the chart resulting from the coastal survey he had undertaken with Strother—and enriched the hint with an order for twenty copies. The next month Price announced in the *Wilmington Gazette* impending publication of the coastal chart from his and Strother's survey. Price supplied plates he had obtained from Philadelphia to William Johnston of New Bern to be used in engraving the coastal chart. It was published in 1798 in two sheets, each measuring 14 by 23 inches, under the dedicatory legend, "To Navigators This Chart, Being an Actual Survey of the Sea Coast and Inland Navigation from Cape Henry to Cape Roman, is most Respectfully Inscribed by Price and Strother." A companion to the coastal chart, and growing out of their survey of the coast, was "A Map of the Cape Fear River and its Vicinity from the Frying Pan Shoals to Wilmington by Actual Survey." This chart, without publication or copyright date, and measuring 13⅞ by 18¾ inches, was not entrusted to a local artisan for engraving. Instead, it was sent to William Barker, of Philadelphia, the skilled engraver of maps and nautical charts employed by Matthew Carey in producing his *General Atlas* of 1796. Joshua Potts, one of the principal merchants of Wilmington, had the chart of the river reengraved (without date and without acknowledging the authorship of Price and Strother) as a charming business card measuring 5¾ by 8 inches by John Scoles, of New York, one of the engravers used by John Payne in his *New and Complete System of Universal Geography* (1798–1800). Publication of Price and Strother's map of North Carolina, however, took ten more years to bring to successful conclusion—so long that Price was obliged to have parts of the plates reengraved in order to show the creation of new counties. By 1808, when "The First Actual Survey of the State of North Carolina" was placed in the hands of the subscribers, Strother had already written his will and left North Carolina for good. No doubt copies of this splendid map were sent to Strother in Tennessee.

The last eight years of Strother's stay in North Carolina were spent essentially in Buncombe County, where he was active on behalf of John Gray Blount and his business associate, David Allison, on behalf of the state, on behalf of local government, and on behalf of his own interests. The decline of American commercial prosperity that set in towards the latter half of 1796 continued to worsen in 1797 after the Bank of England suspended specie payments; it reached its low point during the talk of an impending war between America and France in the middle and latter part of 1798. The great speculators in land, whose schemes and finances were very nearly inextricably linked, began to collapse and then to fall into bankruptcy. The difficulties of the celebrated financier, Robert Morris, created financial woes for David Allison and Judge James Wilson, both of whom were financially committed to John Gray Blount's speculations in land. By late 1796 both Allison and Blount were hard pressed to pay the entry fees on hundreds of thousands of acres they had entered in North Carolina. By 1797 they could not pay the taxes on the hundreds of thousands of acres they held by patent from the state. In 1798 the General Assembly ordered the sale of the speculation lands on which the taxes had not been paid just as Allison was imprisoned for debt in Philadelphia. Allison sent money from prison to Blount to be used by Strother in paying taxes on Allison's land. He further proposed "selling" his land to Strother (so as to defeat the creditors who were trying to ruin him), then sailing to Europe with Strother to sell the three million acres he owned in Georgia and elsewhere. Blount, however, was in no position to let Strother depart for Europe on Allison's behalf. Instead, he sent him to Raleigh with negotiable instruments with which to raise money to pay taxes on the Buncombe lands, then sent Strother on to Buncombe to salvage what he could.

In Buncombe, Strother purchased 546,880 of the more than one million acres of the speculation lands at a tax sale. He took the deed from the sheriff in his own name and immediately began selling the land in small tracts to local buyers, giving personal deeds of title to the purchasers. He was, of course, acting for Blount in these transactions, as is evidenced by the fact that one of the provisions of his will was to return the unsold balance to Blount. From this time Strother became Blount's principal business agent for western affairs. At the same time, he began acquiring tracts in Buncombe on his own account, eventually purchasing 4,440 acres from the state apart from land bought from private persons. Among the latter were the ferry and adjoining lands at Warm Springs, already attracting people during the sickly season from South Carolina and Tennessee. Here Strother laid out the town of Spaightville, incorporated in 1802. (Following earth changes at the time of the Charleston earthquake of 1886, the temperature of the springs rose, causing their name to be altered to Hot Springs in that year.)

In addition to attending to his own and Blount's affairs, Strother was active in public matters. He served in 1799 as one of the surveyors for North Carolina in determining the boundary with Tennessee. In 1800 he was commissioned one of the marshals for taking the U.S. census in Buncombe, Rutherford, Wilkes, and Ashe counties. In 1805 he was named one of the commissioners to procure a public square in Asheville. Strother did not serve under the latter commission, however, for he was on the verge of leaving North Carolina to enter what would prove to be the third and final decade of his adult life.

In 1804 Strother accompanied John Gray Blount, Jr., to Nashville, Tenn., carrying with him a letter of introduction to Andrew Jackson that had been give him by Willie Blount. In 1805 Strother made his brother George his agent for the sale of Buncombe lands. In 1806 he entered into a contract with Henry M. Rutledge of Charleston, S.C., to help survey Rutledge's 75,000 acres on Elk River, Tenn., and to act as his agent in leasing the land. Strother immediately wrote his will and left North Carolina. The opening of a land office for middle Tennessee in 1806, the attraction of Duck River lands, and continuing business for John Gray Blount kept Strother in Nashville and Jefferson for some time.

In the spring of 1812 Strother, at the general's request, accompanied Andrew Jackson to Georgia, where Jackson went to secure from the heirs of David Allison quitclaim deeds to 10,000 acres that had come to him by execution of a judgment levied on lands originally patented by Thomas and John Gray Blount, then sold to Allison. Weeks later, when war was declared against Great Britain, General Jackson employed Strother on a mission to Cherokee Chief John Lowrey, whose help he sought in preventing the spread of British intrigue among the Indians. At the same time, he sent Strother on a scouting expedition to discover Indian strengths. When war against the Creek Indians broke out in earnest following the massacre at Fort Mims on 30 Aug. 1812, Jackson appointed Strother topographic engineer to his army. Strother served well in a triple role of scout, adviser, and topographer. Fort Strother, built on the Coosa River in October 1813, was named as a compliment to him. In February 1814 he resigned as Jackson's topographic engineer in order to return to middle Tennessee on business (apparently for John Gray Blount). As a result, he was not with Jackson at the Battle of the Horseshoe, which ended in capitulation by the Creeks on 24 March.

Following the Treaty of Fort Jackson, Strother was appointed surveyor to the commissioners to settle the boundary between the Creek and Cherokee Indians, and to lay off the 23 million acres of Creek land (half of the present state of Alabama) taken by the United States under terms of the treaty. In the spring of 1815 he returned to Fort Strother prepared to begin the survey. After waiting vainly for the commissioners to arrive, he began surveying a portion of the boundary unlikely to be subject to dispute and was thus engaged at the time of his death in August. A manuscript map of the Creek country that he had started drawing in 1814 was left unfinished at his death. Strother was survived by Flora Inman of Buncombe County and their two natural daughters, Mary Inman (Mrs. Ninian Edmonston) and Caroline Inman (Mrs. Benjamin R. Edmonston).

SEE: John Haywood, *Civil and Political History of Tennessee* (1796); Alice B. Keith and others, eds., *The John Gray Blount Papers*, vols. 2–4 (1959–82); Thomas McAdory Owen, "William Strother of Virginia and His Descendants," *Publications of the Southern History Association* 2 (April 1898); James G. M. Ramsey, *Annals of Tennessee* (1853); Mary Lindsay Thornton, "The Price and Strother 'First Actual Survey of North Carolina,'" *North Carolina Historical Review* 41 (1965); A. P. Whitaker, "The Muscle Shoals Speculation, 1783–1789," *Mississippi Valley Historical Review* 13 (December 1926).

GEORGE STEVENSON

Stroup, Jacob *(d. 8 Oct. 1846)*, **and Moses Stroup** *(1794–1877)*, ironworkers, came from a family of "mechanics," ironworkers, and small businessmen who were among the earliest to engage in the iron industry in North Carolina, South Carolina, Georgia, and South Alabama. As mechanics the Stroups were skilled artisans, possessing the knowledge to engage in the manufacture of iron, yet often lacking the capital to do so without backing from local merchants or planters. As such, they illustrate a phenomenon of antebellum southern industry as well as give the lie to the myth that no self-respecting southerner would engage in manual industry, or that no honor could be derived from such occupations. On the other hand, their frequent successes, failures, and moves within the South illustrate both the risk involved in industrial enterprises and the opportunities available to those not born to wealth. They also demonstrate the advantage of the mechanic—if he went bankrupt, his skills could not be taken from him, and he could start anew elsewhere. If he succeeded in turning an undeveloped site into a prosperous furnace, he could sell it for a profit, and move on to an undeveloped site farther west, develop it with his sweat, knowledge, and the capital from the previous sale, and, with good luck, become a relatively wealthy man.

The Stroups apparently were iron makers from colonial days. David Stroup was a soldier and gunmaker with the Continental army in Pennsylvania. After the war he moved to North Carolina with his fifteen-year-old son, Jacob. David and Jacob are believed to have engaged in the iron business in Lincoln County, but the records are scanty. Jacob served as an officer in the War of 1812.

Sometime in 1815 or before, Jacob moved to South Carolina and founded an iron company at the mouth of Kings Creek, on the Broad River. A flood and the death of his partner sent the company into bankruptcy, though under new ownership it operated until the Civil War. Jacob Stroup married his late partner's widow, a Mrs. Fewell, and began an ironworks nearby. This he sold in 1825 to a group of New York investors and began a new enterprise near Ninety-Nine Islands in the Broad River. While it was yet incomplete, he sold it about 1830 for $17,000. Jacob moved to Habersham County, Ga., and built a pioneer iron plant, which he sold in 1836. In the early 1840s he began a furnace at Cane Creek in Ala., with his own capital. But he reportedly lost heavily in a bad investment in a gold mine. Stroup sold the Alabama furnace in 1842, then built another in Cass County, Ga., containing a blast furnace and forge, and a sawmill. He sold this furnace to his son Moses about 1843 and began another at Altoona, which he operated until his death.

Moses Stroup, the eldest son of Jacob, was born in Lincoln County, N.C. With little formal schooling, he was brought up in the iron business. Many contemporaries considered him to be one of the "most expert furnacemen" in the South and a "remarkable genius" in the iron business, as well as a good money-maker but a "poor keeper." He accompanied his father to South Carolina about 1815, and when Jacob moved to Georgia in the late 1820s, Moses stayed behind. But in 1843 he joined his father at Cass County, Ga., and bought him out. Moses built a rolling mill and rolled some of the first railroad iron made in Georgia, some of which was used on the state-owned Western and Atlantic. In 1847 he sold the Cass County works to Mark Anthony Cooper and Company and shortly moved to Alabama, where he bought ore lands from the government and began the Round Mountain Furnace in 1849. He later moved to Tuscaloosa County, Ala., and started the Tannehill Furnace. In 1862 he sold his interest to his partner and became superintendent and manager of Oxmoor Furnaces in Jefferson County, Ala., no longer owning his own furnace but working for Daniel Pratt and others. The furnace was destroyed in the Civil War. All three of his sons, Alonzo, Henry, and Andrew, were killed in the Civil War, but he was survived by three daughters. In his lifetime he established seven furnaces and five rolling mills and at the time of his death was ready to start again.

SEE: Ethel Armes, *The Story of Coal and Iron in Alabama* (1910); Ernest M. Lander, Jr., "The Iron Industry in Antebellum South Carolina," *Journal of Southern History* 20 (1954).

JOHN R. DETREVILLE

Strowd, William Franklin *(7 Dec. 1832–12 Dec. 1911),* farm leader and congressman, was the son of Bryant and Martha Wilson Strowd, residents of Orange County. As a youth he attended Bingham School, High Hill Academy, and Graham Institute. Although there had not yet been a declaration of war, he and other young men of the area began organizing a company of volunteers on 6 Apr. 1861; on 22 April they met at Chapel Hill and enrolled for six months of active service. On 13 May in Raleigh the company was mustered into the state service with the designation Orange Light Infantry. Under the command of Richard J. Ashe it became Company D of the First Regiment of North Carolina Volunteers, commanded by Colonel D. H. Hill, who in July was promoted to the rank of brigadier general.

During the six months Strowd served with Hill's regiment, it was deployed mainly in the area between Richmond and Yorktown. Because all or most of the enlistments in the First Regiment were for only six months, the regiment was dissolved in the fall of 1861 and replaced by one designated Eleventh Regiment of North Carolina Regulars. In the meantime many of the soldiers had reenlisted in other regiments. Although Strowd is believed to have served—at least intermittently—as a private throughout the war, his name does not appear on any extant muster roll after he mustered out of Company D in November 1861.

On 18 Apr. 1861, on the eve of his departure for military service, Strowd married Louisiana Atwater, the daughter of Jahaza and Sally Stone Atwater. After completing his military service, he and his wife moved across the line into Chatham County to settle on a farm given to the bride by her father. There Strowd applied himself so diligently that he gained recognition both as an outstanding farmer and as a farm leader. In 1875 he was chosen as one of Chatham County's two delegates to the state constitutional convention called to undo some of the work of the carpetbag convention of 1868 and restore white supremacy. Although he was named a member of the Committee on Suffrage and Eligibility, his principal contribution was in the field of agriculture. First he presented a memorial from the State Grange of North Carolina urging the establishment of a State Department of Agriculture and later the report of the committee to which the memorial had been referred. The committee recommended that such a department be established, and in due course one was set up.

Four years of war had left the South prostrate, and all kinds of businesses had a long, hard struggle to recover any substantial degree of economic well-being. This was particularly true of agriculture. Southern farmers were in a critical economic condition continuously from 1868 to 1900. In fact, their condition progressively worsened as the price of the things they had to sell kept getting lower and the cost of the things they had to buy kept increasing. The price paid for cotton, for example, fell from one dollar a pound in 1868 to twelve cents in the seventies, nine cents in the eighties, and seven cents in the nineties.

The farmers attributed their distressed condition to the credit system, high and discriminatory freight rates, the country's tariff policy, the trusts, and unfair taxation. These complaints were not restricted to the South but were nationwide. Eventually the farm leaders became convinced that relief could come only through concerted action. To improve their bargaining position farmers must organize and launch a revolution, and this they did on a national scale. This "agrarian crusade" went through three stages: first, the organization of Granges, which emphasized education; second, the Farmers' Alliance, which promoted joint effort; and third, political action through a Populist (People's) party.

Strowd assumed a leadership role in all three stages of the agrarian movement, first at the county level and then at the state level. On 11 June 1892 a third-party convention in Chatham County, endorsed the Populist party, which had been organized at St. Louis in February. Delegates, including two blacks, were chosen to attend the upcoming Congressional District Convention and instructed to vote for the nomination of W. F. Strowd for Congress. At the convention held on 17 June, Strowd was nominated as the Populist candidate. In the November election, however, he was defeated by the Democratic incumbent. Nevertheless, in 1894 he won a seat in the U.S. House of Representatives as a Populist and was reelected in 1896. But he failed to get on the Fusionist ticket in 1898, this honor going to his brother-in-law, John W. Atwater, who won the election and thus became Strowd's replacement in Congress.

After four years in Congress Strowd returned to his Chatham County farm and gave his full attention to agricultural interests until 1908, when he moved to Chapel Hill to live with his son, Robert L., whose wife was Fannie Headen of Pittsboro. He died there and was buried in the Chapel Hill cemetery.

SEE: *Biog. Dir. Am. Cong.* (1961); Wade Hadley and others, eds., *Chatham County, 1771–1971* (1971); Hugh T. Lefler and Albert R. Newsome, *North Carolina: The History of a Southern State* (1954); Louis H. Manarin, comp., *North Carolina Troops, 1861–1865: A Roster*, vol. 3 (1971).

PAUL W. WAGER

Strudwick, Clement Read *(16 Apr. 1900–26 Feb. 1958)*, portrait artist, was born in Columbia, Tenn., the son of Shepperd and Susan Read Strudwick. His father, a native of Hillsborough, N.C., lived in Tennessee for a few years while phosphate was being mined on land that he owned. His mother was a native of Farmville, Va. The family returned to Hillsborough when Clement was two; he attended Donaldson Military Academy in Fayetteville and served briefly in the Student Army Training Corps during World War I. While enrolled at The University of North Carolina during the period 1918–20, he was on the staff of several student publications. During that time he became acquainted with Jonathan Daniels of Raleigh and prepared illustrations for some of Daniels's writings. Leaving the university without a degree, he worked for six years in the insurance department of the North Carolina inspection and rating bureau.

Aware of his artistic ability, Strudwick was undecided whether to remain in the insurance business or to take art seriously. His father, who was also artistically inclined though never professionally employed in that field, encouraged his son to make the change. At age twenty-six Strudwick began studying drawing at the Art Student's League in New York under Frank Vincent. Afterwards he became a private pupil of the American painter George Luke and also studied under Frank Vincent Du Mond. In time, when confident of his ability, Strudwick began painting portraits and within a few years enjoyed wide acclaim. In 1929 he went to Paris and studied for about a year under M. Louis François Biliul. By 1933 his portraits appeared in Boston, New York, Philadelphia, Richmond, Raleigh, Hillsborough, Columbia, Florence, Birmingham, Savannah, Memphis, and elsewhere. In Raleigh his portraits of the Right Reverend Joseph Blount Cheshire and General Albert L. Cox were greatly admired, as was his depiction of President Edward Kidder Graham in Chapel Hill. On occasion he also produced landscapes and figures.

Returning home to Hillsborough, Strudwick painted in a workshop constructed for that purpose behind his parents' home. At times he worked in the Art Center Studio in Durham, but he accepted commissions all around the country. He organized the North Carolina Artists' Club to display the works of Tar Heel artists, served on the board of directors of the North Carolina State Art Society, and was a life member of the Southern Academy of Design. Strudwick, a Presbyterian, never married. His funeral was held in the Hillsborough Presbyterian Church, and he was buried in the Hillsborough cemetery.

SEE: *Charlotte Observer*, 9 Apr. 1933; *Durham Sun*, 27–28 Feb. 1958; Daniel L. Grant, *Alumni History of the University of North Carolina* (1924); *Greensboro Daily News*, 21 Dec. 1944; Raleigh *News and Observer*, 7 Sept. 1930, 27 Feb. 1958.

WILLIAM S. POWELL

Strudwick, Edmund Charles Fox *(28 Mar. 1802–29 Nov. 1879)*, physician, was born at Long Meadows, the family home near Hillsborough, the second son of William Francis and Martha Shepperd Strudwick, who had three sons and two daughters. His grandfather Samuel Strudwick, the first of the family in America, had come to North Carolina to claim two vast tracts of land deeded to him, his brother, and his sister by George Burrington, a former governor of the province, to cover a debt owed their father, then deceased, an earlier Edmund Strudwick. One tract was 10,000 acres in New Hanover County called Stag Park, the other 30,000 acres in Orange County in the Haw Oldfields (Hawfields), on each of which Samuel Strudwick established a plantation home.

Dr. Edmund Strudwick received his early schooling at William Bingham's Hillsborough Academy. At his father's death in 1810, Dr. James Webb, a physician, became his guardian, a relationship that may have influenced the course of Strudwick's life. He took two years of lectures at the medical school of the University of Pennsylvania, where Webb had studied, and received his degree in 1824. He then spent two additional years in an internship at the Philadelphia Almshouse and Charity Hospital before returning to Hillsborough to practice.

For over fifty years this commanding, handsome, and revered figure rode the muddy country roads at all hours and in all weathers to treat the sick, or he traveled to distant parts of the state for consultations and operations. He also cared for particularly sick or difficult cases at his home (a common practice of the day), where they remained until they recovered or died. Surgery, still in its infancy, was his specialty, though the bulk of his practice was general medicine and obstetrics. Like all doctors of that time he mixed his own prescriptions, often made from medicinal plants of the field, and dispensed his own drugs.

He never held public office and no medical writings of his survive. Only the semi-legendary lore that unusual character attracts remains to tell of him: his faithful attention to his patients, his unfailing cheerfulness of temper, his inveterate tobacco smoking (six pipefuls before breakfast), his indefatigable search for knowledge through the reading of medical literature even as he rode out on his far-reaching rounds, and his unflagging physical stamina despite the heavy demands of his profession.

Strudwick was one of a group who reestablished the long defunct North Carolina Medical Society, which Dr. Webb had founded in 1799, and became the first president of the new organization in 1850. His address to that body contained the fruit of his reading and thinking about his profession. He advocated high qualifications for admission to medical school after long precollegiate schooling, as well as postgraduate study and internship to perfect the physician's training. He stressed the importance of autopsies to medical knowledge and advocated the exchange of information through means of professional societies and publications. Medical laboratories and museums he urged be set up to serve as valuable adjuncts to the study of medicine.

When offered the superintendentship of the State Hospital for the Insane after its establishment in 1849, Strudwick refused the position. He gave freely of his time, however, in advising and supervising during the seven years of the hospital's construction.

In politics he was an ardent Whig and in religion a Presbyterian; he served as an elder in the Hillsborough church. From his father he had inherited over one thousand acres of land and many slaves so that he was comfortably fixed financially until the Civil War, which left him in straitened circumstances. Strudwick refused to take advantage of the homestead act by which he might have salvaged his home and some land. Instead, he moved to very modest quarters, where he lived out his life.

His accidental death at age seventy-seven was a result of poisoning. He drank by mistake from a glass containing atropine, a portion of which had been administered to his sick son, and died the same day. He was buried in the old town cemetery in Hillsborough beside his wife, who had predeceased him. She was Ann Elizabeth Nash (24 Sept. 1808–26 Sept. 1877), the daughter of Judge Frederick Nash and his wife Mary Kollock Nash. The Strudwicks had five children: William Samuel, Frederick Nash, Edmund, Jr., Martha, and Mary. William and Edmund became physicians, but Martha and Mary died in childhood.

A portrait of Dr. Strudwick by an unknown artist was used for the copy painted by Strudwick's granddaughter, Mrs. W. T. M. Van Plancke, which the family presented to the State Hospital in Raleigh.

SEE: Bennehan Cameron Papers and Cameron Family Papers (Southern Historical Collection, University of North Carolina, Chapel Hill); Estate Papers of William F. Strudwick (North Carolina State Archives, Raleigh); Hugh T. Lefler and Paul Wager, eds., *Orange County, 1752–1952* (1953); Hubert A. Royster, "Edmund Strudwick: Surgeon," *North Carolina Booklet* 15 (July 1915); University of Pennsylvania Archives (University of Pennsylvania, Philadelphia, Pa.); Betsy L. Willis and James W. Strudwick, comps., *Genealogy and Letters of the Strudwick, Ashe, Young, and Allied Families* (1971).

JEAN B. ANDERSON

Strudwick, Frederick Nash *(27 June 1833–29 July 1890)*, lawyer and legislator, was born in Hillsborough, Orange County, one of three sons of Dr. Edmund and Ann Nash Strudwick. His father, a well-known physician, helped reestablish and served as first president of the North Carolina Medical Society. Strudwick's grandfather was Francis Nash, a jurist and member of the North Carolina Supreme Court. After schooling in Hillsborough Frederick attended The University of North Carolina, graduating in 1851. He then began a law practice in Hillsborough. On 27 July 1854 he married Mary S. Burwell of Hillsborough, and they had one son, Robert C. Mary died on 3 July 1859 after a long illness. Strudwick later married Rosa Spottswood, and they had one child, Anne.

During Reconstruction Strudwick became active in the Ku Klux Klan in Orange County. Around Christmas in 1869 he organized and led a group of Klansmen who attempted to assassinate Alamance County Republican state senator T. M. Shoffner, who had introduced legislation aimed at curbing Ku Klux Klan activity. The plot failed when a group of Klansmen opposed to the assassination, hearing the news that Shoffner was in Greensboro, intercepted Strudwick and his men at the Orange-Alamance County line and induced them to turn back.

In February 1870 Strudwick, a Democrat, was chosen to fill the unexpired term of J. J. Allison in the North Carolina House of Representatives. He was elected to a full two-year term in August 1870. In Raleigh his most notable action was presenting the motion to impeach Governor W. W. Holden for having called out the militia against the Ku Klux Klan. Following several meetings with Conservative leaders he introduced the impeachment resolution on 9 Dec. 1870. Strudwick was a central figure in guiding the measure through the house judiciary committee and the full house. He was not chosen as a manager for the subsequent senate trial, however, because it was feared that his widely known association with the Ku Klux Klan might make the impeachment proceedings appear to be a Klan prosecution.

After his service in the house Strudwick became solicitor for the Fifth District, a position he held until his voluntary retirement eight years later. On 11 Aug. 1887 he and C. E. Parish became co-owners and editors of the *Hillsborough Recorder*. In their first issue they stated their editorial philosophy as "a firm and conservative stand on all matters affecting the public welfare." They went on to say "that this paper upon all questions of politics will be thoroughly Democratic, but upon all things else, temperate." He left the *Recorder* after the 8 Mar. 1888 issue.

A member of the Presbyterian church, Strudwick died after an illness of several months and was buried in the Hillsborough Cemetery. A special town meeting, led by C. E. Parish, was convened in his honor. He was survived by his second wife and both children.

SEE: Daniel L. Grant, *Alumni History of the University of North Carolina* (1924); J. G. de Roulhac Hamilton, *Reconstruction in North Carolina* (1914); *Hillsborough Recorder*, scattered issues; *Journal of the House of Representatives of the General Assembly of North Carolina, Session of 1869–70, 1870–71* (1870); Francis Nash Papers (Southern Historical Collection, University of North Carolina, Chapel Hill); *New York Times*, 24 Mar. 1871; F. N. Strudwick, Political Opinion Papers (North Carolina Collection, University of North Carolina, Chapel Hill); Allen W. Trelease, *White Terror* (1971); Stephen B. Weeks Scrapbook, vol. 7 (North Carolina Collection, University of North Carolina, Chapel Hill); Betsy L. Willis and James W. Strudwick, comps., *Genealogy and Letters of the Strudwick, Ashe, Young, and Allied Families* (1971).

R. M. CHAMBERS

Strudwick, Samuel *(d. 1797)*, colonial official, was living in a fashionable section of London when he purchased George Burrington's North Carolina holdings in September 1761. The former governor estimated the total acreage at thirty thousand. Strudwick was apparently in North Carolina by late 1764 but spent the following year tending to business matters in Boston. By December 1767 he entered the political life of North Carolina when he took up his commission as a royal councillor. Along with several of his fellow councillors, he served as a lieutenant general in the first Regulator expedition in 1768.

In 1770 Strudwick again spent most of the year out of the colony tending to business affairs. Two years later he became secretary and clerk of pleas in North Carolina, two of the most lucrative fee-paying positions in the colony. Later in 1772 Governor Josiah Martin praised him for eliminating previous "malpractices" in the office of clerk of pleas. Notwithstanding, Martin made an unsuccessful effort to remove Strudwick from that office, as he believed that the appointment of the county clerks of court should be the governor's prerogative rather than that of the clerk of pleas. Martin proposed to compensate Strudwick for the loss of his clerkship by making him receiver general, but the Crown refused to support the compromise. Strudwick remained one of Martin's strongest supporters right up until the time of the American Revolution.

With the outbreak of the Revolution, Strudwick withdrew to his plantation on the Upper Cape Fear. In 1780 he was so fearful of losing his home that he sought the assistance of James Iredell and Thomas Burke, a close personal friend. Burke apparently saved the plantation, but Strudwick did lose some land because of the vagueness of his original deeds from Burrington. Strudwick attempted to visit Burke when Burke was being held prisoner by the British in October 1781 but was denied admittance. At the close of the Revolution in 1783, Strudwick was offered a seat on the Council of State but apparently did not take it.

He died at Hawfields in 1797, three years after making his will. He left a wife named Martha and a son, William Francis. In addition to his North Carolina holdings, Strudwick also owned a house and land in London at the time of his death.

SEE: Walter Clark, ed., *State Records of North Carolina*, vols. 11, 15, 19 (1895–1901); New Hanover County Wills (North Carolina State Archives, Raleigh); William S. Powell, ed., *The Correspondence of William Tryon and Other Selected Papers*, 2 vols. (1980–81); William L. Saunders, ed., *Colonial Records of North Carolina*, vols. 6–10 (1888–90).

WILLIAM S. PRICE, JR.

Strudwick, Shepperd *(22 Sept. 1907–15 Jan. 1983)*, actor, was born in Hillsborough, the son of Shepperd and Susan Nash Read Strudwick. He was graduated from the Virginia Episcopal School in 1925 and from The University of North Carolina in 1928. At the university he was a member of Phi Beta Kappa and the Golden Fleece and active with the Carolina Playmakers, where his first role was in *Pierrot* (1925). After graduation he studied acting in New York and worked in the office of Charles Coburn, who was preparing a revival of *The Yellow Jacket*, for which Strudwick was made an understudy. He made his debut in New York as Wu-Hu-Git in that play in 1928. In the 1930s he toured stock theaters, generally playing juvenile roles; afterwards he appeared on the stage in New York and elsewhere in the United States as well as in London and Paris.

During his career Strudwick played over two hundred parts. He also was artist-in-residence at the University of Michigan and at the University of North Carolina at Greensboro. In addition to his stage roles, beginning in 1938 he appeared in motion pictures for MGM, Twentieth-Century Fox, RKO, Paramount, and United Artists. For television he had important roles in such series as "Studio One," "Kraft Television Theater," "Curtain Call," and "You Are There" and appeared on "The Defendants," "Perry Mason," and "The Name of the Game." He was Dr. Field in "As the World Turns," Jim Matthews in "Another World," and Mr. Gibson in "One Life to Live."

His native state recognized his talent in 1963, when he received a North Carolina Award for "excellence in the performing arts."

By his first wife, Helen Wynne, he was the father of Shepperd, III. His second wife was Jan Straub; his third, Margaret O'Neill; and his fourth, Mary Jeffrey, who survived him. During World War II Strudwick served in the U.S. Navy as a lieutenant, senior grade. He died of cancer at his home in Manhattan and was buried in Hillsborough.

SEE: *Chapel Hill Newspaper*, 16 Jan. 1983; Ian Herbert, ed., *Who's Who in the Theatre*, vol. I (1981); *New York Times*, 16 Jan. 1983; *Notable Names in the American Theatre* (1976); David Ragan, *Who's Who in Hollywood, 1900–1976* (1976); Raleigh *News and Observer*, 17 Jan. 1983; *Who's Who in America* (1982).

WILLIAM S. POWELL

Strudwick, William Francis *(12 May 1770–31 July 1810)*, Orange County legislator, was born at Stag Park, on the Northeast River near Wilmington; his parents were Samuel (will dated 1794) and Martha Williams Strudwick. It was reported that Samuel Strudwick had another son, Edmund.

In 1789 William Francis was an Orange County delegate to the second state constitutional convention (November 17–22) in Fayetteville. He also served in the state senate in 1792–93 at New Bern and in 1797 at Raleigh. Between those two terms he represented the Fourth District in the U.S. Congress (13 Dec. 1796–3 Mar. 1797), completing the term of Absalom Tatom. Returning to the North Carolina General Assembly, he served in the house from 1801 to 1803. Between his legislative terms, he pursued agricultural interests. His name is also found in Orange County records as an executor of deeds in 1804.

In 1793 Strudwick married Martha Shepperd (12 Apr. 1770–16 June 1844) in Orange County (marriage bond issued on 5 Sept. 1793). They had at least five children: Elizabeth Jane (Aug. 1794–19 May 1871), Samuel (12 June 1796–21 Nov. 1872), Edmund Charles Fox (28 Mar. 1802–29 Nov. 1879), Martha Lucia Margaret (1808–64), and William Francis, Jr. (1810–52).

The particulars of his death are uncertain. A Raleigh newspaper of August 1810 reported the death of a Major William E. Strudwick at Stag Park, forty-eight years old, leaving a wife and five children. Elsewhere it was reported that he was buried on his Hawfields estate in Orange County.

SEE: *Biog. Dir. Am. Cong.* (1961); John L. Cheney, Jr., ed., *North Carolina Government, 1585–1974* (1975); Walter Clark, ed., *State Records of North Carolina*, vol. 22 (1907); *Durham Morning Herald*, 26 Sept. 1973; *First Census of the United States, 1790* (1908); John Hampden Hill, "Plantations on the Northeast River," in James Sprunt, *Chronicles of the Cape Fear River*, 2d ed. (1916); Alice Barnwell Keith, ed., *The John Gray Blount Papers*, vol. 1 (1952); Hugh Lefler and Paul Wager, eds., *Orange County, 1752–1952* (1953); Marriage Bonds, Orange County (North Carolina State Archives, Raleigh); Fred A. Olds, *An Abstract of North Carolina Wills from about 1760 to about 1880* (1925); Benjamin Perley Poore, *A Descriptive Catalog of the Government Publications of the United States, September 5, 1774 to March 4, 1881* (1885); *Raleigh Register and North-Carolina State Gazette*, 23 Aug. 1810; Betsy L. Willis and James W. Strudwick, comps., *Genealogy and Letters of the Strudwick, Ashe, Young, and Allied Families* (1971); *Who Was Who in America, 1607–1896* (1963); *Wilmington Gazette*, 17, 24 July 1810.

EVA BURBANK MURPHY

Stuart, John *(25 Sept. 1718–21 Mar. 1779)*, Indian agent, was born in Iverness, Scotland. He went to sea as a young man and then sailed for America in 1748. Like other Scots of the same period, Stuart sought economic opportunity in the bustling mercantile world of Charleston, S.C. Although his first business failed in 1755, he had acquired a place for himself as a member of city society, for there he had married a young lady, Sarah, whose surname is unknown, and had been accepted for membership in the St. Andrew's Society, the Charleston Library Society, the Charleston Masonic Lodge, and the South Carolina militia. By 1757 he held the rank of captain in the militia.

At the outbreak of war with France in 1755, Captain John Stuart volunteered his services to the royal governor, who posted him to Fort Loudoun, a British outpost in the Cherokee country. While serving this frontier duty, Stuart became friends with a number of Cherokee, including the important tribal leader Little Carpenter. The friendship was instrumental in saving Stuart's life in 1760. Angered by the land and trade policy of South Carolina and urged on by the French, the Anglophobe Cherokee besieged Fort Loudoun in the spring of 1760, forced its capitulation, and then fell on the garrison as it withdrew. Stuart managed to use his experience in forest diplomacy to persuade his captor that he should be taken to Little Carpenter, who Stuart knew would protect him. Two years later Stuart's experiences in the Indian country proved even more beneficial when he was appointed British superintendent for the southern Indians. From 1762 until his death, John Stuart had the responsibility of implementing official British diplomacy with all the Indian tribes living south of the Ohio River and east of the Mississippi River. Principally he was to cooperate with the governors in establishing boundaries and purchasing lands and to attempt some control of the still lucrative Indian trade. In time of war with foreign enemies, he was to engage warriors as auxiliaries to royal troops. In the decades after the French and Indian War, all of Superintendent Stuart's time was consumed by the forest diplomacy necessary to achieve these ends.

At the outbreak of the American Revolution, the pressures on Stuart and the duties demanded of him greatly increased. He was of course gratified by support given to his efforts by such royal officials as Governor Josiah Martin of North Carolina. Early in the war he was accused of encouraging the Native Americans to attack the frontiers and kill those who were unfaithful to the king. Stuart did not expressly order the forest soldiers to attack the western settlements, but his sending of thirty pack horses of ammunition into the Cherokee country in the spring of 1776 cannot be called a wise move in light of the volatile situation among the Cherokee along the borders of Virginia, North Carolina, South Carolina, and Georgia. Officially it was his policy to restrain the Indian warriors until royal troops could be brought to act with them. Forced to flee from Charleston to St. Augustine and thence to Pensacola, Stuart soon found that his prewar openhandedness was staggeringly costly in time of war. Natives from all over the South came to visit him with the expectation of receiving hospitality and presents. His bills grew so enormous that they were singled out by the opposition in Parliament; shortly before his death there were even those in England who believed that Stuart and his deputies were drawing out enormous sums in advance and profiting, but the evidence does not support those accusations.

Another reason for the criticism aimed at him was his failure to deliver Indian auxiliaries when British troops arrived on the seacoast. Although he conferred with General Henry Clinton off Cape Fear in the spring of 1776, the superintendent made no commitments. When the Cherokee attacked the Carolinas, Virginia, and Georgia in 1776, Stuart really had little to do with either the beginning or the ending of the war. Late in 1776 and early in 1777 he tried to persuade the Cherokee to keep fighting and the Creeks to join them, but both refused to risk another invasion similar to that launched from North Carolina, South Carolina, and Virginia against the Cherokee in 1776. After the success of the Patriots in the Cherokee war of 1776, Stuart would have little luck in persuading forest soldiers to attack the Americans. His diplomacy had to be satisfied with the less dramatic objective of keeping the Indians from being swung over to the American side and thus exposing the British frontier in the Floridas. To the end of his life Stuart remained convinced that his native friends would support royal military actions under the proper circumstances, but the superintendent died without the proper circumstances ever being realized. He was buried in Pensacola, Fla. He and his wife had four children: Sarah Christiana, Christiana, a daughter who died in infancy, and John Joseph.

SEE: John R. Alden, *John Stuart and the Southern Colonial Frontier* (1944); David Corkran, *The Cherokee Frontier* (1962) and *The Creek Frontier* (1967); Robert Ganyard, "Threat from the West: North Carolina and the Cherokee, 1776–1778," *North Carolina Historical Review* 45 (January 1968); James H. O'Donnell III, *The Cherokees of North Carolina in the American Revolution* (1976) and *Southern Indians in the American Revolution* (1973).

JAMES H. O'DONNELL III

Stuckey, Jasper Leonidas *(24 July 1891–1 Aug. 1979)*, geologist, college professor, and state administrator, was born on a small farm in eastern Johnston County. The oldest of seven children, he was the son of John Haywood, a farmer and rural schoolteacher, and Betty Eliza Bunn Stuckey. As a boy he attended local rural schools and worked on his father's farm. He was graduated from Smithfield High School in May 1914 and entered The University of North Carolina that fall. A chance encounter with Professor Collier Cobb directed him from schoolteaching into geology. During 1917–18 he operated a lime plant for the North Carolina Department of Agriculture at Bridgeport, Tenn., where he completed his B.A. degree requirements by correspondence. In 1918 and 1919 he served in France as a rifleman in the American Expeditionary Forces, and in the spring of 1919 he studied at Grenoble University.

Following his discharge in July 1919, Stuckey reentered The University of North Carolina and obtained an M.A. degree in 1920. Colonel J. H. Pratt employed him as an assistant geologist on the North Carolina Geological and Economic Survey during 1920 and 1921 and in the summers of 1922 and 1923; from January to June 1921 Stuckey was also an instructor in geology at the university. In 1921 he entered Cornell University, where he was a laboratory assistant and instructor in geology before receiving a Ph.D. degree in 1924. His dissertation on the pyrophyllite deposits in Moore and Chatham counties was based on field mapping for the state.

Returning to North Carolina, Stuckey was again employed by the state as an assistant geologist, and Raleigh then became his permanent residence. In 1925 he was appointed state geologist in the newly created Department of Conservation and Development, of which he was acting director from August to December 1925.

In September 1926 he resigned the governmental post

to accept appointment as associate professor of geology in the Agronomy Department at the North Carolina State College of Agriculture and Engineering. In the following year he became professor of geology and head of the newly formed Department of Geology. Except for student laboratory assistants, he was the sole geology teacher until 1935. Stuckey taught the geology courses for a B.S. degree program in geology and special courses for ceramic and mining engineering students, as well as correspondence and extension courses chiefly for teachers. As staff additions permitted, he concentrated his teaching on economic geology, mineralogy, and petrography. Although he also carried a heavy load of administrative and committee work and was active in college organizations, he continued field investigations of mineral deposits and produced numerous publications. In 1954 the Department of Geology was absorbed into another department, and a year later Stuckey took a leave of absence from the college.

In 1940 he had been asked again to become state geologist, on a part-time basis, a post he resumed full-time in 1955. During the 1940s state financial support of the Division of Mineral Resources was meager. In order to meet wartime requests for information on strategic and critical minerals, Stuckey sought collaboration with other agencies. Cooperative projects arranged with the Tennessee Valley Authority, the U.S. Geological Survey, and the U.S. Bureau of Mines concerned a wide range of mineral deposits as well as groundwater supplies across the state. Stuckey served from 1941 to 1943 as federal emergency coordinator of mines for North Carolina. In 1946 he became the first director of the Minerals Research Laboratory in Asheville, established by the Tennessee Valley Authority and the state to provide mineral beneficiation studies to help the region's industry. His experience and good judgment contributed much to its immediate and continuing success. Though responsibility for the laboratory was transferred in 1954 to the Department of Engineering Research at North Carolina State College, Stuckey continued to influence its operation as a member of its advisory committee for the rest of his life. Under his leadership the Division of Mineral Resources was transformed into an effective and respected state geological survey. Numerous useful reports were published; especially important was the 1958 *Geological Map of North Carolina* with explanatory text, compiled under Stuckey's immediate direction.

Stuckey retired as state geologist in July 1964 but remained as a consultant until March 1965. He completed his comprehensive *North Carolina: Its Geology and Mineral Resources* in 1965. During his career he was author or coauthor of more than fifty publications, essentially all of which were devoted to North Carolina geology and nonmetallic minerals. No other person has had so great an effect on promoting knowledge and use of the state's mineral wealth. After his retirement he continued to work at intervals for the Division of Mineral Resources and took on consulting projects, notably regarding groundwater supplies and sites for nuclear power plants.

A member of many professional, civic, and other organizations, Stuckey held local and regional offices in most of them. Among those in which he was most active were the American Institute of Mining and Metallurgical Engineers (chairman, Eastern North Carolina Subsection, 1957 and 1969), Geological Society of America (vice-chairman, Southeastern Section, 1952–53, and chairman, 1964–65), North Carolina Academy of Science (president, 1941), Carolina Geological Society (president, 1947), Society of Economic Geologists, Mineralogical Society of America, Association of American State Geologists (president, 1958–59), Civitan Club of Raleigh (president, 1933–34), Torch Club, and Executives Club. He was a member of Phi Kappa Phi (president, State College chapter, 1934–35), Sigma Xi (president, State College club, 1938–39), Sigma Gamma Epsilon (president, Cornell chapter, 1923–24), Keramos, Sigma Chi, and the Masonic order. He received the North Carolina Distinguished Citizens Award in 1964, was awarded an honorary doctor of science degree in 1965 by North Carolina State University, and was made an honorary member of the Association of Engineering Geologists in 1978. The main building of North Carolina State University's Minerals Research Laboratory in Asheville was dedicated on 2 Oct. 1981 in Stuckey's honor.

After being active in the Methodist church for much of his life, he became converted about 1951 to the Church of Jesus Christ of Latter Day Saints. After 1962 he was patriarch of the Raleigh Stake, and in 1975–76 he served a missionary term at the Mormon Temple in Washington, D.C.

In 1920 Stuckey married Anabel Stephenson of Smithfield. She died in 1935; they had no children. In 1936 he married Gladys I. Brinkley of Stem. They had one son, William Jasper, born in 1942. Stuckey died in a Raleigh hospital at age eighty-eight following a three-month illness and was buried in Montlawn Memorial Park in Raleigh, survived by his wife, his son, a sister, and a brother.

SEE: *American Men of Science, 1967*; John M. Parker III, "Geology at North Carolina State—A History" (typescript, Archives, North Carolina State University, Raleigh); John M. Parker III and Stephen G. Conrad, "Memorial to Jasper Leonidas Stuckey, 1891–1979," Geological Society of America, *Memorials*, vol. 11 (1980 [portrait and bibliography]); Raleigh *News and Observer*, 7 Aug. 1955, 2 Aug. 1979; Jasper L. Stuckey Papers (Archives, North Carolina State University, and Files, Geological Survey Section, North Carolina Department of Natural Resources and Community Development, Raleigh); *Who's Who in America, 1966–1967*.

JOHN M. PARKER III

Suggs, George Franklin *(7 July 1883–4 Apr. 1949)*, professional baseball player, was the first North Carolina–born major league star of the modern era. Born and raised in Kinston, he was the son of John and Winifred Aldridge Suggs. He was educated locally and later attended Oak Ridge Academy.

From 1904 to 1907 Suggs played minor league ball in Jacksonville, Fla., and Memphis, Tenn. In 1908 his contract was purchased by the American League Detroit Tigers, but the Tigers used the young righthander sparingly. That year he pitched in only six games with one win and no losses. He started the next season with Detroit, compiling a 1–3 record in nine games. His contract was then purchased by Mobile of the Southern League, where he finished the season.

After the 1909 season his contract was purchased by the Cincinnati Reds of the National League. Given the chance to pitch, Suggs became one of the outstanding pitchers in the league. Only five feet, seven inches tall, he was a finesse pitcher, with unusually good control and a fortunate facility for picking runners off base. In 1910 he won 18 games against only 11 losses, with a superb earned run average (ERA) of 2.40, and the best walk-per-inning ratio in the league. In 1911 he won 15 games against 13 losses, with an ERA of 3.00. In 1912, still with Cincinnati, he was 19–16 with a 2.94 ERA. That year he finished among the league leaders in complete games, shutouts, and fewest walks allowed per inning.

In 1913 Suggs slumped to 8–15 for the seventh-place Reds, and after the season his contract was sold to the St. Louis Cardinals. Miffed by this treatment he elected to jump to the Baltimore franchise of the new Federal League, a short-lived attempt to form a third major league. Suggs was one of the league's standouts in 1914, winning 25 games and losing only 12, with a 2.90 earned run average in 319 innings. He finished that season in the league's top five in wins, winning percentage, complete games, shutouts, and fewest walks allowed per inning. The next year Suggs was a deceptive 13–17 for a last-place Baltimore team, which lost almost 70 percent of its games.

The Federal League folded after the 1915 season. Although some of its players were welcomed back to the National and American leagues, Suggs never played in the majors again. After spending the 1916 season in the minor leagues in Raleigh, he retired from baseball. He finished his major league career with a record of 100 wins against 88 losses, a record compiled with generally mediocre teams.

Suggs returned to Kinston and for several years operated a sporting goods store. He was later associated for two decades with the E. V. Webb Tobacco Company, first as a storage house manager and then as a factory foreman.

Suggs and his wife Mozelle Cox had no children. He died in Kinston and was buried at the First Baptist Church.

SEE: *Kinston Daily Free Press*, 4 Apr. 1949; Joseph L. Reichler, ed., *The Baseball Encyclopedia*, 6th ed. (1985); *Sporting News*, 13 Apr. 1949; Suggs File, National Baseball Library (Cooperstown, N.Y.).

JIM L. SUMNER

Sumner, Jacky. *See* **Blount, Mary (Jackie) Sumner**.

Sumner, Jethro *(1733–March 1785)*, Revolutionary general, tavern keeper, and planter, was born in Nansemond County, Va., where his grandfather, William, had settled in 1691. He was the son of Jethro and Margaret Sullivan Sumner. Jethro served in the Virginia militia from 1755 to 1761 during the French and Indian War; he rose to the rank of lieutenant and served as commander of Fort Bedford in 1760. Sometime before the fall of 1764 he moved to North Carolina, where he married Mary, the daughter of William and Christian Hurst of Granville County. His wife's sizable inheritance allowed him to establish himself as a tavern keeper and planter at the county seat of Bute (later Warren) County. By 1768 he had risen to justice of the peace, and he served as sheriff from 1772 to 1777.

Sumner represented Bute County in the North Carolina Provincial Congress that met in August–September 1775 and elected him a major of the minutemen of Halifax County. In November he marched to the aid of the Virginians near Norfolk. After his election by the North Carolina Provincial Congress as colonel of the Third Regiment of North Carolina Continentals, he went to the Lower Cape Fear and from there to Charleston, S.C., where in June 1776 he and his troops assisted in that town's defense against the British. Later he joined Major General Charles Lee, commanding general of the Southern Department, on a projected expedition against Florida, but in September he left the troops in Savannah to return to North Carolina for supplies. The following spring he led his regiment north and joined General George Washington's army at Morristown, N.J. He and his regiment served with Washington through the Battles of Brandywine and Germantown and endured the terrible winter at Valley Forge. Illness in the spring of 1778 forced Sumner to return to North Carolina. During the summer he recruited for the North Carolina Continental regiments.

The Continental Congress elected Sumner brigadier general on 9 Jan. 1779. The next spring he led a brigade of newly recruited Continentals to South Carolina, where he commanded the right wing of the assault on the enemy troops at the Battle of Stono Ferry on 20 June. Afterwards he fell into a "low state of Health" and returned to North Carolina, where for more than a year he recruited for the North Carolina regiments. He then was named commanding general of a brigade of militia that he marched to the southern part of the state to aid in the defense against an invasion by Lord Cornwallis. In October, angered at the state legislature's appointment of Brigadier General William Smallwood of Maryland to the command of the state troops, Sumner refused further militia duty. When Nathanael Greene came south in December 1780 to assume command of the Southern Department, he sought Sumner's help in the rehabilitation of the North Carolina Continentals. Sumner recruited in North Carolina until 2 June 1781, when he was ordered to join Greene in South Carolina; shortly after 1 August he reached the Southern army with three small regiments of 350 raw Continentals. On 8 September Sumner's brigades were stationed on the right of the second line at the Battle of Eutaw Springs, where they fought well. During the remainder of the war Sumner was in charge of military forces in North Carolina.

In 1783 he returned to his tavern keeping, his plantation, and his three minor children. On 18 April he presided over the meeting of the North Carolina Society of the Cincinnati at Hillsborough as the first president of that organization. He died at his home in Warren County sometime between 15 and 19 March 1785. At the time of his death he owned 20,000 acres of land and thirty-four slaves.

SEE: *DAB*, vol. 9 (1936); Walter Clark, ed., *State Records of North Carolina*, vols. 9–10 (1890); Hugh F. Rankin, *North Carolina Continentals* (1971); William L. Saunders, ed., *Colonial Records of North Carolina*, vols. 11–18, 22 (1895–1900, 1907).

HUGH F. RANKIN

Surginer, William *(July 1706–18 Feb. 1750)*, General Baptist leader who established churches in present Warren, Halifax, Edgecombe, and Nash counties, was a major figure in North Carolina colonial Baptist history. He is said by Richard Knight to have led surviving members of the General Baptist church at Burley, Va. (when that place was "visited with a wasting pestilential disease") to Kehukee on the Roanoke River in present southeastern Halifax County about 1742, and to have founded General Baptist churches in quick succession in the Roanoke and Tar river valleys during the next few years. In actuality, Surginer moved from Isle of Wight County, Va., to the area of Kehukee as a teenager in the mid-1720s. He arrived with the family of an older kinsman, John Surginer, who was given a grant of 350 acres at Kehukee on 9 Apr. 1725 for the importation of himself and five others.

Upon attaining his majority, William Surginer bought land for himself adjoining that of his kinsman; he made his first purchase at Kehukee in 1729. When he next appears in the records, the General Baptist church at Kehukee had already been established, and Surginer (who donated the land for its meetinghouse) was its pastor and nearing the apogee of his ministry. Morgan Edwards was unable to gather precise data about Surginer and the origin of his church at the time of Edwards's visit in the early 1770s. In his manuscript "Materials Toward a History of the Baptists of North Carolina," Edwards says that the church was formed about 1742 and that its congregants were from Burley in Isle of Wight County. In the earlier version of his collected notes, "Tour . . . to the Baptists of North Carolina, 1772–1773," he states that they began under one William Wallis. Clearly Edwards was unable to obtain answers to his usual interrogatories concerning ministers and their churches: when and where baptized and by whom, when and where ordained and by whom, and (of churches) when constituted and by whom.

The sense of both Edwards's and Knight's accounts is that the area of Kehukee was settled largely by families from southeastern Virginia, among them some who had attended or been members of the General Baptist church in Isle of Wight County pastored by the two Richard Joneses. This church was nearly fifty miles northeast of Kehukee. Despite this distance, some contact appears to have been kept up between the church and its emigrating families. Presumably Surginer was baptized and ordained by the second Richard Jones of Burley during the early 1730s. If so, Surginer no doubt would have attended the yearly meeting of the Virginia and North Carolina General Baptist churches and would have been at the 1734 yearly meeting. That meeting seems to have been extremely important, for either there, or in conference elsewhere at the time, a concord appears to have been reached whereby Paul Palmer agreed to extend his ministry throughout the counties of North Carolina's outer coastal plain while another, presumably Surginer, would minister to the frontier settlements in the inner coastal plain. If this was the case, it may be assumed that Surginer's effective ministry outside his immediate area of Kehukee commenced shortly after 1734. It may also be assumed that the progress of the parallel ministries was the subject of reports in yearly meetings, for Surginer began to attract others who came to his assistance.

By the late 1730s Surginer was joined in the inner coastal plain by a Baptist hatter named Constant Devotion, who, it appears, helped Surginer in his work. Little is known of Devotion, but that little is suggestive. When the General Baptist church in Chowan Precinct wrote to John Comer of Rhode Island presumably in search of a pastor in 1729, Comer delayed his reply to the church for six weeks. The letter was received by Comer on 27 Sept. 1729. On 2 November Comer was visited by Constant Devotion, and on the seventh Comer replied to the church in Chowan. What Comer said in his reply is not known, but Devotion was with Paul Palmer in eastern North Carolina in 1734, that watershed year during which areas of responsibility seem to have been established by General Baptist leaders. Devotion was in Edenton during 1735 and 1736, when he, with another Rhode Island Baptist named Joseph Witter, was assaulted by an angry bricklayer. Later that year Witter returned home to Westerly, R.I., and sometime between 1736 and 1739 Devotion moved west to Kehukee Swamp. In 1739 he sat on a coroner's jury at Kehukee, and in 1740 he purchased a tract adjoining the land of John Surginer. In the spring of 1742 Devotion visited the community on Lower Fishing Creek (where a General Baptist church was gathered in 1748) and that summer met his death there by a fall from his mare. It is not known whether Devotion was an ordained minister or whether he was an exhorter. If ordained, it was after his visit to Comer in 1729. All the same, it is probably significant that the gathering of four General Baptist churches one after another by Surginer on the Roanoke and Tar rivers (Kehukee, ca. 1742; Falls of Tar River, 1744; Fishing Creek, 1745; and Lower Fishing Creek, 1748) fell hard on the heels of Devotion's arrival in Surginer's neighborhood in the late 1730s.

If Surginer's work drew Devotion to the Roanoke and Tar rivers, it attracted others as well. By 1740 Peleg Rogers (who had lived in Palmer's home precinct of Perquimans in 1728, but who had moved into Bertie Precinct by the mid-1730s) had moved to Town Swamp south of Tar River just outside the territory covered by Surginer's ministry. At the beginning of 1744 Rogers, as an Anabaptist, appeared before the Edgecombe County Court and took the oaths prescribed for dissenting ministers by the Toleration Act of 1689. Rogers was probably responsible for extending the area of General Baptist influence and for gathering a church near the headwaters of Town Creek and Toisnot Swamp by or before 1748; that church was subsequently destroyed and a new church erected at Toisnot by the introduction of Calvinist doctrine in 1758, by which time Rogers had moved to Duplin County.

Surginer's ablest coadjutor was Josiah Hart. Hart, a disciple of and successor to Paul Palmer, fostered Palmer's churches in the outer coastal plain from 1740 to 1747. He then joined Surginer in the inner coastal plain. Over the next three years the ministries of Surginer and Hart, like that of Palmer, assumed the characteristics of the office of a General Baptist messenger. Hart, without a family and able to earn his living anywhere as a physician, seems to have had a greater freedom of movement than Surginer. Hart was in southern Bertie County in 1746, at Lower Fishing Creek in Edgecombe in 1747, then at Kehukee, Falls of Tar River, and Toisnot in 1748; in 1749 he was for a while in Isle of Wight County, Va., then back again at Lower Fishing Creek—all the while serving as Tyrrell County clerk of court (1747–49).

Together, Surginer and Hart preached, baptized, and raised up a new generation of ministers. They enjoyed a brilliant success. Then, suddenly, Surginer died and some of the fires in Hart appear to have been dampened. Hart buried Surginer, marked his grave at Kehukee, and stayed in the area through the year 1753. He then returned to the outer coastal plain and to business affairs tangled by inattention during his long stay with Surginer. From 1755 to 1757 Hart was tied down by several concurrent suits in Tyrrell and Beaufort counties. By the spring of 1758 Hart, too, was dead. The final years of Hart's life, when he was absent in the east, were critical years for the General Baptist churches in the inner coastal plain. The Calvinist doctrine—that of the mass of humanity, only the handful selected for salvation by God before the foundation of the world could hope to enter into a state of grace (as opposed to the doctrine held by the General Baptists that any of humankind could enter into a state of grace by believing in Jesus and repenting of one's sins)—was imported into the inner coastal plain. Henry Whitfield's tempest had begun to blow along the banks of the Roanoke and Tar rivers. As the recently ordained General Baptist ministers were swept up by these new winds of doctrine, the same gusts toppled from their places the candlesticks of the General Baptist churches planted by Surginer and his coadjutors. Without settled pastoral care, the congregations of General Baptists first languished, then "dissolved," as Isaac Backus terms it. Nevertheless, Morgan Edwards and all succeeding Baptist historians trace the histories of the Calvinist Baptist churches of the area back to their General Baptist origins and invariably acknowledge Surginer to have been one of the principal founding fathers of Baptists in North Carolina's inner coastal plain.

Surginer married Mary West Boykin, the widowed daughter of William West of Beaufort County, sometime before 1744. He was survived by his wife and their three children: Jacob, Ann, and Tamar.

SEE: C. Edwin Barrows, ed., "Diary of John Comer," *Collections of the Rhode Island Historical Society* 8 (1893); Lemuel Burkitt and Jesse Read, *Concise History of the Kehukee Baptist Association* (1850); Morgan Edwards, "Materials Toward a History of the Baptists of North Carolina" (Furman MS) and "Tour . . . to the Baptists of North Carolina, 1772–1773" (Crozer MS) (microfilm, North Carolina Collection, University of North Carolina, Chapel Hill); Sylvester Hassell, *History of the Church of God from the Creation to A.D. 1885* (1886); Margaret M. Hofmann, comp., *Province of North Carolina, 1663–1729: Abstracts of Land Patents* (1979), *Colony of North Carolina, 1735–1775: Abstracts of Land Patents*, 2 vols. (1982), and *Abstracts of Deeds, Edgecombe Precinct, Edgecombe County, North Carolina* (1969); George W. Paschal, *History of North Carolina Baptists*, vol. 1, 1663–1805 (1930).

GEORGE STEVENSON

Suther, Samuel *(18 May 1722–28 Sept. 1788)*, German Reformed minister, was born in Switzerland and in 1738 with his family embarked for the American colonies. Early the next year, according to tradition, he was his family's sole survivor in a shipwreck off the coast of Virginia. A decade later he was living in Philadelphia, where he advertised his services as a teacher in the "High German language" with the recommendation of the Reverend Michael Slatter, a German Reformed pastor in that city. By 1751 Suther had moved to Orangeburg, S.C., but after his ordination to the Christian ministry he served as preacher and teacher in congregations of the Lutheran and Reformed persuasions in both South Carolina and North Carolina. In 1768, while pastor of Coldwater Church in Mecklenburg County (now Cabarrus), N.C., he attracted the attention of Governor William Tryon, who ordered him to preach to the Rowan and Mecklenburg militia as the Regulator movement became of increasing concern to the royal governor of North Carolina.

In 1771 Suther transferred to Law's (or Low's) Church, a union German Reformed and Lutheran congregation in Orange (now Guilford) County. His outspoken advocacy of colonial rights led to dissension between Reformed and Lutheran groups and ultimately resulted in the withdrawal of Suther and his followers and the establishment of Brick Reformed Church near the site of Alamance Battlefield. Here Suther remained throughout the American Revolution encouraging the Patriot cause and suffering, along with his congregation, from the attacks of Loyalists who drove him from his home and laid waste his farm. After the Revolution he again served churches in Mecklenburg (Cabarrus) County before returning to Orangeburg, S.C., in 1786 to complete his life.

The organization and survival of the German Reformed Church in North Carolina is due, in no small measure, to this dedicated cleric, educator, and Patriot. His efforts to provide spiritual and material assistance to the struggling German congregations took him in 1784 to Pennsylvania, where he endeavored to interest northern members of the German Reformed church in contributing to the financial support of their southern brethren.

Suther and his wife, Elizabeth, had several children, including Johann Henry (b. 2 Oct. 1752), Jacob (b. 3 June 1756), Elizabeth (b. 5 Apr. 1760), and David (b. 1770). He died and was buried in the vicinity of Orangeburg, S.C. In 1975 a monument to his memory was erected near Concord, N.C., at New Gilead Reformed Church (United Church of Christ), successor to the earlier Coldwater Church where the noted Swiss clergyman was pastor.

SEE: Frank K. Bostian and Bernard W. Cruse, *Dutch Buffalo Creek Meeting House* (1974); J. C. Clapp, ed., *Historic Sketch of the Reformed Church in North Carolina* (1908); Jacob C. Leonard, *History of the Southern Synod of the Evangelical and Reformed Church* (1940); Banks J. Peeler, *A Story of the Southern Synod of the Evangelical and Reformed Church* (1968); Records of the North Carolina Classis of the German Reformed Church in the United States (Reformed Church Archives, Salisbury, N.C.); A. S. Sally, Jr., *History of Orange County* [S.C.] (1969); William L. Saunders, ed., *Colonial Records of North Carolina*, vol. 8 (1890); Banks D. Shepherd, *New Gilead Church: A History of the German Reformed People on Coldwater* (1966); George M. Welker, *A Historical Sketch of the Classis of North Carolina* (1895).

ROBERT W. DELP

Sutton, Louis Valvelle *(6 Aug. 1889–5 Jan. 1970)*, engineer and electric utility executive, was born in Richmond, Va., the son of Lee Edwards and Ella Wagner Sutton. His father, a tobacco manufacturer, invited him into the business, and when the son chose electrical engineering instead, his father built for him an electrical workshop behind their home. This encouragement led to a lifetime in electric utilities later to be recognized nationally by fellow power company presidents. Under Sutton's direction, the customers of the Carolina Power and Light Company (CP&L) grew from 62,500 to 530,000, while its assets increased sevenfold and its generating capacity, by a factor of 1,000.

At age fourteen Sutton moved with the family to Petersburg, Va., where he was graduated from Petersburg (formerly McCabe) Academy. In 1910 he received a B.S. degree in electrical engineering from Virginia Polytechnic Institute, where he was a cadet captain, an adjutant, and a varsity football player. He became an apprentice engineer in General Electric's training program at Lynn, Mass., but kept an eye on job opportunities in North Carolina, where he had met Cantey McDowell Venable, the daughter of Dr. Francis Preston Venable, president of The University of North Carolina. They were married on 30 Apr. 1912 and had two children: Louis, Jr., who married Jane Kennedy of Charlotte, and Sarah Manning, who married Lawrence Tomlinson, Jr., also of Charlotte.

In a personal appeal for a job, Sutton visited Paul A. Tillery, chief engineer of CP&L, and took work as a statistician at less than his General Electric wage. Promoted to commercial manager, he supervised local office managers and sales personnel, whom he urged to seek company growth through increased electrical service to domestic customers. Sutton had installed in the Meredith College home economics department one of the first electric ranges ever built and put a similar stove in his home kitchen. While his wife tested recipes, he took notes and published the first "electric cook book." Such initiative won him promotion to the position of assistant to Tillery, who rose to company chief executive.

In August 1924 Sutton moved to Little Rock, Ark., as assistant general manager of the Arkansas Central Power

Company, and three years later he became vice-president and general manager of the newly formed Mississippi Power and Light Company headquartered at Jackson, Miss. He was called back to CP&L as vice-president in 1932, when Tillery became critically ill. After Tillery's death on 14 Jan. 1933, Sutton was elected president and general manager on 23 March. He continued as chief executive officer for more than thirty-five years.

The economy of the thirties drove homeowners to cut their use of electricity at the same time that long-range construction commitments were bringing "on line" more and more generating capacity. Rather than increase rates to cover any deficit, Sutton surprised the industry by reducing rates. His so-called "inducement rate" permitted householders to use more electricity so long as their total bill did not drop below prior years. Exploiting this lower unit price, homeowners doubled their usage within two years despite the severely depressed economy. Sutton's inducement rate outlived the depression and built a broad base of residential usage that became the envy—and the model—of many utilities nationwide.

The early thirties also brought fear of nationalization of electric utilities. As he had in Mississippi, Sutton resisted government competition. His support of investor-owned utilities won him national recognition and election, in 1950, as president of the Edison Electric Institute. In 1944 he was awarded the honorary degree of doctor of engineering by North Carolina State College, and in 1953 he was cited by the North Carolina Society of Engineers for "outstanding engineering achievement." *The State* magazine cover featured him as North Carolinian of 1953, and *Dixie Business Magazine* chose him as Man of the South for 1966. Virginia Polytechnic Institute, his alma mater, awarded him its Distinguished Alumnus citation in 1961.

Political trends in 1933 also shifted the attention of many utility executives from engineering to legislation. Operations and engineering were left to others while chief executives sought ways of competing successfully with the elastic "yardstick" of the Tennessee Valley Authority and other burgeoning tax-financed power entities. Sutton's resistance to nationalized power and his defense of free enterprise won conservatives' acclaim, as typified in a 1953 comment by a panel of judges for *The State* magazine: "he demonstrated that not only could an investor-owned and privately managed utility adequately meet the power needs of a state, but also that a great corporation could be humanized, kept close to the people and be responsive to their aspirations."

Declining invitations to sit on boards of directors of other corporations, Sutton expressed reservations at possible conflicting business interests and steadfastly confined his work to CP&L and its immediately related operations. He was a director and president of Carolinas, Virginia Nuclear Power Association, director and president of Capitan Corporation, board member of the North Carolina State College Engineering Foundation, president and director of the Business Foundation of The University of North Carolina, president and director of the Southeastern Electric Exchange, and director of the Research Triangle Foundation. Sutton served on the vestry of the Church of the Good Shepherd (Episcopal) in Raleigh, held numerous offices in national trade and fraternal organizations, and was a member of the Society of the Cincinnati. Along with his art-oriented wife, he was active in several cultural and social groups. He was buried in Montlawn Memorial Park, Raleigh.

SEE: *Greensboro Daily News*, 10 Jan. 1970; Raleigh *News and Observer*, 25 Mar. 1951, 6–7 Jan. 1970; Jack Riley, *Carolina Power & Light Co., 1908–1958* (1958); *The State* magazine, 9 Jan. 1954.

JACK RILEY

Sutton, Maude Pennell Minish *(1 Feb. 1890–18 July 1936)*, teacher, folklorist, and journalist, was born in Lenoir, one of three children of Anna Pennell and Walter Lafayette Minish. Her father was a prominent local businessman, Methodist layman, and Democratic politician. A teacher at Davenport College in Lenoir awakened Maude's interest in folklore, and she began in 1906 to fill a notebook with the song repertory of a mountain woman who worked for her family. For a decade after 1913 she herself taught school and found many opportunities to record folk songs, particularly while serving as a school supervisor in Avery County. In 1922 she forwarded three notebooks of song texts to George Lyman Kittredge, at Harvard University, who encouraged her work. From that time until her death she was also active in the North Carolina Folklore Society, usually holding office and often speaking at its annual programs.

Her marriage to Dennis H. Sutton in 1924 and the birth of her daughters Susan Elizabeth and Nancy Howard restricted her field work, but she began in 1926 to draw upon her collection for feature articles about folklore and for fictional sketches of mountain life. Some of these more than sixty pieces appeared locally. Others had simultaneous publication in the Charlotte, Greensboro, and Raleigh newspapers. A few were printed in magazines such as the *Progressive Farmer*. Mrs. Sutton's untimely death prevented her from gathering her writings. She was buried in Belleview Cemetery, Lenoir.

Professor Frank C. Brown, who regarded Maude Sutton as "the most loyal, and certainly his most highly valued co-worker," persuaded her to give her song collection to him for use in the projected publication of the Folklore Society. When *The Frank C. Brown Collection of North Carolina Folklore* finally began to appear in print years after her death, its form obscured the importance of her contributions. These consisted of 154 song texts and 112 tunes, and of entries in categories like beliefs and games as well. Equally valuable were her vignettes of singers, partially quoted in the editors' headnotes. Mrs. Sutton was virtually alone in her time in having a keen interest in singers and their view of the folk songs. Her vignettes and fictional sketches, while influenced by the local-color school, offered a humorous and realistic glimpse of mountain customs and attitudes, particularly as these bore on traditional song.

SEE: Frank C. Brown Papers (Manuscript Department, Duke University Library, Durham); Lenoir *News-Topic*, 21 July 1936 (portrait); Daniel W. Patterson, "A Woman of the Hills: The Work of Maude Minish Sutton," *Southern Exposure* 5 (1977); Maude Minish Sutton Papers (Southern Historical Collection, University of North Carolina, Chapel Hill).

DANIEL W. PATTERSON

Sutton, Robert Bean *(29 Jan. 1826–7 Mar. 1896)*, Episcopal priest and teacher, was born in Westmoreland County, Va. He was graduated from St. Mary's College, Baltimore, in 1844. After studying for the ministry, he was ordained deacon in 1851 and priest in 1852 by Bishop Nicholas H. Cobb of Alabama.

Sutton began a long career of service in the Diocese of North Carolina in the fall of 1854, when he became rector of St. Stephen's Church, Oxford. During the next four years he added to his field of work St. Paul's Church, Louisburg, and several mission stations in Granville County. Leaving the diocese in late 1858, he served for two years as rector of St. Mark's parish in Frederick County, Md. Sutton returned to North Carolina in September 1860 to begin a ministry of eighteen years in St. Bartholomew's parish, Pittsboro. In addition to that work, he held monthly services at St. Mark's, Gulf, and at two other mission stations. He also provided a monthly service for the residents of the county home.

Shortly after going to Pittsboro, Sutton was faced with the many problems brought on by the Civil War including a congregation that was increased by refugees from the eastern part of the state. He was untiring in his efforts to care for the sick and the bereaved in his parish. At the direction of Bishop Thomas Atkinson, Sutton spent the month of October 1864 as a missionary to the Army of Northern Virginia ministering to the troops in General James H. Lane's brigade near Petersburg. He also spent part of his time in the Winder Hospital in Richmond. In September 1865 he reported that "since the surrender of General Lee, no collections have been made, in consequence of the almost entire absence of money from the community." He was forced to add teaching to his duties "in order to get bread for my family." It was at this time that Sutton established a school for girls. Locust Hill Seminary, which operated successfully during his rectorate, attracted students not only from Pittsboro but from other parts of the state as well.

When Sutton resigned as rector of St. Bartholomew's in December 1878, his loss was felt by the whole community, which had come to regard him as "the village priest." In resolutions of regret, his vestry declared that he was distinguished by his acts of "Christian charity" and "untiring and devoted attention to the sick and afflicted, and the poor and needy." For the next two years he was rector of St. Barnabas, Greensboro, and in charge of five nearby missions. He then served for four years as rector of St. Paul's Church, Louisburg.

In the fall of 1884 Sutton became principal of St. Augustine Normal School and Collegiate Institute in Raleigh. During his seven-year tenure, the student body grew from 133 to 167, the curriculum was expanded, and a four-story dormitory and classroom building was completed. In 1891 Sutton resigned as principal to become vice-principal and a member of the teaching staff, posts that he occupied until his death.

Sutton had many important committee assignments in the diocesan convention. He was dean of the Convocation of Raleigh from its organization in 1875 until 1893. In 1874 Rutherford College awarded him the degree of D.D. He died at his home on the campus of St. Augustine's and was buried in the churchyard of St. Bartholomew's, Pittsboro. After his death the Raleigh *News and Observer* commented: "As a teacher Dr. Sutton was especially distinguished for his patient and painstaking work, and he had in extraordinary measure the faculty of attaching his pupils to him personally, and of calling forth and stimulating their best efforts."

Sutton married Julia Ann Biscoe of St. Mary's County, Md. Thet had seven children: Robert, Walter, Annie (Mrs. Nathan Steadman), Sally Emory (Mrs. Walter J. Crews), Juliet Biscoe, James Andrew, and Nicholas H. Cobb, who died in infancy.

SEE: Wade Hadley and others, eds., *Chatham County, 1771–1971* (1971); Cecil D. Halliburton, *A History of St. Augustine's College, 1867–1937* (1937); *Journals of the Diocese of North Carolina*, 1855–96; Pittsboro *Chatham Record*, 2 Jan. 1879, 12 Mar. 1896; Raleigh *News and Observer*, 8–9 Mar. 1896; Royal G. Shannonhouse, ed., *History of St. Bartholomew's Parish, Pittsboro*, N.C. (1933).

LAWRENCE F. LONDON

Swaim, Benjamin *(13 May 1798–23 Dec. 1844)*, lawyer, printer, author, and newspaperman, was almost certainly the son of William (10 Mar. 1770–1 June 1850) and Elizabeth Sherwood Swaim (8 Nov. 1773–14 Aug. 1835). They and several other branches of the numerous Swaim clan were residents of the Timber Ridge Community, near Level Cross in Randolph County. Benjamin's early life and education are obscure, although he perhaps attended schools taught by his uncle Moses Swaim.

Benjamin Swaim first appears in the records of the North Carolina Manumission Society when, on 27 Aug. 1819, he attended the society's convention and began a sixteen-year association with the Abolitionist group. In the fall of 1822 he was hired to teach day classes at Mount Ephraim schoolhouse in Guilford County. Swaim, a law student at the time, was considered to be a teacher of great ability. The number of students attracted to this school was so large that an assistant teacher was needed, and his second cousin, William Swaim, was hired for the position. At the school Benjamin and William organized a debating club known as the Polemic Society, which became a forum for local men of all ages to join in oratorical contests. In 1823 Guilford County sheriff and state legislator Colonel William Dickey asked Benjamin to take over Dickey's private school. Swaim, intending instead to open a law practice, successfully recommended William for the job.

Swaim settled in the Randolph County town of New Salem, a crossroads community on the road between Asheboro and Greensboro. In 1827 he was elected president of the North Carolina Manumission Society, as well as a delegate from North Carolina to the national convention of the abolition society. Swaim's opinions on slavery are revealed in his 1829 "Report to the President," as printed in the *Greensboro Patriot*. In the report, he declared that "the hour of Negro Emancipation is fast approaching. It must and will assuredly come. And all that we can do is prepare for its approach by a timely and gradual improvement of their debased condition. . . . Aided by Divine assistance, we may fearlessly encounter all the opposition of our enemies and confidently stand forth, the advocates of truth and justice, with such unyielding firmness and determined purpose as no earthly interest, power or prejudice can successfully resist." Swaim was reelected president of the Manumission Society until its discontinuance in 1835.

Perhaps as early as May 1831, he began planning a serial law publication, *The Man of Business; or, Every Man's Lawbook*, a pioneer reference work of business law and legal forms. He called *The Man of Business* "new in character and design" and worried that those in the legal fraternity might protest the popularizing of the law. Though the work was "calculated to render every man his own counsellor in matters of ordinary business," Swaim stated that he was motivated by the desire "to improve the modes of doing business, and thereby render the ends of justice more easy and accessible to all classes of the community." He publicly appealed for the approbation of other lawyers, for "the prudent and seasonable prevention of ruinous litigation is no less a professional duty than the skillful management of it."

Benjamin's partner in this venture was his cousin William, editor of the *Greensborough Patriot*, who printed the first volume in 1833–34. However, the successful reception of *The Man of Business*, and the trouble involved in traveling repeatedly from his home to the printing office, led Swaim to open his own shop in October 1834. The New Salem operation, staffed by R. J. West, printer, and John Sherwood (a cousin), bookbinder, produced the second volume of *The Man of Business* in 1834–35.

Thereafter Swaim's legal career consisted mainly of writing and publishing form books and digests of North Carolina law. A proposed third volume of *The Man of Business* grew into his 540-page *The North Carolina Justice,* printed in Raleigh in 1839. This popular work "relating to the office and duty of a justice of the peace and other public officers" saw at least two posthumous editions revised and updated by other authors. In 1841 Swaim published at his office in Asheboro his *The North Carolina Executor . . . a Safe Guide to Executors and Administrators in their practical management of Estates . . . ;* in 1842 he wrote and published *The North Carolina Road Law . . . with all the necessary forms and practical observations pertaining to the . . . responsibilities of overseers and road hands.* His works were offered for sale in the catalogue of the Raleigh booksellers Turner and Hughes, and all were still in print at his death.

In February 1836 Swaim began editing and publishing a newspaper from his office in New Salem. Titled *Southern Citizen,* it had been proposed in November 1834 by William Swaim. William's prospectus lamented the low esteem in which southern newspapers were held; he sought to supersede his *Patriot* with a new "splendid, superfine" publication, "the largest and most useful family newspaper . . . devoted . . . to the interest, amusement, and edification of the American people." Within a year enough subscribers had been attracted to begin publication, but the untimely death of William Swaim in December 1835 threw these preparations into disarray. The *Patriot* continued to be published for the benefit of William's estate, while the *Southern Citizen* operation was taken over by Benjamin.

The *Southern Citizen* was of an uncompromising Whig political persuasion, promoting agriculture, internal improvements, universal education, and literature (its motto was, "What do we live for but to improve ourselves and be useful to one another?"). An unusual feature was the "Legal Department," subtitled "Ignorance of the Law Excuseth No Man." Here Swaim, obviously inspired by the success of *The Man of Business,* answered the questions of subscribers on various points of law.

In December 1836 he moved his newspaper, printing business, and law office to Asheboro, the Randolph County seat; there the *Southern Citizen* was issued weekly without interruption until April 1842, when publication was suspended. Either debt and financial instability or the recent death of Swaim's wife following the birth of a daughter may have contributed to the shutdown. Publication was resumed on 4 Oct. 1843 and continued until 17 Oct. 1844, when Swaim sold the newspaper and printing office to John Milton Sherwood. Whether the newspaper continued after that date is not known.

On 7 Feb. 1829 Swaim married Rachel Dicks (August 1808–3 Mar. 1841), the daughter of Peter and Rachel Beals Dicks. They were the parents of five children: Anna Dicks (b. 17 Apr. 1830), Thomas Clarkson (10 May 1832–1 Mar. 1844), Matilda Rosalie (8 Mar. 1835–26 Feb. 1837), Charlotte (b. 9 Dec. 1837), and Rachel Dicks (b. 21 Feb. 1841). Benjamin Swaim's sudden death while on a trip to Raleigh revealed the fact that he was "indebted beyond the account of his personal assets." Although his executors discovered that more than three hundred debtors owed money to Swaim's estate, very little could be collected, and his property was sold in a futile attempt to pay his creditors.

SEE: Ethel Stephens Arnett, *William Swaim: Fighting Editor* (1963); Fannie M. F. Blackwelder, "Legal Practice and Ethics in North Carolina, 1820–1860," *North Carolina Historical Review* 30 (1953); Deeds and Estate Papers (Randolph County Courthouse, Asheboro, and North Carolina State Archives, Raleigh); Raleigh *Register,* 16 Feb. 1836, 16 Mar. 1841, 24 Dec. 1844; Sidney Swaim Robins, *A Letter on Robins Family History* (no date); Swaim family genealogical records (possession of Mrs. Francine Holt Swaim, Liberty, N.C.); Benjamin Swaim's own publications cited in the text; Robert M. Topkins, ed., "Marriage and Death Notices from Extant Asheboro, N.C., Newspapers, 1836–1857," *North Carolina Genealogical Society Journal* 4 (November 1978); H. M. Wagstaff, ed., "Minutes of the N.C. Manumission Society, 1816–1834," James Sprunt Historical Monographs, no. 22 (1934).

L. MCKAY WHATLEY

Swaim, Lyndon *(15 Dec. 1812–26 Mar. 1893),* printer, newspaperman, and architect, was the oldest of eleven children. His father, Moses (31 Dec. 1788–25 Apr. 1870), married Adah Swindell (17 Apr. 1791–2 May 1866) of Hyde County on 13 Feb. 1812. The family had a farm on Deep River in Randolph County's Timber Ridge community. The nearby village of New Salem was incorporated by legislative act in 1816, and Moses Swaim had been appointed one of the five town commissioners. The same year the elder Swaim had helped to found the North Carolina Manumission Society and was elected its first president. Whether Moses practiced law in addition to farming is unknown, although he was clerk of the superior court in Randolph County from 1837 to 1840. In the 1850s Swaim emigrated to Indiana, where he settled on the St. Joseph River, north of South Bend. He died during a subsequent visit to North Carolina.

Lyndon Swaim left home in 1834 at age twenty-two to work for his cousin, William Swaim, in the printing office of the *Greensborough Patriot.* After William's death in 1835, Lyndon returned to New Salem and became employed in the printing office of another cousin, Benjamin Swaim, editor of the *Southern Citizen.* In 1839 a delegation of Greensboro citizens urged Lyndon to take charge of the moribund *Patriot.* "We need a paper amongst us that will be regularly issued, that will be fixed in its Whig principles and that will advocate with spirit and fearlessness the Whig cause," they frankly admitted. Swaim decided to accept their offer and, in partnership with yet another cousin, bought the ailing newspaper. Michael Swaim Sherwood (b. 1816), the son of Benjamin (1783–1865) and Sally Swaim Sherwood (b. 1787), was to handle the mechanical and business affairs of the printing office, while Lyndon attended to editorial matters. In accordance with the call for a strong Whig point of view, Swaim promised in his first editorial to "advance all well-judged plans for the improvement of the internal commerce of the state and that system of school education which may reach every child in the land."

After devoting the next fifteen years to the *Patriot,* Swaim sold out to Sherwood in 1854 in order to work full time as clerk of the county court. He held that office continuously from his initial election in 1853 until it was abolished by the new state constitution of 1868. In addition, he served as a commissioner of Greensboro in 1846, 1850–52, and 1859–62 and was appointed a town commissioner under the provisional government of Governor W. W. Holden. As his final public service, Swaim represented Guilford County in the state legislature in 1876–77.

He temporarily took over the editorial helm of the *Pa-*

triot once again in 1869, when he counseled moderation and reconciliation in the face of Reconstruction turmoil. At the same time, he began to study architecture and subsequently left the newspaper to start a professional practice. Successful in his new career, Swaim became known as the town's leading architect of the 1870s and 1880s. Although the facts of this stage of his life are as yet unclear, he is said to have designed residences as well as commercial buildings in Greensboro and surrounding communities.

On 3 Jan. 1842 Swaim married Abiah Shirley Swaim, the widow of his former employer, William Swaim. Their only child died in infancy. Swaim's stepdaughter, Mary Jane Virginia, became the mother of William Sydney Porter (O. Henry). Abiah Swaim died in January 1858, and on 25 Oct. 1859 Swaim married Isabella Logan (d. 9 Feb. 1900), the daughter of General John M. Logan of Greensboro. They had four children: Isabella, Mary, Lyndon, and Logan; none married. Swaim was one of the ruling elders of the First Presbyterian Church in Greensboro from 1872 until his death at age eighty after several years of declining health.

SEE: Ethel Stephens Arnett, *Greensboro, North Carolina: The County Seat of Guilford* (1955); Bettie D. Caldwell, ed., *Founders and Builders of Greensboro, 1808–1908* (1925 [portrait]); Deeds (Randolph County Courthouse, Asheboro); Swaim family genealogical records (possession of Mrs. Francine Holt Swaim, Liberty, N.C.).

L. MCKAY WHATLEY

Swaim, William *(16 Dec. 1802–31 Dec. 1835)*, newspaper proprietor and editor, was born in the Centre community of Guilford County, the son of Marmaduke and Sarah Fanning (Fannon) Swaim. His father was a large landowner, and William, the oldest boy in the family, worked on the farm until he was twenty.

As a youth he was known for his bright mind, shrewd remarks, and keen sense of humor, but he was twelve before he learned to write. Previously he had attended an old field school for two months and had learned to read well enough to understand the few books available to him. William asked his father, who wrote a bold and plain hand, to make examples for him to copy. Thereafter, while neighborhood boys wandered aimlessly about on Sundays, young Swaim would settle down in some undisturbed place, as he wrote in his diary, to a "laborious day's writing."

His father occasionally took him to Greensboro, and when court was in session he listened intently to the lawyers as they represented clients or talked among themselves. In 1819 he determined to become a lawyer himself and from then on spent every free moment in reading books borrowed from a Quaker neighbor, Nathan Dick. His first selection was Sir Richard Blackmore's *Creation*, a long poem based on the intellectual philosophy of John Locke. The organization of a circulating library in the community gave Swaim access to a greater variety of books—philosophy, history, poetry, law, and medicine—which served his desire "to learn about all subjects."

When he was eighteen he enrolled for a two-month term in a local school. He only attended when the weather was unsuitable for farm work, however, as he felt that his labor was necessary to help support the family's eight children. His interest in learning led to his appointment as a teacher in a newly organized Sabbath School at Bethlehem Church. Based on his work there, he was appointed superintendent of a Sunday school at Mount Ephrim schoolhouse. When his cousin Benjamin Swaim was engaged to teach a day school in the same building, William became his assistant. Declining to accept pay for this work, he asked that instead three of his siblings be permitted to attend the school.

The Mount Ephrim school experience marked a turning point in William Swaim's life. Benjamin, five years older than he, was well educated and owned a good library. He set about to help William with his studies. Together they organized a debating club, the Polemic Society, and men of all ages participated in its programs. Leading questions of the day were debated, and the society became a strong educational influence in William's life.

As the young man began to take part in discussions on slavery, education for all citizens, constitutional reform, and other social questions, he put aside his wish to become a lawyer and instead determined to make printing his profession. In 1824 he joined the Manumission Society of North Carolina and shortly afterwards was made its secretary, a post he filled for six years. During this time he became acquainted with Benjamin Lundy, author of *The Genius of Universal Emancipation*. In March 1828 Swaim went to Baltimore to study the "mysteries of practical printing" under Lundy's direction. Swaim reviewed the publications that came into Lundy's office, visited the city library, listened to conversations in his boardinghouse, observed happenings on the streets, and began to write for publication. Lundy was impressed and in less than two months made Swaim his assistant editor.

Six months later Swaim's father died, and his mother called him home to take charge of the family's affairs. While acting as his father's administrator, William was in the office of *The Patriot and Greensborough Palladium* when the editor, T. Early Strange, proposed that Swaim buy the paper and printing establishment. With only six months of schooling, Swaim pondered with deep concern the move from plowboy to proprietor and editor of a newspaper. After discussing the possibility with intelligent and trustworthy friends, he signed the contract on 11 Mar. 1829 and took over the Greensboro newspaper and printing establishment.

On 4 April he published a "Prospectus" for his forthcoming newspaper, the *Greensborough Patriot*, announcing its purpose: "To spread before the public a faithful account of all the events and transactions, both *foreign* and *domestic*, that may agitate the political world—to scrutinize closely the conduct of men in power, and chastize their misdoings without regard to rank—to pull the mask from the face of corruption and hold up popular vices to view in their 'native deformity'—to break the spell, which has long palsied the energies of the Southern States, and show them the necessity of improving their advantages—and to influence our young countrymen, with warm hearts and 'lips of fire,' to 'plead their Country's cause'—shall constitute the prominent objects of the *GREENSBOROUGH PATRIOT*."

The first issue of Swaim's paper appeared on 23 May 1829, when, in an "Address to Our Patrons," he presented the topics he intended to keep before the public. Among them were education, scientific agriculture, sound banking and currency, social justice, clean politics, and freedom of the press—policies seen by leading men of the state as necessary to lift North Carolina out of its long period of decline.

Although Swaim considered himself to be a political independent, the paper leaned towards the Whigs (following the Civil War, long after Swaim's death, it became Democratic). His editorials were fearless in their attacks, sparkling with wit and humor or burning with sarcasm, and always in a language that could not be misunderstood. Widely read, the paper was later described by Stephen B. Weeks as "a leader of the best thought in its day."

The front page of the first issue also supported the cause of constitutional reform in North Carolina. Representation in state government had become one-sided, with eastern counties tightly holding control. In a subsequent issue Swaim predicted that constitutional revision would come "by peaceful means if possible, by revolution if necessary." At a convention in June and July 1835 the long-anticipated changes were made—a mere five months before Swaim's death from an earlier, undescribed accident in Fayetteville. He was buried in the First Presbyterian Church cemetery, Greensboro.

On 29 Apr. 1830 Swaim married Abiah Shirley of Princess Anne County, Va. In 1832 their only child, Mary Jane Virginia, was born. She married Algernon Sidney Porter, and their son was William Sydney Porter (O. Henry).

SEE: Ethel Stephens Arnett, *William Swaim: Fighting Editor* (1963); *Greensborough Patriot*, 23 May 1829–31 Dec. 1835; Will L. Scott, "The Life of William Swaim: Former Editor of the Greensboro Patriot," *Greensboro Patriot*, 18 May–22 June 1866.

ETHEL STEPHENS ARNETT

Swain, David Lowry *(4 Jan. 1801–29 Aug. 1868),* lawyer, governor, and educator, was born in the Beaverdam area near Asheville in Buncombe County. His father was George Swain, a Massachusetts native who settled in the Georgia frontier, married, and served in the legislature and the constitutional convention of 1795 before moving to the North Carolina mountains for his health. His mother, Caroline Swain, was the daughter of Jesse Lane, member of a well-known North Carolina family, who moved first to Georgia and then farther west. Her first husband, by whom she had four children, was David Lowry, who was killed during an Indian raid in Georgia. She and George Swain had seven children, of whom David Lowry Swain was the youngest.

In North Carolina George Swain was a small farmer before moving into Asheville to become postmaster, hat manufacturer, justice of the peace, academy trustee, town commissioner, and self-taught physician. The boy David was taught by his father until he entered the Newton Academy, conducted in Asheville by successive Presbyterian ministers. He was a good student and after completing the course remained at the academy for a time as instructor of Latin. His father, ambitious though not affluent, encouraged his wish to become a lawyer, and in 1822 David left home to prepare for the bar. He was examined by the faculty of The University of North Carolina and admitted to the junior class. Older than most of the students and somewhat disappointed in the university, as well as impatient to complete his studies and reluctant to spend his family's limited resources unnecessarily, he withdrew after only one week in order to study law in Raleigh at the school of Chief Justice John Louis Taylor.

In 1823 Swain returned to Asheville with a law license and the friendship and favorable opinion of some of the state's leading men, including Taylor, Joseph and Weston Gales of the Raleigh *Register*, and Taylor's brother-in-law, the prominent lawyer-politician, William Gaston. He began to practice in Asheville and the western circuit and soon became active in the political campaigns of his half brother, James Lowry, who was elected to the state House of Commons, and of his friend, Dr. Robert Brank Vance, who won a seat in Congress. Party affiliations were determined chiefly by preferences in the national presidential elections, and Swain followed most of his friends and associates in opposing the People's ticket, which supported first John C. Calhoun and later Andrew Jackson.

The success of the People's ticket in North Carolina placed Swain in the minority of the state and his own county as far as national politics was concerned, and when he ran for a seat in the House of Commons in 1824, he emphasized local issues and avoided the question of the national president. He was successful; Buncombe County voters sent him to the House of Commons five times (1824, 1825, 1826, 1828, and 1829). In 1827, when the General Assembly elected him solicitor of the northeastern circuit, he did not run for the legislature. A year later he resigned as solicitor to return to Asheville because of his father's illness; he then served two more years in the house but declined to be a candidate for a sixth term in 1830.

In the House of Commons, Swain became known as a champion of western interests, which in those years concerned mainly efforts to create new western counties. Also demonstrating his belief in an active government seeking to improve conditions in the state, he initiated or supported measures related to internal improvements. Both as lawyer and as legislator he tried to protect western settlers whose land titles were disputed either by Indian claimants or by holders of large speculative land claims, an undertaking that naturally made him popular in the west. On a number of issues not strictly sectional, however, Swain agreed with a conservative viewpoint more prevalent in the east. He was a "sound money" man who favored conservative banking practices through privately controlled banks. Himself a member of a family active in local government, he did not support the movement to increase the popular election of local officials. His votes on questions related to the control of slaves and free Negroes were in accord with those of eastern slaveholders. Although recognized as a western leader, Swain was moderate, willing to compromise, and friendly with persons of all sections. Unsympathetic with the majority that supported Andrew Jackson, he was noncommittal on national politics.

In February 1826 Swain married Eleanor White, the daughter of the former secretary of state, William White, and of his wife Anna Caswell, whose father was the Revolutionary governor Richard Caswell. The marriage strengthened Swain's ties with eastern and central North Carolina. His wife was unhappy in Asheville, and when the legislature sent Swain to the superior court bench in 1830, she lived in Raleigh with her sisters and widowed mother while her husband traversed the state on his rotating circuits.

In December 1832 the General Assembly tapped Swain to serve a one-year term as governor of North Carolina. His election was a surprise to most people, for he had not been mentioned in the preelection speculation. He was chosen by a coalition of westerners, National Republicans, and advocates of states' rights who were united only by their opposition to the leading candidate, a prominent eastern Democrat. Swain thus had no hope of effective party support during his term.

The governor's powers and duties were slight, and he was expected to be largely a social figurehead. Even for that limited position Swain seemed poorly endowed, for his face was long and homely, his slender figure was ill-shaped and ungainly, and his movements were awkward. His advantages were an imposing height of six feet two inches, a kindly and intelligent face, and a courteous, genial, and witty personality that made him a welcome companion. In addition, he was considered a well-prepared, persuasive debater and public speaker.

By custom the governor could make recommendations in an annual message and other special communications, but the all-powerful legislature was free to ignore them. Without strong party support, Swain would need great personal influence if he were to accomplish anything, and here he proved to be extremely effective, excelling at careful management and negotiation to achieve his objectives. By the end of his year in office, he was highly popular and some informed leaders thought him the most influential man in North Carolina.

During the second half of 1833 Swain led an unprecedented popular campaign on behalf of state aid to railroad construction. He served as president of an internal improvements convention held in Raleigh in July and during the following months traveled throughout the state to speak for the movement at local conventions. In his annual message to the legislature in December 1833, he threw out a challenge for improvement and reform in many areas of state government. He proposed the revision and codification of state laws, practical banking charters, the drainage of swamplands belonging to the Literary Fund and their sale for the benefit of a public school program, and tax reform, including revised assessment laws, a decrease in the poll tax, the adoption of an income tax, and increased revenue to support constructive activity. The message emphasized the need for railroad construction. It was soon followed by the recommendations of a second internal improvements convention, over which Swain presided, and by the report of the Board for Internal Improvements, which he wrote as chairman. In all of these proposals Swain advocated state construction of two basic lines: the central east-west line and a north-south line that would bisect the central line, with feeder lines and canals to be built by private companies in which the state would buy stock. During the legislative session Swain also forwarded with a strong recommendation a western proposal for constitutional reform.

The General Assembly reelected Swain as governor for another year without opposition; passed two measures he had initiated as a legislator, the creation of a new western county from Buncombe and Burke and the establishment of a commission to revise and codify state laws; and adopted the banking system he advocated. These actions were gratifying, but more important needs were ignored. Nothing was done for a state system of railroads, tax revision, public education, or constitutional reform. Concluding that increased legislative power for the underrepresented and dissatisfied west must precede any far-reaching reform, Swain and his supporters made constitutional revision their major aim in 1834. The campaign strategy differed from that of 1833 in that Swain was less openly active, but he and other proponents of change worked all year to win the necessary eastern votes.

In the meantime, the opponents of Andrew Jackson were trying to form a new national Whig party, and in North Carolina the diverse elements of nationalist and states' rights leaders set as their goal the defeat of staunch Jacksonian Bedford Brown for reelection to the U.S. Senate. Swain, their chosen candidate, wanted the office but feared that he would lose. By the time the legislature met, he had correctly assessed its membership as dominated by Democrats; he did not oppose Brown, who was easily reelected.

Swain's message of 1834 reiterated his proposals of 1833 but was notable chiefly for its persuasive argument for constitutional reform. In addition, calling attention to a national issue previously little noticed in North Carolina, he endorsed the policy of distributing to the states the proceeds of national land sales, with North Carolina's share to be used for internal improvements and public schools. This became a Whig policy popular in North Carolina.

The more partisan Democrats endorsed a well-liked eastern Democrat to oppose Swain's candidacy for a third gubernatorial term, and Swain was reelected by a slim majority after three ballots. He in turn abandoned his noncommittal attitude and openly affiliated with the new Whig party even though it was a divided minority. Party feelings ran high as the Democrats used their power to pass resolutions instructing Senator Willie P. Mangum how to vote.

Swain worked with advocates of constitutional reform from both parties and both sections to put together a compromise bill that would allay eastern fears while granting some of the western demands, and the bill calling for a constitutional convention was adopted. After the convention was endorsed by popular vote, Swain was elected a delegate from Buncombe County and was thus able to play a leading role in the convention of 1835. His two major goals at the conference were to achieve for the west the maximum representation that the convention act permitted and to remove from the constitution all religious disqualifications for officeholding. After a powerful speech in which he abandoned his usual moderation to threaten revolution, he won his first point. Swain only partially achieved his second goal; the convention retained the religious test but removed the disqualifications for Roman Catholics. Believing that the west owed a debt to the boroughs for their support of the convention movement and that the borough representatives had been leaders in advocating constructive legislation, he strongly opposed the convention's decision to eliminate borough representation. In spite of his disappointments, Swain endorsed the amendments as a whole because he thought the change in representation was essential to progress in the state.

Governor Swain spent the last few months of his term working with Mangum to win support for the Whig party, but with the Whig strength in the west underrepresented they could not overcome the Democratic lead in the legislature. The General Assembly of 1835, the last under the old system of representation, was hostile to Swain and quickly chose as his successor the Democrat he had defeated in 1832. Even less attention than formerly was paid to Swain's recommendations for constructive action. Nevertheless, he left office with hope for the future, for one of his last official acts as governor was to proclaim the amendment of the constitution by majority vote in the statewide referendum.

In December 1831 the General Assembly elected Swain a member of the board of trustees of The University of North Carolina, an appointment that could last for life if the incumbent remained active. The next year, as governor, Swain became ex officio chairman of the board. He took his duties as trustee seriously and worked with others to improve the institution, which was unpopular, was inadequately financed, and had a small and declining student body. Several effective measures were implemented: the organization of an executive committee of the board improved efficiency; the sale of university-owned land in Tennessee provided the capital for a small but regular income, and standards were raised by new admission requirements. Joseph Caldwell, the university's respected longtime president, died in 1835, and the position was not filled for most of the year. Swain, needing employment as his gubernatorial term ended and reluctant to return to the practice of law on the western circuit, sought the post. He was hardly the "distinguished literary gentleman" the board had hoped to employ, but influential trustees concluded that the institution's real need was for a good manager who could improve its popularity and effectiveness, and Swain was elected.

In January 1836 Swain moved to Chapel Hill to assume his new duties. He thus withdrew from the political field, for he was aware that the university needed bipartisan support and should not be embroiled in political rivalry. His sympathies remained with the Whig party, and he probably intended to return to politics at a later opportunity. Occasionally his friends considered nominating him as a candidate for governor or U.S. senator, but such proposals came to nothing, and Swain remained at the university for the remainder of his life, filling the longest term of any university president.

Most of the faculty, although naturally surprised, even affronted, that their new head was not to be the scholar they expected, soon accepted Swain and came to respect him. The little institution had no place for a president who was solely an administrator, and Swain became professor of national and constitutional law, instructing the seniors in legal and constitutional history, legal and political theory, and ethics, which he called "moral science." Critics charged that under his administration standards of scholarship were low, the institution emphasized the preparation for public life rather than sound education, the library was neglected, laboratory work in the sciences was deficient, the curriculum was old-fashioned and superficial rather than intensive and thorough, and discipline was too restrictive and juvenile in theory and too lax in practice. Yet many of the same critics also thought Swain was efficient, admired him personally, and were fond of him. His administration and renewed prosperity for the university and the state did produce the popularity and growth that the board wanted. By the end of the antebellum period enrollment stood at nearly five hundred, the largest of any southern institution, with students drawn from throughout the South. New buildings were erected, one of them designed by a nationally acclaimed architect; the campus was improved; both curriculum and faculty were enlarged; and the university's loyal alumni filled the most important state offices.

Such scholarly interests as Swain had were in history, where he concentrated on the study of North Carolina and the collection of source materials for the history of the state. He established at the university the North Carolina Historical Society, with the faculty as officers and himself as the moving spirit, and collected important newspapers and manuscripts in the society's name. It was long his intention to visit England to acquire copies of documents related to North Carolina, a plan endorsed by the General Assembly. However, he was unusually dilatory in beginning the project, and with the onset of the Civil War it was forgotten.

Although personally tolerant of opposing political and religious opinions, Swain was anxious to keep the university free from the controversies of the day. Accordingly, with the full support of the board of trustees he insisted that students and faculty alike refrain from public endorsement of controversial political and religious views. When Benjamin S. Hedrick, a faculty member he liked and had aided as a youth, admitted and defended in the newspapers his preference for the Free Soil party in 1856, Swain not only disagreed with the opinion but also disapproved of the expression of it. Although he legalistically protested that the executive committee, in dismissing Hedrick, usurped authority belonging only to the full board and remained friendly with Hedrick then and later, he did not champion, perhaps was not even familiar with, the principle of academic freedom.

As an old-time Whig with Unionist attitudes, Swain was hopeful until the last that secession and civil war might be prevented, and in February 1861 he led a delegation sent by the legislature to meet with representatives of the seceded states in Montgomery, Ala., in order to seek a reconciliation through compromise. By the time the delegation reached Montgomery the Confederacy had been formed, and instead of discussing reconciliation the Confederates tried to win over the commissioners to the Southern cause. The delegation returned home to report failure. During the Civil War Swain was a loyal though reluctant supporter of his state and region and a trusted adviser of his friend and protégé, Zebulon B. Vance, but he devoted most of his efforts to keeping the university alive, seeking exemption from conscription for university students and refusing to cease operations despite hardships. Most of the students left for the war, as did the younger faculty members, and Swain and the older professors remained to teach a few students too young to enlist, exempt because of ill health, or discharged because of war injuries. Through his determination, the university remained open and held commencement exercises every year of the war.

As William T. Sherman's army reached the center of North Carolina, it was Swain and his old friend William A. Graham who met with the general as representatives of Governor Vance to request protection for Raleigh and the university. Sherman was conciliatory to the two old Unionists; Raleigh was not destroyed, and the university was not vandalized.

Swain, always the negotiator and compromiser, expected that Southerners willing to accept the failure of secession and the end of slavery would join with Northerners to restore peace to the warring country. At the invitation of President Andrew Johnson, he went to Washington as one of several consultants on Reconstruction policy, but he opposed Johnson's plan to replace the elected Vance with an appointed governor and could not accept the leadership of William W. Holden, the former Democratic fire-eater who had reversed his position late in the antebellum period to oppose secession and lead the wartime movement for a separate peace.

Even so, Swain hoped for reconciliation with a minimum of difficulty. He attempted to make up for the loss of the university's endowment by securing aid from the state's share of the Morrill Land Grant fund, and he worked well with Jonathan Worth, another former Whig, who was elected governor during presidential Reconstruction. Swain underestimated the force of political extremism. In spite of the largely Unionist board and faculty, the students had been overwhelmingly Southern in sympathy and the Republicans considered the university a hotbed of Secessionists. Many North Carolinians, on the other hand, felt that the university had given little support to the Confederacy; they thought Swain's readiness for peace, his acceptance of a horse as a gift from Sherman, his giving his daughter a wedding to Illinois general Smith D. Atkins, who commanded the troops occupying Chapel Hill, and his invitation of President Johnson to the commencement of 1867 to be betrayals of the South.

Bankrupt, with no effective political support, only a few students, and a handful of loyal but aging professors, the university was in great danger. Some of its trustees and alumni, concluding that a thorough change in the plan of education was required, recommended an elective system based on a number of different schools modeled after the organization of the University of Virginia. Swain and the other faculty members tendered their resignations to facilitate the new plan; the board adopted it, effective in the fall of 1868; and the faculty was asked to remain until replaced or reelected. These efforts to save the university by a change in educational policy were ineffective, for political control proved to be more important. Under congressional, or radical, Reconstruction, a new state constitution was adopted, providing that the old board would be replaced by a new one chosen by the Board of Education. The old board, at its last meeting in June 1868, reelected the old faculty. The new board, at a meeting in July attended by Swain, heard reports of the old officials courteously but met again the next day without them and accepted the faculty resignations despite their withdrawal.

Swain, troubled by deafness, less politically astute than previously, and unable to gauge political animosities so foreign to his own temperament, was shocked and hurt by an outcome he had not foreseen. He wrote a long legalistic protest but was ignored. An accident cut short any further effort at resistance and prevented his forcible ouster. On 11 August he was thrown from a buggy pulled by his "Sherman" horse, severely shaken up, and confined to bed with shock and weakness. He seemed to be recovering and sat up briefly on the twenty-ninth but died shortly after returning to his bed.

Swain's funeral sermon was preached by his old friend and former pupil, Dr. Charles Phillips, professor of mathematics and minister of the Presbyterian church of which Swain was a member. He was buried in the garden of his home in Chapel Hill but was later reinterred in Oakwood Cemetery, Raleigh, survived by his wife, his daughter Eleanor Swain Atkins, and his son Richard Caswell Swain, a physician. Two infant sons and his oldest child, Anna, who died in 1867, had predeceased him. Swain, who had always been a careful manager, had invested his savings and his small inheritance wisely, and had been successful in land purchases, left his widow a substantial estate for his day, valued at approximately $60,000. To his state he left a legacy of constructive political achievements and of devotion to the university and kindliness to its students that earned for him a warm place in the memories of alumni as they struggled to rebuild the university in the years that followed. There are two portraits of Swain at the University of North Carolina at Chapel Hill.

SEE: Kemp P. Battle, *History of the University of North Carolina*, vol. 1 (1907); Battle Family Papers, William A. Graham Papers, and David L. Swain Papers (Southern Historical Collection, University of North Carolina, Chapel Hill); "Epistolary Correspondence of David L. Swain," 5 vols. (North Carolina Collection, University of North Carolina, Chapel Hill); Legislative Papers, Governors Letter Books, Governors Papers, David L. Swain Papers, and Walter Clark Papers (North Carolina State Archives, Raleigh); Carolyn A. Wallace, "David Lowry Swain, 1801–1835" (Ph.D. diss., University of North Carolina, Chapel Hill, 1954) and "David Lowry Swain: The First Whig Governor of North Carolina," *James Sprunt Studies in History and Political Science*, vol. 39 (1957).

CAROLYN A. WALLACE

Swaine Drage, Theodorus. *See* **Drage, Theodorus Swaine.**

Swan (or Swann), John *(1760–3 Mar. 1793)*, political leader and and state senator, was the son of John Swan, a prosperous planter living in Pasquotank County in 1760 and a councillor to Governor Arthur Dobbs. The elder Swan apparently died a year after his son was born. Young John studied at the school in Edenton taught by the Reverend Daniel Earl, an English missionary sent to North Carolina by the Society for the Propagation of the Gospel in Foreign Parts. He then attended the College of William and Mary. A planter in his own right, Swan in time inherited property from two brothers; by 1790 he owned seven hundred acres and sixty slaves.

On 14 Dec. 1787 Governor Richard Caswell appointed Swan a delegate to the Continental Congress to replace John Baptist Ashe, who resigned. He also was a delegate to the convention that met in Fayetteville in 1789 and approved the adoption of the U.S. Constitution on behalf of North Carolina.

Correspondence between Swan and James Iredell reveals an agreement on political ideals and a pleasant social relationship between the two families. Swan congratulated Iredell on his appointment as an associate justice of the U.S. Supreme Court and invited the Iredells to visit him at The Elms, his plantation in Pasquotank County. In another letter Swan mentioned his wife Margaret and his daughter Penny. His will also refers to a daughter Rebecca.

Swan was a member of the state senate for two terms (1791–92 and 1792–93). Because he died just a few weeks after completing his second term, his death must have been unexpected. He was buried on the grounds of The Elms.

SEE: *Biog. Dir. Am. Cong.* (1971); Walter Clark, ed., *State Records of North Carolina*, vols. 11, 23–25 (1895, 1904–6); *Fayetteville Gazette*, 14 Sept. 1789; Halifax, *North-Carolina Journal*, 13 Mar. 1793; Iredell Papers (Manuscript Department, Duke University Library, Durham); Pasquotank County Tax Lists and Wills (North Carolina State Archives, Raleigh); William C. Pool, "An Economic Interpretation of the Ratification of the Federal Constitution in North Carolina," *North Carolina Historical Review* 27 (April–October 1950); William L. Saunders, ed., *Colonial Records of North Carolina*, vols. 3–6 (1886–88).

VERNON O. STUMPF

Swann, John *(25 Apr. 1707–December 1761)*, colonial official, was the youngest son of the great Proprietary social and political leader, Samuel (d. 1707), and Elizabeth Lillington Swann, the daughter of wealthy Albemarle planter Alexander Lillington. After Samuel's death she married Alexander Goodlatt, who died about 1713; she subsequently married Colonel Maurice Moore. John Swann was born and reared in the Albemarle region, but during his youth his family's interests were increasingly looking towards the Lower Cape Fear region. By his marriage to Ann Moore, the daughter of "King Roger" Moore, he underlined the bond between two powerful families that had begun to form in 1713 with his mother's marriage to Ann's uncle.

With the arrival of royal government to North Carolina in 1731 and the consequent growing interest in the Lower Cape Fear, Swann began rising in politics. His first of several terms as a member of the General Assembly began with election in 1733, and subsequent terms following during 1739–40 and 1743–51. He became justice of the peace for New Hanover in November 1734.

In September 1751 Governor Gabriel Johnston elevated

him to the royal Council by means of an emergency appointment, a move approved and confirmed by the Crown the following year. Despite Johnston's frequent clashes with the Swanns and the Moores, he could hardly ignore the enormous esteem accorded John as leader of the forces defending Brunswick during the Spanish Alarm of 1748.

During the administration of Governor Arthur Dobbs, the chief executive sometimes regretted facing the combined forces of John in the Council and his brother Samuel, who was speaker of the lower house. Indeed, Dobbs accused the two of forming an obstructive junto in 1760.

Unlike many other members of the planter elite, John was a colonel in his county's militia and a member of his parish's vestry. He wrote his will in February 1761, and it was probated in April 1762. He and Ann had no children.

SEE: New Hanover County Wills (North Carolina State Archives, Raleigh); William L. Saunders, ed., *Colonial Records of North Carolina*, vols. 4–6 (1886–88).

WILLIAM S. PRICE, JR.

Swann (or Swan), Samuel *(11 May 1653–14 Sept. 1707)*, Council member, secretary, justice in North Carolina, and burgess, justice, and high sheriff in Virginia, was born at his father's plantation, Swann's Point, in Surry County, Va. He was the son of Colonel Thomas Swann (May 1616–16 Sept. 1680) and his second wife, Sarah Cod or Codd (d. 13 Jan. 1654/55). His paternal grandparents were William (ca. 1587–28 Feb. 1637/38) and Judith Swann (5 Feb. 1589/90–16 Mar. 1636/37). William and Judith had migrated to Virginia from the County of Kent, England, before 1635 and settled in the area that became Surry County.

The Swann family had held land in the counties of Kent and Derby since the time of William the Conqueror. In the seventeenth century a number of its members migrated to America, some settling in Virginia and others in New England and elsewhere. A Thomas Swann of Roxbury, Mass., was associated with North Carolina through trade and lived in that colony for a time, but he was not a member of Samuel's immediate family.

Swann's father, Colonel Thomas Swann, was prominent in the political affairs of Virginia. He was a justice of the Surry County Court, served at least four terms in the House of Burgesses, and was a member of the Council from 1659 until his death. He was married five times and had fourteen children, of whom all but four died young. His wives, in addition to Samuel's mother, were Margaret Delton (d. 1646), Sarah Chandler (d. 1662), Ann Brown (d. 1668), and Mary Mansfield, who survived him. All of his surviving children except Samuel were born of his fifth marriage. They were Mary (b. 5 Oct. 1669), who married Richard Bland; Thomas (b. 14 Dec. 1670), who married Eliza Thompson; and Sarah, who married Henry Randolph and later, Giles Webb.

Samuel Swann entered political life in Virginia in 1674, when he became a commissioner for Surry County, an office that carried the powers of justice of the peace. In 1676 he was high sheriff. He was a burgess in the Assembly of 1677 and in nearly all, if not all, subsequent sessions through 1695. In the 1680s he was deputy escheator for an area that included the counties of Surry, Nansemond, and Isle of Wight. Like his father, he was an officer in the militia, attaining the rank of major, a title by which he was designated for the rest of his life. Meanwhile, he acquired extensive landholdings and became well-to-do, aided no doubt by his father, one of the wealthiest men in Surry.

The time that Swann began his association with North Carolina and the reasons for it are not known. Surviving records show only that he was serving on the North Carolina Council and as surveyor general by March 1693/94. It is noteworthy that Philip Ludwell, a fellow Virginian and an acquaintance of Swann, was acting governor of North Carolina at that time. No doubt Ludwell facilitated, if he did not initiate, the move. Swann appears for a time to have regarded his North Carolina connection as temporary or tentative. He retained residence in Virginia for more than a year after assuming office in the neighboring colony and even served in the Virginia Assembly in April 1695. By 1696, however, he had moved his family to North Carolina and appointed an attorney to handle his Virginia affairs.

Swann remained on the North Carolina Council for the rest of his life. As Council member he was ex officio justice of several courts, including the Palatine's court, Court of Chancery, and General Court. Although the General Court was reorganized in 1698 and no longer was held by the entire Council, Swann continued as a justice until July 1703, sitting under commission from the Council.

About 1700 he was appointed secretary of the colony, serving until about 1704. He probably continued as surveyor general until 1703, when another was appointed to that position. In 1696 he was customs collector for Pasquotank and Perquimans, an office that he held for several years.

Swann lived in Perquimans Precinct, where he was a merchant-planter. He was especially interested in distilling, buying, and exporting tar. He also practiced as an attorney before the General Court, stepping down from the bench to handle his cases, as was the custom of the time. He acquired extensive landholdings in North Carolina and appears to have speculated in land. He became one of the wealthiest men in the colony and one of the most powerful politically. A staunch Anglican, he was a leader in the political struggles of the early 1700s that resulted in the establishment of the Anglican church. He also devoted his private efforts and means to his church and was building an Anglican chapel, one of the first in the colony, at the time of his death.

Swann was married twice. His first wife was Sarah Drummond (b. 2 Mar. 1654), the daughter of William Drummond, the first governor of North Carolina, and his wife Sarah. Samuel and Sarah were married on 24 Mar. 1673/74. They had nine children, but four died before the family moved to North Carolina. The surviving children were William (b. 5 Nov. 1678), Samuel (b. 2 May 1681), Sampson (b. 19 Feb. 1684), Henry (b. 16 June 1688), and Thomas (b. 29 Oct. 1689). Sarah died on 18 Apr. 1696 in North Carolina. She was buried in Virginia at Swann's Point, where her mother and Swann's parents and grandparents were buried.

Swann's second wife was Elizabeth Fendall (b. 17 June 1679), the widow of John Fendall and the daughter of Alexander Lillington and his second wife, Elizabeth Cook. That marriage took place on 19 May 1698. The couple had four children: Elizabeth (b. 26 June 1699), Sarah (b. 29 Dec. 1701), Samuel (b. 31 Oct. 1704), and John (b. 25 Apr. 1707).

Swann died at his plantation in Perquimans, where he was buried. He was survived by his wife, Elizabeth, by the four children born of his second marriage, and by four of the sons of his first marriage. Swann's widow was remarried twice, first to Alexander Goodlatt, who died about 1713, and subsequently to Maurice Moore. In the early 1720s she moved with Moore to the Cape Fear region. She died before July 1734 and was buried on Moore's plantation at Rocky Point.

A few years before his death, Swann lost one of his older sons, Samuel, Jr., who was drowned in Roanoke Inlet in 1702. Although he was only twenty-one, Samuel, Jr., was a justice of Perquimans Precinct Court when he died. He left a wife, Mary, who was a daughter of Alexander Lillington and a sister of Elizabeth, the wife of Swann, Sr. Surviving records indicate, but do not explicitly state, that Mary later married Jeremiah Vail and was the mother of Jeremiah, Jr., John, Moseley, and Mary. Records also indicate, but not conclusively, that the Samuel Swann of Perquimans who died in 1753 was the son of Samuel, Jr., and his wife Mary. Some writers have erroneously identified him as the son of Swann, Sr., apparently being unaware of the death of Samuel, Jr.

Much confusion has existed among genealogists and historians respecting the identity of particular members of the Swann family and of families with which they intermarried, especially the Jones family. The confusion is caused in part by duplication in names. Samuel Swann, Sr., had three sons named Samuel: a son who was born in Virginia in 1674 and died there in 1677; a son, born in Virginia in 1681, who moved with his family to North Carolina and died there by drowning in 1702, as stated above; and a son born in Perquimans Precinct in 1704, who had a long, distinguished political career and died in New Hanover County in 1774. The confusion caused by Swann's having more than one son bearing his name is compounded by his having several grandsons and great-grandsons named Samuel, some of whom historians have confused with their fathers or uncles.

Swann's son Sampson appears also to have died in early manhood. He was named in his father's will, but no later reference to him has been found.

All but one of Swann's remaining sons and a number of his grandsons entered public life. Throughout much of the eighteenth century the North Carolina Assembly included two or more members of the Swann family. For nearly a decade in midcentury two of Swann's sons held two of the highest offices in the colony simultaneously, Samuel as speaker of the Assembly and John as a Council member.

Swann's eldest son, William, settled in Currituck, where he was a justice of the precinct court. He served four terms in the Assembly and was speaker in 1711. He was appointed to the Currituck vestry in 1715. He probably died soon after 12 Apr. 1723, when he made a codicil to his will. No record of his marriage has been found, but a Samuel Swann who was justice of the Currituck court in 1720 may have been his son.

Henry Swann lived for a time in Perquimans, where he was a merchant-planter. He later moved to Currituck, where he was living at the time of his death. He died before September 1724. He had at least one son, Thomas, but nothing more is known of his family. He appears to have taken no active part in politics.

Thomas, who settled in Pasquotank Precinct, also was a merchant-planter. In 1716 he was licensed to practice law in the General Court. He was a member of the Assembly for several years in the 1720s and was speaker in 1724 and 1729. He was treasurer for Pasquotank Precinct in 1732. He was married twice. In 1718 he married Demaris Sanderson, the widow of Richard Sanderson, Sr., but she died about a year later. His second wife was named Rebecca. He died in 1733, survived by wife Rebecca and four children: Samuel, William, Rebecca, and Elizabeth.

The children born of Swann's second marriage ranged in age from eight years to five months when their father died. They were reared under the care of their stepfathers and the closely knit Lillington family. Elizabeth, the eldest, married John Baptista Ashe and moved with him to the Cape Fear. She died before November 1731, survived by her husband and three children: John, Samuel, and Mary.

Sarah, next in age, married Thomas Jones, a lawyer of Virginia. He apparently was not related to Chief Justice Frederick Jones of North Carolina, whom some writers have erroneously identified as Sarah's husband. It is uncertain whether or not Sarah and her husband settled in Virginia or in North Carolina.

Swann's son Samuel (b. 1704) probably was the most prominent of his children. He served in the Assembly for almost forty years and was speaker for nearly twenty, retiring in 1762. He spent his early life in Perquimans but moved to New Hanover County about 1731. He married Jane Jones, the eldest daughter of Chief Justice Frederick and Jane Jones. He died in 1774, survived by his wife, Jane, a son, Samuel, and a daughter, Jane.

Swann's youngest son, John, also settled in New Hanover County. Like his brother Samuel, he was active in politics for much of his life. He was a member of the Assembly in 1733 and from 1739 to September 1751, when he was appointed to the Council. He remained on the Council until his death, which occurred about December 1761. He was married twice. His first wife, Elizabeth, was the stepdaughter of Tobias Knight. His second wife was Ann Moore, the daughter of Roger Moore of Orton plantation. He had no children.

SEE: John Bennett Boddie, *Colonial Surry* (1948); William K. Boyd, ed., *William Byrd's Histories of the Dividing Line . . .* (1929); John L. Cheney, Jr., ed., *North Carolina Government, 1585–1974* (1975); Elizabeth T. Davis, comp., *Surry County Records . . . 1652–1684* (no date); Thomas F. Davis, comp., *A Genealogical Record of the Davis, Swann, and Cabell Families of North Carolina and Virginia* (1934); Essex Institute, pub., *Vital Records of Roxbury, Mass. to . . . 1849* (1925); J. Bryan Grimes, ed., *Abstract of North Carolina Wills* (1910) and *North Carolina Wills and Inventories* (1912); J. R. B. Hathaway, ed., *North Carolina Historical and Genealogical Register*, vols. 1–3 (1900–1903); William Waller Hening, ed., *Statutes at Large . . . of Virginia . . . from 1619* (1823); Frank R. Holmes, comp., *Directory of the Ancestral Heads of New England Families, 1620–1700* (1923); Lewis Hampton Jones, *Captain Roger Jones of London and Virginia . . .* (1891); North Carolina State Archives (Raleigh), various documents in Albemarle Book of Warrants and Surveys (1681–1706), Albemarle County Papers (1678–1739), Colonial Court Records (boxes 139, 185, 189, 192), Council Minutes, Wills, and Inventories (1677–1701), New Hanover County Deeds, also Wills (microfilm), North Carolina Wills, Perquimans Births, Marriages, Deaths (1659–1820), Perquimans Deeds (microfilm), and Perquimans Precinct Court Minutes (1698–1706); Nell Marion Nugent, comp., *Cavaliers and Pioneers: Abstracts of Virginia Land Patents and Grants, 1623–1800* (1934, 1977); Mattie Erma E. Parker, ed., *North Carolina Higher-Court Records, 1670–1696* (1968) and *1697–1701* (1971); William S. Price, Jr., ed., *North Carolina Higher-Court Records, 1702–1708* (1974) and *North Carolina Higher-Court Minutes, 1709–1723* (1977); William L. Saunders, ed., *Colonial Records of North Carolina*, vols. 2–9 (1886–90); James Sprunt, *Chronicles of the Cape Fear River, 1660–1916* (1916); William G. Stanard and Mary Newton Stanard, *The Colonial Virginia Register* (1902); *Virginia Magazine of History and Biography* (vols. 1, 3, 5, 11, 14–15, 18–19); John H. Wheeler, ed., *Reminiscences and Memoirs of North Caro-*

lina and Eminent North Carolinians (1966 ed.); *William and Mary Quarterly* (1st ser., vols. 6, 11, 16); Ellen Goode Winslow, *History of Perquimans County* (1931). Note: All secondary sources cited should be used with care.

MATTIE ERMA E. PARKER

Swann, Samuel *(31 Oct. 1704–February or March 1774),* speaker of the Assembly, was the son of Samuel Swann (11 May 1653–14 Sept. 1707) and his second wife, Elizabeth Lillington Fendall (b. 17 June 1679). He was born at his father's plantation in Perquimans Precinct. Swann's father, one of the wealthiest men in the colony, had long served on the Council and held other high offices; he was the son of Thomas Swann, of Virginia, who had served for many years on the Virginia Council. The young Swann's mother, Elizabeth, was the widow of John Fendall and the daughter of Alexander Lillington and his second wife, Elizabeth Cook. Lillington, an early North Carolina settler, was an influential leader and an Assembly member.

Samuel was one of four children born of his father's second marriage. He had two sisters, Elizabeth and Sarah, and a brother, John. He also had four half brothers, born of his father's first marriage: William, Sampson, Henry, and Thomas. A fifth half brother, Samuel, Jr., had died in 1702. The young Samuel, therefore, was the namesake of his deceased brother as well as his father.

When Samuel was about three years old, his father died. His mother married Alexander Goodlatt but was soon widowed again, for Goodlatt died about 1713. She later married Maurice Moore, who had recently come to the colony from South Carolina. In the early 1720s Moore and Elizabeth moved to the Cape Fear region, which Moore was greatly interested in developing. Samuel remained in Perquimans for some years, probably living at the family plantation, which under his father's will was to go to him at his mother's death.

Samuel's childhood and youth are said to have been spent under the guidance of the closely knit Lillington family, which included several leading politicians. In addition to his stepfather, Maurice Moore, who rapidly gained political influence in the colony, Swann was associated with John Lillington, his uncle; Edward Moseley and John Porter, his uncles-in-law; and John Baptista Ashe, his sister Elizabeth's husband. Moreover, his half brothers were men of wealth and prominence. Both William and Thomas Swann became members of the Assembly, and each served as speaker. From his relatives and members of their social circle Samuel no doubt absorbed an understanding of practical politics that helped direct him to a political career and contributed to his success in that career. His more formal studies gave him an excellent education in law. He also received training in practical surveying.

Swann entered public life in 1725, when he became a member of the lower house of the Assembly. He seems to have served in that body with little or no interruption for the next thirty-seven years. In the early portion of that period he represented Perquimans Precinct, but in 1739 and thereafter he represented the recently formed Onslow County. In March 1742/43 he was elected speaker of the Assembly. With the exception of the years 1754–1756, he continued in that post until 1762, when he declined to accept reelection because of his health.

In 1728 Swann put his training as a surveyor to good use, for that year he was employed as surveyor by the commission that located the boundary line between North Carolina and Virginia. He was on the surveying party that ran the line through the Dismal Swamp, which, it is said, had not previously been crossed by white men.

In February or March 1738/39 the Assembly appointed Swann to a commission charged with revising the laws of the colony, which had last been codified in 1715. Swann's brother John and his uncle-in-law Edward Moseley also were on the commission. Samuel, who was chairman, is said to have been the moving force in preparing the revision, which became generally known as Swann's Revisal. Published in 1752, it was the first book printed in North Carolina.

As speaker, Swann led the lower house of the Assembly during a period of nearly constant struggle against the governor and at times against London officials as well. At issue, in the colonists' view, were what the colonists considered their ancient rights and privileges, the constitution of the colony, and the principles of representative government. In the view of the respective governors, however, the point at issue was the establishment and preservation of the royal prerogative. Although the struggle was marked at times by compromise or even defeat for the colonists, the long-run advantage was with the Assembly, which secured control over fiscal affairs and other crucial matters. Swann's skillful leadership as speaker greatly enhanced the office, raising it to a stature that some considered equal to that of governor.

About 1727 Swann married Jane Jones, the eldest daughter of Frederick Jones, a former chief justice of the colony (1718–22), and his wife Jane. About 1731 he moved his family to the Cape Fear region, to which a number of his relatives had moved. He settled on a plantation called The Oaks, not far from his brother John's plantation, which was called Swann's Point. Also nearby was Maurice Moore's plantation, located at Rocky Point. Later, when Anglican parishes were organized in the area, Swann became a communicant of St. James Parish in Wilmington.

Swann no doubt cultivated the plantation on which he lived and perhaps other land that he owned. He also practiced law and, like his stepfather and other relatives, speculated in land on a large scale. He became very wealthy. His home, The Oaks, was said to be the finest in the Cape Fear area. After his retirement from the Assembly, he devoted himself chiefly to his law practice. He died in 1774 between the last day of January, when he made a codicil to his will, and the seventh of April, when the will and codicil were proved. He was survived by his wife Jane, a daughter, Jane, and a son, Samuel.

Swann's daughter Jane (15 Oct. 1740–1801) married her cousin, Frederick Jones of Virginia, who was the son of Thomas Jones of that colony and the nephew of Chief Justice Frederick Jones of North Carolina. She and her husband had one son, John Swann, and five daughters: Elizabeth, Jane, Rebecca, Lucy, and Ann. When he reached maturity, John Swann Jones took Swann as his surname, becoming John Jones Swann, in deference to the wishes of his grandfather's brother, John Swann, who died childless.

Swann's son Samuel (19 June 1747–11 July 1787) married Mildred Lyon, the daughter of John Lyon, a merchant of Wilmington. He was a major in the minute men organized in the New Hanover district in 1775. Killed in a duel, he was survived by his wife, Mildred, and by three children: Elizabeth, Samuel, and Jane.

SEE: William K. Boyd, ed., *William Byrd's Histories of the Dividing Line Betwixt Virginia and North Carolina* (1929); John L. Cheney, Jr., ed., *North Carolina Government, 1585–1974* (1975); R. D. W. Connor, *History of North Carolina: The Colonial and Revolutionary Periods, 1584–1783*

(1919); Thomas Frederick Davis, comp., *A Genealogical Record of the Davis, Swann, and Cabell Families of North Carolina and Virginia* (1934); Lewis Hampton Jones, comp., *Captain Roger Jones of London and Virginia . . .* (1891); E. Lawrence Lee, *The Lower Cape Fear in Colonial Days* (1965); New Hanover County Wills (microfilm, North Carolina State Archives, Raleigh); William L. Saunders, ed., *Colonial Records of North Carolina*, vols. 1–6, 9 (1886–90); James Sprunt, *Chronicles of the Cape Fear River, 1660–1916* (1916); Alexander M. Walker, ed., *Abstracts of New Hanover County Court Minutes, 1738–1769* (1958).

MATTIE ERMA E. PARKER

Swann, William *(ca. 1685–ca. 1723)*, legislator, was the eldest son of powerful Albemarle leader Samuel Swann and his first wife, Sarah Drummond, who had been the widow of North Carolina's early Proprietary governor, William Drummond. In all likelihood William Swann was born in Virginia at Swann's Point near Jamestown. In the fall of 1694 he entered North Carolina with his father; Sarah Drummond had died recently, and Samuel married Elizabeth Lillington, the daughter of a prominent Albemarle planter.

By 1709 Swann had entered North Carolina politics as a member of the lower house of the Assembly from Currituck Precinct. Two years later he was speaker of the house and spearheaded passage of punitive measures against the leaders of Cary's Rebellion, especially Thomas Cary and Edward Moseley. Swann also served in the assemblies of 1715/16 and 1722. He was a vestryman and militia colonel for Currituck in 1715.

After 1722 Swann does not appear in the extant records of North Carolina. It seems likely that he died (probably intestate) around 1723.

SEE: Mattie Erma E. Parker, ed., *North Carolina Higher-Court Records, 1670–1696* (1968); William L. Saunders, ed., *Colonial Records of North Carolina*, vols. 1–2 (1806).

WILLIAM S. PRICE, JR.

Swepson, George William *(23 June 1819–7 Mar. 1883)*, businessman and Republican activist during Reconstruction, was born in Mecklenburg County, Va., but in the early 1840s moved to Caswell County, N.C., where he is said to have taught school. In 1842 he married Virginia Bartlett Yancey, the daughter of Bartlett Yancey, a lawyer and congressman. Swepson enjoyed considerable success as a banker, textile manufacturer, and broker; the town of Swepsonville was named for his cotton mill built there in 1868. He was also a wholesaler and a land speculator. A dreamer and a planner, he met his downfall by using other people's money to finance his projects. Instead of fulfilling his promise of becoming a great industrial statesman, he is remembered as one of the greatest rascals in the history of North Carolina. Swepson became so involved in railroad fraud after the Civil War that he was dubbed "Our Boss Tweed" and was responsible for the coining of the term *swepsonize* to signify whatever evil was current at the moment.

As his business fortunes grew, Swepson moved from Haw River to Raleigh. He became a major stockholder and president of the Raleigh National Bank, a partner in the New York bond firm of Swepson, Mendenhall, and Company, and president of the Western North Carolina Railroad. It was in the latter capacity that he became involved with the notorious carpetbagger Milton Smith Littlefield. Together they defrauded the state of an estimated $4 million in bonds that were intended for a western extension of the Western North Carolina Railroad. This they accomplished through forged proxies, stock manipulation, bribes, crooked bookkeeping, and numerous other intrigues. The two men used the purloined state bonds to purchase an interest in Florida railroads. Swepson envisioned building a railroad empire as Cornelius Vanderbilt had in New York. Legend maintains that he disappeared from Raleigh in the dead of night with the $4 million in bonds in the cab of a Raleigh and Gaston Railroad engine, tipping the young engineer two dollars when he arrived at his Haw River destination.

Swepson was indicted along with Littlefield for embezzlement, but probably due to the influence of highly placed friends, he was never convicted. The state was able to recover some of the funds through the sale of a few Florida railroad bonds. The fraud, however, delayed construction of the eastern extension of the Western North Carolina Railroad until 1880 and thus resulted in substantial economic loss to the region.

Swepson's tarnished reputation was further damaged in 1876, when he fatally shot Adolphus G. Moore in Haw River. Moore was a business partner of Democrat Thomas W. Holt, who later became governor of North Carolina. Moore, also a Democrat, had once been arrested by radical Republican governor William Woods Holden. The killing of Moore apparently was politically motivated, although there is no known record of an investigation or a formal conclusion to the matter. Again, Swepson was free.

At times it was estimated that he had a personal fortune of between $1 and $2 million. To secure that fortune, he kept all of his assets in the names of his wife or agents and out of reach of authorities. Swepson was considered a conservative, "an Old Line Whig." Although not active politically, he was a close friend of Governor Holden and other prominent officials in the Reconstruction Republican regime.

Swepson and his wife had no children. He was buried in Oakwood Cemetery, Raleigh, where his grave is marked by a very tall monument.

SEE: *Asheville Citizen*, 29 Oct. 1950; Richard N. Current, *Those Terrible Carpetbaggers* (1988); Jonathan Daniels, *Prince of Carpetbaggers* (1958); Charles L. Price, "The Railroad Schemes of George W. Swepson," *East Carolina College Publications in History* 1 (1964); James T. Pugh Papers (Southern Historical Collection, University of North Carolina, Chapel Hill); Raleigh *News and Observer*, 28 Sept. 1930; Thomas E. Skinner, *Sermons and Reminiscences* (1894).

ROBERT J. WYLLIE

Swift, Joseph Gardner *(31 Dec. 1783–23 July 1865)*, engineer and soldier, was born on the island of Nantucket, Mass. As the son of Foster and Deborah Delano Swift, he was descended from two distinguished New England families. His physician father served as a naval and an army surgeon. At seventeen Swift became a cadet in the corps of artillerists and engineers at Newport, R.I., was transferred to West Point, N.Y., as the U.S. Military Academy was being organized, and became its first graduate, a second lieutenant of engineers, on 12 Oct. 1802.

Military orders initiated Swift's lifelong association with the state and people of North Carolina. In June 1804 he was at Fort Johnston in Smithville to develop a plan of defense for the Cape Fear harbor and build batteries already contracted for by General Benjamin Smith. He soon was on close terms with Benjamin and Sarah Dry Smith, who sponsored him among the families of the area. Swift was the general's second in his duel with Maurice Moore; fifty years later Swift provided the tombstone for the Smiths' grave at St. Philip's, Brunswick, installed by his namesake, Dr. Swift Miller of Wilmington.

Swift's Cape Fear friends included John Fanning, George Burgwyn, Dr. Daniel McNeill, Dr. Armand J. DeRosset, George Hooper, John and William Hill, the Swanns, Moores, and Ashes, John Bradley, Alexander C. Miller and General Thomas Brown, the Lords and Londons, Toomers, Wrights, and the Reverend Adam Empie. He also met Captain James Walker and his daughter Louisa, whom he married on 6 June 1805 and who died on 15 Nov. 1855. They were the parents of twelve children: James Foster (1806–30); Jonathan Williams (b. 1808); Alexander Joseph (1810–47), an army engineer involved in North Carolina coastal improvements in the 1830s; Thomas Delano (1812–29); Julius Henry (1814–50); Sarah Delano (1816–76); McRee (b. 1819), who in 1846 became an engineer and superintendent of the Wilmington and Weldon Railroad; Louisa Josephine (1821–59); Harriet Walker (1824–26), Charlotte Farquhar (1826–40); James Thomas (b. 1829); and Foster (b. 1833).

The fledgling American military establishment gave splendid advancement opportunities to bright, well-connected young men, and Swift moved rapidly through the ranks to full colonel at age twenty-eight. On 31 July 1812 the U.S. Senate confirmed his appointment as chief engineer of the army over a list of military and civil candidates that included Robert Fulton. Swift spent a great deal of time supervising the development of defenses along the Carolina coast. He was engineer of James Wilkinson's army during its unsuccessful invasion of Canada in 1813 and was breveted brigadier general in 1814. Shock caused by the burning of Washington, D.C., energized the citizenry of New York to volunteer in great numbers to help Swift fortify that city and its approaches, even as a British fleet stood offshore; his reward was to have his portrait painted for the city hall. He again served the city in the great fire of 1835 by directing the demolition of buildings in its way.

After the War of 1812 partisan politics made his position as chief engineer intolerable, although he continued as ex officio superintendent of West Point, a position he had assumed when the superintendent was obliged to leave in April 1807. In November 1807, promoted major, he was in charge of the defense of the Eastern Department, consisting of the coastal regions of Rhode Island, Massachusetts, New Hampshire, and Maine. Swift resigned from the army in 1818. Maintaining his friendships within the military establishment, however, he was an engineering consultant to the army for many years and a frequent associate of such men as General Winfield Scott, who was almost exactly his contemporary.

Swift became surveyor of the port of New York, chief engineer of a number of new railroads, director of harbor and shore developments on Lake Ontario, and, between jobs, a mediocre farmer. He made Geneva, N.Y., his home but traveled widely in North Carolina and elsewhere on various consultations. His active encouragement of many younger men made Swift important to the development of American military and civil engineering.

From very early in life Swift made notes on events and the people he met; from time to time he consolidated these diaries into a journal and made the last entry six months before his death. Covering a span of sixty-five years, the journal is full of anecdotes of persons and movements between the Revolution and the Civil War by one who knew almost everyone of consequence during that time and had strong opinions about almost everything, including the worth of the presidents under whom he served (President James Monroe alone achieved his full approval).

A slave owner, Swift resented abolitionist efforts to disturb his servants but freed them. And though he opposed interference with the institution of slavery in the slave states, he opposed its extension elsewhere; the last words in his journal are a plea for humane treatment of Confederate prisoners and a stern opposition to Southern independence. Swift left the Masonic order because he considered it un-American. He advocated the purchase of Canada and was, successively, a bitterly partisan Federalist/Whig/Republican. He revered family history, the heroes of the Revolution, and especially George Washington: whenever he met a contemporary of Washington, as during the triumphal tour of General Lafayette, he asked whether the general had actually sworn at Charles Lee at the Battle of Monmouth. When the citizens of Wilmington gave him a testimonial dinner, he proposed a toast to "North Carolina and her liberal spirit, as evinced in her *carte blanche* order to Canova for a sculpture of Washington, at an expense limited only by the artist's decision."

An active and opinionated Episcopalian, Swift was a founding trustee of the General Theological Seminary in New York City, a founder of the American and Foreign Bible Society, and a founding officer of the New York City Philharmonic Society. As president of the Handel and Haydn Society, he "got up the first oratorio in the United States, a great improvement to the musical taste of our country."

SEE: George W. Cullum, *Biographical Sketch of Brigadier-General Joseph G. Swift, Chief Engineer of the United States Army, July 31, 1812, to Nov. 12, 1818* (1877 [portrait]); *DAB*, vol. 18 (1936), which states that Swift's military papers are at West Point and that his letters are in the New York Public Library; Harrison Ellery, ed., *The Memoirs of Gen. Joseph Gardner Swift, LL.D., U.S.A., First Graduate of the United States Military Academy, West Point, Chief Engineer U.S.A. from 1812 to 1818, 1800–1865* (1890 [portrait]); Sarah MCulloh Lemmon, *Frustrated Patriots: North Carolina and the War of 1812* (1973).

WILLIAM ELLWOOD CRAIG

Swimmer *(ca. 1835–March 1899)*, Cherokee traditionalist and storyteller, was born in the Cherokee country of southwestern North Carolina. His Cherokee name, Ayunini, meant "he is swimming" or "he is a swimmer." Trained by the masters of his tribe to be a priest, a doctor, and the keeper of tradition, he never learned to speak English but instead maintained his Indian culture and heritage throughout his life. In fact, as it was intended he should be, he became the conservator of the history and traditions of his people. As a youth he learned the Cherokee syllabary from the elders of his tribe and began early to keep a notebook in which he recorded the sacred rights as well as the facts and stories of his people. He also made note of their ways of doing things and identified plants, roots, and barks whose use had proven useful or effective in one way or another. During the Civil War Swimmer enlisted on 9 Apr. 1862 and served as second sergeant of the Cherokee Company A, Sixty-ninth North Carolina Confederate Regiment in Colonel William Thomas's legion.

In 1887 the Smithsonian Institution sent James Mooney, a former newspaperman and afterwards an ethnologist, to the Cherokee country to observe the Native Americans. Mooney had already interviewed and worked in Washington, D.C., with a Cherokee chief, and they had prepared a Cherokee grammar. During three seasons of fieldwork, he came to know Swimmer. From him Mooney collected a vast storehouse of information and in time obtained Swimmer's notebook. Swimmer perhaps recognized in Mooney a successor who would record for all time the material he had spent a lifetime in learning and recording.

Mooney, indeed, became Swimmer's link to the future. In *Myths of the Cherokee* and other publications, he recorded the history and the wisdom of the Cherokee that had been handed down orally for generations, while Swimmer's notebook is preserved at the Smithsonian Institution. Mooney, of course, gathered information from Swimmer's contemporaries as well, but he was careful to note with gratitude what a splendid thing Swimmer had done with his life. Swimmer had taken Mooney to tribal ceremonies, had explained ancient rites and games, had recited legends and stories, and had imitated animal sounds. (In return, Mooney rewarded Swimmer with Irish folk myths from his own childhood.) He wrote that his native friend was "a genuine aboriginal antiquarian and patriot, proud of his people and their ancient system." At dances, ball games, and other tribal functions Swimmer was always present, and he was looked to for guidance and decisions—perhaps as a referee.

At his death at age sixty-five, he was buried on the slope of a high mountain according to the rituals of his people. Among his descendants were a son Tom (t`a.mi) and a grandson called Dancer. A photograph of Swimmer, now at the Smithsonian Institution, shows him holding a gourd rattle, a badge of his authority in the tribe, and wearing his accustomed turban. He also undoubtedly wore moccasins, as Mooney observed that his head and his feet were always covered by these traditional items of dress.

SEE: John R. Finger, *The Eastern Band of Cherokees, 1819–1900* (1984 [portrait]); Sam Gray, *Mythic Maps: An Exhibition of Cherokee Legends in the Appalachian Landscape* (1979 [portrait]); William G. McLoughlin, *Cherokees and Missionaries, 1789–1839* (1984); James Mooney, *Myths of the Cherokee* (1902) and *The Swimmer Manuscript: Cherokee Sacred Formulas and Medicinal Prescriptions* (1932).

WILLIAM S. POWELL

Sydnor, Charles Sackett *(21 July 1898–2 Mar. 1954)*, historian and university administrator, was born in Augusta, Ga., the oldest of five children of Evelyn Aiken Sackett and Giles Granville Sydnor, pastor of the Green Street Presbyterian Church. Both parents were natives of Virginia and were descended from early American settlers of English origin. From 1901 to 1915 Charles lived with his parents in Rome, Ga., where he was admitted to the recently established Darlington School near age eleven. He was remembered as "strikingly good looking, with cheeks as pink as a girl's." As a result, some of the "boys gave him a rough time," but he took it in good humor and went on to demonstrate his manhood by playing guard on the football team, where he was lighter than any opposing player. He entered Hampden-Sydney College in 1915 and was graduated in three years with a degree in classical studies.

In 1919, after serving briefly in the military and teaching in the Rome high school, he became a teacher of mathematics in the McCallie School at Chattanooga, Tenn. Under the influence of James R. McCain, founder of the Darlington School and later president of Agnes Scott College, Sydnor entered the graduate school of Johns Hopkins University in 1920. In good part he supported himself, partly by summer work with a construction gang on the Baltimore and Ohio Railroad. At Hopkins his major interest was medieval and English history; his unpublished dissertation was on the English Tudors. He received a Ph.D. degree in 1923 and then became professor of history and political science at Hampden-Sydney, the sole teacher, he said, in those departments.

On 12 June 1924 he married Betty Brown, a native of Chattanooga and a former student at Agnes Scott College. They became the parents of two boys, Charles Sackett, Jr., and Victor Brown.

In 1925 he went to the University of Mississippi as chairman of the history department. He had declined an offer to teach at Agnes Scott, possibly because he did not wish to teach only women or because he thought research opportunities would be limited. After teaching for two summers at Duke University, he was invited to join that faculty as associate professor in 1936. He was made a full professor in 1938 and chairman of the department in 1952, when he also was appointed dean of the graduate school. In 1953 he was named James B. Duke Professor, the highest academic appointment.

His first book was a school history of Mississippi written with Claude Bennett. Sydnor was the author of four other books, all carefully researched and all illustrating the ability to write with clarity and distinction. He had the ability to view familiar events with a sharpened perspective. He never thought that history was an exact science, but he insisted that historians should try to shed their prejudice and avoid the propaganda uses of history. He was convinced, however, that an understanding of the past was relevant to succeeding eras. Within the field of southern history he published widely; he contributed twenty-three sketches to the *Dictionary of American Biography*.

His first book, *Slavery in Mississippi* (1933), was long considered the most significant of the several studies of slavery that followed the pioneer work of U. B. Phillips. Carter G. Woodson, a black editor and historian, admitted in an unsigned review, after questioning whether whites could write about Negroes without bias, that the author "apparently endeavored to write with restraint and care." Professor J. G. de Roulhac Hamilton considered it "the most complete picture that has so far emerged for any state," and, he added, "it is absorbingly interesting."

Sydnor's next book, *A Gentleman of the Old Natchez Region: Benjamin L. C. Wailes* (1938), was a biography of a versatile Mississippian whose voluminous diaries and letters were used to illustrate plantation life and slavery, travel, movements for agricultural reform, early educational institutions, and the activities of organized social and intellectual societies reminiscent of the seaboard states. The focus was not on politics but on the evolution of a frontier society.

The Development of Southern Sectionalism, 1818–1848 (1948)—the fifth volume in *The History of the South*, edited by E. Merton Coulter and Wendell H. Stephenson—was broader in scope than anything he had previously written. Both the cotton kingdom and the tobacco kingdom were in a difficult transitional period, when economic problems, internal improvements, population shifts, and issues touching on slavery were about to exceed the grasp of the politicians. Sydnor found that the complexities of politics had to be related to personalities, but that much of the motivation was of economic origin. Southern sectionalism, he wrote, was "essentially dictated by self-interest," and the "wall of constitutional arguments" raised by John C. Calhoun and others merely furnished "the righteous garb of legality and high principle." The more intense the political excitement, the more certain it was that the social reforms that the South might have undertaken would be rejected; the promise of enlightened progress seen in the rise of colleges and the evangelical churches gave way to "intellectual provincialism," which characterized almost every phase of southern life. This book was widely acclaimed. *American Literature* called it "the best study of the ante-bellum South in print." Arthur M. Schlesinger, Jr., wrote of "its pervading quality of thoughtful and dispassionate judgment." Similar comments came from other distinguished historians. For this book Sydnor received the Mayflower Cup for the best book of the year by a resident of North Carolina.

He was disturbed by the failure of modern democracy to produce statesmen of a high order, and, in keeping with his notion that history was a useful depository of knowledge, he studied the political system of eighteenth-century Virginia. In *Gentlemen Freeholders: Political Practices in Washington's Virginia* (1952), he found that the contending forces of aristocracy and democracy coexisted in general harmony. The members of the House of Burgesses, the proving ground for political leaders, were chosen in such a way that they were "more or less acceptable both to the leaders and to the rank and file of the voters." They had been doubly screened, "first by the gentry and then by the freeholders." It was this selective process that seemed to hold the secret of leadership. In this book the emphasis was not so much on new information as on a fresh interpretation.

Professor Sydnor received honorary degrees from Washington and Lee University, Davidson College, Princeton University, and Oxford University. He was a visiting professor at leading universities, including The University of North Carolina, Cornell, and Harvard, and held the Harold Vyvyan Harmsworth professorship of American history at Oxford (1950–51), the first southerner to do so. He also lectured at the Salzburg Seminar of American Studies in Austria (1951). Sydnor was president of the Southern Historical Association (1939), the North Carolina Literary and Historical Association (1949), and the Historical Society of North Carolina (1949). He was a member of the executive committee of the Southern Association of Colleges and Secondary Schools and a member of the Council of the Institute of Early American History and Culture (chairman, 1953) and of the advisory committee of the Office of the Chief of Military History, U.S. Department of the Army. In addition, he sat on the editorial boards of the *Journal of Southern History* (1935–38) and the *South Atlantic Quarterly* (1947–54). He was a member of Phi Beta Kappa, Omicron Delta Kappa, and Kappa Sigma.

Sydnor was a meticulous scholar who knew the effort that went into the writing of good history. His personal qualities, however, did not so much suggest the dedicated scholar as the complete gentleman: unfailing courtesy, good humor, and a relaxed manner. The informality of his classroom discussions did not obscure the fact that he was probing for the reality below the surface. His graduate students were apt to find that conferences with him were enlightening experiences rather than times of dull faultfinding. These same gentlemanly qualities helped to make him an efficient administrator. He got along with people because he had a way of dissipating any point of friction.

Remaining true to his Presbyterian heritage, Sydnor was steadfastly active in the work of his church. He was a trustee of Davidson College, a Presbyterian school (1942–46). He had addressed the Mississippi Historical Society at Biloxi before he was admitted to a local hospital and died of a heart attack. He had been scheduled to give the Walter L. Fleming Lectures in Southern History at Louisiana State University on 1–2 Mar. 1954. In 1955 the Southern Historical Association established the Charles S. Sydnor award of $500 to be given in even-numbered years for the best book on southern history. After a funeral service at the First Presbyterian Church, Durham, he was buried in the Forest Hills Cemetery, Chattanooga, Tenn.

SEE: *Duke Alumni Register*, April 1954; *Durham Morning Herald*, 3–5 Mar. 1954; William B. Hamilton Papers and Wendell H. Stephenson Papers (Manuscript Department, Duke University Library, Durham); Raleigh *News and Observer*, 28 Sept. 1952; Charles S. Sydnor Papers (Duke University Archives, Duke University Library, Durham); Mrs. Charles S. Sydnor (Durham), Mrs. Hugh McCormick (Frederick, Md.), and James Ross McCain to Robert H. Woody, 10 Dec. 1954; *Who's Who in America* (1954).

ROBERT H. WOODY

Syme [pronounced *Sim*], John William *(6 Jan. 1811–26 Nov. 1865)*, newspaper editor and legislator, was born in Petersburg, Va., the only child of the Reverend Andrew Syme, rector of St. Paul's Church, and his wife, Jean Matherson Cameron, the sister of Duncan Cameron. His grandfather was the Reverend John Cameron, rector of Bristol Parish. Young Syme was educated at Partridge's Military School in Middletown, Conn., and attended the College of William and Mary during the period 1827–29. He studied law in Hillsborough under Judge Frederick Nash and began to practice in Petersburg, but after a short time he became editor of the *Petersburg Intelligencer*, a leading Whig paper. On 9 July 1838, as a printer, he was elected a member of the Petersburg Benevolent Mechanic Association.

Syme served five consecutive terms in the Virginia Assembly (1845–50), where he was a strong advocate of internal improvements, particularly railroads. He was a popular public speaker and an editor of firm convictions. In December 1856 he purchased the Raleigh *Register* and in late January moved to Raleigh from Petersburg. He pledged to continue to support Whig policies and to promote the prosperity of the state. Moreover, he bought new equipment and improved the format of the newspaper.

During these pre–Civil War years Syme expressed Union sentiments, but with the threat of Federal coercion of a state, he changed completely. From 1861 his was an intense voice supporting the South. He was the official printer to the Secession Convention in Raleigh in 1861, and the journal of that body was issued from his press. The scarcity of paper in 1863 and the need for a newspaper in Petersburg persuaded Syme to move his press and the *Register* to his native city. He maintained that his interests would now be divided, but that North Carolina would still have his support. His family, in fact, remained in Raleigh. Finally in August 1864 he was obliged to cease publication because of the scarcity of supplies, and thereafter he divided his time between Petersburg and Raleigh. He lived for only a little over a year after his paper was shut down.

Syme's wife was Mary C. Madden, a native of North Carolina (probably Orange County). They were the parents of seven children: Jean Cameron (died in infancy), Elizabeth Battle, Mary Louise, Andrew, Duncan Cameron, Mildred Cameron, and John Cameron.

SEE: Robert N. Elliott, Jr., *The Raleigh Register, 1799–1863* (1955); J. G. de Roulhac Hamilton, ed., *The Papers of William A. Graham*, vol. 2 (1959); John G. McCormick, *Personnel of the Convention of 1861* (1900); Petersburg *Daily Index*, 27 Nov. 1865; Alice Read, *The Reads and Their Relatives* (1940); Edward A. Wyatt IV, ed., *Virginia Imprint Series, Number 9, Preliminary Checklist for Petersburg, 1786–1876* (1949); Wake County, N.C., 1860 Census (North Carolina State Archives, Raleigh).

WILLIAM S. POWELL

Symons (or Simons, Symonds), Thomas *(ca. 1649–18 Apr. 1706)*, justice, Council member, Assembly member, and prominent Quaker, settled in the North Carolina colony before 21 Apr. 1669. His earlier history is unknown.

By 6 Jan. 1689/90 Symons was a justice of Pasquotank Precinct Court, on which he also sat in 1694 and probably in the intervening years. He apparently was a member of the lower house of the Assembly in 1695, for in November of that year and through the following October he held one of the Council seats that the lower house filled by election, usually choosing its own members. As a Council member, Symons was ex officio justice of the General Court, which was then held by the Council. In December 1698 he was appointed to the General Court, which at that time was held by justices commissioned by the Council. He remained on the court through October 1704. He also sat on the Admiralty Court in October 1704, when that court was composed of the justices of the General Court. He was again a member of the Assembly about 1705.

Symons lived on Little River in Pasquotank Precinct, where he owned at least four hundred acres of land and a number of slaves. He was a devout Quaker and one of the earliest known members of the Pasquotank Monthly Meeting, later known as the Symons Creek Monthly Meeting. He entertained Thomas Story in his home during the missionary's tour of the colony in 1698.

Symons and his wife, Rebecca, had six children: John (b. 1678), Frances, Thomas, Peter, Mary, and Elizabeth. Several of the children died in childhood. John, the eldest, married Damaris White, the daughter of Henry White, on 8 Aug. 1700. No record of the marriage of the others has been located.

Symons died at age fifty-seven or fifty-eight. He left his estate to his wife and sons John and Peter, who may have been the only surviving children. Peter died in 1731 and John in 1741.

SEE: J. Bryan Grimes, ed., *Abstract of North Carolina Wills* (1910); J. R. B. Hathaway, ed., *North Carolina Historical and Genealogical Register* (1900–1903); William Wade Hinshaw, comp., *Encyclopedia of American Quaker Genealogy* (1936–50); North Carolina State Archives (Raleigh), particularly Albemarle Book of Warrants and Surveys (1681–1706), Albemarle County Papers (1678–1714), Colonial Court Records (boxes 148, 192), and Council Minutes, Wills, Inventories (1677–1701); Mattie Erma E. Parker, ed., *North Carolina Higher-Court Records, 1670–1696* (1968) and *1697–1701* (1971); William S. Price Jr., ed., *North Carolina Higher-Court Records, 1702–1708* (1974); Records of Symons Creek Monthly Meeting of the Society of Friends of North Carolina (Guilford College Library, Greensboro); Thomas Story, *Journal* (1747).

MATTIE ERMA E. PARKER